Dictionary of Hebrew N(

14,000 Hebrew Nouns and Adjectives Classified into 998 Patterns (or Modes of Inflection), with Grammatical Information

By

Shmuel Bolozky

Prof. Emeritus, University of Massachusetts Amherst

Rubin Mass Publishers, Jerusalem

Second corrected edition, 2022
Printed book: ISBN 978-965-09-0360-2

KDP edition

Rubin Mass Ltd., Publishers and Booksellers
POB 7573, Jerusalem 9107402, Israel
Tel +972-2-6277863; Fax +972-2-6277864
Rmass@barak.net.il www.rubinmass.net

Printed in Israel

This book is dedicated
to the memory
of my departed wife
Neta
the love of my life
whose vitality, love and support
inspired me for 55 blissful years

Table of Contents

Including representative examples of sub-categories within each pattern group
(The figures on the left are ID numbers of patterns within each sub-category)

Introduction

The purpose of this dictionary. For language teaching, lexicographers tend to prepare reference textbooks on the verb system, since regular dictionaries usually provide only a base form of any specific verb, and the user needs the whole conjugation. Verb reference books present representative full conjugations, and the index refers each verb entry to the closest conjugation. Although nouns and adjectives are often characterized by affixes, there is no obvious practical need to mark them in a regular dictionary. In Hebrew and in other Semitic languages, nouns and adjectives are also often marked by affixes (see linear derivation below), but in most cases they are derived in root + *mishkal* (pattern) configurations (see discontinuous derivation below), and often (though not always, as explained below) the *mishkal* also helps in comprehending word meaning and in understanding the connection with other words which incorporate a similar semantic trait. Consequently, in languages like Hebrew, a dictionary such as this one has clear advantages over regular dictionaries. As for nouns with possessive pronouns appended (such as *beyti* 'my house,' *beytkha* 'your house, etc.), their usage in normal speech is limited (generally they are replaced by analytic constructions such as *habait sheli* 'the house mine=my house,' *habait shelkha* 'the house yours masc. sing.=your house,' etc.), but in the higher registers they are important, and they also occur in common collocations (especially kinship terms) such as *avi* 'my father,' *avikha* 'your father,' alongside *(ha-)aba sheli*, *(ha-)aba shelkha*, etc. Therefore, forms with possessive suffixes are included in all noun formation patterns (unless there is no declension at all, which occasionaly happens).

The dictionary is appropriate for learners of Hebrew as a second language, as well as for native learners/users. Native learners can use it for reference on noun and adjective patterns and on how they are formed, on precise vowel marking of the entries and declensions, on derivation classes, on pattern meaning – and for enriching their knowledge re parallel collocations in Hebrew and in English.

The structure of the dictionary and the way it is used. Practically, the order in which the patterns are presented is not important, but for those interested in the **types** of patterns, the presentation order starts with verb-related ones, followed by those that generally do not include affixes (prefixes or suffixes), then patterns with affixes. The number next to each entry in the indices refers to the pattern number in the body of the text (not to the page number!). When the learner/user looks up a noun or adjective in order to connect it to a particular pattern, and/or to translate it into English, s/he needs to look it up in the index at the end of the dictionary (which starts on p 613), and click on any item while pressing the CTRL key, to trigger the hyperlink to the relevant pattern in the text. Each pattern contains a few examples; for a **full** list of all forms **in each pattern**, see the section **preceding** the alphabetical index (starting p 720), which includes hyperlinks as well. To prevent the user from inadvertently corrupting the text in a Word version, the online version is in PDF format.

Word formation in Hebrew. New Hebrew words can be coined by means of two word-formation mechanisms, linear or discontinuous. Derivation is linear when affixes (suffixes or prefixes) are appended to the stem without affecting its internal structure, as is normally the case in English, e.g., critic > criticize, weak > weaken, large > enlarge. The other mechanism (root plus *mishkal*) is discontinuous, which means that the process interferes with the syllabic structure of the stem. In English, discontinuous derivation is essentially restricted to small groups of "strong" verbs, as in: drive-drove-driven, write-wrote-written; in Hebrew it is common as well as productive. In fact, in Hebrew **both** types of derivations are productive, and exist alongside each other. As will be shown below, in some cases linear derivation is occasionally accompanied by some phonetic change necessitated by morpheme combination, but as long as the change is automatic, it can still be claimed that we are essentially dealing with linear derivation.

A ***mishkal*** (מִשְׁקָל, a discontinuous morphological pattern of Hebrew nouns and adjectives) is a word formation pattern in which phonemes (distinct sound units) are arranged in a fixed order, including root consonants, identical vowels, identical affixes, and the same stress pattern. Thus, for instance, the first *mishkal* presented here will be *CCiCa*, with each *C* representing a root consonant, the *i* is a stem vowel, and the *a* a suffix, both *i* and *a* constituting fixed elements of the pattern, while the *C*'s are variable root consonants. The *mishkal* string refers to words with the same surface configuration, with possible exceptions: changes that result from the effect of the phonetic or phonological environment, which can be seen either as separate *mishkalim*, or as alternant realizations of "proto"-*mishkalim*, i.e., "deep structure" *mishkalim*. The obvious examples are forms with *Hatafim*. A *Hataf* חֲטָף is an unstressed vowel that originally was shortened (equivalent to a *shva mobile*), which is represented by a combination of a regular vowel mark and a *shva* mark. Forms with *Hatafim* may be regarded as separate *mishkalim*, or may be attributed to their "proto"-*mishkal*. For instance, a form like *'akhila* אֲכִילָה 'eating' can be regarded as belonging to a *CaCiCa mishkal*, or alternatively to its *CCiCa* "proto"-*mishkal*. Some speakers know how to attribute forms with *Hatafim* to their "deep-structure" *mishkalim*, and it seems that for the purpose of attributing a form to a *mishkal*, the *Hataf* is conceived of by such speakers as a *shva quiescent*, i.e., as if the vowel did not exist. It is hard to tell whether this is a natural automatic phenomenon, or a result of realizing the connection with the proto-pattern in spite of the added vowel. Other changes are more complex. Thus, it is possible to attribute a form like *tisa* טִיסָה 'flight' to a *CiCa mishkal*, or to regard it as an offshoot of the *CCiCa mishkal* when the second root consonant (in this case *w*) is a sonorant consonant that got weakened to a vowel or was totally elided. Occasionally, in addition to using *C*'s to represent root consonants, we will use the קט"ל root prototype, with ק' standing for the first consonant of the root, ט' the second, and ל' the third (the prototype פע"ל is used more commonly, but may be a bit misleading owing to the somewhat exceptional status of ע' as a guttural). The occasional use of קט"ל instead of *C*'s is to disambiguate some strings. For instance, to capture the fact that the first and second root consonants in some pattern are reduplicated in third and fourth position, respectively, cannot be accurately represented by a string like *CaCCeCanut*; קְטַקְטָנוּת is a better alternative (two ק's and two ט's in the appropriate positions).
The description of each *mishkal* (or linear derivation pattern) will contain specific comments regarding any tendency to reflect a certain semantic category, or to be related to verb types or to some *binyan* בִּנְיָן (discontinuous verb pattern), but it should be kept

in mind that these are just tendencies, so as to avoid misleading the reader by over-generalizations. A significant number of *mishkalim* have no meaning, but this volume will concentrate mostly on those that can be characterized semantically, at least in part, assuming that the learner will benefit more from acquiring such *mishkalim*. Each *mishkal* introduced here will be assigned a "number ID," and when the user/reader looks for a specific form in the alphabetical list at the end of the volume, s/he be able to examine the *mishkal* to which it belongs in the body of the text. For instance, a form like בְּדִיקָה will be marked with the number 1, which will refer the reader to the *CCiCa mishkal*, whose number is 1 in the body of the text. The forms at the end of the book will be translated into English, including specific meanings that are not automatic:

checking, examining; examination, checkup (esp. medical) 1 בְּדִיקָה

As explained in the text regarding *CCiCa*, the reader will understand that we are dealing with a gerund derived from a *pa`al* (*CaCaC*) verb, which is the default case in this *mishkal* – in our case בָּדַק 'examine, check.' One should remember, however, that in some cases, a parallel verb form simply does not exist. For instance, in a realization such as 1 וְעִידָה 'conference, convention, congress,' no parallel וָעַד* verb is documented. The form is derived directly from the root ועי״ד (originally יעי״ד), whose general meaning is 'designate, appoint, schedule, etc.,' plus the *CCiCa mishkal*. And there are cases where there is no connection to any verb or verbal root, e.g., פְּנִינָה 'pearl,' and ones where the *CCiCa* (or *CaCiCa*) form is derived from a noun, e.g., חֶבֶל 'rope, string' > חֲבִילָה 'parcel.' Pragmatically, the alphabetical index at the end of the dictionary is sufficient to connect each entry to its pattern, and the examples contained in the specific pattern description in the body of the dictionary illustrate the basic meaning of the pattern to the extent that it exists. But if one is looking for in-depth understanding of the *mishkalim*, and discovering by oneself to what extent each of them stands for a particular meaning core, one may check it in the list that is classified by pattern number, examine all related realizations together, and evaluate the extent to which a particular pattern carries a core of meaning. Thus, for instance, one may look up an entry like כְּתִיבָה 'writing N' in the alphabetical index, find that its pattern is #1, and if one wishes, one can go to the pattern group list (preceding the alphabetical index), and easily go over all occurrences of pattern/*mishkal* #1, listed together.

For pragmatic reasons, only (relatively) frequent forms will be listed at the end of the volume – generally in our case only those that appear in Morfix, whose editors' choices were frequency-based (about 14,000 entries out of about 33,000 nouns and adjectives in a comprehensive dictionary like Even-Shoshan's).

Two general comments:

(1) Obviously not every noun has a plural variant, particularly when abstract nouns are concerned, non-countable nouns (mass nouns etc.), and when plural formation is prevented owing to semantic/pragmatic, syntactic, morphological, idiomatic, phonological or phonetic reasons. In some patterns there are no plural forms at all, which is noted within the text, but generally, the absence of plural variants is marked next to the appropriate lexical item in the index, "no pl." Searching the Internet reveals

that the possible existence of plural variants is a dynamic, ever-changing process, affected by historical, social and scientific developments and others, and that new plural forms commonly appear.

(2) Strictly speaking, the terms prefix and suffix should only be used for morphemes denoting grammatical categories in linear derivation, whereas for discontinuous derivation, formative syllables that do not designate grammatical categories are more appropriately designated by terms like preformatives and afformatives. Nevertheless, for the sake of simplicity the terms prefix and suffix will be used for both in the volume.

Some recurring abbreviated forms: Pl. or ר׳ = Plural, Sing. = Singular, M(asc). or ז = Masculine, F(em). or נ = Feminine, זו״נ = Masculine and Feminine, BH or Bibl. = Biblical Hebrew, MH = Modern Hebrew, Const. = Construct State, Lit. = Literary, Col(l). = Colloquial, Sl. = Slang, Obs. = Obsolete, Med. = Medical, Geog. = Geography, Chem. = Chemistry, Math. = Mathematics.

Orthgraphic transciption conventions used in this dictionary: שׁ = *sh*, ח = *H* (cap.), כ (no *dagesh*) = *kh*, צ = *ts*, א = ’, ע = `.

Verb-related Patterns (more or less)

A. *CCiCa* and related *mishkalim*

1. *CCiCa*: generally nominalizations of verbs in *pa`al* (*CaCaC*)

our/your/their	my/your/his/her	const.	Gloss	sing/pl
סְתִימָתֵנוּ/**סְתִימַתְ**כֶם/כֶן/**סְתִימָתָ**ם/ן	**סְתִימָתִ**י/תְךָ/תֵךְ/תוֹ/תָהּ	סְתִימַת-	sealing; a filling	סְתִימָה נ׳
סְתִימוֹתֵינוּ/כֶם/כֶן/הֶם/הֶן	**סְתִימוֹתַ**י/תֶיךָ/תַיִךְ/תָיו/תֶיהָ	סְתִימוֹת-		סְתִימוֹת

CCiCa is often a pattern designating nominalization of verbs, usually in *pa`al*, as in גָּסַס 'die' ~ גְּסִיסָה 'dying (N),' but in many cases the *CCiCa* form also refers to a specific realization of the nominalization. Thus, for instance, סְתִימָה is either the sealing or the clogging action derived from סָתַם 'seal,' or alternatively, a dental filling. יְשִׁיבָה is a general action derived from יָשַׁב 'sit,' or a pre-planned meeting of a group of people, or a Jewish religious academy. Note that although יְשִׁיבָה is tri-syllabic (*yeshiva*), it will be regarded here as bi-syllabic, like סְתִימָה (*stima*), since the insertion of *e* between the first two consonants is fully automatic, stemming from purely phonetic reasons. In many cases, there is connection to some verb, but not necessarily in *pa`al*: נִכְנַס 'enter' ~ כְּנִיסָה 'entering; entrance,' בִּדֵּחַ 'amuse' ~ בְּדִיחָה 'a joke;' in others the *CCiCa* form is verb-related, but the verb is rare, or is hardly ever used, as in חִבֵּת 'make omelet' ~ חֲבִיתָה 'omelet.' And there are cases where there is no connection to any verb or verbal root: פְּנִינָה 'pearl,' גְּלִימָה 'robe, gown,' and ones where the *CCiCa* form is derived from a noun: חֶבֶל 'rope, string' > חֲבִילָה 'parcel.' In some of the realizations there are no plural forms in use. The reason is pragmatic: often there are no plurals of abstract nouns when the noun is non-countable, as in בְּשִׁילָה 'ripening, maturing.' Under certain rare circumstances such cases can be regarded as countable, in this case בְּשִׁילוֹת as types of ripening, say according to different ripening dates of fruit/vegetables (spring, fall, etc.), but it does not happen in the real world. People do specify by attaching "types of" to "ripening," rather than use "ripenings."

Examples

זְרִימַת הנפט לתוך הים נפסקה סוף סוף לאחר **סְתִימַת** פי הקידוח על ידי החברה.
The **flowing** of oil into the sea finally stopped after the **sealing** of the drilling site opening by the company.

סְתִימָה ישנה שנסדקה גרמה לי לכאב שיניים מחריד.
An old **filling** that cracked caused me horrible pain.

יְשִׁיבָה ממושכת קשה מאוד למי שלוקה בטחורים...
Prolonged **sitting** is difficult for whoever suffers from hemorrhoids...

יְשִׁיבַת המנהלים השנתית נמשכה שש שעות רצופות, אבל הם לא הצליחו להגיע לידי החלטה.
The **meeting** of the Board of Directors lasted non-stop for six hours, but they could not reach a decision.

דויד נסע לישראל ללמוד ב**יְשִׁיבַת** הכותל.
David went to Israel to study at the Wailing Wall **Yeshiva**.

בלימוד שפה זרה, בעוד ש**קְרִיאָה** היא מיומנות פסיבית ביסודה, **כְּתִיבָה** היא אקטיבית.
In learning a foreign language, while **reading** is an essentially passive skill, **writing** is active.

מתי כבר המדענים יבינו ש**בְּרִיאַת** העולם לקחה שישה ימים בלבד?
When will scientists finally understand that the **creation** of the world took only six days?

גְּדִילַת עץ זית אורכת שנים רבות.
The **growing** of an olive tree takes many years.

גְּמִילָה מהתמכרות לסמים הרבה יותר קשה מ**גְּמִילַת** תינוק **מִיְּנִיקַת** חלב אימו.
Withdrawal from drug addiction is much harder than **weaning** a baby from **breast-feeding**.

האביב הערבי התחיל עם תקוות גדולות לשינוי, וברוב המקרים הסתיים ב**דְּעִיכָה** ובאכזבה.
The Arab Spring started with great hopes for change, and in most cases ended with **dying out** and with disappointment.

דויד אינו נבון במיוחד, אבל מצליח בלימודיו בזכות **שְׁקִידָתוֹ** הרבה.
David is not particularly intelligent, but is successful at school owing to his great **diligence**.

Special Expressions

בְּרִיאָה ספונטנית abiogenesis
בחור **יְשִׁיבָה** Yeshiva student
יְשִׁיבָה של מעלה divine **assembly** (i.e., heaven)
יְשִׁיבָה מזרחית sitting with folded legs (Middle East style)
כְּתִיבָה יוצרת creative **writing**
כְּתִיבָה תמה penmanship
סְתִימַת הגולל **filling up** grave; end (of plans, hopes)

Additional Examples in this Pattern

בְּגִידָה betrayal
בְּדִיקָה checking, checkup
בְּחִינָה examining; examination
בְּחִירָה choosing; choice
בְּלִיטָה protrusion; bulge
בְּלִיעָה swallowing
בְּעִיטָה kicking; a kick
בְּרִיחָה escaping; escape
גְּבִינָה cheese
גְּזִירָה cutting; differentiation (math); derivation (grammar)
גְּלִישָׁה boiling over; surfing
גְּמִיעָה swallowing drink
גְּמִירָה completing, finishing
גְּנִיזָה archiving; shelving
גְּסִיסָה dying
גְּרִיסָה crushing, grinding
גְּרִירָה dragging; towing
דְּגִימָה sampling; sample
דְּגִירָה hatching; studying hard Coll.
דְּהִירָה galloping

---

2. *CCiCa* = *CaCiCa*: generally nominalizations of verbs in *pa`al* when the first root consonant is guttural

our/your/their	my/your/his/her	const.	Gloss	sing/pl
עֲצִירָתֵנוּ/**עֲצִירַתְ**כֶם/כֶן/**עֲצִירָתָ**ם/ן	**עֲצִירָ**תִי/תְךָ/תֵךְ/תוֹ/תָהּ	עֲצִירַת-	stopping;	עֲצִירָה נ׳
עֲצִירוֹתֵינוּ/כֶם/כֶן/הֶם/הֶן	**עֲצִירוֹ**תַי/תֶיךָ/תַיִךְ/תָיו/תֶיהָ	עֲצִירוֹת-	stop	עֲצִירוֹת

Like סְתִימָה above, but when the first consonant of *CCiCa* is "guttural," it is separated from the next consonant with the vowel *a*, which in this *mishkal* is marked by a *Hataf-pataH*: עֲצִירָה 'stopping; stop,' עֲצִירָתִי etc. Some speakers regard *CaCiCa* as a separate pattern, but most speakers realize that *CaCiCa* is part of the *CCiCa* pattern (perhaps under the influence of the orthography, or because the speaker is aware of the existence of a consonantal slot, even if that slot is not realized phonetically, as in (`)*atsira*.) If we regard the *Hataf* as *shva*-equivalent, attributing these forms to *CCiCa* will be self-evident, at least insofar as the orthography is concerned. However, to facilitate identification for the learner, we are listing the forms with *Hatafim* separately here.

Examples

יש היום מכוניות הבנויות ל**עֲצִירָה** אוטומטית כאשר הנהג מגיע קרוב מדיי למכונית שלפניו.
Today some cars are built with automatic **stopping/braking** when the driver approaches the car ahead of him too closely.

שלטונות ה**הֲגִירָה** במדינות רבות מנסים להתמודד עם ניסיונות של פליטי מלחמה ודיכוי לקבל מקלט מדיני ועם התנגדות חלק גדול מן הציבור לקליטתם.
The **immigration** authorities in many countries are attempting to deal with attempts of refugees of war and of oppression to get political asylum, and with objection of considerable segments of the public to their absorption.

מעניין לבדוק אצל כל נשיא למי הוא מחליט לתת **חֲנִינָה**, ועל בסיס אילו שיקולים.
It is interesting to examine to whom each president grants **amnesty**, and based on what considerations.

אומרים שלא בריא לאכול ב**עֲמִידָה**.. They say that it is not healthy to eat while **standing**.

תפילת ה**עֲמִידָה** קרויה גם תפילת שמונה עשרה.
The **Amidah** (while **standing**) is also called "the Prayer of Eighteen Benedictions".

לעתים קרובות נראה לי שהמשטרה אינה מנסה אפילו ליישם **אֲכִיפָה** של חוקי התנועה על נהיגה באופנוע – אולי משום שהשוטרים יודעים שהסיכוי שלהם להדביק את האופנוענים הוא די קטן...
It often seems to me that the police does not even try to apply **enforcement** of traffic laws on motor bike operators – perhaps because they realize that their chance of catching up with the bikers is slim…

יש מנהיגים פוליטיים המגיבים על כל מצב העומד בפניהם באופן ספונטני, מבלי לתת הזדמנות לתהליך ה**חֲשִׁיבָה** להתחיל לפעול.
Some political leaders react to any situation facing them spontaneously, without giving the **thought process** an opportunity to begin to operate.

המחירים שלוקחים מרבית חנויות המזון ה"טבעי" וה"בריא" נראים לי תמיד כ**עֲשִׁיקָה** של הציבור.
The prices charged by stores of "natural" and "healthy" food always strike me as **exploitation/robbery** of the public.

Special Expressions

deception **אֲחִיזַת** עיניים
over**eating** **אֲכִילָה** גסה
exhaustion **אֲפִיסַת** כוחות
urinary **retention** **אֲצִירַת** שתן
gift **wrapping** **אֲרִיזַת** מתנה
internal **migration** **הֲגִירָה** פנימית
going with the flow **הֲלִיכָה** בתלם
tour **package** **חֲבִילַת** נופש

sight for sore eyes **חֲגִיגָה** לעיניים
bowel **obstruction** **חֲסִימַת** מעיים
systems **thinking** **חֲשִׁיבָה** מערכתית
blood **libel** **עֲלִילַת** דם
middle age גיל **הָעֲמִידָה**
closing of eyes **עֲצִימַת** עיניים
drought (= **stopping** of rain) **עֲצִירַת** גשמים

Additional Examples in this Pattern

hoarding אֲגִירָה
hold, grasp N אֲחִיזָה
eating אֲכִילָה
keeping safe; retention אֲצִירָה
packing, wrapping אֲרִיזָה
migration, immigration הֲגִירָה
walking; a walk הֲלִיכָה
killing הֲרִיגָה
destroying הֲרִיסָה
parcel, package חֲבִילָה

celebration חֲגִיגָה
penetration חֲדִירָה
leasing חֲכִירָה
evasion, escape חֲמִיקָה
pardoning, amnesty חֲנִינָה
blocking; blockade חֲסִימָה
leaving, departure עֲזִיבָה
plot, story עֲלִילָה
closing of eye(s) עֲצִימָה

---

3. *CCiCa* = *CiCa* when the second root consonant is *w/y*

our/your/their	my/your/his/her	const.	Gloss	sing/pl
טִיסָתֵנוּ/**טִיסַתְ**כֶם/כֶן/**טִיסָתָ**ם/ן	**טִיסָ**תִי/תְךָ/תֵךְ/תוֹ/תָהּ	טִיסַת-	flying; flight	טִיסָה נ׳
טִיסוֹתֵינוּ/כֶם/כֶן/הֶם/הֶן	**טִיסוֹ**תַי/תֶיךָ/תַיִךְ/תָיו/תֶיהָ	טִיסוֹת-		טִיסוֹת

When the second consonant of the root is *w* or *y*, the *CCiCa* pattern is realized as (or "weakened" into) *CiCa*. Also included here are items like סִיעָה 'faction; group' and סִירָה 'boat,' which etymologically cannot be related to any root.

Examples

שלוש **טִיסוֹת** של ״אל על״ בוטלו היום בשל מזג האוויר הסוער.
Three El Al **flights** were cancelled today because of the stormy weather.

יתרונו של הטיול המאורגן הוא בכך שהחברה דואגת מראש לסידורי **לִינָה** נאותים.
The advantage of an organized tour is that the company takes care of proper **lodging** arrangements ahead of time.

צִיפָה היא היכולת לצוף על פני המים.
Buoyancy is the capability to float

Special Expressions

בִּיאַת המשיח **coming** of the Messiah
בִּינָה מלאכותית artificial **intelligence**
טִיסָה ישירה direct **flight**
רִיצַת מרתון Marathon (**run**)

Additional Examples in this Pattern

בִּיאָה coming; sexual intercourse
בִּינָה understanding, wisdom
גִּיחָה trip; sortie
טִינָה grudge, bitterness
מִילָה circumcision
מִיתָה death
סִיכָה anointing; lubrication
סִיעָה faction; group
סִירָה boat
קִימָה arising; getting up
רִיצָה running; a run
שִׁיבָה return, homecoming
שִׂיחָה conversation; talk

---

4. *CCiCa* = *CCiya* when the third root consonant is *y*

our/your/their	my/your/his/her	const.	Gloss	sing/pl
בְּנִיָּתֵנוּ/**בְּנִיַּתְ**כֶם/כֶן/**בְּנִיָּתָ**ם/ן	**בְּנִיָּתִ**י/תְךָ/תֵךְ/תוֹ/תָהּ	בְּנִיַּת-	building	בְּנִיָּה נ׳
בְּנִיּוֹתֵינוּ/כֶם/כֶן/הֶם/הֶן	**בְּנִיּוֹ**תַי/תֶיךָ/תַיִךְ/תָיו/תֶיהָ	בְּנִיּוֹת-	(gerund)	בְּנִיּוֹת

When the third consonant of the root is *y* (at the end of the word usually marked by a silent *h*), the *i* of *CCiCa* and the *y* of the root are merged into a single *yod*. The merger is orthographically marked by a *dagesh forte* – a marker of a (historically) longer, or doubled, consonant, a lengthening/doubling which no longer applies in Israeli Hebrew.

Examples

תושבי האזור מתנגדים ל**בְנִיַּת** רבי-קומות בשכונותיהם.
The residents of the region object to the **building** of high rises in their neighborhoods.

נְהִיָּתָם של ההמונים אחרי מנהיגים דמגוגיים מסבירה את הצלחתם של מטורפים כמו היטלר.
The tendency of the masses for **following** demagogic leaders accounts for the success of insane ones like Hitler.

לאחרונה הקימו מרכז **קְנִיּוֹת** גדול לצד הנהר המזרחי במזרח הארלם.
Recently they built a large **shopping** center next to the East River in East Harlem.

Special Expressions

בְּנִיָּה טרומית prefabricated **construction**
בְּכִיָּה לדורות (**crying**=) tragedy forever
כְּפִיָּה דתית religious **coercion**
נְטִיָּה מגנטית magnetic **variation**
סְטִיַּת תקן standard **deviation**
פְּנִיַּת פרסה u-**turn**
קְנִיָּה בהמרה trade-in

Additional Examples in this Pattern

בְּכִיָּה crying, weeping
גְּבִיָּה collection of taxes, dues
דְּאִיָּה gliding
דְּחִיָּה postponement; rejection

winning; win זְכִיָּה
erring, mistaking טְעִיָּה
shot; shooting יְרִיָּה
coercion; compulsion כְּפִיָּה
tendency; trend נְטִיָּה
mongoose; ferret נְמִיָּה

deviation; digression סְטִיָּה
turn; application פְּנִיָּה
grilling, roasting צְלִיָּה
swimming; a swim שְׂחִיָּה
drinking; a drink שְׁתִיָּה

---

5. *CCiya* = *CaCiya* when the 3rd consonant is *y* and the 1st one is a guttural

our/your/their	my/your/his/her	const.	Gloss	sing/pl
עֲלִיָּתֵנוּ/**עֲלִיַּתְ**כֶם/כֶן/**עֲלִיָּתָ**ם/ן	**עֲלִיָּ**תִי/תְךָ/תֵךְ/תוֹ/תָהּ	עֲלִיַּת-	ascent;	עֲלִיָּה נ׳
עֲלִיּוֹתֵינוּ/כֶם/כֶן/הֶם/הֶן	**עֲלִיּוֹ**תַי/תֶיךָ/תַיִךְ/תָיו/תֶיהָ	עֲלִיּוֹת-	immigration	עֲלִיּוֹת

When the third consonant in *CCiCa* is *y*, and the first is guttural, a *Hataf-pataH* hiatus is inserted, i.e., the vowel *a*: עֲלִיָּה < עְלִיָּה* 'ascent; immigration to Israel,' עֲלִיָּתִי, etc.

Examples

ה**עֲלִיָּה** הרוסית לישראל לאחר שברית המועצות פתחה את שעריה נקלטה מהר יותר וטוב יותר ממרבית ה**עֲלִיּוֹת** האחרות.

The Russian **immigration** to Israel after the Soviet Union had opened its gates was absorbed faster and better than most other **immigrations**.

אחת הסיבות המרכזיות להצלחתם של מרכזי הקניות הגדולים היא מגרשי ה**חֲנִיָּה** (~ **חֲנָיָה** בד"כ במדוברת) הגדולים שבצידם.

One of the main reasons for the success of the large shopping centers is the big **parking** lots alongside them (coll. generally חֲנָיָה).

אתם מעדיפים תנור **אֲפִיָּה** חשמלי, או כזה שפועל על גז?

Do you prefer an electric **baking** oven, or one that operates on gas?

Special Expressions

עֲלִיָּה לרגל pilgrimage

עֲלִיָּה לתורה being called to read from the Torah in synagogue

Additional Examples in this Pattern

pronunciation הֲגִיָּה

division, splitting חֲצִיָּה

making, doing עֲשִׂיָּה

B. *CoCeC* and related *mishkalim*

6. *CoCeC* nouns and adjectives, often related to *pa`al* (*CaCaC*)

our/your/their	my/your/his/her	const.	Gloss	sing/pl
שׁוֹמְרֵנוּ/**שׁוֹמֶרְ**כֶם/כֶן/**שׁוֹמְרָ**ם/ן	שׁוֹמְרִי/שׁוֹמֶרְךָ/**שׁוֹמְ**רֵךְ/רוֹ/רָהּ	שׁוֹמֵר-	guard,	שׁוֹמֵר ז׳
שׁוֹמְרֵינוּ/כֶם/כֶן/הֶם/הֶן	**שׁוֹמְ**רַי/רֶיךָ/רַיִךְ/רָיו/רֶיהָ	שׁוֹמְרֵי-	keeper (m.)	שׁוֹמְרִים

our/your/their	my/your/his/her	const.	Gloss	sing/pl
שׁוֹמַרְתֵּנוּ/תְּכֶם/תְּכֶן/תָּם/תָּן	**שׁוֹמַרְ**תִּי/תְּךָ/תֵּךְ/תּוֹ/תָּהּ	-שׁוֹמֶרֶת	guard,	שׁוֹמֶרֶת נ׳
שׁוֹמְרוֹתֵינוּ/כֶם/כֶן/הֶם/הֶן	**שׁוֹמְרוֹ**תַי/תֶיךָ/תַיִךְ/תָיו/תֶיהָ	-שׁוֹמְרוֹת	keeper (f.)	שׁוֹמְרוֹת

CoCeC, usually the present participle of the *pa`al binyan*, is a (mostly) agentive pattern for nouns, as in the illustration above, or for adjectives, as in the case below:

Gloss	const.	Plural	const.	sing.
dark; gloomy; scowling	-קוֹדְרֵי	קוֹדְרִים	-קוֹדֵר	קוֹדֵר ז׳
	-קוֹדְרוֹת	קוֹדְרוֹת	- קוֹדֶרֶת	קוֹדֶרֶת נ׳

And in many cases, it can designate either a noun or an adjective. חוֹזֵר, for instance, is either a noun meaning 'returning person,' or 'a circular,' or functions as an adjective meaning 'repeated,' or 'repeating oneself' (i.e., as in the 'reflexive' grammatical category.) Because of the difficulty of making clear categorical distinctions, all *CoCeC* realizations will be grouped together.

The second vowel of the base undergoes reduction before a stressed suffix. If as a result of reduction, an impermissible sequence of two *shva* mobiles would have been formed, the base vowel will only undergo partial reduction, *tsere* to *seghol* (or *seghol* to *pataH* in the feminine declension), and a closed syllable is formed: -שׁוֹ < שׁוֹ-מְרֶ-ךָ* < שׁוֹמֶרְךָ* מֶרְ-ךָ. When the third root consonant is א׳, that א׳ is "silent" in the fem. Sing. form: קוֹרֵאת 'reader, f.s.'

Examples

בישראל עומד **שׁוֹמֵר** בפתחו של כל מבנה ציבורי.
In today's Israel, a **guard** is posted at the entrance of every public building.

ככל שפוחתים הסיכויים לשלום, כן נעשית האווירה בישראל יותר ויותר **קוֹדֶרֶת**.
The lesser the prospects for peace decrease, the **gloomi**er the atmosphere in Israel gets.

סגן-המנהל שלח לכל העובדים **חוֹזֵר** המפרט את נוהלי העבודה החדשים.
The vice-president sent a **circular** to all employees, with details of the new work procedures.

ממשלת ישראל מעניקה הטבות מיוחדות ל**חוֹזְרִים**, כדי לעודדם לחזור ארצה.
The Israeli government offers special incentives to **returnees**, to encourage them to come back to Israel.

Special Expressions

"ה**שׁוֹמֵר**" Jewish watchmen's org. in pre-Israel Palestine

שׁוֹמֵר חינם trustee, unpaid keeper

שׁוֹמֵר ישראל Watch of Israel (God)

Additional Examples in this Pattern

אוֹגֵר hamster

אוֹיֵב enemy; opponent

אוֹמֵן foster parent

אוֹצֵר curator

weaver אוֹרֵג
packer אוֹרֵז
traitor בּוֹגֵד
graduate בּוֹגֵר
lonely; alone; isolated person בּוֹדֵד
prominent; outstanding; obvious; salient בּוֹלֵט
cowboy בּוֹקֵר
dying person גּוֹסֵס
cause, factor; element גּוֹרֵם
sweeping, comprehensive גּוֹרֵף
tow truck גּוֹרֵר
spokesperson; speaker of a language דּוֹבֵר
fair; reasonable הוֹגֵן
hedonist, licentious person הוֹלֵל

---

7. *CoCeC* nouns and adjectives, often related to *pa`al*, when the second consonant is a guttural

our/your/their	my/your/his/her	const.	Gloss	sing/pl
אוֹהֲבֵנוּ/**אוֹהַבְ**כֶם/כֶן/**אוֹהֲבָ**ם/ן	אוֹהֲבִי/אוֹהַבְךָ/**אוֹהֲ**בֵךְ/בוֹ/בָהּ	אוֹהֵב-	lover,	אוֹהֵב ז'
אוֹהֲבֵינוּ/כֶם/כֶן/הֶם/הֶן	**אוֹהֲ**בַי/בֶיךָ/בַיִךְ/בָיו/בֶיהָ	אוֹהֲבֵי-	devotee	אוֹהֲבִים

When the second consonant of the root is a guttural, the vowel *a* is added after it (orthographically: *Hataf pataH*) when it occurs syllable-finally: אוֹהֵב 'fan' ~ *אוֹהְ-בִים 'lovers' > אוֹ-הֲ-בִים, since it is hard (or was hard historically) to close a syllable (as expected in the declension) with a guttural. Forms like אוֹ-הַבְ-כֶם result from the difficulty of articulating a *Hataf-shva* sequence within the same syllable, but instead of a *seghol*, as in שׁוֹ-מֶרְ-ךָ above, the (originally) low gutturals prefer the low vowel *a*.

Examples

על גדות הסינה ניתן לראות כל ערב הרבה זוגות **אוֹהֲבִים**.
On the banks of the Seine one can see many **lover**-couples every evening.

Special Expressions

belligerent person **אוֹהֵב** מלחמה
peace **lover** **אוֹהֵב** שלום

Additional Examples in this Pattern

supporter, adherent; fan אוֹהֵד
skunk בּוֹאֵשׁ
glittery, shining בּוֹהֵק
examiner, inspector בּוֹחֵן
voter, selector בּוֹחֵר
burning; urgent Coll בּוֹעֵר
savior, redeemer גּוֹאֵל
raging, stormy גּוֹעֵשׁ
cause, factor; element גּוֹרֵם
worried; caring, concerned דּוֹאֵג
reptile זוֹחֵל
angry, furious זוֹעֵם
miller טוֹחֵן
consultant, adviser יוֹעֵץ
painful כּוֹאֵב
fighter, soldier לוֹחֵם
circumciser מוֹהֵל
crushing, smashing; decisive מוֹחֵץ
speaker נוֹאֵם

---

8. ***CoCeC*** nouns/adjectives, often related to *pa`al*, when the third root consonant is א׳

our/your/their	my/your/his/her	const.	Gloss	sing/pl
רוֹפְאֵנוּ/**רוֹפַאֲ**כֶם/כֶן/**רוֹפְאָ**ם/ן	רוֹפְאִי/רוֹפַאֲךָ/**רוֹפְאֵ**ךְ/אוֹ/אָהּ	רוֹפֵא-	doctor,	רוֹפֵא ז׳
רוֹפְאֵינוּ/כֶם/כֶן/הֶם/הֶן	**רוֹפְאַ**י/אֶיךָ/אַיִךְ/אָיו/אֶיהָ	רוֹפְאֵי-	physician	רוֹפְאִים

When the third consonant of the root is א׳, the vowel *a* is added after it (orthographically: *Hataf pataH*) when it occurs syllable-finally: רוֹ-פַ-אֲ-ךָ > רוֹ-פֵא-ךָ*, since it is hard (or was hard historically) to close a syllable with a guttural; the *tsere* assimilates to the *pataH* of the *Hataf-pataH* to facilitate articulation.

Examples

בארצות מתפתחות יש הרבה כפרים שאין בהם אפילו **רוֹפֵא** אחד.
In developing countries there are many villages without even a single **doctor**.

Special Expressions

consult **doctors** דרש **בְּרוֹפְאִים** veterinarian **רוֹפֵא** בהמות witch **doctor** **רוֹפֵא** אליל

Additional Examples in this Pattern

creator בּוֹרֵא
sinner חוֹטֵא
carrier נוֹשֵׂא
reader; type of desert bird קוֹרֵא
hater, enemy שׂוֹנֵא

---

9. ***CoCeC*** nouns/adjectives, often related to *pa`al*, when the 3rd consonant is ה׳, ח׳, ע׳

our/your/their	my/your/his/her	const.	Gloss	sing/pl
רוֹצְחֵנוּ/**רוֹצַחֲ**כֶם/כֶן/**רוֹצְחָ**ם/ן	רוֹצְחִי/רוֹצַחֲךָ/**רוֹצְחֵ**ךְ/חוֹ/חָהּ	רוֹצֵחַ-	murderer	רוֹצֵחַ ז׳
רוֹצְחֵינוּ/כֶם/כֶן/הֶם/הֶן	**רוֹצְחַ**י/חֶיךָ/חַיִךְ/חָיו/חֶיהָ	רוֹצְחֵי-		רוֹצְחִים

As in the case of א׳ above, when the third root consonant of the root is a guttural, the vowel *a* is added after it (orthographically: *Hataf pataH*) when it occurs syllable-finally: רוֹ-צַ-חֲ-ךָ > רוֹ-צֵח-ךָ*, since it is hard to close a syllable with a guttural; the *tsere* assimilates to the *pataH* of the *Hataf-pataH* to facilitate articulation. Additionally, when the third root consonant is ה׳, ח׳, ע׳, and occurs at the end of the word after a vowel that is not *a*, it comes with a "furtive *pataH*": רוֹצֵחַ, פּוֹשֵׁעַ. Note: in the case of word-final א׳ above (רוֹפֵא etc.), no "furtive *pataH*" is added. It was listed separately above, just this time, to show the difference; in other similar patterns, just remember that word-final א׳ is subject to the same rules as the other gutturals, but takes no "furtive *pataH*."

Examples

בארצות שבהן קיים עדיין עונש מוות על רֶצַח, הקושי הגדול הוא להחליט אם להחילו על **רוֹצֵחַ** שאינו שפוי בדעתו.
In countries the death penalty for murder still exists, the biggest difficulty is whether to apply it to an insane **murderer**.

Special Expressions

פּוֹשֵׁעַ מלחמה war **criminal** **שׁוֹמֵעַ** חופשי auditor

Additional Examples in this Pattern

אוֹרֵחַ guest, visitor
מוֹנֵעַ preventative
מוֹתֵחַ thrilling, suspenseful
נוֹבֵעַ flowing; stemming
נוֹכֵחַ attendee
נוֹסֵעַ passenger
צוֹלֵעַ lame, limping
צוֹמֵחַ plants, vegetation
קוֹלֵעַ on-the-mark
רוֹקֵחַ pharmacist

---

10. *CoCeC* = *CoCe*, when the third root consonant is *y*: *CoCe*

our/your/their	my/your/his/her	const.	Gloss	sing/pl
קוֹנֵנוּ/נְכֶם/נְכֶן/נָם/נָן	**קוֹ**נִי/נְךָ/נֵךְ/נוֹ (נֵהוּ) /נָהּ (נֶהָ)	-קוֹנֵה	buyer, customer	קוֹנֶה ז׳
קוֹנֵינוּ/כֶם/כֶן/הֶם/הֶן	**קוֹ**נַי/נֶיךָ/נַיִךְ/נָיו/נֶיהָ	-קוֹנֵי	(m.)	קוֹנִים

When the third consonant of the root is *y* (orthographically represented as a silent *he*), the *CoCeC* pattern is realized as *CoCe*. Here too, a form can function as a noun, as an adjective, or both. קוֹנֶה 'customer' above is a noun, דּוֹחֶה 'repulsive' can only function as an adjective, and שׁוֹטֶה is either 'a fool' or 'idiotic/mad/rabid.'

Examples

בשל המצב הכלכלי הקשה, יש היום הרבה פחות **קוֹנִים** ברוב החנויות.
Because of the difficult economic situation, there are fewer **customers** in most stores today.

כל מי שפוגש אותו בפעם הראשונה, סולד ממראהו ה**דּוֹחֶה**, אבל מי שמכיר אותו היטב מבין שהוא אדם נהדר.
Whoever meets him for the first time is appalled by his **repulsive** appearance, but those who know him well realize that he is a wonderful man.

הנשיא ההוא אולי לא היה מחכמי הדור, אבל בוודאי אינו **שׁוֹטֶה**.
That president may not have been very wise, but he was certainly not **stupid**.

לא ברור בדיוק למה, אבל אלוהים שומר על ה**שׁוֹטִים**...
It is exactly clear why, but God takes care of **fool**s...

Special Expressions

מוֹרֵה דרך tour **guide**
מוֹרֵה הוראה **Rabbi**, **judge**
מוֹרֵה נבוכים **Guide** to the Perplexed (by Maimonides)
מוֹרַי ורבותי addressing an audience (formal)
מוֹרֵנוּ "our **teacher**," respectful form of address to learned Jews

Additional Examples in this Pattern

אוֹפֶה baker
בּוֹנֶה builder; beaver

collector, esp. of taxes גּוֹבֶה
exiled person גּוֹלֶה
thinker, philosopher הוֹגֶה
daydreamer הוֹזֶה
parent הוֹרֶה
seer/prophet; contract חוֹזֶה
patient; sick person חוֹלֶה
bisector חוֹצֶה

miner כּוֹרֶה
borrower לוֹוֶה
immigrant to Israel עוֹלֶה
productive; fruitful פּוֹרֶה
scout, guard צוֹפֶה
shepherd רוֹעֶה
different שׁוֹנֶה

---

11. *CoCéCet: CoCeC+et* (fem.)

our/your/their	my/your/his/her	const.	Gloss	sing/pl
צוֹלַלְתֵּנוּ/תְּכֶם/תְּכֶן/תָּם/תָּן	**צוֹלַלְ**תִּי/תְּךָ/תֵּךְ/תּוֹ/תָּהּ	צוֹלֶלֶת-	submarine	צוֹלֶלֶת נ׳
צוֹלְלוֹתֵינוּ/כֶם/כֶן/הֶם/הֶן	**צוֹלְלוֹ**תַי/תֶיךָ/תַיִךְ/תָיו/תֶיהָ	צוֹלְלוֹת-		צוֹלְלוֹת

Included are only independent forms that do not constitute feminine counterparts of *CoCeC.*

Examples

עד לשלב די מאוחר במלחמת העולם השניה, **הצוֹלְלוֹת** הגרמניות שלטו שליטה מלאה באוקיינוס האטלנטי וגרמו נזקים חמורים לספינות בעלות הברית.
Until fairly late in WWII, German **submarines** virtually ruled the Atlantic Ocean, and caused great damage to Allied ships.

בזמנו, משפחות בעלות אמצעים נהגו להעסיק **אוֹמֶנֶת**; היום אפילו משפחות עשירות משתמשות במעונות יום לילדיהן.
At the time, families of means would often employ a **nanny**; today even well-off families use day care centers for their children.

בישראל יש לפחות שני בתי חולים מיוחדים **ליוֹלְדוֹת** בלבד.
In Israel there are at least two specialized hospitals for **women giving birth**.

לעוֹפֶרֶת יש שימושים חשובים בתעשיה, אבל היום ידוע שהיא רעילה, ושהיא מזיקה למערכת העצבים, בעיקר אצל ילדים.
Lead has important uses in industry, but today it is known that it is toxic, and can cause damage to the nerve system, especially in children.

Special Expressions

nuclear **submarine** **צוֹלֶלֶת** גרעינית

Additional Examples in this Pattern

tugboat גּוֹרֶרֶת
bird hatching eggs דּוֹגֶרֶת

sucker, young shoot (bot.) יוֹנֶקֶת
lead [no pl.] עוֹפֶרֶת

---

12. *CoCéCet*: *CoCeC+et* (fem.), where the second root consonant is guttural

our/your/their	my/your/his/her	const.	Gloss	sing/pl
טוֹחַנְתֵּנוּ/תְּכֶם/תְּכֶן/תָּם/תָּן	**טוֹחַנְ**תִּי/תְּךָ/תֵּךְ/תּוֹ/תָּהּ	טוֹחֶנֶת-	molar	טוֹחֶנֶת נ׳
טוֹחֲנוֹתֵינוּ/כֶם/כֶן/הֶם/הֶן	**טוֹחֲנוֹ**תַי/תֶיךָ/תַיִךְ/תָיו/תֶיהָ	טוֹחֲנוֹת-	tooth	טוֹחֲנוֹת

As in צוֹלֶלֶת above, but when a *shva* is expected with a guttural, it is replaced by *Hataf-pataH.*

Examples

השיניים ה**טוֹחֲנוֹת** מתכלות מהר יחסית, מכיוון שהן עושות את מרבית עבודת הלעיסה.
The **molar teeth** wear out relatively fast, since they do most of the chewing work.

בכל כוורת, תפקיד ה**פּוֹעֲלוֹת** הוא לבנות את חלות הדבש, לאסוף צוף, ולשרת את המלכה.
In every beehive, the role of the **worker bees** is to build the honeycomb, to collect nectar, and to serve the queen.

---

13. *CoCéCet* with *kamats* in the plural isolation form

our/your/their	my/your/his/her	const.	Gloss	sing/pl
כּוֹתַרְתֵּנוּ/תְּכֶם/תְּכֶן/תָּם/תָּן	**כּוֹתַרְ**תִּי/תְּךָ/תֵּךְ/תּוֹ/תָּהּ	כּוֹתֶרֶת-	heading;	כּוֹתֶרֶת נ׳
כּוֹתְרוֹתֵינוּ/כֶם/כֶן/הֶם/הֶן	**כּוֹתְרוֹ**תַי/תֶיךָ/תַיִךְ/תָיו/תֶיהָ	כּוֹתְרוֹת-	corolla	כּוֹתָרוֹת

In the plural isolation form, the second root consonant comes with a *kamats* (like the plural forms of the segholate*s*), which is reduced to *shva* in all other plural forms.

Examples

יש שחקנים שיוצאים מדעתם אם שמם לא מופיע כל שבוע ב**כּוֹתְרוֹת** העיתונים.
There are actors who go nuts if their name does not appear every week in the press **headlines**.

קצהו העליון, המקושט, של עמוד נקרא **כּוֹתֶרֶת**.
The upper part, decorative, of a column is called **כּוֹתֶרֶת**.

מעגל עלי הפרח נקרא **כּוֹתֶרֶת**.
The circle of petals at the head of a flower is called **corolla**.

אספני בולים רציניים תמיד מעדיפים בולים יקרי ערך עם **חוֹתֶמֶת**.
Serious stamp collectors always prefer stamps with postal **stamp**.

ה**בּוֹלֶשֶׁת** ברוסיה של היום מפחידה ומסוכנת היום לא פחות מזו של התקופה הסובייטית.
Today's **secret police** in Russia is just as scary and as dangerous as the one of the Soviet era.

Special Expressions

wax **seal** **חוֹתֶמֶת** שעווה

ball-shaped head of a column; crowning achievement גולת ה**כּוֹתֶרֶת**

hall**mark**; **seal** of approval **חוֹתֶמֶת** איכות

rubber **stamp** **חוֹתֶמֶת** גומי

family tree, genealogy, pedigree **שׁוֹשֶׁלֶת** יוחסין

Additional Examples in this Pattern

legging חוֹתֶלֶת
viola כּוֹנֶרֶת
shoulder strap כּוֹתֶפֶת
palm dove, wild pigeon צוֹצֶלֶת
dynasty שׁוֹשֶׁלֶת
rosette (bot.) שׁוֹשֶׁנֶת

---

14. ***CoCCut***, abstract noun related to *CoCeC*

our/your/their	my/your/his/her	const.	Gloss	sing/pl
סוֹכְנוּתֵנוּ/תְכֶם/תְכֶן/תָם/תָן	**סוֹכְנוּ**תִי/תְךָ/תֵךְ/תוֹ/תָהּ	סוֹכְנוּת-	agency	סוֹכְנוּת נ׳
סוֹכְנוּיוֹתֵינוּ/כֶם/כֶן/הֶם/הֶן	**סוֹכְנוּיוֹ**תַי/תֶיךָ/תַיִךְ/תָיו/תֶיהָ	סוֹכְנוּיוֹת-		סוֹכְנוּיוֹת

The *CoCCut* pattern is a pattern of abstract nouns related to the present participle form of *pa`al*, *CoCeC*, occasionally from *pi`el*, and historically apparently derived linearly from it, with concomitant phonetically-motivated reduction of the *tsere* before a stressed suffix, but one can also argue that since today this reduction is not truly phonetic, we are dealing here with a **discontinuous** derivation in the *CoCCut mishkal*.

Examples

אנשים רבים מעדיפים שלא לרכוש מכוניות היום אלא לשכור אותן; **סוֹכְנוּיוֹת** רבות למכירת מכוניות נמצאות היום במשבר.
Many people today prefer not to buy cars but to rent/lease them; many car sales **agencies** are in trouble.

יונתן הודיע למפקדו שהוא מעוניין לעבור קורס **חוֹבְשׁוּת**; תמיד רצה להיות חובש בשירותו הצבאי.
Jonathan notified his commanding officer that he is interested in taking **medic training course**; he has always wanted to serve as a medic during his army service.

האולימפיאדה נפתחה ב**נוֹכְחוּת** נשיא המדינה, ראש הממשלה וכל חברי הפרלמנט.
The Olympic Games were opened in the **presence** of the President, the Prime Minister, and all members of Parliament.

אנשים שהכירו את סאדאת סיפרו שברגע שהגיע היית מייד חש ב**נוֹכְחוּתוֹ** המרשימה.
Those who knew Sadat reported that as soon as he arrived, you would immediately sense his impressive **presence**.

בכיתות מסוימות באוניברסיטה המרצים מקיימים בדיקת **נוֹכְחוּת**.
In some classes at the university lecturers conduct **attendance** check.

Special Expressions

the Jewish Agency **הסוֹכְנוּת** היהודית

Additional Examples in this Pattern

enmity, hatred, hostility אוֹיְבוּת
prominence, standing out בּוֹלְטוּת
cattle raising בּוֹקְרוּת
unruly conduct (*tsere* stable) הוֹלֵלוּת

seamanship **חוֹבְלוּת**
tutoring, coaching; mentoring **חוֹנְכוּת**
alertness, readiness **כּוֹנְנוּת**
fraud **נוֹכְלוּת**

Jewish guard unit in British police during British mandate **נוֹטְרוּת**
hostility **עוֹיְנוּת**
gold and silver crafting **צוֹרְפוּת**
pharmacy science **רוֹקְחוּת**

C. *CaCuC* and related *mishkalim*

15. *CaCuC*: passive participle often related to *pa`al*

Gloss	const.	Plural	const.	.sing
suntanned	-שְׁזוּפֵי	שְׁזוּפִים	-שְׁזוּף	שָׁזוּף ז'
	שְׁזוּפוֹת	שְׁזוּפוֹת	-שְׁזוּפַת	שְׁזוּפָה נ'

CaCuC is a passive participle form, generally of *pa`al*, serving mostly as an adjective, but occasionally also denotes nouns characterized by these adjectives. פָּצוּעַ, for instance, is both 'wounded (adj.)' or 'a wounded person.' When a stressed suffix is added, the *kamats* is reduced to *shva*.

Examples

בישראל רבים אוכלים בשר בקר **קָפוּא**. בשר בקר טרי יקר למדיי.
In Israel many eat **frozen** beef; fresh beef is rather expensive.

בימי חמישי האוטובוסים בישראל מלאים **וּצְפוּפִים**; המוני חיילים בחופשה חוזרים מבסיסיהם הביתה.
On Thursdays the buses in Israel are full and **crowded**; multitudes of soldiers on leave come back home from their bases.

Special Expressions

the third section of the Hebrew Bible after Pentateuch and Prophets **כְּתוּבִים**
prejudice, preconceived idea דעה **קְדוּמָה**

In some instances, the *CaCuC* form refers to nouns only, as in:

our/your/their	my/your/his/her	const.	Gloss	sing/pl
פְּסוּקֵנוּ/קְכֶם/קְכֶן/קָם/קָן	**פְּסוּ**קִי/קְךָ/קֵךְ/קוֹ/קָהּ	-פְּסוּק	(Bible) verse;	פָּסוּק ז'
פְּסוּקֵינוּ/כֶם/כֶן/הֶם/הֶן	**פְּסוּ**קַי/קֶיךָ/קַיִךְ/קָיו/קֶיהָ	-פְּסוּקֵי	sentence	פְּסוּקִים

Examples

באזכרות בבית הקברות, נהוג לומר **פְּסוּקֵי** תהילים המתחילים בכל אחת מן האותיות של שם הנפטר.
In memorial services at the cemetery, it is customary to recite **verses** from Psalms that start with each of the letters in the name of the deceased.

Special Expressions

Bible scholar בעל **פָּסוּק**

tell me your opinion פסוק לי **פְּסוּקְךָ**

סוף **פָּסוּק** sign marking end of a biblical verse; enough!

פְּסוּקֵי דזמרא psalms recited before morning prayer

When the third consonant is י׳, the sub-*mishkal* will be *CaCuy*, but no separate pattern is needed, since the declension is identical to that of *CaCuC*:

our/your/their	my/your/his/her	const.	Gloss	sing/pl
שְׁבוּיֵנוּ/קֶכֶם/קְכֶן/קָם/קָן	**שְׁבוּ**יִי/יְךָ/יֵךְ/יוֹ/יָהּ	שְׁבוּי-	prisoner; captive	שָׁבוּי ז׳
שְׁבוּיֵינוּ/כֶם/כֶן/הֶם/הֶן	**שְׁבוּ**יַי/יֶיךָ/יַיִךְ/יָיו/יֶיהָ	שְׁבוּיֵי-		שְׁבוּיִים

Examples

ישראל תמיד הייתה מוכנה להקריב הרבה כדי להשיג את שחרורם של **שְׁבוּיֵי** מלחמה.
Israel has always been willing to sacrifice a lot in order to obtain the release of **prisoners** of war.

Special Expressions

פדיון **שְׁבוּיִים** ransom

Additional Examples in this Pattern

בָּדוּק confirmed, checked
בָּנוּי built
בָּרוּךְ blessed
בָּרוּר clear
גָּדוּשׁ full, crammed
גָּזוּר cut; derived
גָּלוּי revealed, open; known
גָּמוּר finished; total
גָּנוּב stolen
גָּרוּר dragged, towed; trailer
גָּרוּשׁ divorced man
גָּשׁוּם rainy
דָּחוּס compressed; tightly packed
זָקוּף erect, straight
טָחוּן ground, minced
טָרוּד busy, occupied

---

16. *CaCuC*: passive participle often related to *pa`al*, when the first consonant is a guttural

our/your/their	my/your/his/her	const.	Gloss	sing/pl
חֲלוּצֵנוּ/צְכֶם/צְכֶן/צָם/צָן	**חֲלוּ**צִי/צְךָ/צֵךְ/צוֹ/צָהּ	חֲלוּץ-	pioneer, first in the	חָלוּץ ז׳
חֲלוּצֵינוּ/כֶם/כֶן/הֶם/הֶן	**חֲלוּ**צַי/צֶיךָ/צַיִךְ/צָיו/צֶיהָ	חֲלוּצֵי-	field; forward (soccer)	חֲלוּצִים

Like שָׁזוּף above, but if the first consonant in *CaCuC* is a guttural, the *shva* expected in the declension will be realized as a *Hataf* in the declension:
חָלוּץ, חֲלוּצִי, חֲלוּצִים, חֲלוּצֵי ‘pioneer.’

Examples

הַ**חֲלוּצִים** הראשונים שבאו לארץ ישראל בשנות השמונים של המאה התשע עשרה קראו לעצמם בילויים, על שם ארגונם, ביל״ו (בית יעקב לכו ונלכה).
The first **pioneers** who came to Palestine in the 1980’s referee to themselves as BILU, after the name of their organization, whose acronym was BILU.

חברת eBay הייתה **חֲלוּצָה** בתחום המכירות הפומביות באינטרנט.
The eBay company was **first in the field** of public auctions on the Internet.

מספר **הַהֲרוּגִים** בתאונות דרכים בישראל ממשיך לעלות כל שנה.
The number of **people killed** in road accidents in Israel continues to climb every year.

בארה״ב וגם בישראל הרבה אנשים טובים מאמצים ומטפלים בכלבים **עֲזוּבִים** או כאלה שבעליהם התעללו בהם.
In the US as well as in Israel, many good people adopt and take care of **abandoned** dogs or those whose owners abused.

Special Expressions

beloved **אֲהוּב** ליבו
heartless **אֲטוּם** לב
do something against one's better judgment **אָנוּס** על-פי הדיבור
wretched people, Les Misérables (French, Hugo) **עֲלוּבֵי** החיים

Additional Examples in this Pattern

lost; hopeless אָבוּד
beloved; popular אָהוּב
sealed; opaque אָטוּם
eaten; corroded אָכוּל
forced; Marrano אָנוּס
mortal, fatal אָנוּשׁ
forbidden אָסוּר
fiancé; engaged אָרוּס
decent, fair; adequate הָגוּן
shocked, stunned הָמוּם
imbued, saturated חָדוּר
kidnapped (person); brief, momentary חָטוּף
wretched, dismal; meager עָלוּב
busy, occupied עָסוּק

---

17. *CaCuC*: passive participle often related to *pa`al*, when the last consonant is a guttural

our/your/their	my/your/his/her	const.	Gloss	sing/pl
פְּצוּעֵנוּ/עֲכֶם/עֲכֶן/עָם/עָן	**פְּצוּ**עִי/עֲךָ/עֵךְ/עוֹ/עָהּ	פְּצוּעַ-	wounded (adj.);	פָּצוּעַ ז׳
פְּצוּעֵינוּ/כֶם/כֶן/הֶם/הֶן	**פְּצוּ**עַי/עֶיךָ/עַיִךְ/עָיו/עֶיהָ	פְּצוּעֵי-	wounded person	פְּצוּעִים
פְּצוּעָתֵנוּ/תְכֶם/תְכֶן/תָם/תָן	**פְּצוּעָ**תִי/תְךָ/תֵךְ/תוֹ/תָהּ	פְּצוּעַת-		פְּצוּעָה נ׳
פְּצוּעוֹתֵינוּ/כֶם/כֶן/הֶם/הֶן	**פְּצוּעוֹ**תַי/תֶיךָ/תַיִךְ/תָיו/תֶיהָ	פְּצוּעוֹת-		פְּצוּעוֹת

Construct	sing/pl	construct	sing/pl	Gloss
שְׁטוּחַת-	שְׁטוּחָה	שְׁטוּחַ-	שָׁטוּחַ ז׳	flat (adj.
שְׁטוּחוֹת-	שְׁטוּחוֹת	שְׁטוּחֵי-	שְׁטוּחִים	only)

When in the *CaCuC mishkal* (שָׁזוּף above) the third root consonant is ה׳, ח׳, ע׳, and it occurs at the end of the word after a vowel that is not *a*, it comes with a "furtive *PataH*": פָּצוּעַ 'wounded; wounded person,' vs. פְּצוּעִי, פְּצוּעִים, פְּצוּעֵי...

Examples

בישראל, מספר ה**פְּצוּעִים** וההרוגים בתאונות דרכים גדול משמעותית ממספר האבדות בפיגועים ובמלחמות.

In Israel, the number of **wounded** and fatalities in road accidents significantly exceeds the number of casualties in terrorist attacks and in wars.

ציידים מקצועיים יודעים שחיה גדולה **פְּצוּעָה** יכולה להיות מסוכנת ביותר, מכיוון שכשהיא נרגזת, שוב אינה מפחדת ונזהרת כמקודם.

Professional hunters know that a large **wounded** animal might be very dangerous, because when angry, it is no longer wary and careful.

Special Expressions

common-law partner **יָדוּעַ** בציבור

in**famous** **יָדוּעַ** לשמצה

herring **דג מָלוּחַ**

brain-**damaged** **פְּגוּעַ** מוחין

a man whose testicles were crushed **פְּצוּעַ** דכה

the **Wild** West המערב ה**פָּרוּעַ**

stable, **fixed** **קָבוּעַ** ועומד

Additional Examples in this Pattern

certain; safe בָּטוּחַ

bad, inferior גָּרוּעַ

known; famous יָדוּעַ

salty, saline מָלוּחַ

stretched, taut; tense, nervous מָתוּחַ

infected, contaminated נָגוּעַ

swollen; inflated נָפוּחַ

damaged, injured; hurt פָּגוּעַ

unkempt; wild, unruly פָּרוּעַ

open פָּתוּחַ

painted; hypocrite; hypocritical צָבוּעַ

modest, humble צָנוּעַ

routine; permanent, fixed קָבוּעַ

torn קָרוּעַ

flat שָׁטוּחַ

---

18. *CCuCa*

our/your/their	my/your/his/her	const.	Gloss	sing/pl
שְׁכוּנָתֵנוּ/**שְׁכוּנַתְ**כֶם/כֶן/**שְׁכוּנָתָ**ם/ן	**שְׁכוּנָ**תִי/תְךָ/תֵךְ/תוֹ/תָהּ	שְׁכוּנַת-	neighborhood	שְׁכוּנָה נ׳
שְׁכוּנוֹתֵינוּ/כֶם/כֶן/הֶם/הֶן	**שְׁכוּנוֹ**תַי/תֶיךָ/תַיִךְ/תָיו/תֶיהָ	שְׁכוּנוֹת-		שְׁכוּנוֹת

CCuCa is used mostly for nouns (feminine). One can generally identify a relationship with some verb form, but the form itself is not always the passive participle of *pa`al*. Automatic feminine counterparts of the *CaCuC* pattern have not been included, unless the masculine base is not obvious (e.g., בְּתוּלָה 'virgin fem.' from rare בָּתוּל).

Examples

ה**שְּׁכוּנָה** הראשונה שהוקמה בתל-אביב היא **שְׁכוּנַת** "נווה צדק".

The first **neighborhood** built in Tel Aviv is the Neve Tsedek **neighborhood**.

ב**שְּׁכוּנָה** שגרתי בה כילד דאגו שלא לעשות רעש בין 2-4 אחרי הצהריים כדי לא להפריע את מנוחת השכנים בזמן ה"סִיֶּסְטָה".

In the **neighborhood** where I lived as a kid, they were careful not to make noise between 2-4 p.m., so as not to disturb the neighbors during their "Siesta" rest.

הרופאים המטפלים בסרטן חוששים יותר מ**גְרוּרוֹת** מאשר מן הגידול עצמו.
Physicians who treat cancer are more worries about **metastases** than they are about the tumor itself.

קְבוּצוֹת תמיכה לחולי סרטן הפכו לחלק אינטגרלי מן הטיפול במחלה.
Support **groups** for cancer patients have become an integral part of the cancer treatment.

קְבוּרָה חילונית נעשית יותר ויותר מקובלת היום בישראל.
Secular **burial** is becoming more and more common in Israel today.

אפילו במדינות דמוקרטיות יש לעיתים מנהיגים הנוהגים כאילו המדינה היא **מְלוּכָה**.
Even in some democracies, there are sometimes leaders who behave as if the state was a **monarchy**.

Special Expressions

גְבוּרָה גדולה very **brave** (sarcastic, Coll.)
צבא הַיְ**שׁוּעָה** the **Salvation** Army
מְלוּכָה פרלמנטרית parliamentary **monarchy**
נְבוּאָה המגשימה את עצמה self-fulfilling **prophecy**
שְׁכוּנוֹת עוני poverty **areas**
פרויקט הַ**שְׁכוּנוֹת** project **Neighborhood** Renewal

Additional Examples in this Pattern

גְבוּרָה courage, bravery
גְלוּיָה postcard
גְלוּלָה tablet, pill
גְלוּפָה plate in printing
יְשׁוּעָה salvation
כְּמוּסָה capsule (med.)
כְּמוּרָה clergy, priesthood
כְּפוּלָה multiple (math)
נְבוּאָה prophesy, prediction
פְּזוּרָה dispersion, diaspora
פְּרוּסָה slice
פְּרוּצָה prostitute

---

19. ***CCuCa* = *CaCuCa***: the realization of *CCuCa* when the first root consonant is a guttural

our/your/their	my/your/his/her	const.	Gloss	sing/pl
אֲרוּחָתֵנוּ/**אֲרוּחַתְ**כֶם/כֶן/**אֲרוּחָתָ**ם/ן	**אֲרוּחָ**תִי/תְךָ/תֵךְ/תוֹ/תָהּ	אֲרוּחַת-	meal	אֲרוּחָה נ'
אֲרוּחוֹתֵינוּ/כֶם/כֶן/הֶם/הֶן	**אֲרוּחוֹ**תַי/תֶיךָ/תַיִךְ/תָיו/תֶיהָ	אֲרוּחוֹת-		אֲרוּחוֹת

Like שְׁכוּנָה above, but when the first consonant in the *CCuCa mishkal* is a guttural, the *shva* is replaced by *Hataf-pataH*: אֲרוּחָה 'meal,' אֲרוּחָתִי...

Examples

חשוב לאכול שלוש **אֲרוּחוֹת** סדירות ביום ולא "לנשנש" ביניהן.
It is important to eat three regular **meals** a day and not to snack between them.

המשרתים ב**עֲתוּדָה** האקדמאית בישראל עוברים את הכשרתם הצבאית בחופשות הקיץ, ומגויסים כקצינים לשירות החובה שלהם לאחר סיום התואר הראשון.
Those who serve in the academic **reserve** (equivalent of the ROTC) in Israel undergo their military training during the summer breaks, and are enlisted as officers for their compulsory army service when they have completed their undergraduate work.

Special Expressions

lunch special **אֲרוּחָה** עסקית
a rich **meal** with high quality food **אֲרוּחַת** שחיתות

Additional Examples in this Pattern

torch אֲבוּקָה
small group of people חֲבוּרָה
option; alternative חֲלוּפָה
tripod חֲצוּבָה
woman unable to get a divorce עֲגוּנָה
neglect עֲזוּבָה
leech עֲלוּקָה
petition עֲצוּמָה
flowerbed עֲרוּגָה

D. *CaCiC* and related *mishkalim*

20. *CaCiC*

Gloss	const.	plural	const.	sing.
breakable, fragile	-שְׁבִירֵי	שְׁבִירִים	-שְׁבִיר	שָׁבִיר ז׳
	-שְׁבִירוֹת	שְׁבִירוֹת	-שְׁבִירַת	שְׁבִירָה נ׳

our/your/their	my/your/his/her	const.	Gloss	sing/pl
פְּקִידֵנוּ/דְכֶם/דְכֶן/דָם/דָן	**פְּקִי**דִי/דְךָ/דֵךְ/דוֹ/דָהּ	-פְּקִיד	clerk, official; (Biblical)	פָּקִיד ז׳
פְּקִידֵינוּ/כֶם/כֶן/הֶם/הֶן	**פְּקִי**דַי/דֶיךָ/דַיִךְ/דָיו/דֶיהָ	-פְּקִידֵי	supervisor, manager	פְּקִידִים
פְּקִידָתֵנוּ/תְכֶם/תְכֶן/תָם/תָן	**פְּקִידָ**תִי/תְךָ/תֵךְ/תוֹ/תָהּ	-פְּקִידַת		פְּקִידָה נ׳
פְּקִידוֹתֵינוּ/כֶם/כֶן/הֶם/הֶן	**פְּקִידוֹ**תַי/תֶיךָ/תַיִךְ/תָיו/תֶיהָ	-פְּקִידוֹת		פְּקִידוֹת

CaCiC often denotes adjectives of the "-able" type, somewhat similar to the passive participle of *pa`al*, meaning "that is subject to the process denoted by the related verb," as in שָׁבַר 'break' > שָׁבִיר 'breakable, fragile.' Occasionally also used for nouns, e.g., יָצִיעַ 'balcony, gallery,' אָרִיחַ 'tile.' When a stressed suffix is added, the *kamats* is reduced to *shva*.

Examples (adjectives)

כששולחים חפצי זכוכית בחבילה באמצעות הדואר, חשוב לכתוב עליה: זהירות, **שָׁבִיר**.
When one sends glass objects by mail, it is important to note on it: **fragile**, handle with care.

חנה נראית רכה ו**שְׁבִירָה**, אבל האמת היא שהיא אישה חזקה מאוד.
Hannah looks soft and **fragile**, but in fact she is a very strong woman.

אורי עובד כמנהל **בָּכִיר** בבנק הפועלים.
Uri works a a **senior** manager in Bank Hapoalim.

בדרך כלל עובדי מוסדות בישראל המשרתים את הציבור יותר **גְּמִישִׁים** מאלה שבארה״ב.
Generally, workers in institutions serving the public in Israel are more **flexible** than their US counterparts.

אנשים המטפלים בחומרים **דְּלִיקִים** חייבים להיות **זְהִירִים** ביותר.
People handling **flammable** materials must be very **careful**.

Special Expressions

בָּרִיא ושלם safe and **sound**
יָחִיד במינו unique

Examples (nouns)

פָּקִיד טוב הוא זה שמכיר ומבין את כל התחומים השונים של פעילות המשרד, לא רק את מה שבתחום ד׳ אמותיו.
A good **clerk** is one who is familiar with all aspects of the office work, not just his own specialized area.

ביקשתי מ**פְּקִידַת** הקבלה במלון שתיתן לנו חדר בקומה הגבוהה ביותר.
I requested of the hotel (fem.) receptionist (lit. the hotel **clerk**) that she give us a room on the highest floor.

לחיים יש הרבה **יְדִידִים** שהכיר בתקופת שירותו הצבאי.
Hayyim has many **friends** whom he met during his army service.

Special Expressions (nouns)

בְּסִיס נתונים data base
גְּבִישׁ נוזלי liquid **crystal**
גְּלִיל צביעה **roller (paint)**
יְדִיד נפש soul **mate,** close **friend**
פְּקִיד שומה assessment clerk (for tax purposes)
פְּקִידַת קבלה receptionist (f.)

Additional Examples in this Pattern

בָּהִיר light, pale; clear
בָּסִיס basis, foundation; base
בָּצִיר grape harvest
בָּקִיא expert, knowledgeable
בָּרִיא healthy
גָּבִישׁ crystal
גָּלִיל cylinder; roll; region
דָּבִיק sticky, adhesive
דָּלִיל thin, sparse; watery, diluted
זָהִיר careful, cautious
זָמִין available
זָמִיר nightingale
זָקִיף sentry; stalagmite
זָרִיז quick, agile, nimble
טָעִים tasty
יָדִיד friend
יָחִיד alone; one

---

21. *CaCiC*, when the first consonant is a guttural

our/your/their	my/your/his/her	const.	Gloss	sing/pl
חֲלִילֵנוּ/לְכֶם/לְכֶן/לָם/לָן	**חֲלִי**לִי/לְךָ/לֵךְ/לוֹ/לָהּ	חֲלִיל-	flute;	חָלִיל ז'
חֲלִילֵינוּ/כֶם/כֶן/הֶם/הֶן	**חֲלִי**לַי/לֶיךָ/לַיִךְ/לָיו/לֶיהָ	חֲלִילֵי-	recorder	חֲלִילִים

As in *CaCiC* (שָׁבִיר) above, but where a *shva* is expected in the declension, owing to stress shift, a *Hataf-pataH* occurs instead: חָלִיל, חֲלִילִים...'flute; recorder.' Note: the plural form of עָתִיד 'future' is עֲתִידוֹת.

Examples

בכפרים במזרח התיכון מייצרים הרועים **חֲלִילִים** בעצמם מקני סוף.
In the Middle East, shepherds produce their own **recorders** from reeds.

נראה שב**עָתִיד**, לא ישתמשו במזומן בכלל – רק בפעולות אלקטרוניות ובכרטיסי אשראי.
It seems that in the **future**, they would no longer use cash at all – only electronic transactions and credit cards.

Special Expressions

Passover חג ה**אָבִיב**
died while still young נפטר ב**אֲבִיב** ימיו
did exactly ...רקד לפי **חֲלִילוֹ** של
what he was told to do by…

a bright future **עָתִיד** ורוד
in the future ל**עָתִיד** לבוא
is going/destined to **עָתִיד** ל-

Additional Examples in this Pattern

spring אָבִיב
hazy אָבִיךְ
polite, courteous אָדִיב
lampshade אָהִיל
uniform; constant; homogeneous אָחִיד
impervious אָטִים
edible אָכִיל
wealthy, affluent אָמִיד
reliable אָמִין
harvest אָסִיף

noble; nobleman אָצִיל
reversible הָפִיךְ
careful, cautious חָבִיב
penetrable חָדִיר
modern, up-to-date, novel חָדִישׁ
delicate; fragile עָדִין
durable עָמִיד
colleague עָמִית
detainee עָצִיר

---

22. *CaCiC*, when the last consonant is a guttural

Gloss	Plural	sing.
negligible	זְנִיחִים	זָנִיחַ ז'
	זְנִיחוֹת	זְנִיחָה נ'

our/your/their	my/your/his/her	const.	Gloss	sing/pl
גְּבִיעֵנוּ/עֲכֶם/עֲכֶן/עָם/עָן	**גְּבִי**עִי/עֲךָ/עֵךְ/עוֹ/עָהּ	גְּבִיעַ-	goblet,	גָּבִיעַ ז'
גְּבִיעֵינוּ/כֶם/כֶן/הֶם/הֶן	**גְּבִי**עַי/עֶיךָ/עַיִךְ/עָיו/עֶיהָ	גְּבִיעֵי-	cup	גְּבִיעִים

As in שָׁבִיר above, but when word-final after a vowel other than *a*, the guttural is preceded by a *pataH gnuva*. A *shva* with the guttural is replaced by *Hataf-pataH* (including א׳ that of course does not take a *pataH gnuva* word-finally, e.g., נְבִיאֲךָ 'your prophet.)'

Examples

מכבי תל אביב זכתה ב**גְּבִיעַ** המדינה בכדורסל.
Maccabi Tel Aviv won the country's basketball **cup**.

למרות שמחירי הטיסות עלו לאחרונה, הייתה לכך השפעה **זְנִיחָה** על מספר היוצאים לחו״ל בחופשת הקיץ.
In spite of the fact that airfares have recently gone up, it has had a **negligible** effect on the number of passengers going abroad in the summer vacation.

Special Expressions

relay race מֵרוֹץ **שְׁלִיחִים** cantor, leader in prayer **שְׁלִיחַ** ציבור false messiah **מְשִׁיחַ** שקר

Additional Examples in this Pattern

balcony, gallery יָצִיעַ	bullet קָלִיעַ
herring; food preserved in salt מָלִיחַ	hard, rigid; strict קָשִׁיחַ
vulnerable; sensitive emotionally פָּגִיעַ	carpet, rug שָׁטִיחַ
preface, opening; that can be opened פָּתִיחַ	common; frequent שָׁכִיחַ
	messenger שָׁלִיחַ

---

23. *CaCiC*, when the first and third consonants are guttural

our/your/their	my/your/his/her	const.	Gloss	sing/pl
אֲרִיחֵנוּ/חֲכֶם/חֲכֶן/חָם/חָן	**אֲרִי**חִי/חֲךָ/חֵךְ/חוֹ/חָהּ	-אֲרִיחַ	tile	אָרִיחַ ז׳
אֲרִיחֵינוּ/כֶם/כֶן/הֶם/הֶן	**אֲרִי**חַי/חֶיךָ/חַיִךְ/חָיו/חֶיהָ	-אֲרִיחֵי		אֲרִיחִים

Like in שָׁבִיר above, but word-finally after a vowel other than *a*, the guttural is preceded by *pataH gnuva*. An expected *shva* with the guttural is replaced by *Hataf-pataH*.

Examples

בישראל מקובל היום לרצף עם **אֲרִיחִים** גדולים במיוחד.
In Israel today they prefer to cover floors with particularly large **tiles**.

---

24. *CCiCut*

our/your/their	my/your/his/her	const.	Gloss	sing/pl
רְגִישׁוּתֵנוּ/תְכֶם/תְכֶן/תָם/תָן	**רְגִישׁוּ**תִי/תְךָ/תֵךְ/תוֹ/תָהּ	-רְגִישׁוּת	sensitivity	רְגִישׁוּת נ׳
רְגִישׁוּיוֹתֵינוּ/כֶם/כֶן/הֶם/הֶן	**רְגִישׁוּיוֹ**תַי/תֶיךָ/תַיִךְ/תָיו/תֶיהָ	-רְגִישׁוּיוֹת		רְגִישׁוּיוֹת

CCiCut denotes abstract nouns, particularly those derived from adjectival (and sometimes nominal) *CaCiC* forms (see above), and to a lesser extent from *CaCuC* bases (also above), but occasionally from other bases as well. In the case of *CaCuC*-related forms, some claim that it is quasi-linear derivation, involving *u+u* > *i+u* (automatic?) dissimilation, e.g., 'dedication' מְסִירוּת < מָסוּר+וּת 'dedicated.' In the plural forms *y* is inserted before the suffix *–ot*, to "bridge" the hiatus between the two vowels. In some cases, the vowel *e* is automatically inserted to facilitate articulation of an initial cluster: */rgishut/* > *regishut*.

Examples

הַיְדִידוּת בין דויד ויונתן הייתה למשל ולדוגמה **לִיְדִידוּת** של אמת.
The **friendship** between David and Jonathan was a model for true **friendship**.

הַיְרִיבוּת בין שירותי הביטחון השונים בארה״ב תרמה לא מעט למחדל של 11 בספטמבר.
The **rivalry** among the different security systems in the US contributed significantly to their failure to prevent the 9/11 catastrophe.

הַמְּהִירוּת המרבית המותרת ברוב הכבישים המהירים בארה״ב היא 65 מילין לשעה.
The maximum **speed** allowed in most highways in the US is 65 MPH.

הַמְּתִיחוּת בגבול עם רצועת עזה נמשכת כבר שנים.
The **tension** on the border with the Gaza Strip has been continuing for years.

לפעמים **הַבְּדִידוּת** קשה יותר מסבל פיסי.
Sometimes **loneliness** is harder than physical suffering.

אחת הסכנות הגדולות בישראל היא **הַבְּטִיחוּת** הירודה בכבישים; מספר ההרוגים בתאונות הדרכים גדול ממספר ההרוגים במלחמות.
One of the greatest dangers in Israel is the low **safety** standards on the road; the number of fatalities in road accidents is greater than the number of casualties in war.

בדיחה ישראלית: איך עושים זאת (סקס...) הקיפודים? **בִּזְהִירוּת בִּזְהִירוּת**...
Israeli joke: how do the porcupines do it (sex…)? With very great **caution**…

זְרִיזוּת היא אחת התכונות החשובות של מלצרים טובים.
Promptness is one of the important qualities of good waiters.

אחת הבעיות הקשות של ארה״ב היום היא העלות העצומה של שירותי **הַבְּרִיאוּת**.
One of the most difficult problems of the US today is the enormous cost of **health** services.

מנהיג טוב הוא זה המסוגל לנהוג ולהגיב **בִּמְתִינוּת**, גם בשעות משבר.
A good leader is one who is capable of acting and reacting with **moderation**, even in times of crisis.

אהרון מדבר שלוש שפות **בִּרְהִיטוּת**: עברית, אנגלית וספרדית.
Aaron speaks three languages with **fluency**: Hebrew, English, and Spanish.

Special Expressions

בְּדִידוּת מַזְהֶרֶת splendid **isolation**
לִבְרִיאוּת! bless you! Gesundheit!
בקו **הַבְּרִיאוּת** in good **health**

העיקר **הַבְּרִיאוּת!** Don't worry, everything will be OK (lit. the main thing is **health**)

generosity, kindheartedness **נְדִיבוּת** לב
hyper**activity** **פְּעִילוּת** יתר
hypersensitivity **רְגִישׁוּת** יתר
auditory **frequency** **תְּדִירוּת** שמע

sonic **speed** **מְהִירוּת** הקול
total **devotion**, self-sacrifice **מְסִירוּת** נפש
virtual **reality** **מְצִיאוּת** מדומה

Additional Examples in this Pattern

tension, anxiety מְתִיחוּת
moderation מְתִינוּת
accessibility נְגִישׁוּת
generosity נְדִיבוּת
rarity נְדִירוּת
necessity, need נְחִיצוּת
regularity סְדִירוּת
activity פְּעִילוּת
preference, priority קְדִימוּת
gossip רְכִילוּת
dampness רְטִיבוּת
corruption שְׁחִיתוּת
frequency, commonness שְׁכִיחוּת
mission שְׁלִיחוּת
transparency שְׁקִיפוּת
frequency תְּדִירוּת
frequency, repetition תְּכִיפוּת

expertise, knowledge בְּקִיאוּת
flexibility גְּמִישׁוּת
stickiness דְּבִיקוּת
urgency דְּחִיפוּת
thinness דְּלִילוּת
preparedness דְּרִיכוּת
availability זְמִינוּת
arrogance יְהִירוּת
effectiveness; efficiency יְעִילוּת
duplication כְּפִילוּת
subordination כְּפִיפוּת
fitness כְּשִׁירוּת
enthusiasm, passion לְהִיטוּת
speed מְהִירוּת
saltiness מְלִיחוּת
devotion מְסִירוּת
reality מְצִיאוּת
bitterness מְרִירוּת

---

25. ***CCiCut* = *CaCiCut*** when the first consonant is a guttural

our/your/their	my/your/his/her	const.	Gloss	sing/pl
עֲדִיפוּתֵנוּ/תְכֶם/תְכֶן/תָם/תָן	**עֲדִיפוּ**תִי/תְךָ/תֵךְ/תוֹ/תָהּ	עֲדִיפוּת-	preference	עֲדִיפוּת נ׳
עֲדִיפוּיוֹתֵינוּ/כֶם/כֶן/הֶם/הֶן	**עֲדִיפוּיוֹ**תַי/תֶיךָ/תַיִךְ/תָיו/תֶיהָ	עֲדִיפוּיוֹת-		עֲדִיפוּיוֹת

As in רְגִישׁוּת above, but when the first consonant in *CCiCut* is a guttural, the *shva* is replaced by a *Hataf-pataH* throughout the declension: עֲדִיפוּת, עֲדִיפוּתִי, etc.

Examples

בארה״ב, שבה קשה להתקבל לאוניברסיטאות פרטיות יוקרתיות כמו הרווארד וייל, ניתנת בכל זאת **עֲדִיפוּת** לילדיהם של תורמים גדולים...
In the US, where it is difficult to be admitted into prestigious private universities like Harvard and Yale, **preference** is nevertheless given to children of big-time donors...

כשרוכשים מכונית חדשה, אחד השיקולים החשובים ביותר הוא **אֲמִינוּתָהּ**, בעיקר מבחינה מכנית. לשיקולים אחרים יש פחות **חֲשִׁיבוּת**.
When purchasing a new car, one of the most important considerations is its **reliability**, especially mechanically. Other considerations are of lesser **importance**.

איך מסבירים מדוע הכריש לא נגע לרעה בעורך הדין ששחה לצידו? **אֲדִיבוּת** מקצועית...
How does one explain why the shark did not touch the lawyer who swam next to him? Professional **courtesy**...

הנאשם לא הגיב כלל לכל מה שהתרחש סביבו בבית המשפט, לא ברור אם מתוך **אֲטִימוּת** או **אֲדִישׁוּת**.
The accused never reacted to anything that was happening around him in court; it is unclear whether it was out of **imperceptiveness** or **indifference**.

למען **הַהֲגִינוּת**, מן הראוי שתדבר איתו ותנסה לברר מה קרה לפני שתגיש עליו תלונה לממונים עליו.
For the sake of **decency**, it would be only fair if you talk to him first and try to find out what happened before you submit a complaint about him to his superiors.

בבית הספר היסודי בישראל ניתן לכל תלמיד ציון על **חֲרִיצוּת**.
In the Israeli elementary schools, they give each student a grade for **diligence**.

Special Expressions

cold-heartedness **אֲטִימוּת** לב
הָאֲצִילוּת מחייבת noblesse oblige (Fr.)
long life **אֲרִיכוּת** ימים
diplomatic **immunity** **חֲסִינוּת** דיפלומטית
self-**importance** **חֲשִׁיבוּת** עצמית

Additional Examples in this Pattern

nobility; aristocracy אֲצִילוּת
length, extent אֲרִיכוּת
friendliness חֲבִיבוּת
penetrability חֲדִירוּת
warmth חֲמִימוּת
sourness חֲמִיצוּת
apprenticeship חֲנִיכוּת
Hassidism; piety חֲסִידוּת
immunity חֲסִינוּת
sharpness חֲרִיפוּת
navigability, passableness עֲבִירוּת
gentleness עֲדִינוּת
durability עֲמִידוּת
vagueness; opacity עֲמִימוּת
constipation עֲצִירוּת

E. *hiCaCCut* and related *mishkalim*

26. *hiCaCCut*: generally for nominalizations of *nif`al*

our/your/their	my/your/his/her	const.	Gloss	sing/pl
הִמָּנְעוּתֵנוּ/**הִמָּנְעוּתְ**כֶם/כֶן/ **הִמָּנְעוּתָ**ם/ן	**הִמָּנְעוּ**תִי/תְךָ/תֵךְ/תוֹ/תָהּ	הִמָּנְעוּת-	abstention	הִמָּנְעוּת נ'
הִמָּנְעוּיוֹתֵינוּ/כֶם/כֶן/הֶם/הֶן	**הִמָּנְעוּיוֹ**תַי/תֶיךָ/תַיִךְ/תָיו/תֶיהָ	הִמָּנְעוּיוֹת-		הִמָּנְעוּיוֹת

hiCaCCut is the pattern of abstract nouns derived from *nif`al* verbs. The derivation is almost always automatic. One should pay attention to the vowel mark under the first root letter: if it is פתח and not קמץ, the form concerned may be a *hitpa`el*-related form in which the ת' has been assimilated: *hiddabrut* (from **hitdaber* > *hiddaber* 'negotiate,' *hitpa`el*) with *pataH* vs. *hiddavrut* (from *nidbar* 'agree, esp. to meet,' *nif`al*) with *kamats*. The *dagesh* in the 2nd root radical in *hitpa`el* is another distinguishing mark.

Examples

הִמָּנְעוּת מהווה בעיה בכל הצבעה שתוצאותיה בעד ונגד שקולות.
Abstention constitutes a problem in every vote in which the ayes and nays are equal.

הִכָּשְׁלוּת בניסיון לפתור את הסכסוך במזרח התיכון היא נחלתו של כל נשיא חדש בארה״ב.
Failing at the attempt to solve the Middle East conflict is the lot of every new US president.

ב**הִתָּקְלוּת** האחרונה בין יחידה של צה״ל וחוליית מחבלים נהרגו שני מחבלים ונפצע חייל.
In the latest **encounter** between an IDF unit and a terrorist cell two terrorist were killed and a soldier was wounded.

תאריך ה**הִכָּנְסוּת** שלנו לדירה החדשה עדיין לא ידוע; הקבלן נקלע לקשיים כספיים ולא ברור מתי תסתיים הבנייה.
The date of our **entering** the new apartment is not known yet; the contractor has encountered some financial difficulties, and it is still unclear when construction will be completed.

לא כל כך ברור לי מה מושך צופים לסדרות טלוויזיה על **הִשָּׂרְדוּת** בתנאים קשים. החיים הם מאבק **הִשָּׂרְדוּת** גדול, והם הרבה יותר מעניינים ככאלה.
I am not at all sure what attracts viewers what attracts viewers to TV series about **survival** in harsh conditions. Life is one big struggle for **survival**, and it is much more interesting as such.

מאז ה**הִפָּצְעוּת** של אביגדור במלחמת לבנון קשה לו ללכת בלי מקל הליכה.
Since Avigdor's **being wounded** in the Lebanon war he requires a walking cane.

Additional Examples in this Pattern

being tested/examined הִבָּדְקוּת
being created הִבָּרְאוּת
weaning, withdrawal הִגָּמְלוּת
being swept הִגָּרְפוּת
becoming known הִוָּדְעוּת
creation הִוָּצְרוּת
being redeemed הִוָּשְׁעוּת
entering הִכָּנְסוּת

being cracked הִסָּדְקוּת
being injured; being offended הִפָּגְעוּת
meeting הִפָּגְשׁוּת
cessation הִפָּסְקוּת
determination, setting הִקָּבְעוּת
absorption הִקָּלְטוּת
encountering הִקָּלְעוּת
being torn הִקָּרְעוּת

---

27. *hiCaCCut* = *heCaCCut* when the first consonant is guttural

our/your/their	my/your/his/her	const.	Gloss	sing/pl
הֵעָרְכוּתֵנוּ/**הֵעָרְכוּתְ**כֶם/כֶן/ **הֵעָרְכוּתָ**ם/ן	**הֵעָרְכוּ**תִי/תְךָ/תֵךְ/תוֹ/תָהּ	הֵעָרְכוּת-	deployment; organization;	הֵעָרְכוּת נ׳
הֵעָרְכוּיוֹתֵינוּ/כֶם/כֶן/הֶם/הֶן	**הֵעָרְכוּיוֹ**תַי/תֶיךָ/תַיִךְ/תָיו/תֶיהָ	הֵעָרְכוּיוֹת-	arranging	הֵעָרְכוּיוֹת

Like הִמָּנְעוּת above, but when the first root consonant is a (former) "guttural," the *tsere* /e/ is attributed to "compensatory lengthening," which allows the existence of an open syllable because the guttural cannot be geminated, and therefore cannot close the syllable: הֵעָרְכוּת ‘deployment, organization; arranging,’ הֵעָרְכוּתִי etc.

Note: in הֵאָחֲזוּת ‘holding on tightly; settlement’ there is also a *Hataf-pataH* where a *shva* was expected (see *hiCaCaCut* below).

Examples

ה**הֵעָרְכוּת** החדשה של הצבא נועדה לספק מענה למצב החדש שנוצר עם איום הטילים מעבר לגבול.
The re-**deployment** of the army is intended to provide a response to the new situation created by the missile threat from across the border.

כבר עברו שלוש שנים מאז **הֵעָלְמוּתָהּ** של הצעירה, והתעלומה עדיין לא נפתרה.
It has been three years since the **disappearance** of the young woman, and the mystery has not been solved yet.

הֵחָלְשׁוּת מפלגות השמאל בישראל היא תהליך שנמשך כבר הרבה שנים.
The **weakening** of the leftist parties in Israel is a process that has been going on for a good number of years now.

דויד נשפט על ידי מפקד הבסיס ונדון לשבועיים בכלא בשל **הֵעָדְרוּת** מן הבסיס שלא אושרה.
David was tried by the base commander and was sentenced to two weeks in jail for unapproved **absence** from the base.

הֵחָסְמוּת הנהר בסחף ובשפוכת שהביא ההוריקן גרמו לו לעלות על גדותיו ולהציף מספר גדול של יישובים.
The **blocking** of the river by silt and debris brought by the hurricane caused it to overflow its banks and flood a number of villages.

התביעה טוענת ש**הֵחָפְזוּתוֹ** של הקבלן לסיים את הבנייה מוקדם גרמה להפרות בטיחות שבעטיין הבניין התמוטט ברעידת אדמה קלה.
The prosecution claims that the contractor’s **haste** to finish the building early resulted in safety violations as a result of which the building collapsed after a light earthquake.

Special Expressions

freestyle **wrestling** חופשית **הֵאָבְקוּת**
military/agr. **settlement** נח״ל **הֵאָחֲזוּת**

Additional Examples in this Pattern

wrestling; struggle N הֵאָבְקוּת
holding on tightly; settlement הֵאָחֲזוּת
becoming sealed/opaque הֵאָטְמוּת
being forced (to) הֵאָלְצוּת
becoming raped/coerced הֵאָנְסוּת
being destroyed הֵהָרְסוּת
extricating self; volunteering הֵחָלְצוּת
being exposed; exposure הֵחָשְׂפוּת
being offended הֵעָלְבוּת
stopping הֵעָצְרוּת
calming down הֵרָגְעוּת
falling asleep הֵרָדְמוּת
being registered הֵרָשְׁמוּת

28. *hiCaCCut* = *hiCaCaCut* when the second consonant is a guttural

our/your/their	my/your/his/her	const.	Gloss	sing/pl
הִדָּחֲפוּתֵנוּ/**הִדָּחֲפוּתְ**כֶם/כֶן/ **הִדָּחֲפוּתָ**ם/ן	**הִדָּחֲפוּ**תִי/תְךָ/תֵךְ/תוֹ/תָהּ	הִדָּחֲפוּת-	being pushed;	הִדָּחֲפוּת נ׳
הִדָּחֲפוּיוֹתֵינוּ/כֶם/כֶן/הֶם/הֶן	**הִדָּחֲפוּיוֹ**תַי/תֶיךָ/תַיִךְ/תָיו/תֶיהָ	הִדָּחֲפוּיוֹת-	pushing	הִדָּחֲפוּיוֹת

Like הִמָּנְעוּת above, but where a *shva* is expected it is replaced by a *Hataf-PataH*: הִדָּחֲפוּת 'being pushed; pushing,' הִדָּחֲפוּתִי etc.

Examples

קשה לי להתרגל בישראל ל**הִדָּחֲפוּת** הנוסעים בכניסה לאוטובוס בימי חמישי וראשון.
I find it hard to get used to **being shoved** while getting on the bus in Israel on Thursday and on Sunday.

ביום חמישי אני הולך ל**הִוָּעֲצוּת** עם רופא אורתופדי בעניין כאבי גב המציקים לי לאחרונה.
On Thursday I am going for **consultation** with an orthopedic expert regarding back pains I have been having recently.

מפיק הסרטים הסכים להתפטר עקב השערוריה סביב התנהגותו עם נשים רק אחרי **הִלָּחֲצוּת** קשה מצד חבר המנהלים של החברה.
The film producer agreed to resign following the scandal around his conduct with women only after strongly **being pressured** by the company's board of directors.

הִסָּחֲבוּת המשא-ומתן על מכירת החברה גורמת ללחץ עצום על חבר המנהלים.
The **dragging** of the negotiations over the sale of the company creates tremendous pressure on the Board of Directors.

משה מתנה את **הִשָּׁאֲרוּתוֹ** בחברה בהעלאה משמעותית במשכורת.
Moshe conditions his **staying** with the company on a significant salary raise.

העובדים דורשים הצמדת משכורותיהם למדד יוקר המחיה בשל **הִשָּׁחֲקוּת** ערך הדולר.
The workers demand that their salaries be attached to the cost-of-living index because of the **erosion** of the value of the dollar.

Special Expressions

immortality of the soul **הִשָּׁאֲרוּת** הנפש

Additional Examples in this Pattern

being examined הִבָּחֲנוּת
being redeemed הִגָּאֲלוּת
being compressed הִדָּחֲסוּת
meeting הִוָּעֲדוּת
caution, care הִזָּהֲרוּת

becoming extinct הִכָּחֲדוּת
being crushed הִמָּחֲצוּת
being carried away הִסָּחֲפוּת
leaning (on) הִשָּׁעֲנוּת

29. *hiCaCCut* = *hiCaCut* when the last root conson. is *y*

our/your/their	my/your/his/her	const.	Gloss	Sing/pl
הִקָּרוּתֵנוּ/**הִקָּרוּת**ְכֶם/כֶן/**הִקָּרוּת**ָם/ן	**הִקָּרוּ**תִי/תְךָ/תֵךְ/תוֹ/תָהּ	הִקָּרוּת-	occurrence	הִקָּרוּת נ׳
הִקָּרוּיוֹתֵינוּ/כֶם/כֶן/הֶם/הֶן	**הִקָּרוּיוֹ**תַי/תֶיךָ/תַיִךְ/תָיו/תֶיהָ	הִקָּרוּיוֹת-		הִקָּרוּיוֹת

hiCaCut is a sub-pattern of *hiCaCCut* above (הִמָּנְעוּת), when the third root consonant is a /y/ (unrealized): הִקָּרוּת 'occurrence,' הִקָּרוּתִי, etc.

Examples

חשבו שהשחֶפֶת נעלמה מן העולם, אבל לאחרונה נתגלו מספר **הִקָּרוּיוֹת** של המחלה.
It was thought that TB no longer exists on earth, but lately some **occurrences** of the disease were discovered.

גם כאשר מדובר בעבירות קלות, השופטים מתייחסים ביתר חומרה כאשר מדובר ב**הִשָּׁנוּת** של עבירה.
Even when dealing with minor infractions, judges regard them with more severity in cases of **recurrence**.

היטלר שאף להגיע למצב של **הִמָּחוּת** הגן היהודי מעל פני האדמה.
Hitler aspired towards a state of the Jewish gene **being obliterated** from the face of the earth.

Special Expressions

alliteration **הִשָּׁנוּת** צלילים

Additional Examples in this Pattern

postponement הִדָּחוּת being built/established הִבָּנוּת

---

30. *hiCaCCut* = *heCaCut* when the third consonant is *y* and the first is a guttural, no plural forms

our/your/their	my/your/his/her	const.	Gloss	sing/pl
הֵעָנוּתֵנוּ/**הֵעָנוּת**ְכֶם/כֶן/**הֵעָנוּת**ָם/ן	**הֵעָנוּ**תִי/תְךָ/תֵךְ/תוֹ/תָהּ	הֵעָנוּת-	response	הֵעָנוּת נ׳

Like *hiCaCut* above (הִקָּרוּת), when the first root consonant is a (former) "guttural." Historically, the *tsere* /e/ is attributed to "compensatory lengthening" which allows the existence of an open syllable because the guttural cannot be geminated, and therefore cannot close the syllable: הֵעָנוּת 'response,' הֵעָנוּתִי etc. The occurrences included here have no plural forms.

Examples

הֵעָנוּת הציבור לקריאה לתרום דם לנפגעים עלתה מעל ומעבר למצופה.
The public's **response** to the call for donation of blood to the injured exceeded all expectations.

Additional Examples in this Pattern

being divided הֵחָצוּת
visibility, appearance הֵרָאוּת
being carried out; becoming הֵעָשׂוּת

F. *niCCaC* and related *mishkalim*

31. *niCCaC*

niCCaC is the pattern of nouns and adjectives originating from the participle of *nif'al* verbs.

our/your/their	my/your/his/her	const.	Gloss	sing/pl
נִבְדָּקֵנוּ/נִבְדַּקְכֶם/ן/נִבְדָּקָם/ן	נִבְדָּקִי/קְךָ/קֵךְ/קוֹ/קָהּ	נִבְדַּק-	subject,	נִבְדָּק ז׳
נִבְדָּקֵינוּ/נִבְדְּקֵיכֶם/כֶן/הֶם/הֶן	נִבְדָּקַי/קֶיךָ/קַיִךְ/קָיו/קֶיהָ	נִבְדְּקֵי-	examinee (m.)	נִבְדָּקִים

our/your/their	my/your/his/her	const.	Gloss	sing/pl
נִבְדַּקְתֵּנוּ/תְּכֶם/תְּכֶן/תָּם/תָּן	נִבְדַּקְתִּי/תְּךָ/תֵּךְ/תּוֹ/תָּהּ	נִבְדֶּקֶת-	subject,	נִבְדֶּקֶת נ׳
נִבְדְּקוֹתֵינוּ/כֶם/כֶן/הֶם/הֶן	נִבְדְּקוֹתַי/תֶיךָ/תַיִךְ/תָיו/תֶיהָ	נִבְדְּקוֹת-	examinee (f.)	נִבְדָּקוֹת

Examples

משרד הבריאות הודיע שהתרופה החדשה לא תאושר לפני שייבָּדקו השפעותיה על כמה מאות **נִבְדָּקִים**.
The Health Ministry announced that the new medication will not be approved before its effects are examined on a few hundred **subjects**.

נִבְחָנִים רבים לא מצליחים לעבור את מבחן הנהיגה שלהם בפעם הראשונה.
Many **examinees** do not manage to pass their driving test on the first try.

זו הייתה הצבעה מוזרה: מספר ה**נִמְנָעִים** עלה על מספר המצביעים בעד הצעת החוק בבית ה**נִבְחָרִים**.
It was a strange vote: the number of **those abstaining** exceeded the number of those who voted for the bill in the House of (**elected**) **Representatives**.

הנשיא שזר היה אדם **נִמְרָץ**, ונואם **נִלְהָב** בעל סגנון לשוני **נִמְלָץ**.
President Shazar was an **energetic** man, and an **enthusiastic** speaker, with **flowery** linguistic style.

Special Expressions

intensive care טיפול **נִמְרָץ**

Additional Examples in this Pattern

separate, different; offside (soccer) נִבְדָּל
alarmed, frightened נִבְהָל
illiterate, uneducated נִבְעָר
layer, level נִדְבָּךְ
astonished נִדְהָם
required; be in demand נִדְרָשׁ
angry, furious Lit נִזְעָם

respected, important; substantial; נִכְבָּד a notable person

disappointed נִכְזָב

enthusiastic נִלְהָב

flowery, poetic נִמְלָץ

energetic; lively; intensive נִמְרָץ

---

32. ***niCCaC* = *neCCaC*** when the first root consonant is *Het*

	Masc.	Fem.	Gloss
Sing.	נֶחְרָץ	נֶחְרָצָה	decisive, firm
Plural	נֶחְרָצִים	נֶחְרָצוֹת	

The *Hirik* becomes *seghol* in front of ח׳.

Examples

אפרים אמר דברים **נֶחְרָצִים** בישיבת חבר המנהלים; רובם נפגעו מאופן דיבורו.
Ephraim spoke some **firm** words at the board-of-directors meeting; most of them were offended by the tone of his speech.

Special Expressions

finished and done with כָּלָה **וְנֶחְרָצָה**

decisively, firmly **נֶחְרָצוֹת**

Additional Examples in this Pattern

nice, pleasant, lovely נֶחְמָד

faltering, lagging נֶחְשָׁל

---

33. ***niCCaC* = *neCeCaC*** when the first root consonant is א׳, ה׳, ע׳

our/your/their	my/your/his/her	const.	Gloss	sing/pl
נֶאֱמָנֵנוּ/**נֶאֱמַנְ**כֶם/כֶן/**נֶאֱמָנָ**ם/ן	**נֶאֱמָ**נִי/נְךָ/נֵךְ/נוֹ/נָהּ	נֶאֱמַן-	trustee	נֶאֱמָן
נֶאֱמָנֵינוּ/**נֶאֱמְנֵי**כֶם/כֶן/הֶם/הֶן	**נֶאֱמָ**נַי/נֶיךָ/נַיִךְ/נָיו/נֶיהָ	נֶאֶמְנֵי-		נֶאֱמָנִים

	Masc.	Fem.	Gloss
Sing.	נֶאֱמָן	נֶאֱמָנָה	loyal, faithful
Plural	נֶאֱמָנִים	נֶאֱמָנוֹת	

Like נִבְדָּק above, but the *Hirik* turns into *seghol*, and the following guttural is followed by a *Hataf-seghol*: נֶאֱמָן, נֶאֱמָנִי..., נֶאֱמָנָה... 'trustee; loyal, faithful'

Examples

אביגדור מכהן כעת כיו״ר חבר ה**נֶאֱמָנִים** של האוניברסיטה.
Avigdor is serving now as the chairman of the university's Board of **Trustees**.

אפרים היה **נֶאֱמָן** לאשתו במשך כל חיי הנישואים שלהם; בשבילו היא הייתה היחידה בעולם.
Ephraim was **faithful** to his wife throughout their marriage; for him she was the only one in the world.

הנֶאֱשָׁם יוצג על ידי עורך דין מתנדב שבית המשפט מינה, מכיוון שלא היה ביכולתו לשכור עורך דין לפי בחירתו.
The **accused** was represented by a *pro bono* lawyer appointed by the court, since he could not afford to hire a lawyer of his choice.

זוכרים את הפעם הראשונה שפתרתם משוואה אלגבראית עם שני **נֶעֱלָמִים**?
Do you remember the first time you solved algebraic equation with two **unknowns**?

Special Expressions

sincere congratulations ברכה **נֶאֱמָנָה**

one who does not insult back when being **insulted** **נֶעֱלָב** ואינו עולב

Additional Examples in this Pattern

beloved Lit נֶאֱהָב

noble, lofty נֶאֱצָל

magnificent; wonderful נֶהֱדָר/נֶהְדָּר

missing, absent; lacking נֶעֱדָר/נֶעְדָּר

abandoned נֶעֱזָב

insulted, offended נֶעֱלָב

---

34. *niCCaC* = *naCaCaC*: possible realization of *niCCaC* when the first root consonant is ע'

	Masc.	*Fem.*	*Gloss*
Sing.	נַעֲרָץ	נַעֲרָצָה	admired, respected
Plural	נַעֲרָצִים	נַעֲרָצוֹת	

In some isolated instances involving ע', the *Hirik* turns into *pataH*, and the following guttural is followed by a *Hataf-pataH*.

Examples

בן-גוריון היה המנהיג ה**נַעֲרָץ** ביותר בישראל במשך שנים רבות.
Ben-Gurion was the most **admired** leader in Israel for many years.

---

35. *niCCaC* = *niCaC* when the first root consonant is *n*, or the first two are *yts*

	Masc.	*Fem.*	*Gloss*
Sing.	נִכָּר	נִכֶּרֶת	noticeable; substantial
Plural	נִכָּרִים	נִכָּרוֹת	

In *niCCaC*, *n* is assimilated when it is the first root consonant, and the same happens to root-initial *y* when followed by *ts*: **ninCaC* > *niCaC*, **niytsaC* > *nitsaC*. The following consonant is geminated.

Examples

החברה סיימה את השנה ברווח **נִכָּר**.
The company finished the year with **considerable** profit.

הרבה משתמשים היום במחשבים **נִשָּׂאִים** גם בשולחן העבודה שלהם בבית.
Today many use **portable** computer even on their work desk at home.

Special Expressions

אדם **נִכָּר** בכוסו, בכיסו ובכעסו.
(The true nature of) a person **can be recognized** when he drinks, how he spends his money, and when he is angry.

Additional Examples in this Pattern

scattered, fallen leaf נִדָּף
perpendicular; hilt, sword handle; extra (cinema) נִצָּב

---

36. *niCCaC* = *niCCe* when the last root consonant is *y*

Gloss	Fem.	Masc.	
revealed, visible, unconcealed	נִגְלֵית	נִגְלֶה	*Sing.*
	נִגְלוֹת	נִגְלִים	*Plural*

In *niCCaC*, when the 3rd root consonant is *y*, the realization is *niCCe*.

Examples

חשבתי שספרו החדש של הפילוסוף הידוע יבהיר לנו כל מה שלא הבנו על משנתו, אבל עדיין רב בו הנִסְתָּר על ה**נִגְלֶה**.
I thought that the new book by the well-known philosopher will clarify whatever we could not understand about his theories, but it still contains more of the concealed than the **revealed**.

החלק ה**נִרְאֶה** של הקרחון הוא רק עשרה אחוזים ממנו ; השאר מתחת לפני המים.
The **visible** part of the glacier/iceberg is only ten per cent of it; the rest is under the water surface.

Special Expressions

the "revealed" written and oral law, as distinguished from the "hidden" or mysterious Kabbalah תורת ה**נִגְלֶה**
visible, obvious things **נִגְלוֹת**

Additional Examples in this Pattern

despicable, loathsome נִבְזֶה
it seems, it is as נִדְמֶה
epileptic נִכְפֶּה
tired נִלְאֶה
accompanying נִלְוֶה
repeated נִשְׁנֶה

---

37. *niCCaC* = *naCaCe* when the third consonant is *y*, and the first is guttural

Gloss	Fem.	Masc.	
lofty, exalted	נַעֲלָה	נַעֲלֶה	*Sing.*
	נַעֲלוֹת	נַעֲלִים	*Plural*

In *niCCaC*, when the third root consonant is *y*, and the first is a guttural, the realization is *naCaCe*, with a *Hataf-pataH* where is *shva* is expected.

Examples

יש לו הרבה מחשבות **נַעֲלוֹת**, אבל מעט מאוד מגיע לידי מימוש.
He has many **lofty** thoughts, but little of it gets to be realized.

---

38. *niCCaC* = *noCaC* when the first root consonant is *y*

Gloss	*Fem.*	*Masc.*	
additional	נוֹסֶפֶת	נוֹסָף	*Sing.*
	נוֹסָפוֹת	נוֹסָפִים	*Plural*

In *niCCaC*, when the third root consonant is *y*, it becomes *o*, and the realization is *noCaC*.

Note: the feminine form of נוֹרָא 'terrible' is נוֹרָאָה.

Examples

שר האוצר מתכנן קיצוצים **נוֹסָפִים** בתקציב של שנת הכספים הבאה, אבל עדיין לא ברור אם ראש הממשלה תומך בהצעותיו.
The Finance Minister is planning **additional** cuts in the budget, but it is still unclear whether the prime minister supports his proposals.

האריה אכל את חלק הארי מן האיילה שטרף; את **הנוֹתָר** אכלו הצבועים, התנים, ולבסוף הנשרים.
The lion ate the lion's share of the gazelle he had caught; the **remaining** meat was eaten by the hyenas, the jackals, and finally the vultures.

Special Expressions

in **addition** to **נוֹסָף על** additions; appendices **נוֹסָפוֹת**

Additional Examples in this Pattern

desperate, hopeless נוֹאָשׁ daring נוֹעָז very old נוֹשָׁן

---

39. *niCCaC* = *naCoC*, when the second root consonant is *w* or *y*

Construct	**f. sing/pl**	**construct**	**m. sing/pl**	**Gloss**
נְבוֹנַת-	נְבוֹנָה נ'	נְבוֹן-	נָבוֹן ז'	wise, intelligent
נְבוֹנוֹת-	נְבוֹנוֹת	נְבוֹנֵי-	נְבוֹנִים	

The *kamats* is reduced to *e* in the declension.

Examples

ההשקעה של יורם במניות גוגל הייתה השקעה **נְבוֹנָה**.
Yoram's investment in Google stocks was a **wise** investment.

כשמדינה מחליטה להשקיע בחינוך יותר מאשר בכלי נשק חדישים, זו החלטה **נְכוֹנָה**.
When a state decides to invest more in education than in new armements, it is a **correct** decision.

אחרי שהיטלר נעצר בשערי סטאלינגרד והצבא **הנָסוֹג** היה בדמורליזציה, השתנתה המערכה כולה, והיה ברור שגרמניה תובס בסופו של דבר.
When Hitler was stopped at the gates of Stalingrad, and the **retreating** army was demoralized, the course of the war changed, and it became clear that Germany will be eventually defeated.

Special Expressions

נְבוֹן דבר a wise person (Lit.)
מָצָא [רָאָה] **לְנָכוֹן** see fit
נָכוֹן כִּנְכוֹן היום very **clear**, without a shadow of a doubt

Additional Examples in this Pattern

נָאוֹר enlightened
נָאוֹת proper, suitable
נָבוֹךְ embarrassed
נָדוֹן being discussed
נָדוֹשׁ banal, commonplace
נָמוֹג dissipated
נָפוֹץ common, widespread

---

40. *niCCaC* = *niCoC* when either the first root consonant is *n*, or the second is *w*

const.	sing/pl	const.	Gloss	sing/pl
נִצּוֹלַת-	נִצּוֹלָה נ׳	נִצּוֹל-	survivor (m.)	נִצּוֹל ז׳
נִצּוֹלוֹת-	נִצּוֹלוֹת	נִצּוֹלֵי-		נִצּוֹלִים

In *niCCaC*, when the first root consonant is *n* and **in some cases** *u/o*, the realization is *niCoC*.

Examples

נִצּוֹלֵי שואה בדרך כלל מעדיפים שלא לדבר על מה שעברו בזמן המלחמה.
Holocaust **survivors** generally prefer not to talk about what they went through during the War.

Additional Examples in this Pattern

נִזּוֹק injured person
נִמּוֹל circumcised person

---

41. *niCCaC* = *niCoC* when either the first root consonant is *n*, or the second is *w*, and when the last consonant is guttural

sing/pl	Gloss	sing/pl
נְנוֹחָה נ׳	calm, relaxed	נְנוֹחַ ז׳
נְנוֹחוֹת		נְנוֹחִים

In *niCCaC*, when the first root consonant is *n* and in some cases *w*, the realization is *niCoC*. In these cases, when the last consonant is a guttural, a "furtive *pataH*" is inserted following a vowel other than *a* when it is in word-final position.

Examples

אחרי כל מה שעבר עליך, אני שמח לראותך שקט ו**נְנוֹחַ**.
After all you have gone through, I am pleased to see you peaceful and **relaxed**.

---

42. *niCCaCut*

our/your/their	my/your/his/her	const.	Gloss	sing/pl
נִפְקָדוּתֵנוּ/**נִפְקָדוּתְ**כֶם/כֶן/ **נִפְקָדוּתָ**ם/ן	**נִפְקָדוּ**תִי/תְךָ/תֵךְ/תוֹ/תָהּ	נִפְקָדוּת-	absenteeism (military)	נִפְקָדוּת נ׳
נִפְקָדוּיוֹתֵינוּ/כֶם/כֶן/הֶם/הֶן	**נִפְקָדוּיוֹ**תַי/תֶיךָ/תַיִךְ/תָיו/תֶיהָ	נִפְקָדוּיוֹת-		נִפְקָדוּיוֹת

niCCaCut **generally** constitutes **linear derivation** of abstract nouns related to adjectives or nouns in the ***niCCaC*** *mishkal*. On occasion it functions as an alternative *mishkal* for abstract nouns derived from *nif`al*, in which the participle form serves as a base (instead of *hiCaCCut*). The *a* vowel of the base does not undergo reduction. Most of the occurrences included do not have plural forms.

Examples

אביגדור לא חזר מחופשתו לבסיס בזמן, ונדון לשלושה ימי מחבוש בגין **נִפְקָדוּת**.
Avigdor did not return from his leave on time, and was sentenced to three days' incarceration owing to **absenteeism**.

למרות התקשורת וזמינותם של מאגרי מידע בימים אלה, עדיין מדהימה לעיתים מידת **נִבְעָרוּתָם** של אנשים רבים.
In spite of the media and the ready availability of data bases, one is still amazed at the **ignorance** of many people today.

מן הרגע הראשון שאתה פוגש את חנן, אתה מתרשם מ**נִמְרָצוּתוֹ**. הוא לא נח לרגע.
From the moment you meet Hanan, you are impressed by his **energy**. He never rests.

Additional Examples in this Pattern

difference, dissimilarity נִבְדָּלוּת
enthusiasm נִלְהָבוּת
ludicrousness נִלְעָגוּת
haste, hurriedness נִמְהָרוּת
tolerability נִסְבָּלוּת
need; poverty נִצְרָכוּת
oppression, persecution נִרְדָּפוּת

---

43. *niCCaCut* = *neCeCaCut* when the first consonant is א׳ ה׳ ע׳

our/your/their	my/your/his/her	const.	Gloss	sing/pl
נֶאֱמָנוּתֵנוּ/**נֶאֱמָנוּ**תְכֶם/כֶן/ **נֶאֱמָנוּתָ**ם/ן	**נֶאֱמָנוּ**תִי/תְךָ/תֵךְ/תוֹ/תָהּ	נֶאֱמָנוּת-	loyalty, faithfulness	נֶאֱמָנוּת נ׳
נֶאֱמָנוּיוֹתֵינוּ/כֶם/כֶן/הֶם/הֶן	**נֶאֱמָנוּיוֹ**תַי/תֶיךָ/תַיִךְ/תָיו/תֶיהָ	נֶאֱמָנוּיוֹת-		נֶאֱמָנוּיוֹת

When the first root consonant in *niCCaCut* is א׳ ה׳ ע׳, the prefix vowel becomes *e* (*seghol*), and another *e* (*Hataf seghol*) follows it: נֶאֱמָנוּת 'loyalty' נֶאֱמָנוּתִי, etc.

Examples

הסיפור של ״לאסי״ הוא סיפור של **נֶאֱמָנוּת** כלב לאדונו.
The story of Lassie is a story of the **loyalty** of a dog to his master.

ארגוני ימין מסוימים מאשימים את הבג״צ ב**נֶאֱלָחוּת** נגד הימין, בטענה שהוא נוקט עמדות שמאלניות קיצוניות.
Certain right wing organization in Israel accuse the Supreme Court of Justice of **vileness** towards the right wing, arguing that the Court adopts extreme left-wing positions.

Additional Examples in this Pattern

abandonment נֶעֱזָבוּת   insult, effrontery נֶעֱלָבוּת

---

44. *niCCaCut* = *neCCaCut* when the first consonant is ח׳

our/your/their	my/your/his/her	const.	Gloss	sing/pl
נֶחְרָצוּתֵנוּ/**נֶחְרָצוּ**תְכֶם/כֶן/ **נֶחְרָצוּתָ**ם/ן	**נֶחְרָצוּ**תִי/תְךָ/תֵךְ/תוֹ/תָהּ	נֶחְרָצוּת-	decisiveness	נֶחְרָצוּת נ׳
נֶחְרָצוּיוֹתֵינוּ/כֶם/כֶן/הֶם/הֶן	**נֶחְרָצוּיוֹ**תַי/תֶיךָ/תַיִךְ/תָיו/תֶיהָ	נֶחְרָצוּיוֹת-		נֶחְרָצוּיוֹת

When the first root consonant in *niCCaCut* is a ח׳, the prefix vowel becomes *e* (*seghol*), but no *e* (*Hataf-seghol*) is inserted after it as in the case of the other gutturals: נֶחְרָצוּת 'decisiveness,' נֶחְרָצוּתִי etc.

Examples

למרבית הצער, מדינות לא מעטות בעולם השלישי עדיין לוקות ב**נֶחְשָׁלוּת**, בעוני ובבערות. מצד שני, כשמבקרים בהן, בדרך כלל התכונה הבולטת בהן היא **נֶחְמָדוּתָם** של האנשים.
Regrettably, many third world countries are still plagued by **backwardness**, poverty and ignorance. On the other hand, when you visit them, generally the most prominent quality you notice is the **pleasantness** of the people.

G. *CiCuC* and related *mishkalim*

45. *CiCuC*: often for nominalization related to *pi`el*

our/your/their	my/your/his/her	const.	Gloss	sing/pl
בִּשּׁוּלֵנוּ/לְכֶם/כֶן/לָם/לָן	**בִּשּׁוּ**לִי/לְךָ/לֵךְ/לוֹ/לָהּ	בִּישּׁוּל-	cooking	בִּשּׁוּל ז׳
בִּשּׁוּלֵינוּ/כֶם/כֶן/הֶם/הֶן	**בִּשּׁוּ**לַי/לֶיךָ/לַיִךְ/לָיו/לֶיהָ	בִּשּׁוּלֵי-		בִּשּׁוּלִים

CiCuC is often a pattern designating nominalization of verbs, usually in *pi`el*, as in בִּשֵּׁל 'cook' ~ בִּשּׁוּל 'cooking,' but in many cases the *CiCuC* form also refers to a specific realization of the nominalization. Thus, for instance, צִיּוּן is abstract nominalization of צִיֵּן meaning 'noting' or 'marking,' or alternatively, a grade (or mark) denoting evaluation; סִדּוּר denotes 'arranging,' or a specific arrangement, e.g., flower arrangement, or an arrangement of prayers. When the second root consonant is ה׳, ח׳, ע׳ it does not take a *dagesh*, of course. The same applies to א׳ and ר׳, but the preceding *Hirik* becomes *tsere* (see בֵּרוּר below).

Examples

אחרי כל **בִּקּוּר** של הנכדים אנחנו עוסקים **בְּסִדּוּר** הבית **וּבְנִקּוּיוֹ** במשך שעתיים לפחות...
Following every **visit** of the grandchildren, we are engaged in **putting** the house **in order** and **cleaning** it for at least two hours…

הבאתי את המכונית **לְטִפּוּל** תקופתי שגרתי, ובסופו של דבר זה נגמר **בְּתִקּוּן** רציני **וּבְשִׁפּוּץ** חלקי של המנוע...
I brought the car for periodical maintenance ("**treatment**"), and when it was all over it ended with serious **repair** and partial **rebuilding** of the engine…

כשגולדה מאיר הייתה ראשת ממשלה, היא הייתה מתייעצת בביתה בערב שלפני ישיבת הממשלה עם אישים בכירים או יועצים לא-פורמליים. כינו את הקבוצה הזאת "המטבח של גולדה", למרות שחבריה לא עסקו **בְּבִשּׁוּל** פיסי... מכאן **הַבִּטּוּי** "מטבח" בפוליטיקה הישראלית.
When Golda Meir was the Prime Minister, she would consult with senior figures or informal advisers at her home in the evening before a government meeting. The group was nicknamed "Golda's kitchen," though its members did not engage in actual **cooking**… This is the origin of the **expression** "kitchen" in Israeli politics.

לכבוד כל חג לאומי בישראל, כמו יום העצמאות, הרשויות המקומיות מארגנות הופעות **בִּדּוּר** ציבוריות להנאת התושבים.
In honor of national holidays, such as Independence Day, cities and towns organize public **entertainment** shows for the enjoyment of their residents.

אומרים ששירותי **הַבִּיּוּן** של ישראל הם מן הטובים בעולם.
They say that the Israeli **intelligence services** are among the world's best.

סכרים בנויים כך שיפשרו אגירה **וְוִסּוּת** של כמויות המים לפי הצורך, אבל לעתים הם לא עומדים בלחץ ונפרצים בעונת הגשמים והשטפונות, וישובים שלמים מוצפים.
Dams are constructed in such a way that allows storage of water and its **regulation** as needed, but sometimes in the rainy and flood seasons they do not withstand the pressure and burst open, and whole towns and villages are flooded.

צה"ל מעדיף להשתמש במונח "**חִיּוּל**" במקום "גִּיּוּס" – אולי משום ש"**חִיּוּל**" מתייחס לגיוס חיילים בלבד, בעוד ש"גיוס" יכול לשמש לכל מטרה אחרת.
The IDF prefers the term **חִיּוּל** for **enlisting** – perhaps because it refers to drafting of new soldiers only, whereas **גִּיּוּס** refers to enlisting for any purpose.

המניע המקורי של הקומוניזם היה להפסיק את **נִצּוּלוֹ** של מעמד הפועלים.
The original motivation for communism was to stop the **exploitation** of the working class.

כל נשיא חדש של ארה״ב מאמין שיצליח להביא ל**תִּווּךְ** בין הצדדים במזרח התיכון.
Every new US president believes that he would be able to bring about **mediation** in the Middle East conflict..

Special Expressions

אִבּוּד הכרה **loss** of consciousness
אִבּוּד לדעת suicide
אִבּוּד עשתונות confusion
בִּקּוּר בית doctor's home **visit**
כרטיס **בִּקּוּר** **visiting** card
גִּבּוּב דברים/מילים babble, drivel, verbosity
דִּגּוּל נשק presenting arms (mil.)
דִּוּוּר ישיר direct **mailing**
וִסּוּת מניות share/stock **regulation/control**

טִפּוּל מונע preventive **care**
טִפּוּל נמרץ intensive **care**
טִפּוּל שורש root canal **treatment**
נִצּוּל מיני sexual **exploitation**
נִקּוּי יבש dry **cleaning**
נִקּוּי ראש **removal** of all concern
תִּקּוּן סופרים **corrections** to the biblical text to circumvent inappropriate language
תִּקּוּן עולם working to "**improve/fix** the world"

Additional Examples in this Pattern

אִבּוּד loss, disappearance
אִגּוּד organization, union
אִגּוּף outflanking
אִזּוּן balance N, balancing
אִיּוּם threat
אִיּוּשׁ manning
אִמּוּן training, exercise
אִמּוּת verification
אִשּׁוּר confirmation
בִּדּוּד isolation; insulation
בִּטּוּל cancellation
בִּיּוּם staging
גִּבּוּב piling, heaping
גִּבּוּי backup, support; backing
גִּיּוּר conversion to Judaism

גִּנּוּי denunciation, condemnation
גִּנּוּן gardening
גִּשּׁוּשׁ groping; initial contact
דִּבּוּר speech
דִּוּוּר mailing
דִּיּוּן discussion
הִסּוּס hesitation
וִדּוּא confirmation
וִסּוּת adjustment, regulation
חִלּוּן converting from holy to secular
נִצּוּל utilization; exploitation
סִפּוּר story, tale
עִכּוּל digestion
תִּוּוּךְ mediation; brokerage
תִּקּוּן repair

---

46. ***CiCuC*** derived from certain nouns without a *dagesh*

our/your/their	my/your/his/her	const.	Gloss	sing/pl
נִכּוּסֵנוּ/סְכֶם/סְכֶן/סָם/סָן	**נִכּוּ**סִי/סְךָ/סֵךְ/סוֹ/סָהּ	נִכּוּס-	appropriating	נִכּוּס ז'
נִכּוּסֵינוּ/כֶם/כֶן/הֶם/הֶן	**נִכּוּ**סַי/סֶיךָ/סַיִךְ/סָיו/סֶיהָ	נִכּוּסֵי-		נִכּוּסִים

The declension is like that of בִּשּׁוּל above, but in order to maintain the transparency of the nominal base for derivation (here נֶכֶס 'property'), one usually does not geminate the second root consonant (נִכּוּס is too formal): נִכּוּס, נִכּוּסִי... 'appropriating.' For the same reason, generally there is no *dagesh forte* in כִּכּוּב (from כּוֹכָב 'star'), and when כ

with a *dagesh lene* is expected to be spirantized after a vowel, it is unaffected (e.g., לְכִכוּב and not the formal לְכִכּוּב).

Examples

היום כל סרט **בִּכִּכוּבָהּ** של קירה נייטלי הוא הצלחה קופתית מובטחת.
Today any movie **starring** Kiera Knightly is a guaranteed box office success.

הערבים מאשימים את הישראלים **בְּנִיכּוּס** מאכלים ערביים מקוריים כמו חומוס ופלאפל.
The Arabs accuse the Israelis of **appropriating** original Arab dishes like hummus and falafel.

---

47. ***CiCuC*** regular, or with *y* without a *dagesh* in nouns from roots with identical 2nd and 3rd consonant

our/your/their	my/your/his/her	const.	Gloss	sing/pl
סִבּוּ/סִיבוּבֵנוּ/בְכֶם/בְכֶן/בָם/בָן	**סִבּוּ/סִיבוּ**בִי/בְךָ/בֵךְ/בוֹ/בָהּ	סִבּוּב/סִיבוּב-	rotation; turn	סִבּוּב/ סִיבוּב ז'
סִבּוּ/סִיבוּבֵינוּ/כֶם/כֶן/הֶם/הֶן	**סִבּוּ/סִיבוּ**בַי/בֶיךָ/בַיִךְ/בָיו/בֶיהָ	סִבּוּבֵי/סִיבוּבֵי-		סִבּוּבִים/ סִיבוּבִים

Regular *CiCuC*, or with an added י' without a *dagesh* in the following consonant, סִבּוּב/סִיבוּב, סִבּוּבֵי/סִיבוּבֵי... 'rotation; turn,' when the 2nd and 3rd root consonants are identical. The form with י' and without a *dagesh* is commoner in speech, and this is also the recommendation of the Hebrew Language Academy for general use when the parallel verb pattern is *CoCeC*: סוֹבֵב, עוֹדֵד. Some speakers separate between two meanings for the alternate form: סִיבוּב for rotation, and סִבּוּב for causation.

Examples

על פי מספר **סִבּוּבֵי** המנוע לדקה יודעים כמה המנוע מתאמץ.
According to the number of **revolutions** per minute (RPM) one knows how hard the motor is working.

Additional Examples in this Pattern

כִּפּוּף/כִּיפוּף bending
עִדּוּד/עִידוּד encouragement
רִצּוּץ/רִיצוּץ shattering, crushing
תִּפּוּף/תִּיפוּף drumming

---

48. ***CiCuC*** with *yod* without a *dagesh* from roots in which the second root consonant is *w/y*

our/your/their	my/your/his/her	const.	Gloss	sing/pl
אִיתוּתֵנוּ/תְכֶם/תְכֶן/תָם/תָן	**אִיתוּ**תִי/תְךָ/תֵךְ/תוֹ/תָהּ	אִיתוּת-	signaling	אִיתוּת ז'
אִיתוּתֵינוּ/כֶם/כֶן/הֶם/הֶן	**אִיתוּ**תַי/תֶיךָ/תַיִךְ/תָיו/תֶיהָ	אִיתוּתֵי-		אִיתוּתִים

CiCuC with י' without a *dagesh* in the second consonant, in certain cases where the second root consonant is ו' (in others the ו' is realized as י'): אִיתוּת 'signaling,' אִיתוּתִי

etc., and the parallel verb pattern is *CoCeC:* אוֹתֵת 'signal V,' מוֹטֵט 'collapse tr.' Note that צִיתוּת 'eavesdropping' from *ts-t-t* 'eavesdrop' also follows the *w/y* pattern.

Examples

מנחם השתתף בקורס ל**אִיתוּת** במסגרת שירותו הצבאי.
Menahem took part in a **signaling** course during his army service.

צִיתוּת חשאי לשיחות טלפון ללא הסכמת המדבר הוא עברה על החוק.
Secret **eavesdropping** on the phone without the speaker's consent is illegal.

Additional Examples in this Pattern

caving; collapse מִיטוּט re-establishment קִימוּם

---

49. *CiCuC* with *y* without a *dagesh* from Greek

sing/pl	Gloss	const.	my/your/his/her	our/your/their
נִימוּס ז'	politeness,	נִימוּס-	**נִימוּ**סִי/סְךָ/סֵךְ/סוֹ/סָהּ	**נִימוּ**סֵנוּ/סְכֶם/סְכֶן/סָם/סָן
נִימוּסִים	manners	נִימוּסֵי-	**נִימוּ**סַי/סֶיךָ/סַיִךְ/סָיו/סֶיהָ	**נִימוּסֵי**נוּ/כֶם/כֶן/הֶם/הֶן

The declension is as in אִיתוּת above: נִימוּס 'politeness, manners,' נִימוּסִים etc.

Examples

ה**נִימוּס** מחייב לשרת נשים לפני שמשרתים גברים.
Manners dictate that women be served before men are.

Special Expressions

נִימוּסֵי שולחן table **manners**

Additional Examples in this Pattern

סִיקוּס node on a plant

---

50. *CiCuC* when the 2nd root consonant is *he*, *Het*, *`ain*

sing/pl	Gloss	const.	my/your/his/her	our/your/their
אִחוּד ז'	unification;	אִחוּד-	**אִחוּ**דִי/דְךָ/דֵךְ/דוֹ/דָהּ	**אִחוּ**דֵנוּ/דְכֶם/דְכֶן/דָם/דָן
אִחוּדִים	merger	אִחוּדֵי-	**אִחוּ**דַי/דֶיךָ/דַיִךְ/דָיו/דֶיהָ	**אִחוּדֵי**נוּ/כֶם/כֶן/הֶם/הֶן

The declension is as in בִּשּׁוּל above, but when the second root consonant is ה', ח', ע' it does not take a *dagesh*, of course: אִחוּד 'unification; merger,' אִחוּדֵי etc.

Examples

אחת הסיבות המרכזיות ליצירת ה**אִחוּד** האירופי הייתה ליצור גוף מאוחד גדול שיוכל להתמודד עם מעצמות כלכליות כמו ארה"ב וסין.
One of the main reasons for the creation of the European **Union** was to form a large united entity that can compete with economic superpowers like the US and China.

בִּעוּר הבערות עמד תמיד על סדר יומה של מדינת ישראל. זהו נושא חשוב בכל מדינה שנוסדה על ידי מהגרים והממשיכה לקבלם.
Eliminating ignorance has always been a priority on Israel's agenda. It is an important topic in any state established by, and open to, immigration.

נהרות לא מעטים בעולם סובלים מ**זִהוּם**, ו**טִהוּרָם** יקר ואיטי.
A good number of the worlds rivers suffer from **pollution**, and **purification** is expensive and slow.

חברות רבות מקבלות **יִעוּץ** כדי להביא ל**יִעוּל** תפעולן, אבל לא תמיד זה עוזר.
Many companies get **advice** how to bring about more **efficiency** in their operations, but it does not always help.

הצלחתה של כל חברה תלויה במידה רבה ב**נִהוּל** נכון.
The success of any company is dependent to a large extent on good **management**.

חיפה היא עיר נהדרת, אבל **רִחוּקָהּ** ממרכז הארץ הוא בעוכריה.
Haifa is a great city, but its **distance** from the center of the country is detrimental.

תִּעוּשׁ של חברה חקלאית הוא לעיתים בלתי נמנע, ולעיתים קרובות יוצר בעיות קשות.
Industrialization of an agricultural society is sometimes unavoidable, but it often creates serious problems.

Special Expressions

removal of leavened bread (on the eve of Passover) **בִּעוּר** חמץ
voice **recognition** (by computer) **זִהוּי** קול
air **pollution** **זִהוּם** אוויר
air **pollution** **זִהוּם** סביבתי
ethnic **cleansing** **טִהוּר** אתני
anemia **מִעוּט** דם
wild **guess** Coll **נִחוּשׁ** פראי/פרוע
gradual **devaluation** (econ.) **פִּחוּת** זוחל

Additional Examples in this Pattern

wish; wishes אִחוּל
delay N אִחוּר
ironing גִּהוּץ
burp, belch N גִּהוּק
giggle, chuckle N גִּחוּךְ
identification זִהוּי
miniaturization זִעוּר
plea law; case; argumentation טִעוּן
uniqueness יִחוּד
pedigree; attribution יִחוּס
assignment, designation יִעוּד
minority מִעוּט
guess נִחוּשׁ
shaking נִעוּר
nursing סִעוּד
yawn N פִּהוּק
reduction; devaluation פִּחוּת

---

51. ***CiCuC = CeCuC***, when the second consonant is א' or ר'

our/your/their	my/your/his/her	const.	Gloss	sing/pl
בֵּרוּרֵנוּ/רְכֶם/רְכֶן/רָם/רָן	**בֵּרוּ**רִי/רְךָ/רֵךְ/רוֹ/רָהּ	בֵּרוּר-	clarification;	בֵּרוּר ז'
בֵּרוּרֵינוּ/כֶם/כֶן/הֶם/הֶן	**בֵּרוּ**רַי/רֶיךָ/רַיִךְ/רָיו/רֶיהָ	בֵּרוּרֵי-	investigation	בֵּרוּרִים

When the second root consonant is א׳ or ר׳, the *Hirik i* is replaced by a *tsere*. The *tsere* /e/ is attributed to historical "compensatory lengthening," which allowed the existence of an open syllable because these consonants cannot be geminated, and therefore cannot close the syllable: בֵּרוּר 'clarification; investigation,' בֵּרוּרִי etc. No "compensatory lengthening" before ה׳, ח׳ ע׳ (see above).

Examples

המנהל זימן אותי למשרדו **לבֵרוּר** בעניין התקלה שחלה הבוקר במערכת התקשורת הפנימית שעליה אני אחראי.
The manager called me into his office for **clarification** re this morning's mishap that occurred in the internal communications system, for which I am responsible.

גֵּרוּשׁ היהודים מספרד היה אחד האירועים הטראומטיים ביותר בתולדות העם היהודי. מעניין שהיסטוריונים ספרדים מסוימים חושבים היום שזו הייתה שגיאה גדולה, שגרמה לא מעט לירידתה של ספרד בזירה הבינלאומית.
The **expulsion** of the Jews from Spain was one of the most traumatic events in Jewish history. Interestingly, some Spanish historians today believe that it was a grave mistake, which was an important factor in the deterioration of Spain in the international arena.

מדי חודש וחודש, מדי שנה בשנה, גובר בי **היֵאוּשׁ** כשאני רואה את הסיכוי לשלום במזרח התיכון הולך ומתרחק, הולך ומתמעט.
With every passing month, and every passing year, my **despair** increases as I see the prospects for peace in the Middle East getting farther and farther away, ever diminishing.

במרבית ארצות העולם, מספר טלפון **החֵרוּם** למשטרה, מכבי האש ושירותי **חֵרוּם** בריאותיים הוא אותו מספר לכולם.
In most countries, the **emergency** telephone number for the police, the fire department and **emergency** medical services is the same number for all.

כשמזמינים יין באמצעות המרשתת, כדאי לוודא שהחבילה נשלחת **בקֵרוּר**.
When one orders wine through the internet, it is a good idea to ascertain that it is sent in **refrigeration** conditions.

ניתן היום לפתור הרבה בעיות **שֵׁרוּת** דרך המרשתת, אבל כאשר מדובר בבעיות הקשורות במחשבים זה לא פשוט, במיוחד כאשר מחלקת **השֵׁרוּת** נמצאת בצד השני של כדור הארץ...
Many **service** problems can be solved today through the Internet, but when dealing with computer difficulties it is not simple, particularly when the **service** department is located in the other side of the globe...

Special Expressions

בֵּרוּר דברים sorting-out discussion
בבֵרוּר clearly
גֵּרוּשׁ שדים exorcism
דֵּרוּג פסיכוטכני ראשוני (דפ״ר) initial pschotechnic **grading** (military)
סֵרוּב פקודה insubordination
קֵרוּר יתר super**cooling** (chem.)
שֵׁרוּת חובה obligatory (military) **service**

Additional Examples in this Pattern

explanation; exegesis בֵּאוּר
scratching; itching Coll. גֵּרוּד
stimulus גֵּרוּי
classification, grading דֵּרוּג
urging זֵרוּז
insanity טֵרוּף
refusal, rejection סֵרוּב
castration; distortion סֵרוּס
divisiveness; schism פֵּרוּד
detailing; breakdown פֵּרוּט
explanation; commentary פֵּרוּשׁ
joining; combination צֵרוּף
bringing close; proximity קֵרוּב
coordination תֵּאוּם
description; describing תֵּאוּר
excuse תֵּרוּץ

---

52. ***CiCuC* = *CiCuC*/*CeCuC***, in some cases when the second consonant is א'

our/your/their	my/your/his/her	const.	Gloss	sing/pl
נִאוּ/נֵאוּפֵנוּ/פְכֶם/פְכֶן/פָם/פָן	**נִאוּ/נֵאוּ**פִי/פְךָ/פֵךְ/פוֹ/פָהּ	נִאוּף/נֵאוּף-	adultery	נִאוּף/נֵאוּף ז'
נִאוּ/נֵאוּפֵינוּ/כֶם/כֶן/הֶם/הֶן	**נִאוּ/נֵאוּ**פַי/פֶיךָ/פַיִךְ/פָיו/פֶיהָ	נִאוּפֵי/נֵאוּפֵי-		נִאוּפִים/נֵאוּפִים

In a few isolated cases, there are two alternative realizations when the second root consonant is א': with *Hirik* or with a *tsere* in the preceding consonant (compensatory lengthening): נִאוּף/נֵאוּף 'adultery,' נִאוּפֵי/נֵאוּפֵי, etc.

Examples

יש הסוברים כי **נִאוּף** הוא פיתרון מעשי סביר לחיי נישואין לא מוצלחים.
Some people believe that **adultery** is a reasonable practical solution to an unsuccessful married life.

Additional Examples in this Pattern

cursing, swearing נִאוּץ/נֵאוּץ

---

53. ***CiCuC***, when the last root consonant is guttural

our/your/their	my/your/his/her	const.	Gloss	sing/pl
נִתּוּחֵנוּ/חֲכֶם/כֶן/חָם/חָן	**נִתּוּ**חִי/חֲךָ/חֵךְ/חוֹ/חָהּ	נִתּוּחַ-	surgery;	נִתּוּחַ ז'
נִתּוּחֵינוּ/כֶם/כֶן/הֶם/הֶן	**נִתּוּ**חַי/חֶיךָ/חַיִךְ/חָיו/חֶיהָ	נִתּוּחֵי-	analysis	נִתּוּחִים

In the sing. masc. form the final guttural is preceded by a *pataH gnuva* after a vowel other than *a*. Where a *shva* is expected with the guttural, it is replaced by *Hataf-pataH*.

Examples

ה**נִתּוּחַ** הצליח, אבל החולה מת...
The **surgery** went well, but the patient died...

זוגות מבוגרים מתקשים לא פעם להחליט כיצד להגן על בן/בת זוגם כאשר אחד מהם ילך לעולמו: לחסוך כמה שיותר, או לקנות **בִּטּוּחַ** חיים על סכום גבוה.
Older couples are often debating as to how to best protect the spouse when one of them dies: save as much as possible, or purchase life **insurance** for substantial coverage.

ה**וִכּוּחַ** המרכזי היום באירופה ובארה״ב הוא איך לטפל בבעיית פליטי מלחמה ורדיפות.
The primary **discussion** in Europe and in the US is how to deal with the problem of war and persecution refugees.

לקראת עונת הגשמים, המדינה החליטה על **קִבּוּעַ** כל הסכרים שבתחומי שיפוטה.
In anticipation of the rainy season, the state decided on **reinforcing** all dams within its borders.

Special Expressions

social security **בִּטּוּחַ** לאומי
comprehensive **insurance** **בִּטּוּחַ** מקיף
specific performance (law) **בִּצּוּעַ** בעין
useless **argument** **וִכּוּחַ** סרק
magic **square** **רִבּוּעַ** קסם

Additional Examples in this Pattern

implementation; performance בִּצּוּעַ
shaving גִּלּוּחַ
reporting; report N דִּוּוּחַ
informing; making definite (grammar) יִדּוּעַ
terminology מִנּוּחַ
aid, assistance; help סִיּוּעַ
terrorist attack פִּגּוּעַ
development פִּתּוּחַ
drilling, boring קִדּוּחַ
wiping, drying; dessert קִנּוּחַ
discrimination קִפּוּחַ
square רִבּוּעַ

---

54. ***CiCCuC***: the counterpart of *CiCuC* with four root consonants

our/your/their	my/your/his/her	const.	Gloss	sing/pl
פִּרְסוּמֵנוּ/מְכֶם/מְכֶן/מָם/מָן	פִּרְסוּמִי/מְךָ/מֵךְ/מוֹ/מָהּ	פִּרְסוּם-	publicity; publication; advertising	פִּרְסוּם ז׳
פִּרְסוּמֵינוּ/כֶם/כֶן/הֶם/הֶן	פִּרְסוּמַי/מֶיךָ/מַיִךְ/מָיו/מֶיהָ	פִּרְסוּמֵי-		פִּרְסוּמִים

Often, like *CiCuC*, *CiCCuC* is also a pattern of gerunds related to verbs, usually *pi`el* ones, and some look at it simply as an expansion of *CiCuC*, which allows incorporating additional consonants within the disyllabic structure of the base. Nevertheless, the syllabic structure itself is different enough to justify presenting *CiCCuC* as a separate pattern. In a significant number of occurrences, *CiCCuC* preceded its *pi`el* counterpart, e.g., אִבְחוּן 'diagnosis' preceded אִבְחֵן 'diagnose.' As in *CiCuC*, in many cases the *CiCCuC* form refers to the action itself, or to a specific realization derived from the gerund, e.g., in אִרְגֵּן ~ אִרְגּוּן : אִרְגּוּן 'organize/organizing' vs. אִרְגּוּן 'organization.' Occasionally we have a sort of sub-pattern, $CiCC_3uC_3$, where the fourth consonant echoes the third, as in אִוְרוּר 'ventilation,' originating from אֲוִיר 'air,' or תִּכְנוּן, 'planning,' originating from תָּכְנִית, and occasionally $C_1iC_2C_1uC_2$, where the third and fourth consonants repeat the first and second ones, respectively, as in גִּלְגּוּל 'rolling up,' קִשְׁקוּשׁ 'scribble.' Note: nouns with five root consonants, like סִנְכְּרוּן 'synchronization,' belong to a separate pattern, but they are few.

Examples

אִרְגּוּנֵי עובדי ה**תִּפְעוּל** של נמלי התעופה בישראל הם חזקים למדיי, ולא פעם מכריזים על **סִכְסוּךְ** עבודה המסתיים בשביתה, וזו עלולה להימשך שבועות רבים.

The workers **organizations** responsible for the **handling operations** at the Israeli ports are rather powerful, and tend to declare a labor **dispute** which ends with a strike, one that can last many weeks.

בהיסטוריה המוקדמת של ה**תִּרְגּוּם** בישראל חלו לא מעט טעויות ו**בִלְבּוּלִים** כאשר תרגמו לעברית, למשל, את שיקספיר מן הגירסה הרוסית...

In the early history of **translation** in Israel there occurred more than a few errors and **mix-ups** when Shakespeare, for instance, was translated from the Russian version…

בעולם האקדמי נהוג בדרך כלל לקדם מרצים באוניברסיטה על פי כמות **פִּרְסוּמֵיהֶם** ואיכותם ולא על פי כישוריהם כמורים.

In the academic world they generally promote professors on the basis of the quantity and quality of their **publications** rather than the quality of their teaching.

בעבר, פסיכולוגים מסוימים האמינו ב**הִפְּנוּט** חולים כדי לרדת לשורש הבעייה.

In the past, some psychologists believed in **hypnotizing** patients so as to understand their problems.

יש האומרים ש**מִשְׁטוּר** יחסים בין בני אדם וחיקוקם הוא מוות לספונטניות...

Some say that **disciplining** relationships among people and legislating them means the end of spontaneity…

מדובר הרבה על אפשרות **בִּנְאוּמָם** של האתרים הקדושים בירושלים, אבל מרבית הישראלים אינם בוטחים באחרים שיבטיחו גישה פתוחה לכותל המערבי, למשל.

The possibility of **internationalization** of the holy sites in Jerusalem is often discussed, however, most Israelis do not trust others to guarantee free access to the Western Wall, for instance.

כשמעצמות מערביות קולוניאליות חשבו שהן מביאות ל**תִּרְבּוּת** העמים שכבשו, התוצאה הייתה בדרך כלל הריסת התרבות המקומית.

When western colonial powers thought they were bringing about **acculturation** of the peoples they had conquered, the result was generally the elimination of local culture.

Special Expressions

re-organization **רֵה-אִרְגּוּן**
oxidation-reduction, redox reaction **חִמְצוּן** חיזור
mixing (in film, TV) **עִרְבּוּל** צליל
advertising in the public domain **פִּרְסוּם**-חוצות
Septuagint **תִּרְגּוּם** השבעים
verbatim **translation** **תִּרְגּוּם** מילולי
loan **translation**, calque **תִּרְגּוּם** שאילה

Additional Examples in this Pattern

boxing אִגְרוּף
accommodation, hosting אִכְסוּן
improvisation אִלְתּוּר
characterization אִפְיוּן
enabling אִפְשׁוּר
hospitalization אִשְׁפּוּז

recitation, declamation דִּקְלוּם
spurring דִּרְבּוּן
oxidization חִמְצוּן
electrification חִשְׁמוּל
buttoning כִּפְתּוּר
centralization מִרְכּוּז
mortgaging מִשְׁכּוּן
neutralization נִטְרוּל
styling סִגְנוּן
centrifugation סִרְכּוּז
update עִדְכּוּן
mixing עִרְבּוּל

blurring עִרְפּוּל
patrolling פִּטְרוּל
supporting, maintaining פִּרְנוּס
catheterization צִנְתּוּר
cataloguing קִטְלוּג
scrubbing קִרְצוּף
armoring; safeguarding שִׁרְיוּן
spicing, seasoning תִּבְלוּן
programming תִּכְנוּת
precis תִּמְצוּת
maneuvering תִּמְרוּן

---

55. *CiCuC > CiCCuC* when the final consonant is guttural

our/your/their	my/your/his/her	const.	Gloss	sing/pl
פִּעְנוּחֵנוּ/חֲכֶם/חֲכֶן/חָם/חָן	**פִּעְנוּ**חִי/חֲךָ/חֵךְ/חוֹ/חָהּ	פִּעְנוּחַ-	decoding	פִּעְנוּחַ ז'
פִּעְנוּחֵינוּ/כֶם/כֶן/הֶם/הֶן	**פִּעְנוּ**חַי/חֶיךָ/חַיִךְ/חָיו/חֶיהָ	פִּעְנוּחֵי-		פִּעְנוּחִים

In the sing. masc. form the final guttural is preceded by a *pataH gnuva* after a vowel other than *a*. Where a *shva mobile* is expected with the guttural, it is replaced by *Hataf-pataH* (פִּעְנוּחֲךָ < פִּעְנוּחְךָ* etc.). In this particular case, there exist alternative realizations in which the *shva quiescent* in the first syllable is replaced by *Hataf-pataH* as well.

Examples

פִּעְנוּחַ צופן ה"אניגמה" הגרמנית עזר משמעותית לבריטים במלחמת העולם השנייה.
The **decoding** of the German Enigma code helped the British significantly in WWII.

---

56. *CiCuC > CiCCuC = 'iCCuC*: sub-pattern of *CiCCuC* derived from a tri-literal root + initial/prefixal א'

our/your/their	my/your/his/her	const.	Gloss	sing/pl
אִבְחוּנֵנוּ/נְכֶם/נְכֶן/נָם/נָן	**אִבְחוּ**נִי/נְךָ/נֵךְ/נוֹ/נָהּ	אִבְחוּן-	diagnosis	אִבְחוּן ז'
אִבְחוּנֵינוּ/כֶם/כֶן/הֶם/הֶן	**אִבְחוּ**נַי/נֶיךָ/נַיִךְ/נָיו/נֶיהָ	אִבְחוּנֵי-		אִבְחוּנִים

Examples

הרופא הזה אינו פופולרי במיוחד, אבל מצטיין **בְּאִבְחוּן** מחלות.
This doctor is not particularly popular, but he excels in the **diagnosis** of illnesses.

הבעייה העיקרית של הזוכים בבחירות היא **אִכְזוּב** חלק מבוחריהם אם אין הם מקיימים את הבטחותיהם מזמן מערכת הבחירות.
The primary problem facing election winners is **disappointing** some of their voters if they do not keep their campaign promises made during the election campaign.

הרבה בעיות במחשב נפתרות מאליהן על ידי **אִתְחוּל** (מחדש).
Many computer problems are resolved on their own by re-**booting**.

Special Expressions

re-**booting**, restarting (מחדש) **אִתְחוּל**

Additional Examples in this Pattern

reference, citation אִזְכּוּר
retrieval (computing) אִחְזוּר
storage אִחְסוּן
coming out of the closet אִחְצוּן
finishing off textile materials אִשְׁפּוּר

---

57. ***CiCuC* > *CiCCuC* = *'iCCuC*** (with a prefixal א׳) when the final consonant is guttural

sing/pl	Gloss	const.	my/your/his/her	our/your/their
אִזְרוּחַ ז׳	naturalization	אִזְרוּחַ-	**אִזְרוּ**חִי/חֲךָ/חֵךְ/חוֹ/חָהּ	**אִזְרוּ**חֵנוּ/חֲכֶם/חֲכֶן/חָם/חָן
אִזְרוּחִים		אִזְרוּחֵי-	**אִזְרוּ**חַי/חֶיךָ/חַיִךְ/חָיו/חֶיהָ	**אִזְרוּחֵי**נוּ/כֶם/כֶן/הֶם/הֶן

The first consonant in *CiCCuC* is prefixal *'alef*, and the last another guttural. In the sing. masc. form the final guttural is preceded by a *pataH gnuva* after a vowel other than *a*. Where a *shva* is expected with the guttural, it is replaced by *Hataf-pataH*. Pragmatically, plural forms are hardly used here.

Examples

דונלד מתנגד ל**אִזְרוּחָם** של מהגרים בלתי-חוקיים ללא קשר לזמן שהותם בארה״ב.
Donald objects to the **naturalization** of illegal immigrants regardless of how long they have been in the US.

Additional Examples in this Pattern

guarding, securing אִבְטוּחַ
fingering (music) אִצְבּוּעַ

---

58. ***CiCuC* > *CiCCuC* = *miCCuC***: sub-pattern of *CiCCuC* derived from a tri-literal root + initial מ׳

sing/pl	Gloss	const.	my/your/his/her	our/your/their
מִחְזוּר ז׳	recycling	מִחְזוּר-	**מִחְזוּ**רִי/רְךָ/רֵךְ/רוֹ/רָהּ	**מִחְזוּ**רֵנוּ/רְכֶם/רְכֶן/רָם/רָן
מִחְזוּרִים		מִחְזוּרֵי-	**מִחְזוּ**רַי/רֶיךָ/רַיִךְ/רָיו/רֶיהָ	**מִחְזוּרֵי**נוּ/כֶם/כֶן/הֶם/הֶן

Examples

ברוב המדינות המתקדמות בעולם **מִחְזוּר** הנייר, הפלסטיק והמתכת משפרים את איכות הסביבה.
In most advanced counties of the world the **recycling** of paper, plastic and metal improve the quality of the environment.

מִסְפּוּר הבתים ברחוב באירופה ובישראל הוא כזה שהמספרים הזוגיים מתחילים ועולים בצד ימין של הרחוב, והאי-זוגיים בצד שמאל. באזורים מסוימים בארה"ב המצב הפוך.
The **numbering** of houses in Europe and in Israel is such that even numbers begin and rise on the right side of the street, and the odd ones on the left. In some regions in the US the situation is reversed.

מִחְשׁוּב המפעל לקח יותר משנה, אבל כשהושלם הוא הביא להתייעלות משמעותית בתהליך הייצור, הפרסום והמשלוחים.
The plant's **computerization** took over a year, but when completed, it brought about significant streamlining of the production process, publicity and delivery.

תהליך המצאתה של תרופה חדשה הוא ארוך ומורכב, אבל גם **מִסְחוּרָהּ** לאחר מכן אינו פשוט.
The invention of a new medication is a long, complex process, but its subsequent **commercialization** is not simple either.

Special Expressions

cloud **computing** **מִחְשׁוּב** ענן

Additional Examples in this Pattern

miniaturization, minimization מִזְעוּר
equipping מִכְשׁוּר
booby-trapping מִלְכּוּד
framing מִסְגּוּר
nailing מִסְמוּר
making shelters מִקְלוּט

---

59. ***CiCuC* > *CiCCuC* = *miCCuC***: sub-pattern of *CiCCuC* derived from a tri-literal root + initial מִ׳ when the final consonant is a guttural

our/your/their	my/your/his/her	const.	Gloss	sing/pl
מִפְתּוּחֵנוּ/חֲכֶם/חֲכֶן/חָם/חָן	**מִפְתּוּ**חִי/חֲךָ/חֵךְ/חוֹ/חָהּ	מִפְתּוּחַ-	indexing	מִפְתּוּחַ ז׳

The singular forms without possessive pronouns end with a "furtive" *pataH* following a vowel other than *a*, and where a *shva* is expected, it is replaced by *Hataf-pataH*. Generally, no plural.

Examples

לאחר שסיימתי לכתוב את הספר, לקח לי כמה שבועות עד שהשלמתי את ה**מִפְתּוּחַ**.
After I had finished writing the book, it took me a few weeks to complete the **indexing**.

---

60. ***CiCuC* > *CiCCuC* = *shiCCuC***: sub-pattern of *CiCCuC* derived from a tri-literal root + initial שִׁ׳

our/your/their	my/your/his/her	const.	Gloss	sing/pl
שִׁדְרוּגֵנוּ/גְכֶם/גְכֶן/גָם/גָן	**שִׁדְרוּ**גִי/גְךָ/גֵךְ/גוֹ/גָהּ	שִׁדְרוּג-	upgrade N	שִׁדְרוּג ז׳
שִׁדְרוּגֵינוּ/כֶם/כֶן/הֶם/הֶן	**שִׁדְרוּ**גַי/גֶיךָ/גַיִךְ/גָיו/גֶיהָ	שִׁדְרוּגֵי-		שִׁדְרוּגִים

The prefix -ש denotes causation, and generally also causing a change of state, or repeated change of state.

Examples

הישראלים הם אלופי הטכנולוגיה. בכל פעם שיוצא מודל חדש של טלפון נייד, למשל, הם מבקשים **שִׁדְרוּג** מיידי.
The Israelis are champions of technology. As soon as a new model of a mobile phone is available, they immediately request an **upgrade**.

אפילו אם אין בכך צורך, רצוי תמיד לבקש **שִׁכְפּוּל** של כל מפתח שבידך.
Even if it does not seem to be necessary, it is always a good idea to request **duplication** of any key you have.

Additional Examples in this Pattern

שִׁחְבּוּר change one type of syntactic structure to another
שִׁחְזוּר reconstruction, restoration
שִׁחְלוּף exchange; recombination genetics
שִׁטְעוּן transshipment; reloading
שִׁכְתּוּב revision, rewriting
שִׁלְהוּב inciting, inflaming
שִׁעְבּוּד slavery; enslaving; subjugation
שִׁעְבּוּר Hebraization
שִׁעְתּוּק reproducing; transcribing
שִׁפְעוּל activation
שִׁתְחוּל restart (computing)

---

61. ***CiCuC > CiCCuC = shiCaCuC*** when the second consonant is guttural

our/your/their	my/your/his/her	const.	Gloss	sing/pl
שְׁעֲרוּכֵנוּ/כְכֶם/כְכֶן/כָם/כָן	**שְׁעֲרוּ**כִי/כְךָ/כֵךְ/כוֹ/כָהּ	-שְׁעֲרוּךְ	revaluation	שְׁעֲרוּךְ ז'
שְׁעֲרוּכֵינוּ/כֶם/כֶן/הֶם/הֶן	**שְׁעֲרוּ**כַי/כֶיךָ/כַיִךְ/כָיו/כֶיהָ	-שְׁעֲרוּכֵי		שְׁעֲרוּכִים

Like שִׁדְרוּג above, but when a *shva* is expected with a guttural, it is generally replaced by *Hataf-pataH*. Note: formally, there is no *Hataf* in שִׁעְבּוּד subjugation, שִׁעְבּוּר Hebraization (see above), to justify the preservation of a *dagesh lene* in the ב', but in normal speech the *Hataf* vowel is actually inserted: *shi`abud*, *shi`abur*.

Examples

המחיר הסופי שיוצע תמורת רכישת החברה ייקבע לאחר קיום **שְׁעֲרוּךְ**.
The final price to be offered for the company purchase will be determined after it undergoes **revaluation**.

ישראלים לא מעטים שנגררו ל**שִׁעְבּוּר/שִׁעֲבוּר/שְׁעֲבּוּר** שמות המשפחה ה"גלותיים" שלהם מתחרטים על כך היום.
A good number of Israelis who were led to the **Hebraization** of their "diasporic" last names regret having done so today.

---

62. ***CiCuC > CiCCuC = shiCCuC*** when the last consonant is guttural

our/your/their	my/your/his/her	const.	Gloss	sing/pl
שִׁכְנוּעֵנוּ/עֲכֶם/עֲכֶן/עָם/עָן	**שִׁכְנוּ**עִי/עֲךָ/עֵךְ/עוֹ/עָהּ	-שִׁכְנוּעַ	convincing, persuading	שִׁכְנוּעַ ז'
שִׁכְנוּעֵינוּ/כֶם/כֶן/הֶם/הֶן	**שִׁכְנוּ**עַי/עֶיךָ/עַיִךְ/עָיו/עֶיהָ	-שִׁכְנוּעֵי		שִׁכְנוּעִים

In final position following a vowel other than *a*, the guttural comes with a "furtive" *pataH*. When a *shva* is expected with a guttural, it is replaced by a *Hataf-pataH*.

Examples

האפקטיביות של מנהיג טוב מושפעת במידה רבה מכוח ה**שִׁכְנוּעַ** שלו.
To a great extent, the effectiveness of a good leader is determined by his **persuading** capability.

Additional Examples in this Pattern

reseeding שִׁזְרוּעַ   replanting שִׁנְטוּעַ

---

63. *CiCuC* > *CiCCuC* = *shiCCuC* when the last two consonants are identical

our/your/their	my/your/his/her	const.	Gloss	sing/pl
שִׁחְרוּרֵנוּ/רְכֶם/רְכֶן/רָם/רָן	**שִׁחְרוּ**רִי/רְךָ/רֵךְ/רוֹ/רָהּ	שִׁחְרוּר-	release,	שִׁחְרוּר ז'
שִׁחְרוּרֵינוּ/כֶם/כֶן/הֶם/הֶן	**שִׁחְרוּ**רַי/רֶיךָ/רַיִךְ/רָיו/רֶיהָ	שִׁחְרוּרֵי-	liberation	שִׁחְרוּרִים

The two last root consonants are identical (שְׁקְטוּט).

Examples

הישראלים קוראים למלחמת 1948 מלחמת ה**שִׁחְרוּר**; הערבים קוראים לה "האסון".
The Israelis call the 1948 war the War of **Liberation**; the Arabs call it The Catastrophe.

Additional Examples in this Pattern

enhancement, improvement; enhancing, improving שִׁכְלוּל

---

64. *CiCuC* > *CiCCuC* = *shiCCuC* when the last two consonants are identical and the second is guttural

our/your/their	my/your/his/her	const.	Gloss	sing/pl
שִׁעֲמוּמֵנוּ/מְכֶם/מְכֶן/מָם/מָן	**שִׁעֲמוּ**מִי/מְךָ/מֵךְ/מוֹ/מָהּ	שִׁעֲמוּם-	boredom	שִׁעֲמוּם ז'

When the second consonant is a ע', in some instances the *shva* is generally replaced by a *Hataf-pataH*: שִׁעֲמוּם < שִׁעְמוּם (שִׁקֲטוּט < שִׁקְטוּט). Pragmatically, plural forms are hardly used here.

Examples

הוא אוכל יותר מדיי לא בגלל שהוא ממש רעב, אלא מתוך **שִׁעֲמוּם**.
He eats too much not because he is really hungry, but out of **boredom**.

---

65. ***CiCuC > CiCCuC = tiCCuC***: sub-pattern of derived from a tri-literal root + initial ת׳

our/your/their	my/your/his/her	const.	Gloss	sing/pl
תִּפְקוּדֵנוּ/דְכֶם/דְכֶן/דָם/דָן	**תִּפְקוּ**דִי/דְךָ/דֵךְ/דוֹ/דָהּ	תִּפְקוּד-	functioning,	תִּפְקוּד ז׳
תִּפְקוּדֵינוּ/כֶם/כֶן/הֶם/הֶן	**תִּפְקוּ**דַי/דֶיךָ/דַיִךְ/דָיו/דֶיהָ	תִּפְקוּדֵי-	function	תִּפְקוּדִים

Pragmatically, most declensions are hardly ever used, particularly not in the plural.

Examples

מזכירה טובה לא רק ממלאת הוראות ממעסיקה, אלא גם משמשת כמנהלת המפקחת באופן כללי על **תִּפְקוּד** המשרד.

A good secretary not only follows her employer's instructions, but also serves as a manager who supervises the general **functioning** of the office.

לקראת כל ביקור של אישיות ציבורית מרכזית, המשטרה המקומית מקבלת **תִּגְבּוֹר** משמעותי מן המדינה, וכל הגורמים המעורבים עוברים **תִּדְרוּךְ** מפורט.

In preparation for any visit by a central public figure, the local police receives significant **reinforcement** from the State, and those involved undergo detailed **briefing**.

בניהול בתים משותפים, **תִּקְצוּב** נבון דורש הקצאה מראש ל**תִחְזוּק** מונע, כדי למזער את הצורך בהחלפת מערכות שלמות (קירור, חימום וכדו׳).

When managing apartment buildings, wise **budgeting** requires prior allocation for preventive **maintenance**, to minimize the need for replacing total systems (cooling, heating etc.).

השלב הסופי בהכנה של פצצה הוא **תִּחְמוּשָׁהּ**.

The final stage in the preparation of a bomb is its **arming**.

Special Expressions

תִּדְלוּק באוויר in-flight **refueling**

Additional Examples in this Pattern

תִּגְמוּל compensation

תִּדְלוּק refueling

תִּזְמוּן timing

תִּזְמוּר orchestration

תִּחְקוּר investigation

תִּחְשׁוּב calculation

תִּסְכּוּל frustration

תִּפְעוּל operation; management

תִּקְשׁוּב teleprocessing

תִּקְשׁוּר communication system

תִּרְגּוּל exercise, drilling

תִּשְׁאוּל preliminary inquiry

---

66. ***CiCuC > CiCCuC*** when the two first consonants are reduplicated (קִטְקוּט)

our/your/their	my/your/his/her	const.	Gloss	sing/pl
פִּטְפּוּטֵנוּ/טְכֶם/טְכֶן/טָם/טָן	**פִּטְפּוּ**טִי/טְךָ/טֵךְ/טוֹ/טָהּ	פִּטְפּוּט-	chatter,	פִּטְפּוּט ז׳
פִּטְפּוּטֵינוּ/כֶם/כֶן/הֶם/הֶן	**פִּטְפּוּ**טַי/טֶיךָ/טַיִךְ/טָיו/טֶיהָ	פִּטְפּוּטֵי-	prattle	פִּטְפּוּטִים

The first two consonants replace the second and third one, respectively. The result is reduplication of the first syllable, though with a different vowel, the *u* of the *CiCCuC* pattern.

Examples

הרקטור החדש הכריז שתם עידן הדיבורים וה**פִּטְפּוּטִים** ונפתח דף חדש של מעשים.
The new provost announced that the age of talking and **prattling** is over, and that a new page of actual deeds has been opened.

עם ההפרטה במרבית הקיבוצים בישראל שמו גם קץ ל**בִּזְבּוּז** בחדר האוכל. כשמשלמים עבור האוכל, לא מבזבזים ולא זורקים.
With the privatization of most kibbutzim in Israel they also put an end to the **waste** in the dining hall. When you pay for your food, you do not waste and you do not throw food out.

ראש הממשלה הודיע על קיצוצים בתקציב של השנה הבאה. כרגיל, ה**צִמְצוּמִים** יהיו בתקציב החינוך.
The Prime Minister announced cuts in next year's budget. As usual, the **reductions** will be in education.

אליהו עייף מאוד לאחר יום ארוך של עבודה; כשהוא מסיים את ארוחת הערב הוא מייד שוקע ב**נִמְנוּם** על הכורסה שממול הטלוויזיה.
Eliyahu is very tired after a long day's work; when he finishes supper falls into a **nap** on the armchair opposite the TV.

Special Expressions

דִּכְדּוּךְ נפש severe **depression**, despair
דִּקְדּוּק גנרטיבי generative **grammar**
דִּקְדּוּקֵי עניות pedantry, pettiness
ראה מ**הִרְהוּרֵי** לבו (he) imagined things

Additional Examples in this Pattern

גִּמְגּוּם stuttering
גִּרְגּוּר gargling
דִּגְדּוּג tickling
דִּכְדּוּךְ depression
דִּפְדּוּף turning pages
דִּקְדּוּק grammar; being precise
דִּשְׁדּוּשׁ stamping, treading
הִבְהוּב flashing, blinking
הִרְהוּר passing thought
זִלְזוּל disrespect
זִמְזוּם buzz, hum N
טִמְטוּם stupidity
טִפְטוּף dripping
טִרְטוּר rattle, din, clatter
טִשְׁטוּשׁ confusion; effacement

---

67. ***CiCuC* > *CiCCuC*** when the two first consonants are reduplicated (קִטְקוּט) and the final one is guttural

our/your/their	my/your/his/her	const.	Gloss	sing/pl
צִחְצוּחֵנוּ/חֲכֶם/חֲכֶן/חָם/חָן	**צִחְצוּ**חִי/חֲךָ/חֵךְ/חוֹ/חָהּ	צִחְצוּחַ-	brushing,	צִחְצוּחַ ז'
צִחְצוּחֵינוּ/כֶם/כֶן/הֶם/הֶן	**צִחְצוּ**חַי/חֶיךָ/חַיִךְ/חָיו/חֶיהָ	צִחְצוּחֵי-	polishing	צִחְצוּחִים

In the sing. masc. form the final guttural is preceded by a *pataH gnuva* when it follows a vowel other than *a*. Instead of an expected *shva* we get *Hataf-pataH*.

Examples

יש גברים החושבים ש**צִחְצוּחַ** נעליים שאינן חדשות עדיף על קניית נעליים חדשות, מכיוון שהרגליים כבר התרגלו להן.
Some men feel that **polishing** used shoes is preferable to purchasing new ones, since one's feet are already used to them.

קִעְקוּעַ, לא רק על הידיים והרגליים אלא גם על כל הגוף, נחשב היום לשיא האופנה אצל הצעירים.
Tattooing, not only on one's hands and feet but also all over the body, is considered to be top fashion among the young today.

אחד העונשים שהורים מטילים לעתים על ילדיהם שסרחו הוא **קִרְקוּעַ** לבית ליום או יומיים.
One type of punishment parents sometimes impose on their kids when they misbehave is **grounding** to the house for a day or two.

הגשם שירד אתמול לא הספיק כדי למזער את נזקי הבצורת, אבל **לִחְלוּחַ** האדמה שהביא הספיק כדי להציל את גינותיהם של אנשים פרטיים.
Yesterday's rain was not sufficient to minimize the drought damages, but the **moistening** of the ground it brought was enough to save private gardens.

Special Expressions

honing of swords; preparation for a verbal battle **צִחְצוּחַ** חרבות

Additional Examples in this Pattern

bubbling N בִּעְבּוּעַ
cackling of geese גִּעְגּוּעַ
shaking; swaying נִעְנוּעַ
bubbling; seeping פִּעְפּוּעַ
sniffing, smelling רִחְרוּחַ

---

68. *CiCuC* > *CiCCuC* = *CiCaCuC* when the two first consonants are reduplicated (קִטְקוּט), and the 2nd consonant and its duplicate are ע'

זִעֲזוּעַ ז'	shaking, destabilizing	-זִעֲזוּעַ

In the sing. masc. form the final guttural is preceded by a *pataH gnuva*. Instead of the expected *shva* we get *Hataf-pataH*. Pragmatically, no declension occurs, except for the construct state.

Examples

התבטאויותיו האחרונות של שר החוץ גרמו ל**זִעֲזוּעַ** מערכת היחסים בין שתי המדינות.
The latest outbursts by the foreign minister brought about **destabilization** of the relationships between the two nations.

---

69. ***CiCuC* > *CiCCuC* = *CaCaCuC***: *CiCCuC* when the two first consonants are reduplicated (קְטַקּוּט), and the second consonant and its duplicate are ע'

our/your/their	my/your/his/her	const.	Gloss	sing/pl
גַּעֲגוּעֵנוּ/עֲכֶם/עֲכֶן/עָם/עָן	**גַּעֲגוּ**עִי/עֲךָ/עֵךְ/עוֹ/עָהּ	גַּעֲגוּעַ-	longing	גַּעֲגוּעַ ז'
גַּעֲגוּעֵינוּ/כֶם/כֶן/הֶם/הֶן	**גַּעֲגוּ**עַי/עֶיךָ/עַיִךְ/עָיו/עֶיהָ	גַּעֲגוּעֵי-		גַּעֲגוּעִים

In the sing. masc. form the final guttural is preceded by a *pataH gnuva*. Instead of the expected *shva* we get *Hataf-pataH*. Occasionally, two forms, *CiCaCuC* and *CaCaCuC*, coexist; *CiCaCuC* is usually the automatic verbal noun, whereas *CaCaCuC* refers to something more tangible or more specific, as in זִעֲזוּעַ is 'shaking,' vs. זַעֲזוּעַ 'shock.' In the case of גִּעֲגוּעַ, it also denotes the gerund 'cackling,' but the counterpart גַּעֲגוּעַ has a different meaning, 'longing.'

Examples

כשהמנהיג הנוכחי של המדינה אינו מסוגל להתמודד עם בעיות פנימיות או חיצוניות, נזכרים תמיד ב**גַעֲגוּעִים** במנהיג של ממש בעבר שידע איך לעשות זאת.
When the current leader of a nation is unable to face internal or external problems, we always remember with **longing** a real leader in the past who could do it so well.

Special Expressions

concussion to the brain **זַעֲזוּעַ** מוח

Additional Examples in this Pattern

shock, turbulence; turmoil; crisis, upheaval זַעֲזוּעַ
entertainment, game שַׁעֲשׁוּעַ

---

70. ***CiCuC* > *CiCCuC*** when the third and fourth consonants are identical (קִטְלוּל)

our/your/their	my/your/his/her	const.	Gloss	sing/pl
תִּכְנוּנֵנוּ/נְכֶם/נְכֶן/נָם/נָן	**תִּכְנוּ**נִי/נְךָ/נֵךְ/נוֹ/נָהּ	תִּכְנוּן-	planning;	תִּכְנוּן ז'
תִּכְנוּנֵינוּ/כֶם/כֶן/הֶם/הֶן	**תִּכְנוּ**נַי/נֶיךָ/נַיִךְ/נָיו/נֶיהָ	תִּכְנוּנֵי-	designing	תִּכְנוּנִים

In most cases, the fourth consonant is derived by duplicating the last consonant in a tri-consonantal root, which resulted in a secondary quadrilateral root. This is its nominal abstract counterpart.

Examples

האדריכל אביגדור מתמחה ב**תִכְנוּן** מבני מגורים רבי קומות.
The architect Avigdor specializes in **designing** high rise residential buildings.

בדרך כלל, **תִּמְרוּר** הדרכים באירופה מתקדם יותר מאשר בארה"ב.
Generally, the **placing of road signs** in Europe is more advanced than it is in the US.

יש אנשים המעדיפים **אִוְרוּר** טבעי על פני מיזוג אוויר מרכזי.
There are people who prefer natural **ventilation** over central air-conditioning.

כמויות המים העצומות שירדו באזור במשך אלפי שנים גרמו ל**נִקְבּוּבָם** של סלעי הגיר הללו.
The enormous amounts of water that rained on the region for thousands of years caused the **perforation** of this limestone.

Special Expressions

frequency **modulation** (FM) **אִפְנוּן** תֶּדֶר
trade-off **שִׁקְלוּל** תמורות
city **planning**, urban design **תִּכְנוּן** ערים
family **planning** **תִּכְנוּן** המשפחה

Additional Examples in this Pattern

making miserable אִמְלוּל
nasal speech אִנְפּוּף
modulation (electronics) אִפְנוּן
ratification אִשְׁרוּר
ruffling דִּבְלוּל
adjustment, tuning כִּוְנוּן
dribbling ball כִּדְרוּר
spin; dizziness סִחְרוּר
numbering סִפְרוּר
mixing; shuffling עִרְבּוּב
giggling צִחְקוּק
adjusted calculation שִׁקְלוּל
insertion in wrong place שִׁרְבּוּב

H. *meCaCeC* and related *mishkalim*

71. ***meCaCeC***: generally the active participle of *pi`el*

our/your/their	my/your/his/her	const.	Gloss	sing/pl
מְלַמְּדֵנוּ/**מְלַמֶּדְ**כֶם/כֶן/**מְלַמְּדָ**ם/ן	מְלַמְּדִי/מְלַמֶּדְךָ/**מְלַמְּ**דֵךְ/דוֹ/דָהּ	מְלַמֵּד-	teacher,	מְלַמֵּד ז'
מְלַמְּדֵינוּ/כֶם/כֶן/הֶם/הֶן	**מְלַמְּ**דַי/דֶיךָ/דַיִךְ/דָיו/דֶיהָ	מְלַמְּדֵי-	tutor	מְלַמְּדִים

The active participle of *pi`el binyan*, *meCaCeC*, may serve as a noun, usually agentive, as in מְהַגֵּר 'immigrant,' מְנַצֵּחַ '(orchestra) conductor,' מְעַצֵּב 'designer,' and occasionally as an instrument, as in מְאַיֵּד 'carburetor,' or as an adjective, as in מְבַדֵּחַ 'amusing, funny,' מְדַכֵּא 'depressing,' מְרַתֵּק 'fascinating, spellbinding.' But one should remember that not every *meCaCeC* form has a parallel *pi`el* verb. Thus, there is no אִהֵב* form alongside מְאַהֵב 'lover.' When reduction may end in a sequence of two *shva*s within the same syllable, the base vowel is replaced by *seghol* instead of by *shva*, and the other *shva* closes the syllable: מְלַמֶּדְ-ךָ.

Examples

למורה הילדים בעיירה היהודית באירופה נהגו לקרוא **מְלַמֵּד**.
In Jewish town in Europe they used to call a children's teacher **tutor (or Heder teacher)**.

עדיין ממשיך הוויכוח: מה עדיף, **מְאַיֵּד** או הזרקת דלק אלקטרונית? מה שבטוח: ה**מְאַיֵּד** זול יותר.
The discussion continues: what is preferable, **carburetor** or electronic fuel injection? Only one thing is certain: the **carburetor** is cheaper.

אזרחי ישראל אוהבים מאוד לטייל. ה**מְטַיְּלִים** מישראל מגיעים לכל מקום בעולם, ומוצאים אין ספור דרכים לעשות זאת בזול.

The Israelis love to travel. Israeli **travelers** reach any corner of the world, and find innumerable ways to do it at low cost.

יש סופרים המעדיפים לכתוב בגוף ראשון, אחרים בגוף שלישי, ויש המשתמשים ב**מְסַפֵּר**, המספק ממד נוסף לרומן.

Some authors prefer to write in first person, others prefer third person writing, and still others use a **narrator**, who provides the novel with an additional dimension.

שלמה חזר מטיול ביפן עם סיפורים **מְרַתְּקִים** על היפנים ועל תרבותם.

Shlomo has returned from a trip to Japan with **fascinating** stories about the Japanese and their culture.

Special Expressions

I have learned something from any one of my **teachers** מכל **מְלַמְּדַי** השכלתי

which means that… ...**מְלַמֵּד** ש

Additional Examples in this Pattern

sorcerer, magician מְכַשֵּׁף	home room teacher; educator מְחַנֵּךְ
player (music) מְנַגֵּן	caregiver; therapist מְטַפֵּל
exploiter מְנַצֵּל	dryer מְיַבֵּשׁ
coefficient (math) מְקַדֵּם	doctor who delivers babies מְיַלֵּד
softener מְרַכֵּךְ	founder מְיַסֵּד
	representative Adj מְיַצֵּג

---

72. *meCaCeC* when the second consonant of the root is ה׳, ח׳ or ע׳

our/your/their	my/your/his/her	const.	Gloss	sing/pl
מְנַהֲלֵנוּ/**מְנַהַלְכֶם**/כֶן/**מְנַהֲלָם**/ן	מְנַהֲלִי/מְנַהַלְךָ/**מְנַהֲלֵךְ**/לוֹ/לָהּ	מְנַהֵל-	manager,	מְנַהֵל ז׳
מְנַהֲלֵינוּ/כֶם/כֶן/הֶם/הֶן	**מְנַהֲלַי**/לֶיךָ/לַיִךְ/לָיו/לֶיהָ	מְנַהֲלֵי-	headmaster	מְנַהֲלִים

When the second root consonant is a “guttural,” a *shva* will be replaced by a *Hataf-pataH* in the declension: מְנַהֲלִים. When a *shva* follows this *Hataf-pataH*, the latter is replaced by a *pataH*, and the second *shva* closes the syllable: מְנַהַלְ-ךָ.

Examples

אחת השערוריות הגדולות בארה״ב היא גודל משכורותיהם של **מְנַהֲלֵי** החברות הגדולות.

One of the major scandals in the US is the salary size of the of the large corporations’ **managers**.

ה**מְנַהֵל** הוא הגורם העיקרי בקביעת אופיו, איכותו ורמתו של בית ספר.

The **principal/headmaster** is the most important factor determining the nature, quality and level of a school.

המלכה ויקטוריה אהבה מאוד את בעלה הנסיך אלברט, אבל לפני שפגשה אותו היו לה לא מעט **מְאַהֲבִים**.

Queen Victoria truly loved her husband Prince Albert, but before she met him, she had had a number of **lovers**.

Special Expressions

foreman **מְנַהֵל** עבודה   bookkeeper **מְנַהֵל** חשבונות/פנקסים

Additional Examples in this Pattern

daydreaming Sl. מְרַחֵף   fortune teller מְנַחֵשׁ   advisory מְיַעֵץ

---

73. *meCaCeC* when the second consonant of the root is א׳ or ר׳

our/your/their	my/your/his/her	const.	Gloss	sing/pl
מְשָׁרְתֵנוּ/**מְשָׁרֶתְ**כֶם/כֶן/ **מְשָׁרְתָ**ם/ן	מְשָׁרְתִי/מְשָׁרֶתְךָ/**מְשָׁרְ**תֵךְ/תוֹ/תָהּ	מְשָׁרֵת-	servant; affix letter; conjunctive accent (bibl.)	מְשָׁרֵת ז׳
מְשָׁרְתֵינוּ/כֶם/כֶן/הֶם/הֶן	**מְשָׁרְ**תַי/תֶיךָ/תַיִךְ/תָיו/תֶיהָ	מְשָׁרְתֵי-		מְשָׁרְתִים

When the second root consonant is א׳ or ר׳, the *pataH* is replace by a *kamats*. The *kamats* is attributed to historical "compensatory lengthening," which allowed the existence of an open syllable because these consonants cannot be geminated, and therefore cannot close the syllable. When a sequence of two *shva*s could arise within the same syllable, the first is replaced by *seghol*: מְשָׁרֶתְךָ.

Examples

כשאריק עבד בוונצואלה, היו להם שני **מְשָׁרְתִים** צמודים בבית.
When Arik worked in Venezuela, they had two live-in **servants** in the house.

מְפָרֵשׁ המקרא המפורסם והפופולרי ביותר היה רש״י (ר׳ שלמה יצחקי).
The best known and most popular Hebrew Bible **commentator** was Rashi (Rabbi Shlomo YitsHaki).

Special Expressions

God's angels **מְשָׁרְתֵי** עליון

Additional Examples in this Pattern

coordinator מְתָאֵם   exhausting מְפָרֵךְ
refrigerator מְקָרֵר

---

74. *meCaCeC* when the 3rd root consonant is guttural

our/your/their	my/your/his/her	const.	Gloss	sing/pl
מְפַקְחֵנוּ/**מְפַקַּחֲ**כֶם/כֶן/**מְפַקְּחָ**ם/ן	מְפַקְּחִי/מְפַקַּחֲךָ/**מְפַקְּ**חֵךְ/חוֹ/חָהּ	מְפַקֵּחַ-	supervisor	מְפַקֵּחַ ז׳
מְפַקְּחֵינוּ/כֶם/כֶן/הֶם/הֶן	**מְפַקְּ**חַי/חֶיךָ/חַיִךְ/חָיו/חֶיהָ	מְפַקְּחֵי-		מְפַקְּחִים

When the third consonant of the root is guttural, after a vowel other than *a* it carries a *furtive pataH* in word-final position. When a *shva* is expected with a guttural, it will be replaced by a *Hataf-pataH*; when an additional *shva* is expected to result from reduction, that *shva* will be replaced by a *pataH*, so as to maintain an open syllable: מְפַקֵּק-חַךְ.

Examples

משרד החינוך ממנה **מְפַקְּחִים** שיוודאו שכל מורה ימלא את תפקידו כראוי בבית ספרו.
The Ministry of Education appoints **supervisors** to ascertain that every teacher performs his/her duties well at their school.

הכנר הוברמן הציל הרבה מוסיקאים יהודיים מאירופה עם משפחותיהם בשנות השלושים בכך שהביא אותם לארץ ישראל כדי להקים שם תזמורת סימפונית. הוא נעזר בכך לא מעט על ידי **המְנַצֵּחַ** הגדול ארטורו טוסקניני.
The violimist Huberman saved many Jewish musicians from Europe in the 1930's by bringing them to Palestine in order to start a symphony orchestra there. He received considerable help from the great **conductor** Arturo Toscanini.

הטיפול במחלות סרטניות הוא עבודת צוות: **מְנַתֵּחַ** עם עוזרים, אונקולוג, מומחה להקרנות, פסיכיאטר או פסיכולוג, מומחה לתזונה, מדריך לסוגים שונים של התעמלות, ואחרים.
Treating cancer is is team-work: a **surgeon** with assistants, an oncologist, a radiation specialist, a psychiatrist or psychologist, a nutritionist, instructor for different types of exercise, and others.

Special Expressions

מְנַתֵּחַ מערכות systems **analyst**

Additional Examples in this Pattern

מְיַגֵּעַ tiring, exhausting

מְשַׂגֵּעַ wonderful, terrific, gorgeous Sl.

---

75. ***meCaCeC* = *meCaCe*** when the 3rd root consonant is *y*

Gloss	*Fem.*	*Masc.*	
enjoyable	מְהַנָּה	מְהַנֶּה	*Sing.*
	מְהַנּוֹת	מְהַנִּים	*Plural*

As in *meCaCeC*, the active participle here – which is generally related to *pi`el* – can serve as a noun, מְלַוֶּה 'escort,' or an adjective, מְהַנֶּה 'enjoyable,' but in most cases as an adjective. If the second consonant of the root is א or ר and consequently not with a *dagesh*, the preceding vowel is signaled by a *kamats* rather than by a *pataH*, see מְגָרֶה below. However, when the second consonant is ה (or ח or ע, but there are no sufficiently common forms to include here), the *pataH* remains.

Examples

הטיול היה **מְהַנֶּה** מאוד, אבל גם מְעַיֵּף. היה קשה מאוד לחזור לעבודה למחרת.
The trip was very **enjoyable**, but also tiring. It was hard to get back to work the following day.

בדרך כלל אין מרשים לילדי בית ספר לצאת לטיולים ארוכים ללא מספר **מְלַוִּים**.
Generally they don't allow schoolchildren to go out on long trips without a few **escorts**.

Special Expressions

lowest common **denominator** **מְכַנֶּה** משותף

Saturday evening meal with songs to **accompany** the departure of "Sabbath the Queen" (note that the construct state ends with a *tsere*, not *seghol*) מְלַוֵּה **מַלְכָּה**

Additional Examples in this Pattern

cleaner, janitor מְנַקֶּה	used for identification מְזַהֶה
condenser מְעַבֶּה	denominator מְכַנֶּה
enticing, tempting מְפַתֶּה	exhaustive מְמַצֶּה

---

76. ***meCaCe*** **=** ***meCaCeC*** when the 3rd root consonant is *y* and the second consonant is א' or ר'

Gloss	Fem.	Masc.	
stimulating	מְגָרָה	מְגָרֶה	*Sing.*
	מְגָרוֹת	מְגָרִים	*Plural*

The active participle of *meCaCeC* here – which is related to *pi`el* – serves as an adjective. If the second consonant of the root is א' or ר' and consequently not marked with a *dagesh*, the preceding vowel is signaled by a *kamats* rather than by a *pataH*: מְגָרֶה.

Examples

A good book **stimulates** the intellect. ספר טוב **מְגָרֶה** את האינטלקט.

---

77. ***meCaCeC*** **=** ***meCoCeC*** when the second root consonant is *w* or *y*, or when the second and third consonants are identical

our/your/their	my/your/his/her	const.	Gloss	sing/pl
מְשׁוֹרְרֵנוּ/**מְשׁוֹרֶרְ**כֶם/כֶן/**מְשׁוֹרְרָ**ם/ן	מְשׁוֹרְרִי/מְשׁוֹרֶרְךָ/**מְשׁוֹרְ**רֵךְ/רוֹ/רָהּ	מְשׁוֹרֵר-	poet;	מְשׁוֹרֵר ז'
מְשׁוֹרְרֵינוּ/כֶם/כֶן/הֶם/הֶן	**מְשׁוֹרְ**רַי/רֶיךָ/רַיִךְ/רָיו/רֶיהָ	מְשׁוֹרְרֵי-	singer	מְשׁוֹרְרִים

meCoCeC (מְקוֹלֵל) is an alternant of *meCaCeC*, when the second consonant of the root is *w* or *y*, or when the second and third consonant of the root are identical, e.g., בד״ד. In the *mishkal* itself, an וֹ follows the first consonant, and the second and third consonants are identical, even when they are not in the root proper (קו״מ, שי״ר). As in *meCaCeC*, the active participle here – which is generally related to *pi`el* – can serve as a noun, מְשׁוֹרֵר 'poet' or an adjective, מְעוֹדֵד 'encouraging.' When a sequence of two *shva*s could arise within the same syllable, the first is replaced by *seghol*: מְשׁוֹרֶרְךָ.

Examples

מקובל לראות בחיים נחמן ביאליק את ה**מְשׁוֹרֵר** הלאומי של ישראל.

H. N. Bialik is generally regarded as Israel's "national **poet**."

אילן הוא **מְשׁוֹרֵר** צעיר וללא הרבה ניסיון בכתיבה, אבל ספר השירים הראשון שלו זכה לביקורות חיוביות ו**מְעוֹדְדוֹת**.
Ilan is a young **poet** with little experience in writing, but his first poetry book garnered positive and **encouraging** reviews.

במדינה דמוקרטית מתוקנת נהוג העיקרון של הפרדת הרשויות, שלפיו יש לפצל את סמכויות השלטון לרשויות נפרדות ועצמאיות. כך, למשל, הרשות המבצעת אינה יכולה להתערב בתחומי אחריותם של בית ה**מְחוֹקְקִים** או של בית המשפט.
In a *bona fide* democratic state there applies the principle of separation of powers, according to which the branches of government must be split into separate independent entities. Thus, for instance, the executive branch cannot intervene in the areas of responsibility of the **legislative** body or the judicial system.

Special Expressions

application **generator** **מְחוֹלֵל** יישומים (comp.)
legislative body, parliament בית ה**מְחוֹקְקִים**
alarm ("waking") clock שעון **מְעוֹרֵר**

Additional Examples in this Pattern

generator מְחוֹלֵל
flying, airborne מְעוֹפֵף
arousing, stimulating מְעוֹרֵר
outrageous מְקוֹמֵם
drummer מְתוֹפֵף

---

78. *meCaCeC* = *meCaCCeC* with four-consonant roots.

our/your/their	my/your/his/her	const.	Gloss	sing/pl
מְתַרְגְּמֵנוּ/גֶּמְכֶם/גֶּמְכֶן/גְּמָם/גְּמָן	**מְתַרְ**גְּמִי/גֶּמְךָ/גְּמֵךְ/גְּמוֹ/גְּמָהּ	מְתַרְגֵּם-	translator	מְתַרְגֵּם ז'
מְתַרְגְּמֵינוּ/כֶם/כֶן/הֶם/הֶן	**מְתַרְגְּ**מַי/מֶיךָ/מַיִךְ/מָיו/מֶיהָ	מְתַרְגְּמֵי-		מְתַרְגְּמִים

As in *meCaCeC*, the active participle here – which is generally related to *pi`el* – can serve as a noun, מְהַנְדֵּס 'engineer' or an adjective, מְעַנְיֵן, מְעַנְיֶנֶת... 'interesting.' When vowel reduction would have resulted in a sequence of two *shva*s within the same syllable, the first becomes a *seghol*: מְהַנְדֶּסְךָ etc.

Examples

החברה של דני מעסיקה חמישה **מְהַנְדְּסֵי** מכונות.
Danny's company employs five mechanical **engineers**.

Special Expressions

the **rodent** family **מְכַרְסְמִים**

Additional Examples in this Pattern

disappointing מְאַכְזֵב
organizer מְאַרְגֵּן
carcinogenic מְסַרְטֵן
cement mixer; blender מְעַרְבֵּל
breadwinner, wage earner מְפַרְנֵס

---

79. *meCaCeC* = *meCaCaCeC*: realization of *meCaCCeC* (expansion of *meCaCeC*) with four-consonant roots, when the second consonant is a guttural

our/your/their	my/your/his/her	const.	Gloss	sing/pl
מְרַאַיְנֵנוּ/יֶנְכֶם/יֶנְכֶן/יֶנָם/יֶנָן	**מְרַאַיְ**נִי/יֶנְךָ/יֶנֵךְ/יְנוֹ/יְנָהּ	-מְרַאֲיַן	interviewer	מְרַאֲיֵן ז׳
מְרַאַיְנֵינוּ/כֶם/כֶן/הֶם/הֶן	**מְרַאַיְ**נַי/נֶיךָ/נַיִךְ/נָיו/נֶיהָ	-מְרַאַיְנֵי		מְרַאַיְנִים

	Gloss	Fem.	Masc.	
	refreshing	מְרַעֲנֶנֶת	מְרַעֲנֵן	*Sing.*
		מְרַעַנְנוֹת	מְרַעַנְנִים	*Plural*

When the second consonant is a guttural, the expected quiescent *shva* is replaced by a *Hataf-pataH*: מְרַאֲיֵן < מְרַאְיֵן*. Since a *Hataf* is regarded as equivalent to a *shva mobile*, and one cannot have two *shva*'s in a sequence within the same syllable, the expected *Hataf-pataH* is replaced by a *pataH*, and the following *shva* closes the syllable: מְרַאְיֵנִים < מְרַאֲיְנִים* < מְרַאַיְנִים*.

Examples

לַ**מְרַאֲיֵן** הזה יש כל שבוע אורחים **מְעַנְיְנִים** מאוד. התוכנית שלו אף פעם לא **מְשַׁעֲמֶמֶת**.

This **interviewer** has very **interesting** guests every week. His program is never **boring**.

---

80. *meCaCeC* > *meCaCCeC* = *memaCCeC* from a trilateral root + prefixal *m*

our/your/their	my/your/his/her	const.	Gloss	sing/pl
מְמַסְפְּרֵנוּ/פֶּרְכֶם/פֶּרְכֶן/פְּרָם/פְּרָן	**מְמַסְ**פְּרִי/פֶּרְךָ/פְּרֵךְ/פְּרוֹ/פְּרָהּ	-מְמַסְפֵּר	numerator	מְמַסְפֵּר ז׳
מְמַסְפְּרֵינוּ/כֶם/כֶן/הֶם/הֶן	**מְמַסְפְּ**רַי/רֶיךָ/רַיִךְ/רָיו/רֶיהָ	-מְמַסְפְּרֵי		מְמַסְפְּרִים

Examples

בכרטיסי כניסה להופעה עם מקומות שאינם מסומנים משתמשים לא פעם ב**מְמַסְפֵּר** כדי להדפיס לפי מספר המקומות באולם.

In ticket for a performance in which there are no assigned seats they often use a **numerator** so as to print according to the number of total seats available.

---

81. *meCaCeC* > *meCaCCeC* = *meshaCaCeC* from a triconsonantal root + prefixal *sh*, when the two last consonants are identical and the second consonant is guttural

	Gloss	Fem.	Masc.	
	boring	מְשַׁעֲמֶמֶת	מְשַׁעֲמֵם	*Sing.*
		מְשַׁעַמְמוֹת	מְשַׁעַמְמִים	*Plural*

Examples

הסטודנטים אומרים שהמרצה הזה **מְשַׁעֲמֵם**, ושהבעיה היא שהוא קורא מן הכתוב במקום לדבר כדבר איש אל רעהו.

The students say that this lecturer is **boring**, and the problem is that he reads from prepared text instead of talking naturally.

82. *meCaCeC* > *meCaCCeC* = *metaCCeC* from a trilateral root + *t* prefix

our/your/their	my/your/his/her	const.	Gloss	sing/pl
מְתַכְנְתֵנוּ/נֶתְכֶם/נֶתְכֶן/נְתָם/נְתָן	**מְתַכְ**נְתִי/נֶתְךָ/נְתֵךְ/נְתוֹ/נְתָהּ	מְתַכְנֶת-	computer	מְתַכְנֶת ז'
מְתַכְנְתֵינוּ/כֶם/כֶן/הֶם/הֶן	**מְתַכְנְ**תַי/תֶיךָ/תַיִךְ/תָיו/תֶיהָ	מְתַכְנְתֵי-	programmer	מְתַכְנְתִים

Examples

מְתַכְנְתִים הם היום בעלי מקצוע מבוקשים ביותר.
Computer programmers are in high demand today.

Additional Examples in this Pattern

gas station attendant מְתַדְלֵק

---

83. *meCaCeC* > *meCaCCeC* when the two first consonants are duplicated in consonantal positions three and four, respectively (מְקַטְקֵט)

our/your/their	my/your/his/her	const.	Gloss	sing/pl
מְדַקְדְּקֵנוּ/דֶּקְכֶם/דֶּקְכֶן/דְּקָם/דְּקָן	**מְדַקְ**דְּקִי/דֶּקְךָ/דְּקֵךְ/דְּקוֹ/דְּקָהּ	מְדַקְדֵּק-	grammarian	מְדַקְדֵּק ז'
מְדַקְדְּקֵינוּ/כֶם/כֶן/הֶם/הֶן	**מְדַקְדְּ**קַי/קֶיךָ/קַיִךְ/קָיו/קֶיהָ	מְדַקְדְּקֵי-		מְדַקְדְּקִים

	Masc.	Fem.	Gloss
Sing.	מְרַשְׁרֵשׁ	מְרַשְׁרֶשֶׁת	rustling
Plural	מְרַשְׁרְשִׁים	מְרַשְׁרְשׁוֹת	

מרבית ההיקרויות הן שמות תואר. Most occurrences are adjectives

Examples

מרבית הסיפורים של אפלפלד הם **מְדַכְדְּכִים**.
Most of Apelfeld's stories are **depressing**.

קיבוצים רבים במצב כלכלי קשה היום, אבל בכל זאת כמה מהם **מְשַׂגְשְׂגִים** – במיוחד אלה שקנו לעצמם שם בתחומי תעשייה שונים, למשל קיבוץ סאסא שבגליל.
Most kibbutzim today are in dire economic situation, but still some of them are **prosperous** – particularly those that have made a name for themselves in various industrial fields, e.g., Sasa in the Galilee.

Special Expressions

money bills **מְרַשְׁרְשִׁים**

Additional Examples in this Pattern

flashing מְהַבְהֵב
instigator, agitator מְחַרְחֵר
drip (medicine) מְטַפְטֵף
rustling מְרַשְׁרֵשׁ
laxative מְשַׁלְשֵׁל

---

84. *meCaCeC* > *meCaCCeC* = *meCaCaCeC*: when the first two consonants are reduplicated, and both second and last consonants are guttural

our/your/their	my/your/his/her	const.	Gloss	sing/pl
מְנַעַנְעֵנוּ/עַנְכֶם/עַנְכֶן/עָם/עָן	**מְנַעַנְ**עִי/נֵעֲךָ/נְעֵךְ/נְעוֹ/נְעָהּ	מְנַעֲנַע-	key in musical instrument	מְנַעֲנֵעַ ז'
מְנַעַנְעֵינוּ/כֶם/כֶן/הֶם/הֶן	**מְנַעַנְ**עַי/עֶיךָ/עַיִךְ/עָיו/עֶיהָ	מְנַעַנְעֵי-		מְנַעַנְעִים

	Masc.	Fem.	Gloss
Sing.	מְשַׁעֲשֵׁעַ	מְשַׁעֲשַׁעַת	amusing
Plural	מְשַׁעַשְׁעִים	מְשַׁעַשְׁעוֹת	

In the sing. masc. form, the final guttural is preceded by a *furtive pataH* after a vowel other than *a*. When the second consonant is a guttural, the expected quiescent *shva* is replaced by a *Hataf-pataH*: ‘amusing’ מְשַׁעֲשֵׁעַ < מְשַׁעְשֵׁעַ *. Since a *Hataf* is regarded as equivalent to a *shva mobile*, and one cannot have two *shva*’s in a sequence within the same syllable, the *Hataf-pataH* is replaced by *pataH*, and the following *shva* closes the syllable: מְשַׁעַשְׁעִים < מְשַׁעֲשְׁעִים* < מְשַׁעְשְׁעִים*.

Examples

המבקרים נחלקו בהערכותיהם את המחזה החדש בברודווי, אך כולם הסכימו שהוא **מְשַׁעֲשֵׁעַ**.
The critics were divided in their reviews of the new Broadway play, but they all agreed that it was **entertaining**.

Additional Examples in this Pattern

shocking, terrifying מְזַעֲזֵעַ

---

85. *meCaCeC* > *meCaCCeC* when the last two consonants are identical (מְקַטְלֵל)

our/your/their	my/your/his/her	const.	Gloss	sing/pl
מְאַוְרְרֵנוּ/**מְאַוְרֶרְ**כֶם/כֶן/**מְאַוְרְרָ**ם/ן	מְאַוְרְרִי/מְאַוְרֶרְךָ/**מְאַוְרְ**רֵךְ/רוֹ/רָהּ	מְאַוְרֵר-	ventilator, fan	מְאַוְרֵר ז'
מְאַוְרְרֵינוּ/כֶם/כֶן/הֶם/הֶן	**מְאַוְ**רְרַי/רֶיךָ/רַיִךְ/רָיו/רֶיהָ	מְאַוְרְרֵי-		מְאַוְרְרִים

Examples

יש אנשים שאינם יכולים לסבול מיזוג אויר, ומעדיפים **מְאַוְרֵר**.
Some people dislike air conditioning, and prefer a **fan**.

Additional Examples in this Pattern

hair-raising, horrifying מְצַמְרֵר

dizzying מְסַחְרֵר

---

86. ***meCaCeC* > *meCaCCeC* = *meshaCCeC*** with a prefixal *sh+* when the last two consonants are identical (מְקַטְלֵל)

our/your/their	my/your/his/her	const.	Gloss	sing/pl
מְשַׁחְרְרֵנוּ/**מְשַׁחְרֶרְ**כֶם/כֶן/ **מְשַׁחְרְרָ**ם/ן	מְשַׁחְרְרִי/מְשַׁחְרֶרְךָ/**מְשַׁחְרְרֵ**ךְ /רוֹ/רָהּ	מְשַׁחְרֵר-	liberator	מְשַׁחְרֵר ז׳
מְשַׁחְרְרֵינוּ/כֶם/כֶן/הֶם/הֶן	**מְשַׁחְ**רְרַי/רֶיךָ/רַיִךְ/רָיו/רֶיהָ	מְשַׁחְרְרֵי-		מְשַׁחְרְרִים

Examples

אברהם לינקולן ייזכר תמיד כ**מְשַׁחְרֵר** העבדים הכושים בארה״ב.
Abraham Lincoln will always be remembered as the **liberator** of the black slaves in the US.

---

87. ***meCaCeC* > *meCaCCeC* = *metaCCeC*** with prefixal *t+* when the last two consonants are identical (מְקַטְלֵל)

our/your/their	my/your/his/her	const.	Gloss	sing/pl
מְתַכְנְנֵנוּ/נֶנְכֶם/נֶנְכֶן/נְנָם/נְנָן	**מְתַכְ**נְנִי/נֶנְךָ/נְנֵךְ/נְנוֹ/נְנָהּ	מְתַכְנֵן-	planner	מְתַכְנֵן ז׳
מְתַכְנְנֵינוּ/כֶם/כֶן/הֶם/הֶן	**מְתַכְנְ**נַי/נֶיךָ/נַיִךְ/נָיו/נֶיהָ	מְתַכְנְנֵי-		מְתַכְנְנִים

Examples

אחד המקצועות המוזרים ביותר בארה״ב הוא **מְתַכְנֵן** חתונות.
One of the strangest professions in the US is a wedding **planner**.

---

88. ***meCaCeC* > *meCaCaCeC*** when the two last consonants are identical (מְקַטְלֵל < מְקַטֲלֵל), and the second is guttural

Gloss	Fem.	Masc.	
refreshing	מְרַעֲנֶנֶת	מְרַעֲנֵן	*Sing.*
	מְרַעַנְנוֹת	מְרַעַנְנִים	*Plural*

When the second consonant is a guttural, the expected quiescent *shva* is replaced by a *Hataf-pataH*: 'boring' מְרַעֲנֵן < מְרַעְנֵן*. Since a *Hataf* is regarded as equivalent to a *shva mobile*, and one cannot have two *shva*'s within the same syllable, the *Hataf-pataH* is replaced by a *pataH* when a *shva* is expected in the third consonant:
*מְרַעְנְנִים < *מְרַעֲנְנִים < מְ-רַ-עַנְ-נִים

Examples

הצטערתי לשמוע שמייקל קרייטון נפטר. בכל ספר חדש שהוציא היה תמיד משהו חדש ו**מְרַעֲנֵן**.
I was sorry to hear that Michael Crichton. In every new book of his there was always something new and **refreshing**.

---

89. ***meCaCéCet***: the feminine alternant of *meCaCeC*

our/your/their	my/your/his/her	const.	Gloss	sing/pl
מְבַשַּׁלְתֵּנוּ/תְּכֶם/תְּכֶן/תָּם/תָּן	**מְבַשַּׁלְ**תִּי/תְּךָ/תֵּךְ/תּוֹ/תָּהּ	מְבַשֶּׁלֶת-	cook (f.);	מְבַשֶּׁלֶת נ׳
מְבַשְּׁלוֹתֵינוּ/כֶם/כֶן/הֶם/הֶן	**מְבַשְּׁלוֹ**תַי/תֶיךָ/תַיִךְ/תָיו/תֶיהָ	מְבַשְּׁלוֹת-	cooker (tool)	מְבַשְּׁלוֹת

The active participle in this pattern usually serves as a noun – generally for instruments performing the activity denoted by the verb, a can be seen from the additional examples below. When reduction of the vowel with with the second root consonant would have created an impermissible sequence of two *shva* mobiles, the first is replaced by *pataH*, the second closes the syllable.

Examples

כולם מרוצים מן ה**מְבַשֶּׁלֶת** החדשה בחדר האוכל שבמעונות.

Everybody's happy with the new **cook (f.)** of the dorm's dining commons.

רצוי לשטוף ירקות בכיור המטבח, דרך **מְסַנֶּנֶת**, לפני חיתוכם לסלט – כך ניתן להסיר חומרי ריסוס רעילים שלא חדרו לתוך הירקות עצמם.

It is a good idea to wash vegetables in a **strainer** in the kitchen sink before chopping them into a salad – this way one can remove carcinogenic spray that has not penetrated the vegetables.

Additional Examples in this Pattern

combine harvester מְאַלֶּמֶת	sorting machine מְמַיֶּנֶת
fertilizing machine מְדַשֶּׁנֶת	snowplow; grader מְפַלֶּסֶת

---

90. ***meCaCéCet* = *meCaCáCat*** when the second root consonant is guttural

our/your/their	my/your/his/her	const.	Gloss	sing/pl
מְכַסַּחְתֵּנוּ/תְּכֶם/תְּכֶן/תָּם/תָּן	**מְכַסַּחְ**תִּי/תְּךָ/תֵּךְ/תּוֹ/תָּהּ	מְכַסַּחַת-	lawn mower	מְכַסַּחַת נ׳
מְכַסְּחוֹתֵינוּ/כֶם/כֶן/הֶם/הֶן	**מְכַסְּחוֹ**תַי/תֶיךָ/תַיִךְ/תָיו/תֶיהָ	מְכַסְּחוֹת-	Coll.	מְכַסְּחוֹת

In the *meCaCeCet* pattern, when the last root consonant is a "guttural," the last two *seghol*s are replaced by two *pataH*s: מְכַסַּחַת 'lawn mower,' מְכַסַּחְתִּי etc. (in the Coll. מְכַסַּחַת, in normative Hebrew מַכְסֵחָה).

Examples

אתה מעדיף **מְכַסַּחַת** חשמלית או כזו המונעת בבנזין?

Do you prefer an electric **lawn mower** or one working on gasoline?

---

91. ***meCaCCut***

meCaCCut constitutes linear derivation of abstract nouns related to nouns in the *meCaCeC mishkal*, the active participle of *pi`el*. The *e* vowel of the base *meCaCeC* is elided. Only a few nouns are realized in this *mishkal*, and all of them refer to professions. Just one of them, מְיַלְּדוּת, is reasonably frequent, but a number of similar nouns, such as מְפַקְּדוּת 'being a commander,' were included, to show that this is a separate *mishkal*. It seems that pragmatically, there are no declension or plurals in this pattern. Note: when a *shva* is expected in the second consonant that is guttural, it is replaced by a *Hataf-pataH*: מְנַהֲלוּת 'directorship.'

Examples

מנחם קיבל את הכשרתו כרופא משפחה, אבל לאחר כמה שנים החליט להתמחות ב**מְיַלְּדוּת**.
Menahem was trained as a family doctor, but after a few years decided to specialize in **obstetrics**.

Additional Examples in this Pattern

the commander's profession מְפַקְּדוּת	sorcery מְכַשְּׁפוּת
	surgery (profession) מְנַתְּחוּת

I. *meCuCaC* and related *mishkalim*

92. *meCuCaC*

meCuCaC is the pattern of adjectives and sometimes nouns originating from the passive participle of *pu`al* verbs.

our/your/their	my/your/his/her	const.	Gloss	sing/pl
מְלֻמָּדֵנוּ/**מְלֻמַּדְ**כֶם/כֶן/**מְלֻמָּדָ**ם/ן	**מְלֻמָּ**דִי/דְךָ/דֵךְ/דוֹ/דָהּ	מְלֻמַּד-	scholar N;	מְלֻמָּד
מְלֻמָּדֵינוּ/**מְלֻמְּדֵי**כֶם/כֶן/הֶם/הֶן	**מְלֻמָּ**דַי/דֶיךָ/דַיִךְ/דָיו/דֶיהָ	מְלֻמְּדֵי-	learned Adj	מְלֻמָּדִים

מְלֻמֶּדֶת-	מְלֻמֶּדֶת נ'	מְלֻמַּד-	מְלֻמָּד ז'	learned
מְלֻמָּדוֹת-	מְלֻמָּדוֹת	מְלֻמְּדֵי-	מְלֻמָּדִים	

The *kubuts* is also maintained before a root-initial *Het*, but without the compensatory lengthening occurring before other gutturals (see below). When stress falls two syllables away, the *kamats* in the second root consonant is reduced to a *pataH* (מְלֻמַּדְכֶם) or to a *shva* (מְלֻמְּדֵי, מְלֻמְּדֵיכֶם). When the third root consonant is א', that א' is "silent" in the feminine singular form: מְדֻכֵּאת 'depressed, f.s.'

Examples

מְלֻמָּדִים לא מעטים עוסקים במחקר באופן עצמאי מחוץ למסגרת האוניברסיטאות.
a significant number of **scholars** are engaged in independent research outside of the university framework.

בגלל הפער הכלכלי בין גרמניה המערבית לגרמניה המזרחית, חשבו בתחילה שתתעוררנה בעיות קשות עם האיחוד, אבל גרמניה ה**מְאֻחֶדֶת** התגברה על הקשיים הראשוניים די מהר.
Becase of the economic gap between West Germany and East Germany, it was initially thought that serious difficulties would arise with the union, but **united** Germany overcame the early difficulties fairly fast.

כבר **מְאֻחָר** – מספיק לעבוד. בוא לישון ; תמשיך לעבוד מחר בבוקר.
It's **late** – you've worked enough. Come to bed and continue to work tomorrow morning.

היא עדיין ילדה, אבל חושבת ומדברת כמו אישה **מְבֻגֶּרֶת**.
She is still a child, but thinks and talks like an **adult**.

החשוד ברצח שנעלם **מְבֻקָּשׁ** על ידי המשטרה ; תמונתו תלויה בכל תחנות המשטרה ובכל סניפי הדואר באזור.
The murder supect who had disappeared is **wanted** by the police; his photo is hanging in all police stations and in all post offices in the region.

Special Expressions

behavior acquired automatically, out of habit מצוות אנשים **מְלֻמָּדָה**
experienced **מְלֻמַּד** ניסיון

Additional Examples in this Pattern

fossil; fossilized מְאֻבָּן
dusty מְאֻבָּק
unionized מְאֻגָּד
balanced מְאֻזָּן
threatened מְאֻיָּם
illustrated מְאֻיָּר
spelled מְאֻיָּת
trained מְאֻלָּף
forced, unnatural מְאֻלָּץ
insured; insured person מְבֻטָּח
cancelled; insignificant מְבֻטָּל
embarrassed מְבֻיָּשׁ
domesticated מְבֻיָּת
cooked, boiled מְבֻשָּׁל
crystallized מְגֻבָּשׁ

---

93. ***meCuCaC* = *meCoCaC*** when the second root consonant is guttural (except for ח׳)

our/your/their	my/your/his/her	const.	Gloss	sing/pl
מְקֹרָבֵנוּ/**מְקֹרַבְ**כֶם/כֶן/**מְקֹרָבָ**ם/ן	**מְקֹרָבִ**י/בְךָ/בֵךְ/בוֹ/בָהּ	מְקֹרַב-	close	מְקֹרָב ז׳
מְקֹרָבֵינוּ/**מְקֹרְבֵי**כֶם/כֶן/הֶם/הֶן	**מְקֹרָבַ**י/בֶיךָ/בַיִךְ/בָיו/בֶיהָ	מְקֹרְבֵי-	associate	מְקֹרָבִים

Construct	sing/pl	Construct	sing/pl	Gloss
מְרֹהֶטֶת-	מְרֹהֶטֶת נ׳	מְרֹהַט-	מְרֹהָט ז׳	furnished
מְרֹהֲטוֹת-	מְרֹהָטוֹת	מְרֹהֲטֵי-	מְרֹהָטִים	

The *kubuts* in the first root consonant becomes a *Holam Haser* to make up for the guttural not being geminated and in order to maintain an open syllable, *meCuCaC* > *meCoCaC* (though not before ח׳, where it is maintained, unmodified, e.g., מְאֻחָד, מְאֻחָר). When stress falls two syllables away, the *kamats* in the second root consonant is reduced to a *pataH* (מְקֹרַבְכֶם) or to a *shva* (מְקֹרְבֵי, מְקֹרְבֵיכֶם). In the case of א׳, ה׳, ע׳, the reduction to *shva* ends with a *Hataf-pataH* (-מְרֹהֲטֵי), but pragmatically, such form rarely ever occur, so no separate pattern was set for them. A similar process occurs when the final consonant is guttural (מְצֹרַעַךְ, מְצֹרַעֲכֶם), but because of the rarity of realizations, here too no separate pattern was set.

Examples

בכתבה של אתמול ב״ידיעות אחרונות״ דווח כי **מְקֹרָבָיו** של השר קיבלו הטבות חריגות במיסוי ובהקלות בנייה.

In yesterday's newspaper "Yedioth Aharonot" it was reported that the minister's **close associates** received exceptional benefits in taxation and in building permits.

שכירת דירה **מְרֹהֶטֶת** בלב תל אביב עולה כמעט כמו שכירת דירה דומה בניו יורק.

Renting a **furnished** apartment in the heart of Tel Aviv costs almost as much a renting a similar apartment in New York City.

נרקיסיסט הוא אדם ה**מְאֹהָב** בעצמו והבטוח שהוא מתנת אלוהים לעולם ולאומה.

A narcissist is a person who is **in love** with himself and who is convinced that s/he is God's gift to the world and to his/her nation.

למרבית הצער, קשה לעיתים להבין שפוליטיקאים מסוימים הם טיפשים או **מְטֹרָפִים**, והציבור בוחר בהם למשרה ציבורית רמה שהם לא מתאימים לה. נבחרים כאלה בדרך כלל משתפרים במהלך כהונתם, אבל לא תמיד.

Unfortunately, it is sometimes difficult to realize that certain politicians are stupid or **crazy**, and the public elects them for high public office to which they are not suited. Such elected office holders sometimes grow into the job, but not always.

Special Expressions

מְאֹהָב עד מעל לראש head over heels **in love**

מְעֹרָב ירושלמי **mixed** grill

השם ה**מְפֹרָשׁ** Tetragrammaton (the ineffable name)

בִּמְשֹׁעָר **approximate**ly

Additional Examples in this Pattern

מְאֹרָס engaged to be married
מְבֹאָר annotated
מְבֹהָל frightened, terrified
מְבֹרָךְ blessed
מְגֹהָץ ironed, pressed
מְגֹרָשׁ exiled person
מְזֹרָז accelerated
מְכֹעָר ugly
מְסֹרָס castrated
מְעֹרָב mixed; involved
מְפֹאָר magnificent
מְפֹרָט detailed
מְפֹרָשׁ explicit
מְצֹרָע leprous; leper

---

94. *meCuCaC* = *meCoCaC* when the 2nd root consonant is guttural and the plural suffix is *-ot*

our/your/their	my/your/his/her	const.	Gloss	sing/pl
מְאֹרָעֵנוּ/**מְאֹרַעֲ**כֶם/כֶן/**מְאֹרָעָ**ם/ן	**מְאֹרָ**עִי/עֲךָ/עֵךְ/עוֹ/עָהּ	מְאֹרַע-	event	מְאֹרָע ז׳
מְאֹרְעוֹתֵינוּ/כֶם/כֶן/הֶם/הֶן	**מְאֹרְעוֹ**תַי/תֶיךָ/תַיִךְ/תָיו/תֶיהָ	מְאֹרְעוֹת-		מְאֹרָעוֹת

When a *shva* is expected with the guttural, it is replaced by Hataf-*pataH*.

Examples

התושבים היהודיים בארץ ישראל קראו למרד הערבי של 1936 "ה**מְאֹרָעוֹת**".
The Jewish inhabitants of Palestine referred to the Arab Revolt of 1936 as "The **Events**."

---

95. *meCuCaC* = *meCuCe* when the third root consonant is *y*

Gloss	*Fem.*	*Masc.*	
strange	מְשֻׁנָּה	מְשֻׁנֶּה	*Sing.*
	מְשֻׁנּוֹת	מְשֻׁנִּים	*Plural*

As in *meCuCaC*, the passive participle here – which is generally related to *pu`al* – can serve as a noun, מְמֻנֶּה 'appointee,' or as an adjective, מְשֻׁנֶּה 'strange,' but most instances of *meCuCe* are adjectives.

Examples

הוא נראה קצת **מְשֻׁנֶּה**, אבל אומרים שהוא מנהל טוב.
He looks a bit **strange**, but they say that he is a good manager.

עניינים כגון אלה אינם בסמכותי; עליך לפנות ל**מְמֻנִּים** עליי.
Such matters are beyond my authority; you need to approach my **supervisors**.

אליעזר היה **מְרֻצֶּה** מאוד מן השיעור שהשתתף בו באוניברסיטה; לשמחתו, ציון העבודה שהגיש היה "**מְעֻלֶּה**".
Eliezer was very **satisfied** with the course he took at the university. Happily, his grade for the paper he submitted was "**excellent**."

מה שמפריע לי אצלו זה החיוך ה**מְעֻשֶּׂה**. אני יודע עד כמה הוא לא אמיתי.
What bothers me with him is his **artificial** smile; I know how ingenuine it is.

Special Expressions

רב ה**מְכֻסֶּה** על ה**מְגֻלֶּה**.
What is **covered/hidden** exceeds what is **revealed**.

Additional Examples in this Pattern

exposed, visible מְגֻלֶּה
offensive, indecent מְגֻנֶּה
fictitious, bogus מְדֻמֶּה
covered מְכֻסֶּה

experienced מְנֻסֶּה
expected מְצֻפֶּה
great, many מְרֻבֶּה
deceived מְרֻמֶּה

---

96. *meCuCaC* = *meCoCaC* when the second root consonant is *w* or *y*, or when the second and third ones are identical (מְקוֹלָל).

Gloss	*Fem.*	*Masc.*	
isolated	מְבוֹדֶדֶת	מְבוֹדָד	*Sing.*
	מְבוֹדָדוֹת	מְבוֹדָדִים	*Plural*

meCoCaC is an alternant of *meCuCaC*, when the second consonant of the root is *w* or *y*, or when the second and third consonant of the root are identical, e.g., בד״ד. In the *mishkal* itself, an וֹ follows the first consonant, and the second and third consonants are identical, even when they are not in the root proper (רו״מ, רי״ש). An isolated occurrence like מְרוֹקָן 'emptied,' where the two are not identical, is derived from the root רק״נ or רוק״נ, which originated from רי״ק. In almost all occurrences, the passive participle here – which is generally related to *pu`al* – serves as an adjective, מְבוֹדָד 'isolated.'

Examples

חיים במצב רוח **מְרוֹמָם** : הוא התקבל עם מלגה נאה לבית הספר ל**מְחוֹנָנִים**.
Hayyim is in a **festive** mood; he has been admitted with a decent scholarship to the school for the **gifted**.

Special Expressions

סיבה ו**מְסוֹבָב** cause and **outcome**

Additional Examples in this Pattern

מְעוֹדָד encouraged
מְרוֹקָן emptied
מְרוֹשָׁשׁ impoverished
מְשׁוֹלָל lacking

---

97. *meCuCaC* = *meCuCCaC* with four-consonant roots.

Gloss	Fem.	Masc.	
interested	מְעֻנְיֶנֶת	מְעֻנְיָן	*Sing.*
	מְעֻנְיָנוֹת	מְעֻנְיָנִים	*Plural*

In almost all occurrences, the passive participle here – which is generally related to *pu`al* – serves as an adjective, מְעֻנְיָן 'interested.'

Examples

תשובה סטנדרטית לצלצול טלפון מסחרי : ״תודה רבה, אבל אני לא **מְעֻנְיָן**״.
A standard response to a commercial phone call: "Thank you very much, but I am not **interested**."

אזור גוש דן (תל אביב והסביבה) **מְאֻכְלָס** בצפיפות רבה – יותר מכל אזור אחר בארץ.
The Dan region (Tel Aviv and environs) is densely **populated** – more than any other region in Israel.

האתגר העיקרי של מרבית המשטרות בעולם הוא ההתמודדות עם הפשע ה**מְאֻרְגָּן**.
The primary challenge of most police forces in the world is how to handle **organized** crime.

משיקולי בריאות וחיי מדף, יש לפסטר חלב ומוצריו, אבל יש הטוענים שגבינה **מְפֻסְטֶרֶת** אינה טעימה כמו גבינה שלא פוסטרה.
For health considerations and shelf life, milk and its products must be pasteurized, but some claim that **pasteurized** cheese is less tasty than unpasteurized cheese.

Special Expressions

organized crime פֶּשַׁע **מְאֻרְגָּן**
a **certified** idiot טיפש (אידיוט) **מְדֻפְלָם**
hair whose color has been lightened chemically (**oxygenated**, bleached) שער **מְחֻמְצָן**
It is a **well-known** fact מן **הַמְּפֻרְסָמוֹת**

Additional Examples in this Pattern

characterized מְאֻפְיָן
galvanized מְגֻלְוָן
hypnotized מְהֻפְנָט
polished, refined מְהֻקְצָע
electrified מְחֻשְׁמָל
diagonal, slanted מְלֻכְסָן
neutralized מְנֻטְרָל
subsidized מְסֻבְסָד
stylized מְסֻגְנָן
curious מְסֻקְרָן
starched מְעֻמְלָן
formatted מְפֻרְמָט
censored מְצֻנְזָר

---

98. ***meCuCaC > meCuCCaC = me'uCCaC*** from a trilateral root expanded to a quadrilateral one by the addition of the prefix+א

	Masc.	Fem.	Gloss
Sing.	מְאֻכְזָב	מְאֻכְזֶבֶת	disappointed
Plural	מְאֻכְזָבִים	מְאֻכְזָבוֹת	

In all occurrences, the passive participle here – which is generally related to *pu`al* – serves as an adjective.

Examples

אני **מְאֻכְזָב** מאוד מכל המועמדים לנשיאות ארה"ב, משתי המפלגות.
I am very **disappointed** with all candidates for the US presidency, from both parties.

הבית הלבן הוא כנראה הבניין **הַמְּאֻבְטָח** ביותר בארה"ב.
The White House is probably the best-**guarded** building in the US.

Additional Examples in this Pattern

retrieved מְאֻחְזָר
stored מְאֻחְסָן

---

99. ***meCuCaC > meCuCCaC = memuCaC*** from a trilateral root expanded to a quadrilateral one by the addition of the prefix+מ

	Masc.	Fem.	Gloss
Sing.	מְמֻחְזָר	מְמֻחְזֶרֶת	recycled
Plural	מְמֻחְזָרִים	מְמֻחְזָרוֹת	

In all occurrences, the passive participle here – which is generally related to *pu`al* – serves as an adjective.

Examples

היום ניתן לייצר כמעט כל דבר מחומר גלם **מְמֻחְזָר**.
Today it is possible to manufacture almost anything from **recycled** raw materials.

רוב המפעלים **מְמֻחְשָׁבִים** היום, ורוב העובדים פשוט משגיחים שהמכונות פועלות כראוי.
Most plants are **computerized** today, and most workers just make sure that the machines work properly.

Additional Examples in this Pattern

commercialized מְמֻסְחָר
nailed מְמֻסְמָר
disciplined מְמֻשְׁמָע
bespectacled מְמֻשְׁקָף

---

100. *meCuCaC > meCuCCaC = meshuCCaC* from a trilateral root expanded to a quadrilateral one by adding the prefix+ש

	Masc.	*Fem.*	*Gloss*
Sing.	מְשֻׁחְזָר	מְשֻׁחְזֶרֶת	reconstructed
Plural	מְשֻׁחְזָרִים	מְשֻׁחְזָרוֹת	

In all occurrences, the passive participle here – which is generally related to *pu`al* – serves as an adjective.

Examples

אחת האטקרציות הפופולריות בירושלים היא מודל **מְשֻׁחְזָר** של בית המקדש.
One of the popular attractions in Jerusalem is a **reconstructed** model of the Temple.

Additional Examples in this Pattern

convinced מְשֻׁכְנָע
excited, riled up, impassioned מְשֻׁלְהָב

---

101. *meCuCaC > meCuCCaC = meshuCCaC* from a trilateral root expanded to a quadrilateral one by the addition of the prefix +ש and when the last two consonants are identical (מְקֻטְלָל)

	Masc.	*Fem.*	*Gloss*
Sing.	מְשֻׁחְרָר	מְשֻׁחְרֶרֶת	freed, released
Plural	מְשֻׁחְרָרִים	מְשֻׁחְרָרוֹת	

In all occurrences, the passive participle here – which is generally related to *pu`al* – serves as an adjective.

Examples

ממשלת ישראל משתדלת לעזור לחיילים **מְשֻׁחְרָרִים** לרכוש דירות.
The Israeli government tries to help veterans ("**released**" soldiers) acquire housing.

---

102. ***meCuCaC > meCuCCaC = metuCCaC*** from a trilateral root expanded to a quadrilateral one by adding the prefix ת+

Gloss	Fem.	Masc.	
refueled	מְתֻדְלֶקֶת	מְתֻדְלָק	Sing.
	מְתֻדְלָקוֹת	מְתֻדְלָקִים	Plural

In all occurrences, the passive participle here – which is generally related to *pu`al* – serves as an adjective.

Examples

המכונית כבר **מְתֻדְלֶקֶת**? אני רוצה להתחיל כבר לנסוע, לפני שיחשיך.
Is the car **refueled** already? I want to hit the road before it gets dark.

---

103. ***meCuCaC = meCuCCaC*** when the two first consonants are duplicated in consonantal positions three and four, respectively (מְקֻטְקָט)

Gloss	Fem.	Masc.	
dirty	מְלֻכְלֶכֶת	מְלֻכְלָךְ	Sing.
	מְלֻכְלָכוֹת	מְלֻכְלָכִים	Plural

In all occurrences, the passive participle here – which is generally related to *pu`al* – serves as an adjective.

Examples

הכלים במדיח עדיין **מְלֻכְלָכִים**, או כבר נשטפו?
Are the dishes in the dishwasher still **dirty**, or were they washed already?

הכל נראה לי **מְטֻשְׁטָשׁ**; כנראה הגיע הזמן להתחיל להרכיב משקפיים.
Everything looks **blurred** to me; apparently it is time to start wearing eyeglasses.

כששירתנו בצבא, דרשו שהנעליים יהיו **מְצֻחְצָחוֹת** כל בוקר.
When we served in the Army, they required that our shoes be **polished** every morning.

Additional Examples in this Pattern

contemplative מְהֻרְהָר
stupid, foolish מְטֻמְטָם
embittered מְמֻרְמָר
sleepy, drowsy מְנֻמְנָם
dizzy; dazed מְסֻחְרָר
curly מְסֻלְסָל
dim, blurry מְעֻמְעָם
unstable, disturbed מְעֻרְעָר
limited, reduced מְצֻמְצָם
broken; rotten (food) מְקֻלְקָל

---

104. *meCuCaC* > *meCuCCaC* = *meCuCaCaC* when the two first consonants are duplicated in consonantal positions three and four, respectively (מְקֻטְקָט), and the second/fourth consonant is guttural

Gloss	Fem.	Masc.	
amused	מְשֻׁעֲשַׁעַת	מְשֻׁעֲשָׁע	Sing.
	מְשֻׁעֲשָׁעוֹת	מְשֻׁעֲשָׁעִים	Plural

In all occurrences, the passive participle here – which is generally related to *pu`al* – serves as an adjective. When a *shva* is expected, it is replaced by *Hataf-pataH*.

Examples

היא הביטה בו בחיוך **מְשֻׁעֲשָׁע** ולא אמרה דבר.
She looked at him with an **amused** smile, and did not say anything.

---

105. *meCuCaC* = *meCuCCaC* when the two last consonants are identical (מְקֻטְלָל)

Gloss	Fem.	Masc.	
ventilated	מְאֻוְרֶרֶת	מְאֻוְרָר	Sing.
	מְאֻוְרָרוֹת	מְאֻוְרָרִים	Plural

all occurrences, the passive participle here – which is generally related to *pu`al* – serves as an adjective.

Examples

בחורף, אם הכל סגור והבית אינו **מְאֻוְרָר**, צפויות לגרים בו סכנות בריאות רבות.
In the winter, if everything is closed and the house is not **ventilated**, people living in it are subjects to many health hazards.

נאום הנשיא נשמע ספונטני, אבל למעשה הוא היה **מְתֻכְנָן** על כל פרטיו, מילה במילה.
The President's speech sounded spontaneous, but in fact it had been **planned** with all its details, word by word.

Additional Examples in this Pattern

ratified מְאֻשְׁרָר
unkempt, tangled מְדֻבְלָל
crazy, "nuts" Sl. מְטֻרְלָל
adjusted, tuned מְכֻוְנָן
weighted מְשֻׁקְלָל

---

106. *meCuCaC* > *meCuCCaC* > *meCuCaCaC* = *meshuCaCaC* from a tri-literal root to which the prefix +שׁ was added, when the two last consonants are identical (מְקֻטְלָל), and the second consonant is a guttural

Gloss	Fem.	Masc.	
bored	מְשֻׁעֲמֶמֶת/מְשֻׁעֲמֶמֶת	מְשֻׁעֲמָם/מְשֻׁעֲמָם	Sing.
	מְשֻׁעֲמָמוֹת	מְשֻׁעֲמָמִים	Plural

Few occurrences. Where a *shva* is expected, it is replaced by *Hataf-pataH*, or alternatively, by a *Hataf-kamats*, preceded by a *kamats katan*, both pronounced [*o*].

Examples

אפרים מורה די טוב, אבל הסטודנטים בכיתה נראים **מְשֻׁעֲמָמִים** למדיי.
Ephraim is a fairly good teacher, but students in his class look pretty **bored**.

---

107. *meCuCaCut*: gerund/nominalization related to *pu`al*

our/your/their	my/your/his/her	const.	Gloss	sing/pl
מְיֻמָּנוּתֵנוּ/תְכֶם/תְכֶן/תָם/תָן	**מְיֻמָּנוּ**תִי/תְךָ/תֵךְ/תוֹ/תָהּ	מְיֻמָּנוּת-	skill,	מְיֻמָּנוּת נ׳
מְיֻמָּנוּיוֹתֵינוּ/כֶם/כֶן/הֶם/הֶן	**מְיֻמָּנוּיוֹ**תַי/תֶיךָ/תַיִךְ/תָיו/תֶיהָ	מְיֻמָּנוּיוֹת-	proficiency	מְיֻמָּנוּיוֹת

meCuCaCut is the pattern of gerunds or nominalizations related to *pu`al*, which are derived from passive participles in the *meCuCaC* pattern. This pattern can be seen either as a *mishkal* or as linear derivation. The *meCuCaC* base is in most cases an adjective, as in מְיֻמָּן 'skilled,' מְיֻחָד 'special,' and in a few cases either an adjective or noun, as in מְרֻבָּע 'quadrangle; square.' Most occurrences in this *mishkal* have no plural forms in use.

Examples

בהוראת שפה נוספת, מקפידים היום על הוראת כל ארבע ה**מְיֻמָּנוּיוֹת** הבסיסיות, דיבור, כתיבה, האזנה וקריאה, ומוסיפים לכך גם הוראת תרבות.
In teaching an additional language, we make sure today that all four basic **proficiencies** are covered, speaking, writing, listening and reading, and we add the teaching of culture as well.

בשל **מְגֻשָּׁמוּתוֹ** של עמוס, אשתו מעדיפה שלא יעזור לה במטבח. כמעט כל יום הוא מפיל ושובר צלחת או כוס.
Because of Amos' **clumsiness**, his wife prefers that he not help her in the kitchen. Almost daily he drops and breaks a plate or a glass.

Additional Examples in this Pattern

obligation מְחֻיָּבוּת
superfluousness מְיֻתָּרוּת
capability מְסֻגָּלוּת
being accepted; popularity מְקֻבָּלוּת
being square; acting strictly by the rule Col. מְרֻבָּעוּת

J. *hitCaCCut* and related *mishkalim*

108. *hitCaCCut*: gerund/nominalization related to *hitpa`el*

our/your/their	my/your/his/her	const.	Gloss	sing/pl
הִתְנַגְּדוּתֵנוּ/תְכֶם/תְכֶן/תָם/תָן	**הִתְנַגְּדוּ**תִי/תְךָ/תֵךְ/תוֹ/תָהּ	הִתְנַגְּדוּת-	objection,	הִתְנַגְּדוּת נ׳
הִתְנַגְּדוּיוֹתֵינוּ/כֶם/כֶן/הֶם/הֶן	**הִתְנַגְּדוּיוֹ**תַי/תֶיךָ/תַיִךְ/תָיו/תֶיהָ	הִתְנַגְּדוּיוֹת-	opposition	הִתְנַגְּדוּיוֹת

hitCaCCut is often a pattern designating nominalization of *hitpa`el* verbs, or gerunds, as in הִתְאַמֵּן 'train' ~ הִתְאַמְּנוּת 'training,' but often the *hitCaCCut* form also refers to a specific realization of the nominalization, as in הִתְנַגֵּד 'object V' ~ הִתְנַגְּדוּת 'objection (rather than 'objecting'), opposition, resistance.' This pattern can be regarded either as a *mishkal*, or as linear derivation with automatic elision of the base vowel.

Note: when the second consonant is guttural or ר׳, it does not come with a *dagesh* (see separate sub-pattern). Before a ר׳ the *pataH* turns into a *kamats*: הִתְפָּרְצוּת.

Examples

פּוּטִין השתלט על חצי האי קְרים ללא כל **הִתְנַגְּדוּת** צבאית.
Putin took over the Crimean Peninsula without any military **resistance**.

יש **הִתְנַגְּדוּת**? אם לא, נעבור לסעיף הבא בסדר היום.
Any **objection**? If not, let's move on to the next item on the agenda.

התחכום של פושעים היום מאפשר להם ליצור עדויות-כביכול שמדובר ב**הִתְאַבְּדוּת**.
The sophistication of criminals today enables them to create fake evidence of **suicide**.

תקופת ה**הִתְאַבְּלוּת** במסורת היהודית היא חודש ימים.
The **mourning** period in the Jewish tradition is a month.

הִתְיַתְּמוּת קשה לכל אחד, אפילו כאשר ההורה זקן.
Becoming an orphan is difficult for everybody, even when the parent is old.

ה**הִתְבַּטְּאוּיוֹת** של מנהיגים פוליטיים מסוימים אינן הולמות אופן הדיבור של אישיות ציבורית.
The **self-expressions** of certain political leaders do not befit the speech style of public figures.

ה**הִתְגַּיְּסוּת** לצבא היא אחת החוויות המרכזיות, לטובה ולרעה, בחיי כל ישראלי צעיר.
Induction to the army as a new recruit is one of the primary experiences, good and bad, in the life of any young Israeli.

הִתְחַדְּשׁוּת העברית המדוברת בשלהי המאה התשע עשרה הייתה מרכיב הכרחי של התגשמות החלום הציוני.
The **revival** of spoken Hebrew at the later part of the nineteenth century was a necessary component in the realization of the Zionist dream.

Special Expressions

mix-up; **reversal** **הִתְהַפְּכוּת** היוצרות

statute of **limitations** חוק ה**הִתְיַשְּׁנוּת**

Additional Examples in this Pattern

petrification הִתְאַבְּנוּת
unionizing; union הִתְאַגְּדוּת
becoming balanced הִתְאַזְּנוּת
training, exercising הִתְאַמְּנוּת
making an effort הִתְאַמְּצוּת
assembling הִתְאַסְּפוּת
putting on makeup הִתְאַפְּרוּת
maturation הִתְבַּגְּרוּת
standing out הִתְבַּלְּטוּת
splitting, cracking הִתְבַּקְּעוּת

הִתְגַּבְּרוּת overcoming
הִתְגַּבְּשׁוּת consolidation
הִתְגַּיְּרוּת converting to Judaism
הִתְגַּלְּמוּת embodiment
הִתְגַּנְּבוּת sneaking into
הִתְגַּשְּׁמוּת being realized; realization

הִתְהַפְּכוּת turning over
הִתְחַבְּקוּת hugging
הִתְחַבְּרוּת joining
הִתְחַיְּבוּת commitment
הִתְחַנְּפוּת flattery

---

109. *hitCaCCut* with *kamats*: gerund/nominalization related to *hitpa`el* when the second consonant is a ר׳

sing/pl	Gloss	const.	my/your/his/her	our/your/their
הִתְפָּרְצוּת נ׳	outburst; outbreak	הִתְפָּרְצוּת-	**הִתְפָּרְצוּ**תִי/תְךָ/תֵךְ/תוֹ/תָהּ	**הִתְפָּרְצוּ**תֵנוּ/תְכֶם/תְכֶן/תָם/תָן
הִתְפָּרְצוּיוֹת		הִתְפָּרְצוּיוֹת-	**הִתְפָּרְצוּיוֹ**תַי/תֶיךָ/תַיִךְ/תָיו/תֶיהָ	**הִתְפָּרְצוּיוֹ**תֵינוּ/כֶם/כֶן/הֶם/הֶן

When the second consonant in the *hit+CaCCut* pattern is *r*, the preceding *pataH* is replaced by *kamats* ("compensatory lengthening" because it cannot take a *dagesh*).

Examples

הִתְפָּרְצוּת המועמד למינוי כחבר בבית המשפט העליון לא הוסיפה לו כבוד.
The **outburst** by the nominee for membership in the Supreme Court did not add to his dignity.

הִתְאָרְחוּת לפרקי זמן ארוכים, אצל בני משפחה או חברים, לעיתים עלולה לשבש יחסים...
Staying as guests with family members or friends for extended periods may sometimes negatively affect relationships…

ה**הִתְחָרְדוּת** המתגברת של חלק ניכר מן האוכלוסיה הדתית בישראל מדאיגה את הציבור החילוני.
The increasing "**orthodoxification**" of large segments of the Israeli population worries the secular public.

בארה״ב קיימת רגישות חזקה למידת ה**הִתְעָרְבוּת** של המדינה בחיי הפרט ובצנעת הפרט.
In the US there is strong sensitivity to **intervention** of the state in the life of the individual and in his/her privacy.

הרבה התפתחויות חשובות חלו במזרח אירופה כתוצאה מ**הִתְפָּרְקוּת** ברית המועצות.
Many important developments occurred in Eastern Europe as a result of the **disintegration** of the Soviet Union.

הרבה חוששים היום מן האפשרות של **הִתְקָרְרוּת** היחסים בין ארה״ב לאירופה, ולא יודעים איך לפרש את ה**הִתְקָרְבוּת**-כביכול בין ארה״ב לצפון-קוריאה.
Many are worried today about possible **cooling** of the relationship between the US and Europe, and are not sure how to interpret the so-called **becoming closer** of the US and North Korea.

Additional Examples in this Pattern

הִתְאָרְכוּת lengthening
הִתְחָרְדוּת becoming ultra-orthodox Coll
הִתְעָרְבוּת bet; interfering, intervening

הִתְפָּרְדוּת splitting, branching out
הִתְפָּרְסוּת spreading; deployment
הִתְפָּרְעוּת unruliness; rampaging

---

110. *hitCaCCut* = *hitCaCaCut*: gerund/nominalization related to *hitpa`el* when the second consonant is a guttural א׳ ה׳ ח׳ ע׳

our/your/their	my/your/his/her	const.	Gloss	sing/pl
הִתְיַעֲצוּתֵנוּ/תְכֶם/תְכֶן/תָם/תָן	**הִתְיַעֲצוּ**תִי/תְךָ/תֵךְ/תוֹ/תָהּ	הִתְיַעֲצוּת-	consultation	הִתְיַעֲצוּת נ׳
הִתְיַעֲצוּיוֹתֵינוּ/כֶם/כֶן/הֶם/הֶן	**הִתְיַעֲצוּיוֹ**תַי/תֶיךָ/תַיִךְ/תָיו/תֶיהָ	הִתְיַעֲצוּיוֹת-		הִתְיַעֲצוּיוֹת

When the second consonant is a guttural, and a *shva* is expected, it is replaced by a *Hataf-pataH*: הִתְיַעֲצוּת, הִתְיַעֲצוּתִי... ‘consultation’

Examples

ראש הממשלה הורה לשגריר ישראל ברוסיה לחזור ארצה ל**הִתְיַעֲצוּיוֹת**.
The Prime Minister instructed the Israeli ambassador to Russia to come back home for **consultations**.

ההתקדמות העצומה בשנים האחרונות בתחום המחשוב הם ממש מעוררֵי **הִתְפַּעֲלוּת**.
The recent progress in computing is indeed cause for **wonder**.

בישראל ממשיך הויכוח בין הימין והשמאל על השאלה האם ה**הִתְנַחֲלוּיוֹת** בגדה המערבית מהוות מכשול בדרך להסכם שלום עם הפלסטינאים.
In Israel the debate between the right and left continues on the question of whether the **settlements** in the West Bank constitute an impediment to a peace agreement with the Palestinians.

על מה שחסר למנהיג הזה באינטליגנציה הוא מפצה ב**הִתְלַהֲבוּתוֹ** הגדולה.
For what he lacks in intelligence, this leader compensates with his great **enthusiasm**.

במדינות רבות מדווחים היום על הידרדרות ה**הִתְנַהֲגוּת** של תלמידים בבתי הספר.
In many countries today they report deterioration of students’ **behavior** in the schools.

הִתְיַעֲלוּת במפעלים תורמת כמובן להבראת החברה, אבל גם גורמת לעלייה באבטלה.
Streamlining in plants obviously contributes to the well-being of companies, but at the same time also causes increase in unemployment.

Special Expressions

adaptive **behavior** **הִתְנַהֲגוּת** מסתגלת
exaggerated **excitement** (expression borrowed from Yiddish) **הִתְפַּעֲלוּת** של עֵגֶל

Additional Examples in this Pattern

falling in love הִתְאַהֲבוּת
unification הִתְאַחֲדוּת
becoming bestialized הִתְבַּהֲמוּת
becoming clear הִתְבַּהֲרוּת
attitude; reference הִתְיַחֲסוּת
denial הִתְכַּחֲשׁוּת
whispering to each other הִתְלַחֲשׁוּת
boasting הִתְפָּאֲרוּת
crowd, gathering הִתְקַהֲלוּת
happening, event הִתְרַחֲשׁוּת

111. *hitCaCCut* = *histaCCut*: gerund/nominalization related to *hitpa`el* when the first root consonant is *s*

our/your/their	my/your/his/her	const.	Gloss	sing/pl
הִסְתַּיְּגוּתֵנוּ/תְכֶם/תְכֶן/תָם/תָן	**הִסְתַּיְּגוּ**תִי/תְךָ/תֵךְ/תוֹ/תָהּ	הִסְתַּיְּגוּת-	reservation, hesitation	הִסְתַּיְּגוּת נ׳
הִסְתַּיְּגוּיוֹתֵינוּ/כֶם/כֶן/הֶם/הֶן	**הִסְתַּיְּגוּיוֹ**תַי/תֶיךָ/תַיִךְ/תָיו/תֶיהָ	הִסְתַּיְּגוּיוֹת-		הִסְתַּיְּגוּיוֹת

When the first consonant of the root is a “sibilant,” the *t* of *hitpa`el* and the sibilant metathesize: \**hitsaklut* > *histaklut* ‘observation.’ *histaCCut* is also often a gerund of *hitpa`el* verbs, as in הִסְתַּכֵּל ‘observe’ ~ הִסְתַּכְּלוּת ‘observation,’ but occasionally the *hitCaCCut* form also refers to a specific realization of the nominalization, as in הִסְתַּדֵּר ‘arrange/organize oneself’ ~ הִסְתַּדְּרוּת ‘union (in Israel it refers to the large General Workers’ Union).’ *sh* (*shin*) or *s* (*sin*) behave like *s*, but to simplify the presentation, will be introduced separately. For *z* and *ts* the process is a bit more complex (see below). As in other *hitpa`el* cases, before ר׳ the *pataH* becomes *qamats*, e.g., הִסְתָּרְקוּת.

Examples

הצעת החוק הועברה בהצלחה בתת-הוועדה ללא כל **הִסְתַּיְּגוּיוֹת**.
The proposed bill was approved by the subcommittee without any **reservations**.

חומת ההפרדה הוקמה כדי למנוע **הִסְתַּנְּנוּת** מחבלים מעבר לגבול.
The separating wall was built in order to prevent **infiltration** of terrorists across the border.

הִסְתַּדְּרוּת העובדים הכללית היא אחד המוסדות החזקים בישראל.
The General Workers **Union** is one of the strongest institutions in Israel.

עיקרון חשוב במערכת המשפט הוא **הִסְתַּמְּכוּת** על תקדימים.
An important principle in the judicial system is **reliance** on precedents.

טענת הרוסים היא ש-95% מתושבי קרים תמכו ב**הִסְתַּפְּחוּת** לרוסיה.
The Russians claim that 95% of the people of Crimea supported its **becoming attached** to it.

Special Expressions

the Israeli workers **union** **הַהִסְתַּדְּרוּת**
arterio**sclerosis** **הִסְתַּיְּדוּת** עורקים
being satisfied with little **הִסְתַּפְּקוּת** במועט

Additional Examples in this Pattern

entangling; entanglement הִסְתַּבְּכוּת
probability הִסְתַּבְּרוּת
adaptation הִסְתַּגְּלוּת
seclusion; introversion הִסְתַּגְּרוּת
calcification (medical) הִסְתַּיְּדוּת
being aided הִסְתַּיְּעוּת
observing; observation הִסְתַּכְּלוּת
taking a risk הִסְתַּכְּנוּת
leaving, making an escape הִסְתַּלְּקוּת
being satisfied with הִסְתַּפְּקוּת
hiding oneself הִסְתַּתְּרוּת

112. *hitCaCCut* = *histaCaCut*: gerund/nominalization related to *hitpa`el* when the first root consonant is *s* and the second is a guttural

our/your/their	my/your/his/her	const.	Gloss	sing/pl
הִסְתַּעֲרוּתֵנוּ/תְכֶם/תְכֶן/תָם/תָן	**הִסְתַּעֲרוּ**תִי/תְךָ/תֵךְ/תוֹ/תָהּ	הִסְתַּעֲרוּת-	attack,	הִסְתַּעֲרוּת נ׳
הִסְתַּעֲרוּיוֹתֵינוּ/כֶם/כֶן/הֶם/הֶן	**הִסְתַּעֲרוּיוֹ**תַי/תֶיךָ/תַיִךְ/תָיו/תֶיהָ	הִסְתַּעֲרוּיוֹת-	storming	הִסְתַּעֲרוּיוֹת

When the first consonant of the root is *s*, the expected *shva* is replaced by a *Hataf-pataH* (in addition to the consonant metathesis – see הִסְתַּיְּגוּת above): הִסְתַּעֲרוּת....

Examples

ב**הִסְתַּעֲרוּת** על הגבעה ההיא נהרגו ארבעה חיילים.
Four soldiers were killed in the **storming** of (assault on) that hill.

Additional Examples in this Pattern

moral corruption הִסְתָּאֲבוּת
branching out, splitting; bifurcation הִסְתַּעֲפוּת

---

113. *hitCCaCut* = *hishtaCCut/histaCCut*: gerund/nominalization related to *hitpa`el* when the first root consonant is *sh* (*shin*) or *s* (*sin*)

our/your/their	my/your/his/her	const.	Gloss	sing/pl
הִשְׁתַּלְמוּתֵנוּ/תְכֶם/תְכֶן/תָם/תָן	**הִשְׁתַּלְמוּ**תִי/תְךָ/תֵךְ/תוֹ/תָהּ	הִשְׁתַּלְמוּת-	continuing	הִשְׁתַּלְמוּת נ׳
הִשְׁתַּלְמוּיוֹתֵינוּ/כֶם/כֶן/הֶם/הֶן	**הִשְׁתַּלְמוּיוֹ**תַי/תֶיךָ/תַיִךְ/תָיו/תֶיהָ	הִשְׁתַּלְמוּיוֹת-	education	הִשְׁתַּלְמוּיוֹת

When the first consonant of the root is a *s(in)* or *sh* (see *s* above), the *t* of *hitpa`el* and the sibilant metathesize ( = change places): \**hitshalmut* > *hishtalmut* 'continuing education.' Here too, *hishtaCCut* is often a pattern designating nominalization of *hitpa`el* verbs, or gerunds, as in הִשְׁתַּדֵּל 'make efforts, lobby' ~ הִשְׁתַּדְּלוּת 'making efforts; lobbying.'

Examples

משרד החינוך מקיים מדי שנה **הִשְׁתַּלְמֻיּוֹת** מיוחדות למורים, אך מצופה **הִשְׁתַּתְּפוּת** של בתי הספר בהם עובדים המורים בהוצאות הכרוכות בקורסי ה**הִשְׁתַּלְמוּת**.
The Ministry of Education holds yearly **continuing education** training for teachers, but **participation** in the expenses involved in **continuing education** courses is expected of the schools in which the teachers work.

חברות הביטוח בדרך כלל דורשות **הִשְׁתַּתְּפוּת**-עצמית של הלקוח כאשר מוגשת תביעה.
The insurance companies usually require clients' deductible (= **participation**) when a claim is submitted.

נרקיס התאהב בעצמו כשראה את **הִשְׁתַּקְּפוּת** דמותו במי האגם.
Narcissus fell in love with himself when he saw the **reflection** of his image in the water of the lake.

בשנים האחרונות ניכרת **הִשְׁתַּפְּרוּת** משמעותית באיכות השירות במסעדות בישראל.
In recent years one could notice significant **improvement** in the quality of service in Israeli restaurants.

תהליך ה**הִשְׁתַּקְּמוּת** של חיילים אמריקאים שאיבדו אברים במסגרת שירותם הצבאי אינו עומד בציפיות, בעיקר בשל אי סדר במערכת בתי החולים של הצבא ובניהולם הכושל.
The process of **rehabilitation** of American soldiers who have lost limbs during their military service is not up to par, primarily owing to disorder in the army's hospital system and its failing management.

Special Expressions

policyholder's **participation**, deductible **הִשְׁתַּתְּפוּת** עצמית
profit-**sharing** **הִשְׁתַּתְּפוּת** ברווחים

Additional Examples in this Pattern

refraction הִשְׁתַּבְּרוּת
disruption; confusion הִשְׁתַּבְּשׁוּת
making efforts הִשְׁתַּדְּלוּת
belonging הִשְׁתַּיְּכוּת
getting drunk הִשְׁתַּכְּרוּת
earning הִשְׁתַּכְּרוּת
becoming integrated הִשְׁתַּלְּבוּת
gaining control; taking over הִשְׁתַּלְּטוּת
shirking, evading הִשְׁתַּמְּטוּת
expressing one's feelings הִשְׁתַּפְּכוּת

---

114. *hitCCaCut = hishtaCCut/histaCCut* with *kamats*: gerund/nominalization related to *hitpa`el* when the 1st root consonant is *sh* (*shin*) or *s* (*sin*), and the 2nd root consonant is *r* [No pl. variants]

our/your/their	my/your/his/her	const.	Gloss	sing/pl
הִשְׁתָּרְשׁוּתֵנוּ/תְכֶם/תְכֶן/תָם/תָן	**הִשְׁתָּרְשׁוּ**תִי/תְךָ/תֵךְ/תוֹ/תָהּ	הִשְׁתָּרְשׁוּת-	enrooting	הִשְׁתָּרְשׁוּת נ׳

When the second consonant in the *hit+CaCCut* pattern is *r*, the preceding *pataH* is replaced by *kamats* ("compensatory lengthening" because it cannot take a *dagesh*).

Examples

הִשְׁתָּרְשׁוּת הרגלי אכילה לא בריאים אצל ילדים מקשים על שינוי הדיאטה שלהם כשהם מתבגרים.
The **enrooting** of unhealthy eating habits in children makes it difficult to change their diet when they become adults.

Additional Examples in this Pattern

lumbering; being dragged; extending (a queue) הִשְׁתָּרְכוּת
sprawling הִשְׁתָּרְעוּת

---

115. ***hitCaCCut = hishtaCaCut/histaCaCut***: gerund/nominalization related to *hitpa`el* when the first root consonant is *sh* (*shin*) or *s* (*sin*) and the second is a guttural א' ה' ח' ע'

our/your/their	my/your/his/her	const.	Gloss	sing/pl
הִשְׁתַּחֲווּתֵנוּ/תְכֶם/תְכֶן/תָם/תָן	**הִשְׁתַּחֲוו**ּתִי/תְךָ/תֵךְ/תוֹ/תָהּ	הִשְׁתַּחֲוּוּת-	bowing	הִשְׁתַּחֲווּת נ'
הִשְׁתַּחֲוּוּיוֹתֵינוּ/כֶם/כֶן/הֶם/הֶן	**הִשְׁתַּחֲוּוּיוֹ**תַי/תֶיךָ/תַיִךְ/תָיו/תֶיהָ	הִשְׁתַּחֲוּוּיוֹת-	down	הִשְׁתַּחֲוּוּיוֹת

When the first consonant of the root is שׁ or שׂ and the second root consonant is guttural, the expected *shva* is replaced by a *Hataf-pataH* (in addition to the consonant metathesis – see above).

Examples

בעבר **הִשְׁתַּחֲווּת** פרושה היה השתטחות אפיים ארצה; היום מסתפקים בקידה...
In the past, **הִשְׁתַּחֲווּת** meant **prostrating** oneself; today a slight bow suffices…

Additional Examples in this Pattern

coughing הִשְׁתַּעֲלוּת

---

116. ***hit+tsaCCut = hitstaCCut***: gerund/nominalization related to *hitpa`el* when the first root consonant is *ts* (*tsadi*)

our/your/their	my/your/his/her	const.	Gloss	sing/pl
הִצְטַדְּקוּתֵנוּ/תְכֶם/תְכֶן/תָם/תָן	**הִצְטַדְּקוּ**תִי/תְךָ/תֵךְ/תוֹ/תָהּ	הִצְטַדְּקוּת-	self-	הִצְטַדְּקוּת נ'
הִצְטַדְּקוּיוֹתֵינוּ/כֶם/כֶן/הֶם/הֶן	**הִצְטַדְּקוּיוֹ**תַי/תֶיךָ/תַיִךְ/תָיו/יהָ	הִצְטַדְּקוּיוֹת-	justification	הִצְטַדְּקוּיוֹת

When the first consonant of the root is a *ts*, the *t* of *hitpa`el* becomes *tet*, and the *tet* and *ts* metathesize ( = change places): \**hit+tsabrut* > *hitstabrut* 'accumulation.' Here too, *hitstaCCut* is often a pattern designating nominalization of *hitpa`el* verbs, or gerunds, as in הִצְטַבֵּר 'accumulate' ~ הִצְטַבְּרוּת 'accumulation.' When the second root consonant is ר', which cannot be geminated, the *pataH* is replaced by a *kamats*: הִצְטָרְפוּת (see below).

Examples

משפטו של הנהג שדרס ילד ופצע אותו קשה נפתח בהבעת צער על מה שקרה, ו**בהִצְטַדְּקוּת**: הנהג טען שהילד רץ אחרי כדור לאמצע הכביש, והוא לא הספיק לעצור את המכונית בזמן.
The trial of the driver who had run over a child and injured him severely opened with expression of sorrow for what happened, and with **self-justification**: The driver claimed that the child had been chasing a ball onto the middle of the road, and that he was unable to brake on time.

עובדים שהבחירה בידם מעדיפים בדרך כלל פנסיה תקציבית על פני פנסיה מצטברת, מכיוון ש**הִצְטַבְּרוּת** הכספים, אפילו בתוספת רבית, מעולם לא תגיע לרמה שתאפשר להם לקיים רמת חיים נאותה אחרי הפרישה.
Workers who have the choice usually prefer defined benefits plan over cumulative pension (401k-type), since the **accumulation** of funds, even with added interest, will never reach a level that will enable them to maintain a reasonable standard of living after retirement.

משה סיים את התואר הראשון שלו באוניברסיטה העברית ב**הִצְטַיְּנוּת**; אהרון סיים ב**הִצְטַיְּנוּת** יתרה.
Moshe graduated with a B.A. from the Hebrew University *magna* ***cum laude***; Aharon graduated *summa* ***cum laude***.

כמעט כל חורף, מיכה לוקה ב**הִצְטַנְּנוּת**, שלפעמים נמשכת במשך כל האביב.
Almost every .winter, Micah is down with a **cold**, which sometimes continues all through the spring season.

לפני שיוצאים למסע רגלי, יש להקפיד על **הִצְטַיְּדוּת** מתאימה.
Before embarking on a trip on foot, one needs to make sure of properly **equipping oneself**.

הִצְטַנְּעוּת אינה התכונה הבולטת של הנשיא הנוכחי.
Being modest is not the current president's most prominent trait.

Special Expressions

magna cum laude **בְּהִצְטַיְּנוּת**

Additional Examples in this Pattern

accumulation הִצְטַבְּרוּת
shrinking הִצְטַמְּקוּת
intersecting; intersection הִצְטַלְּבוּת
being portrayed/perceived הִצְטַיְּרוּת

---

117. *hitCaCCut* = *hitstaCaCut* with *kamats*: gerund/nominalization related to *hitpa`el* when the first root consonant is *ts* (*tsadi*) and the second consonant is *r*

our/your/their	my/your/his/her	const.	Gloss	sing/pl
הִצְטָרְפוּתֵנוּ/תְכֶם/תְכֶן/תָם/תָן	**הִצְטָרְפוּ**תִי/תְךָ/תֵךְ/תוֹ/תָהּ	הִצְטָרְפוּת-	joining	הִצְטָרְפוּת נ'
הִצְטָרְפוּיוֹתֵינוּ/כֶם/כֶן/הֶם/הֶן	**הִצְטָרְפוּיוֹ**תַי/תֶיךָ/תַיִךְ/תָיו/תֶיהָ	הִצְטָרְפוּיוֹת-		הִצְטָרְפוּיוֹת

When the first consonant of the root in the *hitpa`el* verb pattern is *ts* (*tsadi*) and the second root consonant is *r*, the preceding *pataH* is replaced by *kamats* as "compensatory lengthening" in lieu of the expected *dagesh* (in addition to the consonant metathesis – see above).

Examples

קשה לנו להחליט אם **הִצְטָרְפוּת** לטיול מאורגן היא רעיון טוב, או שעדיף לטייל לבד.
We have difficulty deciding if **joining** an organized group tour is a good idea, or we'd be better touring on our own.

Additional Examples in this Pattern

needing, requiring; having to do something הִצְטָרְכוּת

---

118. *hitCaCCut* = *hitstaCaCut*: gerund/nominalization related to *hitpa`el* when the first root consonant is *ts* (*tsadi*) and the second consonant is a guttural א׳ ה׳ ח׳ ע׳

our/your/their	my/your/his/her	const.	Gloss	sing/pl
הִצְטַעֲרוּתֵנוּ/תְכֶם/תְכֶן/תָם/תָן	**הִצְטַעֲרוּ**תִי/תְךָ/תֵךְ/תוֹ/תָהּ	הִצְטַעֲרוּת-	regretting	הִצְטַעֲרוּת נ׳
הִצְטַעֲרוּיוֹתֵינוּ/כֶם/כֶן/הֶם/הֶן	**הִצְטַעֲרוּיוֹ**תַי/תֶיךָ/תַיִךְ/תָיו/תֶיהָ	הִצְטַעֲרוּיוֹת-		הִצְטַעֲרוּיוֹת

When the second consonant of the root is a guttural, the expected *shva* is replaced by a *Hataf-pataH* (in addition to the consonant metathesis – see above).

Examples

הנזק כבר נעשה; **הִצְטַעֲרוּת** כבר לא תעזור ולא תועיל בשלב זה.
The damage has already been made; **regretting** will not help, nor will it be of any use at this point.

---

119. *hitCaCCut* = *hizdaCCut*: gerund/nominalization related to *hitpa`el* when the first root consonant is *z*

our/your/their	my/your/his/her	const.	Gloss	sing/pl
הִזְדַּמְּנוּתֵנוּ/תְכֶם/תְכֶן/תָם/תָן	**הִזְדַּמְּנוּ**תִי/תְךָ/תֵךְ/תוֹ/תָהּ	הִזְדַּמְּנוּת-	opportunity	הִזְדַּמְּנוּת נ׳
הִזְדַּמְּנוּיוֹתֵינוּ/כֶם/כֶן/הֶם/הֶן	**הִזְדַּמְּנוּיוֹ**תַי/תֶיךָ/תַיִךְ/תָיו/תֶיהָ	הִזְדַּמְּנוּיוֹת-		הִזְדַּמְּנוּיוֹת

When the first consonant of the root is a *z*, the *t* of *hitpa`el* becomes *d* (voicing assimilation), and the *d* and *z* metathesize ( = change places): \**hitzamnut* > *hizdamnut* ‘opportunity.’ Here too, *hizdaCCut* is often a pattern designating nominalization of *hitpa`el* verbs, or gerunds, as in הִזְדָּרֵז ‘hurry’ ~ הִזְדָּרְזוּת ‘hurrying.’

Examples

בדרך כלל נהוג לתת לעובד חדש שכשל **הִזְדַּמְּנוּת** נוספת להוכיח את עצמו.
Generally it is customary to give a new worker who stumbled another **opportunity** to prove himself/herself.

פרט למקרה של דוריאן גריי, תהליך ה**הִזְדַּקְּנוּת** הוא בלתי נמנע...
Except for the case of Dorian Gray, the process of **aging** is unavoidable…

הרבה מאמינים שייסורים יתרים מביאים בסופו של דבר ל**הִזְדַּכְּכוּת**.
Many believe that great suffering ultimately brings about **catharsis**.

Special Expressions

golden opportunity **הִזְדַּמְּנוּת** פז

Additional Examples in this Pattern

mating, sexual intercourse הִזְדַּוְּגוּת
arming; having sexual intercourse Sl. הִזְדַּיְּנוּת
tagging along הִזְדַּנְּבוּת
standing erect; straightening one’s back הִזְדַּקְּפוּת
requirement, need הִזְדַּקְּקוּת
standing out, prominence הִזְדַּקְּרוּת

---

120. ***hitCaCCut = hizdaCaCut*** with *kamats*: gerund/nominalization related to *hitpa`el* when the first root consonant is *z*, and the second consonant is *r*

our/your/their	my/your/his/her	const.	Gloss	sing/pl
הִזְדָּרְזוּתֵנוּ/תְכֶם/תְכֶן/תָם/תָן **הִזְדָּרְזוּיוֹתֵי**נוּ/כֶם/כֶן/תָם/תָן	**הִזְדָּרְזוּ**תִי/תְךָ/תֵךְ/תוֹ/תָהּ **הִזְדָּרְזוּיוֹ**תַי/תֶיךָ/תַיִךְ/תָיו/תֶיהָ	הִזְדָּרְזוּת- הִזְדָּרְזוּיוֹת-	hurrying	הִזְדָּרְזוּת נ׳ הִזְדָּרְזוּיוֹת

When the first consonant of the root is a *z*, the *t* of *hitpa`el* becomes *d* (voicing assimilation), and the *d* and *z* metathesize (see above). When the second consonant of the root is *r*, the preceding *pataH* is replaced by *kamats* ("compensatory lengthening").

Examples

בעיתון : **הִזְדָּרְזוּת** משרד ראש הממשלה להכריז על הפרשה כ׳רכילות׳ הינה מוקדמת מדי.
In the paper: The Prime Minister's office **hurrying** to declare the affair as 'gossip' is premature.

בערבית אומרים ש**הִזְדָּרְזוּת**-יתר (או חיפזון) היא מן השטן.
In Arabic they say that **hurrying** (or **rushing**) is from the Devil.

---

121. ***hitCaCCut = hizdaCaCut***: gerund/nominalization related to *hitpa`el* when the first root consonant is *z*, and the second consonant is a guttural א׳ ה׳ ח׳ ע׳

our/your/their	my/your/his/her	const.	Gloss	sing/pl
הִזְדַּהֲמוּתֵנוּ/תְכֶם/תְכֶן/תָם/תָן **הִזְדַּהֲמוּיוֹתֵי**נוּ/כֶם/כֶן/תָם/תָן	**הִזְדַּהֲמוּ**תִי/תְךָ/תֵךְ/תוֹ/תָהּ **הִזְדַּהֲמוּיוֹ**תַי/תֶיךָ/תַיִךְ/תָיו/ תֶיהָ	הִזְדַּהֲמוּת- הִזְדַּהֲמוּיוֹת-	becoming infected	הִזְדַּהֲמוּת נ׳ הִזְדַּהֲמוּיוֹת

When the first consonant of the root is a *z*, the *t* of *hitpa`el* becomes *d* (voicing assimilation), and the *d* and *z* metathesize (see above). When the second consonant of the root is a guttural, the expected *shva* is replaced by *Hataf-pataH*.

Examples

שמתי יוד על הפצע, כדי למנוע **הִזְדַּהֲמוּת**.
I applied iodine on the wound to prevent it from **becoming infected**.

הִזְדַּעֲפוּת היא המקבילה הספרותית של "התרגזות", אבל הקונוטציה שלה היא חריפה יותר.
Raging is the literary counterpart of "being angry," but its connotation is sharper.

Additional Examples in this Pattern

acting like a wolf הִזְדָּאֲבוּת
proceeding slowly הִזְדַּחֲלוּת
screaming; protesting הִזְדַּעֲקוּת

---

122. *hitCaCCut = hittaCCut*: gerund/nominalization related to *hitpa`el* when the first root consonant is *t*

our/your/their	my/your/his/her	const.	Gloss	sing/pl
הִתַּמְמוּתֵנוּ/תְכֶם/תְכֶן/תָם/תָן	**הִתַּמְמוּ**תִי/תְךָ/תֵךְ/תוֹ/תָהּ	הִתַּמְמוּת-	feigning innocence	הִתַּמְמוּת נ׳
הִתַּמְמוּיוֹתֵינוּ/כֶם/כֶן/הֶם/הֶן	**הִתַּמְמוּיוֹ**תַי/תֶיךָ/תַיִךְ/תָיו/תֶיהָ	הִתַּמְמוּיוֹת-		הִתַּמְמוּיוֹת

When the first consonant of the root is a *t*, the *t* of *hitpa`el* merge with it into a single, geminated *t*: הִתַּמְמוּת *hittamemut* 'feigning innocence' (in normal speech, the *tt* sequence is simplified to a non-geminate: *hitamemut*.) Here too, *hittaCCut* is usually a pattern designating nominalization of *hitpa`el* verbs, or gerunds, as in הִתַּמֵּם 'feign innocence' ~ הִתַּמְמוּת 'pretending innocence' above. [Note the phonetically-required *shva* separating between the two *m*'s.]

Examples

הִתַּמְמוּת לא תעזור לך ; המשטרה יודעת שאתה מעורב בעניין.

Feigning innocence won't help you here; the police know that you are involved.

Additional Examples in this Pattern

rising (smoke) הִתַּמְּרוּת

---

123. *hitCaCCut = hiddaCCut*: gerund/nominalization related to *hitpa`el* when the first root consonant is *d*

our/your/their	my/your/his/her	const.	Gloss	sing/pl
הִדַּיְנוּתֵנוּ/תְכֶם/תְכֶן/תָם/תָן	**הִדַּיְנוּ**תִי/תְךָ/תֵךְ/תוֹ/תָהּ	הִדַּיְנוּת-	litigation	הִדַּיְנוּת נ׳
הִדַּיְנוּיוֹתֵינוּ/כֶם/כֶן/הֶם/הֶן	**הִדַּיְנוּיוֹ**תַי/תֶיךָ/תַיִךְ/תָיו/תֶיהָ	הִדַּיְנוּיוֹת-		הִדַּיְנוּיוֹת

When the first consonant of the root is a *d*, the *t* of *hitpa`el* is assimilated and becomes *d* (voicing assimilation), and the two merge into a single, geminated *d*: **hitdaynut* > *hiddaynut* 'litigation' (in normal speech, the *dd* sequence is simplified to a non-geminate: *hidaynut*.) Here too, *hiddaCCut* is usually a pattern designating nominalization of *hitpa`el* verbs, or gerunds, as in הִדַּיֵּן 'litigate' ~ הִדַּיְנוּת 'litigating; litigation' above.

Examples

אריאל הוא עורך דין שהתמחותו **בהִדַּיְנוּת**.

Ariel is a lawyer specializing in **litigation**.

Additional Examples in this Pattern

contagion הִדַּבְּקוּת

knocking repeatedly הִדַּפְּקוּת

parleying, negotiating הִדַּבְּרוּת

---

124. *hitCaCCut = hittaCCut*: gerund/nominalization related to *hitpa`el* when the first root consonant is *tet*

our/your/their	my/your/his/her	const.	Gloss	sing/pl
הִטַּמְעוּתֵנוּ/תְכֶם/תְכֶן/תָם/תָן	**הִטַּמְעוּ**תִי/תְךָ/תֵךְ/תוֹ/תָהּ	הִטַּמְעוּת-	assimilation, being assimilated	הִטַּמְעוּת נ׳
הִטַּמְעוּיוֹתֵינוּ/כֶם/כֶן/תָם/תָן	**הִטַּמְעוּיוֹ**תַי/תֶיךָ/תַיִךְ/תָיו/תֶיהָ	הִטַּמְעוּיוֹת-		הִטַּמְעוּיוֹת

When the first consonant of the root is a *tet*, the *t* of *hitpa`el* is assimilated and becomes *tet*, and the two merge into a single, geminated *tet*: *hittam`ut* ‘assimilation’ (in normal speech, that *tet* is simplified to a non-geminate: *hitam`ut*.)

Examples

במסורת האורתודוקסית נגיעה של מי שאינו יהודי ביין כשר גורמת ל**הִטַּמְּאוּתוֹ** ולפסילתו לשתיה...
In the orthodox tradition a non-Jew touching a kosher wine causes its **contamination** and disqualification for drinking…

לפחות בעבר, שאיפתם של מרבית המהגרים לארה״ב הייתה להגיע ל**הִטַּמְּעוּת** מלאה באוכלוסיה הכללית.
At least in the past, the desire of immigrants to the US was to reach full **assimilation** in the general population.

Additional Examples in this Pattern

getting dirty הִטַּנְּפוּת being fried הִטַּגְּנוּת

---

125. *hitCaCCut = hittaCaCut*: gerund/nominalization related to *hitpa`el* when the first root consonant is *tet* and when the second consonant is a guttural

our/your/their	my/your/his/her	const.	Gloss	sing/pl
הִטַּהֲרוּתֵנוּ/תְכֶם/תְכֶן/תָם/תָן	**הִטַּהֲרוּ**תִי/תְךָ/תֵךְ/תוֹ/תָהּ	הִטַּהֲרוּת-	purification	הִטַּהֲרוּת נ׳
הִטַּהֲרוּיוֹתֵינוּ/כֶם/כֶן/הֶם/הֶן	**הִטַּהֲרוּיוֹ**תַי/תֶיךָ/תַיִךְ/תָיו/תֶיהָ	הִטַּהֲרוּיוֹת-		הִטַּהֲרוּיוֹת

When the first consonant of the root is a *tet*, the *t* of *hitpa`el* is assimilated and becomes *tet*, and the two merge into a single, geminated *tet* (see above). When the second consonant is a guttural, an expected *shva* is replaced by *Hataf-pataH*.

Examples

טבילה במקווה היא סמל או מחווה של **הִטַּהֲרוּת**.
Dipping oneself in a *mikveh* (ritual bath) is a symbol or gesture of **purification**.

---

126. *hitCaCCut = hitCaCut*: gerund/nominalization of *hitpa`el*, when the third consonant of the root is *y*

our/your/their	my/your/his/her	const.	Gloss	sing/pl
הִתְגַּלּוּתֵנוּ/תְכֶם/תְכֶן/תָם/תָן	**הִתְגַּלּוּ**תִי/תְךָ/תֵךְ/תוֹ/תָהּ	הִתְגַּלּוּת-	revelation	הִתְגַּלּוּת נ׳
הִתְגַּלֻּיּוֹתֵינוּ/כֶם/כֶן/הֶם/הֶן	**הִתְגַּלּוּיוֹ**תַי/תֶיךָ/תַיִךְ/תָיו/תֶיהָ	הִתְגַּלּוּיוֹת-		הִתְגַּלּוּיוֹת

hitCaCut is often a pattern designating nominalization of *hitpa`el* verbs, or gerunds, when the third consonant of the root is *y*; in the singular this *y* is not realized. The *hitCaCut* form may also refer to a specific realization of the nominalization, as in הִתְגַּלָּה ‘be revealed’ ~ **הִתְגַּלּוּת** ‘epiphany’ (in addition to ‘revelation’.)

Examples

מדי פעם מופיעות בערוצי התקשורת הנוצריים נשים המדווחות על **הִתְגַּלּוּת** של ישו בחלומן עם מסר כזה או אחר.
From time to time women appear in the Christian media, reporting on a **revelation** with Jesus in their dream with one message or another.

הִתְהַוּוּת איים חדשים באוקיינוס היא אירוע נדיר, אבל עשויה לחול בכל עת ללא התראה מראש.
The **creation** of new islands in the ocean is a rare occurrence, but might happen at any time with no prior warning.

יש אוניברסיטאות המעדיפות סטודנטים מבוגרים יותר שעברו **הִתְנַסֻּיּוֹת** שונות בחייהם על פני צעירים בראשית דרכם.
Some universities prefer older students with various life **experiences** over youths in their initial stage of adult life.

כאשר צפויים שטפונות בארה״ב בתקופת הגשמים, תפקידה הראשון של המשטרה הוא לוודא **הִתְפַּנּוּת** של התושבים באזור העומד להיפגע.
When floods are expected in the US in the rainy season, the first responsibility of the police is to ensure **evacuation** of the residents of the affected area.

כשרוברט משתתף בתפילת יום א׳ בכנסיה הקתולית המקומית, מתעוררת בו תמיד תחושה של **הִתְעַלּוּת**.
When Robert participates in the Sunday mass in the local Catholic church, it arouses in him a feeling of **spiritual elevation**.

Special Expressions

investigating the…(sources of, reasons) for **הִתְחַקּוּת** על שורשֵי...

Additional Examples in this Pattern

evaporation הִתְאַדּוּת
craving, lust הִתְאַוּוּת
healing; joining together הִתְאַחוּת
being proven false הִתְבַּדּוּת
being humiliated הִתְבַּזּוּת
being worn out הִתְבַּלּוּת
confessing הִתְוַדּוּת
impersonating הִתְחַזּוּת
researching, investigating הִתְחַקּוּת
covering self הִתְכַּסּוּת
being appointed הִתְמַנּוּת
suffering הִתְעַנּוּת
giving in to temptation הִתְפַּתּוּת
hardening הִתְקַשּׁוּת
increase; reproduction הִתְרַבּוּת
relaxing הִתְרַפּוּת

---

127. *hitCaCut* = *hitCaCut*: gerund/nominalization related to *hitpa`el*, when the third consonant of the root is *y* and the second guttural ה׳ ח׳ ע׳

our/your/their	my/your/his/her	const.	Gloss	sing/pl
הִתְמַחוּתֵנוּ/תְכֶם/תְכֶן/תָם/תָן	**הִתְמַחוּ**תִי/תְךָ/תֵךְ/תוֹ/תָהּ	הִתְמַחוּת-	specialization;	הִתְמַחוּת נ׳
הִתְמַחֻיּוֹתֵינוּ/כֶם/כֶן/הֶם/הֶן	**הִתְמַחֻיּוֹ**תַי/תֶיךָ/תַיִךְ/תָיו/תֶיהָ	הִתְמַחֻיּוֹת-	expertise	הִתְמַחֻיּוֹת

The declension is like that of הִתְגַּלּוּת above, but when the second root consonant is ה׳ ח׳ ע׳ it does not take a *dagesh*, of course, and the preceding vowel remains *pataH*.

Examples

הַהִתְמַחוּת של עליזה היא בשפות גרמניות, בעיקר סקנדינביות.
Aliza's **specialization** is in Germanic languages, particularly the Scandinavian ones.

Additional Examples in this Pattern

healing; joining together הִתְאַחוּת

---

128. *hitCaCCut* = *hitCaCut* with *kamats*: gerund/nominalization related to *hitpa`el*, when the third consonant of the root is *y* and the second guttural א׳ ר׳

our/your/their	my/your/his/her	const.	Gloss	sing/pl
הִתְחָרוּתֵנוּ/תְכֶם/תְכֶן/תָם/תָן	**הִתְחָרוּ**תִי/תְךָ/תֵךְ/תוֹ/תָהּ	הִתְחָרוּת-	competing; competition	הִתְחָרוּת נ׳
הִתְחָרוּיוֹתֵינוּ/כֶם/כֶן/הֶם/הֶן	**הִתְחָרוּיוֹ**תַי/תֶיךָ/תַיִךְ/תָיו/תֶיהָ	הִתְחָרוּיוֹת-		הִתְחָרוּיוֹת

The declension is like that of הִתְגַּלּוּת above, but when the second root consonant is א׳ or ר׳ it does not take a *dagesh*, of course, and the preceding vowel changes into *kamats* ("compensatory lengthening".)

Examples

הַהִתְחָרוּת בין נבחרות החתירה של הרווארד וייל נמשכת כבר דורות.
The **competition** between the Harvard and Yale rowing teams has been continuing for generations.

הַהִתְגָּאוּת של אל גור שהוא המציא את האינטרנט לא עזרה לו במערכת הבחירות...
Al Gore's **bragging** that he had invented the Internet did not help him in the election campaign...

Additional Examples in this Pattern

being proud, bragging הִתְגָּאוּת
teasing; arousal הִתְגָּרוּת
integrating הִתְעָרוּת
seeing each other, meeting הִתְרָאוּת

---

129. *hitCaCCut* = *hishtaCut*: gerund/nominalization related to *hitpa`el*, when the first consonant of the root is *sh* and the third is *y*

our/your/their	my/your/his/her	const.	Gloss	sing/pl
הִשְׁתַּטוּתֵנוּ/תְכֶם/תְכֶן/תָם/תָן	**הִשְׁתַּטוּ**תִי/תְךָ/תֵךְ/תוֹ/תָהּ	הִשְׁתַּטוּת-	playing the fool	הִשְׁתַּטוּת נ׳
הִשְׁתַּטוּיוֹתֵינוּ/כֶם/כֶן/הֶם/הֶן	**הִשְׁתַּטוּיוֹ**תַי/תֶיךָ/תַיִךְ/תָיו/תֶיהָ	הִשְׁתַּטוּיוֹת-		הִשְׁתַּטוּיוֹת

hishtaCut is often a pattern designating nominalization of *hitpa`el* verbs, or gerunds, when the first consonant of the root is *sh* and the third is *y*. The *sh* and the *t* of *hitpa`el* metathesize. In the singular, the *y* of the root is not realized.

Examples

במקרים מסוימים, **הִשְׁתַּטּוּת** עוזרת להיחלץ מצרה; אם חושבים שאדם שוטה, עוזבים אותו במנוחה.
In certain situations **playing the fool** can help one extricate oneself from getting in trouble; if they think you are a fool, they leave you alone.

המצב נשאר גרוע כשהיה. לא חלה כל **הִשְׁתַּנּוּת**, לא לטובה ולא לרעה.
The situation remains as bad as it was. No **change** has occurred – no better, no worse.

Additional Examples in this Pattern

equalizing הִשְׁתַּוּוּת

---

130. *hitCaCCut* = *hishtaCut*: gerund/nominalization related to *hitpa`el*, when the first consonant of the root is *sh* and the third is *y* and the second ה׳ ח׳ ע׳

our/your/their	my/your/his/her	const.	Gloss	sing/pl
הִשְׁתַּהוּתֵנוּ/תְכֶם/תְכֶן/תָם/תָן	**הִשְׁתַּהוּ**תִי/תְךָ/תֵךְ/תוֹ/תָהּ	הִשְׁתַּהוּת-	delay,	הִשְׁתַּהוּת נ׳
הִשְׁתַּהֲוִיּוֹתֵינוּ/כֶם/כֶן/הֶם/הֶן	**הִשְׁתַּהֲוִיּוֹ**תַי/תֶיךָ/תַיִךְ/תָיו/תֶיהָ	הִשְׁתַּהֲוִיּוֹת-	lateness	הִשְׁתַּהֲוִיּוֹת

The declension is like that of הִשְׁתַּנּוּת above, but when the second root consonant is ה׳ ח׳ ע׳ it does not take a *dagesh*, of course, and the preceding vowel remains *pataH.*

Examples

הקונצרט לא החל בזמן, בשל **הִשְׁתַּהוּת** טיסתו של המנצח.
The concert did not start on time, because of a **delay** in the conductor's flight.

---

131. *hitCaCCut* = *hishtaCut*: gerund/nominalization related to *hitpa`el*, when the first consonant of the root is *sh*, the third is *y*, and the second א׳ ר׳

our/your/their	my/your/his/her	const.	Gloss	sing/pl
הִשְׁתָּאוּתֵנוּ/תְכֶם/תְכֶן/תָם/תָן	**הִשְׁתָּאוּ**תִי/תְךָ/תֵךְ/תוֹ/תָהּ	הִשְׁתָּאוּת-	amazement	הִשְׁתָּאוּת נ׳
הִשְׁתָּאֻוִיּוֹתֵינוּ/כֶם/כֶן/הֶם/הֶן	**הִשְׁתָּאֻוִיּוֹ**תַי/תֶיךָ/תַיִךְ/תָיו/תֶיהָ	הִשְׁתָּאֻוִיּוֹת-		הִשְׁתָּאֻוִיּוֹת

The declension is like that of הִשְׁתַּנּוּת above, but when the second root consonant is א׳ or ר׳ it does not take a *dagesh*, of course, and the preceding vowel changes into *kamats* ("compensatory lengthening".)

Examples

הקהל הגיב **בהִשְׁתָּאוּת** על נאומו המוזר של המנהיג, אבל איש לא אמר דבר.
The audience reacted with **amazement** at the leader's weird speech, but nobody said anything.

---

132. ***hiCaCCut = hizdaCut***: gerund/nominalization related to *hitpa`el*, when the first consonant of the root is *z* and the third is *y*

our/your/their	my/your/his/her	const.	Gloss	sing/pl
הִזְדַּכּוּתֵנוּ/תְכֶם/תְכֶן/תָם/תָן	**הִזְדַּכּוּ**תִי/תְךָ/תֵךְ/תוֹ/תָהּ	הִזְדַּכּוּת-	returning	הִזְדַּכּוּת נ׳
הִזְדַּכּוּיוֹתֵינוּ/כֶם/כֶן/הֶם/הֶן	**הִזְדַּכּוּיוֹ**תַי/תֶיךָ/תַיִךְ/תָיו/תֶיהָ	הִזְדַּכּוּיוֹת-	(equipment)	הִזְדַּכּוּיוֹת

hizdaCut is a pattern designating nominalization of *hitpa`el* verbs, or gerunds, when the first consonant of the root is *z* and the third is *y*. The *t* of *hitpa`el* is assimilated and becomes *d*, and that *d* and *z* metathesize. In the singular, the *y* of the root is not realized.

Examples

בתום התרגיל אסור לשכוח לסדר את **הַהִזְדַּכּוּת** על הציוד שהוחזר.
At the end of the exercise one should not forget to take care of the (**confirmed**) **return** of the equipment.

---

133. ***hitCaCCut = hizdaCut***: gerund/nominalization related to *hitpa`el*, when the first consonant of the root is *z*, the third is *y*, and the second is ה׳ ח׳ ע׳

our/your/their	my/your/his/her	const.	Gloss	sing/pl
הִזְדַּהוּתֵנוּ/תְכֶם/תְכֶן/תָם/תָן	**הִזְדַּהוּ**תִי/תְךָ/תֵךְ/תוֹ/תָהּ	הִזְדַּהוּת-	identification	הִזְדַּהוּת נ׳
הִזְדַּהוּיוֹתֵינוּ/כֶם/כֶן/הֶם/הֶן	**הִזְדַּהוּיוֹ**תַי/תֶיךָ/תַיִךְ/תָיו/תֶיהָ	הִזְדַּהוּיוֹת-		הִזְדַּהוּיוֹת

The declension is like that of הִזְדַּכּוּת above, but when the second root consonant is ה׳ ח׳ ע׳ it does not take a *dagesh*, of course, and the preceding vowel remains *pataH*.

Examples

מן הידועות היא, שלעתים חטופים מגיעים למידה של **הִזְדַּהוּת** עם חוטפיהם.
It is known that occasionally, kidnapped people reach a degree of **identification** with their kidnappers.

---

134. ***hitCaCCut = hiddaCut***: gerund/nominalization related to *hitpa`el*, when the first consonant of the root is *d* and the third is *y*

our/your/their	my/your/his/her	const.	Gloss	sing/pl
הִדַּמּוּתֵנוּ/תְכֶם/תְכֶן/תָם/תָן	**הִדַּמּוּ**תִי/תְךָ/תֵךְ/תוֹ/תָהּ	הִדַּמּוּת-	modeling	הִדַּמּוּת נ׳
הִדַּמּוּיוֹתֵינוּ/כֶם/כֶן/הֶם/הֶן	**הִדַּמּוּיוֹ**תַי/תֶיךָ/תַיִךְ/תָיו/תֶיהָ	הִדַּמּוּיוֹת-	oneself on; assimilation	הִדַּמּוּיוֹת

hiddaCut is a pattern designating nominalization of *hitpa`el* verbs, or gerunds, when the first consonant of the root is *z* and the third is *y*. The *t* of *hitpa`el* is assimilated and becomes *d* (voicing assimilation), and that *d* is assimilated into the root-initial *d*. In normal speech, the *dd* sequence is realized as a single *d*.

Examples

הִדָּמוּת של קוליות היא תופעה פונטית שכיחה בשפות העולם.
Voicing **assimilation** is a common phonetic phenomenon in world languages.

---

135. *hitCaCCut* = *hitCoCeCut*: gerund/nominalization related to *hitpa`el*, when the second consonant of the root is *w* or *y*, or when the second and third consonants are identical (הִתְקוֹלְלוּת)

our/your/their	my/your/his/her	const.	Gloss	sing/pl
הִתְעוֹרְרוּתֵנוּ/תְכֶם/תְכֶן/תָם/תָן	**הִתְעוֹרְרוּ**תִי/תְךָ/תֵךְ/תוֹ/תָהּ	הִתְעוֹרְרוּת-	waking	הִתְעוֹרְרוּת נ׳
הִתְעוֹרְרוּיוֹתֵינוּ/כֶם/כֶן/הֶם/הֶן	**הִתְעוֹרְרוּיוֹ**תַי/תֶיךָ/תַיִךְ/תָיו/תֶיהָ	הִתְעוֹרְרוּיוֹת-	up; arising	הִתְעוֹרְרוּיוֹת

hitCoCeCut is often a pattern designating nominalization of *hitpa`el* verbs, or gerunds, when the second consonant of the root is *w* or *y*, or when the second or third root consonants are identical (e.g., גנ״נ). In the *mishkal* itself, an ו follows the first consonant, and the second and third consonants are identical – even where they are not in the root proper (גו״ר, בי״נ). An isolated case like הִתְרוֹקְנוּת 'becoming empty,' where the two are not identical, is derived from the root רק״נ or רוק״נ, which originated from רי״ק.

Examples

אחרי עבודה מאומצת עד שעה מאוחרת בלילה, תהליך ה**הִתְעוֹרְרוּת** בבוקר אינו קל.
After strenuous work till late at night, **waking up** in the morning is not easy.

הניתוח לא היה קשה במיוחד, אבל תהליך ה**הִתְאוֹשְׁשׁוּת** ארך שלושה חודשים.
The operation was not particularly difficult, but the **recovery** process took three months.

הגעתי למסקנה הזאת לאחר **הִתְבּוֹנְנוּת** של שנים רבות במה שקורה בשטח.
I came to this conclusion after **observing** what has been happening in the field for many years.

מאז ה-11 בספטמבר 2001, **הִתְגּוֹנְנוּת** המערב בפני התקפות טרור הרבה יותר יעילה.
Since September 11, 2001, the West's **(self-) defense** against terrorism is much more efficient.

אחרי שנים רבות של **הִתְגּוֹרְרוּת** בבת-ים הם החליטו לעבור לתל אביב.
After many years of **living** in Bat-Yam they decided to move to Tel Aviv.

אמריקאים מבוגרים לא ישכחו את **הִתְמוֹטְטוּת** הבורסה של 1929 עד יום מותם.
Older Americans will not forget the 1929 **collapse** of the stock exchange until they die.

הִתְנוֹסְסוּת דגל הקונפדרציה באירועים מסוימים בדרום ארה״ב מרגיזה את מרבית האזרחים באזורים אחרים.
The **flying** of the Confederacy flag in some events in the South angers the majority of people elsewhere in the US.

Special Expressions

self-**defense** **הִתְגּוֹנְנוּת** עצמית	human over-population **הִתְפּוֹצְצוּת** אוכלוסין
nervous **breakdown** **הִתְמוֹטְטוּת** עצבים	

Additional Examples in this Pattern

complaining הִתְאוֹנְנוּת	staggering הִתְנוֹדְדוּת
seclusion הִתְבּוֹדְדוּת	flying (of a flag); displaying prominently הִתְנוֹסְסוּת
assimilation הִתְבּוֹלְלוּת	gleaming הִתְנוֹצְצוּת
wrestling הִתְגּוֹשְׁשׁוּת	being encouraged הִתְעוֹדְדוּת
licentiousness הִתְהוֹלְלוּת	flying, fluttering הִתְעוֹפְפוּת
preparing oneself הִתְכּוֹנְנוּת	explosion; exploding הִתְפּוֹצְצוּת
bending over הִתְכּוֹפְפוּת	uprising הִתְקוֹמְמוּת
joking הִתְלוֹצְצוּת	running around הִתְרוֹצְצוּת
competing; coping הִתְמוֹדְדוּת	

---

136. ***hitCaCCut*** **>** ***hitCoCCut*** **=** ***hitCoCaCut***: gerund/nominalization related to *hitpa`el*, when the second consonant of the root is *w* or *y*, or when the second and third consonants are identical, and when the third consonant is a guttural.

our/your/their	my/your/his/her	const.	Gloss	sing/pl
הִתְנוֹעֲעוּתֵנוּ/תְכֶם/תְכֶן/תָם/תָן	**הִתְנוֹעֲעוּ**תִי/תְךָ/תֵךְ/תוֹ/תָהּ	הִתְנוֹעֲעוּת-	swaying	הִתְנוֹעֲעוּת נ׳
הִתְנוֹעֲעוּיוֹתֵינוּ/כֶם/כֶן/הֶם/הֶן	**הִתְנוֹעֲעוּיוֹ**תַי/תֶיךָ/תַיִךְ/תָיו/תֶיהָ	הִתְנוֹעֲעוּיוֹת-		הִתְנוֹעֲעוּיוֹת

hitCoCeCut is often a pattern designating nominalization of *hitpa`el* verbs, or gerunds, when the second consonant of the root is *w* or *y*, or when the second or third root consonants are identical (e.g., רע״ע). In the *mishkal* itself, an וֹ follows the first consonant, and the second and third consonants are identical (הִתְקוֹלְלוּת). When the second or third consonant is a guttural, the expected *shva* is replaced by a *Hataf-pataH*.

Examples

הַהִתְנוֹעֲעוּת הבלתי פוסקת של הנדנדה גורמת לי לסחרחורת.
The continuous **swaying** of the swing causes me dizziness.

Additional Examples in this Pattern

befriending הִתְרוֹעֲעוּת

---

137. ***hitCaCCut*** **=** ***histoCeCut*** when the second consonant of the root is *w* or *y*, or when the second and third consonants are identical (הִתְקוֹלְלוּת) – in cases where the first consonant is *s*

our/your/their	my/your/his/her	const.	Gloss	sing/pl
הִסְתּוֹבְבוּתֵנוּ/תְכֶם/תְכֶן/תָם/תָן	**הִסְתּוֹבְבוּ**תִי/תְךָ/תֵךְ/תוֹ/תָהּ	הִסְתּוֹבְבוּת-	wandering about	הִסְתּוֹבְבוּת נ׳
הִסְתּוֹבְבוּיוֹתֵינוּ/כֶם/כֶן/הֶם/הֶן	**הִסְתּוֹבְבוּיוֹ**תַי/תֶיךָ/תַיִךְ/תָיו/תֶיהָ	הִסְתּוֹבְבוּיוֹת-		הִסְתּוֹבְבוּיוֹת

histoCeCut is generally a pattern designating nominalization of *hitpa`el* verbs, or gerunds, when the second consonant of the root is *w* or *y*, or when the second or third root consonants are identical (e.g., סב״ב), and when the first consonant of the root is *s*. In the *mishkal* itself, the *t* of *hitpa`el* and the *s* metathesize, *t* is followed by וֹ, and the second and third consonants are identical – even when not in the root proper (סו״ד).

Examples

הִסְתּוֹבְבוּת של מובטלים באפס מעשה מסתיימת לא פעם באירועי אלימות.
The **wandering about** of unemployed people sometimes ends with incidents of violence.

הִסְתּוֹפְפוּתָם הבלתי-פוסקת של החברים של דני בביתם מוציאה את אשתו מדעתה.
The **frequent staying** of Danny's friends in their house drives his wife nuts.

Additional Examples in this Pattern

exchanging whispered secrets הִסְתּוֹדְדוּת

---

138. *hitCaCCut = hishtoCeCut*: gerund/nominalization related to *hitpa`el*, when the second consonant of the root is *w* or *y*, or when the second and third consonants are identical (הִתְקוֹלְלוּת) – in cases where the first consonant is *sh*

our/your/their	my/your/his/her	const.	Gloss	sing/pl
הִשְׁתּוֹלְלוּתֵנוּ/תְכֶם/תְכֶן/תָם/תָן	**הִשְׁתּוֹלְלוּ**תִי/תְךָ/תֵךְ/תוֹ/תָהּ	הִשְׁתּוֹלְלוּת-	wild	הִשְׁתּוֹלְלוּת נ׳
הִשְׁתּוֹלְלוּיוֹתֵינוּ/כֶם/כֶן/הֶם/הֶן	**הִשְׁתּוֹלְלוּיוֹ**תַי/תֶיךָ/תַיִךְ/תָיו/תֶיהָ	הִשְׁתּוֹלְלוּיוֹת-	behavior	הִשְׁתּוֹלְלוּיוֹת

hishtoCeCut is generally a pattern designating nominalization of *hitpa`el* verbs, or gerunds, when the second consonant of the root is *w* or *y*, or when the second or third root consonants are identical (e.g., של״ל), and when the first consonant of the root is *sh*. In the *mishkal* itself, the *t* of *hitpa`el* and the *sh* metathesize, *t* is followed by וֹ, and the second and third consonants are identical – even where they are not in the root proper (e.g., שו״ב < הִשְׁתּוֹבֵב).

Examples

בשל ה**הִשְׁתּוֹלְלוּת** הצפויה של האוהדים הגיעו כוחות משטרים מוגברים לאצטדיון.
Because of the anticipated **unruly behavior** of the fans, reinforced police forces arrived at the stadium.

Additional Examples in this Pattern

being mischievous הִשְׁתּוֹבְבוּת
amazement הִשְׁתּוֹמְמוּת

longing הִשְׁתּוֹקְקוּת

---

139. ***hitCaCCut = hitstoCeCut***: gerund/nominalization of *hitpa`el*, when the second consonant of the root is *w* or *y*, or when the second and third consonants are identical (הִתְקוֹלְלוּת) – in cases where the first consonant is *ts*

our/your/their	my/your/his/her	const.	Gloss	sing/pl
הִצְטוֹפְפוּתֵנוּ/תְכֶם/תְכֶן/תָם/תָן	**הִצְטוֹפְפוּ**תִי/תְךָ/תֵךְ/תוֹ/תָהּ	הִצְטוֹפְפוּת-	crowding	הִצְטוֹפְפוּת נ׳
הִצְטוֹפְפוּיוֹתֵינוּ/כֶם/כֶן/הֶם/הֶן	**הִצְטוֹפְפוּיוֹ**תַי/תֶיךָ/תַיִךְ/תָיו/תֶיהָ	הִצְטוֹפְפוּיוֹת-		הִצְטוֹפְפוּיוֹת

hitstoCeCut is generally a pattern designating nominalization of *hitpa`el* verbs, or gerunds, when the second consonant of the root is *w* or *y*, or when the second or third root consonants are identical (e.g., צפ״פ), and when the first consonant of the root is *ts*. In the *mishkal* itself, the *t* of *hitpa`el* becomes *tet*, the *tet* and *ts* metathesize, *tet* is followed by וֹ, and the second and third consonants are identical – even where they are not in the root proper.

Examples

הִצְטוֹפְפוּת-יתר של הצופים ביציעים גרמה להתמוטטותם ולהיפצעות של עשרות מהם.
Over-**crowding** at the bleachers caused their collapse and the injuries to scores of spectators.

---

140. ***hitCaCCut + CuCaC = hitCuCCut***: slang variant of *hitCaCCut*, combining it with *pu`al*

There are only two documented occurrences of slang variants of *hitpa`el* that integrate the passive voice of *pu`al*: הִתְפֻּטַּר 'be forced to resign,' and הִתְנֻדַּב 'be forced to volunteer.' In fact, a new *binyan* (*hitCuCaC*). A derived gerund is documented only for the first, הִתְפֻּטְּרוּת 'being forced to resign.'

Examples

הִתְפֻּטְּרוּתָם של שלושת השרים הייתה צפויה; הם הצביעו נגד הצעתו של ראש הממשלה, ונרמז להם שאם לא יִתְפַּטְּרוּ, הוא ייאלץ לפטרם.
The **forced resignation** of the three ministers was expected; they voted against the prime minister's proposal, and the message was that if they do not resign, he will have no choice but to fire them.

---

141. ***hitCaCCut = hitCaCCeCut***: gerund/nominalization related to *hitpa`el* when the roots are quadriliteral

our/your/their	my/your/his/her	const.	Gloss	sing/pl
הִתְאַרְגְּנוּתֵנוּ/תְכֶם/תְכֶן/תָם/תָן	**הִתְאַרְגְּנוּ**תִי/תְךָ/תֵךְ/ תוֹ/תָהּ	הִתְאַרְגְּנוּת-	getting organized	הִתְאַרְגְּנוּת נ׳
הִתְאַרְגְּנוּיוֹתֵינוּ/כֶם/כֶן/הֶם/הֶן	**הִתְאַרְגְּנוּיוֹ**תַי/תֶיךָ/ תַיִךְ/תָיו/תֶיהָ	הִתְאַרְגְּנוּיוֹת-		הִתְאַרְגְּנוּיוֹת

hitCaCCeCut is similar to *hitCaCCut*, but with four root consonants. An *e* is inserted between the third and fourth consonant to facilitate pronunciation.

Examples

בהרבה ארצות בעולם מתנגדים המעסיקים בכל תוקף ל**הִתְאַרְגְּנוּת** של עובדים.
In many countries across the world, employers are vehemently opposed to workers **being organized**.

הִתְאַכְלְסוּת הנגב הייתה תמיד יעד חשוב במדיניות הפנים של ישראל.
The Negev **becoming populated** has always been an important goal in Israel's internal development policy.

הִתְאַקְלְמוּתָם של מהגרים היא בדרך כלל קשה וארוכה.
The **acclimatization** of immigrants is usually long and hard.

ידוענים שהתמכרו לסמים לא פעם עוברים **הִתְאַשְׁפְּזוּת**-מרצון במכוני גמילה.
Celebrities who are addicted to drug often undergo voluntary **hospitalization** in rehabilitation centers.

הִתְחַשְׁמְלוּת של פועלים באתרי בנייה או שיפוצים היא עדיין אחת הסכנות הגדולות באתרים כאלה.
Electrocution of workers in building and refurbishing sites is still one of the greatest dangers in such sites.

אני מרוצה מאוד מן ה**הִתְעַנְיְנוּת** הגדולה של נכדתי בהיסטוריה של העולם העתיק.
I am very pleased with the great **interest** of my granddaughter in the history of the Ancient World.

ישראל נוסדה על ידי ציונים סוציאליסטים; עם הזמן חלה **הִתְבַּרְגְּנוּת** של החברה הישראלית, כפי שקרה בארצות סוציאליסטיות רבות.
Israel was founded by socialist Zionists; with time, there occurred **bourgeoisification** of Israeli society, similarly to what happened in many socialist countries.

Additional Examples in this Pattern

naturalization הִתְאַזְרְחוּת
staying as guest הִתְאַכְסְנוּת
becoming widowed הִתְאַלְמְנוּת
converting to Islam הִתְאַסְלְמוּת
complaining Sl. הִתְבַּכְיְנוּת
bourgeoisifying הִתְבַּרְגְּנוּת
coquetry הִתְגַּנְדְּרוּת
making an accounting הִתְחַשְׁבְּנוּת
getting updated הִתְעַדְכְּנוּת
becoming annoyed הִתְעַצְבְּנוּת
debating הִתְפַּלְמְסוּת
philosophizing הִתְפַּלְסְפוּת

---

142. ***hitCaCCut* > *hitCaCCeCut* = *hit'aCCeCut*** when a trilateral root was expanded into a quadrilateral one by adding the prefix +א

our/your/their	my/your/his/her	const.	Gloss	sing/pl
הִתְאַכְזְבוּתֵנוּ/תְכֶם/תְכֶן/תָם/תָן	**הִתְאַכְזְבוּ**תִי/תְךָ/תֵךְ/תוֹ/תָהּ	הִתְאַכְזְבוּת-	disappoint-ment	הִתְאַכְזְבוּת נ'
הִתְאַכְזְבוּיוֹתֵינוּ/כֶם/כֶן/הֶם/הֶן	**הִתְאַכְזְבוּיוֹ**תַי/תֶיךָ/תַיִךְ/תָיו/תֶיהָ	הִתְאַכְזְבוּיוֹת-		הִתְאַכְזְבוּיוֹת

Examples

הרבה טוענים היום שהתחזקות הימין נובעת במידה רבה מ**הִתְאַכְזְבוּת** הציבור מאכיפת-יתר של הדרישות לתקינות פוליטית.

Many claim today that the strengthening of the right stems to a large extent from the public's **disappointment** with excessive enforcement of political correctness.

---

143. ***hitCaCCut* > *hitCaCCeCut* = *hitmaCCaCut*** when a trilateral root was expanded into a quadrilateral one by adding the prefix מ+ and the third consonant is a guttural

our/your/their	my/your/his/her	const.	Gloss	sing/pl
הִתְמַסְחֲרוּתֵנוּ/תְכֶם/תְכֶן/תָם/תָן	**הִתְמַסְחֲרוּ**תִי/תְךָ/תֵךְ/תוֹ/תָהּ	הִתְמַסְחֲרוּת-	commercial-ization	הִתְמַסְחֲרוּת נ׳
הִתְמַסְחֲרוּיוֹתֵינוּ/כֶם/כֶן/הֶם/הֶן	**הִתְמַסְחֲרוּיוֹ**תַי/תֶיךָ/תַיִךְ/תָיו/תֶיהָ	הִתְמַסְחֲרוּיוֹת-		הִתְמַסְחֲרוּיוֹת

hitmaCCaCut is similar to *hitCaCCut*, but with four root consonants, and a *shva* is inserted between the third and fourth consonant to facilitate pronunciation. But when the third consonant with the *shva* is a guttural, the *shva* is replaced by a *Hataf-pataH*, as in הִתְמַסְחֲרוּת here, or as in הִתְעַרְעֲרוּת 'weakening' (see below).

Examples

ה**הִתְמַסְחֲרוּת** של אמצעי התקשורת לא פוסחת אפילו אף על הטלוויזיה הציבורית.

The **commercialization** of the media does not skip even public television.

---

144. ***hitCaCCut* > *hitCaCCeCut* = *hitCaCaCCut***: gerund/nominalization related to *hitpa`el* in quadrilateral roots where the second consonant is a guttural

our/your/their	my/your/his/her	const.	Gloss	sing/pl
הִתְמַעַרְבוּתֵנוּ/תְכֶם/תְכֶן/תָם/תָן	**הִתְמַעַרְבוּ**תִי/תְךָ/תֵךְ/תוֹ/תָהּ	הִתְמַעַרְבוּת-	westerni-zation	הִתְמַעַרְבוּת נ׳
הִתְמַעַרְבוּיוֹתֵינוּ/כֶם/כֶן/הֶם/הֶן	**הִתְמַעַרְבוּיוֹ**תַי/תֶיךָ/תַיִךְ/תָיו/תֶיהָ	הִתְמַעַרְבוּיוֹת-		הִתְמַעַרְבוּיוֹת

In the *hitCaCCut > hitCaCCeCut mishkal*, when the second consonant is a guttural, one would expect a *Hataf-pataH*, but as the following consonant was supposed to be followed by a *shva mobile*, and a *Hataf-shva* sequence is not acceptable within the same syllable, the *Hataf* is replaced by *pataH*, followed by a quiescent *shva* (which properly closes the syllable): הִתְמַעַרְבוּת < *הִתְמַעֲרְבוּת < *הִתְמַעְרְבוּת, *hit-ma-`ar-vut*.

Examples

תהליך ה**הִתְמַעַרְבוּת** בארצות המזרח מתחיל בדרך כלל אצל הצעירים.

The process of **westernization** in the east usually starts with the youth.

Additional Examples in this Pattern

refreshing oneself הִתְרַעַנְנוּת

---

145. ***hitCaCCut* = *hitCaCCeCut*** when the two first consonants are reduplicated in consonantal slots three and four, respectively

our/your/their	my/your/his/her	const.	Gloss	sing/pl
הִתְרַבְרְבוּתֵנוּ/תְכֶם/תְכֶן/תָם/תָן	**הִתְרַבְרְבוּ**תִי/תְךָ/תֵךְ/תוֹ/תָהּ	הִתְרַבְרְבוּת-	boasting, bragging	הִתְרַבְרְבוּת נ'
הִתְרַבְרְבוּיוֹתֵינוּ/כֶם/כֶן/הֶם/הֶן	**הִתְרַבְרְבוּיוֹ**תַי/תֶיךָ/תַיִךְ/תָיו/תֶיהָ	הִתְרַבְרְבוּיוֹת-		הִתְרַבְרְבוּיוֹת

This is a sub-pattern of *hitCaCCeCut* (see הִתְאַרְגְּנוּת above) when the first two root consonants are reduplicated in positions three and four, respectively (הִתְקַטְקְטוּת).

Examples

למרות **הִתְרַבְרְבוּתוֹ** של מועמד המפלגה לראשות הממשלה, קשה להאמין שיש לו סיכוי של ממש לנצח.
In spite of the **bragging** of the candidate for the Prime Minister's position, it is hard to believe that he has a real chance to win.

הִתְלַחְלְחוּת העיניים היא תוצאה של התרגשות, עם כמעט דמעות...
Moistening of eyes is a manifestation one of being moved, almost to tears....

פוליטיקאים ממולחים יודעים היטב איך לנצל **הִתְמַרְמְרוּת** של בוחרים המרגישים מופלים לרעה כדי לזכות בקולותיהם.
Clever politician know very well how to exploit the **bitterness** of voters who feel discriminated against so as to win their votes.

Additional Examples in this Pattern

being wasted הִתְבַּזְבְּזוּת
getting confused הִתְבַּלְבְּלוּת
missing הִתְגַּעְגְּעוּת
becoming dirty הִתְלַכְלְכוּת
wavering הִתְנַדְנְדוּת
breaking down, being damaged; becoming spoiled (food) הִתְקַלְקְלוּת

---

146. ***hitCaCCut* > *hitCaCCeCut* = *hitCaCCaCut*** when the two first consonants are reduplicated in consonantal slots three and four, respectively (הִתְקַטְקְטוּת), and the first/third consonant is guttural (הִתְקַטְקֲטוּת)

our/your/their	my/your/his/her	const.	Gloss	sing/pl
הִתְעַרְעֲרוּתֵנוּ/תְכֶם/תְכֶן/תָם/תָן	**הִתְעַרְעֲרוּ**תִי/תְךָ/תֵךְ/תוֹ/תָהּ	הִתְעַרְעֲרוּת-	weakening, loosening	הִתְעַרְעֲרוּת נ'
הִתְעַרְעֲרוּיוֹתֵינוּ/כֶם/כֶן/הֶם/הֶן	**הִתְעַרְעֲרוּיוֹ**תַי/תֶיךָ/תַיִךְ/תָיו/תֶיהָ	הִתְעַרְעֲרוּיוֹת-		הִתְעַרְעֲרוּיוֹת

When a *shva mobile* is expected with a guttural, it is replace by *Hataf-pataH.*

Examples

שטפונות רבים גרמו במשך השנים ל**הִתְעַרְעֲרוּת** יסודות הבית.

During the years, numerous floods have caused the **weakening** of the house's foundations.

Additional Examples in this Pattern

being shocked הִתְחַלְחֲלוּת
coquetry הִתְחַנְחֲנוּת
dimming הִתְעַמְעֲמוּת

---

147. ***hitCaCCut*** **>** ***hitCaCCeCut*** when the last two consonants are identical (הִתְקַטְלְלוּת)

our/your/their	my/your/his/her	const.	Gloss	sing/pl
הִתְאַוְרְרוּתֵנוּ/תְכֶם/תְכֶן/תָם/תָן	**הִתְאַוְרְרוּ**תִי/תְךָ/תֵךְ/תוֹ/תָהּ	הִתְאַוְרְרוּת־	getting fresh air	הִתְאַוְרְרוּת נ׳
הִתְאַוְרְרוּיוֹתֵינוּ/כֶם/כֶן/הֶם/הֶן	**הִתְאַוְרְרוּיוֹ**תַי/תֶיךָ/תַיִךְ/תָיו/תֶיהָ	הִתְאַוְרְרוּיוֹת־		הִתְאַוְרְרוּיוֹת

Examples

אחרי עבודה מאומצת של שמונה שעות ליד המחשב אני זקוק כעת ל**הִתְאַוְרְרוּת**.

After eight hours of strenuous work on the computer I now need some fresh air.

Additional Examples in this Pattern

becoming mixed up; being mixed into הִתְעַרְבְּבוּת

---

148. ***hit+saCCut*** **>** ***hitsaCCeCut*** **=** ***histaCCeCut***: gerund/nominalization related to *hitpa`el* when the roots are quadrilateral, and the first root consonant is *s*

our/your/their	my/your/his/her	const.	Gloss	sing/pl
הִסְתַּקְרְנוּתֵנוּ/תְכֶם/תְכֶן/תָם/תָן	**הִסְתַּקְרְנוּ**תִי/תְךָ/תֵךְ/תוֹ/תָהּ	הִסְתַּקְרְנוּת־	becoming curious	הִסְתַּקְרְנוּת נ׳

When the first consonant is *s*, it metathesizes with the *t* of *hitpa`el*. No plural forms.

Examples

הִסְתַּקְרְנוּת היא מניע חשוב במרבית הגילויים המדעיים.

Being/becoming curious is an important motive in scientific discovery.

Additional Examples in this Pattern

being temporarily blinded, being dazed הִסְתַּנְוְרוּת

---

149. ***hitsaCCut* > *histaCCeCut* > *histaCaCCut***: gerund/nominalization related to *hitpa`el* when the roots are quadrilateral, the first root consonant is *s* and a *shva* is expected with a guttural

our/your/their	my/your/his/her	const.	Gloss	sing/pl
הִסְתַּעַרְבוּתֵנוּ/תְכֶם/תְכֶן/תָם/תָן	**הִסְתַּעַרְבוּ**תִי/תְךָ/תֵךְ/תוֹ/תָהּ	הִסְתַּעַרְבוּת-	pretending to be Arab	הִסְתַּעַרְבוּת נ'
הִסְתַּעַרְבוּיוֹתֵינוּ/כֶם/כֶן/הֶם/הֶן	**הִסְתַּעַרְבוּיוֹ**תַי/תֶיךָ/תַיִךְ/תָיו/תֶיהָ	הִסְתַּעַרְבוּיוֹת-		הִסְתַּעַרְבוּיוֹת

histaCCeCut > *histaCaCCut* is similar to *hitCaCCut* with four root consonants, *hitCaCCeCut*. When the first consonant is *s*, it metathesizes with the *t* of *hitpa`el*. When a *shva* is expected in a guttural, the potential unacceptable *Hataf-shva* sequence within the same syllable results in the *Hataf* being replaced by *pataH*, and the following *shva* closes the syllable: הִסְתַּעַרְבוּת 'pretending to be an Arab,' *his-ta-CaC-Cut*.

Examples

הִסְתַּעַרְבוּת היא אמצעי ביון שהשתמשו בו עוד לפני קום המדינה, בתקופת הפלמ"ח.
Pretending to be an Arab (or **dressing like an Arab**) is an intelligence ploy used already before Israel was born, in the era of the PalmaH (the Haganah commandos).

---

150. ***hitsaCCut* > *hitsaCseCut* = *histaCseCut*** when the first root consonant is *s*, and the two first consonants are reduplicated in consonantal slots three and four, respectively (הִתְקַטְקְטוּת)

our/your/their	my/your/his/her	const.	Gloss	sing/pl
הִסְתַּכְסְכוּתֵנוּ/תְכֶם/תְכֶן/תָם/תָן	**הִסְתַּכְסְכוּ**תִי/תְךָ/תֵךְ/תוֹ/תָהּ	הִסְתַּכְסְכוּת-	arguing	הִסְתַּכְסְכוּת נ'
הִסְתַּכְסְכוּיוֹתֵינוּ/כֶם/כֶן/הֶם/הֶן	**הִסְתַּכְסְכוּיוֹ**תַי/תֶיךָ/תַיִךְ/תָיו/תֶיהָ	הִסְתַּכְסְכוּיוֹת-		הִסְתַּכְסְכוּיוֹת

histaCseCut is similar to *hitCaCCut*, but with four root consonants. When the first consonant is *s*, it metathesizes with the *t* of *hitpa`el*, *histaCseCut*, with reduplication of the first two consonants in positions three and four (הִתְקַטְקְטוּת).

Examples

הִסְתַּכְסְכוּת בין השותפים נגרמה בשל חילוקי דעות על דרך ניהול החברה.
The **arguing** among the partners was caused by disagreement regarding the way the company is run.

Additional Examples in this Pattern

becoming curled הִסְתַּלְסְלוּת

---

151. ***hitCaCCut* > *hitCaCCeCut* = *hishtaCCeCut*/*histaCCeCut***:
gerund/nominalization related to *hitpa`el* when the roots are quadrilateral, and the first root consonant is *sh* or *s* (sin, שׂ)

our/your/their	my/your/his/her	const.	Gloss	sing/pl
הִשְׁתַּחְצְנוּתֵנוּ/תְכֶם/תְכֶן/תָם/תָן	**הִשְׁתַּחְצְנוּ**תִי/תְךָ/תֵךְ/תוֹ/תָהּ	הִשְׁתַּחְצְנוּת-	bragging	הִשְׁתַּחְצְנוּת נ'
הִשְׁתַּחְצְנוּיוֹתֵינוּ/כֶם/כֶן/הֶם/הֶן	**הִשְׁתַּחְצְנוּיוֹ**תַי/תֶיךָ/תַיִךְ/תָיו/תֶיהָ	הִשְׁתַּחְצְנוּיוֹת-		הִשְׁתַּחְצְנוּיוֹת

hishtaCCeCut/*histaCCeCut* is similar to *hitCaCCut*, but with four root consonants. When the first consonant is *sh* or *s*, it metathesizes with the *t* of *hitpa`el*.

Examples

בלשון הדיבור משתמשים לעתים קרובות במונח **הִשְׁתַּחְצְנוּת** במקום התרברבות.
In the colloquial, one often uses the term **'bragging'** instead of 'boasting.'

Additional Examples in this Pattern

being convinced הִשְׁתַּכְנְעוּת   becoming enslaved הִשְׁתַּעְבְּדוּת

---

152. *hitCaCCut* > *hitCaCCeCut* = *hishtaCsheCut* in *hitpa`el* quadriliteralds where the first root consonant is *shin* or *sin*, and when the two first consonants are reduplicated

our/your/their	my/your/his /her	const.	Gloss	sing/pl
הִשְׁתַּלְשְׁלוּתֵנוּ/תְכֶם/תְכֶן/תָם/תָן	**הִשְׁתַּלְשְׁלוּ**תִי/תְךָ/ תֵךְ/תוֹ/תָהּ	הִשְׁתַּלְשְׁלוּת-	descending; development	הִשְׁתַּלְשְׁלוּת נ׳
הִשְׁתַּלְשְׁלוּיוֹתֵינוּ/כֶם/כֶן/הֶם/הֶן	**הִשְׁתַּלְשְׁלוּיוֹ**תַי/ תֶיךָ/תַיִךְ/תָיו/תֶיהָ	הִשְׁתַּלְשְׁלוּיוֹת-		הִשְׁתַּלְשְׁלוּיוֹת

hishtaCCeCut/*histaCCeCut* is similar to *hitCaCCut*, but with four root consonants. When the first consonant is *sh* or *s*, it metathesizes with the *t* of *hitpa`el*. Furthermore, the two first consonants are reduplicated in consonantal slots three and four, respectively (הִתְקַטְקְטוּת).

Examples

הנשיא חושש ש**הִשְׁתַּלְשְׁלוּת** המאורעות במזרח התיכון עלולה להביא למלחמה חדשה.
The President is worried that the **development** of events in the Middle east may bring about a new war.

Additional Examples in this Pattern

having fun הִשְׁתַּעַשְׁעוּת
rubbing (against something); being worn away הִשְׁתַּפְשְׁפוּת

---

153. *hitCaCCut* > *hitCaCCeCut* = *hishtaCCeCut*/*histaCCeCut*:
gerund/nominalization related to *hitpa`el* when the roots are quadrilateral, the first root consonant is *sh* or *s*, and the last two consonants are identical

our/your/their	my/your/his/her	const.	Gloss	sing/pl
הִשְׁתַּחְרְרוּתֵנוּ/תְכֶם/ תְכֶן/תָם/תָן	**הִשְׁתַּחְרְרוּ**תִי/תְךָ/תֵךְ/תוֹ/תָהּ	הִשְׁתַּחְרְרוּת-	being released	הִשְׁתַּחְרְרוּת נ׳
הִשְׁתַּחְרְרוּיוֹתֵינוּ/ כֶם/כֶן/הֶם/הֶן	**הִשְׁתַּחְרְרוּיוֹ**תַי/תֶיךָ/תַיִךְ/תָיו/תֶיהָ	הִשְׁתַּחְרְרוּיוֹת-		הִשְׁתַּחְרְרוּיוֹת

hishtaCCeCut/histaCCeCut is similar to *hitCaCCut*, but with four root consonants. When the first consonant is *sh* or *s*, it metathesizes with the *t* of *hitpa`el*. Furthermore, the last two consonants are identical (הִתְקַטְלְלוּת).

Examples

לעתים, **הִשְׁתַּחְרְרוּת** משלטון קולוניאלי פשוט מחליפה ניצול ועריצות מבחוץ בניצול ושחיתות מבפנים.

Sometimes, **being released** from colonial rule simply replaces external exploitation and tyranny by exploitation and corruption from the inside.

Additional Examples in this Pattern

improvement; technological advancement הִשְׁתַּכְלְלוּת
being put in the wrong place; sticking out הִשְׁתַּרְבְּבוּת

---

154. ***hitCaCCut* > *hitCaCCeCut* = *his(h)taCaCeCut***: nominalization related to *hitpa`el* when the roots are quadrilateral, and the first root consonant is *sh* or *s* and where a *shva* is expected with a guttural, and the last two consonants are identical (הִתְקַטְלְלוּת)

our/your/their	my/your/his/her	const.	Gloss	sing/pl
הִשְׁתַּעַמְמוּתֵנוּ/תְכֶם/תְכֶן/תָם/תָן	**הִשְׁתַּעַמְמוּ**תִי/תְךָ/תֵךְ/תוֹ/תָהּ	הִשְׁתַּעַמְמוּת-	being bored	הִשְׁתַּעַמְמוּת נ׳

hishtaCCeCut/histaCCeCut is similar to *hitCaCCut*, but with four root consonants. When the first consonant is *sh* or *s*, it metathesizes with the *t* of *hitpa`el*. The last two consonants are identical. When a *shva* is expected in a guttural, becoming *Hataf*, a potential unacceptable sequence of *Hataf* followed by *shva* within the same syllable results in the *Hataf* being replaced by *pataH*, הִשְׁתַּעַמְמוּת. No plural form.

Examples

הִשְׁתַּעַמְמוּת של בני נוער גורמת לעתים קרובות לבעיות התנהגות קשות.

Boredom among youth is often a cause of serious behavioral problems.

---

155. ***hitCaCCut* > *hitCaCCeCut* = *hitstaCtseCut***: gerund/nominalization related to *hitpa`el* when the roots are quadrilateral, and the first root consonant is *ts*, and when the two first consonants are reduplicated in consonantal slots three and four, respectively (הִתְקַטְקְטוּת)

our/your/their	my/your/his/her	const.	Gloss	sing/pl
הִצְטַמְצְמוּתֵנוּ/תְכֶם/תְכֶן/תָם/תָן	**הִצְטַמְצְמוּ**תִי/תְךָ/תֵךְ/תוֹ/תָהּ	הִצְטַמְצְמוּת-	being reduced	הִצְטַמְצְמוּת נ׳
הִצְטַמְצְמוּיוֹתֵינוּ/כֶם/כֶן/הֶם/הֶן	**הִצְטַמְצְמוּיוֹ**תַי/תֶיךָ/תַיִךְ/תָיו/תֶיהָ	הִצְטַמְצְמוּיוֹת-		הִצְטַמְצְמוּיוֹת

hitstaCtseCut is similar to *hitCaCCut*, but with four root consonants. When the first consonant is *ts* (*tsadi*), the *t* of *hitpa`el* becomes *tet*, and the two consonants metathesize. Also, the two first consonants are reduplicated in consonantal slots three and four, respectively.

Examples

הִצְטַמְצְמוּת מרחב המחייה של חיות הבר באפריקה נגרמת בעיקר על ידי ברוא יערות עד לצרכי חקלאות והתיישבות בני אדם.
The **reduction** of wild animal living territory in Africa is caused primarily by deforestation of virgin forests to provide for agriculture and human settlement.

---

156. ***hitCaCCut* > *hitCaCCeCut* = *hitstaCats(e)Cut***: gerund/nominalization related to *hitpa`el* when the roots are quadrilateral, and the first root consonant is *ts* and where a *shva* > *Hataf* is expected in a guttural, and when the two first consonants are reduplicated in consonantal slots three and four, respectively.

our/your/their	my/your/his/her	const.	Gloss	sing/pl
הִצְטַעַצְעוּתֵנוּ/תְכֶם/ תְכֶן/תָם/תָן	**הִצְטַעַצְעוּ**תִי/תְךָ/תֵךְ/תוֹ/תָהּ	הִצְטַעַצְעוּת-	adorning oneself	הִצְטַעַצְעוּת נ'
הִצְטַעַצְעוּיוֹתֵינוּ/כֶם /כֶן/הֶם/הֶן	**הִצְטַעַצְעוּיוֹ**תַי/תֶיךָ/תַיִךְ/תָיו /תֶיהָ	הִצְטַעַצְעוּיוֹת-		הִצְטַעַצְעוּיוֹת

hitstaCats(e)Cut is similar to *hitCaCCut*, but with four root consonants. When the first consonant is *ts*, the *t* of *hitpa`el* becomes *tet*, and the two consonants metathesize. When a *shva* is expected in a guttural, becoming *Hataf*, an unacceptable sequence of *Hataf* followed by a *shva* within the same syllable results in the *Hataf* being replaced by *pataH*, and the following *shva* closes the syllable: הִצְטַעַצְעוּת *hits-ta-`ats-`ut*. Also, the two first consonants are reduplicated in consonantal slots three and four, respectively (הִתְקַטְקְטוּת).

Examples

אינני אוהב **הִצְטַעַצְעוּת** של אנשים במילים גבוהות.
I dislike people's **trying to impress** with high-level words.

---

157. ***hitCaCCut* > *hitCaCCeCut* = *hizdaCaz(e)Cut***: gerund/nominalization related to *hitpa`el* when the roots are quadrilateral, the first root consonant is *z* (the only common occurrence…), where a *shva* is expected in a guttural, and when the two first consonants are reduplicated in consonantal slots three and four, respectively.

our/your/their	my/your/his/her	const.	Gloss	sing/pl
הִזְדַּעַזְעוּתֵנוּ/תְכֶם/תְכֶן/תָם/תָן	**הִזְדַּעַזְעוּ**תִי/תְךָ/תֵךְ/תוֹ/תָהּ	הִזְדַּעַזְעוּת-	being	הִזְדַּעַזְעוּת נ'
הִזְדַּעַזְעוּיוֹתֵינוּ/כֶם/כֶן/הֶם/הֶן	**הִזְדַּעַזְעוּיוֹ**תַי/תֶיךָ/תַיִךְ/תָיו/תֶיהָ	הִזְדַּעַזְעוּיוֹת-	shocked	הִזְדַּעַזְעוּיוֹת

hizdaCaz(e)Cut is similar to *hitCaCCut*, but with four root consonants. When the first consonant is *z*, the *t* of *hitpa`el* becomes *d*, and the two consonants metathesize. In the only frequent occurrence there is a guttural where a *shva* is expected, resulting in an unaccceptable sequence of *Hataf-shva* within the same syllable, so the *Hataf* is replaced by *pataH*, the syllable being closed by a quiescent *shva*: הִזְדַּעַזְעוּת *hiz-da-`az-`ut*. The two first consonants are reduplicated in slots three and four, respectively (הִתְקַטְקְטוּת).

Examples

בתחילה נראה היה ש**הִזְדַּעַזְעוּת** העולם מן הטבח תביא להתערבות צבאית, אבל כעבור שנה-שנתיים העולם שכח...

Initially it looked as if the world **being shocked** by the massacre will bring about military intervention, but in a year or two the world forgot…

---

158. ***hitCaCCut > hitCaCCeCut = hiddaCdeCut***: gerund/nominalization related to *hitpa`el* when the roots are quadrilateral, and the first root consonant is *d* and when the two first consonants are reduplicated in consonantal slots three and four, respectively

our/your/their	my/your/his/her	const.	Gloss	sing/pl
הִדַּרְדְּרוּתֵנוּ/תְכֶם/תְכֶן/תָם/תָן	**הִדַּרְדְּרוּ**תִי/תְךָ/תֵךְ/תוֹ/תָהּ	הִדַּרְדְּרוּת-	deterioration	הִדַּרְדְּרוּת נ'
הִדַּרְדְּרוּיוֹתֵינוּ/כֶם/כֶן/הֶם/הֶן	**הִדַּרְדְּרוּיוֹ**תַי/תֶיךָ/תַיִךְ/תָיו/תֶיהָ	הִדַּרְדְּרוּיוֹת-		הִדַּרְדְּרוּיוֹת

hiddaCdeCut is similar to *hitCaCCut*, but with four root consonants. When the first consonant is *d*, the *t* of *hitpa`el* assimilates to that *d*. In normal speech, the geminated *d* is articulated as a single *d*: *hi-dar-de-rut*. Also, the two first consonants are reduplicated in consonantal slots three and four, respectively (הִקַּטְקְטוּת).

Examples

הִדַּרְדְּרוּת במצבו הבריאותי של ראש הממשלה גרמה להקפאה של כל יוזמות החקיקה החדשות שניסה להעביר בכנסת.

The **deterioration** in the prime minister's health resulted in the freezing of all the new legislative initiatives he had been trying to pass through the Knesset.

Additional Examples in this Pattern

shriveling, decline N, waning, weakening הִדַּלְדְּלוּת

---

159. ***hitCaCCut > hitCaCCeCut = hittaCteCut***: gerund/nominalization related to *hitpa`el* when the roots are quadrilateral, and the first root consonant is *tet* and when the two first consonants are reduplicated in consonantal slots three and four, respectively

our/your/their	my/your/his/her	const.	Gloss	sing/pl
הִטַּלְטְלוּתֵנוּ/תְכֶם/תְכֶן/תָם/תָן	**הִטַּלְטְלוּ**תִי/תְךָ/תֵךְ/תוֹ/תָהּ	הִטַּלְטְלוּת-	being tossed	הִטַּלְטְלוּת נ'
הִטַּלְטְלוּיוֹתֵינוּ/כֶם/כֶן/הֶם/הֶן	**הִטַּלְטְלוּיוֹ**תַי/תֶיךָ/תַיִךְ/תָיו/תֶיהָ	הִטַּלְטְלוּיוֹת-		הִטַּלְטְלוּיוֹת

hittaCteCut is similar to *hitCaCCut*, but with four root consonants. When the first consonant is *tet*, the *t* of *hitpa`el* assimilates to that *tet*. In normal speech, the geminated *t* is articulated as a single *t*: *hi-tal-te-lut*. Also, the two first consonants are reduplicated in consonantal slots three and four, respectively (הִקַּטְקְטוּת).

Examples

הִטַּלְטְלוּת של שבוע ימים ברכיבה על גמל התישה אותו לגמרי.
Tossing about on the camel's back for a whole week totally exhausted him .

Additional Examples in this Pattern

blurring, fading הִטַּשְׁטְשׁוּת

K. *mitCaCeC* and related *mishkalim*

160. ***mitCaCeC***: generally the active participle of *hitpa`el*

our/your/their	my/your/his/her	const.	Gloss	sing/pl
מִתְנַגְּדֵנוּ/דְכֶם/דְכֶן/דָם/דָן	**מִתְנַגְּ**דִי/דְךָ/דֵךְ/דוֹ/דָהּ	מִתְנַגֵּד-	opposer,	מִתְנַגֵּד ז'
מִתְנַגְּדֵינוּ/כֶם/כֶן/הֶם/הֶן	**מִתְנַגְּ**דַי/דֶיךָ/דַיִךְ/דָיו/דֶיהָ	מִתְנַגְּדֵי-	opponent	מִתְנַגְּדִים

The active participle of the *hitpa`el binyan*, *mitCaCeC*, may serve as a noun, as in מִתְאַבֵּד 'one committing suicide,' מִתְגַּיֵּס 'recruit,' מִתְעַמֵּל 'gymnast; one doing exercise,' or as an adjective, as in מִתְקַדֵּם 'progressive,' מִתְקַפֵּל 'folding,' and sometimes as both, as in מִתְנַדֵּב 'volunteer; volunteering,' מִתְנַגֵּד 'opposer; opposing.' Note: no separate sub-*mishkal* was included for *mitCaCeC* forms in which the second root consonant is guttural, since they seldom function as either nouns or adjectives. In a case like מִתְנַחֵל 'settler' plural מִתְנַחֲלִים, the *Hataf-pataH* reflects the expected conversion of a *shva* to *Hataf-pataH* when it comes with a guttural.

Examples

במדינות מסוימות בתי הכלא מלאים **בְּמִתְנַגְּדֵי** המשטר.
In some states the prisons are full with **opponents** of the regime.

Additional Examples in this Pattern

wrestler מִתְאַבֵּק
adolescent מִתְבַּגֵּר
smart aleck מִתְחַכֵּם
settler מִתְיַשֵּׁב
apprentice, trainee מִתְלַמֵּד
volunteer מִתְנַדֵּב
worshiper מִתְפַּלֵּל
advanced, progressive מִתְקַדֵּם
folding, collapsible מִתְקַפֵּל

---

161. ***mitCaCeC* = *mistaCeC***, the active participle of *hitpa`el* when the first root consonant is *s*

our/your/their	my/your/his/her	const.	Gloss	sing/pl
מִסְתַּנְּנֵנוּ/נְכֶם/נְכֶן/נָם/נָן	**מִסְתַּנְּ**נִי/נְךָ/נֵךְ/נוֹ/נָהּ	מִסְתַּנֵּן-	infiltrator	מִסְתַּנֵּן ז׳
מִסְתַּנְּנֵינוּ/כֶם/כֶן/הֶם/הֶן	**מִסְתַּנְּנַ**י/נֶיךָ/נַיִךְ/נָיו/נֶיהָ	מִסְתַּנְּנֵי-		מִסְתַּנְּנִים

The active participle usually serves as a noun (מִסְתַּנֵּן ‘infiltrator’). When the first consonant of the root is a *s,* the *t* of *hitpa`el* and that *s* metathesize (= change places): **mitsaber* > *mistaber* ‘reasonable.’

Examples

הרבה **מִסְתַּנְּנִים** מאפריקה חוצים את הגבול עם מצרים ומוצאים מקלט בישראל.
Many **infiltrators** from Africa cross the border with Egypt and find refuge in Israel.

Additional Examples in this Pattern

reasonable; it turns out that…… מִסְתַּבֵּר
ascetic מִסְתַּגֵּף
dissenter מִסְתַּיֵּג

---

162. ***mitCaCeC* = *mishtaCeC***, the active participle of *hitpa`el* when the first root consonant is *shin/sin*

our/your/their	my/your/his/her	const.	Gloss	sing/pl
מִשְׁתַּמְּשֵׁנוּ/שְׁכֶם/שְׁכֶן/שָׁם/שָׁן	**מִשְׁתַּמְּ**שִׁי/שְׁךָ/שֵׁךְ/שׁוֹ/שָׁהּ	מִשְׁתַּמֵּשׁ-	user	מִשְׁתַּמֵּשׁ ז׳
מִשְׁתַּמְּשֵׁינוּ/כֶם/כֶן/הֶם/הֶן	**מִשְׁתַּמְּשַׁ**י/שֶׁיךָ/שַׁיִךְ/שָׁיו/שֶׁיהָ	מִשְׁתַּמְּשֵׁי-		מִשְׁתַּמְּשִׁים

The active participle usually serves as a noun (מִשְׁתַּתֵּף ‘participant’). When the first consonant of the root is a *sh,* the *t* of *hitpa`el* and that *sh* metathesize (= change places): **mitshamesh* ‘user’ > *mishtamesh.*

Examples

מהירות הגלישה האינטרנט באמצעות כבלים תלויה במספר ה**מִשְׁתַּמְּשִׁים** בעת הגלישה.
The speed of surfing on the internet is dependent on the number of **users** at the time of surfing.

בתקופת מלחמת ויאטנאם, מספר ניכר של **מִשְׁתַּמְּטִים** מחובת השירות הצבאי נמלטו מארה״ב לקנדה.
During the Vietnam War, a good number of draft **dodgers** escaped from the US to Canada.

Additional Examples in this Pattern

resident of a new housing complex מִשְׁתַּכֵּן
worthwhile; one attending a continuing education program מִשְׁתַּלֵּם
participant מִשְׁתַּתֵּף

---

163. *mitCaCeC* = *mitCaCe* when the 3rd root consonant is *y*

	Masc.	Fem.	Gloss
Sing.	מִתְחַזֶּה	מִתְחַזָּה	pretender
Plural	מִתְחַזִּים	מִתְחַזּוֹת	

As in *mitCaCeC*, the active participle here – which is generally related to *hitpa`el* – usually serve as a noun, מִתְחָרֶה 'competitor,' or occasionally as an adjective, מִתְכַּלֶּה 'perishable.' Note that although pronunciation is not affected, if the second consonant of the root is א' or ר' and consequently not marked with a *dagesh*, the preceding vowel is signaled by a *kamats* rather than by a *pataH* (מִתְחָרָה).

Examples

בקילומטר האחרון של המרתון נותרו רק ארבעה **מִתְחָרִים** בקבוצה המובילה ; שניים מהם זכו בשני המרתונים הקודמים.
In the last kilometer of the marathon only for **competitors** remained in the leading group; two of them had won the previous two marathons.

כשעברנו לגור בעיר הגדולה, והזדקקתי לרופא, מצאתי **מִתְמַחָה** בבית חולים שטיפלה בי מצוין, אבל כשניסיתי לראותה שוב הסתבר ש**מִתְמַחִים** מועברים ממקום למקום...
When we moved to the big city, and .I needed a doctor, I found a **resident** in a hospital who took excellent care of me, but when I needed her again, it turned out that **residents** are shifted from one facility to another…

Additional Examples in this Pattern

מִתְחַזֶּה pretender, impersonator   מִתְחַלֶּה one who feigns sickness

---

164. *mitCaCeC* = *mitCoCeC*: active participle of *hitpa`el*, when the second consonant of the root is *w* or *y*, or when the second and third consonants are identical (מִתְקוֹלֵל)

	Masc.	Fem.	Gloss
Sing.	מִתְבּוֹדֵד	מִתְבּוֹדֶדֶת	recluse
Plural	מִתְבּוֹדְדִים	מִתְבּוֹדְדוֹת	

mitCoCeC is the realization of the active participle derived from *hitpa`el* when the second consonant of the root is *w* or *y*, or when the second or third root consonants are identical (e.g., בד"ד). In the *mishkal* itself, an וֹ follows the first consonant, and the second and third consonants are identical – even where they are not in the root proper (roots like קו"ם, לי"ן where the second root consonant is *w* or *y*).

Examples

אני דוחה את הטענה שהיהודים הרפורמים הם **מִתְבּוֹלְלִים** שאיבדו את זהותם היהודית.
I reject the claim that reform Jews are **ones who have assimilated** and lost their Jewish identity.

Additional Examples in this Pattern

wrestler מִתְגּוֹשֵׁשׁ
complainant מִתְלוֹנֵן
insurrectionist, mutineer מִתְקוֹמֵם

---

165. ***mitCaCeC* = *mitCaCCeC***: the active participle of *hitpa`el* when the roots are quadriliteral

	Masc.	Fem.	Gloss
Sing.	מִתְאַגְרֵף	מִתְאַגְרֶפֶת	boxer
Plural	מִתְאַגְרְפִים	מִתְאַגְרְפוֹת	

mitCaCCeC is similar to *mitCaCeC*, but with four root consonants.

Examples

מרבית תשומת הלב של ציבור המתעניינים באִגְרוּף מתרכזת **בַּמִּתְאַגְרְפִים** במשקל כבד.
Most of the attention of the boxing fans is concentrated on heavyweight **boxers**.

Additional Examples in this Pattern

philosopher; one who "philosophizes" (derogatory) מִתְפַּלְסֵף

---

166. ***mitCaCeC* = *mitCaCCeC***: the active participle of *hitpa`el* when the roots are quadrilateral and the last two consonants are identical

	Masc.	Fem.	Gloss
Sing.	מִתְכַּוְנֵן	מִתְכַּוְנֶנֶת	adjustable
Plural	מִתְכַּוְנְנִים	מִתְכַּוְנְנוֹת	

mitCaCCeC is similar to *mitCaCeC*, but with four root consonants, when the last two consonants are identical (מִתְקַטְלֵל).

Examples

קנה התותח בטנק חייב להיות **מִתְכַּוְנֵן**, כדי שיוכל לירות לכל כיוון.
The gun barrel in a tank must be **adjustable**, so that it can shoot at any direction..

---

167. ***mitCaCeC* = *mittaCteC***: the active participle of *hitpa`el* when the roots are quadrilateral, the first root consonant is *tet*, and when the two first consonants are reduplicated in consonantal slots three and four, respectively

	Masc.	Fem.	Gloss
Sing.	מִטַּלְטֵל	מִטַּלְטֶלֶת	portable
Plural	מִטַּלְטְלִים	מִטַּלְטְלוֹת	

mittaCteC is similar to *mitCaCeC*, but with four root consonants, and when the first consonant is *tet*, the *t* of *hitpa`el* assimilates to that *tet*. In normal speech, the geminated *t* is articulated as a single *t* (*mi-tal-tel*). Also, the two first consonants are reduplicated in consonantal slots three and four, respectively (מְקַטְקֵט).

Examples

היום מרבית המשתמשים במחשב מעדיפים מחשב **מְטַלְטֵל**.
Today most computer users prefer a **portable** computer.

L. *haCCaCa* and related *mishkalim*

168. *haCCaCa*: gerund/nominalization related to *hif`il*

Our/your/their	my/your/his/her	const.	Gloss	sing/pl
הַכְנָסָתֵנוּ/**הַכְנַסַתְ**כֶם/כֶן/**הַכְנָסָתָ**ם/ן	**הַכְנָסָ**תִי/תְךָ/תֵךְ/תוֹ/תָהּ	הַכְנָסַת-	income,	הַכְנָסָה נ׳
הַכְנָסוֹתֵינוּ/כֶם/כֶן/הֶם/הֶן	**הַכְנָסוֹ**תַי/תֶיךָ/תַיִךְ/תָיו/תֶיהָ	הַכְנָסוֹת-	binging in	הַכְנָסוֹת

haCCaCa is often a pattern designating nominalization of *hif`il* verbs, or gerunds, as in הִדְלִיק 'light V' ~ הַדְלָקָה 'lighting,' but often the *haCCaCa* form can refer in addition to a more specific meaning of the nominalization, as in הִזְמִין 'invite' ~ הַזְמָנָה 'inviting; invitation.'

Examples

כאשר ההוצאות עולות על ה**הַכְנָסוֹת**, מדובר בגירעון.
When expenses exceed **revenues**, we are talking of a deficit.

הַכְנָסַת תביעות נוספות ברגע האחרון שיבשה את המו״מ עם העובדים.
Introducing new demands at the last minute disrupted the negotiations with the workers.

הַבְרָחַת הסמים ממקסיקו לארה״ב נמשכת כסדרה ללא תלות בחילופי ממשל.
Smuggling of drugs from Mexico to the continues uninterrupted, regardless of regime changes.

לעיתים נראה ש**הַגְדָּלַת** פער שאין לה סוף בין העשירים והעניים ביותר היא בלתי נמנעת.
Sometimes it appears that endless **enlargement** (=widening) of the gap between the richest and the poorest is inevitable.

זכייה גדולה ב**הַגְרָלָה** כרוכה בלא מעט סיבוכים, בעיקר בשל ציפיות מצד משפחה ומכרים – והמדינה...
A large **lottery** win involves a few complications, particularly owing to expectations on the part of family and acquaintances – and the State…

על אף המחלוקת הקשה בין מנהיגי שתי המדינות, בסופו של דבר הצליחו להגיע ל**הַסְדָּרַת** היחסים ביניהם.
In spite of the serious controversy involving the two heads of state, they finally managed to reach a **resolution** of their relations.

בדרך כלל, פוליטיקאים מצליחים הם אלה הטובים ב**הַלְהָבַת** ההמונים.
Generally, successful politicians are those who are good in **arousing** the masses.

Special Expressions

fine line; sharp **perception** **הַבְחָנָה** דקה
false **promise** **הַבְטָחַת** שווא
self-**determination** **הַגְדָּרָה** עצמית
self-**realization**/fulfillment **הַגְשָׁמָה** עצמית
income tax מס **הַכְנָסָה**
hospitality **הַכְנָסַת** אורחים
brain**storming** **הַסְעָרַת** [סיעור] מוחות

Additional Examples in this Pattern

differentiating; differentiation הַבְדָּלָה
clarification הַבְהָרָה
differentiation, distinguishing; distinction; perception; observation הַבְחָנָה
promise הַבְטָחָה
restraint, self-restraint הַבְלָגָה
making prominent הַבְלָטָה
breaking through הַבְקָעָה
recuperation הַבְרָאָה
screwing; screw thread הַבְרָגָה
limiting; limitation הַגְבָּלָה
strengthening; amplification הַגְבָּרָה
exaggerating; exaggeration הַגְזָמָה
lottery הַגְרָלָה
realization הַגְשָׁמָה
gluing; spreading infectious disease הַדְבָּקָה
repression (psychoanalysis) הַדְחָקָה
causing a leak הַדְלָפָה
lighting; turning on הַדְלָקָה
stirring up emotions הַסְעָרָה

---

169. ***haCCaCa* > *haCaCaCa:*** gerund/nominalization related to *hif'il*, when the 1st root consonant is a א', ה', ע'

Our/your/their	my/your/his/her	const.	Gloss	sing/pl
הַעֲרָכָתֵנוּ/**הַעֲרַכְתְ**כֶם/כֶן/**הַעֲרָכָתָ**ם/ן	**הַעֲרָכָ**תִי/תְךָ/תֵךְ/תוֹ/תָהּ	הַעֲרָכַת-	estimation,	הַעֲרָכָה נ'
הַעֲרָכוֹתֵינוּ/כֶם/כֶן/הֶם/הֶן	**הַעֲרָכוֹ**תַי/תֶיךָ/תַיִךְ/תָיו/תֶיהָ	הַעֲרָכוֹת-	evaluation	הַעֲרָכוֹת

haCCaCa is often a pattern designating nominalization of *hif'il* verbs, or gerunds (see above). When the first root consonant is א', ה', ע' (but not ח'), a *shva* is replaced by a *Hataf-pataH*.

Examples

בזמנים קשים, חובה על כולנו לקיים **הַעֲרָכַת** מצב לעתים קרובות.
When time are bad, it is everyone's duty to conduct **evaluation** of conditions every so often.

הַעֲצָבָה של בני אדם נגרמת לעתים במתכוון על ידי אחרים, ולעתים על ידי נסיבות קשות.
Saddening of people is sometimes caused intentionally by others, and sometimes is caused by difficult circumstances.

במדינות טוטליטאריות **הַעֲרָצַת** המנהיג היא תנאי הכרחי להישרדות המשטר.
In totalitarian states, **admiration** of the leader is a necessary condition for the regime's survival.

במקרה של כישלון, **הַאֲשָׁמַת** האחרים היא הדרך הקלה ביותר, אבל יש בכל זאת אנשים שיש להם אומץ לקחת את האחריות על עצמם.

In cases of failure, **blaming** others is the easiest way out, but still some people have enough guts to assume responsibility themselves.

Special Expressions

הַעֲרָכַת מצב **evaluation** of the situation
הַאֲזָנַת סתר bugging
הַעֲבָרָה בנקאית **transfer** of funds
הַעֲדָפָה מתקנת affirmative action
הַעֲלָאָה בדרגה **promotion** to a higher rank

Additional Examples in this Pattern

הַאֲבָקָה pollination
הַאֲזָנָה listening
הַאֲחָדָה unification; standardization
הַאֲכָלָה feeding
הַאֲנָשָׁה personification
הַאֲפָלָה black-out
הַהֲדָרָה editing, emendation
הַעֲבָרָה transferring; transfer
הַעֲדָפָה preference, preferring
הַעֲלָאָה raise, raising
הַעֲמָקָה deepening
הַעֲסָקָה employing

---

170. *haCCaCa* = *'aCCaCa*: alternant, secondary gerund/nominalization related to *hif`il* (with א' replacing ה')

Our/your/their	my/your/his/her	const.	Gloss	sing/pl
אַזְעָקָתֵנוּ/**אַזְעַקְתְ**כֶם/כֶן/**אַזְעָקָתָ**ם/ן	**אַזְעָקָ**תִי/תְךָ/תֵךְ/תוֹ/תָהּ	-אַזְעָקַת	alarm	אַזְעָקָה נ׳
אַזְעָקוֹתֵינוּ/כֶם/כֶן/הֶם/הֶן	**אַזְעָקוֹ**תַי/תֶיךָ/תַיִךְ/תָיו/תֶיהָ	-אַזְעָקוֹת		אַזְעָקוֹת

'aCCaCa is a less frequent alternant of the *haCCaCa* pattern, generally also designating nominalization of *hif`il* verbs, or gerunds, and sometimes the two forms are used essentially interchangeably, as in הַחְזָקָה ~ אַחְזָקָה 'maintenance' (for some, הַחְזָקָה refers to 'holding'), but in most cases the *'aCCaCa* reference is less general, designating a specific realization of the nominalization. Thus, for instance, while הַזְעָקָה refers to calling into action, summoning to gather, as well as giving warning of an approaching danger, אַזְעָקָה generally refers to the warning signal itself, such as a siren. And while הַבְחָנָה denotes differentiation and distinguishing, as well as insight, אַבְחָנָה is limited to diagnosis. Occasionally a secondary quadrilateral root is derived from the *'aCCaCa* form, e.g., אבח״נ from אַבְחָנָה, the א' becomes part of the new root, and this secondary root is realized in *pi`el*, *pu`al*, possibly *hitpa`el*, in this case אִבְחֵן 'diagnose,' אֻבְחַן 'be diagnosed.'

Examples

כשמתקבלות **אַתְרָעוֹת** אודות פיגועים אפשריים, מופצת **אַזְעָקָה** בכל כלי התקשורת.

When there are **warnings** re possible terrorist acts, an **alarm** is issued to all the media.

אות **הָאַזְעָקָה** הוא לעתים באמצעות צפירה ולעתים באופן אחר.

The **alarm signal** is sometimes in the form of a siren, sometimes in another manner.

ברוב המבנים הציבוריים בישראל, והיום גם בחלק ממבנים ציבוריים בארצות אחרות, יש סידורי **אַבְטָחָה** 24 שעות.
In most public buildings in Israel, and today also in some public buildings elsewhere, there are 24-hours **security** arrangements.

כאשר שיעור ה**אַבְטָלָה** עולה על 5%, על המדינה לנקוט צעדים מיידיים לשיפור הכלכלה.
When the **unemployment** rate exceeds 5%, the state must take immediate action so as to improve the economy.

כל מורה טוב לשפה זרה עושה הכל כדי להביא ל**אַשְׁגָּרָתָהּ**, בעיקר בתקשורת מדוברת.
Any good foreign language teacher does everything so as to bring about its **fluency**, particularly in oral communication.

Special Expressions

differential **diagnosis** **אַבְחָנָה** מבדלת (med.)
hidden **unemployment** **אַבְטָלָה** סמויה
alarm siren צפירת **אַזְעָקָה**
traveling expenses **אַחְזָקַת** רכב
affirmative action **אַפְלָיָה** מתקנת
racial **discrimination** **אַפְלָיָה** עדתית

Additional Examples in this Pattern

diagnosis אַבְחָנָה
security, protection אַבְטָחָה
warning אַזְהָרָה
memorial אַזְכָּרָה
maintenance אַחְזָקָה
storage אַחְסָנָה
disappointment אַכְזָבָה
public announcement אַכְרָזָה
diphtheria אַסְכָּרָה
supply N אַסְפָּקָה
discrimination אַפְלָיָה
relief, all-clear אַרְגָּעָה

---

171. ***haCCaCa = hoCaCa***: gerund/nominalization related to *hif'il* when the first consonant of the root is *y*

Our/your/their	my/your/his/her	const.	Gloss	sing/pl
הוֹפָעָתֵנוּ/**הוֹפָעַתְ**כֶם/כֶן/**הוֹפָעָתָ**ם/ן	**הוֹפָעָ**תִי/תְךָ/תֵךְ/תוֹ/תָהּ	-הוֹפָעַת	appearance;	הוֹפָעָה נ׳
הוֹפָעוֹתֵינוּ/כֶם/כֶן/הֶם/הֶן	**הוֹפָעוֹ**תַי/תֶיךָ/תַיִךְ/תָיו/תֶיהָ	-הוֹפָעוֹת	performance	הוֹפָעוֹת

When the first consonant of the root in the pattern comparable to *haCCaCa* is *y*, that *y* becomes *o*: *y-p-`* > *hofa`a*. Note an exception: הֲנָקָה < ינ״ק for 'breast-feeding.'

Examples

ה**הוֹפָעָה** האחרונה של ליידי גאגא בתל אביב התקבלה בהתלהבות עצומה.
Lady Gaga's latest **performance** in Tel Aviv was received with the greatest enthusiasm.

בניו יורק יש כמה חברות **הוֹבָלָה** בבעלות ישראלים.
In New York City there are a number of **moving** companies owned by Israelis.

בנימין קיבל **הוֹדָעָה** שעליו לעבור ביקורת של מס הכנסה.
Benjamin received a **notice** that he has to undergo an audit by the Internal Revenue Service.

המו״ל ביקש משמואל להכין **הוֹצָאָה** שלישית של ספר הלימוד שלו.
The publisher asked Shmuel to prepare a third **edition** of his textbook.

Special Expressions

Silence is equivalent to **admission** שתיקה כ**הוֹדָאָה** דמיא
Thanksgiving חג **הַהוֹדָיָה**
circumstantial **evidence** **הוֹכָחָה** נסיבתית
self **deception** **הוֹנָאָה** עצמית
live **performance** **הוֹפָעָה** חיה
publishing **הוֹצָאָה** לאור
execution **הוֹצָאָה** להורג
implementation **הוֹצָאָה** לפועל
arm wrestling **הוֹרָדַת** ידיים

Additional Examples in this Pattern

confession הוֹדָאָה
thanksgiving הוֹדָיָה
proof; evidence הוֹכָחָה
begetting הוֹלָדָה
conducting הוֹלָכָה
fraud, deception הוֹנָאָה
adding; addition הוֹסָפָה
lowering; removal הוֹרָדָה

---

172. ***haCCaCa* = *hoCaCa***: few gerund/nominalizations related to *hif'il* when the second consonant of the root is *w*, which behave as if their first root consonant were *y*

Our/your/their	my/your/his/her	const.	Gloss	sing/pl
הוֹזָלָתֵנוּ/**הוֹזָלַתְ**כֶם/כֶן/**הוֹזָלָתָ**ם/ן	**הוֹזָלָ**תִי/תְךָ/תֵךְ/תוֹ/תָהּ	הוֹזָלַת-	lowering	הוֹזָלָה נ׳
הוֹזָלוֹתֵינוּ/כֶם/כֶן/הֶם/הֶן	**הוֹזָלוֹ**תַי/תֶיךָ/תַיִךְ/תָיו/תֶיהָ	הוֹזָלוֹת-	prices	הוֹזָלוֹת

When the second consonant of the root in the pattern comparable to *haCCaCa* is *w* or *y*, the prefix *h* is followed by *o*, and that *w* or *y* is not realized: *z-w-l* > *hozala* (*hazala* exists too, but is far less common).

Examples

חברת ״סירְס״ הודיעה על **הוֹזָלָה** גדולה של מחירי מוצרי חשמל בתקופת החג.
The Sears company announced a big **price reduction** of electrical appliances during the holiday.

Additional Examples in this Pattern

leaving land uncultivated הוֹבָרָה

---

173. *haCCaCa* = *haCaCa*: gerund/nominalization related to *hif'il* when the first consonant of the root is *n*, or when the first two consonants are *yz* or *yts*.

our/your/their	my/your/his/her	const.	Gloss	sing/pl
הַכָּרָתֵנוּ/**הַכָּרַתְ**כֶם/כֶן/**הַכָּרָתָ**ם/ן	**הַכָּרָ**תִי/תְךָ/תֵךְ/תוֹ/תָהּ	הַכָּרַת-	consciousness;	הַכָּרָה נ׳
הַכָּרוֹתֵינוּ/כֶם/כֶן/הֶם/הֶן	**הַכָּרוֹ**תַי/תֶיךָ/תַיִךְ/תָיו/תֶיהָ	הַכָּרוֹת-	recognition	הַכָּרוֹת

When the first consonant of the root in the pattern comparable to *haCCaCa* is *n*, that *n* is assimilated, and the following consonant is geminated: *n-k-r* > *hakara*. The same happens to *y* before *z* and before *ts*: יז״ע > הַזָּעָה/הֲזָעָה, יצ״ג > הַצָּגָה.

Examples

לאחר התאונה, משה שכב שלושה ימים בבית החולים ללא **הַכָּרָה**.
Following the accident, Moshe lay in the hospital three days without **consciousness**.

יש מרצים שמוכנים לדבר על כל נושא, גם כאשר **הַכָּרָתָם** את החומר מוגבלת ביותר.
There are lecturers who are willing to speak about any subject, even when their **acquaintance** with the subject matter is very limited.

לפי **הַבָּעַת** פניו, נראה לי שראיון הקבלה לעבודה לא בדיוק הצליח.
According to the **expression** on his face, it seems to me that his job interview was not quite successful.

השר מיהר להתפטר מתפקידו – הוא לא חיכה ל**הַדָּחָתוֹ** על ידי ראש הממשלה...
The minister hurried to resign; he did not wait for his **removal** by the Prime Minister...

הנושא הקשה ביותר שעתיד לעמוד על סדר יומו של בית המשפט העליון בארה״ב הוא חוקיות **הַפָּלוֹת**.
The most difficult issue to face the Supreme court of the US is the legality of **abortions**.

Special Expressions

הַבָּעָה בעל-פה oral **expression**, speech
הַטָּיַת דין miscarriage of justice
הַטָּפַת מוסר **preaching**, rebuking
הַכָּרַת טובה/תודה gratitude
לעשות **הַכָּרָה** עם make the **acquaintance** of

הַכָּרַת פנים בדין judicial partiality
תת-**הַכָּרָה** sub-**consciousness**
הַצָּגַת בכורה premiere
הַצָּעָה לסדר היום **motion** for the agenda

Additional Examples in this Pattern

הַבָּטָה looking
הַגָּעָה arrival
הַגָּשָׁה serving, handing in
הַדָּרָה exclusion
הַזָּלָה shedding tears
הַזָּעָה perspiring
הַטָּיָה turning

הַטָּלָה placing, imposing
הַטָּפָה preaching
הַכָּאָה beating
הַסָּעָה transportation
הַצָּגָה showing; show
הַצָּלָה saving, rescuing
הַצָּעָה suggestion; proposal; offer

174. *haCCaCa* = *haCaCa*: gerund/nominalization related to *hif'il* when the 2nd consonant of the root is *w* or *y*

our/your/their	my/your/his/her	const.	Gloss	sing/pl
הֲנָחָתֵנוּ/**הֲנָחַתְ**כֶם/כֶן/**הֲנָחָתָ**ם/ן	**הֲנָחָ**תִי/תְךָ/תֵךְ/תוֹ/תָהּ	הֲנָחַת-	discount; relief;	הֲנָחָה נ׳
הֲנָחוֹתֵינוּ/כֶם/כֶן/הֶם/הֶן	**הֲנָחוֹ**תַי/תֶיךָ/תַיִךְ/תָיו/תֶיהָ	הֲנָחוֹת-	assumption	הֲנָחוֹת

When the second consonant of the root in the pattern comparable to *haCCaCa* is *w* or *y*, that *w/y* is not realized, and the prefix ה׳ is marked with a *Hataf-pataH*, as in הֲבָנָה, or *seghol* before a guttural, as in הֶעָרָה (see below). Occasionally this pattern includes some forms in which the second and third consonants of the root are identical: הֲזָגָה 'glazing' from זג״ג (in some instances, the two alternants coexist: הֲגַנָּה/הֲגָנָה 'defense' from the root גנ״נ). A rare occurrence: realization from a root whose third consonant is *y*: 'hallucination' הֲזָיָה < הז״י.

Examples

כשקונים בכמויות גדולות, ניתן לקבל **הֲנָחָה** ניכרת.
When one buys in large quantities, one can get significant **discount**.

בישראל, אלמנה מקבלת **הֲנָחָה** במיסי העיריה.
In Israel, a widow gets some **relief (rebate)** from municipal taxes.

בעבר שלטה ה**הֲנָחָה/הַנָּחָה** שהאטום הוא יחידה בלתי נחלקת.
In the past, the prevalent **assumption** was that the atom is an indivisible unit.

המשכורות באוניברסיטאות בישראל אינן גבוהות במיוחד, אבל ה**הֲטָבוֹת** מרשימות, בעיקר קרן ההשתלמות.
Salaries at the universities in Israel are not particularly high, but the **benefits** are impressive, particulary the ones for professional development.

הֲטָלַת כידון היא ספורט עתיק, שיש לו המשך במשחקים האולימפיים היום, אבל משום מה אינו פופולרי במיוחד.
Javelin **throwing** is an ancient sport, which continues in the Olympic games today, but for some reason is not particularly popular.

בארה״ב יש בתי ספר תיכוניים פרטיים, חלקם פנימיות, המיועדים בעיקר ל**הֲכָנַת** תלמידים ללימודים באוניברסיטאות.
In the US there are certain private high schools, some of them boarding schools, whose main purpose is the **preparation** of students for university study.

רשות התעופה מתקשה למצוא שיטה יעילה ובטוחה ל**הֲנָסַת** ציפורים מן המסלולים.
The airport authority has difficulty in finding an efficient and safe way of **driving** birds **away** from the runways.

מספר פעילים בתנועה נאו-נאצית מואשמים ב**הֲפָצַת** כרוזים גזעניים וב**הֲסָתָה** לאלימות.
A number of neo-Nazi movement members are accused of the **distribution** of racist leaflets and of **inciting** violence.

Special Expressions

mis**understanding** אי-**הֲבָנָה**
slow on the uptake קְשה-**הֲבָנָה**
forgivingly, sympathetically **בַּהֲבָנָה**
pre**sumption** **הֲנָחָה/הַנָּחָה** מוקדמת

rear-wheel **drive** **הֲנָעָה** אחורית
unveiling **הֲסָרַת** הלוט
spreading rumors **הֲפָצַת** שמועות

Additional Examples in this Pattern

bringing הֲבָאָה
understanding הֲבָנָה
moving tr. הֲזָזָה
feeding הֲזָנָה
flying an aircraft הֲטָסָה
joke, jest הֲלָצָה
exchange הֲמָרָה

putting to death הֲמָתָה
engine ignition; propulsion הֲנָעָה
removal, withdrawal הֲסָרָה
peeking; glancing הֲצָצָה
bothering הֲצָקָה
smelling, sniffing הֲרָחָה

---

175. ***haCCaCa* = *heCaCa***: gerund/nominalization related to *hif'il* when the second consonant of the root is *w* or *y* and the first consonant of the root is a guttural

our/your/their	my/your/his/her	const.	Gloss	sing/pl
הֶעָרָתֵנוּ/**הֶעָרַתְ**כֶם/כֶן/**הֶעָרָתָ**ם/ן	**הֶעָרָ**תִי/תְךָ/תֵךְ/תוֹ/תָהּ	-הֶעָרַת	comment,	הֶעָרָה נ׳
הֶעָרוֹתֵינוּ/כֶם/כֶן/הֶם/הֶן	**הֶעָרוֹ**תַי/תֶיךָ/תַיִךְ/תָיו/תֶיהָ	-הֶעָרוֹת	note	הֶעָרוֹת

When the second consonant of the root in the pattern comparable to *haCCaCa* is *w* or *y*, that *w/y* is not realized, and the prefix ה׳ is marked with a *seghol* before a guttural.

Examples

המאמר מצא חן בעיניי, אבל היו לי כמה **הֶעָרוֹת**.
I liked the article, but I had a few **comments**.

יש כתבי עת שאינם מוכנים לכלול **הֶעָרוֹת** שוליים במאמרים המתפרסמים בהם.
Some journals are unwilling to include **footnotes** in the articles published in them.

תמיד יהיה מי שיתנגד ל**הֶחָלַת** חוק חדש העלול לפגוע בו באופן זה או אחר.
There will always be someone who will object the **application** of a new **law** that might affect him/her one way or another.

Additional Examples in this Pattern

acceleration הֶאָצָה
illumination הֶאָרָה

gathering (esp. of flock, herd) הֶעָזָה

---

176. *haCCaCa* = *haCaCa*: a number of gerunds/nominalizations related to *hif'il* from roots with identical 2nd and 3rd consonants (not the default הֲקַטָּה below)

When the second and third consonants are identical, the default realization of the pattern comparable to *haCCaCa* is in the הֲקַטָּה *mishkal*, but there are some realizations in הֲקָלָה, as if those cases were derived from roots whose second consonant is *w* or *y*, as in הֲזָגָה from זג״ג. In a form like הֲרָעָה it could be the הֲקָלָה pattern or הֲקַטָּה in which the "guttural" caused the change. In some instances, the two alternants coexist: הֲגַנָּה/הֲגָנָה from the root גנ״ן, הֲנַצָּה/הֲנָצָה from נצ״ץ. **For declension and examples, see the הֲקָלָה pattern** above.

Additional Examples in this Pattern

glazing הֲזָגָה	narrowing הֲצָרָה
violating; violation הֲפָרָה	worsening הֲרָעָה

---

177. *haCCaCa* = *haCaCa*: gerund/nominalization related to *hif'il* when the second and third consonants of the root are identical

our/your/their	my/your/his/her	const.	Gloss	sing/pl
הֲגַנָּתֵנוּ/**הֲגַנַּתְ**כֶם/כֶן/**הֲגַנָּתָ**ם/ן	**הֲגַנָּתִ**י/תְךָ/תֵךְ/תוֹ/תָהּ	הֲגַנַּת-	defense,	הֲגַנָּה נ׳
הֲגַנּוֹתֵינוּ/כֶם/כֶן/הֶם/הֶן	**הֲגַנּוֹתַ**י/תֶיךָ/תַיִךְ/תָיו/תֶיהָ	הֲגַנּוֹת-	protection	הֲגַנּוֹת

When the second and third consonants of the root are identical, the pattern comparable to *haCCaCa* is הֲקַטָּה, with the second (single) consonant geminated with a *dagesh*, following a *pataH*. Occasionally one finds an alternant form in הֲקָלָה, as in הֲגַנָּה/הֲגָנָה from the root גנ״ן, and there are cases in which a root with two identical second and third consonants is realized as if it were derived exclusively from a root with *w* or *y*, as in הֲזָגָה from זג״ג, possibly in analogy with the much more common הֲקָלָה pattern.

Examples

מלחמת הַ**הֲתַשָּׁה/הֲתָשָׁה** בסיני בין מצרים וישראל נמשכה בין יוני 1967 ואוגוסט 1970.
The War of **Attrition** between Egypt and Israel continued between June 1967 and August 1970.

Special Expressions

self-**defense** **הֲגַנָּה** עצמית	retaining for a different **הֲסָבָה** מקצועית job, career change
Israel **Defense** צבא הַ**הֲגַנָּה** לישראל Forces	

Additional Examples in this Pattern

refutation of a witness הֲזַמָּה/הֲזָמָה	turning; altering, הֲסַבָּה/הֲסִבָּה converting
melting, dissolving הֲמַסָּה/הֲמָסָה	shading הֲצַלָּה/הֲצָלָה
blossoming; budding הֲנַצָּה/הֲנָצָה	easing, relief הֲקַלָּה/הֲקָלָה

---

178. ***haCCaCa* = *heCaCa***: gerund/nominalization related to *hif'il* when the second and third consonants of the root are identical and where the first root consonant is a guttural

our/your/their	my/your/his/her	const.	Gloss	sing/pl
הֶעָזָּתֵנוּ/**הֶעָזַּתְ**כֶם/כֶן/**הֶעָזָּתָ**ם/ן הַעֲזָּתֵנוּ/**הַעֲזַּתְ**כֶם/כֶן/**הַעֲזָּתָ**ם/ן	**הֶעָזָּ/הַעֲזָּ**תִי/תְךָ/תֵךְ/תוֹ/תָהּ	הֶעָזַּת- /הַעֲזַּת-	daring N	הֶעָזָּה/הַעֲזָּה נ'
הֶעָזּוֹ/הַעֲזּוֹתֵינוּ/כֶם/כֶן/הֶם/הֶן	**הֶעָזּוֹ/הַעֲזּוֹ**תַי/תֶיךָ/תַיִךְ/תָיו/תֶיהָ	הֶעָזּוֹת- /הַעֲזּוֹת-		הֶעָזּוֹת/הַעֲזּוֹת

In some cases when the second and third consonants of the root are identical, and the first root consonant is a guttural, the prefix comes with a *seghol*. The הֶאָטָה form follows the pattern for words derived from roots with a middle *w/y* (without a *pataH* followed by a *dagesh*). The Hebrew Language Academy prefers the latter for all relevant instances.

Examples

דרושה **הֶעָזָּה/הַעֲזָּה** רבה כדי לחלץ אנשים מבית או רכב בוער.
Great **daring** is required in order to extract people out of a burning house or vehicle.

לעתים קרובות, לפני שעובדים משביתים מפעל, הם מנסים לראות אם שביתת **הֶאָטָה** תספיק.
Often, before workers strike down a plant, they first try to find out whether a **slowdown** strike would suffice.

M. *heCCeC* and related *mishkalim*

179. ***heCCeC***: alternative for *haCCaCa* for gerunds or nominalizations related to *hif'il*

our/your/their	my/your/his/her	const.	Gloss	sing/pl
הֶבְדֵּלֵנוּ/לְכֶם/לְכֶן/לָם/לָן	**הֶבְדֵּ**לִי/לְךָ/לֵךְ/לוֹ/לָהּ	הֶבְדֵּל-	difference,	הֶבְדֵּל ז'
הֶבְדֵּלֵינוּ/כֶם/כֶן/הֶם/הֶן	**הֶבְדֵּ**לַי/לֶיךָ/לַיִךְ/לָיו/לֶיהָ	הֶבְדֵּלֵי-	distinction	הֶבְדֵּלִים

heCCeC is an alternative pattern to *haCCaCa* to designate nominalization of *hif'il* verbs, or gerunds, but often the *heCCeC* form refers to a more specific meaning related to the gerund, as in הִסְכִּים 'agree' ~ הַסְכָּמָה 'agreeing' ~ הֶסְכֵּם 'an agreement,' הֶעֱתִיק 'copy V' ~ הַעֲתָקָה 'copying' ~ הֶעְתֵק 'a copy.'

Examples

החתול דומה מאוד לנמר; **הַהֶבְדֵּל** העיקרי הוא בגודל...
Cats are very similar to tigers; the main **difference** is in size...

בית ההוצאה הודיע לי שהספר שהזמנתי אזל; בקרוב אקבל **הֶחְזֵר** דרך כרטיס האשראי.
The publisher informed me that the book I had ordered is out of print; I will soon get a **refund** through my credit card.

דני וחנה נפרדו. על פי ה**הֶסְדֵּר** ביניהם, הילדה תהיה עם אביה שלושה ימים בשבוע.
Danny and Hannah separated. According to the **agreement** between them, the girl will spend three days a week with her father.

נקווה ש**הֶסְכֵּם** השלום עם מצרים ימשיך להחזיק מעמד שנים רבות.
Let's hope that the peace **agreement** with Egypt continue to hold for many years.

בשל ה**הֶפְסֵדִים** הגדולים של החברה לאחרונה, חבר המנהלים החליט לסגרה.
Owing to the company's recent big **losses**, the board of directors decided to close it.

בין 1949 ו-1967 היה בירושלים שטח **הֶפְקֵר** בין השטח הישראלי לשטח הירדני.
Between 1949 and 1967 there was in Jerusalem a **no-man's land** between the Israeli area and the Jordanian area.

Special Expressions

class **distinctions** **הֶבְדֵּלֵי** מעמדות
reimbursement **הֶחְזֵר** הוצאות
later, in the future, in due course **בְּהֶמְשֵׁךְ**
maritime blockade **הֶסְגֵּר** ימי
plea **agreement** **הֶסְדֵּר** טיעון
collective **agreement** **הֶסְכֵּם** קיבוצי
interim **agreement** **הֶסְכֵּם** ביניים

Additional Examples in this Pattern

print N הֶדְפֵּס
authorization; (kashrut) certification הֶכְשֵׁר
compound word הֶלְחֵם
continuation הֶמְשֵׁךְ
explanation הֶסְבֵּר
confinement; blockade הֶסְגֵּר
eulogy הֶסְפֵּד
output, supply הֶסְפֵּק
break הֶפְסֵק
difference הֶפְרֵשׁ
context הֶקְשֵׁר

---

180. ***heCCeC* = *heCeCeC***: alternative for *haCCaCa* for gerund/nominalization related to *hif'il*, when the first root consonant is a guttural

our/your/their	my/your/his/her	const.	Gloss	sing/pl
הֶעֱתֵקֵנוּ/קְכֶם/קְכֶן/קָם/קָן	**הֶעֱתֵ**קִי/קְךָ/קֵךְ/קוֹ/קָהּ	הֶעֱתֵק-	copy	הֶעֱתֵק ז'
הֶעֱתֵקֵינוּ/כֶם/כֶן/הֶם/הֶן	**הֶעֱתֵ**קַי/קֶיךָ/קַיִךְ/קָיו/קֶיהָ	הֶעֱתֵקֵי-		הֶעֱתֵקִים

heCCeC is an alternative pattern to *haCCaCa* to designate nominalization of *hif'il* verbs, or gerunds. When the first root consonant is a guttural, the expected *shva* is usually replaced by a *Hataf-seghol*.

Examples

כל בר דעת יודע שיש לצלם ולשמור **הֶעֱתֵק** של כל מסמך חשוב.
Any sensible person knows that one needs to photocopy and keep a **copy** of each important document.

בְּהֶעְדֵּר הוכחות ברורות לאשמתו של הנאשם, קרוב לוודאי שחבר המושבעים יקבע שהוא זכאי.
In the **absence** of clear evidence pointing to the defendant's guilt, it is very likely that the jury will find him not guilty.

---

181. ***heCeCC***: alternative for *haCCaCa* for gerund/nominalization related to *hif'il*, when the third root consonant is a guttural

our/your/their	my/your/his/her	const.	Gloss	sing/pl
הֶכְרֵעֵנוּ/עֲכֶם/עֲכֶן/עָם/עָן	**הֶכְרֵ**עִי/עֲךָ/עֵךְ/עוֹ/עָהּ	הֶכְרֵעַ-	decision,	הֶכְרֵעַ ז'
הֶכְרֵעֵינוּ/כֶם/כֶן/הֶם/הֶן	**הֶכְרֵ**עַי/עֶיךָ/עַיִךְ/עָיו/עֶיהָ	הֶכְרֵעֵי-	final ruling	הֶכְרֵעִים

In the isolation form of the sing. masc. the final guttural is preceded by a *furtive pataH*. Where a *shva* is expected, it is replaced by a *Hataf-pataH*: הֶכְרֵעֲךָ, הֶכְרֵעֲכֶם.

Examples

לאביגדור קשה מאוד להחליט אם ללמוד באוניברסיטה בארץ או בחו״ל. הוא התקבל לכמה מוסדות יוקרתיים, אבל רגע ה**הֶכְרֵעַ** הגיע; הוא עלול לאבד מלגות לימודים שהוצעו לו אם לא יחליט בקרוב.
It is difficult for Avigdor to decide whether to study at a university in Israel or abroad. He was accepted into some prestigious institutions, but the **decision** moment has arrived; he may lose scholarships that were offered to him if he does not decide soon.

בהרבה ארצות מתפתחות, משפחות שלמות חיות בדירה בת חדר אחד, מתוך **הֶכְרֵחַ**.
In many developing countries, whole families live in a one-room apartment, out of **necessity**.

Special Expressions

necessarily ב**הֶכְרֵחַ**, מן ה**הֶכְרֵחַ**
don't criticize what stems from compulsion ה**הֶכְרֵחַ** לא יגונה

Additional Examples in this Pattern

flicker N הֶבְלֵחַ

---

182. ***heCCeC* = *heCeC*:** gerund/nominalization comparable to *heCCeC* when the first consonant of the root is *n*, or when the first two consonants are *y-ts*

our/your/their	my/your/his/her	const.	Gloss	sing/pl
הֶשֵּׂגֵנוּ/גְכֶם/גְכֶן/גָם/גָן	**הֶשֵּׂ**גִי/גְךָ/גֵךְ/גוֹ/גָהּ	הֶשֵּׂג-	achievement	הֶשֵּׂג ז'
הֶשֵּׂגֵינוּ/כֶם/כֶן/הֶם/הֶן	**הֶשֵּׂ**גַי/גֶיךָ/גַיִךְ/גָיו/גֶיהָ	הֶשֵּׂגֵי-		הֶשֵּׂגִים

When the first consonant of the root in the pattern comparable to *haCCaCa* is *n*, that *n* is assimilated, and the following consonant is geminated: aspect הֶבֵּט < נב״ט. The same occurs to *y* before *ts*: exposition הֶצֵּג < יצ״ג.

Examples

בלמידת שפה, מקובל היום להדגיש את **הֶשֵּׂגֵי** התלמיד במיומנות הדיבור.
In language acquisition today, there is strong emphasis on student **achievement** in oral proficiency.

מרבית האנשים מרגישים שאין ביכולתם לעמוד בעומס **הֶטֵּלִים** החדשים.
The majority of the public feel that they cannot withstand the hardship causes by the new **taxes**.

Special Expressions

within reach **בְּהֶשֵּׂג** יד

in comparison to, in **analogy** with **בְּהֶקֵּשׁ** אל

Additional Examples in this Pattern

aspect הֶבֵּט   perimeter הֶקֵּף   syllogism הֶקֵּשׁ   permit הֶתֵּר

---

183. ***heCCeC = heCeC***: gerund/nominalization comparable to *heCCeC* when the first consonant of the root is *n*, or when the first two consonants are *yts*, and the 3rd root consonant is guttural

our/your/their	my/your/his/her	const.	Gloss	sing/pl
הֶצֵּעֵנוּ/עֲכֶם/עֲכֶן/עָם/עָן	**הֶצֵּעִ**י/עֲךָ/עֵךְ/עוֹ/עָהּ	הֶצֵּעַ-הֶצַּע	supply	הֶצֵּעַ ז'
הֶצֵּעֵינוּ/כֶם/כֶן/הֶם/הֶן	**הֶצֵּעַ**י/עֶיךָ/עַיִךְ/עָיו/עֶיהָ	הֶצֵּעֵי-	(economics)	הֶצֵּעִים

Here too, the first root consonant is assimilated into the next one. When the 3rd root consonant is guttural, the masc. sing. form comes with *furtive pataH* when word-final (since the preceding vowel is not *a*). When a *shva* is expected, it is replaced by *Hataf-pataH*. The singular construct state has a variant form: הֶצֵּעַ-/הֶצַּע.

Examples

בשוק חופשי, מחירי סחורות נקבעים על פי **הֶצֵּעַ** וביקוש.
In a free market, prices of goods are determined by **supply** and demand.

Special Expressions

distractedness, distraction **הֶסֵּחַ** דעת

---

184. ***heCCeC* = *heCeC*:** gerund/nominalization comparable to *heCCeC* when the second root consonant is *w* or *y*

our/your/their	my/your/his/her	const.	Gloss	sing/pl
הֶטֵּלֵנוּ/**הֶטֵּלְ**כֶם/כֶן/**הֶטֵּלָ**ם/ן	הֶטֵּלִי/הֶטֵּלְךָ/**הֶטֵּלֵ**ךְ/לוֹ/לָהּ	הֶטֵּל-	projection	הֶטֵּל ז'
הֶטֵּלֵינוּ/כֶם/כֶן/הֶם/הֶן	**הֶטֵּלַ**י/לֶיךָ/לַיִךְ/לָיו/לֶיהָ	הֶטֵּלֵי-	(geometry)	הֶטֵּלִים

When the second consonant of the root in the pattern comparable to *heCCeC* is *w* or *y*, that *w/y* is not realized, and the first consonant of the root is geminated. Occasionally the plural suffix is *–ot*: הֶסֵּט ~ הֶסֵּטוֹת 'shift.'

Examples

הֶסֵּט קטן במיקום הרהיטים עשוי לעתים לשפר משמעותית את חזות החדר כולו.
A slight **shift** in the position of the furniture may sometimes bring about significant improvement in the look of the whole room.

---

185. ***heCCeC* = *heCeC***: gerund/nominalization comparable to *heCCeC* when the second root consonant is *w* or *y*, and the 3rd root consonant is guttural

our/your/their	my/your/his/her	const.	Gloss	sing/pl
הֶנֵּעֵנוּ/עֲכֶם/עֲכֶן/עָם/עָן	**הֶנֵּ**עִי/עֲךָ/עֵךְ/עוֹ/עָהּ	הֶנֵּעַ-/הֶנַּע	movement,	הֶנֵּעַ ז'
הֶנֵּעֵינוּ/כֶם/כֶן/הֶם/הֶן	**הֶנֵּעַ**י/עֶיךָ/עַיִךְ/עָיו/עֶיהָ	הֶנֵּעֵי-	drive	הֶנֵּעִים

When the 3rd root consonant is guttural, the masc. sing. form comes with *furtive pataH* when word-final (since the preceding vowel is not *a*). When a *shva* is expected, it is replaced by *Hataf-pataH*. The singular construct state has a variant form: הֶנֵּעַ-/הֶנַּע.

Examples

לרוב המכוניות היום יש **הֶנֵּעַ** קדמי.
Most cars today have front **drive**.

---

186. ***heCCeC* = *heCeC***: gerund/nominalization comparable to *heCCeC* when the second and third consonants of the root are identical, no plural

our/your/their	my/your/his/her	const.	Gloss	sing/pl
הֶסֵּבֵנוּ/**הֶסֵּבְ**כֶם/כֶן/**הֶסֵּבָ**ם/ן	הֶסֵּבִי/הֶסֵּבְךָ/**הֶסֵּבֵ**ךְ/בוֹ/בָהּ	הֶסֵּב-	turn; endorsement	הֶסֵּב ז'

When the second and third consonants of the root are identical, the realization in the pattern comparable to *heCCeC* is *heCeC*, as in roots with *w* or *y* as the second consonant of the root – see above. The number of occurrences is quite small, and there are no plural forms in use.

Examples

הֶסֵּב ראש מהיר מדיי עלול לגרום לעווית בשריר הצוואר.
Head **turning** that is too fast may cause a cramp in the neck muscles.

Additional Examples in this Pattern

blossoming הֶנֵּץ

N. *maCCiC* and related *mishkalim*

187. *maCCiC*: generally the active participle of *hif'il*

sing/pl	Gloss	const.	my/your/his/her	our/your/their
מַנְהִיג ז׳	leader	מַנְהִיג-	מַנְהִיגִי/מַנְהִיגְךָ/**מַנְהִיג**ֵךְ/גוֹ/גָהּ	מַנְהִיגֵנוּ/**מַנְהִיג**ְכֶם/כֶן/**מַנְהִיג**ָם/ן
מַנְהִיגִים		מַנְהִיגֵי-	**מַנְהִיג**ַי/גֶיךָ/גַיִךְ/גָיו/גֶיהָ	**מַנְהִיג**ֵינוּ/כֶם/כֶן/הֶם/הֶן

The active participle of *hif'il binyan*, *maCCiC*, may serve as a noun, as in מַבְרִיחַ 'smuggler,' מַדְרִיךְ 'guide,' מַנְהִיג 'leader,' or as an adjective, as in מַבְהִיל 'scary,' מַבְחִיל 'disgusting,' מַכְאִיב 'painful.'

Examples

לעיתים **מַנְהִיג** שאינו החלטי נתפס כחלש, אך עם הזמן מבינים שהוא בעצם נהג בתבונה.
Sometimes a **leader** that is not decisive is regarded as weak, but with time we understand that he had actually acted wisely.

מַדְרִיכֵי הטיולים בארץ הם מעולים; לרובם יש תואר ראשון בהיסטוריה, בגאוגרפיה, או בתחום קשור אחר.
The tour **guides** in Israel are excellent; most of them have a Bachelor's degree in history, in geography, or in some other related field.

מעניין שבעברית, **מַזְכִּירָה** היא פקידה במשרד, בעוד ש**מַזְכִּיר** הוא **מַזְכִּיר** האו״ם וכד׳...
Interestingly in Hebrew, a **secretary** in an office is in the feminine, whereas the masculine form is for higher types of positions: UN secretary, Secretary of State….

המשטרה עצרה כעשרה מן ה**מַפְגִּינִים** ושחררה אותם רק למחרת בבוקר.
The police arrested ten of the **demonstrators** and released them only on the following morning.

יש לו פרצוף קצת **מַפְחִיד**, אבל אחרי שמכירים אותו מתברר שהוא בן אדם **מַקְסִים**.
He has a somewhat **scary** face, but when you know him it turns out that he is a **charming** person.

כשמתייגים מוצרים יש לרשום בראש הרשימה את ה**מַרְכִּיב** הגדול ביותר.
When labeling products, one needs to place the largest **component** at the top of the list.

Special Expressions

telephone **directory** **מַדְרִיךְ** טלפון

Secretary of State (in the US) **מַזְכִּיר** המדינה

hospitable **מַכְנִיס** אורחים

hearing **aid** **מַכְשִׁיר** שמיעה

malignant tumor גִּדּוּל **מַמְאִיר**

parallelly **בְּמַקְבִּיל**

Additional Examples in this Pattern

stinking מַבְאִישׁ
terrifying מַבְהִיל
nauseating מַבְחִיל
shiny; brilliant מַבְרִיק
handbook, field guide מַגְדִּיר
disgusting מַגְעִיל
worrisome מַדְאִיג
amazing מַדְהִים
printer (person) מַדְפִּיס
inviting מַזְמִין
informative מַחְכִּים
substitute מַחְלִיף
shameful מַחְפִּיר
awful מַחְרִיד
painful מַכְאִיב
profitable, lucrative מַכְנִיס
appliance; instrument מַכְשִׁיר
malignant מַמְאִיר
parallel מַקְבִּיל
charming מַקְסִים

---

188. ***maCCiC* = *maCaCiC***, the active participle of *hif`il* when the first root consonant is a guttural

our/your/their	my/your/his/her	const.	Gloss	sing/pl
מַאֲזִינֵנוּ/**מַאֲזִינְ**כֶם/כֶן/**מַאֲזִינָ**ם/ן	מַאֲזִינִי/מַאֲזִינְךָ/**מַאֲזִי**נֵךְ/נוֹ/נָהּ	מַאֲזִין-	listener	מַאֲזִין ז'
מַאֲזִינֵינוּ/כֶם/כֶן/הֶם/הֶן	**מַאֲזִי**נַי/נֶיךָ/נַיִךְ/נָיו/נֶיהָ	מַאֲזִינֵי-		מַאֲזִינִים

The active participle of *hif`il binyan*, *maCCiC*, may serve as a noun or as an adjective (see above). When the first root consonant is a guttural, the *shva* is replaced by *Hataf-pataH*, especially in א' and ע', excluding cases in which the zero *shva* is maintained in normative articulation, in order to justify the following stop (rather than fricative), e.g., מַעְפִּיל 'illegal immigrant to Palestine.'

Examples

לתוכנית השבועית "שישים דקות" של סי בי אס יש קהל **מַאֲזִינִים** גדול ביותר.
"Sixty Minutes," the CBS weekly program, has a very large **audience** (number of **listeners**).

לאחר ניתוח **מַעֲמִיק** של הנתונים הגעתי למסקנה שהנחת היסוד הראשונית שלי הייתה מוטעית.
After **in-depth** analysis of the data, I came to the conclusion that my initial hypothesis was wrong.

מעניין שהמתנגדים הקולניים ביותר להגירה חדשה לארה"ב הם דווקא ה**מַעֲסִיקִים** ששוכרים עובדים בלתי-חוקיים למפעליהם.
It is interesting that the most vocal opponents of new immigration into the US are those **employers** who hire undocumented workers in their plants.

היום לכל זמר או זמרת, אפילו לבינוניים שבהם, יש קהל **מַעֲרִיצִים** עצום.
Today every male or female singer, even mediocre ones, has a huge **fan** club.

Special Expressions

believers (the term Muslims use to distinguish themselves from followers of other religions) **מַאֲמִינִים**

evening prayer תפילת **מַעֲרִיב**

Additional Examples in this Pattern

Mars (planet) מַאֲדִים
believer מַאֲמִין
employer מַעֲבִיד
insulting מַעֲלִיב
saddening מַעֲצִיב
evening prayer מַעֲרִיב
assessor, appraiser מַעֲרִיךְ

---

189. ***maCCiC*** when the third root consonant is guttural

our/your/their	my/your/his/her	const.	Gloss	sing/pl
מַבְרִיחֵנוּ/חֲכֶם/חֲכֶן/חָם/חָן	**מַבְרִי**חִי/חֲךָ/חֵךְ/חוֹ/חָהּ	מַבְרִיחַ-	smuggler	מַבְרִיחַ ז'
מַבְרִיחֵינוּ/כֶם/כֶן/הֶם/הֶן	**מַבְרִי**חַי/חֶיךָ/חַיִךְ/חָיו/חֶיהָ	מַבְרִיחֵי-		מַבְרִיחִים

When the 3rd root consonant is guttural, the masc. sing. form comes with *furtive pataH* when word-final (since the preceding vowel is not *a*). When a *shva* is expected, it is replaced by *Hataf-pataH*.

Examples

רשת מסועפת של **מַבְרִיחִים** מבריחה אלפים רבים של מחוסרי עבודה ממקסיקו לארצות הברית מדי שנה בשנה.
Every year, a wide net of **smugglers** smuggles many thousands of unemployed from Mexico into the United States.

בארצות הברית מנסות המפלגות מדי פעם להגדיר-מחדש גבולות של אזורי בחירה כדי לקבל מספר גדול יותר של **מַצְבִּיעִים** עבור מועמד מטעמן.
In the US the parties occasionally try to redefine the borders of electoral domains in order to get a larger number of **voters** for their own candidate.

חלק גדול מעורכי הדין ה**מַצְלִיחִים** הם "רודפי אמבולנסים", היודעים מתי יש להם סיכוי לקבל שכר טרחה שמֵן.
A large number of **successful** lawyers are "ambulance chasers," who know when they have a good chance of getting a big fat fee.

אחרי צפיה ארוכה בתוכניות טלוויזיה מרגיזות עם פרסומות מטופשות, אני זקוק למשהו **מַרְגִּיעַ**, כמו מוסיקה קלאסית.
Having watched annoying TV programs with stupid commercials for a long time, I need something **soothing**, like classical music.

Special Expressions

tear gas גז **מַדְמִיעַ**
deciding arbitrator בורר **מַכְרִיעַ**
supervisor of kosher food **מַשְׁגִּיחַ** כשרות

Additional Examples in this Pattern

deciding מַכְרִיעַ
stinking מַסְרִיחַ
surprising מַפְתִּיעַ
deterring מַרְתִּיעַ
supervisor מַשְׁגִּיחַ

promising מַבְטִיחַ
person who raises the Torah scroll מַגְבִּיהַּ
tear-causing מַדְמִיעַ
horrible מַזְוִיעַ

---

190. ***maCCiCa***: the feminine of active participle of *hif'il*

our/your/their	my/your/his/her	const.	Gloss	sing/pl
מַקְבִּילָתֵנוּ/לַתְכֶם/לַתְכֶן/לָתָם/לָתָן	**מַקְבִּילָ**תִי/תְךָ/תֵךְ/תוֹ/תָהּ	מַקְבִּילַת-	parallel,	מַקְבִּילָה נ׳
מַקְבִּילוֹתֵינוּ/כֶם/כֶן/הֶם/הֶן	**מַקְבִּילוֹ**תַי/תֶיךָ/תַיִךְ/תָיו/תֶיהָ	מַקְבִּילוֹת-	equivalent	מַקְבִּילוֹת

In a small number of cases, *maCCiCa*, the feminine form of the active participle of *hif'il binyan*, may exist independently of the masculine form, sometimes denoting instruments.

Examples

בישראל, **הַמַּקְבִּילָה** של מחלקת המדינה בארה״ב היא משרד החוץ.
The **equivalent** of the US State Department in Israel is the Foreign Office.

Additional Examples in this Pattern

gutter; eaves מַזְחִילָה

---

191. ***maCCiCa > maCaCiCa***: the feminine of the active participle of *hif'il* when the first root consonant is a guttural

our/your/their	my/your/his/her	const.	Gloss	sing/pl
מַעֲגִילָתֵנוּ/לַתְכֶם/לַתְכֶן/לָתָם/לָתָן	**מַעֲגִילָ**תִי/תְךָ/תֵךְ/תוֹ/תָהּ	מַעֲגִילַת-	roller	מַעֲגִילָה נ׳
מַעֲגִילוֹתֵינוּ/כֶם/כֶן/הֶם/הֶן	**מַעֲגִילוֹ**תַי/תֶיךָ/תַיִךְ/תָיו/תֶיהָ	מַעֲגִילוֹת-		מַעֲגִילוֹת

In a small number of cases, *maCCiCa*, the feminine form of the active participle of *hif'il binyan*, may exist independently of the masculine form, generally denoting instruments (see above). When the first root consonant is a guttural, the *shva* is replaced by *Hataf-pataH*.

Examples

בזמנו היו סוחטים כביסה רטובה **בַּמַּעֲגִילָה**.
In the past, they used to wring wet laundry through a **roller**.

---

192. ***maCCiC*** **=** ***moCiC***: the active participle of *hif'il* when the first consonant of the root is *y*

our/your/their	my/your/his/her	const.	Gloss	sing/pl
מוֹבִילֵנוּ/לְכֶם/כֶן/לָם/לָן	**מוֹבִי**לִי/לְךָ/לֵךְ/לוֹ/לָהּ	מוֹבִיל-	leading;	מוֹבִיל ז'
מוֹבִילֵינוּ/כֶם/כֶן/הֶם/הֶן	**מוֹבִי**לַי/לֶיךָ/לַיִךְ/לָיו/לֶיהָ	מוֹבִילֵי-	mover	מוֹבִילִים

When first root consonant in the active participle of *hif'il* is *y*, that *y* is realized as *o*.

Examples

אֶפֶּל היא עדיין החברה ה**מוֹבִילָה** בתחום הטלפונים הסלולריים, אבל מדי פעם נראה שסַמְסוּנְג עומדת להדביק אותה.
Apple is still the **leading** company in the cellular phone realm, but from time to time Samsung appears to be catching up.

חברת ה**מוֹבִילִים** הישראלית "מוישה" פופולרית מאוד בעיר ניו יורק.
The Israeli movers' company Moishe is very popular in New York City.

Special Expressions

the national (water) aqueduct (from the Sea of Galilee south) **המוֹבִיל** הארצי

Additional Examples in this Pattern

conductor (electricity) מוֹלִיךְ

---

193. ***maCCiC*** **=** ***moCiC*** the active participle of *hif'il* when the 1st root consonant is *y* and the 3rd is guttural

our/your/their	my/your/his/her	const.	Gloss	sing/pl
מוֹשִׁיעֵנוּ/עֲכֶם/עֲכֶן/עָם/עָן	**מוֹשִׁי**עִי/עֲךָ/עֵךְ/עוֹ/עָהּ	מוֹשִׁיעַ-	savior	מוֹשִׁיעַ ז'
מוֹשִׁיעֵינוּ/כֶם/כֶן/הֶם/הֶן	**מוֹשִׁי**עַי/עֶיךָ/עַיִךְ/עָיו/עֶיהָ	מוֹשִׁיעֵי-		מוֹשִׁיעִים

When the 3rd root consonant is guttural, the masc. sing. form comes with *furtive pataH* before a vowel other than *a*. When a *shva* is expected, it is replaced by *Hataf-pataH.*

Examples

כשמישהו מודיע למשטרה על שריפה, למשל, קודם כל הם עוצרים את ה**מוֹדִיעַ**, ליתר ביטחון...
When someone informs the police of a fire, for instance, they first of all detain the **informer**, just in case…

Additional Examples in this Pattern

reprover, preacher מוֹכִיחַ

---

194. ***maCCiC*** **=** ***maCCe***: the active participle of *hif'il* when the third consonant of the root is *y*

our/your/their	my/your/his/her	const.	Gloss	sing/pl
מַרְצֵנוּ/צְכֶם/צְכֶן/צָם/צָן	**מַרְ**צִי/צְךָ/צֵךְ/צוֹ (צֵהוּ)/צָהּ	מַרְצֵה-	lecturer	מַרְצֶה ז'
מַרְצֵינוּ/כֶם/כֶן/הֶם/הֶן	**מַרְצַי**/צֶיךָ/צַיִךְ/צָיו/צֶיהָ	מַרְצֵי-		מַרְצִים

When third root in the active participle of *hif'il* is *y*, that *y* is realized as zero.

Examples

אברהם הוא **מַרְצֶה** מעולה, אבל ללא פרסומים אין לו סיכוי להגיע לקביעות.
Abraham is an excellent **lecturer**, but without publications, he has no chance of getting tenure.

החזות של עדינה **מַטְעָה**; היא נראית ככבשה תמה, אבל כשמכירים אותה מקרוב, רואים שהיא אישה חזקה, היודעת בדיוק מה היא רוצה ואיך להשיג זאת.
Adina's appearance is **misleading**; she looks like an innocent lamb, but when one knows her closely, one can see that she is a strong woman, who knows exactly what she wants and how to achieve it.

Special Expressions

usurer, money**lender** **מַלְוֶה** בריבית

the **Equator** הקו **הַמַּשְׁוֶה**

Additional Examples in this Pattern

exhausting מַלְאֶה
disobedient מַמְרֶה
moderator; show host; MC מַנְחֶה
thirst-quenching מַרְוֶה
client (in law) מַרְשֶׁה
leading astray מַתְעֶה

---

195. ***maCCiC* = *maCiC***: the active participle of *hif'il* when the third consonant of the root is *n*, and when the second and third ones are *y-ts*.

our/your/their	my/your/his/her	const.	Gloss	sing/pl
מַצִּילֵנוּ/לְכֶם/כֶן/לָם/לָן	**מַצִּי**לִי/לְךָ/לֵךְ/לוֹ/לָהּ	-מַצִּיל	lifeguard	מַצִּיל ז'
מַצִּילֵינוּ/כֶם/כֶן/הֶם/הֶן	**מַצִּי**לַי/לֶיךָ/לַיִךְ/לָיו/לֶיהָ	-מַצִּילֵי		מַצִּילִים

When first root consonant in the active participle of *hif'il* is *n* (as in נצ״ל), that *n* is assimilated, and a *dagesh* is placed in the next consonant. Similarly, when the first consonant is *y*, followed by *ts*, the *y* is assimilated into the *ts*, which in turn has a *dagesh*.

Examples

אסור לשחות בים או בבריכה כאשר אין **מַצִּיל** במקום.
It is not allowed to swim on the beach or ion a swimming pool without a **lifeguard** present.

היום טוענים שאפילו פירות וירקות שאינם אורגניים **מַזִּיקִים** לבריאות, מכיוון ששטיפה אינה עוזרת: חומרי ההדברה חודרים מתחת לקליפה.
Today they claim that even fruit and vegetables that are not organically-grown may be **damaging** to one's health, since washing does not help: the pesticides penetrate the shell/peel.

Special Expressions

comprehensive insurance ביטוח **מַקִּיף**

Additional Examples in this Pattern

announcer (radio, TV) מַגִּישׁ
preacher מַטִּיף
acquaintance מַכִּיר
presenter, exhibitor מַצִּיג
lighter, cigarette lighter מַצִּית
comprehensive מַקִּיף
tangent מַשִּׁיק

---

196. ***maCCiC* = *maCiC***: the active participle of *hif'il* when the first consonant of the root is *n* and the 3rd root consonant is guttural

our/your/their	my/your/his/her	const.	Gloss	sing/pl
מַגִּיהֵנוּ/הֲכֶם/הֲכֶן/הָם/הָן	**מַגִּי**הִי/הֲךָ/הֵךְ/הוֹ/הָהּ	מַגִּיהַ-	proofreader	מַגִּיהַ ז'
מַגִּיהֵינוּ/כֶם/כֶן/הֶם/הֶן	**מַגִּי**הַי/הֶיךָ/הַיִךְ/הָיו/הֶיהָ	מַגִּיהֵי-		מַגִּיהִים

When the 3rd root consonant is guttural, the masc. sing. form comes with *furtive pataH* when word-final (since the preceding vowel is not *a*). When a *shva* is expected, it is replaced by *Hataf-pataH*.

Examples

המַגִּיהַ לא גילה אף שגיאה אחת במאמר שנשלח לו.
The **proofreader** did not find a single error in the article sent to him.

Special Expressions

inciting someone to commit an offense **מַדִּיחַ** לדבר עבירה

---

197. ***maCCiC* = *meCiC***: the active participle of *hif'il* when the second consonant of the root is *w* or *y*

our/your/their	my/your/his/her	const.	Gloss	sing/pl
מְפִיקֵנוּ/קְכֶם/קְכֶן/קָם/קָן	**מְפִי**קִי/קְךָ/קֵךְ/קוֹ/קָהּ	מֵפִיק-	producer	מֵפִיק ז'
מְפִיקֵינוּ/כֶם/כֶן/הֶם/הֶן	**מְפִי**קַי/קֶיךָ/קַיִךְ/קָיו/קֶיהָ	מְפִיקֵי-		מְפִיקִים

When second root consonant in the active participle of *hif'il* is *w* or *y*, it is not realized. Two syllables away from the main stress, the *tsere* is reduced to a *shva*.

Examples

הבמאי אחראי לאספקטים האומנותיים והיצירתיים בהצגה או בסרט, אבל את העבודה האדמיניסטרטיבית עושה **המֵפִיק**.
The director is responsible for the artistic and creative aspects of a play or a film, but the administrative work is done by the **producer**.

לעיתים נראה לי שמראיינים בטלוויזיה הישראלית מנסים להראות שהם מבינים בנושא יותר טוב מן המרואיין, ושגישה כזאת היא לא רק לא מתאימה, אלא אפילו **מְבִישָׁה**.
Sometimes it seems to me that interviewers on Israeli TV try to show that they understand the subject matter better than the interviewee. This approach is not only inappropriate; it is actually **shameful**.

אם החלטת להיות טבעוני, חשוב שתוודא שמה שתאכל יהיה **מֵזִין** דיו.
If you have decided to become vegan, it is important to make sure that you eat sufficiently-**nutritious** food.

Special Expressions

fit walkers **מֵיטִיבֵי** לכת
advocate; character reference **מֵלִיץ** יֹשֶׁר
catalytic **converter** **מֵמִיר** קטליטי

Additional Examples in this Pattern

embarrassing מֵבִיךְ
expert מֵבִין
beneficent מֵטִיב/מֵיטִיב
advocate Lit. מֵלִיץ
converter (elect.) מֵמִיר
inciter, instigator מֵסִית
burdensome מֵעִיק
distributor מֵפִיץ
bothersome מֵצִיק
rower מֵשִׁיט

---

198. *meCiC* when the 3rd root consonant is guttural

our/your/their	my/your/his/her	const.	Gloss	sing/pl
מְנִיעֵנוּ/עֲכֶם/עֲכֶן/עָם/עָן	**מְנִי**עִי/עֲךָ/עֵךְ/עוֹ/עָהּ	מֵנִיעַ-	motive,	מֵנִיעַ ז׳
מְנִיעֵינוּ/כֶם/כֶן/הֶם/הֶן	**מְנִי**עַי/עֶיךָ/עַיִךְ/עָיו/עֶיהָ	מְנִיעֵי-	factor	מְנִיעִים

In final position, following a vowel other than *a*, a guttural comes with a furtive *pataH* when word-final (since the preceding vowel is not *a*)..

Examples

אחד היסודות החשובים בבניית כתב אישום הוא זיהוי **הַמֵּנִיעַ** לפשע.
One of the essential elements in preparing an indictment is the establishment of a **motive** for the crime.

Special Expressions

perpetuum **mobile** **מֵנִיעַ** נצחי
God (the **causer** of all) **הַמֵּנִיעַ** הראשון
dish **washer** **מֵדִיחַ** כלים

---

199. *maCCiC* = *meCeC*: the active participle of *hif'il* when the 2nd and 3rd root consonants are identical

our/your/their	my/your/his/her	const.	Gloss	sing/pl
מְגִנֵּנוּ/נְּכֶם/נְּכֶן/נָּם/נָּן	**מְגִ**נִּי/נְּךָ/נֵּךְ/נּוֹ/נָּהּ	מֵגֵן-	defender	מֵגֵן ז׳
מְגִנֵּינוּ/כֶם/כֶן/הֶם/הֶן	**מְגִ**נַּי/נֶּיךָ/נַּיִךְ/נָּיו/נֶּיהָ	מְגִנֵּי-		מְגִנִּים

When second and third root consonant of the root in the active participle of *hif`il* are identical, only one consonant is realized, and when not final, it comes with a *dagesh*.

Examples

מְגִנֵּי מצדה העדיפו להתאבד מאשר להישבות בידי הרומאים.
The **defenders** of Masada preferred to commit suicide rather than to be taken prisoners by the Romans.

Additional Examples in this Pattern

lenient מֵקֵל endorser (banking) מֵסֵב solvent מֵמֵס

O. *muCCaC* and related *mishkalim*

200. *muCCaC*

muCCaC is the pattern of mostly adjectives and some nouns originating from the passive participle of *huf`al* verbs.

	Masc.	*Fem.*	*Gloss*
Sing.	מֻגְזָם	מֻגְזֶמֶת	exaggerated
Plural	מֻגְזָמִים	מֻגְזָמוֹת	

Sometimes we find alternant forms in which the *kubuts* is replaced by a *kamats katan*: *moCCaC*. The alternant form is the normative ones when the first consonant of the root is guttural, as in מָעֳמָד *mo`omad* 'candidate' (see below; note that the prefix vowel and the next one are both *o*), but alongside there also exists an alternant form with a *kubuts*, and the guttural is followed by a *Hataf-pataH*: מֻעֲמָד *mu`amad.*

When the third root consonant is a guttural, the feminine singular form is followed by a *pataH*: מֻפְתַּעַת 'surprised, f.s.'

Examples

קרוב לוודאי ששתייה **מֻגְזֶמֶת** של אלכוהול מזיקה לבריאות, אבל יש רופאים הטוענים שכוסית יין אחת ליום אפילו מועילה.
It is very likely that **exaggerated** (excessive) drinking of alcohol is bad for your health, but some doctors claim that one wineglass a day is actually beneficial.

בסופרמרקט הזה תמצא רק פירות וירקות **מֻבְחָרִים**. הם אינם מכניסים מוצרים סוג ב'.
In this supermarket you will only find **select** fruit and vegetables; they do not take in any Grade B products.

הגינה שבחצרו של מנחם **מֻזְנַחַת**; כבר כמה שנים הוא אינו מטפל בה.
The garden in Menahem's yard is **neglected**; he has not taken care of it for a number of years now.

אני לא חושב שאפרים **מֻפְרָע**, אבל הוא בהחלט **מֻגְבָּל** מבחינה מנטלית.
I do not think that Ephraim is **disturbed**, but he is definitely **handicapped** mentally.

Special Expressions

a **characteristic**, clearly **distinguishing** one entity from all others סימן **מֻבְהָק**

parenthetical clause מאמר **מֻסְגָּר**

the **occupied** territories השטחים ה**מֻחְזָקִים**

Additional Examples in this Pattern

typical; clear מֻבְהָק	worried מֻדְאָג
promised מֻבְטָח	emphasized מֻדְגָּשׁ
unemployed N/Adj מֻבְטָל	absolute מֻחְלָט
highlighted; prominent מֻבְלָט	held, occupied מֻחְזָק
concealed מֻבְלָע	worried מֻטְרָד
enlarged מֻגְדָּל	declared מֻכְרָז
defined מֻגְדָּר	compelled; must מֻכְרָח
exaggerated מֻגְזָם	parenthetical מֻסְגָּר

---

201. *muCCaC* = *moCoCaC* when the first root consonant is guttural

	Masc.	Fem.	Gloss
Sing.	מֻעֲמָד	מֻעֲמֶדֶת	candidate
Plural	מֻעֲמָדִים	מֻעֲמָדוֹת	

moCoCaC (kamats katan followed by Hataf-kamats) is the realization of the pattern *muCCaC* for adjectives and some nouns originating from the passive participle of *huf`al* verbs (see above) when the first root consonant is a guttural.

Although we sometimes find alternant forms in which the *kubuts* is maintained, and the guttural is followed by *Hataf-pataH*: מֻעֲמָד *mu`amad* 'candidate,' מָעֳמָד is the normative high-register alternant.

Examples

לא כולם אוהבים את ה**מָעֳמֶדֶת** הדמוקרטית למשרת המושל.
Not everybody likes the (**fem.**) Democratic **candidate** for the Governor's position.

סוג הספרים ה**מָעֳדָף** עליי לפני השינה הוא ספרי מתח – אבל של סופרים טובים, כמו קרייטון, גרישם, קובן...
My **preferred** type of reading in bed is thrillers – but only by good authors, like Crichton, Grisham, Coben…

Special Expressions

enriched uranium אורניום **מָעֳשָׁר**

Additional Examples in this Pattern

incorporated מְאֻגָּד	confiscated; מֻחְרָם/מָחֳרָם excommunicated
darkened, blacked out מְאֻפָּל	employee מָעֳסָק
elongated מְאֻרָךְ	copied; shifted מָעֳתָק
grounded (elect.) מְאֻרָק	
destroyed מָחֳרָב	

---

202. *muCCéCet*

In some rare occasions the feminine counterpart of *muCCaC*, *muCCéCet*, denotes somewhat different meaning from that of its *muCCaC* base. In the only case that is sufficiently common, מֻבְלַעַת *muvla`at* 'enclave,' the two *seghol*s are replaced by *pataH* owing to the *`ayin* (pl. מֻבְלָעוֹת, pl. constr. מֻבְלְעוֹת).

Examples

יאסר ערפאת ישב שנתיים בהסגר ישראלי ב**מֻבְלַעַת** קטנה ברמאללה, עד שנתערערה בריאותו.
For two years, Yasser Arafat was confined by Israel to a small **enclave** in Ramallah, until his health declined.

---

203. *muCCaCa*

In some rare occasions the feminine counterpart of *muCCaC* is not *muCCeCet* but *muCCaCa*, and it denotes somewhat different meaning from that of its *muCCaC* base. The only realization included here is מֻסְכָּמָה 'convention, consensus,' constr. מֻסְכֶּמֶת, pl. מֻסְכָּמוֹת, constr. מֻסְכְּמוֹת.

Examples

התכונה הבולטת ביותר באמנות המודרנית היא שבירת **מֻסְכָּמוֹת** בנות מאות שנים.
The most prominent characteristic of Modern Art is the breaking of centuries-old **conventions**.

---

204. *muCCaC* = *muCCe*: the passive participle of *huf`al* when the third consonant of the root is *y*

const.	sing/pl	const.	gloss	sing/pl
-מֻבְנֵית	מֻבְנֵית נ׳	-מֻבְנֵה	built in	מֻבְנֶה ז׳
-מֻבְנוֹת	מֻבְנוֹת	-מֻבְנֵי		מֻבְנִים

When third root consonant in the active participle of *hif`il* is *y*, that *y* is realized as zero at the end of the word.

Examples

כושר הדיבור הוא תכונה **מֻבְנֵית** אצל בני האדם מיום היוולדם.
Speech is a **built-in** characteristic of human beings from the day they are born.

רופא המשפחה היום הוא בד״כ רופא פנימי, ולעיתים קרובות הוא מפנה אותך לרופא **מֻמְחֶה**.
A general practitioner is in most cases an internist, and s/he often refers you to a **specialist**.

היהודים האתיופיים בישראל מרגישים שהם **מֻפְלִים** לרעה בחברה הישראלית, אפילו על ידי המשטרה.
The Ethiopean Jews feel that they are **discriminated against** in the Israel society, even by the police.

Special Expressions

loathsome, abominable, despicable **מֻקְצֶה** מחמת מיאוס
authorized signer **מֻרְשֶׁה** חתימה

Additional Examples in this Pattern

mistaken מֻטְעֶה
camouflaged, hidden מֻסְוֶה
directed (towards) מֻפְנֶה
fertilized מֻפְרֶה
acquired מֻקְנֶה
outcast; forbidden מֻקְצֶה
person w/power of attorney מֻרְשֶׁה
suspended מֻשְׁעֶה

---

205. ***muCCaC* = *muCaC***: the passive participle of *huf'al* when the first consonant of the root is *n*, and when the first and second consonants are *y-ts*.

sing/pl	Gloss	sing/pl
מֻגֶּשֶׁת נ׳	presented,	מֻגָּשׁ ז׳
מֻגָּשׁוֹת	served	מֻגָּשִׁים

When first root consonant in the passive participle of *huf'al* is *n*, that *n* is assimilated, and a *dagesh* is placed in the next consonant. When the first consonant is *y*, followed by *ts*, the *y* is assimilated into the *ts*, which in turn has a *dagesh*. When the third root consonant is a guttural, the feminine singular form comes with two *pataH*s: 'expressed' מֻבַּעַת.

Examples

בבאר טוב, בירה מהחבית **מֻגֶּשֶׁת** בכוס צוננת.
In a good bar, draft beer is **served** in a chilled glass.

הנשיא ה**מֻדָּח** ברח וביקש מקלט בשוודיה.
The **ousted** president fled, and requested asylum in Sweden.

הרוצח **מֻכָּר** היטב למשטרה; חבל שלא קוים מעקב אחריו לפני שעשה מה שעשה.
The murderer is well-**known** to the police; it is a pity that he had not been under surveillance before he did what he did.

ישראל תמיד תיארה את עצמה כ״מדינה קטנה **מֻקֶּפֶת** אויבים״. לפחות חלקית, התיאור הזה עדיין נכון.
Israel has always charachterized itself as a "small state **surrounded** by enemies." At least partially, this description still stands.

בדיחה ישראלית: עולה חדש ששאל מישהו "מה השעה?" נענה ב"אין לי **מֻשָּׂג**". כשנשאל אחר כך בעצמו מה השעה, ענה: "ה**מֻשָּׂג** שלי בתיקון".

An Israeli joke: a new immigrant who asked someone “what time is it?” was answered by “I have no **idea** (מֻשָּׂג)”. When asked the same question later, he responded: “My **מֻשָּׂג** is being repaired.”

Special Expressions

doubtful; whose prospect for success is in doubt **מֻטָּל** בספק

Additional Examples in this Pattern

expressed מֻבָּע
proofread מֻגָּה
excluded מֻדָּר
heated, fired מֻסָּק
military post מֻצָּב
saved, rescued מֻצָּל
permitted; loose מֻתָּר

---

206. ***muCCaC* = *muCe***: the passive participle of *huf`al* when the 1st consonant of the root is *n*, and the 3rd is *y*.

sing/pl	gloss	sing/pl
מֻכָּה נ׳	beaten,	מֻכֶּה ז׳
מֻכּוֹת	battered	מֻכִּים

When first root consonant in the passive participle of *huf`al* is *n*, that *n* is assimilated, and a *dagesh* is placed in the next consonant, and when in addition, the last consonant is *y*, that *y* is not realized at the end of the word.

Examples

אחת הבעיות הקשות ביותר שעדיין לא מצאו את פתרונן אפילו בחברות המתקדמות ביותר, היא האלימות בבית ובעיקר בעיית הנשים ה**מֻכּוֹת**.

One of the most difficult problems that have still not been solved even in the most progressive societies is domestic violence, and especially the issue of **battered** women.

Special Expressions

one who has had very bad luck **מֻכֵּה** גורל
moonstruck **מֻכֵּה** ירח

Additional Examples in this Pattern

slanted; biased מֻטֶּה

---

207. ***muCCaC* = *muCaC***: the passive participle of *huf`al* when the first consonant of the root is *y*

our/your/their	my/your/his/her	const.	Gloss	sing/pl
מוּצָרֵנוּ/**מוּצַרְ**כֶם/כֶן/**מוּצָרָ**ם/ן	**מוּצָרִ**י/רְךָ/רֵךְ/רוֹ/רָהּ	מוּצַר-	product	מוּצָר ז׳
מוּצָרֵינוּ/**מוּצְרֵי**כֶם/כֶן/הֶם/הֶן	**מוּצָרַ**י/רֶיךָ/רַיִךְ/רָיו/רֶיהָ	מוּצְרֵי-		מוּצָרִים

When first root consonant in the passive participle of *huf'al* is *y*, that *y* is realized as *u*.

Examples

בישראל מכון התקנים אחראי לפיקוח על איכות ה**מוּצָר**.
In Israel the Standards Institutes is responsible for inspecting **product** quality.

התאונה אירעה בפתאומיות כזו, ששרה לא הייתה **מוּדַעַת** למה שקרה עד שהתעוררה בבית החולים.
The accident was so sudden, that Sarah was not even **aware** of what had happened until she woke up in the hospital.

תמיד אהבתי לקרוא את התפילות ש**במוּסָף** במי החג. זו שירה נפלאה של ימי הביניים.
I have always loved the prayers included in the **supplement** read during the Jewish holidays. Wonderful Medieval Hebrew poetry.

חלק מן הדלק המניע טילים הוא דלק **מוּצָק**, בין השאר מכיוון שהוא בטוח יותר.
Some of the propellant of rockets and missiles is **solid** fuel, among the rest because it is safer.

Special Expressions

מוּסַר השכל moral (of a story, etc.), lesson
מוּסַר כליות regret, remorse, contrition
מוּצַר/תּוֹצַר לוואי by-**product**
מוּצְרֵי חלב dairy **products**
מוּצְרֵי צריכה commodities

Additional Examples in this Pattern

מוּכָח proven, verified
מוּלָד congenital, from birth
מוּסָר ethics, morals
מוּקָע denunciated
מוּרָשׁ inherited

---

208. ***muCCaC* = *muCaC***: the passive participle of *huf'al* when the 2nd and 3rd root consonants are identical

sing/pl	Gloss	sing/pl
מוּגֶנֶת נ׳	protected	מוּגָן ז׳
מוּגַנּוֹת		מוּגַנִּים

When the second and third consonant of the root are identical, the prefix of the passive participle of *huf'al* contains *u*, and the final consonant of the root has a *dagesh* in the plural forms.

Examples

בישראל חייב כל קבלן הבונה בניין חדש לכלול חדר **מוּגָן** בכל דירה.
In Israel any contractor building a new building must include a **protected** room in every apartment.

אחרי עבודה של 12 שעות מול המחשב אני **מוּתָשׁ** לגמרי.
After 12 hours of work at the computer, I am completely **exhausted**.

Additional Examples in this Pattern

shaded מוּצָל faded, dimmed מוּעָם slowed down מוּאָט

---

209. ***muCCaC* = *muCaC***: the passive participle of *huf'al* when the second consonant of the root is *w* or *y*

sing/pl	Gloss	sing/pl
מוּכָנָה נ'	ready	מוּכָן ז'
מוּכָנוֹת		מוּכָנִים

When the second consonant of the root is *w* or *y*, the prefix of the passive participle of *huf'al* contains *u*.

Examples

אם אתם לא **מוּכָנִים** תוך חמש דקות, ניסע בלעדיכם, ותצטרכו להגיע בכוחות עצמכם.
If you are not **ready** in five minutes, we'll need to leave without you, and you will need to get there on your own.

אני אוהב לעבוד בחדר **מוּאָר** היטב.
I like to work in a well-**lit** room.

לא **מוּבָן** לי מדוע שני הצדדים לא **מוּכָנִים** לדבר זה עם זה.
It is un**clear** to me why the two sides are un**willing** to talk to each other.

ההתנהגות שלו **מוּזָרָה**, אבל אומרים שהוא גאון.
His behavior is **strange**, but they say he is a genius.

בעונת השטפונות, מרתפים רבים בארה״ב **מוּצָפִים**, והנזק רציני.
In the flood seasn many cellars in the US are **flooded**, and the damage is serious.

Special Expressions

uncertain **מוּטָל** בספק
hanging in the balance **מוּטָל** על הכף
ready and willing **מוּכָן** ומזומן

it goes without saying **מוּבָן** מאליו
naturally, of course כַּ**מּוּבָן**
in the full **sense** of the word בִּמְלוֹא **מוּבַן** המילה

Additional Examples in this Pattern

accelerated; tangible מוּחָשׁ
left lying מוּטָל
flown, transported by air מוּטָס
powered; motivated מוּנָע
raised, hoisted מוּנָף
annotated מוּעָר

expeditious מוּאָץ
defeated מוּבָס
carbonated מוּגָז
closed מוּגָף
rinsed מוּדָח
moved מוּזָז
discounted מוּזָל

---

210. *muCaCa*

Our/your/their	my/your/his/her	const.	Gloss	sing/pl
מוּבָאָתֵנוּ/תְכֶם/תְכֶן/תָם/תָן	**מוּבָאָ**תִי/תְךָ/תֵךְ/תוֹ/תָהּ	מוּבְאַת-	quote	מוּבָאָה נ׳
מוּבְאוֹתֵינוּ/כֶם/כֶן/הֶם/הֶן	**מוּבְאוֹ**תַי/תֶיךָ/תַיִךְ/תָיו/תֶיהָ	מוּבְאוֹת-		מוּבָאוֹת

In some instances the feminine counterpart of *muCaC* derived from roots with a second consonant *w* or *y*, *muCaCa*, denotes somewhat different meaning from that of its *muCaC* base.

Examples

במאמרים חשוב לציין באופן מדויק את מקור ה**מוּבָאוֹת**.
In articles it is important to precisely note the source of the **quotes**.

Additional Examples in this Pattern

discomfort מוּעָקָה

---

211. *muCCaCut*: gerund/nominalization related to *huf'al*

Our/your/their	my/your/his/her	const.	Gloss	sing/pl
מֻרְכָּבוּתֵנוּ/תְכֶם/תְכֶן/תָם/תָן	**מֻרְכָּבוּ**תִי/תְךָ/תֵךְ/תוֹ/תָהּ	מֻרְכָּבוּת-	complexity	מֻרְכָּבוּת נ׳
מֻרְכָּבוּיוֹתֵינוּ/כֶם/כֶן/הֶם/הֶן	**מֻרְכָּבוּיוֹ**תַי/תֶיךָ/תַיִךְ/תָיו/תֶיהָ	מֻרְכָּבוּיוֹת-		מֻרְכָּבוּיוֹת

This *mishkal* is also linear derivation from *muCCaC*. When the second root consonant is a guttural, the *shva* is replaced by a *Hataf-pataH*. Only one such realization was common enough to include, מֻעֲמָדוּת 'candidacy,' so we will not list it separately.

Examples

בשל **מוּרְכָּבוּתוֹ** של הסכסוך הישראלי-פלסטינאי, עדיין לא נמצא לו פתרון, והרבה מאמינים שיחלפו עוד שנים לא מעטות עד ששני הצדדים יגיעו להסדר ביניהם.
Because of the **complexity** of the Israeli-Palestinian conflict, it is still unsettled, and many believe that it will take a good number of years before the two sides reach an agreement.

מספר ניכר של נשים וגברים כבר הצהירו רשמית על **מֻעֲמָדוּתָם** לנשיאות בבחירות הבאות. יהיה מעניין.
A considerable number of women and men have already formally announced their **candidacy** for President in the coming elections. It will be interesting.

Special Expressions

statistical **significance** **מֻבְהָקוּת** סטטיסטית
intellectual (developmental) **disability** **מֻגְבָּלוּת** שכלית התפתחותית

Additional Examples in this Pattern

typicalness מֻבְהָקוּת	introvertedness מֻפְנָמוּת
restrictiveness; disability מֻגְבָּלוּת	disturbed state (psych.) מֻפְרָעוּת
neglect מֻזְנָחוּת	abstractness מֻפְשָׁטוּת
talent מֻכְשָׁרוּת	perfection מֻשְׁלָמוּת

---

212. ***muCCaCut* = *muCaCut*** when the first root consonant is *y*

Our/your/their	my/your/his/her	const.	Gloss	sing/pl
מוּדָעוּתֵנוּ/תְכֶם/תְכֶן/תָם/תָן	**מוּדָעוּ**תִי/תְךָ/תֵךְ/תוֹ/תָהּ	מוּדָעוּת-	awareness,	מוּדָעוּת נ׳
מוּדָעוּיוֹתֵינוּ/כֶם/כֶן/הֶם/הֶן	**מוּדָעוּיוֹ**תַי/תֶיךָ/תַיִךְ/תָיו/תֶיהָ	מוּדָעוּיוֹת-	consciousness	מוּדָעוּיוֹת

Examples

ה**מוּדָעוּת** לסכנות הכרוכות בהתחממות כדור הארץ הולכת ומתחזקת לאחרונה.
Awareness of the dangers resulting from global warming has been on the increase lately.

Additional Examples in this Pattern

solidity; firmness מוּצָקוּת

---

213. ***muCCaCut* = *muCaCut*** when the 2nd root consonant is w/*y*

Our/your/their	my/your/his/her	const.	Gloss	sing/pl
מוּזָרוּתֵנוּ/תְכֶם/תְכֶן/תָם/תָן	**מוּזָרוּ**תִי/תְךָ/תֵךְ/תוֹ/תָהּ	מוּזָרוּת-	strangeness	מוּזָרוּת נ׳
מוּזָרוּיוֹתֵינוּ/כֶם/כֶן/הֶם/הֶן	**מוּזָרוּיוֹ**תַי/תֶיךָ/תַיִךְ/תָיו/תֶיהָ	מוּזָרוּיוֹת-		מוּזָרוּיוֹת

Examples

ה**מוּזָרוּת** שבהתנהגותו גורמת לי לחשוב שהוא זקוק לטיפול פסיכיאטרי.
The **weirdness** of his behavior causes me to suspect that he may require psychiatric treatment.

Additional Examples in this Pattern

clarity, comprehensibility מוּבָנוּת
tangibility, concreteness, perceptibility מוּחָשׁוּת

Mostly affix-less *mishkalim* which generally are not verb-related, and if there is a relationship, it is not always transparent

We'll start with nouns and adjectives without affixes; nevertheless, we'll include a number of *mishkalim* with an affix that is not that transparent, owing to their resemblance to similar *mishkalim* without affixes, e.g., *CaCon* with the suffix *-on* (חַלּוֹן, from the root חל״ל), which is close to *CaCoC* (אַלּוֹן).

P. Mono-syllabic *mishkalim* without affixes

214. ***CaC***: mono-syllabic nouns and adjectives in which the *kamats* is maintained in most of the declension

our/your/their	my/your/his/her	const.	Gloss	sing/pl
רָצֵנוּ/רַצְכֶם/רַצְכֶן/רָצָם/רָצָן	רָצִי/רָצְךָ/רָצֵךְ/רָצוֹ/רָצָהּ	רַץ-	courier; runner;	רָץ ז׳
רָצֵינוּ/כֶם/כֶן/הֶם/הֶן	רָצַי/רָצֶיךָ/רָצַיִךְ/רָצָיו/רָצֶיהָ	רָצֵי-	half-back;	רָצִים
			bishop (chess)	

When the form is an adjective, the declension is:

sing/pl	Gloss	sing/pl
נָעָה נ׳	mobile	נָע ז׳
נָעוֹת		נָעִים

Most nouns and adjectives in this pattern are derived from roots with a middle *w* or *y* (רָץ > רו״צ). The *kamats* is maintained in most of the declension, and becomes *pataH* in the construct singular and in the second person plural of nouns with possessive pronouns (in a closed, unstressed syllable).

Examples

בשל דחיפות העניין, שלחתי את המסמכים בידי **רָץ** מיוחד .
Owing to the urgency of the matter, I sent the documents through special **courier**.

ה**רָץ** הגדול ביותר בתולדותיה של צ׳כיה היה אמיל זאטופק.
The greatest **runner** in the history of the Czech nation was Emil Zatopek.

ה**רָץ** בשחמט יכול לנוע רק אלכסונית.
The **bishop** in chess can only move diagonally.

במדינות מסוימות התנאים בכלא קשים ביותר. אסירים מבודדים ב**תָּאִים** קטן בתנאים סניטריים מחרידים.
In some countries the conditions in jail are very difficult. Inmates are isolated in small **cells**, in horrifying sanitary conditions.

הקיסר יוזף השני התלונן בפני מוצארט אחרי ששמע את ״נישואי פיגארו״: ״יותר מדיי **תָּוִים**!״
Having heard "the Marriage of Figaro," Emperor Joseph II complained to Mozart: "Too many (musical) **notes**!"

Special Expressions

shva **quiescent** שווא **נָח**	borrowed (**foreign**) word מילה **זָרָה**
shva **mobile** שווא **נָע**	idol (**foreign**) worship עבודה **זָרָה**

Additional Examples in this Pattern

hook N וָו	sum, total סָך
foreign, foreigner זָר	cloud עָב
silent, quiescent נָח	secret Lit. רָז
wandering נָד	tag, badge תָּג
old, elderly; grandfather סָב	

---

215. ***CaC***: feminine mono-syllabic nouns in which the *kamats* is maintained in most of the declension

our/your/their	my/your/his/her	const.	Gloss	sing/pl
דָּתֵנוּ/דַּתְכֶם/דַּתְכֶן/דָּתָם/דָּתָן	דָּתִי/דָּתְךָ/דָּתֵךְ/דָּתוֹ/דָּתָהּ	דַּת-	religion;	דָּת נ׳
דָּתוֹתֵינוּ/כֶם/כֶן/הֶם/הֶן	**דָּתוֹ**תַי/תֶיךָ/תַיִךְ/תָיו/תֶיהָ	דָּתוֹת-	law; faith	דָּתוֹת

Examples

מרקס ראה **בְּדָת** אופיום להמונים.

Marx considered **religion** as opiate for the masses.

״**דָּת** מוחמד בחרב״.

"The **religion/law** of Muhammad is with/by the sword."

Special Expressions

incur the penalty of death אחת **דָּתוֹ** להמית	by Jewish **Law** כְּ**דָת** משה וישראל
converted המיר את **דָּתוֹ**	heavy drinking שתייה **כַּדָּת**

---

216. ***CaC***: mono-syllabic nouns in which the *kamats* becomes *pataH* in a closed syllable, and is reduced to a *shva* two syllables away from the stress

our/your/their	my/your/his/her	const.	Gloss	sing/pl
דָּגֵנוּ/דַּגְכֶם/דַּגְכֶן/דָּגָם/דָּגָן	דָּגִי/דָּגְךָ/דָּגֵךְ/דָּגוֹ/דָּגָהּ	דַּג-	fish	דָּג ז׳
דָּגֵינוּ/**דְּגֵי**כֶם/כֶן/הֶם/הֶן	דָּגַי/דָּגֶיךָ/דָּגַיִךְ/דָּגָיו/דָּגֶיהָ	דְּגֵי-		דָּגִים

Note: If the first consonant is guttural, a *Hataf-pataH* replaces the *shva*: עָשִׁים 'moths' ~ עֲשֵׁי

Examples

את יונה בלע **דָּג** גדול, לא לווייתן.

It was a big **fish** that swallowed Jonah, not a whale.

Special Expressions

feel very comfortable כְּ**דָג** במים	tore him to piece קרע אותו כְּ**דָג**
small **fish**, small fry **דְּגֵי** רְקָק	

Additional Examples in this Pattern

blood; life דָּם — moth סָס, עָשׁ — aspect פָּן

---

217. ***CaC***: mono-syllabic nouns in which the *kamats* becomes *pataH* in front of כֶם√, הֶם√, and is reduced to a *shva* two syllables away from the stress, and the plural form is dual

our/your/their	my/your/his/her	const.	Gloss	sing/pl
יָדֵנוּ/יַדְכֶם/יַדְכֶן/יָדָם/יָדָן	יָדִי/יָדְךָ/יָדֵךְ/יָדוֹ/יָדָהּ	-יַד	arm;	יָד נ'
יָדֵינוּ/ **יְדֵי**כֶם/כֶן/הֶם/הֶן	יָדַי/יָדֶיךָ/יָדַיִךְ/יָדָיו/יָדֶיהָ	-יְדֵי	hand	יָדַיִם

Examples

לפעמים משה שוכח כמה **הַיָּדַיִם** שלו חזקות, וכשהוא לוחץ **יָד**, האדם שממולו מרגיש שעוד מעט **יָדוֹ** תישבר.
Sometimes Moshe forget how strong his **hands** are, and when he shakes **hand**s, the person opposite him feels that **his hand** is about to break.

Special Expressions

יָד שנייה second hand　　**יָדַיִם** עובדות workers, laborers

Additional Examples in this Pattern

שָׁד/שַׁד breast

---

218. ***CaC***: mono-syllabic nouns in which the *kamats* in the unbound singular form turns into a *pataH* throughout the declension (except for the constr. sg., unless immediately followed by a stressed vowel)

our/your/their	my/your/his/her	const.	Gloss	sing/pl
יַמֵּנוּ/יַמְּכֶם/יַמְּכֶן/יַמָּם/יַמָּן	יַמִּי/יַמְּךָ/יַמֵּךְ/יַמּוֹ/יַמָּהּ	-יָם	sea	יָם ז'
יַמֵּינוּ/כֶם/כֶן/הֶם/הֶן	יַמַּי/יַמֶּיךָ/יַמַּיִךְ/יַמָּיו/יַמֶּיהָ	-יַמֵּי		יַמִּים

Most nouns in this pattern are related to roots with identical second and third consonant, which accounts for the historical gemination (*dagesh*) of the consonant following the *pataH*. If the second consonant is ח', it will not be geminated: חַחִים 'nose rings.' Note: the word in isolation does not have a *dagesh* at the end of the word: צַב ~ צַבִּים 'tortoise.'

Examples

ירושלים עיר יפה, אבל יש לה חיסרון גדול: אין לה גישה **לַיָּם**...
Jerusalem is a beautiful city, but it has one disadvantage: no access to the **sea**...

הַצַּבִּים חיים שנים רבות – לעיתים עד 150 שנה!
Tortoises live many years – up to 150 years in some cases.

Special Expressions

יורדי **יָם** sailors, **sea**farers　　מעבר **לַיָּם** over**seas**
יָם התלמוד the (vast) Talmud

Additional Examples in this Pattern

חַח nose ring　　חַף sprocket　　פַּז gold　　תָּם innocent; naïve N & Adj

---

219. ***CaC***: mono-syllabic nouns with *kamats*: special declensions

A small number of kinship terms, in which an historical *y* is realized in the declension.

Our/your/their	my/your/his/her	const.	Gloss	sing/pl
אָחִינוּ/**אֲחִי**כֶם/כֶן/הֶם/הֶן	אָחִי/אָחִיךָ/אָחִיךְ/אָחִיו/אָחִיהָ	-אֲחִי	brother	אָח ז׳
אֲחֵינוּ/כֶם/כֶן/הֶם/הֶן	אַחַי/אַחֶיךָ/אַחַיִךְ/*אֶחָיו/אַחֶיהָ	-אֲחֵי		אַחִים

*The *seghol* here is to dissimilate from the following *kamats*

Examples

למשה יש שני **אַחִים**: **אָחִיו** הצעיר בחטיבת הביניים, ו**אָחִיו** הגדול בצבא.
Moshe has two **brothers**: **his** younger **brother** is at junior high school, and **his** older **brother** is in the army

Special Expressions

There is none like him אין לו **אָח** וָרֵעַ
one sharing suffering and sorrow אָח לצרה

Additional Examples in this Pattern

father-in-law חָם

---

220. ***CaC***: mono-syllabic nouns with *kamats*: special declensions with the plural ending *-ot*

The historical *y* is realized in the declension, but the plural suffix is וֹת-.

Our/your/their	my/your/his/her	const.	Gloss	sing/pl
אָבִינוּ/**אֲבִי**כֶם/כֶן/הֶם/הֶן	אָבִי/אָבִיךָ/אָבִיךְ/אָבִיו/אָבִיהָ	-אֲבִי-/אַב	father; patriarch;	אָב ז׳
אֲבוֹתֵינוּ/כֶם/כֶן/הֶם/הֶן	**אֲבוֹ**תַי/תֶיךָ/תַיִךְ/תָיו/תֶיהָ	-אֲבוֹת	originator; primary	אָבוֹת

Examples

תאמרו מה שתאמרו על ג׳ורג׳ ב׳, דבר אחד ברור: הוא אהב מאוד את **אָבִיו**.
Whatever you think of George B, one thing is clear: he really loved **his father**.

יצחק היה הדמות החיוורת ביותר בין שלושת ה**אָבוֹת**.
Isaac was the least remarkable of the three **forefathers (patriarchs)**.

איינשטיין נחשב ל**אֲבִי** הפיסיקה המודרנית.
Einstein is regarded as the **father (originator)** of modern physics.

Special Expressions

building superintendent **אַב** בית
step**father** **אָב** חורג
prototype **אַב**-טיפוס
city **elders** **אֲבוֹת** העיר
master plan תוכנית **אָב**
nursing home בית **אָבוֹת**

---

221. ***CaC***: mono-syllabic nouns and adjectives in which the *pataH* is maintained throughout the declension

our/your/their	my/your/his/her	const.	Gloss	sing/pl
גַּנֵּנוּ/גַּנְּכֶם/גַּנְּכֶן/גַּנָּם/גַּנָּן	גַּנִּי/גַּנְּךָ/גַּנֵּךְ/גַּנּוֹ/גַּנָּהּ	גַּן-	garden, park;	גַּן ז'
גַּנֵּינוּ/גַּנֵּיכֶם/כֶן/הֶם/הֶן	גַּנַּי/גַּנֶּיךָ/גַּנַּיִךְ/גַּנָּיו/גַּנֶּיהָ	גַּנֵּי-	kindergarten	גַּנִּים

Most nouns in this pattern are related to roots with identical second and third consonant, which accounts for the historical gemination of the consonant following the *pataH*.

When the second consonant is a ח׳, it is not geminated of course: פַּח, פַּחִי... פַּחִים. The same applies to ר׳, except that the *pataH* is replaced by *kamats* in an open syllable – "compensatory lengthening": סַר, סָרָה....

אַף 'nose; anger' has two plural forms: אַפִּים and אַפַּיִם. The former is used today only for 'nose;' אַפַּיִם serves in expressions like ארך אַפַּיִם 'patient,' מנה אחת אַפַּיִם 'a double share.'

Examples

ברחוב שלנו יש **גַּן** ציבורי קטן.
There's a small public **garden/park** in our street.

ילדים רבים לומדים היום לקרוא כבר **בגַּן**.
Many children already learn to read in **kindergarten** today.

צריך להיזהר כשעובדים במטבח עם סכין **חַדָּה**.
One needs to be careful when working in the kitchen with a **sharp** knife.

קֶרְמִיט הצפרדע: לא **קַל** להיות ירוק.
Kermit the Frog: It's not **easy** being green.

Special Expressions

אַף סולד upturned **nose**
גַּן חובה compulsory **kindergarten** (in Israel, ages 5-6, free of charge)
גַּן חיות zoo(logical **garden**)
גַּן ילדים kinder**garten**
גַּן ירק vegetble **garden**
גַּן עדן **Garden** of Eden
גַּן ציבורי public **park/garden**
גַּן שעשועים play**ground**
גַּס רוח uncouth, rude
חַם מזג **hot**-tempered
חַף מפשע innocent
רַךְ בשנים very young

Additional Examples in this Pattern

אַף nose
בַּז falcon
גַּס coarse, rough
דַּל poor; pauper
דַּק thin
זַךְ pure
חַי alive
חַם hot
חַף innocent
עַז strong

tin; snare פַּח
light; easy קַל
much, great רַב
soft רַךְ
bent שַׁח

---

222. ***CaC***: mono-syllabic nouns (fem. or masc.) in which the *pataH* is maintained throughout the declension, and the plural form ends with וֹת-.

our/your/their	My/your/his/her	const.	Gloss	sing/pl
קַתֵּנוּ/תְּכֶם/תְּכֶן/תָּם/תָּן	**קַ**תִּי/תְּךָ/תֵּךְ/תּוֹ/תָּהּ	קַת-	butt of weapon;	קַת נ׳
קַתוֹתֵינוּ/כֶם/כֶן/הֶם/הֶן	**קַתוֹ**תַי/תֶיךָ/תַיִךְ/תָיו/תֶיהָ	קַתוֹת-	handle	

כַּף 'palm of hand; spoon' has two plural forms: כַּפַּיִם/כַּפּוֹת. כַּפַּיִם is used for 'palm of hand' only; כַּפּוֹת serves for palm of hand, for foot, and for spoon.
Note: the plural of the masculine noun גַּג 'roof' also ends with וֹת-: גַּגּוֹת.

Examples

בארה״ב, כל 20 שנה בערך יש להחליף את רעפי הגַּג.
In the US, every 20 years or so one needs to replace the **roof** tiles.

יש לו **כַּפּוֹת** ידיים חזקות כשל דוב.
The **palms** of his hands are as strong as a bear's

Special Expressions

parent organization ארגון **גַּג**
solemn oral promise made by handshake תקיעת **כַּף**

---

223. ***CaC***: mono-syllabic masculine nouns in which the *pataH* of the singular islation form is realized as a *Hirik* in the rest of the declension

Our/your/their	my/your/his/her	const.	Gloss	sing/pl
מִסֵּנוּ/סְּכֶם/סְּכֶן/סָּם/סָּן	**מִ**סִּי/סְּךָ/סֵּךְ/סּוֹ/סָּהּ	מַס-	tax, toll,	מַס ז׳
מִסֵּינוּ/כֶם/כֶן/הֶם/הֶן	**מִ**סַּי/סֶּיךָ/סַּיִךְ/סָּיו/סֶּיהָ	מִסֵּי-	levy	מִסִּים

צַד 'side' has two plural forms: צְדָדִים/צִדִּים. צְדָדִים is the literary alternative.

Examples

בארה״ב **מִסֵּי** העיריה גבוהים מאוד.
In the US, municipal **taxes** are very high.

הגעתי ל**סַף** דלתו של מנהל החברה, אבל היססתי.
I reached the **threshold** of the company manager's door, but I hesitated.

Special Expressions

income **tax** **מַס** הכנסה
membership **fee** **מַס** חבר
value added tax **מַס** ערך מוסף (מע״מ) (VAT)

on the **verge** of death על **סַף** המוות

lip service **מַס** שפתיים

consciousness **threshold** **סַף** ההכרה

Additional Examples in this Pattern

side; aspect; party צַד

---

224. ***CaC***: mono-syllabic feminine nouns in which the *pataH* of the singular is realized as a *Hirik* in the rest of the declension

our/your/their	my/your/his/her	const.	Gloss	sing/pl
פִּתֵּנוּ/תְּכֶם/תְּכֶן/תָּם/תָּן	**פִּ**תִּי/תְּךָ/תֵּךְ/תּוֹ/תָּהּ	פַּת-	bread Lit.	פַּת נ'
פִּתֵּינוּ/כֶם/כֶן/הֶם/הֶן	**פִּ**תַּי/תֶּיךָ/תַּיִךְ/תָּיו/תֶּיהָ	פִּתֵּי-		פִּתִּים

כַּת 'sect' has three plural forms: כִּתִּים/כִּתּוֹת/כַּתּוֹת. Note: in everyday language, כִּתּוֹת is essentially the only one used.

Examples

היום כבר לא כל כך דורכים ענבים ברגליים ב**גַּת** – מסיבות של היגיינה, וגם משיקולי ייעול...
Today they tend not to press grapes with feet in a **wine press** – for reasons of hygiene, but also due to considerations of efficiency...

במצור בווייקו על ה**כַּת** של דיוויד כורש ב-1993 נהרגו 82 אנשים.
82 people were killed in the Waco siege on David Koresh's **sect** in 1993.

---

225. ***CaC***: mono-syllabic feminine nouns in which the *pataH* of the singular is realized as a *Hirik* in the rest of the declension, and the plural suffix is וֹת-

our/your/their	My/your/his/her	const.	Gloss	sing/pl
בִּתֵּנוּ/תְּכֶם/תְּכֶן/תָּם/תָּן	**בִּ**תִּי/תְּךָ/תֵּךְ/תּוֹ/תָּהּ	בַּת-	daughter	בַּת נ'
בְּנוֹתֵינוּ/כֶם/כֶן/הֶם/הֶן	**בְּנוֹ**תַי/תֶיךָ/תַיִךְ/תָיו/תֶיהָ	בְּנוֹת-		בָּנוֹת

When the stress shifts, the *kamats* is reduced to *shva*: בְּנוֹתַי, ... The plural בָּנוֹת suggests that the *n* was part of the stem (cf. comparable Arabic *bint*), and was assimilated to the next consonant in the singular.

Examples

יש עדיין תרבויות בעולם שבהן לידת **בַּת** נחשבת לאסון.
There are still some cultures in the world where the birth of a **daughter** is considered to be a disaster.

---

226. ***CaC***: mono-syllabic nouns and adjectives ending with a guttural, in which the *pataH* of the singular is realized as a *kamats* in the rest of the declension in an open syllable

our/your/their	my/your/his/her	const.	Gloss	sing/pl
פָּרֵנוּ/**פַּ**רְכֶם/כֶן/**פָּ**רָם/ן	**פָּ**רִי/רְךָ/רֵךְ/רוֹ/רָהּ	פַּר-	bull	פַּר ז'
פָּרֵינוּ/כֶם/כֶן/הֶם/הֶן	**פָּ**רַי/רֶיךָ/רַיִךְ/רָיו/רֶיהָ	פָּרֵי-		פָּרִים

When such nouns and adjectives end with a guttural, which cannot be geminated, there are two possibilities: In the case of ח׳ (cf. פַּח and similar cases) the *dagesh* is not there; in the case of ר׳ and ע׳, there occurs a supposed "compensatory lengthening": the *pataH* becomes *kamats* (but not in a closed syllable, in the construct singular or before -כֶםע).

Examples

פָּרִים משמשים היום בעיקר להרבעה.

Bulls are used today mostly for breeding.

כשמטיילים בוורמונט רואים רכסי **הָרִים** בלי סוף.

When traveling in Vermont one sees endless ranges of **mountains**.

אין לי בעייה עם מזג אוויר **קַר**, אבל אם יש רוח חזקה, זה פחות נעים.

I have no problem with **cold** weather, but if a strong wind blows, it is not so pleasant.

Special Expressions

young **bull** **פַּר** בן בקר

Additional Examples in this Pattern

pure, clean בַּר
pillow; meadow כַּר
bitter מַר
narrow; enemy צַר
bad, nasty רַע
minister; ruler שַׂר

---

227. ***CoC***: mono-syllabic nouns in which the *Holam Haser* of the singular is realized as a *kubuts* in the rest of the declension

our/your/their	my/your/his/her	const.	Gloss	sing/pl
תֻּפֵּנוּ/פְּכֶם/פְּכֶן/פָּם/פָּן	**תֻּ**פִּי/פְּךָ/פֵּךְ/פּוֹ/פָּהּ	-תֹּף	drum	תֹּף ז׳
תֻּפֵּינוּ/כֶם/כֶן/הֶם/הֶן	**תֻּ**פַּי/פֶּיךָ/פַּיִךְ/פָּיו/פֶּיהָ	-תֻּפֵּי		תֻּפִּים

When a suffix is appended, the *Holam Haser* is realized as *kubuts* and the second consonant is geminated. There are cases where declensions exist only in part: חֹם 'heat' and זֹךְ 'clarity, purity,' for instance, have no plural (since it is non-countable), and חֹל 'regular weekday' seems to have no alternants with possessive pronouns, for pragmatic reasons (?)…

Note: the plural of פֹּת 'genitalia (female)' as a feminine form ends with ות: פֻּתּוֹת. Since this an old form, replaced today by פּוֹתָה, it is not assigned to a separate *mishkal*.

Examples

רינגו הצטיין בעיקר בנגינה **בַּתֻּפִּים**.

Ringo excelled particularly in **drum** playing.

בַּתֹּף של אקדח תֻּפִּי יש שישה כדורים.

The **drum** of a revolver has six bullets.

הביטוי "לא **דֻּבִּים** ולא יער" מקורו בסיפור על הנביא אלישע, שלפיו כאשר ילדים הציקו לו, אלוהים שלח "שְׁתַּיִם **דֻּבִּים**" מן היער, ואלה הרגו 42 ילדים. הרבנים/פרשנים כתבו שזה לא קרה – זה רק סיפור אזהרה כדי שיתייחסו בכבוד לנביאים. לא היו **דֻּבִּים** ולא היה יער.
The Hebrew expression "no **bears**, no forest," meaning 'it never happened,' or 'it's old wives' tale,' originates from the story about the prophet Elishah, according to which when children tormented him, God sent "two she-**bears**" out of the forest, and they killed 42 kids. The rabbis/commentators wrote that it never happened – it was just a fable, warning people to show respect to prophets. There were no **bears**, there was no forest.

היום ניתן לזהות DNA ייחודי של אדם מטיפה קטנה של **רֹק**.
Today they can identify unique DNA of a person from a drop of **saliva**.

Special Expressions

בְּתֻפִּים ובמחולות with jubilation
תֹּף מרים tambourine
חֹד החנית spear**head**

Additional Examples in this Pattern

אֹם nut of a bolt
עֹל burden; yoke
חֹד sharp tip
רֹב most; majority

---

228. ***CoC***: mono-syllabic nouns in which the *Holam Haser* of the singular is realized as a *kubuts* and sometimes as *kamats katan* [o] in the rest of the declension

Our/your/their	my/your/his/her	const.	Gloss	sing/pl
חֻקֵּנוּ/קְכֶם/קְכֶן/קָּם/קָּן [חָקְכֶם/ן]	**חֻ**קִּי/קְּךָ/קֵּךְ/קּוֹ/קָּהּ [חָקְךָ]	חֹק-[חָק-]	law; custom; allocation	חֹק ז'
חֻקֵּינוּ/כֶם/כֶן/הֶם/הֶן	**חֻ**קַּי/קֶּיךָ/קַּיִךְ/קָּיו/קֶּיהָ	חֻקֵּי-		חֻקִּים

Historically, *CoC* was probably derived from "segholate" *CoCC*, but wil be treated here as *CoC*, for the sake of simplicity Note: in the case of רֹן 'joy,' only a *kamats katan* is realized in the declension: ...רָנִּי, רָנְּךָ (no separate *mishkal* here).

Examples

על פי **החֹק** הישראלי, כל יהודי הרוצה לעלות לישראל זכותו לעשות זאת.
According to Israeli **law**, any Jew who wants to immigrate to Israel is entitled to do so.

בעברית הקלאסית השתמשו במונח "**חֹק**" גם למנהג.
In classical Hebrew they also used the term for **law** for **custom** as well.

Special Expressions

חֹק ההתיישנות **statute** of limitation
חֹק ולא יעבור immutable **law**
חֹק השבות Law of Return (Israel)
לחם **חֻקּוֹ** his daily bread
הועמד מחוץ **לחֹק** was outlawed

Additional Examples in this Pattern

עֹז might, strength
רֹן joy; singing

---

229. ***CoC***: mono-syllabic nouns in which the *Holam Haser* is maintained throughout because the second consonant is ר׳, which takes no *dagesh*

our/your/their	my/your/his/her	const.	Gloss	sing/pl
חֹרֵנוּ/רְכֶם/רְכֶן/רָם/רָן	**חֹ**רִי/רְךָ/רֵךְ/רוֹ/רָהּ	חֹר-	hole	חֹר ז׳
חֹרֵינוּ/כֶם/כֶן/הֶם/הֶן	**חֹ**רַי/רֶיךָ/רַיִךְ/רָיו/רֶיהָ	חֹרֵי-		חֹרִים

Examples

אחרי חורף מושלג בארה״ב יש צורך למלא **חֹרִים** רבים בכבישים כשמגיע האביב.
After a snowy winter in the US, one needs to fill many **holes** in the roads when spring arrives.

בגיל 65 הוא החליט לברוח מן **הקֹר** של מינסוטה ועבר לפלורידה.
At the age of 65 he decided to flee from the Minnesota **cold** and moved to Florida.

Additional Examples in this Pattern

flint צֹר   myrrh מֹר

---

230. ***CoC***: mono-syllabic nouns in which the *Holam Haser* is maintained throughout the declension and the second consonant is guttural, ה׳ ח׳ ע׳ with a "furtive *pataH*."

our/your/their	my/your/his/her	const.	Gloss	sing/pl
כֹּחֵנוּ/חֲכֶם/חֲכֶן/חָם/חָן	**כֹּ**חִי/חֲךָ/חֵךְ/חוֹ/חָהּ	כֹּחַ-	power, force,	כֹּחַ ז׳
כֹּחוֹתֵינוּ/כֶם/כֶן/הֶם/הֶן	**כֹּחוֹ**תַי/תֶיךָ/תַיִךְ/תָיו/תֶיהָ	כֹּחוֹת-	strength; wealth	כֹּחוֹת

When the guttural occurs at the end of the word, a "furtive" *pataH* precedes (since the preceding vowel is not *a*). When a *shva* is expected with the guttural, it is replaced with a *Hataf-pataH*. When a plural form exists, it ends with וֹת-.

Examples

לא תמיד ברור מה חשוב יותר לאנשי הממון הגדולים: כסף או **כֹּחַ**?
It is not always clear what is more important to big financiers: money or **power**?

אין לו כבר **כֹּחַ** לעבוד יותר; הוא רוצה לפרוש.
He has no more **strength** to continue working; he wants to retire.

Special Expressions

authorized representative **בא-כֹּחַ**
power of attorney **ייפוי-כֹּחַ**
potential **בכֹּחַ**
well done! **יישר כֹּחַ!**
sexual potency **כֹּחַ** גברא

Additional Examples in this Pattern

pharynx לֹעַ   yearning; lamentation Lit נֹהַּ   evil רֹעַ

---

231. ***CeC***: mono-syllabic nouns in which the *tsere* is maintained throughout the declension

our/your/their	my/your/his/her	const.	Gloss	sing/pl
עֵדֵנוּ/עֶדְכֶם/עֶדְכֶן/עֵדָם/עֵדָן	עֵדִי/עֶדְךָ/עֵדֵךְ/עֵדוֹ/עֵדָהּ	עֵד-	witness	עֵד ז׳
עֵדֵינוּ/כֶם/כֶן/הֶם/הֶן	עֵדַי/עֵדֶיךָ/עֵדַיִךְ/עֵדָיו/עֵדֶיהָ	עֵדֵי-		עֵדִים

A substantial number of realizations in this pattern are related to roots with *w* or *y* as the second consonant (עו״ד > עֵד), or with *y* as the third consonant (גא״י > גֵּא). Note: the plural of נֵר 'candle' is נֵרוֹת.

Examples

העֵד העיקרי של התביעה סירב להעיד לאחר שמקורביו של הנאשם איימו על בני משפחתו.
The prosecution star **witness** refused to testify after his family had been threatened by cronies of the defendant.

היהדות הייתה הדת הראשונה שדגלה באמונה **באֵל** אחד.
Judaism was the first religion to introduce the belief in a single **god**.

תורת משה מדגישה את החובה שלא להפלות **גֵּרִים** לרעה.
The Mosaic Law emphasizes the obligation not to discriminate against **alien residents**.

חוקי הקבורה ביהדות אינם מתירים להחזיק את גופת **המֵת** (לפני הקבורה) בשבת.
Jewish burial laws do not allow holding the **body** (before burial) over the Sabbath.

Special Expressions

state **witness** **עֵד** המלך/המדינה
hostile **witness** **עֵד** עוין
eye**witness** **עֵד** ראייה
witness to something heard **עֵד** שמיעה
perjurer **עֵד** שקר

Additional Examples in this Pattern

vapor אֵד
spade, shovel אֵת
proud גֵּא
echo הֵד
wreath זֵר
honest, sincere כֵּן
candle נֵר
pen עֵט
awake; alert עֵר
demon שֵׁד

---

232. ***CeC***: mono-syllabic nouns in which the *tsere* is maintained throughout and the second consonant is guttural, ה׳ ח׳ ע׳

our/your/their	my/your/his/her	const.	Gloss	sing/pl
רֵעֵנוּ/רֵעֲכֶם/רֵעֲכֶן/רֵעָם/רֵעָן	רֵעִי/רֵעֲךָ/רֵעֵךְ/רֵעוֹ/רֵעָהּ	רֵעַ-	friend,	רֵעַ ז׳
רֵעֵינוּ/כֶם/כֶן/הֶם/הֶן	רֵעַי/רֵעֶיךָ/רֵעַיִךְ/רֵעָיו/רֵעֶיהָ	רֵעֵי-	comrade	רֵעִים

When the guttural occurs at the end of the word after a non-*a* vowel, a "furtive" *pataH* precedes. When a *shva* is expected with the guttural, it is replaced with a *Hataf-pataH*.

Examples

זאת לא הייתה שיחת **רֵעִים** אלא ויכוח קשה ונוקב בין שני יריבים-בנפש.
This was not conversation between **friends**, but rather a hard, poignant argument between sworn enemies.

Special Expressions

Love thy **neighbor** as thyself ואהבת ל**רֵעֲךָ** כָּמוֹךָ

a sociable person איש **רֵעִים**
There's none like him אין **רֵעַ** לו

Additional Examples in this Pattern

freshness, vitality לֵחַ

marrow מֵחַ/מוֹחַ

---

233. ***CeC***: mono-syllabic nouns in which the *tsere* is maintained in some of the declension

our/your/their	my/your/his/her	const.	Gloss	sing/pl
עֵצֵנוּ/עֶצְכֶם/עֶצְכֶן/עֵצָם/עֵצָן	עֵצִי/עֶצְךָ/עֵצֵךְ/עֵצוֹ/עֵצָהּ	עֵץ-	tree;	עֵץ ז'
עֵצֵינוּ/**עֲצֵי**כֶם/כֶן/הֶם/הֶן	עֵצַי/עֵצֶיךָ/עֵצַיִךְ/עֵצָיו/עֵצֶיהָ	עֲצֵי-	wood	עֵצִים

The *tsere* is reduced to a *shva* or a *Hataf* when stress shifts in the construct state or before -כֶם\ן, -הֶם\ן.

Examples

בזמנו, **עֵץ** השקמה היה נפוץ מאוד בארץ ישראל.
At the time, the fig sycamore **tree** was very common in Palestine.

מעט מאוד רהיטים מיוצרים היום מ**עֵץ** מלא.
Today, very few pieces of furniture are manufactured from solid **wood**.

Special Expressions

the Tree of Knowledge **עֵץ** הדעת
the Tree of Life **עֵץ** החיים
talk to the tree! (i.e., no one pays attention) דבר אל ה**עֵצִים**!

One cannot see the wood for the trees מרוב **עֵצִים** אין רואים את היער

Additional Examples in this Pattern

trunk, torso, back גֵו

---

234. ***CeC***: mono-syllabic nouns in which the *tsere* is reduced to a *shva* or turns into a *Hirik* in in a closed syllable

our/your/their	my/your/his/her	const.	Gloss	sing/pl
בְּנֵנוּ/בִּנְכֶם/בִּנְכֶן/בְּנָם/בְּנָן	בְּנִי/בִּנְךָ/בְּנֵךְ/בְּנוֹ/בְּנָהּ	בֶּן-	son; boy	בֵּן ז'
בָּנֵינוּ/**בְּנֵי**כֶם/כֶן/הֶם/הֶן	בָּנַי/בָּנֶיךָ/בָּנַיִךְ/בָּנָיו/בָּנֶיהָ	בְּנֵי-		בָּנִים

our/your/their	my/your/his/her	const.	Gloss	sing/pl
שְׁמֵנוּ/שִׁמְכֶם/שִׁמְכֶן/שְׁמָם/שְׁמָן	שְׁמִי/שִׁמְךָ/שְׁמֵךְ/שְׁמוֹ/שְׁמָהּ	שֵׁם-/שֶׁם-	name	שֵׁם ז'
שְׁמוֹתֵינוּ/**שְׁמוֹתֵי**כֶם/כֶן/הֶם/הֶן	**שְׁמוֹ**תַי/תֶיךָ/תַיִךְ/תָיו/תֶיהָ	שְׁמוֹת-		שֵׁמוֹת

Examples

שְׁמוֹת בָּנָיו של אדם היו קין והבל.

The **names** of Adam's **sons** were Cain and Abel.

---

235. ***CeC***: mono-syllabic nouns in which the *tsere* of the singular is realized as a *Hirik* in the rest of the declension

our/your/their	my/your/his/her	const.	Gloss	sing/pl
חִצֵּנוּ/חִצְּכֶם/חִצְּכֶן/חִצָּם/חִצָּן	חִצִּי/חִצְּךָ/חִצֵּךְ/חִצּוֹ/חִצָּהּ	חֵץ-	arrow	חֵץ ז'
חִצֵּינוּ/כֶם/כֶן/הֶם/הֶן	חִצַּי/חִצֶּיךָ/חִצַּיִךְ/חִצָּיו/חִצֶּיהָ	חִצֵּי-		חִצִּים

In some of the occurrences, the nouns concerned are related to roots with an identical second and third consonants which merged – hence the gemination (*dagesh forte*). Note: the plural of (feminine) שֵׁן is שִׁנַּיִם (like the dual form). Some of the forms are feminine: אֵשׁ, עֵז, עֵת, שֵׁן.

Examples

יש אזורים בעולם שבהם עדיין משתמשים בקשת ו**בְחִצִּים** בציד ובמלחמה.

There are still some areas in the world in which people still use bow and **arrows** in hunting and in war.

פרומתאוס גנב **אֵשׁ** מן האולימפוס כדי לעזור לבני האדם, אך שילם על כך ביוקר.

Prometheus stole **fire** from Mt. Olympus to give it to humans, but paid for it dearly.

באיסלאם קל מאוד לגבר לתת גֵּט לאישה; כל מה שהוא צריך לעשות הוא לומר לה: "**גֵּט, גֵּט, גֵּט**" בערבית בנוכחותה.

In Islam, it is very easy for a man to grant his wife a **divorce**; all he needs to do is to repeat the Arabic word for "**divorce**" (*Talaaq*) three times in her presence.

הסיבה העיקרית לכך שישראל צריכה לנטוע כל כך הרבה עצים היא **העֵז** הערבית. היא חיסלה יערות שלמים בכך שאכלה כל עלה שהגיעה אליו – ועִזִּים מסוגלות לטפס על עצים!

The main reason why Israel needs to plant that many trees is the Arab **goat**. It had destroyed entire forests by consuming any leaf it could reach – and **goats** can climb trees!

פעם היו עוקרים **שֵׁן** חולה על-ידי משיכת חוט שאליו הייתה קשורה...
Once they used to pull out a sick **tooth** by pulling a string to which it was tied....

לעתים מתייחסים לעולם האקדמי כ"מגדל **שֵׁן**".
Sometimes the academic world is regarded as an "**ivory** tower".

Special Expressions

גֵּט חליצה levirate **divorce**
גֵּט על תנאי provisional **divorce**
כ**חֵץ** מקשת extremely fast
חִצֵּי לעג mocking criticism
חֵךְ שסוע cleft **palate**
שֵׁן בינה wisdom **tooth**

שֵׁן טוחנת molar
הקהה את **שִׁנָּיו** put him to shame
חרק ב**שִׁנָּיו** gnashed his teeth (in anger)
יצא ב**שֵׁן** ועין lost his shirt
גלגל **שִׁנַּיִם** cogwheel

Additional Examples in this Pattern

גֵּץ spark
חֵךְ palate
חֵן grace, charm
נֵס miracle
נֵץ hawk

עֵת time, season
צֵל shadow
קֵן nest
קֵץ end
תֵּל mound

---

236. ***CeC***: mono-syllabic nouns in which the *tsere* of the singular is realized as a *Hirik* in the rest of the declension and the plural suffix is וֹת-

sing/pl	Gloss	const.	my/your/his/her	our/your/their
לֵב ז'	heart; mind; core	לֵב-	לִבִּי/לִבְּךָ/לִבֵּךְ/לִבּוֹ/לִבָּהּ	לִבֵּנוּ/לִבְּכֶם/לִבְּכֶן/לִבָּם/לִבָּן
לִבּוֹת		לִבּוֹת-	**לִבּוֹ**תַי/תֶיךָ/תַיִךְ/תָיו/תֶיהָ	**לִבּוֹתֵי**נוּ/כֶם/כֶן/הֶם/הֶן

Note: an alternative plural form of לֵב 'heart' is לְבָבוֹת. The plural form of אֵם 'mother' is either אִמּוֹת or אִמָּהוֹת.

Examples

למרות שמדובר היום הרבה על סרטן, מחלות ה**לֵּב** השונות הן עדיין הקטלניות ביותר.
Although one talks a lot about cancer today, the various **heart** diseases are still the major killers.

הוא הקשיב בנימוס לטיעון, אבל ב**לִבּוֹ** חשב שהכל הבל ורעות רוח.
He listened politely to the argument, but thought to himself (= in his **heart** = **mind**) that it was total nonsense.

שבב מעבד הנתונים המרכזי הוא **לִבּוֹ** של המחשב כולו.
The CPU is the **core** of the whole computer.

Special Expressions

courage אומץ **לֵב**
frankness גילוי **לֵב**
kind טוֹב **לֵב**
coward מוג **לֵב**

said to himself דיבר אל **לִבּוֹ**
his conscience smote him נקפו **לִבּוֹ**
far away at sea **בְּלֵב** ים
attention תשׂוּמת **לֵב**

---

237. ***Ce***: mono-syllabic nouns with *seghol* and plural suffix ים-.

our/your/their	my/your/his/her	const.	Gloss	sing/pl
שֵׂינוּ/שֵׂיְכֶם/שֵׂיְכֶן/שֵׂיָם/שֵׂיָן	שֵׂיִי/שֵׂיְךָ/שֵׂיֵךְ/שֵׂיוֹ/שֵׂיָהּ	שֵׂה-	lamb	שֶׂה זו״נ
שֵׂיֵינוּ/**שְׂיֵי**כֶם/כֶן/הֶם/הֶן	שֵׂיַי/שֵׂיֶיךָ/שֵׂיַיִךְ/שֵׂיָיו/שֵׂיֶיהָ	שֵׂיֵי-		שֵׂיִים

Apparently a single realization in this declension.

---

238. ***Ce***: mono-syllabic nouns with *seghol* and plural suffix וֹת-.

our/your/their	my/your/his/her	const.	Gloss	sing/pl
פִּינוּ/פִּיכֶם/פִּיכֶן/פִּיהֶם/ פִּיהֶן	פִּי/פִּיךָ/פִּיךְ/פִּיו(פִּיהוּ)/ פִּיהָ	פִּי-	mouth; opening	פֶּה ז׳
פִּיּוֹתֵינוּ/כֶם/כֶן/הֶם/הֶן	**פִּיּוֹ**תַי/תֶיךָ/תַיִךְ/תָיו/תֶיהָ	פִּיּוֹת-		פִּיּוֹת

Apparently a single realization in this declension.

---

239. ***Ci***: mono-syllabic nouns ending with *i*

our/your/their	my/your/his/her	const.	gloss	sing/pl
אִיֵּנוּ/**אִי**כֶם/כֶן/**אִיָּ**ם/ן	אִיִּי/אִיךָ/אִיֵּךְ/אִיּוֹ/אִיָּהּ	אִי-	island	אִי ז׳
אִיֵּינוּ/כֶם/כֶן/הֶם/הֶן	אִיַּי/אִיֶּיךָ/אִיַּיִךְ/אִיָּיו/אִיֶּיהָ	אִיֵּי-		אִיִּים

Note: when a *y* with a *shva* is expected after a *Hiriq*, that *y* is muted, without a *shva* and of course without a *dagesh*: אִיךָ < אִיְּךָ.

Examples

את חופשתי האחרונה ביליתי **בְּאִיֵּי** יוון.
I spent my last vacation in the Greek **islands**.

אנשים אוהבים להשקיע במדינה הזאת כי הם רואים בה **אִי** של יציבות באזור לא יציב.
People like to invest in this state because they regard it as an **island** of stability in an unstable region.

הַצִּי השישי ביקר פעמים רבות בישראל.
The Sixth **Fleet** visited Israel many times.

Special Expressions

peninsula חֲצִי-**אִי**

median strip in road **אִי**-תְנוּעָה

Additional Examples in this Pattern

heap or mound of ruins Lit. עִי

---

240. ***CoC***: mono-syllabic nouns in which וֹ is maintained throughout the declension and the plural ending is ־ים.

our/your/their	my/your/his/her	const.	Gloss	sing/pl
דּוֹדֵנוּ/דּוֹדְכֶם/דּוֹדְכֶן/דּוֹדָם/דּוֹדָן	דּוֹדִי/דּוֹדְךָ/דּוֹדֵךְ/דּוֹדוֹ/דּוֹדָהּ	דּוֹד-	uncle;	דּוֹד* ז'
דּוֹדֵינוּ/כֶם/כֶן/הֶם/הֶן	דּוֹדַי/דּוֹדֶיךָ/דּוֹדַיִךְ/דּוֹדָיו/דּוֹדֶיהָ	דּוֹדֵי-	lover	דּוֹדִים**

*In Biblical Hebrew: 'lover;' in child language: 'any adult other than parents'
**In BH: 'lovemaking'

Some of these nouns are related to roots with *w* or *y* as a second consonant: זוֹב < זו״ב, טוֹב < טו״ב, etc. Included in this pattern are a number of adjectives, like זוֹל 'cheap, inexpensive,' נוֹחַ 'comfortable, convenient,' and the declension is as it is with adjectives in general: זוֹל, זוֹלָה, זוֹלִים, זוֹלוֹת. The plural form of יוֹם 'day' is יָמִים, construct state יְמֵי-, and see also יְמֵיכֶם etc. The plural form of שׁוֹק 'shin; leg' is dual: שׁוֹקַיִם.

Examples

יש לי שני **דּוֹדִים**, אחד בארץ ואחד בארה״ב. **דּוֹדִי** האמריקאי מלמד באוניברסיטה של מישיגן.
I have two **uncles**, one in Israel, another one in the US. **My** American **uncle** teaches at the Univ. of Michigan.

״**דּוֹדִי** לי ואני לו״ (שיר השירים 2:16)
My beloved is mine, and I am his (Song of Songs 2:16)

אני מבין שבארץ חופשית כמו ארה״ב טבעי הוא ש**הוֹן** עתק מרוכז בידי מספר קטן של אנשים, ואני לא חושב שהם צריכים לשלם 70% מס, אבל בארצות רבות באירופה המס המרבי הוא 50%, ולעיתים אפילו 60%, כדי לוודא שאפילו החלשים ביותר לא ירעבו ויקבלו טיפול רפואי במחיר שווה לכל נפש.
I understand that in a free country like the US it is natural for huge **capital** to be concentrated in the hands of a small number of people, and I do not think that they should pay 70% tax, but in many countries in Europe the maximum tax rate is 50%, sometimes even 60%, to make sure that even the weakest do not go hungry and receive medical treatment at a price they can afford.

בארה״ב כמעט הכל יותר **זוֹל** מאשר בישראל, פרט לפירות וירקות בעונה, ולטיפול רפואי.
In the US, almost everything is **cheap**er than in Israel, except for fruit and vegetables in season, and medical costs.

בגלל מזג האוויר הנוח ברוב ימי השנה, בדרך כלל ה**חוֹפִים** בישראל הומים מבני אדם, ישראלים ותיירים.
Because of the confortable weather for most of the year, the **beaches** in Israel are generally swarming with people, Israelis as well as tourists.

Special Expressions

cousin **בֶּן-דּוֹד**
non-Jew who performs tasks on Sabbath that are forbidden to (orthodox) Jews **גּוֹי** של שבת
black (undeclared) **capital** **הוֹן** שחור
safe **harbor** **חוֹף** מבטחים
independence **day** **יוֹם** העצמאות

week**end** **סוֹף** שבוע
the **end** result, conclusion **סוֹף** דבר
the **end** of the road Col.; excellent Sl. **סוֹף** הדרך
finally! **סוֹף** (כל) **סוֹף**
biblical cantillation symbol; the **final** word Col **סוֹף** פסוק

Additional Examples in this Pattern

power, vitality אוֹן
gentile; nation גּוֹי
glory הוֹד
good טוֹב
day יוֹם

wandering נוֹד
view נוֹף
end סוֹף
monkey, ape קוֹף
whip שׁוֹט

---

241. ***CoC***: mono-syllabic nouns in which וֹ is maintained throughout the declension and when the second consonant is a guttural

our/your/their	my/your/his/her	const.	gloss	sing/pl
חוֹחֵנוּ/חוֹחֲכֶם/חוֹחֲכֶן/חוֹחָם/חוֹחָן	חוֹחִי/חוֹחֲךָ/חוֹחֵךְ/חוֹחוֹ/חוֹחָהּ	חוֹחַ-	thistle,	חוֹחַ ז'
חוֹחֵינוּ/כֶם/כֶן/הֶם/הֶן	חוֹחַי/חוֹחֶיךָ/חוֹחַיִךְ/חוֹחָיו/חוֹחֶיהָ	חוֹחֵי-	thorn	חוֹחִים

When the guttural occurs at the end of the word, without a suffix, a "furtive" *pataH* is inserted (since the preceding vowel is not *a*). When a *shva* is expected with the guttural, it is replaced with a *Hataf-pataH*.

Examples

קשה לי לנהוג במכונית הזו, כיוון שהמושבים בה אינם **נוֹחִים**.
It is hard for me to drive this car, since its seats are not **comfortable**.

Special Expressions

Like a rose among the **briars** (something fine in a coarse environment) כשושנה בין ה**חוֹחִים**

Additional Examples in this Pattern

movement נוֹעַ

wealthy person שׁוֹעַ

---

242. ***CoC***: mono-syllabic nouns in which וֹ is maintained throughout the declension and the plural ending is וֹת-

our/your/their	my/your/his/her	const.	Gloss	sing/pl
קוֹלֵנוּ/לְכֶם/לְכֶן/לָם/לָן	קוֹלִי/קוֹלְךָ/קוֹלֵךְ/קוֹלוֹ/קוֹלָהּ	קוֹל-	voice, sound;	קוֹל ז׳
קוֹלוֹתֵינוּ/כֶם/כֶן/הֶם/הֶן	**קוֹלוֹ**תַי/תֶיךָ/תַיִךְ/תָיו/תֶיהָ	קוֹלוֹת-	opinion, vote	קוֹלוֹת

Some of these nouns are related to roots with *w* or *y* as a second consonant: חוֹב < חו״ב, עוֹף < עו״פ, etc.

In some occurrences there also exists an alternative plural form, less frequent, with the suffix ־ִים: אוֹר ~ אוֹרוֹת/אוֹרִים, דּוֹר ~ דּוֹרוֹת/דּוֹרִים. The plural form of אוֹת 'sign, signal' is אוֹתוֹת, and of אוֹת 'letter' is אוֹתִיּוֹת.

Examples

אני מכיר את **קוֹלוֹ** של הקריין הזה, אבל לא זוכר את שמו.
I know the **voice** of this news announcer, but do not remember his name.

בשעות הצוהריים במנהטן, שומעים בעיקר **קוֹל** קשקוש של סכינים ומזלגות.
In Manhattan at lunchtime, one hears mainly the clinging **sound** of knives and forks.

בתום המלחמה נשמעו **קוֹלוֹת** רבים נגד הכיבוש.
At the end of the war, many **voices (= opinions)** were heard against the occupation.

אם אתה אוהב לקרוא במיטה, תדאג שיהיה לך **אוֹר** מתאים, ושלא יפריע לבת-זוגך.
If you like to read in bed, make sure you have an appropriate **light**, which will also not disturb your spouse.

למתחם המוגן של המטכ״ל ומשרד הביטחון בקריה בתל-אביב העם קורא ״**הבּוֹר**״.
The protected peremeter of the general staff of the military and the depense ministry in Tel Aviv is popularly referred to as the "**pit**."

מה יעשה **הדּוֹר** הצעיר אם פתאום יקחו לו את כל הסמרטפונים?
What will the young **generation** do if all of a sudden their smartphones will be taken away?

Special Expressions

The secret **עוֹף** השמים הוליך את **הקוֹל** became public knowledge
the (mythological) phoenix **עוֹף** החוֹל
a rare **bird**, a strange person **עוֹף** מוזר

There's no response אין **קוֹל** ואין עונה
voice crying in the wilderness **קוֹל** קורא במדבר
did as he was told שמע **בְּקוֹלוֹ** של...

Additional Examples in this Pattern

sign, signal אוֹת
hole, pit בּוֹר
debt חוֹב
sand חוֹל

glass, cup כּוֹס
pole, rod מוֹט
bird; poultry עוֹף
fast; fasting צוֹם

243. ***CoC***: mono-syllabic nouns in which וֹ is maintained throughout the declension and the plural ending is וֹת-, when the last consonant is guttural

our/your/their	my/your/his/her	const.	Gloss	sing/pl
מוֹחֵנוּ/חֲכֶם/חֲכֶן/חָם/חָן	מוֹחִי/מוֹחֲךָ/מוֹחֵךְ/מוֹחוֹ/מוֹחָהּ	מוֹחַ-	brain	מוֹחַ ז'
מוֹחוֹתֵינוּ/כֶם/כֶן/הֶם/הֶן	**מוֹחוֹ**תַי/תֶיךָ/תַיִךְ/תָיו/תֶיהָ	מוֹחוֹת-		מוֹחוֹת

When the guttural occurs word-finally, a "furtive" *pataH* precedes, since it follows a non-*a* vowel. When a *shva* is expected with that guttural, it is replaced with a *Hataf-pataH*.

Examples

גופו הולך ונחלש, אבל **מוֹחוֹ** נשאר מבריק כשהיה.
His body is getting weaker and weaker, but **his brain** remains as brilliant as it has always been.

Special Expressions

brainwashing שטיפת **מוֹחַ**   feather **brain**ed **מוֹחַ** של אפרוח

---

244. ***CoC***: mono-syllabic nouns in which *Holam Haser* with a mute א' is maintained throughout, and the plural suffix is ים-

our/your/their	my/your/his/her	const.	Gloss	sing/pl
רֹאשֵׁנוּ/שְׁכֶם/שְׁכֶן/שָׁם/שָׁן	רֹאשִׁי/רֹאשְׁךָ/רֹאשֵׁךְ/רֹאשׁוֹ/רֹאשָׁהּ	רֹאשׁ-	head	רֹאשׁ ז'
רָאשֵׁינוּ/כֶם/כֶן/הֶם/הֶן	**רָא**שַׁי/שֶׁיךָ/שַׁיִךְ/תָיו/תֶיהָ	רָאשֵׁי-		רָאשִׁים

Examples

ד"ר דוליטל קיבל במתנה סוס עם שני **רָאשִׁים** : דְחוֹף-מְשׁוֹךְ.
Dr. Dolittle received a horse with two **heads** as a present: push-me-pull-you.

Special Expressions

the prime minister **ראש** הממשלה   **first** of all **בראש** ובראשונה
he brought it upon himself דמו **בראשו**   **ahead** of time **מֵראש**

---

245. ***CoC***: mono-syllabic nouns in which *Holam Haser* with a mute א is maintained throughout, and the plural suffix is וֹת-

our/your/their	my/your/his/her	const.	Gloss	sing/pl
נֹאדֵנוּ/דְכֶם/דְכֶן/דָם/דָן	נֹאדִי/נֹאדְךָ/נֹאדֵךְ/נֹאדוֹ/נֹאדָהּ	נֹאד-	leather bottle;	נֹאד ז'
נֹאדוֹתֵינוּ/כֶם/כֶן/הֶם/הֶן	**נֹאדוֹ**תַי/תֶיךָ/תַיִךְ/תָיו/תֶיהָ	נֹאדוֹת-	fart (Col.);	נֹאדוֹת
			pompous pers.	

Examples

הבדואים משתמשים עדיין **בנֹאדות** לנשיאת מים.
The Bedouins still use **leather bottles** to transport water.

יכול להיות שהוא אינטליגנטי, אבל הוא מתנהג כמו **נֹאד** נפוח.
He may be intelligent, but he behaves like a **pompous** ass.

Additional Examples in this Pattern

צֹאן sheep and goats [no plural]

---

246. ***CuC***: mono-syllabic nouns where ו is maintained throughout the declension and the plural ending is *-im*

our/your/their	my/your/his/her	const.	Gloss	sing/pl
סוּסֵנוּ/סְכֶם/סְכֶן/סָם/סָן	סוּסִי/סוּסְךָ/סוּסֵךְ/סוּסוֹ/סוּסָהּ	סוּס-	horse	סוּס ז׳
סוּסֵינוּ/כֶם/כֶן/הֶם/הֶן	סוּסַי/סוּסֶיךָ/סוּסַיִךְ/סוּסָיו/סוּסֶיהָ	סוּסֵי-		סוּסִים

Some of these nouns are related to roots with *w* or *y* as a second consonant: בּוּז > בו״ז, חוּשׁ > חו״ש, etc.

Note: גּוּף 'body' has two plural forms, גּוּפִים and גּוּפוֹת. Generally גּוּפִים is used for inanimate objects, and גּוּפוֹת for animate ones. When referring to dead humans and animals, the plural גּוּפוֹת is identical, of course, to the plural of גּוּפָה 'corpse.' The plural form of שׁוּל 'margin' is dual, שׁוּלַיִם.

Examples

יש ארצות שבהן **סוּס** ועגלה הם עדיין אמצעי התחבורה השכיח ביותר.
There are countries in which **horse**-and-carriage are still the commonest means of transportation.

הרעיון של "**בּוּל** תמיד" הוא רעיון מעולה. היום, כשתקשורת אלקטרונית מספקת את רוב הצרכים, לא צריך לרוץ לסניף הדואר כשבכל זאת צריך לשלוח מכתב רגיל ויש בבית כבר **בּוּלִים** שרכשת מזמן.
The idea of a "forever" **stamp** is great. Today, with electronic communication fulfilling most needs, when you still need to send a regular letter, you do not have to rush to the post office, since you already have **stamps** at home that you had bought long ago.

אפילו בגיל תשעים היה למקס **גוּף** של בחור בן שלושים. מזל, אבל גם פעילות גופנית...
Even at the age of ninety, Max had the **body** of a thirty-year-old young man. Luck, but also physical exercise…

לדני יש **חוּשׁ** טכני מצוין. מספיק לו תרשים של המתקן המסובך ביותר, ותוך שעה הוא יתקין אותו באופן מושלם.
Danny has an excellent technical **sense**. All he needs is a chart of even the most complex device, and within an hour he will install it perfectly.

החדר החשוב ביותר בכל **חוג** באוניברסיטה הוא חדר לשימוש כללי: ישיבות, פגישות אישיות בין מרצים לתלמידים ובין תלמידים בינם לבין עצמם, וכד'.

The most important room in any **university department** is a general use room (the so-called conference room): for general meetings, for meetings between professors and students and for students meeting with other students, and so on.

Special Expressions

heating **element** **גוף** חימום
judicial **body** **גוף** משפטי
obstructive **block** (politics) **גוש** חוסם
congenital **defect** **מום** מולד

horse power כּוֹחַ **סוס**
hippopotamus **סוס** יאור
Trojan **horse** **סוס** טרויאני
walrus **סוס** ים

Additional Examples in this Pattern

firebrand אוּד
scorn, disdain בּוּז
ignoramus בּוּר
dwarf גּוּץ
cub גּוּר
lump, chunk גּוּשׁ
string חוּט
brown חוּם

row; column טוּר
nook כּוּךְ
furnace; reactor כּוּר
chicken coop לוּל
defect מוּם
loom נוּל
margin שׁוּל

---

247. ***CuC***: mono-syllabic nouns where ו is maintained throughout the declension and the plural ending is *-ot*

our/your/their	my/your/his/her	const.	Gloss	sing/pl
זוּגֵנוּ/גְכֶם/גְכֶן/גָם/גָן	זוּגִי/זוּגְךָ/זוּגֵךְ/זוּגוֹ/זוּגָהּ	זוּג-	pair,	זוּג ז'
זוּגוֹתֵינוּ/כֶם/כֶן/הֶם/הֶן	**זוּגוֹ**תַי/תֶיךָ/תַיִךְ/תָיו/תֶיהָ	זוּגוֹת-	couple	זוּגוֹת

Examples

יעקב ורחל היו אחד ה**זוגות** הרומנטיים ביותר בהיסטוריה.

Jacob and Rachel were one of the most romantic **couples** in history.

Special Expressions

like a **pair** of doves (in love and harmony) כמו **זוג** יונים
abroad **חוּץ**-לָאָרֶץ

Additional Examples in this Pattern

outside חוּץ

---

248. ***CuC***: mono-syllabic nouns in which ו is maintained throughout the declension, the plural ending is וֹת-, and the final consonant is guttural

our/your/their	my/your/his/her	const.	gloss	sing/pl
לוּחֵנוּ/חֲכֶם/חֲכֶן/חָם/חָן	לוּחִי/לוּחֲךָ/לוּחֵךְ/לוּחוֹ/לוּחָהּ	לוּחַ-	board	לוּחַ ז'
לוּחוֹתֵינוּ/כֶם/כֶן/הֶם/הֶן	**לוּחוֹ**תַי/תֶיךָ/תַיִךְ/תָיו/תֶיהָ	לוּחוֹת-		לוּחוֹת

When the word ends with a guttural, a "furtive" *pataH* precedes a non-*a* vowel. When a *shva* is expected with the guttural, it is replaced with a *Hataf-pataH.*

Note: רוּחַ could originally be either masculine or feminine. Today the tendency is to regard it as a feminine form, but some differentiate: רוּחַ as movement of air in the feminine, and רוּחַ as spirit in the masculine.

Examples

כשלמדתי בבית הספר היסודי מוּנָּה כל שבוע תורן אחר, שתפקידו היה לנקות את **הלוּחַ** לפני בוא המורה.
Went I went to elementary school, every week a new "student on duty" was appointed, whose responsibility was to clean the **blackboard** before the teacher came in.

Special Expressions

the life of the party **הרוּחַ** החיה
ghost **רוּחַ** רפאים
the Holy **Ghost** **רוּחַ** הקודש
crazy, demented חולה **רוּחַ**

Additional Examples in this Pattern

report דוּחַ
wind, breeze; soul; spirit; essence רוּחַ

---

249. ***CuC***: mono-syllabic nouns in which וּ is maintained throughout and the plural form follows the same pattern as the segholates

our/your/their	my/your/his/her	const.	Gloss	sing/pl
שׁוּקֵנוּ/קְכֶם/קְכֶן/קָם/קָן	שׁוּקִי/שׁוּקְךָ/שׁוּקֵךְ/שׁוּקוֹ/שׁוּקָהּ	שׁוּק-	market	שׁוּק ז'
שְׁוָקֵינוּ/**שׁוּקֵי**כֶם/כֶן/הֶם/הֶן	**שְׁוָ**קַי/קֶיךָ/קַיִךְ/קָיו/קֶיהָ	שׁוּקֵי-		שְׁוָקִים

In the plural form, *u* turns into the consonant *v*, in a pattern that characterizes segholate forms, except where it occurs two syllables away from the main stress: שׁוּקֵיכֶם etc.

Notes: Although שׁוֹר has וֹ and not וּ, its declension is similar. Alongside דְּוָדִים one also encounters דּוּדִים.

Examples

בכל יום שבת מתקיים כאן **שוּק** של איכרים המוכרים את מוצריהם החקלאיים.
Every Saturday there's a farmers' **market** here, where agricultural products are sold.

כאשר **שוּק** המניות אינו יציב, רבים מעדיפים להשקיע בנכסי דלא-ניידי.
When the stock **market** is unstable, many prefer to invest in real estate.

Special Expressions

market share פֶּלח **שוּק**
capital **market** **שוּק** ההון
black **market** **שוּק** שחור
flea **market** **שוּק** פִּשְׁפְּשִׁים

Additional Examples in this Pattern

ox שׁוֹר   vat; water tank; boiler דּוּד

---

250. ***CuC_iiC_i***: bisyllabic nouns derived from monosyllabic nouns in which the last consonant is reduplicated

our/your/their	my/your/his/her	const.	gloss	sing/pl
גוּפִיֵנוּ/פְּכֶם/פְּכֶן/פָּם/פָּן	גוּפִיפִי/גוּפִיפְךָ/גוּפִיפֵךְ/גוּפִיפוֹ/גוּפִיפָהּ	גוּפִיף-	cell,	גוּפִיף ז׳
גוּפִיֵינוּ/כֶם/כֶן/הֶם/הֶן	**גוּפִי**פַי/פֶיךָ/פַיִךְ/פָיו/פֶיהָ	גוּפִיפֵי-	corpuscle	גוּפִיפִים

Examples

בדמו של כל יצור חי מצויים **גוּפִיפִים** אדומים ו**גוּפִיפִים** לבנים.
In the blood of any living being there are red **corpuscles** and white **corpuscles**.

---

251. ***CiC***: mono-syllabic nouns in which a *Hirik male* ִי is maintained throughout

our/your/their	my/your/his/her	const.	Gloss	sing/pl
מִיֵנוּ/נְכֶם/נְכֶן/נָם/נָן	מִינִי/מִינְךָ/מִינֵךְ/מִינוֹ/מִינָהּ	מִין-	kind; gender,	מִין ז׳
מִינֵינוּ/כֶם/כֶן/הֶם/הֶן	מִינַי/מִינֶיךָ/מִינַיִךְ/מִינָיו/מִינֶיהָ	מִינֵי-	sex; heretic	מִינִים

Some exceptions in plural forms: אִישׁ ~ אֲנָשִׁים 'man ~ people (rather than 'men'),' עִיר ~ עָרִים 'city,' and at least one item which can end with either ִים– or וֹת–:
רִיב 'quarrel' ~ רִיבִים ~ רִיבוֹת

Examples

השפן והארנב הם שני **מִינִים** שונים של יונקים.
The hyrax and the rabbit are two different **kinds/species** of mammals.

המילה 'עיר' היא מ**מִין** נקבה, למרות שאינה מסתיימת ב-ה'.
The word for 'town' is of the feminine **gender**, although it does not end with ה׳.

הספרים הפופולאריים ביותר היום הם אלה העוסקים ב**מִין** בעולם הפוליטיקה.
The most popular books today are those dealing with **sex** in the world of politics.

מגילה שכתבה גוי או **מִין** פסולה.
A scroll written by a non-Jew or **heretic** is disqualified.

התחלתי לקרוא ספרות קלאסית ב**גִיל** מוקדם מאוד. בכיתה ו' כבר קראתי את "מלחמה ושלום" של טולסטוי.
I began to read classical literature at a very early **age**. When in sixth grade I already read Tolstoy's "War and Peace."

היה לנו מורה אחד בבית הספר היסודי, שאם מישהו לא היה מקשיב בזמן השיעור, הוא היה זורק עליו חתיכת **גִיר**.
We had a teacher at elementary school who, if any was not paying attention in class, he would throw a piece of **chalk** at him.

ארה״ב מעוניינת לרכוש את ״כיפת ברזל״, מערכת ההגנה נגד **טִילִים** שפותחה בישראל.
The US is interested in buying “Iron Dome”, the anti-**missile** defense system developed in Israel.

אומרים ש**מִיץ** רימונים טוב מאוד לבריאות, אבל עוד יותר טוב לאכול את הפרי עצמו.
They say that pomegranate **juice** is very good for your health, but it is even healthier to eat the fruit itself.

Special Expressions

argument **דִּין** ודברים
report, account **דִּין** וחשבון
disciplinary **trial** **דִּין** משמעתי
divine **justice** **דִּין** שמיים
guided **missile** **טִיל** מונחה
homing **missile** **טִיל** מתביית

four **species**, varieties ארבעת **הַמִּינִים** (Sukkoth)
the human **species** **הַמִּין** האנושי
of the same **kind** בן-**מִינוֹ**
one of a **kind** יחיד **בְּמִינוֹ**

Additional Examples in this Pattern

man (pl. *'anashim*, from אִישׁ ר׳ אֲנָשִׁים *'enosh > 'insh > 'ish*
sewer, drain בִּיב
tendon גִּיד
brother-in-law גִּיס
law דִּין
pen (for animals) דִּיר
protuberance זִיז
gill זִים
bristle N זִיף
spark זִיק
pocket כִּיס
great-grandson נִין
fiber סִיב
cooking pot סִיר

---

252. ***CiC***: mono-syllabic nouns in which a *Hirik male* ִי is maintained throughout and the final consonant is a guttural

our/your/their	my/your/his/her	const.	Gloss	sing/pl
שִׂיחֵנוּ/חֲכֶם/חֲכֶן/חָם/חָן	שִׂיחִי/שִׂיחֲךָ/שִׂיחֵךְ/שִׂיחוֹ/שִׂיחָהּ	שִׂיחַ-	bush;	שִׂיחַ ז׳
שִׂיחֵינוּ/כֶם/כֶן/הֶם/הֶן	שִׂיחַי/שִׂיחֶיךָ/שִׂיחַיִךְ/שִׂיחָיו/שִׂיחֶיהָ	שִׂיחֵי-	discourse	שִׂיחִים

Word-finally, a “furtive” *pataH* precedes a guttural (since the preceding vowel is not *a*). When a *shva* is expected with the guttural, it is replaced with a *Hataf-pataH*.

Examples

אחרי חיפושים רבים מצאתי את החתולה רובצת מתחת **לְשִׂיחַ**.
After considerable search, I found the cat lying underneath a **bush**.

בלשנים רבים עוסקים היום בחקר **הַשִּׂיחַ**.
Many linguists today work on **discourse** analysis.

Special Expressions

dialogue דּוּ-**שִׂיחַ**
exchange of words שִׂיג **וָשִׂיחַ**

Additional Examples in this Pattern

movement Lit. נִיעַ phlegm כִּיחַ plaster N טִיחַ flutter זִיעַ

---

253. ***CiC***: mono-syllabic nouns in which *Hirik male* ִי is maintained throughout, and the plural suffix is *-ot*

our/your/their	my/your/his/her	const.	gloss	sing/pl
קִירֵנוּ/קִירְכֶם/ן/קִירָם/ן	קִירִי/קִירְךָ/קִירֵךְ/קִירוֹ/קִירָהּ	קִיר-	wall	קִיר ז'
קִירוֹתֵינוּ/כֶם/כֶן/הֶם/הֶן	**קִירוֹ**תַי/תֶיךָ/תַיִךְ/תָיו/תֶיהָ	קִירוֹת-		קִירוֹת

Examples

כשמשפצים דירה טרומית, יש לוודא שלא יוסרו **קִירוֹת** תומכים.
When remodeling a prefabricated apartment, one needs to make sure that no supporting **walls** be removed.

Special Expressions

warning כתובת על ה**קִיר**
gave him no options לחץ אותו אל ה**קִיר**
made every possible effort; had no idea what else to do טיפס על **קִירוֹת**

---

254. ***CeyC***: nouns in which *tsere male* ֵי is maintained throughout the declension

our/your/their	my/your/his/her	const.	Gloss	sing/pl
אֵידֵנוּ/דְכֶם/דְכֶן/דָם/דָן	אֵידִי/אֵידְךָ/אֵידֵךְ/אֵידוֹ/אֵידָהּ	אֵיד-	misfortune;	אֵיד ז'
אֵידֵינוּ/כֶם/כֶן/הֶם/הֶן	אֵידַי/אֵידֶיךָ/אֵידַיִךְ/אֵידָיו/אֵידֶיהָ	אֵידֵי-	gentile holiday	אֵידִים

Examples

"בנפול אויבך אל תשמח" – המקרא שולל שמחה ל**אֵיד**, אפילו שמחה ל**אֵידוֹ** של האויב.
"Do not rejoice when your enemy falls" – the Bible rejects rejoicing at ones **demise**, even at the **misfortune** of the enemy.

"כנענים עובדי כוכבים ומזלות הם, ויום ראשון הוא יום **אֵידָם**" (רמב"ם)
"Canaanites are star worshippers, and Sunday is their **holiday**" (Maimonides)

Additional Examples in this Pattern

bosom חֵיק

---

255. ***CeyC***: nouns in which ֵי is maintained throughout the declension, when the plural suffix is וֹת- and the final consonant is guttural

our/your/their	my/your/his/her	const.	Gloss	sing/pl
רֵיחֵנוּ/חֲכֶם/חֲכֶן/חָם/חָן	רֵיחִי/רֵיחֲךָ/רֵיחֵךְ/רֵיחוֹ/רֵיחָהּ	רֵיחַ-	smell; odor;	רֵיחַ ז'
רֵיחוֹתֵינוּ/כֶם/כֶן/הֶם/הֶן	**רֵיחוֹ**תַי/תֶיךָ/תַיִךְ/תָיו/תֶיהָ	רֵיחוֹת-	smattering	רֵיחוֹת

The final guttural is preceded by a *furtive pataH*, since the preceding vowel is not *a*. Where a *shva* is expected with the guttural, it is replaced by a *Hataf-pataH*.

Examples

הבוֹאֶשׁ הוא בעל חיים יפהפה, אבל **הָרֵיחַ** שהוא מפיק...
The skunk is a very pretty animal, but the **odor** it produces...

חוש הטעם קשור לחוש **הָרֵיחַ**.
The sense of taste is related to the sense of **smell**.

כאשר פוליטיקאי נוסע נסיעות פרטיות על חשבון הציבור, יש בכך **רֵיחַ** של שחיתות.
When a politician travels privately at the public's expense, it has a **smattering** of corruption.

Special Expressions

בלי טעם ובלי **רֵיחַ** tasteless, boring
חוש **הָרֵיחַ** the sense of **smell**
הבאיש את **רֵיחוֹ** של... besmirch someone
רֵיחַ ניחוחַ very pleasant **smell**

Q. Bi-syllabic *mishkalim*
(but also including monosyllabic ones with an initial cluster and some isolated tri-syllabic ones) without affixes, or with non-transparent ones

256. ***CaCi***: nouns ending with ִי and where the preceding *kamats* is reduced in the declension

sing/pl	Gloss	const.	my/your/his/her	our/your/their
צְלִי ז'	roast	צְלִי-	צְלִיִי/צְלִיךָ/צְלִיֵךְ/צְלִיוֹ/צְלִיָהּ	צְלִיֵנוּ/צְלִיכֶם/כֶן/צְלִיָם/ן
צְלָיִים	meat	צְלָיֵי-	**צְלָ**יַי/יֶיךָ/יַיִךְ/יָיו/יֶיהָ	**צְלָיֵי**נוּ/כֶם/כֶן/הֶם/הֶן

Most of the forms are derived from roots in which the third consonant is י. The *kamats* is reduced to *shva* two syllables before the main stress. When a quiescent *shva* is expected in a י, that י is weakened to a vowel: צְלִיךָ < צְלְיְךָ*. When the first consonant is a guttural, the *kamats* is reduced to a *Hataf-pataH*: עֲנִי- < עְנִי-*, etc.

Examples

צְלִי כבש הוא מאכל אהוב במזרח התיכון.
Lamb **roast** is a popular dish in the Middle East.

Special Expressions

צְלִי אֵשׁ roast meat (on fire)
צְלִי שפוד kebab
צְלִי קְדֵרה pot roast (no liquid added)

Additional Examples in this Pattern

עָנִי pauper; poor
קָלִי toast N
שָׁנִי scarlet

---

257. ***CCi/CeCi***: bi-consonantal nouns ending with ִי and where the first consonant is, generally, followed by a *shva* or *seghol*, and in the declension by a *Hiriq Haser* or *seghol*

our/your/their	my/your/his/her	const.	gloss	sing/pl
גְּדְיֵנוּ/**גֶּדְיְכֶם**/כֶן (**גְּדִיכֶם**/כֶן)/גִּדְיָם/ן	גִּדְיִי/גֶּדְיְךָ/**גִּדְיֵךְ**/יוֹ/יָהּ	-גְּדִי	kid	גְּדִי ז'
גְּדָיֵינוּ/כֶם/כֶן/הֶם/הֶן	**גְּדָיַי**/יֶיךָ/יַיִךְ/יָיו/יֶיהָ	-גְּדָיֵי	(m.)	גְּדָיִים

Most of the forms are derived from roots in which the third consonant is י. The *Hiriq Haser* is replaced by *seghol* in some 2nd person forms with stress shift. In most cases, the plural form (when it exists) follows the segholate plural pattern. In speech, at least in two forms, the pausal form also sometimes alternates with the isolation form: בְּכִי/בֶּכִי 'crying,' תְּלִי/תֶּלִי 'hanger.' An initial *seghol* is stressed when pre-pausal.

Examples

הַגְּדִי הוא מטפורה שכיחה לילד.
The **kid** is a common metaphor for a child.

Special Expressions

גְּדָיִים נעשו תְּיָשִׁים the **kids** have grown up

מזל **גְּדִי** Capricorn

חוג הַ**גְּדִי** Tropic of Capricorn

Special declension with a different plural form: כְּלִי ~ כֵּלִים 'tool,' פְּרִי ~ פֵּרוֹת 'fruit.'

our/your/their	my/your/his/her	const.	Gloss	sing/pl
כֶּלְיֵנוּ/**כֶּלְיְכֶם**/כֶן (**כְּלִיכֶם**/כֶן) /**כֶּלְיָם**/ן	כֶּלְיִי/כֶּלְיְךָ/**כֶּלְיֵךְ**/יוֹ/יָהּ	-כְּלִי	tool; article;	כְּלִי ז'
כֵּלֵינוּ/**כְּלֵיכֶם**/כֶן/הֶם/הֶן	**כֵּלַי**/לֶיךָ/לַיִךְ/לָיו/לֶיהָ	-כְּלֵי	vessel	כֵּלִים

Note: In the declension of דְּלִי 'bucket,' a *kamats* surfaces in singular forms with possessive suffixes: ...דָּלְיוֹ

Examples

קשה לעשות עבודה מקצועית ללא **כְּלֵי** עבודה מתאימים.
It is hard to do a professional job without appropriate work **tools**.

אני מחפש **כְּלִי** מתאים להחזיק בו את מה שנשאר מן הארוחה הגדולה של הערב.
I am looking for an appropriate **vessel** to hold the leftovers from tonight's big meal.

Special Expressions

כְּלֵי בית house**wares**

כְּלֵי מיתר string **instruments**

כְּלֵי זין weapon

כְּלֵי קודש sacred **objects**; religious officials

Special declension with a different plural form with א׳ instead of י׳:
צְבִי ~ צְבָאִים 'deer,' פֶּתִי ~ פְּתָאִים 'naïve, gullible person.'

sing/pl	Gloss	const.	my/your/his/her	our/your/their
צְבִי ז׳	deer;	צְבִי-	צִבְיִי/צֶבְיְךָ/**צִבְיֵ**ךְ/יוֹ/יָהּ	צִבְיֵנוּ/**צֶבְיְ**כֶם/כֶן (**צְבִי**כֶם/כֶן) /**צִבְיָ**ם/ן
צְבָאִים	splendor	צִבְאֵי-	**צְבָ**אַי/אֶיךָ/אַיִךְ/אָיו/אֶיהָ	**צִבְאֵי**נוּ/כֶם/כֶן/הֶם/הֶן

Examples

מקום מגורנו מוקף יער, ומסתובבים בו לא מעט **צְבָאִים**.
Our place of residence is surrounded by forest, in which a number of **deer** roam.

ארץ ישראל כונתה גם בעבר "ארץ **הַצְּבִי**".
The Land of Israel was also referred to as "The Land of **Splendor**".

Special Expressions

attribute for the Land of Israel ארץ **הַצְּבִי**
invested money in a doubtful enterprise הניח מעותיו על קרן **הַצְּבִי**

Additional Examples in this Pattern

- crying בְּכִי/בֶּכִי
- bucket דְּלִי
- dropper טְפִי
- rebellion מְרִי
- silk מֶשִׁי
- fruit פְּרִי
- gullible, naïve person פֶּתִי
- accidental ejection of sperm קֶרִי
- captivity שְׁבִי
- warp (weaving) שְׁתִי
- hanger; arrow quiver תְּלִי/תֶּלִי

---

258. *CCi/CeCi/CaCi*: bi-consonantal nouns ending with ִי and where the first consonant is a guttural

sing/pl	Gloss	const.	my/your/his/her	our/your/their
עֲדִי ז׳	adornment,	עֲדִי-	**עֶדְ**יִי/יְךָ/יֵךְ/יוֹ/יָהּ	**עֶדְ**יֵנוּ/יְכֶם/יְכֶן (**עֲדִי**כֶם/כֶן) /**עֶדְ**יָם/ן
עֲדָיִים	jewel	עֲדָיֵי-	**עֲדָ**יַי/יֶיךָ/יַיִךְ/יָיו/יֶיהָ	**עֲדָיֵי**נוּ/כֶם/כֶן/הֶם/הֶן

sing/pl	Gloss	const.	my/your/his/her	our/your/their
אֲרִי ז׳	lion	אֲרִי-	**אַרְ**יִי/יְךָ/יֵךְ/יוֹ/יָהּ	**אַרְ**יֵנוּ/יְכֶם/יְכֶן (**אֲרִי**כֶם/כֶן) /**אַרְ**יָם/ן
אֲרָיוֹת		אַרְיוֹת-	**אַרְיוֹ**תַי/תֶיךָ/תַיִךְ/תָיו/תֶיהָ	**אַרְיוֹתֵי**נוּ/כֶם/כֶן/הֶם/הֶן

Most of the forms are derived from roots in which the third consonant is י׳. The *shva* expected with the guttural is replaced by a *Hataf pataH*, and in the forms with possessive pronouns, a *Hiriq* is replaced by a *seghol* or by a *pataH*. In most cases, the plural form (when it exists) follows the segholate plural pattern.

Notes: In the form עֱלִי 'pestle, pistil,' the *shva* expected with the guttural is replaced by a *Hataf-seghol*. The plural form of אֲרִי 'lion' is אֲרָיוֹת. The plural form of חֲצִי 'half' is חֲצָאִים or חֲצָיִים. In pausal position, the singular form is penultimately-stressed חֵצִי.

Examples

בעברית הספרותית משתמשים במונח "**עֲדָיִים**" במקום "תכשיטים".
In literary Hebrew they use the term "**adornments**" for "jewelry."

Special Expressions

precious **jewels** **עֲדִי עֲדָיִים**

Additional Examples in this Pattern

half חֲצִי/חֵצִי

pestle; pistil (Bot.) עֱלִי

---

259. ***CCi/CeCi***: bi-consonantal nouns ending with ִי and where the second consonant is a guttural

our/your/their	my/your/his/her	const.	Gloss	sing/pl
לֶחְיֵנוּ/יְכֶם/יְכֶן/יָם/יָן	**לֶחְ**יִי/יְךָ/יֵךְ/יוֹ/יָהּ	לְחִי-	cheek; jaw;	לְחִי/לֶחִי ז'
לְחָיֵינוּ/כֶם/כֶן/הֶם/הֶן	**לְחָ**יַי/יֶיךָ/יַיִךְ/יָיו/יֶיהָ	לְחָיֵי-	yoke-rope	לְחָיַיִם

Most of the forms are derived from roots in which the third consonant is י״. When the second consonant is a guttural, the *Hiriq* is replaced by a *seghol* in a closed syllable. The plural form of שֶׁחִי 'armpit' is שְׁחָיִים; and the plural forms of לְחִי 'cheek' and of מְעִי 'intestine' follow the dual pattern: לְחָיַיִם , מֵעַיִים.

Examples

למרות שהוא צעיר מאוד, נראית כבר חתימת זקן על **לְחָיָיו**.
Although he is very young, one already sees signs of a beard on his **cheeks**.

Special Expressions

he will never live so long **יעלו עשבים בִּלְחָיָיו**

slap in the face **סטירת לֶחִי**

Additional Examples in this Pattern

failure (דְּחִי(/דֶּחִי

clap, stroke מְחִי

intestine מְעִי

lamentation נְהִי

filth סְחִי

mirror רְאִי

grazing; grazing cattle רְעִי

armpit שֶׁחִי

---

260. ***CeCe***: generally adjectives and some nouns related to roots whose last consonant is *y*

our/your/their	my/your/his/her	const.	Gloss	sing/pl
גֵּאֵנוּ/**גְּאֵ**כֶם/כֶן/**גֵּאָ**ם/ן	**גֵּ**אִי/אֲךָ/אֵךְ/אוֹ (אֵהוּ) /אָהּ (אֶהָ)	גְּאֵה-	gay; proud	גֵּאֶה ז'
גֵּאֵינוּ/**גְּאֵי**כֶם/כֶן/הֶם/הֶן	**גֵּ**אַי/אֶיךָ/אַיִךְ/אָיו/אֶיהָ	גְּאֵי-	person	גֵּאִים

Most of the forms are derived from roots in which the third consonant is י. When a *shva* is expected with a guttural, it is replaced by *Hataf-pataH*. When the form is an adjective, the declension is:

Construct	f. sing/pl	Construct	m. sing/pl	Gloss
גְּאַת-	גֵּאָה נ׳	גְּאֵה-	גֵּאֶה ז׳	proud
גְּאוֹת-	גֵּאוֹת	גְּאֵי-	גֵּאִים	

Examples

גֵּאִים כמוהו תמיד בטוחים שהם יודעים הכל טוב מכולם.
Conceited people like him are always sure that they know everything better than anybody.

מצעד הגאווה של **הַגֵּאִים** מתקיים כל שנה גם בישראל.
The pride parade of the **gay community** takes place annually in Israel as well.

אין לו ״גרוש על הנשמה״, אבל הוא **גֵּאֶה** מדיי מכדי לקבל נדבה.
He does not have a penny to his name, but he is too **proud** to accept a handout.

אפילו תאומים בדרך כלל אינם **זֵהִים** בכל פן; לפחות באישיות ניתן להבחין בהבדלים.
Even twins are not totally **identical** in every facet; one can notice differences at least in personality.

טוענים שלבוש בהיר או **כֵּהֶה** מְשַׁנֶּה אם אדם עשוי להיראות בעיני אחרים כשמן או רזה יותר מכפי שהוא באמת.
It is claimed that being dressed in light or **dark** clothing affects whether one is seen by others as fatter or thinner than s/he actually is.

Additional Examples in this Pattern

blunt, dull קֵהֶה   tired לֵאֶה

---

261. ***CaCe***: nouns with the plural ending *-im*

our/your/their	my/your/his/her	const.	Gloss	sing/pl
קָנֵנוּ/**קְנֵ**כֶם/כֶן/**קָנָ**ם/ן	**קָנִ**י/נְךָ/נֵךְ/נוֹ (נֵהוּ) /נָהּ (נֶהָ)	קְנֵה-	stalk; barrel;	קָנֶה ז׳
קָנֵינוּ/**קְנֵי**כֶם/כֶן/הֶם/הֶן	**קָנַ**י/נֶיךָ/נַיִךְ/נָיו/נֶיהָ	קְנֵי-	windpipe; cane	קָנִים

Most of the forms are derived from roots in which the third consonant is ״י. In the construct state and when two syllables away from the main stress, the *kamats* is reduced to *shva*.
Note: the plural of טָלֶה 'lamb' is טְלָאִים (טְלָאֵי-, טְלָאַי...)

Examples

בדגניים, **הַקָּנֶה** הוא הגבעול הנושא את הפרחים.
In the wheat family, the **stalk** carries the flowers.

קְנֵה הרובה חייב להיות נקי ויבש כדי לפעול כראוי.
The **barrel** of the gun must be clean and dry in order to function properly.

נְוֵה מדבר הוא שטח בלב המדבר שיש בו מקור מים, המשמש בית גידול לבעלי חיים ומוקד משיכה לאדם.
An **oasis** is an area in the heart of the desert with a water source, which serves as a habitat for animals and attracts humans.

כל מלחמה משאירה אחריה **נְכִים** רבים.
Every war leaves many **hadicapped persons** behind it.

Special Expressions

scale, measuring **rod** **קְנֵה** מידה

gun **barrel** **קְנֵה** רובה

sugar **cane** **קְנֵה** סוכר

undistinguished person קוטל **קָנִים**

Additional Examples in this Pattern

shovel, dustpan יָעֶה

---

262. ***CaCe***: nouns with the plural ending ים-, when the first consonant is guttural

sing/pl	Gloss	const.	my/your/his/her	our/your/their
עָלֶה ז׳	leaf	עֲלֵה-	**עָ**לִי/לְךָ/לֵךְ/לוֹ (לֵהוּ) /לָהּ (לֶהָ)	עָלֵנוּ/**עֲ**לֵכֶם/כֶן/**עָ**לָם/ן
עָלִים		עֲלֵי-	**עָ**לַי/לֶיךָ/לַיִךְ/לָיו/לֶיהָ	עָלֵינוּ/**עֲלֵי**כֶם/כֶן/הֶם/הֶן

When a *shva* is expected, a *Hataf* will show up instead: עֲלֵה-, עֲלֵי-, עֲלֵיכֶם.

Examples

בארה״ב ובאירופה כמות ה**עָלִים** שיש לפנות בסתיו היא עצומה.
In the US and in Europe, one needs to clear huge amounts of **leaves** in the fall.

Special Expressions

petal **עֲלֵה** כותרת

fig **leaf**, covering, mask **עֲלֵה** תאנה

Additional Examples in this Pattern

bract (Bot.) חָפֶה

sacrum עָצֶה

---

263. ***CaCe***: nouns with the plural suffix *-ot*

sing/pl	Gloss	const.	my/your/his/her	our/your/their
שָׂדֶה ז׳	field	שְׂדֵה-	**שָׂ**דִי/דְךָ/דֵךְ/דוֹ (דֵהוּ) /דָהּ (דֶהָ)	שָׂדֵנוּ/**שְׂדֵ**כֶם/כֶן/**שָׂדָ**ם/ן
שָׂדוֹת		שְׂדוֹת-	**שְׂדוֹ**תַי/תֶיךָ/תַיִךְ/תָיו/תֶיהָ	**שְׂדוֹתֵי**נוּ/כֶם/כֶן/הֶם/הֶן

Most of the forms are derived from roots in which the 3rd consonant is *y*.
Note: קָצֶה edge, end, extremity, pl. קְצָווֹת, קְצוֹת-/קַצְוֵי-

Examples

שָׂדוֹת רבים בישראל הפכו עם השנים לאזורי בנייה.
Many **fields** in Israel have become development areas through the years.

הוא היה מוכן ללכת אחריה עד **קְצֵה** העולם.
He was willing to follow her to the **end** of the world.

Special Expressions

שְׂדֵה בּוּר fallow **land**
חיית **הַשָּׂדֶה** wild animals
שְׂדֵה קרב/קטל battle**field**
שְׂדֵה תעופה air**field**

---

264. *CaCe*: nouns with the plural ending *-ot*, when the first root consonant is guttural

our/your/their	my/your/his/her	const.	Gloss	sing/pl
חָזֵנוּ/**חֲזֵ**כֶם/כֶן/**חָזָ**ם/ן	**חָזִ**י/זְךָ/זֵךְ/זוֹ (זֵהוּ) /זָהּ (זֶהָ)	-חֲזֵה	chest,	חָזֶה ז׳
חֲזוֹתֵינוּ/כֶם/כֶן/הֶם/הֶן	**חֲזוֹתַ**י/תֶיךָ/תַיִךְ/תָיו/תֶיהָ	-חֲזוֹת	breast	חָזוֹת

As in שָׂדֶה above, but when a *shva* is expected with a guttural, a *Hataf* will replace it.

Examples

דוקטור, יש לי כאבים חזקים **בֶּחָזֶה**!
Doctor, I have strong pains in my **chest**!

Special Expressions

בית **הֶחָזֶה** thorax
עצם **הֶחָזֶה** breast bone

---

265. *CaCe*: adjectives derived from verbs with *y* as the last root consonant

Construct	f. sing/pl	Construct	m. sing/pl	Gloss
-יְפַת	יָפָה נ׳	-יְפֵה	יָפֶה ז׳	beautiful
-יְפוֹת	יָפוֹת	-יְפֵי	יָפִים	

Examples

...ורחל הייתה יְפַת-תואר ויפַת מראה (בראשית כט:יז).
And Rachel was pretty and good looking (Gen 29:17).

ראיתי הרבה נשים **יָפוֹת** בטיול האחרון שלנו באירופה.
I saw many **beautiful** women during our last trip to Europe.

אומרים שהמועמד החדש לראשות הממשלה הוא גבר **נָאֶה**. על טעם וריח אין להתווכח...
They say that the new candidate for the Prime Minister's position is a **hansome** man. Everyone has their taste...

קָשֶׁה להאמין עד כמה מצבה הכלכלי של ונצואלה **קָשֶׁה** – מדינה שבעבר הייתה כה עשירה.
It is **hard** to believe how **difficult** the economic situation in Venezuela is – a country which used to be so rich in the past.

מתוך מאבק מתמיד כדי להישאר **רָזוֹת**, יש דוגמניות שחולות באנורקסיה.
Owing to a continuous struggle to stay **slim**, some models get sick with anorexia.

Special Expressions

belles-lettres, fiction ספרות **יָפָה**
generously (ב)עין **יָפָה**
good looking **יְפֵה** תואר
he **likes** it **יָפֶה** בעיניו
sensitive, delicate; gentle soul; bleeding heart **יְפֵה**-נפש
slow-witted **קְשֵׁה** הבנה/תפיסה
work **weary**, downtrodden **קְשֵׁה** יום

unbearable **קָשֶׁה** מנשוא
stiff-necked, stubborn **קְשֵׁה** עורף
hard of hearing **קְשֵׁה** שמיעה
having **equal** rights **שְׁוֵה** זכויות
apathetic **שְׁוֵה** נפש
suitable for everyone; affordable **שָׁוֶה** לכל נפש
money's worth; valuable **שְׁוֵה** כסף

Additional Examples in this Pattern

worn out Lit. בָּלֶה
painful דָּוֶה
befitting יָאֶה
short-lived; yearning כָּלֶה

swollen צָבֶה
quenched רָוֶה
weak, limp; lax רָפֶה
equal; worth שָׁוֶה

---

266. ***CaCe***: adjectives, when the 1st root consonant is guttural

Construct	f. sing/pl	construct	m. sing/pl	Gloss
עֲבַת-	עָבָה נ'	עֲבֵה-	עָבֶה ז'	thick
עֲבוֹת-	עָבוֹת	עֲבֵי-	עָבִים	

When a *shva* is expected with a guttural, a *Hataf* will replace it.

Examples

כשהתקרב, ראה שפניה מכוסות בשכבה **עָבָה** של איפור.
When he got closer, he saw that her face was covered with a **thick** layer of makeup.

Special Expressions

low (= **thick**) voice, consisting mostly of low tones קול **עָבֶה**

---

267. ***CaCaC***: nouns and some adjectives with the plural suffix *–im* where the first *kamats* is reduced in the declension

our/your/their	my/your/his/her	const.	Gloss	sing/pl
דְּבָרֵנוּ/**דְּבַרְ**כֶם/כֶן/**דְּבָרָ**ם/ן	**דְּבָ**רִי/רְךָ/רֵךְ/רוֹ/רָהּ	-דְּבַר	thing, object;	דָּבָר ז'
דְּבָרֵינוּ/**דִּבְרֵי**כֶם/כֶן/הֶם/הֶן	**דְּבָ**רַי/רֶיךָ/רַיִךְ/רָיו/רֶיהָ	-דִּבְרֵי	word, saying	דְּבָרִים

Construct	f. sing/pl	construct	m. sing/pl	Gloss
-שִׁפְלַת	שְׁפָלָה נ'	-שְׁפַל	שָׁפָל ז'	low;
-שִׁפְלוֹת	שְׁפָלוֹת	-שִׁפְלֵי	שְׁפָלִים	worthless

In nouns and adjectives there is a strong tendency to the reduce or completely elide the vowel *a* in an unstressed syllable two syllables away from the main stress, **davarím* 'things' > *dvarím*, *shafalá* 'low, f.s.' > *shfalá*. The reduction also applies to the construct state, since the construct is considered as non-stress-bearing morpheme. The *a* or *i* split an impermissible sequence of two *shva* mobiles; the first is replaced by *pataH* or *Hirik*, and the second closes the syllable: **dv*^{e}*r*^{e}*khem* > *dvar-khem*, **sh*^{e}*f*^{e}*lat-* > *shif-lat-*, etc. The historical motivation for reduction has lost some of its phonetic validity, but the phonological rule is maintained. In Israeli Hebrew reduction means complete vowel loss, except for cases in which we need to split a consonant cluster that is impossible, or very difficult, to articulate, with the "minimal" vowel *e*, as in **nHashim* 'snakes' > *neHashim*, **lvanim* 'white, m.pl.' > *levanim*.

Note: the plural of כָּנָף 'wing (fem.)' is a dual, כְּנָפַיִם, or כְּנָפוֹת (כַּנְפוֹת-).

Examples

על שלושה **דְּבָרִים** העולם עומד: על התורה, על העבודה, ועל גמילות חסדים.
The world stands on three **things** (principles): learning, work (worship?) and charity.

הוא הקשיב ל**דְבָרַי**, אבל נראה לי שלא הבין **דָּבָר**.
He listened to **my words**, but I do not think he understood **anything**.

חלק מן השרפות הגדולות נגרמו על ידי השלכה חסרת-אחריות של **בְּדָל** סיגריה שלא כובה.
Some of the largest fires were caused by irresponsible throwing of an unextinguished cigarette **butt**.

הנשק שבו השתמש זאוס כאמצעי ענישה היה ה**בָּרָק**.
The weapon Zeus used as a means of punishment was **lightning**.

קשה לי להבין את אופנת ה**זְּקָנִים** הנהוגה היום, במיוחד זו המזכירה את הטאליבאן.
It is difficult for me to appreciate the **beards** fashion of today, especially that which reminds one of the Taliban.

הנעליים הטובות ביותר מיוצרות באיטליה, אך הן גם **יְקָרוֹת** מדיי לאמריקאי הממוצע.
The best shoes are mamufactured in Italy, but there are also too **expensive** for average American.

בדרך כלל, ככל שיין אדום **יָשָׁן** יותר הוא טוב יותר – כל עוד הוא נשמר בטמפרטורה מתאימה.
Generally, the **old**er red wine the better it is – as long as it is kept in appropriate temperature.

Special Expressions

בְּדַל סיגריה cigarette **butt**
בְּשַׂר ודם human being, flesh and **blood**
בְּשַׂר מבשרו relative, kinsman
אין **דָּבָר** never mind
דְּבַר מה **something**, a trifle
דְּבָרִים שבינו לבינה **matters** between a man and a woman
לאמיתו של **דָּבָר** the truth of the **matter** is
על לא **דָּבָר** not at all (reply to thanks), for **nothing**
יְקַר המציאות **rare**, hard to find

יְקַר ערך precious
יָשָׁן נושן ancient, very **old**
יָשָׁר לעניין **straight** to the point
לָבָן כשלג **white** as snow
קָצָר ולעניין/וקולע **short** and sweet
קָצָר המצע מהשתרע it is impossible to cover it all
רְחַב ידיים **wide** open, expansive
רְחַב אופקים **broad**-minded
שְׁפַל קוֹמָה **short** (of short height)
שְׁפַל רוח modest, unassuming

Additional Examples in this Pattern

בָּצָל onion
בָּשָׂר flesh; meat
דָּגָן cereal; grain
זָכָר male
טָרָף blade (Bot.)
יָבָם brother-in-law Lit
יָשָׁר straight; honest
נָדָל centipede
כָּזָב lie N

לָבָן white
מָרָק soup
מָשָׁל fable
פָּרָג poppy
צָלָף caper (plant)
קָצָר short
רָחָב broad
רָשָׁע evil person
שָׁפָל low; despicable

---

268. ***CaCaC***: nouns and some adjectives with the plural suffix *–im* where the first *kamats* following a guttural is reduced in the declension to a *Hataf pataH*

our/your/their	my/your/his/her	const.	Gloss	sing/pl
אֲסָמֵנוּ/**אֲסַמְ**כֶם/כֶן/**אֲסָמָ**ם/ן	**אֲסָ**מִי/מְךָ/מֵךְ/מוֹ/מָהּ	אֲסָם-	granary	אָסָם ז'
אֲסָמֵינוּ/**אַסְמֵי**כֶם/כֶן/הֶם/הֶן	**אֲסָ**מַי/מֶיךָ/מַיִךְ/מָיו/מֶיהָ	אַסְמֵי-		אֲסָמִים

Construct	f. sing/pl	Construct	m. sing/pl	Gloss
חִזְקַת -	חֲזָקָה נ'	חֲזַק -	חָזָק ז'	strong
חִזְקוֹת -	חֲזָקוֹת	חִזְקֵי -	חֲזָקִים	

In nouns and adjectives there is a strong tendency to the reduce the vowel *a* in an unstressed syllable two syllables away from the main stress (see above). When the first consonant is a guttural, the expected *shva* is replaced by a *Hataf-pataH*, אְסָמִים* < אֲסָמִים. When, as a consequence of reduction, one expects a hard-to-articulate sequence of *Hataf* immediately followed by a *shva* the *Hataf* is replaced by *pataH* in a syllable closed by a *shva* quiescent: אַסְ-מֵי-כֶם < אֲסְמֵיכֶם* < אֲסָמֵיכֶם*.

Examples

מלאו **אֲסָמֵינוּ** בר, יקבינו יין... (מתוך פזמון ישראלי)
Our **granaries** are full of wheat, our wine cellars (full of) wine… (from an Israeli song)

הרבה עולים **חֲדָשִׁים** הגיעו לישראל ממזרח אירופה כשנפתחו שערי הגוש הסובייטי.
Many **new** immigrants from Eastern Europe arrived in Israel when the gates of the Soviet Union opened.

המתאגרף הזה כבר מבוגר למדי, אבל עדיין **חָזָק** מאוד.
This boxer is pretty old by now, but he is still very **strong**.

בחברות המסורתיות זקני העדה נחשבו תמיד לאנשים **חֲכָמִים**, בשל ניסיון חייהם.
In traditional societies, the community elders were always regarded as **wise** people, due to their life experience.

כשבישראל היו עוד הרבה שִׁקְמִים, אהבנו כילדים לטפס עליהם, ולכל **עָנָף** המצאנו שם, על פי צורתו: "הגמל", "קיר המוות"...
When there were still many sycamores in Israel, we loved to climb them as kids, and we named each **branch** according to its shape: "the Camel," "the Death wall…"

Special Expressions

אֲבַק אדם riffraff, rabble
אֲבַק שוחד **hint** of bribery
אֲבַק שריפה gun**powder**
מֵ**חָדָשׁ** from the beginning, a**new**
חֲדָשִׁים לַבְּקָרים (repeated) every day
חֲזַק אופי having a **strong** character
דגש **חָזָק** gemination mark (long conson.)
חָכָם בלילה "**wise** guy" Coll.
חָכָם לאחר מעשה **wise** after the event
חָלָב עמיד **milk** not requiring refrigeration
חָלָב דל-שומן low-fat/skimmed **milk**
חָלָל ריק vacuum
עָפָר וָאֵפֶר dust = earth and ashes Lit.

Additional Examples in this Pattern

אָבָק dust
אָשָׁם guilt
הָדָר glory
חָגָב grasshopper
חָוָק rung
חָטָט boil, pimp
חָלָב milk
חָלָל outer space; space
חָלָק smooth
עָנָו humble
עָנָן cloud
עָנָף branch
עָפָר earth
עָקָר sterile; futile
עָשָׁן smoke

---

269. ***CaCaC***: nouns with the plural suffix *–im* when the second consonant is a guttural

our/your/their	my/your/his/her	const.	Gloss	sing/pl
נְחָשֵׁנוּ/**נְחַשְׁ**כֶם/כֶן/**נְחָשָׁ**ם/ן	**נְחָ**שִׁי/שְׁךָ/שֵׁךְ/שׁוֹ/שָׁהּ	נְחַשׁ-	snake,	נָחָשׁ ז׳
נְחָשֵׁינוּ/**נַחֲשֵׁי**כֶם/כֶן/הֶם/הֶן	**נְחָ**שַׁי/שֶׁיךָ/שַׁיִךְ/שָׁיו/שֶׁיהָ	נַחֲשֵׁי-	serpent	נְחָשִׁים

In nouns and adjectives there is a strong tendency to the reduce the vowel *a* in an unstressed syllable two syllables away from the main stress (see above). When the second consonant is a guttural, the expected *shva* in the declension of the plural is replaced by a *Hataf-pataH*, נַחֲשֵׁי < -נְחֲשֵׁי* < -נְחָשֵׁי* ‘snakes of’ (The *pataH* in the נ׳ is an echo of the *pataH* in the *Hataf-pataH*, to facilitate articulation). Also, an initial cluster in which the second member is guttural requires *e*-insertion to facilate articulation: /*nHashim*/ > *neHashim*.

Examples

בישראל הצֶפַע הוא **הנָחָשׁ** הארסי והמסוכן ביותר.
In Israel, the most poisonous and most dangerous **snake** is the viper/adder.

הקָהָל מחא כף לשחקנים בתום ההצגה, אבל נראה שעשו זאת מתוך נימוס. ההצגה הייתה גרועה.
The **audience** applauded the actors at the end of the play, but it seems that they did it to be polite. The performance was bad.

Special Expressions

עָרוּם **כְּנָחָשׁ** as cunning and as crafty as a **snake**

קְהַל יעד target **audience**

זְהַב פרוויים the very best Lit.

טוב **שבנְחָשִׁים**, רצץ את מוחו Even (in the case of) the best of **snakes**, smash its brains

Additional Examples in this Pattern

זָהָב gold — קָאָק jackdaw (bird) — רָעָב hunger

---

270. ***CaCaC***: nouns with the plural suffix *-ot* where the first *kamats* is reduced in the declension

our/your/their	my/your/his/her	const.	Gloss	sing/pl
זְנָבֵנוּ/**זְנַבְ**כֶם/כֶן/**זְנָבָ**ם/ן	**זְנָבִ**י/בְךָ/בֵךְ/בוֹ/בָהּ	-זְנַב	tail; end,	זָנָב ז׳
זַנְבוֹתֵינוּ/כֶם/כֶן/הֶם/הֶן	**זַנְבוֹ**תַי/תֶיךָ/תַיִךְ/תָיו/תֶיהָ	-זַנְבוֹת	stump	זְנָבוֹת

our/your/their	my/your/his/her	const.	Gloss	sing/pl
מְטָרֵנוּ/**מְטַרְ**כֶם/כֶן/**מְטָרָ**ם/ן	**מְטָרִ**י/רְךָ/רֵךְ/רוֹ/רָהּ	-מְטַר	rain,	מָטָר
מִטְרוֹתֵינוּ/כֶם/כֶן/הֶם/הֶן	**מִטְרוֹ**תַי/תֶיךָ/תַיִךְ/תָיו/תֶיהָ	-מִטְרוֹת	shower	מְטָרוֹת

In nouns and adjectives there is a strong tendency to the reduce the vowel *a* in an unstressed syllable two syllables away from the main stress, and if, as a result of reduction, an impermissible sequence of two *shva* mobiles might be formed, that sequence is replaced by a *pataH* followed by *shva* (see above): -זַנְבוֹת < -זְנְבוֹת*. The construct form of the plural is also the base for the declension with possessive pronouns, sometimes with a *pataH*, sometimes with a *Hirik*.

Examples

הפרה משתמשת **בזְנָבָהּ** בעיקר כדי לגרש זבובים.
The cow uses its **tail** mostly to drive away flies.

על פי התחזית יֵרדו בסוף השבוע **מְטָרוֹת** כבדים באזור המרכז.
According to the forecast, it will rain heavily in the central region over the weekend (= heavy **showers** will fall).

Special Expressions

הוֵוי **זָנָב** לאריות ואל תהא ראש לשועלים better be a follower of the great than a leader of the lesser

ישב לו על ה**זָנָב**/נצמד ל**זָנָב** שלו attach oneself closely to someone (col.)

retreat (col.) קיפל את ה**זָנָב**

humiliated (col.) עם ה**זָנָב** בין הרגלים

torrential **rain** **מְטָר** סוחֵף

heavy **rains** **מִטְרוֹת** עוֹז

Additional Examples in this Pattern

young of an animal וָלָד   vegetable יָרָק

---

271. ***CaCaC***: nouns with the plural suffix *–ot* where the first *kamats* is reduced in the declension, when the second consonant is a guttural

our/your/their	my/your/his/her	const.	Gloss	sing/pl
נְהָרֵנוּ/**נְהַרְ**כֶם/כֶן/**נְהָרָ**ם/ן	**נְהָרִ**י/רְךָ/רֵךְ/רוֹ/רָהּ	נְהַר-	river	נָהָר ז'
נַהֲרוֹתֵינוּ/כֶם/כֶן/הֶם/הֶן	**נַהֲרוֹ**תַי/תֶיךָ/תַיִךְ/תָיו/תֶיהָ	נַהֲרוֹת-		נְהָרוֹת

In nouns and adjectives there is a strong tendency to the reduce the vowel *a* in an unstressed syllable two syllables away from the main stress (see above). When a *shva* is expected with the (second) guttural, it is replaced by a *Hataf-pataH*.

Examples

נְהַר הירדן משתפך לים המלח.
The Jordan **river** flows into the Dead Sea.

Special Expressions

Mesopotamia (two rivers) ארם **נַהֲרַיִם**

the Milky Way (lit. a river of fire) **נְהַר** די-נוּר

---

272. ***CaCaC***: nouns with the plural suffix *-ot* where the first *kamats* is reduced in the declension, when the third consonant is a guttural

our/your/their	my/your/his/her	const.	Gloss	sing/pl
צְבָאֵנוּ/**צְבַאֲ**כֶם/כֶן/**צְבָאָ**ם/ן	**צְבָאִ**י/אֲךָ/אֵךְ/אוֹ/אָהּ	צְבָא-	army,	צָבָא ז'
צִבְאוֹתֵינוּ/כֶם/כֶן/הֶם/הֶן	**צִבְאוֹ**תַי/תֶיךָ/תַיִךְ/תָיו/תֶיהָ	צִבְאוֹת-	host	צְבָאוֹת

In nouns and adjectives there is a strong tendency to the reduce the vowel *a* in an unstressed syllable two syllables away from the main stress (see above). When a *shva* is expected with a guttural as the third consonant, it is replaced by a *Hataf-pataH*.

Examples

הַצָּבָא הישראלי מורכב ברובו מחיילי מילואים.

The bulk of the Israeli **army** is made up of reserve soldiers.

Special Expressions

soldier איש **צָבָא**

person subject to military service יוצא **צָבָא**

Israel Defense Forces **צְבָא** הגנה לישראל

regular **army** **צְבָא** קבע

the **host** of heaven (starts) **צְבָא** השמיים

army commander שַׂר **צָבָא**

Additional Examples in this Pattern

(pl. with *-ot*, but no declension ר׳ בָּבוֹת) gate בָּבָא

---

273. ***CaCaC***: nouns with the plural suffix *–im* where the *kamats* is not reduced

our/your/their	my/your/his/her	const.	Gloss	sing/pl
פָּנָסֵנוּ/**פְּנַסְ**כֶם/כֶן/**פָּנָסָ**ם/ן	**פָּנָסִ**י/סְךָ/סֵךְ/סוֹ/סָהּ	פְּנַס-	flashlight,	פָּנָס ז׳
פָּנָסֵינוּ/כֶם/כֶן/הֶם/הֶן	**פָּנָסַ**י/סֶיךָ/סַיִךְ/סָיו/סֶיהָ	פָּנָסֵי-	torch	פָּנָסִים

Examples

כדאי תמיד לשמור **פָּנָס** אחד או שניים בבית, למקרה של הפסקת חשמל.

It is always a good idea to keep a **flashlight** or two at home in case of power failure.

Special Expressions

a small ("pocket") **flashlight** **פָּנַס** כיס

overhead projector (Obs.?) **פָּנַס** קֶסֶם

Additional Examples in this Pattern

pagan; a rustic פָּגָן

---

274. *CaCaC ~ CCaC-*: nouns (and occasionally adjectives) with the plural suffix *-im* in which the second *kamats* turns into a *pataH* in the declension, and the next consonant is geminated

our/your/their	my/your/his/her	const.	Gloss	sing/pl
גְּמַלֵּנוּ/**גְּמַלְ**כֶם/כֶן/**גְּמַלָּ**ם/ן	**גְּמַלִּ**י/לְּךָ/לֵּךְ/לוֹ/לָהּ	גְּמַל-	camel	גָּמָל ז׳
גְּמַלֵּינוּ/כֶם/כֶן/הֶם/הֶן	**גְּמַלַּ**י/לֶּיךָ/לַּיִךְ/לָּיו/לֶּיהָ	גְּמַלֵּי-		גְּמַלִּים

Construct	f. sing/pl	Construct	m. sing/pl	Gloss
קְטַנַּת -	קְטַנָּה נ׳	קְטַן -	קָטָן ז׳	small,
קְטַנּוֹת -	קְטַנּוֹת	קְטַנֵּי -	קְטַנִּים	little

Before suffixes the stem-final vowel is *pataH*, followed by a geminated consonant: גְּמַלִּים vs. גָּמָל. When the first root consonant is a guttural, an expected *shva* is replaced by *Hataf-pataH*: עָצָב 'nerve' ~ עֲצַבִּים 'nerves,' חָרָךְ 'slit' ~ חֲרַכִּים 'slits.' In מָסָךְ 'screen, curtain' (plural מָסַכִּים) the *kamats* in the מ׳ is maintained throughout the declension, since this מ׳ is not an element of the root. Owing to the small mumber of occurrences, no separate sub-patterns were listed here.

Examples

הַגָּמָל מחזיק מעמד ימים רבים בלי מים, מכיוון שכשהוא שותה, הוא אוגר בגופו כמויות עצומות של נוזלים.
The **camel** can hold out very long without water, because when it drinks, he can store huge quantities of liquid in its body.

אחד התפקידים של מערכת **הָעֲצַבִּים** בגוף הוא לשדר למוח כאבים כמנגנון אזהרה.
One of the functions of the **nerve** system in the body is to broadcast pain to the brain as a warning mechanism.

הסרט החדש על פוליצר יוקרן בקרוב על **מָסַכֵּי** הקולנוע.
The new film about Pulitzer will be shown soon on the cinema **screen(s)**.

הַשָּׁפָן, למרות גודלו, שייך בעצם למשפחת הפילים.
The **hyrax**, in spite of its small size, is actually related to the elephant family.

Special Expressions

גָּמָל חד-דבשתי Arabian **camel**, single-humped **camel**
גָּמָל דו-דבשתי Asian **camel**, double-humped **camel**, Bactrian **camel**
הקש ששבר את גב **הַגָּמָל** the straw that broke the **camel**'s back
חֲרַךְ יְרִי embrasure, crenel
מָסַךְ הברזל the Iron **Curtain** (Soviet bloc till 1989)
מָסַךְ עשן smoke screen
עָצָב תחושתי afferent neuron
עָצָב תנועתי efferent neuron
שְׁפַן ניסיון/ניסיונות guinea pig, subject of an **experiment**; laboratory animal (note: from the colloquial reading of this word as 'rabbit,' not 'hyrax')

Additional Examples in this Pattern

חָרָךְ crack, slit
שָׁלָב rung, stage, phase

---

275. ***CaCaC*=קַטָּל**: nouns (and occasionally adjectives) with the plural suffix *-im*, designating mainly professionals, occasionally instruments and animals, in which a geminate closes the syllable with the *pataH*

sing/pl	Gloss	const.	my/your/his/her	our/your/their
חַיָּט ז׳	tailor	חַיַּט-	**חַיָּטִי**/טְךָ/טֵךְ/טוֹ/טָהּ	חַיָּטֵנוּ/**חַיָּטְכֶם**/כֶן/**חַיָּטָם**/ן
חַיָּטִים		חַיָּטֵי-	**חַיָּטַי**/טֶיךָ/טַיִךְ/טָיו/טֶיהָ	**חַיָּטֵינוּ**/כֶם/כֶן/הֶם/הֶן

In a number of cases, where the reference is not to a professional or a characteristic quality, the *kamats* may be reduced in the plural declension with stress shift: אַיָּלִים ~ אַיְּלֵי-, אַיְּלֵיכֶם... The feminine suffix may be ־ֶת (זַמֶּרֶת), ־ִית (זַבָּנִית), or (less commonly) ־ָה (אַיָּלָה). The realization of the feminine suffix will be noted for each form in the detailed index, unless it is difficult to determine it with a reasonable degree of certainty (possibly because many of the professions concerned have been traditionally male?). Since a different declension means a different pattern, it would have been better to classify into three sub-patterns, but owing to some difficulty in determining the feminine form in a significant number of cases, no such division will take place here.

our/your/their	my/your/his/her	const.	Gloss	sing/pl
חַיַּלְתֵּנוּ/תְּכֶם/תְּכֶן/תָּם/תָּן	**חַיַּלְ**תִּי/תְּךָ/תֵּךְ/תּוֹ/תָּהּ	חַיֶּלֶת-	fem.	חַיֶּלֶת נ׳
חַיְּלוֹתֵינוּ/כֶם/כֶן/הֶם/הֶן	**חַיְּלוֹ**תַי/תֶיךָ/תַיִךְ/תָיו/תֶיהָ	חַיְּלוֹת-	soldier	חַיָּלוֹת

our/your/their	my/your/his/her	const.	Gloss	sing/pl
סַפָּרִיתֵנוּ/תְכֶם/תְכֶן/תָם/תָן	**סַפָּרִי**תִי/תְךָ/תֵךְ/תוֹ/תָהּ	סַפָּרִית-	hair-	סַפָּרִית נ׳
סַפָּרִיּוֹתֵינוּ/כֶם/כֶן/הֶם/הֶן	**סַפָּרִיּוֹ**תַי/תֶיךָ/תַיִךְ/תָיו/תֶיהָ	סַפָּרִיּוֹת-	dresser	סַפָּרִיּוֹת

Examples

יהודים רבים באירופה עבדו במשך מאות שנים כ**חַיָּטִים** וכסנדלרים.

In Europe, many Jews worked for hundreds of years as **tailors** and as shoemakers.

חנה היא **סַפָּרִית** מצוינת, לנשים וגם לגברים.

Hannah is an excellent **hairdresser/barber**, for women a well as for men.

רוב הגברים הישראליים עד גיל 48 הם **חַיָּלִים** בחופשה 10-11 חודשים בשנה...

Most Israeli men up to the age 48 are **soldiers** on leave 10-11 months a year …

ריקי עבד כ**בַלָּשׁ** משטרה, בישראל ובארה״ב, על לפרישתו לפני כמה שנים.

Ricky worked as a police **detective**, in Israel and in the US, until his retirement a few years ago.

אימרה בעברית: הגונב מ**גַּנָּב** פטור.

Hebrew saying: stealing from a **thief** is permissible.

בעברית: **גַּנָּן** הוא מי שעובד בגינון בגן; **גַּנֶּנֶת** היא מי שעובדת בגן ילדים.

In Hebrew: **גַּנָּן** is a man who does gardening in a garden (**gardener**); **גַּנֶּנֶת** is a **kindergarden teacher**.

חמותי נולדה בפולין, שנתיים אחרי שאחיה בן ה-14 היגר לארה״ב, וחי שם עם קרובים. כל המשפחה נספתה בשואה, וכל מה שהיא זכרה הוא שהוא גר בברונקס. היא שלחה מכתב לארה״ב עם שמו וברונקס בלבד. הוא כבר לא היה אז בברונקס, אבל קרה נס: **דַּוָּר** אחד בברונקס זכר אותו, והמכתב הגיע לתעודתו.

My mother-in-law was born in Poland, two years after her 14-year-old brother had immigrated to the US, and lived there with relatives. The rest of the family perished in the Holocaust, and all she remembered was that he lived in the Bronx. She sent a leter to the US with only his name and The Bronx. He was no longer in the Bronx then, but a miracle happened: a **postman** in the Bronx remembered him, and the letter reached its destination.

יש לנו דירה בישראל, ולמזלנו יש לנו בה **דַּיָּרִים** פחות-או-יותר קבועים השמחים לשכור אותה בתקופות שבהן אנחנו לא מבקרים בארץ.

We have an apartment in Israel, and luckily we have more-or-less regular **tenants** who are happy to rent it in periods when we are not visiting.

Special Expressions

the Mediterranean **basin** **אַגַּן** הים התיכון
drainage **basin** **אַגַּן** ניקוז
rein**deer** **אַיַּל** הצפון
chef **אַשַּׁף** מטבח
protected **tenant** **דַּיַּר** מוגן
sub-**tenant** **דַּיַּר** מִשְׁנֶה
lone **soldier** (with no family in Israel) **חַיַּל** בודד
regular soldier, serviceman **חַיַּל** סדיר
reservist **חַיַּל** מילואים
discharged **soldier**, veteran **חַיַּל** משוחרר
combat **soldier** **חַיַּל** קרבי

Additional Examples in this Pattern

bowl, basin; pelvis אַגָּן
pear אַגָּס
deer אַיָּל
rapist אַנָּס
expert, wiz אַשָּׁף
signalman אַתָּת
defender, back (sports) בַּלָּם
enlistment officer גַּיָּס
engraver גַּלָּף
dwarf, midget גַּמָּד
camel driver גַּמָּל
tracker, scout גַּשָּׁשׁ
fisherman דַּיָּג
host, steward דַּיָּל
rabbinical judge דַּיָּן
printer (person) דַּפָּס
salesperson זַבָּן
glazier זַגָּג

---

276. קֶטָל = קַטָּל: nouns (and occasionally adj.) with the plural suffix *-im*, generally designating professionals, occasionally instruments and animals, where the second consonant is ה׳ or ח׳

our/your/their	my/your/his/her	const.	Gloss	sing/pl
נֶהָגֵנוּ/**נֶהַגְ**כֶם/כֶן/**נֶהָגָ**ם/ן	**נֶהָ**גִי/גְךָ/גֵךְ/גוֹ/גָהּ	נֶהַג-/נַהַג-	driver	נֶהָג/נַהָג ז׳
נַהָגֵנוּ/**נַהַגְ**כֶם/כֶן/**נַהָגָ**ם/ן	**נַהָ**גִי/גְךָ/גֵךְ/גוֹ/גָהּ			
נֶהָגֵינוּ/כֶם/כֶן/הֶם/הֶן	**נֶהָ**גַי/גֶיךָ/גַיִךְ/גָיו/גֶיהָ	נֶהָגֵי-		נֶהָגִים/נַהָגִים
נַהָגֵינוּ/כֶם/כֶן/הֶם/הֶן	**נַהָ**גַי/גֶיךָ/גַיִךְ/גָיו/גֶיהָ	/נַהָגֵי-		

When the second consonant is ה׳ or ח׳, the *pataH* remains as is, without gemination, of course. In the past the rule was that the *pataH* becomes a *seghol* (dissimilation?), נֶהָג/נַהָג 'driver,' פֶּחָח/פַּחָח 'tinsmith,' but such pronunciation is no longer common today.

Examples

נֶהָגִים ישראליים נוטים לִטּוֹל סיכונים גדולים בכבישים כשהם עוקפים כלי רכב אחרים.
Israeli **drivers** tend to take great risks on the road when they overtake other cars.

Special Expressions

marine corps חֵיל **נַחָתִים**

Additional Examples in this Pattern

marine (military) נַחָת/נֶחָת
metal worker; car body repairman פַּחָח/פֶּחָח

---

277. ***CaCaC***: nouns with the plural suffix *-im* in which a *kamats* that originates from compensatory lengthening before *r* in the "professionals" pattern is not reduced

sing/pl	Gloss	const.	my/your/his/her	our/your/their
חָרָשׁ ז׳	craftsman,	חָרַשׁ-	**חָרָ**שִׁי/שְׁךָ/שֵׁךְ/שׁוֹ/שָׁהּ	חָרָשֵׁנוּ/**חָרַשְׁ**כֶם/כֶן/**חָרָשָׁ**ם/ן
חָרָשִׁים	artisan	חָרָשֵׁי-	**חָרָ**שַׁי/שֶׁיךָ/שַׁיִךְ/שָׁיו/שֶׁיהָ	**חָרָשֵׁי**נוּ/כֶם/כֶן/הֶם/הֶן

The קַטָּל pattern generally refers to professionals; when the second consonant is ר׳, which cannot be geminated, the *pataH* turns into *kamats* by "compensatory lengthening."

Examples

״**חָרָשׁ**״ הוא מונח גבוה המתייחס לכל בעל מלאכה או אומן.

חָרָשׁ is a high-register term referring to any craftsman or artisan.

אני עדיין זוכר את הימים שאחד האנשים הבולטים בבית הספר היה ה**שָּׁרָת**. בין השאר, הוא היה מצלצל בפעמון כשהגיע הזמן להיכנס לכיתה וכאשר תם השיעור.

I still remember the days when one of the most prominent people at the school was the **janitor**. Among his other duties, he would ring a hand-held bell when it was time to go into the classroom, and when class ended.

Special Expressions

חָרַשׁ ברזל blacksmith, smith (Lit.)   **חָרַשׁ** עץ carpenter (Lit.)

Additional Examples in this Pattern

חָרָט engraver   פָּרָשׁ horseman   קָרָר refrigerant

---

278. ***CaCaC*=קַטָּל**: nouns with the plural suffix *-ot*, in which a geminate closes the syllable with the *pataH*

sing/pl	Gloss	const.	my/your/his/her	our/your/their
שַׁבָּת	Sabbath;	שַׁבַּת-	**שַׁבָּ**תִּי/תְּךָ/תֵּךְ/תּוֹ/תָּהּ	שַׁבָּתֵנוּ/**שַׁבַּתְּ**כֶם/כֶן/**שַׁבָּתָּ**ם/ן
שַׁבָּתוֹת	Saturday	שַׁבְּתוֹת-	**שַׁבְּתוֹ**תַי/תֶיךָ/תַיִךְ/תָיו/תֶיהָ	**שַׁבְּתוֹתֵי**נוּ/כֶם/כֶן/הֶם/הֶן

The number of occurrences is small: שַׁבָּת is fem., מַזָּל 'luck; zodiac sign masc.'

Examples

אפילו במשפחות לא-מסורתיות בישראל משתדלים בדרך כלל לציין את ה**שַּׁבָּת** בארוחה משפחתית מיוחדת.

Even in non-traditional families in Israel they generally try to note the **Sabbath** in a special family dinner.

Special Expressions

מַזָּל טוב! Congratulations!   בַּר **מַזָּל** a lucky, successful person

שִׂחֵק לו **מַזָּלוֹ** he was lucky, he was successful

---

279. ***CaCeC***: adjectives and nouns with the plural suffix *-im*

Construct	f. sing/pl	Construct	m. sing/pl	Gloss
כִּבְדַת-	כְּבֵדָה נ׳	כְּבַד-	כָּבֵד ז׳	heavy
כִּבְדוֹת-	כְּבֵדוֹת	כִּבְדֵי-	כְּבֵדִים	

our/your/their	my/your/his/her	const.	Gloss	sing/pl
שְׁכֵנֵנוּ/**שְׁכַנְ**כֶם/כֶן/**שְׁכֵנָ**ם/ן	**שְׁכֵ**נִי/נְךָ/נֵךְ/נוֹ/נָהּ	שְׁכַן-	neighbor	שָׁכֵן ז׳
שְׁכֵנֵינוּ/**שִׁכְנֵי**כֶם/כֶן/הֶם/הֶן	**שְׁכֵ**נַי/נֶיךָ/נַיִךְ/נָיו/נֶיהָ	שְׁכֵנֵי-		שְׁכֵנִים

The *kamats* is reduced to *shva* two syllables away from the main stress, שְׁכֵנִי < שָׁכֵנִי*, and the following *tsere* to *pataH* when it occurs in a closed syllable, שְׁכַנְכֶם < שְׁכֵנְכֶם*. If the last root consonant is א׳, the *tsere* remains: -צְמֵא, -תְּאֵב (constr.).
Note: The construct forms of forms like שָׁמֵן 'fat Adj.' may follow those of זָקֵן 'old' or כָּבֵד 'heavy,' i.e., -זִקְנֵי, -כִּבְדֵי, or those of יָשֵׁן 'asleep' or שָׁכֵן 'neighbor,' i.e., -יְשֵׁנֵי, שְׁכֵנֵי. Both alternatives seem to be acceptable, but most Hebrew speakers would (correctly) opt for -שְׁמֵנֵי over -שִׁמְנֵי, and preserve the base *tsere* to keep the שְׁמֵנִים paradigm uniform. Also note: when the 3rd root radical is ה׳, ח׳, ע׳ in final position, it takes a "furtive" *pataH*, e.g., תָּמֵהַּ.

Examples

בדרך כלל, אנשים **שְׁמֵנִים** מתעייפים מהר יותר מאנשים רזים בשעת פעולה מאומצת.
Generally, **fat** people tire faster than thin ones during strenuous activity.

הגולדמנים הם **שְׁכֵנִים** שלנו כבר ארבעים שנה.
The Goldmans have been our **neighbors** for forty years now.

בחנות הירקות בשכונתנו הירקן היה מוכר פירות וירקות **בְּשֵׁלִים** מדיי בכל יום חמישי אחרי הצוהריים בעשירית ממחירם המקורי. אימא הייתה שולחת אותי לקנות את כל פירות האבוקדו **הַבְּשֵׁלִים** ועושה סלט אבוקדו נהדר.
In the neighborhood greengrocer's store the greengrocer would sell over**ripe** fruit and vegetables every Thursday afternoon for about a tenth of their orginal price. Mom would send me to buy all the **ripe** avocados and make terrific avocado salad.

דומני שמיי ווסט אמרה: להיות **זָקֵן** זה לא פיקניק. היא צדקה!
I believe Mae West said: Being **old** is no picnic. She was right!

נכון שלירושלים אין חוף ים, אבל מצד שני **יָבֵשׁ** ונעים שם בקיץ, בעוד שבתל אביב אז לח וחם מאוד.
It is true that Jerusalem has no beach, but on the other hand, in the summer it is **dry** there, whereas in Tel Aviv it is humid and hot then.

Special Expressions

hard of hearing **כְּבַד** שמיעה
kosher in accordance with the stringent Jewish law **כָּשֵׁר** למהדרין
blood**thirsty** **צְמֵא** דם
a close **neighbor** is preferable to a distant brother טוב **שָׁכֵן** טוב מאח רחוק
money-**hungry**, greedy **תְּאֵב** בצע

negligible, insignificant **בָּטֵל** בשישים
null and **void** **בָּטֵל** ומבוטל
flaky **pastry**, Filo **dough** **בָּצֵק** עלים
shortcrust **pastry** **בָּצֵק** פריך
a dirty/wicked **old man** **זָקֵן** אַשְׁמַאי
the city **elders** **זִקְנֵי** העיר
stuttering **כְּבַד** לשון
stammerer **כְּבַד** פֶּה

Additional Examples in this Pattern

invalid; idle בָּטֵל
dough; swollen בָּצֵק
dagesh (gemination sign); emphasis דָּגֵשׁ
fertile, rich דָּשֵׁן
impure טָמֵא
subordinate טָפֵל
barefoot יָחֵף
ibex יָעֵל
ostrich יָעֵן
stake, peg יָתֵד

heavy; liver כָּבֵד
kosher; valid; fit for כָּשֵׁר
port נָמֵל
thirsty צָמֵא
ewe רָחֵל
complete שָׁלֵם
quiet שָׁקֵט
craving תָּאֵב
bland תָּפֵל
valid תָּקֵף

---

280. ***CaCeC***: nouns and adjectives with the plural suffix *-im* where the first root consonant is guttural

Construct	f. sing/pl	Construct	m. sing/pl	Gloss
חַסְרַת-	חֲסֵרָה נ׳	חֲסַר-	חָסֵר ז׳	deficient,
חַסְרוֹת-	חֲסֵרוֹת	חַסְרֵי-	חֲסֵרִים	lacking

our/your/their	my/your/his/her	const.	Gloss	sing/pl
חֲבֵרֵנוּ/**חֲבֶרְ**כֶם/כֶן/**חֲבֵרָ**ם/ן	**חֲבֵ**רִי/רְךָ/רֵךְ/רוֹ/רָהּ	חֲבֵר-	friend,	חָבֵר ז׳
חֲבֵרֵינוּ/**חַבְרֵי**כֶם/כֶן/הֶם/הֶן	**חֲבֵ**רַי/רֶיךָ/רַיִךְ/רָיו/רֶיהָ	חַבְרֵי-	member	חֲבֵרִים

As already noted, in nouns and adjectives there is a strong tendency to reduce the vowel *a* in an unstressed syllable two syllables away from the main stress. When the first consonant is a guttural, the expected *shva* is replaced by a *Hataf-pataH*, חֲבֵרִים < חְבֵרִים*. When, as a consequence of reduction, one expects a hard-to-articulate sequence of *Hataf* immediately followed by a *shva*, the result is a *pataH* in a syllable closed by a *shva quiescent*: חַבְרֵיכֶם < חֲבְרֵיכֶם* < חֲבֵרֵיכֶם*.

Examples

לדבר עם **חָבֵר** טוב עוזר לא פחות מאשר ללכת לפסיכולוג.
Talking to a good **friend** is just as helpful as going to a psychologist.

הגולדמנים הם זוג מאושר; הדבר היחיד ש**חָסֵר** להם הוא נכד או נכדה.
The Goldmans are a happy couple. The only that's **lacking** is a grandchild.

אחת הבעיות הקשות של מי ששרד אסון שבו נהרגו כל יקיריו היא ההרגשה שאיכשהו הוא **אָשֵׁם**: למה דווקא אני היחיד ששרד?
A major problem facing a person who is the only survivor of a disaster in which all those who were dear to him were killed is the feeling that somehow he is **guilty**: Why am I the only one to have survived?

אם אתה מרגיש שאתה רוב הזמן **עָיֵף**, כדאי שתלך להיבדק על-ידי רופא המשפחה שלך.
If you feel that you are **tired** most of the time, it's a good idea for you to be examined by your family doctor.

Special Expressions

without precedent **חֲסַר** תקדים
That's all I need… (= is **lacking**) רק זה **חָסֵר** לי...
everybody benefits from it (none comes out **lacking**) זה נהנה וזה לא **חָסֵר**

mortified, chastened **אָבֵל** וחפוי ראש
Knesset **member** **חֲבֵר** כנסת
membership fee מס **חָבֵר**
help**less** **חֲסַר** אונים
homeless **חֲסַר** בית

Additional Examples in this Pattern

branched; diverse עָנֵף
lazy, idle; loafer עָצֵל
guarantor; pleasant עָרֵב
inattentive Lit.; uncircumcised עָרֵל
smoking Adj עָשֵׁן

mourner; mourning אָבֵל
dark אָפֵל
anxious; ultra-orthodox person חָרֵד
moldy עָבֵשׁ
laborer עָמֵל

---

281. ***CaCeC***: nouns with the plural suffix *-im* or *-ot* where the *kamats* is reduced in the declension

our/your/their	my/your/his/her	const.	Gloss	sing/pl
גְּדֵרֵנוּ/**גְּדֶרְ**כֶם/כֶן/**גְּדֵרָ**ם/ן	**גְּדֵרִ**י/רְךָ/רֵךְ/רוֹ/רָהּ	גֶּדֶר-	fence,	גָּדֵר נ׳
גִּדְרוֹתֵינוּ/כֶם/כֶן/הֶם/הֶן	**גִּדְרוֹ**תַי/תֶיךָ/תַיִךְ/תָיו/תֶיהָ	גִּדְרוֹת-	border	גְּדֵרוֹת/
גְּדֵרֵינוּ/**גִּדְרֵי**כֶם/כֶן/הֶם/הֶן	**גְּדֵרַ**י/רֶיךָ/רַיִךְ/רָיו/רֶיהָ	גִּדְרֵי-/		גְּדֵרִים

When as a result of reduction a closed syllable is formed, the *tsere* becomes *seghol* (גְּדֶרְכֶם), or the *kamats* becomes *Hirik* (גִּדְרוֹתַי).

Examples

כשהייתי ילד, אמי הייתה נוהגת לדבר כל יום עם השכנה מעבר **לַגָּדֵר**.
When I was a kid, my mother used to talk every day with the (fem.) neighbor across the **fence**.

Special Expressions

lost his cool יצא **מִגִּדְרוֹ**

hedge, hedgerow **גָּדֵר** חיה

Additional Examples in this Pattern

potbelly כָּרֵס

---

282. ***CaCeC***: nouns with the plural suffix *-im* or *-ot* where the *kamats* is reduced in the declension and the first root consonant is guttural

our/your/their	my/your/his/her	const.	Gloss	sing/pl
חֲצֵרֵנוּ/**חֲצַרְ**כֶם/כֶן/**חֲצֵרָ**ם/ן	**חֲצֵרִ**י/רְךָ/רֵךְ/רוֹ/רָהּ	חֲצַר-	yard,	חָצֵר נ׳
חַצְרוֹתֵינוּ/כֶם/כֶן/הֶם/הֶן	**חַצְרוֹ**תַי/תֶיךָ/תַיִךְ/תָיו/תֶיהָ	חַצְרוֹת-	court	חֲצֵרוֹת/
חֲצֵרֵינוּ/**חַצְרֵי**כֶם/כֶן/הֶם/הֶן	**חֲצֵרַ**י/רֶיךָ/רַיִךְ/רָיו/רֶיהָ	חַצְרֵי-/		חֲצֵרִים

As already noted, in nouns and adjectives there is a strong tendency to the reduce the vowel *a* in an unstressed syllable two syllables away from the main stress. When the first consonant is a guttural, the expected *shva* is replaced by a *Hataf-pataH*, *חָצֵרִים > חֲצֵרִים. Moreover, as a result of *tsere* reduction with further stress shift, the *tsere* in the next syllable is reduced to *pataH* if it occurs in a closed syllable: *חָצֵרְכֶם > חֲצַרְכֶם. When, as a consequence of reduction, one expects a hard-to-articulate sequence of *Hataf* immediately followed by a *shva* within the same syllable, the *Hataf* is replaced by *pataH* in a syllable closed by a *shva* quiescent: *חֲצֵרֵיכֶם > *חֲצְרֵיכֶם > חַצְרֵיכֶם.

Examples

בחָצֵר בית הספר שלנו היו קוראים כל בוקר מפרשת השבוע.

In our school **court** they would read a section from the Torah portion of the week every morning.

כשאישה עוברת בנעליים עם **עֲקֵבִים** גבוהים, גם בלי לראות אותה אפשר להסיק כמה מסקנות אודותיה על פי קצב נקישת **העֲקֵבִים** ועל פי עוצמת הנקישה.

When a woman passes with high-**heel**-shoes, one can tell a lot about her without even seeing her by the rhythm of the clicking of the **heels** and by the energy of the click.

Special Expressions

אנשי **החָצֵר** courtiers

עֲקֵב אכילס Achilles **heel**

בעִקְבוֹת- following…, in the **footsteps** of…

---

283. ***CiCeC***: Adjectives and nouns

our/your/their	my/your/his/her	const.	Gloss	sing/pl
אִלְמֵנוּ/**אִלֶמְכֶם**/כֶן/**אִלְמָם**/ן	אִלְמִי/אִלֶמְךָ/**אִלְמֵךְ**/מוֹ/מָהּ	אִלֵּם-	mute N.	אִלֵּם ז׳
אִלְמֵינוּ/כֶם/כֶן/הֶם/הֶן	**אִלְמַי**/מֶיךָ/מַיִךְ/מָיו/מֶיהָ	אִלְמֵי-		אִלְמִים

Construct	f. sing/pl	Construct	m. sing/pl	Gloss
אִלֶּמֶת-	אִלֶּמֶת נ׳	אִלֵּם-	אִלֵּם ז׳	mute Adj
אִלְמוֹת-	אִלְמוֹת	אִלְמֵי-	אִלְמִים	

Most realizations in this *mishkal* serve either as nouns or as adjectives: אִלֵּם is a mute person or an adjective describing such a person. The *tsere* is elided in the syllable preceding a stressed suffix (אִלְמִי), or reduced to a *seghol* in a closed syllable (אִלֶּמְכֶם) (in earlier vocalization traditions, the *shva* was considered quiescent in some cases, and the *dagesh forte* was dropped, e.g., עִוְרִים, פִּקְחִים, but not always, e.g., אִלְּמִים).

Examples

בהרבה מִקְרִים, **אִלְּמִים** הם גם חֵרְשִׁים.

In many cases, **mute persons** are also deaf.

כנראה שהייתה לריצ׳ארד השלישי בעיית גב, אבל קרוב לוודאי שהוא לא היה ממש **גִּבֵּן**. ייתכן ששיקספיר תיאר אותו כך כדי לשקף את רוע ליבו.

Apparently Richard III had a back/spine problem, but it is unlikely that he was actually **hunchbacked**. Shakespeare probably portrayed him so in order to reflect the inner evil in him.

יש **טִפְּשִׁים** המודעים לטפשותם, ויכולים להימנע מלחשוף את טפשותם באמצעות שתיקה, אבל מרבית ה**טִפְּשִׁים** אינם מסוגלים לשתוק.
Some **fools** are aware of their stupidity, and can avoid exposing their stupidity by keeping silent, but most **fools** are incapable of shutting up.

Special Expressions

לְטִפֵּשׁ אין מראים חצי עבודה You don't show a half-finished job to **a fool**
כִּסֵּא/מושב מפלט ejection **seat**
כִּסֵּא הכבוד the heavenly **throne**

לפני **עִוֵּר** לא תתן מכשול Do not place an obstacle in a **blind man**'s way
עִוֵּר צבעים color-**blind**

Additional Examples in this Pattern

אִטֵּר left-handed person
גִּדֵּם one whose hand has been amputated
דִּבֵּר (pl. דִּבְּרוֹת) commandment
חִגֵּר lame; lame person

חִוֵּר pale
כִּסֵּא (pl. כִּסְאוֹת) chair
עִוֵּר blind; blind person
עִקֵּשׁ stubborn

---

284. ***CiCeC* = *CiCeaC*:** Adjectives & nouns, when the 3rd consonant is guttural

our/your/their	my/your/his/her	const.	Gloss	sing/pl
פִּכְּחֵנוּ/**פִּכַּחֲ**כֶם/כֶן/**פִּכְּחָ**ם/ן	פִּכְּחִי/פִּכַּחֲךָ/**פִּכְּחֵ**ךְ/חוֹ/חָהּ	פִּכֵּחַ-	sober; sober	פִּכֵּחַ ז'
פִּכְּחֵינוּ/כֶם/כֶן/הֶם/הֶן	**פִּכְּחַ**י/חֶיךָ/חַיִךְ/חָיו/חֶיהָ	פִּכְּחֵי-	person	פִּכְּחִים

The final guttural is preceded by a *furtive pataH* (after a vowel other than *a*). Where a *shva* is expected with the guttural, it is replaced by a *Hataf*-pataH, and the preceding *tsere* echoes it by turning into *pataH* (פִּכַּחֲךָ). Note: in the declension of פִּקֵּחַ 'clever' there is no *dagesh forte* in the second root consonant in a closed syllable: פִּקְחִים etc.

Examples

בדיחה מוונצואלה: אם אדם נוסע ישר בכביש, המשטרה עוצרת אותו בעוון שכרות בזמן נהיגה; אדם **פִּכֵּחַ** זוכר שכל הדרכים בונצואלה מלאות בורות...
A joke from Venezuela: if a person drives strainght ahead, the police would stop him for driving under the influence; a **sober** man remembers that all roads in Venezuela are full of potholes…

לא ייתכן ש**פִּקֵּחַ** כמוהו יעשה שטות כזו.
I do not believe that a **clever man** like him would do such nonsense.

Special Expressions

השוחד יעוור **פִּקְחִים** (שמות כג:ח)
A bribe makes **clever/seeing persons** blind (Ex. 23:8).

Additional Examples in this Pattern

bald גִּבֵּחַ
one whose hand was amputated גִּדֵּעַ
very tall Lit. קִפֵּחַ
obstinate Lit. קִשֵּׁחַ
great-grandson Lit. (רִבֵּעַ (ר׳ רִבֵּעִים

---

285. ***CiCeC* = *CeCeC***, when the 2nd root consonant is *alef* or *r*

Construct	f. sing/pl	Construct	m. sing/pl	Gloss
-חֵרֶשֶׁת	חֵרֶשֶׁת נ׳	-חֵרֵשׁ	חֵרֵשׁ ז׳	deaf; deaf
-חֵרְשׁוֹת	חֵרְשׁוֹת	-חֵרְשֵׁי	חֵרְשִׁים	person

When the second root consonant is א׳ or ר׳, the *i* is replace by a *tsere*. The *tsere* /e/ is attributed to historical "compensatory lengthening," which allowed the existence of an open syllable because these consonants cannot be geminated, and therefore cannot close the syllable. קֵרֵחַ 'bald' also ends with a 'furtive' *pataH*.

Examples

מרבית הַ**חֵרְשִׁים** הם **חֵרְשִׁים** מלידה.
Most of the **deaf** are **deaf** from their day of birth.

״לילה על הר **קֵרֵחַ**״ היא אחת מיצירותיו הידועות של של רימסקי-קורסקוב (המבוססת על יצירה קודמת של מוסורגסקי).
"Night on a **Bald** Mountain" is one of Rimsky-Korsakov's best known composions (based on asn earlier composition by Mussorgsky).

Special Expressions

deaf-mute **חֵרֵשׁ**-אילם
discussion in which neither side listens or responds to the other דו-שיח של **חֵרְשִׁים**
lose out both ways (when trying to obtain two things at the same time) **קֵרֵחַ** מכאן ומכאן

Additional Examples in this Pattern

bald; bald person קֵרֵחַ

---

286. ***CiCaC***: nouns

our/your/their	my/your/his/her	const.	Gloss	sing/pl
אִכָּרֵנוּ/**אִכָּרְ**כֶם/כֶן/**אִכָּרָ**ם/ן	**אִכָּרִ**י/רְךָ/רֵךְ/רוֹ/רָהּ	-אִכַּר	peasant,	אִכָּר
אִכָּרֵינוּ/כֶם/כֶן/הֶם/הֶן	**אִכָּרַ**י/רֶיךָ/רַיִךְ/רָיו/רֶיהָ	-אִכָּרֵי	farmer	אִכָּרִים

The vowel in the syllable preceding a stressed suffix is not reduced. Note: the plural form of כִּכָּר 'square' is כִּכָּרוֹת.

Examples

העלייה הראשונה לארץ ישראל הייתה של חלוצים שמטרתם הייתה להפוך ל**אִכָּרִים**.
The first immigration to Palestine was of pioneers whose goal was to become **farmers**.

בעשורים האחרונים התחילו להבין שמבחינת יעילות התנועה, **כִּכָּר** עדיפה על רמזור.
In the last few decades, they began to understand that in terms of traffic efficiency, a **roundabout** is better than a traffic light.

ההרצאה הייתה תיאורטית ומורכבת, אבל את **עִקַּר** הטיעון הבנתי.
The lecture was theoretical and complex, but I did understand the **essence** of the argument.

Special Expressions

כִּכַּר לחם **loaf** of bread
כִּכַּר השוק market **square**
בְּעִקָּר **main**ly
עִקַּר הָעִקָּרִים the **main** thing

Additional Examples in this Pattern

כִּכָּר square; roundabout (כִּכָּרוֹת, כִּכְּרוֹת- (pl.
נִצָּן bud
קֵבָר bran, course flour
רֵבָס rhubarb

---

287. ***CeCaC***: nouns

our/your/their	my/your/his/her	const.	Gloss	sing/pl
לְבָבֵנוּ/**לְבַבְ**כֶם/כֶן/**לְבָבָ**ם/ן	**לְבָבִ**י/בְךָ/בֵךְ/בוֹ/בָהּ	לְבַב-	heart	לֵבָב ז׳
לִבְבוֹתֵינוּ/כֶם/כֶן/הֶם/הֶן	**לִבְבוֹ**תַי/תֶיךָ/תַיִךְ/תָיו/תֶיהָ	לִבְבוֹת-		לְבָבוֹת

our/your/their	my/your/his/her	const.	Gloss	sing/pl
שְׂעָרֵנוּ/**שְׂעַרְ**כֶם/כֶן/**שְׂעָרָ**ם/ן	**שְׂעָרִ**י/רְךָ/רֵךְ/רוֹ/רָהּ	שְׂעַר-	hair	שֵׂעָר ז׳
שַׂעֲרָתֵנוּ/**שַׂעֲרַתְ**כֶם/כֶן/**שַׂעֲרָתָ**ם/ן	**שַׂעֲרָ**תִי/תְךָ/תֵךְ/תוֹ/תָהּ	שַׂעֲרַת-	a hair	שַׂעֲרָה נ׳
שַׂעֲרוֹתֵינוּ/כֶם/כֶן/הֶם/הֶן	**שַׂעֲרוֹ**תַי/תֶיךָ/תַיִךְ/תָיו/תֶיהָ	שַׂעֲרוֹת-		ר׳ שְׂעָרוֹת

our/your/their	my/your/his/her	const.	Gloss	sing/pl
עֲנָבֵנוּ/**עֲנַבְ**כֶם/כֶן/**עֲנָבָ**ם/ן	**עֲנָבִ**י/בְךָ/בֵךְ/בוֹ/בָהּ	עֲנַב-	grape;	עֵנָב ז׳
עֲנָבֵינוּ/**עִנְבֵי**כֶם/כֶן/הֶם/הֶן	**עֲנָבַ**י/בֶיךָ/בַיִךְ/בָיו/בֶיהָ	עִנְבֵי-	berry	עֲנָבִים

This is a small group of nouns, but varied. The plural ending may be וֹת- or ִים–. In some cases there is no declension (except for the construct state): חֵמָר 'clay,' שֵׁכָר 'liquor,' נֵכָר 'diaspora.' The *tsere* is reduced in the declension, or turns into a *Hataf pataH* with a guttural consonant. When a *shva quiescent* is expected in the second consonant, the consonant is followed by a *Hataf pataH* (שַׂעֲרָתִי etc.).

Examples

״מי האיש הירא ורך ה**לֵּבָב** ילך וישוב לביתו״ (מדיני המלחמה בתורה, דב׳ כ:ח).
"He who is faint-**hearted** should go back and return to his home" (from the Rules of War, Deut. 20:8.)

נחמה מגדלת **שֵׂעָר** ארוך. כשהיא יושבת, **שַׂעֲרוֹתֶיהָ** נוגעות ברצפה.
Nehama is growing long **hair**. When she sits, her **hairs** touch the floor.

מ**עִנְּבֵי** הגולן מייצרים יין מצוין.
They make excellent wine from the **grapes** of the Golan.

על פי הספרות הרבנית, יש בגוף האדם רמ״ח **אֲבָרִים/אֵיבָרִים** ושס״ה גידים, המקבילים למספר המצוות החיוביות והשליליות בתורה, בהתאמה (בסך הכל תרי״ג מצוות)
According to the rabbinic literature, there are 248 **organs** and 365 tendons in the human body, corresponding to the number off positive and negative commandments, respectively, in the Torah (a total of 613 commandments).

Special Expressions

בכל רמ״ח **אֲבָרָיו/אֵיבָרָיו** (ושס״ה גידיו) with all one's might/being
בכל **לְבָבוֹ** whole**heart**edly
בר **לֵבָב** pure **heart**ed
רך **לֵבָב** faint **heart**ed
כִּלְבָבוֹ as one wishes/likes
עִנְּבֵי רוש poisonous **grapes**
עִנְּבֵי שועל goose**berries**
אדרת **שֵׂעָר** **fur** coat
מְסַמֵּר **שֵׂעָר** **hair** raising

Additional Examples in this Pattern

אֵבָר/אֵיבָר (ר׳ אֲבָרִים/אֵיבָרִים)/ אֵבֶר limb, organ
חֵמָר clay
נֵכָר foreign country, diaspora

---

288. ***CaCoC*: nouns**

our/your/their	my/your/his/her	const.	Gloss	sing/pl
יְתוֹמֵנוּ/מְכֶם/מְכֶן/מָם/מָן	**יְתוֹ**מִי/מְךָ/מֵךְ/מוֹ/מָהּ	-יְתוֹם	orphan	יָתוֹם ז׳
יְתוֹמֵינוּ/כֶם/כֶן/הֶם/הֶן	**יְתוֹ**מַי/מֶיךָ/מַיִךְ/מָיו/מֶיהָ	-יְתוֹמֵי		יְתוֹמִים

The *kamats* is reduced two syllables before the main stress. The plural ending is ־ִים. In some cases, there is no declension (except for the construct state), דָּרוֹם 'south,' צָפוֹן 'north,' and sometimes no plural, כָּבוֹד 'honor, respect; dignity.'

Examples

אחד החובות החשובים המצוינים בתורה הוא להגן על **יְתוֹמִים** ואלמנות.
One of the important duties mentioned in the Torah is to protect **orphans** and widows.

תושבי **דָּרוֹם** הארץ סבלו מאוד לאחרונה מפעולות טרור שמקורן ברצועת עזה.
Residents of the **south** of Israel have suffered a lot lately from terror acts orginating in the Gaza Strip.

לאורך כל ההיסטוריה האנושית, תפיסה מעוותת של מושג **הַכָּבוֹד** גרמה לרצח, לשנאה תהומית בין אנשים ובין עמים, ואפילו למלחמות (מלחמת טרויה היא רק דוגמה אחת).
Throughout human history, a distorted concept of **honor** has been the cause of murder, deeply-ingrained hatred between individuls and nations, and even wars (the Trojan War is just one illustration).

מדברים הרבה על **שָׁלוֹם** במזרח התיכון, אבל מחודש לחודש ומשנה לשנה הסיכוי **לְשָׁלוֹם** במזרח התיכון מתרחק והולך.
They talk a great deal about **peace** in the Middle East, but from month to month and from year to year the prospect of **peace** in the Middle East is getting farther and farther.

Special Expressions

tank belly **גְּחוֹן** הטנק
well done! Way to go! כל **הַכָּבוֹד**!
with all due respect… עם כל **הַכָּבוֹד**...
respectfully, **בְּכָבוֹד** רב,
honorary citizen אזרח **כָּבוֹד**

true **peace** **שָׁלוֹם** אמת
domestic **peace**, marital harmony; good relations **שְׁלוֹם** בית
Hellow! Welcome! **שָׁלוֹם** עליכם!

Additional Examples in this Pattern

belly, underbelly Lit. גָּחוֹן
south דָּרוֹם

corset, girdle מָחוֹךְ
north צָפוֹן

---

289. ***CaCoC***: nouns, when the first root letter is a guttural

our/your/their	my/your/his/her	const.	Gloss	sing/pl
אֲדוֹנֵנוּ/נְכֶם/נְכֶן/נָם/נָן	**אֲדוֹ**נִי/נְךָ/נֵךְ/נוֹ/נָהּ	אֲדוֹן-	Sir, Mr., gentleman;	אָדוֹן ז'
אֲדוֹנֵינוּ/כֶם/כֶן/הֶם/הֶן	**אֲדוֹ**נַי/נֶיךָ/נַיִךְ/נָיו/נֶיהָ	אֲדוֹנֵי-	lord, master; owner	אֲדוֹנִים

The plural ending ִ–ים, and in the case of אָחוֹר it is dual: אָחוֹר ‘back’ ~ אֲחוֹרַיִם ‘buttocks.’ When the first consonant is a guttural, the expected *shva* is replaced by a *Hataf-pataH.*

Examples

סליחה, **אֲדוֹנִי**, אתה יכול לומר לי מה השעה?
Excuse me, **Sir**, can you tell me what time it is?

אָדוֹן אחד שנתקלתי בו ברחוב טוען שהוא הכיר את אבי.
A certain **gentleman** that I bumped into in the street claims that he knew my father.

אפרים הוא בנו הממזר של **אֲדוֹן** האחוזה.
Ephraim is the illegitimate child of the **lord** of the manor.

בַּעֲשׂוֹרִים האחרונים הסְמַרְטְפוֹנִים השתלטו על חיינו, בעיקר על חיי הדור הצעיר.
In the last few **decades** the smartphones have taken over our lives, particularly the lives of the young.

Special Expressions

Lord of the Earth (God) **אֲדוֹן** כל הארץ

Lord of all works (God) **אֲדוֹן** כל המעשים

Lord of the World (God) **אֲדוֹן** עולם

Dear **Sir,** **אָדוֹן** נכבד,

Additional Examples in this Pattern

back (N) אָחוֹר

African wild ass עָרוֹד

---

290. ***CaCoC***: nouns, when the plural suffix is *-ot*

our/your/their	my/your/his/her	const.	Gloss	sing/pl
לְשׁוֹנֵנוּ/נְכֶם/נְכֶן/נָם/נָן	**לְשׁוֹ**נִי/נְךָ/נֵךְ/נוֹ/נָהּ	לְשׁוֹן-	tongue;	לָשׁוֹן זו״נ
לְשׁוֹנוֹתֵינוּ/כֶם/כֶן/הֶם/הֶן	**לְשׁוֹנוֹ**תַי/תֶיךָ/תַיִךְ/תָיו/תֶיהָ	לְשׁוֹנוֹת-	language	לְשׁוֹנוֹת

The *kamats* is reduced two syllables before the main stress.

Examples

העברית שייכת למשפחת ה**לְשׁוֹנוֹת** השמיות, והעברית הקלאסית היא אחת מן ה**לְשׁוֹנוֹת** הכנעניות, המהוות ענף של השפות השמיות הצְפוֹן-מערביות.

Hebrew belongs to the Semitic **language** family, and Classical Hebrew is one of the Canaanite **languages**, which constitute a branch of North-Western Semitic.

אימי הייתה עושה מטעמים מ**גְרוֹנוֹת** של תרנגולי הודו שהייתה קונה בזול אצל הקצב.

My mother used to make delicacies out of the **necks** of turkey she would buy cheap at the butcher's.

Special Expressions

hold one by the **throat**, put one in an impossible situation תפס אותו ב**גָּרוֹן**

a pain in the neck, like a bone stuck in the **throat** כעצם ב**גָּרוֹן**

in other words **לָשׁוֹן** אחֵר

mother **tongue** **לְשׁוֹן** אם

libel; evil gossip **לְשׁוֹן** הרע

stutterer; **tongue**-tied כבד **לָשׁוֹן**

someone's destination **מְחוֹז** חפצו

Additional Examples in this Pattern

larynx; throat; neck גָּרוֹן

district מָחוֹז

car (of train); wagon קָרוֹן

---

291. ***CaCoC***: nouns, when the plural suffix is וֹת- and the first root consonant is guttural

our/your/their	my/your/his/her	.const	Gloss	sing/pl
אֲסוֹנֵנוּ/נְכֶם/נְכֶן/נָם/נָן	**אֲסוֹ**נִי/נְךָ/נֵךְ/נוֹ/נָהּ	אֲסוֹן-	disaster	אָסוֹן ז׳
אֲסוֹנוֹתֵינוּ/כֶם/כֶן/הֶם/הֶן	**אֲסוֹנוֹ**תַי/תֶיךָ/תַיִךְ/תָיו/תֶיהָ	אֲסוֹנוֹת-		אֲסוֹנוֹת

When the first consonant is a guttural, the expected *shva* is replaced by a *Hataf-pataH*: אֲסוֹנוֹת < אְסוֹנוֹת*.

Examples

רוב הָ**אֲסוֹנוֹת** בכבישים הם תוצאה של נהיגה חסרת-זהירות או נהיגה במהירות מופרזת.
Most **disasters** on the road result from careless driving or from driving at excessive speed.

כשמישהו מצהיר שהוא הומוסקסואל, אומרים עליו שהוא יצא מן הָ**אָרוֹן**.
When one declares that he is homosexual, they say that he has come out of the **closet**.

שאול יצא לחפש את הָ**אֲתוֹנוֹת** של אביו שאבדו, ומצא מלוכה.
Saul searched for his fathers' **asses** that got lost, and found a kingdom.

Special Expressions

אֲסוֹן-טֶבַע a **disaster** caused by nature; Coll.: an intolerable person

אֲרוֹן הקודש the Holy **Ark** (in a synagogue)

אֲרוֹן הברית **Ark** of the Covenant

אֲרוֹן בגדים **closet**, wardrobe

אֲרוֹן מֵתִים **coffin**

אֲרוֹן ספרים book**case**

אֲרוֹן קיר wardrobe

---

292. ***CaCon***: nouns derived from roots with a 3rd third consonant י, & a generally non-transparent suffix וֹן-

our/your/their	my/your/his/her	const.	Gloss	sing/pl
גְּאוֹנֵנוּ/נְכֶם/נְכֶן/נָם/נָן	**גְּאוֹ**נִי/נְךָ/נֵךְ/נוֹ/נָהּ	גְּאוֹן-	genius; grandeur;	גָּאוֹן ז'
גְּאוֹנֵינוּ/כֶם/כֶן/הֶם/הֶן	**גְּאוֹ**נַי/נֶיךָ/נַיִךְ/נָיו/נֶיהָ	גְּאוֹנֵי-	pride; swelling	גְּאוֹנִים

The *kamats* undergoes reduction.

Examples

ראש הנבחרת האולימפית של אַנדורה צעד בראש משלחתו, כשהוא נושא בְּ**גָאוֹן** את הדגל הלאומי...
The head of the Andorran Olympic team marched at the head of his delegation, carrying the national flag with **pride**…

גָּאוֹן (היום: אדם בעל אינטליגנציה ויצירתיות גבוהות) היה התואר של ראשי ישיבות בבבל ובארץ ישראל מסוף המאה השישית ועד אמצע המאה האחת עשרה. מתקופת הַ**גְּאוֹנִים** נותרה ספרות ענפה של שאלות שנשלחו לַ**גְּאוֹנִים** ותשובותיהם.
גָּאוֹן (today a person of high intelligence and creativity) was the title of the heads of *yeshiva*s in Babylon and in Palestine from the end of the sixth century to the middle of the eleventh. From the Geonic period there remained extensive literature composed of questions sent to the Geonim and their answers ("respona").

הַ**דְּאוֹנִים** הראשונים פותחו בתקופת מלחמת העולם הראשונה.
The first **drones** were developed during WWI.

Special Expressions

area adjacent to the river bank which is flooded during tide **גְּאוֹן** הנהר

Additional Examples in this Pattern

wickedness, malice זָדוֹן
grief Lit. יָגוֹן
shame, disgrace N קָלוֹן
thinness רָזוֹן
tumult, noise Lit שָׁאוֹן

---

293. ***CaCon***: nouns derived from roots in which the third consonant is י', plus a non-transparent suffix וֹן-, when the first root consonant is guttural

our/your/their	my/your/his/her	const.	Gloss	sing/pl
עֲלוֹנֵנוּ/נְכֶם/נְכֶן/נָם/נָן	**עֲלוֹ**נִי/נְךָ/נֵךְ/נוֹ/נָהּ	עֲלוֹן-	pamphlet	עָלוֹן ז'
עֲלוֹנֵינוּ/כֶם/כֶן/הֶם/הֶן	**עֲלוֹ**נַי/נֶיךָ/נַיִךְ/נָיו/נֶיהָ	עֲלוֹנֵי-		עֲלוֹנִים

The *shva* expected with a guttural is replaced by *Hataf pataH*: עֲלוֹנִים < עָלוֹנִים*

Examples

לקראת הבחירות, ניתן למצוא **עֲלוֹנֵי** תעמולה של המפלגות השונות בכל מקום.
Towards the elections, one can find propaganda **pamphlets** of the various parties everywhere.

למרבית הצער, לעיתים קרובות קולות **הֶהָמוֹן** מעלים דמגוגים מסוכנים לשלטון.
Unfortunately, the votes of **the masses** often raise dangerous demagogues to power.

Special Expressions

Public opinion matters ("the voice of the **masses** is like the voice of God") קול **הָמוֹן** כקול שדי
great anger, fury **חֲרוֹן** אף

Additional Examples in this Pattern

crowd, mob, masses; tumult, noise Lit הָמוֹן
anger, wrath חָרוֹן

---

294. ***CaCon***: nouns derived from roots in which the third consonant is י, plus a generally non-transparent suffix וֹן-, when the plural suffix is *-ot*

our/your/their	my/your/his/her	const.	Gloss	sing/pl
רְצוֹנֵנוּ/נְכֶם/נְכֶן/נָם/נָן	**רְצוֹ**נִי/נְךָ/נֵךְ/נוֹ/נָהּ	רְצוֹן-	will,	רָצוֹן ז'
רְצוֹנוֹתֵינוּ/כֶם/כֶן/הֶם/הֶן	**רְצוֹנוֹ**תַי/תֶיךָ/תַיִךְ/תָיו/תֶיהָ	רְצוֹנוֹת-	wish	רְצוֹנוֹת

Examples

בוודאי שאשמח לעזור ; אעשה זאת **בְּרָצוֹן**.
Of course I'll be happy to help; I'll do it willingly ("with **will**").

Special Expressions

people's **wish**es should be respected **רְצוֹנוֹ** של אדם כבודו
if you **will** it, it will happen אין דבר העומד בפני **הָרָצוֹן**

---

295. ***CaCon***: nouns derived from roots in which the third consonant is י, plus a generally non-transparent suffix וֹן-, when the plural suffix is וֹת- and the first consonant is guttural

our/your/their	my/your/his/her	const.	Gloss	sing/pl
חֲזוֹנֵנוּ/נְכֶם/נְכֶן/נָם/נָן	**חֲזוֹ**נִי/נְךָ/נֵךְ/נוֹ/נָהּ	חֲזוֹן-	vision	חָזוֹן ז'
חֶזְיוֹנוֹתֵינוּ/כֶם/כֶן/הֶם/הֶן	**חֲזוֹנוֹ**תַי/תֶיךָ/תַיִךְ/תָיו/תֶיהָ	חֲזוֹנוֹת-		חֲזוֹנוֹת

The expected *shva* is replaced by a *Hataf-pataH*: חֲזוֹנוֹת < חְזוֹנוֹת*.

Examples

כשבוחרים נשיא חדש לאוניברסיטה, מצפים שיידע לגייס כספים, ושיהיה גם איש **חָזוֹן**.
When we elect a new president for the university, we expect him not only to be good at fundraising, but also to be a man of **vision**.

Special Expressions

a common phenomenon **חָזוֹן** נִפְרָץ
material achievements without ideals may lead to stagnation and corruption. באין **חָזוֹן** ייפָּרע עם

Additional Examples in this Pattern

sin, transgression Lit עָווֹן

---

296. ***CaCoC***: nouns in which the *kamats* does not reduce

our/your/their	my/your/his/her	const.	Gloss	sing/pl
כָּרוֹזֵנוּ/זְכֶם/זְכֶן/זָם/זָן	**כָּרוֹ**זִי/זְךָ/זֵךְ/זוֹ/זָהּ	כָּרוֹז-	herald,	כָּרוֹז ז'
כָּרוֹזֵינוּ/כֶם/כֶן/הֶם/הֶן	**כָּרוֹ**זַי/זֶיךָ/זַיִךְ/זָיו/זֶיהָ	כָּרוֹזֵי-	announcer	כָּרוֹזִים

Examples

בנמל התעופה נשמעה הזהרה של **כָּרוֹז** שאין להשאיר תיקים ללא השגחה.
A warning was broadcast by an **announcer** at the airport that bags should not be left unattended.

Additional Examples in this Pattern

probe, tester בָּחוֹן
ferret חָמוֹס
probe (esp. in dentistry); calipers גָּשׁוֹשׁ

---

297. ***CaCoC***: nouns in which the *kamats* does not undergo reduction and the plural suffix is וֹת-

our/your/their	my/your/his/her	const.	Gloss	sing/pl
מָמוֹנֵנוּ/נְכֶם/נְכֶן/נָם/נָן	**מָמוֹ**נִי/נְךָ/נֵךְ/נוֹ/נָהּ	מָמוֹן-	money,	מָמוֹן ז׳
מָמוֹנוֹתֵינוּ/כֶם/כֶן/הֶם/הֶן	**מָמוֹנוֹ**תַי/תֶיךָ/תַיִךְ/תָיו/תֶיהָ	מָמוֹנוֹת-	capital	מָמוֹנוֹת

If the last consonant of the root is guttural, it it will be realized with a furtive *pataH* at the end of the word: לָקוֹחַ.

Examples

אברהם השקיע את כל **מָמוֹנוֹ** בנכסי דלא ניידי.
Abraham invested all of his **money** in real estate.

במזרח התיכון, בשעות שבהן אין הרבה **לָקוֹחוֹת**, בעלי החנויות אוהבים לשבת בחוץ ולפטפט עם בעלי החנויות הסמוכות.
In the Middle East, in times when there are few **customers**, store owners like to sit outside and chat with owners of nearby stores.

במכונית המודרנית, **פָּגוֹשׁ** המתכת הקשיח מצופה בדרך כלל בשכבת פלסטיק.
In a modern car, the rigid metal **bumper** is generally covered with a layer of plastic.

Special Expressions

a rich man בעל **מָמוֹן**
civil law, **monetary** law דיני **מָמוֹנוֹת**

Additional Examples in this Pattern

candlestick פָּמוֹט
toddler פָּעוֹט

---

298. ***CaCoC***: adjectives (which sometimes function as nouns as well) in which the *kamats* undergoes reduction

Construct	f. sing/pl	Construct	m. sing/pl	Gloss
קְדוֹשַׁת-	קְדוֹשָׁה נ׳	קְדוֹשׁ-	קָדוֹשׁ ז׳	holy
קְדוֹשׁוֹת-	קְדוֹשׁוֹת	קְדוֹשֵׁי-	קְדוֹשִׁים	

our/your/their	my/your/his/her	const.	Gloss	sing/pl
קְדוֹשֵׁנוּ/שְׁכֶם/שְׁכֶן/שָׁם/שָׁן	**קְדוֹ**שִׁי/שְׁךָ/שֵׁךְ/שׁוֹ/שָׁהּ	קְדוֹשׁ-	holy	קָדוֹשׁ ז׳
קְדוֹשֵׁינוּ/כֶם/כֶן/הֶם/הֶן	**קְדוֹ**שַׁי/שֶׁיךָ/שַׁיִךְ/שָׁיו/שֶׁיהָ	קְדוֹשֵׁי-	man	קְדוֹשִׁים

Examples

לכל אחת משלוש הדתות ה**גְּדוֹלוֹת** יש אתרים **קְדוֹשִׁים** בירושלים.
Each one of the three **major** religions has **holy** sites in Jerusalem.

ילדים בדרך כלל מחכים בכיליון עיניים לרגע שבו יהיו **גְּדוֹלִים**; כשהם מבוגרים, הם מתגעגעים לילדותם...
Children generally cannot wait for the moment when they become **big** = **adults**; when they are adults, they miss their childhood…

יש לחיים **קְרוֹבִים רְחוֹקִים** בתל אביב; הדירה שלהם **קְרוֹבָה** לחוף הים.
Hayyim has **distant relatives** in Tel Aviv; their apartment is **close** to the beach.

Special Expressions

גְּדוֹל הדור **outstanding** rabbi of the generation
גָּדוֹל מהחיים **larg**er than life
גָּדוֹל עליו beyond him
גְּדוֹלוֹת ונצורות wonderful things
גְּדוֹלָה מזו moreover
קְדוֹשׁ מְעוּנֶּה martyr
אחרי מות **קְדוֹשִׁים** אֱמוֹר Do not speak ill of the dead (interpreting names of three consecutive Torah portions)
קָרוֹב לוודאי more than likely
קָרוֹב לצלחת well connected Col.
בְּקָרוֹב soon
רְחוֹק ראייה/רואי **far**-sighted

Additional Examples in this Pattern

יָכוֹל able   רָחוֹק far   שָׁחוֹחַ bent, hunched

---

299. ***CaCoC***: adjectives in which the first root consonant is guttural

Construct	f. sing/pl	Construct	m. sing/pl	Gloss
-חֲסוֹנַת	חֲסוֹנָה נ׳	-חֲסוֹן	חָסוֹן ז׳	strong,
-חֲסוֹנוֹת	חֲסוֹנוֹת	-חֲסוֹנֵי	חֲסוֹנִים	powerful

When reduction of the *kamats* is expected in a syllable with a guttural is expected, it is replaced by a *Hataf-pataH*.

Examples

חיים נמוך קומה, אך יש לו ידיים **חֲסוֹנוֹת**.
Hayyim is short of stature, but his hands are **strong**.

---

300. ***CaCoC***: adjectives in which the *Holam* becomes *shuruk* in the declension

Construct	f. sing/pl	Construct	m. sing/pl	Gloss
-מְתוּקַת	מְתוּקָה נ׳	-מְתוֹק	מָתוֹק ז׳	sweet
-מְתוּקוֹת	מְתוּקוֹת	-מְתוּקֵי	מְתוּקִים	

The *kamats* is reduced to *shva* throughout the declension, and the *shuruk* appears in all forms other than the singular masculine.

Examples

כולנו יודעים שכדי למזער את הסיכון שנחלה בסכרת, עלינו להימנע מאכילת יותר של פחמימות, ובעיקר דברי מאפה **מְתוּקִים**, ממתקים, וכו', אך הפיתוי הוא גדול...
We all know that in order to minimize the risk of becoming diabetic, we should avoid consuming too much carbohydrates, and particularly **sweet** baked goods, sweets, etc., but the temptation is great...

Special Expressions

blessing in disguise, all for the best מעז יצא **מָתוֹק**

---

301. ***CaCoC***: adjectives whose basic form is *CaCuC* (with *kubuts*) and the *kamats* undergoes reduction

Construct	f. sing/pl	Construct	m. sing/pl	Gloss
סְגֻלַּת-	סְגֻלָּה	סְגֹל-	סָגֹל ז'	purple,
סְגֻלּוֹת-	סְגֻלּוֹת	סְגֻלֵּי-	סְגֻלִּים	violet

The vowel *u* is maintained as a *kubuts* (followed by a *dagesh*) before a suffix, but lowered to *o* (*Holam Haser*) in the unsuffixed form. The *kamats* is fully reduced, as in *sgula* 'purple, f.s.,' or reduced to the minimal vowel *e* if the first consonant is a sonorant: *yerukim* 'green, m.pl.' A prominent group in this pattern is of color adjectives. Note: in the form רָטֹב/רָטוּב 'wet' *kubuts* and *shuruk* exist alongside each other: רְטֻבָּה etc. and רְטוּבָה etc. (the forms with *shuruk* are the common variants used in speech). The form רָטוּב is listed twice: here, and under the *CaCuC mishkal*.

Examples

לדעת רוב הרופאים, בריא יותר לאכול ירקות ופירות אורגניים צבעוניים, בעיקר **סְגֻלִּים** וַאֲדֻמִּים, כמו סלק ופלפל אָדֹם.
Most doctors believe that it is healthier to eat colored organic vegetables and fruit, especially **purple** and red, such as beets and red peppers.

מעניין איך נולדה התפיסה שילדות קטנות צריכות ללבוש בגדים בצבע **וָרֹד** – אולי מכיוון **שהוָרֹד** נתפס כצבע עדין?
Interesting how the conception that little girls need to wear **pink** clothing came about – perhaps because **pink** is regarded as a delicate color?

רצוי לא להשתמש במכשירים חשמליים עם ידיים **רְטֻבּוֹת/רְטוּבוֹת**.
It is advisable not to use electrical appliances with **wet** hands.

Special Expressions

green light, OK to process אור **יָרֹק**   evergreen **יְרֹק**-עד
dollar bills (of any denominations) Coll **יְרֻקִּים**

Additional Examples in this Pattern

golden זָהֹב
green יָרֹק
orange כָּתֹם
spotted, speckled נָקֹד
yellow צָהֹב
brown, cinnamon-color קָנֹם
brownish, dark brown שָׁחֹם/שָׁחוּם

---

302. ***CaCoC***: adjectives in *CaCuC* when the first consonant is guttural

Construct	f. sing/pl	Construct	m. sing/pl	Gloss
אֲדֻמַּת-	אֲדֻמָּה	אֲדֹם-	אָדֹם ז'	red
אֲדֻמּוֹת-	אֲדֻמּוֹת	אֲדֻמֵּי-	אֲדֻמִּים	

The vowel *u* (*kubuts*) is maintained before a suffix, but lowered to *o* (*Holam Haser*) in the unsuffixed form. The *kamats* is replaced by a *Hataf-pataH* when a *shva* is expected as a result of reduction two syllables away from the main stress.

Examples

קשה לדעת אם פניו **אֲדֻמִּים** [או **אֲדֻמּוֹת**] ממאמץ, מחשיפה לשמש, או מעודף שתייה...
It is hard to say whether his **red** face is due to physical effort, to exposure to the sun, or to excessive drinking…

כשמגלים תבניות **עֲגֻלּוֹת** במקומות לא צפויים, נוטים לא פעם לייחס את יצירתן לחייזרים...
When **round** patterns are discovered in unexpected places, people sometimes tend to attribute their formation to aliens…

באגמים רבים המים **עֲמֻקִּים** ממה שחושבים, ויש להיזהר כשרוחצים בהם.
In some lakes the water is **deep**er than one tends to think, so one needs to be careful when bathing in them.

Special Expressions

Israeli EMS מגן דוד **אָדֹם**
red light, warning אור **אָדֹם**
redbreast robin **אֲדֹם** החזה
terrible! **אָיֹם** ונורא!
curve **עֲקֻמָּה**

Additional Examples in this Pattern

terrible אָיֹם
gray Lit. אָמֹץ
soft, delicate עָנֹג
curved, twisted עָקֹם
naked עָרֹם

---

303. ***CaCoC***: adjectives whose *o* vowel does not change in the declension because the final *r* cannot be geminated after *u,* but the *kamats* undergoes reduction

Construct	f. sing/pl	Construct	m. sing/pl	Gloss
שְׁחֹרַת-	שְׁחֹרָה	שְׁחֹר-	שָׁחֹר ז'	black
שְׁחֹרוֹת-	שְׁחֹרוֹת	שְׁחֹרֵי-	שְׁחֹרִים	

The *kamats* is fully reduced two syllables away from the main stress, or reduced to a *Hataf-pataH* if the first consonant is a guttural (אֲפֹרִים ‘gray m.pl.’ etc.).

Examples

השמים התכסו בעננים **שְׁחֹרִים**, והחל לרדת גשם זלעפות.
The sky filled up with **black** clouds, and torrential rain fell.

יש מקומות שבגלל ערפל כמעט תמידי וגשם תמיד נראים **אֲפֹרִים**.
Some places always appear to be **gray**, because of almost-constant fog and rain.

Special Expressions

pitch black (or black as a raven) **שָׁחֹר** כזפת/כעורב
melancholy ("**black** spleen") מרה **שְׁחֹרָה**
pessimist, regarding everything as bad רואה **שְׁחֹרוֹת**

Additional Examples in this Pattern

white, pure צָחֹר   of the color of earth Lit. עָפֹר   gray אָפֹר

---

304. ***CuCaC***: nouns with *kubuts* in which the *kamats* does not undergo reduction in most of the declension

our/your/their	my/your/his/her	const.	Gloss	sing/pl
שֻׁתָּפֵנוּ/פְכֶם/פְכֶן/פָם/פָן	**שֻׁתָּ**פִי/פְךָ/פֵךְ/פוֹ/פָהּ	שֻׁתַּף-	partner	שֻׁתָּף ז'
שֻׁתָּפֵינוּ/כֶם/כֶן/הֶם/הֶן	**שֻׁתָּ**פַי/פֶיךָ/פַיִךְ/פָיו/פֶיהָ	שֻׁתְּפֵי-		שֻׁתָּפִים

The *kamats* is maintained in most of the declension, except for the construct singular, where it is repaced by a *pataH*.

Examples

יזמים המחפשים **שֻׁתָּפִים** עושים זאת בדרך כלל כשאין להם מספיק אמצעים למימון עצמי.
Entrepreneurs who look for **partners** often do so because they do not have enough capital of their own.

מובן שגם היהדות, ככל הדתות, אינה מעודדת הפלות, אבל **העֻבָּר** כשלעצמו אינו נחשב כאדם לפני שנולד.
Judaism, like all other religions, of course does not encourage abortion, but in itself, the **fetus** is not considered a human being before actually being born.

Special Expressions

accessory to a felony **שֻׁתָּף** לדבר עבירה

Additional Examples in this Pattern

saddle אֻכָּף
craftsman, artisan אֻמָּן
the five books of the Pentateuch חֻמָּשׁ
French fried potato chip טֻגָּן
fennel שֻׁמָּר

---

305. ***CuCaC***: nouns with *kubuts* in which the *kamats* does not undergo reduction in most of the declension, and the plural suffix is וֹת-

our/your/their	my/your/his/her	const.	Gloss	sing/pl
סֻלָּמֵנוּ/מְכֶם/מְכֶן/מָם/מָן	**סֻלָּ**מִי/מְךָ/מֵךְ/מוֹ/מָהּ	סֻלַּם-	ladder;	סֻלָּם ז'
סֻלָּמוֹתֵינוּ/כֶם/כֶן/הֶם/הֶן	**סֻלָּמוֹ**תַי/תֶיךָ/תַיִךְ/תָיו/תֶיהָ	סֻלָּמוֹת-	scale	סֻלָּמוֹת

Examples

על פי חלום יעקב, מלאכים אינם עפים אלא משתמשים **בְּסֻלָּם**...
According to Jacob's dream, angels do not fly, but use a **ladder**…

Special Expressions

musical scale **סֻלַּם** הקולות

---

306. ***CoCaC***: nouns with *kamats katan* [pronounced *o*] that is maintained throughout the declension

our/your/their	my/your/his/her	const.	Gloss	sing/pl
אָמָּנֵנוּ/נְכֶם/נְכֶן/נָם/נָן	**אָמָּ**נִי/נְךָ/נֵךְ/נוֹ/נָהּ	אָמַּן-	artist	אָמָּן ז'
אָמָּנֵינוּ/כֶם/כֶן/הֶם/הֶן	**אָמָּ**נַי/נֶיךָ/נַיִךְ/נָיו/נֶיהָ	אָמָּנֵי-		אָמָּנִים

Examples

רוב **הָאָמָּנִים** חייבים גם לעבוד בעבודות אחרות ; מעטים מתפרנסים מאמנות.
Most **artists** have to work at other jobs; only a few can make a living from art.

Special Expressions

master class כיתת **אָמָּן**

---

307. ***CCeC***: nouns with a *tsere* that is maintained throughout

our/your/their	my/your/his/her	const.	Gloss	sing/pl
זְאֵבֵנוּ/בְכֶם/בְכֶן/בָם/בָן	**זְאֵ**בִי/בְךָ/בֵךְ/בוֹ/בָהּ	זְאֵב-	wolf	זְאֵב ז'
זְאֵבֵינוּ/כֶם/כֶן/הֶם/הֶן	**זְאֵ**בַי/בֶיךָ/בַיִךְ/בָיו/בֶיהָ	זְאֵבֵי-		זְאֵבִים

Examples

Wolves generally live and hunt in packs. **זְאֵבִים** בדרך כלל חיים וצדים בלהקות.

יכולתו של אדם לשאת **כְּאֵב** עומדת במבחן קשה כשמענים אותו פיסית.
A person's tolerance for **pain** is severely tested when s/he is physically tortured.

Special Expressions

German shepherd **כלב זְאֵב** dog-eat-dog **אדם לאדם זְאֵב**

Additional Examples in this Pattern

relative שְׁאֵר splendor פְּאֵר
strength שְׂאֵת oryx רְאֵם

---

308. ***CCeC* = *CaCeC*** nouns with *tsere* that is maintained throughout and when the 1st consonant is a guttural

our/your/their	my/your/his/her	const.	gloss	sing/pl
אֲפֵרֵנוּ/רְכֶם/רְכֶן/רָם/רָן	**אֲפֵ**רִי/רְךָ/רֵךְ/רוֹ/רָהּ	-אֲפֵר	eye-	אֲפֵר ז'
אֲפֵרֵינוּ/כֶם/כֶן/הֶם/הֶן	**אֲפֵ**רַי/רֶיךָ/רַיִךְ/רָיו/רֶיהָ	-אֲפֵרֵי	mask	אֲפֵרִים

The expected *shva* with a guttural is replaced by a *Hataf-pataH*.

---

309. ***C(e)CeC***: feminine nouns with a *tsere* that is maintained throughout, with the plural ending וֹת-

our/your/their	my/your/his/her	const.	gloss	sing/pl
בְּאֵרֵנוּ/רְכֶם/רְכֶן/רָם/רָן	**בְּאֵ**רִי/רְךָ/רֵךְ/רוֹ/רָהּ	-בְּאֵר	well	בְּאֵר נ'
בְּאֵרוֹתֵינוּ/כֶם/כֶן/הֶם/הֶן	**בְּאֵרוֹ**תַי/תֶיךָ/תַיִךְ/תָיו/תֶיהָ	-בְּאֵרוֹת		בְּאֵרוֹת

Examples

בְּאֵר המים הייתה המרכז החברתי של מרבית היישובים הכפריים בעולם העתיק.
The water(ing) **well** was the social center of most rural villages in the ancient world.

Special Expressions

the underworld, hell; tomb Lit. **בְּאֵר** שחת

---

310. ***CCaC***: nouns with *kamats* that is maintained in most of the declension

our/your/their	my/your/his/her	const.	Gloss	sing/pl
פְּרָטֵנוּ/**פְּרַטְ**כֶם/כֶן/**פְּרָטָ**ם/ן	פְּרָטִי/פְּרָטְךָ/פְּרָטֵךְ/פְּרָטוֹ/פְּרָטָהּ	-פְּרַט	detail;	פְּרָט ז'
פְּרָטֵינוּ/כֶם/כֶן/הֶם/הֶן	**פְּרָ**טַי/טֶיךָ/טַיִךְ/טָיו/טֶיהָ	-פְּרָטֵי	individual	פְּרָטִים

This *mishkal* is monosyllabic, but since the initial *shva*, which is not realized in Israeli Hebrew, was originally a *shva mobile*, we will treat it here as a bisyllabic *mishkal*. In a closed syllable and in the construct singular, a *kamats* becomes *pataH*.

Examples

אל תחתום על החוזה לפני שאתה קורא את כל ה**פְּרָטִים** שבאותיות הקטנות.
Do not sign the contract before you read all the **details** in the small print.

תמיד יתקיים המתח שבין חירות ה**פְּרָט** וטובת הכלל.
There will always be the tension between **individual** liberties and the common good.

פוטין הבטיח לטרמפ ש**טְוַח** הטילים של צפון קוריאה אינו מגיע לארה"ב.
Putin assured Trump that the North Korean missile **range** does not reach the US.

כְּלָלֵי הדקדוק של המישלב המדובר לא תמיד זהים לאלה של המישלב הגבוה.
The grammatical **rules** of the spoken register are not always the same as those of the higher register.

בדרך כלל, במרכז כל **כְּפָר** ערבי (מוסלמי) ניצב מסגד.
Generally, at the center of any (Muslim) Arab **village** stands a mosque.

משחקי **קְלָפִים**, כמו פוקר ואחרים, פופולריים בישראל לא פחות מאשר בארה"ב.
Card games, like poker etc., are no less popular in Israel than they are in the US.

Special Expressions

final (in sports) **גְּמַר** גביע

public works projects for the unemployed עבודות **דְּחָק**

hearing **range** **טְוַח** שמיעה

iron-clad **rule** **כְּלָל** ברזל

bill of indictment **כְּתַב** אישום

traffic **jam** **פְּקַק** תנועה

not for personal gain שלא על מנת לקבל **פְּרָס**

except for **פְּרָט** ל-

in particular **בִּפְרָט**

in great **detail** **בִּפְרָטֵי פְּרָטִים**

in the fullest possible **detail** לכל **פְּרָטָיו** ודקדוקיו

protocol **פְּרָטֵי** כל/פרוטוקול

swastika **צְלַב** קרס

bargaining **chip** **קְלַף** מיקוח

un**tarnish**ed ללא **רְבָב**

Additional Examples in this Pattern

sentence, judgment גְּזָר

end גְּמָר/גֶּמֶר

tow truck גְּרָר

pattern, design, model דְּגָם

social stress דְּחָק

homiletic exegesis דְּרָשׁ

moss טְחָב

honor, glory יְקָר

writing כְּתָב

deputy סְגָן

restriction סְיָג

foal, colt סְיָח

the covering of a sukkah סְכָךְ

border, edge, frontier סְפָר

depreciation פְּחָת

cork, stopper, plug; traffic jam פְּקָק

prize פְּרָס

cross צְלָב

spot, stain; fault רְבָב

chip שְׁבָב

311. ***CCaC* = *CaCaC*** nouns with *kamats* that is maintained in most of the declension when the first consonant is a guttural

our/your/their	my/your/his/her	const.	Gloss	sing/pl
עֲנָקֵנוּ/**עֲנַקְ**כֶם/כֶן/**עֲנָקָ**ם/ן	**עֲנָ**קִי/קְךָ/קֵךְ/קוֹ/קָהּ	עֲנַק-	giant;	עֲנָק ז'
עֲנָקֵינוּ/כֶם/כֶן/הֶם/הֶן	**עֲנָ**קַי/קֶיךָ/קַיִךְ/קָיו/קֶיהָ	עַנְקֵי-	necklace	עֲנָקִים

When the first consonant is a guttural, the *shva* is replaced by a *Hataf-pataH*, and in the case of אֱיָל, by a *Hataf-seghol*. The *kamats* becomes *pataH* only in the construct sing.

our/your/their	my/your/his/her	const.	Gloss	sing/pl
חֲשָׁדֵנוּ/**חֲשַׁדְ**כֶם/כֶן/**חֲשָׁדָ**ם/ן	**חֲשָׁ**דִי/דְךָ/דֵךְ/דוֹ/דָהּ	חֲשַׁד-	suspicion	חֲשָׁד ז'
חֲשָׁדוֹתֵינוּ/כֶם/כֶן/הֶם/הֶן	**חֲשָׁ**דוֹתַי/תֶיךָ/תַיִךְ/תָיו/תֶיהָ	חַשְׁדוֹת-		חֲשָׁדוֹת

The plural forms of חֲשָׁד and חֲשָׁשׁ use the *-ot* plural suffix (in earlier stages of Hebrew the form חֲשָׁדִים was used as well).

Examples

גוליבר ביקר לא רק בארץ הגמדים, אלא גם בארץ ה**עֲנָקִים**.
Gulliver visited not only the land of the little people, but that of the **giants** as well.

עֲנָקֵי פנינים יש לחרוז מחדש מדי כמה שנים ; קל לאבד פנינים פנינים אם החוט נקרע.
Pearl **necklaces** should be re-strung every few years; pearls are easily lost once the string breaks.

משטרת ישראל אינה פוחדת מאף אחד, וגם כשעולים **חֲשָׁדוֹת** לשחיתות במערכת הפוליטית, היא מכינה כתבי אישום ללא היסוס.
The Israeli police is not afraid of anybody, and even when **suspicions** of corruption arise in the political arena, it prepares indictments with no hesitation.

מספרים ש**אֲוָזִים** הצילו את רומא, אבל זה לא סייע להם לקבל חנינה במטבח...
They say that **geese** saved Rome, but it did not help then get a pardon in the kitchen…

Special Expressions

אֲתַר בנייה construction **site**

חֲתַךְ רוחב cross-**section**

Additional Examples in this Pattern

אֲנָךְ vertical, perpendicular N.; plumb line

אֲתָר site

חֲטָף *Hataf* (shortened vowel in Classical Hebrew)

חֲשָׁשׁ fear, concern

חֲתָךְ cut; cross-section

עֲרָר appeal

312. ***CCaC***: nouns with *a* that is maintained through most of the declension when the plural suffix is *-ot* (feminine or masculine)

our/your/their	my/your/his/her	const.	Gloss	sing/pl
קְרָבֵנוּ/**קְרַבְ**כֶם/כֶן/**קְרָבָ**ם/ן	**קְרָ**בִי/בְךָ/בֵךְ/בוֹ/בָהּ	קְרַב-	battle;	קְרָב ז'
קְרָבוֹתֵינוּ/כֶם/כֶן/הֶם/הֶן	**קְרָבוֹ**תַי/תֶיךָ/תַיִךְ/תָיו/תֶיהָ	קְרָבוֹת-	match	קְרָבוֹת

This *mishkal* is monosyllabic, but since the initial *shva*, which is not realized in Israeli Hebrew, was originally a *shva mobile*, we will treat it here as a bisyllabic *mishkal*. In a closed syllable and in the construct singular, a *kamats* becomes *pataH.*

Examples

הקְרָב על הבליטה היה אחד **הקְרָבוֹת** הקשים האחרונים של מלחמת העולם השנייה.
The **Battle** of the Bulge was one of the toughest last **battles** of WWII.

המונח העברי לדֶקָתְלוֹן הוא "**קְרַב** עשר/עשור".
The Hebrew term for the decathlon is '**battle** of ten'.

בתל אביב אנשים רבים חונים על המדרכה, והמשטרה אינה מטילה עליהם **קְנָסוֹת**.
In Tel aviv many people park on the sidewalk, and the police does not impose **fines** on them.

לדעתי אי אפשר לעשות כל עבודת תיקון בבית, אפילו הקטנה ביותר, ללא **צְבָת**.
In my opinion, it is impossible to do any repair job at home, even the smallest, without **pliers**.

Special Expressions

tin **foil** **נְיַר** כסף
face to face **קְרָב** מגע/פנים אל פנים **combat**
duel; match דו-**קְרָב**
battlefield שדה **קְרָב**

eager to fight שש אלי **קְרָב**
promissory **note** **שְׁטַר** חוב
paper money, bank**note** **שְׁטַר** כסף
bill of sale **שְׁטַר** מכר

Additional Examples in this Pattern

paper נְיָר   bill, banknote שְׁטָר

---

313. ***CCaC***: nouns with a *pataH* followed by a *dagesh*

our/your/their	my/your/his/her	const.	Gloss	sing/pl
זְמַנֵּנוּ/נְּכֶם/נְּכֶן/נָּם/נָּן	**זְמַ**נִּי/נְּךָ/נֵּךְ/נּוֹ/נָּהּ	זְמַן-	time; season,	זְמַן ז'
זְמַנֵּינוּ/כֶם/כֶן/הֶם/הֶן	**זְמַ**נַּי/נֶּיךָ/נַּיִךְ/נָּיו/נֶּיהָ	זְמַנֵּי-	term	זְמַנִּים

This *mishkal* is monosyllabic, but since the initial *shva*, which is not realized in Israeli Hebrew, was originally a *shva mobile*, we will treat it here as a bisyllabic *mishkal*.

Examples

אין לי **זְמַן** היום ; בוא ניפגש מחר.
I have no **time** today; let's meet tomorrow.

Special Expressions

lately **בִּזְמַן** האחרון
when, while **בִּזְמַן** ש...
at the **time** **בִּזְמַנּוֹ**
between **terms** בין **הַזְּמַנִּים**
in course of **time** בִּמרוצת/במשך **הַזְּמַן**
as long as כל **זְמַן** ש...
there's a **time** for everything לכל **זְמַן** ועת לכל חפץ

in the spirit of the **time** בְּרוח **הַזְּמַן**, לפי רוח **הַזְּמַן**
a long **time** ago מִזְּמַן
before his **time** קודם **זְמַנּוֹ**
very little Lit. **מְעַט** מזעיר
bone **marrow**; the innermost part Lit. **לְשַׁד** עצם

Additional Examples in this Pattern

large city כְּרַךְ   juice, essence לְשַׁד   little, few מְעַט

---

314. ***CCaC* = *CaCaC*** nouns with a *pataH* followed by a *dagesh*, when the first root consonant is guttural

our/your/their	my/your/his/her	const.	Gloss	sing/pl
אֲגַפֵּנוּ/פְּכֶם/פְּכֶן/פָּם/פָּן	**אֲגַפִּ**י/פְּךָ/פֵּךְ/פּוֹ/פָּהּ	אֲגַף-	wing, department,	אֲגַף ז'
אֲגַפֵּינוּ/כֶם/כֶן/הֶם/הֶן	**אֲגַפַּ**י/פֶּיךָ/פַּיִךְ/פָּיו/פֶּיהָ	אֲגַפֵּי-	branch; flank	אֲגַפִּים

The expected *shva* is replaced by a *Hataf-pataH*

Examples

הָאֲגַף השמאלי של הבניין נהרס כליל.
The left **wing** of the building was completely destroyed.

דני עובד **בַּאֲגַף** האפסנאות.
Danny works in the storekeeping **department**.

הָאֲגַם המפורסם בארץ הוא **אֲגַם**/ים הכינרת, בשל הקשר עם ישו.
The best known **lake** in Israel is the Sea of Galilee, because of the association with Jesus.

Special Expressions

Operations **Branch** at GHQ **אֲגַף** המטה
Department of Antiquities **אֲגַף** העתיקות

Additional Examples in this Pattern

fodder, straw חֲשַׁשׁ   myrtle הֲדַס

---

315. ***CCaC***: nouns with a *pataH* without a *dagesh*, with a segholate-type declension (base with *i*)

our/your/their	my/your/his/her	const.	Gloss	sing/pl
סִבְכֵנוּ/כְכֶם/כְכֶן/כָם/כָן	**סִבְ**כִי/כְךָ/כֵךְ/כוֹ/כָהּ	סְבַךְ-	entanglement;	סְבַךְ ז׳
סְבָכֵינוּ/**סִבְכֵי**כֶם/כֶן/הֶם/הֶן	**סְבָ**כַי/כֶיךָ/כַיִךְ/כָיו/כֶיהָ	סִבְכֵי-	thicket	סְבָכִים

This *mishkal* is monosyllabic, but since the initial *shva*, which is not realized in Israeli Hebrew, was originally a *shva mobile*, we will treat it here as a bisyllabic *mishkal*. In a closed syllable, the first consonant is followed by a *Hirik*.

Examples

חבר המושבעים התקשה להגיע להחלטה בשל **סְבַךְ** העדויות הסותרות.
The jury had difficulty reaching a verdict owing to the **complicated situation** involving contradictory testimonies.

״איל... נאחז **בִּסְבַךְ** בקרניו״ (בר׳ כב :יג)
"A ram… with his horns entangled in the **thicket**" (Gen 22:13)

Additional Examples in this Pattern

honey דְּבַשׁ

---

316. ***CCoC***: nouns with a *CCuC* base

our/your/their	my/your/his/her	const.	Gloss	sing/pl
לְאֻמֵּנוּ/מְּכֶם/מְּכֶן/מָּם/מָּן	**לְאֻ**מִּי/מְּךָ/מֵּךְ/מּוֹ/מָּהּ	לְאֹם-	nation,	לְאֹם ז׳
לְאֻמֵּינוּ/כֶם/כֶן/הֶם/הֶן	**לְאֻ**מַּי/מֶּיךָ/מַּיִךְ/מָּיו/מֶּיהָ	לְאֻמֵּי-	people	לְאֻמִּים

The vowel *u* is maintained before a suffix, but lowered to *o* in an unsuffixed form. The consonant following *u* takes a *dagesh*.

Examples

ביהדות לא תמיד קל להבדיל ביו הדת היהודית **לַלְאֹם** היהודי.
In Judaism it not that easy to distinguish between the Jewish religion and the Jewish **nation**.

Special Expressions

the League of **Nations** חֶבֶר הַ**לְאֻמִּים**

---

317. ***CéCeC***: segholate (penultimately stressed) nouns with a *CiCC* base

our/your/their	my/your/his/her	const.	Gloss	sing/pl
דִּגְלֵנוּ/לְכֶם/לְכֶן/לָם/לָן	**דִּגְ**לִי/לְךָ/לֵךְ/לוֹ/לָהּ	דֶּגֶל-	flag,	דֶּגֶל ז'
דְּגָלֵינוּ/**דִּגְלֵי**כֶם/כֶן/הֶם/הֶן	**דְּגָ**לַי/לֶיךָ/לַיִךְ/לָיו/לֶיהָ	דִּגְלֵי-	banner	דְּגָלִים

One can classify nouns in the penultimately-stressed *CeCeC mishkal* based on their assumed historical base, as realized when a suffix is added: *dégel* 'flag' ~ *diglon* 'small flag,' *degel* ~ *digli* 'my flag…' The historical explanation: when the base, in this case *CiCC*, did not have a suffix appended to it, the final consonant cluster was hard for speakers of Classical Hebrew to articulate, and they consequently split it with a *seghol*; afterwards the base vowel assimilated to the following *seghol*, to facilitate articulation, but stress stayed on the base vowel, as it was before the split, which accounts for the penultimate stress. Clearly, when suffixes were appended, there was no articulation problem, since re-syllabification eliminated final clusters, e.g., *dig-lon*. The plural form is by itself a kind of *mishkal* on its own: *CCaCim* (קְטָלִים).

Examples

בהרבה מקומות מניפים **דְּגָלִים** מיוחדים בחצי התורן להזדהות עם חיילים שבויים ונעדרים.
In many places they fly special **flags** at half-mast as a mark of identification with prisoners of war and soldiers missing in action.

בקהילות היהודיות בגולה מקובל היה שעל הציבור לדאוג לכך שלכל חבר בקהילה יהיה לחם לאכול ו**בֶגֶד** ללבוש.
The Jewish communities in the diaspora it was accepted that the community should make sure that every member has bread to eat and **clothing** to wear.

בישראל יורד שלג רק במספר מקומות; ברוב הארץ החורף הוא עונת ה**גְּשָׁמִים**.
It Israel it snows only in a few places; in most of the country winter is the **rain**y season.

אחד ה**גְּשָׁרִים** היפים בעולם הוא ה**גֶּשֶׁר** המוזהב של סן-פרנציסקו.
One of the most beautiful **bridges** in the world is the Golden Gate **Bridge** of San Francisco.

ה**דֶּגֶם** המרהיב של בית המקדש הועבר ממקומו המקורי ליד מלון "הולילנד" למוזיאון ישראל.
The very impressive **model** of the Temple was transferred from its original location next to the Holyland Hotel to the Israel Museum.

ה**דֶּקֶל** ששימש מקור השראה לשירה המפורסם של רחל "כינרת" קרס בסערה ב-2018.
The **palm tree** that inspired the poetess Rachel in her famous poem "Kinneret" collapsed in a storm in 2018.

טֶקֶס יום הזיכרון השנתי לשואה ולגבורה, הנערך כל שנה בין פסח ליום העצמאות, הוא אחד **הטְקָסִים** המרשימים ביותר בארץ.

The annual memorial **ceremony** for the Holocaust and Resistance, which takes place every year between Passover and Israel Independence Day, is one of the most impressive **ceremonies** in Israel.

Special Expressions

swim **suit** **בֶּגֶד** ים
bountiful **rain** **גֶּשֶׁם** ברכה, **גֶּשֶׁם** נדבות
raft **bridge** **גֶּשֶׁר** דוברות
rope **bridge** **גֶּשֶׁר** חבלים
contact **glue** **דֶּבֶק** מגע
every man to his post איש על **דִּגְלוֹ**
was called to the colors נקרא אל **הדֶּגֶל**
proto**type** **דֶּגֶם** אב
palm oil tree **דֶּקֶל** השמן

stream of consciousness **זֶרֶם** התודעה
rite of passage **טֶקֶס** מעבר
swearing-in/induction **ceremony** **טֶקֶס** השבעה
hypertension **יֶתֶר** לחץ דם
double taxation **כֶּפֶל** מס
many **times** more **כֶּפֶל** כפליים
nuclear **weapon** **נֶשֶׁק** גרעיני
public opinion **poll** **סֶקֶר** דעת קהל

Additional Examples in this Pattern

abdomen, belly בֶּטֶן
faucet, tap בֶּרֶז
gypsum גֶּבֶס
glue דֶּבֶק
model דֶּגֶם
songs, singing זֶמֶר
flow; electric current זֶרֶם
winery יֶקֶב
remainder; excess יֶתֶר

sheep; mutton כֶּבֶשׂ
assembly, conference כֶּנֶס
multiplication; double כֶּפֶל
stain כֶּתֶם
message מֶסֶר
farm; economy מֶשֶׁק
weapon נֶשֶׁק
survey סֶקֶר
ribbon; movie, film סֶרֶט

---

318. ***CéCeC***: segholate (penultimately stressed) nouns with a *CiCC* base when the first consonant is guttural

const.	Gloss	sing/pl
-עֶנֶד	decoration;	עֶנֶד ז'
-עִנְדֵי	knot	עֲנָדִים

See above explanation for declensions of *CeCeC* whose base is *CiCC*, as exemplified by the דֶּגֶל 'flag' declension. When the first consonant is a guttural, the expected *shva* is replaced by a *Hataf-pataH*. The only occurrence that is not obsolete is the word עֶנֶד 'decoration; knot,' for which no alternants with possessive suffixes can be documented.

Examples

הגנרל הופיע בטקס כשעשרות **עִנְּדֵי** כבוד על חזהו.
The general appeared at the ceremony with scores of honorary **decorations** on breast.

---

319. ***CéCeC***: segholate (penultimately stressed) nouns with a *CiCC* base when the final consonant is guttural

our/your/their	my/your/his/her	const.	Gloss	sing/pl
פִּתְחֵנוּ/**פִּתְ**חֲכֶם/חֲכֶן/חָם/חָן	**פִּתְ**חִי/חֲךָ/חֵךְ/חוֹ/חָהּ	פֶּתַח-	doorway,	פֶּתַח ז'
פְּתָחֵינוּ/**פִּתְחֵי**כֶם/כֶן/הֶם/הֶן	**פְּתָ**חַי/חֶיךָ/חַיִךְ/חָיו/חֶיהָ	פִּתְחֵי-	entrance; opening	פְּתָחִים

See above explanation for declensions of *CeCeC* whose base is *CiCC*, as exemplified by the דֶּגֶל 'flag' declension. If a *shva* is expected, it is replaced by a *Hataf-pataH*. In the isolation form and in the singular construct of ה' ח' ע' (but not א'), the expected *seghol* is replaced by a *pataH* (word-final gutturals prefer low vowels before them).

Examples

הוא עמד **בְּפֶתַח** הבית אבל לא העז להיכנס.
He stood at the **entrance** to the house but dared not come in.

הַפֶּתַח הזה צר מדיי. לא נוכל לעבור דרכו.
This **opening** is too narrow; we won't be able to pass through it.

יש הטוענים שהסוציאליזם מנוגד **לְטֶבַע** האדם. נראה לי שלא. אולי הקומוניזם, אבל לא הסוציאליזם.
Some claim that socialism is against the **nature** of man. I believe it is not. Pehaps communism is, but not socialism.

מה לדעתכם חשוב יותר בחיים: **יֶדַע** או אינטליגנציה?
What do you think is more important in life, **knowledge** or intelligence?

הנמלים והדבורים חיים בחברות מאורגנות למופת ובשיתוף פעולה מלא; **הַפֶּלֶא** הוא שהם לא השתלטו על העולם.
Ants and bees live in highly organized societies and in full cooperation among themselves; the **wonder** is that they have not taken over the world.

Special Expressions

גֶּזַע המוח brain**stem**
טֶבַע דומם still **life** (in painting)
פֶּלַח שוק market **segment**
פֶּרֶא אדם **wild**, savage person
פֶּרַח קצונה cadet
פִּשְׁעֵי מלחמה war **crimes**
חזר על **הַפְּתָחִים** went from house to house (begging)
פֶּתַח דבר preface

Additional Examples in this Pattern

peace, security Lit. בֶּטַח	slice פֶּלַח
small hill גֶּבַע	wound פֶּצַע
trunk (of tree); race גֶּזַע	savage פֶּרֶא
jail כֶּלֶא	flower פֶּרַח
a lesson לֶקַח	crime פֶּשַׁע
volume נֶפַח	

---

320. *CéCeC*: segholate (penultimately stressed) nouns with a *CiCC* base and the plural suffix is a dual

our/your/their	my/your/his/her	const.	Gloss	sing/pl
בִּרְכֵּנוּ/כְּכֶם/כְּכֶן/כָּם/כָּן	**בִּרְ**כִּי/כְּךָ/כֵּךְ/כּוֹ/כָּהּ	בֶּרֶךְ-	knee; knee-	בֶּרֶךְ נ׳
בִּרְכֵּינוּ/כֶם/כֶן/הֶם/הֶן	**בִּרְ**כַּי/כֶּיךָ/כַּיִךְ/כָּיו/כֶּיהָ	בִּרְכֵּי-	shaped pipe	בִּרְכַּיִם

See above explanation for declensions of *CeCeC* whose base is *CiCC*, as exemplified by the דֶּגֶל 'flag' declension. The plural suffix is the dual form ַ–יִם.

Examples

אם יש לך ארתיטיס ב**בִּרְכַּיִם**, נסה לקחת גלוקוסמין.
If you have arthritis in your knees, try to take glucosamine.

Special Expressions

בִּרְכַּיִם כושלות/פיק **בִּרְכַּיִם** faint-heartedness	מֵי **בִּרְכַּיִם** knee-deep water
	שְׁפַל **בֶּרֶךְ** humble, lowly

Additional Examples in this Pattern

apostrophe גֶּרֶשׁ/גֵּרֵשׁ

---

321. *CéCeC*: segholate (penultimately stressed) feminine nouns with a *CiCC* base

our/your/their	my/your/his/her	const.	Gloss	sing/pl
שִׁמְשֵׁנוּ/שְׁכֶם/שְׁכֶן/שָׁם/שָׁן	**שִׁמְ**שִׁי/שְׁךָ/שֵׁךְ/שׁוֹ/שָׁהּ	שֶׁמֶשׁ-	sun	שֶׁמֶשׁ נ׳
שִׁמְשׁוֹתֵינוּ/כֶם/כֶן/הֶם/הֶן	**שִׁמְשׁוֹ**תַי/תֶיךָ/תַיִךְ/תָיו/תֶיהָ	שִׁמְשׁוֹת-		שְׁמָשׁוֹת

In Classical Hebrew, שֶׁמֶשׁ also functions as masculine. Most forms in this *mishkal* end with ׳תי: שֶׁנֶת, רֶשֶׁת, רֶפֶת, לֶפֶת, לֶסֶת, כֶּסֶת, זֶרֶת, וֶסֶת, גֶּפֶת. Note: רֶגֶשׁ is a masculine form, but its declension is like that of the rest of the forms here.

Examples

חשיפה יתירה ל**שֶׁמֶשׁ** מפריעה לי; בקיץ אני מעדיף להסתובב עם כובע.
I am uncomfortable with excessive exposure to the **sun**; in the summer I wear a cap.

בישראל מצפים את גגות הבטון ב**זֶפֶת**, כדי שמי הגשם לא יחדרו לבניין.
In Israel they cover the concrete roofs of buildings with **tar**, to prevent rain water from penetrating inside.

בקיבוץ שלו, אפריים אחראי על ה**רֶפֶת**. הפרות מכירות אותו ואוהבות אותו, והוא מאמין שהן נותנות יותר חלב מפרות שבקיבוצים אחרים בזכות הטיפול המסור שלו.
In his kibbutz, Ephraim is responsible for the **cowshed**. The cows know him and like him, and he believes that they yield more milk than cows in other kibbutzim owing to his dedicated treatment of them.

Special Expressions

רֶשֶׁת ביטחון safety **net**
רֶשֶׁת מזון food **chain**
רֶשֶׁת חברתית social **network**
בין ה**שְּׁמָשׁוֹת** twi**light**
ברור כ**שֶּׁמֶשׁ** clear as **daylight**
מזרח ה**שֶּׁמֶשׁ** the east
מכת **שֶׁמֶשׁ** **sun**stroke
משקפי **שֶׁמֶשׁ** **sun**glasses
תחת ה**שֶּׁמֶשׁ** under the **sun**

Additional Examples in this Pattern

גֶּפֶת olive waste
זֶרֶת little finger
לֶסֶת jaw
לֶפֶת turnip
רֶשֶׁת net

---

322. ***CéCeC***: segholate (penultimately stressed) nouns with a *CiCC* base in which the first vowel is a *tsere*

our/your/their	my/your/his/her	const.	Gloss	sing/pl
סִפְרֵנוּ/רְכֶם/רְכֶן/רָם/רָן	**סִפְ**רִי/רְךָ/רֵךְ/רוֹ/רָהּ	סֵפֶר-	book; ledger;	סֵפֶר ז'
סְפָרֵינוּ/**סִפְרֵי**כֶם/כֶן/הֶם/הֶן	**סְפָ**רַי/רֶיךָ/רַיִךְ/רָיו/רֶיהָ	סִפְרֵי-	letter (ancient)	סְפָרִים

Examples

אם משה לא קורא לפחות **סֵפֶר** אחד בשבוע, הוא מרגיש אומלל.
If Moshe does not read at least one **book** a week, he feels miserable.

רואה החשבון עדיין לא עבר על ה**סְּפָרִים** של החברה.
The accountant has still not gone over the company's **books/ledgers**.

מרוב המשפחות של הורי כולנו שנשארו באירופה לא נשאר **זֵכֶר**.
Of the families of most of us who remained in Europe no **remnant** was left.

אנחנו מדליקים נר ל**זֵכֶר** כל אחד מהורינו ביום השנה לפטירתם. אם אנחנו אז בארץ, אנחנו עושים זאת כשאנו עורכים אזכרות על קברותיהם.
We light a candle in **memory** of each one of our parents on the anniversary of their passing away. If we are in Israel then, we do it when we hold memorials at their graves.

אחת השאלות שקשה לענות עליהן היא מה יותר חזק, **יֵצֶר** הקיום או **יֵצֶר** המשך הדורות? במצב נואש, האם תקריב את עצמך כדי שילדך ישרוד? נראה שרוב בני האדם יעשו זאת.
One of the questions that are difficult to answer is what is stronger, the **instinct** of survival, or the **instinct** of preseving the species? In a desparate situation, will you sacrifice yourself so that your child survive? It appears that most people would.

כל מי שיש לו ספריה של ממש יודע שאין מנוס מלקיים **סֵדֶר** **בִּסְפָרִים**.
Whoever has a decent library knows that there is no escape from maintaining **order** among the **books**.

אימרה המיוחסת לצ׳רצ׳יל (לא בדוק סופית): מי שלא היה ליברלי או סוציאליסט בצעירותו, אין לו לב, ומי שנשאר ליברלי או סוציאליסט כשהתבגר, אין לו **שֵׂכֶל**.
A saying attributed to Churchill (not confirmed…): He who was not a liberal or socialist in his youth, has no heart, and he who has remained liberal or socialist as an adult has no **brain/common sense**.

Special Expressions

evil **inclination** (nature) **יֵצֶר** הרע
instinct **יֵצֶר** בסיסי
list of priorities **סֵדֶר** עדיפויות
order of magnitude; size, scope, value **סֵדֶר** גודל
daily **routine**, agenda **סֵדֶר** יום
trade**mark** **סֵמֶל** מסחרי
school בית-**סֵפֶר**
the Apocrypha **הַסְּפָרִים** החיצוניים
scholar יודע **סֵפֶר**
like a sealed **book** כ**סֵפֶר** החתום
the Bible **סֵפֶר** הספרים
memorial **volume** **סֵפֶר** זיכרון
annals; memoirs **סֵפֶר** זיכרונות
bill of divorce **סֵפֶר** כריתות
the people of the book (Jews) עם ה**סֵפֶר**
the **lowest** rung; the **worst** situation **שֵׁפֶל** המדרגה

Additional Examples in this Pattern

inclination; instinct; urge יֵצֶר
harp נֵבֶל/נֶבֶל
order; the Passover Seder סֵדֶר
symbol סֵמֶל
mug סֵפֶל
tribe, clan שֵׁבֶט
ebb; low point שֵׁפֶל

---

323. ***CéCeC***: segholate (penultimately stressed) nouns in which the first vowel is a *tsere* with a *CiCC* base, when the first consonant is a guttural

our/your/their	my/your/his/her	const.	Gloss	sing/pl
חֶלְקֵנוּ/קְכֶם/קְכֶן/קָם/קָן	**חֶלְ**קִי/קְךָ/קֵךְ/קוֹ/קָהּ	חֵלֶק-	part; fate; region;	חֵלֶק ז׳
חֲלָקֵינוּ/**חֶלְקֵי**כֶם/כֶן/הֶם/הֶן	**חֲלָ**קַי/קֶיךָ/קַיִךְ/קָיו/קֶיהָ	חֶלְקֵי-	smoothness	חֲלָקִים

In a closed syllable the *Hirik* of the base becomes a *seghol*, and in an open stressed one a *tsere*. When a *shva* is expected, it is replaced by a *Hataf-pataH*.

Examples

על פי הצוואה, רכושם של ההורים יחולק לאחר פטירתם לשלושה **חֲלָקִים** שווים בין שלושת ילדיהם.
According to the will, the parents' estate will be divided after their death into three equal **parts** among their three children.

בתקופת המקרא, עושרו ומעמדו של אדם נקבעו בעיקר על פי גודל **עֲדָרָיו**.
In Biblical times, a person's wealth and stature were determined primarily by the size of his **flocks/herds**.

הבדואים נודדים עם **עֶדְרֵיהֶם** ממקום למקום בחיפוש אחר שדות מרעה טובים.
The Bedouins wander with their **herds** from place to place in search of good pastures.

אֵבֶל גדול ירד על הארץ כשיצחק רבין נרצח ב-1995.
All Israel was in **mourning** when Yitzhak Rabin was assassinated in 1995.

זה מפתיע, אבל לפעמים דווקא אנשים שנראים **הֲפָכִים** גמורים מסתדרים טוב זה עם זה.
It is surprising, but sometimes it is just those people who look like complete **opposites** of each other get along well together.

Special Expressions

חֶבְלֵי לידה labor **pains**
חֵלֶק הארי the lion's **share**
חֵלֶק חילוף spare **part**
חֵלֶק כחֵלֶק equal **parts**
יהי **חֶלְקִי** עמכם may I share your fortune
לקח **חֵלֶק** ב... took part in
נפל **בחֶלְקוֹ** was fortunate to win
איזהו עשיר? השמח **בחֶלְקוֹ** Who is rich? He who is content with his **lot**

עֵבֶר הירדן **Trans**-Jordan (former name of Jordan)
עֵגֶל הזהב the golden **calf**
עֵרֶב רב **rabble**, mob
שְׁתִי **וערֶב** horizontally and vertically
עֵרֶךְ מוסף added **value**
עֵרֶךְ נקוב face **value**
עֵרֶךְ מילוני lexical **entry**

Additional Examples in this Pattern

אֵדֶר hide of stuffed animal
אֵבֶר limb, organ
אֵפֶר ash
הֵלֶךְ wanderer
הֵפֶךְ/הֶפֶךְ opposite, contrary N
חֵבֶל pang, pain
חֵטְא sin; offense
חֵלֶב animal fat; candle wax
חֵפֶץ object, article; desire, want, wish Lit.
חֵרֶם excommunication; boycott; fishing net (biblical)
עֵבֶר side, direction
עֵגֶל calf (male)
עֵזֶר aid, assistance; aid(s)
עֵרֶב mix; rabble; woof (weaving)
עֵרֶךְ value; dictionary entry

324. ***CéCeC***: segholate (penultimately stressed) nouns in which the first vowel is a *tsere* with a *CiCC* base, when the last consonant is a guttural

Our/your/their	my/your/his/her	const.	Gloss	sing/pl
מִצְחֵנוּ/חֲכֶם/חֲכֶן/חָם/חָן	**מִצְ**חִי/חֲךָ/חֵךְ/חוֹ/חָהּ	מֵצַח-	forehead,	מֵצַח ז׳
מְצָחֵינוּ/**מִצְחֵי**כֶם/כֶן/הֶם/הֶן	**מְצָ**חַי/חֶיךָ/חַיִךְ/חָיו/חֶיהָ	מִצְחֵי/מִצְחוֹת-	brow	מְצָחִים/וֹת
מִצְחוֹתֵינוּ/כֶם/כֶן/הֶם/הֶן	**מִצְחוֹ**תַי/חֶיךָ/חַיִךְ/חָיו/חֶיהָ			

The *seghol* preceding a final guttural turns into a *pataH*. When a *shva* is expected with the guttural, it is replaced by a *Hataf-pataH*. Historically, מֵצַח could also be regarded feminine.

Examples

בלשון נקייה מתייחסים בסלנג הישראלי לקרחת כ״**מֵצַח** גבוה״.
In Israeli slang, they sometimes use a euphemism for baldness, referring to it as a "high **forehead**."

Special Expressions

התקפת **מֵצַח** **frontal** attack
חרות על **מִצְחוֹ** written on his face
מֵצַח נחושה hardened impudence
עזות **מֵצַח** effrontery
קימט את ה**מֵצַח** knit his **brows** (in thought)

---

325. ***CéCeC***: segholate (penultimately stressed) nouns in which the first vowel is a *tsere* with a *CiCC* base and whose plural suffix is וֹת-

our/your/their	my/your/his/her	const.	Gloss	sing/pl
סִבְלֵנוּ/לְכֶם/לְכֶן/לָם/לָן	**סִבְ**לִי/לְךָ/לֵךְ/לוֹ/לָהּ	סֵבֶל-	load, burden;	סֵבֶל ז׳
סִבְלוֹתֵינוּ/כֶם/כֶן/הֶם/הֶן	**סִבְלוֹ**תַי/תֶיךָ/תַיִךְ/תָיו/תֶיהָ	סִבְלוֹת-	suffering	סְבָלוֹת

Examples

בני מזדהה עם **סִבְלָם** של כל המדוכאים שבעולם.
Benny identifies with the **suffering** of all the oppressed of the world.

---

326. ***CéCeC***: segholate (penultimately stressed) nouns with a *CaCC* base

our/your/their	my/your/his/her	const.	Gloss	sing/pl
דַּרְכֵּנוּ/כְּכֶם/כְּכֶן/כָּם/כָּן	**דַּרְ**כִּי/כְּךָ/כֵּךְ/כּוֹ/כָּהּ	דֶּרֶךְ-	road, way;	דֶּרֶךְ זו״נ
דְּרָכֵינוּ/**דַּרְכֵי**כֶם/כֶן/הֶם/הֶן	**דְּרָ**כַי/כֶיךָ/כַיִךְ/כָיו/כֶיהָ	דַּרְכֵי-	manner; custom	דְּרָכִים

Examples

הרומאים סללו **דְּרָכִים** ישרות כמעוף הדבורה.
The Romans paved straight bee-line **roads**.

לא תצליח להשיג דבר אם תמשיך להתנהג **בְּדֶרֶךְ** הזאת.
You won't be able to achieve anything if you continue to behave in this **manner**.

זו **דַּרְכָּם** של היפנים, ועליך להבין זאת אם רצונך לחיות ביפן.
This is the **custom** of the Japanese, and you need to understand it if you wish to live in Japan.

למרבית הצער, למרות היומרות לשיוויון בין המינים, במרבית הארצות משכורות **הַגְּבָרִים** עדיין גבוהות ממשכורות נשים באותה משרה.
Unfortunately, in spite of the pretenses of equality between the sexes, in most countries **men**'s salaries are still higher that women's salaries for the same position.

הרבה תנאים נחוצים כדי לייצר יין משובח; הראשון שבהם הוא איכותה של **הַגֶּפֶן**.
There are many reuirements fpor the production of high-quality wine; the first is the quality of the **grapevine**.

בישראל יש משפחות מרובות **יְלָדִים** בשני מגזרים: המגזר הערבי והמגזר היהודי החרדי; נראה שהיום מספר **הַיְלָדִים** גדול יותר באחרון.
In Israel there are families with many **children** in two sectors: the Arab sector and the ultra-orthodox Jewish sector; it seems that today the number of **children** is higher in the latter.

תמיד היו לנו חתולים בבית. היום, לאור הכרותנו עם **הַכֶּלֶב** של נכדתנו, ברור לנו שיש הבדל גדול. **הַכְּלָבִים** יותר אינטליגנטיים וכמובן יותר נאמנים.
We always has cats in the house. Today, having become acquainted with out our granddaughter's **dog**, it is clear to us that there is a big difference. **Dogs** are more intelligent, and of course more loyal.

Special Expressions

אם **הַדֶּרֶךְ** cross**roads**
פרשת **דְּרָכִים** cross**road**
בְּדֶרֶךְ כל הארץ the **way** of all flesh
דֶּרֶךְ אגב incidentally
דֶּרֶךְ ארץ good manners
דֶּרֶךְ הַמֶּלֶךְ main **road**, highway
דֶּרֶךְ צְלֵחָה! bon **voyage!**
קפיצת **הַדֶּרֶךְ** miraculous shortcut
וֶרֶד הצלע entrecote
יֶלֶד/בן זְקוּנִים youngest child in family
כֶּסֶף/הון שחור black/undeclared **capital**
כֶּסֶף קטן small change
כֶּסֶף מזומן cash
לֶחֶם חוק daily bread; daily occurrence
לֶחֶם ושעשועים **bread** and circus
מֶלֶךְ העולם **king** of the world (God)
צֶלֶם אלוהים the **image** of God
צֶמֶר גפן cotton **wool**
צֶמֶר פלדה steel **wool**
שֶׁמֶן סיכה lubricating **oil**
שֶׁמֶן חריע safflower **oil**
הלך **בַּתֶּלֶם** tow the **line**

Additional Examples in this Pattern

דֶּרֶג scale, rank
וֶרֶד rose
כֶּסֶף money; silver
כֶּרֶם vineyard
לֶחֶם bread
מֶלֶךְ king
פֶּלֶג brook; part
צֶלֶם image; idol
צֶמֶר wool

one time, once; one of three (biblical) pilgrimages רֶגֶל	oil שֶׁמֶן
	furrow תֶּלֶם

---

327. ***CéCeC***: segholate (penultimately stressed) nouns with a *CaCC* base and where the first consonant is a guttural

our/your/their	my/your/his/her	const.	Gloss	sing/pl
עַבְדֵּנוּ/דְּכֶם/דְּכֶן/דָּם/דָּן	**עַבְ**דִּי/דְּךָ/דֵּךְ/דּוֹ/דָּהּ	עֶבֶד-	slave; servant;	עֶבֶד ז׳
עֲבָדֵינוּ/**עַבְדֵי**כֶם/כֶן/הֶם/הֶן	**עֲבָ**דַי/דֶיךָ/דַיִךְ/דָיו/דֶיהָ	עַבְדֵי-	subject	עֲבָדִים

When a *shva* is expected with a guttural, it is replaced by a *Hataf-pataH.*

Examples

עד מלחמת האזרחים בארה״ב, כלכלת הדרום נבנתה בעיקר על עבודת ה**עֲבָדִים**.
Until the Civil War in the US, Southern economy was dependent on **slave** labor.

התורה מזהירה מפני פולחן עצים **וַאֲבָנִים**.
The Torah warns against the worship of trees and **stones**.

אַלְפֵי אנשים השתתפו בהפגנה למען שיוויון זכויות מלא לנשים.
Thousands of people participated in the demobstration for full equality for women.

הביקורות של מבקר התיאטרון הזה תמיד מלאות **אֶרֶס**.
The reviews of this theater critic are always full of **poison**.

לאור מספר תקריות שארעו לאחרונה, חיילי צה״ל מוזהרים שלא למהר ללחוץ על ה**הֶדֶק**.
In view of a number of incidents that have occurred recently, IDF soldiers have been warned not to rush to squeeze the **trigger**.

הדירות הפופולריות ביותר בניו יורק היום הן של שני **חַדְרֵי** שינה.
The most popular apartments in New York City today are those with two bed**rooms**.

Special Expressions

mile**stone** **אֶבֶן** דֶּרֶךְ	when a **slave** reigns **עֶבֶד** כי ימלוך
criterion, acid test **אֶבֶן** בוחן	Canaanite **slave** (for life) **עֶבֶד** כנעני
lime**stone** **אֶבֶן** גיר	willing **slave** (for life from choice) **עֶבֶד** נרצע
Thousand and One Nights (the Arabic folk tale) **אֶלֶף** לילה ולילה	breast**bone** **עֶצֶם** החזה
dining **room** **חֲדַר** אוכל	one's own fleash and blood **עֶצֶם** מעצמיו
walk-in wardrobe **חֲדַר** אֲרוֹנוֹת	toward **evening** לפנות **עֶרֶב**
servant of God (esp. prophet) **עֶבֶד** ה׳	

Additional Examples in this Pattern

windowsill אֶדֶן	killing הֶרֶג
clothespin; clip N אֶטֶב	kindness; charity; grace חֶסֶד
zero; nothing אֶפֶס	young man עֶלֶם
opposite N הֶפֶךְ	sadness עֶצֶב

evening עֶרֶב

thing; essence עֶצֶם

---

328. ***CéCeC***: segholate (penultimately stressed) nouns with a *CaCC* base and where the second consonant is a guttural

our/your/their	my/your/his/her	const.	Gloss	sing/pl
בַּעֲלֵנוּ/**בַּעַלְ**כֶם/כֶן/**בַּעְלָ**ם/ן	בַּעֲלִי/בַּעַלְךָ/**בַּעְלֵ**ךְ/לוֹ/לָהּ	בַּעַל-	husband; owner;	בַּעַל ז'
בְּעָלֵינוּ/**בַּעֲלֵי**כֶם/כֶן/הֶם/הֶן	**בְּעָ**לַי/לֶיךָ/לַיִךְ/לָיו/לֶיהָ	בַּעֲלֵי-	lord; Baal	בְּעָלִים

When a *shva* is expected with a guttural, it is replaced by a *Hataf-pataH*: בַּעֲלִי my husband. When such *Hataf-pataH* is expected before a *shva*, it is replaced by *pataH*, which closes the open syllable: בַּעַלְךָ < בַּעֲלְךָ*.

Examples

בַּעְלָהּ עובד כל היום וכמעט לא נמצא בבית.
Her husband works all day, and is hardly ever at home.

נפגשנו עם **בַּעַל** הדירה, אבל שכר הדירה שהוא דורש גבוה מדיי.
We had a meeting with the land**lord**, but the rent he demands is too steep.

יש אנשים שאינם מסוגלים לשלוט **בְּזַעֲמָם**.
Some people cannot control their **anger**.

על **טַעַם** וריח אין להתווכח.
There is no accounting for **taste**.

הַיְחָסִים בין עליזה לבעלה-לשעבר אינם טובים. הם נפרדו לאחר מריבה גדולה.
The **relations** between Aliza and her ex-husband are not good. They separated after a big fight.

ליד ביתם של דניאל וחביבה זורם **נַחַל** קטן. לעיתים הם מעלים בחכתם דג לארוחת הערב.
A small **river** flows next to Daniel and Haviva's house. Occasionally they catch a small fish for dinner.

Special Expressions

inverse **ratio** **יַחַס** הפוך
eye of a **needle** קוף **הַמַּחַט**
perennial **spring** **נַחַל** איתן
seasonal **spring** **נַחַל** אכזב
slipers **נַעֲלֵי** בית
sneakers **נַעֲלֵי** התעמלות/ספורט
elevator **boy** **נַעַר** מעלית
crescent, half-**moon** חצי-**סַהַר**
the Israeli SPCA **צַעַר** בעלי חיים

land**lord** **בַּעַל** בית
ally **בַּעַל** ברית
a corpulent person **בַּעַל** בשר
burly person **בַּעַל** גוף
capitalist **בַּעַל** הון
living creature **בַּעַל** חיים
person with initiative **בַּעַל** יוזמה
bird **בַּעַל** כנף
skilled professional **בַּעַל** מקצוע
experienced person **בַּעַל** ניסיון

Additional Examples in this Pattern

ignoramus בַּעַר
knowledge; wisdom דַּעַת
objective; destination יַעַד
blade; tongue of flame לַהַב
flock; squadron לַהַק
tune, melody לַחַן

needle מַחַט
shoe נַעַל
youth, youngster נַעַר
.moon, crescent Lit סַהַר
sorrow צַעַר

---

329. ***CéCeC***: segholate (penultimately stressed) nouns with a *CaCC* base and where the third consonant is a guttural

our/your/their	my/your/his/her	const.	Gloss	sing/pl
סַלְעֵנוּ/**סַלְ**עֲכֶם/עֲכֶן/עָם/עָן	**סַלְ**עִי/עֲךָ/עֵךְ/עוֹ/עָהּ	סֶלַע-	rock; boulder,	סֶלַע ז׳
סְלָעֵינוּ/**סַלְעֵי**כֶם/כֶן/הֶם/הֶן	**סְלָ**עַי/עֶיךָ/עַיִךְ/עָיו/עֶיהָ	סַלְעֵי-	ancient coin	סְלָעִים

The *seghol* preceding a final guttural turns into a *pataH* (The low gutturals prefer low vowels.)

Examples

קשה מאוד לעבד את האדמה הזאת מכיוון שהיא מלאה **סְלָעִים**.
It is very difficult to cultivate this soil because it is full of **rocks**.

זה נוח מאוד שהמקררים החדשים מייצרים אוטומטית קוביות **קֶרַח**.
It is very convenient that the nrew refigerators produce **ice** cubes.

Special Expressions

Petra **הַסֶּלַע** הָאָדוֹם
Rock of Edom (Petra) **סֶלַע** אֱדוֹם
the **bone** of contention **סֶלַע** המחלוקת

If a word is worth one **coin**, silence is worth two מילה **בְּסֶלַע**, שתיקה בשניים
honey**moon** **יֶרַח** דבש
slingstone אבן **קֶלַע**

Additional Examples in this Pattern

seed; semen; sperm זֶרַע
month Lit. יֶרַח

slingshot, catapult קֶלַע

---

330. ***CéCeC***: segholate (penultimately stressed) nouns with a *CaCC* base and the plural suffix is וֹת-

our/your/their	my/your/his/her	const.	Gloss	sing/pl
נַפְשֵׁנוּ/שְׁכֶם/שְׁכֶן/שָׁם/שָׁן	**נַפְ**שִׁי/שְׁךָ/שֵׁךְ/שׁוֹ/שָׁהּ	נֶפֶשׁ-	soul, life;	נֶפֶשׁ נ׳
נַפְשׁוֹתֵינוּ/כֶם/כֶן/הֶם/הֶן	**נַפְשׁוֹ**תַי/תֶיךָ/תַיִךְ/תָיו/תֶיהָ	נַפְשׁוֹת-	person	נְפָשׁוֹת

Examples

העבודה הטובה ביותר היא זו שמספקת גם את צורכי הגוף וגם את צורכי ה**נֶּפֶשׁ**.
The best job is one that satisfies the needs of both body and **soul**.

אוכלוסיית העולם מונה היום למעלה מ-6.5 מיליארד **נֶפֶשׁ**.
The world population now exceeds 6.5 billion **persons**.

ה**נְפָשׁוֹת** הפועלות במחזה הן...
The **characters** in the play are...

היא נעלה את ה**דֶּלֶת**, אבל הוא הצליח להיכנס לבית מאחור.
She locked the **door**, but he managed to enter the house from the back.

בישראל יש **קֶרֶן** מיוחדת לעידוד הקולנוע הישראלי.
Israel has a special **fund** supporting original Israeli films.

Special Expressions

דֶּלֶת הזזה sliding **door**
דֶּלֶת מסתובבת revolving **door**
בחירוף **נֶפֶשׁ** at the risk of one's **life**
באו מים עד **נֶפֶשׁ** became unbearable
דיני **נְפָשׁוֹת** criminal law
חשקה **נַפְשׁוֹ** ב... he longed for...
ידיד **נֶפֶשׁ** bosom friend
כל עוד **נַפְשׁוֹ** בו at his last **gasp**
מְחייה **נְפָשׁוֹת** refreshing

מפח **נֶפֶשׁ** disappointment
מר **נֶפֶשׁ** embittered
משאת) **נֶפֶשׁ**) ideal
סכנת **נְפָשׁוֹת** mortal danger
עגמת **נֶפֶשׁ** sorrow
קֶרֶן המטבע הבין-לאומית International Monetary **Fund**
כחץ מ**קֶשֶׁת** very fast

Additional Examples in this Pattern

יֶרֶק vegetation, greenery
קֶסֶת inkstand
קֶשֶׁת bow; rainbow; arc

---

331. ***CéCeC***: segholate (penultimately stressed) nouns with a *CaCC* base and the plural suffix is וֹת- when the first consonant is a guttural.

sing/pl	Gloss	const.	my/your/his/her	our/your/their
אֶרֶץ נ׳	country, land;	אֶרֶץ-	**אַרְ**צִי/צְךָ/צֵךְ/צוֹ/צָהּ	**אַרְ**צֵנוּ/צְכֶם/צְכֶן/צָם/צָן
אֲרָצוֹת	earth; ground	אַרְצוֹת-	**אַרְצוֹ**תַי/תֶיךָ/תַיִךְ/תָיו/תֶיהָ	**אַרְצוֹתֵי**נוּ/כֶם/כֶן/הֶם/הֶן

When a *shva* is expected with a guttural, it is replaced by a *Hataf-pataH.*

Examples

כל קיץ עזריאל נוסע לבקר ב**אֶרֶץ** אחרת.
Every summer, Azriel travels to visit another **country**.

התפוחים הבשלים כבר נשרו ; צריך לאסוף אותם מן ה**אָרֶץ**.
The ripe apples have already fallen. We need to pick them up from the **ground**.

טוענים שכדור ה**אָרֶץ** הולך ומתחמם בהדרגה.
It is claimed that (the planet) **Earth** is gradually warming.

בימי הביניים סיסמת האיסלאם הייתה: "דת מוחמד ב**חֶרֶב**".
In the Middle Ages, the motto of Islam was: "Muhammad's religion/law is with/by the **sword**."

כלבים אוהבים מאוד **עֲצָמוֹת**, אבל אם הם מרסקים ובולעים אותן, זה מסכן את קיבתם.
Dogs like **bones** a lot, but if they crush and swallow them, it endangers their stomach.

Special Expressions

אֶרֶץ אבות father**land**
אֶרֶץ גזירה **country** of exile
אֶרֶץ הקודש the Holy **Land**
אֶרֶץ ישראל the **Land** of Israel, Palestine
אַרְצוֹת הברית the United **States**
דֶּרֶךְ **אֶרֶץ** good manners
הלך בדרך כל ה**אָרֶץ** went the way of all flesh (died)
חוץ ל**אָרֶץ** abroad
עם ה**אָרֶץ** ignoramus
ה**אָרֶץ** Israel (familiar use)
חֶרֶב פיפיות double-edged **sword**
חֶרֶב דמוקלס **sword** of Damocles
עֶרֶשׂ דווי death**bed**

Additional Examples in this Pattern

חֶשֶׁד/חֲשָׁד suspicion   עֶרֶשׂ cradle; bed

---

332. ***CéCeC***: segholate (penultimately stressed) nouns with a *CaCC* base and the plural suffix is וֹת- when the second consonant is a guttural

our/your/their	my/your/his/her	const.	Gloss	sing/pl
יַעֲרֵנוּ/**יַעַרְ**כֶם/כֶן/**יַעֲרָ**ם/ן	יַעֲרִי/יַעַרְךָ/**יַעֲרֵ**ךְ/רוֹ/רָהּ	יַעַר-	wood, forest	יַעַר ז'
יַעֲרוֹתֵינוּ/כֶם/כֶן/הֶם/הֶן	**יַעֲרוֹ**תַי/תֶיךָ/תַיִךְ/תָיו/תֶיהָ	יַעֲרוֹת-		יְעָרוֹת

When a *shva* is expected with a guttural, it is replaced by a *Hataf-pataH*; if another *shva* follows, the *Hataf* is replaced by *pataH* in a closed syllable (no *Hataf-shva* sequence allowed).

Examples

הם גרים בכפר קטן, בלב **יַעַר** גדול.
They live in a small village, in the heart of a large **forest**.

Special Expressions

יַעַר עד/בראשית virgin **forest**
לא דובים ולא **יַעַר** nothing of the sort

Additional Examples in this Pattern

שַׁחַת pit; grave, hell Lit.; hay

---

333. ***CéCeC***: segholate (penultimately stressed) nouns with a *CaCC* base and the plural suffix is וֹת- when the third consonant is a guttural

our/your/their	my/your/his/her	const.	Gloss	sing/pl
צַלְעֵנוּ/**צַלְ**עֲכֶם/עֲכֶן/עָם/עָן	**צַלְ**עִי/עֲךָ/עֵךְ/עוֹ/עָהּ	צֶלַע-/צֶלַע-	rib; slope;	צֶלַע/צֵלָע ז׳
סְלָעֵינוּ/**צַלְעֵי**כֶם/כֶן/הֶם/הֶן	**צְלָ**עַי/עֶיךָ/עַיִךְ/עָיו/עֶיהָ	צַלְעוֹת-	side, edge	צְלָעוֹת

The *seghol* preceding a final guttural turns into a *pataH.*

Examples

״ויבן ה׳ אלהים את-הַ**צֵּלָע** אשר לקח מן-האדם לאִשה״ (ברי ב:כב).
"And the **rib**, which the Lord God has taken from man, made he a woman" (Gen 2:22).

Special Expressions

צֶלַע ההר mountain**side/slope**

שְׁוֵה **צְלָעוֹת** of equal sides (triangle, etc.)

---

334. ***CéCeC***: segholate (penultimately stressed) nouns with a *CaCC* base and the plural suffix is the dual *-áyim*

our/your/their	my/your/his/her	const.	Gloss	sing/pl
רַגְלֵנוּ/לְכֶם/לְכֶן/לָם/לָן	**רַגְ**לִי/לְךָ/לֵךְ/לוֹ/לָהּ	רֶגֶל-	leg; foot; measure of	רֶגֶל נ׳
רַגְלֵינוּ/כֶם/כֶן/הֶם/הֶן	**רַגְ**לַי/לֶיךָ/לַיִךְ/לָיו/לֶיהָ	רַגְלֵי-	length	רַגְלַיִם

Examples

בלרינות מפורסמות נוהגות לבטח את **רַגְלֵיהֶן** בסכומי עתק.
Famous ballerinas often insure their **legs** for huge sums.

מרבית מטוסי הנוסעים טסים בגבהים שבין שלושים לשלושים ושישה אלף **רֶגֶל**.
Most passenger planes fly at heights between thirty and thirty six thousand **feet**.

אני גורב **גַּרְבַּיִם** גם כאשר אני נועל סנדלים בקייץ.
I wear **socks** even when I only have sandals on.

כואב הלב לראות איך ציידים באפריקה הורגים קרנפים רק בשביל **הַקֶּרֶן**, שאותה הם מוכרים לשוק הסיני.
It pains me to see how hunters in Africa kill rhinos just for their **horn**, which they then sell to the Chinese market.

Special Expressions

גַּרְבֵּי ניילון nylon **stockings**

מחלת הפה וה**טְלָפַיִם** **hoof** and mouth disease

בְּרֶגֶל on **foot**

דריסת **רֶגֶל** right of entry

דחק את **רַגְלָיו** ousted him

כיתת את **רַגְלָיו** wear one's **feet** out

פשט את **הָרֶגֶל** went bankrupt

due to **לְרֶגֶל**
centi**pede** מרבה **רַגְלַיִם**
hastily על **רֶגֶל** אחת
light **foot**ed קל **רַגְלַיִם**
flat **foot** **רֶגֶל** שטוחה

Additional Examples in this Pattern

hoof טֶלֶף

---

335. ***CéCeC=CéCaC***: segholate (penultimately stressed) nouns with a *CaCC* base and the plural suffix is the dual *-áyim* when the third consonant is a guttural

our/your/their	my/your/his/her	const.	Gloss	sing/pl
כַּרְעֵנוּ/**כַּרְ**עֲכֶם/עֲכֶן/עָם/עָן	**כַּרְ**עִי/עֲךָ/עֵךְ/עוֹ/עָהּ	כֶּרַע-	thigh; leg of	כֶּרַע ז'
כְּרָעֵינוּ/**כַּרְעֵי**כֶם/כֶן/הֶם/הֶן	**כְּרָ**עַי/עֶיךָ/עַיִךְ/עָיו/עֶיהָ	כַּרְעֵי-	animal; leg of furniture Lit.	כְּרָעַיִם

The *seghol* preceding a final guttural turns into a *pataH*. When a *shva* is expected with the guttural, it is replaced by a *Hataf-pataH*.

Examples

"ואת האיל תנתח לנתחיו, ורחצת קרבו **וּכְרָעָיו**" (שמ' כט יז).
"And you shall cut the ram in pieces, and wash its entrails, and its **legs**" (Ex 29:17).

Special Expressions

shaky, unstable על **כַּרְעֵי** תרנגולת
the whole thing על **כְּרָעָיו** ועל קרבו

---

336. ***CéCeC***: segholate (penult. stressed) nouns with a *CeCC* base

our/your/their	my/your/his/her	const.	Gloss	sing/pl
נֶכְדֵּנוּ/דְּכֶם/דְּכֶן/דָּם/דָּן	**נֶכְ**דִּי/דְּךָ/דֵּךְ/דּוֹ/דָּהּ	נֶכֶד-	grandchild;	נֶכֶד ז'
נְכָדֵינוּ/**נֶכְדֵי**כֶם/כֶן/הֶם/הֶן	**נְכָ**דַי/דֶיךָ/דַיִךְ/דָיו/דֶיהָ	נֶכְדֵי-	grandson	נְכָדִים

Examples

יעקוב ועשו היו **נְכָדָיו** של אברהם.
Jacob and Esau were Abraham's **grandsons**.

Special Expressions

descendant נִין **וָנֶכֶד**

Additional Examples in this Pattern

against; opposite נֶגֶד

---

337. ***CéCeC***: segholate (penultimately stressed) nouns with a *CeCC* base, when the first consonant is a guttural

our/your/their	my/your/his/her	const.	Gloss	sing/pl
הֶבְלֵנוּ/לְכֶם/לְכֶן/לָם/לָן	**הֶבְ**לִי/לְךָ/לֵךְ/לוֹ/לָהּ	הֶבֶל-	vapor; breath;	הֶבֶל ז'
הֲבָלֵינוּ/**הַבְלֵי**כֶם/כֶן/הֶם/הֶן	**הֲבָ**לַי/לֶיךָ/לַיִךְ/לָיו/לֶיהָ	הַבְלֵי-	foolishness	הֲבָלִים

The expected *shva* with the guttural is replaced by *Hataf-pataH*. Note: In הַבְלֵי- and הַבְלֵיכֶם etc. the *seghol* is replaced by *pataH*.

Examples

ישעיהו הוא איש רוח, ש**הַבְלֵי** העולם הזה אינם מעניינים אותו.
Yesha`ayau is a spiritual person; this world's **vanities** do not interest him.

Special Expressions

absolute **nonsense** **הֶבֶל** ורעות רוח/דברי **הֶבֶל** just by **talking** **בְּהֶבֶל** פיו

Additional Examples in this Pattern

grace, charm, beauty, loveliness חֶמֶד universe, world Lit. חֶלֶד

---

338. ***CéCeC***: segholate (penultimately stressed) nouns with a *CeCC* base, when the third consonant of the root is *y* and the first is guttural

our/your/their	my/your/his/her	const.	Gloss	sing/pl
הֶגְיֵנוּ/יְכֶם/יְכֶן/יָם/יָן	**הֶגְ**יִי/יְךָ/יֵךְ/יוֹ/יָהּ	הֶגֶה-	utterance;	הֶגֶה ז'
הֲגָיֵינוּ/**הַגְיֵי**כֶם/כֶן/הֶם/הֶן	**הֲגָ**יַי/יֶיךָ/יַיִךְ/יָיו/יֶיהָ	הַגְיֵי-	steering	הֲגָיִים/הֲגָאִים
הֲגָאֵינוּ/**הַגְאֵי**כֶם/כֶן/הֶם/הֶן	**הֲגָאַ**י/אֶיךָ/אַיִךְ/אָיו/אֶיהָ	/הַגְאֵי-	wheel	

Examples

בכל תקופת משפטו, הנאשם לא הוציא **הֶגֶה** מפיו.
Throughout his trial, the defendant never made a single **utterance**.

Special Expressions

a fricative **sound/segment** הֶגֶה חוכך phonology תורת **הַהֲגָאִים**

---

339. ***CéCeC***: segholate (penultimately stressed) nouns with an initial guttural, with a *CiCC* base in which the *i* of the isolation form becomes a *tsere*

our/your/their	my/your/his/her	const.	Gloss	sing/pl
עִמְקֵנוּ/קְכֶם/קְכֶן/קָם/קָן	**עִמְ**קִי/קְךָ/קֵךְ/קוֹ/קָהּ	עֵמֶק-	valley	עֵמֶק ז'
עֲמָקֵינוּ/**עִמְקֵי**כֶם/כֶן/הֶם/הֶן	**עֲמָ**קַי/קֶיךָ/קַיִךְ/קָיו/קֶיהָ	עִמְקֵי-		עֲמָקִים

Unlike the larger group in which the *Hirik* following an initial guttural turns into *seghol* in a closed syllable (see חֵלֶק part, חֶלְקִי, חֲלָקֵי above), in this group the *Hirik* is maintained – except for the unsuffixed form with an open syllable, in which it becomes a *tsere*. The expected *shva* with the guttural is replaced by *Hataf-pataH*.

Examples

עֵמֶק יזרעאל הוא **העֵמֶק** הפורה ביותר בישראל.
The Jezre'el **Valley** is Israel's most fertile **valley**.

משקיעים היום הרבה כספים ב**חֵקֶר** הסרטן.
They invest a lot today in cancer **research**.

עִסְקֵי נדל"ן הם בראש מעייניהם של פוליטיקאים רבים.
Many politicians highly value real estate **business deals**.

Additional Examples in this Pattern

business עֵסֶק	desire חֵשֶׁק

---

340. ***CéCeC***: segholate (penultimately stressed) feminine nouns with an initial guttural with a *CeCC* base and the unsuffixed form starts with a *tsere*

our/your/their	my/your/his/her	const.	Gloss	sing/pl
חֶמְתֵּנוּ/תְּכֶם/תְּכֶן/תָּם/תָּן	**חֶמְ**תִּי/תְּךָ/תֵּךְ/תּוֹ/תָּהּ	-חֵמֶת	gourd, vessel for liquid Lit.	חֵמֶת נ'
חֶמְתוֹתֵינוּ/כֶם/כֶן/הֶם/הֶן	**חֶמְתוֹ**תַי/תֶיךָ/תַיִךְ/תָיו/תֶיהָ	-חֶמְתוֹת		חֲמָתוֹת

The first vowel in all suffixed form is *seghol*, which when stressed in the unsuffixed form becomes *tsere*. The expected *shva* with the guttural is replaced by *Hataf-pataH*.

Special Expressions

bagpipes חֵמֶת חלילים

This is the only instance found.

---

341. ***CóCeC***: segholate (penultimately stressed) nouns with a *CoCC* base

our/your/their	my/your/his/her	const.	Gloss	sing/pl
כָּתְלֵנוּ/לְכֶם/לְכֶן/לָם/לָן	**כָּתְ**לִי/לְךָ/לֵךְ/לוֹ/לָהּ	-כֹּתֶל	wall; side	כֹּתֶל ז'
כָּתְלֵינוּ/**כָּתְלֵי**כֶם/כֶן/הֶם/הֶן	**כְּתָ**לַי/לֶיךָ/לַיִךְ/לָיו/לֶיהָ	-כָּתְלֵי		כְּתָלִים

The *kamats* in the base is a *kamats katan* (pronounced [o]). It is realized as a *Holam Haser* (also pronounced [o]) in the isolation form. A significant number of occurrences have no plural forms. Note: the plural form of שֹׁרֶשׁ 'root' is שָׁרָשִׁים (or שֳׁרָשִׁים), and that of קֹדֶשׁ 'sacredness' is קֳדָשִׁים (or קֳדָשִׁים).

Examples

מעניין מה עושים עם כל פתקאות הבקשה והתפילה שאנשים תוחבים לתוך סדקי **הכֹּתֶל**...
It would be interesting to know what they do with all the request and prayer notes that people shove into the cracks of the (Wailing) **Wall**...

מכיוון שנראה שאין הסכמה באשר לקשר בין קפה ובריאות, החלטתי שבינתיים אסתפק בכוס קפה אחת בלבד ביום, בשעות ה**בֹּקֶר**.
Since it seems that there is no agreement regarding the connection between coffee and health, I decided that in the meantime, I will settle for only one cup of coffee a day, in the **morning**.

כשמסדרים את הספרים בספרייה שבבית, חשוב לסדרם על פי נושאים ועל פי מחברים, לא על פי **גֹּדֶל** הספר וגובה המדף.
When arranging books in the home library, one should go by subject and author, not by book **size** and shelf height.

כשה**גֹּלֶם** הופך לפרפר, זוהי אחת הטרנספורמציות המרשימות ביותר בטבע.
When the **pupa** turns into a butterfly, it is one of the most impressive transformations in nature.

טָפְסֵי הבקשה להתקבל לאוניברסיטה בארה״ב הם ארוכים ומייגעים ביותר.
The application **forms** for admission into an American university are long and tiring to fill out.

כָּבְדוֹ של ה״ניו יורק טיימס״ ביום ראשון הוא כה גדול, שמספרים שפעם הוא הוטל ממטוס קטן עבור מנוי באזור כפרי והרג פרה.
The **weight** of the New York Times on Sunday is so substantial, that they say it was once dropped from a small plane for a subscriber in a rural area and killed a cow.

Special Expressions

every now and then חדשות **לִבְקָרִים**
first thing in the **morning** **בַּבֹּקֶר בַּבֹּקֶר** Col.
You don't say! (sarcastic) **בֹּקֶר** טוב אליהו
altruism, self-sacrifice **גֹּדֶל** רוח
with close supervision עם יד על **הַדֹּפֶק**
walls have ears אוזניים **לַכֹּתֶל**
within the institution בין **כָּתְלֵי** המוסד
to talk to a brick wall לדבר אל **הַכֹּתֶל**

hams (**sides** of…) **כָּתְלֵי** חזיר
the Wailing (or Western) **Wall** (of the Temple) **הַכֹּתֶל** המערבי
physical **fitness** **כֹּשֶׁר** גופני
intersection **צֹמֶת** דרכים
present **need** **צֹרֶךְ** השעה
Holy of Holies **קֹדֶשׁ הַקֳּדָשִׁים**
square **root** **שֹׁרֶשׁ** ריבועי/מרובע
table of **contents** **תֹּכֶן** העניינים

Additional Examples in this Pattern

perfume; scent בֹּשֶׂם
plane tree דֹּלֶב
pulse דֹּפֶק
dryness יֹבֶשׁ
ability, capability כֹּשֶׁר
whiteness לֹבֶן
intersection צֹמֶת

need; necessity צֹרֶךְ
sacredness קֹדֶשׁ
diameter קֹטֶר
level, layer רֹבֶד
impression רֹשֶׁם
root שֹׁרֶשׁ
contents; gist תֹּכֶן

342. ***CóCeC***: segholate (penultimately stressed) nouns with a *CoCC* base and the first consonant is a guttural

our/your/their	my/your/his/her	const.	Gloss	sing/pl
חָדְשֵׁנוּ/שְׁכֶם/שְׁכֶן/שָׁם/שָׁן	**חָדְ**שִׁי/שְׁךָ/שֵׁךְ/שׁוֹ/שָׁהּ	חֹדֶשׁ-	month; new	חֹדֶשׁ ז׳
חֳדָשֵׁינוּ/**חָדְשֵׁי**כֶם/כֶן/הֶם/הֶן	**חֳדָ**שַׁי/שֶׁיךָ/שַׁיִךְ/שָׁיו/שֶׁיהָ	חָדְשֵׁי-	moon	חֳדָשִׁים

In the unsuffixed form, the *kamats katan* is replaced by *Holam Haser*. The *shva* expected with the guttural is replaced by *Hataf-kamats* (or, rarely, by *Hataf-pataH*, אֹמֶר ~ אֲמָרִים utterance).

Examples

עבודתם של המורים קשה, אבל לפחות יש להם כשלושה **חָדְשֵׁי** חופשה.
The teachers' job is hard, but at least they have about three **months**' vacation.

בני אדם יכולים לשרוד כמה ימים ללא **אֹכֶל**, אבל לא ללא מים.
People can survive a few days without **food**, but not without water.

למרטי יש **אֹסֶף** של בולים נדירים, הכולל את סדרת בולי הצֶפֶּלִין.
Marty has a **collection** of rare stamps, which includes the Zeppelin stamp series.

האדריכל הסביר לנו שאפשר לתכנן את המבנה הפנימי של הדירה בשלושה **אֳפָנִים** שונים.
The architect explained to us that it is possible to plan the internal structure of the apartment in three different **modes**.

יש פַּסָּלִים היוצרים פְּסָלִים מרשימים מ**חֳמָרִים** שאנשים השליכו החוצה כפסולת.
Some sculptors create impressive sculptures from **materials** that others have thrown away as garbage.

Special Expressions

broad **horizons** **אֳפָקִים** רחבים
event **horizon** **אֹפֶק** האירועים
longevity **אֹרֶךְ** ימים
patience **אֹרֶךְ** רוח
short **month** (29 days) **חֹדֶשׁ** חסר
full **month** (30 days) **חֹדֶשׁ** מלא
feast of the new **moon**, first day of the **month** ראש **חֹדֶשׁ**
overweight **עֹדֶף** משקל
death **penalty** **עֹנֶשׁ** מוות

Additional Examples in this Pattern

utterance, word אֹמֶר
horizon אֹפֶק
length אֹרֶךְ
strength חֹזֶק
winter חֹרֶף
grove חֹרֶשׁ
change; surplus, excess עֹדֶף
depth עֹמֶק
punishment עֹנֶשׁ
sting עֹקֶץ
nape; home front; (mil.) rear עֹרֶף

343. ***CóCeC=CóCaC***: segholate (penultimately stressed) nouns with a *CoCC* base and the second consonant is a guttural

our/your/their	my/your/his/her	const.	Gloss	sing/pl
פָּעֳלֵנוּ/פָּעָלְכֶם/כֶן/**פָּעֳלָם**/ן	פָּעֳלִי/פָּעָלְךָ/**פָּעֳלֵךְ**/לוֹ/לָהּ	פֹּעַל-	work, action;	פֹּעַל ז׳
פְּעָלֵינוּ/**פָּעֳלֵי**כֶם/כֶן/הֶם/הֶן	**פְּעָלַי**/לֶיךָ/לַיִךְ/לָיו/לֶיהָ	פָּעֳלֵי-	wages; verb	פְּעָלִים

In the unsuffixed form, the *kamats katan* is replaced by *Holam Haser*. The *shva* expected with the guttural is replaced by *Hataf-pataH*, and if a *shva* follows, the *Hataf-kamats* is replaced by a *kamats katan*.

Examples

מוקדם עדיין להעריך את **פָּעֳלוֹ** של הנשיא הנוכחי של ארה״ב.
It is still too early to evaluate the **work** of the current US president.

מערכת **הפֹּעַל** בעברית דומה לזו של ערבית, אבל יש בה פחות בניינים.
The Hebrew **verb** system is similar to that of Arabic, except that it has fewer patterns.

יש מורים לעברית המאמינים שהדרך הטובה ביותר לוודא שהתלמידים באים מוכנים לשיעור היא לקיים **בֹּחַן** בתחילת כל שיעור.
Some Hebrew teachers believe that the best way of ascertaining that the students come to class prepared is to hold a **quiz** at the beginning of each class.

למרות השימוש הנרחב **בדֹּאַר** אלקטרוני היום, עדיין יש מצבים שבהם אין תחליף **לדֹּאַר** הרגיל.
In spite of the extensive use of electronic **mail** today, there are still situations where there is no substitute for regular **mail**.

אוניברסיטאות רבות מעניקות **תָּאֳרֵי** כבוד לכמה אנשים ראויים מדי שנה בשנה.
Many universities confer honorary **degrees** to a few deserving people every year.

Special Expressions

בפֹּעַל actually; acting (e.g. acting VP)
הפֹּעַל היוצא the conclusion
פֹּעַל יוצא transitive **verb**
פֹּעַל עומד intransitive **verb**
להוציא אל **הפֹּעַל** put into execution
פֹּעַל ידיים/כפיים handiwork
רב **פְּעָלִים** person active in many fields
שילם לו **כפָעֳלוֹ** rewarded him according to his deserts

בֹּחַן פתע unannounced **quiz**
דֹּאַר אוויר air **mail**
דֹּאַר נכנס incoming **mail**, inbox
רֹחַב יד generosity
רֹחַק ראייה **far**-sightedness
תֹּאַר אצולה **title** of nobility
תֹּאַר שלישי doctorate

Additional Examples in this Pattern

נֹהַל regulation; procedure　　רֹחַב width　　רֹחַק distance

---

344. ***CóCeC=CóCaC***: segholate (penultimately stressed) nouns with a *CoCC* base and the third consonant is a guttural

our/your/their	my/your/his/her	const.	Gloss	sing/pl
גָּבְהֵנוּ/גָּבְהֲכֶם/כֶן/**גָּבְהָ**ם/ן	גָּבְהִי/גָּבְהֲךָ/**גָּבְ**הֵךְ/הוֹ/הָהּ	גֹּבַהּ-	height;	גֹּבַהּ ז'
גָּבְהֵינוּ/**גָּבְהֵי**כֶם/כֶן/הֶם/הֶן	**גָּבָ**הַי/הֶיךָ/הַיִךְ/הָיו/הֶיהָ	גָּבְהֵי-	extent, level	גְּבָהִים

In the unsuffixed form, the *kamats katan* is replaced by *Holam Haser*. The *shva* expected with the guttural is replaced by *Hataf-pataH.*

Examples

גֹּבַהּ התקרה של דירה רגילה הא בדרך כלל 2.70 מטרים, אבל נעים יותר לגור בדירה שתקרתה גבוהה יותר.
The **height** of ceilings is generally 2.70 meters, but is feels nicer to live in an apartment whose ceiling is higher.

החייל מילא את הפקודה **בכֹּרַח**, למרות שהיה מודע לכך שהיא אינה מוסרית.
The soldier followed the order by **compulsion**, although he was aware that it was immoral.

Special Expressions

גֹּבַהּ אף/לב/רוח arrogance Lit.
ב**גֹבַהּ** העיניים without condescension
גֹּבַהּ פני הים sea **level**
על ה**גֹּבַהּ** of very high quality Coll.
כֹּרַח המציאות inevitability

Additional Examples in this Pattern

נֹגַהּ gleam, glow
נֹסַח/נֻסָּח wording; version
רֹגַע calm, serenity
שֹׂבַע satiation

---

345. ***CóCeC***: masculine segholate (penultimately stressed) nouns with a *CoCC* base where the plural suffix is the dual form

our/your/their	my/your/his/her	const.	Gloss	sing/pl
מָתְנֵנוּ/נְכֶם/נְכֶן/נָם/נָן	**מָתְ**נִי/נְךָ/נֵךְ/נוֹ/נָהּ	מֹתֶן-	waist, hip	מֹתֶן ז'
מָתְנֵינוּ/**מָתְנֵי**כֶם/כֶן/הֶם/הֶן	**מָתְ**נַי/נֶיךָ/נַיִךְ/נָיו/נֶיהָ	מָתְנֵי-		מָתְנַיִם

The *kamats* in the base is a *kamats katan* (becoming Holam in the unsuffixed form), and the plural suffix is the dual form ַיִם.

Examples

קשה למצוא חגורה מספיק ארוכה שתתאים להיקף ה**מָּתְנַיִם** שלו.
It is hard to find a long-enough belt that will fit the circumference of his **waist**.

Special Expressions

כוחו **בְּמָתְנָיו** he is powerful
שלף מה**מֹּתֶן** acted spontaneously

---

346. ***CóCeC*: feminine** segholate (penultimately stressed) nouns with a *CoCC* base

our/your/their	my/your/his/her	const.	Gloss	sing/pl
גָּרְנֵנוּ/נְכֶם/נְכֶן/נָם/נָן	**גָּרְ**נִי/נְךָ/נֵךְ/נוֹ/נָהּ	גֹּרֶן-	thrashing floor;	גֹּרֶן נ׳
גָּרְנוֹתֵינוּ/כֶם/כֶן/הֶם/הֶן	**גָּרְנוֹתַ**י/תֶיךָ/תַיִךְ/תָיו/תֶיהָ	גָּרְנוֹת-	open space	גְּרָנוֹת

Examples

בגֹּרֶן היו דשים את החיטה כדי להפריד את המוץ מן הגרגרים.
In the **thrashing floor** they used to thrash the wheat in order to separate the chafe from the wheat kernels.

לעיתים מרפדים את **דָּפְנוֹת** הקירות בבתי חולים לחולי רוח, כדי שלא יזיקו לעצמם.
Sometimes they pad the **walls** in insane aylums, so that the patients do not harm themselves.

Special Expressions

בית **בֹּשֶׁת** brothel
דֹּפֶן התא cell **wall** (bot.)
סָלְתָּהּ ושמנה the choicest, the best; top quality; elite

המן הגֹּרֶן או מן היקב? where on earth from? (out of the **thrashing floor**? or wine press?)
חצי **גֹּרֶן** עגולה semicircle
בֹּשֶׁת פנים **shame**, disgrace

Additional Examples in this Pattern

סֹלֶת semolina; finely sifted flour
בֹּשֶׁת shame, disgrace

---

347. ***CóCeC***: feminine segholate (penultimately stressed) nouns with a *CoCC* base and the second consonant is a guttural

our/your/their	my/your/his/her	const.	Gloss	sing/pl
בָּהֳנֵנוּ/**בָּהָ**נְכֶם/נְכֶן/**בָּהֳ**נָם/נָן	בָּהֳנִי/בָּהָנְךָ/**בָּהֳ**נֵךְ/נוֹ/נָהּ	בֹּהֶן-	big toe;	בֹּהֶן זו״נ
בְּהוֹנוֹתֵינוּ/כֶם/כֶן/הֶם/הֶן	**בְּהוֹנוֹתַ**י/תֶיךָ/תַיִךְ/תָיו/תֶיהָ	בְּהוֹנוֹת-	thumb	בְּהוֹנוֹת

In the unsuffixed form, the *kamats katan* is replaced by *Holam Haser*. The *shva* expected with the guttural is replaced by *Hataf-kamats*, and if a *shva* is expected to follow, the *Hataf-kamats* is replaced by a *kamats katan*, to avoid a *Hataf-shva* sequence: בָּהָנְכֶם < בָּ-הֳנְ-כֶם*.

Examples

חיים צולע מכיוון שאתמול בלילה נתקלה **בָּהֳנוֹ** באחת מרגלי המיטה וכמעט נשברה.
Hayyim is limping because last night his **toe** bumped into one of the legs of his bed and almost broke.

Special Expressions

הולך על **בְּהוֹנוֹת** רגליו tip**toe**ing

---

348. ***CóCeC***: feminine segholate (penultimately stressed) nouns with a *CoCC* base and the plural form is the dual one

our/your/their	my/your/his/her	const.	Gloss	sing/pl
אָזְנֵנוּ/נְכֶם/נְכֶן/נָם/נָן	**אָזְ**נִי/נְךָ/נֵךְ/נוֹ/נָהּ	אֹזֶן-	ear	אֹזֶן נ׳
אָזְנֵינוּ/כֶם/כֶן/הֶם/הֶן	**אָזְ**נַי/נֶיךָ/נַיִךְ/נָיו/נֶיהָ	אָזְנֵי-		אָזְנַיִם

In the unsuffixed form, the *kamats katan* is replaced by *Holam Haser*.

Examples

אָזְנֵי כלב שומעות צלילים גבוהים ש**אֹזֶן** אדם אינה מסוגלת לשמוע.
A dog **ears** can hear high sounds that a human **ear** is incapable of hearing.

Special Expressions

Haman's **ear** (cake eaten at Purim) **אֹזֶן** המן
give a simple and clear explanation סַבֵּר אֶת הָ**אֹזֶן**
be shocked, be outraged צָלְלוּ (שְׁתֵּי) **אָזְנָיו**

---

349. ***CóCi***: (penultimately stressed) nouns with a *CoCC* base and the third consonant is *y*

our/your/their	my/your/his/her	const.	Gloss	sing/pl
קָשְׁיֵנוּ/יְכֶם/יְכֶן/יָם/יָן	**קָשְׁ**יִי/יְךָ/יֵךְ/יוֹ/יָהּ	קֹשִׁי-	hardness; difficulty;	קֹשִׁי ז׳
קְשָׁיֵינוּ/כֶם/כֶן/הֶם/הֶן	**קְשָׁ**יַי/יֶיךָ/יַיִךְ/יָיו/יֶיהָ	קְשָׁיֵי-	obduracy	קְשָׁיִים

Most of the forms are derived from roots in which the third consonant is י׳. In the unsuffixed form, the *kamats katan* is replaced by *Holam Haser*. The plural form (when it exists) follows the segholate plural pattern.

Examples

קְשָׁיִים גדולים עמדו בפניהם של החלוצים הראשונים.
Great **difficulties** faced the early settlers.

קֹשִׁי המתכת ומשקלה קובעים ממה יִיוּצר טנק.
The **hardness** of the metal and its weight determine what a tank will be made of.

על **יָפְיָהּ** של הלנה מטרויה נכתב: ״הפנים שהשיקו אלף ספינות״.
About the **beauty** of Helen of Troy it was written: "The face that launched a thousand ships."

לפני שמוכרים דירה, ראוי לבדוק אם כדאי להשקיע בתיקונים כדי להעלות את **שָׁוְיָהּ**, או שעדיף להוריד מן המחיר במשא ומתן עם הקונה.
When planning to sell an apartment, one should consider repairs to raise its **value**, or to reduce the selling price when negotiating with the buyer.

Special Expressions

with **difficulty**, **hard**ly **בְּקֹשִׁי**
obstinacy **קְשִׁי** עורף
perfect, impeccable ללא **דֹּפִי**

Additional Examples in this Pattern

silence דְּמִי/דֹּמִי　　value, worth שֹׁוִי
blemish, fault, defect דֹּפִי　　difference שֹׁנִי
beauty יֹפִי

---

350. ***CóCi***: bi-consonantal nouns ending with י׳, where the first consonant is a guttural

our/your/their	my/your/his/her	const.	Gloss	sing/pl
חָלְיֵנוּ/יְכֶם/יְכֶן/יָם/יָן	**חָלְ**יִי/יְךָ/יֵךְ/יוֹ/יָהּ	חֳלִי-	illness, sickness	חֹלִי ז׳
חֳלָיֵינוּ/כֶם/כֶן/הֶם/הֶן	**חֳלָ**יַי/יֶיךָ/יַיִךְ/יָיו/יֶיהָ	חֳלָיֵי-		חֳלָיִים

Most of the forms are derived from roots in which the third consonant is י׳. In the unsuffixed form, the *kamats katan* is replaced by *Holam Haser*. In the construct and in the plural forms the *kamats katan* is reduced to a *Hataf kamats*. In most cases, the plural form (when it exists) follows the segholate plural pattern.

Examples

אידיאליסטים שואפים תמיד לרפא את החברה האנושית מ**חֳלָיֶיהָ** הרבים.
Idealists always aspire to cure human society of its numerous **maladies**.

Special Expressions

epilepsy **חֳלִי** נֵפֶל/נִכְפֶּה　　cholera **חֳלִי** רע　　**sick**ly person יְדוּעַ **חֹלִי**

Additional Examples in this Pattern

character אֹפִי　　thickness עֹבִי
videotape, VCR חֹזִי　　poverty עֹנִי

---

351. ***CóCi***: bi-consonantal nouns ending with י׳ and where the first consonant is a guttural, and א׳ replaces י׳ in the plural forms:

our/your/their	my/your/his/her	const.	Gloss	sing/pl
עָפְיֵנוּ/יְכֶם/יְכֶן/יָם/יָן	**עָפְ**יִי/יְךָ/יֵךְ/יוֹ/יָהּ	עֳפִי-	branch	עֹפִי ז׳
עֳפָאֵינוּ/כֶם/כֶן/הֶם/הֶן	**עֳפָ**אַי/אֶיךָ/אַיִךְ/אָיו/אֶיהָ	עֳפָאֵי-		עֳפָאִים

The forms is derived from a root in which the third consonant is י׳. In the unsuffixed form, the *kamats katan* is replaced by *Holam Haser*. In the construct and in the plural forms the *kamats katan* is reduced to a *Hataf kamats*. The plural form follows the segholate plural pattern with א׳ replacing י׳.

Examples

בעברית הספרותית משתמשים לעתים במונח "**עֳפָאִים**" במקום "ענפים".
In literary Hebrew they sometimes use the term **עֳפָאִים** instead of עֲנָפִים for ‘branches.’

---

352. ***CuCC=CóCeC***: segholate (penult. stressed) nouns with a *CuCC* base

our/your/their	my/your/his/her	const.	Gloss	sing/pl
קֻמְצֵנוּ/צְכֶם/צְכֶן/צָם/צָן	**קֻמְ**צִי/צְךָ/צֵךְ/צוֹ/צָהּ	קֹמֶץ-	handful	קֹמֶץ ז'
קְמָצֵינוּ/**קֻמְצֵי**כֶם/כֶן/הֶם/הֶן	**קְמָ**צַי/צֶיךָ/צַיִךְ/צָיו/צֶיהָ	קֻמְצֵי-		קְמָצִים

The *u* in the segholate base turns to *o* in an open syllable when there are no suffixes.

Examples

בסוף המאה ה-19 ובתחילת המאה ה20 התיישבו בארץ ישראל רק **קֹמֶץ** חלוצים.
At the end of the 19th century and in the beginning of the 20th century only a **handful** of pioneers settled in Palestine.

Special Expressions

אין ה**קֹמֶץ** משביע את הארי.
it's a drop in the ocean (a **handful** won't satisfy a lion).

Additional Examples in this Pattern

סֹמֶק redness; blush   רֹכֶס/רֶכֶס mountain range

---

353. ***CóCeC***: segholate (penultimately stressed) nouns with a *CuCC* base, and the first consonant is a guttural

our/your/their	my/your/his/her	const.	Gloss	sing/pl
חֻלְדֵּנוּ/דְּכֶם/דְּכֶן/דָּם/דָּן	**חֻלְ**דִּי/דְּךָ/דֵּךְ/דּוֹ/דָּהּ	חֹלֶד-	mole	חֹלֶד ז'
חֲלָדֵינוּ/**חֻלְדֵי**כֶם/כֶן/הֶם/הֶן	**חֲלָ**דַי/דֶיךָ/דַיִךְ/דָיו/דֶיהָ	חֻלְדֵי-		חֲלָדִים

The *u* in the segholate base turns to *o* in an open syllable when there are no suffixes. The *shva* expected with the guttural is replaced by *Hataf-kamats*.

Examples

ה**חֹלֶד** חי באדמה, וניזון משרשי צמחים.
The **mole** lives underground, and feeds on plant roots.

Additional Examples in this Pattern

חֹמֶץ vinegar   חֹמֶשׁ five-year (plan etc.)   עֹקֶם twistedness; distortion

---

354. ***CáCeC~CoC***: (penultimately stressed) nouns with a *CaCeC* base, the second consonant is *w* or *y*, and the *ave* sequence is reduced to a single vowel [o] in the declension

our/your/their	my/your/his/her	const.	Gloss	sing/pl
אוֹנֵנוּ/נְכֶם/נְכֶן/נָם/נָן	**אוֹ**נִי/נְךָ/נֵךְ/נוֹ/נָהּ	אוֹן-	evil;	אָוֶן ז'
אוֹנֵינוּ/כֶם/כֶן/הֶם/הֶן	**אוֹ**נַי/נֶיךָ/נַיִךְ/נָיו/נֶיהָ	אוֹנֵי-	affliction	אוֹנִים

Examples

"לב חורש מחשבות **אָוֶן**..." (מִשְׁלֵי ו׳:יח)

A mind that hatches **evil** plots... (Proverbs 6:18)

בית המשפט גזר על המחבל גזר דין **מָוֶת**, אבל עורך דינו ערער, בטענה שלא היו הוכחות מספיקות לאשמתו, ושנעשה לו **עָוֶל**.

The court gave the terrorist a **death** sentence, but his lawyer appealed, arguing that there was no sufficient evidence to his guilt, and that it was an **injustice**.

Special Expressions

brain **death** **מָוֶת** מוֹחִי **evil** doer איש **אָוֶן**, פועל **אָוֶן**

while innocent of any **crime** על לא **עָוֶל** בכפו

Additional Examples in this Pattern

[Note: consonantal *vav* is maintained in *`avlo* etc; no plural.] injustice עָוֶל

---

355. ***CáCeC~CoC***: (penultimately stressed) nouns with a *CaCeC* base, the second consonant is *w* or *y*, the *ave* sequence (originally a diphthong) is reduced to a single vowel in the declension; the plural suffix is *-im* or *-ot*

our/your/their	my/your/his/her	const.	Gloss	sing/pl
תּוֹכֵנוּ/כְכֶם/כְכֶן/כָם/כָן	**תּוֹ**כִי/כְךָ/כֵךְ/כוֹ/כָהּ	תּוֹךְ-	center;	תָּוֶךְ ז׳
תּוֹכוֹתֵינוּ/כֶם/כֶן/הֶם/הֶן	**תּוֹכוֹ**תַי/תֶיךָ/תַיִךְ/תָיו/תֶיהָ	תּוֹכוֹת-/	inside,	תּוֹכוֹת/
תּוֹכֵינוּ/כֶם/כֶן/הֶם/הֶן	**תּוֹ**כַי/כֶיךָ/כַיִךְ/כָיו/כֶיהָ	תּוֹכֵי-	interior	תּוֹכִים

Examples

מאז שהיה ילד, תמיד עניין אותו מה מתרחש **בְּתוֹךְ** מכונות ומכשירים.

Since he was a child, he has been interested in what occurs **inside** machines and instruments.

Special Expressions

the main stay עמוד **הַתָּוֶךְ** within a week **תּוֹךְ** שבוע

in the course of **תּוֹךְ** כדי hypocrite אין **תּוֹכוֹ** כברו

in his innermost heart **בתוֹךְ** תּוֹכוֹ

---

356. ***CáCeC~CoC***: (penultimately stressed) nouns with a *CaCeC* base, the second consonant is *w* or *y*, the *ave* sequence (originally a diphthong) is reduced to a single vowel in part of the declension (note: גְּוָנַי, but גּוֹנֵינוּ), and the stand-alone plural form is as in the other segholate patterns

our/your/their	my/your/his/her	const.	Gloss	sing/pl
גּוֹנֵנוּ/נְכֶם/נְכֶן/נָם/נָן	**גּוֹ**נִי/נְךָ/נֵךְ/נוֹ/נָהּ	גּוֹן-	color; hue;	גָּוֶן ז׳
גּוֹנֵינוּ/כֶם/כֶן/הֶם/הֶן	**גְּוָ**נַי/נֶיךָ/נַיִךְ/נָיו/נֶיהָ	גּוֹנֵי-	nuance	גְּוָנִים

Examples

כל קיר בדירתה של דליה צבוע בצבע אחר. התוצאה בית עם כל **גּוֹנֵי** הקשת.
Each wall in Dalia's apartment is painted with a different color. The result is an apartment with all the **shades** of the rainbow.

Special Expressions

many shades of **color** **גּוֹנֵי גְּוָנִים**

---

357. *CáCiC* (or *CáyiC*)~*CeyC* (or *CeC-*): (penultimately stressed) nouns with a *CaCiC* base, the second consonant is *y*, and the string *ayi* is reduced to the diphthong *ey* or to *e* in the declension

our/your/their	my/your/his/her	const.	gloss	sing/pl
זֵיתֵנוּ/תְכֶם/תְכֶן/תָם/תָן	**זֵי**תִי/תְךָ/תֵךְ/תוֹ/תָהּ	זֵית-	olive (tree,	זַיִת ז'
זֵיתֵינוּ/כֶם/כֶן/הֶם/הֶן	**זֵי**תַי/תֶיךָ/תַיִךְ/תָיו/תֶיהָ	זֵיתֵי-	wood, fruit)	זֵיתִים

Note: the plural of *báyit* 'home, house' is *batim*.

Examples

מכל סוגי הַ**זֵּיתִים**, אני מעדיף **זֵיתִים** ירוקים דפוקים.
Of all the types of **olives**, I prefer green cracked ones.

גם אחרי שנים רבות של חיים בחו"ל, חלק גדול מן הישראלים עדיין מרגיש שישראל היא **בֵּיתָם**.
Even after having lived for many years abroad, many Israelis still feel that Israel is their **home**.

כשאימי עלתה ארצה בשנות השלושים, היא הייתה חלק מגרעין שהקים קיבוץ שעסק **בְּדַיִג**.
When my mother immigrated to Israel in the 1930's, she was part of a group that founded a kibbutz that specialized in **fishing**.

בצה"ל, הטייסים היו העילית. אמרו: "הטובים **לַטַּיִס**". ואני הייתי מעדיף: "הטובים להוראה"...
In the IDF, the pilots were the elite. They said: "the best for **flying**." I would have preferred: "The best for teaching…"

האדם הקדמון עסק **בְּצַיִד**, ואכל פירות וירקות שמצא. החקלאות התפתחה יותר מאוחר.
Early man was engaged in **hunting**, and ate fruit and vegetables that he found. Agriculture developed only later.

Special Expressions

school (**house**) **בֵּית** ספר
clan **בֵּית** אב
Mount of Olives (Jerusalem) הר הַ**זֵּיתִים**
olive oil שמן **זַיִת**
very small amount כ**זַיִת**
witch **hunt** **צֵיד** מכשפות
barbed **wire** **תַּיִל** דוקרני

Additional Examples in this Pattern

ram (male sheep) אַיִל	summer vacation קַיִט
threshing דַּיִשׁ	boating; sailing שַׁיִט
arms, weapons; penis (vulg.) זַיִן	marble שַׁיִשׁ
partition, barrier; division חַיִץ	wire תַּיִל
eagle (not vulture, as popularly assumed) עַיִט	

---

358. ***CáCiC* (or *CáyiC*)~*CeyC* (or *CeC-*)**: (penultimately stressed) nouns with a *CaCiC* base, the second consonant is *y*, the string *ayi* is reduced to the diphthong *ey* in the declension, and the plural suffix is וֹת- (note: לַיִל is Lit.; in Coll. Heb. it is לַיְלָה ז׳)

Our/your/their	my/your/his/her	const.	Gloss	sing/pl
לֵילֵנוּ/לְכֶם/לְכֶן/לָם/לָן	**לֵי**לִי/לְךָ/לֵךְ/לוֹ/לָהּ	-לֵיל	night,	לַיִל/לַיְלָה ז׳
לֵילוֹתֵינוּ/כֶם/כֶן/הֶם/הֶן	**לֵילוֹ**תַי/תֶיךָ/תַיִךְ/תָיו/תֶיהָ	-לֵילוֹת	darkness	לֵילוֹת

Examples

לאכזבתנו הגדולה, הלילה הראשון של הטיול היה **לֵיל** סערה.

To our great disappointment, the first **night** of the trip was a stormy **night**.

Special Expressions

in the middle of the **night** באישון **לַיְלָה**	**nocturnal** emission מקרה **לַיְלָה**
over**night** בִּן **לַיְלָה**	chamber pot, bed-pan סיר **לַיְלָה**
sleepless **night** **לֵיל** שימורים	

Additional Examples in this Pattern

[גֵּיאָיוֹת plural] valley, gorge, ravine, gulch גַּיְא/גַּי

---

359. ***CáCiC* (or *CáyiC*)~*CeyC* (or *CeC-*)**: (penultimately stressed) nouns with a *CaCiC* base, the second consonant is *y*, the string *ayi* is reduced to the diphthong *ey* or *e* in part of the declension, but the plural form in isolation follows the regular segholate pattern

our/your/their	my/your/his/her	const.	Gloss	sing/pl
תֵּישֵׁנוּ/שְׁכֶם/שְׁכֶן/שָׁם/שָׁן	**תֵּי**שִׁי/שְׁךָ/שֵׁךְ/שׁוֹ/שָׁהּ	-תֵּישׁ	he-goat	תַּיִשׁ ז׳
תְּיָשֵׁינוּ/**תֵּישֵׁי**כֶם/כֶן/הֶם/הֶן	**תְּיָ**שַׁי/שֶׁיךָ/שַׁיִךְ/שָׁיו/שֶׁיהָ	-תֵּישֵׁי		תְּיָשִׁים

Examples

לא ברור בדיוק, למה ל**תַּיִשׁ** יש זקן...

It is not exactly clear, why the **he-goat** has a beard...

Special Expressions

the young have made their mark (kids have become **goats**) הגדיים נעשו **תְּיָשִׁים**

goatee זְקַן **תַּיִשׁ**

Additional Examples in this Pattern

foil, fencing sword; fencing (sports) סַיִף　　　lion (biblical) לַיִשׁ

---

360. ***CáCiC* (or *CáyiC*)~*CeyC***: (penultimately stressed) nouns with a *CaCiC* base, the second consonant is *y*, the string *ayi* is reduced to the diphthong *ey* in part of the declension, but the plural form follows the segholate pattern with the suffix וֹת-

our/your/their	my/your/his/her	const.	Gloss	sing/pl
גֵּיסֵנוּ/סְכֶם/סְכֶן/סָם/סָן	גֵּיסִי/סְךָ/סֵךְ/סוֹ/סָהּ	גֵּיס-	corps	גַּיִס ז׳
גֵּיסוֹתֵינוּ/כֶם/כֶן/הֶם/הֶן	גֵּיסוֹתַי/תֶיךָ/תַיִךְ/תָיו/תֶיהָ	גֵּיסוֹת-	(military)	גְּיָסוֹת

Examples

במרבית מלחמות ישראל, ל**גֵיסוֹת** השריון היה תפקיד מרכזי במערכה.
In most of Israel's wars the armor **corps** had a central role.

Special Expressions

fifth **column** **גַּיִס** חֲמִישִׁי

---

361. ***CáCiC* (or *CáyiC*)~*CeyC***: (penult. stressed) fem. nouns with a *CaCiC* base, the second consonant is *y*, in part of the declension the string *ayi* is reduced to the diphthong *ey*, but the plural form follows a version of the segholate pattern for feminine nouns

our/your/their	my/your/his/her	const.	Gloss	sing/pl
עֵינֵנוּ/נְכֶם/נְכֶן/נָם/נָן	עֵינִי/נְךָ/נֵךְ/נוֹ/נָהּ	עֵין-	spring,	עַיִן נ׳
עֵינוֹתֵינוּ/כֶם/כֶן/הֶם/הֶן	עֵינוֹתַי/תֶיךָ/תַיִךְ/תָיו/תֶיהָ	עֵינוֹת-	fountain	עֲיָנוֹת

Examples

המילה "**עַיִן**" היא תחליף ספרותי ל"מעיין".
The word *`áyin* is a literary alternant of *ma`ayan* '**spring**.'

מקורות הירקון נקראים "ראש ה**עַיִן**".
The sources of the Yarkon River are called "the **Fountain**head".

---

362. ***CáCiC* (or *CáyiC*)~*CeyC***: (penultimately stressed) nouns with a *CaCiC* base, the second consonant is *y*, the string *ayi* is reduced to the diphthong *ey* in part of the declension, and the plural form is either וֹת- or ים-

our/your/their	my/your/his/her	const.	Gloss	sing/pl
פֵּיסֵנוּ/סְכֶם/סְכֶן/סָם/סָן	פֵּיסִי/סְךָ/סֵךְ/סוֹ/סָהּ	פֵּיס-	lottery ticket;	פַּיִס ז׳
פֵּיסֵינוּ/כֶם/כֶן/הֶם/הֶן	פֵּיסַי/סֶיךָ/סַיִךְ/סָיו/סֶיהָ	פֵּיסֵי-/	lot, fate	פְּיָסִים/
פֵּיסוֹתֵינוּ/כֶם/כֶן/הֶם/הֶן	פֵּיסוֹתַי/תֶיךָ/תַיִךְ/תָיו/תֶיהָ	פֵּיסוֹת-	(Talmudic)	פְּיָסוֹת

Examples

בישראל, מפעל ה**פַּיִס** משתתף בהקמת הרבה מוסדות חברתיים חשובים ובתפעולם.
In Israel, the state **lottery** participates in the establishment of many important social institutions, and in their maintenance.

---

363. ***CáCiC* (or *CáyiC*)~*CeyC***: (penultimately stressed) nouns with a *CaCiC* base, the second consonant is *y*, the string *ayi* is reduced to the diphthong *ey* in part of the declension, the plural form is either ־ות or ־ים, and the first consonant is a guttural

our/your/their	my/your/his/her	const.	Gloss	sing/pl
חֵילֵנוּ/לְכֶם/לְכֶן/לָם/לָן	**חֵי**לִי/לְךָ/לֵךְ/לוֹ/לָהּ	־חֵיל	strength;	חַיִל ז'
חֲיָלֵינוּ/**חֵילֵי**כֶם/כֶן/הֶם/הֶן	**חֲיָ**לַי/לֶיךָ/לַיִךְ/לָיו/לֶיהָ	־/חֵילֵי	bravery;	חֲיָלִים/חֵילוֹת
חֵילוֹתֵינוּ/כֶם/כֶן/הֶם/הֶן	**חֵילוֹ**תַי/תֶיךָ/תַיִךְ/תָיו/תֶיהָ	־חֵילוֹת	force; wealth	/חֲיָלוֹת

Where a *shva* is expected with the guttural, it is replaced by *Hataf-pataH*.

Examples

בארה״ב, ה**חֵילוֹת** השונים (**חֵיל** האוויר, **חֵיל** הים, **חֵילוֹת** היבשה השונים) מתחרים ביניהם ולא תמיד משתפים פעולה.
In the US, the different **branches of the military** (the Air **Force**, the Navy, the various Army **Corps**) compete with one another, and do not always cooperate.

להפתעת כולנו, הוא דווקא עשה **חַיִל** בלימודיו.
We were all surprised, but he actually **excelled** in his studies.

Special Expressions

brave/worthy man איש **חַיִל**
smart/worthy woman אשת **חַיִל**
smart man בן **חַיִל**
went from **strength** to **strength** הלך מחַיִל אל **חַיִל**
excel at… ...עשה **חַיִל** ב
get stronger, overcome אזר **חַיִל**
Navy **חֵיל** הים
Army (lit. foot soldiers) **חֵיל** הרַגְלים
Air **Force** **חֵיל** האוויר
Corps of Engineers **חֵיל** ההנדסה

Additional Examples in this Pattern

tailoring of clothes Lit חַיִט

---

364. ***CáCiC* (or *CáyiC*)~*CeyC***: (penultimately stressed) nouns with a *CaCiC* base, the second consonant is *y*, the string *ayi* is reduced to the diphthong *ey* in the declension, but the plural form is the dual form

our/your/their	my/your/his/her	const.	Gloss	sing/pl
עֵינֵנוּ/נְכֶם/נְכֶן/נָם/נָן	**עֵי**נִי/נְךָ/נֵךְ/נוֹ/נָהּ	־עֵין	eye; shade, color;	עַיִן נ'
עֵינֵינוּ/כֶם/כֶן/הֶם/הֶן	**עֵי**נַי/נֶיךָ/נַיִךְ/נָיו/נֶיהָ	־עֵינֵי	appearance	עֵינַיִם

Examples

הראיה שלי הידרדרה ; אני צריך ללכת לרופא **עֵינַיִם**.
My eyesight is deteriorating; I need to go to an **eye** doctor.

למראית **עַיִן**, הכל נראה בסדר אצלו, אבל האמת היא שהוא חולה מאוד.
Everything **appears** to be OK with him, but the truth is that he is very sick.

Special Expressions

he felt relief אורו **עֵינָיו**
trickery אחיזת **עֵינַיִם**
with great impatience בכליון **עֵינַיִם**
touch wood! בלי **עַיִן** הרע!
favorably; generously **בעַיִן** יפה
still the same **בעֵינוֹ** עומד
with great vigilance בשבע **עֵינַיִם**
glanced העיף **עַיִן**
turn a blind **eye** to העלים **עַיִן** מ...
he was stunned חשכו **עֵינָיו**
perspicacity טביעת **עַיִן**
lost heavily יצא בשן **ועַיִן**
in a flash כהרף **עַיִן**
as he pleases כטוב **בעֵינָיו**
did not take his **eyes** off לא גרע **עַיִן** מ...
stared לטש את **עֵינָיו**
on the face of it למראית **עַיִן**
openly **לעֵינֵי** השמש
a kind of **מעֵין**
he liked it מצא חן **בעֵינָיו**
looked up נשא את **עֵינָיו**
got drunk נתן **עֵינוֹ** בכוס
eye for an **eye** **עַיִן** תחת **עַיִן**
was jealous of him **עֵינוֹ** צרה בו
attend to שם **עַיִן** על
looked/looked up at תלה **עֵינָיו** ב...

---

365. *CáCiC* (or *CáyiC*)~*CiC*: (penultimately stressed) nouns with a *CaCiC* base, the second consonant is *y*, the string *ayi* is reduced to *i* in part of the declension, but the plural form is a segholate pattern

our/your/their	my/your/his/her	const.	Gloss	sing/pl
עִירֵנוּ/רְכֶם/רְכֶן/רָם/רָן	**עִי**רִי/רְךָ/רֵךְ/רוֹ/רָהּ	עִיר-	young	עַיִר ז'
עֲיָרֵינוּ/**עִירֵי**כֶם/כֶן/הֶם/הֶן	**עֲיָ**רַי/רֶיךָ/רַיִךְ/רָיו/רֶיהָ	עִירֵי-	ass	עֲיָרִים

Examples

מרבית הילדים בעולם המערבי לא ראו מימיהם חמור או **עַיִר**, למרות שהמונחים מוכרים.
Most children in the western world have never seen a donkey or a **young ass**, although they are familiar with the terms.

---

366. *CoCaC*

our/your/their	my/your/his/her	const.	Gloss	sing/pl
גּוֹזָלֵנוּ/**גּוֹזַלְ**כֶם/כֶן/**גּוֹזָלָ**ם/ן	**גּוֹזָ**לִי/לְךָ/לֵךְ/לוֹ/לָהּ	גּוֹזַל-	chick,	גּוֹזָל ז'
גּוֹזָלֵינוּ/**גּוֹזְלֵי**כֶם/כֶן/הֶם/הֶן	**גּוֹזָ**לַי/לֶיךָ/לַיִךְ/לָיו/לֶיהָ	גּוֹזְלֵי-	fledgling	גּוֹזָלִים

The initial וֹ is maintained throughout the declension. The following *kamats* is elided when two syllables away from the main stress, or turns into a *pataH* in a closed syllable.

Examples

בנים ובנות עוזבים את בית הוריהם כשמגיע הזמן, כשם ש**גוֹזָלִים** פורחים מן הקן.
Sons and daughters leave their parents' home, just like **chicks** fly out of the nest.

בישראל, כשהייתי ילד, ה**אוֹלָר** היה לא רק מכשיר לגלף ולקלף, אלא גם כלי מרכזי במשחקים שונים, בעיקר בין הבנים.
In Israel when I was a kid, the **penknife** was not only an instrument of sculpting and peeling, but also the centeriece of different games, especially among boys.

״ה**כּוֹכָבִים** רימו אותי״, כתב ביאליק בשיר על אהבה, או העדרה...
"The **stars** cheated me," wrote Bialik in a poem about love, or its absence...

פעמיים בשנה נשמע קול **צוֹפָר** בכל רחבי הארץ, ביום הזיכרון לשואה וגבורה וביום הזיכרון לחללי מלחמות ישראל בערב יום העצמאות.
Twice a year a general **siren** sounds throughout Israel, on Holocaust Memorial Day and on Memorial Day for Israel's Fallen Soldiers on the eve of Israel's Independence Day.

״כשה**תּוֹתָחִים** רועמים, המוזות שותקות.״
"When the **cannons** thunder, the muses are silent".

Special Expressions

אוֹלָר קפיצי switchblade **knife**
כּוֹכַב לֶכֶת planet
כּוֹכַב הצפון north **star**, Polaris
שִׁניים **תּוֹתָבוֹת** dentures
תּוֹתַח לא-רֶתע recoilless **cannon**
תּוֹתָח מִתְנייע self-propelled **cannon**

Additional Examples in this Pattern

גּוֹפָן font (in printing)
כּוֹנָן disk drive (computers); stand, rack
כּוֹתָר title (of book, etc.)
לוֹלָב bolt
עוֹלָל babe
קוֹלָב hanger
קוֹלָר collar
שׁוֹבָב mischievous; naughty
שׁוֹבָךְ dovecote
שׁוֹשָׁן lily
תּוֹתָב prosthetic, artificial
תּוֹלָע red, scarlet (biblical)

---

367. ***CoCaC***: plural suffix: ות-/-ים-

our/your/their	my/your/his/her	const.	Gloss	sing/pl
עוֹלָמֵנוּ/**עוֹלַמְ**כֶם/כֶן/**עוֹלָמָ**ם/ן	**עוֹלָמִ**י/מְךָ/מֵךְ/מוֹ/מָהּ	עוֹלַם-	world;	עוֹלָם ז׳
עוֹלָמֵינוּ/**עוֹלְמֵי**כֶם/כֶן/הֶם/הֶן	**עוֹלָמַ**י/מֶיךָ/מַיִךְ/מָיו/מֶיהָ	**עוֹלְ**מוֹת/מֵי-	eternity	**עוֹלָ**מוֹת/מִים

The initial וֹ is maintained throughout the declension. The following *kamats* is elided when two syllables away from the main stress, or turns into a *pataH* in a closed syllable. The plural suffix is ים- or וֹת-.

Examples

אנשים רבים מצפים בכיליון עיניים לפרישה, כדי שיוכלו לטייל ברחבי **העוֹלָם**.
Many people cannot wait to retire, so that they can travel around the **world**.

גדעון נשבע **שלְעוֹלָם** לא יחזור להודו.
Gideon swore that he would **never** return to India.

Special Expressions

the next **world** **העוֹלָם** הבא
this **world** **העוֹלָם** הזה
out of this **world** לא **מהעוֹלָם** הזה
social reform תיקון **עוֹלָם**
the whole **universe** **עוֹלָם** ומלואו
for**ever** **לעוֹלָם** (וָעֶד)
never (in future) **לעוֹלָם** לא
never (in past) **מעוֹלָם** לא
the under**world** **העוֹלָם** התחתון
philosophy of life השקפת **עוֹלָם**
it's a complete fabrication לא היו דברים **מעוֹלָם** (להד"ם)
from the beginning of days מאז **ומעוֹלָם**

---

368. ***CoCaC*** when the plural suffix is *-ot*

our/your/their	my/your/his/her	const.	Gloss	sing/pl
גּוֹרָלֵנוּ/**גּוֹרַלְ**כֶם/כֶן/**גּוֹרָלָ**ם/ן	**גּוֹרָלִ**י/לְךָ/לֵךְ/לוֹ/לָהּ	גּוֹרַל-	fate; casting	גּוֹרָל ז'
גּוֹרְלוֹתֵינוּ/כֶם/כֶן/הֶם/הֶן	**גּוֹרְלוֹ**תַי/תֶיךָ/תַיִךְ/תָיו/תֶיהָ	**גּוֹרְ**לוֹת	lots	גּוֹרָלוֹת

The initial וֹ is maintained throughout the declension. The following *kamats* is elided when two syllables away from the main stress, or turns into a *pataH* in a closed syllable. The plural suffix is וֹת-.

Examples

עדיין לא ברור מה **גּוֹרַל** הצעת החוק שהקונגרס הגיש לנשיא.
The **fate** of the bill Congress presented to the President is still uncertain.

Special Expressions

cast **lots** הטיל **גּוֹרָל**
determined by **fate** יד **הגּוֹרָל**
determined his **fate** חרץ את **גּוֹרָלוֹ**
unexpected turn of events/**fate** צחוק **הגּוֹרָל**
blowing of the **shofar** תקיעת **שׁוֹפָר**

Additional Examples in this Pattern

wrapper, envelope; sack; container (Talmudic) חוֹתָל
seal, impression; influence חוֹתָם
ram's horn שׁוֹפָר
belt loop; rosette תּוֹבָר

---

369. ***CoCaC***: *pataH* in the isolation form becomes *kamats* w/ stress shift in open syll.

our/your/their	my/your/his/her	const.	Gloss	sing/pl
כּוֹבָעֵנוּ/**כּוֹבַעְ**כֶם/כֶן/**כּוֹבָעָ**ם/ן	**כּוֹבָ**עִי/עֲךָ/עֵךְ/עוֹ/עָהּ	-כּוֹבַע	hat, cap;	כּוֹבַע ז'
כּוֹבָעֵינוּ/**כּוֹבְעֵי**כֶם/כֶן/הֶם/הֶן	**כּוֹבָ**עַי/עֶיךָ/עַיִךְ/עָיו/עֶיהָ	-כּוֹבְעֵי	helmet	כּוֹבָעִים

The initial וֹ is maintained throughout the declension. An apparently original *kamats* is maintained in an open syllable, is elided two syllables away from the main stress, but is realized as *pataH* in a closed syllable, including the unsufixed form. An expected *shva* with ע' is replaced by *Hataf-pataH*.

Examples

היום **כּוֹבְעֵי** נשים אינם אופנתיים כפי שהיו בעבר.
Today, ladies' **hats** are not as fashionable as they used to be.

Special Expressions

steel **helmet** **כּוֹבַע** פלדה

toque, knitted **hat** **כּוֹבַע** גֶּרֶב

Additional Examples in this Pattern

beeswax; ear wax דּוֹנַג
ancient threshing implement מוֹרַג
helmet, steel helmet (archaic) קוֹבַע

---

370. ***CuCaC***

our/your/their	my/your/his/her	const.	Gloss	sing/pl
דּוּכָנֵנוּ/**דּוּכַנְ**כֶם/כֶן/**דּוּכָנָ**ם/ן	**דּוּכָ**נִי/נְךָ/נֵךְ/נוֹ/נָהּ	- דּוּכַן	stall;	דּוּכָן ז'
דּוּכָנֵינוּ/**דּוּכְנֵי**כֶם/כֶן/הֶם/הֶן	**דּוּכָ**נַי/נֶיךָ/נַיִךְ/נָיו/נֶיהָ	-דּוּכְנֵי	dais	דּוּכָנִים

The initial וּ is maintained throughout the declension. The following *kamats* is elided when two syllables away from the main stress, or turns into a *pataH* in a closed syllable.

Examples

למנחם יש **דּוּכַן** ירקות גדול ב״שוק הכרמל״ בתל אביב.
Menahem has a large vegetable **stall** at the Carmel Market of Tel Aviv.

Special Expressions

went up to the **dais** (to bless the congregation); took a leadership position עלה לַ**דּוּכָן**

Additional Examples in this Pattern

lulav, ceremonial palm frond לוּלָב
water lily נוּפָר
scarf, shawl sweater (Rare); סוּדָר
pipe organ עוּגָב
fat N שׁוּמָן/שֻׁמָּן

---

371. ***CuCaC***: when the second consonant is a guttural

our/your/their	my/your/his/her	const.	Gloss	sing/pl
שׁוּעָלֵנוּ/**שׁוּעַלְ**כֶם/כֶן/**שׁוּעָלָ**ם/ן	**שׁוּעָ**לִי/לְךָ/לֵךְ/לוֹ/לָהּ	שׁוּעַל-	fox	שׁוּעָל
שׁוּעָלֵינוּ/**שׁוּעֲלֵי**כֶם/כֶן/הֶם/הֶן	**שׁוּעָ**לַי/לֶיךָ/לַיִךְ/לָיו/לֶיהָ	שׁוּעֲלֵי-		שׁוּעָלִים

The initial וּ is maintained throughout the declension. The following *kamats* is elided when two syllables away from the main stress, or turns into a *pataH* in a closed syllable. An expected *shva* with a guttural is replaced by *Hataf-pataH*.

Examples

בבריטניה מוחים אזרחים רבים על ציד **שׁוּעָלִים**, הספורט החביב על המעמדות העליונים.
In Britain many citizens protest **fox** hunting, the favorite sport of the upper classes.

Special Expressions

הווי זנב לאריות ואל תהי ראש ל**שׁוּעָלִים**
Better be a follower of the great than a leader of the insignificant

שיבולת **שׁוּעָל** oats
ערום כ**שׁוּעָל** cunning as a **fox**

Additional Examples in this Pattern

דּוּחַל chat (bird)

---

372. ***CuCaC***: a stable *pataH*

our/your/their	my/your/his/her	const.	Gloss	sing/pl
יוּבַלֵּנוּ/**יוּבַלְ**כֶם/כֶן/**יוּבַלָּ**ם/ן	**יוּבַ**לִּי/לְּךָ/לֵּךְ/לּוֹ/לָּהּ	יוּבַל -	river; tributary;	יוּבַל ז׳
יוּבַלֵּינוּ/כֶם/כֶן/הֶם/הֶן	**יוּבַ**לַּי/לֶּיךָ/לַּיִךְ/לָּיו/לֶּיהָ	יוּבַלֵּי-	creek	יוּבַלִּים

The initial וּ is maintained throughout the declension. When a suffix is added, the syllable with the *pataH* is closed by a *dagesh forte*, which is also maintained throughout the declension.

Examples

לנהר הירדן מספר **יוּבַלִּים** משני עבריו.
The Jordan River has a few **tributaries** from either bank.

---

373. ***CuCaC***: *pataH* changes to *kamats* in most of the declension

our/your/their	my/your/his/her	const.	Gloss	sing/pl
סוּגָרֵנוּ/**סוּגַרְ**כֶם/כֶן/**סוּגָרָ**ם/ן	**סוּגָ**רִי/רְךָ/רֵךְ/רוֹ/רָהּ	סוּגַר -	cage	סוּגַר ז׳
סוּגָרֵינוּ/**סוּגְרֵי**כֶם/כֶן/הֶם/הֶן	**סוּגָ**רַי/רֶיךָ/רַיִךְ/רָיו/רֶיהָ	סוּגְרֵי-		סוּגָרִים

The initial ו is maintained throughout the declension. When a suffix is added, the *pataH* is replaced by a *kamats* in open syllables, but is maintained in closed ones.

Examples

הוא מסתובב כל היום בחוסר מנוחה כארי ב**סוּגַר**.
He is walking restlessly all day like a lion in a **cage**.

---

374. *CeyCaC*

our/your/their	my/your/his/her	const.	Gloss	sing/pl
הֵיכָלֵנוּ/**הֵיכַלְ**כֶם/כֶן/**הֵיכָלָ**ם/ן	**הֵיכָ**לִי/לְךָ/לֵךְ/לוֹ/לָהּ	הֵיכַל-	palace;	הֵיכָל
הֵיכָלֵינוּ/**הֵיכְלֵי**כֶם/כֶן/הֶם/הֶן	**הֵיכָ**לַי/לֶיךָ/לַיִךְ/לָיו/לֶיהָ	הֵיכְלֵי/וֹת-	temple	**הֵיכָ**לִים/לוֹת

The initial *ey* is maintained throughout the declension. The following *kamats* is elided when two syllables away from the main stress, or turns into a *pataH* in a closed syllable.

Examples

התזמורת הפילהרמונית הישראלית מרבה להופיע ב"**הֵיכַל** התרבות" בתל-אביב.
The Israel Philharmonic Orchestra performs a lot at the Tel Aviv "**Palace** of Culture."

המונח המקובל במקרא ל"בית המקדש" הוא "ה**הֵיכָל**".
The common term for the **Temple** in the Bible is "ה**הֵיכָל**".

Special Expressions

the **Templ**ar Knights אבירי ה**הֵיכָל**

Additional Examples in this Pattern

limb, organ אֵיבָר
zoo, menagerie Lit. בֵּיבָר
sliver; toothpick קֵיסָם
jujube (tree, fruit) שֵׁיזָף

---

375. *CeyCaC*: *kamats* > *pataH* followed by *dagesh* in the declension; the plural ending is וֹת-

our/your/their	my/your/his/her	const.	Gloss	sing/pl
כֵּילַפֵּנוּ/פְּכֶם/פְּכֶן/פָּם/פָּן	**כֵּילַ**פִּי/פְּךָ/פֵּךְ/פּוֹ/פָּהּ	כֵּילַף-	hatchet	כֵּילָף ז'
כֵּילַפּוֹתֵינוּ/כֶם/כֶן/הֶם/הֶן	**כֵּילַפּוֹ**תַי/תֶיךָ/תַיִךְ/תָיו/תֶיהָ	כֵּילַפּוֹת-		כֵּילַפּוֹת

ey is maintained throughout the declension. When a suffix is added, the *kamats* is replaced by *pataH*, and the syllable is closed by a *dagesh forte*, which is also maintained throughout the declension. The plural suffix is וֹת-.

Examples

ה**כֵּילָף** של תקופת המקרא שימש בעיקר להריסה ולחפירה.
The biblical **hatchet** was used mostly in demolition and in digging.

---

376. ***CaCuC***: Noun, when the *kamats* undergoes no reduction at all

our/your/their	my/your/his/her	const.	Gloss	sing/pl
חָרוּבֵנוּ/בְכֶם/בְכֶן/בָם/בָן	**חָרוּ**בִי/בְךָ/בֵךְ/בוֹ/בָהּ	חָרוּב -	carob	חָרוּב ז'
חָרוּבֵינוּ/כֶם/כֶן/הֶם/הֶן	**חָרוּ**בַי/בֶיךָ/בַיִךְ/בָיו/בֶיהָ	חָרוּבֵי-		חָרוּבִים

Examples

יחידת הקָרָט נקבעה לראשונה על פי גרעין ה**חָרוּב** – בשל משקלו הקל אך אחיד יחסית, ומשום שנפחו אינו משתנה.

The carat (= karat) unit weight was originally determined based on the **carob** bean (pit) – owing to its light but relatively uniform weight, and because its volume never changes.

Special Expressions

crutch of **carobs** (= a small quantity) קב **חָרוּבִין**

---

377. ***CaCuC***: Noun, when the *kamats* undergoes reduction only in the construct state; the plural suffix is וֹת-

our/your/their	my/your/his/her	const.	Gloss	sing/pl
שָׁבוּעֵנוּ/עֲכֶם/עֲכֶן/עָם/עָן	**שָׁבוּ**עִי/עֲךָ/עֵךְ/עוֹ/עָהּ	שְׁבוּעַ -	week	שָׁבוּעַ ז'
שָׁבוּעוֹתֵינוּ/כֶם/כֶן/הֶם/הֶן	**שָׁבוּעוֹ**תַי/תֶיךָ/תַיִךְ/תָיו/תֶיהָ	שְׁבוּעוֹת-		שָׁבוּעוֹת

Examples

בשנה יש כ-52 **שָׁבוּעוֹת**.

In a year there are about 52 **weeks**.

חג ה**שָׁבוּעוֹת** נחוג שבעה **שָׁבוּעוֹת** ממחרת היום הראשון של פסח.

The Feast of **Weeks** (or Pentecost) is celebrated seven **weeks** after the first day of Passover.

Special Expressions

Have a good week! (Saturday night greeting) **שָׁבוּעַ** טוב!

weekend סוף **שָׁבוּעַ**

---

378. ***CaCuC***: the *pataH* is stable

our/your/their	my/your/his/her	const.	Gloss	sing/pl
כַּדּוּרֵנוּ/רְכֶם/רְכֶן/רָם/רָן	**כַּדּוּ**רִי/רְךָ/רֵךְ/רוֹ/רָהּ	כַּדּוּר-	ball, sphere;	כַּדּוּר ז'
כַּדּוּרֵינוּ/כֶם/כֶן/הֶם/הֶן	**כַּדּוּ**רַי/רֶיךָ/רַיִךְ/רָיו/רֶיהָ	כַּדּוּרֵי-	pill; bullet	כַּדּוּרִים

The *pataH* is maintained throughout the declension, and is followed by a *dagesh forte*.

Examples

לעתים **כַּדּוּר** הבסיס נחבט בכוח כזה, שהוא מגיע ליציע הצופים ופוגע במישהו בקהל...
Occasionally, a base**ball** is hit with such force, that it reaches the bleachers and hits a spectator…

מרבית המבוגרים בולעים מספר ניכר של **כַּדּוּרִים** מדי יום ביומו מכל מיני סיבות.
Most adults swallow a large number of **pills** daily, for all kinds of reasons.

כַּדּוּר "טו-טו" הוא אמנם קטן מאוד, אבל בכל זאת עלול להרוג.
A 2.2 caliber **bullet** is indeed small, but it can still kill.

ב-1972 בובי פישר היה **לְאַלּוּף** העולם ה-11 בשחמט.
In 1972 Bobby Fischer became the 11th World chess **champion**.

תמיד נראה לי שהעיר ניו יורק היא **טַבּוּר** העולם.
It has always seemed to me that New York City is the **navel** of the world.

מנהיגים מסוימים מוּנָעים על ידי שני משפטים בצרפתית: "המדינה זה אני" ו"אחרַי – **הַמַּבּוּל**".
Some leaders are motivated by two French sentences: "L'état c'est moi," and "Après moi le **déluge**."

הַתַּפּוּזִים הישראלים לא פחות טובים מאלה של פלורידה.
The Israeli **oranges** are just as good as the Florida ones.

Special Expressions

אַלּוּף מִשְׁנֶה colonel
אַלּוּף פיקוד דרום **Commander** of the Southern Command (IDF)
חַלּוּקֵי אבן/נחל pebbles
טַבּוּר האופן/הגלגל **hub** (of wheel)
יַתּוּשׁ בראש bee in the bonnet Sl.
כַּדּוּר הארץ planet Earth
כַּדּוּרֶגֶל soccer

כַּדּוּרֶגֶל אמריקני American foot**ball**
כַּדּוּרְסַל basket**ball**
כַּדּוּרְעָף volley**ball**
כַּדּוּר בסיס base**ball**
כַּדּוּר פורח hot-air **balloon**
כַּדּוּר נותב tracer **bullet**
עַמּוּד השִׁדרה spinal **column**

Additional Examples in this Pattern

אַבּוּב oboe
בַּלּוּט acorn
דַּבּוּר hornet Coll.
חַבּוּשׁ quince
חַלּוּק smooth stone
חַמּוּק curve (of body)
חַנּוּן merciful

יַתּוּשׁ mosquito
סַמּוּר weasel
עַכּוּז buttocks
עַמּוּד post, pole, pillar
שַׁכּוּל bereaved
תַּנּוּר oven, stove
תַּפּוּד potato

---

379. ***CaCuC***: the *pataH* is stable, and the last consonant is guttural

our/your/their	my/your/his/her	const.	Gloss	sing/pl
תַּפּוּחֵנוּ/חֲכֶם/חֲכֶן/חָם/חָן	**תַּפּוּ**חִי/חֲךָ/חֵךְ/חוֹ/חָהּ	-תַּפּוּחַ	apple; ball,	תַּפּוּחַ ז'
תַּפּוּחֵינוּ/כֶם/כֶן/הֶם/הֶן	**תַּפּוּ**חַי/חֶיךָ/חַיִךְ/חָיו/חֶיהָ	-תַּפּוּחֵי	knob	תַּפּוּחִים

The *pataH* is maintained throughout the declension and is followed by a *dagesh forte*. Where a *shva* is expect following a guttural, it is replaced by *Hataf-pataH*. The unsuffixed form comes with a *furtive pataH* since the preceding vowel is not *a*.

Examples

פאי **תַּפּוּחִים** הוא מאפה אמריקאי טיפוסי, בעיקר בניו-אינגלנד.
Apple pie is a typical American dish, particularly in New England.

תַּפּוּחַ הבריח נקרא כך משום שברובה הקלאסי הייתה לו צורת כדור.
The bolt **knob** (lit. 'apple' in Hebrew) in a rifle is called so because in the classical rifle it was ball-shaped.

Special Expressions

תַּפּוּחַ אדמה potato　　**תַּפּוּחַ** זהב = תַּפּוּ״ז orange N

Additional Examples in this Pattern

אֲשׁוּחַ fir tree　　מַדּוּחַ temptation Lit.　　מַלּוּחַ orache (plant)

---

380. *CaCoC*: the *pataH* is stable

our/your/their	my/your/his/her	const.	Gloss	sing/pl
אַלּוֹנֵנוּ/נְכֶם/נְכֶן/נָם/נָן	**אַלּוֹ**נִי/נְךָ/נֵךְ/נוֹ/נָהּ	אַלּוֹן-	oak	אַלּוֹן ז׳
אַלּוֹנֵינוּ/כֶם/כֶן/הֶם/הֶן	**אַלּוֹ**נַי/נֶיךָ/נַיִךְ/נָיו/נֶיהָ	אַלּוֹנֵי-	(tree)	אַלּוֹנִים

The *pataH* is maintained throughout the declension, and is followed by a *dagesh forte*.

Examples

קיימים הרבה סוגי **אַלּוֹנִים** בישראל, חלקם אפילו לא נשירים.
There exist many types of **oak(s)** in Israel, some of them not even deciduous.

Special Expressions

חסון **כָּאַלּוֹן** as sturdy as an oak

Additional Examples in this Pattern

כַּמּוֹן cumin (plant, spice)　　רַתּוֹק chain, cable

---

381. *CaCon*: the *pataH* is stable, derived from identical 2nd and 3rd consonants, plus the affix וֹן-, plural suffix וֹת-

our/your/their	my/your/his/her	const.	Gloss	sing/pl
חַלּוֹנֵנוּ/נְכֶם/נְכֶן/נָם/נָן	**חַלּוֹ**נִי/נְךָ/נֵךְ/נוֹ/נָהּ	חַלּוֹן-	window	חַלּוֹן ז׳
חַלּוֹנוֹתֵינוּ/כֶם/כֶן/הֶם/הֶן	**חַלּוֹנוֹ**תַי/תֶיךָ/תַיִךְ/תָיו/תֶיהָ	חַלּוֹנוֹת-		חַלּוֹנוֹת

The *pataH* is maintained throughout the declension, and is followed be a *dagesh forte*. Derived from roots with identical 2nd and 3rd consonants, plus the affix ון-, and the plural suffix is ות-.

Examples

ב**חַלּוֹנוֹת** בקומת הקרקע או בקומה הראשונה רצוי להתקין סורגים, מטעמי בטיחות.
In **windows** on the ground floor or on the first floor it is a good idea to install grating, for security reasons.

Special Expressions

the **Windows** operating system **חַלּוֹנוֹת** display window **חַלּוֹן** ראווה

---

382. ***CiCoC***: the *Hirik* is stable

our/your/their	my/your/his/her	const.	Gloss	sing/pl
גִּבּוֹרֵנוּ/רְכֶם/רְכֶן/רָם/רָן	**גִּבּוֹ**רִי/רְךָ/רֵךְ/רוֹ/רָהּ	גִּבּוֹר-	hero; central figure,	גִּבּוֹר ז'
גִּבּוֹרֵינוּ/כֶם/כֶן/הֶם/הֶן	**גִּבּוֹ**רַי/רֶיךָ/רַיִךְ/רָיו/רֶיהָ	גִּבּוֹרֵי-	protagonist	גִּבּוֹרִים

The *Hirik* is maintained throughout the declension, and is followed be a *dagesh forte*. Note: צִפּוֹר 'bird' is feminine.

Examples

מכבי האש שנספו בנסותם להציל נפשות ב-11 בספטמבר היו **גִּבּוֹרִים** אמיתיים.
The firefighters who died while trying to save people on September 11 were real **heroes**.

התקשורת לא פסקה מלעסוק בעניין, אבל **גִּבּוֹר** הפרשה סירב להתראיין.
The media were constantly dealing with the matters, but the **hero** of the affair refused to be interviewed.

ברומנים של היום, ה**גִּבּוֹר** הוא לעתים קרובות אנטי-**גִּבּוֹר**...
In today's novels, the **protagonist** is often an anti-**hero**...

הטראומה של **נִצּוֹלֵי** שואה לא פעם מונחלת גם לדור הבא.
The trauma of Holocaust **survivors** may sometimes be passed on to the next generation.

אחת ה**צִפּוֹרִים** שאהבתי בישראל כילד הייתה החוחית. אחת מהן קיננה אצלנו בגינה.
As a kid, one of the **birds** I loved in Israel was the goldfinch. One of them nested in our garden.

אומרים היום שאחד הפירות הבריאים ביותר הוא ה**רִמּוֹן**.
Today they say that the **pomegranate** is one of the healthiest fruits to eat.

כששאלו את רבי מאיר מדוע הוא ממשיך להיפגש עם אלישע בן אבויה, תלמיד חכם שהפך מומר, ענה: "**רִמּוֹן** מצאתי, תוכו אכלתי, קליפתו זרקתי".
When they asked Rabbi Meir why he continued to meet with Elisha Ben Avuya, a Jewish scholar who became an apostate, he answered: "I found a **pomegranate**, ate its inside, and threw away the shell."

Special Expressions

Who's a **hero**? he who controls (lit. conquers) his passions איזהו **גִּבּוֹר**? הכובש את יצרו.
hero of the day **גִּבּוֹר** היום
anti-**hero** אנטי-**גִּבּוֹר**
brave **warrior** **גִּבּוֹר** חַיִל
mighty hunter **גִּבּוֹר** צַיִד
free spirit **צִפּוֹר** דרור
the most precious thing **צִפּוֹר** הנפש
sea urchin **קִפּוֹד** ים
(hand) **grenade** **רִמּוֹן** יד
as **drunk** as Lot **שִׁכּוֹר** כלוט

Additional Examples in this Pattern

convert to Judaism גִּיּוֹר
newborn יִלּוֹד
sink; basin כִּיּוֹר
hedgehog קִפּוֹד
pomegranate; grenade רִמּוֹן
drunk, drunkard שִׁכּוֹר
rye שִׁפּוֹן/שִׁיפּוֹן

---

383. ***CiCoC***: the *Hirik* is stable, the plural suffix is *-ot*

our/your/their	my/your/his/her	const.	Gloss	sing/pl
צִנּוֹרֵנוּ/רְכֶם/רְכֶן/רָם/רָן	**צִנּוֹ**רִי/רְךָ/רֵךְ/רוֹ/רָהּ	צִנּוֹר-	pipe, tube,	צִנּוֹר ז'
צִנּוֹרוֹתֵינוּ/כֶם/כֶן/הֶם/הֶן	**צִנּוֹרוֹ**תַי/תֶיךָ/תַיִךְ/תָיו/תֶיהָ	צִנּוֹרוֹת-	channel	צִנּוֹרוֹת

The *Hirik* is maintained throughout the declension, and is followed be a *dagesh forte*. The plural suffix is -וֹת.

Examples

כל **צִנּוֹרוֹת** המים בבית הזה חלודים ; יש להחליפם בהקדם האפשרי.
All water **pipes** in this house are rusty; they should be replaced ASAP.

Special Expressions

first **violin** (music) **כִּנּוֹר** ראשון
spanner מפתח **צִנּוֹרוֹת**
the official **channels** ה**צִּנּוֹרוֹת** הרשמיים
blood vessel **צִנּוֹר** דם
exhaust **pipe** **צִנּוֹר** פליטה

Additional Examples in this Pattern

violin כִּנּוֹר

---

384. ***niCoC***: the *Hirik* is stable, form derived from roots with ו' as a second consonant

our/your/their	my/your/his/her	const.	Gloss	sing/pl
נִשּׁוֹמֵנוּ/מְכֶם/מְכֶן/מָם/מָן	**נִשּׁוֹ**מִי/מְךָ/מֵךְ/מוֹ/מָהּ	נִשּׁוֹם-	assessee,	נִשּׁוֹם ז'
נִשּׁוֹמֵינוּ/כֶם/כֶן/הֶם/הֶן	**נִשּׁוֹ**מַי/מֶיךָ/מַיִךְ/מָיו/מֶיהָ	נִשּׁוֹמֵי-	taxpayer	נִשּׁוֹמִים

The *pataH* is maintained throughout the declension, and is followed be a *dagesh forte*. Forms are derived from roots with a medial ו consonant, and are related to the *niCCaC* verb pattern.

Examples

בארה״ב כל מי שיש לו הכנסה, בין אם הוא שכיר או עצמאי, נחשב ל**נִשּׁוֹם** וחייב בדיווח כל שנה על כל הכנסותיו.

In the US, everyone who has income, be it an employee or a business owner, is regarded as an **assessee/taxpayer**, and is required to report his annual income every year.

Special Expressions

list of all **taxpayers** ספר ה**נִשּׁוֹמִים**

Additional Examples in this Pattern

circumcised נִמּוֹל

---

385. ***CiCon***: the *Hirik* is stable, the form includes the affix וֹן-

our/your/their	my/your/his/her	const.	Gloss	sing/pl
מִלּוֹנֵנוּ/נְכֶם/נְכֶן/נָם/נָן	**מִלּוֹ**נִי/נְךָ/נֵךְ/נוֹ/נָהּ	מִלּוֹן-	dictionary	מִלּוֹן ז׳
מִלּוֹנֵינוּ/כֶם/כֶן/הֶם/הֶן	**מִלּוֹ**נַי/נֶיךָ/נַיִךְ/נָיו/נֶיהָ	מִלּוֹנֵי-		מִלּוֹנִים

The *Hirik* is maintained throughout the declension, and is followed be a *dagesh forte*. The form includes the affix וֹן-.

Examples

מִלּוֹן אבן-שושן הוא ה**מִלּוֹן** הפופולרי ביותר היום בישראל.

The Even-Shoshan **Dictionary** is the most popular **dictionary** in Israel today.

Special Expressions

bilingual **dictionary** **מִלּוֹן** דו-לשוני

pocket **dictionary** **מִלּוֹן** כיס

Good Lord! (expressing amazement); **Master** of the Universe (entreaty) **רִבּוֹנוֹ** של עולם

Additional Examples in this Pattern

broadside of ship צִדּוֹן   ruler, overlord רִבּוֹן

---

386. ***CeCoC/'eCoC***: the *tsere* is generally reduced to *Hataf-pataH*

our/your/their	my/your/his/her	const.	Gloss	sing/pl
אֲזוֹרֵנוּ/רְכֶם/רְכֶן/רָם/רָן	**אֲזוֹ**רִי/רְךָ/רֵךְ/רוֹ/רָהּ	אֵזוֹר-	zone,	אֵזוֹר ז׳
אֲזוֹרֵינוּ/כֶם/כֶן/הֶם/הֶן	**אֲזוֹ**רַי/רֶיךָ/רַיִךְ/רָיו/רֶיהָ	אֲזוֹרֵי-	region; belt	אֲזוֹרִים

The *tsere* of the isolation form is maintained only in the construct state of the singular. Elsewhere it is reduced to a *Hataf-pataH* (and not to a *shva*, because of the guttural).

Examples

בארה״ב יש ארבעה **אֲזוֹרֵי** זמן : **אֵזוֹר** המזרח, **אֵזוֹר** המרכז, **אֵזוֹר** ההרים, ו**אֵזוֹר** חוף האוקיאנוס השקט.
There are four time zones in the US: Eastern, Central, Mountain, and Pacific.

Special Expressions

אֵזוֹר חיוג **area** dialing code
אֵזוֹר מפורז demilitarized **zone**
אֵזוֹר סגור restricted **zone**
אֵזוֹר פיתוח development **zone**
אֵזוֹר תעשיה industrial **zone**

Additional Examples in this Pattern

אֵזוֹב hyssop
אֵפוֹד vest of Jewish high priest; bullet-proof vest

---

387. *CiCoC*

sing/pl	Gloss	const.	my/your/his/her	our/your/their
כִּידוֹן ז׳	spear; bayonet;	כִּידוֹן-	**כִּידוֹ**נִי/נְךָ/נֵךְ/נוֹ/נָהּ	**כִּידוֹ**נֵנוּ/נְכֶם/נְכֶן/נָם/נָן
כִּידוֹנִים	javelin	כִּידוֹנֵי-	**כִּידוֹ**נַי/נֶיךָ/נַיִךְ/נָיו/נֶיהָ	**כִּידוֹנֵי**נוּ/כֶם/כֶן/הֶם/הֶן

Some of the realizations have no plural forms.

Examples

פעם ה**כִּידוֹן** היה בעיקר כלי נשק ; היום הוא משמש בעיקר בספורט.
The **spear** used to be mainly a weapon; today it is used mainly in sports (**javelin**).

היחס ל**טִירוֹנִים** בצה״ל הוא מעורב : יש בסיסים שבהם נוהגים בהם באופן סביר, ויש כאלה שבהם מאמינים שכדי שיהיו חיילים ממושמעים יש קודם לדכאם ולהשפילם.
The attitude to **recruits** in the IDF is mixed: In some bases they treat them decently; in others they believe that in ordrer to make disciplined soldiers out of them, they should first be suppressed and humiliated.

היום, קטרי **קִיטוֹר** נמצאים רק במוזיאונים ; כל הקטרים מונעים בדיזל.
Today, **steam** engines can only be found in museums; all locomotives are diesel-driven.

Special Expressions

זריקת/הטלת **כִּידוֹן** **javelin** throw

Additional Examples in this Pattern

דִּישׁוֹן antelope
טִירוֹן recruit (military); beginner, greenhorn
כִּישׁוֹר spindle
לִימוֹן lemon
פִּיתוֹם ventriloquist

solitary confinement צִינוֹק
ivy קִיסוֹס
[Coll שִׁפּוֹן] rye שִׁיפּוֹן
grape juice תִּירוֹשׁ

---

388. ***CiCoC***: the plural suffix is *-ot*

our/your/their	my/your/his/her	const.	Gloss	sing/pl
וִילוֹנֵנוּ/נְכֶם/נְכֶן/נָם/נָן	**וִילוֹ**נִי/נְךָ/נֵךְ/נוֹ/נָהּ	וִילוֹן-	curtain,	וִילוֹן ז'
וִילוֹנוֹתֵינוּ/כֶם/כֶן/הֶם/הֶן	**וִילוֹנוֹ**תַי/תֶיךָ/תַיִךְ/תָיו/תֶיהָ	וִילוֹנוֹת-	drape, shade	וִילוֹנוֹת

Examples

בחלונות הפונים דרומה ראוי להתקין **וִילוֹנוֹת** אטומים, כדי להפחית את החשיפה לשמש.
It is a good idea to install opaque **drapes** in southern windows, to prevent excessive exposure to the sun.

השימוש במטוסי **סִילוֹן** במלחמת העולם השנייה היה מוגבל; תרומתם הקרבית המשמעותית החלה במלחמת קוריאה.
The use of **jet** planes in WWII was limited; their significant battle contribution began in the Korean War.

Additional Examples in this Pattern

spark נִיצוֹץ
סִילוֹן/סִילוֹן jetstream; jet (ר' סִילוֹנוֹת או סִילוֹנִים)
small bedchamber קִיטוֹן
ewer קִיתוֹן

---

389. ***miCoC***: the form is derived from a root with initial י'

our/your/their	my/your/his/her	const.	Gloss	sing/pl
מִישׁוֹרֵנוּ/רְכֶם/רְכֶן/רָם/רָן	**מִישׁוֹ**רִי/רְךָ/רֵךְ/רוֹ/רָהּ	מִישׁוֹר-	plain, plateau;	מִישׁוֹר ז'
מִישׁוֹרֵינוּ/כֶם/כֶן/הֶם/הֶן	**מִישׁוֹ**רַי/רֶיךָ/רַיִךְ/רָיו/רֶיהָ	מִישׁוֹרֵי-	plane	מִישׁוֹרִים

Examples

מרבית האוכלוסיה בישראל מרוכזת ב**מִישׁוֹר** החוף.
Most of the population in Israel is concentrated in the **coastal** plain.

Special Expressions

inclined plane **מִישׁוֹר** משופע

---

390. ***tiCoC***: the form is derived from a root with initial י, the plural suffix is *-ot*.

our/your/their	my/your/his/her	const.	Gloss	sing/pl
תִּינוֹקֵנוּ/קְכֶם/קְכֶן/קָם/קָן	**תִּינוֹ**קִי/קְךָ/קֵךְ/קוֹ/קָהּ	תִּינוֹק-	baby	תִּינוֹק ז'
תִּינוֹקוֹתֵינוּ/כֶם/כֶן/הֶם/הֶן	**תִּינוֹקוֹ**תַי/תֶיךָ/תַיִךְ/תָיו/תֶיהָ	תִּינוֹקוֹת-		תִּינוֹקוֹת

Examples

תִּינוֹקוֹת רבים נולדים היום לנשים בסוף שנות השלושים שלהן.
Many **babies** are born today to mothers in their late thirties.

Special Expressions

infants, schoolchildren **תִּינוֹקוֹת** של בית רבן

---

391. ***CeCuC/'eCuC***: the *tsere* is generally reduced to *Hataf-pataH*

our/your/their	my/your/his/her	const.	Gloss	sing/pl
אֲבוּסֵנוּ/סְכֶם/סְכֶן/סָם/סָן	**אֲבוּ**סִי/סְךָ/סֵךְ/סוֹ/סָהּ	אֵבוּס-	manger;	אֵבוּס ז'
אֲבוּסֵינוּ/כֶם/כֶן/הֶם/הֶן	**אֲבוּ**סַי/סֶיךָ/סַיִךְ/סָיו/סֶיהָ	אֲבוּסֵי-	trough	אֲבוּסִים

The *tsere* of the isolation form is maintained only in the construct state of the singular. Elsewhere it is reduced to a *Hataf-pataH* (not to *shva*, owing to the guttural).

Examples

אין החמור נואק אלא מתוך **אֵבוּס** מלא.
It is those who have enough who always complain (lit. a donkey grunts only when the **trough** is full).

---

392. ***CeCuC/'eCuC***: the *tsere* in the initial א' is reduced to *Hataf-seghol*

our/your/their	my/your/his/her	const.	Gloss	sing/pl
אֱמוּנֵנוּ/נְכֶם/נְכֶן/נָם/נָן	**אֱמוּ**נִי/נְךָ/נֵךְ/נוֹ/נָהּ	אֵמוּן-	trust,	אֵמוּן ז'
אֱמוּנֵינוּ/כֶם/כֶן/הֶם/הֶן	**אֱמוּ**נַי/נֶיךָ/נַיִךְ/נָיו/נֶיהָ	אֱמוּנֵי-	confidence, faith	אֱמוּנִים

The *tsere* in the א' of the isolation form is maintained only in the construct state of the singular. Elsewhere it is reduced to a *Hataf-seghol* (not to *shva*, owing to the guttural).

Examples

ישנן חברות שבהן אין צורך בחוזים – הכל מבוסס על **אֵמוּן** הדדי.
There are societies in which contracts are not required – everything is based on mutual **trust**.

Special Expressions

no-**confidence** vote הצבעת אי-**אֵמוּן**

---

393. ***CCoC***

our/your/their	my/your/his/her	const.	Gloss	sing/pl
בְּכוֹרֵנוּ/רְכֶם/רְכֶן/רָם/רָן	**בְּכוֹ**רִי/רְךָ/רֵךְ/רוֹ/רָהּ	בְּכוֹר-	first-	בְּכוֹר ז'
בְּכוֹרֵינוּ/כֶם/כֶן/הֶם/הֶן	**בְּכוֹ**רַי/רֶיךָ/רַיִךְ/רָיו/רֶיהָ	בְּכוֹרֵי-	born	בְּכוֹרִים (בְּכוֹרוֹת)

This *mishkal* is monosyllabic, but since the initial *shva*, which is not realized in Israeli Hebrew, was originally a *shva mobile*, we will treat it here as a bisyllabic *mishkal*.

Examples

בתרבויות רבות (הבן) **הַבְּכוֹר** יורש את כל רכושו של האב לאחר מותו.
In many cultures, the **firstborn** (son) inherits all his father's possessions after his death.

כשצפוי **כְּפוֹר** בלילה, רצוי להכניס את העציצים הביתה.
When **frost** is expected at night, it is advisable to bring the flowerpots inside the house.

מכיוון שמצב רוח טוב ואופטימיות עוזרים להתגבר על מחלות קשות, **הַצְּחוֹק** הוא טוב לבריאות.
Since a good mood and optimism help one overcome serious illness, **laughter** is good for one's health.

הרבה צעירים מסתובבים עם **שְׂרוֹכֵי** נעליים שאינם קשורים, ובכל זאת אינם מועדים.
Many young people go around with untied **shoelaces**, and still they do not stumble.

Special Expressions

"little devil" **בְּכוֹר** שטן
tenth plague (smiting of **firstborn**) מכת **בְּכוֹרוֹת**
sponge cake עוגת **סְפוֹג**

the **irony** of fate **צְחוֹק** הגורל
the **worst place** **שְׁאוֹל** תחתיות
the **best/main** part **הַשְּׂאוֹר** שבעיסה

Additional Examples in this Pattern

failure, disaster, foul-up Sl. בְּרוֹךְ
cypress בְּרוֹשׁ
freedom; sparrow דְּרוֹר
spleen טְחוֹל
fullness Lit. מְלוֹא
wandering נְדוֹד/נְדֹד
noise Lit. סְאוֹן
closure, seal סְגוֹר

sponge סְפוֹג
exemption פְּטוֹר
whiteness צְחוֹר
netherworld שְׁאוֹל
leaven שְׂאוֹר
blackness שְׁחוֹר
bereavement שְׁכוֹל
twin תְּאוֹם

---

394. ***CCoC*** = ***CeCoC*** when the first consonant is *'alef*

our/your/their	my/your/his/her	const.	Gloss	sing/pl
אֱגוֹזֵנוּ/זְכֶם/זְכֶן/זָם/זָן	**אֱגוֹ**זִי/זְךָ/זֵךְ/זוֹ/זָהּ	אֱגוֹז-	nut	אֱגוֹז ז'
אֱגוֹזֵינוּ/כֶם/כֶן/הֶם/הֶן	**אֱגוֹ**זַי/זֶיךָ/זַיִךְ/זָיו/זֶיהָ	אֱגוֹזֵי-	(fruit)	אֱגוֹזִים

When the first consonant is *'alef*, a *shva* is replaced by a *Hataf-seghol.*

Examples

אֱגוֹזִים הם מקור מצוין לחלבונים עבור מי שאינו צורך בשר.
Nuts are an excellent source of protein for whoever does not consume meat.

Special Expressions

A stubborn person whose opinions it is hard to change **אֱגוֹז** קשה

wal**nut** **אֱגוֹז** מלך   pea**nut** **אֱגוֹז** אדמה

Additional Examples in this Pattern

man, person Lit. אֱנוֹשׁ

---

395. ***CCoC*** **=** ***CaCoC*** when the first consonant is ה׳ ח׳ ע׳, thus always *Hataf*

our/your/their	my/your/his/her	const.	Gloss	sing/pl
חֲמוֹרֵנוּ/רְכֶם/רְכֶן/רָם/רָן	**חֲמוֹ**רִי/רְךָ/רֵךְ/רוֹ/רָהּ	חֲמוֹר-	donkey	חֲמוֹר ז׳
חֲמוֹרֵינוּ/כֶם/כֶן/הֶם/הֶן	**חֲמוֹ**רַי/רֶיךָ/רַיִךְ/רָיו/רֶיהָ	חֲמוֹרֵי-		חֲמוֹרִים

Examples

ה**חֲמוֹר** ידוע בעקשנותו, בכוח סבילותו, ולדעת רבים גם בטפשותו.

The **donkey** is known for his stubbornness, for his endurance, and in popular belief for stupidity as well.

Special Expressions

an absolute fool **חֲמוֹר חֲמוֹרָתַיִם**

Additional Examples in this Pattern

pawn עֲבוֹט   foot-rest; stool (רגליים) הֲדוֹם

load-bearing equipment (military) חֲגוֹר

---

396. ***C(e)CoC***: the plural suffix is *-ot*

our/your/their	my/your/his/her	const.	Gloss	sing/pl
רְחוֹבֵנוּ/בְכֶם/בְכֶן/בָם/בָן	**רְחוֹ**בִי/בְךָ/בֵךְ/בוֹ/בָהּ	רְחוֹב-	street,	רְחוֹב ז׳
רְחוֹבוֹתֵינוּ/כֶם/כֶן/הֶם/הֶן	**רְחוֹבוֹ**תַי/תֶיךָ/תַיִךְ/תָיו/תֶיהָ	רְחוֹבוֹת-	road	רְחוֹבוֹת

This *mishkal* is monosyllabic, but since the initial *shva*, which is realized in Israeli Hebrew only when required phonetically (e.g., *rHov* 'street' > *reHov*) was originally a *shva mobile*, we will treat it here as a bisyllabic *mishkal*.

Examples

בהרבה כפרים קטנים באירופה ה**רְחוֹבוֹת** כה צרים, שרק מכונית קטנה אחת יכולה לנוע בהם.

In many small villages in Europe the **streets** are so narrow, that only a small single car can move in them.

יש מי שמנסה לערער את **יְסוֹדוֹת** הדמוקרטיה במדינות המערב על ידי מניפולציה של הרשתות החברתיות במרשתת כדי להשפיע על תוצאות הבחירות בהן.

There are ones who are trying to shake the **foundations** of democracy in Western states by manipulating the social networks on the Internet so as to affect the elections results.

Special Expressions

one-way **street** **רְחוֹב** חד-סטרי
street children/urchins ילדי **רְחוֹב**
hematoma **צְרוֹר** דם
oblivion Lit. **תְּהוֹם** הנשייה

Additional Examples in this Pattern

basis, foundation; element (chem.) יְסוֹד
bundle; (gunfire) burst צְרוֹר
abyss תְּהוֹם

---

397. ***CCoC* > *CaCoC*** when the pl. suffix is וֹת- and the 1st conson. is guttural

our/your/their	my/your/his/her	const.	Gloss	sing/pl
חֲלוֹמֵנוּ/מְכֶם/מְכֶן/מָם/מָן	**חֲלוֹ**מִי/מְךָ/מֵךְ/מוֹ/מָהּ	חֲלוֹם-	dream	חֲלוֹם ז׳
חֲלוֹמוֹתֵינוּ/כֶם/כֶן/הֶם/הֶן	**חֲלוֹמוֹ**תַי/תֶיךָ/תַיִךְ/תָיו/תֶיהָ	חֲלוֹמוֹת-		חֲלוֹמוֹת

Examples

כולנו חולמים מספר **חֲלוֹמוֹת** כל לילה, אבל בדרך כלל לא זוכרים הרבה בבוקר.
We all dream a few **dreams** every night, but usually remember much in the morning.

Special Expressions

nightmare **חֲלוֹם** בלהות
day**dreams** **חֲלוֹמוֹת** בהקיץ
pleasant **dream** **חֲלוֹם** פז
dreamer בעל **חֲלוֹמוֹת**
baseless **dream** **חֲלוֹם** באספמיא

Additional Examples in this Pattern

strong rope Lit. עֲבוֹת

---

398. ***CCoC***: feminine nouns, when the last consonant is a guttural

our/your/their	my/your/his/her	const.	Gloss	sing/pl
זְרוֹעֵנוּ/עֲכֶם/עֲכֶן/עָם/עָן	**זְרוֹ**עִי/עֲךָ/עֵךְ/עוֹ/עָהּ	זְרוֹעַ-	arm	זְרוֹעַ נ׳
זְרוֹעוֹתֵינוּ/כֶם/כֶן/הֶם/הֶן	**זְרוֹעוֹ**תַי/תֶיךָ/תַיִךְ/תָיו/תֶיהָ	זְרוֹעוֹת-		זְרוֹעוֹת

This *mishkal* is monosyllabic, but since the initial *shva*, which is not realized in Israeli Hebrew, was originally a *shva mobile*, we will treat it here as a bisyllabic *mishkal*. When a *shva* is expected with a guttural, it is replaced by a *Hataf-pataH*. When no suffix follows, a guttural with a preceding vowel other than *a* requires "furtive" *pataH*.

Examples

משה שרד את תאונת הדרכים הנוראה שעבר, אבל הרופאים נאלצו לקטוע את **זְרוֹעוֹ** השמאלית.
Moshe survived the horrible road accident, but the doctors had to amputate **his** left **arm**.

Special Expressions

by force בכוח הַ**זְּרוֹעַ**
welcomingly, with open **arms** בִּ**זְרוֹעוֹת** פתוחות
arm in **arm** (demonstration of closeness, friendship) שְׁלוּבֵי **זְרוֹעַ**

---

399. ***CCuC***: no vowel changes

our/your/their	my/your/his/her	const.	Gloss	sing/pl
גְּדוּדֵנוּ/דְכֶם/דְכֶן/דָם/דָן	**גְּדוּ**דִי/דְךָ/דֵךְ/דוֹ/דָהּ	גְּדוּד-	battalion,	גְּדוּד ז׳
גְּדוּדֵינוּ/כֶם/כֶן/הֶם/הֶן	**גְּדוּ**דַי/דֶיךָ/דַיִךְ/דָיו/דֶיהָ	גְּדוּדֵי-	regiment	גְּדוּדִים

This *mishkal* is monosyllabic, but since the initial *shva*, which is realized in Israeli Hebrew only when required phonetically (e.g., *yvul* 'yield' > *yevul*), was originally a *shva mobile*, we will treat it here as a bisyllabic *mishkal*.

Examples

בְּ**גְדוּד** בחיל הרגלים יש בדרך כלל שלוש פלוגות.
In an infantry **battalion** there are usually three companies.

כבר הרבה שנים לא משתמשים בעופרת בבתי הַ**דְּפוּס**.
For many years now, they have not been using lead in **printing** houses.

נראה שתפקידו העיקרי של זנב הפרה הוא לגרש **זְבוּבִים**...
It seems that the main function of the cow's tail is to drive away **flies**…

יְבוּל התפוזים היה קטן השנה – אולי בגלל מזג האוויר הקר יותר בפלורידה.
The orange **yield** this year was smaller – perhaps because of the cooler weather in Florida.

בדרך כלל, כשערך הַ**יְּצוּא** השנתי עולה משמעותית על ערך הַ**יְּבוּא**, זה מצביע על כך שמצבה הכלכלי של המדינה שפיר.
Generally, when the annual **export** value is significantly greater than that of the **import**, it usually indicates that the economic state of the nation is good.

Special Expressions

"הַ**גְּדוּד** העברי" a mule drivers **battalion** of Jewish volunteers from Palestine in WWI
דְּפוּס שֶׁקַע photogravure
דְּפוּס בֶּלֶט relief **printing**
דְּפוּסֵי חיים lifestyle
זְבוּב הבית house **fly**, common **fly**

יְבוּא אישי personal importing
יְצוּר כלאיים hybrid; amalgam
כְּלוּב של זהב gilded **cage**
כְּרוּב ניצנים Brussels sprout
נְאוּם בכורה maiden **speech**
פְּסוּל דין incompetent (law)

Additional Examples in this Pattern

גְּמוּל reward, recompense; payback, retaliation
גְּרוּשׁ obsolete Israeli currency
יְצוּר creature; organism

יְקוּם universe
כְּלוּב cage
כְּלוּם nothing; anything
כְּרוּב cabbage; cherub
כְּרוּז written proclamation or announcement
לְבוּשׁ clothing
נְאוּם speech
סְחוּס cartilage
סְכוּם sum of money; sum, total
פְּסוּל flaw, defect

---

400. *CCuC* = *CaCuC*, with the first consonant *Het*

our/your/their	my/your/his/her	const.	Gloss	sing/pl
חֲבוּרֵנוּ/רְכֶם/רְכֶן/רָם/רָן	**חֲבוּ**רִי/רְךָ/רֵךְ/רוֹ/רָהּ	חֲבוּר-	stub,	חֲבוּר ז׳
חֲבוּרֵינוּ/כֶם/כֶן/הֶם/הֶן	**חֲבוּ**רַי/רֶיךָ/רַיִךְ/רָיו/רֶיהָ	חֲבוּרֵי-	butt	חֲבוּרִים

When the first consonant is ח׳, the *shva* is replaced by *Hataf-pataH*. In the case of א׳ or ע׳, it will be replaced by *Hataf-seghol*, but the occurrences concerned, אֱשׁוּן and עֱזוּז, are obsolete.

Examples

בעברית המדוברת, הַ**חֲבוּר** נקרא תְּלוּשׁ.
In colloquial Hebrew, the **stub** is called "detachable," or "coupon".

---

401. *CCuC*: no vowel changes when the plural suffix is וֹת-

our/your/their	my/your/his/her	const.	Gloss	sing/pl
גְּבוּלֵנוּ/לְכֶם/לְכֶן/לָם/לָן	**גְּבוּ**לִי/לְךָ/לֵךְ/לוֹ/לָהּ	גְּבוּל-	border;	גְּבוּל ז׳
גְּבוּלוֹתֵינוּ/כֶם/כֶן/הֶם/הֶן	**גְּבוּ**לַי/לֶיךָ/לַיִךְ/לָיו/לֶיהָ	גְּבוּלוֹת-	limit	גְּבוּלוֹת

This *mishkal* is monosyllabic, but since the initial *shva*, which is not realized in Israeli Hebrew, was originally a *shva mobile*, we will treat it here as a bisyllabic *mishkal*.

Examples

בדרך כלל **גְּבוּלוֹת** טבעיים כמו נהרות מפחיתים את הסיכון לסכסוך בין מדינות שכנות.
Generally, natural **borders** like rivers reduce the risk of conflict between neighboring nations.

Special Expressions

בלי/ללא **גְּבוּל** no **end**, **end**less

הסיג **גְּבוּל** trespass

---

402. *CaCiC* with *pataH* followed by *dagesh*, adjectives and nouns

our/your/their	my/your/his/her	const.	Gloss	sing/pl
סַכִּינֵנוּ/נְכֶם/נְכֶן/נָם/נָן	**סַכִּי**נִי/נְךָ/נֵךְ/נוֹ/נָהּ	סַכִּין-	knife	סַכִּין זו״נ
סַכִּינֵינוּ/כֶם/כֶן/הֶם/הֶן	**סַכִּי**נַי/נֶיךָ/נַיִךְ/נָיו/נֶיהָ	סַכִּינֵי-		סַכִּינִים

Construct	f. sing/pl	Construct	m.sing/pl	Gloss
אַמִּיצַת-	אַמִּיצָה	אַמִּיץ-	אַמִּיץ	brave
אַמִּיצוֹת-	אַמִּיצוֹת	אַמִּיצֵי-	אַמִּיצִים	

In this pattern adjectives and nouns are distributed more-or-less equally, though there are some realizations that can denote both, e.g., צַדִּיק is either 'righteous' or 'a righteous person.' Owing to the presence of a *pataH* followed by a *dagesh*, no reduction occurs in the declension.

Examples

בְסַכִּין מטבח בעלת ידית עץ, רצוי שיהיו שלושה פינים, אחרת הידית עלולה להישבר.
A kitchen **knife** with a wooden handle should be held together by three pins, otherwise the handle may break.

סאדאת ורבין היו אנשים **אַמִּיצִים**; הם ידעו שחייהם תמיד בסכנה, ובכל זאת ניסו להביא שלום.
Sadat and Rabin were **brave** men; they knew they were risking their lives, but were still determined to seek peace.

בימי הביניים **אַבִּירִים** היו לוחמים רכובים על סוס ועטויי שריון. היום **אַבִּיר** הוא תואר מכובד המוענק לאדם על שירותו לממלכה.
In the Middle Ages, **knights** were warriors mounted on horses and clad in armor. Today "**knight**" is an honorific title bestowed on a person for his service to the kingdom.

נחשול **אַדִּיר** התרומם פתאום, ובכוח עצום נחת על הספינה והטביעה.
A **mighty** breaker rose all of a sudden, and landed with great force upon the boat and sunk it.

אילן הוא אדם **אַלִּים** ביותר, המטיל את מוראו על כל השכונה.
Ilan is a very **violent** person, who terrorized the whole neighborhood.

Special Expressions

the **strong** dominate כל ד**אַלִּים** גבר
life **prisoner**, "lifer" **אַסִּיר** עולם
razor **blade** **סַכִּין** גילוח
switch**blade** **סַכִּין** קְפיצית

a non-migrating bird ציפור **יַצִּיבָה**
ancient **עַתִּיק** יומין
capital-intensive **עַתִּיר** הון
pneumatic **drill** **פַּטִּישׁ** אוויר

Additional Examples in this Pattern

flask (in chemistry) אַבִּיק
prisoner אַסִּיר/אָסִיר
parasite טַפִּיל
tapir טַפִּיר
fixed, firm; stable יַצִּיב
redundant יַתִּיר
tremendous, enormous כַּבִּיר
torch לַפִּיד

gauge מַדִּיד
sapphire סַפִּיר
happy, cheerful עַלִּיז
ancient עַתִּיק
rich, abundant עַתִּיר
hammer פַּטִּישׁ
righteous צַדִּיק

403. ***CaCiC*** without reduction

our/your/their	my/your/his/her	const.	Gloss	sing/pl
עָרִיצֵנוּ/צְכֶם/צְכֶן/צָם/צָן	**עָרִי**צִי/צְךָ/צֵךְ/צוֹ/צָהּ	עָרִיץ-	tyrant,	עָרִיץ ז׳
עָרִיצֵינוּ/כֶם/כֶן/הֶם/הֶן	**עָרִי**צַי/צֶיךָ/צַיִךְ/צָיו/צֶיהָ	עָרִיצֵי-	despot	עָרִיצִים

The *kamats* does not undergo reduction in the declension, and the lexical item is generally not verb-related.

Examples

סטאלין היה אחד ה**עָרִיצִים** הגדולים ביותר בהיסטוריה.
Stalin was one of the greatest **tyrants** in history.

במדינות "מתקדמות" כמו האימפריה העותומנית ל**סָרִיסִים** היה תפקיד חשוב, מכיוון שהייתה להם גישה ישירה לנשותיו המועדפות של הסולטאן.
In "progressive" states like the Ottoman Empire the **eunuchs** had an important role, since they had direct contact with the Sultan's favorite wives.

יש כל כך הרבה חנויות **רָהִיטִים** טובות בארה"ב, שצריך לערוך מחקר מקיף לפני שקונים **רָהִיט** כלשהו במחיר סביר.
There are so many good **furniture** stores in the US, that one needs to conduct thorough research before buying a **piece of furniture** for a reasonable price.

Special Expressions

senior citizen אזרח **וָתִיק**

Additional Examples in this Pattern

old-timer וָתִיק
Polish landowner/nobleman פָּרִיץ
fireplace קָמִין
adjutant שָׁלִישׁ
twig, shoot, tendril שָׂרִיג

---

404. ***CaCiC*** as an adjectival diminution pattern, with reduction and reduplication

Construct	f. sing/pl	Construct	m. ing/pl	Gloss
דְּקִיקַת-	דְּקִיקָה	דְּקִיק-	דָּקִיק	very
דְּקִיקוֹת-	דְּקִיקוֹת	דְּקִיקֵי-	דְּקִיקִים	thin

All forms in this pattern denote diminution of the derivation base; the base itself is usually regarded as related to a tri-literal root with identical second and third consonant, e.g. דַּק 'thin' and דק"ק.

Examples

אני אוהב כל דבר מאפה מבצק עלים; בצק עלים **דָּקִיק** ופריך, ואין טוב מזה.
I love any baked goods baked from Filo dough; Filo dough is **very thin** and crunchy, and there is nothing better.

הישראלים בד״כ אוהבים שוקולד **מָרִיר** יותר מאשר שוקולד חלב.
Israelis usually prefer **bitter**-sweet chocolate to milk chocolate.

Special Expressions

downtrodden **מְרִיר** יום

Additional Examples in this Pattern

warm חָמִים
(somewhat) bitter מָרִיר
very light קָלִיל
cool קָרִיר

---

405. ***CCiC***

our/your/their	my/your/his/her	const.	Gloss	sing/pl
שְׁבִילֵנוּ/לְכֶם/לְכֶן/לָם/לָן	**שְׁבִי**לִי/לְךָ/לֵךְ/לוֹ/לָהּ	שְׁבִיל-	path,	שְׁבִיל ז׳
שְׁבִילֵינוּ/כֶם/כֶן/הֶם/הֶן	**שְׁבִי**לַי/לֶיךָ/לַיִךְ/לָיו/לֶיהָ	שְׁבִילֵי-	trail	שְׁבִילִים

This *mishkal* is monosyllabic, but since the initial *shva*, which is not realized in Israeli Hebrew, was originally a *shva mobile*, we will treat it here as a bisyllabic *mishkal*. It is a noun pattern. The vowel *i* is maintained throughout the declension.

Examples

כמעט כל תלמיד תיכון בישראל מטפס ב**שְׁבִיל** הנחש כדי לעלות לפסגת מצדה.
Almost every high school student in Israel climbs the "snake **trail**" to reach the top of Masada.

כילדים בארץ, היינו חורטים תבנית של מטוס בלְבֵנה, ממסים שפופרות שיניים מ**בְּדִיל** על האש, ויוצקים לתוך התבנית שבלבנה, והרי מודל מטוס יצוק.
As kids in Israel, we used to carve a mold in the form of a plane in a brick, melt **tin** on the fire, and pour it into the mold in the brick, and the result was a tin plane model.

להרבה אנשים יש **וְרִידִים** בולטים ברגליים; זה לא יפה במיוחד, אבל גם לא מסוכן.
Many people have varicose **veins** in their legs; it is not that attractive, but is not dangerous either.

יש בישראל כמה **כְּבִישִׁים** מהירים, אבל הם בדרך כלל כה עמוסים, שקשה לנסוע מהר.
There are some fast **roadways** in Israel, but they are usually so crowded, that it is hard to travel fast.

Special Expressions

medley of tongues **בְּלִיל** לשונות
one can burn books, but their content stays forever **גְּוִילִים** נשרפים ואותיות פורחות
pearl **barley** **גְּרִיסֵי** פנינה
drive a **wedge** between... ...תקע **טְרִיז** בין
made by his own hands **יְצִיר** כפיו
plene **writing** **כְּתִיב** מלא
at any **price** בכל **מְחִיר**
the Milky **Way** **שְׁבִיל** החלב
thyroid gland בלוטת ה**תְּרִיס**

Additional Examples in this Pattern

rod בְּדִיד
mixture בְּלִיל
master, lord; rich man גְּבִיר
tassel, fringe; strand גְּדִיל
parchment גְּוִיל
icicle גְּלִיד
groats, grits גְּרִיס
wedge טְרִיז
creature, product Lit. יְצִיר
fair, exhibition, market יְרִיד/יָרִיד
staple כְּלִיב
fool כְּסִיל
young lion Lit. כְּפִיר
spelling כְּתִיב
price מְחִיר
ingot, bar מְטִיל
coat, cloak מְעִיל
virus נְגִיף

---

406. ***CCiC = CaCiC*** when the first consonant is guttural

sing/pl	Gloss	const.	my/your/his/her	our/your/their
עֲצִיץ ז׳	flowerpot,	עֲצִיץ־	**עֲצִי**צִי/צְךָ/צֵךְ/צוֹ/צָהּ	**עֲצִי**צֵנוּ/צְכֶם/צְכֶן/צָם/צָן
עֲצִיצִים	planter	עֲצִיצֵי־	**עֲצִי**צַי/צֶיךָ/צַיִךְ/צָיו/צֶיהָ	**עֲצִיצֵי**נוּ/כֶם/כֶן/הֶם/הֶן

When the first consonant in the *CCiC* pattern is guttural, the (zero) *shva* is replaced by a *Hataf-pataH*, and in the case of א׳ also by *Hataf-seghol* (אֱוִיל, אֱלִיל).

Examples

כאשר הטמפרטורה יורדת ויש חשש לקרה, חשוב להכניס את כל ה**עֲצִיצִים** הביתה.
When the temperature falls and frost is likely, it is important to bring in all **flowerpots** inside the house.

איכות ה**אֲוִיר** בערים כמו לוס אנג׳לס ובֵּייג׳ינְג היא גרועה ביותר בשל זיהום תעשייתי ופליטת מכוניות.
The **air** quality in cities such as Los Angeles and Beijing is very bad owing to industrial pollution and car emissions.

קיבוץ מזרע התפרסם בכך שמגדלים שם **חֲזִירִים** ומייצרים מוצרי **חֲזִיר**.
Kibbutz Mizra` is known for raising **pigs** and for the production of **pork** products.

Special Expressions

compressed **air** **אֲוִיר** דחוס
idolatry עבודת **אֱלִילִים**
legal **proceedings** **הֲלִיכִים** משפטיים
cast pearls before **swine** נזם זהב באף **חֲזִיר**
eye of the needle **חֲרִיר** המחט
sole of hashish Sl. סוליית **חֲשִׁישׁ**

Additional Examples in this Pattern

fool אֱוִיל
idol; deity אֱלִיל
proceeding (law), rocedure הֲלִיךְ
lightening (biblical); firecracker חֲזִיז
snack חֲטִיף
wedge חֲפִיר
hole, aperture חֲרִיר
hashish חֲשִׁישׁ

---

407. ***CCiC*** **when the last consonant is guttural**

our/your/their	my/your/his/her	const.	Gloss	sing/pl
בְּרִיחֵנוּ/חֲכֶם/חֲכֶן/חָם/חָן	**בְּרִי**חִי/חֲךָ/חֵךְ/חוֹ/חָהּ	בְּרִיחַ-	bolt	בְּרִיחַ ז׳
בְּרִיחֵינוּ/כֶם/כֶן/הֶם/הֶן	**בְּרִי**חַי/חֶיךָ/חַיִךְ/חָיו/חֶיהָ	בְּרִיחֵי-		בְּרִיחִים

This *mishkal* is monosyllabic (ignoring the inserted "furtive" *pataH*), but since the initial *shva*, which is not realized in Israeli Hebrew, was originally a *shva mobile*, we will treat it here as a bisyllabic *mishkal*. When the last consonant is guttural, and the preceding vowel is not *a*, the unsuffixed form it comes with a "furtive" *pataH*, and when a *shva* is expected with the guttural, it is replaced by a *Hataf-pataH* (בְּרִיחֲךָ).

Examples

חברת "רב **בְּרִיחַ**" הישראלית מייצרת **בְּרִיחִים** מעולים הנמכרים היטב בכל העולם.
The Israeli company Multi**Lock** (/Multi**Bolt**?) manufactures excellent **locks/bolts** which sell well throughout the world.

צְרִיחַ הוא: 1. מגדל שמירה מבוצר. 2. ראש הטנק המסתובב שאליו מחובר קנה התותח. 3. אחד מכלי השחמט, הנע בקווים ישרים בלבד.
צְרִיחַ has three meanings: 1. A fortified guard tower. 2. The revolving head of a tank to which the gun barrel is attached. 3. A chess piece (rook) which can only move in a straight line.

Special Expressions

behind bars, under **lock** and key מאחורי סורג **וּבְרִיחַ**
very **hard work** **יְגִיעַ** כפיים

Additional Examples in this Pattern

.quarter Lit רְבִיעַ hard work יְגִיעַ crack, breach בְּקִיעַ

---

408. ***CCiC*** **when the plural form is a dual**

our/your/their	my/your/his/her	const.	Gloss	sing/pl
נְחִירֵנוּ/רְכֶם/רְכֶן/רָם/רָן	**נְחִי**רִי/רְךָ/רֵךְ/רוֹ/רָהּ	נְחִיר-	nostril	נְחִיר ז׳
נְחִירֵינוּ/כֶם/כֶן/הֶם/הֶן	**נְחִי**רַי/רֶיךָ/רַיִךְ/רָיו/רֶיהָ	נְחִירֵי-		נְחִירַיִם

Identical to the *CCiC* pattern, but the plural form is the dual *-áyim.*

Examples

בנשימה נורמלית נושמים דרך **נְחִירֵי** האף ופולטים אויר דרך הפה.
In normal breathing one inhales through the nose's **nostrils** and exhales through the mouth.

---

409. *CaCCaC*

our/your/their	my/your/his/her	const.	Gloss	sing/pl
עַכְבָּרֵנוּ/**עַכְבַּרְ**כֶם/כֶן/**עַכְבָּרָ**ם/ן	**עַכְבָּרִ**י/רְךָ/רֵךְ/רוֹ/רָהּ	עַכְבַּר-	mouse	עַכְבָּר
עַכְבָּרֵינוּ/**עַכְבְּרֵי**כֶם/כֶן/הֶם/הֶן	**עַכְבָּרַ**י/רֶיךָ/רַיִךְ/רָיו/רֶיהָ	עַכְבְּרֵי-		עַכְבָּרִים

This is a quadriliteral noun pattern; in some cases they can also be used as adjectives (אַכְזָרִי is an adjective, but אַכְזָר is either 'a cruel person' or alternatively used for the adjective 'cruel' in daily usage.) In the declension, when the second syllable is closed, the *kamats* becomes *pataH* (עַכְבַּרְכֶם), and when the second syllable is open and is located two syllables away from the final, stressed syllable, the *kamats* is reduced to *shva* (עַכְבְּרֵיכֶם).

Examples

אין שום תועלת בחתול הזה; אפילו **עַכְבָּרִים** הוא לא תופס.
This cat is useless; it does not even catch **mice**.

יש "האקֶרים" שבלחיצת **עַכְבָּר** אחת מסוגלים למוטט מערכות שלמות ולחולל פאניקה עצומה.
There are hackers who with one click of the **mouse** are capable of causing complete systems to collapse and generating horrible panic.

בישראל בזמנו, כדי לוודא שהקרפיון לשבת יהיה טרי, עקרות בית היו קונות אותו חי, מבריכה בחנות הדגים, ומטילות אותו בבית לתוך **אַמְבָּט** מלא למחצה, שישחה בו עד יום שישי...
In Israel at the time, to make sure that the carp for the sabbath is fresh, housewives would buy it alive at the fish shop (which had a large water tank), and dump it at home into a half-full **bathtub**, to swim in until Friday...

במוקדי משיכה לתיירים רואים לעיתים קרובות שלטים: "היזהרו מכייסים". מסתבר שבחלק מהם הכייסים עצמם תולים את השלטים: כשתייר רואה שלט כזה הוא בודק אינסטינקטיבית את **אַרְנָקוֹ**, ואז הכייס יודע איפה הוא.
In tourist attractions there are often signs: "Beware of pickpockets." It turns out that in some cases, it is the pickpockets themselves who post these signs: When a tourist sees such sign, he instinctively checks his **wallet**, and the pickpocket then knows where it is.

בשר **הַבַּרְוָז** פופולרי בצרפת, ובעיקר במסעדות סיניות, בסין ובכל העולם.
Duck meat is popular in France, and particularly in Chinese retaurants, in China and throughout the world.

Special Expressions

אַלְמָן קש grass **widower**
אַמְבָּט קש sitz/hip **bath**
אַרְגַּז חול sand **box**; litter box
בַּרְוָז עיתונאי journalistic fabrication

עַכְבַּר העיר **וְעַכְבַּר** הכפר the city **mouse** and the country **mouse** (from the fable)
ההר הוליד **עַכְבָּר** when prior expectations are great, but the result is meager

Additional Examples in this Pattern

buckle (of belt) אַבְזָם
accessory אַבְזָר
cruel; cruel person אַכְזָר
widower אַלְמָן
halter אַפְסָר
crate אַרְגָּז
hare (male) אַרְנָב
courier בַּלְדָּר
mite בַּרְחָשׁ
guy, chap, bloke בַּרְנָשׁ
bench, board דַּרְגָּשׁ
porcupine דַּרְבָּן
half-track זַחְלָ״ם
mustard חַרְדָּל
parking meter מַדְחָן
sandal סַנְדָּל
godfather סַנְדָּק
bench סַפְסָל
middleman; speculator סַפְסָר
overall; coverall סַרְבָּל

---

410. ***CaCCaC* =*'aCCaC*** when a trilateral root was expanded by the addition of the prefix +א

No declension in occurrences listed here.

Examples

ישראל מפיקה כמויות עצומות של **אַשְׁלָג** מים המלח.
Israel extracts huge quantities of **potash** from the Dead Sea.

Special Expre ssions

seasonal river (with water flowing in it only during the rainy season) נחל **אַכְזָב**

Additional Examples in this Pattern

seasonal (only for stream, river) אַכְזָב

---

411. ***CaCCaC*** when the two last consonants are identical (קַטְלָל)

our/your/their	my/your/his/her	const.	Gloss	sing/pl
סַרְטָטֵנוּ/**סַרְטַטְ**כֶם/כֶן/**סַרְטָטָ**ם/ן	**סַרְטָ**טִי/טְךָ/טֵךְ/טוֹ/טָהּ	סַרְטָט-	draftsman	סַרְטָט
סַרְטָטֵינוּ/**סַרְטְטֵי**כֶם/כֶן/הֶם/הֶן	**סַרְטָ**טַי/טֶיךָ/טַיִךְ/טָיו/טֶיהָ	סַרְטְטֵי-		סַרְטָטִים

In the declension, when the second syllable is closed, the *kamats* becomes *pataH* (סַרְטַטְכֶם), and when the second syllable is open and is located two syllables away from the final, stressed, syllable, the *kamats* is reduced to *shva* (סַרְטְטֵיכֶם).

Examples

דרושים : **סַרְטָטִים** לחברת אדריכלים גדולה בתל-אביב.
Needed: **draftsmen** for a large architectural firm in Tel Aviv.

Additional Examples in this Pattern

vent, ventilation opening אַוְרָר

---

412. ***CaCCaC*** when the *kamats* in the second syllable of the isolation form corresponds to a *pataH* that is followed by *dagesh* in the declension

our/your/their	My/your/his/her	const.	Gloss	sing/pl
עַקְרַבֵּנוּ/עַקְרַבְּכֶם/כֶן/עַקְרַבָּם/ן	עַקְרַבִּי/בְּךָ/בֵּךְ/בּוֹ/בָּהּ	עַקְרַב-	scorpion;	עַקְרָב
עַקְרַבֵּינוּ/כֶם/כֶן/הֶם/הֶן	עַקְרַבַּי/בֶּיךָ/בַּיִךְ/בָּיו/בֶּיהָ	עַקְרַבֵּי-	thorn (Bibl.)	עַקְרַבִּים

It appears that the forms with the *pataH* and the following *dagesh* constitute the base, which in isolation becomes a *kamats*.

Examples

כשהופכים אבן במזרח התיכון, צריך תמיד לקחת בחשבון שמתחתיה עלול להתחבא **עַקְרָב**.
When you turn over a rock in the Middle East, you should always remember that a **scorpion** might be hiding underneath.

Special Expressions

surrounded by hostile neighbors יושב אל **עַקְרַבִּים**

Additional Examples in this Pattern

cardinal חַשְׁמָן — stone, pit, pip (of fruit) חַרְצָן

---

413. ***CaCCaC > CaCaCaC*** when the *kamats* in the second syllable is replaced by *pataH* and is followed by *dagesh*, the two last consonants are identical (קַטְלָל), and the second consonant is guttural

f. sing/pl	m. sing/pl	Gloss
שַׁאֲנַנָּה	שַׁאֲנָן	tranquil;
שַׁאֲנַנּוֹת	שַׁאֲנַנִּים	complacent

The only common occurrence is an adjective. The *kamats* in the second syllable is replaced by *pataH* and is followed by *dagesh* when a suffix is added. An expected *shva* with a guttural is replaced by *Hataf-pataH*: קַטְלָל < קַטֲלָל.

Examples

אירועי 11 בספטמבר 2001 הוכיחו בעליל כי שירותי הביטחון של ארה"ב היו **שַׁאֲנַנִּים** מדיי.
The events of September 11th 2001 indicated clearly that the American security services were too **complacent**.

---

414. ***CaCCaC*** with *pataH* in both syllables

our/your/their	my/your/his/her	const.	Gloss	sing/pl
קַרְנַפֵּנוּ/פְּכֶם/פְּכֶן/פָּם/פָּן	קַרְנַפִּי/פְּךָ/פֵּךְ/פּוֹ/פָּהּ	קַרְנַף-	rhinoceros	קַרְנַף ז'
קַרְנַפֵּינוּ/כֶם/כֶן/הֶם/הֶן	קַרְנַפַּי/פֶּיךָ/פַּיִךְ/פָּיו/פֶּיהָ	קַרְנַפֵּי-		קַרְנַפִּים

The second *pataH* is followed by a *dagesh forte*; the geminated consonant that follows makes sure that the second syllable remain closed. [Note: in this particular item, the פ׳ of קַרְנַף remains without *dagesh* throughout the declension in the colloquial (קַרְנָפִים etc.), making the paradigm unified.]

Examples

הַקַּרְנַף מצוי באזורים הטרופיים של אפריקה ואסיה.
The **rhinoceros** is found in the tropical regions of Africa and Asia.

על **חַיְדַּקִּים** ניתן בדרך כלל להתגבר באמצעות אנטיביוטיקה, אבל לא על וירוסים.
It is generally possible to overcome **germs** with antibiotics, but viruses.

השכבות החלשות של החברה הישראלית הן הנפגעות העיקריות כל אימת שחלות עליות במחירי **הַחַשְׁמַל**.
The lower classes in the Israeli society are affected the most by raises in **electricity** charges.

Special Expressions

גַּנְזַךְ המדינה state **archives**
חַיְדַּקֵּי קולי coliform **bacteria**
חַשְׁמַל סטטי static **electricity**

Additional Examples in this Pattern

גַּנְזַךְ archive N
דַּרְדַּק young child Lit.
כַּרְפַּס celery

---

415. ***CaCCaC*** with the plural suffix -וֹת and the second *pataH* becomes *kamats* in an open syllable and the final consonant is guttural

our/your/their	my/your/his/her	const.	Gloss	sing/pl
קַרְקָעֵנוּ/**קַרְקַעֲ**כֶם/כֶן/**קַרְקָעָ**ם/ן	**קַרְקָ**עִי/עֲךָ/עֵךְ/עוֹ/עָהּ	קַרְקַע-	bottom; soil;	קַרְקַע נ׳
קַרְקְעוֹתֵינוּ/כֶם/כֶן/הֶם/הֶן	**קַרְקְעוֹ**תַי/תֶיךָ/תַיִךְ/תָיו/תֶיהָ	קַרְקְעוֹת-	land	קַרְקָעוֹת

An apparently original *kamats* is maintained in an open syllable, is elided two syllables away from the main stress, but is realized as *pataH* in a closed syllable, including the unsufixed form. A *shva* expected with the guttural is replaced by *Hataf pataH*.

Examples

הוא פוחד להיכנס לבריכה אם רגליו אינן מגיעות **לַקַּרְקַע**.
He is afraid to enter the pool if his feet do not reach the **bottom**.

הַקַּרְקַע בחצרנו גרועה ביותר; שום דבר אינו צומח בה.
The **soil** in our yard is very bad; nothing grows in it.

חקרן הקיימת קנתה הרבה **קַרְקָעוֹת** בארץ ישראל כדי ליישב עליהן יהודים.
The Jewish National Fund bought many plots of **land** in Palestine to settle Jews on them.

Special Expressions

ground crops גידולי **קַרְקַע**
lower head in shame כבש פניו **בְּקַרְקַע**
settle on the land עלה על **הַקַּרְקַע**
ground floor קומת **קַרְקַע**
virgin soil **קַרְקַע** בתולה

Additional Examples in this Pattern

נַעְנַע/נַעֲנָה mint (ר׳ נַעֲנוֹת)

---

416. ***CaCCaC*** when the two first consonants are reduplicated in consonantal slots three and four, respectively (קַטְקַט)

sing/pl	Gloss	const.	my/your/his/her	our/your/their
גַּלְגַּל ז׳	wheel	גַּלְגַּל-	**גַּלְגַּ**לִי/לְךָ/לֵךְ/לוֹ/לָהּ	**גַּלְגַּ**לֵּנוּ/לְכֶם/לְכֶן/לָם/לָן
גַּלְגַּלִּים		גַּלְגַּלֵּי-	**גַּלְגַּ**לַּי/לֶּיךָ/לַּיִךְ/לָּיו/לֶּיהָ	**גַּלְגַּלֵּי**נוּ/כֶם/כֶן/הֶם/הֶן

The third consonant, which identical to the first, is followed by a *pataH*, and the following consonant is geminated, so as to make sure that the second syllable remain closed.

Examples

רכב עם הנעה של ארבעה **גַּלְגַּלִּים** פופולרי מאוד בעשורים האחרונים.
Vehicles with four-**wheel** (here wheels) drive have been very popular in the last few decades.

״צנח לו **זַלְזַל**״ הוא אחד משיריו הלירייים הטובים ביותר של ביאליק.
"A **Sprig** is Stooping Down" is one of Bialik's best lyrical poems.

Special Expressions

life preserver **גַּלְגַּל** הצלה
spare **tire** **גַּלְגַּל** חילוף
the zodiac **גַּלְגַּל** המזלות
Ferris wheel **גַּלְגַּל** ענק
judge by what's inside, not by appearance אל תסתכל **בַּקַּנְקַן**, אלא במה שיש בו

Additional Examples in this Pattern

buzzer זַמְזַם
connecting rod טַלְטַל
pancreas לַבְלַב
dimmer עַמְעַם
aperture adjuster (photog.) צַמְצַם
clog קַבְקַב
jar, jug, flask קַנְקַן
fish scale; dandruff קַשְׂקַשׂ
curl (of hair) תַּלְתַּל

---

417. ***CaCCaC*** when the two first consonants are reduplicated in consonantal slots three and four, respectively (קַטְקַט), and the second vowel becomes *kamats* in the declension

our/your/their	my/your/his/her	const.	Gloss	sing/pl
פַּרְפָּרֵנוּ/רְכֶם/רְכֶן/רָם/רָן	**פַּרְפָּ**רִי/רְךָ/רֵךְ/רוֹ/רָהּ	פַּרְפַּר-	butterfly	פַּרְפַּר ז׳
פַּרְפְּרֵינוּ/כֶם/כֶן/הֶם/הֶן	**פַּרְפָּ**רַי/רֶיךָ/רַיִךְ/רָיו/רֶיהָ	פַּרְפְּרֵי-		פַּרְפָּרִים

The third consonant, which is identical to the first, is followed by a *pataH*, and the following consonant should have been geminated, so as to make sure that the second syllable remain closed, but when the consonant is guttural and thus cannot be geminated, the preceding *pataH* becomes *kamats*. Only occurrences with ר׳ were found; it is hard to say regarding א׳, ה׳ ח׳ ע׳, since the only other occurrence with a guttural is קַעְקַע 'tatoo,' which has no declension other than the construct singular, and has no plural.

Examples

פַּרְפָּרִים מסוימים נודדים מרחקים עצומים בדומה לציפורים נודדות.
Some **butterflies** travel huge distances, just like migrating birds.

Special Expressions

bow tie עניבת **פַּרְפַּר**

Additional Examples in this Pattern

tattoo קַעְקַע/קַעֲקַע juniper עַרְעָר thistle דַּרְדַּר

---

418. ***CaCCaC*** when the two first consonants are reduplicated in consonantal slots three and four, respectively (קַטְקַט), and the plural form is dual

our/your/their	my/your/his/her	const.	Gloss	sing/pl
עַפְעַפֵּנוּ/פְּכֶם/פְּכֶן/פָּם/פָּן	**עַפְעַ**פִּי/פְּךָ/פֵּךְ/פּוֹ/פָּהּ	עַפְעַף-	eyelid	עַפְעַף ז׳
עַפְעַפֵּינוּ/כֶם/כֶן/הֶם/הֶן	**עַפְעַפַּ**י/פֶּיךָ/פַּיִךְ/פָּיו/פֶּיהָ	עַפְעַפֵּי-		עַפְעַפַּיִם

The third consonant, which is identical to the first, is followed by a *pataH*, and the following consonant is geminated, so as to make sure that the second syllable remain closed. The plural form is the dual ־ַיִם.

Examples

When one sleeps, the eyelids are closed. בזמן השנה ה**עַפְעַפַּיִם** סגורים.

Special Expressions

did not move an **eyelid** לא הניד **עַפְעַף**

---

419. *CaCCeC*

our/your/their	my/your/his/her	const.	Gloss	sing/pl
אַבְנֵטֵנוּ/טְכֶם/טְכֶן/טָם/טָן	**אַבְנֵ**טִי/טְךָ/טֵךְ/טוֹ/טָהּ	-אַבְנֵט	sash,	אַבְנֵט ז'
אַבְנֵטֵינוּ/כֶם/כֶן/הֶם/הֶן	**אַבְנֵ**טַי/טֶיךָ/טַיִךְ/טָיו/טֶיהָ	-אַבְנֵטֵי	girdle	אַבְנֵטִים

The *tsere* does not reduce to a *shva* in the declension.

Examples

הלבוש המסורתי של הגבר הערבי כולל מכנסיים תפוחים עם **אַבְנֵט** רחב.
The traditional costume of the Arab man includes wide pants with broad **sash**.

אחת השאלות המורכבות העומדות בפני החברה הישראלית היא האם לחייב **אַבְרְכִים** לשרת בצבא כמו כל אזרח צעיר אחר, או לחייבם בשירות לאומי אחר, או להמשיך להיכנע לתכתיבים קואליציוניים.
One of the complex questions facing Israeli society is whether to require **Yeshiva students** to serve in the army like any other young citizen, or to require another form of national service of them, or to continue to bow down to coalition dictates.

Special Expressions

a spoiled **young man** (usually refers to Yeshiva atudents) **אַבְרֵךְ** משי

Additional Examples in this Pattern

monument, memorial גַּלְעֵד athlete אַתְלֵט

---

420. *CaCCeC* when the *tsere* is reduced in the declension

Our/your/their	my/your/his/her	const.	Gloss	sing/pl
גַּרְגְּרֵנוּ/**גַּרְגֶּרְ**כֶם/כֶן/**גַּרְגְּרָ**ם/ן	גַּרְגְּרִי/גַּרְגֶּרְךָ/**גַּרְגְּרֵ**ךְ/רוֹ/רָהּ	-גַּרְגֵּר	cress	גַּרְגֵּר ז'
גַּרְגְּרֵינוּ/כֶם/כֶן/הֶם/הֶן	**גַּרְגְּ**רַי/רֶיךָ/רַיִךְ/רָיו/רֶיהָ	-גַּרְגְּרֵי	(botany)	גַּרְגְּרִים

The *tsere* is reduced to a *shva* in an open syllable, גַּרְגְּרִי < גַּרְגֵּרִי*, and to a *seghol* in a closed one, גַּרְגֶּרְךָ < גַּרְגֵּרְךָ*.

Examples

גַּרְגֵּר הוא צמח בר ממשפחת המצליבים.
Cress is a wild plant of the Cruciferae family.

---

421. *CiCCeC*

our/your/their	my/your/his/her	const.	Gloss	sing/pl
לִזְבְּזֵנוּ/זְכֶם/זְכֶן/זָם/זָן	**לִזְבְּ**זִי/זְךָ/זֵךְ/זוֹ/זָהּ	-לִזְבֵּז	frame,	לִזְבֵּז ז'
לִזְבְּזֵינוּ/כֶם/כֶן/הֶם/הֶן	**לִזְבְּ**זַי/זֶיךָ/זַיִךְ/זָיו/זֶיהָ	-לִזְבְּזֵי	ledgde	לִזְבְּזִים

The *tsere* is reduced to a *shva* in the declension with stress shift.

Examples

לִזְבֵּז הוא מונח מתקופת התלמוד המציין שפה או מסגרת (לכלי וכו')
לִזְבֵּז is a term from the Talmudic term denoting **rim, edge** or **frame** (of vessel, etc.)

---

422. ***CaCCeC*** with seghol

our/your/their	my/your/his/her	const.	Gloss	sing/pl
גַּרְזִנֵּנוּ/נְּכֶם/נְּכֶן/נָּם/נָּן	**גַּרְזִ**נִּי/נְּךָ/נֵּךְ/נּוֹ/נָּהּ	-גַּרְזֶן	axe,	גַּרְזֶן ז'
גַּרְזִנֵּינוּ/כֶם/כֶן/הֶם/הֶן	**גַּרְזִ**נַּי/נֶּיךָ/נַּיִךְ/נָּיו/נֶּיהָ	-גַּרְזְנֵי	hatchet	גַּרְזִנִּים

In the declension the *seghol* is replaced by *Hirik*, which is followed by *dagesh Hazak*.

Examples

ברגע שהומצא המסור החשמלי והחליף את הַ**גַּרְזֶן**, נגזר דינם של יערות העד.
The moment the chain saw was invented and replaced the **axe**, the jungles were doomed.

תקופת הַ**בַּרְזֶל** החלה לפני כשלושת אלפים שנה, כשהאדם גילה את הַ**בַּרְזֶל** ותכונותיו.
The **iron** age began about three thousand years ago, when man discovered **iron** and its qualities.

Special Expressions

infinite patience סבלנות של **בַּרְזֶל** **railroad** track מסילת **בַּרְזֶל**

Additional Examples in this Pattern

fertile agricultural area (biblical); toasted young wheat (biblical) כַּרְמֶל

---

423. ***CaCCoC*** with *Holam Haser*

our/your/their	my/your/his/her	const.	Gloss	sing/pl
גַּרְדֻּמֵּנוּ/מְּכֶם/מְּכֶן/מָּם/מָּן	**גַּרְדֻּ**מִּי/מְּךָ/מֵּךְ/מּוֹ/מָּהּ	-גַּרְדֹּם	scaffold,	גַּרְדֹּם ז'
גַּרְדֻּמֵּינוּ/כֶם/כֶן/הֶם/הֶן	**גַּרְדֻּ**מַּי/מֶּיךָ/מַּיִךְ/מָּיו/מֶּיהָ	-גַּרְדֻּמֵּי	gallows	גַּרְדֻּמִּים

In the declension the *Holam* is replaced by *kubuts* (possibly the original vowel?), and is followed by *dagesh Hazak*.

Examples

גַּרְדֹּם הוא במה שעליה מוצאים להורג נידונים למוות.
Gallows are a stage on which those sentenced to death are executed.

באילת יש שונית **אַלְמֻגִּים** יפהפיה שניתן לצפות בה גם מבלי לצלול, דרך קיר זכוכית ענק, במבנה גדול שהוקם בתוך מי ים סוף.
In Eilat there is a magnificent **coral** reef that can be observed without diving, through a huge glass wall in a large structure that was built inside the water of the Red Sea.

Special Expressions

was executed **עלה לַגַּרְדֹּם**

Irgun/Stern Gang members **עולי הַגַּרְדֹּם** executed by the British in the Mandatory period

Egyptian hieroglyphs; **כְּתב חַרְטֻמִּים** illegible handwriting Coll.

Additional Examples in this Pattern

coral; sandalwood אַלְמֹג/אַלְגֹּם

ancient Egyptian priest or חַרְטֹם magician

jacinth, ruby Bibl. כַּדְכֹּד

border, edge; cornice; rim כַּרְכֹּב (architecture)

crocus; saffron כַּרְכֹּם

milling cutter כַּרְסֹם

thermometer מַדְחֹם

---

424. ***CaCCoC*** with dual plural

our/your/their	my/your/his/her	const.	Gloss	sing/pl
קַרְסֻלֵּנוּ/לְּכֶם/לְּכֶן/לָּם/לָּן	**קַרְסֻ**לִּי/לְּךָ/לֵּךְ/לּוֹ/לָּהּ	קַרְסֹל-	ankle	קַרְסֹל ז'
קַרְסֻלֵּינוּ/כֶם/כֶן/הֶם/הֶן	**קַרְסֻ**לַּי/לֶּיךָ/לַּיִךְ/לָּיו/לֶּיהָ	קַרְסֻלֵּי-		קַרְסֻלַּיִם

In the declension the *Holam* is replaced by *kubuts* (possibly the original vowel?), and is followed by *dagesh Hazak*. The plural form is dual.

Examples

כשנופלים, לעתים קרובות נוקעים את **הַקַּרְסֹל**.
When one falls, one often sprains one's **ankle**.

Special Expressions

is not in the same league (does not even reach his **ankles**) **לא מגיע לְקַרְסֻלָּיו**

---

425. ***CaCCoC*** with dual plural *-ot/-im*

our/your/their	my/your/his/her	const.	Gloss	sing/pl
קַרְדֻּמֵּנוּ/מְּכֶם/מְּכֶן/מָּם/מָּן	קַרְדֻּמִּי/מְּךָ/מֵּךְ/מּוֹ/מָּהּ	קַרְדֹּם-	axe,	קַרְדֹּם ז'
קַרְדֻּמּוֹתֵינוּ/כֶם/כֶן/הֶם/הֶן	קַרְדֻּמּוֹתַי/תֶיךָ/תַיִךְ/תָיו/תֶיהָ	קַרְדֻּמּוֹת-	hatchet	קַרְדֻּמּוֹת/...מִּים

In the declension the *Holam* is replaced by *kubuts* (possibly the original vowel?), and is followed by *dagesh Hazak*. The plural suffix is *–ot* (possibly also *-im*).

Examples

קַרְדֹּם הוא מכשיר חפירה הדומה למכוש.
A **pickaxe** is a tool for digging that combines a hoe with an axe...

Special Expressions

קַרְדֹּם לחפור בו a means for one's benefit/profit

---

426. ***CeCCaC* = *'eCCaC*** where the first consonant is *'alef*

our/your/their	my/your/his/her	const.	Gloss	sing/pl
אֶתְגָּרֵנוּ/אֶתְגַּרְכֶם/כֶן/אֶתְגָּרָם/ן	אֶתְגָּרִי/רְךָ/רֵךְ/רוֹ/רָהּ	אֶתְגַּר-	challenge	אֶתְגָּר ז'
אֶתְגָּרֵינוּ/אֶתְגְּרֵיכֶם/כֶן/הֶם/הֶן	אֶתְגָּרַי/רֶיךָ/רַיִךְ/רָיו/רֶיהָ	אֶתְגְּרֵי-	N	אֶתְגָּרִים

In some of the occurrences, the א' is a derivational prefix, but not in all. In a closed syllable the *kamats* becomes *pataH* when the stress shifts, אֶתְגַּרְכֶם, and in an open syllable two syllables away from the stress it is reduced to a *shva*, אֶתְגְּרֵיכֶם.

Examples

עידן המחשבים מעמיד את כולנו בפני הרבה **אֶתְגָּרִים** חדשים.
The computer era causes us to face numerous new **challenges**.

Additional Examples in this Pattern

dispatch אֶשְׁגָּר

---

427. ***CeCCaC*** = *'eCCaC* where the first consonant is *'alef* and when the last consonant is guttural

our/your/their	my/your/his/her	const.	Gloss	sing/pl
אֶזְרָחֵנוּ/אֶזְרַחֲכֶם/כֶן/אֶזְרָחָם/ן	אֶזְרָחִי/חֲךָ/חֵךְ/חוֹ/חָהּ	אֶזְרַח-	citizen;	אֶזְרָח ז'
אֶזְרָחֵינוּ/אֶזְרְחֵיכֶם/כֶן/הֶם/הֶן	אֶזְרָחַי/חֶיךָ/חַיִךְ/חָיו/חֶיהָ	אֶזְרְחֵי-	civilian	אֶזְרָחִים

As in אֶתְגָּר above, and when a *shva* is expected with a guttural, it is replaced by *Hataf-pataH*: אֶזְרָחֵךְ, אֶזְרַחֲכֶם.

Examples

שאיפתם הגדולה של מהגרים לארה״ב היא להפוך ל**אֶזְרָחִים** בעלי זכויות מלאות בה.
The greatest wish of immigrants to the US is to become **citizens** with full rights and privileges.

משה השתחרר מן הצבא כבר לפני שנה, אבל עדיין אינו מצליח להסתגל לחייו החדשים כ**אֶזְרָח**.
Moshe was (honorably) discharged from the Army a year ago, but still cannot adjust to his new life as a **civilian**.

Special Expressions

cosmopolitan person **אֶזְרָח** העולם
senior **citizen** **אֶזְרָח** ותיק
honorary **citizen** **אֶזְרָח** כבוד
civil war מלחמת **אֶזְרָחִים**

water **pistol** **אֶקְדַּח** מים
nail **gun** **אֶקְדַּח** מסמרים
stapling **gun** **אֶקְדַּח** סיכות
revolver **אֶקְדַּח** תֻּפִּי

Additional Examples in this Pattern

pistol, handgun; red precious stone Bibl. אֶקְדָּח

---

428. ***CeCCaC*** = *'eCCaC* when the *kamats* becomes *pataH* in the declension, and is followed by *dagesh*

our/your/their	My/your/his/her	const.	Gloss	sing/pl
אֶשְׁנַבֵּנוּ/**אֶשְׁנַבְּ**כֶם/כֶן/**אֶשְׁנַבָּ**ם/ן	**אֶשְׁנַבִּ**י/בְּךָ/בֵּךְ/בּוֹ/בָּהּ	אֶשְׁנַב-	small	אֶשְׁנָב ז׳
אֶשְׁנַבֵּינוּ/כֶם/כֶן/הֶם/הֶן	**אֶשְׁנַבַּ**י/בֶּיךָ/בַּיִךְ/בָּיו/בֶּיהָ	אֶשְׁנַבֵּי-	window	אֶשְׁנַבִּים

No vowel changes in the declension. The *kamats* does not change to *pataH* before a guttural: אֶתְנָחִים etc.

Examples

הפקיד סגר את **אֶשְׁנַב**-הקבלה להפסקת צהריים בדיוק כשהגיע תורי.
The clerk closed the reception **window** exactly when my turn came.

כדי להגן על הפילים, העומדים היום בפני סכנת הכחדה, נאסר סחר ה**שֶׁנְהָב** במרבית המדינות בעולם.
In order to protect the elephants, which are facing extinction today, **ivory** trade has been declared illegal in most of the countries of the world.

Additional Examples in this Pattern

pause; a pause cantillation mark אֶתְנָח

prostitute's fee אֶתְנָן

---

429. ***CeCCaC*** = *'eCCaC* when the *pataH* becomes *kamats* in the declension, and the last consonant is ע'

our/your/their	my/your/his/her	const.	Gloss	sing/pl
אֶמְצָעֵנוּ/**אֶמְצַעֲ**כֶם/כֶן/**אֶמְצָעָ**ם/ן	**אֶמְצָ**עִי/עֲךָ/עֵךְ/עוֹ/עָהּ	אֶמְצַע-	center,	אֶמְצַע ז'
אֶמְצָעֵינוּ/**אֶמְצְעֵי**כֶם/כֶן/הֶם/הֶן	**אֶמְצָ**עַי/עֶיךָ/עַיִךְ/עָיו/עֶיהָ	אֶמְצְעֵי-	middle	אֶמְצָעִים

An apparently original *kamats* is maintained in an open syllable, is elided two syllables away from the main stress, but is realized as *pataH* in a closed syllable, including the unsufixed form. A *shva* expected with the guttural is replaced by *Hataf pataH.*

Examples

יש לי שני כרטיסים ל"המלט", במקום טוב ב**אֶמְצַע**.

I have two tickets for Hamlet, at a good place in the **middle**.

---

430. ***CeCCaC*** = ***'eCCaC*** when the *pataH* becomes *kamats* in the declension, the last consonant is *`ayin*, and the plural suffix is *-ot*

our/your/their	my/your/his/her	const.	Gloss	sing/pl
אֶצְבָּעֵנוּ/**אֶצְבַּעֲ**כֶם/כֶן/ **אֶצְבָּעָ**ם/ן	**אֶצְבָּ**עִי/עֲךָ/עֵךְ/עוֹ/עָהּ	אֶצְבַּע-	finger; index	אֶצְבַּע נ'
אֶצְבְּעוֹתֵינוּ/כֶם/כֶן/הֶם/הֶן	**אֶצְבְּעוֹ**תַי/תֶיךָ/תַיִךְ/ תָיו/תֶיהָ	אֶצְבְּעוֹת -	finger	אֶצְבָּעוֹת

An apparently original *kamats* is maintained in an open syllable, is elided two syllables away from the main stress, but is realized as *pataH* in a closed syllable, including the unsufixed form. A *shva* expected with the guttural is replaced by *Hataf pataH.*

Examples

מדי פעם נולדים תינוקות בעלי **אֶצְבַּע** שישית.

Sometimes babies are born with a sixth **finger** .

Special Expressions

prayed for his success החזיק לו אֶצְבָּעוֹת
totally סובב אותו על ה**אֶצְבַּע** הקטנה שלו
manipulated him to do his bidding

does not lift a **finger** אינו נוקף **אֶצְבַּע**
all by himself בעשר אֶצְבְּעוֹתָיו
has no base in reality מצוץ מן ה**אֶצְבַּע**

---

431. ***CiCCaC***

our/your/their	my/your/his/her	const.	Gloss	sing/pl
פִּנְקָסֵנוּ/**פִּנְקַסְ**כֶם/כֶן/**פִּנְקָסָ**ם/ן	**פִּנְקָ**סִי/סְךָ/סֵךְ/סוֹ/סָהּ	פִּנְקַס-	notebook;	פִּנְקָס ז'
פִּנְקָסֵינוּ/**פִּנְקְסֵי**כֶם/כֶן/הֶם/הֶן	**פִּנְקָ**סַי/סֶיךָ/סַיִךְ/סָיו/סֶיהָ	פִּנְקְסֵי-	registry	פִּנְקָסִים

In a closed syllable the *kamats* becomes *pataH* when the stress shifts, פִּנְקַסְכֶם, and in an open syllable two syllables away from the stress it is reduced to a *shva*, פִּנְקְסֵיכֶם.

Examples

מנשה לא יכול היה להצביע בבחירות האחרונות; בשל טעות אדמיניסטרטיבית, שמו לא נכלל **בפִּנְקַס** הבוחרים.
Menashe could not vote in the last elections. Owing to an administrative error, his name was not included in the voter **registry**.

כשבניין משותף מנוהל על ידי דייריו, הדיירים בוחרים ועד בית, הכולל בדרך כלל נשיא **וגִזְבָּר**.
When an apartment building is managed by its residents, they elect board, which generally includes a president and a **treasurer**.

אומרים ש**העִנְבָּר** המשובח ביותר מצוי בפולין.
They say that the best **amber** can be found in Poland.

פִּתְגָמִים רבים בעברית הישראלית מקורם במקרא ובמשנה.
Many **proverbs/sayings** in Israeli Hebrew originated in the Bible and in the Mishnah.

Special Expressions

פִּנְקַס חבר membership card

הנהלת **פִּנְקָסִים** bookkeeping

Additional Examples in this Pattern

אִלְפָּס casserole, stew-pot
חִזְרָן bamboo
סִכְסָךְ zigzag
סִרְפָּד nettle
עִנְבָּל clapper, tongue of bell; uvula
פִּרְחָח street urchin
פִּשְׁפָּשׁ small/narrow gate or door
צִלְצָל harpoon; ancient cymbals-like instrument
קִרְקָס circus
תִּמְסָח crocodile

---

432. *CiCCeC*

our/your/their	my/your/his/her	const.	Gloss	sing/pl
אִזְמֵלֵנוּ/לְכֶם/לְכֶן/לָם/לָן	**אִזְמֵל**ִי/לְךָ/לֵךְ/לוֹ/לָהּ	אִזְמֵל-	chisel,	אִזְמֵל ז'
אִזְמֵלֵינוּ/כֶם/כֶן/הֶם/הֶן	**אִזְמֵל**ַי/לֶיךָ/לַיִךְ/לָיו/לֶיהָ	אִזְמְלֵי-	scalpel	אִזְמֵלִים

The *tsere* is maintained throughout the declension.

Examples

פַּסָּלִים המגלפים בעץ עושים שימוש רב **באִזְמֵל**.
Sculptors who carve wood make extensive use of a **chisel**.

Additional Examples in this Pattern

קִנְרֵס artichoke

---

433. *CeCCeC*

our/your/their	my/your/his/her	const.	Gloss	sing/pl
חֶרְמֵשֵׁנוּ/שְׁכֶם/שְׁכֶן/שָׁם/שָׁן	**חֶרְמֵ**שִׁי/שְׁךָ/שֵׁךְ/שׁוֹ/שָׁהּ	חֶרְמֵשׁ-	scythe	חֶרְמֵשׁ ז׳
חֶרְמֵשֵׁינוּ/כֶם/כֶן/הֶם/הֶן	**חֶרְמֵ**שַׁי/שֶׁיךָ/שַׁיִךְ/שָׁיו/שֶׁיהָ	חֶרְמְשֵׁי-		חֶרְמֵשִׁים

The *tsere* is maintained throughout the declension.

Examples

עד סוף המאה התשע עשרה, מרבית החקלאים בעולם קצרו את תבואתם ב**חֶרְמֵשׁ**.
Till the end of the 19th century, most farmers in the world reaped grain with a **scythe**.

Special Expressions

crescent moon **חֶרְמֵשׁ** הירח

---

434. *CoCCe*

our/your/their	my/your/his/her	const.	Gloss	sing/pl
בָּטְנֵנוּ/נְכֶם/נְכֶן/נָם/נָן	**בָּטְ**נִי/נְךָ/נֵךְ/נוֹ /נָהּ	בָּטְנֵה-	pistachio	בָּטְנֶה ז׳
בָּטְנֵינוּ/כֶם/כֶן/הֶם/הֶן	**בָּטְ**נַי/נֶיךָ/נַיִךְ/נָיו/נֶיהָ	בָּטְנֵי-		בָּטְנִים

Examples

עץ ה**בָּטְנָה** הוא עץ הפיסטוקים ; בלשון הדיבור ה**בָּטְנִים** הם אגוזי אדמה.
The **pistachio** tree produces **pistachios**. [In colloquial Hebrew, the term for **pistachio** is often confused with peanuts.]

Additional Examples in this Pattern

ebony (tree) הָבְנֶה

---

435. *CuCCaC*

our/your/their	my/your/his/her	const.	Gloss	sing/pl
פֻּנְדָּקֵנוּ/**פֻּנְדַּקְ**כֶם/כֶן/**פֻּנְדָּקָ**ם/ן	**פֻּנְדָּ**קִי/קְךָ/קֵךְ/קוֹ/קָהּ	פֻּנְדַּק-	inn,	פֻּנְדָּק ז׳
פֻּנְדָּקֵינוּ/**פֻּנְדְקֵי**כֶם/כֶן/הֶם/הֶן	**פֻּנְדָּ**קַי/קֶיךָ/קַיִךְ/קָיו/קֶיהָ	פֻּנְדְּקֵי-	hostel	פֻּנְדָּקִים

In a closed syllable the *kamats* becomes *pataH* when the stress shifts, פֻּנְדַּקְכֶם, and in an open syllable two syllables away from the stress it is reduced to a *shva*, פֻּנְדְּקֵיכֶם.

Examples

בחפירות בעכו נתגלו **פֻּנְדְּקֵי** ענק מתקופת הצלבנים.
Huge **inns** from the crusaders period were uncovered during excavations in Acre.

הַכֻּסְבָּר (שאול מארמית, או כֻּסְבָּרָה בעברית המדוברת – שאילה מערבית) פופלרי מאוד בישראל, לא פחות מפטרוזיליה.
Coriander is very popular in Israel, at least as popular as parsley.

בלשון הסלנג, כשאדם נראה לא טבעי, והתנהגותו מאולצת, מכנים אותו **פֻּחְלָץ**.
In Israeli Hebrew slang, when a person looks unnatural, and his behavior forced, he is characterized as a **stuffed animal**.

Special Expressions

happened to meet (unplanned) נזדמנו **לְפֻנְדָּק** אחד

Additional Examples in this Pattern

artichoke חֻרְשָׁף
type of citrus, used for grafting and jam חֻשְׁחָשׁ
aeolianite (type of sandstone) כֻּרְכָּר
crab apple עֻזְרָד/עֻזְרָר
street urchin קֻנְדָּס
sledgehammer, mallet קֻרְנָס

---

436. ***CuCCaC*** with plural suffix *–ot*

our/your/their	my/your/his/her	const.	Gloss	sing/pl
פֻּזְמָקֵנוּ/פֻּזְמַקְכֶם/כֶן/פֻּזְמָקָם/ן	פֻּזְמָקִי/קְךָ/קֵךְ/קוֹ/קָהּ	פֻּזְמַק-	sock	פֻּזְמָק ז'
פֻּזְמְקוֹתֵינוּ/כֶם/כֶן/הֶם/הֶן	פֻּזְמְקוֹתַי/תֶיךָ/קַיִךְ/קָיו/קֶיהָ	פֻּזְמְקוֹת-	Lit.	פֻּזְמָקוֹת/ פֻּזְמְקָאוֹת

In a closed syllable the *kamats* becomes *pataH* when the stress shifts, פֻּזְמַקְכֶם, and in an open syllable two syllables away from the stress it is reduced to a *shva*, פֻּזְמְקוֹתַי.

Examples

המילה **פֻּזְמָק** נשאלה מפרסית בתקופת התלמוד.
The word *puzmak* was borrowed from Persian in the Talmudic period.

---

437. ***CCaCaC***

our/your/their	my/your/his/her	const.	Gloss	sing/pl
צִלְצַלֵנוּ/לְכֶם/לְכֶן/לָם/לָן	צִלְצַלִי/לְךָ/לֵךְ/לוֹ/לָהּ	צִלְצַל-	kind of	צְלָצַל ז'
צִלְצַלֵינוּ/כֶם/כֶן/הֶם/הֶן	צִלְצַלַי/לֶיךָ/לַיִךְ/לָיו/לֶיהָ	צִלְצְלֵי-	locust	צִלְצָלִים

our/your/their	my/your/his/her	const.	Gloss	sing/pl
צִרְצָרֵנוּ/רְכֶם/רְכֶן/רָם/רָן	צִרְצָרִי/רְךָ/רֵךְ/רוֹ/רָהּ	צְרָצַר-	cricket	צְרָצַר ז'
צִרְצָרֵינוּ/כֶם/כֶן/הֶם/הֶן	צִרְצָרַי/רֶיךָ/רַיִךְ/רָיו/רֶיהָ	צִרְצְרֵי-		צִרְצָרִים

The *pataH* is maintained throughout the declension, and is followed by *dagesh Hazak*. When the following consonant is ר', which does not take a *dagesh*, the *pataH* is replaced by a *kamats*. When the first syllable is closed with a *shva quiescent* two syllables away from the main stress, the original *shva mobile* is replaced by a *Hirik*: צִלְצְלֵי etc.

Examples

הצְלָצַל הוא אחד מסוגי הארבה הנזכרים במקרא.
The *tslatsal* is one of the types of locust mentioned in the Bible.

Additional Examples in this Pattern

nascent fruit סְמָדַר

---

438. *'aCaCCaC*

our/your/their	my/your/his/her	const.	Gloss	sing/pl
אֲגַרְטָלֵנוּ/**אֲגַרְטַלְ**כֶם/כֶן/**אֲגַרְטָלָ**ם/ן	**אֲגַרְטָ**לִי/לְךָ/לֵךְ/לוֹ/לָהּ	אֲגַרְטַל-	vase	אֲגַרְטָל ז'
אֲגַרְטָלֵינוּ/**אֲגַרְטְלֵי**כֶם/כֶן/הֶם/הֶן	**אֲגַרְטָ**לַי/לֶיךָ/לַיִךְ/לָיו/לֶיהָ	אֲגַרְטְלֵי-		אֲגַרְטָלִים

In a closed syllable the *kamats* becomes *pataH* when the stress shifts, אֲגַרְטַלְכֶם, and in an open syllable two syllables away from the stress it is reduced to a *shva*, אֲגַרְטְלֵיכֶם.

Examples

בחדר האורחים של משה מוצגים לראווה שני **אֲגַרְטָלִים** סיניים נדירים.
Two rare Chinese **vases** are displayed in Moshe's living room.

לא פעם, הצלחתו של אמן (זמר וכו') נזקפת לזכותו של **אֲמַרְגָּנוֹ** המוכשר.
More than once, the success of a performing artist (such as a singer) is credited to his/her **agent/impresario**.

Additional Examples in this Pattern

administrator אֲמַרְכָּל

---

439. *CiCCeC* with reduplication

our/your/their	my/your/his/her	const.	Gloss	sing/pl
פִּשְׁפְּשֵׁנוּ/**פִּשְׁפֶּשְׁ**כֶם/כֶן/**פִּשְׁפְּשָׁ**ם/ן	**פִּשְׁפְּ**שִׁי/פֶּשְׁךָ/**פִּשְׁפְּ**שֵׁךְ/שׁוֹ/שָׁהּ	פִּשְׁפֵּשׁ-	bug;	פִּשְׁפֵּשׁ ז'
פִּשְׁפְּשֵׁינוּ/כֶם/כֶן/הֶם/הֶן	**פִּשְׁפְּ**שַׁי/שֶׁיךָ/שַׁיִךְ/שָׁיו/שֶׁיהָ	פִּשְׁפְּשֵׁי-	flea	פִּשְׁפְּשִׁים

The first two consonants are reduplicated in the second syllable (קְטַקֵט). In a closed syllable the *tsere* becomes *seghol* when the stress shifts, פִּשְׁפֶּשְׁכֶם, and in an open syllable two syllables away from the stress it is reduced to a *shva*, פִּשְׁפְּשֵׁי.

Examples

פזמון ישראלי סאטירי: "איך קרה שה**פִּשְׁפֵּשׁ** עלה למעלה?...טיפס, טיפס, עלה, עלה – עד שעלה לממשלה".
A satirical Israeli song: "How did it happen that the **bug** climbed to the top?.. He climbed and climbed and went all the way up, till he got up (=rose) to the government."

לא כל עקרת בית בטוחה כמה מלח ו**פִלְפֵּל** להוסיף לתבשיל כשבאים אורחים, ולכן היא משאירה זאת לבחירתו של כל אורח.
Not every housewife is sure how much salt and **pepper** to add to a dish when guests arrive, so she leaves it to each guest to add.

Special Expressions

black **pepper** **פִּלְפֵּל** שחור

bed bug **פִּשְׁפֵּשׁ** מיטה

flea market שוק **פִּשְׁפְּשִׁים**

Additional Examples in this Pattern

pepper פִּלְפֵּל

---

440. *CiCCoC*

our/your/their	my/your/his/her	const.	Gloss	sing/pl
גִּבְעוֹלֵנוּ/לְכֶם/לְכֶן/לָם/לָן	**גִּבְעוֹ**לִי/לְךָ/לֵךְ/לוֹ/לָהּ	-גִּבְעוֹל	stalk,	גִּבְעוֹל ז׳
גִּבְעוֹלֵינוּ/כֶם/כֶן/הֶם/הֶן	**גִּבְעוֹ**לַי/לֶיךָ/לַיִךְ/לָיו/לֶיהָ	-גִּבְעוֹלֵי	stem	גִּבְעוֹלִים

Examples

המים, המלחים וכל חמרי המזון עוברים לכל חלקי הצמח דרך ה**גִּבְעוֹל**.
Water, salts/minerals and all nutrients pass through the **stem** to all parts of the plant.

הזמר המפורסם טען שהוא הותקף בלילה על ידי **בִּרְיוֹנִים**.
The famous singer claimed that he had been attacked by **thugs** at night.

Special Expressions

strong, muscular person Sl. **בִּרְיוֹן** קַשְׁקַשִּׁים

went down the drain, came to nothing (from 'went to the (king's) treasury') ירד ל**טִמְיוֹן**

Additional Examples in this Pattern

treasury (Talmudic) טִמְיוֹן   multi-layered stalk/stem גִּזְעוֹל

---

441. *CiCCoC* (*CiCCon?*) pl. -ot

our/your/their	my/your/his/her	const.	Gloss	sing/pl
פִּגְיוֹנֵנוּ/נְכֶם/נְכֶן/נָם/נָן	**פִּגְיוֹ**נִי/נְךָ/נֵךְ/נוֹ/נָהּ	-פִּגְיוֹן	dagger	פִּגְיוֹן ז׳
פִּגְיוֹנֵינוּ/כֶם/כֶן/הֶם/הֶן	**פִּגְיוֹ**נַי/נֶיךָ/נַיִךְ/נָיו/נֶיהָ	-פִּגְיוֹנוֹת		פִּגְיוֹנוֹת

Examples

כלי ההתנקשות הנפוץ ביותר בעבר היה ה**פִּגְיוֹן**; היום זה האקדח.
In the past the commonest assassination tool was the **dagger**; today it is the handgun.

Additional Examples in this Pattern

bag, sack Lit. צִקְלוֹן

---

442. *CiCCoC = 'eCCoC*

our/your/their	my/your/his/her	const.	Gloss	sing/pl
אֶגְרוֹפֵנוּ/פְכֶם/פְכֶן/פָם/פָן	**אֶגְרוֹ**פִי/פְךָ/פֵךְ/פוֹ/פָהּ	-אֶגְרוֹף	fist,	אֶגְרוֹף ז׳
אֶגְרוֹפֵינוּ/כֶם/כֶן/הֶם/הֶן	**אֶגְרוֹ**פַי/פֶיךָ/פַיִךְ/פָיו/פֶיהָ	-אֶגְרוֹפֵי	punch	אֶגְרוֹפִים

Examples

אביגדור קיבל זעזוע מוח קשה ממכת **אֶגְרוֹף** אדירה בתחרות האיגרוף הראשונה והאחרונה שלו...
Avigdor got a severe concussion from a stupendous **fist** blow in his first and last boxing match...

חרדים מקפידים מאוד שלא יהיה כל פגם **בְּאֶתְרוֹג** לסוכות; כל פגם פוסל אותו הלכתית.
When purchasing an **etrog (citron)** for Sukkoth, the orthodox check it very carefully for any imperfection; any imperfection disqualifies it according to the Halakhah (Jewish religious law).

Additional Examples in this Pattern

pauper Lit. אֶבְיוֹן

spadix (botany) אֶשְׁבּוֹל

---

443. *CiCCoC = 'eCCoC* with a final guttural

our/your/their	my/your/his/her	const.	Gloss	sing/pl
אֶפְרֹחֵנוּ/חֲכֶם/חֲכֶן/חָם/חָן	**אֶפְרֹ**חִי/חֲךָ/חֵךְ/חוֹ/חָהּ	אֶפְרֹחַ-	chick, young	אֶפְרֹחַ ז'
אֶפְרֹחֵינוּ/כֶם/כֶן/הֶם/הֶן	**אֶפְרֹ**חַי/חֶיךָ/חַיִךְ/חָיו/חֶיהָ	אֶפְרֹחֵי-	bird	אֶפְרֹחִים

The א' is prefixal. When the last consonant is a guttural, and a *shva* is expected, that *shva* will be replaced by a *Hataf-pataH*. When the guttural word-final after a vowel other that *a*, a furtive *pataH* occurs.

Examples

לציפורים הגדולות יש בדרך כלל רק **אֶפְרֹחַ** אחד באותו זמן.
Large birds usually have only a single **chick** at a time.

Additional Examples in this Pattern

pistol, handgun (variant of the standard form *'ekdaH*) אֶקְדּוֹחַ

---

444. *CaCCoC* with *Holam male*

our/your/their	my/your/his/her	const.	Gloss	sing/pl
כַּפְתּוֹרֵנוּ/רְכֶם/רְכֶן/רָם/רָן	**כַּפְתּוֹ**רִי/רְךָ/רֵךְ/רוֹ/רָהּ	כַּפְתּוֹר-	button,	כַּפְתּוֹר ז'
כַּפְתּוֹרֵינוּ/כֶם/כֶן/הֶם/הֶן	**כַּפְתּוֹ**רַי/רֶיךָ/רַיִךְ/רָיו/רֶיהָ	כַּפְתּוֹרֵי-	switch	כַּפְתּוֹרִים

The *Holam male* is maintained throughout the declension.

Examples

אתה מעדיף סוודר עם **כַּפְתּוֹרִים** או עם רוכסן?
Do you prefer a sweater with **buttons** or with a zipper?

בדרך כלל ישראל שולחת **דַּחְפּוֹרִים** להרוס את בתיהם של מְחַבְּלִים שהרגו אנשים. לא כולם מסכימים עם המדיניות הזאת.

Generally, Israel sends **bulldozers** to pull down the houses of terrorists who had killed people. Not everyone agrees with this policy.

חַרְטוֹם הספינה ניזוק קשות בעת ההתנגשות עם הצוללת.

The ship's **bow** was severely damaged during the collision with the submarine.

קיימים אלפי סוגים של **סַבְיוֹנִים**; שישה סוגים מצויים בישראל, שבה הם גדלים בעיקר בחורף ובאביב בחודשים שבין דצמבר למאי.

There exist thousands of types of **dandelions**; six of them are found in Israel, where they grow primarily in the winter and spring, between December and May.

הסרט המדבר הראשון, המסונכרן עם **פַּסְקוֹל**, הוצג לציבור לראשונה בשנת 1930.

The first speaking movie, synchronized with a **soundtrack**, was introduced to the public in 1930.

Special Expressions

memorial album **אַלְבּוֹם** זיכרון

toe of shoe **חַרְטוֹם** הנעל

wonderful, fantastic, terrific **כַּפְתּוֹר** וָפֶרַח (exclamations of wonder)

tsunami **נַחְשׁוֹל** סייסמי

one cannot testify as to the quality of his own goods אין **נַחְתּוֹם** מעיד על עיסתו

behind closed doors, behind the scenes, covertly מאחורי **הַפַּרְגּוֹד**

Additional Examples in this Pattern

album אַלְבּוֹם

hook אַנְקוֹל

sparrow אַנְקוֹר

pauper דַּלְפוֹן

spotlight, floodlight זַרְקוֹר

grasshopper חַרְגּוֹל

starred agama lizard חַרְדּוֹן

light meter מַדְאוֹר

breaker, large wave נַחְשׁוֹל

baker Lit. נַחְתּוֹם

storm; whirlwind Lit. עַלְעוֹל

screen, divider פַּרְגּוֹד

flea פַּרְעוֹשׁ

traffic light רַמְזוֹר

loudspeaker רַמְקוֹל

valve שַׁסְתּוֹם

---

445. ***CaCCoC = CaCaCoC*** with *Holam male* when the second root consonant is guttural

our/your/their	my/your/his/her	const.	Gloss	sing/pl
יַהֲלוֹמֵנוּ/מְכֶם/מְכֶן/מָם/מָן	**יַהֲלוֹ**מִי/מְךָ/מֵךְ/מוֹ/מָהּ	יַהֲלוֹם-	diamond	יַהֲלוֹם ז'
יַהֲלוֹמֵינוּ/כֶם/כֶן/הֶם/הֶן	**יַהֲלוֹ**מַי/מֶיךָ/מַיִךְ/מָיו/מֶיהָ	יַהֲלוֹמֵי-		יַהֲלוֹמִים

The *Holam male* is maintained throughout the declension. Where a *shva* is expected with a guttural, it is replaced by a *Hataf-pataH*.

Examples

ישראל היא מן המרכזים החשובים בעולם בעיבוד **יַהֲלוֹמִים**.

Israel is an important center for processing and cutting **diamonds**.

Special Expressions

the jewel in the crown, the greatest achievement/asset **הַיַּהֲלוֹם** שבכתר

Additional Examples in this Pattern

thorn (biblical) נַהֲלוֹל

---

446. *CaCCoC*, pl –ot

our/your/their	my/your/his/her	const.	Gloss	sing/pl
אַרְמוֹנֵנוּ/נְכֶם/נְכֶן/נָם/נָן	**אַרְמוֹ**נִי/נְךָ/נֵךְ/נוֹ/נָהּ	אַרְמוֹן-	palace	אַרְמוֹן ז׳
אַרְמוֹנוֹתֵינוּ/כֶם/כֶן/הֶם/הֶן	**אַרְמוֹנוֹ**תַי/תֶיךָ/תַיִךְ/תָיו/תֶיהָ	אַרְמוֹנוֹת-		אַרְמוֹנוֹת

Examples

בעזרת הצבא, המורדים השתלטו אתמול על **אַרְמוֹן** הנשיא.
With the Army's help, the rebels took over the President's **Palace** yesterday.

Additional Examples in this Pattern

harem הַרְמוֹן

---

447. *CaCCuC*

our/your/their	my/your/his/her	const.	Gloss	sing/pl
יַלְקוּטֵנוּ/טְכֶם/טְכֶן/טָם/טָן	**יַלְקוּ**טִי/טְךָ/טֵךְ/טוֹ/טָהּ	יַלְקוּט-	bag;	יַלְקוּט ז׳
יַלְקוּטֵינוּ/כֶם/כֶן/הֶם/הֶן	**יַלְקוּ**טַי/טֶיךָ/טַיִךְ/טָיו/טֶיהָ	יַלְקוּטֵי-	collection	יַלְקוּטִים

Examples

ההורים מתלוננים על כך שילדיהם נושאים **יַלְקוּטִים** כבדים מדיי בדרכם לבית הספר.
Parents complain that their children carry **bags** that are too heavy when going to school.

לאנתולוגיה, או לקובץ של ערכים או מאמרים, נהוג לקרוא לעתים "**יַלְקוּט**", למשל "ילקוט שירי מלחמת העצמאות".
An anthology, or a collection of entries or articles is sometimes called "***yalkut***," e.g., "an **anthology** of the songs of the War of Independence."

הַיַּנְשׁוּף הוא ציפור טרף מתוחכמת, העטה על טרפה במעוף מהיר ושקט להפליא.
The **owl** is a sophisticated bird of prey, which swoops on its prey in a remarkably swift and noiseless flight.

אומרים ש**פַּרְצוּפוֹ** כה מכוער, שהוא מפחיד ילדים קטנים.
They say that his **face** is so ugly, that it scares little children.

Special Expressions

radio silence דְּמָמַת **אַלְחוּט**
personal file in army **יַלְקוּט** שירות
showed his real **face** גילה את **פַּרְצוּפוֹ** האמיתי
person in a bad mood **פַּרְצוּף** חמוץ
a very sad **face** **פַּרְצוּף** של תשעה באב

Additional Examples in this Pattern

anesthesia אַלְחוּשׁ	petrel, shearwater יַסְעוּר
wireless N אַלְחוּט	serum, blood serum נַסְיוּב
lonesome, lonely גַּלְמוּד	curve N, bend N נַפְתּוּל
hose, nozzle זַרְנוּק	sun spider עַכְשׁוּב
gnat, midge יַבְחוּשׁ	lasso פַּלְצוּר
fallow deer יַחְמוּר	

---

448. ***CaCCuC*** with final *`ayin*

our/your/their	my/your/his/her	const.	Gloss	sing/pl
שַׁרְתוּעֵנוּ/עֲכֶם/עֲכֶן/עָם/עָן	**שַׁרְתוּ**עִי/עֲךָ/עֵךְ/עוֹ/עָהּ	שַׁרְתּוּעַ-	strut	שַׁרְתּוּעַ ז׳
שַׁרְתוּעֵינוּ/כֶם/כֶן/הֶם/הֶן	**שַׁרְתוּ**עַי/עֶיךָ/עַיִךְ/עָיו/עֶיהָ	שַׁרְתּוּעֵי-		שַׁרְתּוּעִים

The final (guttural) consonant comes with a "furtive" *pataH*. When a *shva* is expected with a guttural consonant, it is replaced by a *Hataf-pataH*. When word-final after a vowel other that *a*, a furtive *pataH* occurs.

---

449. ***CaCCuC*** when the first two consonants are reduplicated in positions three and four, respectively

our/your/their	my/your/his/her	const.	Gloss	sing/pl
בַּקְבּוּקֵנוּ/קְכֶם/קְכֶן/קָם/קָן	**בַּקְבּוּ**קִי/קְךָ/קֵךְ/קוֹ/קָהּ	בַּקְבּוּק-	bottle	בַּקְבּוּק ז׳
בַּקְבּוּקֵינוּ/כֶם/כֶן/הֶם/הֶן	**בַּקְבּוּ**קַי/קֶיךָ/קַיִךְ/קָיו/קֶיהָ	בַּקְבּוּקֵי-		בַּקְבּוּקִים

The basic pattern is *CaCCuC*, but in all of these cases, the first and second consonants are reduplicated in the third and fourth consonant slots, respectively (קַטְקוּט), and thus may be regarded as a sub-pattern.

Examples

אחד הצעדים הפשוטים שכולנו יכולים לנקוט כדי להגן על הסביבה הוא למחזר **בַּקְבּוּקִים**.
One of the simplest steps we could all take to protect the environment is to recycle **bottles**.

הַבַּרְבּוּר נחשב תמיד לסמל של יופי ואלגנטיות.
The **swan** has always been regarded as a symbol of beauty and elegance.

Special Expressions

a hot water **bottle** **בַּקְבּוּק** חם	**swan** song שירת **הַבַּרְבּוּר**
Molotov cocktail **בַּקְבּוּק** מולוטוב	**pimp, panderer** **סַרְסוּר** לדבר עבירה
bottleneck צוואר **בַּקְבּוּק**	

Additional Examples in this Pattern

serin (bird) בַּזְבּוּז	cartilage חַסְחוּס/סְחוּס
percolator חַלְחוּל	pimp; broker סַרְסוּר

tapeworm שַׁרְשׁוּר

clay jug (Talmudic) צַרְצוּר

---

450. ***CaCCuC*** with the third consonant repeated in fourth position

our/your/their	my/your/his/her	const.	Gloss	sing/pl
גַּפְרוּרֵנוּ/רְכֶם/רְכֶן/רָם/רָן	**גַּפְרוּ**רִי/רְךָ/רֵךְ/רוֹ/רָהּ	גַּפְרוּר-	match (for lighting)	גַּפְרוּר ז׳
גַּפְרוּרֵינוּ/כֶם/כֶן/הֶם/הֶן	**גַּפְרוּ**רַי/רֶיךָ/רַיִךְ/רָיו/רֶיהָ	גַּפְרוּרֵי-		גַּפְרוּרִים

The basic pattern is *CaCCuC*, but in all of these cases, the third consonant is repeated in the fourth consonant slot (קַטְלוּל), and thus may be regarded as a sub-pattern. Some of the occurrences add a shade of diminution, e.g. סַפְלוּל 'small cup; cupule (botany).'

Examples

קשה היום למצוא קופסאות **גַּפְרוּרִים** עם **גַּפְרוּרֵי** עץ כמו שייצרו אותם פעם.
It is difficult today to find **match** boxes with wood **matches** the way they used to manufacture them in the past.

הרופא אמר שה**גַּבְשׁוּשִׁים** בגבו של החולה הם תסמין של מחלה מסוכנת.
The doctor said that the **lumps** in the patient's back are a symptom of a dangerous illness.

קשה לי להתרגל למחשבה שאפשר לאכול **שַׁבְּלוּלִים**.
It is hard for me to get used to the idea that one can eat **snails**.

אי-עצירה ב**תַמְרוּר** "עצור" היא אחד הגורמים העיקריים לתאונות דרכים.
Not stopping at a stop **sign** is one of the major causes of road accidents.

Special Expressions

stop **sign** **תַּמְרוּר** עצור

Additional Examples in this Pattern

whisper, murmur לַחְשׁוּשׁ
deception Lit. נַכְלוּל
small cup; cupule (botany) סַפְלוּל
pinch, smidgen קַמְצוּץ

contrabass בַּטְנוּן
hunchback גַּבְנוּן
shading, variation גַּוְנוּן
frayed ends דַּבְלוּל
bleak (fish) לַבְנוּן

---

451. ***CaCCuC = CaCaCuC*** with the third consonant repeated in fourth position, and the second consonant is guttural

our/your/their	my/your/his/her	const.	Gloss	sing/pl
לַהֲטוּטֵנוּ/טְכֶם/טְכֶן/טָם/טָן	**לַהֲטוּ**טִי/טְךָ/טֵךְ/טוֹ/טָהּ	לַהֲטוּט-	juggling trick, sleight of hand	לַהֲטוּט ז׳
לַהֲטוּטֵינוּ/כֶם/כֶן/הֶם/הֶן	**לַהֲטוּ**טַי/טֶיךָ/טַיִךְ/טָיו/טֶיהָ	לַהֲטוּטֵי-		לַהֲטוּטִים

The basic pattern is *CaCCuC*, when the third consonant is repeated in the fourth consonant slot, and the second consonant is guttural, with a *Hataf-pataH* instead of a *shva* (קַטְלוּל < קַטֲלוּל).

Examples

בדרך כלל **לַהֲטוּט** טוב מצליח מכיוון שרוב האנשים אינם מתבוננים היטב במקום הנכון.
Generally, a good **magic trick** succeeds because most people are not locking carefully at the right place.

Additional Examples in this Pattern

effect (in film, radio etc.) פַּעֲלוּל infant, toddler זַאֲטוּט

---

452. *CaCCiC*

our/your/their	my/your/his/her	const.	Gloss	sing/pl
כַּרְטִיסֵנוּ/סְכֶם/סְכֶן/סָם/סָן	**כַּרְטִי**סִי/סְךָ/סֵךְ/סוֹ/סָהּ	כַּרְטִיס-	ticket;	כַּרְטִיס ז׳
כַּרְטִיסֵינוּ/כֶם/כֶן/הֶם/הֶן	**כַּרְטִי**סַי/סֶיךָ/סַיִךְ/סָיו/סֶיהָ	כַּרְטִיסֵי-	card	כַּרְטִיסִים

Examples

יש היום תוכנות שבעזרתן קונים ספסרים אלפי **כַּרְטִיסִים** למופעים פופולריים מייד עם פרסום ההופעה, ולאחר מכן מוכרים אותם במחירים מופקעים.
Today there is software which makes it possible for scalpers to purchase thousands of **tickets** as soon as a show is open for sale, and then sell them for exorbitant prices.

יש סוחרים שאינם מכבדים **כַּרְטִיסֵי** אשראי של "אמריקן אקספרס" מכיוון שהעמלות שנגבות הן גבוהות מדיי.
Some merchants do not accept American Express credit **cards** because their charges to the merchants are too high.

למרבית הצער, לא מעט אנשים, כולל מנהיגים בעמדות מפתח, אינם מאמינים שזיהום האוויר גורם לשינויים קיצוניים ב**אַקְלִים** כדור הארץ.
Unfortunately, a good number of people, including leaders in key positions, do not believe that air pollution causes extreme changes in the **climate** of Planet Earth.

על פי סרטי המערב הפרוע, ערכו של אדם נמדד במהירות שבה הוא שולף אקדח מ**נַּרְתִּיקוֹ**.
According to the Wild West movies, a person's value is determined by the speed with which he draws a handgun from its **holster**.

היו תקופות בהיסטוריה שבהן **תַּבְלִינִים** יקרי מציאות הועדפו על פני כסף וזהב.
There were times in history when rare **spices** were valued higher than silver and gold.

Special Expressions

credit **card** **כַּרְטִיס** אשראי
business **card**, calling **card** **כַּרְטִיס** ביקור

temperate **climate** **אַקְלִים** ממוזג
core of the earth **גַּלְעִין** כדור הארץ
atomic **nucleus** **גַּרְעִין** האטום

Additional Examples in this Pattern

pit (of fruit) גַּלְעִין
seed, kernel; nucleus; grain גַּרְעִין
drizzle זַרְזִיף
limerick חַמְשִׁיר
jasmine יַסְמִין

daffodil נַרְקִיס
smog (note furtive *pataH* in עַרְפִּיחַ isolation form)
scepter; wand; baton שַׁרְבִיט

---

453. ***CaCCiC***, where the first and second consonants are reduplicated in third and fourth position, respectively (קַטְקִיט)

our/your/their	my/your/his/her	const.	Gloss	sing/pl
גַּרְגִּירֵנוּ/רְכֶם/רְכֶן/רָם/רָן	**גַּרְגִּי**רִי/רְךָ/רֵךְ/רוֹ/רָהּ	גַּרְגִּיר-	grain; crumb,	גַּרְגִּיר ז׳
גַּרְגִּירֵינוּ/כֶם/כֶן/הֶם/הֶן	**גַּרְגִּי**רַי/רֶיךָ/רַיִךְ/רָיו/רֶיהָ	גַּרְגִּירֵי-	tiny particle	גַּרְגִּירִים

Examples

יש זקנים שאוהבים לשבת בפארק ולפזר **גַּרְגִּירִים** לציפורים או לסנאים.
There are old people who like to sit in the park and spread **grains** or **crumbs** for birds or squirrels.

אִמְרָה יהודית מן המקורות: הלך **זַרְזִיר** אצל עורב משום שהוא בן מינו.
A Jewish saying from the sources: The **starling** seeks the company of the raven, because they are related (i.e., everyone seeks his own kind).

Special Expressions

wild **berries** **גַּרְגִּירֵי** יער

Additional Examples in this Pattern

teal שַׁרְשִׁיר

---

454. ***CaCCiC***, where the third consonant is reduplicated in the fourth consonant position (קַטְלִיל)

our/your/their	my/your/his/her	const.	Gloss	sing/pl
שַׁגְרִירֵנוּ/רְכֶם/רְכֶן/רָם/רָן	**שַׁגְרִי**רִי/רְךָ/רֵךְ/רוֹ/רָהּ	שַׁגְרִיר-	ambassador,	שַׁגְרִיר ז׳
שַׁגְרִירֵינוּ/כֶם/כֶן/הֶם/הֶן	**שַׁגְרִי**רַי/רֶיךָ/רַיִךְ/רָיו/רֶיהָ	שַׁגְרִירֵי-	delegate	שַׁגְרִירִים

Examples

בשל המצב הפוליטי המורכב במזרח התיכון, ה**שַּׁגְרִירִים** הנשלחים לשם חייבים להיות בעלי כישורים מיוחדים.
Owing to the complex political situation in the Middle East, **ambassadors** sent there must have special qualifications.

דַּחְלִילִים מיועדים להפחיד ציפורים כדי שלא יאכלו את היבול שבשדה, אבל מרבית הציפורים מתעלמות מהם.

Scarecrows are intended to scare away birds so that they do not eat the crops in the field, but most birds just ignore them.

Special Expressions

a good-will **ambassador** **שַׁגְרִיר** של רצון טוב

Additional Examples in this Pattern

wood sorrel חַמְצִיץ	heavy rain סַגְרִיר
cabbage butterfly לַבְנִין	shred, fraction שַׁבְרִיר

---

455. ***CCaCCuC***, with the 2nd and 3rd consonants reduplicated in positions four and five, respectively (קְטַלְטוּל)

our/your/their	my/your/his/her	const.	Gloss	sing/pl
בְּצַלְצוּלֵנוּ/לְכֶם/לְכֶן/לָם/לָן	**בְּצַלְצוּ**לִי/לְךָ/לֵךְ/לוֹ/לָהּ	בְּצַלְצוּל-	bulbil,	בְּצַלְצוּל ז׳
בְּצַלְצוּלֵינוּ/כֶם/כֶן/הֶם/הֶן	**בְּצַלְצוּ**לַי/לֶיךָ/לַיִךְ/לָיו/לֶיהָ	בְּצַלְצוּלֵי-	shallot	בְּצַלְצוּלִים

In the reduplication process, the second and third consonants are reduplicated in positions four and five, respectively. Semantically, the derivation is generally intended to create a diminutive version of the base.

Examples

בְּצַלְצוּל הוא פקעת משנית המסתעפת מן הפקעת הראשית.

Bulbil is a secondary, smaller bulb, splitting off the primary bulb.

---

456. ***CCaCCuC > CaCaCCuC***, when the second and third consonants are reduplicated in positions four and five, respectively, and the first consonant is guttural

our/your/their	my/your/his/her	const.	Gloss	sing/pl
חֲתַלְתּוּלֵנוּ/לְכֶם/לְכֶן/לָם/לָן	**חֲתַלְתּוּ**לִי/לְךָ/לֵךְ/לוֹ/לָהּ	חֲתַלְתּוּל-	kitten	חֲתַלְתּוּל ז׳
חֲתַלְתּוּלֵינוּ/כֶם/כֶן/הֶם/הֶן	**חֲתַלְתּוּ**לַי/לֶיךָ/לַיִךְ/לָיו/לֶיהָ	חֲתַלְתּוּלֵי-		חֲתַלְתּוּלִים

In the reduplication process, the second and third consonants are reduplicated in positions four and five, respectively. When the first consonant is guttural, the *shva* is replaced by *Hataf-pataH* (קְטַלְטוּל < קֲטַלְטוּל). Semantically, the derivation is generally intended to create a diminutive version of the base.

Examples

החֲתוּלָה שלנו המליטה השבוע ארבעה **חֲתַלְתּוּלִים**.

Our cat had a four-**kitten** litter this week.

---

457. ***CCaCCiC* > *CaCaCCiC*** when the second and third consonants are reduplicated in positions four and five, respectively, and the first consonant is guttural

our/your/their	my/your/his/her	const.	Gloss	sing/pl
חֲזַרְזִירֵנוּ/רְכֶם/רְכֶן/רָם/רָן	**חֲזַרְזִיר**ִי/רְךָ/רֵךְ/רוֹ/רָהּ	-חֲזַרְזִיר	piglet	חֲזַרְזִיר ז׳
חֲזַרְזִירֵינוּ/כֶם/כֶן/הֶם/הֶן	**חֲזַרְזִיר**ַי/רֶיךָ/רַיִךְ/רָיו/רֶיהָ	-חֲזַרְזִירֵי		חֲזַרְזִירִים

In the reduplication process, the second and third consonants are reduplicated in positions four and five, respectively. When the first consonant is guttural, the *shva* is replaced by *Hataf-pataH* (קְטַלְטִיל < קֲטַלְטִיל). Semantically, the derivation is generally intended to create a diminutive of the base.

Examples

יש אנשים המגדלים **חֲזַרְזִיר** בבית כחיית מחמד.

Some people raise a **piglet** at home as a pet.

---

458. ***CCaCCaC***, when the second and third consonants are reduplicated in positions four and five, respectively

our/your/their	my/your/his/her	const.	Gloss	sing/pl
זְקַנְקַנֵּנוּ/נְּכֶם/נְּכֶן/נָּם/נָּן	**זְקַנְקַ**נִּי/נְּךָ/נֵּךְ/נּוֹ/נָּהּ	-זְקַנְקַן	small	זְקַנְקַן ז׳
זְקַנְקַנֵּינוּ/כֶם/כֶן/הֶם/הֶן	**זְקַנְקַ**נַּי/נֶּיךָ/נַּיִךְ/נָּיו/נֶּיהָ	-זְקַנְקַנֵּי	beard	זְקַנְקַנִּים

f. sing/pl	m. sing/pl	Gloss
יְרַקְרַקָּה/יְרַקְרֶקֶת/יְרַקְרֹקֶת	יְרַקְרַק	greenish
יְרַקְרַקּוֹת	יְרַקְרַקִּים	

In the reduplication process, the second and third consonants are reduplicated in positions four and five, respectively (קְטַלְטַל). Semantically, the derivation is generally intended to create a diminutive of the base. The forms can be either nouns or adjectives. Generally, we can also find a segholate variant in the feminine singular: יְרַקְרֶקֶת, עֲגַלְגֶּלֶת etc. (stress falls on the penultimate syllable.) In some forms, the final vowel of the stem is alternatively realized as [o], קְטַנְטַן/טֹן, שְׁחַרְחַר/חֹר, שְׁמַנְמַן/מֹן, but practically, it usually occurs in the feminine singular (and that [o] is stressed): קְטַנְטֹנֶת, שְׁחַרְחֹרֶת, שְׁמַנְמֹנֶת ?זְעַרְעֹרֶת, ?יְרַקְרֹקֶת.

Examples

יש לו **זְקַנְקַן** כמו לתַיִשׁ.

He has a **small beard** (a "goatee") like a goat's.

במשך הסתיו, העלים הירוקים של העצים הנשירים בהדרגה הופכים **יְרַקְרַקִּים**, ועם הזמן צהובים, אדומים, או חומים.

During the fall, the green leaves of the deciduous trees gradually become **greenish**, and with time, yellow, or red, or brown.

הכלבה של השכנים ילדה השבוע ארבעה **כְּלַבְלַבִּים** (במדוברת **כְּלַבְלָבִים**), וכולם הובטחו כבר לבני משפחה וחברים.
The neighbors' female dog gave birth this week to four **puppies**, all of which have already been promised to family members and friends.

המוסיקה שהוא כותב טובה, אבל לדעתי קצת סנטימנטלית **וּמְתַקְתַּקָּה**.
The music he writes is good, but in my opinion a bit sentimental and **on the sweet side**.

הוא לא ממש שמן, אבל בהחלט **שְׁמַנְמַן**.

He is not really fat, but definitely **chubby**.

Additional Examples in this Pattern

small onion בְּצַלְצַל
young person trying to act גְּבַרְבַּר/גְּבַרְבַר "grown up" (Coll.)
pinkish וְרַדְרַד
golden, golden-brown זְהַבְהַב
small tail זְנַבְנַב
very tiny זְעַרְעַר

bluish כְּחַלְחַל
orangish; small spot כְּתַמְתַּם
whitish לְבַנְבַּן
purplish; oval סְגַלְגַּל
dizzy סְחַרְחַר
yellowish צְהַבְהַב
very short קְצַרְצַר

---

459. ***CCaCCaC* > *CaCaCCaC***, when the second and third consonants are reduplicated in positions four and five, respectively, and the first consonant is guttural (קְטַלְטַל > קֲטַלְטַל)

sing/pl	Gloss	const.	my/your/his/her	our/your/their
חֲבַלְבַּל ז׳	bindweed,	חֲבַלְבַּל-	**חֲבַלְבַּ**לִּי/לְּךָ/לֵּךְ/לּוֹ/לָּהּ	**חֲבַלְבַּ**לֵּנוּ/לְּכֶם/לְּכֶן/לָּם/לָּן
חֲבַלְבַּלִּים	convolvulus	חֲבַלְבַּלֵּי-	**חֲבַלְבַּ**לַּי/לֶּיךָ/לַּיִךְ/לָּיו/לֶּיהָ	**חֲבַלְבַּלֵּי**נוּ/כֶם/כֶן/הֶם/הֶן

Gloss	m. sing/pl	f. sing/pl
reddish	אֲדַמְדַּם	אֲדַמְדַּמָּה/אֲדַמְדֶּמֶת
	אֲדַמְדַּמִּים	אֲדַמְדַּמּוֹת

In the reduplication process, the second and third consonants are reduplicated in positions four and five, respectively. Semantically, the derivation is generally intended to create a diminutive of the base. Most forms are adjectives. Generally, we can also find a segholate variant in the feminine singular: אֲדַמְדֶּמֶת etc. (stress falls on the penultimate syllable.) An expected *shva* with the 1st root consonant is replaced by *Hataf-pataH*.

Examples

ג׳ינְג׳י הוא כינוי או שם תואר בעברית המדוברת לאדם ששערו **אֲדַמְדַּם**.
"Ginger" is a colloquial Hebrew term, or adjective, referring to a person whose hair is **reddish**.

קשה לפעמים לדעת אם סוכן המנסה למכור לך משהו הוא אמין, או אדם **חֲלַקְלַק** שעליך להיזהר מפניו.
Sometimes it is hard to tell whether a salesman who tries to sell you something is trustworthy, or a **very smooth** person and that you should watch out.

Additional Examples in this Pattern

grayish אֲפַרְפַּר
striped (animal) חֲבַרְבַּר
slightly pale Lit. חֲוַרְוַר
slightly sour חֲמַצְמַץ
evasive, slippery חֲמַקְמַק
rounded, roundish עֲגַלְגַּל
twisting, winding; crooked, underhanded עֲקַלְקַל

---

460. *'aCCaCCa*

our/your/their	my/your/his/her	const.	Gloss	sing/pl
אַכְסַנְיָתֵנוּ/**אַכְסַנְיַתְ**כֶם/כֶן/**אַכְסַנְיָתָ**ם/ן	**אַכְסַנְיָ**תִי/תְךָ/תֵךְ/תוֹ/תָהּ	אַכְסַנְיַת-	hostel, inn; gathering place	אַכְסַנְיָה/א נ'
אַכְסַנְיוֹתֵינוּ/כֶם/כֶן/הֶם/הֶן	**אַכְסַנְיוֹ**תַי/תֶיךָ/תַיִךְ/תָיו/תֶיהָ	אַכְסַנְיוֹת-		אַכְסַנְיוֹת

All occurrences in the pattern are borrowed – mostly from Greek, some from Aramaic.

Examples

בעל ה**אַכְסַנְיָה** הזאת הוא גם הטבח שלה.
The **inn**keeper here is also the chef.

המלון הזה ישמש **אַכְסַנְיָה** מצוינת לכנס שלנו.
This hotel will provide excellent **accommodation** for our conference.

תמיד יותר נוח כשיש בדירה יותר מחדר **אַמְבַּטְיָה** אחד.
It is always more convenient when there is more than one **bathroom** in an apartment.

ה**אַנְדַּרְטָה** לזכר השואה בבוסטון היא אחת הפשוטות אך המרשימות ביותר שראיתי.
The Holocaust Memorial **Monument** in Boston is one of the simplest but still most impressive **monuments** I have seen.

Special Expressions

youth **hostel** **אַכְסַנְיַת** נוער

Additional Examples in this Pattern

vestibule, corridor אַכְסַדְרָה
reference, support אַסְמַכְתָּה/א
beginning אַתְחַלְתָּא

Patterns with affixes

R. Patterns with the prefix *m-*, without or with a suffix

461. *moCaC*

our/your/their	my/your/his/her	const.	Gloss	sing/pl
מוֹשָׁבֵנוּ/**מוֹשַׁבְ**כֶם/כֶן/**מוֹשָׁבָ**ם/ן	**מוֹשָׁ**בִי/בְךָ/בֵךְ/בוֹ/בָהּ	מוֹשַׁב-	seat;	מוֹשָׁב ז׳
מוֹשָׁבֵינוּ/**מוֹשְׁבֵי**כֶם/כֶן/הֶם/הֶן	**מוֹשָׁ**בַי/בֶיךָ/בַיִךְ/בָיו/בֶיהָ	מוֹשְׁבֵי-	session	מוֹשָׁבִים

All forms are derived from roots whose first radical is *y* (replaced by וֹ). The *kamats* is replaced by *pataH* in an unstressed closed syllable: מוֹשַׁבְכֶם etc.

Examples

המוֹשָׁבִים במטוס היו נוחים למדיי, אבל ללא מרחב מספיק לרגליים.
The **seats** on the plane were fairly comfortable, but there was insufficient leg space.

המוֹשָׁבִים האחרונים של הקונגרס הם בדרך כלל עמוסים לעייפה; המחוקקים מנסים להעביר הצעות חוק רבות ככל האפשר לפני הפגרה.
The last **sessions** of Congress are heavily scheduled; the legislators try to pass as many bills as possible before recess.

חג **המוֹלָד** הוא החג המרכזי בכל המדינות שמרבית אוכלוסייתן נוצרית.
Christmas is the central holiday in all coutries where the majority of the population is Christian.

Special Expressions

חג **המוֹלָד** Christmas (**birth** of Christ)
מוֹשַׁב עובדים/**מוֹשָׁב** שיתופי forms of cooperative **settlement** in Israel
מוֹשַׁב זקנים old people's **home**
תחום **המוֹשָׁב** the pale of **settlement**
מוֹשַׁב לצים **gathering** (= **session**) of clowns

Additional Examples in this Pattern

מוֹבָל canal, duct
מוֹלָד birth
מוֹתָב formal panel of judges, consultants, etc.

---

462. *moCaC*, when the third root consonant is guttural

our/your/their	my/your/his/her	const.	Gloss	sing/pl
מוֹפָעֵנוּ/**מוֹפַעֲ**כֶם/כֶן/**מוֹפָעָ**ם/ן	**מוֹפָ**עִי/עֲךָ/עֵךְ/עוֹ/עָהּ	מוֹפַע-	performance,	מוֹפָע ז׳
מוֹפָעֵינוּ/**מוֹפְעֵי**כֶם/כֶן/הֶם/הֶן	**מוֹפָ**עַי/עֶיךָ/עַיִךְ/עָיו/עֶיהָ	מוֹפְעֵי-	show	מוֹפָעִים

All forms are derived from roots whose first radical is *y*. When a *shva* is expected, it is replaced by *Hataf-pataH*.

Examples

בכל יום עצמאות, העיריה או המועצה המקומית מספקת **מוֹפְעֵי** תרבות לתושבים.
On every Independence Day, the city or local council provides cultural **performances** to the public.

Special Expressions

מוֹפָע אורקולי audio-visual **show**

Additional Examples in this Pattern

מוֹדָע acquaintance Lit.

---

463. *moCaC* pl. -ot

our/your/their	my/your/his/her	const.	Gloss	sing/pl
מוֹסָדֵנוּ/**מוֹסַדְ**כֶם/כֶן/**מוֹסָדָ**ם/ן	**מוֹסָ**דִי/דְךָ/דֵךְ/דוֹ/דָהּ	מוֹסַד-	institution;	מוֹסָד ז'
מוֹסְדוֹתֵינוּ/כֶם/כֶן/הֶם/הֶן	**מוֹסְדוֹ**תַי/תֶיךָ/תַיִךְ/תָיו/תֶיהָ	מוֹסְדוֹת-	basis	מוֹסָדוֹת

All forms are derived from roots whose first radical is *y*. The plural suffix is *-ot*. Note: while the plural of מוֹלָד 'birth' is מוֹלָדִים, that of מוֹלָד 'new moon' is מוֹלָדוֹת.

Examples

ממשלת ישראל תומכת בכל ה**מוֹסָדוֹת** המוכרים להשכלה גבוהה, כולל המכללות השונות.
The Israeli government supports all recognized **institutions** of higher education, including the various community colleges.

במשלב הגבוה, "**מוֹסָד**" הוא תחלופה ל"בסיס, יסוד".
In the upper register, **מוֹסָד** is an alternate for '**base**, **foundation**.'

Special Expressions

המוֹסָד the Israeli CIA/secret service

מוֹלַד הירח/הלבנה **new** moon

Additional Examples in this Pattern

מוֹלָד (birth of the) new moon
מוֹרָד slope, hillside
מוֹתָר advantage; extra

---

464. *muCaC*

our/your/their	my/your/his/her	const.	Gloss	sing/pl
מוּסַכֵּנוּ/כְּכֶם/כְּכֶן/כָּם/כָּן	**מוּסַ**כִּי/כְּךָ/כֵּךְ/כּוֹ/כָּהּ	מוּסַךְ-	garage;	מוּסַךְ ז'
מוּסַכֵּינוּ/כֶם/כֶן/הֶם/הֶן	**מוּסַ**כַּי/כֶּיךָ/כַּיִךְ/כָּיו/כֶּיהָ	מוּסַכֵּי-	hangar	מוּסַכִּים

The base form is *musak*, but at the end of the word: *musakh*; in speech the form is realized with *kh* only: *musakhim* rather than *musakim*, etc., for paradigm uniformity.

Examples

אני יכול לנסוע איתך לעבודה? המכונית שלי **במוּסָךְ**.
Can I get a ride with you to work? My car is the **garage**.

---

465. ***meyCaC***

our/your/their	my/your/his/her	const.	Gloss	sing/pl
מֵיתָרֵנוּ/**מֵיתַרְ**כֶם/כֶן/**מֵיתָרָ**ם/ן	**מֵיתָרִ**י/רְךָ/רֵךְ/רוֹ/רָהּ	מֵיתַר-	string	מֵיתָר ז'
מֵיתָרֵינוּ/**מֵיתְרֵי**כֶם/כֶן/הֶם/הֶן	**מֵיתָרַ**י/רֶיךָ/רַיִךְ/רָיו/רֶיהָ	מֵיתְרֵי-		מֵיתָרִים

Most realizations in this *mishkal* are related to roots the first radical of which is *y*. The *kamats* is reduced to zero two syllables before the main stress, and in the construct state of the plural form: מֵיתְרֵיכֶם etc., מֵיתְרֵי-.

Examples

הרבה מופתעים לשמוע שהפסנתר הוא כלי **מֵיתָר**...
Many are surprised to hear that the piano is a **string** instrument...

העברת **מֵידָע** חסוי למדינה זרה נחשבת לעבירה לחמורה, אפילו לבגידה.
Transferring confidential **information** to a foreign state is regarded as a serious felony, even as an act of treason.

Special Expressions

to the **best** of my knowledge **לְמֵיטַב** ידיעתי

vocal **cords** **מֵיתְרֵי** הקול

Additional Examples in this Pattern

project, initiative מֵיזָם
sweater, sweatshirt מֵיזָע
utmost, best מֵיטָב
installation (art) מֵיצָב
performance, display מֵיצָג
screw anchor מֵיתָד

---

466. ***meCiCa***

our/your/their	my/your/his/her	const.	Gloss	sing/pl
מְסִבָּתֵנוּ/**מְסִבַּתְ**כֶם/כֶן/**מְסִבָּתָ**ם/ן	**מְסִבָּ**תִי/תְךָ/תֵךְ/תוֹ/תָהּ	מְסִבַּת-	party	מְסִבָּה נ'
מְסִבּוֹתֵינוּ/כֶם/כֶן/הֶם/הֶן	**מְסִבּוֹ**תַי/תֶיךָ/תַיִךְ/תָיו/תֶיהָ	מְסִבּוֹת-		מְסִבּוֹת

Most realizations in this *mishkal* are related to roots in which the second and third radical are identical. The two identical consonants merge into a single geminate consonant.

Examples

כאשר מתכננים **מְסִבָּה** לכבוד מישהו לרגל אירוע מיוחד, כמו יום הולדת ״עגול״, **מְסִבָּה** כזו היא מוצלחת במיוחד כאשר היא הפתעה מוחלטת ל״חתן השמחה״.
When one plans a **party** for someone on special occasions, like a "round birthday," such **party** is particularly successful when it is a complete surprise for the person in whose honor it is prepared.

לאחרונה התגלתה **מְגִלָּה** נוספת במדבר יהודה ליד חוף ים המלח.
Lately an additional **scroll** was discovered in the Judean Desert next to Dead Sea shore.

צריך להיזהר מאוד כשחוצים **מְסִלַּת** ברזל ברכב בהצטלבות שאין בה מחסום.
One needs to be very careful when crossing **railroad tracks** in an intersection without a barrier.

Special Expressions

the Dead Sea **scrolls** **הַמְּגִלּוֹת** הגנוזות
five **books in the Bible** read in the synagogue on holidays חמש **מְגִלּוֹת**
the **Book of Esther** **הַמְּגִלָּה**
an excuse to **celebrate** Coll. סיבה ל**מְסִבָּה**
railroad **tracks** **מְסִלַּת** ברזל

Additional Examples in this Pattern

plot, conspiracy מְזִמָּה
burrow, tunnel מְחִלָּה
partition מְחִצָּה
shard Lit. מְכִתָּה
railroad track; track; orbit מְסִלָּה
small bell; cymbal מְצִלָּה

---

467. ***meCaC***

our/your/their	my/your/his/her	const.	Gloss	sing/pl
מְמַדֵּנוּ/**מְמַדְּ**כֶם/כֶן/**מְמַדָּ**ם/ן	**מְמַדִּ**י/דְּךָ/דֵּךְ/דּוֹ/דָּהּ	מֵמַד-	dimension	מֵמַד ז׳
מְמַדֵּינוּ/כֶם/כֶן/הֶם/הֶן	**מְמַדַּ**י/דֶּיךָ/דַּיִךְ/דָּיו/דֶּיהָ	מְמַדֵּי-		מְמַדִּים

Most realizations in this *mishkal* are related to roots in which the second and third radical are identical. The two identical consonants merge into a single geminate consonant. The *tsere* is reduced to shva two syllables before the main stress.

Examples

למעצבי פנים קל הרבה יותר היום להציג את תוכניותיהם מכיוון שהם יכולים להראותם ללקוחותיהם בשלושה **מְמַדִּים**.
It is easier for interior designers today to display their plans since they can demonstrate them to their clients in three **dimensions**.

Special Expressions

the fourth **dimension** (time) **הַמֵּמַד** הרביעי

Additional Examples in this Pattern

samovar מֵחַם	strait; isthmus מֵצַר
bearing (mechanics) מֵסַב	maximum מֵרַב

---

468. *maCeC*

our/your/their	my/your/his/her	const.	Gloss	sing/pl
מַגְּבֵנוּ/**מַגֶּבְ**כֶם/כֶן/**מַגְּבָ**ם/ן	מַגְּבִי/מַגֶּבְךָ/**מַגְּבֵ**ךְ/בוֹ/בָהּ	מַגֵּב-	wiper	מַגֵּב ז׳
מַגְּבֵינוּ/כֶם/כֶן/הֶם/הֶן	**מַגְּבַ**י/בֶיךָ/בַיִךְ/בָיו/בֶיהָ	מַגְּבֵי-		מַגְּבִים

Result of the assimilation of a root-initial *n* (in this case *n-g-b* 'wipe'); thus the *dagesh forte* throughout the declension. Similar assimilation occurs with root-initial *yts*, as in מַצֵּת 'spark plug' (< *y-ts-t*). This is probably a development of the *maCCeC* pattern below (generally for instruments). With stress shift, the *tsere* is reduced to *shva*, or to *seghol* in a closed syllable.

Examples

כשהגשם הוא בעצם טפטוף קל, אני מעדיף להשתמש במנגנון ההשהיה של ה**מַגֵּב**.
When the rain is actually a drizzle, I prefer to use the intermittent function of the **windshield wiper**.

---

469. *maCeC* pl. -ot

our/your/their	my/your/his/her	const.	Gloss	sing/pl
מַקְלֵנוּ/**מַקֶּלְ**כֶם/כֶן/**מַקְּלָ**ם/ן	מַקְּלִי/מַקֶּלְךָ/**מַקְּלֵ**ךְ/לוֹ/לָהּ	מַקֵּל-	stick	מַקֵּל ז׳
מַקְּלוֹתֵינוּ/כֶם/כֶן/הֶם/הֶן	**מַקְּלוֹ**תַי/תֶיךָ/תַיִךְ/תָיו/תֶיהָ	מַקְּלוֹת-		מַקְּלוֹת

It is not clear that this *m* is indeed a prefix here. The **dagesh forte** is maintained throughout the declension (in earlier vocalization traditions, the *shva* was considered quiescent, and the *dagesh forte* was dropped, e.g., מַקְלוֹת).

Examples

מנחם הולך עם **מַקֵּל** שהוא מטייל, כדי להבריח כלבים.
Menahem uses a **cane** when he walks in order to drive away dogs.

Special Expressions

cudgel, bat **מַקֵּל** חובלים	the **stick** and carrot שיטת ה**מַקֵּל** והגזר method of punishment/reward
educating with a gentle hand **מַקֵּל** נועם	
with all his (meager) possessions **בְּמַקְלוֹ** ובתרמילו	

---

470. *maCeCa*

our/your/their	my/your/his/her	const.	Gloss	sing/pl
מַגֵּפָתֵנוּ/**מַגֵּפַתְ**כֶם/כֶן/**מַגֵּפָתָ**ם/ן	**מַגֵּפָ**תִי/תְךָ/תֵךְ/תוֹ/תָהּ	מַגֵּפַת-	epidemic;	מַגֵּפָה נ׳
מַגֵּפוֹתֵינוּ/כֶם/כֶן/הֶם/הֶן	**מַגֵּפוֹ**תַי/תֶיךָ/תַיִךְ/תָיו/תֶיהָ	מַגֵּפוֹת-	plague	מַגֵּפוֹת

The gemination reflects the assimilation of a root-initial נ׳, or י׳ followed by צ׳, and it is maintained throughout the declension. Probably a development of *maCCeCa* below.

Examples

אחת ה**מַגֵּפוֹת** שהעולם כולו חושש ממנה בעת האחרונה היא **מַגֵּפַת** נגיף הקורונה.
One of the most feared **epidemics** that the whole world has been worried about lately is the Covid-19 **pandemic**.

בישראל נוהגים לגלות **מַצֵּבָה** חודש לאחר פטירתו של אדם או ביום השנה לפטירה.
In Israel they unveil a **tombstone** either a month after one passes, or on the first year anniversary.

Special Expressions

the Black **Plague** **הַמַּגֵּפָה** השחורה

oxygen **mask** **מַסֵּכַת** חמצן

Additional Examples in this Pattern

mask; disguise מַסֵּכָה

---

471. *maCaCa*

our/your/their	my/your/his/her	const.	Gloss	sing/pl
מַתְּנָתֵנוּ/**מַתְּנַתְ**כֶם/כֶן/**מַתְּנָתָ**ם/ן	**מַתְּנָ**תִי/תְךָ/תֵךְ/תוֹ/תָהּ	מַתְּנַת-	gift	מַתָּנָה נ׳
מַתְּנוֹתֵינוּ/כֶם/כֶן/הֶם/הֶן	**מַתְּנוֹ**תַי/תֶיךָ/תַיִךְ/תָיו/תֶיהָ	מַתְּנוֹת-		מַתָּנוֹת

The gemination reflects the assimilation of a root-initial נ׳, or י׳ followed by צ׳, and it is maintained throughout the declension. Two syllables away from the main stress and in the construct state the *kamats* is reduced to a zero *shva*, and > *pataH* in a closed syll.

Examples

מַטְּרָתוֹ של בנימין היא להמשיך לכהן כראש ממשלה עד גיל 110 לפחות.
Benjamin's **goal** is to continue to serve as prime minister at least until the age of 110.

Special Expressions

It is better (and safer?) not to accept **gifts** שונא **מַתָּנוֹת** יחיה

Additional Examples in this Pattern

task, assignment מַטָּלָה

purpose, goal; target מַטָּרָה

workforce; (military) strength; inventory מַצָּבָה

---

472. *maCaCa* segholate-like decl.

our/your/their	my/your/his/her	const.	Gloss	sing/pl
מַפַּלְתֵּנוּ/תְּכֶם/תְּכֶן/תָּם/ן	**מַפַּלְ**תִּי/תְּךָ/תֵּךְ/תּוֹ/תָּהּ	מַפֶּלֶת-	defeat,	מַפָּלָה נ׳
מַפְּלוֹתֵינוּ/כֶם/כֶן/הֶם/הֶן	**מַפְּלוֹ**תַי/תֶיךָ/תַיִךְ/תָיו/תֶיהָ	מַפְּלוֹת-	downfall	מַפָּלוֹת

In the single case included here, the *dagesh* results from the assimilation of a root-initial *n* (*n-p-l* 'fall'.) The construct state (-מַפֶּלֶת) is penultimately stressed, like the segholate nouns. The *kamats* is reduced to *shva*, or > *pataH* in a closed syllable: **מַפַּלְ**תִּי etc.

Examples

כאשר מנהיג פוליטי נתפס ומורשע בעבירות שחיתות, **מַפַּלְתּוֹ** היא אדירה ומוחלטת, אלא אם כן...
When a political leader is caught and convicted on corruption charges, his **downfall** is huge and complete – unless…

---

473. *moCa*

our/your/their	my/your/his/her	const.	Gloss	sing/pl
מוֹצָאֵנוּ/**מוֹצָאֲ**כֶם/כֶן/**מוֹצָאָ**ם/ן	**מוֹצָאִ**י/אֲךָ/אֵךְ/אוֹ/אָהּ	מוֹצָא-	outlet;	מוֹצָא ז׳
מוֹצָאֵינוּ/כֶם/כֶן/הֶם/הֶן	**מוֹצָאַ**י/אֶיךָ/אַיִךְ/אָיו/אֶיהָ	מוֹצָאֵי-	origin	מוֹצָאִים

Forms in this pattern are derived from roots with an initial *yod* and a final *'alef*. The *yod* is realized as וֹ, and the *'alef* is muted at the end of the word. When a *shva* is expected with the *'alef*, it is replaced by *Hataf-pataH*: מוֹצָאֲכֶם. Note some differences with מוֹפָע above.

Examples

המשבר במזרח התיכון נמשך שנים רבות, ורבים חושבים שאין **מוֹצָא** מן המצב הזה.
The crisis in the Middle East has been continuing for many years, and many think that there is no **way out** of this situation.

לירושלים איו **מוֹצָא** אל הַיָּם.
Jerusalem has no **access** to the sea.

ספרו החשוב של דרווין נקרא "**מוֹצָא** המינים".
Darwin's important book is called "The **origin** of the Species".

Special Expressions

word, utterance **מוֹצָא** פה/שפתיים　　Saturday evening **מוֹצָאֵי** שבת

Additional Examples in this Pattern

fear מוֹרָא

---

474. *moCaCa*

our/your/their	my/your/his/her	const.	Gloss	sing/pl
מוֹשַׁבְתֵּנוּ/תְּכֶם/תְּכֶן/תָּם/תָּן	**מוֹשַׁבְ**תִּי/תְּךָ/תֵּךְ/תּוֹ/תָּהּ	מוֹשֶׁבֶת-	farming	מוֹשָׁבָה נ׳
מוֹשְׁבוֹתֵינוּ/כֶם/כֶן/הֶם/הֶן	**מוֹשְׁבוֹ**תַי/תֶיךָ/תַיִךְ/תָיו/תֶיהָ	מוֹשְׁבוֹת-	community	מוֹשָׁבוֹת

Forms in this pattern are derived from roots with an initial *yod*; the *yod* is realized as וֹ. A *kamats* is reduced to *shva* two syllables away from the main stress, מוֹשְׁבוֹתַי, and if its reduction would have resulted in an unacceptable a sequence of two *shva* mobiles, its first *shva* is realized as *pataH* in a closed syllable: מוֹשַׁבְתִּי. The constr. sing. is penultimately stressed as in the segholates.

Examples

המוֹשָׁבָה הראשונה בארץ ישראל הייתה פתח תקווה, ולכן היא קרויה גם אֵם **המוֹשָׁבוֹת**.
The first Jewish ***moshava*** settlement in Palestine was PetaH Tikva, which why it is also called the "mother of all ***moshavot***".

Special Expressions

the **heritage/inheritance** of our (fore)fathers **מוֹרֶשֶׁת** אבות

Additional Examples in this Pattern

heritage, legacy מוֹרָשָׁה

---

475. *moCaCa* when the 2nd root consonant is guttural

our/your/their	my/your/his/her	const.	Gloss	sing/pl
מוֹעַצְתֵּנוּ/תְּכֶם/תְּכֶן/תָּם/תָּן	**מוֹעַצְ**תִּי/תְּךָ/תֵּךְ/תּוֹ/תָּהּ	מוֹעֶצֶת-	council	מוֹעָצָה נ׳
מוֹעֲצוֹתֵינוּ/כֶם/כֶן/הֶם/הֶן	**מוֹעֲצוֹ**תַי/תֶיךָ/תַיִךְ/תָיו/תֶיהָ	מוֹעֲצוֹת-		מוֹעָצוֹת

Forms in this pattern are derived from roots with an initial *yod*; the *yod* is realized as וֹ. A *kamats* becomes *pataH* in a closed syllable two syllables away from the main stress: מוֹעַצְתִּי etc. When a *shva* is expected, it is replaced by a *Hataf-pataH*: מוֹעֲצוֹת-. The constr. sing. is segholate.

Examples

בישובים רבים בארץ ל**מוֹעֲצוֹת** הפועלים יש תפקיד חשוב בהפצת תרבות לעם.
In many settlements/towns in Israel the workers' **councils** have an important role in disseminating culture to the people.

Special Expressions

the (UN) security **council** **מוֹעֶצֶת** הביטחון
board of directors **מוֹעֶצֶת** מנהלים
the Soviet Union ברית **המוֹעָצוֹת**

regional **council** **מוֹעָצָה** אזורית
legislative **council** **מוֹעָצָה** מחוקקת
local **council** **מוֹעָצָה** מקומית

---

476. ***moCaCa*** when the third root consonant is guttural

our/your/their	my/your/his/her	const.	Gloss	sing/pl
מוֹדַעְתֵּנוּ/תְּכֶם/תְּכֶן/תָּם/תָּן	**מוֹדַעְ**תִּי/תְּךָ/תֵּךְ/תּוֹ/תָּהּ	מוֹדַעַת-	notice	מוֹדָעָה נ'
מוֹדְעוֹתֵינוּ/כֶם/כֶן/הֶם/הֶן	**מוֹדְעוֹ**תַי/תֶיךָ/תַיִךְ/תָיו/תֶיהָ	מוֹדְעוֹת-		מוֹדָעוֹת

Forms in this pattern are derived from roots with an initial *yod*; the *yod* is realized as וֹ. A *kamats* becomes *pataH* in a closed syllable two syllables away from the main stress: מוֹדַעְתִּי. Because of the guttural, the construct state (sing.) is with two *pataHs* rather than with two *seghols*: מוֹדַעַת-. Following the tradition, the quiescent (zero) *shva* is maintained with the ע', but not with א', thus מוֹרָאֲתִי etc.

Examples

כשהייתי ילד, מידע על סרטים בבתי הקולנוע נמצא כמעט בלעדית על לוחות **מוֹדָעוֹת**.
When I was a child, information regarding shows in movie theatres was available almost exclusively on **bulletin/advertising** boards.

Special Expressions

notice announcing the death/funeral of a departed person **מוֹדַעַת** אֵבֶל

Additional Examples in this Pattern

fear Lit. מוֹרָאָה

---

477. ***maCoC***

our/your/their	my/your/his/her	const.	Gloss	sing/pl
מְטוֹסֵנוּ/סְכֶם/סְכֶן/סָם/סָן	**מְטוֹ**סִי/סְךָ/סֵךְ/סוֹ/סָהּ	מְטוֹס-	airplane	מָטוֹס ז'
מְטוֹסֵינוּ/כֶם/כֶן/הֶם/הֶן	**מְטוֹ**סַי/סֶיךָ/סַיִךְ/סָיו/סֶיהָ	מְטוֹסֵי-		מְטוֹסִים

Most nouns in this pattern are related to "hollow" roots with a middle *w* (or *y*); they can refer to instruments, locations, abstract nouns… The *kamats* is reduced two syllables before the main stress (constr. sing. included).

Examples

לחברת "אל על" אין הרבה **מְטוֹסִים**, אבל הם משתמשים בהם ברציפות, כך שנראה כאילו זו חברת תעופה עצומה...
El Al does not have that many **planes**, but it uses them continuously, so that it looks as if it were a huge airline company…

באוניברסיטה שלימדתי בה עיצבו **מָבוֹךְ** מגדר חייה להנאתם של הסטודנטים ושל ילדי העובדים.
At the university in which I taught they designed a hedgerow **maze** to the delight of students and children of the employees.

היום, כשהכל משתמשים במקרן נתונים, **מְטוֹל** השקפים עבר ובטל מן העולם.
Today, when everybody uses data projectors, the overhead **projector** is obsolete.

מְכוֹן וייצמן למדע ברחובות הוא אחד ממוסדות המחקר הבולטים בעולם.
The Weizmann **Institute** in Rehovot (Israel) is one of the most prominent research institutions in the world.

לפני כמה שנים נפל במנהטן **מָנוֹף** ענק ומספר אנשים נהרגו.
A few years ago a giant **crane** fell and a number of people were killed.

Special Expressions

jet **airplane** **מְטוֹס** סילון
drone **מְטוֹס** זעיר ללא טייס (מזל״ט) (small plane without a pilot)
missle **launcher** **מְטוֹל** רקטות
research **institute** **מְכוֹן** מחקר
fitness **club** **מְכוֹן** כושר
there is no other way ...אין **מָנוֹס** מ
irresistible pressure **מָנוֹף** לחץ

Additional Examples in this Pattern

sprint N מָאוֹץ
contention, quarrel Lit. מָדוֹן
reactor (electricity) מָגוֹב
valve; tap מָגוֹף
fear, terror Lit. מָגוֹר
resonator מָהוֹד
cure, medicine מָזוֹר
hand (on clock) מָחוֹג
antenna, feeler, tentacle מָחוֹשׁ
overhead projector; missile launcher מָטוֹל
swab מָטוֹשׁ
escape מָנוֹס
weaver's beam מָנוֹר
terminal מָסוֹף
chase מָצוֹד

---

478. ***maCoC*** pl. *-ot* - also mostly from roots with a middle *w* (or *y*)

our/your/their	my/your/his/her	const.	Gloss	sing/pl
מְאוֹרֵנוּ/רְכֶם/רְכֶן/רָם/רָן	**מְאוֹ**רִי/רְךָ/רֵךְ/רוֹ/רָהּ	מְאוֹר-	light; luminary;	מָאוֹר ז'
מְאוֹרוֹתֵינוּ/כֶם/כֶן/הֶם/הֶן	**מְאוֹרוֹ**תַי/תֶיךָ/תַיִךְ/תָיו/תֶיהָ	מְאוֹרוֹת-	sun/moon Lit.	מְאוֹרוֹת

Examples

הבית הזה מלא **מָאוֹר**, תרתי משמע: יש בו אור רב, ובעליו מסבירי פנים.
This house is full of **light**, in two senses: it is full of light, and the owners are very welcoming (see *Special Expressions* below).

הביטוי ״ליקוי **מְאוֹרוֹת**״ מתייחס גם לשמש וגם לירח.
The expression "eclipse" refers to the moon as well as to the sun.

לעיתים, ה**מָבוֹא** לספר חשוב לא פחות מן הספר עצמו.
Sometimes, a book's **preface** is not less important than the book proper.

בעלי חיים הנמצאים בסביבה אחת מקיימים ביניהם אינטראקציות רבות, ניזונים מתפריט מגוון, ומהווים **מָזוֹן** להרבה יצורים חיים אחרים – ובכך מהווים מארג של מספר שרשרות **מָזוֹן** בסביבה כלשהי.
Animals located in one environment maintain many interactions, feed on various foods, and themselves constitute **food** for other animals – and thus form a net of a number of **food** chains in a particular environment.

חדר **במָלון** בתל-אביב או בירושלים יקר כמעט כמו כמו חדר מקביל בניו יורק.
A **hotel** room in Tel Aviv or in Jerusalem is almost as expensive as a similar room in New York City.

מגורים **במְעוֹנוֹת** הסטודנטים הם חלק חיוני מחוויית הלימודים לתואר הראשון.
Living in student **dorms** is an essential part of the undergraduate experience.

Special Expressions

sun **המָאוֹר** הגדול
moon **המָאוֹר** הקטן
hospitality, welcome **מְאוֹר** פנים
eyesight; smiling face, fine welcome; blind man (euphemism) **מְאוֹר** עיניים
light of the diaspora (title given to rabbis in the Middle Ages) **מְאוֹר** הגולה
the entrances to the city **מְבוֹאוֹת** העיר
royal jelly (bee queen **food**) **מְזוֹן** מלכות
aerobics **מָחוֹל** אירובי
witch-hunt **מְחוֹל** שֵׁדים
address, dwelling **place** **מְקוֹם** מגורים
public **place** **מָקוֹם** ציבורי
reserved seat **מָקוֹם** שמור

Additional Examples in this Pattern

dance מָחוֹל
source, origin; spring מָקוֹר
place; space; spot, position; seat מָקוֹם

---

479. ***meCoCa***

sing/pl	Gloss	const.	my/your/his/her	our/your/their
מְנוֹרָה נ׳	light	מְנוֹרַת-	**מְנוֹרָ**תִי/תְךָ/תֵךְ/תוֹ/תָהּ	מְנוֹרָתֵנוּ/**מְנוֹרַתְ**כֶם/כֶן/**מְנוֹרָתָ**ם/ן
מְנוֹרוֹת	fixture	מְנוֹרוֹת-	**מְנוֹרוֹ**תַי/תֶיךָ/תַיִךְ/תָיו/תֶיהָ	**מְנוֹרוֹתֵ**ינוּ/כֶם/כֶן/הֶם/הֶן

Examples

המְנוֹרוֹת היפות ביותר מיוצרות באיטליה.
The most beautiful **lamps/chandeliers** are manufactured in Italy.

השטיח הזה נארג ביד; הוא לא עבודת **מְכוֹנָה**.
This rug was woven by hand; it is not **machine**-made.

Special Expressions

deliberate thoroughly Lit. ישב על **המְדוֹכָה**
typewriter **מְכוֹנַת** כתיבה
light socket בית **מְנוֹרָה**
ultra-violet **lamp** **מְנוֹרָה** כחולה

Additional Examples in this Pattern

mortar; seat; canister launcher מְדוֹכָה
homeland, native land Lit. מְכוֹרָה

---

480. *meCuCa*

our/your/their	my/your/his/her	const.	Gloss	sing/pl
מְצוּדָתֵנוּ/מְצוּדַתְכֶם/כֶן/מְצוּדָתָם/ן	מְצוּדָתִי/תְךָ/תֵךְ/תוֹ/תָהּ	מְצוּדַת-	fortress,	מְצוּדָה נ׳
מְצוּדוֹתֵינוּ/כֶם/כֶן/הֶם/הֶן	מְצוּדוֹתַי/תֶיךָ/תַיִךְ/תָיו/תֶיהָ	מְצוּדוֹת-	citadel	מְצוּדוֹת

Most nouns in this pattern are related to "hollow" roots with a middle *w* (or *y*).

Examples

המבנה הקרוי **מְצוּדַת** דויד הוא סימן הכר מובהק של ירושלים.
The building called David's **Citadel** is a known marker of Jerusalem, known to all.

דובים שקועים בתרדמת חורף ב**מְאוּרָתָם** בחודשים הקרים של השנה.
Bears hibernate in their **den** during the cold months of the year.

יש פוליטיקאים ש"מצפצפים" על דעת הקהל ועל התקשורת, וחושבים שלעולם אינם טועים; אף פעם אי אפשר לראותם במצב של **מְבוּכָה**.
Some politicians don't "give a damn" about public opinion or the media, and believe that they are never wrong. You can never catch then in an **embarrassment** situation.

כשהיינו ילדים היינו בונים ומדליקים **מְדוּרוֹת** ענק כל שנה בל"ג בעומר.
As kids we would build up and kindle huge **bonfires** every year on Lag Ba`Omer.

מהפכות בדרך כלל הן תוצאה של **מְצוּקָה** כלכלית הפוגעת קשות בשכבות החלשות, וה**מְהוּמוֹת** הפורצות בעקבותיה.
Revolutions are usually the result of economic **distress** that mostly affect the lower classes, and the **riots** that follow.

Special Expressions

מְאוּרַת נחשים snake pit

הוסיף שמן ל**מְדוּרָה** add fuel to the **fire** (aggravate a situation)

רוב **מְהוּמָה** על לא **מאומה** much **ado** about **nothing**

מְנוּחַת עולמים eternal **rest**, burial

Additional Examples in this Pattern

anything, nothing Lit. מְאוּמָה
plug, cork, stopper מְגוּפָה
(shipping) compartment מְגוּרָה
commotion; riot מְהוּמָה
mezuzah; doorpost מְזוּזָה
pair of compasses מְחוּגָה

shipping container מְכוּלָה
kennel, doghouse מְלוּנָה
rest N מְנוּחָה
flight מְנוּסָה
deep water מְצוּלָה
running מְרוּצָה

---

481. *meCiCa*

Our/your/their	my/your/his/her	const.	Gloss	sing/pl
מְדִינָתֵנוּ/מְדִינַתְכֶם/כֶן/מְדִינָתָם/ן	מְדִינָתִי/תְךָ/תֵךְ/תוֹ/תָהּ	מְדִינַת-	state, nation	מְדִינָה נ׳
מְדִינוֹתֵינוּ/כֶם/כֶן/הֶם/הֶן	מְדִינוֹתַי/תֶיךָ/תַיִךְ/תָיו/תֶיהָ	מְדִינוֹת-		מְדִינוֹת

Nouns in this pattern are related to “hollow” roots with a middle *w* (or *y*).

Examples

בארה״ב תושבים לא מעטים הם אזרחי שתי **מְדִינוֹת**, למשל ארה״ב וישראל.
In the US, a good number of residents are citizens of two **states**, e.g., the US and Israel.

כדי להגדיל את סיכוייהם להתקבל לאוניברסיטה טובה, לא מעט תלמידים נרשמים ל**מְכִינָה** קְדַם-אוניברסיטאית.
To increase their chances of being admitted into a good university, a good number of students enroll in a pre-academic **preparatory program**.

בזמנו, **מְרִיבוֹת** אידיאולוגיות בקרב מפלגות השמאל בישראל גרמו להתפלגויות, גם בתוך הקיבוצים.
At the time, ideological **disputes** within the socialist parties in Israel caused splits, even within the kibbutzim.

ה**מְשִׂימָה** שהוטלה על הגדוד הייתה להגיע לגשר בלילה ולפוצץ אותו.
The **task** assigned to the battalion was to reach the bridge at night and blow it up.

Special Expressions

trouble affecting everybody מכת **מְדִינָה** welfare state **מְדִינַת** סעד/רווחה

Additional Examples in this Pattern

wheelbarrow מְרִיצָה hand-held fan מְנִיפָה flowery phrase מְלִיצָה

---

482. *miCCoC*

our/your/their	my/your/his/her	const.	Gloss	sing/pl
מִכְשׁוֹלֵנוּ/לְכֶם/לְכֶן/לָם/לָן	**מִכְשׁוֹ**לִי/לְךָ/לֵךְ/לוֹ/לָהּ	מִכְשׁוֹל-	obstacle,	מִכְשׁוֹל ז׳
מִכְשׁוֹלֵינוּ/כֶם/כֶן/הֶם/הֶן	**מִכְשׁוֹ**לַי/לֶיךָ/לַיִךְ/לָיו/לֶיהָ	מִכְשׁוֹלֵי-	impediment	מִכְשׁוֹלִים

Examples

כולם מקווים כי למרות כל ה**מִכְשׁוֹלִים**, יימצא בסופו של דבר פתרון לסכסוך במזה״ת.
Everyone is hoping that in spite of all the **obstacles**, a solution will eventually be found to the conflict in the Middle East.

כשבונים בית ב**מִדְרוֹן** ההר, הסכנה היא של מפולת בוץ כאשר יורדים גשמים חזקים.
When one builds a house of a mountain **slope**, the danger is a mudslide in case of heavy rain.

האוכל ב**מִזְנוֹן** הכנסת אינו טוב במיוחד, אבל הוא מהווה מקום מפלט לחברי כנסת עייפים.
The food in the Knesset **cafetria** is not that good, but it provides a refuge for weary Knesset members.

Special Expressions

dry **dock** (shipping) **מִבְדּוֹק** יבש

surmount the **obstacles** להתגבר על ה**מִכְשׁוֹלִים**

obstacle course מסלול **מִכְשׁוֹלִים**

do not mislead the ignorant (lit. put no **obstacle** in the way of the blind) לפני עיוור לא תיתֵן **מִכְשׁוֹל**

Additional Examples in this Pattern

shipyard מִבְדּוֹק

slope, gradient מִדְרוֹן

psalm; song מִזְמוֹר

mattress (Coll.; normative מִזְרָן) מִזְרוֹן

paintbrush מִכְחוֹל

whole N מִכְלוֹל

hiding place מִסְתּוֹר

stockpile מִצְבּוֹר

tone (music) מִצְלוֹל

mountain viewpoint מִצְפּוֹר

path Lit. מִשְׁעוֹל

escarpment מִתְלוֹל

---

483. ***miCCoC*** when the last C is *'alef*

our/your/their	my/your/his/her	const.	Gloss	sing/pl
מִכְלוֹאֵנוּ/אֲכֶם/אֲכֶן/אָםע	**מִכְלוֹ**אִי/אֲךָ/אֵךְ/אוֹ/אָהּ	-מִכְלוֹא	hybrid	מִכְלוֹא ז׳
מִכְלוֹאֵינוּ/כֶם/כֶן/הֶם/הֶן	**מִכְלוֹ**אַי/אֶיךָ/אַיִךְ/אָיו/אֶיהָ	מִכְלוֹאֵי		מִכְלוֹאִים

When a *shva* is expected with *'alef*, it is replaced by a *Hataf-pataH.*

Additional Examples in this Pattern

animal feed מִסְפּוֹא

---

484. ***miCCoC*** = ***maCaCoC*** when the first C is *he* or *`áyin*

our/your/their	my/your/his/her	const.	Gloss	sing/pl
מַעֲצוֹרֵנוּ/רְכֶם/רְכֶן/רָם/רָן	**מַעֲצוֹ**רִי/רְךָ/רֵךְ/רוֹ/רָהּ	-מַעֲצוֹר	mental block;	מַעֲצוֹר ז׳
מַעֲצוֹרֵינוּ/כֶם/כֶן/הֶם/הֶן	**מַעֲצוֹ**רַי/רֶיךָ/רַיִךְ/רָיו/רֶיהָ	-מַעֲצוֹרֵי	brake(s)	מַעֲצוֹרִים

When a *shva* is expected with *he* or *`ayin*, it is replaced by a *Hataf-pataH*. The *Hirik* of the prefix *mi-* preceding *he* or *`ayin* is replaced by *pataH*; it is an assimilation intended to facilitate articulation of two different consecutive vowels.

Examples

יש אנשים, שכאשר הם כותבים בדוא״ל או ״מצייצים״, הם מאבדים את כל ה**מַעֲצוֹרִים** שהם מציבים לעצמם בדיבור.

Some people, when the use email or "tweet," lose all **inhibitions** they place on themselves when they speak.

Special Expressions

brakes **מַעֲצוֹרִים** = בלמים

air **brakes** **מַעֲצוֹרֵי** אוויר

Additional Examples in this Pattern

rolling pin מַעֲרוֹךְ electric shocker מַהֲלוֹם

---

485. ***miCCoC = maCCoC*** when the first *C* is *Het*

our/your/their	my/your/his/her	const.	gloss	sing/pl
מַחְסוֹמֵנוּ/מְכֶם/מְכֶן/מָם/מָן	**מַחְסוֹ**מִי/מְךָ/מֵךְ/מוֹ/מָהּ	מַחְסוֹם-	barrier;	מַחְסוֹם ז׳
מַחְסוֹמֵינוּ/כֶם/כֶן/הֶם/הֶן	**מַחְסוֹ**מַי/מֶיךָ/מַיִךְ/מָיו/מֶיהָ	מַחְסוֹמֵי-	obstacle	מַחְסוֹמִים

The *Hirik* preceding the *Het* is replaced by a *pataH*. A low vowel is easier to articulate before a low consonant.

Examples

הַמַּחְסוֹמִים המווסתים את התנועה בין ישראל והגדה המערבית או עזה הפכו עם הזמן לסמל של כיבוש, אך יש לזכור שקיומם הוא הכרחי.
The **barriers** (here: checkpoints) between Israel and the west Bank or Gaza have become symbols of occupation, but one needs to remember that they are inevitable.

בעת האחרונה גבר בישראל **הַמַּחְסוֹר** במיטות בבתי החולים.
Lately, the **shortage** of beds in the Israeli hospitals has increased.

Additional Examples in this Pattern

cleavage מַחְשׂוֹף incarceration (military) מַחְבּוֹשׁ

---

486. ***miCCoC = maCCo(C)*** when the first C is *Het* and the last is *'álef*

our/your/their	my/your/his/her	const.	Gloss	sing/pl
מַחְבּוֹאֵנוּ/אֲכֶם/אֲכֶן/אָם/אָן	**מַחְבּוֹ**אִי/אֲךָ/אֵךְ/אוֹ/אָהּ	מַחְבּוֹא-	hiding	מַחְבּוֹא ז׳
מַחְבּוֹאֵינוּ/כֶם/כֶן/הֶם/הֶן	**מַחְבּוֹאַ**י/אֶיךָ/אַיִךְ/אָיו/אֶיהָ	מַחְבּוֹאֵי-	place	מַחְבּוֹאִים

The *Hirik* preceding the *Het* is replaced by a *pataH*, and the *shva* expected with the *'álef* is replaced by a *Hataf-pataH.*

Examples

מַחְבּוֹאֵי הנשק של ה״הגנה״ בתקופת המנדט הבריטי בארץ ישראל נקראו ״סְלִיקִים״.
The weapon **caches** of the Haganah during the British mandatory rule of Palestine were referred to as "slicks."

---

487. ***miCCoC*** when the last consonant is guttural

our/your/their	my/your/his/her	const.	Gloss	sing/pl
מִשְׁלוֹחֵנוּ/חֲכֶם/חֲכֶן/חָם/חָן	**מִשְׁלוֹ**חִי/חֲךָ/חֵךְ/חוֹ/חָהּ	מִשְׁלוֹחַ-	delivery,	מִשְׁלוֹחַ ז׳
מִשְׁלוֹחֵינוּ/כֶם/כֶן/הֶם/הֶן	**מִשְׁלוֹ**חַי/חֶיךָ/חַיִךְ/חָיו/חֶיהָ	מִשְׁלוֹחֵי-	shipment	מִשְׁלוֹחִים

A "furtive" *pataH* is inserted before a word-final guttural when preceded by a non-low vowel, and the *shva* expected with the guttural is replaced by a *Hataf-pataH.*

Examples

אנשים רבים מעדיפים היום לשלם עבור **מִשְׁלוֹחֵי** מזון לביתם.
Many people today prefer to pay for food **deliveries** to their home.

---

488. *maCCoC*

our/your/their	my/your/his/her	const.	Gloss	sing/pl
מַתְכּוֹנֵנוּ/נְכֶם/נְכֶן/נָם/נָן	**מַתְכּוֹ**נִי/נְךָ/נֵךְ/נוֹ/נָהּ	מַתְכּוֹן-	recipe	מַתְכּוֹן ז׳
מַתְכּוֹנֵינוּ/כֶם/כֶן/הֶם/הֶן	**מַתְכּוֹ**נַי/נֶיךָ/נַיִךְ/נָיו/נֶיהָ	מַתְכּוֹנֵי-		מַתְכּוֹנִים

Examples

אנשים רבים היו מעדיפים לבשל על פי **מַתְכּוֹנִים** של האימא או הסבתא שלהם, אבל כשהם נזכרים להקליט ולרשום, זה כבר מאוחר מדיי...
Many people would have preferred to cook by **recipes** of their mothers or grandmothers, but by the time they remember to record and write down, it is too late…

מדי פעם מתגלה **מַטְמוֹן** מטבעות בחפירות בישראל; חשיבותו בכך שהוא מספק עדויות היסטוריות על התקופה שבה הוטבעו.
Occasionally a **buried** coin **treasure** is discovered in excavations in Israel. Its importance is in providing historical evidence on the period in which the coins were minted.

Additional Examples in this Pattern

pain, suffering מַכְאוֹב
last rain of rainy season מַלְקוֹשׁ
fuse מַרְעוֹם
collateral מַשְׁכּוֹן
doorpost מַשְׁקוֹף

---

489. *maCCoC* when the last consonant is guttural

our/your/their	my/your/his/her	const.	Gloss	sing/pl
מַשְׁגּוֹחֵנוּ/חֲכֶם/חֲכֶן/חָם/חָן	**מַשְׁגּוֹ**חִי/חֲךָ/חֵךְ/חוֹ/חָהּ	מַשְׁגּוֹחַ-	monitor	מַשְׁגּוֹחַ ז׳
מַשְׁגּוֹחֵינוּ/כֶם/כֶן/הֶם/הֶן	**מַשְׁגּוֹ**חַי/חֶיךָ/חַיִךְ/חָיו/חֶיהָ	מַשְׁגּוֹחֵי-		מַשְׁגּוֹחִים

A "furtive" *pataH* is inserted before a word-final guttural when preceded by a non-low vowel, and the *shva* expected with the guttural is replaced by a *Hataf-pataH.*

Examples

הקרדיולוג הזמין עבורי **מַשְׁגּוֹחַ** שיבדוק את פעולת הלב במשך עשרה ימים רצופים.
The cardiologist ordered for me a **monitor** that will record my heart's activities for ten consecutive days.

Additional Examples in this Pattern

rest, peace, relaxation מַרְגּוֹעַ

---

490. ***maCCuC*** nouns

our/your/their	my/your/his/her	const.	Gloss	sing/pl
מַנְעוּלֵנוּ/לְכֶם/לְכֶן/לָם/לָן	**מַנְעוּ**לִי/לְךָ/לֵךְ/לוֹ/לָהּ	מַנְעוּל-	lock	מַנְעוּל ז׳
מַנְעוּלֵינוּ/כֶם/כֶן/הֶם/הֶן	**מַנְעוּ**לַי/לֶיךָ/לַיִךְ/לָיו/לֶיהָ	מַנְעוּלֵי-		מַנְעוּלִים

This pattern contains only a limited number of nouns; compare with a similar pattern of adjectives borrowed from Arabic – see below.

Examples

״רב-בריח״, אחד ה**מַּנְעוּלִים** המשוכללים בעולם, הוא המצאה ישראלית.
"Multi-lock," one of the most sophisticated **locks** in the world, is an Israeli invention.

במדינות רבות מנסים להקל את התנועה בכבישים בכך שמקצים **מַסְלוּלִים** מיוחדים למכוניות שנוסעים בהן מספר אנשים.
In many countries they try to alleviate traffic congestion by apportioning special **lanes** for multi-passenger cars.

Special Expressions

runway (takeoff **lane**) **מַסְלוּל** המראה
get back to one's **routine** חזר ל**מַּסְלוּל**
pangs of **conscience** ייסורי **מַצְפּוּן**
clear **conscience** **מַצְפּוּן** נקי

Additional Examples in this Pattern

retractable tape measure מַגְלוּל
clothing, garment מַלְבּוּשׁ
conscience מַצְפּוּן

---

491. ***maCCuC*** adjectives

This *mishkal*, which is limited to the colloquial, generally designates adjectives, and occasionally also persons characterized by these adjectives, and it exists separately from the *maCCuC* patterns for nouns above (*man`ul*, *maslul*). The *mishkal* is borrowed from Arabic – probably under the influence of borrowed lexical items such as *mabsut* 'happy, satisfied,' *majnun* 'crazy,' *mastul* 'drunk; drugged' – and in this respect it has a special standing, since it is rare for one language to borrow a *mishkal* from another language and also maintain a degree of productivity in the borrowing language independently of the language of origin. In some cases there exists a homonymous Arabic word but with a different meaning (*maHlū`* 'wild; immoral; outcast; coward,' whereas in Colloquial Hebrew *maHlu* or *maHlúa* – assuming a lost *`áyin* – means 'neglected, ugly,' perhaps owing the similarity with *maHli* 'sickening'); in other cases there exists an Arabic counterpart, but in a different *mishkal* (*miskīn* 'poor, miserable' vs. Colloquial Hebrew *maskun*, cf. normative *misken*); and in a significant number of cases, realizations have no parallel in Arabic (*mafluts(a)* 'monstrous; disgusting,' inspired by *miflétset* 'monster'), which is a clear indication of productivity. Still, the connection with Arabic probably still exists in the speaker's consciousness: a significant segment of the result of this productivity originated from the 1948 generation, many of them knowing Arabic, and with their passing away this productivity declined somewhat – a decline probably also due to today's Hebrew-speaking generation not knowing Arabic. Still, a degree of productivity continues to be maintained even now (e.g., *masHut* as an alternant of *saHut* 'exhausted, literally "squeezed"'). The connection to Arabic is also manifest in the stable placement of stress, regardless of any suffixation (for some reasons, perhaps pragmatic, in some of these, only the *-a* feminine suffix is documented, e.g., *maflútsa*; all feminine forms are stressed penultimately).

Examples

כבר יומיים שיש לי יום **מְבָאוּס**, לא יודעת, לא מסתדר, והכי מתסכל שאתה יודע מה לא בסדר, ואין מה לעשות (מן המרשתת).

For two days now I've been having a **depressing** day, and the most frustrating thing is that you know what's wrong, and there's nothing you can do about it (extracted from the Internet).

אבי חשב שייצא מדעתו כשיפרוש, אבל הוא התרגל מהר והוא **מְבָסוּט**: ישן יותר, אוכל ושותה יין טוב בניחותא, ומטייל בכל העולם.

Avi thought that he would go nuts when he retires, but he go used to it fast, and he is **happy**: sleeps longer, eats and drinks good wine at leisure, and travels all over.

Additional Examples in this Pattern

great, superb Sl. מַגְנוּב
disgusting Sl. מַגְעוּל
excited by, turned on by Sl. מַדְלוּק
miserable Sl. מַדְרוּב
stupid Sl. מַהְבּוּל
neglected; ugly Sl. מַחְלוּא/מַחְלוּעַ
hollow-headed Sl. מַחְלוּל(ה)
ugly; shriveled Sl. מַחְנוּט(ה)
stupid Sl. מַלְטוּךְ
cursed; unlucky Sl. מַנְחוּס
overly muscular Sl. מַנְפוּח
exhausted Sl. מַסְחוּט
poor, miserable Sl. מַסְכּוּן
puny, miserable Sl. מַסְרוּח
monstrous Sl. מַפְלוּצ(ה)
no longer virgin Sl. מַפְתּוּח(ה)

---

492. ***maCCuC = maCuC*** when first root *C* is *n* and the last *C* is guttural

our/your/their	my/your/his/her	const.	Gloss	sing/pl
מַפּוּחֵנוּ/חֲכֶם/חֲכֶן/חָם/חָן	**מַפּוּ**חִי/חֲךָ/חֵךְ/חוֹ/חָהּ	מַפּוּחַ-	bellows	מַפּוּחַ ז'
מַפּוּחֵינוּ/כֶם/כֶן/הֶם/הֶן	**מַפּוּ**חַי/חֶיךָ/חַיִךְ/חָיו/חֶיהָ	מַפּוּחֵי-		מַפּוּחִים

When the first root consonant is *n*, it is assimilated (in MH deleted), as expected, at the end of the syllable (here it happens throughout the paradigm), and in the two realizations found in the corpus, a guttural appears in the third position in the root, which means a "furtive" *pataH* when it occurs at the end of the word (after a vowel other than *a*).

Examples

מַפּוּחַ הוא מכשיר המספק זרם אוויר חזק לליבוי אש בעבודת הנַפָּח, ולניפוּחַ זכוכית; היום משתמשים במונח גם לציון כלי גינון המפיק זרם אוויר חזק לערימת עלים (כדי שייקל לפנותם).

Bellows is an instrument that provides a strong stream of air in a blacksmith's work, and in glass blowing; today one uses this term also to designate a leaf blower.

Additional Examples in this Pattern

spring Lit. מַבּוּעַ

---

493. *maCCoC* = *maCoC* when first root *C* is *n*

our/your/their	my/your/his/her	const.	Gloss	sing/pl
מַסּוֹרֵנוּ/רְכֶם/רְכֶן/רָם/רָן	**מַסּוֹר**ִי/רְךָ/רֵךְ/רוֹ/רָהּ	מַסּוֹר-	saw	מַסּוֹר ז׳
מַסּוֹרֵינוּ/כֶם/כֶן/הֶם/הֶן	**מַסּוֹר**ַי/רֶיךָ/רַיִךְ/רָיו/רֶיהָ	מַסּוֹרֵי-		מַסּוֹרִים

When the first root consonant is *n*, it is assimilated (in MH deleted), as expected, at the end of the syllable (here it happens throughout the paradigm). Some of the realizations are instruments: מַסּוֹר 'saw,' מַכּוֹשׁ 'pick-axe,' מַסּוֹעַ 'conveyor belt.' Note the "furtive" *pataH*.

Examples

המצאת ה**מַסּוֹר** החשמלי היא אחד הגורמים העיקריים בהאצת התהליך של בירוא יערות בעולם.
The invention of the electric **saw** is one of the main factors causing the accelerated process of deforestation in the world.

מכיוון שבמרבית הצבאות בעולם משתמשים יותר ויותר ב**מַסּוֹקִים** להובלת גייסות, פחתה חשיבותה של הצניחה לתוך שטח האויב.
Since in many of the world's armies they increasingly use **helicopters** to transport troops, the importance of parachuting soldiers into enemy territory has been decreasing.

מַקּוֹרוֹ של התוּכִּי עבה וחזק, כדי שיוכל לפצח אגוזים.
The parrot's **beak** is thick and strong, so that he can easily crack nuts.

Special Expressions

moving walkway **מַסּוֹעַ** לֶכֶת
police patrolman שׁוֹטֵר **מַקּוֹף**
erodium (plant) **מַקּוֹר** חֲסִידָה

Additional Examples in this Pattern

pick, pick-axe מַכּוֹשׁ
conveyor belt מַסּוֹעַ
district מַקּוֹף
beak מַקּוֹר
drumstick, hammer מַקּוֹשׁ
favoritism; bias (פָּנִים) מַשּׂוֹא

---

494. *maCCuCa*

our/your/their	my/your/his/her	const.	Gloss	sing/pl
מַמְגּוּרָתֵנוּ/**מַמְגּוּרַתְ**כֶם/כֶן/**מַמְגּוּרָתָ**ם/ן	**מַמְגּוּרָ**תִי/תְךָ/תֵךְ/תוֹ/תָהּ	מַמְגּוּרַת-	granary, silo	מַמְגּוּרָה נ׳
מַמְגּוּרוֹתֵינוּ/כֶם/כֶן/הֶם/הֶן	**מַמְגּוּרוֹ**תַי/תֶיךָ/תַיִךְ/תָיו/תֶיהָ	מַמְגּוּרוֹת-		מַמְגּוּרוֹת

Examples

מַמְגּוּרוֹת דגון הן מסוף הגרעינים הנמלי של מדינת ישראל, והן נמצאות במערבו של נמל חיפה. כ-75% מכלל יבוא הגרעינים (כ-3 מיליון טון גרעיני דגנים) מיובאים לישראל מדי שנה דרך ה**מַמְגּוּרוֹת**.
The Dagon **granaries** are the terminal port of Israel, located at the western section of the Haifa port. About 75% of the whole grain import into Israel (about 3 million ton of grain) are imported to Israel every year through these **granaries**.

Additional Examples in this Pattern

cache, subterranean granary מַטְמוּרָה   plane (carpentry) מַקְצוּעָה

---

495. ***maCCuCa* = *maCaCuCa*** when the first root consonant is a guttural

our/your/their	my/your/his/her	const.	Gloss	sing/pl
מַהֲדוּרָתֵנוּ/**מַהֲדוּרַתְ**כֶם/כֶן/ **מַהֲדוּרָתָ**ם/ן	**מַהֲדוּרָ**תִי/תְךָ/תֵךְ/תוֹ/תָהּ	מַהֲדוּרַת-	edition	מַהֲדוּרָה נ'
מַהֲדוּרוֹתֵינוּ/כֶם/כֶן/הֶם/הֶן	**מַהֲדוּרוֹ**תַי/תֶיךָ/תַיִךְ/תָיו/תֶיהָ	מַהֲדוּרוֹת-		מַהֲדוּרוֹת

When the first root consonant is a guttural, the *shva* expected with it is replaced by a *Hataf-pataH.*

Examples

כל בית הוצאה ראוי לשמו המוציא לאור מילון מוציא כל כמה שנים **מַהֲדוּרָה** חדשה שלו כדי לשקף את השינויים שחלו בלקסיקון עם הזמן.
A publisher of a dictionary issues every few years a new **edition** of it so as to reflect changes that have occurred in the lexicon with time.

---

496. ***miCCaC***

our/your/their	my/your/his/her	const.	Gloss	sing/pl
מִכְתָּבֵנוּ/**מִכְתַּבְ**כֶם/כֶן/**מִכְתָּבָ**ם/ן	**מִכְתָּ**בִי/בְךָ/בֵךְ/בוֹ/בָהּ	מִכְתַּב-	letter,	מִכְתָּב ז'
מִכְתָּבֵינוּ/**מִכְתְּבֵי**כֶם/כֶן/הֶם/הֶן	**מִכְתָּ**בַי/בֶיךָ/בַיִךְ/בָיו/בֶיהָ	מִכְתְּבֵי-	message	מִכְתָּבִים

Two syllables away from the main stress the *kamats* is reduced to *shva*, < *מִכְתָּבֵיכֶם מִכְתְּבֵיכֶם, and in a closed syllable to *pataH*, to avoid a sequence of two *shva* mobiles: מִכְתַּבְכֶם < *מִכְ-תְּבְ-כֶם < *מִכְתָּבְכֶם. The *mishkal* has numerous realizations, and some of them share some general semantic features, such as locations/places (מִגְדָּל tower, מִבְצָר fortress, מִפְרָץ bay), abstract nouns (מִפְלָט escape, מִבְצָע operation, מִגְדָּר gender, etc.).

Examples

בעידן האינטרנט פחות כותבים היום **מִכְתָּבִים** כפי שכתבו בעבר, אבל למסר בדוא"ל יש פחות-או-יותר אותו תפקיד, למרות שהוא בדרך כלל קצר יותר ופחות פורמאלי.
In the Internet age one writes less **letters** than one did in the past, but an electronic message has more-or-less the same role, although it is generally shorter and less formal.

בזמנו, הודעות חשובות דחופות היו נשלחות באמצעות **מִבְרָק**. בקיץ 2013 נשלח **הַמִּבְרָק** האחרון...
At the time, important, urgent messages were sent by **telegram**. The last **telegram** ever was sent in summer 2013…

מעניין מתי ייבנה "**מִגְדַּל** טרמפ" הראשון בצפון קוריאה...
An interesting question: when will the first "Trump **Tower**" be built in North Korea?

ברוח הזמן, גם הבלשנים עוסקים הרבה היום במחקר **הַמִּגְדָּר** (בשפה).
Following current trends, linguists are also engaged in the study of **gender** (in language).

בשימוש מטפורי, קוראים לגמל "ספינת **הַמִּדְבָּר**".
Metaphorically, they call the camel "the ship of the **desert**".

ההיפים של שנות השישים והשבעים לחמו מלחמת חורמה **בַּמִּמְסָד**, אבל כשהתבגרו, רובם הפכו חלק אינטגראלי ממנו.
The hippies of the sixties and seventies were committed to a struggle against the **establishment**, but when they became adults, most of them became well-integrated in it.

Special Expressions

מִגְדַּל אור = מִגְדָּלוֹר lighthouse
מִגְדַּל קלפים house of cards
מִגְדָּל הפורח באוויר something of no real substance, something imaginary
נווה **מִדְבָּר** oasis
קול קורא **בַּמִּדְבָּר** unanswered call
מִכְרָז תפור "tailored" **bid**, to fit only one particular person/company
מִקָּח **וּמִמְכָּר** trade, commerce; negotiation, bargaining (= negotiating and **selling**)
מִסְפָּר אי-זוגי odd **number**
מִפְגַּן כוח **show** of force
מִפְקַד אוכלוסין population **census**
מִקְלָט מדיני political **asylum**
מִשְׁטָר נשיאותי presidential **form of government** (as in the U.S.)
מִשְׁפָּט בינלאומי international **law**
מִשְׂרַד החינוך Department of Education

Additional Examples in this Pattern

מִבְדָּק examination, test
מִבְזָק news flash
מִבְצָר fortress
מִבְרָץ spillway
מִבְתָּר hilly area
מִגְבָּשׁ conglomeration
מִגְוָן variety; color range
מִגְזָר sector
מִגְרָשׁ lot; yard; field
מִדְגָּם sample N
מִדְרָס insole
מִדְרָשׁ homiletical exegesis
מִטְרָד nuisance
מִכְנָס trouser
מִכְרָז bid; auction
מִמְטָר shower
מִמְכָּר selling
מִמְסָר relay N
מִמְשָׁל regime
מִמְשָׁק interface (computing)
מִנְזָר monastery
מִנְשָׁר manifest
מִסְדָּר roll call; order (monks, etc.)
מִסְמָךְ document
מִפְגָּשׁ gathering

---

497. ***miCCaC*** when the 2nd root consonant is a guttural

our/your/their	my/your/his/her	const.	Gloss	sing/pl
מִפְעָלֵנוּ/**מִפְעַלְ**כֶם/כֶן/**מִפְעָלָ**ם/ן	**מִפְעָלִ**י/לְךָ/לֵךְ/לוֹ/לָהּ	מִפְעַל-	project;	מִפְעָל
מִפְעָלֵינוּ/**מִפְעֲלֵי**כֶם/כֶן/הֶם/הֶן	**מִפְעָלַ**י/לֶיךָ/לַיִךְ/לָיו/לֶיהָ	מִפְעֲלֵי-	factory	מִפְעָלִים

When the second root consonant is a guttural, the *shva* expected with it is replaced by a *Hataf-pataH*, מִפְעֲלֵיכֶם < מִפְעָלֵיכֶם*, and in a closed syllable the *kamats* is replaced by *pataH*, מִפְעַלְכֶם < מִפְעָלְכֶם*.

Examples

מִפְעָלִים לא מעטים מוקמים באזורים שאינם עירוניים ובארצות מתפתחות, בעיקר כדי להעסיק פועלים זולים וכדי לקבל הקלות מס מן הממשלה.
A good number of **factories** are built in non-urban areas and in developing countries, mostly in order to employ cheaper workforce and to obtain tax incentives from government.

מרבית האנשים אינם עוברים בהצלחה את **מִבְחַן** הנהיגה בפעם הראשונה...
Most people do not pass the driving **test** on their first try…

למרות שהקלרינט אינו כלי נגינה גדול, **מִנְעַד** הצלילים שלו רחב ביותר.
Although the clarinet is not a large instrument, its sound **range** is quite wide.

המִסְחָר בבורסה התחדש היום, לאחר שהופסק אתמול בשל התראה על פעולת טרור.
Trade in the stock exchange resumed this morning, after it had been suspended yesterday owing to a terrorist threat.

Special Expressions

מִבְחַן בד screen **test**
מִטְעַן חבלה explosive device/**charge**
מִנְהַג המקום local **custom**
מִנְהַל מקרקעי ישראל Israel Lands **Administration**
מִפְעַל חיים lifetime **work/achievement**
מִשְׁאַל עַם **referendum**

Additional Examples in this Pattern

מִבְחָר choice
מִטְעָן load N
מִנְהָג custom, habit
מִנְהָל administration
מִנְחָת landing pad
מִפְעָם tempo
מִצְעָד march, parade
מִצְעָר small quantity
מִשְׁאָל poll, survey
מִשְׂחָק game; acting; play
מִשְׁעָן support
מִתְאָר outline

---

498. ***miCCaC*** when the 3rd root consonant is a guttural

our/your/their	my/your/his/her	const.	Gloss	sing/pl
מִבְצָעֵנוּ/**מִבְצַעֲ**כֶם/כֶן/**מִבְצָעָ**ם/ן	**מִבְצָעִ**י/עֲךָ/עֵךְ/עוֹ/עָהּ	מִבְצַע-	operation; sale	מִבְצָע
מִבְצָעֵינוּ/**מִבְצְעֵי**כֶם/כֶן/הֶם/הֶן	**מִבְצָעַ**י/עֶיךָ/עַיִךְ/עָיו/עֶיהָ	מִבְצְעֵי-		מִבְצָעִים

When the third root consonant is a guttural, the *shva* expected with it is replaced by a *Hataf-pataH*.

Examples

מִבְצָע סיני (או קָדֵשׁ) ב-1956 היה הקונפליקט הצבאי הגדול הראשון בין ישראל ומדינה ערבית כלשהי אחרי 1948.
The Sinai (or Kadesh) **campaign** in 1956 was the first large military conflict between Israel and any Arab state since 1948.

מִבְצָע הוא בדרך כלל **מִבְצָע** צבאי, אבל איכשהו החלו, כבר לפני שנים רבות, להשתמש בו גם לציון מכירה מיוחדת, בהנחה.
מִבְצָע is generally a **military operation**, but somehow they started, a while ago, to also use it for a special **sale**, at discount.

מרבית היהודים שעלו ארצה מגרמניה, פרט לילדים, שמרו על **מִבְטָא** גרמני מובהק, גם אחרי שנים רבות בארץ.
Except for children, most of the Jews who immigrated to Israel from Germany maintained their German **accent**, even after many years in Israel.

בדירות רבות היום אנשים מעדיפים שלא להפריד בין ה**מִטְבָּח** לבין חדר האוכל או חדר האורחים.
In many apartments today people prefer not to separate between the **kitchen** and the dining room or the living room.

Special Expressions

heavy **accent** **מִבְטָא** כבד
Middle-**Eastern** **מִזְרָח**-תיכוני
public health **hazard** **מִפְגָּע** תברואתי
touch **pad** **מִשְׁטַח** מגע

Additional Examples in this Pattern

safe haven Lit. מִבְטָח
east מִזְרָח
shooting practice; firing range מִטְוָח
finding, evidence מִמְצָא
spread N מִמְרָח
span מִמְתָּח
carrier, baby sling מִנְשָׂא
hazard מִפְגָּע
parachute jump מִצְנָח
slingshot מִקְלָע
the Bible; legend, key מִקְרָא
flat surface מִשְׁטָח

---

499. ***miCCaC > miCCa*** when the last root consonant is *y*

our/your/their	my/your/his/her	const.	Gloss	sing/pl
מִשְׂרָתֵנוּ/**מִשְׂרַתְ**כֶם/כֶן/**מִשְׂרָתָ**ם/ן	**מִשְׂרָ**תִי/תְךָ/תֵךְ/תוֹ/תָהּ	מִשְׂרַת-	post,	מִשְׂרָה נ׳
מִשְׂרוֹתֵינוּ/כֶם/כֶן/הֶם/הֶן	**מִשְׂרוֹ**תַי/תֶיךָ/תַיִךְ/תָיו/תֶיהָ	מִשְׂרוֹת-	position	מִשְׂרוֹת

The *miCCaC* pattern when the last consonant of the root is *y* (orthographically ה).

Examples

החוג שלנו קיבל שלוש **מִשְׂרוֹת** חדשות בחמש השנים האחרונות.
Our department received three new **positions** in the last five years.

הממשלה מודאגת בשל העלייה החדה לאחרונה ביוקר **הַמִּחְיָה**.
The government has been worried about the recent sharp rise in the cost of **living**.

תרי״ג **מִצְווֹת** מפורטות בספרי המקרא.
613 **commandments** are specified in the Hebrew Bible.

Special Expressions

מִשְׁנָה סדורה well-ordered, well organized **studies** and/or knowledge
מרחב **מִחְיָה** **living** space

מצא את **מִחְיָתוֹ** found a way to make a **living**
מאזני **מִרְמָה** crooked scales intended to deceive ("scales of **deceit**/cheating")

Additional Examples in this Pattern

מִכְסָה allotment; quota
מִצְוָה commandment; good deed
מִקְוָה/מִקְוֶה ritual bath
מִקְשָׁה field (esp. of watermelons)

מִרְמָה fraud
מִשְׁנָה Mishna (Jewish oral law); doctrine, theory
מִתְוָה draft, sketch; layout

---

500. *miCCaC* = *miCaC* when root starts with נ or יצ

our/your/their	my/your/his/her	const.	Gloss	sing/pl
מִצָּבֵנוּ/**מִצַּבְכֶם**/כֶן/**מִצָּבָם**/ן	**מִצָּבִי**/בְךָ/בֵךְ/בוֹ/בָהּ	מִצַּב-	status	מִצָּב
מִצָּבֵינוּ/**מִצְּבֵי**כֶם/כֶן/הֶם/הֶן	**מִצָּבַי**/בֶיךָ/בַיִךְ/בָיו/בֶיהָ	מִצְּבֵי-		מִצָּבִים

When in the *miCCaC* pattern, the first *C* of the root is is *n*, or is *y* followed by *ts*, either one is fully assimilated into the second root consonant.

Examples

מִצָּב הוא מעמדו של פרט בחברה יחסית לשאר חברי קבוצתו.
Status is the standing of a particular individual vis-à-vis the rest of the members of his group.

Additional Examples in this Pattern

מִשָּׁק joint (carpentry, building)

---

501. *miCCaC* when *kamats* > *pataH,* followed by a *dagesh*

our/your/their	My/your/his/her	const.	Gloss	sing/pl
מִכְמַנֵּנוּ/**מִכְמַנְּכֶם**/כֶן/**מִכְמַנָּם**/ן	**מִכְמַנִּי**/נְּךָ/נֵּךְ/נּוֹ/נָּהּ	מִכְמַן-	hidden thing;	מִכְמָן
מִכְמַנֵּינוּ/כֶם/כֶן/הֶם/הֶן	**מִכְמַנַּי**/נֶּיךָ/נַּיִךְ/נָּיו/נֶּיהָ	מִכְמַנֵּי-	treasure Lit.	מִכְמַנִּים

In the base form, the last vowel is a *kamats*. In the declension, with the shift in stress, the *kamats* is replaced by *pataH*, and the syllable is closed with a *dagesh forte*.

Examples

למרות שלמד אנגלית בגיל מאוחר, הסופר הפולני ג'וזף קונרד שלט היטב ב**מִכְמַנֵּי** השפה האנגלית.
Although he learned English only late in life, the Polish author Joseph Conrad had excellent command of the **secrets** (**treasures**?) of the English language.

Additional Examples in this Pattern

being fat; being fertile Lit. מִשְׁמָן

---

502. *miCCeC*

Our/your/their	my/your/his/her	const.	Gloss	sing/pl
מִסְפְּדֵנוּ/**מִסְפֶּדְ**כֶם/כֶן/**מִסְפְּדָ**ם/ן	מִסְפְּדִי/מִסְפֶּדְךָ/**מִסְפְּד**ֵךְ/דוֹ/דָהּ	מִסְפַּד-	eulogy	מִסְפֵּד ז'
מִסְפְּדֵינוּ/כֶם/כֶן/הֶם/הֶן	**מִסְפְּדַ**י/דֶיךָ/דַיִךְ/דָיו/דֶיהָ	מִסְפְּדֵי-		מִסְפְּדִים

The *tsere* is reduced throughout the declension (to *shva*, or to *seghol* before another *shva*).

Examples

הַמִּסְפֵּד שנשא הנשיא לזכרו של המשורר האהוב שנפטר היה מרגש מאוד.
The **eulogy** delivered by the President in memory of the beloved poet who passed away was very moving.

Additional Examples in this Pattern

apricot מִשְׁמֵשׁ

---

503. *miCCeC* plural suffix *–ot*

our/your/their	my/your/his/her	const.	Gloss	sing/pl
מִזְבְּחֵנוּ/**מִזְבַּחֲ**כֶם/כֶן/**מִזְבְּחָ**ם/ן	מִזְבְּחִי/מִזְבַּחֲךָ/**מִזְבְּ**חֵךְ/חוֹ/חָהּ	מִזְבַּח-	altar	מִזְבֵּחַ ז'
מִזְבְּחוֹתֵינוּ/כֶם/כֶן/הֶם/הֶן	**מִזְבְּחוֹ**תַי/תֶיךָ/תַיִךְ/תָיו/תֶיהָ	מִזְבְּחוֹת-		מִזְבְּחוֹת

The *tsere* is reduced to *shva* mobile, but when the next consonant is a guttural with *Hataf*, the potential impermissible sequence causes the *shva* to be replaced by *pataH*.

Examples

אליהו חיסל 400 נביאי בעל לאחר שלא הצליחו להעלות אש **בַּמִּזְבֵּחַ**...
Elijah slaughtered 400 Ba`al prophets when they were unsuccessful in causing fire to start at the **altar**.

מיליוני רוסים אבדו את חייהם על **מִזְבַּח** הקומוניזם הסטאליניסטי.
Millions of Russians lost their lives in the cause of (lit. at the **altar** of) Stalinist communism.

Special Expressions

החזיק בקרנות ה**מִּזְבֵּחַ**
seize any means of escape (lit. grasp the horns/corners of the altar), seek sanctuary

---

504. ***miCCeC* = *miCCe*** when the last root consonant is *y*

our/your/their	my/your/his/her	const.	Gloss	sing/pl
מִקְרֵנוּ/רְכֶם/רְכֶן/רָם/רָן	**מִקְ**רִי/רְךָ/רֵךְ/רוֹ (רֵהוּ) /רֵהּ (רֶהָ)	מִקְרֵה-	incident;	מִקְרֶה ז'
מִקְרֵינוּ/כֶם/כֶן/הֶם/הֶן	**מִקְ**רַי/רֶיךָ/רַיִךְ/רָיו/רֶיהָ	מִקְרֵי-	chance; case	מִקְרִים

The *miCCeC* pattern when the last consonant of the root is *y* (orthographically ה'). Note: the plural form of מִכְרֶה is מִכְרוֹת.

Examples

לעולם לא אשכח **מִקְרֶה** שקרה לי לפני עשר שנים.
I'll never forget an **incident** that happened to me ten years ago.

נתגלו **מִקְרִים** נוספים של שפעת העופות.
Additional **cases** of the bird flu have been discovered.

בית הספר לעברית שוכן ב**מִבְנֶה** נפרד בתוך מתחם המרכז הקהילתי היהודי בעיר.
The Hebrew school was housed in a separate **building** within the Jewish Community Center complex in town.

מלחמת ששת הימים ב-1967 היוותה נקודת **מִפְנֶה** בהיסטוריה של מדינת ישראל.
The Six Day war of 1967 constituted a **turning** point in the history of the state of Israel.

Special Expressions

deep **structure** **מִבְנֶה** עומק
turning point נקודת **מִפְנֶה**
by **chance** ב**מִקְרֶה**
in case that… ב**מִקְרֶה** ש...
at all **events** בכל **מִקְרֶה**
nocturnal emission **מִקְרֶה** לילה

Additional Examples in this Pattern

fishing farm מִדְגֶּה
cover, lid מִכְסֶה
mine (coal etc.) מִכְרֶה
loan מִלְוֶה
lookout מִצְפֶּה
ritual bath; small basin of collected water מִקְוֶה
livestock מִקְנֶה
heat (sports) מִקְצֶה
pasture מִרְעֶה
deputy מִשְׁנֶה
feast מִשְׁתֶּה

---

505. *miCCaCa*

our/your/their	my/your/his/her	const.	Gloss	sing/pl
מִשְׁטַרְתֵּנוּ/תְּכֶם/תְּכֶן/תָּם/תָּן	**מִשְׁטַרְ**תִּי/תְּךָ/תֵּךְ/תּוֹ/תָּהּ	מִשְׁטֶרֶת-	police	מִשְׁטָרָה נ'
מִשְׁטְרוֹתֵינוּ/כֶם/כֶן/הֶם/הֶן	**מִשְׁטְרוֹ**תַי/תֶיךָ/תַיִךְ/תָיו/תֶיהָ	מִשְׁטְרוֹת-		מִשְׁטָרוֹת

The *miCCaCa* pattern tends to have a few meanings, such as 'locations in which one is engaged in a well-defined activity,' such as מִסְעָדָה 'restaurant,' or which have a characteristic quality, like מִדְשָׁאָה 'lawn,' institutions, like מִשְׁטָרָה 'police,' abstract nouns like מִלְחָמָה 'war,' and so on. Two syllables away from the main stress and in the construct state the first *kamats* is replaced by a *shva*: *מִשְׁטָרוֹתַי > מִשְׁטְרוֹתַי, *מִשְׁטָרוֹת- > מִשְׁטְרוֹת-, and in a closed syllable the *kamats* is replaced by a *pataH*, to avoid a sequence of two *shva* mobiles: *מִשְׁטָרְתִּי > *מִשְׁ-טָרְ-תִּי > מִשְׁטַרְתִּי. The construct state in the singular is characterized by two *seghol*s, and is penultimately stressed: מִשְׁטֶרֶת-.

Examples

מִשְׁטֶרֶת ישראל היא מן **הַמִּשְׁטָרוֹת** האמיצות בעולם; היא אינה מפחדת להגיש כתב אישום נגד אף אחד, כולל ראשי ממשלה ונשיאים.
The Israeli **police** is one of the bravest **police institutions** in the world; it is not afraid of indicting anybody, including prime ministers and presidents.

בבקשה לא לדרוך על הדשא; המבקרים בפארק מתבקשים ללכת על **הַמִּדְרָכוֹת**.
Please do not step on the grass; visitors to the park are requested to walk on the **sidewalks**.

הַמִּזְבָּלָה העירונית כבר מלאה עד גדותיה; העיר מחפשת מקום נוסף.
The municipal **garbage dump** is full to the brim; the city is looking for an additional location.

בוא ניפגש בשעה חמש ליד **הַמִּזְרָקָה** שבכיכר המרכזית של העיר.
Let's meet at 5 o'clock next to the **fountain** in the town's main square.

מכיוון שצעירים רבים בישראל אינם מצליחים להתקבל לאוניברסיאות הרגילות, נפתחו במקביל **מִכְלָלוֹת** שתנאי הקבלה שלהן אינם כה מחמירים.
Since a large number of young people in Israel are not successful in being admitted to the regular universities, a number of **community colleges** were opened whose admission requirements are not as high.

בבחירות הבאות בישראל יתמודדו מספר גדול של **מִפְלָגוֹת**, רובן קטנות, ללא סיכוי להשיג הישגים של ממש.
A large number of small **parties** will compete in the next elections in Israel, most of them small, with little chance of making significant gains.

Special Expressions

מִשְׁטָרָה חשאית secret **police**
מִשְׁטָרָה צבאית military **police** (MP)
יושב על **הַמִּזְוָודוֹת** ready to go/leave/travel on a moment's notice
מִפְלְגוֹת הימין the right (wing) **parties**
מִתְקֶפֶת נגד counter**attack**

Additional Examples in this Pattern

מִבְשָׁלָה brewery
מִבְרָקָה telegraph station
מִגְבָּלָה limitation
מִגְנָנָה defense system
מִגְרָרָה sled, sleigh
מִדְרָשָׁה college

suitcase מִזְוָדָה	shipping dock מִסְפָּנָה
fast food restaurant Coll. מִזְלָלָה	barber shop, hairdresser shop מִסְפָּרָה
distillery מִזְקָקָה	headquarters מִפְקָדָה
laundry facility מִכְבָּסָה	advance payment מִקְדָּמָה
writing desk מִכְתָּבָה	incinerator; crematorium מִשְׂרָפָה
gear (mech.) מִמְסָרָה	nursery (gardening) מִשְׁתָּלָה
prism מִנְסָרָה	offensive N מִתְקָפָה

---

506. ***miCCaCa*** when the second root consonant is a guttural

our/your/their	my/your/his/her	const.	Gloss	sing/pl
מִלְחַמְתֵּנוּ/תְּכֶם/תְּכֶן/תָּם/תָּן	**מִלְחַמְ**תִּי/תְּךָ/תֵּךְ/תּוֹ/תָּהּ	מִלְחֶמֶת-	war;	מִלְחָמָה נ׳
מִלְחֲמוֹתֵינוּ/כֶם/כֶן/הֶם/הֶן	**מִלְחֲמוֹ**תַי/תֶיךָ/תַיִךְ/תָיו/תֶיהָ	מִלְחֲמוֹת-	controversy	מִלְחָמוֹת

For vowel changes, see מִשְׁטָרָה above. When a *shva* is expected with the second consonant of the root, it is replaced by a *Hataf-pataH*.

Examples

אין עוד **מִלְחָמָה** בין ישראל למצרים, אבל גם אין בין שתי המדינות שלום אמיתי.
There is no longer a state of **war** between Israel and Egypt, but there is no real peace between the two states either.

מטבע הדברים, הבניין החשוב ביותר בכל אוניברסיטה הוא בניין ה**מִנְהָלָה**...
Naturally, the most important building in any University is the **Administration** Building…

לפעמים, האוכל ב**מִסְעֶדֶת** פועלים יכול להיות טעים יותר מאשר ארוחות שהוכנו על ידי שֶף מהולל ב**מִסְעָדָה** יוקרתית.
Sometimes, the food in a workers' **restaurant** can be tastier than meals that have been prepared by a highly-regarded chef in a prestigious **restaurant**.

Special Expressions

warrior איש **מִלְחָמָה**	wind **tunnel** **מִנְהֶרֶת** אוויר/רוח
religious/holy **war** **מִלְחֶמֶת** מצווה	vegetarian **restaurant** **מִסְעָדָה** צמחונית
declare **war** on הכריז **מִלְחָמָה** על	**desire**, **wish** **מִשְׁאֶלֶת** לב

Additional Examples in this Pattern

pressing/ironing room מִגְהָצָה	wish N מִשְׁאָלָה
handkerchief מִמְחָטָה	slaughterhouse מִשְׁחָטָה
tunnel מִנְהָרָה	

---

507. ***miCCaCa*** when the third root consonant is a guttural (other than 'א)

our/your/their	my/your/his/her	const.	Gloss	sing/pl
מִשְׁפַּחְתֵּנוּ/תְּכֶם/תְּכֶן/תָּם/תָּן	**מִשְׁפַּחְ**תִּי/תְּךָ/תֵּךְ/תּוֹ/תָּהּ	מִשְׁפַּחַת-	family	מִשְׁפָּחָה נ׳
מִשְׁפְּחוֹתֵינוּ/כֶם/כֶן/הֶם/הֶן	**מִשְׁפְּחוֹ**תַי/תֶיךָ/תַיִךְ/תָיו/תֶיהָ	מִשְׁפְּחוֹת-		מִשְׁפָּחוֹת

When the third root consonant is guttural (other than 'א), the two *seghol*s in the singular construct form are replaced by two *pataH*s.

Examples

משה הוא הבן הצעיר ביותר ב**מִשְׁפָּחָה** גדולה עם שבעה ילדים.
Moshe is the youngest son in a large **family** with seven children.

Special Expressions

מִשְׁפָּחָה אומנת foster **family**
מִשְׁפָּחָה חד-הורית single-parent **family**
בן **מִשְׁפָּחָה** **family** member
שם **מִשְׁפָּחָה** last name, surname

Additional Examples in this Pattern

מִמְלָחָה salt shaker
מִסְלָעָה rockery (gardening)
מִפְרָעָה payment on account
מִפְשָׂעָה crotch, groin

---

508. ***miCCaCa*** when the 3rd root consonant is *'alef*

Our/your/their	my/your/his/her	const.	Gloss	sing/pl
מִרְפְּאָתֵנוּ/**מִרְפְּאַתְ**כֶם/כֶן/**מִרְפְּאָתָ**ם/ן	**מִרְפְּאָ**תִי/תְךָ/תֵךְ/תוֹ/תָהּ	מִרְפְּאַת-	clinic	מִרְפָּאָה נ׳
מִרְפְּאוֹתֵינוּ/כֶם/כֶן/הֶם/הֶן	**מִרְפְּאוֹ**תַי/תֶיךָ/תַיִךְ/תָיו/תֶיהָ	מִרְפְּאוֹת-		מִרְפָּאוֹת

Each *kamats* undergoes reduction to a *shva* two syllables before a stressed syllable, like regular *miCCaCa*, but the singular form of the construct state does not come with two *seghol*s or two *pataH*s, but rather undergoes normal *kamats* reduction: *מִרְפָּאָה- < מִרְפְּאַת-.

Examples

ב**מִרְפָּאָה** השכונתית שלנו יש רופאים כלליים מצוינים.
Our neighborhood **clinic** has excellent general practitioners.

אפשר לראות את משה כל ערב ב**מִסְבָּאָה** האירית שבמרכז העיר.
You can see Moshe every evening at the Irish **pub** in the center of town.

Special Expressions

מִרְפֶּאֶת חוץ outpatient **clinic**
מִשְׁוָאָה ריבועית quadratic **equation**

Additional Examples in this Pattern

lawn מִדְשָׁאָה
spinning mill מִטְוָאָה
corral; temp. prison camp מִכְלָאָה
anthology of readings מִקְרָאָה
equation מִשְׁוָאָה

---

509. *miCCéCet*

our/your/their	my/your/his/her	const.	Gloss	sing/pl
מִשְׁמַרְתֵּנוּ/תְּכֶם/תְּכֶן/תָּם/תָּן	**מִשְׁמַרְ**תִּי/תְּךָ/תֵּךְ/תּוֹ/תָּהּ	מִשְׁמֶרֶת-	watch; shift;	מִשְׁמֶרֶת נ׳
מִשְׁמְרוֹתֵינוּ/כֶם/כֶן/הֶם/הֶן	**מִשְׁמְרוֹ**תַי/תֶיךָ/תַיִךְ/תָיו/תֶיהָ	מִשְׁמְרוֹת-	safekeeping	מִשְׁמָרוֹת

This is a segholate noun pattern, penultimately stressed; as in the case of bi-syllabic segholates, the base *miCCaCt* (מִשְׁמַרְת) stays as is when a suffix is added, but in isolation becomes *miCCéCet* (מִשְׁמֶרֶת).

Examples

הוא לא הבין איך הם הצליחו להיכנס; הוא לא עזב את **מִשְׁמַרְתּוֹ** אפילו לרגע.
He could not understand how they managed to get in; he never left **his watch** even for a moment.

כשלא היו מספיק חדרי לימוד בבית הספר, חלקנו למדנו ב**מִשְׁמֶרֶת** שנייה.
When there were not enough classrooms at school, some of us studied at second **shift.**

כשהיא יצאה לטיול, היא השאירה בידיי את תכשיטיה ל**מִשְׁמֶרֶת**.
When she went on a trip, she left her jewelry with me for **safekeeping**.

קיבלנו במתנה רישום נפלא של צייר ידוע; כעת עלינו לחפש בשבילו **מִסְגֶּרֶת** מתאימה.
We got a wonderful drawing by a well-known artist; now we need to look for an appropriate **frame** for it.

אהרון אוהב לשבת ב**מִרְפֶּסֶת** ולקרוא ספר.
Aaron loves to sit on the **balcony** and read a book.

אם יושבים באופרה רחוק מן הבמה, תמיד אפשר להשתמש ב**מִשְׁקֶפֶת**.
If you sit far from the stage in an opera, you can always use **binoculars**.

Special Expressions

חרג מן ה**מִסְגֶּרֶת** went beyond what he was supposed to do
מִקְטֶרֶת השלום peace **pipe**
ה**מִשְׁמֶרֶת** הצעירה the Young Guard
מִשְׁמֶרֶת לילה night **shift**

Additional Examples in this Pattern

brush מִבְרֶשֶׁת
stenciled cutout מִגְזֶרֶת
shtreimel מִזְנֶבֶת
sugar bowl מִסְכֶּרֶת
strainer; colander מִסְנֶנֶת
monster מִפְלֶצֶת

aneurism מִפְרֶצֶת
conical hat מִצְנֶפֶת
(smoking) pipe מִקְטֶרֶת
keyboard מִקְלֶדֶת
telephone exchange מִרְכֶּזֶת
tiles; pavement מִרְצֶפֶת
square; rubric מִשְׁבֶּצֶת

---

510. ***miCCéCet*** when the second root consonant is a guttural

our/your/their	my/your/his/her	const.	Gloss	sing/pl
מִשְׁעַנְתֵּנוּ/תְּכֶם/תְּכֶן/תָּם/תָּן	**מִשְׁעַנְ**תִּי/תְּךָ/תֵּךְ/תּוֹ/תָּהּ	מִשְׁעֶנֶת-	back rest	מִשְׁעֶנֶת נ׳
מִשְׁעֲנוֹתֵינוּ/כֶם/כֶן/הֶם/הֶן	**מִשְׁעֲנוֹ**תַי/תֶיךָ/תַיִךְ/תָיו/תֶיהָ	מִשְׁעֲנוֹת-		מִשְׁעָנוֹת

When the second root consonant is guttural, an expected *shva* is replaced by a *Hataf-pataH*.

Examples

התקנתי את ה**מִשְׁעֶנֶת** המיוחדת לכיסא שהרופא המליץ עליה וישבתי לעבוד.
I installed the special **head rest** that the doctor recommended and sat down to work.

Special Expressions

someone or something that cannot be depended upon **מִשְׁעֶנֶת** קנה רצוץ

Additional Examples in this Pattern

sled, sleigh מִזְחֶלֶת
large bowl for dough to rise מִשְׁאֶרֶת/מִשְׁאֶרֶת

---

511. ***miCCéCet* = *miCCáCat*** when the third root consonant is a guttural

our/your/their	my/your/his/her	const.	Gloss	sing/pl
מִטְפַּחְתֵּנוּ/תְּכֶם/תְּכֶן/תָּם/תָּן	**מִטְפַּחְ**תִּי/תְּךָ/תֵּךְ/תּוֹ/תָּהּ	מִטְפַּחַת-	handkerchief;	מִטְפַּחַת נ׳
מִטְפְּחוֹתֵינוּ/כֶם/כֶן/הֶם/הֶן	**מִטְפְּחוֹ**תַי/תֶיךָ/תַיִךְ/תָיו/תֶיהָ	מִטְפְּחוֹת-	shawl; cover	מִטְפָּחוֹת

When the third root consonant is a guttural, the two *seghol*s in the singular form of the construct state are replaced by two *pataH*s.

Examples

בכיסי השמאלי אני מחזיק תמיד **מִטְפַּחַת**.
In my left pocket I always keep a **handkerchief**.

נשים אורתודוקסיות רבות עוטפות את ראשן ב**מִטְפַּחַת**.
Many orthodox women cover their head with a **shawl**.

כשעייפים, **מִקְלַחַת** תמיד מרעננת ועוזרת להישאר ער.
When one is tired, a **shower** always refreshes one and helps keep one awake.

מיכאל היה חבר ב**מִשְׁלַחַת** ישראל באו״ם שנים רבות.
Michael was a member of the Israeli **delegation** to the U.N. for many years.

Special Expressions

מִטְפַּחַת אף **handkerchief**

מִטְפַּחַת ספרים cover for Torah scroll

קיבל **מִקְלַחַת** (קרה) was severely reprimanded

Additional Examples in this Pattern

מִטְבַּעַת die N, swage

מִקְלַעַת braid

מִרְקַחַת concoction Lit.

מִרְשַׁעַת wicked woman

מִשְׁמַעַת discipline

---

512. *miCCóCet*

our/your/their	my/your/his/her	const.	Gloss	sing/pl
מִשְׁקָלְתֵּנוּ/תְּכֶם/תְּכֶן/תָּם/תָּן	**מִשְׁקָלְ**תִּי/תְּךָ/תֵּךְ/תּוֹ/תָּהּ	מִשְׁקֶלֶת-	weight	מִשְׁקֹלֶת נ׳
מִשְׁקוֹלוֹתֵינוּ/כֶם/כֶן/הֶם/הֶן	**מִשְׁקוֹלוֹ**תַי/תֶיךָ/תַיִךְ/תָיו/תֶיהָ	מִשְׁקוֹלוֹת-		מִשְׁקוֹלוֹת

The isolation form is penultimately stressed, as in other segholates. In a closed syllable, a *Holam Haser* is replaced by a *kamats katan* (or the reverse: the *kamats katan* of the base is replaced by *Holam* in an open syllable…)

Examples

מִשְׁקוֹלוֹת משמשות כיחידות משקל בשקילת מזון וכו׳, כיחידות כובד שמֵרים ספורטאי, ולבדיקה (בקצה חוט) אם קיר הוא אמנם מאונך.

Weights are used as units of measuring weight (of food etc.), as weight units lifted by athletes, and to check (at the end of a string) whether a wall is indeed vertical.

Special Expressions

הרמת **מִשְׁקוֹלוֹת** **weight** lifting

Additional Examples in this Pattern

מִכְמֹנֶת speed trap

מִכְמֹרֶת fishing net

מִשְׁחֹלֶת device for cleaning rifle barrel

מִשְׁמֹרֶת guardianship, custody

---

513. *meCCaC*

our/your/their	my/your/his/her	const.	Gloss	sing/pl
מֶרְכָּזֵנוּ/**מֶרְכַּזְ**כֶם/כֶן/**מֶרְכָּזָ**ם/ן	**מֶרְכָּ**זִי/זְךָ/זֵךְ/זוֹ/זָהּ	מֶרְכַּז-	center	מֶרְכָּז ז׳
מֶרְכָּזֵינוּ/**מֶרְכְּזֵי**כֶם/כֶן/הֶם/הֶן	**מֶרְכָּ**זַי/זֶיךָ/זַיִךְ/זָיו/זֶיהָ	מֶרְכְּזֵי-		מֶרְכָּזִים

The *kamats* is reduced to a *shva* two syllables before the stress and in the construct state, and in a closed syllable it is replaced by a *pataH*.

Examples

בארצות רבות היום **מֶרְכְּזֵי** הקניות, בעיקר הקניונים, הפכו למוקדי בידור בשעות הפנאי, בעיקר לצעירים.

In many countries today shopping **centers**, particularly shopping malls, have become entertainment center at leisure time, particularly among the young.

במלחמת יום-כיפור של 1973, כשישראל הותקפה בהפתעה גמורה, היותה של ישראל לא מוכנה כלל לאפשרות כזו כונתה "**הַמֶּחְדָּל**".

In the 1973 Yom Kippur war, when Israel was attacked by surprise, its not being ready at all for such eventuality was referred to as "the **failure**" (to do something).

Special Expressions

center of gravity **מֶרְכַּז** הכובד

Additional Examples in this Pattern

ramp, connecting road מֶחְבָּר
intrusion (geology) מֶחְדָּר
interchange, junction מֶחְלָף
dept. of police מֶחְלָק
public bath house (בית) מֶרְחָץ
body (of a vehicle etc.) מֶרְכָּב

---

514. ***meCCaC***, when the 2nd root radical is a guttural

our/your/their	my/your/his/her	const.	Gloss	sing/pl
מֶרְחָבֵנוּ/**מֶרְחַבְ**כֶם/כֶן/**מֶרְחָבָ**ם/ן	**מֶרְחָ**בִי/בְךָ/בֵךְ/בוֹ/בָהּ	מֶרְחַב-	wide	מֶרְחָב ז'
מֶרְחָבֵינוּ/**מֶרְחֲבֵי**כֶם/כֶן/הֶם/הֶן	**מֶרְחָ**בַי/בֶיךָ/בַיִךְ/בָיו/בֶיהָ	מֶרְחֲבֵי-	space	מֶרְחָבִים

When a *shva* is expected with a guttural, the *kamats* is replaced by a *Hataf-pataH*, and in a closed syllable the *kamats* is replaced by a *pataH*.

Examples

מרבית אימוני הצבא בישראל נערכים ב**מֶרְחַב** הדרום.

Most military exercises in Israel are conducted in its southern **space**.

Special Expressions

lebens**raum** (Ger.) **מֶרְחַב** מחיה

certain freedom of action **מֶרְחַב** תמרון

---

515. ***meCCaC*** *kamats > pataH, dagesh*

our/your/their	My/your/his/her	const.	Gloss	sing/pl
מֶרְחַקֵּנוּ/**מֶרְחַקְּ**כֶם/כֶן/**מֶרְחַקָּ**ם/ן	**מֶרְחַ**קִּי/קְּךָ/קֵּךְ/קּוֹ/קָּהּ	מֶרְחַק-	distance	מֶרְחָק ז'
מֶרְחַקֵּינוּ/כֶם/כֶן/הֶם/הֶן	**מֶרְחַ**קַּי/קֶּיךָ/קַּיִךְ/קָּיו/קֶּיהָ	מֶרְחַקֵּי-		מֶרְחַקִּים

In the whole declension except for the singular, the *kamats* is replaced by *pataH*, followed by a *dagesh forte*.

Examples

הַמֶּרְחָק בקילומטרים בין תל אביב לירושלים אינו גדול, אבל ההבדלים באופיין של שתי הערים הם עצומים.

The **distance** in kilometers between Tel Aviv and Jerusalem is minor, but the differences between the characters of these two cities are huge.

---

516. *meCCa*

our/your/their	my/your/his/her	const.	Gloss	sing/pl
מֶחְצָתֵנוּ/**מֶחְצַתְ**כֶם/כֶן/**מֶחְצָתָ**ם/ן	**מֶחְצָ**תִי/תְךָ/תֵךְ/תוֹ/תָהּ	מֶחְצַת-	half (lit.)	מֶחְצָה/מֶחֱצָה נ׳
מֶחְצוֹתֵינוּ/כֶם/כֶן/הֶם/הֶן	**מֶחְצוֹ**תַי/תֶיךָ/תַיִךְ/תָיו/תֶיהָ	מֶחְצוֹת-		מֶחְצוֹת

Nouns realized in this *mishkal* are derived from roots with a final *y*.

Examples

משה הודיע שאינו מסוגל לעשות את עבודתו **לְמֶחְצָה** ; הוא דרש שיאפשרו לו לסיימה.

Moshe announced that he is incapable of doing **half**-a-job; he demanded to be allowed to finish it.

Special Expressions

semi-automatic אוטומטי **לְמֶחְצָה**
half-track זחל **לְמֶחְצָה**
half-brother אח **לְמֶחְצָה**

Additional Examples in this Pattern

tribute; gesture מֶחְוָה/מֶחֱוָה

---

517. *meCCaCa*

our/your/their	my/your/his/her	const.	Gloss	sing/pl
מֶמְשַׁלְתֵּנוּ/תְּכֶם/תְּכֶן/תָּם/תָּן	**מֶמְשַׁלְ**תִּי/תְּךָ/תֵּךְ/תּוֹ/תָּהּ	מֶמְשֶׁלֶת-	government	מֶמְשָׁלָה נ׳
מֶמְשְׁלוֹתֵינוּ/כֶם/כֶן/הֶם/הֶן	**מֶמְשְׁלוֹ**תַי/תֶיךָ/תַיִךְ/תָיו/תֶיהָ	מֶמְשְׁלוֹת-		מֶמְשָׁלוֹת

The declensions and vowel changes are similar to those in the *miCCaCa* pattern above.

Examples

מכיוון שמעולם לא זכתה מפלגה כלשהי ברוב באף אחת מן הבחירות בתולדות המדינה, כל **הַמֶּמְשָׁלוֹת** בישראל הן **מֶמְשָׁלוֹת** קואליציה.

Since no government in the history of the State of Israel has ever won a majority in any election, all Israeli **governments** are coalition **governments**.

היום משתמשים ב**מֶרְכָּבָה** רק לצרכים טקסיים, למשל כשהמלכה אליזבת חוגגת יום הולדת עגול, ונתיניה מריעים לה משני צידי הדרך.

Today they use a **carriage** only for ceremonial purposes, for instance, when Queen Elizabeth celebrates a "round" birthday, and her subjects cheer on both sides of the road.

Special Expressions

מֶמְשֶׁלֶת בובות puppet **government**
מֶמְשֶׁלֶת צללים shadow **government**
ראש **מֶמְשָׁלָה** prime minister

Additional Examples in this Pattern

מֶלְתָּחָה coat check; dressing room; wardrobe
מֶרְקָחָה concoction; mix-up, confusion

---

518. ***maCCaC***

sing/pl	Gloss	const.	my/your/his/her	our/your/their
מַחְסָן	storeroom;	מַחְסַן-	**מַחְסָנ**ִי/נְךָ/נֵךְ/נוֹ/נָהּ	מַחְסָנֵנוּ/**מַחְסַנְ**כֶם/כֶן/**מַחְסָנָ**ם/ן
מַחְסָנִים	warehouse	מַחְסְנֵי-	**מַחְסָנַ**י/נֶיךָ/נַיִךְ/נָיו/נֶיהָ	מַחְסָנֵינוּ/**מַחְסְנֵי**כֶם/כֶן/הֶם/הֶן

Two syllables away from the main stress the *kamats* is reduced to *shva*, מַחְסְנֵיכֶם < *מַחְסָנֵיכֶם, and in a closed syllable to *pataH*, מַחְסַנְכֶם < *מַחְסָנְכֶם.

Examples

כשגרים בבית משותף, אין מספיק מקום בדירה לכל החפצים שאוגרים במשך הזמן; מורידים אותם ל**מַחְסָן** שבקומת הקרקע.

When one lives in an apartment building, there is no space in one's apartments to all objects that have accumulated with time; one takes them down to the **storeroom** on the ground floor.

למה שקרה בישראל אחרי בחירות 1977, שהביאו לשלטון הימין לאחר כמעט שלושים שנה של ממשלות השמאל, קראו "ה**מַהְפָּךְ**".

What took place after the 1977 elections in Israel, which led to a right-wing government after almost thirty years of a left-wing government, was referred to as "the **upset**."

Special Expressions

מַחְסַן חירום emergency **storage**
מַחְסַן ערובה bonded **warehouse**
חיית **מַחְמָד** pet

Additional Examples in this Pattern

מַחְמָד darling; precious thing Lit.
מַחְמָל beloved person Lit.
מַחְנָק/מַחֲנָק suffocation
מַעְפָּל a daring action Lit.
מַרְגָּשׁ mood, general feeling Coll.
מַשְׁמָע meaning
מַתְחָל spathe (bot.)

---

519. ***maCCaC* = *maCaCaC***, when the 1st root consonant is guttural (only in some instances in the case of *Het*)

our/your/their	my/your/his/her	const.	Gloss	sing/pl
מַאֲכָלֵנוּ/**מַאֲכַלְכֶם**/כֶן/**מַאֲכָלָם**/ן	**מַאֲכָלִי**/לְךָ/לֵךְ/לוֹ/לָהּ	מַאֲכַל-	food	מַאֲכָל
מַאֲכָלֵינוּ/**מַאַכְלֵיכֶם**/כֶן/הֶם/הֶן	**מַאֲכָלַי**/לֶיךָ/לַיִךְ/לָיו/לֶיהָ	מַאַכְלֵי-	(item); dish	מַאֲכָלִים

When a *shva* is expected with a guttural, it is replaced by *Hataf-pataH*; if a *shva* is expected immediately before another *shva*, the first *shva* is replaced not by a *Hataf*, but by a *pataH*: מַאַכְלֵיכֶם < מַאֲכְלֵיכֶם* < מַאְכָלֵיכֶם*.

Examples

קשה ליורם להתרגל ל**מַאֲכָלִים** ההודיים, בשל חריפותם הרבה.
Yoram finds it difficult to get used to Indian **dishes**, because of their being so hot.

ה**מַאֲבָקִים** הקשים של היום הם בין הורים לילדים, סביב השימוש הבלתי-פוסק של הילדים בסְמַרְטפון.
Today's hard **struggles** are between parents and children, regarding the children's incessant use of smartphones.

חלק גדול מן המחקר הלשוני היום מתבסס על **מַאַגְרֵי** לשון גדולים, כתובים ומדוברים.
A large part of linguistic research today is based on large language **corpora**, written and spoken.

מַאֲמָרִים רבים נכתבים היום על אכילה נכונה שעשויה לעכב או למנוע את התפשטות הסרטן.
Many **articles** today discuss healthy eating habits that may delay or prevent the spread of cancer.

הנשיא שסרח והורשע בהטרדות ותקיפות מיניות נדון לשבע שנות **מַאֲסָר** (ושוחרר אחרי חמש – לא ברור למה, מכיוון שלעולם לא הביע חרטה).
The president who transgressed and was convicted for sexual molestations and attacks was sentenced to seven years **imprisonment** (of which he served only five – unclear why, since he never expressed any contrition).

Special Expressions

מַאֲכַל מלכים **food** fit for a king
מַאֲכַל תאווה delicious **dish**
מַאֲבָק איתנים continuous strenuous **struggle**
מַאֲגַר נתונים data **base**
מַאֲזַן אֵימה mutual assured destruction
מַאֲזַן תשלומים **balance** of payments
מַאֲמַר מערכת main **editorial**
מַאֲסַר עולם life **sentence**

מַאֲסַר בית house **arrest**
מַאֲסָר על תנאי suspended **sentence**
מַהֲלַךְ/תולדות חיים life story, biography
מַעֲבַר חֲצָיָה/חֲצִיָּה pedestrian **crossing**
מַעֲבָר מפולש covered **passageway**
מַעְגָּל חשמלי electrical **circuit**
מַעְגָּל קסמים vicious **circle**
מַעֲמַד הביניים Middle **class**

Additional Examples in this Pattern

consortium מַאֲגָד
tent encampment מַאֲהָל
balance (sheet) מַאֲזָן
outpost; handhold מַאֲחָז
ambush מַאֲרָב
process, step מַהֲלָךְ
frying pan מַחֲבַת
passageway מַעֲבָר
circle; cycle; scope מַעֲגָל/מַעְגָּל

anchorage מַעֲגָן
position; status; class מַעֲמָד
grant מַעֲנָק
surveillance; tracking מַעֲקָב
bypass מַעֲקָף
west מַעֲרָב
alignment, arrangement מַעֲרָךְ
shift מַעֲתָק

---

520. ***maCCaC* = *maCaC***, with assimilation of root-initial *n* and the *y* of *yts* to the following consonant

our/your/their	my/your/his/her	const.	Gloss	sing/pl
מַבָּטֵנוּ/**מַבָּטְ**כֶם/כֶן/**מַבָּטָ**ם/ן	**מַבָּ**טִי/טְךָ/טֵךְ/טוֹ/טָהּ	מַבַּט-	glance,	מַבָּט
מַבָּטֵינוּ/**מַבְּטֵי**כֶם/כֶן/הֶם/הֶן	**מַבָּ**טַי/טֶיךָ/טַיִךְ/טָיו/טֶיהָ	מַבְּטֵי-	look, gaze	מַבָּטִים

Note: the *kamats* is maintained in the plural forms of מַכָּר 'acquaintance': מַכָּרֵי-, מַכָּרֵיכֶם...

Examples

קשה היה לי להבין אם ה**מַבָּט** המוזר שהעיף בי מכוון היה להראות אי שביעות רצון מהתנהגותי, או שמשהו לא בסדר איתו.
It was difficult for me to determine whether the strange **glance** he cast at me was intended to display dissatisfaction with my behavior, or there is something wrong with him.

כמה מן ה**מַכָּרִים** שלך הם באמת ידידים?
How many of your **acquaintances** are truly friends?

הרבה ונצואלנים עוזבים את המדינה בגלל ה**מַצָּב** הכלכלי הקשה.
Many Venezuelans leave their country because of the difficult economic **situation**. there.

Special Expressions

point of **view** נקודת **מַבָּט**
on first **impression** ב**מַבָּט** ראשון
love at first **sight** אהבה מ**מַבָּט** ראשון

instrument **tray** **מַגַּשׁ** טיפולים
standby **מַצַּב** הִכּוֹן

Additional Examples in this Pattern

tray מַגָּשׁ
waterfall מַפָּל
bang, explosion מַפָּץ

lighter מַצָּת
hyphen מַקָּף/מַקֵּף
wing-clap Lit. מַשָּׁק

---

521. ***maCCaC* = *maCaC*,** with assimilation of root-initial *n* and the *y* of *yts* to the following consonant, and the last consonant is guttural

our/your/their	my/your/his/her	const.	Gloss	sing/pl
מַבָּעֵנוּ/מַבַּעֲכֶם/כֶן/מַבָּעָם/ן	מַבָּעִי/עֲךָ/עֵךְ/עוֹ/עָהּ	מַבַּע-	expression;	מַבָּע
מַבָּעֵינוּ/מַבְּעֵיכֶם/כֶן/הֶם/הֶן	מַבָּעַי/עֶיךָ/עַיִךְ/עָיו/עֶיהָ	מַבְּעֵי-	utterance	מַבָּעִים

When a *shva* is expected, it is replaced by *Hataf-pataH*. Note: the *kamats* is maintained in the plural forms of מַטָּע 'orchad': מַטָּעֵי, מַטָּעֵיכֶם...

Examples

הוא לא הצליח ליצור **מַגָּע** עם הקהל. פניו היו מאובנים, ללא כל **מַבָּע**, ובדקות הראשונות אף **מַבָּע** לא יצא מפיו.
He was unable to establish **contact** with the audience. His face was stony, **expression**less, and in the first few moments not a single **utterance** came out of his mouth.

באזור השרון קיימים עדיין הרבה **מַטָּעֵי** תפוזים, למרות פיתוח הבנייה העצום שעבר.
In the Sharon region there still exist many orange **orchards**, in spite of the vast building development it underwent.

Special Expressions

establish **contact** with בא **בְּמַגָּע** עם
sexual intercourse **מַגָּע** מיני
political **negotiation** **מַגָּע** דיפלומטי
ramjet **מַגַּח** סילון
bitter **disappointment** **מַפַּח** נפש

Additional Examples in this Pattern

butt, gore Lit.-rare מַגָּח
salvo; barrage מַטָּח
frustration (נפש) מַפָּח
platform; bed; bedding מַצָּע

---

522. ***maCCaC* > *maCaC***, with assimilation of root-initial *n* or *y* of *yts* to the following consonant, the last consonant is guttural, and the plural suffix is *-ot*.

our/your/their	my/your/his/her	const.	Gloss	sing/pl
מַסָּעֵנוּ/מַסַּעֲכֶם/כֶן/מַסָּעָם/ן	מַסָּעִי/עֲךָ/עֵךְ/עוֹ/עָהּ	מַסַּע-	journey; campaign;	מַסָּע
מַסְּעוֹתֵינוּ/כֶם/כֶן/הֶם/הֶן	מַסְּעוֹתַי/עֶיךָ/עַיִךְ/עָיו/עֶיהָ	מַסְּעוֹת-	march	מַסָּעוֹת

When a *shva* is expected, it is replaced by *Hataf-pataH*. An alternative (older) form of the plural of מַסָּע is מַסָּעִים.

Examples

הוא חשב, שעם מתן התעודה נסתיים הסיוט, אבל במהרה נתברר לו **שמַסַּע** היסורים שלו רק החל...
He assumed that with the granting of the diploma, the nightmare was over, but he soon found out that his **via** dolorosa has just started.

Special Expressions

propaganda campaign **מַסָּע** הסברה

punitive **expedition** **מַסָּע** עונשין

the Crusades **מַסְּעֵי** הצלב

travel document; passport תעודת **מַסָּע**

travel books ספרי **מַסָּעוֹת**

Additional Examples in this Pattern

load מַשָּׂא

---

523. ***maCCaC* = *maCaC*,** when the second root consonant is *w* or the first one is *y*

our/your/their	my/your/his/her	const.	Gloss	sing/pl
מַטָּסֵנוּ/**מַטָּסְ**כֶם/כֶן/**מַטָּסָ**ם/ן	**מַטָּ**סִי/סְךָ/סֵךְ/סוֹ/סָהּ	מַטַּס-	flyover, aerial demo.	מַטָּס
מַטָּסֵינוּ/**מַטְּסֵי**כֶם/כֶן/הֶם/הֶן	**מַטָּ**סַי/סֶיךָ/סַיִךְ/סָיו/סֶיהָ	מַטְּסֵי-		מַטָּסִים

There is no difference between the declensions in this sub-pattern and those of the other *maCaC* groups above. Thus, no separation was made between forms derived from roots with a middle *w* and initial *y* (like מַדָּע from *y-d-`*), nor between those in which the final consonant is guttural (מַדָּע, מַנָּח).

Examples

המַטָּס השנתי של חיל האוויר ביום העצמאות הוא אחת האטרקציות המרכזיות של החג.
The annual **overfly** of the Israeli Air Force is one of the holiday's main attractions.

יש בתי ספר תיכוניים מיוחדים בישראל לנוער שוחֵר **מַדָּע**.
There are special highschools in Israel for **science**-loving youth.

Special Expressions

science fiction **מַדָּע** בידיוני

the Humanities **מַדְּעֵי** הרוח

the Social **Sciences** **מַדְּעֵי** החברה

Additional Examples in this Pattern

boot מַגָּף (ר' זוגי מַגָּפַיִם)

position מַנָּח

---

524. ***maCCaC*** where a final *kamats* > *pataH* plus *dagesh* medially

our/your/their	My/your/his/her	const.	Gloss	sing/pl
מַמְתַּקֵּנוּ/**מַמְתַּקְּ**כֶם/כֶן/**מַמְתַּקָּ**ם/ן	**מַמְתַּ**קִּי/קְּךָ/קֵּךְ/קּוֹ/קָּהּ	מַמְתַּק-	sweet, candy	מַמְתָּק
מַמְתַּקֵּינוּ/כֶם/כֶן/הֶם/הֶן	**מַמְתַּ**קַּי/קֶּיךָ/קַּיִךְ/קָּיו/קֶּיהָ	מַמְתַּקֵּי-		מַמְתַּקִּים

PataH followed by *dagesh* in all suffixed forms.

Examples

מקובל היום על כל הקהילה הרפואית שאכילה מופרזת של **מַמְתַּקִּים** מסוכנת לבריאות: היא גורמת להשמנת-יתר, ומזיקה לבריאות השיניים.

There is general agreement in the medical community today that excessive consumption of **sweets** is dangerous to one's health: it causes obesity, and damages one's teeth.

ים המלח הוא מקור חשוב ל**מַחְצָבִים**, שאותם מפיקים ישראל וירדן, ובשל הפקת-יתר מביאים גם להידרדרותו.

The Dead Sea is an important source of **minerals**, which both Israel and Jordan extract, but over-extracting also causes its demise.

Special Expressions

מַשְׁאַבֵּי אנוש human **resources**

מַרְבַד קסמים magic carpet

Additional Examples in this Pattern

מַחְשָׁךְ deep darkness Lit.

מַרְבָד carpet, rug

מַטְעָם delicacy

מַשְׁאָב resource

---

525. ***maCCaC > maCaCaC*** where a final *kamats* > pataH plus *dagesh* medially, and when the first root consonant is guttural (only in some occurrences of *Het*)

our/your/their	My/your/his/her	const.	Gloss	sing/pl
מַאֲמַצֵּנוּ/**מַאֲמַצְּ**כֶם/כֶן/**מַאֲמַצָּ**ם/ן	**מַאֲמַ**צִּי/צְּךָ/צֵּךְ/צּוֹ/צָּהּ	-מַאֲמַץ	effort	מַאֲמָץ
מַאֲמַצֵּינוּ/כֶם/כֶן/הֶם/הֶן	**מַאֲמַ**צַּי/צֶּיךָ/צַּיִךְ/צָּיו/צֶּיהָ	-מַאֲמַצֵּי		מַאֲמַצִּים

PataH followed by *dagesh* throughout. The *shva* expected with a guttural in the first root consonant is replaced by *Hataf-pataH*.

Examples

כל נשיא חדש של ארה״ב עושה **מַאֲמָץ** ניכר לקדם את השלום במזרח התיכון, ובינתיים אף נשיא לא הצליח להביא להתקדמות של ממש בנושא.

Every US president has been making considerable **effort** to advance the cause of peace in the Middle East, and so far, no president has been able to bring about significant progress in this matter.

יש תרבויות שבהן נמלים נחשבות ל**מַעֲדָן**.

There are cultures in which ants are considered a **delicacy**.

Special Expressions

מַעֲדַנֵּי מלך wonderful **delicacies**

מ**מַּעֲמַקֵּי** הלב from the **depth** of one's heart

Additional Examples in this Pattern

מַעֲמָק depth Lit.

מַעֲקָשׁ obstacle, difficulty Lit.

---

526. *maCCaCa*

our/your/their	my/your/his/her	const.	Gloss	sing/pl
מַחְלַבְתֵּנוּ/תְּכֶם/תְּכֶן/תָּם/תָּן	**מַחְלַבְ**תִּי/תְּךָ/תֵּךְ/תּוֹ/תָּהּ	מַחְלֶבֶת-	dairy	מַחְלָבָה נ׳
מַחְלְבוֹתֵינוּ/כֶם/כֶן/הֶם/הֶן	**מַחְלְבוֹ**תַי/תֶיךָ/תַיִךְ/תָיו/תֶיהָ	מַחְלְבוֹת-	plant	מַחְלָבוֹת

Two syllables away from the main stress and in the construct state the first *kamats* is replaced by a *shva*, מַחְלְבוֹתַי etc., and in a closed syllable the *kamats* is replaced by a *pataH*: מַחְלַבְתִּי. The construct state in the singular is characterized by two *seghol*s, and is penultimately stressed: מַחְלֶבֶת-.

Examples

בזמנו, **מַחְלֶבֶת** "תנובה" שלטה פחות-או-יותר בתחום מוצרי החלב בארץ. היום יש לפחות שבע **מַחְלָבוֹת** גדולות, ומספר רב של "**מַחְלְבוֹת** בוטיק".

At the time, the Tnuva **dairy plant** more-or-less controlled the dairy products field in Israel. Today there are at least seven large **dairies** there, and a large number of "boutique **dairies**."

פעמיים או שלוש קרה ששידרגו אותי ל**מַחְלֶקֶת** עסקים ללא תשלום נוסף. זאת חוויה שתמיד זוכרים אותה, בעיקר בטיסות ארוכות...

Twice or three times I was upgraded (for feee) to business **class**. It was an experience to remember, particularly in long flights…

Special Expressions

the UK **הַמַּמְלָכָה** המאוחדת
the plant **kingdom**, flora **מַמְלֶכֶת** הצומח
space **lab** **מַעְבֶּדֶת** חלל

first **class** (in travel) **מַחְלָקָה** ראשונה
Jewish **thought** **מַחְשֶׁבֶת** ישראל
intentionally, deliberately **בְּמַחְשָׁבָה** תחילה

Additional Examples in this Pattern

kingdom מַמְלָכָה
lab מַעְבָּדָה
transit camp מַעְבָּרָה

quarry מַחְצָבָה
lathe shop מַחְרָטָה
thought מַחְשָׁבָה

---

527. ***maCCaCa* = *maCaCaCa***, when the first root consonant is guttural (not in all instances of *Het* and *`ayin*)

our/your/their	my/your/his/her	const.	Gloss	sing/pl
מַעֲטַפְתֵּנוּ/תְּכֶם/תְּכֶן/תָּם/תָּן	**מַעֲטַפְ**תִּי/תְּךָ/תֵּךְ/תּוֹ/תָּהּ	מַעֲטֶפֶת-	envelope	מַעֲטָפָה נ׳
מַעַטְפוֹתֵינוּ/כֶם/כֶן/הֶם/הֶן	**מַעַטְפוֹ**תַי/תֶיךָ/תַיִךְ/תָיו/תֶיהָ	מַעַטְפוֹת-		מַעֲטָפוֹת

Where a *shva* is expected with a guttural, it is replaced by a *Hataf-pataH*. Note: מַעֲרֶכֶת is an alternant of מַעֲרָכָה (see below), and also an independent term referring to an editorial board. Both refer to systems and sets, but in spoken Hebrew people tend to use מַעֲרָכָה only for battle.

Examples

כשהיינו ילדים, אספנו **מַעֲטָפוֹת** של היום הראשון שניפקה המדינה לרגל חגים ומועדים. מי ששמר על כולן יצא ברכוש גדול...

When we were kids, we used to collect **envelopes** of the first day of issue sold by the government to commemorate special days and holidays. Those who kept them all now have something of real value…

Special Expressions

מַעֲטֶפֶת נפץ letter bomb

מַעֲצֶמֶת-על super-**power**

המַעֲצָמָה השביעית the press (the "seventh **power**")

מַעֲרֶכֶת הפעלה operating **system**

מַעֲרֶכֶת השמש the solar **system**

Additional Examples in this Pattern

מַעֲמָסָה burden

מַעֲצָמָה (world) power

מַעֲרָכָה war, battle; system; act

---

528. ***maCCaCa***, when the last root consonant is guttural

The declension is the same as in regular *maCCaCa*; the only difference is in the singular of the construct state, owing to the guttural: -מַלְתַּעַת.

Examples

אחד הסרטים הפופולריים ביותר בשנות השבעים היה "**מַלְתָּעוֹת**", סרט זוועות על כריש העושה שמות במתרחצים בחוף נופש בניו אינגלנד...

One of the most popular movies in the seventies was "**Jaws**," a horror movie about a shark wreaking havoc on bathers in a New England resort beach…

---

529. ***maCCaCa*** with regular vowel reduction (no segholate-like alternants)

our/your/their	my/your/his/her	const.	Gloss	sing/pl
מַסְקָנָתֵנוּ/תְכֶם/תְכֶן/תָם/תָן	**מַסְקָנָ**תִי/תְךָ/תֵךְ/תוֹ/תָהּ	-מַסְקֶנֶת	conclusion	מַסְקָנָה נ׳
מַסְקְנוֹתֵינוּ/כֶם/כֶן/הֶם/הֶן	**מַסְקְנוֹ**תַי/תֶיךָ/תַיִךְ/תָיו/תֶיהָ	-מַסְקְנוֹת		מַסְקָנוֹת

Examples

כשעוקבים אחרי הקריירות של אמנים, בעיקר זמרים, **המַסְקָנָה** החשובה היא שאמן טוב חייב גם להבין מתי עליו להפסיק, לפני הוא לגמרי מאבד את קולו.

When one follows the careers of artists, particularly singers, the important **conclusion** is that a good artist also needs to understand at what stage he should quit, before he completely loses his voice.

Additional Examples in this Pattern

מַחְמָאָה compliment

מַחְרָאָה latrine, privy

---

530. ***maCCaCa* = *maCaCaCa*** with a dagesh in the last root consonant, and the first root consonant is a guttural

our/your/their	my/your/his/her	const.	Gloss	sing/pl
מַהֲתַלָּתֵנוּ/תְכֶם/תְכֶן/תָם/תָן	**מַהֲתַלָּ**תִי/תְךָ/תֵךְ/תוֹ/תָהּ	מַהֲתַלַּת-	joke	מַהֲתַלָּה נ׳
מַהֲתַלּוֹתֵינוּ/כֶם/כֶן/הֶם/הֶן	**מַהֲתַלּוֹ**תַי/תֶיךָ/תַיִךְ/תָיו/תֶיהָ	מַהֲתַלּוֹת-		מַהֲתַלּוֹת

The *dagesh* is preceded by (an expected) *pataH*. Where a *shva* is expected with a guttural, it is replaced by a *Hataf-pataH*.

Examples

כולם צחקו מן ה**מַהֲתַלָּה** של הקומיקאי הידוע שעשה חוכא ואיטלולא מן המנהיג, אבל נושא ה**מַהֲתַלָּה** כלל לא חשב שזה מצחיק.

Everybody laughed at the **joke** of the famous comedian, who made fun of the leader, but the subject of the **joke** did not find it funny at all.

---

531. ***maCCéCet***

our/your/their	my/your/his/her	const.	Gloss	sing/pl
מַזְכַּרְתֵּנוּ/תְּכֶם/תְּכֶן/תָּם/תָּן	**מַזְכַּרְ**תִּי/תְּךָ/תֵּךְ/תּוֹ/תָּהּ	מַזְכֶּרֶת-	souvenir,	מַזְכֶּרֶת נ׳
מַזְכְּרוֹתֵינוּ/כֶם/כֶן/הֶם/הֶן	**מַזְכְּרוֹ**תַי/תֶיךָ/תַיִךְ/תָיו/תֶיהָ	מַזְכְּרוֹת-	memento	מַזְכָּרוֹת

As in the segholate nouns without a prefix (cf. כַּלְבִּי ~ כֶּלֶב), stress falls on the penultimate syllable. In the declension the two *seghol*s are replaced by a *pataH* and a quiescent *shva* (which actually reflect the historical base). Some of the nouns in this *mishkal* denote instruments.

Examples

מבקרים באתרים ארכיאולוגיים לעתים ״סוחבים״ פריטים שנתקלו בהם בסיור כ**מַזְכָּרוֹת** מן הטיול.

Visitors to archeological sites occasionally "lift" items they bump into during their tour to serve as **souvenirs** of the trip.

בשל השימוש הנרחב היום במחשבים ניידים קטנים, תלמידי בתי הספר משתמשים הרבה פחות ב**מַחְבָּרוֹת**.

Owing to increased use of small portable computers, school pupils make much lesser use of (actual) **notebooks** today…

כשמדברים על ה**מַחְתָּרוֹת** שפעלו בארץ ישראל בתקופת המנדט הבריטי, מתכוונים בדרך כלל לאצ״ל (״ארגון לוחמי ישראלי״) וללח״י (״לוחמי חירות ישראל״).

When referring to the **underground organizations** operating in Mandatory Palestine, one usually refers to Begin's Irgun and to the Stern Gang.

Special Expressions

formulaic dedication inscribed on object presented as token of friendship, etc — **לְמַזְכֶּרֶת** נצח/עולם

Additional Examples in this Pattern

mat מַחְצֶלֶת
clamp (carpentry) מַלְחֶצֶת
polishing machine מַלְטֶשֶׁת
sculpting tool מַפְסֶלֶת
destroyer (navy) מַשְׁחֶתֶת

---

532. ***maCCéCet = maCaCéCet*** when the first root consonant is guttural

our/your/their	my/your/his/her	const.	Gloss	sing/pl
מַעַרַכְתֵּנוּ/תְּכֶם/תְּכֶן/תָּם/תָּן	**מַעֲרַכְ**תִּי/תְּךָ/תֵּךְ/תּוֹ/תָּהּ	מַעֲרֶכֶת-	set, system;	מַעֲרֶכֶת נ׳
מַעַרְכוֹתֵינוּ/כֶם/כֶן/הֶם/הֶן	**מַעַרְכוֹ**תַי/תֶיךָ/תַיִךְ/תָיו/תֶיהָ	מַעַרְכוֹת-	editorial board	מַעֲרָכוֹת

A *shva* with a guttural is replaced by a *Hataf-pataH*. If the following vowel is reduced to a *shva* in the declension, the *Hataf* with the guttural is replaced by a *pataH*, since a *Hataf-shva* sequence is hard to articulate: -מַעְרְכוֹת* > -מַעֲרְכוֹת* > מַ-עַרְ-כוֹת-.

Examples

בחברות גדולות או במפעלים המורכבים מאלפי מרכיבים התלויים זה בזה, כשלון של מרכיב אחד עלול למוטט את כל ה**מַעֲרֶכֶת**.
In large companies or plants that consist of thousands of interdependent components, the failure of one component may bring about the collapse of the whole **system**.

Special Expressions

the journal's **editorial board** **מַעֲרֶכֶת** העיתון
operating **system** **מַעֲרֶכֶת** הפעלה
the solar **system** **מַעֲרֶכֶת** השמש
information **system** **מַעֲרֶכֶת** מידע
class **schedule** **מַעֲרֶכֶת** שיעורים
changing and replacing the old **systems** שידוד **מַעֲרָכוֹת**

Additional Examples in this Pattern

slaughtering/carving knife Lit. מַאֲכֶלֶת
mantle; casing; surround; dura מַעֲטֶפֶת

---

533. ***maCCéCet = maCCáCat*** when the third root consonant is guttural

our/your/their	my/your/his/her	const.	Gloss	sing/pl
מַטְבַּעְתֵּנוּ/תְּכֶם/תְּכֶן/תָּם/תָּן	**מַטְבַּעְ**תִּי/תְּךָ/תֵּךְ/תּוֹ/תָּהּ	מַטְבַּעַת-	die,	מַטְבַּעַת נ׳
מַטְבְּעוֹתֵינוּ/כֶם/כֶן/הֶם/הֶן	**מַטְבְּעוֹ**תַי/תֶיךָ/תַיִךְ/תָיו/תֶיהָ	מַטְבְּעוֹת-	swage	מַטְבָּעוֹת

When the third root consonant is ה׳, ח׳, ע׳, the two *seghol*s are replaced by two *pataH*s.

Examples

מכונה המייצרת צורות שונות במתכת על פי תבנית (״שְׁטַנְץ״) קרויה **מַטְבַּעַת**.
A machine that reproduces different forms in metal is called **מַטְבַּעַת**.

Special Expressions

a machine that produces letter casts for printing **מַטְבַּעַת** אותיות

Additional Examples in this Pattern

saddlecloth מַרְדַּעַת

---

534. *maCCóCet*

our/your/their	my/your/his/her	const.	Gloss	sing/pl
מַשְׂכֻּרְתֵּנוּ/תְּכֶם/תְּכֶן/תָּם/תָּן	**מַשְׂכֻּרְ**תִּי/תְּךָ/תֵּךְ/תּוֹ/תָּהּ	מַשְׂכֹּרֶת-	salary,	מַשְׂכֹּרֶת נ׳
מַשְׂכּוֹרוֹתֵינוּ/כֶם/כֶן/הֶם/הֶן	**מַשְׂכּוֹרוֹ**תַי/תֶיךָ/תַיִךְ/תָיו/תֶיהָ	מַשְׂכּוֹרוֹת-	wages	מַשְׂכּוֹרוֹת

In the singular isolation form and in the singular construct, stress falls on the penultimate syllable. In the declension the historical *kubuts* resurfaces in closed syllables.

Examples

ועד הפועלים במפעל איים להשביתו אם לא תינתן לעובדים העלאה של 5% **בַּמַּשְׂכֹּרֶת**.
The workers' union threatened to strike it if the workers are not granted a 5% **salary** increase.

אחת **המַּחְלוֹקוֹת** ההולכות ומחריפות בארה״ב, היא האם ראוי להתייחס לאוניברסיטה כעסק ככל העסקים, או שיש לראות באוניברסיטה נשאית של תרבות וקידמה, ולתמוך בה מבחוץ אם אינה מצליחה לשאת את עצמה כלכלית.
One of the sharp **controversies** getting worse and worse in the US, is whether one should treat a university like any other business, or to regard it as a carrier of culture and progress, and support it with outside funds if it cannot fully support itself.

Special Expressions

may he be תהי **מַשְׂכֻּרְתּוֹ** שלמה paid/rewarded in full

a **controversial** issue סלע **המַּחְלֹקֶת**

booby **trap** **מַלְכֹּדֶת** פתאים

space **shuttle** **מַעְבֹּרֶת** חלל

Additional Examples in this Pattern

trap מַלְכֹּדֶת

ferry מַעְבֹּרֶת

structure, format, framework מַתְכֹּנֶת

---

535. *maCCe*, from roots in which the third consonant is *y*

our/your/their	my/your/his/her	const.	Gloss	sing/pl
מַקְלֵנוּ/לְכֶם/לְכֶן/לָם/לָן	**מַקְ**לִי/לְךָ/לֵךְ/לוֹ (לֵהוּ) לָהּ (לֶהָ)	מַקְלֵה-	toaster	מַקְלֶה ז׳
מַקְלֵינוּ/כֶם/כֶן/הֶם/הֶן	**מַקְ**לַי/לֶיךָ/לַיִךְ/לָיו/לֶיהָ	מַקְלֵי-		מַקְלִים

The *y* at the end of the root is not realized. Most realizations denote instruments.

Examples

בין מכשירי המטבח, **המַקְלֶה** היה תמיד אחד ממכשירי החשמל השווים לכל נפש.
Among the electrical kitchen appliances, the **toaster** has always been one of the least expensive.

בכל כלי תחבורה ציבורי, או בבניין ציבורי, חייב להיות לפחות **מַטְפֶּה** אחד.
In any public means of transportation, as well as in any public building, there must be at least one **fire extinguisher**.

Special Expressions

shelter (for homeless people, battered women, etc.) בית **מַחְסֶה**

Additional Examples in this Pattern

pointer מַחְוֶה
shelter מַחְסֶה
blender מַמְחֶה
mask, guise מַסְוֶה
loop on clothing to hang on hook מַתְלֶה

---

536. ***maCCe***, from roots in which the third consonant is *y* and the plural suffix is *-ot*

our/your/their	my/your/his/her	const.	Gloss	sing/pl
מַרְאֵנוּ/אֲכֶם/אֲכֶן/אָם/אָן	**מַרְ**אִי/אֲךָ/אֵךְ/אוֹ (אֵהוּ) אָהּ (אֶהָ)	מַרְאֵה-	view,	מַרְאֶה ז׳
מַרְאוֹתֵינוּ/כֶם/כֶן/הֶם/הֶן	**מַרְאוֹ**תַי/תֶיךָ/תַיִךְ/תָיו/תֶיהָ	מַרְאוֹת-	sight	מַרְאוֹת

There is also the plural alternant מַרְאִים, but in current Hebrew one only uses מַרְאוֹת. In this case, because of the א׳, a *shva* with the א׳ is replaced by a *Hataf-pataH*.

Examples

אחד היתרונות של נסיעה ברכבת הוא **המַרְאוֹת** היפים החולפים לצד המסילה.
One of the advantages of train travel is the beautiful **sights** one passes by along the rail.

---

537. ***maCCe***, from roots in which the third consonant is *y* and the plural ending is -אוֹת,

our/your/their	my/your/his/her	const.	Gloss	sing/pl
מַשְׁקֵנוּ/קְכֶם/קְכֶן/קָם/קָן	**מַשְׁקִ**י/קְךָ/קֵךְ/קוֹ (קֵהוּ) קָהּ (קֶהָ)	מַשְׁקֵה-	beverage	מַשְׁקֶה ז׳
מַשְׁקְאוֹתֵינוּ/כֶם/כֶן/הֶם/הֶן	**מַשְׁקְאוֹ**תַי/תֶיךָ/תַיִךְ/תָיו/תֶיהָ	מַשְׁקְאוֹת-		מַשְׁקָאוֹת

מַשְׁקֶה denotes beverage or drink, and in the past also the server of drinks. The plural suffix of the server is ים-, and of the drink – at least today – is ות- (with א׳, of course).

Examples

המַשְׁקֶה האלכוהולי החביב עליי הוא בְּרֶנְדִּי התפוחים הצרפתי קַלְבָדוֹס.
My favorite alcoholic **drink** is the French apple brandy Calvados.

Special Expressions

non-alcoholic **beverage** **מַשְׁקֶה** קל

alcoholic **beverages/drinks** **מַשְׁקָאוֹת** חריפים

---

538. ***maCCe*** = ***maCaCe*** from roots in which the third consonant is *y* and the first root consonant is guttural

our/your/their	my/your/his/her	const.	Gloss	sing/pl
מַעֲשֵׂנוּ/**מַעַשְׂ**כֶם/כֶן/**מַעֲשָׂ**ם/ן	מַעֲשִׂי/מַעַשְׂךָ/**מַעֲשֵׂ**ךְ/שׂוֹ (שֵׂהוּ)/שָׂהּ (שֶׂהָ)	מַעֲשֵׂה-	deed, thing made; event; tale	מַעֲשֶׂה ז׳
מַעֲשֵׂינוּ/כֶם/כֶן/הֶם/הֶן	**מַעֲשַׂ**י/שֶׂיךָ/שַׂיִךְ/שָׂיו/שֶׂיהָ	מַעֲשֵׂי-		מַעֲשִׂים

A *shva* with a guttural is replaced by a *Hataf-pataH*. If the following vowel is a *shva* (which results from reduction), the *Hataf* with the guttural is replaced by a *pataH*: מַעַשְׂךָ < מַעֲשְׂךָ* (unacceptable sequence of a *Hataf* and *shva*). Note the *seghol* > *tsere* in the construct state.

Examples

מַעֲשִׂים טובים חשובים יותר מכוונות טובות.

Good **deeds** are more important than good intentions.

העוגה הזאת היא ממש **מַעֲשֵׂה** אומנות.

This cake is a true **work** of art.

בעברית ספרותית, סיפורים מתחילים לעתים קרובות ב״**מַעֲשֶׂה** ב...״

In literary Hebrew, stories often start with "this is a **story/tale** about..."

Special Expressions

in the **act** בשעת **מַעֲשֶׂה**

instructions put into actual practice הלכה **לְמַעֲשֶׂה**

sitting idle, unemployed יושב באפס **מַעֲשֶׂה**

actually, in fact **לְמַעֲשֶׂה**

What do you do? מה **מַעֲשֶׂיךָ**?

something to be proud of **מַעֲשֵׂה** ידיו להתפאר

miracle **מַעֲשֵׂה** ניסים

prank **מַעֲשֵׂה** קונדס

a true **story** **מַעֲשֶׂה** שהיה

Additional Examples in this Pattern

pastry מַאֲפֶה　　thick N Lit. מַעֲבֶה　　cover; cloak מַעֲטֶה

---

539. ***maCCe*** = ***maCaCe***, from roots in which the 3rd consonant is *y*, the 1st root consonant guttural, and the plural suffix is *-ot*.

our/your/their	my/your/his/her	const.	Gloss	sing/pl
מַחֲנֵנוּ/**מַחֲנְ**כֶם/כֶן/**מַחֲנָ**ם/ן	מַחֲנִי/מַחַנְךָ/**מַחֲנֵ**ךְ/נוֹ (נֵהוּ) /נָהּ (נֶהָ)	מַחֲנֵה-	camp, encampment	מַחֲנֶה ז׳
מַחֲנֵינוּ/כֶם/כֶן/הֶם/הֶן	**מַחֲנַ**י/נֶיךָ/נַיִךְ/נָיו/נֶיהָ	מַחֲנוֹת-		מַחֲנוֹת

A *shva* with a guttural is replaced by a *Hataf-pataH*. If the following vowel is a *shva* (which results from reduction), the *Hataf* with the guttural is replaced by a *pataH*: מַחַנְךָ < מַחֲנְךָ* (a *Hataf-shva* sequence is difficult to articulate).

Examples

השומר בשער אינו נותן לאיש להיכנס **לַמַּחֲנֶה** ללא סיסמה.
The MP at the gate does not allow anyone to enter the **camp** without a password.

בארה״ב ילדים רבים מבלים חלק מחופשת הקיץ **בְּמַחֲנוֹת** – חופש לילדים, חופש להורים...
In the US many children spend some of their summer vacation in **camps** – vacation for kids, vacation for parents...

Special Expressions

concentration **camp** **מַחֲנֵה** ריכוז
refugee **camp** **מַחֲנֵה** פליטים
dodge ball (game) **מַחֲנַיִם**
horror **show** **מַחֲזֵה** אימים

Additional Examples in this Pattern

play; show מַחֲזֶה
incline, slope; rise, ascent מַעֲלֶה

---

540. ***maCCe* = *maCe***, from roots in which the third consonant is *y*, and the first root consonant is an assimilated *n*.

our/your/their	my/your/his/her	const.	Gloss	sing/pl
מַטֵּנוּ/טְּכֶם/טְּכֶן/טָּם/טָּן	**מַ**טִּי/טְּךָ/טֵּךְ/טּוֹ (טֵּהוּ)/טָּהּ (טֶּהָ)	מַטֵּה-	walking	מַטֶּה ז׳
מַטּוֹתֵינוּ/כֶם/כֶן/הֶם/הֶן	**מַטּוֹ**תַי/תֶיךָ/תַיִךְ/תָיו/תֶיהָ	מַטּוֹת-	stick; staff	מַטּוֹת

The root here is *n-t-y*, and the root-initial *n* is totally assimilated into the 2nd root consonant. The plural form is מַטּוֹת.

Examples

כשמשה השליך את **מַטֵּהוּ** לפני פרעה, הוא הפך לנחש.
When Moses threw his **staff** in front of Pharaoh, it turned into a snake.

המקום בו ממוקם **הַמַּטֶּה** הכללי בתל אביב מכונה בלשון עממית ״הבור״.
The place in which the general **staff** in Tel Aviv is located is colloquially referred to as “the hole,” or “the pit.”

Special Expressions

the General **Staff** **הַמַּטֶּה** הכללי (מטכ״ל)
the Chief of the General **Staff** ראש **הַמַּטֶּה** הכללי (רמטכ״ל)

---

541. *maCCeC*

Our/your/their	my/your/his/her	const.	Gloss	sing/pl
מַסְמְרֵנוּ/**מַסְמֶרְכֶם**/כֶן/**מַסְמְרָם**/ן	מַסְמְרִי/מַסְמֶרְךָ/**מַסְמְרֵךְ**/רוֹ/רָהּ	מַסְמֵר-	nail;	מַסְמֵר ז׳
מַסְמְרֵינוּ/כֶם/כֶן/הֶם/הֶן	**מַסְמְרַי**/רֶיךָ/רַיִךְ/רָיו/רֶיהָ	מַסְמְרֵי-	center	מַסְמְרִים

Many realizations in this *mishkal* denote instruments. Where reduction is expected and the following vowel is a *shva*, the reduction of the *tsere* is to a *seghol*, not to a *shva*.

Examples

אם תוקעים בקיר **מַסְמֵר** ללא ראש, קשה מאוד להוציאו משם אם יש צורך בכך.
If one sticks a headless **nail** in the wall, it is very difficult it remove it later should it become necessary.

עוזי היה במצב רוח מצוין אתמול, ועם כל הסיפורים והבדיחות הוא הפך **לְמַסְמֵר** המסיבה.
Uzi was in excellent mood last night, and with all his stories and jokes, he became the **center** of the party.

באוכלו, האמריקאי הטיפוסי משתמש בסכין רק כשאין ברירה וצריך לחתוך. משחתך, הוא מניח את הסכין, נוטל את **הַמַּזְלֵג** לבדו ביד ימין, ומשתמש בו כקִלשון.
While eating, the typical American uses a knife only when needed for cutting. Once s/he has cut, s/he lifts the **fork** alone in the right hand, and uses it as a pitchfork.

בבדיקות דם, אחת האחיות בקליניקה של האוניברסיטה הייתה תוקעת את **הַמַּזְרֵק** לתוך הווריד בזווית של 90 מעלות, ותמיד גורמת לחולה לקריש דם בווריד.
In drawing blood, one of the nurses in the university clinic would stick the **syringe** in a 90 degree angle, and always cause the patient a blood clot in the vein.

קשה להאמין שפעם כתבנו וחיפשנו מידע ללא **מַחְשֵׁב**.
It is hard to believe that once we wrote and looked for information without a **computer**.

חברת קטרפילר מייצרת את **הַמַּכְבֵּשִׁים** הטובים והפופולריים ביותר שניתן לרכוש.
The Caterpillar company produces the best and most popular **steamrollers** one can acquire.

הַמַּשְׁבֵּר בבורסה האמריקאית ב-1929 היה הקשה ביותר בתולדות ארה״ב.
The 1929 stock exchange **crisis** in 1929 was the worst in the history of the US.

Special Expressions

stuck, immobile **כְּמַסְמֵר** תקוע
cannot be extracted **כְּמַסְמֵר** בלי ראש
the **center** (of attention) of the evening **מַסְמֵר** הערב
arrived at a critical point בא עד **מַשְׁבֵּר**

whatever comes, whatever is readily available כל אשר יעלה **הַמַּזְלֵג**
very little, just a small sample על קצה **הַמַּזְלֵג**
PC **מַחְשֵׁב** אישי
tablet computer **מַחְשֵׁב** לוח

Additional Examples in this Pattern

מַבְרֵג screwdriver
מַגְבֵּר amplifier
מַחְבֵּט bat, baseball bat
מַחְלֵץ corkscrew
מַכְלֵב stapler
מַכְתֵּשׁ crater
מַלְבֵּן rectangle
מַסְרֵק comb
מַפְלֵג distributor
מַפְלֵט exhaust pipe
מַפְסֵק switch
מַצְבֵּר battery
מַצְמֵד clutch
מַצְנֵם toaster
מַצְפֵּן compass
מַקְלֵט (radio) receiver
מַקְרֵן projector

---

542. *maCCeC* = *maCaCeC* when the first root consonant is a guttural

sing/pl	Gloss	const.	my/your/his/her	Our/your/their
מַהֲדֵק ז׳	paper clip,	מַהֲדֵק-	מַהְדְּקִי/מַהֲדֶקְךָ/**מַהֲדְ**קֵךְ/קוֹ/קָהּ	מַהְדְּקֵנוּ/**מַהֲדֶקְ**כֶם/כֶן/**מַהֲדְקָ**ם/ן
מַהְדְּקִים	stapler	מַהְדְּקֵי-	**מַהְדְּ**קַי/קֶיךָ/קַיִךְ/קָיו/קֶיהָ	**מַהְדְּקֵי**נוּ/כֶם/כֶן/הֶם/הֶן

A *shva* with a guttural is replaced by a *Hataf-pataH*. When the reduction of the *tsere* to *shva* would have created an unacceptable *Hataf-shva* sequence, the *Hataf* is replaced by *seghol* in מַהֲדֶקְךָ < *מַהֲדְקְךָ < *מַהֲדֵקְךָ etc., but in מַהְדְּקֵי < *מַהֲדְקֵי etc. it is replaced by *pataH*. In both cases a quiescent *shva* closes the syllable.

Examples

יש אנשים שיכולים לפרוץ מנעול בעזרת **מַהֲדֵק** שיישרו את התיל שלו.
There are people who can open a lock by using a **paper clip** whose wire has been straightened.

Additional Examples in this Pattern

מַעֲדֵר/מַעְדֵּר hoe

---

543. *maCCeC* = *maCaCeC* when the first root consonant is a guttural and the plural suffix is -וֹת

sing/pl	Gloss	const.	my/your/his/her	Our/your/their
מַעֲשֵׂר ז׳	tithing	מַעֲשַׂר-	מַעַשְׂרִי/מַעֲשֶׂרְךָ/**מַעַשְׂ**רֵךְ/רוֹ/רָהּ	מַעַשְׂרֵנוּ/**מַעֲשֶׂרְ**כֶם/כֶן/**מַעַשְׂרָ**ם/ן
מַעַשְׂרוֹת		מַעַשְׂרוֹת-	**מַעַשְׂרוֹ**תַי/תֶיךָ/תַיִךְ/תָיו/תֶיהָ	**מַעַשְׂרוֹתֵי**נוּ/כֶם/כֶן/הֶם/הֶן

A *shva* with a guttural is replaced by a *Hataf-pataH*. When the reduction of the *tsere* to *shva* would have created an unacceptable *Hataf-shva* sequence, the *Hataf* is replaced by *seghol* in מַעֲשֶׂרְךָ < *מַעֲשְׂרְךָ < *מַעֲשֵׂרְךָ etc., but in מַ-עַשְׂ-רוֹת < *מַעֲשְׂרוֹת etc. it is replaced by *pataH*. In both cases a quiescent *shva* closes the syllable.

Examples

אצל המורמונים, כמו אצל היהודים בעת העתיקה, נהוג להפריש **מַעֲשֵׂר** מן ההכנסות האישיות לקופת הציבור, לעזרה לנצרכים.

Among the Mormons, like among the Jews in ancient times, it is customary to pay **tithing** (a tenth) of one's personal income to the public coffers, to help the needy.

---

544. ***maCCeC*** when the second root consonant is guttural

our/your/their	my/your/his/her	const.	Gloss	sing/pl
מַגְהֵצֵנוּ/**מַגְהֶצְכֶם**/כֶן/**מַגְהֵצָם**/ן	מַגְהֵצִי/מַגְהֶצְךָ/**מַגְהֵצֵךְ**/צוֹ/צָהּ	מַגְהֵץ-	iron	מַגְהֵץ ז׳
מַגְהֲצֵינוּ/כֶם/כֶן/הֶם/הֶן	**מַגְהֲצַי**/צֶיךָ/צַיִךְ/צָיו/צֶיהָ	מַגְהֲצֵי-		מַגְהֲצִים

A *shva* with a guttural is replaced by a *Hataf-pataH*. If the following vowel is a *shva*, the *Hataf* of the guttural is replaced by a *pataH*: מַגְ-הַצְ-ךָ > *מַגְהֲצְךָ, to avoid an unacceptable *pataH-shva* sequence.

Examples

בלשון הדיבור משתמשים בדרך כלל בצורה מְגַהֵץ במקום **מַגְהֵץ**, מכיוון שמרבית הדוברים אינם מבחינים בין אדם ומכשיר המבצעים את אותה הפעולה, וייתכן שאמנם אין הצדקה של ממש להבחנה מסוג זה...

In spoken Hebrew one usually uses the form מְגַהֵץ (for **iron**) instead of the (normative) מַגְהֵץ, since most speakers do not distinguish between a person and an instrument performing the same function, and it is possible that indeed there is no real need for such a distinction…

למרות שמרבית המטוסים היום הם מטוסי סילון, עדיין יש לא מעט מטוסים מונעי-**מַדְחֵף** – רובם קטנים יותר, אבל עדיין יש גם מטוסי תובלה ומטוסים קטנים עם **מַדְחֵף**.

Although most planes today are jet planes, there are still a good number of **propeller**-driven ones – most of them smaller, but there are also transport planes and small planes that have a **propeller**.

Special Expressions

מַבְעֵר אחורי after**burner**

מַגְהֵץ אדים steam **iron**

Additional Examples in this Pattern

מַבְעֵר burner; lighter

מַדְחֵס compressor

מַטְעֵן charger

מַלְחֵם soldering iron; blowtorch

מַפְחֵת reducer (of noise etc.)

מַשְׁאֵף inhaler

מַשְׁחֵז knife sharpener

מַתְאֵם adapter (electronics)

---

545. ***maCCeC*** when the third root consonant is *'alef*

our/your/their	my/your/his/her	const.	Gloss	sing/pl
מַקְפְּאֵנוּ/**מַקְפַּאֲכֶם**/כֶן/**מַקְפְּאָם**/ן	מַקְפְּאִי/מַקְפַּאֲךָ/**מַקְפְּאֵךְ**/אוֹ/אָהּ	מַקְפֵּא-	freezer	מַקְפֵּא ז׳
מַקְפְּאֵינוּ/כֶם/כֶן/הֶם/הֶן	**מַקְפְּאַי**/אֶיךָ/אַיִךְ/אָיו/אֶיהָ	מַקְפְּאֵי-		מַקְפְּאִים

A *shva* with a guttural is replaced by a *Hataf-pataH*. If the preceding vowel is expected to undergo reduction, it is replaced by a *pataH*: מַקְפֵּאֲךָ < מַקְפַּאֲךָ*.

Examples

אם קונים מוצרי מזון בכמויות גדולות כדי לשלם פחות, מחזיקים את חלקם **בַּמַּקְפֵּא**.
If one buys large quantities of food so as to pay less, one can keep some in the **freezer**.

Additional Examples in this Pattern

cure מַרְפֵּא

---

546. ***maCCeC*** when the third root consonant is ה׳ ח׳ ע׳

our/your/their	my/your/his/her	const.	Gloss	sing/pl
מַצְנְחֵנוּ/**מַצְנַחֲ**כֶם/כֶן/**מַצְנְחָ**ם/ן	מַצְנְחִי/מַצְנַחֲךָ/**מַצְנְחֵ**ךְ/חוֹ/חָהּ	מַצְנֵחַ-	parachute	מַצְנֵחַ ז׳
מַצְנְחֵינוּ/כֶם/כֶן/הֶם/הֶן	**מַצְנְחַ**י/חֶיךָ/חַיִךְ/חָיו/חֶיהָ	מַצְנְחֵי-		מַצְנְחִים

In the isolation form, the guttural is preceded by a *furtive pataH* before a vowel other than *a*. A *shva* with a guttural is replaced by a *Hataf-pataH*. If the preceding vowel is expected to undergo reduction, it is reduced to a *pataH*, to avoid a *Hataf-shva* sequence: מַצְנֵחֲךָ < מַצְנְחֲךָ* < מַצְנַחֲךָ.

Examples

מַצְנֵחַ שאינו נפתח הוא סיוטו הגדול ביותר של כל צנחן.
A **parachute** that does not open is the worst nightmare of any parachutist.

להב **מַקְדֵּחַ** הבטון, הנקרא בארץ "**מַקְדֵּחַ** וידיה" (בהשפעת הגרמנית), עשוי מקרביד הטונגסטן.
The blade of the concrete **drill**, called "vidia **drill**" (from German) in Israel, is made of tungsten carbide.

הַמַּקְלֵעַ הומצא כבר בשנות השמונים של המאה התשע עשרה, והיה לו תפקיד חשוב בכל המלחמות מאז. כבר במלחמת העולם הראשונה השתמשו בו כל הצבאות.
The **machine gun** was invented in the 1880's, and has had an important role in all wars that have taken place since then. Already in WWI all armies used it.

Special Expressions

glider parachute **מַצְנֵחַ** רחיפה
sub-**machine gun** תת-**מַקְלֵעַ**
the truth was exposed יצא **הַמַּרְצֵעַ** מן השק

Additional Examples in this Pattern

jack מַגְבֵּהַ
nutcracker מַפְצֵחַ
machine gun מַקְלֵעַ
pub, tavern מַרְזֵחַ
punch, awl מַרְצֵעַ
starter (of car) מַתְנֵעַ

---

547. ***maCCeC*** when the third root consonant is ה׳ ח׳ ע׳, plural suffix *-ot*

sing/pl	Gloss	const.	my/your/his/her	our/your/their
מַפְתֵּחַ ז׳	key; index;	מַפְתֵּחַ-	מַפְתְּחִי/מַפְתַּחֲךָ/**מַפְתְּ**חֵךְ/חוֹ/חָהּ	מַפְתְּחֵנוּ/**מַפְתַּחֲ**כֶם/כֶן/**מַפְתְּחָ**ם/ן
מַפְתְּחוֹת	spanner	מַפְתְּחוֹת-	**מַפְתְּחוֹ**תַי/תֶיךָ/תַיִךְ/תָיו/תֶיהָ	**מַפְתְּחוֹתֵי**נוּ/כֶם/כֶן/הֶם/הֶן

In the isolation form, the guttural is preceded by a *furtive pataH* (since the preceding vowel is not *a*). A *shva* with a guttural is replaced by a *Hataf-pataH*. If the preceding vowel is expected to undergo reduction, it is replaced by a *pataH*, to avoid a *Hataf-shva* sequence: מַפְ-תַּ-חֲ-ךָ < מַפְתְּחֲךָ* < מַפְתֵּחֲךָ*.

Examples

בבניינים משותפים יש בדרך כלל היום שני **מַפְתְּחוֹת** לכל דייר: לבניין ולדירה.
In apartment buildings today each tenant usually has two **keys**: to the building and to the apartment.

קשה להתמצא בספר מדעי אם אין בסופו **מַפְתֵּחַ** מפורט.
It is hard to find your way around in a scientific book without a detailed **index**.

מכשירו החשוב ביותר של השרברב הוא **מַפְתֵּחַ** צינורות.
The plumber's most important tool is the pipe **spanner**.

Special Expressions

מַטְבֵּעַ זר foreign **currency**
מַטְבֵּעַ לשון idiomatic phrase
מַפְתֵּחַ גנבים burglar **key**/tool
מַפְתֵּחַ שוודי adjustable **spanner**

מַפְתֵּחַ סול music **key**
עמדת **מַפְתֵּחַ** **key** (= essential) position
דמי **מַפְתֵּחַ** **key** fee (for guaranteeing use of dwelling at a fixed reduced rent)

Additional Examples in this Pattern

מַטְבֵּעַ coin

---

548. ***maCCeC* = *maCeC***: when the second and third root consonants are identical

sing/pl	Gloss	const.	my/your/his/her	our/your/their
מָגֵן ז׳	shield	מָגֵן-	**מָגִנִּ**י/נְּךָ/נֵּךְ/נּוֹ/נָּהּ	מָגִנֵּנוּ/**מָגִנְּ**כֶם/כֶן/**מָגִנָּ**ם/ן
מָגִנִּים		מָגִנֵּי-	**מָגִנַּ**י/נֶּיךָ/נַּיִךְ/נָּיו/נֶּיהָ	**מָגִנֵּי**נוּ/כֶם/כֶן/הֶם/הֶן

The *kamats* is maintained throughout the declension. The merger of the two identical root consonants (here *g-n-n*) is reflected in a *dagesh forte*.

Examples

לפני שהומצא הנשק החם, אמצעי ההגנה העיקרי של הלוחם היה **המָגֵן**, שהגן עליו בעיקר מפני חיצים.
Before the invention of firearms, the primary means of protection for soldiers was the **shield**, which protected him mostly against arrows.

Special Expressions

sun visor **מָגֵן** שמש

tariff to protect local products from the competition of imports מכס **מָגֵן**

the thyroid gland בלוטת ה**מָגֵן**

David's shield, ancient Jewish symbol, now drawn on the Israeli flag **מָגֵן** דויד

the Israeli equivalent of the Red Cross **מָגֵן** דויד אדום

---

549. ***maCC(a)CeC*** when the first two root consonants are reduplicated in positions three and four, and the second is guttural

our/your/their	my/your/his/her	const.	Gloss	sing/pl
מַטְאַטְאֵנוּ/**מַטְאֲטַאֲ**כֶם/כֶן/ **מַטְאַטְאָ**ם/ן	מַטְאַטְאִי/מַטְאֲטַאֲךָ/**מַטְאַטְא**ֵךְ /אוֹ/אָהּ	מַטְאֲטֵא-	broom	מַטְאֲטֵא ז׳
מַטְאַטְאֵינוּ/כֶם/כֶן/הֶם/הֶן	**מַטְאַטְא**ַי/אֶיךָ/אַיִךְ/אָיו/אֶיהָ	מַטְאַטְאֵי-		מַטְאַטְאִים

A *shva* with a guttural is replaced by a *Hataf-pataH*. If the preceding vowel is expected to undergo reduction, it is replaced by a *pataH*, to avoid a *Hataf-shva* sequence: מַטְ-אַטְ-אִי < *מַטְאֲטְאִי < *מְטְאֲטְאִי.

Examples

״פתגם״ יידישאי: אם אלוהים רוצה, גם **מַטְאֲטֵא** יורה.
A Yiddish saying: If God wills it, even a **broom** can shoot.

Special Expressions

mocking description of a new manager trying to impose a new order **מַטְאֲטֵא** חדש

---

550. ***maCCeCa***

Our/your/their	my/your/his/her	const.	Gloss	sing/pl
מַדְרֵגָתֵנוּ/**מַדְרֵגַתְ**כֶם/כֶן/**מַדְרֵגָתָ**ם/ן	**מַדְרֵגָ**תִי/תְךָ/תֵךְ/תוֹ/תָהּ	מַדְרֵגַת-	step, stair; terrace; rank; level	מַדְרֵגָה נ׳
מַדְרֵגוֹתֵינוּ/כֶם/כֶן/הֶם/הֶן	**מַדְרֵגוֹ**תַי/תֶיךָ/תַיִךְ/תָיו/תֶיהָ	מַדְרֵגוֹת-		מַדְרֵגוֹת

The *tsere* is maintained throughout the declension; the *kamats* is replaced by a *pataH* in a closed syllable. Many realizations denote instruments.

Examples

כדי להגיע לדירתם יש לטפס כמאה **מַדְרֵגוֹת**.
In order to reach their apartment, one needs to climb about one hundred **stairs**.

את מדרון ההר הזה ניתן לעבד אך ורק ב**מַדְרֵגוֹת**.
The slope of this mountain can only be cultivated in **terraces**.

כדי להבין חשבון דיפרנציאלי ואינטגראלי, יש להגיע ל**מַדְרֵגָה** גבוהה של תפיסה מתמטית.
To understand calculus, one needs to reach a high **level** of mathematical conception.

לילדים שנהרו בהפרייה חוץ-גופית קוראים בלשון הדיבור ילדי **מַבְחֵנָה**.
In the colloquial, children who were conceived through invitro fertilization are referred to as **test tube** kids.

המַגְלֵשָׁה היא אבזר המשחק הפופולרי ביותר במגרש המשחקים.
The **slide** is the most popular item in the playground.

המַהְפֵּכָה הצרפתית של 1789 הייתה אחד האירועים החשובים והמשפיעים ביותר בהיסטוריה האנושית.
The French **revolution** of 1789 was one of the most important and most influential events in human history.

Special Expressions

emergency **staircase** **מַדְרֵגוֹת** חירום
spiral **staircase** **מַדְרֵגוֹת** לולייניות
tax **bracket** **מַדְרֵגַת** מס
escalator **מַדְרֵגוֹת** נעות
industrial revolution **מַהְפֵּכָה** תעשייתית
hidden/candid **camera** **מַצְלֵמָה** נסתרת

Additional Examples in this Pattern

crusher, grinder; paper shredder מַגְרֵסָה
rake מַגְרֵפָה
hatchery, incubator מַדְגֵּרָה
pruning shears מַזְמֵרָה
distillery, refinery מַזְקֵקָה
lathe מַחְרֵטָה
plough מַחְרֵשָׁה
food grinder מַטְחֵנָה
product (math) מַכְפֵּלָה
water sprinkler מַמְטֵרָה
juice extractor, juicer מַסְחֵטָה
video camera מַסְרֵטָה
camera מַצְלֵמָה

---

551. ***maCCeCa* = *maCaCeCa*** when the first root consonant is guttural

Our/your/their	my/your/his/her	const.	Gloss	sing/pl
מַאֲפֵרָתֵנוּ/**מַאֲפֵרַתְ**כֶם/כֶן/**מַאֲפֵרָתָ**ם/ן	**מַאֲפֵרָ**תִי/תְךָ/תֵךְ/תוֹ/תָהּ	מַאֲפֵרַת-	ashtray	מַאֲפֵרָה נ׳
מַאֲפֵרוֹתֵינוּ/כֶם/כֶן/הֶם/הֶן	**מַאֲפֵרוֹ**תַי/תֶיךָ/תַיִךְ/תָיו/תֶיהָ	מַאֲפֵרוֹת-		מַאֲפֵרוֹת

The *tsere* is maintained throughout the declension; the *kamats* is replaced by a *pataH* in a closed syllable. A *shva* with a guttural is replaced by a *Hataf-pataH*.

Examples

מכיוון שהרבה פחות אנשים מעשנים היום, מסיבות בריאות, רואים רק **מַאֲפֵרוֹת** מועטות במקומות ציבוריים.
Since much fewer people smoke today, for health reasons, one sees fewer **ashtrays** in public spaces.

Additional Examples in this Pattern

neglect, aimlessness Lit. מַעֲצֵבָה
meat smoker; chimney (arch.) מַעֲשֵׁנָה

---

552. ***moCeC*** from roots in which the first consonant is *y*

our/your/their	my/your/his/her	const.	Gloss	sing/pl
מוֹקְשֵׁנוּ/**מוֹקֶשְׁ**כֶם/כֶן/**מוֹקְשָׁ**ם/ן	מוֹקְשִׁי/מוֹקֶשְׁךָ/**מוֹקְשֵׁ**ךְ/שׁוֹ/שָׁהּ	מוֹקֵשׁ-	(land) mine,	מוֹקֵשׁ ז׳
מוֹקְשֵׁינוּ/כֶם/כֶן/הֶם/הֶן	**מוֹקְשַׁ**י/שֶׁיךָ/שַׁיִךְ/שָׁיו/שֶׁיהָ	מוֹקְשֵׁי-	obstacle	מוֹקְשִׁים

When reduction occurs and a *Hataf* is expected, and the following vowel is a *shva*, the reduction of the *tsere* is to a *seghol* (to avoid a sequence of a sequence of two *shva* mobiles): מוֹ-קֶשְׁ-ךָ < מוֹקֶשְׁךָ* < מוֹקֵשְׁךָ*.

Examples

לצואת כלבים על המדרכה שלא נאספה על ידי בעליהם קוראים בישראל "**מוֹקֵשׁ**".
In Israeli slang dog poop that is not collected by the dog owner is called "(land) **mine.**"

Additional Examples in this Pattern

focus, center; bonfire, pyre מוֹקֵד

---

553. ***moCeC*** from roots in which the first consonant is *y*, and the second consonant of the root is guttural

our/your/their	my/your/his/her	const.	Gloss	sing/pl
מוֹעֲדֵנוּ/**מוֹעַדְ**כֶם/כֶן/**מוֹעֲדָ**ם/ן	מוֹעֲדִי/מוֹעַדְךָ/**מוֹעֲדֵ**ךְ/דוֹ/דָהּ	מוֹעֵד-	time;	מוֹעֵד ז׳
מוֹעֲדֵינוּ/כֶם/כֶן/הֶם/הֶן	**מוֹעֲדַ**י/דֶיךָ/דַיִךְ/דָיו/דֶיהָ	מוֹעֲדֵי-	holiday	מוֹעֲדִים

A *shva* with a guttural is replaced by a *Hataf-pataH*. If the next vowel is a *shva*, the reduction of the basic *tsere* is to a *pataH*, not to a *Hataf* (to avoid a *Hataf-shva* sequence): מוֹ-עַדְ-ךָ < מוֹעֲדְךָ* < מוֹעֵדְךָ*.

Examples

מה **מוֹעֵד** הפירעון של איגרת החוב הזאת?
What is the **due date** of this bond?

Special Expressions

Happy Holidays! **מוֹעֲדִים** לשמחה!
at the **appointed time** **לַמּוֹעֵד**
short-**term** (loan etc.) קצר **מוֹעֵד**
on **time**, before it is too late בעוד **מוֹעֵד**
was too late איחר את ה**מוֹעֵד**
there is still **time** עוד חזון לַ**מּוֹעֵד**

---

554. ***moCéCet*** from roots in which the first consonant is *y*

our/your/their	my/your/his/her	const.	Gloss	sing/pl
מוֹלַדְתֵּנוּ/תְּכֶם/תְּכֶן/תָּם/תָּן	**מוֹלַדְ**תִּי/תְּךָ/תֵּךְ/תּוֹ/תָּהּ	מוֹלֶדֶת-	native land,	מוֹלֶדֶת נ׳
מוֹלְדוֹתֵינוּ/כֶם/כֶן/הֶם/הֶן	**מוֹלְדוֹ**תַי/תֶיךָ/תַיִךְ/תָיו/תֶיהָ	מוֹלְדוֹת-	homeland	מוֹלָדוֹת

Stress falls on the penultimate syllable in unsuffixed forms, as in all segholates. The historical base surfaces in the singular declension: ...מולַד.

Examples

ארץ ישראל היא **מוֹלֶדֶת** האומה העברית.
The Land of Israel (Palestine) is the **birthplace** of the Hebrew nation.

---

555. *maCoC* from roots whose second and third consonants are identical

our/your/their	my/your/his/her	const.	Gloss	sing/pl
מָעֻזֵּנוּ/זְּכֶם/זְּכֶן/זָּם/זָּן	**מָעֻ**זִּי/זְּךָ/זֵּךְ/זּוֹ/זָּהּ	מָעוֹז-	stronghold	מָעוֹז ז׳
מָעֻזֵּינוּ/כֶם/כֶן/הֶם/הֶן	**מָעֻ**זַּי/זֶּיךָ/זַּיִךְ/זָּיו/זֶּיהָ	מָעֻזֵּי-		מָעֻזִּים

The *kamats* is maintained throughout the declension. The merger of the two identical consonants is reflected in a *dagesh forte*.

Examples

ישראל מחזיקה במספר גדול של **מָעֻזִּים** בגבול הצפון, בעיקר בגלל הבעיות עם חזבאללה.
Israel maintains a large number of **strongholds** in its northern border, particularly because of the problems with Hizballah.

---

556. *meCoC* from roots whose second and third consonants are identical

our/your/their	my/your/his/her	const.	Gloss	sing/pl
מְתֻמֵּנוּ/מְּכֶם/מְּכֶן/מָּם/מָּן	**מְתֻ**מִּי/מְּךָ/מֵּךְ/מּוֹ/מָּהּ	מְתֹם-	whole; healthy	מְתֹם ז׳

The only form included here does not have a plural declension that is in use.

Special Expressions

He does not have a **healthy limb** in his body; his whole body is injured אין בו **מְתֹם**

---

557. *meCaC* from roots whose second consonant is *w*

our/your/their	my/your/his/her	const.	Gloss	sing/pl
מְכָלֵנוּ/**מְכַלְ**כֶם/כֶן/**מְכָלָ**ם/ן	**מְכָ**לִי/לְךָ/לֵךְ/לוֹ/לָהּ	מְכַל-	tank	מְכָל ז׳
מְכָלֵינוּ/כֶם/כֶן/הֶם/הֶן	**מְכָ**לַי/לֶיךָ/לַיִךְ/לָיו/לֶיהָ	מְכָלֵי-		מְכָלִים

In a closed syllable the *kamats* is reduced to *pataH*: מְכַלְכֶם < מְכָלְכֶם*.

Examples

על גגות של בניינים ישנים גדולים בניו יורק רואים עדיין מדי פעם **מְכָלֵי** מים ענקיים...
On the roofs of some old large buildings in New York one still sometimes sees huge water **tanks**.

Additional Examples in this Pattern

stronghold Lit. מְצָד

S. Patterns with the prefix *t-*, without or with a suffix

558. *taCCiC*

our/your/their	my/your/his/her	const.	Gloss	sing/pl
תַּבְשִׁילֵנוּ/לְכֶם/לְכֶן/לָם/לָן	**תַּבְשִׁי**לִי/לְךָ/לֵךְ/לוֹ/לָהּ	תַּבְשִׁיל-	cooked	תַּבְשִׁיל ז׳
תַּבְשִׁילֵינוּ/כֶם/כֶן/הֶם/הֶן	**תַּבְשִׁי**לַי/לֶיךָ/לַיִךְ/לָיו/לֶיהָ	תַּבְשִׁילֵי-	food, dish	תַּבְשִׁילִים

There are no vowel changes in the declension.

Examples

רוב האנשים שאני מכיר מתגעגעים ל**תַּבְשִׁילִים** של אימא...
Most people I know miss mom's **dishes**...

בכל אדם מתקנא, חוץ מבנו ו**תַלְמִידוֹ** (בבלי/סנהדרין)
A man can envy anybody, except for his son and his **student**.

מכיוון שלעתים קרובות הטכנולוגיה נכשלת, אני תמיד מביא **תַּמְסִירִים** להרצאותיי.
Since technology often fails, I always bring **handouts** to my talks.

מי שאוהב את עבודתו אינו חייב למצוא לו **תַּחְבִּיב** – עיסוקו הוא בעצם **תַּחְבִּיבוֹ**.
Whoever loves his job does not necessarily require a **hobby** – his occupation is also his **hobby**.

תמיד קל יותר לממשלה לקצץ ב**תַּקְצִיב** החינוך, אבל לטווח ארוך, זה תמיד רעיון גרוע.
It is always easier for governments to cut the education **budget**, but in the long run, it is always a bad idea.

Special Expressions

behaved improperly (lit. "burned his dish in public") הקדיח **תַּבְשִׁילוֹ** ברבים
scholar **תַּלְמִיד** חכם
negative **incentive** **תַּמְרִיץ** שלילי
Oedipal **complex** **תַּסְבִּיךְ** אדיפוס
inferiority **complex** **תַּסְבִּיךְ** נחיתות
he is on (official) duty הוא ב**תַפְקִיד**

Additional Examples in this Pattern

shape of the surface, relief תַּבְלִיט
newspaper cutting תַּגְזִיר
printout תַּדְפִּיס
memorandum תַּזְכִּיר
syntax תַּחְבִּיר
trick, tactics תַּכְסִיס
piece of jewelry תַּכְשִׁיט
dictate N תַּכְתִּיב
incentive תַּמְרִיץ
complex (psych.) תַּסְבִּיךְ
radio play תַּסְכִּית
symptom תַּסְמִין
screenplay תַּסְרִיט
duty, task, job; function; part, role תַּפְקִיד
precedent תַּקְדִּים

---

559. *taCCiC* = *taCaCiC* when the 1st root consonant is guttural

our/your/their	my/your/his/her	const.	Gloss	sing/pl
תַּעֲרִיפֵנוּ/פְכֶם/פְכֶן/פָם/פָן	**תַּעֲרִי**פִי/פְךָ/פֵךְ/פוֹ/פָהּ	תַּעֲרִיף-	tariff, rate, cost	תַּעֲרִיף ז׳
תַּעֲרִיפֵינוּ/כֶם/כֶן/הֶם/הֶן	**תַּעֲרִי**פַי/פֶיךָ/פַיִךְ/פָיו/פֶיהָ	תַּעֲרִיפֵי-		תַּעֲרִיפִים

Where a *shva* is expected with a guttural, it is replaced by *Hataf pataH.*

Examples

בדרך כלל, **תַּעֲרִיפֵי** הנסיעה ברכבת גבוהים מאלה של נסיעה באוטובוס.
Generally, **rates** of travel by train are higher than rates of travel by bus.

לצערי, לא אוכל להצטרף אליכם לטיול; יש לי כנס בדיוק בין אותם ה**תַּאֲרִיכִים**.
Unfortunately, I won't be able to join you on the trip; I have a conference on exactly the same **dates**.

תַּהֲלִיךְ קבלת אזרחות במדינה אחרת אינו פשוט, ונמשך זמן רב.
The **process** of getting citizenship in another country is not simple, and takes a long time.

Special Expressions

תַּאֲרִיךְ יעד target **date**
תַּאֲרִיךְ לועזי Gregorian **date**
תַּאֲרִיךְ תפוגה expiration **date**

Additional Examples in this Pattern

תַּאֲגִיד corporation
תַּעֲתִיק transcription

---

560. ***taCCiCa* = *taCaCiCa*** when the first root consonant is guttural

sing/pl	gloss	const.	my/your/his/her	our/your/their
תַּאֲחִיזָה נ׳	adhesion	תַּאֲחִיזַת-	**תַּאֲחִיזָ**תִי/תְךָ/תֵךְ/תוֹ/תָהּ	**תַּאֲחִיזָ**תֵנוּ/תְכֶם/תְכֶן/תָם/תָן

Where a *shva* is expected with a guttural, it is replaced by *Hataf-pataH*. The only case included here is not used in the plural.

Examples

תַּאֲחִיזָה היא כוח ההידבקות וההיצמדות של פרודות החומר זו לזו.
Adhesion is the force attaching material molecules to one another.

---

561. ***taCCit***

sing/pl	Gloss	const.	my/your/his/her	our/your/their
תַּבְנִית נ׳	mold;	תַּבְנִית-	**תַּבְנִי**תִי/תְךָ/תֵךְ/תוֹ/תָהּ	**תַּבְנִי**תֵנוּ/תְכֶם/תְכֶן/תָם/תָן
תַּבְנִיּוֹת	pattern	תַּבְנִיּוֹת-	**תַּבְנִיּוֹ**תַי/תֶיךָ/תַיִךְ/תָיו/תֶיהָ	**תַּבְנִיּוֹתֵי**נוּ/כֶם/כֶן/הֶם/הֶן

All realizations are derived from roots in which the third consonant is *y*.

Examples

פסלים רבים מייצרים לפסליהם **תַּבְנִיּוֹת** יציקה מגבס.
Many sculptors manufacture gypsum **molds** for their sculptures.

המשקלים בעברית הם **תַּבְנִיּוֹת** של תצורת מלים.
The Hebrew *mishkalim* are word formation **patterns**.

הַתַּגְלִיּוֹת החשובות ביותר במאה העשרים היו של אלברט איינשטיין: שמושג הזמן הוא יחסי, שאפשר להפוך חומר לאנרגיה ולהפך, ועוד.
The most important **discoveries** in the Twentieth Century were by Albert Einstein: the time is relative, that it is possible to convert matter to energy and vice versa, and more.

הצלחתם של אישי ציבור ושל חברות מסחריות תלויה לא מעט **בְּתַדְמִית** שלהם בעיני הציבור. **הַתַּדְמִית** מקודמת גם על ידי חברות המתמחות בקידום **תַּדְמִית**.
The success of public figures and of commercial companies is dependent to a considerable extent by their **image** in the eyes of the public. The **image** is also promoted by companies who specialize in **image** building.

יש אנשים שכשהכל נראה להם חסר **תַּכְלִית** ושאין שום משמעות לכלום, הם מנסים להתרחק מן העולם באמצעות דמיון.
When it looks to some people that everything is **purpose**-less and that nothing has meaning, they try to use their imagination to get away from the world.

Special Expressions

תַּבְנִית התנהגות behavior **pattern**
חסר/ללא **תַּכְלִית** having no **purpose**
תַּפְנִית של 180 מעלות total **shift**
תַּצְפִּית אוויר aerial **observation**

Additional Examples in this Pattern

תַּמְצִית essence
תַּפְנִית turn about
תַּצְפִּית observation (point)
תַּקְרִית incident
תַּרְמִית deceit, fraud
תַּשְׁתִּית infrastructure

---

562. ***taCCit = taCaCit*** when the 1st root consonant is guttural

our/your/their	my/your/his/her	const.	Gloss	sing/pl
תַּעֲנִיתֵנוּ/תְכֶם/תְכֶן/תָם/תָן	**תַּעֲנִי**תִי/תְךָ/תֵךְ/תוֹ/תָהּ	תַּעֲנִית-	fast	תַּעֲנִית נ׳
תַּעֲנִיּוֹתֵינוּ/כֶם/כֶן/הֶם/הֶן	**תַּעֲנִיּוֹ**תַי/תֶיךָ/תַיִךְ/תָיו/תֶיהָ	תַּעֲנִיּוֹת-		תַּעֲנִיּוֹת

Where a *shva* is expected with a guttural, it is replaced by *Hataf-pataH.*

Examples

בדתות רבות מאמינים כי כשקורה אסון, **תַּעֲנִית** היא הדרך להעביר את רוע הגזירה.
In many religions they believe that when disaster occurs, **fasting** is the way to reverse it.

Special Expressions

תַּחֲזִית מזג האוויר weather **forecast**
תַּעֲנִית אסתר the **fast** of Esther
תַּעֲנִית יחיד private **fast**
תַּעֲנִית ציבור public **fast**

Additional Examples in this Pattern

forecast תַּחֲזִית

---

563. *taCCuC*

our/your/their	my/your/his/her	const.	Gloss	sing/pl
תַּגְמוּלֵנוּ/לְכֶם/לְכֶן/לָם/לָן	**תַּגְמוּ**לִי/לְךָ/לֵךְ/לוֹ/לָהּ	תַּגְמוּל-	remuneration;	תַּגְמוּל ז׳
תַּגְמוּלֵינוּ/כֶם/כֶן/הֶם/הֶן	**תַּגְמוּ**לַי/לֶיךָ/לַיִךְ/לָיו/לֶיהָ	תַּגְמוּלֵי-	retaliation	תַּגְמוּלִים

Examples

הנשיא הודיע שהוא מתכוון להטיל מכס גבוה על מוצרי יבוא מסוימים כ**תַּגְמוּל** על הטלת מכס מקביל על יצוא מארה״ב.

The President announced that he intends to impose high custom duty on certain products as **retaliation** for the imposition of comparable duties on exports from the US.

בעת שיטפון גדול במדינה מסוימת, הוכרה אם כגיבורה לאומית לאחר שחשה להציל **תַּצְלוּם** של המנהיג הנערץ במקום להציל את תינוקה הטובע.

During a flood in a certain country, a mother was recognized as a national heroine after she had rushed to save a **photograph** of the venerated leader instead of saving her drowning baby.

Special Expressions

retaliatory act פעולת **תַּגְמוּל**

pension payment, golden handshake **תַּגְמוּלִים**

accumulated **pension/retirement** plan קרן **תַּגְמוּלִים**

aerial photograph **תַּצְלוּם** אוויר

payment by installments **תַּשְׁלוּמִים** לשיעורים

Additional Examples in this Pattern

Talmud, Oral Law תַּלְמוּד

cosmetics, perfumes תַּמְרוּק

payment תַּשְׁלוּם

---

564. *taCCuC* = *taCaCuC* when the first root consonant is guttural

our/your/their	my/your/his/her	const.	gloss	sing/pl
תַּעֲנוּגֵנוּ/גְכֶם/גְכֶן/גָם/גָן	**תַּעֲנוּ**גִי/גְךָ/גֵךְ/גוֹ/גָהּ	תַּעֲנוּג-	pleasure,	תַּעֲנוּג ז׳
תַּעֲנוּגוֹתֵינוּ/כֶם/כֶן/הֶם/הֶן	**תַּעֲנוּגוֹ**תַי/תֶיךָ/תַיִךְ/תָיו/תֶיהָ	תַּעֲנוּגוֹת-	delight	תַּעֲנוּגוֹת

Where a *shva* is expected with a guttural, it is replaced by *Hataf-pataH*.

Examples

שינה בשבת – **תַּעֲנוּג**.

Sleeping on the sabbath is a **delight**.

דני אוהב לבצע **תַּעֲלוּלִים**. בדרך כלל הם לא מזיקים.
Danny loves to perform **practical jokes**. Generally they are harmless.

Special Expressions

sexual relations **תַּעֲנוּגוֹת**-בשרים

Additional Examples in this Pattern

strength (lit.) תַּעֲצוּם

supplicatory prayer; plea, entreaty תַּחֲנוּן

---

565. ***taCCuCa***

our/your/their	my/your/his/her	const.	Gloss	sing/pl
תַּחְבּוּלָתֵנוּ/**תַּחְבּוּלַתְ**כֶם/כֶן/ **תַּחְבּוּלָתָ**ם/ן	**תַּחְבּוּלָ**תִי/תְךָ/תֵךְ/תוֹ/תָהּ	תַּחְבּוּלַת-	trick, ruse	תַּחְבּוּלָה נ׳
תַּחְבּוּלוֹתֵינוּ/כֶם/כֶן/הֶם/הֶן	**תַּחְבּוּלוֹ**תַי/תֶיךָ/תַיִךְ/תָיו/תֶיהָ	תַּחְבּוּלוֹת-		תַּחְבּוּלוֹת

Examples

תַּחְבּוּלָה שכיחה שמשתמשים בה נוכלים בעלי שם היא לגייס כספי משקיעים תמימים ולאחר זמן מה להכריז על פשיטת רגל, כדי שלא להחזיר את הכספים שגויסו.
A common **ruse** used by famous crooks is to raise funds from naïve investors, and after a while to declare bankruptcy, so that they do not have to refund the raised investments.

מערכת ה**תַּבְרוּאָה** במנהטן היא מן הגרועות בארה״ב; העירייה אינה משתלטת על כמויות האשפה האדירות, והמדרכות באזורים מסוימים של העיר נראות כמו לאחר יריד פרוע.
The **sanitation** system in Manhattan is one of the worst in the US; the City does not manage to control the huge amounts of trash, and the sidewalks in some of the areas of the city look like the aftermath of a wild fair.

מערכת ה**תַּחְבּוּרָה** הציבורית ביפן הרשימה אותי כאחת הטובות בעולם.
The **transportation** system in Japam impressed as one of the best in the world.

Special Expressions

public **transportation** **תַּחְבּוּרָה** ציבורית

Additional Examples in this Pattern

turnover תַּחְלוּפָה

maintenance תַּחְזוּקָה

set (theater), decoration, decor תַּפְאוּרָה

morbidity תַּחְלוּאָה

---

566. ***taCCuCa* = *taCaCuCa*** when the first root consonant is guttural (except for *Het*)

our/your/their	my/your/his/her	const.	Gloss	sing/pl
תַּעֲרוּכָתֵנוּ/**תַּעֲרוּכַתְ**כֶם/כֶן/ **תַּעֲרוּכָתָ**ם/ן	**תַּעֲרוּכָ**תִי/תְךָ/תֵךְ/תוֹ/תָהּ	תַּעֲרוּכַת-	exhibition, exhibit	תַּעֲרוּכָה נ׳
תַּעֲרוּכוֹתֵינוּ/כֶם/כֶן/הֶם/הֶן	**תַּעֲרוּכוֹ**תַי/תֶיךָ/תַיִךְ/תָיו/תֶיהָ	תַּעֲרוּכוֹת-		תַּעֲרוּכוֹת

Where a *shva* is expected with a guttural, it is replaced by *Hataf-pataH.*

Examples

בארה״ב נבנים מדי פעם מוזיאונים גדולים מחוץ לערים הגדולות, שניתן להציג בם **תַּעֲרוּכוֹת** הדורשות שטח תצוגה נרחב ממה שקיים בתוך העיר עצמה.
In the US they sometimes build large museums outside of the big cities in which one can display **exhibits** that require larger display spaces than what the city can provide.

מצב ה**תַּעֲסוּקָה** הוא בדרך כלל מדד טוב לחוסנו של המשק.
The **employment** situation is generally a good measure of the nation's economic state.

בעבר, בישראל הסוציאליסטית, קוימו כל שנה **תַּהֲלוּכוֹת** פועלים באחד במאי.
In the past, in socialist Israel, workers **parades** were held yearly on May 1st.

Special Expressions

תַּהֲלוּכַת ניצחון victory **parade**
תַּעֲצוּמוֹת נפש mental **strength**
שירות ה**תַּעֲסוּקָה** **employment** office

Additional Examples in this Pattern

תַּעֲבוּרָה traffic
תַּעֲצוּמָה strength Lit.
תַּעֲמוּלָה propaganda
תַּעֲרוּבָה warranty Lit.

---

567. ***toCaC*** when the first root consonant is *y*

sing/pl	Gloss	const.	my/your/his/her	our/your/their
תּוֹצָר ז'	product;	תּוֹצַר-	**תּוֹצָרִ**י/רְךָ/רֵךְ/רוֹ/רָהּ	תּוֹצָרֵנוּ/**תּוֹצַרְ**כֶם/כֶן/**תּוֹצָרָ**ם/ן
תּוֹצָרִים	outcome	תּוֹצְרֵי-	**תּוֹצָרַ**י/רֶיךָ/רַיִךְ/רָיו/רֶיהָ	תּוֹצָרֵינוּ/**תּוֹצְרֵי**כֶם/כֶן/הֶם/הֶן

The *kamats* is reduced to *shva* two syllables away from the stress, תּוֹצְרֵיכֶם, תּוֹצְרֵי-, and is replaced by *pataH* in a closed syllable, תּוֹצַרְכֶם, תּוֹצַר-. Note: except for the singular construct (תּוֹשַׁב-), the *kamats* does **not** reduce in the declension of תּוֹשָׁב: תּוֹשָׁבִים, תּוֹשָׁבֵי- תּוֹשָׁבֵיכֶם. Owing to the final א', the *kamats* does not reduce in the construct singular of תּוֹצָא 'effect.'

Examples

חוסנה של מדינה נִקְבָּע במידה לא מעטה על פי גודל ה**תּוֹצָר** הלאומי הגולמי שלה.
The strength of a nation is determined to consiserable extent by the size of its gross national **product**.

חלומם הגדול של מהגרים בתי-חוקיים בארה״ב הוא להגיע למעמד של **תּוֹשָׁבֵי** קבע, ובסופו של דבר להפוך לאזרחים.
The big dream of illegal immigrants in the US is to reach the status of permanent **residents**, and eventually become citizens.

Special Expressions

food **additive** **תּוֹסָף** מזון
nutritional **supplement** **תּוֹסָף** תזונה
Doppler **effect** **תּוֹצָא** דופלר
by**product** **תּוֹצָר** לוואי
the national **product** ה**תּוֹצָר** הלאומי
gross national **product** **תּוֹצָר** לאומי גולמי
permanent **resident** **תּוֹשָׁב** קֶבַע

Additional Examples in this Pattern

additive תּוֹסָף
effect תּוֹצָא
resident (see note above re תּוֹשָׁב exception)

---

568. ***toCaCa*** when the first root consonant is *y*

sing/pl	Gloss	const.	my/your/his/her	our/your/their
תּוֹרָשָׁה נ׳	heredity	תּוֹרֶשֶׁת-	**תּוֹרַשְׁ**תִּי/תְּךָ/תֵּךְ/תּוֹ/תָּהּ	**תּוֹרַשְׁ**תֵּנוּ/תְּכֶם/תְּכֶן/תָּם/תָּן
תּוֹרָשׁוֹת		תּוֹרְשׁוֹת-	**תּוֹרְשׁוֹ**תַי/תֶיךָ/תַיִךְ/תָיו/תֶיהָ	**תּוֹרְשׁוֹתֵי**נוּ/כֶם/כֶן/הֶם/הֶן

The *kamats* is reduced to *shva* two syllables away from the stress, תּוֹרְשׁוֹתַי, and is replaced by *pataH* in a closed syllable, תּוֹרַשְׁתִּי.

Examples

את כישרונו המוסיקלי קיבל ב**תּוֹרָשָׁה** מאמו ; מאביו קיבל את קומתו הגבוהה.
He got his musical talent by **heredity** from his mother; from his father he inherited his tall stature.

Additional Examples in this Pattern

transport תּוֹבָלָה
outcome תּוֹלָדָה

---

569. ***toCaCa*** when the first root consonant is *y* and the last ח׳/ע׳

sing/pl	Gloss	const.	my/your/his/her	our/your/their
תּוֹפָעָה נ׳	phenomenon	תּוֹפַעַת-	**תּוֹפַעְ**תִּי/תְּךָ/תֵּךְ/תּוֹ/תָּהּ	**תּוֹפַעְ**תֵּנוּ/תְּכֶם/תְּכֶן/תָּם/תָּן
תּוֹפָעוֹת		תּוֹפְעוֹת-	**תּוֹפְעוֹ**תַי/תֶיךָ/תַיִךְ/תָיו/תֶיהָ	**תּוֹפְעוֹתֵי**נוּ/כֶם/כֶן/הֶם/הֶן

The declension is the same as that of תּוֹרָשָׁה above, but the sing. construct is with two *pataH*s, owing to the gutturals. Note: when the guttural is א׳, the sing. construct is different, and the *kamats* undergoes regular reduction: תּוֹצְאַת-.

Examples

גשם בישראל בקיץ זו **תּוֹפָעָה** נדירה, אבל מדי פעם זה קורה.
Rain in Israel in the summer is a rare **phenomenon**, but occasionally it does happen.

Additional Examples in this Pattern

consciousness תּוֹדָעָה
reproof תּוֹכָחָה
outcome (see note above) תּוֹצָאָה

---

570. ***toCaCa*** when the second root consonant is *y*

The only form introduced here is תּוֹבָנָה, a popular spontaneous translation of 'insight.' The form belongs to a *mishkal* derived from roots whose first consonant is *y*, but it is clear that the neologizer's intention was to relate this form to the root *b-y-n* 'understand.' The normative Hebrew Language Academy term is בּוֹנְנוּת, but the public continues to prefer תּוֹבָנָה, which is why it is listed separately here. It appears that only the isolation forms of the singular and of the plural, תּוֹבָנוֹת, are in actual use.

---

571. ***toCéCet*** when the first root consonant is *y*

our/your/their	my/your/his/her	const.	Gloss	sing/pl
תּוֹסַפְתֵּנוּ/תְּכֶם/תְּכֶן/תָּם/תָּן	**תּוֹסַפְ**תִּי/תְּךָ/תֵּךְ/תּוֹ/תָּהּ	-תּוֹסֶפֶת	addition,	תּוֹסֶפֶת נ׳
תּוֹסְפוֹתֵינוּ/כֶם/כֶן/הֶם/הֶן	**תּוֹסְפוֹ**תַי/תֶיךָ/תַיִךְ/תָיו/תֶיהָ	-תּוֹסְפוֹת	increase	תּוֹסָפוֹת

The singular declension follows the segholate model, and the base with *pataH* (in a closed syllable) surfaces before suffixes. The plural forms are regular, with reduction to *shva* two syllables away from the stress.

Examples

קשה לפעמים לראות את ה**תּוֹעֶלֶת** המיידית של השקעות לטווח ארוך.
It is sometimes difficult to see the immediate **benefit** of long-term investments.

תודות לחמי, שהיה סנדלר מוכשר, זכיתי מדי פעם בנעליים מ**תּוֹצֶרֶת** עצמית.
Thanks to my father-in-law, who was a talented shoemaker, I was occasionally privileged to get **handmade** shoes.

Special Expressions

life **expectancy** **תּוֹחֶלֶת** חיים
marginal/decreasing **benefit** **תּוֹעֶלֶת** שולית
produced in Israel **תּוֹצֶרֶת** הארץ

Additional Examples in this Pattern

expectation, hope; expectancy Lit תּוֹחֶלֶת
base, seating תּוֹשֶׁבֶת

---

572. ***tCuCa***

our/your/their	my/your/his/her	const.	Gloss	sing/pl
תְּשׁוּבָתֵנוּ/**תְּשׁוּבַתְ**כֶם/כֶן/ **תְּשׁוּבָתָ**ם/ן	**תְּשׁוּבָ**תִי/תְךָ/תֵךְ/תוֹ/תָהּ	-תְּשׁוּבַת	answer; return; repentance	תְּשׁוּבָה נ׳
תְּשׁוּבוֹתֵינוּ/כֶם/כֶן/הֶם/הֶן	**תְּשׁוּבוֹ**תַי/תֶיךָ/תַיִךְ/תָיו/תֶיהָ	-תְּשׁוּבוֹת		תְּשׁוּבוֹת

Most occurrences are derived from roots in which the second consonant is ו׳.

Examples

הילד הזה נבון; לכל דבר יש לו **תְּשׁוּבָה**.
This child is smart; he has an **answer** for everything.

עשרת ״הימים הנוראים״ נקראים גם ״עשרת ימי **תְּשׁוּבָה**״.
The ten Days of Awe are also called the ten Days of **Repentance**.

את **תְּבוּסָתוֹ** הגדולה הראשונה נחל היטלר בסטאלינגרד.
Hitler was dealt his first great **defeat** in Stalingrad.

לא קל למכור בית, ולעיתים קשה לא פחות למכור את **תְּכוּלָתוֹ** אם המוכרים אינם זקוקים לה במקום מגוריהם החדש.
It is not easy to sell a house, and sometimes it is not less difficult to sell its **contents** if the sellers do not need it in their new residence.

בארצות מסוימות בעולם השלישי שיעור **תְּמוּתַת** הילדים הוא גבוה מעל ומעבר לכל קנה מידה מקובל בעולם.
In some third world countries the rate of child **mortality** goes way beyond what can be regarded as acceptable anywhere.

Special Expressions

road **accident** **תְּאוּנַת** דרכים
manual **skill**, dexterity **תְּבוּנַת** כפיים
chain **reaction** **תְּגוּבַת** שרשרת
got **involved** נכנס ל**תְּמוּנָה**
repentant person בעל **תְּשׁוּבָה**
repented חזר בִּ**תְשׁוּבָה**/עשה **תְּשׁוּבָה**

Additional Examples in this Pattern

accident תְּאוּנָה
acceleration תְּאוּצָה
lighting תְּאוּרָה
crops; grains תְּבוּאָה
understanding, wisdom תְּבוּנָה
reaction תְּגוּבָה
resonance תְּהוּדָה
movement, motion תְּזוּזָה
nutrition תְּזוּנָה
sensation; feeling תְּחוּשָׁה
complaint תְּלוּנָה
picture, photograph תְּמוּנָה
produce, yield תְּנוּבָה
posture, position of body תְּנוּחָה
document תְּעוּדָה
flight, aviation תְּעוּפָה
capacity תְּפוּסָה
distribution תְּפוּצָה

573. *taCCeCa*

our/your/their	my/your/his/her	const.	Gloss	sing/pl
תַּרְדֵּמָתֵנוּ/**תַּרְדֵּמַתְ**כֶם/כֶן/ **תַּרְדֵּמָתָ**ם/ן	**תַּרְדֵּמָ**תִי/תְךָ/תֵךְ/תוֹ/תָהּ	תַּרְדֵּמַת-	deep sleep, hibernation	תַּרְדֵּמָה נ׳
תַּרְדֵּמוֹתֵינוּ/כֶם/כֶן/הֶם/הֶן	**תַּרְדֵּמוֹ**תַי/תֶיךָ/תַיִךְ/תָיו/תֶיהָ	תַּרְדֵּמוֹת-		תַּרְדֵּמוֹת

In a closed syllable, the *kamats* is replaced by *pataH.*

Examples

דניאל היה שקוע ב**תַּרְדֵּמָה** כה עמוקה, שרעידת האדמה אפילו לא העירה אותו.
Daniel was in such **deep sleep**, that the earthquake did not even wake him up.

Special Expressions

תַּרְדֵּמַת חורף hibernation
תַּרְדֵּמַת מרמוטה very **deep sleep**
פצצת **תַּבְעֵרָה** napalm bomb
שתה את כוס ה**תַּרְעֵלָה** suffered a great deal

Additional Examples in this Pattern

תַּבְהֵלָה panic, consternation Lit.
תַּבְעֵרָה conflagration, fire
תַּדְהֵמָה amazement, astonishment
תַּרְעֵלָה poison Lit.

---

574. *tiCCéCet*

our/your/their	my/your/his/her	const.	Gloss	sing/pl
תִּפְאַרְתֵּנוּ/תְּכֶם/תְּכֶן/תָּם/תָּן	**תִּפְאַרְ**תִּי/תְּךָ/תֵּךְ/תּוֹ/תָּהּ	תִּפְאֶרֶת-	glory, splendor	תִּפְאֶרֶת נ׳
תִּפְאֲרוֹתֵינוּ/כֶם/כֶן/הֶם/הֶן	**תִּפְאֲרוֹ**תַי/תֶיךָ/תַיִךְ/תָיו/תֶיהָ	תִּפְאֲרוֹת-		תִּפְאָרוֹת

The declension follows that of the segholates .

Examples

לאחר ששופץ על ידי הורדוס, עלה בית המקדש השני ב**תִפְאַרְתּוֹ** על הראשון.
After it was renovated by Herod, the Second Temple's **splendor** exceeded that of the First.

Special Expressions

ל**תִפְאֶרֶת** המליצה for the glory of words, not for their content
לא תהיה **תִּפְאַרְתְּךָ** על הדרך הזאת the way you are going will bring you no glory

Additional Examples in this Pattern

תִּנְשֶׁמֶת barn owl
תִּפְלֶצֶת horror, something horrible; monster

---

575. ***tiCCéCet* = *tiCCáCat*** when the 3rd consonant is guttural

our/your/their	my/your/his/her	const.	Gloss	sing/pl
תִּגְלַחְתֵּנוּ/תְּכֶם/תְּכֶן/תָּם/תָּן	**תִּגְלַחְ**תִּי/תְּךָ/תֵּךְ/תּוֹ/תָּהּ	תִּגְלַחַת-	shave	תִּגְלַחַת נ׳
תִּגְלְחוֹתֵינוּ/כֶם/כֶן/הֶם/הֶן	**תִּגְלְחוֹ**תַי/תֶיךָ/תַיִךְ/תָיו/תֶיהָ	תִּגְלְחוֹת-		תִּגְלָחוֹת

The two *seghol*s are replaced by two *pataH*'s because of the presence of a guttural. The *kamats* is reduced to *shva* two syllables away from the stress, תִּגְלְחוֹתַי, and is replaced by *pataH* in a closed syllable, תִּגְלַחְתִּי.

Examples

תִּפְרַחַת היא קבוצת פרחים על גבעול משותף.
Inflorescence is the complete flower head of a plant including stems, stalks, bracts, and flowers.

Additional Examples in this Pattern

תִּמְלַחַת brine
תִּפְרַחַת inflorescence (bot.); flowering Lit.
תִּשְׁבַּחַת praise Lit.

---

576. ***tiCCóCet***

our/your/their	my/your/his/her	const.	Gloss	sing/pl
תִּזְמָרְתֵּנוּ/תְּכֶם/תְּכֶן/תָּם/תָּן	**תִּזְמָרְ**תִּי/תְּךָ/תֵּךְ/תּוֹ/תָּהּ	תִּזְמֹרֶת-	orchestra	תִּזְמֹרֶת נ׳
תִּזְמוֹרוֹתֵינוּ/כֶם/כֶן/הֶם/הֶן	**תִּזְמוֹרוֹ**תַי/תֶיךָ/תַיִךְ/תָיו/תֶיהָ	תִּזְמוֹרוֹת-		תִּזְמוֹרוֹת

The declension follows the segholate pattern (cf. בֹּקֶר ~ בָּקְרוֹ), and in a closed syllable a *kamats katan* [o] (prob. the historical base) replaces the *Holam* of the isolation form.

Examples

ישראל קטנה, אבל מייצרת וצורכת הרבה תרבות; כמעט לכל עיר, למשל, יש **תִּזְמֹרֶת** סימפונית משלה...
Israel is small, but produces and consumes a great deal of culture; most towns, for instance, have their own symphony **orchestra**...

לשוטר בודד או לזוג שוטרים יש בדרך כלל הוראות לא להתעמת עם פושעים מבלי לחכות קודם **לְתִגְבֹּרֶת**.
Single policemen or even partners are generally instructed not to confront criminals before **reinforcement** arrives.

בבתי ספר רבים דורשים **תִּלְבֹּשֶׁת** אחידה, כדי שתלמידים מעוטי יכולת לא ירגישו אי נוחות בלבושם.
In many schools they require uniform **clothing/outfit**, so that students of limited means would not feel uncomfortable with the way they are dressed.

אם אתה מעוניין ב**תִסְפֹּרֶת** כמו של מנהיגה הנערץ של צפון-קוריאה, אני מכיר ספרים שיסדרו לך את זה בקלות.

If you are interested in a **haircut** like that of North Korea's worshipped leader, I know a few barbers who will easily take care of it for you.

כאשר ה**תִקְשֹׁרֶת** מבקרת את השלטון, אפשר תמיד להאשים אותה בשמאלנות.

When **the media** criticize the government, it is always possible to blame it as having leftist leanings.

Special Expressions

תִזְמֹרֶת פילהרמונית philharmonic **orchestra**

תִזְמֹרֶת בצורת lipsynching Coll.

תִלְבֹּשֶׁת אחידה uniform (**clothing**)

תִלְבֹּשֶׁת ערב evening **wear**

תִסְמֹנֶת דאון Down's **syndrome**

תִרְכֹּבֶת יציבה stable **compound**

ה**תִקְשֹׁרֶת** the **media**

Additional Examples in this Pattern

תִכְתֹּבֶת correspondence

תִמְסֹרֶת transmission (mech.)

תִסְבֹּכֶת complication, complexity

תִסְמֹנֶת syndrome (medic.)

תִסְרֹקֶת hair style, hairdo

תִפְזֹרֶת bulk

תִצְרֹכֶת consumption, utilization

תִרְכֹּבֶת chemical compound

תִשְׁלֹבֶת concern, group, complex; gearing (mech.)

---

577. ***tiCCóCet* = *taCCóCet*** when the first root consonant is ח׳, ר׳

our/your/their	my/your/his/her	const.	Gloss	sing/pl
תַחְבָּשְׁתֵּנוּ/תְּכֶם/תְּכֶן/תָּם/תָּן	**תַחְבָּשְׁ**תִּי/תְּךָ/תֵּךְ/תּוֹ/תָּהּ	-תַחְבֹּשֶׁת	dressing,	תַחְבֹּשֶׁת נ׳
תַחְבּוֹשׁוֹתֵינוּ/כֶם/כֶן/הֶם/הֶן	**תַחְבּוֹשׁוֹ**תַי/תֶיךָ/תַיִךְ/תָיו/תֶיהָ	-תַחְבּוֹשׁוֹת	bandage	תַחְבּוֹשׁוֹת

The declension is identical to that of תִזְמֹרֶת above, except that the *Hirik* is converted to *pataH*. In a closed syllable a *kamats katan* [o] parallels the *Holam* of the isolation form.

Examples

החלפת **תַחְבֹּשֶׁת** לפני שהפצע החלים לחלוטין עלולה להיות מכאיבה למדיי.

Replacing a **bandage** before the wound has fully healed may be fairly painful.

תַחְפּוֹשׂוֹת הילדים הפופולריות ביותר בפורים הן של אסתר המלכה והמלך אחשוורוש.

The most popular children's **costumes** for Purim are of Queen Esther and King Achashverosh.

Special Expressions

תַחְמֹשֶׁת חיה live **ammunition**

Additional Examples in this Pattern

תַחְמֹצֶת oxide (chem.)

תַחְמֹשֶׁת ammunition

תַרְעֹמֶת grudge, complaint

---

578. ***tiCCóCet = taCaCóCat*** when the first root consonant is 'ע

our/your/their	my/your/his/her	const.	Gloss	sing/pl
תַּעֲרָבְתֵּנוּ/תְּכֶם/תְּכֶן/תָּם/תָּן	**תַּעֲרָבְ**תִּי/תְּךָ/תֵּךְ/תּוֹ/תָּהּ	תַּעֲרֹבֶת-	mixture,	תַּעֲרֹבֶת נ'
תַּעֲרוֹבוֹתֵינוּ/כֶם/כֶן/הֶם/הֶן	**תַּעֲרוֹבוֹ**תַי/תֶיךָ/תַיִךְ/תָיו/תֶיהָ	תַּעֲרוֹבוֹת-	blend	תַּעֲרוֹבוֹת

The declension is identical to that of תִּזְמֹרֶת above, except that where a *shva* is expected with 'ע, it is converted to *Hataf-pataH*. In a closed syllable a *kamats katan* [o] is the counterpart of the *Holam* of the isolation form.

Examples

המוסיקה של עידן רייכל מהווה **תַּעֲרֹבֶת** מעניינת של מרכיבים מתרבויות שונות בעולם.
Idan Reichel's music constitutes an interesting **blend** of elements from different cultures around the globe.

Special Expressions

half-breed, cross-breed בן-**תַּעֲרֹבֶת**   **mixed** marriage נישואי **תַּעֲרֹבֶת**

---

579. ***tiCCa***

our/your/their	my/your/his/her	const.	Gloss	sing/pl
תִּקְרָתֵנוּ/**תִּקְרַתְ**כֶם/כֶן/**תִּקְרָתָ**ם/ן	**תִּקְרָ**תִי/תְךָ/תֵךְ/תוֹ/תָהּ	תִּקְרַת-	ceiling	תִּקְרָה נ'
תִּקְרוֹתֵינוּ/כֶם/כֶן/הֶם/הֶן	**תִּקְרוֹ**תַי/תֶיךָ/תַיִךְ/תָיו/תֶיהָ	תִּקְרוֹת-		תִּקְרוֹת

In a closed syllable, the *kamats* is replaced by *pataH*: תִּקְרַתְכֶם. Since the -ת here is a prefix and not part of the root, the plural form is תִּקְרוֹת and not תְּקָרוֹת* (for the feminine form of segholate nouns see שִׂמְלָה 'dress; tunic' below).

Examples

בדירות החדשות, ה**תִּקְרָה** היא בדרך כלל נמוכה-יחסית. התחושה הרבה יותר נעימה כשה**תִּקְרָה** גבוהה.
In new apartments, the **ceiling** is generally relatively-low. Where the **ceiling** high, it feels nicer.

יש מדינות שבהן **תִּקְרַת** מס ההכנסה מגיעה ל-60%.
In some countries, the **ceiling** for income tax reaches 60%.

ההמנון של מדינת ישראל נקרא "ה**תִּקְוָה**"; המילים הן של נפתלי הרץ אימבר.
The Israeli national anthem is called "the **Hope**," lyrics were by Naftali Hertz Imber.

Special Expressions

he **despaired** אבדה **תִּקְוָתוֹ**

Additional Examples in this Pattern

tastelessness, frivolity Lit. תִּפְלָה   end, limit Lit. תִּכְלָה

---

580. *tCiCa*

our/your/their	my/your/his/her	const.	Gloss	sing/pl
תְּפִלָּתֵנוּ/**תְּפִלַּתְ**כֶם/כֶן/**תְּפִלָּתָ**ם/ן	**תְּפִלָּ**תִי/תְךָ/תֵךְ/תוֹ/תָהּ	תְּפִלַּת-	prayer	תְּפִלָּה נ'
תְּפִלּוֹתֵינוּ/כֶם/כֶן/הֶם/הֶן	**תְּפִלּוֹ**תַי/תֶיךָ/תַיִךְ/תָיו/תֶיהָ	תְּפִלּוֹת-		תְּפִלּוֹת

A *dagesh Hazak* is maintained throughout. Most forms are derived from roots whose 2nd and 3rd consonants are identical, hence the geminated consonant.

Examples

מוסלמי אדוק חייב להתפלל חמש **תְּפִלּוֹת** ביום.
A devout Muslim is required to pray five **prayers** a day.

כשמדברים על **תְּחִיַּת** השפה העברית בעת החדשה מתכוונים לשפה המדוברת. העברית הכתובה המשיכה להתקיים לאורך הדורות.
When we talk of the **revival** of Hebrew in the Modern period, we refer to the spoken language. Written Hebrew has continued to exist throughout the ages.

תְּחִקָּה במדינת ישראל אינה עניין פשוט, מכיוון שבמציאות הישראלית הפוליטית ההפרדה בין דת ומדינה אינה מוחלטת.
In the state of Israel **legislation** is not simple, because in the Israeli political reality, the separation between state and religion is not complete.

Special Expressions

prayer said when going on long trip **תְּפִלַּת** הדרך
I pray אני **תְּפִלָּה**
empty **prayer** **תְּפִלַּת** שווא
prayer leader, cantor בעל **תְּפִלָּה**

song of praise שיר **תְּהִלָּה**
he became very famous שמו יצא ל**תְּהִלָּה**
resurrection **תְּחִיַּת** המתים
from the **outset** מלכ**תְּחִלָּה**
from **beginning** to end מ**תְּחִלָּה** ועד סוף

Additional Examples in this Pattern

beginning, opening תְּחִלָּה
solution (chem.) תְּמִסָּה

praise, adoration תְּהִלָּה
plea, cry for help תְּחִנָּה

---

581. *taCCeC*

Our/your/their	my/your/his/her	const.	Gloss	sing/pl
תַּשְׁבְּצֵנוּ/**תַּשְׁבֶּצְ**כֶם/כֶן/**תַּשְׁבְּצָ**ם/ן	תַּשְׁבְּצִי/תַּשְׁבֶּצְךָ/**תַּשְׁבְּ**צֵךְ/צוֹ/צָהּ	תַּשְׁבֵּץ-	crossword	תַּשְׁבֵּץ ז'
תַּשְׁבְּצֵינוּ/כֶם/כֶן/הֶם/הֶן	**תַּשְׁבְּ**צַי/צֶיךָ/צַיִךְ/צָיו/צֶיהָ	תַּשְׁבְּצֵי-	puzzle	תַּשְׁבְּצִים

Except for the singular construct, the *tsere* is reduced to *shva* in an open syllable, תַּשְׁבְּצִי, and in a closed one is replaced by *seghol*, תַּשְׁבֶּצְךָ.

Examples

יש אנשים שפתרון **תַּשְׁבְּצִים** הוא עיסוקם העיקרי בשעות הפנאי.
For some people, solving **crossword puzzles** is their main leisure activity.

Additional Examples in this Pattern

arrow crossword puzzle, Swedish crossword תַּשְׁחֵץ jigsaw puzzle תַּצְרֵף

T. Patterns ending with the suffix *-a* (including some with the e suffix)

582. *CaCa*

Our/your/their	my/your/his/her	const.	Gloss	sing/pl
רָמָתֵנוּ/**רָמַתְ**כֶם/כֶן/**רָמָתָ**ם/ן	**רָמָ**תִי/תְךָ/תֵךְ/תוֹ/תָהּ	רָמַת-	high plateau;	רָמָה נ׳
רָמוֹתֵינוּ/כֶם/כֶן/הֶם/הֶן	**רָמוֹ**תַי/תֶיךָ/תַיִךְ/תָיו/תֶיהָ	רָמוֹת-	level	רָמוֹת

The *kamats* stays stable throughout the declension.

Examples

יינות **רָמַת** הגולן הם מהטובים בארץ היום.
Wines of the Golan **Heights** are of the best in Israel.

משרד החינוך מודאג מאוד מן הירידה **בְּרָמַת** המשמעת בבתי הספר.
The Education Ministry is quite worried about the decline in the discipline **level** at school.

הזמרת הזאת אינה מרשימה כלל כשרואים אותה ברחוב, אבל על **הַבָּמָה** הופעתה ממש מחשמלת.
This singer is not at all impressive when you see here on the street, but on **stage** her appearance is truly electrifying.

הַפָּרוֹת של **רָמַת** הגולן הן מהיפות והבריאות שראיתי בישראל.
The **cows** of the Golan **Heights** are some of the best looking and heathiest I have seen in Israel.

Special Expressions

entertainment **stage** **בָּמַת** בידור
depression, melancholy **מָרָה** שחורה
dire straits, deep trouble **צָרָה** צרורה
standard of living **רָמַת** החיים
level of education **רָמַת** השכלה
loudly **בְּרָמָה**
barometric pressure **רָמָה** ברומטרית

Additional Examples in this Pattern

kite (bird) דָּאָה
sifter, sieve נָפָה
slang, jargon עָגָה
gall, bile מָרָה
trouble, difficulty צָרָה
cold front קָרָה
evil רָעָה

---

583. ***CaCa*** with reduction

Our/your/their	my/your/his/her	const.	Gloss	sing/pl
שְׁעָתֵנוּ/**שְׁעַתְ**כֶם/כֶן/**שְׁעָתָ**ם/ן	**שְׁעָ**תִי/תְךָ/תֵךְ/תוֹ/תָהּ	שְׁעַת-	hour,	שָׁעָה נ׳
שְׁעוֹתֵינוּ/כֶם/כֶן/הֶם/הֶן	**שְׁעוֹ**תַי/תֶיךָ/תַיִךְ/תָיו/תֶיהָ	שְׁעוֹת-	time	שָׁעוֹת

The *kamats* is reduced to *shva* two syllables away from the stress, and is replaced by *pataH* in a closed syllable. Note: the plural form of שָׁנָה 'year, f.' is שָׁנִים.

Examples

טיסה מארה״ב לישראל נמשכת כעשר וחצי **שָׁעוֹת**, ובכיוון ההפוך כשתים עשרה (נגד הרוח).
A flight from the US to Israel lasts about ten and a half **hours**, and in the opposite direction about twelve (against the wind).

נקווה ש**השָּׁנָה** הבאה תהיה טובה יותר מקודמתה.
Let's hope that next **year** would be better than the previous one.

אומרים שלאדם המדבר שתי **שָׂפוֹת** קוראים דו-לשוני, ולמי שמדבר שפה אחת אמריקאי...
They that a person who speaks two **languages** is called bi-lingual, and one who speaks one language American...

Special Expressions

anniversary יום **הַשָּׁנָה**
each and every **year** (מדי) **שָׁנָה בְּשָׁנָה**
completely full, overflowing עובר על **גְּדוֹתָיו**
for **hours** **שָׁעָה** ארוכה
It's time! הגיעה **הַשָּׁעָה**!
Good luck! בְּ**שָׁעָה** טובה!
the right time **שְׁעַת** הכושר
at least for now לפי **שָׁעָה**
foreign **language** **שָׂפָה** זרה
mother **tongue** **שְׂפַת** אם
body **language** **שְׂפַת** גוף

twice as much **מָנָה** אחת אפיים
unit of blood **מְנַת** דם
his lot, his fate **מְנַת** חלקו
IQ **מְנַת** משכל
battle **ration** **מְנַת** קרב
civil year (solar) **שָׁנָה** אזרחית
leap **year** **שָׁנָה** מעוברת
non-leap **year** **שָׁנָה** פשוטה
fiscal **year** **שְׁנַת** הכספים
this **year** **הַשָּׁנָה**
calendar לוח **שָׁנָה**
A Happy (Jewish) New **year**! לְ**שָׁנָה** טובה תיכתבו ותיחתמו!

Additional Examples in this Pattern

coin Lit. מָעָה
lip שָׂפָה (ר׳ שְׂפָתַיִם)
language שָׂפָה (ר׳ שָׂפוֹת)

bank (of river) גָּדָה
fish (general) דָּגָה
portion; dose; ration; quotient מָנָה

---

584. ***CaCa*** with reduction when the first root consonant is guttural

Our/your/their	my/your/his/her	const.	Gloss	sing/pl
אֲמָתֵנוּ/**אֲמַתְ**כֶם/כֶן/**אֲמָתָ**ם/ן	**אֲמָ**תִי/תְךָ/תֵךְ/תוֹ/תָהּ	אֲמַת-	female	אָמָה נ׳
אַמְהוֹתֵינוּ/כֶם/כֶן/הֶם/הֶן	**אַמְהוֹ**תַי/תֶיךָ/תַיִךְ/תָיו/תֶיהָ	אַמְהוֹת-	servant Lit.	אֲמָהוֹת

The *kamats* is reduced to *Hataf-pataH* two syllables away from the stress, and is replaced by *pataH* in a closed syllable. When a sequence of *Hataf-shva* would have been formed, the first is replaced by *pataH* and the second closes the syllable. Only one realization, literary, is included here.

---

585. *CaCa* with *dagesh forte*

our/your/their	my/your/his/her	const.	Gloss	sing/pl
חַלָּתֵנוּ/**חַלַּתְ**כֶם/כֶן/**חַלָּתָ**ם/ן	**חַלָּ**תִי/תְךָ/תֵךְ/תוֹ/תָהּ	חַלַּת-	challah;	חַלָּה נ׳
חַלּוֹתֵינוּ/כֶם/כֶן/הֶם/הֶן	**חַלּוֹ**תַי/תֶיךָ/תַיִךְ/תָיו/תֶיהָ	חַלּוֹת-	priest's share of dough	חַלּוֹת

The *dagesh forte* is maintained throughout, mostly from roots with identical second and third consonants, occasionally others (e.g. roots with initial *n* or final *y*).

Examples

הרבה מעדיפים **חַלָּה** אפילו על פני עוגה.
Many prefer a **challah** even over cake.

שיר הילדים ״למקדונלד הזקן הייתה **חַוָּה**״ תורגם לעברית כ״לדוד משה הייתה **חַוָּה**״.
The children's song "old McDonald had a **farm**" was translated into Hebrew as "Uncle Moses had a **farm**."

בחתונה בדרך כלל נשים משתדלות לא להיראות יותר יפות מן ה**כַּלָּה**...
In weddings women generally try not to look prettier than the **brid**e...

כל מי שמנסה למצוא את דרכו בשטח לא מוכר על פי **מַפָּה** טופוגרפית יודע שזה לא תמיד קל.
Anyone who tries to find his way with the help of a topographical **map** knows that it is not always easy.

Special Expressions

ד׳ **אַמּוֹת** minimal distance
אַמַּת מידה criterion
בַּדַּקָּה התשעים at the very last moment
חַיַּת טרף animal of prey
חַלַּה של שבת a Sabbath **challah**
חַלַּת דבש honeycomb
ליקוי **חַמָּה** **solar** eclipse

Additional Examples in this Pattern

אַיָּה buzzard
אַלָּה club, cudgel
אַמָּה forearm; cubit; middle finger
גַּבָּה eyebrow
דַּיָּה kite (bird)
דַּקָּה minute
חַיָּה animal
חַכָּה fishing rod
חַמָּה sun Lit.
חַסָּה/א lettuce
יַמָּה lake, inland sea
מַכָּה blow
מַסָּה essay; despair Lit.
מַצָּה Matzah
סַפָּה sofa
צַמָּה braid
רַקָּה temple (side of head)
שַׁמָּה wilderness

---

586. *CiCa* with *dagesh forte*

our/your/their	my/your/his/her	const.	Gloss	sing/pl
כִּתָּתֵנוּ/**כִּתַּתְ**כֶם/כֶן/**כִּתָּתָ**ם/ן	**כִּתָּ**תִי/תְךָ/תֵךְ/תוֹ/תָהּ	כִּתַּת-	class;	כִּתָּה נ'
כִּתּוֹתֵינוּ/כֶם/כֶן/הֶם/הֶן	**כִּתּוֹ**תַי/תֶיךָ/תַיִךְ/תָיו/תֶיהָ	כִּתּוֹת-	classroom; section (military)	כִּתּוֹת

The *dagesh forte* is maintained throughout. Mostly forms derived from roots with identical second and third consonants – the *dagesh* results from the historical merger.

Examples

נעמי מספרת ש**בכִּתָּה** שלה בבית הספר היסודי היו כמה ילדים של אנשים מפורסמים.
Naomi says that in her elementary school **class** there were some children of famous people.

כשלומדים שפה זרה בארץ שבה היא מדוברת, רוכשים מיומנות בדיבור מחוץ **לכִּתָּה** לא פחות מאשר בתוכה.
When one studies a foreign language in the country in which it is spoken, one acquires oral proficiency outside of class as much as one does in the **classroom**.

ייבוש **בִּצּוֹת** עוזר בחיסול יתושים המפיצים קדחת, אבל לעתים גם פוגע באיכות הסביבה.
Drying up **swamps** helps in elimination malaria-spreading mosquitoes, but at the same time sometimes negatively affects the environment.

הכלכלנים מנסים להבין את ה**סִּבּוֹת** למפולת האחרונה של הבורסה.
The economists are trying to understand the **reasons** for the latest collapse of the stock exchange.

לכובע שלי שלוש **פִּנּוֹת**...
My hat has three **corners**...

Special Expressions

משפט **זִקָּה** attributive clause
חִבַּת ציון **love** of Zion; 19th Cent. term for Zionism
כִּפַּת הסלע **Dome** of the Rock, main mosque on Jerusalem's Temple Mount
כִּפַּת השמים sky Lit.
כִּתַּת אָמָן master **class**
כִּתַּת יורים firing **squad**
מִדָּה טובה virtue
במִדָּה רבה to a great **extent**
סִכַּת ביטחון safety **pin**
סִכַּת ראש hair**pin**

Additional Examples in this Pattern

הִלָּה halo; corona; areola
זִמָּה lust
זִקָּה affinity, attachment; linkage
חִבָּה affection
כִּפָּה skullcap; cupola, dome
לִבָּה core; kernel
מִדָּה measurement; size; extent
סִכָּה pin; brooch; hair clip; staple
עִלָּה excuse
פִּנָּה corner
פִּסָּה snippet; slice
צִיָּה desert, wilderness
רִבָּה jam, jelly
שִׁדָּה dresser, chest of drawers

---

587. ***CiCa*** when the plural suffix is *-im*

our/your/their	my/your/his/her	const.	Gloss	sing/pl
חִטָּתֵנוּ/**חִטַּתְ**כֶם/כֶן/**חִטָּתָ**ם/ן	**חִטָּ**תִי/תְךָ/תֵךְ/תוֹ/תָהּ	חִטַּת-	wheat	חִטָּה נ׳
חִטֵּינוּ/כֶם/כֶן/הֶם/הֶן	חִטַּי/חִטֶּיךָ/חִטַּיִךְ/חִטָּיו/חִטֶּיהָ	חִטֵּי-		חִטִּים

Examples

ה**חִטָּה** היא המקור החשוב ביותר בעולם ללחם.
Wheat is the most important source for bread in the world.

על פי המקרא, העולם נברא ב**מִלָּה**.
According to the Bible, the world was created with a **word**.

Special Expressions

חִטָּה מלאה **wheat** from which fiber was not removed

מִלַּת כבוד **word** of honor

מִלָּה נרדפת synonym

מִלִּים של שבת fancy **words**

מִלָּה בסלע, שתיקה בתרי silence is golden

Additional Examples in this Pattern

אִשָּׁה woman (from *'enosh* 'human being > *'insh* > *'insha* > *'isha*)

כִּנָּה flea שִׁטָּה acacia

---

588. ***CeCa***

our/your/their	my/your/his/her	const.	Gloss	sing/pl
תֵּבָתֵנוּ/**תֵּבַתְ**כֶם/כֶן/**תֵּבָתָ**ם/ן	**תֵּבָ**תִי/תְךָ/תֵךְ/תוֹ/תָהּ	תֵּבַת-	chest/box;	תֵּבָה נ׳
תֵּבוֹתֵינוּ/כֶם/כֶן/הֶם/הֶן	**תֵּבוֹ**תַי/תֶיךָ/תַיִךְ/תָיו/תֶיהָ	תֵּבוֹת-	word; bar	תֵּבוֹת

The *tsere* is maintained throughout the declension.

Examples

מכיוון שלא היינו בבית שבוע, כשחזרנו **תֵּבַת** הדואר שלנו הייתה מלאה עד אפס מקום.
Since we were away from home for a week, our mail **box** was full when we returned.

כנראה שאכלתי משהו לא טרי אתמול; יש לי כאבים חזקים ב**קֵבָה**.
I must have eaten something stale yesterday; I have strong **stomach** pain.

בדיני כשרות ביהדות, פגם קטן ב**רֵאָה** פוסל את הפרה כולה.
In Jewish Kosher laws, a small defect in the **lung** disqualifies the whole cow.

Special Expressions

ב**זֵעַת** אפיו by the **sweat** of his brow

לֵדַת מלקחיים forceps **birth**

רֵאָה ירוקה urban open (green) space

ראשי תֵּבוֹת initials, acronym

תֵּבַת הילוכים gear **box**

תֵּבַת נוח Noah's **ark**

תֵּבַת תהודה sound **box** (music)

Additional Examples in this Pattern

birth לֵדָה   sweat זֵעָה   terebinth (tree) אֵלָה

---

589. ***CeCa*** where *tsere* is reduced to *shva*

our/your/their	my/your/his/her	const.	Gloss	sing/pl
פְּאָתֵנוּ/**פְּאַתְ**כֶם/כֶן/**פְּאָתָ**ם/ן	**פְּאָ**תִי/תְךָ/תֵךְ/תוֹ/תָהּ	פְּאַת-	edge; side-	פֵּאָה נ׳
פְּאוֹתֵינוּ/כֶם/כֶן/הֶם/הֶן	**פְּאוֹ**תַי/תֶיךָ/תַיִךְ/תָיו/תֶיהָ	פְּאוֹת-	lock; wig	פֵּאוֹת

Examples

בארץ ישראל ההיסטורית נהוג היה להשאיר תבואה **בִּפְאַת** השדה לעניים.
In the historical Land of Israel they used to leave wheat at the **edge** of the field for the poor.

בני החסידים נוטים לטפח **פֵּאוֹת** לתפארה.
Hassidic boys tend to grow magnificent **side-locks**.

נשים אורתודוקסיות חובשת לעתים **פֵּאָה** (נוכרית), משום ש״שיער באישה ערווה״.
Orthodox Jewish women sometimes wear a **wig**, since the sight of a woman's hair is considered by some to be indecent (as if she was naked).

חוסר **שֵׁנָה** הוא מן הגורמים העיקריים לתאונות בדרכים ובעבודה.
Insufficient **sleep** is one of the main causes of accidents on the road and at work.

Special Expressions

wig **פֵּאָה** נוכרית   broken/troubled **sleep** **שֵׁנָה** טרופה

due to **מִפְּאַת**   **sleep** of the just **שְׁנַת** ישרים

---

590. ***CeCa*** where *tsere* is replaced by *Hataf*

Our/your/their	my/your/his/her	const.	Gloss	sing/pl
עֲצָתֵנוּ/**עֲצַתְ**כֶם/כֶן/**עֲצָתָ**ם/ן	**עֲצָ**תִי/תְךָ/תֵךְ/תוֹ/תָהּ	עֲצַת-	piece of advice;	עֵצָה נ׳
עֲצוֹתֵינוּ/כֶם/כֶן/הֶם/הֶן	**עֲצוֹ**תַי/תֶיךָ/תַיִךְ/תָיו/תֶיהָ	עֲצוֹת-	sagacity; timber	עֵצוֹת

When a *shva* is expected with a guttural, it is replaced by *Hataf-pataH.*

Examples

מכיוון ששמעתי **לַעֲצָתוֹ** של מנהל ההשקעות, הפסדתי 50% מחסכונותיי...
Since I listened to the **advice** of the investment advisor, I lost 50% of my savings…

בעברית ספרותית, במקום לומר ״מצא פיתרון חכם לבעייה״, אומרים ״מצא **עֵצָה**״.
In literary Hebrew, instead of saying "find a clever solution to the problem," one says "find **advice**" (i.e., "employ sagacity.")

Special Expressions

bewildered אובד **עֵצוֹת**
ask for his advice שאל **בַּעֲצָתוֹ**
in full agreement **בְּעֵצָה** אחת

bad advice, **עֲצַת** אחיתופל (שמ׳ ב׳ טו:לא) intended to cause harm (II Sam 15:31)
trunk wood **עֲצַת** הגזע

Additional Examples in this Pattern

ethnic group; group עֵדָה

---

591. ***CeCa*** sing. following *da`at*

sing/pl	Gloss	const.	my/your/his/her	our/your/their
דֵּעָה נ׳	opinion	דַּעַת-	דַּעְתִּי/תְּךָ/תֵּךְ/תּוֹ/תָּהּ	דַּעְתֵּנוּ/דַּעַתְכֶם/כֶן/דַּעְתָּם/ן
דֵּעוֹת		דֵּעוֹת-	דֵּעוֹתַי/תֶיךָ/תַיִךְ/תָיו/תֶיהָ	דֵּעוֹתֵינוּ/כֶם/כֶן/הֶם/הֶן

Exceptional form. Either with *Hataf* or *shva* (דַּעֲתִי ~ דַּעְתִּי etc.).

Examples

בציבור האמריקאי היום נשמעות **דֵּעוֹת** שונות כיצד לטפל במהגרים שנכנסו לארה״ב באופן שאינו חוקי.
In the American public there are many **opinions** today as to how to deal with illegal immigrants.

Special Expressions

with the majority of people agreeing ברוב **דֵּעוֹת**

of sound **mind** **בְּדֵעָה** צלולה
prejudice **דֵּעָה** קדומה

---

592. ***CuCa***

sing/pl	Gloss	const.	my/your/his/her	our/your/their
סֻכָּה נ׳	temporary	סֻכַּת-	סֻכָּתִי/תְךָ/תֵךְ/תוֹ/תָהּ	סֻכָּתֵנוּ/סֻכַּתְכֶם/כֶן/סֻכָּתָם/ן
סֻכּוֹת	structure to live in; succah	סֻכּוֹת-	סֻכּוֹתַי/תֶיךָ/תַיִךְ/תָיו/תֶיהָ	סֻכּוֹתֵינוּ/כֶם/כֶן/הֶם/הֶן

The *dagesh* is maintained throughout. Some of the forms are derived from roots with identical second and third consonants (חֻקָּה, סֻכָּה), or where the first consonant is an assimilated *n* (מֻטָּה) - thus the *dagesh* – but the declension is the same.

Examples

יהודים אדוקים מקפידים לאכול את כל ארוחותיהם **בַּסֻּכָּה** בכל ימי חג הסֻכּוֹת.
Orthodox Jews eat all their meals in a **succah** during the Feast of the Tabernacles.

מכיוון שבישראל הדתיים הם תמיד חלק מן הקואליציה, אין בה **חֻקָּה** – רק חוקי יסוד.
Since in Israel the religious are always part of the coalition, it has no **constitution** – only basic laws.

תמיד אפשר להזמין כרטיסים מראש להצגה או לקולנוע, ולאסוף אותם בערב ב**קֻפָּה**.
One can always order tickets ahead of time for a show or a movie, and pick them up later at the **box office**.

Special Expressions

masterpiece, climax **גֻּלַּת** הכותרת
Jewish marriage ceremony **חֻפָּה** וְקִדּוּשִׁין
Feast of the **Tabernacles** (חג ה)**סֻכּוֹת**
petty **cash box** **קֻפָּה** קטנה

can of worms trailing behind him (= has a bad history) **קֻפָּה** של שרצים תלויה לו מאחוריו

Additional Examples in this Pattern

nation, people אֻמָּה
lobe (anatomy) אֻנָּה
puppet בֻּבָּה
small ball, marble גֻּלָּה
pit, hole, dimple גֻּמָּה

canopy; canopy used at Jewish wedding חֻפָּה
span, extent מֻטָּה
money box; cash register; box office; treasury קֻפָּה

---

593. ***CoCa***

our/your/their	my/your/his/her	const.	Gloss	sing/pl
קוֹמָתֵנוּ/**קוֹמַתְ**כֶם/כֶן/**קוֹמָתָ**ם/ן	**קוֹמָ**תִי/תְךָ/תֵךְ/תוֹ/תָהּ	קוֹמַת-	height;	קוֹמָה נ'
קוֹמוֹתֵינוּ/כֶם/כֶן/הֶם/הֶן	**קוֹמוֹ**תַי/תֶיךָ/תַיִךְ/תָיו/תֶיהָ	קוֹמוֹת-	floor	קוֹמוֹת

The *kamats* is maintained throughout the declension, except for a closed syllable, where it is converted to *pataH*, קוֹמַתְכֶם. The roots from which the forms were derived are varied: first consonant *y*, second *w*, third *y*, but the declension is the same for all.

Examples

באמסטרדם, למשל, בתי ה**זוֹנוֹת** הם חוקיים לגמרי.
In Amsterdam, for instance, brothels ("**prostitutes**' houses") are completely legal.

שירות צבאי הוא **חוֹבָתוֹ** הבסיסית של כל אזרח ישראלי.
Army service is a basic **duty** of every Israeli citizen.

יש עדיין שכונות במרבית הערים בעולם שבהן בעלי כלבים אינם טורחים לאסוף את **צוֹאָתָם**.
There are still neighborhoods in many of the world's cities in which dog owners do not bother to collect their **excrement**.

יש אנשים הטוענים ש**השׁוֹאָה** לא הייתה ולא נבראה, ושהיא פרי דימיונם של היהודים.
Some people claim that the **Holocaust** never happened, and that it is a myth generated by the Jews.

Special Expressions

brothel **בית זונות**/בית בושת

Great wall of China **חוֹמַת** סין

the **good** of the public **טוֹבַת** הכלל

humdrum **period** Coll. **עוֹנַת** המלפפונים

home, shelter, a **roof** over one's head **קוֹרַת** גג

thanks a lot! **תּוֹדָה** רבה!

gospel truth **תּוֹרָה** מסיני

Additional Examples in this Pattern

wall חוֹמָה

good N; favor N טוֹבָה

feather נוֹצָה

season עוֹנָה

vagina; sleeve for hinge פּוֹתָה

beam קוֹרָה

thanks, gratitude תּוֹדָה

Torah; theory; doctrine תּוֹרָה

---

594. ***CoCa*** when the plural suffix is *-im*

our/your/their	my/your/his/her	const.	Gloss	sing/pl
יוֹנָתֵנוּ/**יוֹנַתְ**כֶם/כֶן/**יוֹנָתָ**ם/ן	**יוֹנָ**תִי/תְךָ/תֵךְ/תוֹ/תָהּ	-יוֹנַת	pigeon,	יוֹנָה נ׳
יוֹנֵינוּ/כֶם/כֶן/הֶם/הֶן	**יוֹנַ**י/נֶיךָ/נַיִךְ/נָיו/נֶיהָ	-יוֹנֵי	dove	יוֹנִים

As in the קוֹמָה declension above, except that the plural suffix is *-im*. A single illustration (a similar illustration in a different *mishkal*: דְּבוֹרָה – דְּבוֹרִים 'bee').

Examples

אחד הסמלים של השלום הוא **יוֹנָה** לבנה, לעתים כשהיא מחזיקה במקורה עלה או ענף של עץ זית – כנראה מספר "בראשית": **היוֹנָה** נשלחה על ידי נוח בתום המבול למצוא יבשה.

One of the symbols of peace is a white **dove**, sometimes holding an olive leaf or branch in her beak – apparently from Genesis: the **dove** was sent by Noah at the end of the deluge to look for dry land.

Special Expressions

carrier **pigeon** **יוֹנַת** דואר

---

595. ***CuCa***

our/your/their	my/your/his/her	const.	Gloss	sing/pl
שׁוּרָתֵנוּ/**שׁוּרַתְ**כֶם/כֶן/**שׁוּרָתָ**ם/ן	**שׁוּרָ**תִי/תְךָ/תֵךְ/תוֹ/תָהּ	-שׁוּרַת	line;	שׁוּרָה נ׳
שׁוּרוֹתֵינוּ/כֶם/כֶן/הֶם/הֶן	**שׁוּרוֹ**תַי/תֶיךָ/תַיִךְ/תָיו/תֶיהָ	-שׁוּרוֹת	series	שׁוּרוֹת

The *kamats* is maintained throughout the declension, except for a closed syllable, where it is converted to *pataH*, שׁוּרַתְכֶם. The roots from which the forms are derived are often with *w* as a second consonant, but regardless, the declension is the same for all.

Examples

כאשר הנשיא יוצא לשחק גולף, מתלווה אליו **שׁוּרַת** מכוניות ארוכה של השירות החשאי.

When the President goes out to play golf, he is accompanied by a long **line** of secret service cars.

זו **בּוּשָׁה** לראות כמה חסרי בית יש בארץ כה עשירה כמו ארה"ב.
It is a **shame** to see how many homeless people there are in a country as rich as the US.

בסוּפָה האחרונה נותרו מאות רבות של אנשים ללא קורת גג.
In the last **storm** hundreds of people found themselves without a roof over their heads.

ביתו של מארק טוויין בהרטפורד נבנה **בצוּרָה** של ספינה.
Mark Twain's house in Hartford was built in the **shape** of a boat.

Special Expressions

over my (dead) body על **גוּפָתִי** (המתה) Coll.
morphology **תּוֹרַת הצוּרוֹת**
the bottom line **השּׁוּרָה** התחתונה/האחרונה
in order, properly **כַּשּׁוּרָה**
strict law, letter of the law **שׁוּרַת** הדין
the punch line **שׁוּרַת** המחץ

Additional Examples in this Pattern

(dead) body, cadaver גוּפָה
light bulb נוּרָה
genre סוּגָה
cake עוּגָה
trench שׁוּחָה
tax assessment; evaluation שׁוּמָה
sadness תּוּגָה

---

596. *CeyCa*

sing/pl	Gloss	const.	my/your/his/her	Our/your/their
אֵימָה נ'	dread,	אֵימַת-	**אֵימָ**תִי/תְךָ/תֵךְ/תוֹ/תָהּ	אֵימָתֵנוּ/**אֵימַתְ**כֶם/כֶן/**אֵימָתָ**ם/ן
אֵימוֹת/אֵימִים	awe	אֵימוֹת-	**אֵימוֹ**תַי/תֶיךָ/תַיִךְ/תָיו/תֶיהָ	**אֵימוֹתֵי**נוּ/כֶם/כֶן/הֶם/הֶן

Examples

הטרור הוא הטלת **אֵימָה** על הציבור כאמצעי להשגת מטרות פוליטיות, חברתיות או כלכליות.
Terror is the imposing of **dread** on the public in order to achieve political, social or economic goals.

האֵיבָה שבין הנוודים לעובדי האדמה היא **אֵיבָה** עתיקה כתולדות האנושות.
The **enmity** between the nomads and settled agricultural communities is as old as human civilization.

Special Expressions

great **fear** **אֵימָה** חשכה
stage **fright** **אֵימַת** הבימה/הציבור
deadly **terror** **אֵימַת** מוות
strike **terror** into him הלך/הילך עליו **אֵימִים**
eternal **loathing** **אֵיבַת** עולם
ripe **old age** **שֵׂיבָה** טובה

Additional Examples in this Pattern

end, final section סֵיפָה	introduction, preface; beginning רֵישָׁה
supplies צֵידָה	old age; white hair שֵׂיבָה

---

597. ***CeyCa*** plural suffix *-im*

Our/your/their	my/your/his/her	const.	Gloss	sing/pl
בֵּיצָתֵנוּ/**בֵּיצַתְ**כֶם/כֶן/**בֵּיצָתָ**ם/ן	**בֵּיצָ**תִי/תְךָ/תֵךְ/תוֹ/תָהּ	בֵּיצַת-	egg	בֵּיצָה נ׳
בֵּיצֵינוּ/כֶם/כֶן/הֶם/הֶן	**בֵּי**צַי/צֶיךָ/צַיִךְ/צָיו/צֶיהָ	בֵּיצֵי-		בֵּיצִים

The singular as in the אֵימָה declension above, but the plural suffix is *–im*, and the plural declension follows it. A single illustration.

Examples

שאלה קלאסית: מה קדם למה, ה**בֵּיצָה** או התרנגולת?
A classical question: what came first, the **egg** or the chicken?

Special Expressions

something that does not yet exist, but might in the future **בֵּיצָה** שלא נולדה

---

598. ***CiCCa*** with segholate-type plural

our/your/their	my/your/his/her	const.	Gloss	sing/pl
שִׂמְלָתֵנוּ/**שִׂמְלַתְ**כֶם/כֶן/**שִׂמְלָתָ**ם/ן	**שִׂמְלָ**תִי/תְךָ/תֵךְ/תוֹ/תָהּ	שִׂמְלַת-	dress; tunic	שִׂמְלָה נ׳
שִׂמְלוֹתֵינוּ/כֶם/כֶן/הֶם/הֶן	**שִׂמְלוֹ**תַי/תֶיךָ/תַיִךְ/תָיו/תֶיהָ	שִׂמְלוֹת-	(Bibl.)	שְׂמָלוֹת

As shown above, penultimately-stressed masculine nouns ending with a *seghol* originated from splitting of final consonant clusters in bases such as *CaCC*, *CiCC*, etc. by a *seghol*, since speakers of Classical Hebrew had difficulty articulating final clusters. When the feminine suffix *-a* is appended to comparable bases, the articulation difficulty is gone, owing to the different syllabification: *sim-la*. Regardless of whether it is appropriate to assume a "segholate" base such as *siml-* or not, the plural formation pattern of forms like *simla*, like that of masculine segholate nouns, is an independent *mishkal* with a similar base, *CCaC-*, but with the suffix *-ot*: *CCaCot* instead of *CCaCim*. In a closed syllable, the *kamats* is replaced by *pataH*: שִׂמְלַתְכֶם.

Examples

כבר שלושה חודשים היא מחפשת **שִׂמְלָה** לחתונת בִּתָּהּ אך אינה מצליחה למצוא משהו מתאים.
For three months now she has been looking for a **dress** for her daughter's wedding, but cannot find anything appropriate.

שִׂמְלָה לך, קצין תהיה לנו (ישעי׳ ג:ו).
If you have a **tunic** (mantle), you shall be our leader (Is 3:6).

הגדרה מילונית ל"**גִּבְעָה**": הר שגובהו אינו עולה על 300 מטר מעל פני הים.
Dictionary definition of a "**hill**": a mountain whose height does not exceed 300 meters above sea level..

הרבה פולנים נשבעים שראו את פסל המדונה השחורה בצ'נסטוחובה מזיל **דְּמָעוֹת**.
Many Poles swear that they saw the statue of the Black Madonna in Czestochowa shed **tears**.

אברהם תמיד נראה לי צעיר, אבל לאחרונה ניכרים בו כבר סימנים ראשונים של **זִקְנָה**.
Avraham has always looked young to me, but lately one can notice first indications in him of **old age**.

לא אהבנו את שיעורי **הזִמְרָה** שלנו בבית הספר היסודי, אבל בדיעבד, השירים נטמעו בנו, ורובנו שמחים על כך.
We did not like our **singing** classes at elementary school, but in retrospect, we assimilated those songs, and most of us are glad that we did.

בסוף החודש **היִתְרָה** בחשבוננו בבנק שואפת לאפס...
At the end of the month the **balance** in our bank account is pretty close to zero…

כולם מחכים לראות מה יקרה בוועידת **הפִּסְגָּה** בין הנשיא האמריקאי ונשיא רוסיה.
Everybody is waiting to see what will happen in the summit meeting between the American President and the President of Russia.

אני לא נוגע ב"פייסבוק", בעיקר בגלל שהאתר אינו מקפיד כראוי בשמירה על **צִנְעַת** הפרט.
I never touch Facebook, primarily because they are not sufficiently careful to maintain privacy.

אם גילית קן **צְרָעוֹת** בחצר, אל תנסה להיפטר ממנו בעצמך; קרא למדביר מקצועי.
If you discover a hornets' nest in the yard, do not try to get rid of it on your own. Call a professional exterminator.

עמנואל מקפיד לקיים **שִׁגְרָה** יומיומית המשלבת פעילות אינטלקטואלית וגופנית כדי לשמור על בריאותו הפיסית והנפשית.
Immanuel maintains a strict daily **routine** that combines intellectual and physical activity in order to preserve his mental and physical health.

Special Expressions

בִּקְעַת הירדן the Jordan Valley (part of the Syrian-African fault)
גִּבְעַת התחמושת Ammunition Hill (in Jerusalem)
דִּמְעוֹת תנין crocodile **tears**
שכר **טִרְחָה** fee for professional services
יִרְאַת שמיים religiosity, piety
יִרְאַת כבוד **respect, reverence, awe**
יִתְרָה מועברת **balance** brought forward
כִּבְרַת דרך a good part of the way
מוסר **כְּלָיוֹת** pangs of conscience
סִדְרַת (פס) ייצור production **line**
פִּרְצָה קוראת לגנב **lack of supervision** encourages theft
קִנְאַת סופרים תרבה חוכמה rivalry among scholars promotes wisdom/scholarship
קִצְבַּת **זִקְנָה** **old age** pension
קִרְבַת משפחה **kin**ship
בעידנא **דרִתְחָא** in a moment of **extreme anger**
שִׂמְחָה לְאֵיד **rejoicing** in another person's failure

Additional Examples in this Pattern

lining (of clothing) בִּטְנָה
valley בִּקְעָה
shack, hut בִּקְתָּה
sector; figure גִּזְרָה
bother, nuisance טִרְדָּה
effort טִרְחָה
awe, fear יִרְאָה
a certain distance כִּבְרָה
kidney כִּלְיָה
office, bureau לִשְׁכָּה
ointment מִשְׁחָה
safety catch נִצְרָה
tunnel נִקְבָּה
cave, grotto נִקְרָה
series סִדְרָה
digit סִפְרָה
nipple פִּטְמָה
breach, opening; loophole פִּרְצָה
mollusk צִדְפָּה
progress קִדְמָה
jealousy קִנְאָה
proximity; relationship; similarity קִרְבָה
city, town קִרְיָה
floor רִצְפָּה
boiling; great anger רִתְחָה
layer שִׁכְבָה
forgetfulness שִׁכְחָה
chassis שִׁלְדָּה
happiness שִׂמְחָה
windowpane שִׁמְשָׁה
hatred שִׂנְאָה

---

599. ***CiCCa*** with segholate-type plural when the first root consonant is guttural

our/your/their	my/your/his/her	const.	Gloss	sing/pl
אִמְרָתֵנוּ/**אִמְרַתְ**כֶם/כֶן/**אִמְרָתָ**ם/ן	**אִמְרָ**תִי/תְךָ/תֵךְ/תוֹ/תָהּ	אִמְרַת-	saying	אִמְרָה נ׳
אִמְרוֹתֵינוּ/כֶם/כֶן/הֶם/הֶן	**אִמְרוֹ**תַי/תֶיךָ/תַיִךְ/תָיו/תֶיהָ	אִמְרוֹת-		אֲמָרוֹת

The declension is as in שִׂמְלָה above, except that where a *shva* is expected with a guttural, it is replaced by *Hataf-pataH*. In a closed syllable, the *kamats* is replaced by *pataH*: אִמְרַתְכֶם.

Examples

אִמְרָה נפוצה בערבית: כל כלב בא יומו.
An Arabic **saying**: Every dog has his day.

Special Expressions

a commonly used, poignant **saying** **אִמְרַת** כנף

Additional Examples in this Pattern

thrust (e.g., of sword) אִבְחָה
fishbone; fish skeleton אִדְרָה
trace; memory trace (note: no *dagesh kal* in last root consonant) עִקְבָה

---

600. ***CiCCa*** plural regular (not segholate-like)

our/your/their	my/your/his/her	const.	Gloss	sing/pl
אִוְשָׁתֵנוּ/**אִוְשַׁתְ**כֶם/כֶן/**אִוְשָׁתָ**ם/ן	**אִוְשָׁ**תִי/תְךָ/תֵךְ/תוֹ/תָהּ	אִוְשַׁת-	murmur,	אִוְשָׁה נ׳
אִוְשׁוֹתֵינוּ/כֶם/כֶן/הֶם/הֶן	**אִוְשׁוֹ**תַי/תֶיךָ/תַיִךְ/תָיו/תֶיהָ	אִוְשׁוֹת-	undertone	אִוְשׁוֹת

The plural form is regular – not as in segholate nouns . In a closed syllable, the *kamats* is replaced by *pataH*: אִוְשַׁתְכֶם.

Examples

אִוְשָׁה בלב פירושה בדרך כלל שיש פגם כלשהו באחד השסתומים.
A **murmur** in the heart usually means that there is some defect in one of the valves.

Special Expressions

תִּגְרֶת ידיים **scuffle**

Additional Examples in this Pattern

חִמְצָה chick-pea, garbanzo
חִגְגָּה celebration, feast
מִנְתָּה mint, peppermint
שִׁקְצָה gentile (fem.) Lit.
תִּגְרָה skirmish, fracas

---

601. ***CiCCa*** plural *-a'ot*

our/your/their	my/your/his/her	const.	Gloss	sing/pl
גִּמְלָתֵנוּ/**גִּמְלַתְ**כֶם/כֶן/**גִּמְלָתָ**ם/ן	**גִּמְלָ**תִי/תְךָ/תֵךְ/תוֹ/תָהּ	גִּמְלַת-	pension,	גִּמְלָה נ׳
גִּמְלְאוֹתֵינוּ/כֶם/כֶן/הֶם/הֶן	**גִּמְלְאוֹ**תַי/תֶיךָ/תַיִךְ/תָיו/תֶיהָ	גִּמְלְאוֹת-	benefit	גִּמְלָאוֹת

The plural form is regular, not as in segholate nouns, but the suffix is ָ-אוֹת. Two syllables away from the stress, the *kamats* of ָ-אוֹת is reduced to *shva*: גִּמְלְאוֹתַי.

Examples

יש **גִּמְלָאוֹת** תקציביות, ויש כאלה המתבססות על חסכונות בתוספת תרומת המעביד.
There are defined benefits **pensions,** and ones that are based on savings plus the employer's contribution.

פוליטיקאים רבים מאמינים שאין קונפליקט שאי אפשר לפתרו באמצעות **עִסְקָה**.
Many politicians believe that there exists no conflict that cannot be resolved by means of a **deal**.

Special Expressions

גִּמְלָה (פנסיה) מוקדמת early **pension**
עִסְקַת חבילה package deal
עִסְקַת טיעון plea bargain, plea agreement (law)

Additional Examples in this Pattern

note, message פִּתְקָה   disk, disc דִּסְקָה

---

602. ***CiCCa*** plural *-a'ot* or segholate-type

our/your/their	my/your/his/her	const.	Gloss	sing/pl
מִלְגָּתֵנוּ/**מִלְגַּתְ**כֶם/כֶן/**מִלְגָּתָ**ם/ן	**מִלְגָּתִ**י/תְךָ/תֵךְ/תוֹ/תָהּ	מִלְגַּת-	fellow-	מִלְגָּה נ׳
מִלְגוֹתֵינוּ/כֶם/כֶן/הֶם/הֶן	**מִלְגוֹ**תַי/תֶיךָ/תַיִךְ/תָיו/תֶיהָ	מִלְגוֹת-	ship	מִלְגָּאוֹת/מְלָגוֹת

The plural form is either with ָאוֹת- or as in segholate nouns, but when the suffix is ָאוֹת- it is generally maintained only in the isolation form; in the plural declension with possessive pronouns the segholate pattern (מִלְגוֹתַי...) is normally followed.

Examples

בנימין בר מזל; הוענקה לו **מִלְגָּה** ממשלתית נדיבה שאיפשרה לו לסיים בהצטיינות את התואר הראשון באוניברסיטה יוקרתית במזרח ארה״ב.
Benjamin is lucky; he was awarded a generous governmental fellowship that enabled him to graduate magna cum laude from a prestigious university in the Eastern US.

בבתי ספר יסודיים בארה״ב שבהם מלמדים מחזות של שייקספיר, מציעים לתלמידים בחירה בין **הַגִּרְסָה** המקורית לבין עיבוד לאנגלית מודרנית.
In elementary schools in the US where they teach plays by Shakespeare, they offer the students a choice between the original **version** and its adaptation into modern English.

Special Expressions

knowledge acquired in childhood **גִּרְסָא** דינקותא

Additional Examples in this Pattern

spine שִׁדְרָה   section, paragraph פִּסְקָה

---

603. ***CiCCa*** plural *-a'ot* or regular plural, not segholate-type

our/your/their	my/your/his/her	const.	Gloss	sing/pl
סִמְטָתֵנוּ/**סִמְטַתְ**כֶם/כֶן/**סִמְטָתָ**ם/ן	**סִמְטָתִ**י/תְךָ/תֵךְ/תוֹ/תָהּ	סִמְטַת-	alley	סִמְטָה נ׳
סִמְטוֹתֵינוּ/כֶם/כֶן/הֶם/הֶן	**סִמְטוֹ**תַי/תֶיךָ/תַיִךְ/תָיו/תֶיהָ	סִמְטוֹת-		סְמָטָאוֹת/סִמְטוֹת

The plural form is either with -ָאוֹת, or as in regular plural formation, but when the suffix is -ָאוֹת, it is generally maintained only in the isolation form; in the plural declension with possessive pronouns the regular plural pattern is normally followed.

Examples

בערים עתיקות יש הרבה **סְמָטָאוֹת** צרות; בערים חדשות יותר הרחובות בדרך כלל יותר רחבים.
In ancient cities there are many narrow **alleys**; in newer cities the streets are generally wider.

---

604. ***CiCCa*** plural *-im* regular

our/your/their	my/your/his/her	const.	Gloss	sing/pl
פִּשְׁתָּתֵנוּ/**פִּשְׁתַּתְ**כֶם/כֶן/**פִּשְׁתָּתָ**ם/ן	**פִּשְׁתָּ**תִי/תְךָ/תֵךְ/תוֹ/תָהּ	פִּשְׁתַּת-	flax	פִּשְׁתָּה נ׳
פִּשְׁתֵּינוּ/כֶם/כֶן/הֶם/הֶן	**פִּשְׁ**תַּי/תֶיךָ/תַיִךְ/תָיו/תֶיהָ	פִּשְׁתֵּי-		פִּשְׁתִּים

The plural form is regular, but with the suffix *-im.*

Examples

ההלכה היהודית אוסרת על לבישת בגדים העשויים מצמר **ופִּשְׁתִּים** יחדיו – משום שבסוג זה של בד השתמשו כוהני מצריים העתיקה...

Jewish law forbids wearing clothes made of a mixture of wool and **flax** – because priests of ancient Egypt used such cloth….

---

605. ***CiCCa*** plural regular *-im* or *-ot*

our/your/their	my/your/his/her	const.	Gloss	sing/pl
שִׁקְמָתֵנוּ/**שִׁקְמַתְ**כֶם/כֶן/**שִׁקְמָתָ**ם/ן	**שִׁקְמָ**תִי/תְךָ/תֵךְ/תוֹ/תָהּ	שִׁקְמַת-	sycamore	שִׁקְמָה נ׳
שִׁקְמֵינוּ/כֶם/כֶן/הֶם/הֶן	**שִׁקְמַ**י/מֶיךָ/מַיִךְ/מָיו/מֶיהָ	שִׁקְמֵי-		שִׁקְמִים/שִׁקְמוֹת

The plural form is regular, with the suffix *-im* or *-ot.*

Examples

השִׁקְמִים היו נפוצות מאוד בארץ ישראל, אך למרבית הצער רובן נגדעו עם התרחבות הבנייה.

The **sycamore fig trees** were very common in Israel/Palestine, but unfortunately most of them were cut down with the expansion of building.

---

606. ***CiCCa=CeCCa*** with segholate-type plural when the first root consonant is guttural

our/your/their	my/your/his/her	const.	Gloss	sing/pl
עֶמְדָּתֵנוּ/**עֶמְדַּתְ**כֶם/כֶן/**עֶמְדָּתָ**ם/ן	**עֶמְדָּ**תִי/תְךָ/תֵךְ/תוֹ/תָהּ	עֶמְדַּת-	position	עֶמְדָּה נ׳
עֶמְדוֹתֵינוּ/כֶם/כֶן/הֶם/הֶן	**עֶמְדוֹ**תַי/תֶיךָ/תַיִךְ/תָיו/תֶיהָ	עֶמְדוֹת-		עֲמָדוֹת

The declension is segholate, as in שִׂמְלָה above, except that the first vowel is *seghol* because of the guttural, and where a *shva* is expected with a guttural, it is replaced by *Hataf-pataH*. In a closed syllable, the *kamats* is replaced by *pataH*: עֶמְדַּתְכֶם.

Examples

אנשים רבים מאמינים שארה״ב נשלטת על ידי **הַחֲבָרוֹת** הגדולות.

Many people believe that the US is controlled by the big **companies**.

לפני שנים רבות אבי קנה **חֶלְקַת** אדמה קטנה כהשקעה לעתיד ילדיו.

Many years ago, my father bought a small **lot** as an investment for his children’s future.

כבר מזה זמן רב מייצרים כל מיני תחליפים "בריאים" ל**חֶמְאָה**, אבל היום כבר לא ברור אם התחליפים עצמם אינם מזיקים לבריאות.
For a while they have been producing all kinds of "healthy" substitutes for **butter**, but today it is no longer clear whether the substitutes themselves may be damaging to one's health.

אנשים רבים מתנגדים לעונש מוות, אך לאו דווקא מתוך תחושה של **חֶמְלָה** כלפי הפושע.
Many people object to the death penalty, but not necessarily out of a feeling of **pity** for the perpetrator.

יש אנשים שתמיד מוכנים לעזור, אבל אינם מוכנים לעולם לבקש **עֶזְרָה** מאחרים.
There are people who are always willing to help, but can never bring themselves to ask for **help** from others.

Special Expressions

חֶבְרָה בע"מ proprietary limited **company**
חֶבְרָה לתועלת הציבור public-benefit **company**
חֶלְקַת אלוהים הקטנה God's little acre
עֶזְרָה הדדית mutual **aid**
עֶזְרָה ראשונה first **aid**
עֶמְדַּת כוח **position** of power
עירום **ועֶרְיָה** stark naked; destitute
עֶרְכַּת מגן protection **kit** (e.g., in chemical warfare)

Additional Examples in this Pattern

חֶזְקָה power (math)
חֶלְאָה scum
חֶמְדָּה desire; precious thing
חֶרְפָּה shame
עֶדְנָה gentleness
עֶרְגָּה yearning
עֶרְיָה nakedness; genitalia
עֶרְכָּה set, kit

---

607. *CeCCa* plural regular (not segholate)

sing/pl	Gloss	const.	my/your/his/her	our/your/their
חֶדְוָה נ׳	joy	חֶדְוַת-	**חֶדְוָ**תִי/תְךָ/תֵךְ/תוֹ/תָהּ	חֶדְוָתֵנוּ/**חֶדְוַתְ**כֶם/כֶן/**חֶדְוָתָ**ם/ן
חֶדְווֹת		חֶדְווֹת-	**חֶדְווֹ**תַי/תֶיךָ/תַיִךְ/תָיו/תֶיהָ	**חֶדְווֹתֵי**נוּ/כֶם/כֶן/הֶם/הֶן

The plural form is regular – not as in segholate nouns . In a closed syllable, the *kamats* is replaced by *pataH*: חֶדְוַתְכֶם

Examples

המילה **חֶדְוָה** היא המקבילה הספרותית הגבוהה לשמחה.
The word ***Hedva*** is the literary counterpart of *simHa* 'joy.'

Additional Examples in this Pattern

נֶגְדָּה wife, woman Lit. (only case of *seghol* here that is not due to a guttural?)
עֶרְוָה (עֲרָוֹת/עֲרָיוֹת) nakedness; genitalia

---

608. *CiCCe*

our/your/their	my/your/his/her	const.	Gloss	sing/pl
לִבְנֵנוּ/נְכֶם/נְכֶן/נָם/נָן	**לִבְ**נִי/נְךָ/נֵךְ/נוֹ(נֵהוּ)/נָהּ(נֶהָ)	לִבְנֵה-	birch	לִבְנֶה ז׳
לִבְנֵינוּ/כֶם/כֶן/הֶם/הֶן	**לִבְ**נַי/נֶיךָ/נַיִךְ/נָיו/נֶיהָ	לִבְנֵי-	(tree)	לִבְנִים

The suffix הֶ is not the suffix *-a*, of course. It was inserted here because of similarity to other patterns listed here.
Note: The Hebrew name for the birch tree is derived from *lavan* 'white.'

---

609. *CeCCe*

our/your/their	my/your/his/her	const.	Gloss	sing/pl
אֶפְעֵנוּ/עֲכֶם/עֲכֶן/עָם/עָן	**אֶפְ**עִי/עֲךָ/עֵךְ/עוֹ(עֵהוּ)/עָהּ(עֶהָ)	אֶפְעֵה-	adder	אֶפְעֶה ז׳
אֶפְעֵינוּ/כֶם/כֶן/הֶם/הֶן	**אֶפְ**עַי/עֶיךָ/עַיִךְ/עָיו/עֶיהָ	אֶפְעֵי-	(snake)	אֶפְעִים

Here too, the suffix הֶ is not the suffix *-a*, and was inserted here because of similarity to other patterns listed here. It is actually a sub-pattern of *CiCCe* above; the *shva* expected with a guttural is replaced by *Hataf-pataH.*

Examples

בישראל **האֶפְעֶה** מצוי בסביבות ים המלח.
In Israel the **adder** is found around the Dead Sea.

---

610. *CaCCa* segholate-like plural

our/your/their	my/your/his/her	const.	Gloss	sing/pl
דַּרְגָּתֵנוּ/**דַּרְגַּתְ**כֶם/כֶן/**דַּרְגָּתָ**ם/ן	**דַּרְגָּ**תִי/תְךָ/תֵךְ/תוֹ/תָהּ	דַּרְגַּת-	rank,	דַּרְגָּה נ׳
דַּרְגוֹתֵינוּ/כֶם/כֶן/הֶם/הֶן	**דַּרְגוֹ**תַי/תֶיךָ/תַיִךְ/תָיו/תֶיהָ	דַּרְגוֹת-	level	דְּרָגוֹת

The declension is as in שִׂמְלָה above. In a closed syllable, the *kamats* is replaced by *pataH*: דַּרְגַּתְכֶם.

Examples

הדַּרְגָּה הגבוהה ביותר בצה״ל (צבא הגנה לישראל) היא רב-אלוף.
The highest **rank** in the IDF (Israel Defense Forces) is major general.

במכונית, **דַּוְשַׁת** הבלמים חשובה יותר **מדַּוְשַׁת** הדלק – מסיבות בטיחות.
In a car, the brake **pedal** is more important than the gas **pedal** – for safety reasons.

היום כבר לא רואים אנשים לבושים **בפַּרְוָה** כמו פעם – מרבית האנשים מבינים שאין היום הצדקה להריגת בעלי חיים רק כדי להשתמש **בפַּרְוָתָם** ללבוש ראוותני.
Today one does not see people wearing a **fur** as they used to – most people realize that there is no justification today for killing animals merely so as to use their **furs** in ostentatious display of dressing.

בדיני כשרות, בהמה כשרה היא זו שמפרסת **פַּרְסָה**, שוסעת שסע ומעלה גרה.
In Jewish law, a kosher beast is one that has a split **hoof** and chews cud.

Special Expressions

brevet **rank** **דַּרְגַּת** ייצוג U-turn סיבוב **פַּרְסָה**

Additional Examples in this Pattern

phosphate זַרְחָה
carbonate פַּחְמָה
hoof; horseshoe פַּרְסָה
helmet קַסְדָּה

---

611. ***CaCCa*** with segholate-type plural when the 1st root consonant is guttural

sing/pl	Gloss	const.	my/your/his/her	our/your/their
אַשְׁמָה נ׳	guilt, fault	אַשְׁמַת-	**אַשְׁמָ**תִי/תְךָ/תֵךְ/תוֹ/תָהּ	אַשְׁמָתֵנוּ/**אַשְׁמַתְ**כֶם/כֶן/**אַשְׁמָתָ**ם/ן
אֲשָׁמוֹת		אַשְׁמוֹת-	**אַשְׁמוֹ**תַי/תֶיךָ/תַיִךְ/תָיו/תֶיהָ	**אַשְׁמוֹתֵי**נוּ/כֶם/כֶן/הֶם/הֶן

The declension is as in דַּרְגָּה above, except that where a *shva* is expected with a guttural, it is replaced by *Hataf-pataH*. In a closed syllable, the *kamats* is replaced by *pataH*: אַשְׁמַתְכֶם.

Examples

לפעמים אנו נדהמים מטיפשותם, בהמיותם וחוסר אחריותם של מנהיגי האומה, אבל זו לא **אַשְׁמָתָם** – זו **אַשְׁמָתֵנוּ**-שלנו ; בחרנו אותם בתהליך דמוקרטי...
Sometimes we are appalled by the stupidity, vulgarity and irresponsibility of the nation's leaders, but it is not their **fault** – it is our own **fault**; we elected them in a democratic process...

המשטרה מצאה שרידי **אַבְקָה** על בגדיו של החשוד, אבל בדיעבד הסתבר שמדובר לא בקוקאין אלא **באַבְקַת** אפייה...
The police found **powder** residues on the suspect's clothes, but later it turned out that it was not cocaine but baking **powder**...

מאז הפלת מגדלי התאומים בניו יורק, הרבה יותר קשה לקבל **אַשְׁרַת** כניסה לארה״ב.
Since the bombing of the Twin Towers in NYC, it has been harder to get an entry **visa** into the US.

נשמנו לרווחה כשהמרצה נתן לנו **אַרְכָּה** של שבוע להגשת עבודת הסמינר.
We breathed in relief when the lecturer gave us a week's **extension** on before submitting the seminar paper.

חבר טוב מישראל אמר לי שהמראה המרהיב ביותר שראה בביקורו בארה״ב הוא **העַלְוָה** בסתיו בניו-אינגלנד.
A good friend from Israel told him that the most splendid view he saw on his visit to the US was the autumn **foliage** in New England.

Special Expressions

baking **powder** **אַבְקַת** אפייה
detergent, washing **powder** **אַבְקַת** כביסה

אֲסדַּת קידוח off-shore drilling **rig**
אַשְׁרַת מעבר transit **visa**
אַשְׁרַת עבודה work **permit**
אַשְׁמַת שווא false **accusation**
חַשְׁרַת עבים gathering of thick clouds
עַפְרוֹת ברזל iron **ore**

Additional Examples in this Pattern

אַסְדָּה raft
אַסְלָה toilet bowl
חַנְקָה nitrate
עַמְלָה commission
עַפְרָה ore
חַשְׁרָה gathering of thick clouds

---

612. ***CaCCa* = *CaCaCa*** with segholate-type plural when the second root consonant is guttural

our/your/their	my/your/his/her	const.	Gloss	sing/pl
טַחֲנָתֵנוּ/**טַחֲנַתְ**כֶם/כֶן/**טַחֲנָתָ**ם/ן	**טַחֲנָ**תִי/תְךָ/תֵךְ/תוֹ/תָהּ	טַחֲנַת-	mill	טַחֲנָה נ׳
טַחֲנוֹתֵינוּ/כֶם/כֶן/הֶם/הֶן	**טַחֲנוֹ**תַי/תֶיךָ/תַיִךְ/תָיו/תֶיהָ	טַחֲנוֹת-		טְחָנוֹת

The declension is as in דַּרְגָּה above, except that where a *shva* is expected with a guttural, it is replaced by *Hataf-pataH*: טַחֲנָה.

Examples

אזור מקורות הירקון קרוי "שבע **טְחָנוֹת**", מכיוון שבזמנו היו שם אמנם שבע **טַחֲנוֹת** מים.
The region of the Yarkon river origins is called "Seven **Mills**" because at the time, there were indeed seven water **mills** there.

מרבית העבודה החשובה בכל מוסד פרלמנטרי (כמו הכנסת או הקונגרס) נעשית **בוַעֲדוֹת**-מִשְׁנֶה לנושאים ספציפיים.
Most of the important work in any parliamentary institution (such as the Knesset or Congress) is conducted in sub-**committees** for specific issues.

במשך שנים רבות **הלַהֲקוֹת** הצבאיות היו גורמי הבידור הבולטים בארץ.
For many years, the army **troupes** were the most prominent entertainment components in Israel.

היו זמנים שבהם **רַעֲמַת** שיער הייתה סימן היכר של משורר...
There were times when a **mane** of hair was a marker of a poet...

מרבית הדתות מתייחסות **לגַאֲוָה** כחטא.
Most religions regard **pride** as a sin.

סנגורו של הנאשם מקווה שחבר המושבעים יתייחס **באַהֲדָה** לנאשם בשל כל מה שעבר עליו בילדותו.
The defense attorney of the accused is hoping that the jury will treat him with **sympathy** in view of his difficult childhood.

Special Expressions

וַעֲדָה מייעצת advisory **committee**
וַעֲדָה רפואית medical **committee**

טַחֲנַת חשמל electric power **plant**
טַחֲנַת מים water **mill**
טַחֲנַת רוח wind**mill**
נלחם ב**טַחֲנוֹת** רוח fight imaginary enemies
טַחֲנוֹת הצדק טוחנות לאט the **mills** of justice grind slowly
יַחֲסַת הקניין possessive **case**
לַהֲקַת מחול dance **troupe**
שַׁעֲוַת האוזן cerumen (ear**wax**)

Additional Examples in this Pattern

יַחֲסָה case (syntax)
יַעֲרָה honeycomb
לַהֲקָה choir, band, troupe; flock (birds), school (fish)
נַחֲרָה snore N
פַּעֲמָה beat
צַחֲנָה stench
רַחֲצָה bathing
רַעֲיָה wife; consort
רַעֲמָה mane
שַׁעֲוָה wax
שַׁחֲלָה ovary
שַׂעֲרָה hair

---

613. ***CaCCa* = *CaCaCa*** with segholate-type plural when the first and second root consonants are guttural

our/your/their	my/your/his/her	const.	Gloss	sing/pl
אַהֲבָתֵנוּ/**אַהֲבַתְ**כֶם/כֶן/**אַהֲבָתָ**ם/ן	**אַהֲבָ**תִי/תְךָ/תֵךְ/תוֹ/תָהּ	אַהֲבַת-	love	אַהֲבָה נ׳
אַהֲבוֹתֵינוּ/כֶם/כֶן/הֶם/הֶן	**אַהֲבוֹ**תַי/תֶיךָ/תַיִךְ/תָיו/תֶיהָ	אַהֲבוֹת-		אֲהָבוֹת

The declension is as in דַּרְגָּה above, except that where a *shva* is expected with a guttural, it is replaced by *Hataf-pataH*: אַהֲבָה, אֲהָבוֹת.

Examples

במקרים של **אַהֲבָה** עזה, לעתים קורה שעם אכזבה קשה ממנה היא הופכת לשנאה קיצונית.
In cases of intense **love**, it sometimes happens that with frustration and disappointment with it, it turns into extreme hate.

Special Expressions

אַהֲבַת בצע greed
אַהֲבַת הבריות **love** of humanity/mankind
אַהֲבָה חצרונית courtly **love**
אַהֲבָה נכזבת unrequited **love**
אַהֲבַת נפש profound **love**
אַהֲבָה עצמית narcissism
אַהֲבַת שמיים **love** of God, piety
אַהֲבָה התלויה בדבר conditional/dependent **love**

Additional Examples in this Pattern

אַהֲדָה sympathy

---

614. ***CaCCa*** plural regular (not segholate-like)

our/your/their	my/your/his/her	const.	Gloss	sing/pl
שַׁלְוָתֵנוּ/**שַׁלְוַתְ**כֶם/כֶן/**שַׁלְוָתָ**ם/ן	**שַׁלְוָ**תִי/תְךָ/תֵךְ/תוֹ/תָהּ	שַׁלְוַת-	calm,	שַׁלְוָה נ׳
שַׁלְווֹתֵינוּ/כֶם/כֶן/הֶם/הֶן	**שַׁלְווֹ**תַי/תֶיךָ/תַיִךְ/תָיו/תֶיהָ	שַׁלְווֹת-	serenity	שַׁלְווֹת

The plural form is regular – not as in segholate nouns . In a closed syllable, the *kamats* is replaced by *pataH*: שַׁלְוַתְכֶם.

Examples

שַׁלְוָה אמיתית היא לשבת ולקרוא ספר על שפת הים, עם כוסית גדולה של קלבדוס.
True **serenity** is sitting on the beach, reading a book with a large drink of Calvados.

כבישי הָ**אַגְרָה** באירופה ואפילו בישראל מתקדמים יותר מאשר בארה״ב. אין אף פעם צורך לחכות למחסום שייפתח.
Toll roads in Europe and even in Israel are more advanced than in the US. One never needs to wait for a toll gate to open.

כשהיינו ילדים הרבו להאכיל אותנו **בַּדַּיְסָה**. רובנו שנאנו את המרקם והטעם, אבל יש שממשיכים היום לאכלה, בעיקר כשהקיבה רגישה.
When we were kids they fed us **porridge** a lot. Most of us hated the texture and taste, but some continue to eat it today, particularly because it is easy on the stomach.

Special Expressions

אַגְרַת רישוי licensing **fee;** vehicle license **fee**

כביש **אַגְרָה** **toll** road

פַּגְרַת קיץ summer **vacation**

Additional Examples in this Pattern

אַרְבָּה barge

חַמְרָה red loam

עַוְלָה injustice

פַּגְרָה recess, vacation

תַּחְרָה/תַּחֲרָה lace

---

615. ***CaCCa/maCCa*** plural regular (not segholate-like); the last root consonant is *y*

our/your/their	my/your/his/her	const.	Gloss	sing/pl
מַרְאָתֵנוּ/**מַרְאַתְ**כֶם/כֶן/**מַרְאָתָ**ם/ן	**מַרְאָ**תִי/תְךָ/תֵךְ/תוֹ/תָהּ	מַרְאַת-	mirror	מַרְאָה נ׳
מַרְאוֹתֵינוּ/כֶם/כֶן/הֶם/הֶן	**מַרְאוֹ**תַי/תֶיךָ/תַיִךְ/תָיו/תֶיהָ	מַרְאוֹת-		מַרְאוֹת

The plural form is regular – not as in segholate nouns . In a closed syllable, the *kamats* is replaced by *pataH*: מַרְאַתְכֶם.

Examples

מַרְאוֹת רבות בדירה נותנות תחושה של גודל.
Many **mirrors** in an apartment give one a sense of larger size.

Special Expressions

panoramic **mirror** מַרְאָה פנורמית

Additional Examples in this Pattern

firepan; brazier מַחְתָּה

---

616. ***CaCCa/maCCa/taCCa = CaCaCa*** plural regular (not segholate-like); the last root consonant is *y* and the first is guttural

our/your/their	my/your/his/her	const.	Gloss	sing/pl
תַּחֲנָתֵנוּ/**תַּחֲנַתְ**כֶם/כֶן/**תַּחֲנָתָ**ם/ן	**תַּחֲנָ**תִי/תְךָ/תֵךְ/תוֹ/תָהּ	תַּחֲנַת-	stop N,	תַּחֲנָה נ׳
תַּחֲנוֹתֵינוּ/כֶם/כֶן/הֶם/הֶן	**תַּחֲנוֹ**תַי/תֶיךָ/תַיִךְ/תָיו/תֶיהָ	תַּחֲנוֹת-	station	תַּחֲנוֹת

The plural form is regular – not as in segholate nouns. In a closed syllable, the *kamats* is replaced by *pataH*: תַּחֲנַתְכֶם. Where a *shva* is expected with a guttural, it is replaced by *Hataf-pataH*.

Examples

תַּחֲנַת האוטובוסים המרכזית בתל-אביב הייתה אחד המקומות הסואנים בעיר. היום, מסיבות שונות, היא איבדה במקצת מחשיבותה.
The central bus **station** in Tel Aviv was one of the busiest locations in the city. Today, for a variety of reasons, it has lost some of its importance.

מַחֲלַת הסרטן, לסוגיה השונים, היא כה שכיחה היום, שנראה כאילו היא ממש מגפה.
The cancer **illness**, in its different manifestations, is so common today, that it looks like an epidemic.

Special Expressions

intermediate **station/stop** **תַּחֲנַת** ביניים
sight for sore eyes **תַּאֲוָה** לעיניים

Additional Examples in this Pattern

desire תַּאֲוָה   advantage; degree מַעֲלָה

---

617. ***CaCCa = CaCaCa*** plural segholate-like; the last root consonant is *y* and the second is guttural

our/your/their	my/your/his/her	const.	Gloss	sing/pl
רַאֲוָתֵנוּ/**רַאֲוַתְ**כֶם/כֶן/**רַאֲוָתָ**ם/ן	**רַאֲוָ**תִי/תְךָ/תֵךְ/תוֹ/תָהּ	רַאֲוַת-	showcase,	רַאֲוָה נ׳
רַאֲווֹתֵינוּ/כֶם/כֶן/הֶם/הֶן	**רַאֲווֹ**תַי/תֶיךָ/תַיִךְ/תָיו/תֶיהָ	רַאֲווֹת-	display	רְאָווֹת

The declension is identical to that of טַחֲנָה above, when the last root consonant is *y*.

Examples

המעצב הנודע החליט שמעתה יציג ל**רַאֲוָה** גירסאות עממיות יותר של מוצריו בחנויות כולבו שונות כדי שגם המעמד הבינוני יוכל לרכשם.

The famous designer decided that from now on he will put on **display** popular versions of his products in various department stores, so that the middle classes will be able to purchase them as well.

Special Expressions

חלון **רַאֲוָה** **display** window

---

618. ***CaCCa*** plural segholate-like or *-a'ot* and the 2nd root consonant is guttural

our/your/their	my/your/his/her	const.	Gloss	sing/pl
נַחֲלָתֵנוּ/**נַחֲלַתְ**כֶם/כֶן/**נַחֲלָתָ**ם/ן	**נַחֲלָ**תִי/תְךָ/תֵךְ/תוֹ/תָהּ	נַחֲלַת-	estate,	נַחֲלָה נ׳
נַחֲלוֹתֵינוּ/כֶם/כֶן/הֶם/הֶן	**נַחֲלוֹ**תַי/תֶיךָ/תַיִךְ/תָיו/תֶיהָ	נַחֲלוֹת-	inheritance	נְחָלוֹת/נַחֲלָאוֹת

Examples

כשארץ ישראל חולקה בין השבטים, **נַחֲלַת** כל שבט הייתה פחות-או-יותר יחסית לגודלו.

When the land of Israel was divided among the tribes, the **inheritance/estate** of each tribe was more-or-less proportional to its size.

Special Expressions

נַחֲלַת אבות patrimony

נַחֲלַת הכלל common knowledge; common property

---

619. ***CaCCa*** plural regular (not segholate-like), or *–a'ot*

our/your/their	my/your/his/her	const.	Gloss	sing/pl
סַדְנָתֵנוּ/**סַדְנַתְ**כֶם/כֶן/**סַדְנָתָ**ם/ן	**סַדְנָ**תִי/תְךָ/תֵךְ/תוֹ/תָהּ	סַדְנַת-	workshop	סַדְנָה נ׳
סַדְנוֹתֵינוּ/כֶם/כֶן/הֶם/הֶן	**סַדְנוֹ**תַי/תֶיךָ/תַיִךְ/תָיו/תֶיהָ	סַדְנוֹת-		סַדְנוֹת/סַדְנָאוֹת

The plural form is regular, not as in segholate nouns, or with *–a'ot.*

Examples

בדרך כלל לומדים יותר טוב במסגרת **סַדְנָה** מאשר בהרצאה פרונטאלית.

One generally learns better in the framework of a **workshop** than through frontal lectures.

Additional Examples in this Pattern

טַבְלָה table, tabulation

---

620. *CaCaCa*

our/your/their	my/your/his/her	const.	Gloss	sing/pl
בַּקָּשָׁתֵנוּ/**בַּקָּשַׁתְ**כֶם/כֶן/**בַּקָּשָׁתָ**ם/ן	**בַּקָּשָׁ**תִי/תְךָ/תֵךְ/תוֹ/תָהּ	-בַּקָּשַׁת	request,	בַּקָּשָׁה נ׳
בַּקָּשׁוֹתֵינוּ/כֶם/כֶן/הֶם/הֶן	**בַּקָּשׁוֹ**תַי/תֶיךָ/תַיִךְ/תָיו/תֶיהָ	-בַּקָּשׁוֹת	application	בַּקָּשׁוֹת

Throughout, the first consonant is followed by a *pataH*, and the next one takes a *dagesh forte* and is followed by a *kamats*.

Examples

יש לי רק **בַּקָּשָׁה** אחת: אל תדרכו על הדשא.
I have only one **request**: do not step on the grass.

ברוב האוניברסיטאות, טופסי ה**בַּקָּשָׁה** לקבלה הם ארוכים ומורכבים ביותר.
In most universities, the admission **application** forms are very long and complex.

בַּקָּרַת איכות היא יסוד חשוב בכל חברת ייצור.
Quality **control** is an important component in any production company.

המשטרה עדיין אינה יודעת אם ההתפוצצות האחרונה במרכז העיר הייתה תוצאה של תאונה או **חַבָּלָה**.
The police still does not knowwhether the recent explosion in town was the result of an accident or **sabotage**.

אימרה ידועה: הדרך לגהינום רצופה **כַּוָּנוֹת** טובות.
A familiar saying: the way to hell is paved with good **intentions**.

נראה לי ש**כַּתָּבָה** טיפוסית בטלוויזיה הישראלית מעמיקה יותר מ**כַּתָּבוֹת** דומות בארה״ב.
It appears to me that a typical **report** on Israeli TV is more insightful than similar **reports** in the US.

Special Expressions

wasted effort ברכה ל**בַטָּלָה**
please! if you please **בְּבַקָּשָׁה**!
would you **please**... **בְּבַקָּשָׁה** ממך
the **search** for truth **בַּקָּשַׁת** האמת
what is your **wish**? מה **בַּקָּשָׁתְךָ**?
letter of **application** מכתב **בַּקָּשָׁה**
remote **control** **בַּקָּרָה** מרחוק

criminal **intent** (law) **כַּוָּנָה** פלילית
investigative **reporting** **כַּתָּבַת** תחקיר
mortal **danger** **סַכָּנַת** נפשות
acceptance of one's punishment **קַבָּלַת** הדין
decision making **קַבָּלַת** החלטות
public policy **תַּקָּנַת** הציבור

Additional Examples in this Pattern

idleness בַּטָּלָה
atonement כַּפָּרָה
danger סַכָּנָה
inhibition עַכָּבָה

(last) will צַוָּאָה
(written) receipt; acceptance קַבָּלָה
mishap, hitch תַּקָּלָה
regulation תַּקָּנָה

621. ***CaCaCa*** when the second root consonant is *r*

our/your/their	my/your/his/her	const.	Gloss	sing/pl
פָּרָשָׁתֵנוּ/**פָּרָשַׁתְ**כֶם/כֶן/**פָּרָשָׁתָ**ם/ן	**פָּרָשָׁ**תִי/תְךָ/תֵךְ/תוֹ/תָהּ	פָּרָשַׁת-	affair;	פָּרָשָׁה נ׳
פָּרָשׁוֹתֵינוּ/כֶם/כֶן/הֶם/הֶן	**פָּרָשׁוֹ**תַי/תֶיךָ/תַיִךְ/תָיו/תֶיהָ	פָּרָשׁוֹת-	separation	פָּרָשׁוֹת

When the second root consonant is ר׳, there is no *dagesh* and the previous vowel is replaced by a *kamats*.

Examples

כשדיברו בישראל על ה**פָּרָשָׁה** בשנות החמישים, התכוונו ל**פָּרָשַׁת** לבון, ״העסק הביש״ במצרים.
In the 1950's in Israel, when they discussed "the **Affair**," they referred to the Lavon **Affair**, the "unfortunate incident" in Egypt.

Special Expressions

love **affair** **פָּרָשַׁת** אהבים
intersection, junction **פָּרָשַׁת** דרכים
watershed line קו **פָּרָשַׁת** המים

Additional Examples in this Pattern

dry land Bibl. חָרָבָה

---

622. ***CaCaCa = CeCaCa*** when the second root consonant is *he*

our/your/their	my/your/his/her	const.	Gloss	sing/pl
בֶּהָלָתֵנוּ/**בֶּהָלַתְ**כֶם/כֶן/**בֶּהָלָתָ**ם/ן	**בֶּהָלָ**תִי/תְךָ/תֵךְ/תוֹ/תָהּ	בֶּהָלַת-	panic;	בֶּהָלָה נ׳
בֶּהָלוֹתֵינוּ/כֶם/כֶן/הֶם/הֶן	**בֶּהָלוֹ**תַי/תֶיךָ/תַיִךְ/תָיו/תֶיהָ	בַּהֲלוֹת-	rush	בֶּהָלוֹת

When the second root consonant is ה׳, there is no *dagesh* and the previous vowel is replaced by a *seghol*. In the construct plural the *seghol* is replaced by *pataH*.

Examples

במקרים של אסון טבע או פעולת טרור, המשטרה משתדלת למנוע **בֶּהָלָה**, כדי למנוע אסון גדול יותר.
In cases of a natural disaster, or a terror act, the police try to prevent **panic**, on order to prevent an even greater disaster.

Special Expressions

the Gold **Rush** ה**בֶּהָלָה** לזהב

---

623. ***CaCaCa ~ CaCéCet***

our/your/their	my/your/his/her	const.	Gloss	sing/pl
שַׁיַּרְתֵּנוּ/**שַׁיַּרְתְּ**כֶם/כֶן/**שַׁיַּרְתָּ**ם/ן	**שַׁיַּרְ**תִּי/תְּךָ/תֵּךְ/תּוֹ/תָּהּ	שַׁיֶּרֶת-	caravan	שַׁיָּרָה/שַׁיֶּרֶת נ׳
שַׁיְּרוֹתֵינוּ/כֶם/כֶן/הֶם/הֶן	**שַׁיְּרוֹ**תַי/תֶיךָ/תַיִךְ/תָיו/תֶיהָ	שַׁיְּרוֹת-		שַׁיָּרוֹת

The singular construct form is *CaCéCet.*

Examples

במשך מאות רבות של שנים, המסחר במזרח התיכון התבסס על **שַׁיָּרוֹת** גמלים.
For many centuries, trade in the Middle East relied on camel **caravans**.

Additional Examples in this Pattern

dry land; continent יַבָּשָׁה/יַבֶּשֶׁת

---

624. ***CuCCa*** plural regular (not segholate-like)

sing/pl	Gloss	const.	my/your/his/her	our/your/their
חֻלְצָה נ׳	shirt,	חֻלְצַת-	**חֻלְצָ**תִי/תְךָ/תֵךְ/תוֹ/תָהּ	חֻלְצָתֵנוּ/**חֻלְצַתְ**כֶם/כֶן/**חֻלְצָתָ**ם/ן
חֻלְצוֹת	blouse	חֻלְצוֹת-	**חֻלְצוֹ**תַי/תֶיךָ/תַיִךְ/תָיו/תֶיהָ	**חֻלְצוֹתֵי**נוּ/כֶם/כֶן/הֶם/הֶן

The plural form is regular – not as in segholate nouns . In a closed syllable, the *kamats* is replaced by *pataH*: חֻלְצַתְכֶם.

Examples

כשמגיע הקיץ רוב הגברים מעדיפים **חֻלְצוֹת** עם שרוולים קצרים, לעיתים אפילו ללא גופיה מתחתן.
With the arrival of summer, most men prefer **shirts** with short sleeves, sometimes even without undershirts underneath them.

שנים רבות תהו תושבי מנהטן אם יש יותר אנשים או יותר **חֻלְדּוֹת** בעיר. לפני כשנה-שנתיים נשמו כולם לרווחה: עדיין יש יותר בני אדם, אבל לא הרבה יותר...
For many years, the residents of Manhattan were wondering if there are more people or mare **rats** in town. About a year ago all sighed in relief: there are more people, but the margin is not that large...

יש לי **חֻלְשָׁה** ל"מציאות", בעיקר לחפצים ישנים יפים. תוכלו למצוא אותי לעתים קרובות בשוק הפשפשים.
I have a **weakness** for "bargains," particularly for old beautiful items. You can often find me in the flea market.

בישראל נוטים להתייחס למוצרי יבוא כמוצרי **יֻקְרָה**, גם אם איכותם אינה גבוהה.
In Israel they tend to regard imported products as **prestige** products, even when their quality is not high.

Special Expressions

חֻמְצָה אמינית amino **acid**
חֻמְצָה חנקתית nitric **acid**
חֻפְשָׁה ללא תשלום unpaid leave
סֻלְיַת חשיש **sole** of hashish Sl.

עֻבְדָּה קיימת/מוגדרת established **fact**, **fait** accompli
נקודת **תֻּרְפָּה** **weak** point/spot

Additional Examples in this Pattern

division (military) אֻגְדָּה
steak אֻמְצָה

stable N אֻרְוָה
piston בֻּכְנָה

niche, alcove גֻּמְחָה
link; part; vertebra חֻלְיָה
acid N חֻמְצָה
severity, rigidity חֻמְרָה
vacation חֻפְשָׁה
grove, small forest חֻרְשָׁה
pretension יֻמְרָה
beret כֻּמְתָּה
issue, matter סֻגְיָה
sole סֻלְיָה
fact עֻבְדָּה
question, problem קֻשְׁיָה
anger, fury רֻגְזָה
cheek, insolence, impertinence חֻצְפָּה
weakness תֻּרְפָּה

---

625. ***CuCCa*** plural regular suffix *-im*

our/your/their	my/your/his/her	const.	Gloss	sing/pl
כֻּסְפָּתֵנוּ/**כֻּסְפַּתְ**כֶם/כֶן/**כֻּסְפָּתָ**ם/ן	**כֻּסְפָּ**תִי/תְךָ/תֵךְ/תוֹ/תָהּ	כֻּסְפַּת-	pulp,	כֻּסְפָּה נ'
כֻּסְפֵּינוּ/כֶם/כֶן/הֶם/הֶן	**כֻּסְפַּ**י/פֶּיךָ/פַּיִךְ/פָּיו/פֶּיהָ	כֻּסְפֵּי-	oil cake	כֻּסְפִּים

Plural form regular, but with the suffix *-im.*

---

626. ***CuCCa* = *CuCaCa*** plural regular, second root consonant guttural

our/your/their	my/your/his/her	const.	Gloss	sing/pl
זֻהֲמָתֵנוּ/**זֻהֲמַתְ**כֶם/כֶן/**זֻהֲמָתָ**ם/ן	**זֻהֲמָ**תִי/תְךָ/תֵךְ/תוֹ/תָהּ	זֻהֲמַת-	filth,	זֻהֲמָה נ'
זֻהֲמוֹתֵינוּ/כֶם/כֶן/הֶם/הֶן	**זֻהֲמוֹ**תַי/תֶיךָ/תַיִךְ/תָיו/תֶיהָ	זֻהֲמוֹת -	dirt	זֻהֲמוֹת

When a *shva* is expected with a guttural, it is replaced by *Hataf-pataH.*

Examples

זֻהֲמָה אינה בהכרח תוצאה של עוני; יש שכונות עוני השומרות על ניקיון מופתי.
Filth is not necessarily a corollary of poverty. There are poor neighborhoods that maintain exemplary cleanliness.

פוליטיקאים רבים נכשלים לא בגלל טיפשותם אלא בגלל **יֻהֲרָתָם/יָהֳרָתָם**.
Many politicians fail not because of their stupidity but because of their **arrogance**.

---

627. ***CuCCa*** plural regular or *–a'ot*

our/your/their	my/your/his/her	const.	Gloss	sing/pl
דֻּגְמָתֵנוּ/**דֻּגְמַתְ**כֶם/כֶן/**דֻּגְמָתָ**ם/ן	**דֻּגְמָ**תִי/תְךָ/תֵךְ/תוֹ/תָהּ	דֻּגְמַת-	sample;	דֻּגְמָה נ'
דֻּגְמוֹתֵינוּ/כֶם/כֶן/הֶם/הֶן	**דֻּגְמוֹ**תַי/תֶיךָ/תַיִךְ/תָיו/תֶיהָ	דֻּגְמוֹת-	example; model	דֻּגְמ(א)וֹת

The plural form is either דֻּגְמוֹת or דֻּגְמָאוֹת. When the form is דֻּגְמָאוֹת, there is also the option of a related declension: דֻּגְמְאוֹת-, דֻּגְמְאוֹתַי, etc.

Examples

תני לי בבקשה **דֻּגְמָה** מכל אחד מסוגי השוקולד שלכם.
Please give me a **sample** of each of the types of chocolate you carry.

אינדוקציה היא הכללה המתקבלת מהתבוננות בהרבה **דֻּגְמוֹת (דֻּגְמָאוֹת)**.
Induction is a generalization arrived at by observing many examples.

התנהגותו מהווה **דֻּגְמָה** חיובית לבני הנוער.
His behavior constitutes a good **example** for young people.

זו חוצפה שאין **כְּדֻגְמָתָהּ**.
This is impudence that has no parallel (i.e. incomparable).

יש לי בבית **כֻּרְסָה** נפתחת נפלאה של נָטוּצִי; אחרי חמש דקות של מנוחה עליה אני מרגיש כמו אדם חדש.
At home I have an **armchair** that opens Lazy-Boy-style by Natucci. After five minutes of rest on it I feel like a new person.

פרשתי מן האוניברסיטה לפני כשלוש שנים, אבל חדר עבודתי בביתנו עדיין מלא **קֻפְסָאוֹת** של ספרים ממשרדי שם שאין לי מושג איפה לשים אותם.
I retired from the university about three years ago, but my study at home is still filled with **boxes** of books from my office there that I have no idea where to place.

Special Expressions

for **instance** **לְדֻגְמָה**
magic **formula** **נֻסְחַת** קסם
black **box**, flight recorder **קֻפְסָה** שחורה
match**box** **קֻפְסַת** גפרורים

Additional Examples in this Pattern

exaggeration, hyperbole גֻּזְמָה
dumpling, matzo ball כֻּפְתָּה
formula נֻסְחָה

---

628. ***CoCCa*** (w *kamats katan*), plural regular (not segholate-like)

sing/pl	Gloss	const.	my/your/his/her	Our/your/their
חָכְמָה נ׳	wisdom; skill;	חָכְמַת-	**חָכְמָ**תִי/תְךָ/תֵךְ/תוֹ/תָהּ	חָכְמָתֵנוּ/**חָכְמַתְ**כֶם/כֶן/**חָכְמָתָ**ם/ן
חָכְמוֹת	study, science	חָכְמוֹת-	**חָכְמוֹ**תַי/תֶיךָ/תַיִךְ/תָיו/תֶיהָ	**חָכְמוֹתֵי**נוּ/כֶם/כֶן/הֶם/הֶן

Examples

הרבה נכתב על ההבדל שבין **חָכְמָה** לאינטליגנציה.
A lot has been written about the difference between **wisdom** and intelligence.

מה שנקרא היום "לימודי ..." נקרא בעבר "**חָכְמַת** ..."
The term "… Studies" was referred to in the past as "the **Wisdom/Science** of ..."

ברוב ארצות המערב יש היום הרבה בתי ספר גבוהים **לְאָפְנָה**.
In most Western countries there are today higher education schools in **fashion**.

כמעט כל נשיא בארה״ב ניסה לקדם **יָזְמַת** שלום במזה״ת, וכמעט תמיד נכשל.
Almost every US president tried to advance some peace **initiative** in the Middle East, and almost always failed.

המכבים הצליחו לעמוד בפני צבא יוון ואפילו להביסו בקרבות מסוימים בזכות טקטיקות של **לְחִמַת** גרילה.
The Maccabees were able to face the Greek army and even defeat it in some battles owing to guerilla **warfare** tactics.

עָצְמָה כלכלית של מדינה חשובה לא פחות מ**עָצְמָה** צבאית.
The economic **strength** of a country is just as important as its military **strength**.

בארצות מסוימות מאמינים ש**עָרְמָה** היא מידה טובה.
In some countries they believe that **cunning** is a virtue.

Special Expressions

חָכְמָה חיצונית secular studies (lit. external)
חָכְמַת החשבון arithmetic
חָכְמַת חיים wisdom emanation from life experience
חָכְמַת הטבע the natural sciences
חָכְמָה נסתרה (ח״ן) Kabbalah (lit. secret/hidden)

חָכְמַת ישראל Jewish Studies
בקי בכל שבע ה**חָכְמוֹת** erudite
מלחמת **חָרְמָה** **total** war, **all-ou**t war
לָחְמָה בשטח בנוי urban **warfare**
לָחְמָה אלקטרונית electronic **warfare**
תָּכְנָה ציבורית public domain software, freeware

Additional Examples in this Pattern

אָמְנָה fostering (a child)
אָשְׁיָה foundation; prominent person
גָּנְבָה pirated software Sl.
גָּפְרָה sulfate
חָגְלָה partridge
חָזְקָה firmness, strength
חָמְרָה hardware
חָפְזָה haste

חָרְמָה destruction, annihilation
חָרְשָׁה/חֹרְשָׁה/חֳרְשָׁה grove, small forest
לָמְדָה courseware
עָפְרָה lead of a pencil
עָרְלָה foreskin
שָׂבְעָה satiation (of hunger)
תָּכְנָה computer program

---

629. ***CoCCa*** plural segholate

Our/your/their	my/your/his/her	const.	Gloss	sing/pl
שָׁפְכָתֵנוּ/**שָׁפְכַתְ**כֶם/כֶן/**שָׁפְכָתָ**ם/ן	**שָׁפְכָ**תִי/תְךָ/תֵךְ/תוֹ/תָהּ	שָׁפְכַת-	urethra	שָׁפְכָה נ׳
שָׁפְכוֹתֵינוּ/כֶם/כֶן/הֶם/הֶן	**שָׁפְכוֹ**תַי/תֶיךָ/תַיִךְ/תָיו/תֶיהָ	שָׁפְכוֹת-		שְׁפָכוֹת

Examples

תפקיד ה**שָׁפְכָה** הוא להוביל את השתן משלפוחית השתן אל מחוץ לגוף.
The role of the **urethra** is to conduct the urine from the urine bladder out of the body.

---

630. ***CoCCa*** plural segholate, the first root consonant is guttural

Our/your/their	my/your/his/her	const.	Gloss	sing/pl
חָרְבָּתֵנוּ/**חָרְבַּתְ**כֶם/כֶן/**חָרְבָּתָ**ם/ן	**חָרְבָּ**תִי/תְךָ/תֵךְ/תוֹ/תָהּ	חָרְבַּת-/חֳרְבַּת-	ruin,	חָרְבָּה/חֳרְבָּה נ׳
חָרְבוֹתֵינוּ/כֶם/כֶן/הֶם/הֶן	**חָרְבוֹ**תַי/תֶיךָ/תַיִךְ/תָיו/תֶיהָ	חָרְבוֹת-	destruction	חֳרָבוֹת

When a *shva* is expected owing to reduction, and when it comes with a guttural in this pattern, it is replaced by a *Hataf-kamats*.

Examples

לאחר שאחרי 70 לספירה נשארו מירושלים רק **חֳרָבוֹת**, בנו הרומאים על **חָרְבוֹת** העיר את איליה קפיטולינה.
When all was left of Jerusalem after 70 CE were just **ruins**, the Romans built Aeliea Capitolina on top of the city **ruins**.

---

631. ***CoCCa = CoCoCa*** plural segholate, the second root consonant is guttural

Our/your/their	my/your/his/her	const.	Gloss	sing/pl
טָהֳרָתֵנוּ/**טָהֳרַתְ**כֶם/כֶן/**טָהֳרָתָ**ם/ן	**טָהֳרָ**תִי/תְךָ/תֵךְ/תוֹ/תָהּ	טָהֳרַת-	purity,	טָהֳרָה נ׳
טָהֳרוֹתֵינוּ/כֶם/כֶן/הֶם/הֶן	**טָהֳרוֹ**תַי/תֶיךָ/תַיִךְ/תָיו/תֶיהָ	טָהֳרוֹת-	purification	טָהֳרוֹת

When a *shva* is expected with a guttural, in this pattern it is replaced by a *Hataf-kamats*.

Examples

בלשנים העוסקים בתיאור השפה המדוברת ובניתוחה אינם מאמינים בהקפדה על **טָהֳרַת** הלשון.
Linguists describing and analyzing the colloquial language do not believe in insisting on the "**purity**" of the language.

Additional Examples in this Pattern

joy, rejoicing; cry of joy צָהֳלָה

---

632. ***CCaCa*** regular

our/your/their	my/your/his/her	const.	Gloss	sing/pl
דְּרָשָׁתֵנוּ/**דְּרָשַׁתְ**כֶם/כֶן/**דְּרָשָׁתָ**ם/ן	**דְּרָשָׁ**תִי/תְךָ/תֵךְ/תוֹ/תָהּ	דְּרָשַׁת-	sermon;	דְּרָשָׁה נ׳
דְּרָשׁוֹתֵינוּ/כֶם/כֶן/הֶם/הֶן	**דְּרָשׁוֹ**תַי/תֶיךָ/תַיִךְ/תָיו/תֶיהָ	דְּרָשׁוֹת-	homiletic interpretation	דְּרָשׁוֹת

The first *kamats* is maintained throughout.

Examples

הדְּרָשָׁה שנשא הרב בשבת שעברה הייתה כה משעממת, שמחצית משומעיו נמנמו.
The **sermon** the rabbi delivered last Saturday was so boring, that half of his audience napped.

הבניין הזה לא נבנה כראוי, ולדייריו יש **בְּעָיוֹת** תחזוקה בלתי פוסקות.
This building was not built properly, and its tenants have constant maintenance **problems**.

גְּבָבָה היא שארית הקש אחרי איסוף תבואה שנקצרה, או כל מה שנגזם.
Stubble is the straw remaining after reaped wheat has been gathered, or any pruning/shearing.

נבחרת הנוער של תאילנד בכדורגל כבר לא תטייל יותר **בִּמְעָרוֹת**...
The Thai soccer team will no longer visit underground **caves**...

אחרי דיונים ארוכים הגיעו שני הצדדים **לִפְשָׁרָה** שהשביעה את רצון כולם.
After long negotiations the two sides reached a **compromise** that satisfied everybody.

Special Expressions

מְעָרַת המכפלה the **cave (tomb)** of the forefathers
מְעָרַת פריצים **den** of iniquity Lit.
פְּלָדַת אל-חלד stainless **steel**
קש **וּגְבָבָה** nonsense, worthless stuff
רְאָיָה נסיבתית circumstantial **evidence**

Additional Examples in this Pattern

בְּדָיָה lie, fabrication
בְּלָיָה weathering
כְּלָיָה extinction
כְּסָיָה glove
כְּפָפָה glove
כְּרָזָה poster, placard
לְטָאָה lizard
מְחָאָה protest
מְנָיָה stock, share
מְעָרָה cave
סְחָבָה rag
סְכָכָה shed
פְּלָדָה steel
פְּשָׁרָה compromise N
קְטָטָה quarrel
רְאָיָה evidence
רְעָלָה veil
שְׂרָרָה authority

---

633. ***CCaCa* = *CaCaCa*** regular, first root consonant is guttural

sing/pl	Gloss	const.	my/your/his/her	our/your/their
חֲזָרָה נ׳	return; repeat;	חֲזָרַת-	**חֲזָרָ**תִי/תְךָ/תֵךְ/תוֹ/תָהּ	חֲזָרָתֵנוּ/**חֲזָרַתְ**כֶם/כֶן/**חֲזָרָתָ**ם/ן
חֲזָרוֹת	rehearsal	חֲזָרוֹת-	**חֲזָרוֹ**תַי/תֶיךָ/תַיִךְ/תָיו/תֶיהָ	**חֲזָרוֹתֵי**נוּ/כֶם/כֶן/הֶם/הֶן

The first *kamats* is maintained throughout. Where a *shva* is expected with a guttural, it is replaced by a *Hataf-pataH*.

Examples

לעתים קרובות, כאשר הציבור מאוכזב מן הדרך שבה המדינה מנוהלת, עולה מחדש הציפייה **לַחֲזָרָתָם** של מנהיגים חזקים שפרשו מן החיים הפוליטיים.
Often, when the public is disappointed with .the way the country is run, there arises the anticipation for the **return** of strong leaders who withdrew from political life.

לפעמים אפשר להשיג כרטיסים יותר בזול להצגה אם מוכנים לראות את **הַחֲזָרָה** הכללית.
Sometimes one can obtain cheaper tickets for a show if one is willing to see the general **rehearsal**.

גברים רבים מביעים היום **חֲרָטָה** על התנהגותם בעבר כלפי נשים, אבל נראה שזה מאוחר מדיי...
Many men today express **regret** re their past behavior towards women, but it seems that it is too late…

העיר הגדולה נמאסה בסופו של דבר על משה, והוא עבר לגור ב**עֲיָרָה** קטנה בנגב.
Moshe got tired of the big city, and he moved to a **small town** in the Negev.

Special Expressions

אֲמָנָה חברתית social contract
הֲוָיוֹת העולם the world as it **exists** Lit.
חֲבָטַת הגשה serve (tennis, volleyball)
עֲיָרַת פיתוח development **town**

Additional Examples in this Pattern

אֲמָנָה treaty
הֲוָיָה being
הֲזָיָה hallucination
הֲנָאָה pleasure
חֲבָטָה blow, thump
חֲוָיָה experience
חֲמָמָה greenhouse
חֲנָיָה parking
חֲצָיָה crossing
עֲוָיָה grimace N

---

634. ***CCaCa*** **with *Hirik* in the declension**

our/your/their	my/your/his/her	const.	Gloss	sing/pl
נִדְבָתֵנוּ/**נִדְבַתְ**כֶם/כֶן/**נִדְבָתָ**ם/ן	**נִדְבָ**תִי/תְךָ/תֵךְ/תוֹ/תָהּ	נִדְבַת-	donation;	נְדָבָה נ׳
נִדְבוֹתֵינוּ/כֶם/כֶן/הֶם/הֶן	**נִדְבוֹ**תַי/תֶיךָ/תַיִךְ/תָיו/תֶיהָ	נִדְבוֹת-	alms	נְדָבוֹת

Throughout the declension, the first *kamats* is reduced to a *shva quiescent* with stress shift, and the *shva* preceding it is replaced by a *Hirik* (a sequence of two *shva* mobiles not allowed); the second *kamats* turns into *pataH* in a closed syllable. Exception: a *dagesh lene* in the singular form of the construct of בְּרָכָה , בִּרְכַּת- 'the blessing of.'

Examples

הבניין החדש להנדסת חשמל הוא **נִדְבַת** משפחת גולדמן.
The new Electrical Engineering Building is the **donation** of the Goldman family.

בכל הדתות, נתינת **נְדָבָה** לעני היא מצווה.
In all religions, giving **alms** to the poor is a commandment.

דְּמָמָה מוחלטת שררה באולם בזמן ההספד.
Complete **silence** was maintained in the hall during the eulogy.

כפי שכתב ביאליק, עוד לא נברא **נְקָמָה** מתאימה על רציחת ילד קטן.
As Bialik wrote, an appropriate **revenge** for the murder of a small child has not been invented yet.

שְׁמָמָה היא לא רק מושג פיסי ; מדברים גם על **שְׁמָמָה** רוחנית.
Wilderness is no only a physical concept; it can also refer to spiritual **emptiness**.

Special Expressions

blessing recited unnecessarily; wasted effort **בְּרָכָה** לבטלה	beggar מקבץ **נְדָבוֹת**
willing donation **נִדְבַת** יד	vendetta **נִקְמַת** דם
generosity **נִדְבַת** לב	kind person (sometimes used ironically) **נְשָׁמָה** טובה
plentiful rain גשם **נְדָבוֹת**	alive **נְשָׁמָה** באפו

Additional Examples in this Pattern

blessing בְּרָכָה	soul נְשָׁמָה
wail N יְבָבָה	charity צְדָקָה
24-hour period יְמָמָה	scream צְוָחָה
moon Lit. לְבָנָה	curse קְלָלָה
funeral לְוָיָה	ten thousand רְבָבָה

---

635. ***CCaCa*** with *Hirik* in the declension, the first root consonant is guttural

our/your/their	my/your/his/her	const.	Gloss	sing/pl
הִלְכָתֵנוּ/**הִלְכַתְ**כֶם/כֶן/**הִלְכָתָ**ם/ן	**הִלְכָ**תִי/תְךָ/תֵךְ/תוֹ/תָהּ	הִלְכַת-	Jewish	הֲלָכָה נ'
הִלְכוֹתֵינוּ/כֶם/כֶן/הֶם/הֶן	**הִלְכוֹ**תַי/תֶיךָ/תַיִךְ/תָיו/תֶיהָ	הִלְכוֹת-	law	הֲלָכוֹת

Throughout the declension, the first *kamats* is reduced to a *shva quiescent* with stress shift, and the *shva* preceding it is replaced by a *Hirik* (a sequence of two *shva* mobiles not allowed); the second *kamats* turns into *pataH* in a closed syllable. When the first consonant is guttural, if a *shva* is expected it is replaced by *Hataf-pataH.*

Examples

על פי ה**הֲלָכָה**, כל מי שאימו יהודיה הוא יהודי.
According to **Jewish law**, whoever is born to a Jewish mother is Jewish.

Special Expressions

in practice **הֲלָכָה** למעשה
rule or **regulation** that must not be trespassed or questioned **הֲלָכָה** למשה מסיני

---

636. ***CCaCa*** regular or with *Hirik* in the declension

our/your/their	my/your/his/her	const.	Gloss	sing/pl
פִּצְצָתֵנוּ/**פִּצְצַתְ**כֶם/כֶן/**פִּצְצָתָ**ם/ן	**פִּצְצָ**תִי/תְךָ/תֵךְ/תוֹ/תָהּ	פְּצָצַת- /פִּצְצַת-	bomb	פְּצָצָה נ'
פִּצְצוֹתֵינוּ/כֶם/כֶן/הֶם/הֶן	**פִּצְצוֹ**תַי/תֶיךָ/תַיִךְ/תָיו/תֶיהָ	פְּצָצוֹת- /פִּצְצוֹת-		פְּצָצוֹת

As in נְדָבָה above, since no two *shva* mobiles sequences are allowed, but still, options without a *Hirik,* ...פְּצָצָתִי, ...פְּצָצוֹתַי, co-exist as well.

Examples

מן ה**פְּצָצוֹת** הקונבנציונאליות, **פְּצָצַת** תבערה היא אחת הגרועות ביותר.
Of the conventional **bombs**, the napalm **bomb** is one of the worst.

Special Expressions

פְּצָצָה גרעינית nuclear **bomb** **פְּצָצָה** מתקתקת ticking **bomb**

---

637. ***CCaCa*** with *Hirik* in the declension plural *-im*

sing/pl	Gloss	const.	my/your/his/her	our/your/their
נְמָלָה נ׳	ant	נְמַלַת-	**נְמָלָ**תִי/תְךָ/תֵךְ/תוֹ/תָהּ	נְמָלָתֵנוּ/**נְמַלַתְ**כֶם/כֶן/**נְמְלָתָ**ם/ן
נְמָלִים		נְמָלֵי-	**נְמָלַ**י/לֶיךָ/לַיִךְ/לָיו/לֶיהָ	**נְמָלֵי**נוּ/כֶם/כֶן/הֶם/הֶן

As in נְדָבָה above, the first *kamats* is reduced to *shva*, the preceding one is replaced by *Hirik*, and the second *kamats* is replaced by *pataH* in a closed syllable.

Examples

חברת ה**נְמָלִים** היא מן החברות המאורגנות והמפותחות ביותר בטבע.
Ant society is one of the best organized and best developed societies in nature.

Special Expressions

עבודת **נְמָלִים** slow, tedious job **נְמָלָה** לבנה termite

---

638. *CCaCa* with *pataH* in the declension

sing/pl	Gloss	const.	my/your/his/her	our/your/their
זְוָעָה נ׳	horror	זַוְעַת-	**זַוְעָ**תִי/תְךָ/תֵךְ/תוֹ/תָהּ	זַוְעָתֵנוּ/**זַוְעַתְ**כֶם/כֶן/**זַוְעָתָ**ם/ן
זְוָעוֹת		זַוְעוֹת-	**זְוָעוֹ**תַי/תֶיךָ/תַיִךְ/תָיו/תֶיהָ	**זְוָעוֹתֵי**נוּ/כֶם/כֶן/הֶם/הֶן

Except for the declension of the plural with possessive suffixes, the first *kamats* is reduced to a *shva quiescent* with stress shift, and the *shva* preceding it is replaced by a *pataH*; the second *kamats* turns into *pataH* in a closed syllable.

Examples

המשטרה הזדעזעה לראות את ה**זְוָעָה** במקלט לחיות מחמד שבעליהם נטשום.
The police were shocked to see the **horror** in a shelter for pets abandoned by their owners.

מעניין שדווקא קלינטון הליברלי צמצם את שירותי ה**רְוָחָה**.
Interestingly, it was the liberal Clinton who reduced **welfare** benefits.

---

639. ***CCaCa* = *CaCaCa*** with *pataH* in the declension, when the first root consonant is guttural

our/your/their	my/your/his/her	const.	Gloss	sing/pl
אַדְמָתֵנוּ/**אַדְמַתְ**כֶם/כֶן/**אַדְמָתָ**ם/ן	**אַדְמָ**תִי/תְךָ/תֵךְ/תוֹ/תָהּ	אַדְמַת-	earth,	אֲדָמָה נ׳
אַדְמוֹתֵינוּ/כֶם/כֶן/הֶם/הֶן	**אַדְמוֹ**תַי/תֶיךָ/תַיִךְ/תָיו/תֶיהָ	אַדְמוֹת-	soil; land	אֲדָמוֹת

In the isolation forms, when the first root consonant is guttural, the *shva* is replaced by *Hataf-pataH*. The first *kamats* is reduced to a *shva quiescent* with stress shift, and the *shva* preceding it is replaced by a *pataH*; the second *kamats* turns into *pataH* in a closed syllable.

Examples

הָאֲדָמָה הטובה ביותר בישראל היא זו של עמק יזרעאל.
The best **soil** in Israel is that of the Valley of Jezreel.

מרבית הפלסטינאים אינם מוכנים לוותר על אף שעל **אֲדָמָה** שהייתה בידם לפני 1967.
Most Palestinians are not willing to give up an inch of the **land** they held before 1967.

יש שפות, כמו יפנית, שלדובריהן קשה להגות צרורות עיצורים בתוך **הַהֲבָרָה**.
There are languages, such as Japanese, whose speakers find it hard to pronounce consonant clusters within a **syllable**.

הַחֲדָשׁוֹת מגבול רצועת עזה אינן טובות. נראה שהחמאס מנסה לגרור את ישראל למלחמה.
The **news** from the Gaza Strip border is not good. It seems that Hamas is trying to provoke Israel into a war.

עֲנָוָה אינה מתכונותיו הבולטות של נשיאנו הנוכחי.
Modesty is not one of the prominent qualities of our current president.

Special Expressions

אַדְמַת בּוּר fallow soil
אַדְמַת טרשים stony soil
אַדְמַת הקודש the Holy Land
אַדְמַת נכר foreign land
אַדְמַת שְׁלחין irrigated soil
אגוז **אֲדָמָה** peanut
עבודת **אֲדָמָה** farming
עובד **אֲדָמָה** farmer

פרי **הָאֲדָמָה** farm products
תפוח **אֲדָמָה** potato
אַנְחַת רווחה sigh of relief
הֲבָרָה מוטעמת stressed syllable
חֲדָשׁוֹת לבקרים every other day, frequently
עַדְשׁוֹת מגע contact lenses

Additional Examples in this Pattern

אֲנָחָה sigh
עֲדָשָׁה lens
עֲמָלָה commission

עֲנָנָה gloom; cloud Lit.
עֲרָבָה wilderness, steppe, plain

640. ***CCaCa*** with *pataH* in the declension, the second root consonant is guttural

our/your/their	my/your/his/her	const.	Gloss	sing/pl
קַעֲרָתֵנוּ/**קַעֲרַתְ**כֶם/כֶן/**קַעֲרָתָ**ם/ן	**קַעֲרָ**תִי/תְךָ/תֵךְ/תוֹ/תָהּ	קַעֲרַת-	bowl,	קְעָרָה נ׳
קַעֲרוֹתֵינוּ/כֶם/כֶן/הֶם/הֶן	**קַעֲרוֹ**תַי/תֶיךָ/תַיִךְ/תָיו/תֶיהָ	קַעֲרוֹת-	basin	קְעָרוֹת

Throughout the declension, the first *kamats* is reduced to a *Hataf-pataH* with stress shift, and the *shva* preceding it is replaced by a *pataH*; the second *kamats* turns into *pataH* in a closed syllable.

Examples

אוליבר הרים את **קַעֲרַת** האוכל שלו וביקש תוספת.
Oliver lifted his food **bowl** and asked for more.

אומרים ש״מרבה נכסים מרבה **דְּאָגָה**״, אבל רוב בני האדם היו מעדיפים שיהיו להם **דְּאָגוֹת** כאלה...
They say that "he who has lots of property has much **worry**," but most people would prefer to have such **worries**....

רחל (מתוך ״עקרה״): ״אורי אקרא לו, אורי שלי! רך וצלול הוא השם הקצר. רסיס **נְהָרָה**.״
The poet Rachel (from "Childless"): "I will name him Uri, my Uri! Soft and clear is this short name. A splinter of **brightness**."

ב**סְעָרָה** קטרינה ב-2005 נהרגו יותר מ-1800 איש.
More than 1,800 people died in the **storm** Katrina of 2005.

הרבה אירועים היסטוריים חשובים קרו ב**רְחָבוֹת** מרכזיות של ערים גדולות ברחבי העולם.
Many important historical events took place in central **squares** of large cities throughout the world.

שַׁאֲגַת האריה נשמעת למרחקים ארוכים ומפחידה את מרבית החיות האחרות.
The lion's **roar** sounds across large distances and scares most other animals.

Special Expressions

battle cry **זַעֲקַת** קרב
change the whole situation drastically הפך את ה**קְעָרָה** על פיה
storm in a teacup **סְעָרָה** בכוס מים

flared tempers **סַעֲרַת** רוחות
parking area **רַחֲבַת** חנייה
fear and trepidation Lit. חיל **וּרְעָדָה**

Additional Examples in this Pattern

reprimand, scolding גְּעָרָה
worry דְּאָגָה
gallop N דְּהָרָה
shout, yell N זְעָקָה
growl(ing), roar(ing) N נְהָמָה
bray N נְעָרָה

march N צְעָדָה
cry, shout N צְעָקָה
shivering רְעָדָה
galloping, hoof beats שְׁעָטָה
alternant of *se`ara* 'storm, gale' שְׂעָרָה נ

---

641. ***CCaCa* = *CaCaCa*** with *seghol* in the declension, when the first root consonant is guttural

our/your/their	my/your/his/her	const.	Gloss	sing/pl
עֶגְלָתֵנוּ/**עֶגְלַתְ**כֶם/כֶן/**עֶגְלָתָ**ם/ן	**עֶגְלָתִ**י/תְךָ/תֵךְ/תוֹ/תָהּ	עֶגְלַת-	cart, wagon	עֲגָלָה נ׳
עֶגְלוֹתֵינוּ/כֶם/כֶן/הֶם/הֶן	**עֶגְלוֹ**תַי/תֶיךָ/תַיִךְ/תָיו/תֶיהָ	עֶגְלוֹת-		עֲגָלוֹת

Throughout the declension, the first *kamats* is reduced to a *shva quiescent* with stress shift, and the *shva* preceding it is replaced by a *seghol*; the second *kamats* turns into *pataH* in a closed syllable.

Examples

כשהייתי ילד בישראל, היו מוכרים בלוקים של קרח ונפט ברחוב, מ**עֲגָלָה** עם סוס.
When I was a kid in Israel, they would sell ice blocks and kerosene in the street, from a horse-drawn **cart**.

רוב הבדואים גרים במבנים ארעיים או באוהלים, אבל הם מרגישים שיש להם **חֲזָקָה** על מקום מושבם, גם אם אין להם תעודות בעלות עליו.
Most Bedouins live in temporary structures, or in tents, but they still feel that they have **right of possession** where they are, even if they do not have formal title to it.

לילדים יש התקפות **חֲרָדָה** לא פחות קשות מאשר מבוגרים.
Children have **anxiety** attacks just as much as adults do.

Special Expressions

חֲזָקָה עליו ש... one can be confident that he…
חֲזָקָה היא (בידינו) ש... it is accepted among us that…
חֶרְדַּת אלוהים panic, terror
עֶזְרַת נשים ladies' **section** in an orthodox Jewish synagogue

העֲגָלָה הגדולה Ursa Major
העֲגָלָה הקטנה Ursa Minor
עֶגְלַת חורף sleigh
עֶגְלַת יד hand **cart**
עֶגְלַת ילדים stroller, pram
עֶגְלַת תה tea **cart**

Additional Examples in this Pattern

עֲזָרָה separate section (e.g. women's in synagogue)

---

642. ***CCaCa* = *CaCaCa*** with construct state singular feminine segholate, when the 1st root consonant guttural

our/your/their	my/your/his/her	const.	Gloss	sing/pl
עֲטַרְתֵּנוּ/תְּכֶם/תְּכֶן/תָּם/תָּן	**עֲטַרְ**תִּי/תְּךָ/תֵּךְ/תּוֹ/תָּהּ	עֲטֶרֶת-	crown; garland; corona	עֲטָרָה נ׳
עַטְרוֹתֵינוּ/כֶם/כֶן/הֶם/הֶן	**עַטְרוֹ**תַי/תֶיךָ/תַיִךְ/תָיו/תֶיהָ	עַטְרוֹת-		עֲטָרוֹת

The singular feminine construct state form follows the segholate pattern, and consequently the other forms also take the characteristic form of the segholate base: ...עֲטַרְתִּי..., עַטְרוֹתַי etc.

Examples

ביוון וברומא העתיקות, נהגו להניח על ראש המנצח בתחרות ספורט **עֲטָרָה** של דפנה.
In ancient Greece and Rome they used to place a **garland** of laurel on the head of the winner in sports competitions.

שרה הייתה **עֲקָרָה** עד גיל תשעים...
Sarah was **barren** until the age of ninety...

Special Expressions

החזיר **עֲטָרָה** ליושנה restore to its former glory

נטל **עֲטָרָה** לעצמו give oneself airs

עֲטָרָה שאינה הולמתו an honor that ill becomes him

נפלה **עֲטֶרֶת** ראשנו said upon loss of a great person

Additional Examples in this Pattern

עֲלָטָה darkness, gloom Lit.

---

643. ***tCaCa***

our/your/their	my/your/his/her	const.	Gloss	sing/pl
תְּלָאָתֵנוּ/**תְּלָאַתְ**כֶם/כֶן/**תְּלָאָתָ**ם/ן	**תְּלָאָ**תִי/תְךָ/תֵךְ/תוֹ/תָהּ	תְּלָאַת-	suffering, hardship	תְּלָאָה נ'
תְּלָאוֹתֵינוּ/כֶם/כֶן/הֶם/הֶן	**תְּלָאוֹ**תַי/תֶיךָ/תַיִךְ/תָיו/תֶיהָ	תְּלָאוֹת-		תְּלָאוֹת

The declension is the same as *CCaCa* – see *drasha* above.

Examples

הרבה **תְּלָאוֹת** עברו על העולים בדרכם הארוכה והקשה לארץ ישראל.
The immigrants to Palestine endured many **hardships** on their long, arduous way.

---

644. ***CCaCa* = *CeCaCa*** with *seghol* > *pataH*, construct state singular feminine segholate

our/your/their	my/your/his/her	const.	Gloss	sing/pl
לַהַבְתֵּנוּ/תְּכֶם/תְּכֶן/תָּם/תָּן	**לַהַבְ**תִּי/תְּךָ/תֵּךְ/תוֹ/תָּהּ	לַהֶבֶת-	flame	לֶהָבָה נ'
לֶהָבוֹתֵינוּ/כֶם/כֶן/הֶם/הֶן	**לֶהָבוֹ**תַי/תֶיךָ/תַיִךְ/תָיו/תֶיהָ	לַהֲבוֹת-		לֶהָבוֹת

The singular feminine construct state form follows the segholate pattern, and consequently the other singular forms also take the characteristic form of the segholate base: ...לַהַבְתִּי etc.

Examples

בחתונה מפוארת שנכחתי בה בישראל הקיפו את האורחים ב**לֶהָבוֹת**-אש ובמזרקות מים לצידן. כביכול סגנון רומי?

In a fancy wedding I attended in Israel, they surrounded the guests with **flames** and water-fountains alongside them – supposedly Roman style?

Special Expressions

go up in **flames** עלה ב**לֶהָבוֹת**

highly inspiring (speech, speaker) חוצב **לֶהָבוֹת**

---

645. ***CCaCa* = *CeCaCa*** with *seghol* throughout

our/your/their	my/your/his/her	const.	Gloss	sing/pl
נֶחָמָתֵנוּ/**נֶחָמַתְ**כֶם/כֶן/**נֶחָמָ**תָם/תָן	**נֶחָמָ**תִי/תְךָ/תֵךְ/תוֹ/תָהּ	נֶחָמַת-	consolation	נֶחָמָה נ׳
נֶחָמוֹתֵינוּ/כֶם/כֶן/הֶם/הֶן	**נֶחָמוֹ**תַי/תֶיךָ/תַיִךְ/תָיו/תֶיהָ	נֶחָמוֹת-		נֶחָמוֹת

Examples

עליזה אינה מרוצה מכך שבנה "יצא מן הארון"; **נֶחָמָתָהּ** היחידה היא שהוא רופא מצליח.

Aliza is not happy with her son "coming out of the closet;" her only **consolation** is that he is a successful physician.

Special Expressions

cold **comfort**, limited **consolation** **נֶחָמָה** פורתא

---

646. ***C(e)CiCa*** with *Hirik* followed by *dagesh*

our/your/their	my/your/his/her	const.	Gloss	sing/pl
קְהִלָּתֵנוּ/**קְהִלַּתְ**כֶם/כֶן/**קְהִלָּתָ**ם/ן	**קְהִלָּ**תִי/תְךָ/תֵךְ/תוֹ/תָהּ	קְהִלַּת-	community	קְהִלָּה נ׳
קְהִלּוֹתֵינוּ/כֶם/כֶן/הֶם/הֶן	**קְהִלּוֹ**תַי/תֶיךָ/תַיִךְ/תָיו/תֶיהָ	קְהִלּוֹת-		קְהִלּוֹת

Examples

עד עתה, ה**קְהִלָּה** הלהט"בית בישראל הצליחה להגיע להישגים ניכרים. היום הם מקווים שיצליחו לבטל את חוק הפונדקאות.

The LGTB **community** in Israel has already achieved a great deal. Today they are trying to abolish the Surrogacy Law.

רוב האפרוחים כבר יצאו מביצתם, אבל אחד עדיין לא הצליח לבקוע את **קְלִפַּת** הביצה.

Most chicks are out of the eggs by now, but one has not managed to break the egg **shell** yet.

Special Expressions

Jewish **community** Lit. **קְהִלָּה** קדושה (literally: holy **community**)

shame on you! בושה ו**כְלִמָּה**!

cancellation of debts **שְׁמִטַּת** חובות

Additional Examples in this Pattern

shame כְּלִמָּה
Shmita (Jewish law): 7th year land fallow and debts canceled שְׁמִטָּה

---

647. ***CCiCa*** w/*Hirik* + *dagesh* when the first root consonant is guttural

our/your/their	my/your/his/her	const.	Gloss	sing/pl
אֲמִתָּתֵנוּ/**אֲמִתַּתְ**כֶם/כֶן/**אֲמִתָּתָ**ם/ן	**אֲמִתָּ**תִי/תְךָ/תֵךְ/תוֹ/תָהּ	אֲמִתַּת-	truth;	אֲמִתָּה נ'
אֲמִתּוֹתֵינוּ/כֶם/כֶן/הֶם/הֶן	**אֲמִתּוֹ**תַי/תֶיךָ/תַיִךְ/תָיו/תֶיהָ	אֲמִתּוֹת-	axiom	אֲמִתּוֹת

When the first root consonant is guttural, the *shva* is replaced by *Hataf-PataH*.

Examples

אֲמִתָּה בהנדסה : בין שתי נקודות יכול לעבור רק קו ישר אחד.
An **axiom** in geometry: only one straight line can pass through two dots.

Special Expressions

the naked truth, the absolute truth האמת **לַאֲמִתָּה**

---

648. ***neCiCa*** when the second and third root consonants are identical

our/your/their	my/your/his/her	const.	Gloss	sing/pl
נְסִבָּתֵנוּ/**נְסִבַּתְ**כֶם/כֶן/**נְסִבָּתָ**ם/ן	**נְסִבָּ**תִי/תְךָ/תֵךְ/תוֹ/תָהּ	נְסִבַּת-	circumstance	נְסִבָּה נ'
נְסִבּוֹתֵינוּ/כֶם/כֶן/הֶם/הֶן	**נְסִבּוֹ**תַי/תֶיךָ/תַיִךְ/תָיו/תֶיהָ	נְסִבּוֹת-		נְסִבּוֹת

The *n-* is prefixal, and the two identical root consonants of ס-ב-ב are merged into one, hence the *dagesh*.

Examples

בִּנְסִבּוֹת אחרות הייתי שמח להכיר אותו מקרוב, אבל דעותיו הפוליטיות מעבירות אותי על דעתי.
In different **circumstances** I would have been happy to be better acquainted with him, but his political opinions drive me nuts.

Special Expressions

extenuating **circumstances** **נְסִבּוֹת** מקילות

---

649. ***CCeCa***

our/your/their	my/your/his/her	const.	Gloss	sing/pl
בְּרֵכָתֵנוּ/**בְּרֵכַתְ**כֶם/כֶן/**בְּרֵכָתָ**ם/ן	**בְּרֵכָ**תִי/תְךָ/תֵךְ/תוֹ/תָהּ	בְּרֵכַת-	pool,	בְּרֵכָה נ'
בְּרֵכוֹתֵינוּ/כֶם/כֶן/הֶם/הֶן	**בְּרֵכוֹ**תַי/תֶיךָ/תַיִךְ/תָיו/תֶיהָ	בְּרֵכוֹת-	pond	בְּרֵכוֹת

The *tsere* is maintained throughout.

Examples

בבתים רבים בפלורידה יש **בְּרֵכַת** שחייה בחצר.
Many houses in Florida have a swimming **pool** in the yard.

שיר היתולי ישראלי: "אין **בְּרֵרָה**, אין **בְּרֵרָה**, צריך למות באופרה".
A comic Israeli song: "There is no **choice**, one needs to die in an opera."

בזמנו, מקובל היה שמלחינים שואלים זה מזה נעימות ומנגינות. היום זה נחשב ל**גְנֵבָה**.
At the time, it was acceptable for composers to borrow tunes and melodies from each other; today it is considered **piracy/theft**.

בעולם החי, הזכר בדרך כלל נאה מן ה**נְקֵבָה** – כדי למשוך את תשומת ליבה.
In the natural world, the male is generally more handsome than the **female** – in order to attract her attention.

במדע צריך לדעת איך לשאול את ה**שְׁאֵלוֹת** הנכונות.
In science one needs to know how to ask the right **questions**.

Special Expressions

בְּרֵכַת דגים fish **pond**
בְּרֵרַת מחדל default **choice**
בְּרֵרָה טבעית natural **selection**
גְּזֵרָה היא מלפניו irrevocable **decree**
גְּנֵבָה ספרותית **plagiarism**
גְּנֵבַת דעת deceit

Additional Examples in this Pattern

בְּעֵרָה conflagration
גְּזֵלָה theft; stolen object
גְּזֵרָה decree
דְּלֵקָה fire
טְרֵפָה food ritually unfit for eating
מְגֵרָה drawer
פְּרֵדָה departure
קְדֵרָה casserole, cauldron
שְׂדֵרָה avenue
שְׁפֵלָה plain
שְׂרֵפָה fire

---

650. ***CCeCa = CaCeCa*** when the first root consonant is guttural

our/your/their	my/your/his/her	const.	Gloss	sing/pl
אֲבֵדָתֵנוּ/**אֲבֵדַתְ**כֶם/כֶן/**אֲבֵדָתָ**ם/ן	**אֲבֵדָ**תִי/תְךָ/תֵךְ/תוֹ/תָהּ	אֲבֵדַת-	loss	אֲבֵדָה נ׳
אֲבֵדוֹתֵינוּ/כֶם/כֶן/הֶם/הֶן	**אֲבֵדוֹ**תַי/תֶיךָ/תַיִךְ/תָיו/תֶיהָ	אֲבֵדוֹת-		אֲבֵדוֹת

When the first root consonant is guttural, the accompanying *shva* is replaced by *Hataf-pataH*.

Examples

אֲסֵפָה מְכוֹנֶנֶת היא גוף נבחר אשר מטרתו העיקרית היא לנסח טיוטה, או אף לאמץ, חוקה למדינה בהתהוותה.
A constituent **assembly** is an elected body whose primary mandate is to formulate a draft, or even adopt, a constitution for a founded state.

אחרי שישבנו כל הלילה **בַּאֲפֵלָה**, תוקנה בסופו של דבר התקלה וזרימת החשמל התחדשה.
After we had been sitting all night in **darkness**, the malfunction was fixed and the electric current resumed.

מדי פעם חלה **הֲפֵכָה** שאינה מלווה בשפיכות דמים.
Occasionally there occurs a **coup d'état** that is not accompanied by bloodshed.

במדינות רבות מחמירים בעונשו של מי שעבר שלוש **עֲבֵרוֹת**.
In many states they increase the punishment of those who committed three **violations**.

Special Expressions

valley of **death** Lit. גיא **הַהֲרֵגָה** constituent **assembly** **אֲסֵפָה** מְכוֹנֶנֶת

Additional Examples in this Pattern

heap עֲרֵמָה (the) binding (of Isaac) עֲקֵדָה mass killing הֲרֵגָה

---

651. ***CeCeCa***, pl. suffix *-im/-ot*

our/your/their	my/your/his/her	const.	Gloss	sing/pl
תְּאֵנָתֵנוּ/**תְּאֵנַתְ**כֶם/כֶן/**תְּאֵנָתָ**ם/ן	**תְּאֵנָ**תִי/תְךָ/תֵךְ/תוֹ/תָהּ	תְּאֵנַת-	fig	תְּאֵנָה נ'
תְּאֵנֵינוּ/כֶם/כֶן/הֶם/הֶן	**תְּאֵנַ**י/נֶיךָ/נַיִךְ/נָיו/נֶיהָ	תְּאֵנֵי-		תְּאֵנִים

The plural suffix is *+im*, especially for the fruit; תְּאֵנוֹת is used especially for the tree. The *shva* is articulated as *e* here because of a cluster with א'.

Examples

עץ ה**תְּאֵנָה** הוא ממשפחת עצי הפיקוס.
The **fig** tree belongs to the ficus plant family.

---

652. ***CCeCa*** with *Hirik* in the declension

our/your/their	my/your/his/her	const.	Gloss	sing/pl
נִבְלָתֵנוּ/**נִבְלַתְ**כֶם/כֶן/**נִבְלָתָ**ם/ן	**נִבְלָ**תִי/תְךָ/תֵךְ/תוֹ/תָהּ	נִבְלַת-	carcass;	נְבֵלָה נ'
נִבְלוֹתֵינוּ/כֶם/כֶן/הֶם/הֶן	**נִבְלוֹ**תַי/תֶיךָ/תַיִךְ/תָיו/תֶיהָ	נִבְלוֹת-	corpse; "bastard"	נְבֵלוֹת

With the shift in stress, the *tsere* is reduced to a zero *shva*, and the preceding *shva* is replaced by a *Hirik*.

Examples

נִבְלַת הפרה שנפגעה במחלת "הפרה המשוגעת" נשרפה כליל.
The **carcass** of the cow that was affected by the "Mad Cow" disease was totally burned.

הנֵבֵלָה הזה אביגדור הוציא את כספי הפנסיה של כולנו וברח לדרום-אמריקה.
This **bastard** Avigdor withdrew the pension funds of us all and fled to South America (Note: when the colloquial use 'bastard' is intended for a male, masc. gender is allowed)

Special Expressions

נְבֵלָה סרוחה a disgusting person

זה **נְבֵלָה** וזה טרפה they are equally bad

פשוט **נְבֵלָה** בשוק ואל תצטרך לבריות work hard and don't be dependent on anybody

Additional Examples in this Pattern

כְּתֵפָה shoulder strap Lit.

---

653. *CCeCa* with *Hirik* in the declension, pl *-im*

our/your/their	my/your/his/her	const.	Gloss	sing/pl
לִבְנָתֵנוּ/**לִבְנַתְ**כֶם/כֶן/**לִבְנָתָ**ם/ן	**לִבְנָ**תִי/תְךָ/תֵךְ/תוֹ/תָהּ	-לִבְנַת	brick,	לְבֵנָה נ׳
לִבְנֵינוּ/כֶם/כֶן/הֶם/הֶן	**לְבֵנַ**י/נֶיךָ/נַיִךְ/נָיו/נֶיהָ	-לִבְנֵי	block	לְבֵנִים

The declension is like *nevela* above, but the plural suffix is *-im.*

Examples

בערים קטנות ובכפרים בארה״ב בונים בד״כ בתי עץ; אמידים יותר בונים בית **לְבֵנִים**.
In small towns and villages in the US they usually build wood houses; well-off folks build **brick** ones.

Special Expressions

לִבְנַת חבלה demolition **block**

---

654. *CCeCa = CaCeCa* with *seghol* in the declension, no plural, when the first root consonant is guttural

our/your/their	my/your/his/her	const.	Gloss	sing/pl
חֶשְׁכָתֵנוּ/**חֶשְׁכַתְ**כֶם/כֶן/**חֶשְׁכָתָ**ם/ן	**חֶשְׁכָ**תִי/תְךָ/תֵךְ/תוֹ/תָהּ	-חֶשְׁכַת	darkness	חֲשֵׁכָה נ׳

With the shift in stress, the *tsere* is reduced to a zero *shva*, and the preceding *shva* is replaced by a *seghol*. In the isolation form, the *shva* is replaced by *Hataf-pataH* owing to the guttural.

Examples

העיירה שלנו אינה מוארת כראוי בלילה, ומאוד לא נעים להסתובב בה בלילה ב**חֲשֵׁכָה**.
Our little town is not properly lit at night, and it is very unpleasant to walk around in it at night in **darkness**.

---

655. ***CCeCa*** with *seghol* in the declension, second root consonant guttural

our/your/their	my/your/his/her	const.	Gloss	sing/pl
בְּהֶמְתֵּנוּ/תְכֶם/תְכֶן/תָּם/תָּן	**בְּהֶמְ**תִּי/תְּךָ/תֵּךְ/תּוֹ/תָּהּ	בֶּהֱמַת-	beast	בְּהֵמָה נ׳
בַּהֲמוֹתֵינוּ/כֶם/כֶן/הֶם/הֶן	**בַּהֲמוֹ**תַי/תֶיךָ/תַיִךְ/תָיו/תֶיהָ	בַּהֲמוֹת-		בְּהֵמוֹת

With the shift in stress, the *kamats* in the singular declension is elided into a zero *shva*, and in the closed syllable that is formed the *tsere* is replaced by *seghol*: בְּהֶמְתִּי. In the plural declension the *tsere* is reduced to *Hataf-pataH* owing to the guttural, and the preceding *shva* copies it by becoming a *pataH* (easier to pronounce): בַּהֲמוֹתַי. A similar process occurs in the singular construct form, except that here the *tsere* is reduced to *Hataf-seghol*, and the preceding *shva* consequently copies it with a *seghol*: -בֶּהֱמַת.

Examples

מי יודע נפש האדם העולה היא למעלה ונפש ה**בְּהֵמָה** היורדת היא למטה (קֹהֶלֶת).
Who knows whether the spirit of man goes upward, and the spirit of the **beast** goes downward? (Ecclesiastes).

Special Expressions

sheep and goats **בְּהֵמָה** דקה cattle; vulgar person Coll. **בְּהֵמָה** גסה

---

656. ***CCeCa*** with *pataH* in the declension

our/your/their	my/your/his/her	const.	Gloss	sing/pl
שַׂדְמָתֵנוּ/**שַׂדְמַתְ**כֶם/כֶן/ **שַׂדְמָתָ**ם/ן	**שַׂדְמָ**תִי/תְךָ/תֵךְ/תוֹ/תָהּ	שַׂדְמַת-	field, cultivated land Lit.	שְׂדֵמָה נ׳
שַׂדְמוֹתֵינוּ/כֶם/כֶן/הֶם/הֶן	**שַׂדְמוֹ**תַי/תֶיךָ/תַיִךְ/תָיו/תֶיהָ	שַׂדְמוֹת-		שְׂדֵמוֹת

With the shift in stress, the *tsere* is reduced to a zero *shva*, and the preceding *shva* is replaced by a *pataH*. The *kamats* is replaced by *pataH* in a closed syllable.

Examples

המונח המקראי **שְׂדֵמָה** מתייחס בדרך כלל לשדה תבואה או לכרם.
The Biblical term שְׂדֵמָה generally refers to a wheat field or a vineyard.

---

657. ***CCeCa = CaCeCa*** with pataH in the declension, when the first root consonant is guttural

our/your/their	my/your/his/her	const.	Gloss	sing/pl
אַשְׁדָּתֵנוּ/**אַשְׁדַּתְ**כֶם/כֶן/**אַשְׁדָּתָ**ם/ן	**אַשְׁדָּ**תִי/תְךָ/תֵךְ/תוֹ/תָהּ	אַשְׁדַּת-	slope Bibl.	אֲשֵׁדָה נ׳
אַשְׁדוֹתֵינוּ/כֶם/כֶן/הֶם/הֶן	**אַשְׁדוֹ**תַי/תֶיךָ/תַיִךְ/תָיו/תֶיהָ	אַשְׁדוֹת-		אֲשֵׁדוֹת

With the shift in stress, the *tsere* is reduced to a zero *shva*, and the preceding *shva* is replaced by a *pataH*. When a *shva* is expected in a first root consonant that is guttural, it is replaced by a *Hataf-pataH*. The *kamats* is replaced by *pataH* in a closed syllable.

Examples

אַשְׁדּוֹת הרי יהודה אל עבר ים המלח הן תלולות מאוד.
The **slopes** of the Judean hills towards the Dead Sea are very steep.

---

658. ***CCuCa*** with *kubuts* plus *dagesh*

our/your/their	my/your/his/her	const.	Gloss	sing/pl
נְקֻדָּתֵנוּ/**נְקֻדַּתְ**כֶם/כֶן/**נְקֻדָּתָ**ם/ן	**נְקֻדָּ**תִי/תְךָ/תֵךְ/תוֹ/תָהּ	נְקֻדַּת-	point; dot	נְקֻדָּה נ׳
נְקֻדּוֹתֵינוּ/כֶם/כֶן/הֶם/הֶן	**נְקֻדּוֹ**תַי/תֶיךָ/תַיִךְ/תָיו/תֶיהָ	נְקֻדּוֹת-		נְקֻדּוֹת

Examples

יש מורים שמעדיפים לתת ציונים באותיות, מ-A עד F ; אחרים מעדיפים **נְקֻדּוֹת**, מ-0 עד 100.
Some teachers prefer to assign letter-grades, between A-F; other prefer **points**, on a 0-100 scale.

המרחק הקצר ביותר בין שתי **נְקֻדּוֹת** הוא קו ישר.
The shortest distance between two **dots** is a straight line.

שיעור **הַיְלֻדָּה** בקרב המשפחות החרדיות בישראל גבוה היום מזה של המשפחות הערביות.
The **birthrate** among ultra-orthodox families in Israel today is higher than that of the Arab families.

בִּפְלֻגַּת חי״ר בצבאות העולם יכולות להיות בין 2-8 מחלקות, ומספר החיילים בין 80-250.
In an infantry **company** in the armies of the world there can be between 2-8 platoons, totaling 80-250 soldiers.

חייל טוב ונבון יודע שאין למלא אחר **פְּקֻדָּה** שבעליל אינה מוסרית.
A good, intelligent soldier know that s/he cannot follow an **order** which is clearly immoral.

Special Expressions

blood **vengeance** **גְּאֻלַּת** דם
redemption of the land **גְּאֻלַּת** אדמות
hand **luggage** **כְּבֻדַּת** יד
high **priesthood** **כְּהֻנָּה** גדולה
proven **remedy** **סְגֻלָּה** בדוקה
final **meal** before a fast **סְעֻדָּה** מפסקת
storm **troops** (Nazi militia) **פְּלֻגּוֹת** סער
acts of hostility **פְּעֻלּוֹת** איבה
standing **orders** **פְּקֻדּוֹת** קבע

Additional Examples in this Pattern

redemption, salvation גְּאֻלָּה
greatness גְּדֻלָּה
inheritance יְרֻשָּׁה
luggage כְּבֻדָּה

senior position; priesthood כְּהֻנָּה
Jewish marriage contract כְּתֻבָּה
unique quality; folk remedy סְגֻלָּה
meal סְעֻדָּה
action פְּעֻלָּה
holiness קְדֻשָּׁה
military officers (collectively); officer's rank קְצֻנָּה
lobby שְׁדֻלָּה

---

659. ***CCuCa* = *CaCuCa*** when the first root consonant is guttural

our/your/their	my/your/his/her	const.	Gloss	sing/pl
אֲגֻדָּתֵנוּ/**אֲגֻדַּתְ**כֶם/כֶן/**אֲגֻדָּתָ**ם/ן	**אֲגֻדָּ**תִי/תְךָ/תֵךְ/תוֹ/תָהּ	-אֲגֻדַּת	association;	אֲגֻדָּה נ׳
אֲגֻדּוֹתֵינוּ/כֶם/כֶן/הֶם/הֶן	**אֲגֻדּוֹ**תַי/תֶיךָ/תַיִךְ/תָיו/תֶיהָ	-אֲגֻדּוֹת	bundle	אֲגֻדּוֹת

Examples

אֲגֻדַּת הסוחרים בעיר החליטה לשכור חברת אבטחה מקצועית לכל שכונה.

The town's Merchants **Association** decided to hire a professional security outfit for each neighborhood.

באירופה ובישראל, כשפרופסור מגיע לגיל מתקדם, עמיתים ותלמידים-לשעבר בדרך כלל עורכים **אֲסֻפַּת** מאמרים לכבודו.

In Europe and in Israel, when a Professor reaches an advanced age, colleagues and former students often edit a **collection** of articles in his honor.

במדינות שבהן קיים פער גדול בין העניים והמעמד הגבוה, פוליטיקאים רבים מבטיחים **חֲלֻקָּה** צודקת יותר של המשאבים הלאומיים, אבל רובם לא מקיימים את הבטחותיהם לאחר שנבחרו.

In countries where there exist a huge gap between the poor and the higher classes, many politicians promise more just **division** of the nation's resources, but most of them do not keep their promise after they have been elected.

ב**חֲתֻנָּה** טיפוסית בישראל נוכחים בדרך כלל מאות אורחים.

In a typical Israeli **wedding** there are usually hundreds of guests.

Special Expressions

a cooperative **אֲגֻדָּה** שיתופית
an ultra-orthodox party in Israel **אֲגֻדַּת** ישראל
.burial plot, family grave Lit **אֲחֻזַּת** קבר
the wealthy class **אֲצֻלַּת** הממון
eye socket **אֲרֻבַּת** העין
house warming **חֲנֻכַּת** הבית
golden wedding anniversary **חֲתֻנַּת** הזהב
registered association **עֲמֻתָּה** רשומה

Additional Examples in this Pattern

estate אֲחֻזָּה
sheaf (of wheat) אֲלֻמָּה
vest אֲפֻדָּה
aristocracy אֲצֻלָּה
chimney אֲרֻבָּה
commotion הֲמֻלָּה
rust חֲלֻדָּה
consecration, dedication חֲנֻכָּה
flattery חֲנֻפָּה
non-profit organization עֲמֻתָּה
curve עֲקֻמָּה
guarantee עֲרֻבָּה

---

660. *CoCCa*

our/your/their	my/your/his/her	const.	Gloss	sing/pl
מוֹשְׁכָתֵנוּ/**מוֹשְׁכַתְ**כֶם/כֶן/**מוֹשְׁכָתָ**ם/ן	**מוֹשְׁכָ**תִי/תְךָ/תֵךְ/תוֹ/תָהּ	מוֹשְׁכַת-	rein	מוֹשְׁכָה נ׳
מוֹשְׁכוֹתֵינוּ/כֶם/כֶן/הֶם/הֶן	**מוֹשְׁכוֹ**תַי/תֶיךָ/תַיִךְ/תָיו/תֶיהָ	מוֹשְׁכוֹת-		מוֹשְׁכוֹת

Examples

השימוש העיקרי ב**מוֹשְׁכוֹת** הוא לכוון את הסוס ימינה או שמאלה לפי הצורך.
The primary use of the **reins** is to direct the horse to the right or left as needed.

היום מייצרים **סוֹלְלוֹת** שמחזיקות הרבה יותר זמן מאשר בעבר.
Today they produce **batteries** that last much longer than in the past.

במצדה ניתן עדיין לראות את שרידי ה**סוֹלְלָה** שהקימו הרומאים בזמן המצור בשנת 70.
In Masada one can still observe the remains of the **rampart** the Romans erected during their siege of the fortress in 70 CE.

Additional Examples in this Pattern

support, armrest Lit. סוֹמְכָה

---

661. *CoCeC+a* > *CoCCa* when the 3rd root consonant is א׳

our/your/their	my/your/his/her	const.	Gloss	sing/pl
רוֹפְאָתֵנוּ/**רוֹפֵאתְ**כֶם/כֶן/**רוֹפֵאתָ**ם/ן	**רוֹפֵא**תִי/תְךָ/תֵךְ/תוֹ/תָהּ	רוֹפֵאת-	doctor	רוֹפְאָה נ׳
רוֹפְאוֹתֵינוּ/כֶם/כֶן/הֶם/הֶן	**רוֹפְאוֹ**תַי/תֶיךָ/תַיִךְ/תָיו/תֶיהָ	רוֹפְאוֹת-	fem.	רוֹפְאוֹת

In the isolation form, the *tsere* is of the masculine base is elided, רוֹפֵא+ה > רוֹפְאָה, but is maintained in the singular declension, with a muted א׳. It is elided in all plural forms.

Examples

חנה היא **רוֹפֵאת** הילדים הטובה ביותר בבית החולים הזה.
Hannah is the best children's **(fem.) doctor** in this hospital.

Additional Examples in this Pattern

hater, enemy f. שׂוֹנְאָה

---

662. *CoCeCa*

our/your/their	my/your/his/her	const.	Gloss	sing/pl
יוֹלַדְתֵּנוּ/**יוֹלַדְתְּ**כֶם/כֶן/**יוֹלַדְתָּ**ם/ן	**יוֹלַדְ**תִּי/תְּךָ/תֵּךְ/תּוֹ/תָּהּ	יוֹלֶדֶת-	woman giving birth	יוֹלֵדָה/יוֹלֶדֶת נ׳
יוֹלְדוֹתֵינוּ/כֶם/כֶן/הֶם/הֶן	**יוֹלְדוֹ**תַי/תֶיךָ/תַיִךְ/תָיו/תֶיהָ	יוֹלְדוֹת-		יוֹלְדוֹת

In the singular, the *tsere* is reduced and replaced by *pataH* in a closed syllable. יוֹלֶדֶת, the construct form, serves as as isolation form as well, a less formal variant of יוֹלֵדָה.

Examples

בתי נולדה בבית החולים ל**יוֹלְדוֹת** בכפר סבא.
My daughter was born in a maternity hospital (for **women giving birth**) in Kfar Saba.

---

663. ***CoCeCa*** with *cere* that is elided throughout, except in the uninflected plural form

our/your/their	my/your/his/her	const.	Gloss	sing/pl
מוֹסַרְתֵּנוּ/**מוֹסַרְתְּ**כֶם/כֶן/**מוֹסַרְתָּ**ם/ן	**מוֹסַרְ**תִּי/תְּךָ/תֵּךְ/תּוֹ/תָּהּ	מוֹסֶרֶת-	rein Lit.	מוֹסֵרָה נ׳
מוֹסְרוֹתֵינוּ/כֶם/כֶן/הֶם/הֶן	**מוֹסְרוֹ**תַי/תֶיךָ/תַיִךְ/תָיו/תֶיהָ	מוֹסְרוֹת-		מוֹסֵרוֹת

Examples

מוֹשְׁכוֹת היא המילה המקובלת בלשון יום יום ; בעברית הספרותית משתמשים ב**מוֹסֵרוֹת**.
For **reins** one normally uses מוֹשְׁכוֹת; in literary Hebrew the word מוֹסֵרוֹת is used.

Additional Examples in this Pattern

choice vine (Bibl.) שׂוֹרֵקָה gleaning (of grapes), secondary crops עוֹלֵלָה (סמי׳ עוֹלֶלֶת-)

---

664. ***CoCeCa*** when the second root consonant is guttural

our/your/their	my/your/his/her	const.	Gloss	sing/pl
תּוֹעֲבָתֵנוּ/**תּוֹעֲבַתְ**כֶם/כֶן/**תּוֹעֲבָתָ**ם/ן	**תּוֹעֲבָ**תִי/תְךָ/תֵךְ/תוֹ/תָהּ	תּוֹעֲבַת-	abomination	תּוֹעֵבָה נ׳
תּוֹעֲבוֹתֵינוּ/כֶם/כֶן/הֶם/הֶן	**תּוֹעֲבוֹ**תַי/תֶיךָ/תַיִךְ/תָיו/תֶיהָ	תּוֹעֲבוֹת-		תּוֹעֵבוֹת

The declension is as in מוֹסֵרָה above, but when the second root consonant is guttural, the expected *shva* is replaced by *Hataf-pataH.*

Examples

בעברית ספרותית מיושנת-קצת ספרות פורנוגראפית מכונה ספרות **תּוֹעֵבָה**.
In somewhat-outdated literary Hebrew, pornographic literature is referred to as **abomination** literature.

---

665. ***toCeCa*** when the 3rd root consonant is guttural

our/your/their	my/your/his/her	const.	Gloss	sing/pl
תּוֹכַחְתֵּנוּ/תְּכֶם/תְּכֶן/תָּם/תָּן	**תּוֹכַחְ**תִּי/תְּךָ/תֵּךְ/תּוֹ/תָּהּ	תּוֹכַחַת-	chastisement,	תּוֹכֵחָה נ׳
תּוֹכְחוֹתֵינוּ/כֶם/כֶן/הֶם/הֶן	**תּוֹכְחוֹ**תַי/תֶיךָ/תַיִךְ/תָיו/תֶיהָ	תּוֹכְחוֹת-	punishment	תּוֹכֵחוֹת

With stress shift, the *tsere* is reduced to a *shva*, and in the resulting sequence of two *shva* mobiles, the first becomes *pataH*, the second closes the syllable. Const. form with *a-a* sequence.

Examples

תפקידו של הנביא היה להשמיע דברי **תּוֹכֵחָה** לעם בתקופה של הידרדרות מוסרית.
The role of the prophet was to chastise (= say words of **chastisement**) the people in periods of moral decline.

---

666. ***CoCeCa*** when the last root consonant is ע׳ and the plural suffix is ים-

our/your/their	my/your/his/her	const.	Gloss	sing/pl
תּוֹלַעְתֵּנוּ/**תּוֹלַעַתְ**כֶם/כֶן/**תּוֹלַעְתָּ**ם/ן	**תּוֹלַעְ**תִּי/תְּךָ/תֵּךְ/תּוֹ/תָּהּ	תּוֹלַעַת-	worm,	תּוֹלֵעָה/ תּוֹלַעַת נ׳
תּוֹלְעוֹתֵינוּ/כֶם/כֶן/הֶם/הֶן	**תּוֹלְעוֹ**תַי/תֶיךָ/תַיִךְ/תָיו/תֶיהָ	תּוֹלְעֵי-	maggot	תּוֹלָעִים

Examples

בעברית מכנים אדם חלש שתמיד מושפל ונרמס על ידי אחרים "**תּוֹלַעַת** אדם".
In Hebrew they refer to a person often humiliated and trampled by others as "human **worm**".

---

667. *CaCoCa*

our/your/their	my/your/his/her	const.	Gloss	sing/pl
מָסוֹרָתֵנוּ/מָסוֹרַתְכֶם/כֶן/מָסוֹרָתָם/ן	מָסוֹרָתִי/תְךָ/תֵךְ/תוֹ/תָהּ	מָסוֹרַת-	Masorah	מָסוֹרָה נ׳
מָסוֹרוֹתֵינוּ/כֶם/כֶן/הֶם/הֶן	מָסוֹרוֹתַי/תֶיךָ/תַיִךְ/תָיו/תֶיהָ	מָסוֹרוֹת-		מָסוֹרוֹת

The first *kamats* is stable throughout the declension.

Examples

בעלי **הַמָּסוֹרָה** מטבריה הם אלה שגירסתם שרדה והתקבלה על ידי מרבית קהילות ישראל.
The Tiberian **Masorah** scholars are those whose version survived and was accepted by most Jewish communities.

Additional Examples in this Pattern

support, stake סָמוֹכָה

---

668. *CaCuCa* with *pataH* plus *dagesh*

our/your/their	my/your/his/her	const.	Gloss	sing/pl
חַבּוּרָתֵנוּ/חַבּוּרַתְכֶם/כֶן/חַבּוּרָתָם/ן	חַבּוּרָתִי/תְךָ/תֵךְ/תוֹ/תָהּ	חַבּוּרַת-	bruise N	חַבּוּרָה נ׳
חַבּוּרוֹתֵינוּ/כֶם/כֶן/הֶם/הֶן	חַבּוּרוֹתַי/תֶיךָ/תַיִךְ/תָיו/תֶיהָ	חַבּוּרוֹת-		חַבּוּרוֹת

The *pataH* and *dagesh* are maintained throughout the declension. מַשּׂוּאָה and מַשּׁוּאָה are derived from roots with an initial *n*, which is totally assimilated, but the declension is the same, which is why they are included here.

Examples

גופו מלא **חַבּוּרוֹת** מתאונת הדרכים שהיה מעורב בה.
His body is full of **bruises** from the road accident in which he was involved.

Additional Examples in this Pattern

collateral, security (for loan) בַּטּוּחָה
early ripening fig בַּכּוּרָה
gland בַּלּוּטָה
mushroom פַּקּוּעָה
destruction Lit. מַשּׁוּאָה
torch מַשּׂוּאָה

---

669. ***CiCoCa*** with Hirik plus dagesh

our/your/their	my/your/his/her	const.	Gloss	sing/pl
צִנּוֹרָתֵנוּ/**צִנּוֹרַתְ**כֶם/כֶן/**צִנּוֹרָתָ**ם/ן	**צִנּוֹרָ**תִי/תְךָ/תֵךְ/תוֹ/תָהּ	צִנּוֹרַת-	crochet	צִנּוֹרָה נ׳
צִנּוֹרוֹתֵינוּ/כֶם/כֶן/הֶם/הֶן	**צִנּוֹרוֹ**תַי/תֶיךָ/תַיִךְ/תָיו/תֶיהָ	צִנּוֹרוֹת-	hook	צִנּוֹרוֹת

The *Hirik* and *dagesh* are maintained throughout the declension.

Examples

צִנּוֹרָה היא מחט סריגה עם וו בקצה לסריגת קְרוֹשֶׁה.
צִנּוֹרָה is a **crochet hook** – a type of knitting needle with a hook at its end.

Additional Examples in this Pattern

rim, brim תִּתּוֹרָה　　　bird Lit-Rare צִפּוֹרָה

---

670. ***CiCuCa***

our/your/their	my/your/his/her	const.	Gloss	sing/pl
הִלּוּלָתֵנוּ/**הִלּוּלַתְ**כֶם/כֶן/**הִלּוּלָתָ**ם/ן	**הִלּוּלָ**תִי/תְךָ/תֵךְ/תוֹ/תָהּ	הִלּוּלַת-	celebration in memory	הִלּוּלָה נ׳
הִלּוּלוֹתֵינוּ/כֶם/כֶן/הֶם/הֶן	**הִלּוּלוֹ**תַי/תֶיךָ/תַיִךְ/תָיו/תֶיהָ	הִלּוּלוֹת-	of a saintly rabbi	הִלּוּלוֹת

The *Hirik* and *dagesh* are maintained throughout the declension.

Examples

ההִלּוּלָה על קברו של ר׳ שמעון בר יוחאי היא אולי הגדולה ביותר בישראל.
The **celebration in memory** of Rabbi Shim`on Bar-YoHay is possibly the largest one in Israel.

Additional Examples in this Pattern

bezel (bibl.); panel (arch.); inlay, inlay (dental) מִלּוּאָה

---

671. ***CCoCa***

our/your/their	my/your/his/her	const.	Gloss	sing/pl
סְחוֹרָתֵנוּ/**סְחוֹרַתְ**כֶם/כֶן/**סְחוֹרָתָ**ם/ן	**סְחוֹרָ**תִי/תְךָ/תֵךְ/תוֹ/תָהּ	סְחוֹרַת-	merchandise,	סְחוֹרָה נ׳
סְחוֹרוֹתֵינוּ/כֶם/כֶן/הֶם/הֶן	**סְחוֹרוֹ**תַי/תֶיךָ/תַיִךְ/תָיו/תֶיהָ	סְחוֹרוֹת-	goods	סְחוֹרוֹת

No vowel changes in the declension.

Examples

מדי פעם, כשהחמאס נוקט בפעולות איבה נגד ישראל, הצבא מעכב מעבר **סְחוֹרוֹת** לרצועה.
Occasionally, when Hamas initiates hostilities against Israel, the army delays passage of **goods** into the Gaza strip.

בְּשׂוֹרָה טובה : נבחרת הכדורסל של ישראל מדורגת במקום ה-35 בעולם...
Good **tidings**: the Israeli basketball team is ranked number 35th in the world...

Special Expressions

the plague of the **firstborn** (the tenth of the ten plagues) מכת **בְּכוֹרוֹת**
tragic news **בְּשׂוֹרַת** איוב
bookend **תְּמוֹכַת** ספרים

Additional Examples in this Pattern

firstborn birthright; precedence בְּכוֹרָה
frankincense לְבוֹנָה
inkwell דְּיוֹתָה
antenna מְשׂוֹשָׁה
branch (esp. of grapevine) זְמוֹרָה
supporting beam תְּמוֹכָה

---

672. ***CCoCa* = *CaCoCa*** when the first root consonant is guttural

our/your/their	my/your/his/her	const.	Gloss	sing/pl
חֲגוֹרָתֵנוּ/**חֲגוֹרַתְ**כֶם/כֶן/**חֲגוֹרָתָ**ם/ן	**חֲגוֹרָ**תִי/תְךָ/תֵךְ/תוֹ/תָהּ	חֲגוֹרַת-	belt	חֲגוֹרָה נ׳
חֲגוֹרוֹתֵינוּ/כֶם/כֶן/הֶם/הֶן	**חֲגוֹרוֹ**תַי/תֶיךָ/תַיִךְ/תָיו/תֶיהָ	חֲגוֹרוֹת-		חֲגוֹרוֹת

No vowel changes in the declension. When a *shva* is expected with the guttural, it is replaced by *Hataf-pataH.*

Examples

ב״חדר״ האולטרה-אורתודוקסי בישראל, המלמד מעניש את הילדים בהכאה בסרגל, במקל, או ב**חֲגוֹרָה**.
In the ultra-orthodox Heder, the teacher punishes the children by beating them with a ruler, a stick, or a **belt**.

Special Expressions

valueless **coin** **אֲגוֹרָה** שחוקה
piece**work** **עֲבוֹדָה** בקבלנות
black belt (martial arts) **חֲגוֹרָה** שחורה
practical **work** **עֲבוֹדָה** מעשית

Additional Examples in this Pattern

smallest Israeli coin אֲגוֹרָה
work; job עֲבוֹדָה

---

673. ***CCoCa*** when the plural suffix is *-im*

our/your/their	my/your/his/her	const.	Gloss	sing/pl
דְּבוֹרָתֵנוּ/**דְּבוֹרַתְ**כֶם/כֶן/**דְּבוֹרָתָ**ם/ן	**דְּבוֹרָ**תִי/תְךָ/תֵךְ/תוֹ/תָהּ	דְּבוֹרַת-	bee	דְּבוֹרָה נ׳
דְּבוֹרֵינוּ/כֶם/כֶן/הֶם/הֶן	**דְּבוֹ**רַי/רֶיךָ/רַיִךְ/רָיו/רֶיהָ	דְּבוֹרֵי-		דְּבוֹרִים

Examples

עקיצת **דְּבוֹרָה** מכאיבה אך אינה מסוכנת – אלא אם כן לנעקץ יש אלרגיה.
The stinging of a **bee** is painful but not dangerous – unless the person stung has allergy.

Additional Examples in this Pattern

barley שְׂעוֹרָה

---

674. *CaCiya* with *Hirik* plus *dagesh*

our/your/their	my/your/his/her	const.	Gloss	sing/pl
דְּלִיָּתֵנוּ/**דְּלִיַּתְ**כֶם/כֶן/**דְּלִיָּתָ**ם/ן	**דְּלִיָּ**תִי/תְךָ/תֵךְ/תוֹ/תָהּ	-דְּלִיַּת	tendril	דְּלִיָּה נ׳
דְּלִיּוֹתֵינוּ/כֶם/כֶן/הֶם/הֶן	**דְּלִיּוֹ**תַי/תֶיךָ/תַיִךְ/תָיו/תֶיהָ	-דְּלִיּוֹת		דְּלִיּוֹת

Examples

ב**דְּלִיּוֹת** הדקות של העצים החלו להופיע ניצני פרחים.
Flower buds began to sprout in the thin **tendrils** of the trees.

---

675. *CaCCuCa* with *kubuts* plus *dagesh*

our/your/their	my/your/his/her	const.	Gloss	sing/pl
חַרְצֻבָּתֵנוּ/**חַרְצֻבַּתְ**כֶם/כֶן/**חַרְצֻבָּתָ**ם/ן	**חַרְצֻבָּ**תִי/תְךָ/תֵךְ/תוֹ/תָהּ	-חַרְצֻבַּת	knot,	חַרְצֻבָּה נ׳
חַרְצֻבּוֹתֵינוּ/כֶם/כֶן/הֶם/הֶן	**חַרְצֻבּוֹ**תַי/תֶיךָ/תַיִךְ/תָיו/תֶיהָ	-חַרְצֻבּוֹת	chain Lit.	חַרְצֻבּוֹת

Special Expressions

restraints one places on what one says **חַרְצֻבּוֹת** לשון
one who does not resist ill-treatment by others, a "**door mat**" **אַסְקֻפָּה** נדרסת

Additional Examples in this Pattern

threshold, doorsill Lit. אַסְקֻפָּה

---

676. *maCCuCa=maCaCuCa* when the first root consonant is guttural

our/your/their	my/your/his/her	const.	Gloss	sing/pl
מַהֲלֻמָּתֵנוּ/**מַהֲלֻמַּתְ**כֶם/כֶן/**מַהֲלֻמָּתָ**ם/ן	**מַהֲלֻמָּ**תִי/תְךָ/תֵךְ/תוֹ/תָהּ	-מַהֲלֻמַּת	blow	מַהֲלֻמָּה נ׳
מַהֲלֻמּוֹתֵינוּ/כֶם/כֶן/הֶם/הֶן	**מַהֲלֻמּוֹ**תַי/תֶיךָ/תַיִךְ/תָיו/תֶיהָ	-מַהֲלֻמּוֹת		מַהֲלֻמּוֹת

When a *shva* is expected with the guttural, it is replaced by *Hataf-pataH*.

Examples

המתאגרף האנגלי לא יכול היה לעמוד במטר ה**מַּהֲלֻמּוֹת** שהונחתו עליו והתמוטט כבר בסיבוב הראשון.
The English boxer could not withstand the barrage of **blows** that were landed on him and collapsed already on the first round.

Special Expressions

first **strike** **מַהֲלֻמָּה** ראשונה

---

677. *CuCCaCa*

our/your/their	my/your/his/her	const.	Gloss	sing/pl
קֻבְלָנָתֵנוּ/**קֻבְלַנְתְ**כֶם/כֶן/**קֻבְלָנָתָ**ם/ן	**קֻבְלָנָ**תִי/תְךָ/תֵךְ/תוֹ/תָהּ	קֻבְלַנַת-	complaint	קֻבְלָנָה נ׳
קֻבְלָנוֹתֵינוּ/כֶם/כֶן/הֶם/הֶן	**קֻבְלָנוֹ**תַי/תֶיךָ/תַיִךְ/תָיו/תֶיהָ	קֻבְלָנוֹת-		קֻבְלָנוֹת

Examples

קֻבְלָנָה היא אישום שבו המאשים הוא אדם פרטי, בניגוד לאישום רגיל, שבו המאשימה היא המדינה.

A **complaint** is an indictment made by an individual, whereas a regular indictment is presented by the state.

Special Expressions

criminal **complaint** **קֻבְלָנָה** פלילית

Additional Examples in this Pattern

action, complaint, proceeding (law) תֻּבְעָנָה

---

678. *CCuCCa*

our/your/their	my/your/his/her	const.	Gloss	sing/pl
כְּנֻפְיָתֵנוּ/**כְּנֻפְיַתְ**כֶם/כֶן/**כְּנֻפְיָתָ**ם/ן	**כְּנֻפְיָ**תִי/תְךָ/תֵךְ/תוֹ/תָהּ	כְּנֻפְיַת-	gang	כְּנֻפְיָה נ׳
כְּנֻפְיוֹתֵינוּ/כֶם/כֶן/הֶם/הֶן	**כְּנֻפְיוֹ**תַי/תֶיךָ/תַיִךְ/תָיו/תֶיהָ	כְּנֻפְיוֹת-		כְּנֻפְיוֹת

Examples

אחד האתגרים הגדולים בערים הגדולות היא כיצד לשכנע את הנוער לא להצטרף ל**כְּנֻפְיוֹת**.

One of the major challenges in the big cities is how to convince the youth not to join **gangs**.

Additional Examples in this Pattern

roll, bun, cake Lit. גְּלֻסְקָה

dowry נְדוּנְיָה/נְדֻנְיָה

---

679. *CCuCCa=CaCuCCa* when the first root consonant is guttural

our/your/their	my/your/his/her	const.	Gloss	sing/pl
אֲלֻנְקָתֵנוּ/**אֲלֻנְקַתְ**כֶם/כֶן/**אֲלֻנְקָתָ**ם/ן	**אֲלֻנְקָ**תִי/תְךָ/תֵךְ/תוֹ/תָהּ	אֲלֻנְקַת-	stretcher	אֲלֻנְקָה נ׳
אֲלֻנְקוֹתֵינוּ/כֶם/כֶן/הֶם/הֶן	**אֲלֻנְקוֹ**תַי/תֶיךָ/תַיִךְ/תָיו/תֶיהָ	אֲלֻנְקוֹת-		אֲלֻנְקוֹת

When a *shva* is expected with the guttural, it is replaced by *Hataf-pataH.*

Examples

הָאֲלֻנְקָה היא אולי פריט הציוד החשוב ביותר בקרב – אי אפשר לפנות פצועים בלעדיה.
The **stretcher** is perhaps the most important equipment item in battle – one cannot evacuate the wounded without it.

---

680. *CaCCeCa*

our/your/their	my/your/his/her	const.	Gloss	sing/pl
נַדְנֵדָתֵנוּ/**נַדְנֵדַתְ**כֶם/כֶן/**נַדְנֵדָתָ**ם/ן	**נַדְנֵדָ**תִי/תְךָ/תֵךְ/תוֹ/תָהּ	נַדְנֵדַת-	swing	נַדְנֵדָה נ׳
נַדְנֵדוֹתֵינוּ/כֶם/כֶן/הֶם/הֶן	**נַדְנֵדוֹ**תַי/תֶיךָ/תַיִךְ/תָיו/תֶיהָ	נַדְנֵדוֹת-		נַדְנֵדוֹת

The *tsere* is maintained throughout the declension. The *mishkal* is quadriliteral, *CaCCeCa*, but the first root consonant is copied in position three, and the second in position four, so that in fact we are dealing here with two root consonants – but in a quadrilateral *mishkal*, which is more appropriately captured in the designation קַטְקֵטָה.

Examples

בעברית משתמשים במונח **נַדְנֵדָה** גם ל-swing וגם ל-seesaw.
In Hebrew the use the same word, נַדְנֵדָה, for both '**swing**' and '**seesaw**.'

Additional Examples in this Pattern

flinging, shaking, hurling טַלְטֵלָה   whistle N צַפְצֵפָה

---

681. *CaCCaCa*

our/your/their	my/your/his/her	const.	Gloss	sing/pl
קַיְטָנָתֵנוּ/**קַיְטַנְתְּ**כֶם/כֶן/**קַיְטָנָתָ**ם/ן	**קַיְטָנָ**תִי/תְךָ/תֵךְ/תוֹ/תָהּ	קַיְטָנַת-	summer day	קַיְטָנָה נ׳
קַיְטָנוֹתֵינוּ/כֶם/כֶן/הֶם/הֶן	**קַיְטָנוֹ**תַי/תֶיךָ/תַיִךְ/תָיו/תֶיהָ	קַיְטָנוֹת-	camp	קַיְטָנוֹת

The *kamats* is maintained throughout – except for the const. plural of פַּרְנָסָה, 'livelihood,' פַּרְנְסוֹת-.

Examples

לא תמיד ברור אם מטרתן של **קַיְטָנוֹת** הקיץ היא בעיקר שהילדים לא ישתעממו בחופש הגדול, או כדי שלהוריהם תהיה קצת מנוחה מהם.
It is not always clear whether the main purpose of **summer day camps** is to keep the kids from getting bored during the summer vacation, or to allow their parents some peace and quiet without them.

איזהו מאושר? מי שאוהב את עבודתו כאילו הייתה תחביבו, ולא רק מקור **פַּרְנָסָתוֹ**.
Who is a happy person? He who loves his work as if it were his hobby, and not just his source of **livelihood**.

Special Expressions

court of appeals **עַרְכָּאַת** ערעור

Additional Examples in this Pattern

proceeding (law); court (law) עַרְכָּאָה

female toad קַרְפָּדָה

---

682. ***CaCCaCa*** with reduplication

sing/pl	Gloss	const.	my/your/his/her	our/your/their
קַלְקָלָה נ׳	failure,	קַלְקֶלֶת-	**קַלְקָלָ**תִי/תְךָ/תֵךְ/תוֹ/תָהּ	קַלְקָלָתֵנוּ/**קַלְקַלְתְ**כֶם/כֶן/**קַלְקָלָתָ**ם/ן
קַלְקָלוֹת	corruption	קַלְקְלוֹת -	**קַלְקְלוֹ**תַי/תֶיךָ/תַיִךְ/תָיו/תֶיהָ	**קַלְקְלוֹתֵי**נוּ/כֶם/כֶן/הֶם/הֶן

The *tsere* is maintained throughout the declension. The *mishkal* is quadriliteral, *CaCCaCa*, but the first root consonant is copied in position three, and the second in position four, so that in fact we are dealing here with two root consonants – but in a quadrilateral *mishkal*, which is more appropriately captured in the designation קַטְקָטָה.

Examples

לא קל לראות ידידים בשעת **קַלְקָלָתָם**.
It is not easy to watch friends in their hour of **iniquity**.

פוליטיקאים רבים לא מבינים הרבה **בְּכַלְכָּלָה**, וכשהם מגיעים לעמדת כוח הם עושים לעיתים טעויות כלכליות חמורות.
Many politicians do not understand much in **economics**, and when they reach a position of power, they sometimes commit serious economic mistakes.

Special Expressions

free market **economy** **כַּלְכָּלָה** חופשית

black economy (unreported financial transactions, often related to criminal activity, moonlighting, etc.) **כַּלְכָּלָה** שחורה

Additional Examples in this Pattern

horror, fear, aversion חַלְחָלָה

poplar צַפְצָפָה

U. Patterns with suffixes including *-t (including -ut, -it)*

683. ***maCéCet*** when the first root consonants are *n* or *yts*

sing/pl	Gloss	const.	my/your/his/her	our/your/their
מַגֶּבֶת נ׳	towel	מַגֶּבֶת-	**מַגַּבְ**תִּי/תְּךָ/תֵּךְ/תּוֹ/תָּהּ	**מַגַּבְ**תֵּנוּ/תְּכֶם/תְּכֶן/תָּם/תָּן
מַגָּבוֹת		מַגְּבוֹת-	**מַגְּבוֹ**תַי/תֶיךָ/תַיִךְ/תָיו/תֶיהָ	**מַגְּבוֹתֵ**ינוּ/כֶם/כֶן/הֶם/הֶן

The *m-* is a derivational prefix, and the נ׳ or י׳ (in the יצ sequence) at the beginning of the root is totally assimilated into the second root consonant. The two derivational sub-classes share the same declension. The declension essentially follows the segholate model, and the base with *pataH* (in a closed syllable) surfaces before suffixes. In the plural the *kamats* is reduced to *shva* two syllables away from the stress.

Examples

קשה לי להיות חשוף לשמש זמן רב, כך שכשאני על חוף הים, אני מתעטף רוב הזמן **בְּמַגֶּבֶת**.
It is difficult for me to be exposed to the sun for too long, so when I am on the beach, most of the time I wrap myself in a **towel**.

זהב הוא **מַתֶּכֶת** אצילה, שאינה מחלידה.
Gold is a precious **metal,** which does not rust.

כשאני מרצה בכנסים, אני מעדיף לחלק תמסירים. אסור לסמוך על **מַצֶּגֶת**, כי לעתים קרובות הטכנולוגיה אינה פועלת כראוי.
When I give talks in conferences, I prefer to use handouts. One should not depend on computer-**presentation**, since technology often fails.

Special Expressions

מַסֶּכֶת ייסורים trouble, suffering

מַצֶּבֶת זיכרון memorial **monument**

Additional Examples in this Pattern

מַסֶּכֶת tractate (of the Mishna); revue, review

מַצֶּבֶת tombstone Rare; position Lit.

מַצֶּקֶת ladle

מַקֶּבֶת sledgehammer Lit.

---

684. *maCéCet* = *maCáCat* when the first root consonant is *n*, the third guttural

our/your/their	my/your/his/her	const.	Gloss	sing/pl
מַגַּעְתֵּנוּ/תְּכֶם/תְּכֶן/תָּם/תָּן	**מַגַּעְ**תִּי/תְּךָ/תֵּךְ/תּוֹ/תָּהּ	מַגַּעַת-	contact	מַגַּעַת נ׳
מַגְּעוֹתֵינוּ/כֶם/כֶן/הֶם/הֶן	**מַגְּעוֹ**תַי/תֶיךָ/תַיִךְ/תָיו/תֶיהָ	מַגְּעוֹת-	(elec.)	מַגָּעוֹת

The *m-* is a derivational prefix, and the *n* at the beginning of the root is totally assimilated into the second root consonant. The declension essentially follows the segholate model, and the base with *pataH* (in a closed syllable) surfaces before suffixes, but because of the guttural in root-position-three, the singular isolation form and the singular construct form come with two *pataH*s rather than with two *seghol*s. In the plural forms the *kamats* is reduced to *shva* two syllables away from the stress. This is the only instance found in the non-obsolete lexicon.

---

685. *CaCéCet*

our/your/their	my/your/his/her	const.	Gloss	sing/pl
צַמַּרְתֵּנוּ/תְּכֶם/תְּכֶן/תָּם/תָּן	**צַמַּרְ**תִּי/תְּךָ/תֵּךְ/תּוֹ/תָּהּ	צַמֶּרֶת-	tree-top; top,	צַמֶּרֶת נ׳
צַמְּרוֹתֵינוּ/כֶם/כֶן/הֶם/הֶן	**צַמְּרוֹ**תַי/תֶיךָ/תַיִךְ/תָיו/תֶיהָ	צַמְּרוֹת-	upper ranks	צַמָּרוֹת

The singular declension follows a segholate-like model, and the base with *pataH* (in a closed syllable) surfaces before suffixes. In the plural forms the *kamats* is reduced to *shva* two syllables away from the stress. A significant number of cases denote sicknesses and a few carry some negative connotation, but by no means all (צַמֶּרֶת above clearly does not). In most cases, items designating sicknesses do not have plural forms.

Examples

אלה עצים גבוהים מאוד; **צַמְּרוֹתֵיהֶם** מגיעות לגובה של שלושים או ארבעים מטר.
These are very tall trees; **their tops** reach a height of thirty or forty meters.

ההתחלה שלה הייתה צנועה למדיי, אבל היום היא נמצאת **בַּצַּמֶּרֶת** של תעשיית האופנה הישראלית.
Her beginnings were pretty modest, but today she is at the **top** of the Israeli fashion industry.

במדינות מסוימות בארה״ב נתגלו מקרים רבים של **חַצֶּבֶת** אצל ילדים שהוריהם סירבו לחסנם.
In certain states in the US a good number of **measles** were discovered among children whose parents refused to vaccinate.

מקור המושג **דַּלֶּקֶת** במילה דְלֵיקה (בעירה, שריפה), בשל החום הנוצר במקום **הַדַּלֶּקֶת**, ולעיתים אף בכל הגוף.
The origin of the Hebrew term דַּלֶּקֶת is the word דְלֵיקה (fire, **inflammation**), because of the heat formed around it, and sometimes in the whole body.

המונח העברי **חַזֶּרֶת** מקורו בנפיחות הפנים הכרוכה במחלה – נפיחות המזכירה פני חזיר.
The Hebrew term for **mumps**, חַזֶּרֶת, comes from the face being swollen by the sickness, reminding one of a pig's face (חזיר).

כַּלֶּבֶת נגרמת כל ידי נשיכת חיה שוטה, בעיקר כלב שוטה.
Rabies is caused by the bite of a rabid animal, often a rabid dog. [If the term were derived from 'dog' as in Hebrew, it would probably have been named 'dogitis'…]

כששוטר אינו נוהג כראוי בעת מילוי תפקידו, לעיתים קרובות שולפים אותו מן עבודת המקוף ומגבילים אותו לעבודת **נַיֶּרֶת**.
When a policeman behaves improperly on a job on his beat, he is often pulled out from patrolling the streets and is reassigned to **paperwork** (office work).

Special Expressions

צַמֶּרֶת השלטון **upper ranks** of government
זונת **צַמֶּרֶת** **high class** prostitute
דַּבֶּשֶׁת הגל **crest** of wave
דַּלֶּקֶת ריאות pneumonia (**inflammation** of the lungs)
דַּלֶּקֶת המוח encephalitis (brain **inflammation**)
כַּוֶּנֶת אחורית rear-**sight** (weaponry)
רַכֶּבֶת אוויר airlift
רַכֶּבֶת משא freight **train**

Additional Examples in this Pattern

German measles אֲדֶמֶת
robe, cloak אַדֶּרֶת
edema בַּצֶּקֶת
garrulousness, "verbal diarrhea" דַּבֶּרֶת Coll.
camel's hump דַּבֶּשֶׁת
hemophilia דַּמֶּמֶת
acne חַטֶּטֶת
promenade, esplanade טַיֶּלֶת
squadron (military) טַיֶּסֶת
wart יַבֶּלֶת
sight (of rifle etc.) כַּוֶּנֶת
beehive כַּוֶּרֶת
safe; deposit box כַּסֶּפֶת
lumbago מַתֶּנֶת
runny nose נַזֶּלֶת
syphilis עַגֶּבֶת
caries (dentistry) עַשֶּׁשֶׁת
fungal infection פַּטֶּרֶת
thrombosis פַּקֶּקֶת
scar צַלֶּקֶת
tetanus צַפֶּדֶת
cassette קַלֶּטֶת
asthma קַצֶּרֶת
lethargy רַדֶּמֶת
train רַכֶּבֶת
flotilla שַׁיֶּטֶת
fall (of autumn leaves) שַׁלֶּכֶת
aphasia שַׁתֶּקֶת

---

686. ***CaCéCet*** when the second root consonant is 'ה or 'ח or 'ע

our/your/their	my/your/his/her	const.	Gloss	sing/pl
רַחַפְתֵּנוּ/תְּכֶם/תְּכֶן/תָּם/תָּן	**רַחַפְ**תִּי/תְּךָ/תֵּךְ/תּוֹ/תָּהּ	רַחֶפֶת-	hovercraft	רַחֶפֶת נ'
רַחְפוֹתֵינוּ/כֶם/כֶן/הֶם/הֶן	**רַחְפוֹ**תַי/תֶיךָ/תַיִךְ/תָיו/תֶיהָ	רַחְפוֹת-		רַחָפוֹת

The declension is similar to that of *tsameret* above, but without a *dagesh.*

Examples

רַחֶפֶת היא ספינה עם מתקנים מיוחדים המסייעים לה להחליק על פני הגלים וכמעט לרחף על פני המים.
A **hovercraft** is a boat with special devices that enable it to glide over the waves and almost hover above the water.

הרבה מנהלים של מוסדות ממשלתיים העומדים בפני בעיות קשות מאמינים ש**סַחֶבֶת** תפתור את הכל. בסוף יימאס למגישי בקשות, עתירות ותלונות והם יוותרו, וכך הבעיות ייפתרו מעצמן.
Many directors of government institutions who are facing serious problems believe that **foot-dragging** will eventually solve everything. Presenters of requests, petitions and complaints will be tired of waiting and give up, and thus the problems will disappear on their own.

חשבו שה**שַּׁחֶפֶת** עברה ובטלה מן העולם, אבל לאחרונה נראה שהיא חוזרת שוב.
It was believed that **tuberculosis** no longer exists, but recently it seems to have returned.

Additional Examples in this Pattern

vitiligo (medic.) בַּהֶקֶת/בַּהֶרֶת
freckle בַּהֶרֶת
landing craft נַחֶתֶת
manifold; impetigo סַעֶפֶת

jaundice צַהֶבֶת
toxemia רַעֶלֶת
cirrhosis שַׁחֶמֶת
whooping cough שַׁעֶלֶת

---

687. ***CaCéCet*** when the second root consonant is 'ה or 'ח or 'ע, and the plural suffix is *-im*

our/your/their	my/your/his/her	const.	Gloss	sing/pl
גַּחַלְתֵּנוּ/תְּכֶם/תְּכֶן/תָּם/תָּן	**גַּחַלְ**תִּי/תְּךָ/תֵּךְ/תּוֹ/תָּהּ	גַּחֶלֶת-	ember;	גַּחֶלֶת נ'
גַּחֲלֵינוּ/כֶם/כֶן/הֶם/הֶן	**גַּחֲ**לַי/לֶיךָ/לַיִךְ/לָיו/לֶיהָ	גַּחֲלֵי-	remnant	גֶּחָלִים

The declension is similar to that of צַמֶּרֶת above, but without a *dagesh*, and the plural suffix is *-im*. When a *shva* is expected with the ח', it is replaced by *Hataf-pataH*.

Examples

יש הטוענים שגַּחֶלֶת יהדותם של יהודי ארה״ב בסכנה, אבל זה בהחלט לא נכון.
Some claim that the **remnant** of the Judaism of American Jewry is in danger, but the claim is wrong.

Special Expressions

an **ember** that continues to burn, that is still "alive" **גַּחֶלֶת** לוחשת

---

688. ***CaCéCet*** when the second root consonant is 'א or 'ר

our/your/their	my/your/his/her	const.	Gloss	sing/pl
צָרַבְתֵּנוּ/תְּכֶם/תְּכֶן/תָּם/תָּן	**צָרַבְ**תִּי/תְּךָ/תֵּךְ/תּוֹ/תָּהּ	צָרֶבֶת-	heartburn	צָרֶבֶת נ'
צָרְבוֹתֵינוּ/כֶם/כֶן/הֶם/הֶן	**צָרְבוֹ**תַי/תֶיךָ/תַיִךְ/תָיו/תֶיהָ	צָרְבוֹת-		צָרָבוֹת

The declension is similar to that of צַמֶּרֶת above, but without a *dagesh*, and the *pataH* is replaced by *kamats* (in "compensation" for the lost *dagesh*.) Here too most cases denote sicknesses and some negative connotation, and do not have plural variants.

Examples

מיכאל סובל מ**צָרָבוֹת** קשות מכיוון שהוא מרבה לאכול מאכלים מטוגנים.
Michael suffers from serious **heartburns** because he eats a lot of fried food.

טָרֶשֶׁת נפוצה היא מחלה כרונית של מערכת העצבים, הפוגעת בתפקודם של תאי העצב.
Multiple sclerosis is a chronic disease of the nervous system, which affects the functioning of nerve cells.

כשאדם נוטה לנאום נאומים ארוכים ללא הרף, מתייחסים לזה כאל מחלה, **נָאֶמֶת**.
When a person displays a **tendency to make non-stop speeches**, they regard it as a sickness.

Additional Examples in this Pattern

halitosis בָּאֶשֶׁת
agate; emerald בָּרֶקֶת
scabies גָּרֶדֶת
diphtheria קָרֶמֶת
scratch, cut שָׂרֶטֶת

---

689. ***CaCéCet* = *CaCáCat*** when the third root consonant is ח'

our/your/their	my/your/his/her	const.	Gloss	sing/pl
צַלַּחְתֵּנוּ/תְּכֶם/תְּכֶן/תָּם/תָּן	**צַלַּחְ**תִּי/תְּךָ/תֵּךְ/תּוֹ/תָּהּ	-צַלַּחַת	plate, dish,	צַלַּחַת נ'
צַלְּחוֹתֵינוּ/כֶם/כֶן/הֶם/הֶן	**צַלְּחוֹ**תַי/תֶיךָ/תַיִךְ/תָיו/תֶיהָ	-צַלְּחוֹת	bowl, saucer	צַלָּחוֹת

The declension is similar to that of צַמֶּרֶת above, but the singular isolation form and the singular construct are with two *pataH*s instead of two *seghol*s, owing to the presence of the guttural.

Examples

אימא לא אוהבת לראות שמשאירים משהו ב**צַלַּחַת**.
Mom does not like to see us leave anything on our **plate**.

כשהיינו ילדים, תמיד היה נטפל אלינו כ**סַפַּחַת** ילד לא פופולרי שרצה לשחק איתנו ; עד היום יש לי רגש אשמה על שעשינו הכל כדי להיפטר ממנו...
When we kids, an unpopular boy would stick to us as a **tag-along**; to this day I feel guilty because we did all we could to get rid of him…

העדיפות הראשונה של החלוצים שהגיעו לארץ ישראל הייתה לייבש ביצות, כדי לחסל את היתושים שהפיצו את מחלת ה**קַדַּחַת**.
The first priority of the pioneers when they came to Palestine was to dry the swamps, in order to eliminate the mosquitoes that spread **malaria**.

Special Expressions

did not remain idle לא טמן ידו ב**צַלַּחַת**
flying **saucer** **צַלַּחַת** מעופפת
with a job or connections that allow one to benefit more than others from public funds or assets קרוב ל**צַלַּחַת**
hay **fever** **קַדַּחַת** השחת
election **turmoil** **קַלַּחַת** בחירות

Additional Examples in this Pattern

frontal baldness Lit. גַּבַּחַת
asthma גַּנַּחַת
emphysema נַפַּחַת
psoriasis; "tag-along," nuisance Coll. סַפַּחַת
forehead Lit. פַּדַּחַת
flask, bottle, jug צַפַּחַת
turmoil; cauldron (biblical) קַלַּחַת

---

690. *CaCéCet* = *CaCáCat* when the third root consonant is 'ע

our/your/their	my/your/his/her	const.	Gloss	sing/pl
טַבַּעְתֵּנוּ/תְּכֶם/תְּכֶן/תָּם/תָּן	**טַבַּעְ**תִּי/תְּךָ/תֵּךְ/תּוֹ/תָּהּ	-טַבַּעַת	ring,	טַבַּעַת נ'
טַבְּעוֹתֵינוּ/כֶם/כֶן/הֶם/הֶן	**טַבְּעוֹ**תַי/תֶיךָ/תַיִךְ/תָיו/תֶיהָ	-טַבְּעוֹת	signet ring	טַבָּעוֹת

The singular isolation form and the singular construct are with two *pataH*s, owing to the presence of the 'ע. The declension is similar to that of צַלַּחַת above, but today the preference is for *Hataf-pataH* under the 'ע – which reflects the common pronunciation.

Examples

בעבר, המלך היה חותם על מסמכים רשמיים ב**טַבַּעַת** חותם מיוחדת.
In the past, the king used to sign official documents with a **signet ring**.

חשוב לזכור ש**שַׁפַּעַת** והצטננות הן שתי תופעות שונות. נגיף ה**שַׁפַּעַת** מסוכן הרבה יותר ועלול להתפתח לדלקת ריאות.
One should remember that the **flu** and a common cold are different phenomena. The **influenza** virus is much more dangerous and may develop into pneumonia.

Special Expressions

swine **flu** **שַׁפַּעַת** החזירים
avian/bird **flu** **שַׁפַּעַת** העופות
wedding ring **טַבַּעַת** קידושין/נישואין
anus פי ה**טַבַּעַת**

Additional Examples in this Pattern

schizophrenia שַׁסַּעַת

---

691. *CaCéCet* = *CaCáCat* when the second root consonant is 'א or 'ר and the third is 'ח

our/your/their	my/your/his/her	const.	Gloss	sing/pl
קָרַחְתֵּנוּ/תְּכֶם/תְּכֶן/תָּם/תָּן	**קָרַחְ**תִּי/תְּךָ/תֵּךְ/תּוֹ/תָּהּ	-קָרַחַת	bald spot	קָרַחַת נ'
קָרְחוֹתֵינוּ/כֶם/כֶן/הֶם/הֶן	**קָרְחוֹ**תַי/תֶיךָ/תַיִךְ/תָיו/תֶיהָ	-קָרְחוֹת		קָרָחוֹת

The declension is similar to that of צַמֶּרֶת above, but the singular isolation form and the singular construct are with two *pataH*s instead of two *seghol*s, owing to the presence of the guttural.

Examples

בלשון הסלנג אומרים לעיתים על בעל **קָרַחַת** שיש לו מצח גבוה...
In Hebrew slang they sometimes say of a person with a **bald spot** that he has a high forehead.

Special Expressions

clearing (in a forest) **קָרַחַת** יער

---

692. ***CaCéCet* = *CaCáCat*** when the second root consonant is 'א or 'ר and the third is guttural, no plural

our/your/their	my/your/his/her	const.	Gloss	sing/pl
צָרַעְתֵּנוּ/תְּכֶם/תְּכֶן/תָּם/תָּן	**צָרַעְ**תִּי/תְּךָ/תֵּךְ/תּוֹ/תָּהּ	צָרַעַת-	leprosy	צָרַעַת נ'

The singular isolation form and the singular construct are with two *pataH*s, owing to the presence of the ע'. The declension is similar to that of קָרַחַת above, but today the preference is for *Hataf-pataH* under the ע' – which reflects the common pronunciation. This form has no plural variant.

Examples

בימינו ניתן לטפל טיפול תרופתי במחלת ה**צָרַעַת**, ולרפא את החולים בה ריפוי שלם.
Today it is possible to treat **leprosy** with medication, and reach complete recovery.

---

693. ***taCCéCet***

our/your/their	my/your/his/her	const.	Gloss	sing/pl
תַּרְדַּמְתֵּנוּ/תְּכֶם/תְּכֶן/תָּם/תָּן	**תַּרְדַּמְ**תִּי/תְּךָ/תֵּךְ/תּוֹ/תָּהּ	תַּרְדֶּמֶת-	coma	תַּרְדֶּמֶת נ'
תַּרְדְּמוֹתֵינוּ/כֶם/כֶן/הֶם/הֶן	**תַּרְדְּמוֹ**תַי/תֶיךָ/תַיִךְ/תָיו/תֶיהָ	תַּרְדְּמוֹת-		תַּרְדָּמוֹת

The declension essentially follows the segholate model, and the base with *pataH* (in a closed syllable) surfaces before suffixes. In the plural forms the *kamats* is reduced to *shva* two syllables away from the stress. Clearly, this specific word was formed in analogy with *CaCéCet*, which very often designates sicknesses.

Examples

אין אפשרות לנבא מתי אדם יתעורר מ**תַּרְדֶּמֶת**. ידועים מקרים של חולים שהתעוררו מ**תַּרְדֶּמֶת** אחרי שנים...
It is impossible to tell how long a person could last while in **coma**. There were cases in which patients woke up from coma after **years**…

---

694. ***CiCéCet***

our/your/their	my/your/his/her	const.	Gloss	sing/pl
אִגַּרְתֵּנוּ/תְּכֶם/תְּכֶן/תָּם/תָּן	**אִגַּרְ**תִּי/תְּךָ/תֵּךְ/תּוֹ/תָּהּ	אִגֶּרֶת-	letter,	אִגֶּרֶת נ'
אִגְּרוֹתֵינוּ/כֶם/כֶן/הֶם/הֶן	**אִגְּרוֹ**תַי/תֶיךָ/תַיִךְ/תָיו/תֶיהָ	אִגְּרוֹת-	missive	אִגְּרוֹת

The singular declension essentially follows the segholate model, and the base with *pataH* (in a closed syllable) surfaces before suffixes. In the plural forms the *kamats* is reduced to *shva* two syllables away from the stress – also in the isolation form. Sicknesses and other items that carry negative connotation do not have plural forms.

Examples

מימי הביניים, כשהעברית שימשה רק כשפה כתובה, שרדו **אִגְּרוֹת** רבות ששלחו רבנים וגדולי תורה, בינם לבין עצמם וכתשובות לשאלות מן הציבור.

From the medieval period, when Hebrew only served as a written language, there survived many **letters/missives** sent by rabbis and authorities on Jewish law, among themselves and in response to queries from the public.

את ריצ׳רד השלישי זוכרים היום בעיקר כמי שרצח את שני אחייניו, ואת **הגַּבֶּנֶת** שלו... בקשר לרציחות, היסטוריונים אומרים היום שלא הכל נכון.

Richard the Third is remembered today mainly for his murdering his two nephews, as well as for his **hump**… As for the murders, historians today say that only part of them are true.

Special Expressions

אִגֶּרֶת אוויר airmail **letter** — **אִגֶּרֶת** חוב **bond**

Additional Examples in this Pattern

אִוֶּלֶת stupidity, foolishness — כִּנֶּמֶת pediculosis, presence of lice on head/body

---

695. *CaCóCet*

our/your/their	my/your/his/her	const.	Gloss	sing/pl
בַּצָּרְתֵּנוּ/תְּכֶם/תְּכֶן/תָּם/תָּן	**בַּצָּרְ**תִּי/תְּךָ/תֵּךְ/תּוֹ/תָּהּ	בַּצֹּרֶת-	drought	בַּצֹּרֶת נ׳
בַּצְּרוֹתֵינוּ/כֶם/כֶן/הֶם/הֶן	**בַּצְּרוֹ**תַי/תֶיךָ/תַיִךְ/תָיו/תֶיהָ	בַּצְּרוֹת-		בַּצָּרוֹת

The declension essentially follows the segholate model, and the base with *kamats katan* (in a closed syllable) surfaces before suffixes. In the plural forms the *kamats* is reduced to *shva* two syllables away from the stress. Note: מַכֹּלֶת comes from the root אכ״ל with an initial א׳, and מַפֹּלֶת from a root with initial *n* (*n-p-l*), but the declension is identical to that of *CaCóCet*.

Examples

מספר שנים של **בַּצֹּרֶת** יכולות להביא אומה חקלאית שלמה למצב של רעב ללחם.

a number of years of **drought** can cause a whole agricultural nation to starve.

האם צפויה לנו **מַפֹּלֶת** כלכלית חדשה בשל מלחמת מיסי המגן הניטשת עתה?

Should we expect a new economic **collapse** as a result of the protective tariffs war being waged now?

Special Expressions

שנת **בַּצֹּרֶת** a year of drought — **מַפֹּלֶת** שלגים avalanche

Additional Examples in this Pattern

כַּדֹּרֶת bowling — כַּפֹּרֶת covering of the holy ark (biblical)

מַכֹּלֶת grocery, convenience store

---

696. *CaCóCet*

our/your/their	my/your/his/her	const.	Gloss	sing/pl
מָסָרְתֵּנוּ/תְּכֶם/תְּכֶן/תָּם/תָּן	**מָסָרְ**תִּי/תְּךָ/תֵּךְ/תּוֹ/תָּהּ	מָסֹרֶת-	tradition	מָסֹרֶת נ׳
מָסוֹרוֹתֵינוּ/כֶם/כֶן/הֶם/הֶן	**מָסוֹרוֹ**תַי/תֶיךָ/תַיִךְ/תָיו/תֶיהָ	מָסוֹרוֹת-		מָסוֹרוֹת

The *kamats* with the first consonant is maintained throughout; no *dagesh* follows. The singular declension essentially follows the segholate model, and the base with *kamats katan* (in a closed syllable) surfaces before suffixes, but in the plural forms there occur no vowel changes.

Examples

ביחידות מסוימות של צה״ל השבעת טירונים שזה עתה התגייסו על פסגת הר מצדה הפכה ל**מָסֹרֶת**.
In certain units of the IDF, swearing in of new recruits on Masada mountain has become a **tradition**.

Special Expressions

legend, myth; traditional belief (Talmudic) **מָסֹרֶת** אגדה

Additional Examples in this Pattern

covering of the (holy) ark in the synagogue פָּרֹכֶת

---

697. *CiCóCet*

our/your/their	my/your/his/her	const.	Gloss	sing/pl
בִּקָּרְתֵּנוּ/תְּכֶם/תְּכֶן/תָּם/תָּן	**בִּקָּרְ**תִּי/תְּךָ/תֵּךְ/תּוֹ/תָּהּ	בִּקֹּרֶת-	criticism, review; inspection	בִּקֹּרֶת נ׳
בִּקּוֹרוֹתֵינוּ/כֶם/כֶן/הֶם/הֶן	**בִּקּוֹרוֹ**תַי/תֶיךָ/תַיִךְ/תָיו/תֶיהָ	בִּקּוֹרוֹת-		בִּקּוֹרוֹת

The declension of singular forms essentially follows the segholate model, and the base with *kamats katan* (in a closed syllable) surfaces before suffixes.

Examples

המאמר לא עבר את ה**בִּקֹּרֶת** של הקוראים המקצועיים.
The article did not pass the professional readers' **review**.

המסעדה לא עברה את ה**בִּקֹּרֶת** של משרד הבריאות.
The restaurant did not pass the **inspection** of the Health Ministry.

ה**סִּיּוֹמוֹת** –ים ו-ות לא תמיד מעידות על מינו של שם העצם, זכר או נקבה.
The **suffixes** *-im* and *-ot* do not necessarily indicate the noun gender, masculine or feminine.

קִדֹּמֶת הטלפון של ישראל היא 972.
The **telephone code** ("prefix") of Israel is 972.

pecial Expressions

בִּקֹּרֶת הספרות literary **criticism**

מתח **בִּקֹּרֶת** על criticize

למטה מכל **בִּקֹּרֶת**, beneath **criticism**, atrocious

Additional Examples in this Pattern

טִנֹּפֶת filth

סִפֹּרֶת fiction writing

נִצֹּלֶת utilization

קִבֹּלֶת capacity

סִיֹּמֶת suffix

קִדֹּמֶת prefix; telephone area code

---

698. ***CiCóCet*** with the plural suffix is *-im*

sing/pl	Gloss	const.	my/your/his/her	our/your/their
שִׁבֹּלֶת נ׳	stalk (of	-שִׁבֹּלֶת	**שִׁבָּלְ**תִּי/תְּךָ/תֵּךְ/תּוֹ/תָּהּ	**שִׁבָּלְ**תֵּנוּ/תְּכֶם/תְּכֶן/תָּם/תָּן
שִׁבּוֹלִים	grain)	-שִׁבּוֹלֵי	**שִׁבּוֹ**לַי/לֶיךָ/לַיִךְ/לָיו/לֶיהָ	**שִׁבּוֹלֵי**נוּ/כֶם/כֶן/הֶם/הֶן

The declension of singular forms essentially follows the segholate model, and the base with *kamats katan* (in a closed syllable) surfaces before suffix. The plural suffix is *–im*.

Examples

החקלאי בדק את מצב החיטה, ושמח לראות שה**שִׁבּוֹלִים** בשלות ומלאות גרגירים גדולים.
The farmer checked the wheat's growth, and was pleased to see that the **stalks** are ripe and full of large grains.

Special Expressions

שִׁבֹּלֶת שועל oats, oatmeal

---

699. ***CuCéCet***, no plural

sing/pl	Gloss	const.	my/your/his/her	our/your/their
הֻלֶּדֶת נ׳	birth	-הֻלֶּדֶת	**הֻלַּדְ**תִּי/תְּךָ/תֵּךְ/תּוֹ/תָּהּ	**הֻלַּדְ**תֵּנוּ/תְּכֶם/תְּכֶן/תָּם/תָּן

The declension essentially follows the segholate model, and the base with *pataH* (in a closed syllable) surfaces before suffixes. No plural forms.

Examples

את **הֻלֶּדֶת** הרעיון של מדינת היהודים נוהגים לייחס לקונגרס הציוני הראשון בבאזל ב-1897.
They usually attribute the **birth** of the notion of a Jewish state to the First Zionist Congress in Basel in 1897.

Special Expressions

יום **הֻלֶּדֶת** **birth**day

סֻכֶּרֶת נעורים juvenile onset **diabetes**

Additional Examples in this Pattern

diabetes סֻכֶּרֶת

---

700. *CuCéCet* plural *-im*

our/your/their	my/your/his/her	const.	Gloss	sing/pl
כֻּסַּמְתֵּנוּ/תְּכֶם/תְּכֶן/תָּם/תָּן	**כֻּסַּמְ**תִּי/תְּךָ/תֵּךְ/תּוֹ/תָּהּ	כֻּסֶּמֶת-	buckwheat	כֻּסֶּמֶת נ'
כֻּסְּמֵינוּ/כֶם/כֶן/הֶם/הֶן	**כֻּסְּ**מַי/מֶיךָ/מַיִךְ/מָיו/מֶיהָ	כֻּסְּמֵי-		כֻּסְּמִים

The singular declension essentially follows the segholate model, and the base with *pataH* (in a closed syllable) surfaces before suffixes. The plural suffix is *–im.*

Examples

ה**כֻּסֶּמֶת** ושיבולת השועל נחשבות לדגנים בריאים.
Buckwheat and oats are considered to be healthy cereals.

---

701. *CuCéCet* = *CuCáCat*, 3rd root consonant is *`ayin*

our/your/their	my/your/his/her	const.	Gloss	sing/pl
קֻבַּעֲתֵּנוּ/תְּכֶם/תְּכֶן/תָּם/תָּן	**קֻבַּעֲ**תִּי/תְּךָ/תֵּךְ/תּוֹ/תָּהּ	קֻבַּעַת-	cup Lit.-	קֻבַּעַת נ'
קֻבְּעוֹתֵינוּ/כֶם/כֶן/הֶם/הֶן	**קֻבְּעוֹ**תַי/תֶיךָ/תַיִךְ/תָיו/תֶיהָ	קֻבְּעוֹת-	Rare	קֻבָּעוֹת

The singular isolation form and the singular construct are with two *pataH*s, owing to the presence of the ע'. The declension is similar to that of צַלַּחַת above (but with *kubuts*), but today the preference is for *Hataf-pataH* under the ע' – which reflects the common pronunciation.

Special Expressions

of sorrow (flowery) cup **קֻבַּעַת** כוס התרעלה

---

702. *CCéCet* with *i* in the declension

our/your/their	my/your/his/her	const.	Gloss	sing/pl
גְּבִרְתֵּנוּ/תְּכֶם/תְּכֶן/תָּם/תָּן	**גְּבִרְ**תִּי/תְּךָ/תֵּךְ/תּוֹ/תָּהּ	גְּבֶרֶת-	lady, madame;	גְּבֶרֶת נ'
גְּבִירוֹתֵינוּ/כֶם/כֶן/הֶם/הֶן	**גְּבִירוֹ**תַי/תֶיךָ/תַיִךְ/תָיו/תֶיהָ	גְּבִירוֹת-	Mrs., Miss, Ms.	גְּבָרוֹת

The declension of singular forms essentially follows the segholate model, and the base is realized with *Hirik* (in a closed syllable) before a suffix. גְּבָרוֹת itself looks like a segholate, but the other plural forms do not. The plural of כְּנֶסֶת has two alternative realizations: כְּנָסוֹת, כְּנֶסֶת-, כְּנֶסֶת, כְּנָסוֹתַי..., or כְּנֵסִיּוֹת, כְּנֵסִיּוֹת-, כְּנֵסִיּוֹתַי...

Examples

גְּבֶרֶת גולדמן מעולם לא יוצאת מן הבית.
Mrs. Goldman never leaves the house.
חדר השירותים ל**גְבָרוֹת** נמצא בסוף המסדרון, בצד ימין.

The **ladies**' room is at the end of the corridor, on the right

בַּכְּנֶסֶת של מדינת ישראל יש 120 נציגים.
In the Israeli **parliament (Knesset)** there are 120 representatives.

Special Expressions

גְּבִירוֹתַי ורבותי ladies and gentlemen
גְּבֶרֶת נכבדה Dear **Lady** (in letter)
ה**גְּבֶרֶת** הראשונה the First **Lady**
אותה **גְּבֶרֶת** בשינוי אדרת It's the same thing, even if it looks different

כְּנֶסֶת ישראל the Jewish people (flowery); the Israeli parliament
כְּנֶסֶת הגדולה the Great Assembly (supreme council during Second Temple period)

---

703. ***CCéCet* = *CaCéCet*** with *pataH* in the declension, 1st root cons. guttural

our/your/their	my/your/his/her	const.	Gloss	sing/pl
עֲצַרְתֵּנוּ/תְּכֶם/תְּכֶן/תָּם/תָּן	**עֲצַרְ**תִּי/תְּךָ/תֵּךְ/תּוֹ/תָּהּ	עֲצֶרֶת-	assembly; last day of some Jewish holidays	עֲצֶרֶת נ׳
עַצְרוֹתֵינוּ/כֶם/כֶן/הֶם/הֶן	**עַצְרוֹ**תַי/תֶיךָ/תַיִךְ/תָיו/תֶיהָ	עַצְרוֹת-		עֲצָרוֹת

When a *shva* is expected with a guttural, it is replaced by *Hataf-pataH*. The declension essentially follows the segholate model: in the singular the base is realized with *pataH* (in a closed syllable) before a suffix. In the plural the *kamats* is reduced to *shva* two syllables before the stress, but consequently the preceding *Hataf* is replaced by *pataH*: a *Hataf-shva* sequence is hard to articulate.

Examples

מנהיג האופוזיציה קרא לכינוס **עֲצֶרֶת** עם להבעת מחאה על עליית מחירי הדלק.
The leader of the opposition called for the convening of a mass **assembly** to protest the rise in gasoline prices.

כשפניו של אדם אינם מפגינים כל רגשות כלפי חוץ, קוראים ל**אֲרֶשֶׁת** פניו פני פּוֹקֶר.
When a person's face does not reflect any emotions, they call his **expression** "poker face."

בליל הסדר, ה**חֲזֶרֶת** מייצגת את המרור.
In the Passover evening meal, **horse radish** represents the bitter herb.

Special Expressions

אֲרֶשֶׁת פנים appearance, expression
עֲצֶרֶת האו״ם the UN General Assembly
עֲצֶרֶת עם mass assembly

שמיני **עֲצֶרֶת** last day of the Feast of Tabernacles
עֲקֶרֶת בית housewife

Additional Examples in this Pattern

חֲזֶרֶת horse radish | עֲקֶרֶת housewife | עֲשֶׂרֶת group of ten

---

704. ***CCéCet*** with *e* in the declension, no plural

our/your/their	my/your/his/her	const.	Gloss	sing/pl
תְּכֶלְתֵּנוּ/תְּכֶם/תְּכֶן/תָּם/תָּן	**תְּכֶלְ**תִּי/תְּךָ/תֵּךְ/תּוֹ/תָּהּ	תְּכֵלֶת-	pale blue, azure	תְּכֵלֶת נ׳

The declension of singular forms essentially follows the segholate model, and the base is realized with *seghol* (in a closed syllable) before suffix. No plural.

Examples

צבעי דגל של מדינת ישראל מבוססים על ה**תְּכֵלֶת**, צבע המעיל שהיה חלק מבגדי הכהן הגדול, ועל צבעי הטלית והציצית.

The colors of the flag of the state of Israel are based on the **blue/azure**, which was the color of the cloak that was part of the garments of the high priest (in the Temple) and on the colors of the prayer shawl and its fringes.

Special Expressions

Côte d'**Azur**, the French Riviera חוף ה**תְּכֵלֶת**

---

705. ***CCéCet = CCáCat*** when the 3rd root consonant is ח'

our/your/their	my/your/his/her	const.	Gloss	sing/pl
מְלַחְתֵּנוּ/תְּכֶם/תְּכֶן/תָּם/תָּן	**מְלַחְ**תִּי/תְּךָ/תֵּךְ/תּוֹ/תָּהּ	מְלַחַת-	saltpeter	מְלַחַת נ׳
מַלְחוֹתֵינוּ/כֶם/כֶן/הֶם/הֶן	**מַלְחוֹ**תַי/תֶיךָ/תַיִךְ/תָיו/תֶיהָ	מַלְחוֹת-		מְלָחוֹת

The declension more-or-less follows the segholate*s*; the singular isolation form and the singular construct are with two *pataH*s instead of two *seghol*s, owing to the presence of the guttural.

---

706. ***CCéCet = CCáCat*** when the third root consonant is ע'

our/your/their	my/your/his/her	const.	Gloss	sing/pl
פְּקַעֲתֵנוּ/תְכֶם/תְכֶן/תָם/תָן	**פְּקַעֲ**תִי/תְךָ/תֵךְ/תוֹ/תָהּ	פְּקַעַת-	bulb	פְּקַעַת נ׳
פַּקְעוֹתֵינוּ/כֶם/כֶן/הֶם/הֶן	**פַּקְעוֹ**תַי/תֶיךָ/תַיִךְ/תָיו/תֶיהָ	פַּקְעוֹת-		פְּקָעוֹת

The singular isolation form and the singular construct are with two *pataH*s, owing to the presence of the ע׳. The declension is similar to that of מְלַחַת above, but today the preference is for *Hataf-pataH* under the ע׳ – which reflects the common pronunciation.

Examples

פְּקַעַת היא אבר תת-קרקעי לאגירת מזון בצמחים רב-שנתיים מסוימים.

A **bulb** is an under-the-ground food storage part of some perennial plants.

Special Expressions

bundle of nerves **פְּקַעַת** עצבים

---

707. *CCéCet* = *CCáCat* when the 3rd root cons. is 'ע, plural *-im*

our/your/their	my/your/his/her	const.	Gloss	sing/pl
דְּלַעְתֵּנוּ/תְכֶם/תְכֶן/תָם/תָן	**דְּלַעְ**תִּי/תְךָ/תֵךְ/תוֹ/תָהּ	דְּלַעַת-	pumpkin	דְּלַעַת נ'
דְּלָעֵינוּ/כֶם/כֶן/הֶם/הֶן	**דְּלָעַ**י/עֶיךָ/עַיִךְ/עָיו/עֶיהָ	דְּלוּעֵי-		דְּלוּעִים

The singular isolation form and the singular construct are with two *pataHs*, owing to the presence of the 'ע. The declension is similar to that of פְּקַעַת above, but the plural suffix is ים-.

Examples

ה**דְּלַעַת** פופולרית בבישול, ומשמשת לפיסול (ג'יק-או-לנטרן) כחלק מחגיגות ליל כל הקדושים.
The **pumpkin** is popular in cooking, and when carved (jack-o'-lantern) is part of the Halloween celebration.

---

708. *CCóCet*

our/your/their	my/your/his/her	const.	Gloss	sing/pl
כְּתָבְתֵּנוּ/תְּכֶם/תְּכֶן/תָּם/תָּן	**כְּתָבְ**תִּי/תְּךָ/תֵּךְ/תּוֹ/תָּהּ	כְּתֹבֶת-	address;	כְּתֹבֶת נ'
כְּתוֹבוֹתֵינוּ/כֶם/כֶן/הֶם/הֶן	**כְּתוֹבוֹ**תַי/תֶיךָ/תַיִךְ/תָיו/תֶיהָ	כְּתוֹבוֹת-	inscription	כְּתוֹבוֹת

The declension of singular forms essentially follows the segholate model, and the base with *kamats katan* (in a closed syllable) surfaces before a suffix. A significant number of the occurrences do not have plural forms in use.

Examples

מהי **כְּתֹבֶת** הדואר האלקטרוני שלך?
What is your email address?

כל פעם שמתגלית **כְּתֹבֶת** שמית עתיקה, זוהי חגיגה גדולה לחוקרי השפות השמיות העתיקות.
Any time a new Semitic **inscription** is discovered, it is a cause for celebration for researchers of ancient Semitic languages.

אחת הבעיות הקשות ביותר של עיר גדולה היא מה לעשות עם כמויות ה**פְּסֹלֶת** האדירות המצטברות בה בדי יום ביומו.
One of the most difficult problems of a large city is what to do with the huge quantities of **garbage** accumulated in it every single day.

פועלי מנסרות ונגרים משתמשים בדרך כלל במסכות כדי לא לנשום יותר מדיי **נְסֹרֶת**.
Sawmill workers and carpenters often use masks so as not to breathe in too much **sawdust**.

הסכנה בפצצה גרעינית היא לא רק בפיצוץ האדיר עצמו, אלא גם ב**נְפֹלֶת** הרדיואקטיבית שבעקבותיה.
The danger of a nuclear bomb is not just in the huge blast itself, but also in the radioactive **fallout** the follows it.

רוכלים בדוכני רחוב לעתים מדליקים מקלות **קְטֹרֶת** כדי למשוך תשומת לב למרכולתם.
Street vendors sometimes light **incense** sticks in order to attract attention to their wares.

Special Expressions

כְּתֹבֶת קעקע tattoo
כְּתֹבֶת על הקיר warning **sign**
יְכֹלֶת כל omni**potence**

Additional Examples in this Pattern

גְּרֹפֶת silt, alluvium, sediment
גְּרֹדֶת grated citrus peel
יְבֹשֶׁת dryness, indifference
יְכֹלֶת capacity
יְרֹקֶת scum (stagnant water); patina
נְעֹרֶת chaff
נְצֹלֶת manufacturing reusable waste; salvage
נְשֹׁרֶת fallout; waste
פְּסֹקֶת part, parting (hairdressing)
רְשֹׁמֶת sketch; epigraph
שְׁפֹכֶת debris

---

709. *CCóCet* = *CaCóCet* when the first root consonant is guttural

our/your/their	my/your/his/her	const.	Gloss	sing/pl
חֲרָסְתֵּנוּ/תְּכֶם/תְּכֶן/תָּם/תָּן	**חֲרָסְ**תִּי/תְּךָ/תֵּךְ/תּוֹ/תָּהּ	חֲרֹסֶת-	Haroset (eaten at	חֲרֹסֶת נ׳
חֲרוֹסוֹתֵינוּ/כֶם/כֶן/הֶם/הֶן	**חֲרוֹסוֹ**תַי/תֶיךָ/תַיִךְ/תָיו/תֶיהָ	חֲרוֹסוֹת-	Passover Seder)	חֲרוֹסוֹת

The declension of singular forms essentially follows the segholate model, and the base with *kamats katan* (in a closed syllable) surfaces before suffix. When a *shva* is expected with a guttural, it is replaced by *Hataf-pataH*.

Examples

מכיוון שה**חֲרֹסֶת** מתוקה, היא המאכל החביב ביותר על הילדים בליל הסדר.
Since the **Haroset** is sweet, it is the children's favorite item on Passover night.

חֲרֹשֶׁת היא תעשיית ייצור, וכן מלאכה הנעשית בסדנה, בעיקר בעבודת מכונות.
Haroshet is **production industry**, as well as any workshop production, particularly where machines are used.

Special Expressions

בית **חֲרֹשֶׁת** factory, plant
חֲרֹשֶׁת של שמועות rumors going around

Additional Examples in this Pattern

חֲרֹתֶת graffito (archeol.), engraved inscription

---

710. *C(e)CóCet* with *kubuts* in the declension, no plural

our/your/their	my/your/his/her	const.	Gloss	sing/pl
נְחֻשְׁתֵּנוּ/תְּכֶם/תְּכֶן/תָּם/תָּן	**נְחֻשְׁ**תִּי/תְּךָ/תֵּךְ/תּוֹ/תָּהּ	נְחֹשֶׁת-	copper	נְחֹשֶׁת נ׳

The declension of singular forms essentially follows the segholate model, and the base with *kubuts* (in a closed syllable) surfaces before suffix. No plural.

Examples

חשיבותה הגדולה של ה**נְחֹשֶׁת** היא בהיותה מוליכה מצוינת של חשמל.
The great importance of **copper** is its being an excellent conductor of electricity.

Special Expressions

(biblical) burnished brass; (archaic) bronze **נְחֹשֶׁת** קלל

---

711. *niCCéCet*

our/your/their	my/your/his/her	const.	Gloss	sing/pl
נִגְזַרְתֵּנוּ/תְּכֶם/תְּכֶן/תָּם/תָּן	**נִגְזַרְ**תִּי/תְּךָ/תֵּךְ/תּוֹ/תָּהּ	נִגְזֶרֶת-	derivative;	נִגְזֶרֶת נ'
נִגְזְרוֹתֵינוּ/כֶם/כֶן/הֶם/הֶן	**נִגְזְרוֹ**תַי/תֶיךָ/תַיִךְ/תָיו/תֶיהָ	נִגְזְרוֹת-	by-product	נִגְזָרוֹת

This is an independent feminine form of the present participle of *nif'al*. The declension essentially follows the segholate model, and the base with *pataH* (in a closed syllable) surfaces before suffixes. In the plural forms the *kamats* is reduced to *shva* two syllables away from the stress.

Examples

המילה ״יַלְדּוּתִי״ היא **נִגְזֶרֶת** של ״יַלְדוּת״; ״יַלְדוּתִיוּת״ היא **נִגְזֶרֶת** של ״יַלְדוּתִי״.
yalduti 'childish' is a derivative of *yaldut* 'childhood'; *yaldutiyut* 'childishness' is a derivative of *yalduti* 'childish.'

Additional Examples in this Pattern

trailer נִגְרֶרֶת

---

712. *niCCéCet*, when the second root consonant is guttural

our/your/their	my/your/his/her	const.	Gloss	sing/pl
נִבְחַרְתֵּנוּ/תְּכֶם/תְּכֶן/תָּם/תָּן	**נִבְחַרְ**תִּי/תְּךָ/תֵּךְ/תּוֹ/תָּהּ	נִבְחֶרֶת-	team (usu.	נִבְחֶרֶת נ'
נִבְחֲרוֹתֵינוּ/כֶם/כֶן/הֶם/הֶן	**נִבְחֲרוֹ**תַי/תֶיךָ/תַיִךְ/תָיו/תֶיהָ	נִבְחֲרוֹת-	in sports)	נִבְחָרוֹת

This is an independent feminine form of the present participle of *nif'al*. The declension essentially follows the segholate model, and the base with *pataH* (in a closed syllable) surfaces before suffixes. In the plural forms the *kamats* is reduced to *shva* two syllables away from the stress. When a *shva* is expected with a guttural, it is replaced by *Hataf-pataH*.

Examples

ה**נִבְחֶרֶת** הישראלית בכדורגל מעולם לא הגיעה אפילו לשלבי הגמר במונדיאל.
The Israeli soccer **team** has never even made it to the finals of the world championship.

Special Expressions

youth **team** **נִבְחֶרֶת** נוער

---

713. *CiCCéCet*

our/your/their	my/your/his/her	const.	Gloss	sing/pl
נִבְרַשְׁתֵּנוּ/תְּכֶם/תְּכֶן/תָּם/תָּן	**נִבְרַשְׁ**תִּי/תְּךָ/תֵּךְ/תּוֹ/תָּהּ	נִבְרֶשֶׁת-	chandelier	נִבְרֶשֶׁת נ׳
נִבְרְשׁוֹתֵינוּ/כֶם/כֶן/הֶם/הֶן	**נִבְרְשׁוֹ**תַי/תֶיךָ/תַיִךְ/תָיו/תֶיהָ	נִבְרְשׁוֹת-		נִבְרָשׁוֹת

The derivational class is quadrilateral. The declension essentially follows the segholate model, and the base with *pataH* (in a closed syllable) surfaces before suffixes. In the plural forms the *kamats* is reduced to *shva* two syllables away from the stress.

Examples

נִבְרֶשֶׁת היא מנורה גדולה הנתלית בתקרה, המכילה בדרך כלל כמה מנורות קטנות.
A **chandelier** is a large lamp hanging from the ceiling, which generally includes a number of smaller lamps.

Additional Examples in this Pattern

urticaria, nettle rash סִרְפֶּדֶת

---

714. *CiCCéCet* with reduplication

our/your/their	my/your/his/her	const.	Gloss	sing/pl
צִנְצַנְתֵּנוּ/תְּכֶם/תְּכֶן/תָּם/תָּן	**צִנְצַנְ**תִּי/תְּךָ/תֵּךְ/תּוֹ/תָּהּ	צִנְצֶנֶת-	jar	צִנְצֶנֶת נ׳
צִנְצְנוֹתֵינוּ/כֶם/כֶן/הֶם/הֶן	**צִנְצְנוֹ**תַי/תֶיךָ/תַיִךְ/תָיו/תֶיהָ	צִנְצְנוֹת-		צִנְצָנוֹת

The derivational class is quadrilateral, i.e., *CiCCéCet*, but since the first root consonant is reduplicated in position three, and the second in position four, the representation קִטְקֶטֶת is more appropriate. The declension, as in *CiCCéCet* above, essentially follows the segholate model, and the base with *pataH* (in a closed syllable) surfaces before suffixes. In the plural forms the *kamats* is reduced to *shva* two syllables away from the stress.

Examples

להכנת ביתית של שימורי ירקות ופירות, הפופולרית באזורים הכפריים של ארה״ב, דרושות הרבה **צִנְצָנוֹת**...
For home preparation of vegetable and fruit preserves, which is popular in the rural areas of the US, many **jars** are needed...

Additional Examples in this Pattern

paprika, pepper פִּלְפֶּלֶת

---

715. *CaCCéCet*

our/your/their	my/your/his/her	const.	Gloss	sing/pl
אַרְנַבְתֵּנוּ/תְּכֶם/תְּכֶן/תָּם/תָּן	**אַרְנַבְ**תִּי/תְּךָ/תֵּךְ/תּוֹ/תָּהּ	אַרְנֶבֶת-	rabbit,	אַרְנֶבֶת נ'
אַרְנְבוֹתֵינוּ/כֶם/כֶן/הֶם/הֶן	**אַרְנְבוֹ**תַי/תֶיךָ/תַיִךְ/תָיו/תֶיהָ	אַרְנְבוֹת-	hare (fm.)	אַרְנָבוֹת

The derivational class is quadriliteral. The declension essentially follows the segholate model, and the base with *pataH* (in a closed syllable) surfaces before suffixes. In the plural forms the *kamats* is reduced to *shva* two syllables away from the stress.

Examples

בדיחה ישראלית: איך תופסים **אַרְנֶבֶת**? משמיעים קולות של כרוב.
Israeli joke: How do you catch a **rabbit**? You make cabbage noises.

הָאַסְפֶּסֶת שייכת למשפחת הקטניות, ומשמשת למאכל בהמות ולשחת.
The **lucerne** is a member of the bean family, and serves as food and hay for cattle.

במלחמת העולם השנייה קנדי היה מפקד **טַרְפֶּדֶת** באוקיינוס השקט.
In WWII, Kennedy was a **torpedo boat** commander in the Pacific.

היום, כשהמחשבים והסמרטפונים מכילים מידע כה רב, אין כל כך צורך **בְּכַּרְטֶסוֹת**.
Today, when commuters and smartphones contain so much information, there is less of a need for **card indices**.

הסרת **הַקַּרְקֶפֶת** על ידי הלוחמים האינדיאנים בצפון אמריקה הייתה הרבה פחות נפוצה ממה שנהוג לחשוב.
Removal of **scalps** by Indian warriors in North America was far less common than what people believe.

Special Expressions

שַׁלְבֶּקֶת חוגרת shingles, herpes zoster

Additional Examples in this Pattern

גַּרְעֶנֶת trachoma
סַנְוֶרֶת visor
סַרְכֶּזֶת centrifuge
סַרְעֶפֶת diaphragm
שַׁלְבֶּקֶת herpes
שַׁלְהֶבֶת flame

---

716. *CaCCéCet* = *CaCCáCat*, last consonant is guttural

our/your/their	my/your/his/her	const.	Gloss	sing/pl
אַמְתַּחְתֵּנוּ/תְּכֶם/תְּכֶן/תָּם/תָּן	**אַמְתַּחְ**תִּי/תְּךָ/תֵּךְ/תּוֹ/תָּהּ	אַמְתַּחַת-	sack, bag	אַמְתַּחַת נ'
אַמְתְּחוֹתֵינוּ/כֶם/כֶן/הֶם/הֶן	**אַמְתְּחוֹ**תַי/תֶיךָ/תַיִךְ/תָיו/תֶיהָ	אַמְתְּחוֹת-		אַמְתָּחוֹת

The declension is as in *CaCCéCet* above, but the two *seghol*s in the singular, in the isolation form as well as in the construct, are replaced by two *pataH*s owing to the guttural.

Examples

אַמְתַּחַת היא תחליף ספרותי לתרמיל או שק.
amtaHat is a literary variant of the common word for **bag** or **sack**.

---

717. ***CaCCéCet*** **with reduplication (קַטְקֶטֶת)**

our/your/their	my/your/his/her	const.	Gloss	sing/pl
גַּרְגַּרְתֵּנוּ/תְּכֶם/תְּכֶן/תָּם/תָּן	**גַּרְגַּרְ**תִּי/תְּךָ/תֵּךְ/תּוֹ/תָּהּ	-גַּרְגֶּרֶת	trachea,	גַּרְגֶּרֶת נ׳
גַּרְגְּרוֹתֵינוּ/כֶם/כֶן/הֶם/הֶן	**גַּרְגְּרוֹ**תַי/תֶיךָ/תַיִךְ/תָיו/תֶיהָ	-גַּרְגְּרוֹת	windpipe	גַּרְגָּרוֹת

The derivational class is quadrilateral, i.e., *CaCCeCet*, but since the first root consonant is reduplicated in position three, and the second in position four, the representation קַטְקֶטֶת is more appropriate. The declension, as in *CaCCeCet* above, essentially follows the segholate model, and the base with *pataH* (in a closed syllable) surfaces before suffixes. In the plural forms the *kamats* is reduced to *shva* two syllables away from the stress.

Examples

בדרך כלל, פיקת ה**גַּרְגֶּרֶת** בולטת יותר אצל גברים רזים.
In general, Adam's apple (of the **windpipe**) is more prominent in thin men.

ישראל חלוצה בנושא של **טַפְטָפוֹת** בהשקייה.
Israel has been doing pioneering work in the area of **drip irrigation systems**.

דיברו הרבה בפגישה הזו, הרבה **קַשְׁקֶשֶׁת**, אבל לא הושגה כל התקדמות.
They talked a lot during that meeting, a lot of **prattle**, but no progress was made.

נעים תמיד לסיים ארוחה עם **רַפְרֶפֶת**.
It is always nice to finish a meal with a **mousse dessert**.

Additional Examples in this Pattern

chatter, babble Sl. בַּרְבֶּרֶת
pulley block גַּלְגֶּלֶת
loose-leaf folder דַּפְדֶּפֶת
bird droppings לַשְׁלֶשֶׁת
dandruff; fish scales קַשְׂקֶשֶׂת
weather vane שַׁבְשֶׁבֶת
jock itch; door mat שַׁפְשֶׁפֶת

---

718. ***CaCCéCet*** **with reduplication (קַטְקֶטֶת), plural either regular, or with** ***–a'ot***

our/your/their	my/your/his/her	const.	Gloss	sing/pl
שַׁלְשַׁלְתֵּנוּ/תְּכֶם/תְּכֶן/תָּם/תָּן	**שַׁלְשַׁלְ**תִּי/תְּךָ/תֵּךְ/תּוֹ/תָּהּ	-שַׁלְשֶׁלֶת	heavy	שַׁלְשֶׁלֶת נ׳
שַׁלְשְׁלוֹתֵינוּ/כֶם/כֶן/הֶם/הֶן	**שַׁלְשְׁלוֹ**תַי/תֶיךָ/תַיִךְ/תָיו/תֶיהָ/	-שַׁלְשְׁלוֹת/	chain	שַׁלְשָׁלוֹת/
שַׁלְשְׁלָאוֹתֵינוּ/כֶם/כֶן/הֶם/הֶן	**שַׁלְשְׁלָאוֹ**תַי/תֶיךָ/תַיִךְ/תָיו/תֶיהָ	-שַׁלְשְׁלָאוֹת		שַׁלְשְׁלָאוֹת

The declension is as in קַטְקֶטֶת above; the plural suffix is either regular, or *–a'ot*.

Examples

תמורות היסטוריות בדרך כלל לא מתרחשות בבת אחת; קודמים להם **שַׁלְשֶׁלֶת** אירועים והתפתחויות שונות – כלכליות, חברתיות, וכו'.

Historical transformations generally do not occur all of a sudden; they are preceded by a **chain** of events and different developments – economic, social, etc..

Special Expressions

family tree, genealogy, pedigree **שַׁלְשֶׁלֶת** יוחסין

---

719. ***CaCCéCet*** with reduplication (קַטְקֶטֶת) plural with *–a'ot*

our/your/their	my/your/his/her	const.	Gloss	sing/pl
שַׁרְשַׁרְתֵּנוּ/תְּכֶם/תְּכֶן/תָּם/תָּן	**שַׁרְשַׁרְ**תִּי/תְּךָ/תֵּךְ/תּוֹ/תָּהּ	שַׁרְשֶׁרֶת-	chain	שַׁרְשֶׁרֶת נ'
שַׁרְשְׁרָאוֹתֵינוּ/כֶם/כֶן/הֶם/הֶן	**שַׁרְשְׁרָאוֹ**תַי/תֶיךָ/תַיִךְ/תָיו/תֶיהָ	שַׁרְשְׁרָאוֹת-		שַׁרְשְׁרָאוֹת

The declension is as in קַטְקֶטֶת above; the plural suffix is *–a'ot*.

Examples

בביקורים של מנהיגים פוליטיים ואחרים בערים גדולות, מפרידים בדרך כלל בין המנהיגים והציבור באמצעות **שַׁרְשְׁרָאוֹת**.

During visits of political figures and others in big cities, they usually separate between the leaders and the public by means of **chains**.

Special Expressions

human chain **שַׁרְשֶׁרֶת** אדם/אנושית

---

720. ***CaCCóCet***

our/your/their	my/your/his/her	const.	Gloss	sing/pl
כַּרְבָּלְתֵּנוּ/תְּכֶם/תְּכֶן/תָּם/תָּן	**כַּרְבָּלְ**תִּי/תְּךָ/תֵּךְ/תּוֹ/תָּהּ	כַּרְבֹּלֶת-	crest (of	כַּרְבֹּלֶת נ'
כַּרְבּוֹלוֹתֵינוּ/כֶם/כֶן/הֶם/הֶן	**כַּרְבּוֹלוֹ**תַי/תֶיךָ/תַיִךְ/תָיו/תֶיהָ	כַּרְבּוֹלוֹת-	a bird)	כַּרְבּוֹלוֹת

The derivational class is quadrilateral. The declension essentially follows the segholate model, and in the singular forms the base with *kamats katan* (in a closed syllable) surfaces before suffixes.

Examples

כַּרְבָּלְתּוֹ של התרנגול זקופה וגדולה מזו של התרנגולת.

A rooster's **crest** is more erect and larger than that of the hen.

Additional Examples in this Pattern

milling machine כַּרְסֹמֶת

---

721. ***CaCCóCet*** **with reduplication (קַטְקֹטֶת)**

our/your/their	my/your/his/her	const.	Gloss	sing/pl
סַגְסָגְתֵּנוּ/תְּכֶם/תְּכֶן/תָּם/תָּן	**סַגְסָגְ**תִּי/תְּךָ/תֵּךְ/תּוֹ/תָּהּ	סַגְסֹגֶת-	alloy	סַגְסֹגֶת נ׳
סַגְסוּגוֹתֵינוּ/כֶם/כֶן/הֶם/הֶן	**סַגְסוּגוֹ**תַי/תֶיךָ/תַיִךְ/תָיו/תֶיהָ	סַגְסוּגוֹת-		סַגְסוּגוֹת

The derivational class is quadrilateral, i.e., *CaCCóCet*, but since the first root consonant is reduplicated in position three, and the second in position four, the representation קַטְקֹטֶת is more appropriate. The declension of the singular, as in *CaCCóCet* above, essentially follows the segholate model, and the base with *kamats katan* (in a closed syllable) surfaces before suffixes.

Examples

מרבית המטבעות מיוצרות מ**סַגְסֹגֶת** של מתכות שונות.
Most coins are produced from an **alloy** made of a few metals.

Additional Examples in this Pattern

חַלְחֹלֶת rectum

---

722. ***CiCCóCet***

our/your/their	my/your/his/her	const.	Gloss	sing/pl
פִּרְסָמְתֵּנוּ/תְּכֶם/תְּכֶן/תָּם/תָּן	**פִּרְסָמְ**תִּי/תְּךָ/תֵּךְ/תּוֹ/תָּהּ	פִּרְסֹמֶת-	advertise-	פִּרְסֹמֶת נ׳
פִּרְסוֹמוֹתֵינוּ/כֶם/כֶן/הֶם/הֶן	**פִּרְסוֹמוֹ**תַי/תֶיךָ/תַיִךְ/תָיו/תֶיהָ	פִּרְסוֹמוֹת-	ment	פִּרְסוֹמוֹת

The derivational class is quadrilateral. The declension essentially follows the segholate model, and in the singular forms the base with *kamats katan* (in a closed syllable) surfaces before suffixes.

Examples

מפיק של סדרת טלוויזיה מצליחה בארה״ב אמר פעם שתפקיד כל תוכנית בטלוויזיה הוא בסך הכל לשמור על התעניינות הציבור בין ה**פִּרְסוֹמוֹת**, שימשיכו לצפות.
A producer of a successful TV series in the US said once that the purpose of any TV program is simply just to keep the public interested between the **commercials**, so that they continue to watch.

---

723. ***CiCCóCet*** **with reduplication, no plural**

our/your/their	my/your/his/her	const.	Gloss	sing/pl
בִּלְבָּלְתֵּנוּ/תְּכֶם/תְּכֶן/תָּם/תָּן	**בִּלְבָּלְ**תִּי/תְּךָ/תֵּךְ/תּוֹ/תָּהּ	בִּלְבֹּלֶת-	confusion, mix-up	בִּלְבֹּלֶת נ׳

The derivational class is quadrilateral, i.e., *CiCCóCet*, but since the first root consonant is reduplicated in position three, and the second in position four, the representation קִטְקֹטֶת is more appropriate. The declension essentially follows the segholate model, and the base with *kamats katan* (in a closed syllable) surfaces before suffixes.

Examples

יש מחזות מודרניים שה**בִּלְבֹּלֶת** בעלילתם היא כה גדולה, שאי אפשר להבין דבר וחצי דבר.
There are some modern plays in which the **confusion** in their story-line is so great, that one cannot understand anything at all.

---

724. *CuCCóCet* with reduplication

our/your/their	my/your/his/her	const.	Gloss	sing/pl
גֻּלְגָּלְתֵּנוּ/תְּכֶם/תְּכֶן/תָּם/תָּן	**גֻּלְגָּלְ**תִּי/תְּךָ/תֵּךְ/תּוֹ/תָּהּ	גֻּלְגֹּלֶת-	skull,	גֻּלְגֹּלֶת נ'
גֻּלְגְּלוֹתֵינוּ/כֶם/כֶן/הֶם/הֶן	**גֻּלְגְּלוֹ**תַי/תֶיךָ/תַיִךְ/תָיו/תֶיהָ	גֻּלְגְּלוֹת-	head	גֻּלְגָּלוֹת

The derivational class is quadrilateral, i.e., *CuCCóCet*, but since the first root consonant is reduplicated in position three, and the second in position four, the representation קֻטְקֹטֶת is more appropriate. The declension essentially follows the segholate model, and the base with *kamats katan* (in a closed syllable) surfaces before suffixes. In the plural forms the *kamats* is reduced to *shva* two syllables away from the stress.

Examples

הַמְלֶט התרגש כשראה את ה**גֻּלְגֹּלֶת** של יוריק.
Hamlet was moved when he saw Yorick's **skull**.

Special Expressions

per **capita** **לְגֻלְגֹּלֶת**

---

725. *CCoCéCet*

our/your/their	my/your/his/her	const.	Gloss	sing/pl
שְׁפוֹפַרְתֵּנוּ/תְּכֶם/תְּכֶן/תָּם/תָּן	**שְׁפוֹפַרְ**תִּי/תְּךָ/תֵּךְ/תּוֹ/תָּהּ	שְׁפוֹפֶרֶת-	tube; phone	שְׁפוֹפֶרֶת נ'
שְׁפוֹפְרוֹתֵינוּ/כֶם/כֶן/הֶם/הֶן	**שְׁפוֹפְרוֹ**תַי/תֶיךָ/תַיִךְ/תָיו/תֶיהָ	שְׁפוֹפְרוֹת-	receiver	שְׁפוֹפָרוֹת

The declension essentially follows the segholate model, and the base with *pataH* (in a closed syllable) surfaces before suffixes. In the plural forms the *kamats* is reduced to *shva* two syllables away from the stress.

Examples

בזמנו, **שְׁפוֹפְרוֹת** משחות השיניים היו עשויות ממתכת; היום רק מפלסטיק.
At the time, toothpaste **tubes** were made of metal; today they are made only of plastic.

שְׁפוֹפֶרֶת הטלפון משמשת היום בעיקר בטלפון קווי; היא אינה מתאימה לטלפון סלולרי.
Today the **telephone receiver** is used primarily for line phones; it is not appropriate for a cellular phone.

Additional Examples in this Pattern

punch, sharp blow Lit. סְנוֹקֶרֶת

---

726. *CCoCéCet* with reduplication

our/your/their	my/your/his/her	const.	Gloss	sing/pl
גְּנוֹגַנְתֵּנוּ/תְּכֶם/תְּכֶן/תָּם/תָּן	**גְּנוֹגַנְ**תִּי/תְּךָ/תֵּךְ/תּוֹ/תָּהּ	גְּנוֹגֶנֶת-	awning	גְּנוֹגֶנֶת נ׳
גְּנוֹגְנוֹתֵינוּ/כֶם/כֶן/הֶם/הֶן	**גְּנוֹגְנוֹ**תַי/תֶיךָ/תַיִךְ/תָיו/תֶיהָ	גְּנוֹגְנוֹת-		גְּנוֹגָנוֹת

The derivational class is quadrilateral, i.e., *CCoCéCet*, but since the first root consonant is reduplicated in position three, and the second in position four, the representation קְטוֹקֶטֶת is more appropriate. The declension essentially follows the segholate model, and the base with *pataH* (in a closed syllable) surfaces before suffixes. In the plural forms the *kamats* is reduced to *shva* two syllables away from the stress.

Examples

ה**גְּנוֹגֶנֶת** משמשת בעיקר להגנה מפני שמש וגשם כיושבים בשטח פתוח צמוד לבית.
An **awning** is used primarily for protection from sun and rain when sitting in an open space next to the house.

Additional Examples in this Pattern

גְּרוֹגֶרֶת dried fig (Talmudic) | קְנוֹקֶנֶת tendril

---

727. *CCoCéCet* = *CaCoCéCet* when the first root consonant is guttural

our/your/their	my/your/his/her	const.	Gloss	sing/pl
חֲטוֹטַרְתֵּנוּ/תְּכֶם/תְּכֶן/תָּם/תָּן	**חֲטוֹטַרְ**תִּי/תְּךָ/תֵּךְ/תּוֹ/תָּהּ	חֲטוֹטֶרֶת-	hump,	חֲטוֹטֶרֶת נ׳
חֲטוֹטְרוֹתֵינוּ/כֶם/כֶן/הֶם/הֶן	**חֲטוֹטְרוֹ**תַי/תֶיךָ/תַיִךְ/תָיו/תֶיהָ	חֲטוֹטְרוֹת-	gibbous	חֲטוֹטָרוֹת

The declension essentially follows the segholate model, and the base with *pataH* (in a closed syllable) surfaces before suffixes. In the plural forms the *kamats* is reduced to *shva* two syllables away from the stress. When a *shva* is expected with a guttural, it is replaced by *Hataf-pataH*.

Examples

האסוציאציה הראשונה של **חֲטוֹטֶרֶת** היא הגיבן מנוטר-דם.
The initial association of **hump** is the Hunchback of Notre Dame.

---

728. *CCaCCéCet* with reduplication, no plural

our/your/their	my/your/his/her	const.	Gloss	sing/pl
כְּלַבְלַבְתֵּנוּ/תְּכֶם/תְּכֶן/תָּם/תָּן	**כְּלַבְלַבְ**תִּי/תְּךָ/תֵּךְ/תּוֹ/תָּהּ	כְּלַבְלֶבֶת-	distemper	כְּלַבְלֶבֶת נ׳

Since the second root consonant is reduplicated in position four, and the third in position five, the representation is *CCaCCéCet*, or קְטַלְטֶלֶת. The declension essentially follows the segholate model, and the base with *pataH* (in a closed syllable) surfaces before suffixes.

Examples

כְּלַבְלֶבֶת היא מחלת כלבים פחות חמורה מאשר כלבת.
Distemper is a less serious sickness than rabies is.

---

729. ***CCaCéCet* = *CaCaCéCet*** with reduplication, when the first root consonant is guttural

our/your/their	my/your/his/her	const.	Gloss	sing/pl
חֲפַרְפַּרְתֵּנוּ/תְּכֶם/תְּכֶן/תָּם/תָּן	**חֲפַרְפַּרְ**תִּי/תְּךָ/תֵּךְ/תּוֹ/תָּהּ	חֲפַרְפֶּרֶת-	mole	חֲפַרְפֶּרֶת נ׳
חֲפַרְפְּרוֹתֵינוּ/כֶם/כֶן/הֶם/הֶן	**חֲפַרְפְּרוֹ**תַי/תֶיךָ/תַיִךְ/תָיו/תֶיהָ	חֲפַרְפְּרוֹת-		חֲפַרְפָּרוֹת

Since the second root consonant is reduplicated in position four, and the third in position five, the representation is קְטַלְטֶלֶת. The declension essentially follows the segholate model, and the base with *pataH* (in a closed syllable) surfaces before suffixes. In the plural forms the *kamats* is reduced to *shva* two syllables away from the stress. When a *shva* is expected with a guttural, it is replaced by *Hataf-pataH*. Hence: קֲטַלְטֶלֶת.

Examples

ל**חֲפַרְפֶּרֶת** יש יכולת חפירה מפותחת יותר מאשר לרוב בעלי החיים החופרים.
The **mole** is one of the most skillful diggers in the animal world.

---

730. ***CCaCCóCet*** with reduplication

our/your/their	my/your/his/her	const.	Gloss	sing/pl
סְחַרְחָרְתֵּנוּ/תְּכֶם/תְּכֶן/תָּם/תָּן	**סְחַרְחָרְ**תִּי/תְּךָ/תֵּךְ/תּוֹ/תָּהּ	סְחַרְחֹרֶת-	vertigo,	סְחַרְחֹרֶת נ׳
סְחַרְחוֹרוֹתֵינוּ/כֶם/כֶן/הֶם/הֶן	**סְחַרְחוֹרוֹ**תַי/תֶיךָ/תַיִךְ/תָיו/תֶיהָ	סְחַרְחוֹרוֹת-	dizziness	סְחַרְחוֹרוֹת

Since the second root consonant is reduplicated in position four, and the third in position five, the representation is קְטַלְטֹלֶת. The singular declension essentially follows the segholate model, and the base with *kamats katan* (in a closed syllable) surfaces before suffixes (in the singular).

Examples

ירידה מהירה מדיי מן המיטה גורמת לעתים ל**סְחַרְחֹרֶת**.
Getting too fast out of bed may sometimes cause **dizziness**.

Additional Examples in this Pattern

shivering, shuddering צְמַרְמֹרֶת   shuddering Lit. סְמַרְמֹרֶת

---

731. *CaCut*

our/your/their	my/your/his/her	const.	Gloss	sing/pl
כַּמוּתֵנוּ/תְכֶם/תְכֶן/תָם/תָן	**כַּמוּ**תִי/תְךָ/תֵךְ/תוֹ/תָהּ	כַּמוּת-	quantity,	כַּמוּת נ'
כַּמוּיוֹתֵינוּ/כֶם/כֶן/הֶם/הֶן	**כַּמוּיוֹ**תַי/תֶיךָ/תַיִךְ/תָיו/תֶיהָ	כַּמוּיוֹת-	amount	כַּמוּיוֹת

In most realizations (though not in all – see, for instance, כַּמוּת originating from כְּ-מָה) the *dagesh* originates from the merger of two identical consonants in positions two and three of the root (דל״ל, חד״ד). In the plural form with *+ot*, probably in order to avoid the sequence *…*utot*, the *t* of the singular (which is not a root consonant) is elided, and a transition *y*-glide is inserted, since a sequence of two vowels without a transition glide is not optimal. In earlier vocalization traditions the *y* itself had a *dagesh*, and therefore was preceded by *kubuts*, (e.g., כַּמֻּיּוֹת), but in 2009 the Hebrew Language Academy determined that a *shuruk* followed by *y* without *dagesh* will be more appropriate before *+ot* (e.g. כַּמוּיוֹת). The same applies to all other patterns ending with the suffix *+ut*, but note that a significant number of forms with *+ut* have no plural forms in actual use.

Examples

החוק קובע כי כאשר יצרני מזון מפרטים את מרכיבי המוצר, סדר הפירוט הוא על פי ה**כַּמוּת** היחסית של כל מרכיב.
The law says that when producers of food list the ingredients of a product, they should order them by the relative **quantity** of each ingredient.

ביאליק הגדיר את הצרצר כ״משורר ה**דַּלּוּת**״.
The poet Bialik called the cricket “the poet of **poverty**”.

הקומיקאים הטובים ביותר מצטיינים ב**חַדּוּת** לשונם.
The best comedians excel in the **sharpness** of their tongue.

המורים הגרועים ביותר הם אלה המתייחסים ב**גַסּוּת** לתלמידים ומשפילים אותם.
The worst teachers are those who treat their students with **rudeness** and humiliate them.

בפוליטיקה **רַכּוּת** בדיבור ובנאומים ציבוריים נתפסת כסימן של חולשה.
In politics, **softness** in speech and in political addresses is regarded as an indication of weakness.

Special Expressions

a negligible **amount** **כַּמוּת** מבוטלת
uncouthness, **rudeness** **גַסּוּת** רוח
impertinence, arrogance, vulgarity **עַזּוּת** מצח/פנים

lightheadedness, **recklessness** **קַלּוּת** דעת
frivolousness **קַלּוּת** ראש
fleet-footedness **קַלּוּת** רגליים
quick perceptiveness **קַלּוּת** תפיסה

Additional Examples in this Pattern

position אַיּוּת
thinness, fineness דַּקּוּת
innocence חַפּוּת

audacity; power, strength Lit.עַזּוּת
ease, easiness; lightness קַלּוּת
naiveté, innocence תַּמּוּת

732. *CaCut* with *h*, *H*, no *dagesh*

our/your/their	my/your/his/her	const.	Gloss	sing/pl
מַהוּתֵנוּ/תְכֶם/תְכֶן/תָם/תָן	**מַהוּ**תִי/תְךָ/תֵךְ/תוֹ/תָהּ	מַהוּת-	essence;	מַהוּת נ׳
מַהוּיוֹתֵינוּ/כֶם/כֶן/הֶם/הֶן	**מַהוּיוֹ**תַי/תֶיךָ/תַיִךְ/תָיו/תֶיהָ	מַהוּיוֹת-	being	מַהוּיוֹת

The declension is like כַּמּוּת above (including the transitional glide *y* in plural forms), but because of the ה׳ and the ח׳ there is no *dagesh*.

Examples

אומרים שדרך העיניים ניתן לגלות את **מַהוּתוֹ** הפנימית של אדם. אולי...
They say that one can discover the internal true **essence** of a person. Possibly…

בערי חוף כמו תל אביב ה**לַחוּת** הגבוהה בקיץ מקשה על הנשימה יותר מאשר החום הכבד.
In coastal cities like Tel Aviv the high **humidity** makes it harder to breathe than the heavy heat does.

בתרבויות מסוימות **צַחוּת** הדיבור נחשבת לחשובה יותר מן התוכן.
In some cultures the "**purity**" of language is regarded as more important than its content.

Special Expressions

relative **humidity** **לַחוּת** יחסית

---

733. *CaCut*

our/your/their	my/your/his/her	const.	Gloss	sing/pl
גָּלוּתֵנוּ/תְכֶם/תְכֶן/תָם/תָן	**גָּלוּ**תִי/תְךָ/תֵךְ/תוֹ/תָהּ	גָּלוּת-	exile;	גָּלוּת נ׳
גָּלוּיוֹתֵינוּ/כֶם/כֶן/הֶם/הֶן	**גָּלוּיוֹ**תַי/תֶיךָ/תַיִךְ/תָיו/תֶיהָ	גָּלוּיוֹת-	diaspora	גָּלוּיוֹת

The declension is like כַּמּוּת above (including the transitional glide *y* in plural forms), but with *kamats* instead of *pataH*, and there is no *dagesh*. Many of the forms are derived from roots with final *y* (orthographically *h*), some from roots with middle *w* or *y*. A good number of occurrences have no plural forms in actual use.

Examples

גָּלוּת בבל נמשכה שבעים שנה, עד שכורש הרשה לגולים לחזור לארצם.
The Babylonian **exile** lasted for seventy years, until Cyrus allowed the exiled Judeans to return to their homeland.

בתקופת מלחמת העולם השניה, כשבפולין שלטו הגרמנים, ישבה בלונדון ממשלה פולנית ב**גָּלוּת**.
During WWII, when Poland was occupied by the German, a Polish government in **exile** was in residence in London.

חָלוּת החוק תקפה לגבי כל אחד, כולל נשיא וראש ממשלה.
The **application** of the law is valid for everyone, including the President and the Prime Minister.

ערים מסוימות בארה״ב נותנות **חָסוּת** לפליטים שנכנסו למדינה אופן לא חוקי.
Certain cities in the US provide **protection** to refugees who enter the country illegally.

במדינות דמוקרטיות אמיתיות מקפידים מאוד על הפרדה בין שלוש ה**רָשׁוּיוֹת**.
In truly democratic countries they strictly separate between **authorities** (here: branches of government).

Special Expressions

גָּלוּת אשור the Assyrian **captivity**
גָּלוּת בבל the Babylonian **captivity**
יום טוב שני של **גָּלוּיוֹת** 2nd day of a festival, only in the **Diaspora**
כאורך ה**גָּלוּת** extremely long (lit. as long as the period of **exile**)
מיזוג **גָּלוּיוֹת** intermingling of the **exiles**

קיבוץ **גָּלוּיוֹת** ingathering of the **exiled**
רְשׁוּת השידור Israel Broadcasting Authority
רְשׁוּת מבצעת executive **authority**
רְשׁוּת מחוקקת legislative **authority**
רְשׁוּת שיפוטית judicial **authority**

Additional Examples in this Pattern

בָּרוּת diet
זָלוּת meanness, baseness, pettiness Lit.
הָגוּת meditation, contemplation
זָרוּת alienage, strangeness
חָבוּת liability, indebtedness (formal)
חָזוּת appearance

טָעוּת error
מָרוּת authority
נָכוּת disability, handicap
צָרוּת narrowness
רָאשׁוּת chairmanship, leadership

---

734. ***CCut***

our/your/their	my/your/his/her	const.	Gloss	sing/pl
זְכוּתֵנוּ/תְכֶם/תְכֶן/תָם/תָן	**זְכוּ**תִי/תְךָ/תֵךְ/תוֹ/תָהּ	-זְכוּת	right; merit;	זְכוּת נ׳
זְכוּיוֹתֵינוּ/כֶם/כֶן/הֶם/הֶן	**זְכוּיוֹ**תַי/תֶיךָ/תַיִךְ/תָיו/תֶיהָ	-זְכוּיוֹת	credit side	זְכוּיוֹת

The declension is like גָּלוּת above (including the transitional glide *y* in plural forms), but the first consonant comes with a *shva* instead of *kamats*.

Examples

לבעל הבית אין **זְכוּת** להיכנס לדירה שהשכיר למישהו אחר ללא הודעה מוקדמת ותיאום מראש.
A landlord has no **right** to enter an apartment he has rented to someone else without prior notice and prior arrangements.

על פי המסורת היהודית, העולם ממשיך להתקיים ב**זְכוּתָם** של ל״ו צדיקים החיים בו בכל נקודת זמן.
According to Jewish tradition, the world continues to exist thanks to (lit. based on the **merit** of) 36 righteous people who exist in it at any point in time.

כשמאזנים חשבון בנק, בעמודה אחת מציינים פעולות **זְכוּת**, ובשני פעולות חובה.
When one balances one's checkbook, one notes **credit** transactions in one column, and debit transactions in another.

דְּמוּת האימא (או האישה) הפולנייה היא במרכזן של הרבה בדיחות ישראליות.
The **figure** of the Polish mother/wife is at the center of many Israeli jokes.

שחקן טוב יודע לגלם **דְּמוּיוֹת** רבות ושונות באותה מידה של מהימנות והצלחה.
A good actor can play various different **characters** with the same degree of credibility and success.

יש ערים מסוימות, כמו אמסטרדם, למשל, שבהן עיסוק ב**זְנוּת** אינו נחשב לעבירה.
There are certain cities, such as Amsterdam, where **prostitution** is legal.

רציתי להגיד לו שהוא מדבר **שְׁטוּיוֹת**, אבל זה לא יעזור; הוא לא מוכן להקשיב לאף אחד.
I wanted to tell him that what he was saying was **nonsense**, but it won't help; he is not willing to listen to anybody.

מספר רבנים אשכנזים טוענים, בחוכמה, שלמרות שהראשונים היו גדולים מכולם בתורה, יש לנו היום יתרון אחד: אנחנו ננסים על כתפי ענקים, ולכן **רְאוּתֵנוּ** רחוקה יותר.
Some Ashkenazi rabbis wisely im that although the early Torah scholars were the greatest, we have one advantage today: we are dwarfs on the shoulders of giants, and thus our **visibility** goes even farther.

יש ילדים ש**תְּלוּתָם** בהורים ממשיכה גם בשנות העשרים של חייהם.
There are children whose **dependence** on their parents continues even in their twenties.

Special Expressions

thanks to **בִּזְכוּת**
hereditary **privilege** **זְכוּת** אבות
equal **rights** שיוויון **זְכוּיוֹת**
copy**right** **זְכוּת** יוצרים
all **rights** reserved כל ה**זְכוּיוֹת** שמורות
privilege **זְכוּת** יתר
human **rights** **זְכוּיוֹת** האדם

see one's **good side** לדון אותו לכף **זְכוּת**
may his **virtue** defend us **זְכוּתוֹ** יגן עלינו (when mentioning a dead sage)
to defend him ללמד **זְכוּת** עליו
the **right** not to answer so as not to incriminate oneself **זְכוּת** השתיקה
interdependence **תְּלוּת** גומלין

Additional Examples in this Pattern

disgrace, defamation גְּנוּת
clothing; cover כְּסוּת
hop (plant) כְּשׁוּת
impairment, disability, deficiency לְקוּת

salvation, liberation Lit. פְּדוּת
return N שְׁבוּת
stay N, sojourn שְׁהוּת

---

735. ***CCut*** **=** ***CaCut*** when the first root consonant is guttural

our/your/their	my/your/his/her	const.	Gloss	sing/pl
חֲנוּתֵנוּ/תְכֶם/תְכֶן/תָם/תָן	**חֲנוּ**תִי/תְךָ/תֵךְ/תוֹ/תָהּ	חֲנוּת-	store,	חֲנוּת נ׳
חֲנוּיוֹתֵינוּ/כֶם/כֶן/הֶם/הֶן	**חֲנוּיוֹ**תַי/תֶיךָ/תַיִךְ/תָיו/תֶיהָ	חֲנוּיוֹת-	shop	חֲנוּיוֹת

The declension is like זְכוּת above (including the transitional glide *y* in plural forms), but the first consonant comes with a *Hataf-pataH* instead of *shva* because of the guttural.

Examples

באזורים עניים של ערים גדולות קשה למצוא **חֲנֻיּוֹת** איכות; מכיוון שמרבית התושבים מעוטי יכולת, לא משתלם לרשתות הטובות לפתוח שם סניפים.

In poor areas within large cities it is difficult to find quality **stores**; since most of the residents have very limited means, it is not profitable for the good chains to open branches there.

לפני שפותחים עסק חדש, יש לבדוק את **העֲלֻיּוֹת** הכרוכות בהקמתו ובאחזקתו, ואת הסיכוי שיתפתח בסביבה שבה הוא מיועד להיות מוקם.

Before opening a new business, one needs to check the **costs** involved in starting it and its maintenance, as well as the prospect for its development in the neighborhood in which it is intended to be opened.

Special Expressions

outlet **store**, factory outlet **חֲנוּת** מפעל

---

736. *CaCCut*

our/your/their	my/your/his/her	const.	Gloss	sing/pl
סַמְכוּתֵנוּ/תְכֶם/תְכֶן/תָם/תָן	**סַמְכוּ**תִי/תְךָ/תֵךְ/תוֹ/תָהּ	סַמְכוּת-	authority	סַמְכוּת נ'
סַמְכוּיוֹתֵינוּ/כֶם/כֶן/הֶם/הֶן	**סַמְכוּיוֹ**תַי/תֶיךָ/תַיִךְ/תָיו/תֶיהָ	סַמְכוּיוֹת-		סַמְכוּיוֹת

As in most words ending with *–ut*, in the plural the *t* of the singular is elided, and a transition *y*-glide is inserted. A significant number of occurrences have no actual plural forms in use. Also included here is the form תַּרְבּוּת culture, the first ת׳ of which is prefixal, but the whose declension is similar.

Examples

סַמְכוּתוֹ של נשיא ארה״ב אינה בלתי-מוגבלת, אבל היא רחבה ביותר.

The **authority** of the American President is not unlimited, but it is quite broad.

מלחמת האזרחים בארה״ב בשנות הששים של המאה התשע עשרה הייתה בעיקר סביב מוסד **הַעַבְדוּת** ואינטרסים כלכליים, אבל הצפון רצה גם לשמור על **אַחְדוּת** האומה.

The American Civil war in the sixties of the nineteenth century was mainly about the institution of **slavery** and about economic interests, but the North also wanted to maintain the **unity** of the nation.

הדור הצעיר של היום מגיע **לבַגְרוּת** הרבה יותר מהר, מכל מיני סיבות.

Today's younger generation reaches **maturity** much faster, for all kinds of reasons.

רוב הסופרים והמשוררים מביטים לאחור בגעגועים לתקופת **יַלְדוּתָם**, אבל ניסיונם של מרבית בני האדם הוא שחברת הילדים יכולה להיות הרבה יותר קשה ואכזרית מחברת המבוגרים.

Most authors and poets look back with longing to their **childhood**, but most people's experience is that child society can be tougher and more cruel than adult society.

השחיטה על פי דיני ה**כַּשְׁרוּת** מחייבת ניקוז כל הדם בעוד בעל החיים עודו חי. האורתודוקסים טוענים שהשחיטה אינה כרוכה בסבל מיותר, מכיוון שכשהדם אינו מגיע למוח, בעל החיים אינו חש דבר. אני מסופק אם זה נכון.
Slaughtering according to **Jewish dietary law** requires that all blood be drained while the animal is still alive. The orthodox claim that when blood does not reach the brain, the animal feels nothing. I doubt that this is correct.

מַלְכוּת יהודה נכבשה על ידי הבבלים ב-586 לפני הספירה.
The **kingdom** of Judea was conquered by the Babylonians on 586 BCE.

במשך שתי המאות הראשונות לספירה, היהדות וה**נַצְרוּת** נאבקו על עשיית נפשות בקרב עובדי האלילים. לאחר מכן היהדות ויתרה.
During the first two centuries CE, Judaism and **Christianity** both strove to convert the pagans. Afterwards Judaism gave up.

מוסלמים פונדמנטליסטיים מרבים לדבר על מלחמת **תַּרְבּוּיוֹת**, בין **תַּרְבּוּת** האיסלאם ל**תַּרְבּוּת** המערב.
Muslim fundamentalists talk often of a war between **cultures**: Islamic **culture** and Western **culture**.

כשמדברים על **תַּרְבּוּת** האכילה, הכוונה היא בעצם לנימוס ולחינוך טוב בזמן הארוחה.
When one talks of the **culture** of eating, one actually refers to good manners and good breeding as manifest in one's behavior at the table.

Special Expressions

ממשלת **אַחְדוּת** **unity** government
בחינת **בַּגְרוּת** **matri**culation exam
שגעון **גַּדְלוּת** superiority **complex**
גַּדְלוּת נפש altruism, self-sacrificing
הַלְמוּת לב heart**beat**, pulse
תַּרְבּוּת בקטריות bacteria **culture**
תַּרְבּוּת הגוף sports, gym
תַּרְבּוּת הפנאי **culture** of leisure

בן-**תַּרְבּוּת** cultured person
חדר **תַּרְבּוּת** **cultural** activities room
יצא ל**תַּרְבּוּת** רעה was corrupted
צמחי **תַּרְבּוּת** **cultured** plants
רב-**תַּרְבּוּתִי** multi-**cultural**
משרד ה**תַּרְבּוּת** Ministry of **Culture**
האציל **סַמְכוּיוֹת** delegate **authority**

Additional Examples in this Pattern

גַּבְרוּת masculinity
גַּדְלוּת greatness
הַלְמוּת beat N
הַבְלוּת folly, unimportance
יַנְקוּת infancy
יַתְמוּת orphanhood; sense of loss
כַּשְׁרוּת Jewish dietary law; validity, legality

נַבְלוּת villainousness Lit.
עַצְבוּת sadness
עַצְלוּת laziness
עַרְבוּת guarantee; collateral
פַּשְׁטוּת simplicity
קַדְרוּת darkness; gloom
קַטְנוּת smallness; pettiness

---

737. ***CaCCut* = *CaCaCut***, when the second root consonant is guttural

our/your/their	my/your/his/her	const.	Gloss	sing/pl
בַּעֲלוּתֵנוּ/תְכֶם/תְכֶן/תָם/תָן	**בַּעֲלוּ**תִי/תְךָ/תֵךְ/תוֹ/תָהּ	בַּעֲלוּת-	ownership	בַּעֲלוּת נ׳
בַּעֲלוּיוֹתֵינוּ/כֶם/כֶן/הֶם/הֶן	**בַּעֲלוּיוֹ**תַי/תֶיךָ/תַיִךְ/תָיו/תֶיהָ	בַּעֲלוּיוֹת-		בַּעֲלוּיוֹת

The declension as in סַמְכוּת above, but where a *shva* is expected with a guttural, it is replaced by *Hataf-pataH*. Most occurrences have no plural forms in actual use. Also included here is the form תַּחֲרוּת competition, the first ת׳ of which is (probably) prefixal, but whose declension is similar.

Examples

על פי החוק העות׳מאני שעדיין תקף (חלקית) במדינת ישראל, זכאית המדינה לממש **בַּעֲלוּת** על שטחים חקלאיים שלא עובדו לפחות שלוש שנים.
According to Ottoman Law, that still (partly) applies in the State of Israel, the State is entitled to claim **ownership** of agricultural lands that have not been cultivated at least three years.

כדי לקדם אוריינות באזורים החלשים של הארץ, מקיימת מדינת ישראל מדי פעם מבצעים לביעור ה**בַּעֲרוּת**.
In order to advance literacy in the weaker regions in the country, from time to time the State of Israel conducts projects of "Eliminating **Ignorance**."

בארה״ב מוחים הזרמים השונים ב**יַהֲדוּת** על השתלטות התנועה האורתודוקסית בישראל.
In the US the various streams within **Judaism** protest the orthodox movement taking over in Israel.

תורת ה**יַחֲסוּת** הכללית של איינשטיין חוללה מהפכה של ממש בעולם המדע.
Einstein's General **Relativity** theory brought about a true revolution in the world of science.

במדינות רבות מנסים למנוע היווצרות מונופולים, כדי ש**תַּחֲרוּת** תביא להורדת מחירים.
In many countries they try to prevent the formation of monopolies, so that **competition** lead to decrease in prices.

Special Expressions

בַּעֲלוּת פרטית private **ownership**
בַּעֲלוּת ציבורית public **ownership/property**
תַּחֲרוּת חופשית free (market) **competition**
תַּחֲרוּת רעים friendly **competition**

Additional Examples in this Pattern

בַּחֲרוּת adolescence
יַחֲפוּת being barefoot Lit.
נַעֲרוּת youth, adolescence

---

738. *CiCCut*

our/your/their	my/your/his/her	const.	Gloss	sing/pl
סִפְרוּתֵנוּ/תְכֶם/תְכֶן/תָם/תָן	**סִפְרוּ**תִי/תְךָ/תֵךְ/תוֹ/תָהּ	סִפְרוּת-	literature	סִפְרוּת נ׳
סִפְרוּיוֹתֵינוּ/כֶם/כֶן/הֶם/הֶן	**סִפְרוּיוֹ**תַי/תֶיךָ/תַיִךְ/תָיו/תֶיהָ	סִפְרוּיוֹת-		סִפְרוּיוֹת

The declension as in סַמְכוּת above, but with *Hirik* instead of *pataH*. A significant number of occurrences have no actual plural forms in use.

Examples

קשה לי להירדם מבלי לקרוא קצת קודם – משהו ב**סִפְרוּת** יפה, או אפילו **סִפְרוּת** מתח.
I find it difficult to fall asleep without having read something first – a piece of **fiction**, or even a thriller.

עִבְרוּת שמות היה נפוץ למדיי בתקופת בן-גוריון ; למעשה, לא הרשו לייצג את ישראל בחו״ל עם שם שאינו עברי.
Hebraization of names was fairly common in the Ben-Gurion era; in fact, one was not allowed to represent Israel abroad with a non-Hebrew name.

כשחיים ודינה יוצאים עם זוג חברים מסוים לטיול, חיים תמיד מתנדב להסיע את כולם במכוניתו ; החבר נוהג ב**פִּרְאוּת** כזו, שחיים פשוט מפחד.
When Hayyim and Dina go on a trip with another certain couple, Hayyim always volunteers to drive them all in his car; their friend drives with such **wildness**, that Hayyim is simply afraid.

מה לדעתכם יותר מסוכן – נהיגה במצב של **שִׁכְרוּת**, או שליחת טקסט בזמן נהיגה?
What do you think is more dangerous: driving while in a state of **drunkenness**, or driving and texting?

Special Expressions

belles-lettres, fiction **סִפְרוּת** יפה
humility, modesty, humbleness **שִׁפְלוּת** רוח

Additional Examples in this Pattern

old age זִקְנוּת
socialization חִבְרוּת
despicableness, contemptibleness נִבְזוּת
being epileptic נִכְפּוּת
inferiority נִקְלוּת
indolence; weariness נִרְפּוּת
stupidity, naiveté סִכְלוּת
wickedness רִשְׁעוּת
baseness, despicableness שִׁפְלוּת

---

739. *CiCCut*, with dagesh in the second root consonant

our/your/their	my/your/his/her	const.	Gloss	sing/pl
טִפְּשׁוּתֵנוּ/תְכֶם/תְכֶן/תָם/תָן	**טִפְּשׁוּ**תִי/תְךָ/תֵךְ/תוֹ/תָהּ	טִפְּשׁוּת-	stupidity,	טִפְּשׁוּת נ׳
טִפְּשׁוּיוֹתֵינוּ/כֶם/כֶן/הֶם/הֶן	**טִפְּשׁוּיוֹ**תַי/תֶיךָ/תַיִךְ/תָיו/תֶיהָ	טִפְּשׁוּיוֹת-	foolishness	טִפְּשׁוּיוֹת

The declension as in סִפְרוּת above, but with *dagesh* in the second root consonant. Note: in פִּקְחוּת 'intelligence' there is no *dagesh forte* in the second root consonant. Almost all occurrences have no plural forms in actual use.

Examples

זאת **טִפְּשׁוּת** מסוכנת להכחיש שאמנם קיימת תופעה מדאיגה של התחממות עולמית.
It is dangerous **foolishness** to deny that there indeed exists a worrying phenomenon of global warming.

הילד הזה נראה קטן פיסית לגילו, אבל **פִּקְחוּתוֹ** מפצה על קומתו הנמוכה.
This child looks small for his age, but his **intelligence** makes up for his small stature.

קשה למנחם לעבוד עם אחרים בצוות, בגלל **עִקְּשׁוּתוֹ** וסירובו התמידי לשנות את דעתו.
It is difficult for Menahem to work with others in a team, because of his **stubbornness** and his constant refusal to change his opinions.

Additional Examples in this Pattern

אִלְּמוּת muteness	עִוְּרוּת blindness
גִּדְּמוּת amputatedness	עִלְּגוּת stammering, mumbling
חִגְּרוּת lameness	

---

740. Linear derivation Noun + *ut*

sing/pl	Gloss	const.	my/your/his/her	our/your/their
אֶפְשָׁרוּת נ׳	possibility	אֶפְשָׁרוּת-	**אֶפְשָׁרוּ**תִי/תְךָ/תֵךְ/תוֹ/תָהּ	**אֶפְשָׁרוּ**תֵנוּ/תְכֶם/תְכֶן/תָם/תָן
אֶפְשָׁרוּיוֹת		אֶפְשָׁרוּיוֹת-	**אֶפְשָׁרוּיוֹ**תַי/תֶיךָ/תַיִךְ/תָיו/תֶיהָ	**אֶפְשָׁרוּיוֹתֵי**נוּ/כֶם/כֶן/הֶם/הֶן

As in most words ending with *–ut*, in the plural the *t* of the singular is elided, and a transition *y*-glide is inserted. The derivation is linear: אֶפְשָׁר 'possible' + *ut* > אֶפְשָׁרוּת 'possibility,' occasionally with automatic vowel change/deletion, but as will be shown below, some of them may be classified into sub-groups, which may also be regarded as realizations of discontinuous patterns (root+*mishkal*). Most realizations do not have plural forms in use.

Examples

אל תמהרו להתייאש: תמיד יש **אֶפְשָׁרוּיוֹת** נוספות להיחלץ ממצבים שנראים ללא מוצא.
Do not rush to give up: there are always additional **possibilities** to survive situations that appear to be desperate.

מספר ישראלים עשו לעצמם שם עולמי **בַּאֲדְרִיכָלוּת**. אחד הבולטים שבהם הוא משה ספדי.
A number of Israelis have acquired an international reputation in **architecture**. One of the most prominent of those is Moshe Safdie.

בישראל, שנוסדה כמדינת מקלט לעם היהודי, מוענקת לכל עולה יהודי **אֶזְרָחוּת** באופן אוטומטי.
In Israel, founded as a safe haven to the Jewish people, **citizenship** is automatically granted to any Jewish immigrant.

פוליטיקאי שהגיע לעמדת כוח בדרך כלל אינו מקבל **אַחְרָיוּת** על כישלונות; הוא תמיד מאשים את קודמיו בתפקיד.
A politician who has reached a position of power usually does not take **responsibility** for failures; he always places the blame on former holders of the position.

מרבית העוסקים ב**אָמָּנוּת** עושים זאת לשמה, אבל לא מעטים גם מתפרנסים בכבוד ממנה.
Most of those engaged in **art** do it for art's sake, but a good number also derive a nice livelihood from it.

ה**גִּזְבָּרוּת** היא אחת המחלקות החשובות בכל חברה.
The **accounts department** is one of the most important in any company.

כל צעיר ישראלי המתגייס לצבא חייב לעבור **טִירוֹנוּת**. האימונים לא קלים, אבל לרוב החיילים יש זיכרונות טובים מן התקופה הזאת של שירותם.
Every Israeli youth enlisting in the army must undergo **basic training**. The training is not easy, but most soldiers have good memories from that period of their service.

יש פוליטיקאים הטוענים שה**עִתּוֹנוּת** רודפת אותם ומפרסמת חדשות שקריות אודותם.
Some politicians claim that **the press** persecutes them and publicizes fake news about them.

אחד הקשיים הגדולים במשא ומתן שהביא להסכם אוסלו היה שאלת ה**רִבּוֹנוּת** באזורים השונים של הגדה המערבית.
One of the great difficulties in the negotiations that resulted in the Oslo Agreement was the question of **sovereignty** in the different regions of the West Bank.

Special Expressions

אֶזְרָחוּת טובה good **citizenship**
אֶזְרָחוּת כבוד honorary **citizenship**
אֶזְרָחוּת כפולה dual **citizenship**
אַחְרָיוּת מקצועית professional **liability**
אַחְרָיוּת פלילית criminal **liability**
אַחְרָיוּת קולקטיבית collective **liability**
אֵיכוּת הסביבה **quality** of the environment
אֵיכוּת חיים **quality** of life
אָמָּנוּת לחימה martial **art**
בּוּרוּת מחשב computer **illiteracy**
זֶהוּת מינית gender **identity**
זֶהוּת שאולה borrowed **identity**
עִתּוֹנוּת צהובה tabloids

Additional Examples in this Pattern

אַבָהוּת/אֲבָהוּת paternity, fatherhood
אֶגְרוֹפָנוּת boxing
אֵיכוּת quality
אֻמְלָלוּת misery
אֻמָּנוּת craft
בּוּרוּת ignorance
הַרְפַּתְקָנוּת adventurousness
מוּקְיוֹנוּת clowning
מִלּוֹנוּת lexicography
עֶלְיוֹנוּת superiority
עֲתִידָנוּת futurology
פַּטְרוֹנוּת patronage
צִיּוֹנוּת Zionism
רִאשׁוֹנוּת precedence, priority
שְׁנָנוּת dental hygiene
תְּקֵפוּת validity

741. Linear derivation Noun + *ut* / *maCCiCut*

our/your/their	my/your/his/her	const.	Gloss	sing/pl
מַנְהִיגוּתֵנוּ/תְכֶם/תְכֶן/תָם/תָן	**מַנְהִיגוּ**תִי/תְךָ/תֵךְ/תוֹ/תָהּ	מַנְהִיגוּת-	leadership	מַנְהִיגוּת נ׳
מַנְהִיגוּיוֹתֵינוּ/כֶם/כֶן/הֶם/הֶן	**מַנְהִיגוּיוֹ**תַי/תֶיךָ/תַיִךְ/תָיו/תֶיהָ	מַנְהִיגוּיוֹת-		מַנְהִיגוּיוֹת

Although generally we are dealing here with linear derivation of N+*ut*, מַנְהִיג 'leader' + *ut*, such realizations also constitute discontinuous derivation in the *maCCiCut mishkal*.

Examples

האם **מַנְהִיגוּת** נמדדת ביכולתו של מנהיג לשכנע את האומה ללכת אחריו בנאומים חוצבי להבות, או בהישגיו בתחומים הכלכליים והחברתיים?

Is **leadership** measured by the capability of a leader to convince the nation to follow him by using fiery speeches, or by his achievements in the economic and social realms?

בבתי ספר טובים יש ל**מַזְכִּירוּת** תפקיד חשוב, לא פחות מאשר להנהלה.

In good schools, the **office** has an important role, at least as important as the principal's.

יש **מַקְבִּילוּת** רבה בהתנהלותם של שני המנהיגים הללו, אבל יש פער גדול ביניהם ביכולת אינטלקטואלית.

There is considerable **parallelism** in the way these two leaders conduct themselves, but there is a big difference in their intellectual capabilities.

Special Expressions

spiritual **leadership** **מַנְהִיגוּת** רוחנית

---

742. Linear derivation Noun + *ut* / *neCoCut*

our/your/their	my/your/his/her	const.	Gloss	sing/pl
נְכוֹנוּתֵנוּ/תְכֶם/תְכֶן/תָם/תָן	**נְכוֹנוּ**תִי/תְךָ/תֵךְ/תוֹ/תָהּ	נְכוֹנוּת-	readiness,	נְכוֹנוּת נ׳
נְכוֹנוּיוֹתֵינוּ/כֶם/כֶן/הֶם/הֶן	**נְכוֹנוּיוֹ**תַי/תֶיךָ/תַיִךְ/תָיו/תֶיהָ	נְכוֹנוּיוֹת-	willingness	נְכוֹנוּיוֹת

This is linear derivation of N+*ut*, נָכוֹן 'ready' + *ut* (after automatic reduction to *shva*), or alternatively discontinuous derivation in the *neCoCut mishkal*. In most realizations no plural forms exist.

Examples

אחרי שהחשוד בניסיון לרצח הביע **נְכוֹנוּת** להעיד נגד מי ששילם לו כדי לחסל את המנהיג, התובע חתם על הסכם שיקל בעונשו תמורת עדותו.

After the suspect of a murder attempt expressed **willingness** to testify against the person who paid him to assassinate the leader, the DA signed a plea bargain to reduce the charges against him in lieu of his testimony.

Additional Examples in this Pattern

enlightenment, progressiveness נְאוֹרוּת
propriety, being proper/suitable נְאוֹתוּת
wisdom, wit נְבוֹנוּת
corruptness, immorality נְלוֹזוּת

---

743. Linear derivation Noun + *ut* / *CCaCCaCut*, with reduplication, no plural

our/your/their	my/your/his/her	const.	Gloss	sing/pl
צְהַבְהַבּוּתֵנוּ/תְכֶם/תְכֶן/תָם/תָן	**צְהַבְהַבּוּ**תִי/תְךָ/תֵךְ/תוֹ/תָהּ	-צְהַבְהַבּוּת	yellow-ishness	צְהַבְהַבּוּת נ׳

This is linear derivation of N+*ut*, צְהַבְהַב 'yellow' + *ut* (note the *dagesh* when the -*ut* suffix is added), but such realizations also constitute discontinuous derivation in the *CCaCCaCut mishkal*, with reduplication (קְטַלְטַלּוּת). No plural forms exist.

Examples

צְהַבְהַבּוּת (במדוברת **צְהַבְהָבוּת**) של העור וגירוד קשה עלולים להיות תסמינים של צהבת, או גרוע מזה, של סרטן הלבלב.

Yellowishness of the skin and strong itching might be symptoms of jaundice, or worse, of pancreatic cancer.

Additional Examples in this Pattern

כְּחַלְחַלּוּת bluishness

לְבַנְבַּנּוּת (במדוברת לְבַנְבָנוּת) whiteness, pallor

שְׁרַבְרַבּוּת (במדוברת שְׁרַבְרָבוּת) plumbing

---

744. Linear derivation Noun + *ut* / *CCaCCut* > *CaCaCCaCut*, with reduplication, the first root consonant is guttural, no plural

our/your/their	my/your/his/her	const.	Gloss	sing/pl
אֲפַרְפָּרוּתֵנוּ/תְכֶם/תְכֶן/תָם/תָן	**אֲפַרְפָּרוּ**תִי/תְךָ/תֵךְ/תוֹ/תָהּ	-אֲפַרְפָּרוּת	grayness	אֲפַרְפָּרוּת נ׳

This is linear derivation of N+*ut*, אֲפַרְפַּר 'gray' + *ut*, or alternatively discontinuous derivation in the *CCaCCaCut* > *CaCaCCaCut mishkal*, with reduplication (קֲטַלְטַלּוּת). When a *shva* is expected with a guttural, it is replaced by *Hataf-pataH*. No plural forms exist.

Examples

סימנים ראשונים של **אֲפַרְפָּרוּת** כבר עלו בשערו עוד לפני היותו בן ארבעים.

First signs of **grayness** could already be seen in his hair before he was forty.

Additional Examples in this Pattern

עֲקַלְקַלּוּת being crooked

---

745. Linear derivation Noun + *ut* / *CCaCCanut*, no plural

our/your/their	my/your/his/her	const.	Gloss	sing/pl
רַהַבְתָנוּתֵנוּ/תְכֶם/תְכֶן/תָם/תָן	**רַהַבְתָנוּ**תִי/תְךָ/תֵךְ/תוֹ/תָהּ	-רַהַבְתָנוּת	arrogance, haughtiness	רַהַבְתָנוּת נ׳

This is linear derivation of N+*ut*, רְהַבְתָן 'arrogant (person)' + *ut*, or alternatively discontinuous derivation in the *CCaCCanut mishkal*. No plural forms exist.

Examples

רְהַבְתָנוּת של מנהיגי מדינות במשא ומתן ביניהם היא בדרך כלל מכשול בדרך להסכם.
Arrogance of leaders of states while negotiating is generally a handicap on the way to agreement.

Additional Examples in this Pattern

muscular strength, toughness גְּבַרְתָּנוּת

---

746. Linear derivation Noun + *ut* / *CaCaCCanut*, no plural

our/your/their	my/your/his/her	const.	Gloss	sing/pl
גַּאַוְתָנוּתֵנוּ/תְכֶם/תְכֶן/תָם/תָן	**גַּאַוְתָנוּ**תִי/תְךָ/תֵךְ/תוֹ/תָהּ	-גַּאַוְתָנוּת	arrogance	גַּאַוְתָנוּת נ׳

The declension is close to that of רְהַבְתָנוּת above, except for a *pataH* instead of the first *shva*. No plural forms exist.

Examples

בנצרות, **גַּאַוְתָנוּת** ו**רַעַבְתָנוּת** הם שניים משבעת החטאים (הקטלניים), שהם החטאים החמורים ביותר שאדם יכול לעשות, ושהעונש עליהם הוא מות הנפש.
In Christianity, **arrogance** and **gluttony** are two of the Seven Deadly Sins, which are the most serious ones that man may commit, and for which the punishment is death of one's soul.

Additional Examples in this Pattern

gluttony, voracity רַעַבְתָנוּת

---

747. Linear derivation Noun + *ut* / *CiCConut*, no plural

our/your/their	my/your/his/her	const.	Gloss	sing/pl
טִבְעוֹנוּתֵנוּ/תְכֶם/תְכֶן/תָם/תָן	**טִבְעוֹנוּ**תִי/תְךָ/תֵךְ/תוֹ/תָהּ	-טִבְעוֹנוּת	being vegan	טִבְעוֹנוּת נ׳

This is linear derivation of N+*ut*, טִבְעוֹנ(י) 'vegan' + *ut*, but at the same time also discontinuous derivation in the *CiCConut mishkal*. No plural forms exist.

Examples

בעבר ה**צִמְחוֹנוּת** הייתה באופנה ; היום מדברים הרבה יותר על **טִבְעוֹנוּת**.
In the past, **vegetarianism** was in fashion; today people speak more about **being vegan**.

ברוסיה יש היום הרבה תופעות **בִּרְיוֹנוּת**, שחלקן הגדול הוא ביוזמת המשטר או בעידודו.
In Russia today there occur many instances of **hooliganism**, many of them generated or encouraged by the regime.

Additional Examples in this Pattern

weirdness, strangeness תְּמְהוֹנוּת   vegetarianism צִמְחוֹנוּת

---

748. Linear derivation Noun + *ut* /*CiCut*

our/your/their	my/your/his/her	const.	Gloss	sing/pl
צִירוּתֵנוּ/תְכֶם/תְכֶן/תָם/תָן	**צִירוּ**תִי/תְךָ/תֵךְ/תוֹ/תָהּ	צִירוּת-	legation,	צִירוּת נ׳
צִירוּיוֹתֵינוּ/כֶם/כֶן/הֶם/הֶן	**צִירוּיוֹ**תַי/תֶיךָ/תַיִךְ/תָיו/תֶיהָ	צִירוּיוֹת-	representation	צִירוּיוֹת

This is linear derivation of N+*ut*, צִיר 'legate, representative' + *ut*, or alternatively discontinuous derivation in the *CiCut mishkal*. Most realizations have no plural forms in use.

Examples

בין ארצות מסוימות אין יחסים דיפלומטיים סדירים, אבל לפחות יש **צִירוּת** המטפלת בצרכים המינימליים הדורשים מענה.

Between certain countries there are no regular diplomatic relations, but at least there is a **legation** that takes care of basic needs that require response.

מכיוון שבישראל לאף מפלגה אין רוב כדי להקים ממשלה לבדה, הממשלה היא תמיד ממשלת קואליציה, ומכיוון שהאורתודוקסים מהווים תמיד חלק ממשלות כאלה, הם דורשים שדיני **אִישׁוּת** של ההלכה יהיו אוטומטית חוקי מדינת ישראל.

Since in Israel no party has ever had a majority that would enable it to form a government, the government has always been a coalition government, and since the orthodox are always members of such coalitions, they require that the **marital** laws of the Jewish Halakha automatically be the laws of the State of Israel.

Additional Examples in this Pattern

miserliness, Lit. כִּילוּת   contempt, disrespect זִילוּת

---

749. Linear derivation Noun + *ut* / *CaCCeCanut*, with reduplication, no plural

our/your/their	my/your/his/her	const.	Gloss	sing/pl
בַּזְבְּזָנוּתֵנוּ/תְכֶם/תְכֶן/תָם/תָן	**בַּזְבְּזָנוּ**תִי/תְךָ/תֵךְ/תוֹ/תָהּ	בַּזְבְּזָנוּת-	squandering, wasting	בַּזְבְּזָנוּת נ׳

This is linear derivation of N+*ut*, בַּזְבְּזָן+וּת 'squanderer' + *ut*, but at the same time also discontinuous derivation in the *CaCCeCanut mishkal* (קַטְקְטָנוּת), in which the first and second consonants of the root are reduplicated in positions three and four, respectively. Most realizations have no plural forms in use.

Examples

במרבית הארצות או האזורים הסובלים ממחסור במים מעלים מדי פעם את תעריפי המים, כדי למתן את ה**בַּזְבְּזָנוּת** בשימוש בהם.

In most countries or regions that suffer from water shortage they occasionally raise the water fee use (by meter), so as to reduce **wasting** of water by excessive use.

יש המאשימים את האקדמיה ללשון העברית ב**דַּקְדְּקָנוּת**-יתר, אבל האקדמיה יותר ליברלית ממה שנהוג לחשוב.
Some accuse the Hebrew Language Academy of excessive **pedantry**, but the Academy is actually more liberal than people assume it is.

Additional Examples in this Pattern

גַּמְגְּמָנוּת stammering גַּרְגְּרָנוּת gluttony

---

750. Linear derivation Noun + *ut* / *CaCCiCut*, with reduplication

our/your/their	my/your/his/her	const.	Gloss	sing/pl
שַׁגְרִירוּתֵנוּ/תְכֶם/תְכֶן/תָם/תָן	**שַׁגְרִירוּ**תִי/תְךָ/תֵךְ/תוֹ/תָהּ	שַׁגְרִירוּת-	embassy	שַׁגְרִירוּת נ׳
שַׁגְרִירוּיוֹתֵינוּ/כֶם/כֶן/הֶם/הֶן	**שַׁגְרִירוּיוֹ**תַי/תֶיךָ/תַיִךְ/תָיו/תֶיהָ	שַׁגְרִירוּיוֹת-		שַׁגְרִירוּיוֹת

שַׁגְרִיר 'ambassador' + *ut* is linear derivation of N+*ut*, but also constitutes discontinuous derivation in the *CaCCiCut mishkal* (קַטְלִילוּת), in which the third consonant of the root is reduplicated in position four. עֲקְמִימוּת and עֲרְמִימוּת below are probably just discontinuous *CaCCiCut* forms, since linear derivation from עֲקְמוּמִי 'curved, crooked,' and עֲרְמוּמִי 'cunning Adj' is hard to motivate – there are no parallel עֲקְמִים* and עֲרְמִים* forms (עֲקְמוּמִי ~ עֲקְמוּמִיּוּת and עֲרְמוּמִי ~ עֲרְמוּמִיּוּת do exist, though).

Examples

הַשַּׁגְרִירוּת האמריקאית בישראל הועברה מתל-אביב לירושלים.
The American **embassy** to Israel was moved from Tel Aviv to Jerusalem.

Additional Examples in this Pattern

עֲקְמִימוּת curvature עֲרְמִימוּת cunning N (Talmudic)

---

751. Linear derivation Noun + *ut* / *CaCCaCut* = *CaCaCaCut*, with reduplication, when the second root consonant is guttural, no plural

our/your/their	my/your/his/her	const.	Gloss	sing/pl
רַעֲנַנוּתֵנוּ/תְכֶם/תְכֶן/תָם/תָן	**רַעֲנַנוּ**תִי/תְךָ/תֵךְ/תוֹ/תָהּ	רַעֲנַנוּת-	freshness	רַעֲנַנוּת נ׳

This is linear derivation of N+*ut*, רַעֲנָן 'fresh' + *ut*, but at the same time also discontinuous derivation in the *CaCCaCut* > *CaCaCaCut mishkal*, in which the third consonant of the root is reduplicated in position four (קַטְלָלוּת). When a *shva* is expected with a guttural, it is replaced by *Hataf-pataH*. There are no plural forms in use.

Examples

התכונות המרשימות של ראש העיר החדש הן **רַעֲנַנּוּתוֹ** ומרצו.
The impressive qualities of the new mayor are his **freshness** and his energy.

Additional Examples in this Pattern

complacence; serenity שַׁאֲנַנּוּת

---

752. Linear derivation Noun + *ut* / *CaCCanut*, no plural

our/your/their	my/your/his/her	const.	Gloss	sing/pl
בַּטְלָנוּתֵנוּ/תְכֶם/תְכֶן/תָם/תָן	**בַּטְלָנוּ**תִי/תְךָ/תֵךְ/תוֹ/תָהּ	בַּטְלָנוּת-	idleness, laziness	בַּטְלָנוּת נ׳

This is linear derivation of N+*ut*, בַּטְלָן 'idle, lazy' + *ut*, but such realizations also constitute discontinuous derivation in the *CaCCanut mishkal*. There are no plural forms in use.

Examples

רבים טוענים כי ההקצבות הגדולות מתקציב המדינה לישיבות החרדיות מהוות למעשה תשלום לתלמידיהן עבור **בַּטְלָנוּתָם**.
Many argue that the large allocations to ultra-orthodox yeshivas from the state budget actually constitute payments to their students for their **idleness**.

עד למלחמת העולם הראשונה האשימו האירופאים את ארה״ב ב**בַּדְלָנוּת**.
Until WWI the Europeans accused the US of **isolationism**.

בַּיְשָׁנוּת אינה תכונה שניתן למצוא אצל פוליטיקאים...
Shyness is not a quality you can find in politicians...

אני חושש שבשל **בַּרְרָנוּתוֹ**, מנשה לעולם לא ימצא אישה שלדעתו מתאימה לו.
I am afraid that because of his **selectiveness**, Menashe will never find a woman he feels would be suitable to become his wife.

Special Expressions

computational **linguistics** **בַּלְשָׁנוּת** חישובית
applied **linguistics** **בַּלְשָׁנוּת** שימושית

Additional Examples in this Pattern

gluttony אַכְלָנוּת
collecting, hoarding אַסְפָנוּת
tendency to be a cry-baby בַּכְיָנוּת
linguistics בַּלְשָׁנוּת
precision דַּיְקָנוּת
exegesis, preaching, sermonizing דַּרְשָׁנוּת

---

753. Linear derivation Noun + *ut* / *CaCCanut* = *CaCaCanut*, the second root consonant is guttural, no plural

our/your/their	my/your/his/her	const.	Gloss	sing/pl
דַּאֲגָנוּתֵנוּ/תְכֶם/תְכֶן/תָם/תָן	**דַּאֲגָנוּ**תִי/תְךָ/תֵךְ/תוֹ/תָהּ	דַּאֲגָנוּת-	anxiety, worrying	דַּאֲגָנוּת נ׳

This is linear derivation of N+*ut*, דַּאֲגָן 'one who always worries' + *ut*, but such realizations also constitute discontinuous derivation in the *CaCCanut* > *CaCaCanut mishkal*. When a *shva* is expected with a guttural, it is replaced by *Hataf-pataH*. There are no plural forms in use.

Examples

תמיד התקנאתי בטיפוסים כמו אלפרד א. ניומן, שה**דַּאֲגָנוּת** הייתה תמיד ממנו והלאה: "אני דואג? מה פתאום!"

I have always envied characters like Alfred E. Newman, who never knew the meaning of **worrying**: "what, me worry?"

Special Expressions

excessive **anxiety** **דַּאֲגָנוּת**-יתר

Additional Examples in this Pattern

rebelliousness בַּעֲטָנוּת

---

754. Linear derivation Noun + *ut* ? / *CaCiCut*

our/your/their	my/your/his/her	const.	Gloss	sing/pl
אַלִּימוּתֵנוּ/תְכֶם/תְכֶן/תָם/תָן	**אַלִּימוּ**תִי/תְךָ/תֵךְ/תוֹ/תָהּ	אַלִּימוּת-	violence	אַלִּימוּת נ'

This is linear derivation of N+*ut*, אַלִּים violent + *ut*. In cases like אַלִּיפוּת 'championship' one could argue for linear derivation of N+*ut* as well, אַלּוּף champion + *ut* > אַלִּיפוּת, with internal vowel change (dissimilation of *u*+*u* > *i*+*u*?), but it is more likely to be discontinuous derivation in the *CaCiCut mishkal*. The first consonant is followed by a *pataH* and by a *dagesh forte* in the second. Most occurrences have no plural forms in actual use, but אַלִּיפוּיוֹת 'championships' (...אַלִּיפוּיוֹתַי 'my championships') does exist.

Examples

הישראלים אוהבים מאוד כדורגל, אבל נבחרת ישראל מעולם לא זכתה ב**אַלִּיפוּת** העולם או ב**אַלִּיפוּת** אירופה, ורק פעם אחת זכתה ב**אַלִּיפוּת** אסיה. הסיבה: שחקניה אף פעם אינם מתאמנים מספיק; הם פשוט עצלנים.

The Israelis love soccer, but the Israeli team never won the world **championship** or the European **championship**, and only once won the Asian **championship**. The reason: its players never train enough; they are simply lazy.

כשהייתי סטודנט לתואר הראשון, ניסיתי לעזור בבחינה לסטודנטית חמודה שישבה לידי. הפרופסור ניגש אליי ואמר: "איש צעיר, ימי ה**אַבִּירוּת** כבר חלפו מן העולם!".

When I was an undergraduate student, I tried to help a cute female student sitting next to me during an exam. The professor approached me and said: "young man, the days of **chivalry** are over!"

למרבית הצער, אנשים רבים מאמינים שבעיות ניתן לפתור רק באמצעות **אַלִּימוּת**.

Unfortunately, many people believe that problems can be resolved only through **violence**.

קשה לקיים **יַצִּיבוּת** של משטר בתקופות של משבר כלכלי.
It is difficult to maintain the **stability** of a regime in a period of economic crisis.

Special Expressions

אֲלִיפוּת העולם world **championship**
אַלִּימוּת מילולית verbal **abuse/violence**
תַּקִּינוּת פוליטית political **correctness**

Additional Examples in this Pattern

דַּקִּיקוּת thinness
תַּקִּינוּת being in order; being undamaged
טַפִּילוּת parasitism
תַּקִּיפוּת firmness

---

755. Linear derivation Noun + *ut* / *CaCiCut* with *kamats*, no plural

our/your/their	my/your/his/her	const.	Gloss	sing/pl
עָרִיצוּתֵנוּ/תְכֶם/תְכֶן/תָם/תָן	**עָרִיצוּ**תִי/תְךָ/תֵךְ/תוֹ/תָהּ	עָרִיצוּת-	tyranny	עָרִיצוּת נ׳

This is linear derivation of N+*ut*, עָרִיץ 'tyrant' + *ut*, but such realizations also constitute discontinuous derivation in the *CaCiCut mishkal* (especially in the case of חָרִיצוּת; it is not clear to what extent derivation from חָרוּץ can be considered linear, with quasi-automatic vowel change, *u*+*u* > *i*+*u* dissimilation?). There are no plural forms in use.

Examples

מרבית הרוסים אהבו את סטאלין, למרות **עָרִיצוּתוֹ** והמיליונים שרצח או גרם למותם.
Most Russians loved Stalin, in pite of his terrible **tyranny** and the millions he had murdered or had caused to die.

איני יודע אם ה**שָּׁלִישׁוּת** הצבאית עדיין שם, אבל בזמנו כל חייל ידע שהיא ברמת גן.
I am not sure whether this is still the case, but any soldier knew that the military **adjutant's office** was located in Ramat Gan.

Additional Examples in this Pattern

וָתִיקוּת seniority Rare
חָרִיצוּת diligence
שָׁלִישׁוּת adjutancy (military)

---

756. Linear derivation Noun + *ut* / *CaCa'ut*

our/your/their	my/your/his/her	const.	Gloss	sing/pl
זַכָּאוּתֵנוּ/תְכֶם/תְכֶן/תָם/תָן	**זַכָּאוּ**תִי/תְךָ/תֵךְ/תוֹ/תָהּ	זַכָּאוּת-	entitlement	זַכָּאוּת נ׳
זַכָּאוּיוֹתֵינוּ/כֶם/כֶן/הֶם/הֶן	**זַכָּאוּיוֹ**תַי/תֶיךָ/תַיִךְ/תָיו/תֶיהָ	זַכָּאוּיוֹת-		זַכָּאוּיוֹת

This is linear derivation of N/Adj+*ut*, זַכָּאִי 'one who is entitled' + *ut*, but such realizations also constitute discontinuous derivation in the *CaCa'ut mishkal*. All forms are derived from roots with *yod* as the third root consonant (זכ״י etc.). Most occurrences have no plural forms in actual use.

Examples

סעיפי ה**זַכָּאוּיוֹת** בתקציב כל מדינה הם הסעיפים הגדולים והיקרים ביותר, ולכן מדינות רבות מנסות לצמצמן.
The **entitlements** lines in the budget of any state are the largest and most expensive, which is why many states try to cut them in size.

שחקני קולנוע טובים מנסים לעיתים קרובות לנצל את כשרונותיהם גם ב**בַמָּאוּת**.
Good film actors often try to use their talents in movie **directing** as well.

Additional Examples in this Pattern

fabricating, lying בַּדָּאוּת

building trade בַּנָּאוּת

---

757. Linear derivation Noun + *ut* / *CaCaCut*, no plural forms

our/your/their	my/your/his/her	const.	Gloss	sing/pl
		-גַּנָּנוּת	gardening	גַּנָּנוּת נ׳

This is linear derivation of N/Adj+*ut*, גַּנָּן ‘gardener’ + *ut*, but at the same time also discontinuous derivation in the *CaCaCut mishkal*. Most forms refer to professions. There no inflected forms in actual use (other than the singular construct form).

Examples

גַּנָּנוּת היא מקצוע מבוקש, מכיוון שמרבית האנשים אינם יודעים כיצד לתחזק את גינתם כראוי.
Gardening is in high demand, because most people do not know how to maintain their garden properly.

בזמנו עסקו ב**דַיָּלוּת** רק נשים. היום יש כבר לא מעט דיילים-גברים.
At the time, only women were engaged in **airline stewarding**. Today there quite a few men-stewards.

Additional Examples in this Pattern

detective work בַּלָּשׁוּת

short stature גַּמָּדוּת

tracking, scouting גַּשָּׁשׁוּת

being a soldier חַיָּלוּת

pickpocketing כַּיָּסוּת

---

758. Linear derivation Noun + *ut* / *CuCCaCut*, no plural

our/your/their	my/your/his/her	const.	Gloss	sing/pl
קֻנְדָּסוּתֵנוּ/תְכֶם/תְכֶן/תָם/תָן	**קֻנְדָּסוּ**תִי/תְךָ/תֵךְ/תוֹ/תָהּ	-קֻנְדָּסוּת	mischievousness	קֻנְדָּסוּת נ׳

This is linear derivation of N+*ut*, קֻנְדָּס 'prankster; mischief' + *ut*, but such realizations also constitute discontinuous derivation in the *CuCCaCut mishkal*. There are no plural forms in use.

Examples

בבית הספר היסודי בישראל, העונש על מעשי **קֻנְדָּסוּת** בכיתה היה העמדת הקונדס בפינה, עם הפנים לקיר...
In the elementary school in Israel, the punishment for **mischief** or **prank** was having the prankster stand in the corner, facing the wall…

במדינות הקומוניסטיות, בסופו של דבר משתלטת ה**בֻּרְגָּנוּת**. זהו טבע האדם, כנראה.
In the communist countries, the **bourgeoisie** ultimately takes over. The nature of man, apparently.

Additional Examples in this Pattern

modeling דֻּגְמָנוּת   assessment, evaluation אֻמְדָּנוּת

---

759. Linear derivation Noun + *ut* / *CoCCanut*, no plural

our/your/their	my/your/his/her	const.	Gloss	sing/pl
בּוֹגְדָנוּתֵנוּ/תְכֶם/תְכֶן/תָם/תָן	**בּוֹגְדָנוּ**תִי/תְךָ/תֵךְ/תוֹ/תָהּ	בּוֹגְדָנוּת-	treachery	בּוֹגְדָנוּת נ׳

This is linear derivation of N/Adj+*ut*, בּוֹגְדָנ(י) 'treacherous' + *ut*, but such realizations also constitute discontinuous derivation in the *CaCCanut mishkal*. There are no plural forms in use.

Examples

עם עליית הלאומנות במדינות רבות בעולם, מתחזקת גם הנטייה לראות בשמאלנות **בּוֹגְדָנוּת**.
With the rise of nationalism in many of the worlds' countries, there increases the tendency to view left wing leanings as **treachery**.

רבים בציבור מייחסים **פּוֹסְקָנוּת**-יתר לאקדמיה ללשון העברית, אבל הנחתם אינה נכונה.
Many in the public attribute excessive **normativism** to the Hebrew Language Academy, but their assumption is incorrect.

Special Expressions

computer **literacy** **אוֹרְיָנוּת** מחשב

Additional Examples in this Pattern

daydreaming חוֹלְמָנוּת   literacy אוֹרְיָנוּת
swampiness, bogginess טוֹבְעָנוּת   prickliness דּוֹקְרָנוּת
recklessness, destructiveness דּוֹרְסָנוּת

---

760. Linear derivation Noun + *ut* / *CoCanut*, no plural

our/your/their	my/your/his/her	const.	Gloss	sing/pl
כּוֹחְנוּתֵנוּ/תְכֶם/תְכֶן/תָם/תָן	**כּוֹחְנוּ**תִי/תְךָ/תֵךְ/תוֹ/תָהּ	כּוֹחְנוּת-	aggressiveness	כּוֹחְנוּת נ׳

This is linear derivation of N/Adj+*ut*, כּוֹחָנ(י) 'aggressive' + *ut*, but such realizations also constitute discontinuous derivation in the *CoCanut mishkal*. There are no plural forms in use.

Examples

יש מנהיגים החושבים שהפגנת **כּוֹחְנוּת** היא הדרך היחידה לפתור בעיות פוליטיות קשות.
There are some leaders who believe that exhibiting **aggressiveness** is the only way of solving difficult political problems.

---

761. Linear derivation Noun + *ut* / *CoCut*, no plural

our/your/their	my/your/his/her	const.	Gloss	sing/pl
הוֹרוּתֵנוּ/תְכֶם/תְכֶן/תָם/תָן	**הוֹרוּ**תִי/תְךָ/תֵךְ/תוֹ/תָהּ	הוֹרוּת-	parenthood	הוֹרוּת נ׳

This is linear derivation of N+*ut*, הוֹרֶה 'parent' + *ut*, but such realizations also constitute discontinuous derivation in the *CoCut mishkal*. There are no plural forms in use.

Examples

כמעט כל ההורים מצהירים שאין חוויה נהדרת מזו של **הוֹרוּת**.
Almost all parents declare that there is no experience more wonderful than that of **parenthood**.

למרות עליית הלאומנות בעולם, אנשים רבים עדיין מאמינים בחשיבותה של ה**שׁוֹנוּת** האתנית והחברתית של החברה בה הם חיים.
In spite of the rise in nationalism in the world, many still believe in the importance of ethnic and cultural **diversity** in the society in which they live.

Additional Examples in this Pattern

sexual potency אוֹנוּת — cheapness; vulgarity זוֹלוּת

---

762. Linear derivation Noun +*i* +*ut*, no declension, no plural

our/your/their	my/your/his/her	const.	Gloss	sing/pl
אִטִּיּוּתֵנוּ/תְכֶם/תְכֶן/תָם/תָן	**אִטִּיּוּ**תִי/תְךָ/תֵךְ/תוֹ/תָהּ	אִטִּיּוּת-	slowness	אִטִּיּוּת נ׳

This is linear derivation of N/Adj+*i*+*ut*, אִטִּי 'slow'+*ut*. There are no plural forms in use (in **any** form ending with +*i*+*ut*).

Examples

הערבים אומרים: "החיפזון מן השטן". אין לי מושג אם יש להם גם פתגם מקביל על **אִטִּיּוּת**...
The Arabs say: "Rush is from the Devil." I have no idea whether they have a counterpart saying about **slowness**…

המועמד לראשות המפלגה הוא אדם ישר ומעורר כבוד, אבל למרבית הצער **אִישִׁיּוּת** כזו אינה מספיקה כדי להיות פוליטיקאי מצליח.
The candidate for the party leadership is an honest person, and commands respect, but unfortunately this type of **personality** is insufficient to make him a successful politician.

נרקיסיסטיות היא אולי הדרגה הגבוהה ביותר של **אָנוֹכִיּוּת**.
Narcissism is possibly the highest degree of **egotism**.

מקורות **הָאַנְטִישֵׁמִיּוּת** הם רבים ושונים: דתיים, כלכליים ואחרים.
The reasons for **anti-semitism** are numerous and varied: religious, economic, and others.

בִּקָּרְתִּיּוּת על הממשלה מתפרשת לעיתים קרובות כביטוי של אי-נאמנות למדינה בכלל.
Criticism of the government is often interpreted as expression of lack of loyalty to the state in general.

Special Expressions

אִישִׁיּוּת בלתי רצויה **persona** non-grata

אִישִׁיּוּת משפטית legal person (law)

Additional Examples in this Pattern

אִכְפַּתִּיּוּת caring
אַלְמוֹנִיּוּת anonymity
אֱנוֹשִׁיּוּת humaneness, compassion
בֵּינוֹנִיּוּת mediocrity
בִּלְעָדִיּוּת exclusivity
בַּרְבָּרִיּוּת barbarism
גָּלוּתִיּוּת ghetto manner
הֶשֵּׂגִיּוּת ambitiousness
זֶהוּתִיּוּת similar identity
זוּגִיּוּת relationship of a couple
זְמַנִּיּוּת temporariness
חַדְגּוֹנִיּוּת monotony
חִיצוֹנִיּוּת external appearance
חֲלוּצִיּוּת pioneering

---

763. Linear derivation Noun +*i* +*ut* / *heCCeCiyut*, no plural

sing/pl	Gloss	const.	my/your/his/her	our/your/their
הֶחְלֵטִיּוּת נ׳	determination	הֶחְלֵטִיּוּת-	**הֶחְלֵטִיּוּ**תִי/תְךָ/תֵךְ/תוֹ/תָהּ	**הֶחְלֵטִיּוּ**תֵנוּ/תְכֶם/תְכֶן/תָם/תָן

This is linear derivation of N/Adj+*i*+*ut*, הֶחְלֵטִי 'determined, decisive'+*ut*, but such realizations also constitute discontinuous derivation in the *heCCeCiyut mishkal*. There are no plural forms in use.

Examples

מנהיג מנוסה יודע שמסוכן להסס, ולעיתים פועל **בְּהֶחְלֵטִיּוּת** גם כאשר הוא יודע שייתכן שהוא טועה.
An experienced leader knows that it is risky to hesitate, and sometimes acts with **determination** even when he realizes that he may be wrong.

דני מסיים את חטיבת הביניים, ולדעת הוריו רצוי שיעבור לבית-ספר תיכון שנחשב לטוב יותר, אבל הוא מעדיף להישאר באותו בית ספר, כדי לקיים **הֶמְשֵׁכִיּוּת**.
Danny is about to finish Junior High, and his parents feel that he should move to a high school that is regarded as better, but he prefers to stay at the same school, to maintain **continuity**.

Additional Examples in this Pattern

necessity הֶכְרֵחִיּוּת

---

764. Linear derivation Noun +*i* +*ut* / *haCCaCatiyut*, no declension

const.	Gloss	sing/pl
הַדְרָגָתִיּוּת-	gradualness	הַדְרָגָתִיּוּת נ׳

This is with linear derivation of N/Adj+*ut*, הַדְרָגָתִי 'gradual'+*i*+*ut*, but such realizations also constitute discontinuous derivation in the *haCCaCatiyut mishkal*. There are no declension forms in use.

Examples

כדי לשרוד באוויר דל-חמצן, מעפילי האוורסט חייבים לטפס בשלבים. **הַדְרָגָתִיּוּת** בטיפוס מאפשרת לגוף להסתגל.
To survive in an atmosphere of reduced oxygen, Everest climbers must climb in stages. **Gradualness** in climbing enables the body to adjust.

Additional Examples in this Pattern

demonstrativeness הַפְגָּנָתִיּוּת

---

765. Linear derivation Noun +*i* +*ut* / *miCCaCtiyut*, no plural or no declension at all

our/your/their	my/your/his/her	const.	Gloss	sing/pl
מִפְלַגְתִּיּוּתֵנוּ/תְכֶם/תְכֶן/תָם/תָן	**מִפְלַגְתִּיּוּ**תִי/תְךָ/תֵךְ/תוֹ/תָהּ	מִפְלַגְתִּיּוּת-	partisanship	מִפְלַגְתִּיּוּת נ׳

This is linear derivation of N/Adj+*i*+*ut*, מִפְלַגְתִּי 'partisan'+*ut*, but such realizations also constitute discontinuous derivation in the *miCCaCtiyut mishkal*. There are no plural forms in use, or there is no declension at all.

Examples

המִפְלַגְתִּיּוּת הקיצונית בחברה הישראלית מקשה מאוד על הרכבת ממשלה יציבה.
The extreme **partisanship** in the Israeli society makes the formation of a stable government very difficult.

Additional Examples in this Pattern

family feeling/conduct מִשְׁפַּחְתִּיּוּת belligerence מִלְחַמְתִּיּוּת

---

766. Linear derivation Noun +*i* +*ut* / *miCCoCiyut*, no plural

our/your/their	my/your/his/her	const.	Gloss	sing/pl
מִקְצוֹעִיּוּתֵנוּ/תְכֶם/תְכֶן/תָם/תָן	**מִקְצוֹעִיּוּ**תִי/תְךָ/תֵךְ/תוֹ/תָהּ	מִקְצוֹעִיּוּת-	professionalism	מִקְצוֹעִיּוּת נ׳

This is linear derivation of N/Adj+*i*+*ut*, מִקְצוֹעִי 'professional' + *ut*, but such realizations also constitute discontinuous derivation in the *miCCoCiyut mishkal*. There are no plural forms in use.

Examples

לא נדרשת כל **מִקְצוֹעִיּוּת** כדי להיות שר בממשלת ישראל; כמעט כל המינויים הם מפלגתיים/פוליטיים גרידא.
No **professionalism** is required of a minister (secretary of…) in Israel; almost all appointments are purely partisan/political.

Additional Examples in this Pattern

mystery מִסְתּוֹרִיּוּת

---

767. Linear derivation Noun +*i* +*ut* / *muCaCiyut*, no plural

our/your/their	my/your/his/her	const.	Gloss	sing/pl
מוּסָרִיּוּתֵנוּ/תְכֶם/תְכֶן/תָם/תָן	**מוּסָרִיּוּ**תִי/תְךָ/תֵךְ/תוֹ/תָהּ	מוּסָרִיּוּת-	morality	מוּסָרִיּוּת נ׳

This is linear derivation of N/Adj+*i*+*ut*, מוּסָרִי 'moral' + *ut*, but such realizations also constitute discontinuous derivation in the *muCaCiyut mishkal*. There are no plural forms in use.

Examples

הגדרה אפשרית של **מוּסָרִיּוּת**: הבחנה בין התנהגויות שנחשבות ״טובות״ לבין אלה שנחשבות ״רעות״.
One possible definition of **morality**: the distinction between modes of behavior that are regarded as "good" and those that are considered "bad."

Additional Examples in this Pattern

tangibility, concreteness מוּחָשִׁיּוּת

---

768. Linear derivation Noun +*i* +*ut* / *CCiCiyut*, no plural

our/your/their	my/your/his/her	const.	Gloss	sing/pl
מְדִינִיּוּתֵנוּ/תְכֶם/תְכֶן/תָם/תָן	**מְדִינִיּוּ**תִי/תְךָ/תֵךְ/תוֹ/תָהּ	מְדִינִיּוּת-	policy	מְדִינִיּוּת נ׳

This is linear derivation of N/Adj+*i*+*ut*, מְדִינִי 'political; of the state' + *ut*, but such realizations also constitute discontinuous derivation in the *CCiCiyut mishkal*. There are no plural forms in use.

Examples

עד מלחמת העולם הראשונה, **מְדִינִיּוּת** החוץ של ארה״ב גרסה בדרך כלל אי-התערבות בסכסוכים ומלחמות בחו״ל.

Until WWI, the US foreign **policy** was generally of non-interference in conflicts and wars abroad.

דני אוהב את ה**קְפִיצִיּוּת** של המזרן של מיטת הוריו. הוא מקפץ עליו כמו על טרמפולינה.

Danny loves the **springiness** of his parents' mattress. He jumps on it as if it were a trampoline.

Additional Examples in this Pattern

גְּבִישִׁיּוּת crystallization
מְלִיצִיּוּת using flowery language
פְּנִימִיּוּת internalness
תְּמִידִיּוּת constancy, continuity

---

769. Linear derivation Noun +*i* +*ut* / *CCiCiyut*, with reduplication, no plural

our/your/their	my/your/his/her	const.	Gloss	sing/pl
שְׁלִילִיּוּתֵנוּ/תְכֶם/תְכֶן/תָם/תָן	**שְׁלִילִיּוּ**תִי/תְךָ/תֵךְ/תוֹ/תָהּ	שְׁלִילִיּוּת-	negativity	שְׁלִילִיּוּת נ׳

This is linear derivation of N/Adj+*i*+*ut*, שְׁלִילִי 'negative' + *ut*, but such realizations also constitute discontinuous derivation in the *CCiCiyut mishkal*, in which the second and third consonants are identical (קְטִיטִיּוּת). There are no plural forms in use.

Examples

אפרים טיפוס פסימי; הוא מדגיש תמיד את ה**שְׁלִילִיּוּת** בכל דבר.

Ephraim is a pessimistic person; he always emphasizes the **negativity** in everything.

אי אפשר להבין כראוי את מבנה ההברה מבלי להבין את סולם ה**צְלִילִיּוּת** של העיצורים.

One cannot properly understand the structure of the syllable without understanding the consonantal **sonority** scale.

Additional Examples in this Pattern

בְּסִיסִיּוּת basicity; centrality
גְּלִילִיּוּת cylindricalness
פְּלִילִיּוּת criminality

---

770. Linear derivation Noun *+i +ut* / *CCiCiyut* = *CaCiCiyut* (קֲטִיטִיּוּת), with reduplication, when the first consonant is guttural, no plural

our/your/their	my/your/his/her	const.	Gloss	sing/pl
חֲגִיגִיוּתֵנוּ/תְכֶם/תְכֶן/תָם/תָן	**חֲגִיגִיוּ**תִי/תְךָ/תֵךְ/תוֹ/תָהּ	-חֲגִיגִיּוּת	festivity; formality	חֲגִיגִיּוּת נ׳

This is linear derivation of N/Adj+*i*+*ut*, חֲגִיגִי 'festive' + *ut*, but such realizations also constitute discontinuous derivation in the *CCiCiyut* > *CaCiCiyut mishkal*, in which the second and third consonants are identical, and the first consonant is guttural – and since it is always followed by *shva*, the *shva* is replaced by *Hataf-pataH*. There are no plural forms in use.

Examples

טקס העברת השגרירות האמריקאית לירושלים נערך ב**חֲגִיגִיּוּת** גדולה.
The formal transferring of the American embassy to Jerusalem was conducted with great **festivity**.

Additional Examples in this Pattern

אֲבִיבִיּוּת spring-like feeling

עֲסִיסִיּוּת juiciness; vivaciousness

---

771. Linear derivation Noun *+i +ut* / *CCaCiyut*, no plural

our/your/their	my/your/his/her	const.	Gloss	sing/pl
פְּרָטִיוּתֵנוּ/תְכֶם/תְכֶן/תָם/תָן	**פְּרָטִיוּ**תִי/תְךָ/תֵךְ/תוֹ/תָהּ	-פְּרָטִיּוּת	privacy	פְּרָטִיּוּת נ׳

This is linear derivation of N/Adj+*i*+*ut*, פְּרָטִי 'private' + *ut*, but such realizations also constitute discontinuous derivation in the *CCaCiyut mishkal*. There are no plural forms in use.

Examples

האמריקאי הטיפוסי שומר בקנאות על **פְּרָטִיּוּתוֹ**.
The typical American zealously guards **his privacy**.

באזורים עניים של ערים גדולות בדרך כלל לא פותחים חנויות יוקרה, משיקולי **כְּדָאִיּוּת**.
In poor areas of large cities they usually do not open upscale stores, for reasons of **profitability** (or lack of it…).

ראש הממשלה התקבל ב**לְבָבִיּוּת** על ידי נשיא ארה״ב. לשניהם אותה נטייה פוליטית...
The Prime Minister was received with **warm-heartedness** by the US President. They have the same political leanings...

Additional Examples in this Pattern

יְמָנִיּוּת being right-wing

סְתָמִיּוּת vagueness; impersonality

כְּלָלִיּוּת generalness

צְבָאִיּוּת militarism

marginality; sidedness צְדָדִיּוּת
being combatant קְרָבִיּוּת
devilry שְׂטָנִיּוּת

---

772. Linear derivation Noun +*i* +*ut* / *CCaCiyut* = *CaCaCiyut*, when the first consonant is guttural, no plural

our/your/their	my/your/his/her	const.	Gloss	sing/pl
חֲשָׁאִיּוּתֵנוּ/תְכֶם/תְכֶן/תָם/תָן	**חֲשָׁאִיּוּ**תִי/תְךָ/תֵךְ/תוֹ/תָהּ	-חֲשָׁאִיּוּת	secrecy	חֲשָׁאִיּוּת נ׳

This is linear derivation of N/Adj+*i*+*ut*, חֲשָׁאִי 'secret' + *ut*, but such realizations also constitute discontinuous derivation in the *CCaCiyut* > *CaCaCiyut mishkal*, and the first consonant is guttural – and since it is always followed by *shva*, the *shva* is replaced by *Hataf-pataH*. There are no plural forms in use.

Examples

רוברט מילר, החוקר המיוחד, שמר על **חֲשָׁאִיּוּת** מוחלטת בחקירת ההתערבות הרוסית בבחירות 2016 בארה״ב.
Robert Mueller, the Special Counsel, maintained complete **secrecy** in the investigation of the Russian meddling in the 2016 US elections.

בטבע יש לא מעט יחסי **הֲדָדִיּוּת**, למשל, חרקים ניזונים מצוף של פרחים, ותוך כדי מעבר מפרח לפרח הם מפרים את הצמחים.
In nature there are quite a few **reciprocity** relationships; for instance, insects feed on one flower nectar, and while moving from one flower to another they pollinate plants.

למרבית הצער, פוליטיקאים ישראליים מסוימים מלבים את בעיית ה**עֲדָתִיּוּת** ואת תחושת הקיפוח של עדות מסוימות כדי לקדם את שאיפותיהם הפוליטיות.
Unfortunately, certain Israeli politicians aggravate the **ethnicity** issue and the feeling of being discriminated of certain ethnic groups in order to advance their own political aspirations.

Additional Examples in this Pattern

temporariness אֲרָעִיּוּת/עֲרָאִיּוּת
simplicity, popularity עֲמָמִיּוּת

---

773. Linear derivation Noun +*i* +*ut* / *C(e)CoCiyut*, no plural

our/your/their	my/your/his/her	const.	Gloss	sing/pl
גְּאוֹנִיּוּתֵנוּ/תְכֶם/תְכֶן/תָם/תָן	**גְּאוֹנִיּוּ**תִי/תְךָ/תֵךְ/תוֹ/תָהּ	-גְּאוֹנִיּוּת	genius	גְּאוֹנִיּוּת נ׳

This is linear derivation of N/Adj+*i*+*ut*, גָּאוֹן 'genius N' +*i* + *ut* (the base *a* being reduced to *shva* or zero), but such realizations also constitute discontinuous derivation in the *C(e)CoCiyut mishkal*. There are no plural forms in use.

Examples

יש מספר לא קטן של גאונים בעולם, אבל **גְאוֹנִיּוּתוֹ** של איינשטיין הייתה תופעה יחידה במינה.
There are a number of geniuses in the world, but the genius of Einstein was unique.

Additional Examples in this Pattern

wickedness, malice, evil זְדוֹנִיּוּת	thoroughness יְסוֹדִיּוּת

---

774. Linear derivation Noun *+i +ut* / *CCoCiyut* = *CaCoCiyut*, the first root consonant is guttural, no plural

sing/pl	Gloss	const.	my/your/his/her	our/your/their
הֲמוֹנִיּוּת נ׳	vulgarity, commonness	-הֲמוֹנִיּוּת	**הֲמוֹנִיּוּ**תִי/תְךָ/תֵךְ/תוֹ/תָהּ	**הֲמוֹנִיּוּ**תֵנוּ/תְכֶם/תְכֶן/ תָם/תָן

This is linear derivation of N/Adj+*i*+*ut*, הֲמוֹנִי 'vulgar, common' + *ut* (the *shva* is replaced by *Hataf-pataH* because of the guttural), but such realizations also constitute discontinuous derivation in a *CCoCiyut* > *CaCoCiyut mishkal*. There are no plural forms in use.

Examples

קומיקאים לא מעטים ידועים **בַּהֲמוֹנִיּוּתָם** יותר מאשר בחוש ההומור שלהם.
A good number of comedians are better known their **vulgarity** than for their sense of humor.

---

775. Linear derivation Noun *+i +ut* / *CCuCiyut*, no plural

sing/pl	Gloss	const.	my/your/his/her	our/your/their
בְּתוּלִיּוּת נ׳	virginity, purity	-בְּתוּלִיּוּת	**בְּתוּלִיּוּ**תִי/תְךָ/תֵךְ/תוֹ/תָהּ	**בְּתוּלִיּוּ**תֵנוּ/תְכֶם/תְכֶן /תָם/תָן

This is linear derivation of N/Adj+*i*+*ut*, בְּתוּלִי 'virginal' + *ut*, but such realizations also constitute discontinuous derivation in the *CCuCiyut mishkal*. There are no plural forms in use.

Examples

הנוצרים מקשרים את **בְּתוּלִיּוּתָהּ** של מרים אם ישו לפסוק בישעיהו: "והנה העלמה יולדת בן..."
The Christians attribute the **virginity** of Mary, Jesus' mother, to a verse in Isaiah, "and here is the maiden (erroneously translated into Greek as 'virgin') giving birth to a son..."

Additional Examples in this Pattern

glassiness זְגוּגִיּוּת

---

776. Linear derivation Noun +*i* +*ut* / *CiCCiyut*, no plural

our/your/their	my/your/his/her	const.	Gloss	sing/pl
עִקְבִיּותֵנוּ/תְכֶם/תְכֶן/תָם/תָן	**עִקְבִיּו**תִי/תְךָ/תֵךְ/תוֹ/תָהּ	עִקְבִיּוּת-	consistency	עִקְבִיּוּת נ׳

This is linear derivation of N/Adj+*i*+*ut*, עִקְבִי 'consistent' + *ut*, but such realizations also constitute discontinuous derivation in the *CiCCiyut mishkal*. There are no plural forms in use.

Examples

הרבה טוענים שהמכשול הגדול ביותר העומד בפני בני אדם בדרך להשגת מטרותיהם הוא היעדר **עִקְבִיּוּת**.
Many claim that the greatest handicap people face on the way to achieving their goals is lack of **consistency**.

משה התחיל לנהוג בגיל 16. הוא למד נהיגה בקלות ובמהירות, וכבר אז נהג **בְטִבְעִיּוּת** כאילו נולד עם הגה...
Moshe began to drive at the age of 16. He learned to drive easily and quickly, and already then was driving with **naturalness** as if he had been born with a steering wheel…

כשארה״ב בחרה בברק אובמה לנשיא האפרו-אמריקאי הראשון, הייתה בכך הרבה **סִמְלִיּוּת**!
When the US elected Barack Obama as its first Afro-American president, there was considerable **symbolism** in it!

כאשר מדינה משקיעה משאבים בתשתית ובשירותי ציבור, בדרך כלל אין היא מונעת על ידי שיקולים של **רְוְחִיּוּת**.
When a state invests resources in infrastructure and public services, it is generally not motivated by considerations of **profitability**.

Additional Examples in this Pattern

גִּזְעִיּוּת pedigree
טִקְסִיּוּת pomp, ceremony
יִצְרִיּוּת following one's urges
נִצְחִיּוּת eternity
קִצְבִּיּוּת rhythm
רִגְעִיּוּת temporariness
רִגְשִׁיּוּת emotionality
רִשְׁמִיּוּת formality
שִׁטְחִיּוּת superficiality

---

777. Linear derivation Noun +*i* +*ut* / *CiCCaCiyut*, no plural

our/your/their	my/your/his/her	const.	Gloss	sing/pl
עִנְיָנִיּותֵנוּ/תְכֶם/תְכֶן/תָם/תָן	**עִנְיָנִיּו**תִי/תְךָ/תֵךְ/תוֹ/תָהּ	עִנְיָנִיּוּת-	matter-of-factness	עִנְיָנִיּוּת נ׳

This is linear derivation of N/Adj+*i*+*ut*, עִנְיָנִי 'matter-of-fact' + *ut*, but such realizations also constitute discontinuous derivation in the *CiCCaCiyut mishkal*. There are no plural forms in use.

Examples

ראש החברה אינו כריזמטי, אבל את עסקי חברתו הוא מנהל **בעִנְיָנִיּוּת** וביעילות.
The company's head is not charismatic, but he manages the company business with **matter-of-factness** and efficiency.

---

778. Linear derivation Noun *+i +ut* / *CiCCatiyut*, no plural

our/your/their	my/your/his/her	const.	Gloss	sing/pl
שִׁגְרָתִיּוּתֵנוּ/תְכֶם/תְכֶן/תָם/תָן	**שִׁגְרָתִיּוּ**תִי/תְךָ/תֵךְ/תוֹ/תָהּ	שִׁגְרָתִיּוּת-	routineness	שִׁגְרָתִיּוּת נ'

This is linear derivation of N/Adj+*i*+*ut*, שִׁגְרָתִי 'routine Adj' + *ut*, but such realizations also constitute discontinuous derivation in the *CiCCatiyut mishkal*. There are no plural forms in use.

Examples

יש אנשים ש**שִׁגְרָתִיּוּת** עוזרת להם לתפקד היטב בחיי היום-יום ; אחרים יוצאים מדעתם אם אינם יכולים לחרוג מן השגרה.
There are people whom **routineness** helps to function well in daily life; others go nuts if they cannot deviate from their daily routine.

---

779. Linear derivation Noun *+i +ut* / *CiCConiyut*, no plural

our/your/their	my/your/his/her	const.	Gloss	sing/pl
צִבְעוֹנִיּוּתֵנוּ/תְכֶם/תְכֶן/תָם/תָן	**צִבְעוֹנִיּוּ**תִי/תְךָ/תֵךְ/תוֹ/תָהּ	צִבְעוֹנִיּוּת-	colorfulness	צִבְעוֹנִיּוּת נ'

This is linear derivation of N/Adj+*i*+*ut*, צִבְעוֹנִי 'colorful' + *ut*, but such realizations also constitute discontinuous derivation in the *CiCConiyut mishkal*. There are no plural forms in use.

Examples

ה**צִבְעוֹנִיּוּת** של התוכים האלה ממש מהממת.
The **colorfulness** of these parrots is simply striking.

Additional Examples in this Pattern

נִסְיוֹנִיּוּת experimentalness   שִׁוְיוֹנִיּוּת equality

---

780. Linear derivation Noun +*i* +*ut* / *CiCoCiyut*, no plural

our/your/their	my/your/his/her	const.	Gloss	sing/pl
חִלּוֹנִיּוֹתֵנוּ/תְכֶם/תְכֶן/תָם/תָן	**חִלּוֹנִיּוֹ**תִי/תְךָ/תֵךְ/תוֹ/תָהּ	חִלּוֹנִיּוּת-	secularity	חִלּוֹנִיּוּת נ׳

This is linear derivation of N/Adj+*i*+*ut*, חִלּוֹנִי 'secular' + *ut*, but such realizations also constitute discontinuous derivation in the *CiCoCiyut mishkal*. There are no plural forms in use.

Examples

המאבק בין ה**חִלּוֹנִיּוּת** והדתיות בישראל הולך ומחריף.
The struggle between **secularism** and religiosity in Israel keeps getting worse.

Additional Examples in this Pattern

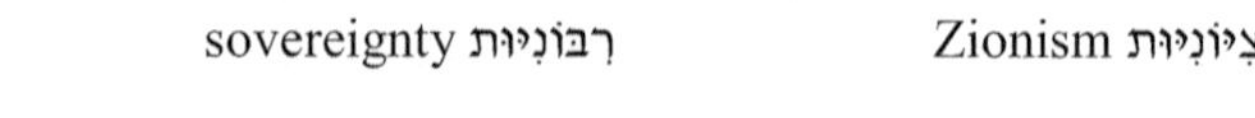

צִיּוֹנִיּוּת Zionism

רִבּוֹנִיּוּת sovereignty

---

781. Linear derivation Noun +*i* +*ut* / *CiCuCiyut*, no plural

our/your/their	my/your/his/her	const.	Gloss	sing/pl
חִיּוּנִיּוֹתֵנוּ/תְכֶם/תְכֶן/תָם/תָן	**חִיּוּנִיּוֹ**תִי/תְךָ/תֵךְ/תוֹ/תָהּ	חִיּוּנִיּוּת-	vitality	חִיּוּנִיּוּת נ׳

This is linear derivation of N/Adj+*i*+*ut*, חִיּוּנִי 'vital' + *ut*, but such realizations also constitute discontinuous derivation in the *CiCuCiyut mishkal*. There are no plural forms in use.

Examples

אני מאמין שעם ה**חִיּוּנִיּוּת** העצומה שלה היא תתגבר בסופו של דבר על המחלה.
I believe that with her tremendous **vitality** she will overcome her illness.

מי היה מאמין לפני כמה עשרות שנים שה**שִׁמּוּשִׁיּוּת** של המחשב האישי תהיה כה עצומה...
Who would have believed just a few decades ago that the **usefulness** of the personal computer would be so huge...?

דיקטטורות מחזיקות מעמד רק כאשר מידת ה**רִכּוּזִיּוּת** שבניהולן היא גבוהה.
Dictatorships hold out only when the degree of **centralization** in their running is high.

Additional Examples in this Pattern

חִיּוּבִיּוּת positiveness
מִלּוּלִיּוּת literalness
נִגּוּדִיּוּת difference, oppositeness
צִבּוּרִיּוּת public nature, universality
צִיּוּרִיּוּת picturesqueness
קִבּוּצִיּוּת collectivity; collectivism
שִׁתּוּפִיּוּת cooperativeness; collectiveness

---

782. Linear derivation Noun +*i* +*ut* / *CiConiyut*, no plural

our/your/their	my/your/his/her	const.	Gloss	sing/pl
קִיצוֹנִיּוּתֵנוּ/תְכֶם/תְכֶן/תָם/תָן	**קִיצוֹנִיּוּ**תִי/תְךָ/תֵךְ/תוֹ/תָהּ	-קִיצוֹנִיּוּת	extremism	קִיצוֹנִיּוּת נ'

This is linear derivation of N/Adj+*i*+*ut*, קִיצוֹנִי 'extreme' + *ut*, but such realizations also constitute discontinuous derivation in the *CiConiyut mishkal*. There are no plural forms in use.

Examples

קִיצוֹנִיּוּת פוליטית מביאה לא פעם לרצח ממניעים פוליטיים.
Political **extremism** sometimes brings about politically-motivated murder.

---

783. Linear derivation Noun +*i* +*ut* / *CeCCiyut*, no plural

our/your/their	my/your/his/her	const.	Gloss	sing/pl
חֶלְקִיּוּתֵנוּ/תְכֶם/תְכֶן/תָם/תָן	**חֶלְקִיּוּ**תִי/תְךָ/תֵךְ/תוֹ/תָהּ	-חֶלְקִיּוּת	partialness	חֶלְקִיּוּת נ'

This is linear derivation of N/Adj+*i*+*ut*, חֶלְקִי 'partial' + *ut*, but such realizations also constitute discontinuous derivation in the *CeCCiyut mishkal*. There are no plural forms in use.

Examples

הבעייה עם הסדרי ביניים בין מדינות בסכסוך היא **חֶלְקִיּוּתָם** של ההסדרים.
The problem with interim arrangements between nations in conflict is the **partialness** of such arrangements.

Additional Examples in this Pattern

moral standard; valence, valency עֶרְכִּיּוּת　　　contradiction, opposition נֶגְדִּיּוּת

---

784. Linear derivation Noun +*i* +*ut* / *CeCConiyut*, no plural

our/your/their	my/your/his/her	const.	Gloss	sing/pl
עֶקְרוֹנִיּוּתֵנוּ/תְכֶם/תְכֶן/תָם/תָן	**עֶקְרוֹנִיּוּ**תִי/תְךָ/תֵךְ/תוֹ/תָהּ	-עֶקְרוֹנִיּוּת	behavior by principle	עֶקְרוֹנִיּוּת נ'

This is linear derivation of N/Adj+*i*+*ut*, עֶקְרוֹנִי 'of principle' + *ut*, but such realizations also constitute discontinuous derivation in the *CeCConiyut mishkal*. There are no plural forms in use.

Examples

הטלתי ספק ב**עֶקְרוֹנִיּוּת** שבעמדתו.
I doubted the "**principledness**" of his stand/position.

---

785. Linear derivation Noun *+i +ut* / *CaCCiyut*, no plural

our/your/their	my/your/his/her	const.	Gloss	sing/pl
גַּבְרִיּוּתֵנוּ/תְכֶם/תְכֶן/תָם/תָן	**גַּבְרִיּוּ**תִי/תְךָ/תֵךְ/תוֹ/תָהּ	-גַּבְרִיּוּת	manhood, manliness	גַּבְרִיּוּת נ׳

This is linear derivation of N/Adj+*i*+*ut*, גַּבְרִי 'manly' + *ut*, but such realizations also constitute discontinuous derivation in the *CaCCiyut mishkal*. There are no plural forms in use.

Examples

חבל שיש לא מעט גברים המאמינים ש**גַּבְרִיּוּת** מתבטאת באלימות, לא פעם נגד נשים.
It is a pity that quite a few men believe that **manhood** expresses itself in violence, in some cases against women.

יש מבקרי ספרות, תיאטרון וקולנוע שכתיבתם נוטפת **אַרְסִיּוּת**.
There are literary, theater and film critics whose writing is drenched with **poisonousness**.

יש דמויות, למשל גנדי, שהן כל כך רוחניות, שקשה לחשוב עליהן במונחים של **גַּשְׁמִיּוּת**.
There are figures, such as Gandhi, that are so spiritual, that it is hard to think of them in terms of **corporeality**.

Additional Examples in this Pattern

nothingness אַפְסִיּוּת
earthliness אַרְצִיּוּת
rockiness טַרְשִׁיּוּת
country life כַּפְרִיּוּת
rockiness סַלְעִיּוּת
identity, self-concept עַצְמִיּוּת

---

786. Linear derivation Noun *+i +ut* / *CaCCiyut* = *CaCaCiyut*, the second root consonant is guttural, no plural

our/your/their	my/your/his/her	const.	Gloss	sing/pl
יַחֲסִיּוּתֵנוּ/תְכֶם/תְכֶן/תָם/תָן	**יַחֲסִיּוּ**תִי/תְךָ/תֵךְ/תוֹ/תָהּ	-יַחֲסִיּוּת	relativity	יַחֲסִיּוּת נ׳

This is linear derivation of N/Adj+*i*+*ut*, יַחֲסִי 'relative' + *ut*, but such realizations also constitute discontinuous derivation in the *CaCCiyut = CaCaCiyut mishkal*. When a *shva* is expected with the guttural, it is replaced by *Hataf-pataH*. There are no plural forms in use.

Examples

תורת ה**יַּחֲסִיּוּת** הכללית של איינשטיין שינתה את תפיסת הפיסיקה המודרנית יותר מכל תורה אחרת.
Einstein's General **Relativity** theory affected the conception of modern physics more than any other theory.

Additional Examples in this Pattern

brutishness, vulgarity בַּהֲמִיּוּת
volcanism גַּעֲשִׁיּוּת

---

787. Linear derivation Noun +*i* +*ut* / *CaCCiCiyut*, with reduplication, no plural

our/your/their	my/your/his/her	const.	Gloss	sing/pl
שַׁבְרִירִיּותֵנוּ/תְכֶם/תְכֶן/תָם/תָן	**שַׁבְרִירִיּו**תִי/תְךָ/תֵךְ/תוֹ/תָהּ	שַׁבְרִירִיּוּת-	fragility	שַׁבְרִירִיּוּת נ׳

This is linear derivation of N/Adj+*i*+*ut*, שַׁבְרִירִי 'fragile' + *ut*, but such realizations also constitute discontinuous derivation in the *CaCCiCiyut mishkal*. The third root consonant is reduplicated in position four (קַטְלִילִיּוּת). There are no plural forms in use.

Examples

גבריאל אוהב נשים קטנות שישותן מקרינה **שַׁבְרִירִיּוּת** ומשוועת להגנה.
Gabriel likes small women whose presence emanates **fragility** and cries out to be protected.

Additional Examples in this Pattern

redness, reddishness Lit. חַכְלִילִיּוּת lightness, airiness אַוְרִירִיּוּת

---

788. Linear derivation Noun +*i* +*ut* / *CaCCaCiyut*, no plural

our/your/their	my/your/his/her	const.	Gloss	sing/pl
אַכְזָרִיּותֵנוּ/תְכֶם/תְכֶן/תָם/תָן	**אַכְזָרִיּו**תִי/תְךָ/תֵךְ/תוֹ/תָהּ	אַכְזָרִיּוּת-	cruelty	אַכְזָרִיּוּת נ׳

This is linear derivation of N/Adj+*i*+*ut*, אַכְזָרִי 'cruel' + *ut*, but such realizations also constitute discontinuous derivation in the *CaCCaCiyut mishkal*. There are no plural forms in use.

Examples

קשה לי מאוד לראות אנשים נוהגים ב**אַכְזָרִיּוּת** כלפי חיות.
I find it very difficult tom watch people treat animals with **cruelty**.

Additional Examples in this Pattern

wheeling-dealing (esp. in politics) עַסְקָנִיּוּת being updated עַדְכָּנִיּוּת

---

789. Linear derivation Noun +*i* +*ut* / *CaCConiyut*, no plural

our/your/their	my/your/his/her	const.	Gloss	sing/pl
קַדְמוֹנִיּותֵנוּ/תְכֶם/תְכֶן/תָם/תָן	**קַדְמוֹנִיּו**תִי/תְךָ/תֵךְ/תוֹ/תָהּ	קַדְמוֹנִיּוּת-	antiquity	קַדְמוֹנִיּוּת נ׳

This is linear derivation of N/Adj+*i*+*ut*, קַדְמוֹנִי 'ancient' + *ut*, but such realizations also constitute discontinuous derivation in the *CaCConiyut mishkal*. There are no plural forms in use.

Examples

ספרו החשוב של יוסף בן-מתתיהו על תולדות עם ישראל נקרא "**קַדְמוֹנִיּוֹת** היהודים".
Josephus' important book on the history of the Jewish people is called "The **Antiquity** of the Jews."

---

790. Linear derivation Noun *+i +ut* / *CaCCuCiyut*, with reduplication, no plural

our/your/their	my/your/his/her	const.	Gloss	sing/pl
קַטְנוּנִיּוּתֵנוּ/תְכֶם/תְכֶן/תָם/תָן	**קַטְנוּנִיּוּ**תִי/תְךָ/תֵךְ/תוֹ/תָהּ	קַטְנוּנִיּוּת-	pettiness	קַטְנוּנִיּוּת נ'

This is linear derivation of N/Adj*+i+ut*, קַטְנוּנִי 'petty' + *ut*, but such realizations also constitute discontinuous derivation in the *CaCCuCiyut mishkal*. The third root consonant is reduplicated in position four (קַטְלוּלִיּוּת). There are no plural forms in use.

Examples

קַטְנוּנִיּוּת היא הקפדה על פרטים קטנים, חסרי ערך, וביחסי אנוש היא בדרך כלל מצביעה גם על העדר נדיבות.
Pettiness is excessive dealing with small, insignificant details, and in human relations it generally also indicates lack of generosity.

אם נקעה נפשך במה שנראה לך כ**אַפְרוּרִיּוּת** של העיר הגדולה, טייל קצת באחד הגנים הנפלאים שלה.
If you feel fed up with the **grayness** of the big city, walk a bit in one of its wonderful gardens/parks.

במזרח התיכון, ה**עַרְמוּמִיּוּת** נחשבת לתכונה חיובית, המראה על פיקחות; המרומה על ידי הערמומי נתפס כטיפש ומוצא עצמו מבודד חברתית.
In the Middle East, **cunning** is regarded as a positive quality, which demonstrates cleverness. The person cheated by the cunning one is regarded as a fool, and is isolated socially.

הבעייה עם משחת ההגנה על העור שאני משתמש בה היא **שַׁמְנוּנִיּוּתָהּ** הרַבָּה מדיי.
The problem with the skin protection cream I am using is its excessive **oiliness**.

Additional Examples in this Pattern

redness, ruddiness אַדְמוּמִיּוּת
dimness, vagueness אַפְלוּלִיּוּת
porousness נַקְבוּבִיּוּת
sadness עַגְמוּמִיּוּת
being crooked, twisted עַקְמוּמִיּוּת
spinelessness רַכְרוּכִיּוּת
oiliness שַׁמְנוּנִיּוּת

---

791. Linear derivation Noun +*i* +*ut* /*CaCCuCiyut* = *CaCaCuCiyut*, with reduplication, the second root consonant is guttural, no plural

our/your/their	my/your/his/her	const.	Gloss	sing/pl
סַהֲרוּרִיוּתֵנוּ/תְכֶם/תְכֶן/תָם/תָן	**סַהֲרוּרִיוּ**תִי/תְךָ/תֵךְ/תוֹ/תָהּ	-סַהֲרוּרִיּוּת	somnambulism; daydreaming	סַהֲרוּרִיּוּת נ׳

This is linear derivation of N/Adj+*i*+*ut*, סַהֲרוּרִי 'somnambulant; daydreaming' + *ut*, but such realizations also constitute discontinuous derivation in the *CaCCuCiyut* = *CaCaCuCiyut mishkal*. The third root consonant is reduplicated in position four (קְטַלוּלִיּוּת). When a *shva* is expected with the guttural, it is replaced by *Hataf-PataH* (קְטֲלוּלִיּוּת). There are no plural forms in use.

Examples

כשידידים אומרים לי שפתרון הסכסוך הפלסטיני-ישראלי מתקרב, אני עונה להם שיפה שהם מאמינים בזה, אבל שבמציאות של היום זו **סַהֲרוּרִיּוּת** להאמין בכך.

When friends tell me that the resolution of Palestinian-Israeli conflict is imminent, I respond that I appreciate their believing it, but that in today's reality it is **daydreaming** to think so.

Additional Examples in this Pattern

tininess זַעֲרוּרִיּוּת

---

792. Linear derivation Noun +*i* +*ut* / *CaCCutiyut*, no plural

our/your/their	my/your/his/her	const.	Gloss	sing/pl
יַלְדוּתִיוּתֵנוּ/תְכֶם/תְכֶן/תָם/תָן	**יַלְדוּתִיוּ**תִי/תְךָ/תֵךְ/תוֹ/תָהּ	-יַלְדוּתִיּוּת	childishness	יַלְדוּתִיּוּת נ׳

This is linear derivation of N/Adj+*i*+*ut*, יַלְדוּתִי 'childish' + *ut*, but such realizations also constitute discontinuous derivation in the *CaCCutiyut mishkal*. There are no plural forms in use. With only one *CiCCutiyut* occurrence, סִפְרוּתִיּוּת is listed under *CaCCatiyut*.

Examples

אנשים מסוימים, אפילו האינטלקטואלים שבהם, שומרים על מידה של **יַלְדוּתִיּוּת** אפילו בגיל מבוגר. יש בזה לא מעט קסם.

Some people, even the intellectual among them, maintain a degree of **childishness**. It adds to their charm.

Additional Examples in this Pattern

friendliness, sociability חַבְרוּתִיּוּת　　authoritarianism סַמְכוּתִיּוּת

---

793. Linear derivation Noun +*i* +*ut* / *CaCuCiyut*, no plural

our/your/their	my/your/his/her	const.	Gloss	sing/pl
כַּדּוּרִיוּתֵנוּ/תְכֶם/תְכֶן/תָם/תָן	**כַּדּוּרִיוּ**תִי/תְךָ/תֵךְ/תוֹ/תָהּ	-כַּדּוּרִיּוּת	roundness	כַּדּוּרִיּוּת נ׳

This is linear derivation of N/Adj+*i*+*ut*, כַּדּוּרִי 'round' + *ut*, but such realizations also constitute discontinuous derivation in the *CaCuCiyut mishkal*. There are no plural forms in use.

Examples

מעניין אם יש עדיין אנשים שאינם מאמינים ב**כַּדּוּרִיּוּתוֹ** של כדור הארץ...
It is interesting: are there still people who do not believe in the **roundness** of Earth?

Additional Examples in this Pattern

quantitativeness כַּמּוּתִיּוּת

---

794. Linear derivation Noun +*i* +*ut* / *CoCCiyut*, no plural

sing/pl	Gloss	const.	my/your/his/her	our/your/their
שָׁרְשִׁיּוּת נ׳	rootedness	שָׁרְשִׁיּוּת-	**שָׁרְשִׁיּוּ**תִי/תְךָ/תֵךְ/תוֹ/תָהּ	**שָׁרְשִׁיּוּ**תֵנוּ/תְכֶם/תְכֶן/תָם/תָן

This is linear derivation of N/Adj+*i*+*ut*, שָׁרְשִׁי 'rooted' + *ut* (with *kamats katan* [o]), but such realizations also constitute discontinuous derivation in the *CoCCiyut mishkal*. There are no plural forms in use.

Examples

כשמבקרים באזורים החקלאיים של המערב התיכון, מתרשמים מ**שָׁרְשִׁיּוּתָם** של האיכרים.
When one visits the agricultural regions of the Mid-West, one is impressed with the **rootedness** of the farmers.

בהודו הפרות עדיין מסתובבות ב**חָפְשִׁיּוּת** אפילו בערים הגדולות.
In India cows still roam with **freedom** even in the large cities.

Additional Examples in this Pattern

rawness, amorphousness גָּלְמִיּוּת
materialism חָמְרִיּוּת
foreignness נָכְרִיּוּת
polarity קָטְבִּיּוּת

---

795. Linear derivation Noun +*i* +*ut* / *CoCCiyut* = *CoCoCiyut*, the second root consonant is guttural, no plural

sing/pl	Gloss	const.	my/your/his/her	our/your/their
כָּהֳלִיּוּת נ׳	alcohol content	כָּהֳלִיּוּת-	**כָּהֳלִיּוּ**תִי/תְךָ/תֵךְ/תוֹ/תָהּ	**כָּהֳלִיּוּ**תֵנוּ/תְכֶם/תְכֶן/תָם/תָן

This is linear derivation of N/Adj+*i*+*ut*, כָּהֳלִי 'of alcohol' + *ut*, but such realizations also constitute discontinuous derivation in the *CoCCiyut* = *CoCoCiyut mishkal*. When a *shva* is expected with a guttural, it is replaced by *Hataf-kamats*. There are no plural forms in use.

Examples

יצרני משקאות חריפים חייבים לציין על כל בקבוק את אחוזי **כָּהֳלִיּוּתוֹ**.
Manufacturers of alcoholic drinks must note on each bottle what the **alcohol content** is.

Additional Examples in this Pattern

disgustingness, loathsomeness Col. גָּעֳלִיּוּת

---

796. Linear derivation Noun +*i* +*ut* / *CoCCatiyut*, no plural

our/your/their	my/your/his/her	const.	Gloss	sing/pl
אָפְנָתִיּוּתֵנוּ/תְכֶם/תְכֶן/תָם/תָן	**אָפְנָתִיּוּ**תִי/תְךָ/תֵךְ/תוֹ/תָהּ	אָפְנָתִיּוּת-	being fashionable	אָפְנָתִיּוּת נ׳

This is linear derivation of N/Adj+*i*+*ut*, אָפְנָתִי 'fashionable' + *ut*, but such realizations also constitute discontinuous derivation in the *CoCCatiyut mishkal*. There are no plural forms in use.

Examples

אשתו ובתו של הנשיא מתלבשות **באָפְנָתִיּוּת** ובטוב טעם.
The President's wife and daughter dress in a **fashionable manner** and in good taste.

---

797. Linear derivation Noun +*i* +*ut* / *CaCiyut*, no plural

our/your/their	my/your/his/her	const.	Gloss	sing/pl
דָּתִיּוּתֵנוּ/תְכֶם/תְכֶן/תָם/תָן	**דָּתִיּוּ**תִי/תְךָ/תֵךְ/תוֹ/תָהּ	דָּתִיּוּת-	religiosity	דָּתִיּוּת נ׳

This is with linear derivation of N/Adj+*i*+*ut*, דָּתִי 'religious' + *ut*, but such realizations also constitute discontinuous derivation in the *CaCiyut mishkal*. There are no plural forms in use.

Examples

מדינת ישראל הוקמה כמדינה ציונית חילונית, אבל מדי שנה בשנה מתגברת בה **הדָּתִיּוּת** למגינת לבם של אזרחיה החילוניים.
Israel was founded as a secular Zionist state, but year by year **religiosity** in it is getting stronger, which worries its secular citizens.

Additional Examples in this Pattern

varicosity דָּלִיּוּת

---

798. Linear derivation Noun +*i* +*ut* / *CoCCaniyut*, no plural

our/your/their	my/your/his/her	const.	Gloss	sing/pl
חוֹלְמָנִיּוּתֵנוּ/תְכֶם/תְכֶן/תָם/תָן	**חוֹלְמָנִיּוּ**תִי/תְךָ/תֵךְ/תוֹ/תָהּ	חוֹלְמָנִיּוּת-	dreaminess	חוֹלְמָנִיּוּת נ׳

This is linear derivation of N/Adj+*i*+*ut*, חוֹלְמָנִי 'dreamy' + *ut*, but such realizations also constitute discontinuous derivation in the *CoCCaniyut mishkal*. There are no plural forms in use.

Examples

חוֹלְמָנִיּוּת היא תכונה שמורים לא כל כך אוהבים אצל תלמידים בזמן השיעור...
Dreaminess is a quality that teachers do not particularly like in students in class…

---

799. Linear derivation Noun +*i* +*ut* / *CoCiyut*, no plural

our/your/their	my/your/his/her	const.	Gloss	sing/pl
סוֹדִיּוּתֵנוּ/תְכֶם/תְכֶן/תָם/תָן	**סוֹדִיּוּ**תִי/תְךָ/תֵךְ/תוֹ/תָהּ	סוֹדִיּוּת-	secrecy	סוֹדִיּוּת נ׳

This is linear derivation of N/Adj+*i*+*ut*, סוֹדִי 'secret Adj' + *ut*, but such realizations also constitute discontinuous derivation in the *CoCiyut mishkal*. There are no plural forms in use.

Examples

תאריך פלישת בנות הברית ומיקומה נשמרו ב**סוֹדִיּוּת** מוחלטת.
The date and exact date of the Allies' invasion were kept in complete **secrecy**.

Additional Examples in this Pattern

finality סוֹפִיּוּת

---

800. Linear derivation Noun +*i* +*ut* / *CoCaniyut*, no plural

our/your/their	my/your/his/her	const.	Gloss	sing/pl
קוֹצָנִיּוּתֵנוּ/תְכֶם/תְכֶן/תָם/תָן	**קוֹצָנִיּוּ**תִי/תְךָ/תֵךְ/תוֹ/תָהּ	קוֹצָנִיּוּת-	thorniness	קוֹצָנִיּוּת נ׳

This is linear derivation of N/Adj+*i*+*ut*, קוֹצָנִי 'thorny' + *ut*, but such realizations also constitute discontinuous derivation in the *CoCaniyut mishkal*. There are no plural forms in use.

Examples

ה**קוֹצָנִיּוּת** שבאופן דיבורו מרגיזה הרבה אנשים.
The **thorniness** of his manner of speaking annoys many people.

---

801. Linear derivation Noun +*i* +*ut* / *CuCaniyut*, no plural

our/your/their	my/your/his/her	const.	Gloss	sing/pl
חוּשָׁנִיּוּתֵנוּ/תְכֶם/תְכֶן/תָם/תָן	**חוּשָׁנִיּוּ**תִי/תְךָ/תֵךְ/תוֹ/תָהּ	חוּשָׁנִיּוּת-	sensuality	חוּשָׁנִיּוּת נ׳

This is linear derivation of N/Adj+*i*+*ut*, חוּשָׁנִי 'sensual' + *ut*, but such realizations also constitute discontinuous derivation in the *CuCaniyut mishkal*. There are no plural forms in use.

Examples

החוּשָׁנִיּוּת בקולה מושכת מאוד ; זה חלק חשוב מקסמה.
The **sensuality** of her voice is very attractive; it is an important aspect of her charm.

Additional Examples in this Pattern

חוּצָנִיּוּת extraterritoriality

---

802. Linear derivation Noun +*i* +*ut* / *tCuCatiyut*, no plural

our/your/their	my/your/his/her	const.	Gloss	sing/pl
תְּנוּדָתִיּותֵנוּ/תְכֶם/תְכֶן/תָם/תָן	**תְּנוּדָתִיּו**תִי/תְךָ/תֵךְ/תוֹ/תָהּ	-תְּנוּדָתִיּוּת	fluctuation	תְּנוּדָתִיּוּת נ׳

This is linear derivation of N/Adj+*i*+*ut*, תְּנוּדָתִי 'fluctuating' + *ut*, but such realizations also constitute discontinuous derivation in the *tCuCatiyut mishkal*. There are no plural forms in use.

Examples

התְּנוּדָתִיּוּת המתמדת בשוק המניות מבלבלת את מרבית האנשים ומרתיעה אותם מלהשקיע בה.
The constant **fluctuation** of the stock exchange confuses most people and deters them from investing in it.

Additional Examples in this Pattern

תְּנוּעָתִיּוּת mobility

---

803. Linear derivation Noun +*i* +*ut* / *taCCutiyut*, no plural

our/your/their	my/your/his/her	const.	Gloss	sing/pl
תַּרְבּוּתִיּותֵנוּ/תְכֶם/תְכֶן/תָם/תָן	**תַּרְבּוּתִיּו**תִי/תְךָ/תֵךְ/תוֹ/תָהּ	-תַּרְבּוּתִיּוּת	culture, sophistication	תַּרְבּוּתִיּוּת נ׳

This is linear derivation of N/Adj+*i*+*ut*, תַּרְבּוּתִי 'cultural' + *ut*, but such realizations also constitute discontinuous derivation in the *taCCutiyut mishkal*. There are no plural forms in use.

Examples

השלכת אשפה ברשות הרבים היא סימן מובהק להיעדר **תַּרְבּוּתִיּוּת**.
Throwing garbage in the public domain is a clear indication of lack of **culture**.

---

804. Linear derivation Noun +*i* +*ut* / *toCaCtiyut*, no plural

our/your/their	my/your/his/her	const.	Gloss	sing/pl
תּוֹעַלְתִּיוּתֵנוּ/תְכֶם/ תְכֶן/תָם/תָן	**תּוֹעַלְתִּיוּ**תִי/תְךָ/תֵךְ/תוֹ/תָהּ	תּוֹעַלְתִּיוּת-	usefulness; practicability	תּוֹעַלְתִּיוּת נ׳

This is linear derivation of N/Adj+*i*+*ut*, תּוֹעַלְתִּי 'useful' + *ut*, but such realizations also constitute discontinuous derivation in the *toCaCtiyut mishkal*. There are no plural forms in use.

Examples

בכל בית יש הרבה חפצים שאין בהם כל **תּוֹעַלְתִּיוּת**, אך אנו מחזיקים בהם מסיבות אסתטיות או נוסטלגיות.

In every home there are many objects that have no **usefulness**, but we keep hold of them for aesthetic or nostalgic reasons.

Additional Examples in this Pattern

heritability, heredity תּוֹרַשְׁתִּיוּת

---

805. ***CCit***, pl. *-ot*

our/your/their	my/your/his/her	const.	Gloss	sing/pl
בְּרִיתֵנוּ/תְכֶם/תְכֶן/תָם/תָן	**בְּרִי**תִי/תְךָ/תֵךְ/תוֹ/תָהּ	בְּרִית-	treaty;	בְּרִית נ׳
בְּרִיתוֹתֵינוּ/כֶם/כֶן/הֶם/הֶן	**בְּרִיתוֹ**תַי/תֶיךָ/תַיִךְ/תָיו/תֶיהָ	בְּרִיתוֹת-	circumcision	בְּרִיתוֹת

The base suffix is *-it*, the plural suffix is *-ot.*

Examples

חלק ניכר מארצות אירופה הן חברות היום בארגון **בְּרִית** הארצות הצפון אטלנטיות.

A significant number of the countries of Europe are members of the North Atlantic **Treaty** Organization.

Special Expressions

very strong **covenant** **בְּרִית** דמים

the Soviet **Union** **בְּרִית** המועצות

the United States ארצות ה**בְּרִית**

defense **treaty** **בְּרִית** הגנה

ritual **circumcision** **בְּרִית** מילה

celebration of female infant birth corresponding to male circumcision (Coll.) **בְּרִיתָה**

very strong **bond** **בְּרִית** אחים

Additional Examples in this Pattern

(borrowed from Latin; in its source, this *-it* is not a suffix.) sardine טְרִית

---

806. ***CCit* = *CaCit***, the first root consonant is guttural, pl. *-ot*

our/your/their	my/your/his/her	const.	Gloss	sing/pl
חֲנִיתֵנוּ/תְכֶם/תְכֶן/תָם/תָן	**חֲנִי**תִי/תְךָ/תֵךְ/תוֹ/תָהּ	חֲנִית-	spear,	חֲנִית נ'
חֲנִיתוֹתֵינוּ/כֶם/כֶן/הֶם/הֶן	**חֲנִיתוֹ**תַי/תֶיךָ/תַיִךְ/תָיו/תֶיהָ	חֲנִיתוֹת-	javelin	חֲנִיתוֹת

The base suffix is *-it*, the plural suffix is *-ot*. When a *shva* is expected with a guttural, it is replaced by *Hataf-pataH*. It is not clear whether the *-it* in חֲנִית is indeed a suffix.

Examples

חֲנִית היא כלי נשק, להגנה או לתקיפה, המורכב ממקל ארוך שבקצהו חוד העשוי מתכת, אבן או עצם. ה**חֲנִית** קלה וקצרה מרומח.

A **spear** is a weapon, for defense or attack, made of a pole with a pointed edge made of metal, stone or bone. It is lighter and shorter than a pike.

Additional Examples in this Pattern

spasm עֲוִית

---

807. ***CCit*, pl. *-iyot***

our/your/their	my/your/his/her	const.	Gloss	sing/pl
מְחִיתֵנוּ/תְכֶם/תְכֶן/תָם/תָן	**מְחִי**תִי/תְךָ/תֵךְ/תוֹ/תָהּ	מְחִית-	puree	מְחִית נ'
מְחִיּוֹתֵינוּ/כֶם/כֶן/הֶם/הֶן	**מְחִיּוֹ**תַי/תֶיךָ/תַיִךְ/תָיו/תֶיהָ	מְחִיּוֹת-		מְחִיּוֹת

The base suffix is *-it*, the plural suffix is *-iyot*. The forms are derived from roots with final *y* or *'*.

Examples

בעברית המדוברת, במקום **מְחִית** משתמשים במילה השאולה פִּירֶה.

In colloquial Hebrew, instead of מְחִית, they use the borrowing פִּירֶה, pronounced close to the French source *puree*.

Additional Examples in this Pattern

filling (in cooking/baking) מְלִית

---

808. ***CaCCit*** (from segholates etc.)

our/your/their	my/your/his/her	const.	Gloss	sing/pl
אַלְפִּיתֵנוּ/תְכֶם/תְכֶן/תָם/תָן	**אַלְפִּי**תִי/תְךָ/תֵךְ/תוֹ/תָהּ	אַלְפִּית-	a thous-	אַלְפִּית נ'
אַלְפִּיּוֹתֵינוּ/כֶם/כֶן/הֶם/הֶן	**אַלְפִּיּוֹ**תַי/תֶיךָ/תַיִךְ/תָיו/תֶיהָ	אַלְפִּיּוֹת-	andth	אַלְפִּיּוֹת

The base suffix is *-it*, and the plural suffix, when it exists, is *-iyot*. In some of the cases, the base is “segholate,” e.g., אֶבֶן/אַבְנ+ית < אַבְנִית, אֶלֶף/אַלְפּ+ית < אַלְפִּית. In some of the occurrences, the ending *-it* suggests diminution.

Examples

הגדרה ישראלית ל**אַלְפִּית** שנייה: פסק הזמן בין האור הצהוב ברמזור והצפירה מאחוריך.
An Israeli definition for **a thousandth** of a second: the time that elapses between the yellow light ("get ready" in Israel, before the green light) and the honk behind you.

הַחַרְצִית מחזיקה מעמד במזג אוויר קר יותר טוב ממרבית צמחי הנוי האחרים.
The **chrysanthemum** holds out in cold weather better than most other flower plants.

מרבית האנשים מעדיפים היום להשתמש ב**טַבְלִיּוֹת** במדיח הכלים במקום באבקה.
Today most people today prefer to use **tablets** in dishwashers in lieu of powder.

בעוד שהאמריקאים בדרך כלל מחפשים את העוף הגדול ביותר, הישראלים והערבים מעדיפים את **הַפַּרְגִּית** הקטנה יותר, מפני שבשרה רך יותר.
While Americans usually look for the biggest chicken, the Israelis and the Arabs prefer the smaller **young chicken**, because its meat is more tender.

Special Expressions

אַבְנִית שִׁנַּיִם tartar (teeth)
כַּסְפִּית רועמת fulminating **mercury** (munitions)

Additional Examples in this Pattern

אַבְנִית scale (in kettle, etc.)
בַּרְקִית glaucoma
דַּלְגִּית skipping rope
זַרְעִית skylark
חַרְסִית clay, red soil; clay shards
יַבְלִית couch grass, couch grass plant
יַרְכִּית tunic
כַּסְפִּית mercury
לַחְמִית conjunctiva (of eye)
סַלְעִית wheateater, oenanthe (bird)
צַלְמִית figurine, statuette; icon (comp.)
קַרְנִית cornea
קַרְצִית tick (insect)
קַשְׁתִּית iris (of eye)
רַגְלִית kickstand; short leg of furniture, machine

---

809. ***CaCCit* (from segholates etc.) > *CaCaCit***, the second root consonant is guttural

our/your/their	my/your/his/her	const.	Gloss	sing/pl
קַעֲרִיתֵנוּ/תְכֶם/תְכֶן/תָם/תָן	**קַעֲרִי**תִי/תְךָ/תֵךְ/תוֹ/תָהּ	קַעֲרִית-	small	קַעֲרִית נ'
קַעֲרִיּוֹתֵינוּ/כֶם/כֶן/הֶם/הֶן	**קַעֲרִיּוֹ**תַי/תֶיךָ/תַיִךְ/תָיו/תֶיהָ	קַעֲרִיּוֹת-	bowl	קַעֲרִיּוֹת

The base suffix is *-it*, and the plural suffix is *-iyot*. In some of the cases, the base is "segholate," e.g., זַחֲלִית < זַחַל+ית. In some of the occurrences, the ending *-it* suggests diminution. When a *shva* is expected with the guttural, it is replaced by *Hataf-pataH*.

Examples

משה רגיל לפתוח כל ארוחת ערב, בבית או במסעדה, עם **קַעֲרִית** מרק.
Moshe is used to starting any dinner, at home or in a restaurant, with a **small bowl** of soup.

Additional Examples in this Pattern

carbuncle גַּחֲלִית
tracked carrier (military) זַחֲלִית
tern (bird) שַׁחֲפִית
morning prayer שַׁחֲרִית

---

810. *maCCit*

our/your/their	my/your/his/her	const.	Gloss	sing/pl
מַגְבִּיתֵנוּ/תְכֶם/תְכֶן/תָם/תָן	**מַגְבִּי**תִי/תְךָ/תֵךְ/תוֹ/תָהּ	-מַגְבִּית	fundraising	מַגְבִּית נ׳
מַגְבִּיוֹתֵינוּ/כֶם/כֶן/הֶם/הֶן	**מַגְבִּיוֹ**תַי/תֶיךָ/תַיִךְ/תָיו/תֶיהָ	-מַגְבִּיוֹת	campaign	מַגְבִּיוֹת

The base comes with the prefix -מ, its suffix is *-it*, and the plural suffix (if it exists) is -*iyot*. Most forms are derived from roots with a final *y*.

Examples

כל שנה לפני חג המולד עורכים בארה״ב **מַגְבִּית** כדי לאפשר לילדים חולי סרטן לבקר בפארק של דיסני עם משפחותיהם מעוטות היכולת.
In the US, every year before Christmas they hold **fundraiser** to enable children to visit Disney World with their low-income families.

מחקרים מראים ש**מַרְבִּית** האנשים עדיין מעדיפים גלידת וניל...
Research shows that **most** people still prefer vanilla ice cream...

Special Expressions

apparent, superficial **מַרְאִית** עין

Additional Examples in this Pattern

rag מַטְלִית
vision; view; point of view מַרְאִית
image; ornament, locket Lit. מַשְׂכִּית
stroma (animal tissue); support מַשְׁתִּית
layer

---

811. *maCCit* = *maCaCit*, the 2nd root consonant is guttural

our/your/their	my/your/his/her	const.	Gloss	sing/pl
מַעֲלִיתֵנוּ/תְכֶם/תְכֶן/תָם/תָן	**מַעֲלִי**תִי/תְךָ/תֵךְ/תוֹ/תָהּ	-מַעֲלִית	elevator	מַעֲלִית נ׳
מַעֲלִיוֹתֵינוּ/כֶם/כֶן/הֶם/הֶן	**מַעֲלִיוֹ**תַי/תֶיךָ/תַיִךְ/תָיו/תֶיהָ	-מַעֲלִיוֹת		מַעֲלִיוֹת

The base comes with the prefix suffix -מ, its suffix is *-it*, and the plural suffix is *-iyot*. The forms are derived from roots with a final *y*. When a *shva* is expected with the guttural, it is replaced by *Hataf-pataH*.

Examples

ה**מַעֲלִיוֹת** בבניין שלנו הן מתוצרת החברה הגרמנית תיסנקרופ.
The **elevators** in our buildings were manufactured by the German company Thyssenkrupp.

Additional Examples in this Pattern

half מַחֲצִית

---

812. *CiCCit* (from segholate*s* etc.)

our/your/their	my/your/his/her	const.	Gloss	sing/pl
דִּסְקִיתֵנוּ/תְכֶם/תְכֶן/תָם/תָן	**דִּסְקִי**תִי/תְךָ/תֵךְ/תוֹ/תָהּ	דִּסְקִית-	dog tag,	דִּסְקִית נ׳
דִּסְקִיּוֹתֵינוּ/כֶם/כֶן/הֶם/הֶן	**דִּסְקִיּוֹ**תַי/תֶיךָ/תַיִךְ/תָיו/תֶיהָ	דִּסְקִיּוֹת-	ID tag	דִּסְקִיּוֹת

The base suffix is *-it*, and the plural suffix, when it exists, is *-iyot*. In some of the cases, the base is “segholate,” e.g., bridge of musical instrument גֶּשֶׁר/גִּשְׁר+ית > גִּשְׁרִית bridge. In some of the occurrences, the ending *-it* suggests diminution.

Examples

כל חייל חייב לענוד **דִּסְקִית** בזמן שירותו – זוהי הדרך הבטוחה ביותר לזהותו במקרה של פגיעה.
Every soldier must wear a **dog tag** during his/her service; it is the safest and easiest way of identifying him/her in case he is hit.

קרע **בִּרְשִׁתִית** העין עלול לגרום לעיוורון אם לא מטפלים מייד בבעייה.
A tear in the eye’s **retina** can cause blindness if not taken care of right away.

Additional Examples in this Pattern

bridge (of string instrument) גִּשְׁרִית
gelatin מִקְפִּית
lamium (plant) נִזְמִית
Hebrew עִבְרִית
keel שִׁדְרִית

---

813. *CoCCit* (from segholates etc.)

our/your/their	my/your/his/her	const.	Gloss	sing/pl
תָּכְנִיתֵנוּ/תְכֶם/תְכֶן/תָם/תָן	**תָּכְנִי**תִי/תְךָ/תֵךְ/תוֹ/תָהּ	תָּכְנִית-	plan	תָּכְנִית נ׳
תָּכְנִיּוֹתֵינוּ/כֶם/כֶן/הֶם/הֶן	**תָּכְנִיּוֹ**תַי/תֶיךָ/תַיִךְ/תָיו/תֶיהָ	תָּכְנִיּוֹת-		תָּכְנִיּוֹת

The first vowel is *kamats katan* [o]. The base suffix is *-it*, and the plural suffix, when it exists, is *-iyot*. In some of the cases, the base is “segholate,” e.g., אֹזֶן/אָזְנ+ית > אָזְנִית. In some of the occurrences, the ending *-it* suggests diminution.

Examples

אמרה ישראלית: כל **תָּכְנִית** היא בסיס לשינויים...
An Israeli saying: every **plan** is a base for changes...

גָּפְרִית היא חומר חיוני לכל היצורים החיים, ויש לה גם שימושים חשובים בתעשייה.
Sulphur is an essential element for all forms of life, and also has important uses in industry.

Special Expressions

תָּכְנִית אב master **plan** | **תָּכְנִית** מְגֵרה contingency **plan**

Additional Examples in this Pattern

אָזְנִית earphone, headphone
הָבְנִית vulcanite, ebonite
חָטְמִית althea, hollyhock, rose of Sharon
כָּתְלִית pellitory (plant)
מָתְנִית filet, porterhouse steak; belt, sash; battledress

---

814. N/Adj + *-it*, generally linear

our/your/their	my/your/his/her	const.	Gloss	sing/pl
מַפִּיתֵנוּ/תְכֶם/תְכֶן/תָם/תָן	**מַפִּי**תִי/תְךָ/תֵךְ/תוֹ/תָהּ	מַפִּית-	napkin	מַפִּית נ׳
מַפִּיוֹתֵינוּ/כֶם/כֶן/הֶם/הֶן	**מַפִּיוֹ**תַי/תֶיךָ/תַיִךְ/תָיו/תֶיהָ	מַפִּיוֹת-		מַפִּיוֹת

The suffix is *-it*, and the plural suffix, when it exists, is *-iyot*. Most forms are linearly derived, but in some of them there is no clear evidence that the derivation is indeed linear. In some of the occurrences, the ending *-it* suggests diminution.

Examples

יש מסעדות המגישות **מַפִּיוֹת** יפהפיות לכל סועד.
There are restaurants that set tables with beautiful **napkins**.

הַבֵּיצִיּוֹת של האישה גם הן מזדקנות עם הגיל...
A woman's **ova** also get older with age...

בבתי עסק מסוימים ניתן לקבל הנחה ניכרת כאשר משלמים במזומן, ללא **חֶשְׁבּוֹנִית**.
In some businesses one can get a significant discount when one pays with cash, without **invoice**.

הַחַשְׁמַלִּיּוֹת פופולריות מאוד ברוב הערים הגדולות באירופה.
Tramcars are very popular in most big cities in Europe.

אנשים רבים אוהבים לשתות לפחות **כּוֹסִית** אחת של אלכוהול לפני השינה.
Many people like to drink at least one **glass** of alcohol before going to bed.

היום משתמשים **בִּפְנִימִית** רק בצמיגי אופניים.
Today they use **inner tube**s only in bicycle tires.

Special Expressions

חֶשְׁבּוֹנִית מס tax **invoice**
יָדִית הילוכים gear stick
כָּרִית אוויר air bag
לוּחִית זיהוי dog **tag**, ID **tag**, license **plat**e
מַקְבִּילִית הכוחות **parallelogram** of forces

Additional Examples in this Pattern

tree frog אִילָנִית
small cupboard, chest אֲרוֹנִית
vesicle, globule בּוּעִית
skate N גַּלְגִּלִּית
delphinium (plant) דָּרְבָנִית
small hook וָוִית
computing pane חַלּוֹנִית
recorder (musical instrument) חֲלִילִית
handle יָדִית
corpuscle, blood cell כַּדּוּרִית
asterisk כּוֹכָבִית
teaspoon כַּפִּית
cauliflower כְּרוּבִית
small pillow כָּרִית
plate, tag לוּחִית
a hundred's part מֵאִית
magazine (weaponry) מַחְסָנִית
harmonica מַפּוּחִית
parallelogram מַקְבִּילִית
capillary (anat.) נִימִית
suffix סוֹפִית
particle board, chip board סִיבִית (carpentry)
hydrofoil סְנַפִּירִית
eyepiece (of microscope, etc.) עֵינִית
buckeye (tree); castanets; עַרְמוֹנִית prostate
small can פַּחִית
slop bowl צְבוּרִית
picnic cooler צֵידָנִית

---

815. N/Adj + *-it/meCoCit*

our/your/their	my/your/his/her	const.	Gloss	sing/pl
מְכוֹנִיתֵנוּ/תְכֶם/תְכֶן/תָם/תָן	**מְכוֹנִי**תִי/תְךָ/תֵךְ/תוֹ/תָהּ	מְכוֹנִית-	car	מְכוֹנִית נ׳
מְכוֹנִיוֹתֵינוּ/כֶם/כֶן/הֶם/הֶן	**מְכוֹנִיוֹ**תַי/תֶיךָ/תַיִךְ/תָיו/תֶיהָ	מְכוֹנִיּוֹת-		מְכוֹנִיּוֹת

This is linear derivation of N+*it*, מְכוֹנָה 'machine' + *it*, but such realizations also constitute discontinuous derivation in the *meCoCit mishkal*. The base suffix is *-it*, and the plural suffix *-iyot*. The ending *-it* may suggest diminution.

Examples

אורי מחליף את **מְכוֹנִיתוֹ** ב**מְכוֹנִית** חדשה כל שנתיים, לפני שיידרשו תיקונים...
Uri replaces his **car** with a new **car** after two years, before repairs are required...

Special Expressions

commercial **car/van/truck** **מְכוֹנִית** מסחרית

Additional Examples in this Pattern

chorea, St. Vitus' dance (medic.) מְחוֹלִית

---

816. N/Adj + -it/*miCCaCit*

our/your/their	my/your/his/her	const.	Gloss	sing/pl
מִפְרָשִׂיתֵנוּ/תְכֶם/תְכֶן/תָם/תָן	**מִפְרָשִׂי**תִי/תְךָ/תֵךְ/תוֹ/תָהּ	מִפְרָשִׂית-	sail-	מִפְרָשִׂית נ׳
מִפְרָשִׂיּוֹתֵינוּ/כֶם/כֶן/הֶם/הֶן	**מִפְרָשִׂיּוֹ**תַי/תֶיךָ/תַיִךְ/תָיו/תֶיהָ	מִפְרָשִׂיּוֹת-	boat	מִפְרָשִׂיּוֹת

This is linear derivation of N+*it*, מִפְרָשׂ 'sail' + *it*, but such realizations also constitute discontinuous derivation in the *miCCaCit mishkal*. The base suffix is -*it*, and the plural suffix -*iyot*. The ending -*it* may suggest diminution.

Examples

בימי הקיץ ניתן לראות בישראל מספר ניכר של **מִפְרָשִׂיּוֹת** בחוף הים התיכון ואפילו בכינרת.
In the summer in Israel one can see a significant number of **sailboats** on the Mediterranean coast and even on the sea of Galilee.

Additional Examples in this Pattern

pad מִשְׁטַחִית covered pickup truck מִטְעָנִית

---

817. N/Adj + -*it*/*maCaCit*

our/your/their	my/your/his/her	const.	Gloss	sing/pl
מַשָּׂאִיתֵנוּ/תְכֶם/תְכֶן/תָם/תָן	**מַשָּׂאִי**תִי/תְךָ/תֵךְ/תוֹ/תָהּ	-מַשָּׂאִית	truck	מַשָּׂאִית נ׳
מַשָּׂאִיוֹתֵינוּ/כֶם/כֶן/הֶם/הֶן	**מַשָּׂאִיוֹ**תַי/תֶיךָ/תַיִךְ/תָיו/תֶיהָ	-מַשָּׂאִיּוֹת		מַשָּׂאִיּוֹת

This is linear derivation of N+*it*, מַשָּׂא 'load' + *it*, but such realizations also constitute discontinuous derivation in the *maCaCit mishkal*. All forms are derived from roots whose first consonant is *n*, or *y* (followed by *ts*), which is assimilated into the following consonant. The base suffix is -*it*, and the plural suffix -*iyot*. The ending -*it* may suggest diminution.

Examples

יוסי הוא נהג **מַשָּׂאִית** מקצועי. הוא רגיל לנהוג ב**מַשָּׂאִיתוֹ** 4-5 שעות ללא הפסקה.
Yossi is a professional **truck** driver. He is used to driving **his truck** for 4-5 hours non-stop.

Additional Examples in this Pattern

receptacle (bot.); placemat מַצָּעִית small tray מַגָּשִׁית

---

818. N/Adj + -*it*/*maCoCit*

our/your/their	my/your/his/her	const.	Gloss	sing/pl
מַסּוֹרִיתֵנוּ/תְכֶם/תְכֶן/תָם/תָן	**מַסּוֹרִי**תִי/תְךָ/תֵךְ/תוֹ/תָהּ	-מַסּוֹרִית	hacksaw	מַסּוֹרִית נ׳
מַסּוֹרִיּוֹתֵינוּ/כֶם/כֶן/הֶם/הֶן	**מַסּוֹרִיּוֹ**תַי/תֶיךָ/תַיִךְ/תָיו/תֶיהָ	-מַסּוֹרִיּוֹת		מַסּוֹרִיּוֹת

This is linear derivation of N+*it*, מַסּוֹר 'saw' + *it*, but such realizations also constitute discontinuous derivation in the *maCoCit mishkal*. All forms are derived from roots whose first consonant is *n*, where this *n* is assimilated into the following consonant. The base suffix is -*it*, and the plural suffix -*iyot*. The ending -*it* may suggest diminution.

Examples

הַמַּסּוֹרִית מתאימה יותר לעבודות קטנות בבית, הדורשות דיוק רב יותר ממה שניתן לבצע במַסּוֹר רגיל.
The **hacksaw** is more suitable for small jobs at home, which require more accuracy than can be achieved with a regular saw.

Additional Examples in this Pattern

xylophone מַקּוֹשִׁית

---

819. N/Adj + *-it/maCCoCit*

our/your/their	my/your/his/her	const.	Gloss	sing/pl
מַרְכּוֹלִיתֵנוּ/תְכֶם/תְכֶן/תָם/תָן	**מַרְכּוֹלִי**תִי/תְךָ/תֵךְ/תוֹ/תָהּ	מַרְכּוֹלִית-	mini-	מַרְכּוֹלִית נ׳
מַרְכּוֹלִיּוֹתֵינוּ/כֶם/כֶן/הֶם/הֶן	**מַרְכּוֹלִיּוֹ**תַי/תֶיךָ/תַיִךְ/תָיו/תֶיהָ	מַרְכּוֹלִיּוֹת-	market	מַרְכּוֹלִיּוֹת

This is linear derivation of N+*it*, מַרְכּוֹל 'supermarket' + *it*, but such realizations also constitute discontinuous derivation in the *maCoCit mishkal* (in the case of מַשְׁרוֹקִית 'whistle,' it is not clear that the derivation is actually linear; the form may have been borrowed from Aramaic). The base suffix is *-it*, and the plural suffix *-iyot*. The ending *-it* may suggest diminution.

Examples

כדי להישאר בממשלת הקואליציה, האורתודוקסים דורשים לסגור את כל **הַמַּרְכּוֹלִיּוֹת** בשבת.
In order to stay in the coalition government, the orthodox demand that all **minimarkets** be closed on the Sabbath.

Additional Examples in this Pattern

whistle מַשְׁרוֹקִית

---

820. N/Adj + *-it/CCiCit*

our/your/their	my/your/his/her	const.	gloss	sing/pl
(**שְׁמִינִי**תֵנוּ/תְכֶם/תְכֶן/תָם/תָן)	(**שְׁמִינִי**תִי/תְךָ/תֵךְ/תוֹ/תָהּ)	שְׁמִינִית-	eighth	שְׁמִינִית נ׳
(**שְׁמִינִיּוֹתֵי**נוּ/כֶם/כֶן/הֶם/הֶן)	(**שְׁמִינִיּוֹ**תַי/תֶיךָ/תַיִךְ/תָיו/תֶיהָ)	שְׁמִינִיּוֹת-	(part)	שְׁמִינִיּוֹת

This is linear derivation of N+*it*, שְׁמוֹנֶה eight + *it*, with some vowel change, but such realizations also constitute discontinuous derivation in the *CCiCit mishkal*. The base suffix is *-it*, and the plural suffix *-iyot*. The ending *-it* may suggest diminution. The forms with possessive pronouns potentially exist, but are hardly ever in use.

Examples

בעברית ספרותית, כשאומרים "**שְׁמִינִית** שבִּ**שְׁמִינִית**" מתכוונים לחלק קטן ביותר (1 מ-64).
In literary Hebrew, "**eighth** of an **eighth**" means a very small part (1 out of 64).

Additional Examples in this Pattern

a fourth (part) רְבִיעִית	a third (part) שְׁלִישִׁית
a seventh (part) שְׁבִיעִית	a ninth (part) תְּשִׁיעִית

---

821. N/Adj + *-it*/*CCiCit* = *CaCiCit* when the first root consonant is guttural

our/your/their	my/your/his/her	const.	Gloss	sing/pl
(**עֲשִׂירִי**תֵנוּ/תְכֶם/תְכֶן/תָם/תָן)	(**עֲשִׂירִי**תִי/תְךָ/תֵךְ/תוֹ/תָהּ	-עֲשִׂירִית	tenth	עֲשִׂירִית נ׳
(**עֲשִׂירִיּוֹתֵי**נוּ/כֶם/כֶן/הֶם/הֶן)	(**עֲשִׂירִיּוֹ**תַי/תֶיךָ/תַיִךְ/תָיו/תֶיהָ	-עֲשִׂירִיּוֹת	(part)	עֲשִׂירִיּוֹת

This is linear derivation of N+*it*, עֲשָׂרָה 'ten' + *it*, occasionally with automatic vowel change, but such realizations also constitute discontinuous derivation in the *CCiCit* = *CaCiCit mishkal*. The base suffix is *-it*, and the plural suffix *-iyot*. The ending *-it* may suggest diminution. The forms with possessive pronouns potentially exist, but are hardly ever in use. When a *shva* is expected with a guttural, it is replaced by *Hataf-pataH*.

Examples

המורמונים מפרישים **עֲשִׂירִית** מהכנסתם (על פי המַעֲשֵׂר במקרא) לקופת הקהילה, כדי לעזור למעוטי יכולת.

The Mormons allocate **a tenth** of their income (tithing, as in Biblical times) to help the needy in their community.

Additional Examples in this Pattern

wafer, waffle אֲפִיפִית	a fifth (part) חֲמִישִׁית
scrofula (medic.) חֲזִירִית	

---

822. N/Adj + *-it*/*CCaCit*

our/your/their	my/your/his/her	const.	Gloss	sing/pl
צְלָלִיתֵנוּ/תְכֶם/תְכֶן/תָם/תָן	**צְלָלִי**תִי/תְךָ/תֵךְ/תוֹ/תָהּ	-צְלָלִית	silhouette	צְלָלִית נ׳
צְלָלִיּוֹתֵינוּ/כֶם/כֶן/הֶם/הֶן	**צְלָלִיּוֹ**תַי/תֶיךָ/תַיִךְ/תָיו/תֶיהָ	-צְלָלִיּוֹת		צְלָלִיּוֹת

This is linear derivation of N+*it*, צֵל/צְלָלִ(ים) 'shadow(s)' + *it*, but such realizations also constitute discontinuous derivation in the *CCaCit mishkal*. In some of the forms the second and third root consonants are identical. The base suffix is *-it*, and the plural suffix *-iyot*. The ending *-it* may suggest diminution.

Examples

כשהיינו ילדים אהבנו להטיל **צְלָלִיּוֹת** על הקיר באמצעות תצורות של ידיים ואצבעות.

When we were kids, we loved to project **silhouettes** on the wall by means of and finger configuration.

Additional Examples in this Pattern

gagea (plant) זְהָבִית
basis point רְבָבִית
craziness, hysteria תְּזָזִית

---

823. N/Adj + *-it/CCaCit* = *CaCaCit* when the first root consonant is guttural

our/your/their	my/your/his/her	const.	Gloss	sing/pl
חֲלָלִיתֵנוּ/תְכֶם/תְכֶן/תָם/תָן)	(**חֲלָלִי**תִי/תְךָ/תֵךְ/תוֹ/תָהּ	חֲלָלִית-	space-	חֲלָלִית נ׳
חֲלָלִיּוֹתֵינוּ/כֶם/כֶן/הֶם/הֶן)	(**חֲלָלִיּוֹ**תַי/תֶיךָ/תַיִךְ/תָיו/תֶיהָ	חֲלָלִיּוֹת-	ship	חֲלָלִיּוֹת

This is linear derivation of N+*it*, חָלָל 'space' + *it*, but such realizations also constitute discontinuous derivation in the *CCaCit* = *CaCaCit mishkal*. In some of the forms the second and third root consonants are identical. The base suffix is *-it*, and the plural suffix *-iyot*. The ending *-it* may suggest diminution. The forms with possessive pronouns potentially exist, but are hardly ever in use. When a *shva* is expected with a guttural, it is replaced by *Hataf-pataH*.

Examples

מעניין כמה שנים יעברו עד ש**חֲלָלִית** כמו "אנטרפרייז" תיבנה במציאות.
One wonders how many years it will take until a **spaceship** like the Enterprise will actually be built.

Additional Examples in this Pattern

planter, window box אֲדָנִית
lichen (bot.) חֲזָזִית

---

824. N/Adj + *-it/CCoCit*

our/your/their	my/your/his/her	const.	Gloss	sing/pl
שְׁעוֹנִיתֵנוּ/תְכֶם/תְכֶן/תָם/תָן	**שְׁעוֹנִי**תִי/תְךָ/תֵךְ/תוֹ/תָהּ	שְׁעוֹנִית-	passion-	שְׁעוֹנִית נ׳
שְׁעוֹנִיּוֹתֵינוּ/כֶם/כֶן/הֶם/הֶן	**שְׁעוֹנִיּוֹ**תַי/תֶיךָ/תַיִךְ/תָיו/תֶיהָ	שְׁעוֹנִיּוֹת-	flower	שְׁעוֹנִיּוֹת

This is linear derivation of N+*it*, שָׁעוֹן 'clock' + *it* (after *a* > *e* reduction two syllables away from the main stress), but such realizations also constitute discontinuous derivation in the *CCoCit mishkal*. The base suffix is *-it*, and the plural suffix *-iyot*. The ending *-it* may suggest diminution.

Examples

ל**שְׁעוֹנִית** יש שימושים רפואיים, והפירות של אחד מסוגיה משמשים למאכל.
Passionflower has medical applications, and the fruit of one of its sub-types is edible.

Additional Examples in this Pattern

rayon; crimson, crimson cloth Lit. זְהוֹרִית

---

825. N/Adj + *-it/CCuCit*

our/your/their	my/your/his/her	const.	Gloss	sing/pl
שְׁקוּפִיתֵנוּ/תְכֶם/תְכֶן/תָם/תָן	**שְׁקוּפִי**תִי/תְךָ/תֵךְ/תוֹ/תָהּ	שְׁקוּפִית-	slide	שְׁקוּפִית נ׳
שְׁקוּפִיּוֹתֵינוּ/כֶם/כֶן/הֶם/הֶן	**שְׁקוּפִיּוֹ**תַי/תֶיךָ/תַיִךְ/תָיו/תֶיהָ	שְׁקוּפִיּוֹת-		שְׁקוּפִיּוֹת

This is linear derivation of N/Adj+*it*, שָׁקוּף 'transparent' + *it*, occasionally with some automatic vowel change, but such realizations also constitute discontinuous derivation in the *CCuCit mishkal*. In some of the forms the second and third root consonants are identical. The base suffix is -*it*, and the plural suffix -*iyot*. The ending -*it* may suggest diminution.

Examples

במשך הרבה שנים אמצעי ההמחשה העיקרי היה מטול **שְׁקוּפִיּוֹת**; היום הכל נעשה באמצעות מחשב ומקרן נתונים.

For many years the primary means of visualizing was the **slide** projector; today everything is done by means of computer and a data projector.

אני לא רואה דבר. אתה מוכן לזוז קצת? אתה לא עשוי מִ**זְּכוּכִית**...

I cannot see anything. Will you move aside a bit? You are not made of **glass**...

הרבה אמריקאים הצופים בסרט בריטי בטלוויזיה מעלים **כְּתוּבִיּוֹת**; אפילו להם קשה לפעמים להבין אנגלית בריטית...

Many Americans who watch a British movie on TV put on **subtitles**; even they sometimes hard to follow British English...

כשאוכלים הרבה **שְׁעוּעִית**, צריך לזכור שלפעמים יש לכך תופעות לוואי לא נעימות...

When one eats a lot of **beans**, one should remember that it sometimes has unpleasant side effects...

Additional Examples in this Pattern

small fishing boat דְּגוּגִית
glass panel זְגוּגִית
at; @ strudel (Internet) כְּרוּכִית
clause (syntax) פְּסוּקִית

profile, side view צְדוּדִית
puddle שְׁלוּלִית
mound, heap תְּלוּלִית

---

826. N/Adj + *-it/CiCCaCit/CiCCanit*

our/your/their	my/your/his/her	const.	Gloss	sing/pl
שִׂמְלָנִיתֵנוּ/תְכֶם/תְכֶן/תָם/תָן	**שִׂמְלָנִי**תִי/תְךָ/תֵךְ/תוֹ/תָהּ	שִׂמְלָנִית-	skirt	שִׂמְלָנִית נ׳
שִׂמְלָנִיּוֹתֵינוּ/כֶם/כֶן/הֶם/הֶן	**שִׂמְלָנִיּוֹ**תַי/תֶיךָ/תַיִךְ/תָיו/תֶיהָ	שִׂמְלָנִיּוֹת-	Lit.	שִׂמְלָנִיּוֹת

This is linear derivation of N+*it*, שִׂמְלָה dress + *it*, with a transition onset *n*, but such realizations also constitute discontinuous derivation in the *CiCCaCit/CiCCanit mishkal*. The base suffix is -*it*, and the plural suffix -*iyot*. The ending -*it* may suggest diminution.

Examples

בעברית ספרותית משתמשים לעתים בצורה **שִׂמְלָנִית** במקום חצאית.
In literary Hebrew they sometimes use the form שִׂמְלָנִית for **skirt**.

Additional Examples in this Pattern

linaria (plant) פִּשְׁתָּנִית

---

827. N/Adj + -*it*/*CiCCoCit*/*CiCConit*

our/your/their	my/your/his/her	const.	Gloss	sing/pl
שִׁרְיוֹנִיתֵנוּ/תְכֶם/תְכֶן/תָם/תָן	**שִׁרְיוֹנִי**תִי/תְךָ/תֵךְ/תוֹ/תָהּ	שִׁרְיוֹנִית-	armored	שִׁרְיוֹנִית נ׳
שִׁרְיוֹנִיּוֹתֵינוּ/כֶם/כֶן/הֶם/הֶן	**שִׁרְיוֹנִיּוֹ**תַי/תֶיךָ/תַיִךְ/תָיו/תֶיהָ	שִׁרְיוֹנִיּוֹת-	car	שִׁרְיוֹנִיּוֹת

This is linear derivation of N+*it*, שִׁרְיוֹן 'armor' + *it* (or linear-like, the case of חִדְקוֹנִית below, which may have been derived from חֵדֶק 'notch; thorn),' but such realizations also constitute discontinuous derivation in the *CiCCoCit*/*CiCConit mishkal*. The base suffix is -*it*, and the plural suffix -*iyot*. The ending -*it* may suggest diminution.

Examples

לַשִּׁרְיוֹנִיּוֹת היה תמיד תפקיד חשוב במלחמות ישראל.
Armored cars have always had an important role in the wars of Israel.

Additional Examples in this Pattern

weevil (beetle) חִדְקוֹנִית

---

828. N/Adj + -*it*/*CiCit*

our/your/their	my/your/his/her	const.	Gloss	sing/pl
צִפִּיתֵנוּ/תְכֶם/תְכֶן/תָם/תָן	**צִפִּי**תִי/תְךָ/תֵךְ/תוֹ/תָהּ	צִפִּית-	pillow	צִפִּית נ׳
צִפִּיּוֹתֵינוּ/כֶם/כֶן/הֶם/הֶן	**צִפִּיּוֹ**תַי/תֶיךָ/תַיִךְ/תָיו/תֶיהָ	צִפִּיּוֹת-	case	צִפִּיּוֹת

In some of the cases this is linear derivation of N/Adj+*it*, צִפָּה 'comforter cover' + *it*, but those and some others also constitute discontinuous derivation in the *CiCit mishkal*. The base suffix is -*it*, and the plural suffix -*iyot*. The ending -*it* may suggest diminution. In most cases the potential forms with possessive pronouns are rarely used.

Examples

בקיץ רצוי להחליף את **צִפִּיּוֹת** הכרים בחדר השינה לעיתים קרובות, בשל הזיעה.
In the summer it is advisable to replace the **pillow cases** in the bedroom fairly often because of sweat.

בכל מדינה הבנק הממשלתי מתאים מדי פעם את אחוז **הרִבִּית** כדי לווסת את הפעילות הכלכלית לרמה סבירה.
In all countries the central governmental bank adjusts **interest** rates occasionally so as to regulate economic activity and bring it to a reasonable level.

Additional Examples in this Pattern

elite; top quality עִלִּית
interest (banking) רִבִּית

a sixth (part) שִׁשִּׁית

---

829. N/Adj + *-it/CiCaCit*

our/your/their	my/your/his/her	const.	Gloss	sing/pl
חִנָּנִיתֵנוּ/תְכֶם/תְכֶן/תָם/תָן	**חִנָּנִי**תִי/תְךָ/תֵךְ/תוֹ/תָהּ	חִנָּנִית-	daisy	חִנָּנִית נ׳
חִנָּנִיּוֹתֵינוּ/כֶם/כֶן/הֶם/הֶן	**חִנָּנִיּוֹ**תַי/תֶיךָ/תַיִךְ/תָיו/תֶיהָ	חִנָּנִיּוֹת-		חִנָּנִיּוֹת

This is linear derivation of N/Adj+*it*, חִנָּנִי 'graceful' + *it*, but such realizations also constitute discontinuous derivation in the *CiCaCit mishkal*. The second and third root consonants are identical (קִטָּטִית). The base suffix is *-it*, and the plural suffix *-iyot*. The ending *-it* may suggest diminution. The potential forms with possessive pronouns are rarely used.

Examples

ה**חִנָּנִית** היא צמח רב-שנתי הפורח בתחילת החורף.
The **daisy** is a perennial plant that blooms in the beginning of winter.

Additional Examples in this Pattern

dental hygienist (fem.) שִׁנָּנִית

---

830. N/Adj + *-it/CiCuCit*

our/your/their	my/your/his/her	const.	Gloss	sing/pl
אִתּוּרִיתֵנוּ/תְכֶם/תְכֶן/תָם/תָן	**אִתּוּרִי**תִי/תְךָ/תֵךְ/תוֹ/תָהּ	אִתּוּרִית-	beeper,	אִתּוּרִית נ׳
אִתּוּרִיּוֹתֵינוּ/כֶם/כֶן/הֶם/הֶן	**אִתּוּרִיּוֹ**תַי/תֶיךָ/תַיִךְ/תָיו/תֶיהָ	אִתּוּרִיּוֹת-	pager	אִתּוּרִיּוֹת

This is linear derivation of N/Adj+*it*, אִתּוּר 'locating N' + *it*, but such realizations also constitute discontinuous derivation in the *CiCuCit mishkal*. The base suffix is *-it*, and the plural suffix *-iyot*. The ending *-it* may suggest diminution.

Examples

מעניין לדעת אם השימוש הרב בטלפונים הסלולריים הביא לירידה בשימוש ב**אִתּוּרִית**.
It would be interesting to know whether the widespread use of cellular phones has caused decline in the use of **pager**s.

Additional Examples in this Pattern

ameba חִלּוּפִית
tour bus תִּיּוּרִית

---

831. N/Adj + *-it/CaCCiCit*

our/your/their	my/your/his/her	const.	Gloss	sing/pl
בַּרְזִלִיתֵנוּ/תְכֶם/תְכֶן/תָם/תָן	**בַּרְזִלִי**תִי/תְךָ/תֵךְ/תוֹ/תָהּ	-בַּרְזִלִית	steel	בַּרְזִלִית נ׳
בַּרְזִלִיּוֹתֵינוּ/כֶם/כֶן/הֶם/הֶן	**בַּרְזִלִיּוֹ**תַי/תֶיךָ/תַיִךְ/תָיו/תֶיהָ	-בַּרְזִלִיּוֹת	wool	בַּרְזִלִיּוֹת

This is with linear derivation of N/Adj+*it*, בַּרְזֶל 'iron' + *it* (with automatic vowel change), but such realizations also constitute discontinuous derivation in the *CaCCiCit mishkal*. The base suffix is *-it*, and the plural suffix *-iyot*. The ending *-it* may suggest diminution.

Examples

בַּרְזִלִית יעילה מאוד בהורדת מה שנדבק למחבתות וסירים, אבל למחבתות טפלון היא עלולה להזיק.

Steel wool is very effective in removing what has stuck to frying pans and pots, but it may also cause damage to Teflon pans.

Additional Examples in this Pattern

nebula עֲרָפִלִית

---

832. N/Adj + *-it/CaCCiCit*, with reduplication

our/your/their	my/your/his/her	const.	Gloss	sing/pl
גַּחְלִילִיתֵנוּ/תְכֶם/תְכֶן/תָם/תָן	**גַּחְלִילִי**תִי/תְךָ/תֵךְ/תוֹ/תָהּ	-גַּחְלִילִית	firefly	גַּחְלִילִית נ׳
גַּחְלִילִיּוֹתֵינוּ/כֶם/כֶן/הֶם/הֶן	**גַּחְלִילִיּוֹ**תַי/תֶיךָ/תַיִךְ/תָיו/תֶיהָ	-גַּחְלִילִיּוֹת		גַּחְלִילִיּוֹת

This is linear derivation of N/Adj+*it*, גַּחְלִיל 'small ember' + *it*, but such realizations also constitute discontinuous derivation in the *CaCCiCit mishkal*. The third root consonant is reduplicated in position four (קַטְלִילִית). The base suffix is *-it*, and the plural suffix *-iyot*. The ending *-it* may suggest diminution.

Examples

כילד אהבתי לשבת בחוץ בלילות הקיץ ולהתבונן בנצנוצי הַ**גַּחְלִילִיּוֹת**.

As a child I loved to sit outside on summer nights and watch the twinkles of **fireflies**.

Additional Examples in this Pattern

redstart (bird) חַכְלִילִית

---

833. N/Adj + *-it/CaCCaCit/CaCCanit*

our/your/their	my/your/his/her	const.	Gloss	sing/pl
פַּחְזָנִיתֵנוּ/תְכֶם/תְכֶן/תָם/תָן	**פַּחְזָנִי**תִי/תְךָ/תֵךְ/תוֹ/תָהּ	-פַּחְזָנִית	cream	פַּחְזָנִית נ׳
פַּחְזָנִיּוֹתֵינוּ/כֶם/כֶן/הֶם/הֶן	**פַּחְזָנִיּוֹ**תַי/תֶיךָ/תַיִךְ/תָיו/תֶיהָ	-פַּחְזָנִיּוֹת	puff	פַּחְזָנִיּוֹת

This is linear derivation of N/Adj+*it*, פַּחְזָן 'swift, rushed' + *it*, but such realizations also constitute discontinuous derivation in the *CaCCaCit*/*CaCCanit mishkal*. The base suffix is *-it*, and the plural suffix *-iyot*. The ending *-it* may suggest diminution.

Examples

יעקב אוהב מאוד **פַּחְזָנִיּוֹת**. הוא מסוגל לאכול עשר מהן תוך שתי דקות.
Yaakov loves **cream puffs** a lot. He can gobble ten of them in two minutes.

Additional Examples in this Pattern

phlomis (plant) שַׁלְהֶבִית

---

834. N/Adj + *-it*/*CaCCaCit* > *CaCaCaCit*/*CaCCanit* > *CaCaCanit*, the second root consonant is guttural

our/your/their	my/your/his/her	const.	Gloss	sing/pl
שַׁעֲוָנִיתֵנוּ/תְכֶם/תְכֶן/תָם/תָן	**שַׁעֲוָנִי**תִי/תְךָ/תֵךְ/תוֹ/תָהּ	שַׁעֲוָנִית-	oilcloth	שַׁעֲוָנִית נ׳
שַׁעֲוָנִיּוֹתֵינוּ/כֶם/כֶן/הֶם/הֶן	**שַׁעֲוָנִיּוֹ**תַי/תֶיךָ/תַיִךְ/תָיו/תֶיהָ	שַׁעֲוָנִיּוֹת-		שַׁעֲוָנִיּוֹת

This is linear derivation of N/Adj+*it*, שַׁעֲוָה 'wax' + *it*, with transitional *n*, but such realizations also constitute discontinuous derivation in the *CaCCaCit* > *CaCaCaCit*/*CaCCanit* = *CaCaCanit mishkal*. The base suffix is *-it*, and the plural suffix *-iyot*. The ending *-it* may suggest diminution. When a *shva* is expected with a guttural, it is replaced by *Hataf-pataH*.

Examples

ה**שַּׁעֲוָנִית** היא הכיסוי המעשי והיעיל ביותר לשולחן. היא אינה אלגנטית במיוחד, אבל קלה ביותר לניקוי.
The **oilcloth** is the most pragmatic and efficient table cover. It is not particularly elegant, but is the easiest to clean.

---

835. N/Adj + *-it*/*CaCCuCit*

our/your/their	my/your/his/her	const.	Gloss	sing/pl
שַׁלְפּוּחִיתֵנוּ/תְכֶם/תְכֶן/תָם/תָן	**שַׁלְפּוּחִי**תִי/תְךָ/תֵךְ/תוֹ/תָהּ	שַׁלְפּוּחִית-	blister,	שַׁלְפּוּחִית נ׳
שַׁלְפּוּחִיּוֹתֵינוּ/כֶם/כֶן/הֶם/הֶן	**שַׁלְפּוּחִיּוֹ**תַי/תֶיךָ/תַיִךְ/תָיו/תֶיהָ	שַׁלְפּוּחִיּוֹת-	bladder	שַׁלְפּוּחִיּוֹת

It is not clear that we are dealing with linear derivation here, since this form was apparently borrowed from Aramaic. Obviously such realizations may also constitute discontinuous derivation in the *CaCCuCit mishkal*. The base suffix is *-it*, and the plural suffix *-iyot*. The ending *-it* appears to suggest diminution.

Examples

מאוד לא נעים להסתובב עם **שַׁלְפּוּחִית** שתן מלאה כשאין שירותים בסביבה.
It is quite unpleasant to walk around with a full urinary **bladder** where there are no restrooms around.

Additional Examples in this Pattern

blister, vesicle (medic.) שַׁלְחוּפִית

---

836. N/Adj + *-it*/*CaCCuCit*, with reduplication

our/your/their	my/your/his/her	const.	Gloss	sing/pl
נַקְבּוּבִיתֵנוּ/תְכֶם/תְכֶן/תָם/תָן	**נַקְבּוּבִי**תִי/תְךָ/תֵךְ/תוֹ/תָהּ	נַקְבּוּבִית-	tiny hole;	נַקְבּוּבִית נ׳
נַקְבּוּבִיּוֹתֵינוּ/כֶם/כֶן/הֶם/הֶן	**נַקְבּוּבִיּוֹ**תַי/תֶיךָ/תַיִךְ/תָיו/תֶיהָ	נַקְבּוּבִיּוֹת-	pore	נַקְבּוּבִיּוֹת

This is with linear derivation of N/Adj+*it*, נַקְבּוּבִי 'porous' + *it*, but such realizations also constitute discontinuous derivation in the *CaCCuCit mishkal*. The third root consonant is reduplicated in position four (קַטְלוּלִית). The base suffix is *-it*, and the plural suffix *-iyot*. The ending *-it* may suggest diminution.

Examples

הזיעה הנודפת מן ה**נַקְבּוּבִיּוֹת** בעור מסייעת בקירור מסוים של הגוף בימי החום.
The sweat evaporating through **pores** in the skin helps cool the body in hot days.

אַדְמוּמִית בפנים אינה נובעת תמיד מסומק בלחיים. במקרים רבים, הסיבה ל**אַדְמוּמִית** הקבועה היא מחלת עור בשם רוזציאה.
Redness on the face us not always the result of blushing. In many cases, the reason for the **redness** that does not go away is the skin disease rosacea.

טוב להוסיף **רַקְבּוּבִית** לאדמה שבה שותלים צמחים – כדי להקל חלחול מים, וכדי להוסיף תזונה לצמח.
It is a good idea to add **humus** to the earth in which one plants – to allow better water absorption, and to add nutrients.

Additional Examples in this Pattern

dimness, obscurity אַפְלוּלִית
gray N אַפְרוּרִית
hump, protuberance גַּבְנוּנִית
bump N; lump גַּבְשׁוּשִׁית
spout; snout זַרְבּוּבִית
whiteness, pallor לַבְנוּנִית
curvature עַקְמוּמִית

---

837. N/Adj + *-it*/*CaCCuCit* = ***CaCaCuCit***, with reduplication, the second root consonant is guttural

our/your/their	my/your/his/her	const.	Gloss	sing/pl
קַעֲרוּרִיתֵנוּ/תְכֶם/תְכֶן/תָם/תָן	**קַעֲרוּרִי**תִי/תְךָ/תֵךְ/תוֹ/תָהּ	קַעֲרוּרִית-	skullcap (flower);	קַעֲרוּרִית נ׳
קַעֲרוּרִיּוֹתֵינוּ/כֶם/כֶן/הֶם/הֶן	**קַעֲרוּרִיּוֹ**תַי/תֶיךָ/תַיִךְ/תָיו/תֶיהָ	קַעֲרוּרִיּוֹת-	depression	קַעֲרוּרִיּוֹת

This is linear derivation of N/Adj+*it*, קַעֲרוּרִי 'bowl-shaped' + *it*, but such realizations also constitute discontinuous derivation in the *CaCaCuCit mishkal*. The third root consonant is reduplicated in position four (קַטְלוּלִית). The base suffix is *-it*, and the plural suffix -*iyot*. The ending -*it* may suggest diminution. When a *shva* is expected with a guttural, it is replaced by *Hataf-pataH* (קֲטָלוּלִית).

Examples

הַקְעֲרוּרִית נקראת כך בשל צורת הפרח שלה, המזכירה קערית.
The **skullcap** is named like that because its flower is shaped like a little bowl.

Additional Examples in this Pattern

radiance, glow Lit. זַהֲרוּרִית

---

838. N/Adj + -*it*/*CaCCuCit*, with reduplication

our/your/their	my/your/his/her	const.	Gloss	sing/pl
זַמְזוּמִיתֵנוּ/תְכֶם/תְכֶן/תָם/תָן	**זַמְזוּמִי**תִי/תְךָ/תֵךְ/תוֹ/תָהּ	זַמְזוּמִית-	bellevalia	זַמְזוּמִית נ׳
זַמְזוּמִיּוֹתֵינוּ/כֶם/כֶן/הֶם/הֶן	**זַמְזוּמִיּוֹ**תַי/תֶיךָ/תַיִךְ/תָיו/תֶיהָ	זַמְזוּמִיּוֹת-	(plant)	זַמְזוּמִיּוֹת

This is linear derivation of N/Adj+*it*, זִמְזוּם 'buzz' + *it* (with *i* > *a* change), but it also constitutes discontinuous derivation in the *CaCCuCit mishkal*. The first and second root consonants are reduplicated in positions three and four, respectively (קַטְקוּטִית). The base suffix is -*it*, and the plural suffix -*iyot*. The ending -*it* may suggest diminution.

Examples

שם הצמח **זַמְזוּמִית** מקורו בזמזום הנשמע כשמועכים את פרחיו ביד.
The plant name in Hebrew זַמְזוּמִית 'little buzzer' derives from the buzz generated when its flowers are crushed by hand...

Additional Examples in this Pattern

moisture; vitality לַחְלוּחִית

---

839. N/Adj + -*it*/*CaCCuCit* > *CaCaCuCit*, with reduplication, the second root consonant is guttural

our/your/their	my/your/his/her	const.	Gloss	sing/pl
זַעֲזוּעִיתֵנוּ/תְכֶם/תְכֶן/תָם/תָן	**זַעֲזוּעִי**תִי/תְךָ/תֵךְ/תוֹ/תָהּ	זַעֲזוּעִית-	quaking grass	זַעֲזוּעִית נ׳
זַעֲזוּעִיּוֹתֵינוּ/כֶם/כֶן/הֶם/הֶן	**זַעֲזוּעִיּוֹ**תַי/תֶיךָ/תַיִךְ/תָיו/תֶיהָ	זַעֲזוּעִיּוֹת-	(plant)	זַעֲזוּעִיּוֹת

This is linear derivation of N/Adj+*it*, זַעֲזוּעַ 'quake' + *it*, but such realizations also constitute discontinuous derivation in the *CaCaCuCit mishkal*. The first and second root consonants are reduplicated in positions three and four, respectively. The base suffix is -*it*, and the plural suffix -*iyot*. The ending -*it* may suggest diminution. When a *shva* is expected with the guttural, it is replaced by *Hataf-pataH* (קַטֲקוּטִית).

Examples

שם הצמח **זַעֲזוּעִית** נובע מכך שהוא נע הלוך ושוב עם כל בריזה קלה.

The plant name in Hebrew **זַעֲזוּעִית** 'quaker/quaking grass' derives from its flowers quaking even with the slightest breeze.

---

840. N/Adj + *-it/CaCaCit/CaCa'it/CaCanit*

our/your/their	my/your/his/her	const.	Gloss	sing/pl
כַּבָּאִיתֵנוּ/תְכֶם/תְכֶן/תָם/תָן	**כַּבָּאִי**תִי/תְךָ/תֵךְ/תוֹ/תָהּ	כַּבָּאִית-	fire	כַּבָּאִית נ'
כַּבָּאִיּוֹתֵינוּ/כֶם/כֶן/הֶם/הֶן	**כַּבָּאִיּוֹ**תַי/תֶיךָ/תַיִךְ/תָיו/תֶיהָ	כַּבָּאִיּוֹת-	truck	כַּבָּאִיּוֹת

This is linear derivation of N/Adj+*it*, כַּבָּאי 'firefighter' + *it*, but such realizations also constitute discontinuous derivation in the *CaCaCit/CaCa'it/CaCanit mishkal*. The base suffix is *-it*, and the plural suffix *-iyot*. The ending *-it* may suggest diminution.

Examples

כששלוש **כַּבָּאִיּוֹת** הגיעו לבניין תוך חמש דקות מרגע הפעלת האזעקה, הסתבר שאחד הדיירים פשוט שכח לכבות את הגאז בכיריים והסטייקים שלו נשרפו...

When three **fire trucks** arrived at the building five minutes after the alarm came on, it turned out that one of the tenants simply forgot to turn off the flame on the gas range, and his steaks burned...

Additional Examples in this Pattern

sunflower חַמָּנִית   European spadefoot toad חַפָּרִית

---

841. ?N/Adj + *-it/ CCa'it/CaCa'it*, when the first root consonant is guttural

our/your/their	my/your/his/her	const.	Gloss	sing/pl
חֲצָאִיתֵנוּ/תְכֶם/תְכֶן/תָם/תָן	**חֲצָאִי**תִי/תְךָ/תֵךְ/תוֹ/תָהּ	חֲצָאִית-	skirt	חֲצָאִית נ'
חֲצָאִיּוֹתֵינוּ/כֶם/כֶן/הֶם/הֶן	**חֲצָאִיּוֹ**תַי/תֶיךָ/תַיִךְ/תָיו/תֶיהָ	חֲצָאִיּוֹת-		חֲצָאִיּוֹת

This may be regarded as linear derivation of N/Adj+*it*, חֲצִי(א) 'half' + *it*, but because of the vowel change and the surfacing of א', is more likely to constitute discontinuous derivation in the *CCa'it > CaCa'it mishkal*. The base suffix is *-it*, and the plural suffix *-iyot*. The ending *-it* suggests diminution. The *shva* is replaced by *Hataf-pataH* owing to the guttural.

Examples

האורתודוקסים אינם מרשים לבנותיהם ללבוש **חֲצָאִיּוֹת** – אלא אם כן ה**חֲצָאִית** ארוכה ומכסה היטב את הרגליים.

The orthodox do not allow their daughters to wear **skirts** – unless the **skirt** is long and well-covers the legs.

---

842. N/Adj + *-it/CaCit*

our/your/their	my/your/his/her	const.	Gloss	sing/pl
דָּלִיתֵנוּ/תְכֶם/תְכֶן/תָם/תָן	**דָּלִי**תִי/תְךָ/תֵךְ/תוֹ/תָהּ	-דָּלִית	vine	דָּלִית נ׳
דָּלִיּוֹתֵינוּ/כֶם/כֶן/הֶם/הֶן	**דָּלִיּוֹ**תַי/תֶיךָ/תַיִךְ/תָיו/תֶיהָ	-דָּלִיּוֹת	tendril	דָּלִיּוֹת

This is linear derivation of N/Adj+*it*, דָּלִיָּה 'branch' + *it*, but such realizations also constitute discontinuous derivation in the *CaCit mishkal*. The base suffix is -*it*, and the plural suffix -*iyot*. The ending -*it* may suggest diminution, and some illnesses.

Examples

דָּלִית היא ענף או זלזל של גפן הנסמך על גזע עץ או עמודים.
דָּלִית is a **tendril** of a vine that is supported by a (tree) trunk or posts.

Additional Examples in this Pattern

choroid (anat.) דָּמִית
bract, bracteole (bot.) חָפִית
sciatica נָשִׁית
acrosephalus (bird) קָנִית
scarlet fever שָׁנִית
labellum (plant) שָׂפִית

---

843. N/Adj + *-it/CuCCeCanit*, with reduplication

our/your/their	my/your/his/her	const.	Gloss	sing/pl
שֻׁמְשְׁמָנִיתֵנוּ/תְכֶם/תְכֶן/תָם/תָן	**שֻׁמְשְׁמָנִי**תִי/תְךָ/תֵךְ/תוֹ/תָהּ	-שֻׁמְשְׁמָנִית	sesame	שֻׁמְשְׁמָנִית נ׳
שֻׁמְשְׁמָנִיּוֹתֵינוּ/כֶם/כֶן/הֶם/הֶן	**שֻׁמְשְׁמָנִיּוֹ**תַי/תֶיךָ/תַיִךְ/תָיו/תֶיהָ	-שֻׁמְשְׁמָנִיּוֹת	cookie	שֻׁמְשְׁמָנִיּוֹת

This is linear derivation of N/Adj+*it*, (שֻׁמְשֻׁם(ן 'sesame' + *it* (after *u* > *e* reduction plus a transitional *n*), but such realizations also constitute discontinuous derivation in the *CuCCeCanit mishkal*. The first and second root consonants are reduplicated in positions three and four, respectively (קֻטְקְטָנִית). The base suffix is -*it*, and the plural suffix -*iyot*. The ending -*it* may suggest diminution.

Examples

הַשֻּׁמְשְׁמָנִיּוֹת הן עוגיות פופולריות ביותר במזרח התיכון.
Sesame cookies are very popular in the Middle East.

Additional Examples in this Pattern

red currant, ribes דֻּמְדְּמָנִית

---

844. N/Adj + *-it/CoCit*

our/your/their	my/your/his/her	const.	Gloss	sing/pl
חוֹחִיתֵנוּ/תְכֶם/תְכֶן/תָם/תָן	**חוֹחִי**תִי/תְךָ/תֵךְ/תוֹ/תָהּ	-חוֹחִית	finch,	חוֹחִית נ׳
חוֹחִיּוֹתֵינוּ/כֶם/כֶן/הֶם/הֶן	**חוֹחִיּוֹ**תַי/תֶיךָ/תַיִךְ/תָיו/תֶיהָ	-חוֹחִיּוֹת	goldfinch	חוֹחִיּוֹת

This is linear derivation of N/Adj+*it*, חוֹחַ 'thistle' + *it*, but such realizations also constitute discontinuous derivation in the *CoCit mishkal*. The base suffix is *-it*, and the plural suffix *-iyot*. The ending *-it* may suggest diminution.

Examples

החוֹחִית היא ציפור שיר יציבה בארץ ישראל. מזונה העיקרי הוא זרעי קוצים למיניהם.
The **(gold)finch** is a stable (i.e., non-migrating) songbird in Israel. Its main food is seeds of various thorns.

Additional Examples in this Pattern

nuance גּוֹנִית
dune חוֹלִית
stint (bird), dunlin חוֹפִית
fibula (bone) שׁוֹקִית
infix תּוֹכִית

---

845. N/Adj + *-it/CuCit*

our/your/their	my/your/his/her	const.	Gloss	sing/pl
דוּגִיתֵנוּ/תְכֶם/תְכֶן/תָם/תָן	**דוּגִי**תִי/תְךָ/תֵךְ/תוֹ/תָהּ	דוּגִית-	dinghy,	דוּגִית נ׳
דוּגִיּוֹתֵינוּ/כֶם/כֶן/הֶם/הֶן	**דוּגִיּוֹ**תַי/תֶיךָ/תַיִךְ/תָיו/תֶיהָ	דוּגִיּוֹת-	skiff	דוּגִיּוֹת

This is linear derivation of N/Adj/V+*it*, דוּג 'fish V (or gerund?)' + *it*, but such realizations also constitute discontinuous derivation in the *CuCit mishkal*. The base suffix is *-it*, and the plural suffix *-iyot*. The ending *-it* may suggest diminution.

Examples

הדוּגִית פופולרית מאוד בישראל, בחוף הים התיכון ובכינרת.
The **dinghy** is very popular in Israel, on the Mediterranean coast and on the Sea of Galilee.

Additional Examples in this Pattern

honey-sucker, sunbird צוּפִית
creeping jack (plant) צוּרִית
strawberry shortcake תּוּתִית

V. Patterns with suffixes including *-n (-an, -on)*

846. *CaCCan*

our/your/their	my/your/his/her	const.	Gloss	sing/pl
גַּלְשָׁנֵנוּ/**גַּלְשַׁנְ**כֶם/כֶן/**גַּלְשָׁנָ**ם/ן	**גַּלְשָׁ**נִי/נְךָ/נֵךְ/נוֹ/נָהּ	גַּלְשַׁן-	surfboard	גַּלְשָׁן ז׳
גַּלְשָׁנֵינוּ/כֶם/כֶן/הֶם/הֶן	**גַּלְשָׁ**נַי/נֶיךָ/נַיִךְ/נָיו/נֶיהָ	גַּלְשָׁנֵי-		גַּלְשָׁנִים

The suffix is *-an*. Forms in this pattern generally refer to an agent (a person controlling the action), especially when the action denoted by the base characterizes his/her occupation (בַּלְשָׁן 'linguist,' יַצְרָן 'manufacturer'), or an instrument (גַּלְשָׁן 'surfboard,' הַלְמָן 'mallet,'), or a noun/adjective denoting a characteristic quality of an agent (דַּיְקָן 'punctual, punctilious person,' דַּגְרָן 'bookish, studious person'). [Note: in the formal register, *CaCCan* only denotes nouns; parallel adjectives require an added *-i*, but in spoken Hebrew *CaCCan* is generally used for both.] Sometimes the form is not agentive, but rather relates one way or another to some action (יַשְׁבָן 'buttocks'), or to some noun (אַבְקָן 'stamen bot.'). Note: in forms such as אַסְפָן, בַּלְפָן, גַּדְפָן, זַיְפָן, זַנְבָן, חַיְכָן, חַלְפָן and others there is no *dagesh lene* in the last root consonant, probably so as to preserve the transparency of the derivation base.

Examples

כשרואים את רוברט מפגין את כישורי הגלישה שלו, **הַגַּלְשָׁן** נראה כחלק אינטגרלי מגופו.
When one sees Robert demonstrating his surfing skill, the **surfboard** looks like an integral part of his body.

צ׳רלס הוא אחד **מאַסְפָנֵי** הבולים הגדולים בחוף המזרחי של ארה״ב.
Charles is one of the biggest stamp **collector**s in the US.

בזמנו, סאמי דיוויס ג׳וניור היה **הַבַּדְרָן** המפורסם ביותר בארה״ב.
At the time, Sammy Davis Jr. was the most celebrated **entertainer** in the US.

אומרים שראש העיר הנוכחי של ניו יורק הוא ראש העיר **הַבַּטְלָן** ביותר שידעה העיר.
They say that the current mayor of new York City is the greatest **loafer** in the city's history.

משנה, פרקי אבות: ״לא **הַבַּיְשָׁן** למד ולא **הַקַּפְּדָן** מלמד״.
The Mishnah (Pirkey Avot): "A **shy person** won't learn, and the **strict/pedantic** one should not teach."

כשהיינו בטירונות, קראנו לרוכל שמכר לנו מיני מתיקה ״**גַּזְלָן**״.
When we were in basic training, we called the peddler who sold us sweets "**robber**."

אין **דַּיְקָן** כמו אביגדור. אם הוא מאחר, סימן שהייתה לו תאונה.
Nobody is as punctual as Avigdor. If he is late, he must have been in an accident.

Special Expressions

sailboard **גַּלְשָׁן** רוח/מפרש
snowboard **גַּלְשָׁן** שלג
court jester, clown **בַּדְחָן**/לֵיצָן החצר

Additional Examples in this Pattern

hoarder אַגְרָן
glutton אַכְלָן
joker בַּדְחָן
cry baby בַּכְיָן
thistle בַּרְקָן
choosy בַּרְרָן
bookish, studious person דַּגְרָן
preacher, sermonizer דַּרְשָׁן
someone hesitant, irresolute הַסְסָן

one who gives up, conceder; lenient וַתְּרָן
forger זַיְּפָן
glutton זַלְלָן
phosphorus זַרְחָן
chamber-man חַדְרָן
innovator חַדְשָׁן
interferer חַטְטָן
dialer חַיְגָן
smiler חַיְכָן
sensor חַיְשָׁן
money changer חַלְפָן
greedy person חַמְדָן
oxygen חַמְצָן
flatterer חַנְפָן
frugal person חַסְכָן
janitor, caretaker חַצְרָן
imitator, mimic חַקְיָן
horny person Coll. חַרְמָן

---

847. ***CaCCan*** when the second root consonant is geminated

Our/your/their	my/your/his/her	const.	Gloss	sing/pl
קַבְּלָנֵנוּ/**קַבְּלַנְ**כֶם/כֶן/**קַבְּלָנָ**ם/ן	**קַבְּלָנִ**י/נְךָ/נֵךְ/נוֹ/נָהּ	קַבְּלַן-	contractor	קַבְּלָן ז׳
קַבְּלָנֵינוּ/כֶם/כֶן/הֶם/הֶן	**קַבְּלָנַ**י/נֶיךָ/נַיִךְ/נָיו/נֶיהָ	קַבְּלָנֵי-		קַבְּלָנִים

This pattern belongs to the general *CaCCan* category above, which primarily denotes performers of actions or their characteristic quality, except that in this sub-group are included forms in which the second root consonant is geminated – generally because the corresponding consonant in the base for derivation is geminated: קִבֵּל 'receive, accept' > קַבְּלָן 'contractor.' Note: קַבְּרָן 'gravedigger' is derived not from the common verb קָבַר 'bury,' but from the less common *pi`el* form קִבֵּר 'bury (over and over),' because among the rest, *pi`el* also designates a repeated action; the derivation base for וַכְּחָן 'argumentative person' is הִתְוַכֵּחַ 'argue;' etc.

Examples

יזמי בנייה עובדים עם אדריכל ועם **קַבְּלָן** או **קַבְּלָנֵי**-משנה.
Builders work with an architect and with a **contractor** or sub-**contractors**.

לצבא ולמשטרה יש יחידות מיוחדות של **חַבְּלָנִים** המטפלים בפצצות או מתקינים אותן.
The army and the police have special units of **sappers/bomb experts** who deal with bombs or install them.

ברכבת התחתית של ניו יורק מסתובבים הרבה **קַבְּצָנִים**.
There are many **beggars** roaming in the New York subway system.

נראה לי שמרבית תלמידי בתי הספר מעריכים מורים **קַפְּדָנִים**.
It seems to me that most students at school appreciate **strict** teachers.

Special Expressions

construction **contractor** **קַבְּלָן** בניין
sub-**contractor** **קַבְּלַן** מִשְׁנֶה

Additional Examples in this Pattern

a talkative person דַּבְּרָן
argumentative person וַכְּחָן
one who tends to make matters worse סַבְּכָן
gravedigger קַבְּרָן
strict, meticulous (person) קַפְּדָן/קַפְדָן

---

848. ***CaCCan*** when the third root consonant is a stop

Our/your/their	my/your/his/her	const.	Gloss	sing/pl
טַלְפָּנֵנוּ/**טַלְפַּנְ**כֶם/כֶן/**טַלְפָּנָ**ם/ן	**טַלְפָּנִ**י/נְךָ/נֵךְ/נוֹ/נָהּ	טַלְפַּן-	switchboard	טַלְפָּן ז׳
טַלְפָּנֵינוּ/כֶם/כֶן/הֶם/הֶן	**טַלְפָּנַ**י/נֶיךָ/נַיִךְ/נָיו/נֶיהָ	טַלְפְּנֵי-	operator	טַלְפָּנִים

This pattern belongs to the general *CaCCan* category above, which primarily denotes performers of actions or their characteristic quality, except that in this sub-group are included forms in which the third root consonant is a stop. The *n* of טַלְפָּן is originally part of טלפון, but is reinterpreted as the *n* of *-an*. Instead of טַלְפָּן one usually uses מרכזנ(ית) טלפון 'telephone operator,' and the colloquial חַלְבָּן form is replaced by חַלְבָן (which better preserves the base חָלָב 'milk') in the higher registers and as חוֹלֵב in the translation into Hebrew of Shalom Aleichem's *Tuvia the Dairyman*.

Examples

בתנאי הטכנולוגיה של היום כבר אין יותר צורך ב**טַלְפָּנִים**, ואנשים ״חשובים״ מסננים או מתעלים את שיחות הטלפון דרך מזכירות.

In today's technology there is no longer any need for **telephone operators**, and "important" people sift or channel their phone conversations through secretaries.

Additional Examples in this Pattern

חַלְבָּן/חַלְבָן milkman

---

849. ***CaCCan = CaCaCan***, when the 2nd root consonant is guttural

Our/your/their	my/your/his/her	const.	Gloss	sing/pl
דַּאֲגָנֵנוּ/**דַּאֲגַנְ**כֶם/כֶן/**דַּאֲגָנָ**ם/ן	**דַּאֲגָנִ**י/נְךָ/נֵךְ/נוֹ/נָהּ	דַּאֲגַן-	worrier	דַּאֲגָן ז׳
דַּאֲגָנֵינוּ/כֶם/כֶן/הֶם/הֶן	**דַּאֲגָנַ**י/נֶיךָ/נַיִךְ/נָיו/נֶיהָ	דַּאֲגָנֵי-		דַּאֲגָנִים

This pattern belongs to the general *CaCCan* category above, which primarily denotes performers of actions or their characteristic quality; in this sub-group are included forms in which the second root consonant is guttural. When a *shva* is expected with the guttural, it is placed by *Hataf-pataH*.

Examples

דויד הוא **דַּאֲגָן** גדול. גם כאשר הכל מתנהל כשורה, הוא עדיין דואג.

David is a great **worrier**. Even when everything goes well, he still worries.

טַהֲרָנֵי הלשון בישראל אינם מכירים בלגיטימיות של העברית המדוברת אם אינה שומרת על כל כללי הדקדוק של המשלב הגבוה.

The language **purists** in Israel are not willing to recognize the legitimacy of spoken Hebrew unless it conforms to all the grammatical rules of the higher registers.

בשל מספרם וגודלם של הפארקים הלאומיים בארה״ב, **לַיַּעֲרָנִים** בה יש הרבה מאוד עבודה.

Because of the number and size of the national parks in the US, **forest rangers** have a lot of work there.

אביגדור הוא **כַּעֲסָן** גדול, אבל תוך כמה שניות נרגע, כאילו לא קרה דבר.
Avidgor is **hot-headed**, but a few seconds afterwards he calms down, as if nothing has happened.

פתחתי את החלון, ומשב רוח **רַעֲנָן** טיהר את האוויר בחדר.
I opened the window, and a **fresh** gust of wind refreshed the room.

Additional Examples in this Pattern

kicker, rebel, dissenter בַּעֲטָן	quick-tempered זַעֲפָן
ironer גַּהֲצָן	adulterer נַאֲפָן
one who often scolds גַּעֲרָן	shouter צַעֲקָן
coluber (type of snake) זַעֲמָן	rattle, noise maker רַעֲשָׁן

---

850. ***CaCC(e)Can***

Our/your/their	my/your/his/her	const.	Gloss	sing/pl
גַּנְדְּרָנֵנוּ/**גַּנְדְּרַנְ**כֶם/כֶן/**גַּנְדְּרָנָ**ם/ן	**גַּנְדְּרָ**נִי/נְךָ/נֵךְ/נוֹ/נָהּ	גַּנְדְּרַן-	dandy	גַּנְדְּרָן ז׳
גַּנְדְּרָנֵינוּ/כֶם/כֶן/הֶם/הֶן	**גַּנְדְּרָ**נַי/נֶיךָ/נַיִךְ/נָיו/נֶיהָ	גַּנְדְּרָנֵי-		גַּנְדְּרָנִים

This pattern is parallel to the general *CaCCan* category above, which primarily denotes performers of actions or their characteristic quality, but here it is extended to forms derived from quadriliteral roots. The vowel *e* is inserted only when required to facilitate articulation, e.g., in *karseman* 'rodent,' but not in *gandran* 'dandy,' where syllable division dispenses with the need for *e*-insertion: *gan-dran* vs. *kar-se-man*.

Examples

מקובל לחשוב שנשים מייחסות חשיבות גדולה להופעתן, אבל יש גם לא מעט גברים **גַּנְדְּרָנִים** המקפידים על לבושם ומפגינים את גבריותם ואת אלגנטיותם.
It is customary to think that women attribute great importance to their appearance, but there are also **dandy** men who take pride in the way they are dressed and who exhibit their manhood and their elegance.

הגדרת חז״ל: מי שמעביר ביקורת על מנת לפגוע בחברו הרי זה **קַנְטְרָן**.
According to the sages, a **spiteful** person is he who criticizes others in order to hurt them.

Additional Examples in this Pattern

rodent כַּרְסְמָן	thick-bearded (man) עַבְדְּקָן

---

851. ***CaCCeCan*** with reduplication

Our/your/their	my/your/his/her	const.	Gloss	sing/pl
בַּזְבְּזָנֵנוּ/**בַּזְבְּזַנְ**כֶם/כֶן/**בַּזְבְּזָנָ**ם/ן	**בַּזְבְּזָ**נִי/נְךָ/נֵךְ/נוֹ/נָהּ	בַּזְבְּזַן-	squanderer	בַּזְבְּזָן ז׳
בַּזְבְּזָנֵינוּ/כֶם/כֶן/הֶם/הֶן	**בַּזְבְּזָ**נַי/נֶיךָ/נַיִךְ/נָיו/נֶיהָ	בַּזְבְּזָנֵי-		בַּזְבְּזָנִים

This pattern is parallel to the *CaCC(e)Can* pattern above, which primarily denotes performers of actions or their characteristic quality, when the first and second root consonants are reduplicated in positions three and four, respectively (קַטְקְטָן).

Examples

פוליטיקאים לא מעטים שאינם ממהרים לתרום לצדקה מכספם-שלהם מתגלים כ**בַזְבְּזָנִים** גדולים של כספי ציבור בהגיעם לשלטון.
A good number of politicians who do not rush to donate their own money to charity turn out to be great **squanderers** of public funds when they get to positions of power.

איזה **דַפְדְּפָן** אתה מעדיף? פיירפוקס או גוגל כרום?
Which **browser** do you prefer? Firefox or Google Chrome?

רוב ה**כַלְכְּלָנִים** בעולם חושבים שהבנק המרכזי של כל מדינה צריך לווסת את שערי הריבית על פי שיקולים כלכליים ולא פוליטיים.
Most **economists** in the world believe that the central bank of any nation should regulate interest rates based on economic considerations, not political.

הנשיא ה**רַבְרְבָן** הכריז שהוא מבין בענייני ביטחון יותר מאשר כל הגנרלים.
The **braggart** president declared that he understand security matters better than all the generals.

Additional Examples in this Pattern

בַּלְבְּלָן one who easily gets confused
גַּמְגְּמָן stammerer
דַּגְדְּגָן clitoris
דַּקְדְּקָן pedantic (person)
זַלְזְלָן one who is disparaging
חַרְחְרָן provocateur
לַגְלְגָן ridiculer
לַכְלְכָן one who gets himself dirty; one who speaks derogatorily about others
נַמְנְמָן slumberer
סַכְסְכָן contentious (man)
פַּטְפְּטָן chatterbox, prattler
פַּקְפְּקָן doubter, skeptic
קַשְׁקְשָׁן chatterbox, prattler

---

852. ***CCaCtan***

Our/your/their	my/your/his/her	const.	Gloss	sing/pl
גְּבַרְתָּנֵנוּ/**גְּבַרְתַּנְ**כֶם/כֶן/**גְּבַרְתָּנָ**ם/ן	**גְּבַרְתָּ**נִי/נְךָ/נֵךְ/נוֹ/נָהּ	גְּבַרְתַּן-	tough	גְּבַרְתָּן ז׳
גְּבַרְתָּנֵינוּ/כֶם/כֶן/הֶם/הֶן	**גְּבַרְתָּ**נַי/נֶיךָ/נַיִךְ/נָיו/נֶיהָ	גְּבַרְתָּנֵי-	guy	גְּבַרְתָּנִים

This pattern primarily denotes people with characteristic qualities, and the quadriliteral base is formed by the addition of a *t* to a triliteral root.

Examples

שומרי ראש, בעיקר של עשירים מופלגים ושל ראשי כנופיות פשע, הם בדרך כלל **גְּבַרְתָּנִים** שבעצם הופעתם מרתיעים כל תוקף-בכוח.
Bodyguards, especially of very rich people and of heads of criminal gangs, are generally **tough guys** whose mere presence deters any potential attacker.

פוליטיקאי שאינו **שְׁאַפְתָן** בד"כ אינו מגיע רחוק.
A politician who is not **ambitious** generally does not get very far.

Additional Examples in this Pattern

glutton רְעַבְתָּן/רַעַבְתָן	potbellied; obese person כְּרֵסְתָן
	arrogant, boastful רַהַבְתָן

---

853. *CaCCetan*

Our/your/their	my/your/his/her	const.	Gloss	sing/pl
עַנְוְתָנֵנוּ/**עַנְוְתַנְ**כֶם/כֶן/**עַנְוְתָנָ**ם/ן	**עַנְוְתָ**נִי/נְךָ/נֵךְ/נוֹ/נָהּ	עַנְוְתַן-	modest	עַנְוְתָן ז׳
עַנְוְתָנֵינוּ/כֶם/כֶן/הֶם/הֶן	**עַנְוְתָ**נַי/נֶיךָ/נַיִךְ/נָיו/נֶיהָ	עַנְוְתָנֵי-	(person)	עַנְוְתָנִים

Like *CCaCCan* above, his pattern primarily denotes people with characteristic qualities, and the quadriliteral base is formed by the addition of a *t* to a triliteral root, but the consonant-vowel configuration is somewhat different. Only one case found.

Examples

למרות הצלחתה הגדולה של החברה שהקים, משה נשאר **עַנְוְתָן**, וחוזר וטוען שההצלחה היא עבודת צוות, שהוא רק חלק ממנו.
In spite of the great success of the company he built, Moshe remains a **modest person**, and repeatedly argues that success is due to team work, and that he is only a team member.

---

854. *shtaCCan*

Our/your/their	my/your/his/her	const.	Gloss	sing/pl
שְׁתַלְטָנֵנוּ/**שְׁתַלְטַנְ**כֶם/כֶן/**שְׁתַלְטָנָ**ם/ן	**שְׁתַלְטָ**נִי/נְךָ/נֵךְ/נוֹ/נָהּ	שְׁתַלְטַן-	domineering	שְׁתַלְטָן ז׳
שְׁתַלְטָנֵינוּ/כֶם/כֶן/הֶם/הֶן	**שְׁתַלְטָ**נַי/נֶיךָ/נַיִךְ/נָיו/נֶיהָ	שְׁתַלְטָנֵי-		שְׁתַלְטָנִים

Like *CCaCCan* above, this pattern primarily denotes people with characteristic qualities, and the quadriliteral base is formed by the addition of a *t* to a triliteral root, but the added *t*, which originates from the base for derivation, הִשְׁתַּלֵּט 'take over,' is located in position two, as a result of the consonant metathesis of *t* and *sh* in the *hitpa`el binyan*.

Examples

יוסי טוען שחיה אישה **שְׁתַלְטָנִית**, ושקשה לו מאוד לעבוד איתה יחד.
Yossi claims that Haya is a **domineering woman**, and that it is very difficult for him to work together with her.

---

855. *CoC(e)Can*

our/your/their	my/your/his/her	const.	Gloss	sing/pl
צוֹלְלָנֵנוּ/**צוֹלְלַנְ**כֶם/כֶן/**צוֹלְלָנָ**ם/ן	**צוֹלְלָ**נִי/נְךָ/נֵךְ/נוֹ/נָהּ	צוֹלְלַן-	submariner	צוֹלְלָן ז׳
צוֹלְלָנֵינוּ/**צוֹלְלְנֵי**כֶם/כֶן/הֶם/הֶן	**צוֹלְלָ**נַי/נֶיךָ/נַיִךְ/נָיו/נֶיהָ	צוֹלְלְנֵי-		צוֹלְלָנִים

The suffix is -*an*. As in *CaCCan* above, forms in this pattern refer to a person with a characteristic quality (תּוֹקְפָן 'aggressive person') or to his occupation (צוֹלְלָן 'submariner') or to an instrument/other noun (פּוֹתְחָן 'bottle/can opener,' כּוֹרְכָן 'file folder, binder'), generally through a verb suggesting the characteristic quality. Most of the forms belong to the higher register, whereas those of *CaCCan* can be found at all registers. For some reason, the percentage of instruments/nouns in *CoCCan* is larger than their percentage in *CaCCan* (Note the large number the Academy coined terms for different types of office folders…) Since most forms have parallels in the *CoCeC* present participle pattern of the *pa`al binyan*, one can also regard most of them as linear derivation from *CoCeC* + *an*, but not all. When the 2nd and 3rd root consonants are identical, *e* is inserted, or alternatively, is maintained, to facilitate articulation: *tsolelan*, *Hovevan*.

Examples

חיילים המשרתים כ**צוֹלְלָנִים** בצה״ל מהווים יחידת עילית, ונבחרים בקפידה רבה.
Soldiers who serve as **submariners** in the IDF form an elite unit, and are very carefully selected.

בישראל אוהבים מאוד כדורגל. הבעייה היא ששחקני הכדורגל בארץ, למרות משכורותיהם הגבוהות, משחקים כמו **חוֹבְבָנִים**; הם עצלנים מדיי, וכמעט אינם מתאמנים.
In Israel they love soccer. The problem is that soccer players in Israel, in spite of their high salaries, play like **amateurs**; they are too lazy, and hardly train.

קשה לי להירדם לפני שאני קורא שעה או שעתיים במיטה, בדרך כלל **מוֹתְחָנִים**.
It is hard for me to fall asleep before I read an hour or two in bed, generally **thrillers**.

אליהו סיפר לי שפעם היה בחתונה בקיבוץ, ואי אפשר היה לשתות את היין – לא נמצא אפילו **פּוֹתְחָן** בקבוקים אחד...
Eliyahu told me that he once attended a wedding in a kibbutz where one could not drink the wine – not a single bottle **opener** was available...

הבעייה עם המעיל הזה היא שלעתים קרובות ה**רוֹכְסָן** נתקע.
The problem with this coat is that the **zipper** often gets stuck.

Additional Examples in this Pattern

ring binder; folder (computing) אוֹגְדָן
sinkhole בּוֹלְעָן
spike; sear דּוֹקְרָן
glutton זוֹלְלָן
folder חוֹבְקָן
pestering, nagging (person) טוֹרְדָן
file folder, binder כּוֹרְכָן
salesperson מוֹכְרָן
antibody (medic.) נוֹגְדָן
forgiving person סוֹלְחָן
folder עוֹטְפָן
binder עוֹקְדָן
normativist פּוֹסְקָן
antecedent קוֹדְמָן
aggressive person תּוֹקְפָן

856. ***CoCCan* = *CoCaCan*** when the 2nd root consonant is guttural

our/your/their	my/your/his/her	const.	Gloss	sing/pl
תּוֹאֲמָנֵנוּ/**תּוֹאֲמַנְ**כֶם/כֶן/**תּוֹאֲמָנָ**ם/ן	**תּוֹאֲמָ**נִי/נְךָ/נֵךְ/נוֹ/נָהּ	תּוֹאֲמַן-	conformist	תּוֹאֲמָן ז׳
תּוֹאֲמָנֵינוּ/כֶם/כֶן/הֶם/הֶן	**תּוֹאֲמָ**נַי/נֶיךָ/נַיִךְ/נָיו/נֶיהָ	תּוֹאֲמָנֵי-		תּוֹאֲמָנִים

The pattern is the same as in *CaCCan* above, but when a *shva* is expected with a guttural, it is replaced by *Hataf-pataH*.

Examples

המילה **תּוֹאֲמָן** היא המקבילה הגבוהה יותר של סְתַגְלָן.
to'aman 'conformist' is the higher-register counterpart of *staglan*.

---

857. ***CiCCan*** (from segholates etc.)

our/your/their	my/your/his/her	const.	Gloss	sing/pl
כִּבְשָׁנֵנוּ/**כִּבְשַׁ**נְכֶם/נְכֶן/**כִּבְשָׁ**נָם/נָן	**כִּבְשָׁ**נִי/נְךָ/נֵךְ/נוֹ/נָהּ	כִּבְשַׁן-	furnace	כִּבְשָׁן ז׳
כִּבְשָׁנֵינוּ/**כִּבְשְׁנֵי**כֶם/כֶן/הֶם/הֶן	**כִּבְשָׁ**נַי/נֶיךָ/נַיִךְ/נָיו/נֶיהָ	כִּבְשְׁנֵי-		כִּבְשָׁנִים

The suffix is *-an*. In some of the cases, the base is "segholate," e.g., גֶּזַע/גִּזְעְ+ָן < גִּזְעָן. In some of the occurrences, the ending *-an* suggests a characteristic quality denoted by the base.

Examples

היום ארובה של **כִּבְשָׁן** של בית חרושת חייבת לעמוד בתנאים מסוימים כדי למזער את זיהום הסביבה שהיא גורמת.
Today a **furnace** chimney of a factory must follow certain standards so as to minimize the environmental pollution it causes.

צ'רלי טוען שהוא אינו **גִּזְעָן**; הוא פשוט לא אוהב אנשים שאינם לבנים...
Charlie claims that he is not a **racist**; he simply does not like people who are not white…

יוסי הסביר לי שאינו יכול לסיים את הארוחה העיקרית ללא **לִפְתָּן**.
Yossi explained to me that he cannot conclude the main meal of the day without **compote**.

יהודים שומרי מצוות אינם לובשים בגדים העשויים מצמר **וּפִשְׁתָּן** יחדיו.
Observant Jews do not wear clothes made of wool and **flax** together.

ה**תִּלְתָּן** נקרא כך בשל צורת העלה שלו, המורכב משלושה (תלת) עלעלים.
The **clover** is called so because of the shape of its leaf, which is composed of three (תלת) sections.

Additional Examples in this Pattern

sturgeon חִדְקָן
sweet, candy מִגְדָּן
tar עִטְרָן
glasswort (plant) פִּרְקָן
pigment צִבְעָן

---

858. ***CiCCan***, when the third root consonant is *y*

our/your/their	my/your/his/her	const.	Gloss	sing/pl
בִּנְיָנֵנוּ/**בִּנְיַ**נְכֶם/נְכֶן/**בִּנְיָ**נָם/נָן	**בִּנְיָ**נִי/נְךָ/נֵךְ/נוֹ/נָהּ	בִּנְיַן-	building	בִּנְיָן ז׳
בִּנְיָנֵינוּ/**בִּנְיְנֵי**כֶם/כֶן/הֶם/הֶן	**בִּנְיָ**נַי/נֶיךָ/נַיִךְ/נָיו/נֶיהָ	בִּנְיְנֵי-		בִּנְיָנִים

The suffix is *-an*. The third root consonant is always *y*.

Examples

כולנו מכירים יזם בנייה מסוים הדורש שכל **בִּנְיָן** שהוא בונה ייקרא על שמו.
We all know a certain builder who insists that every **building** he initiates will be named after him.

ליהודים שומרי מצוות חשוב לקיים תפילה בציבור שכשנוכחים לפחות **מִנְיָן** גברים.
For observant Jews it is important to hold public prayers with at least **ten men** present.

יש עדיין חברות בעולם שבהן האישה היא **קִנְיָן** הבעל.
There are still some societies in the world in which a wife is her husband's **property**.

Special Expressions

basic rule, precedent **בִּנְיַן** אב (Talmudic)

a **matter** to deal with/of interest **עִנְיָן** לענות בו

intellectual **property** **קִנְיָן** רוחני

Additional Examples in this Pattern

number amount; quorum for Jewish public prayer (ten) מִנְיָן
matter; interest עִנְיָן

---

859. ***CeCCan*** (from segholates)

our/your/their	my/your/his/her	const.	Gloss	sing/pl
נֶכְדָּנֵנוּ/**נֶכְדַּ**נְכֶם/נְכֶן/**נֶכְדָּ**נָם/נָן	**נֶכְדָּ**נִי/נְךָ/נֵךְ/נוֹ/נָהּ	נֶכְדַּן-	grand-	נֶכְדָּן ז׳
נֶכְדָּנֵינוּ/כֶם/כֶן/הֶם/הֶן	**נֶכְדָּ**נַי/נֶיךָ/נַיִךְ/נָיו/נֶיהָ	נֶכְדְּנֵי-	nephew	נֶכְדָּנִים

The suffix is *-an*; the base is "segholate," נֶכְדָּן < נֶכֶד/נֶכְד+ַן.

Examples

דני מאושר: יש הרבה ילדים במשפחה, נכדים **וּנֶכְדָּנִים**.
Danny is a happy person: there many children in the family, grandchildren and **grand-nephews**.

---

860. *CuCCan*

our/your/their	my/your/his/her	const.	Gloss	sing/pl
אֻלְפָּנֵנוּ/**אֻלְפַּנְ**כֶם/כֶן/**אֻלְפָּ**נָם/נָן	**אֻלְפָּ**נִי/נְךָ/נֵךְ/נוֹ/נָהּ	אֻלְפַּן-	studio; Hebrew	אֻלְפָּן ז'
אֻלְפָּנֵינוּ/**אֻלְפְּנֵי**כֶם/כֶן/הֶם/הֶן	**אֻלְפָּ**נַי/נֶיךָ/נַיִךְ/נָיו/נֶיהָ	אֻלְפְּנֵי-	school	אֻלְפָּנִים

The suffix is *-an*, and it points to a noun or verb denoting a quality of the base. When the third root consonant is guttural, the *shva* that resulted from reduction is replaced by *Hataf-pataH*: ...פֻּלְחָן ... פֻּלְחֲנֵיכֶם

Examples

בזמנו היה רק **אֻלְפָּן** סרטים אחד בארץ ; היום יש כבר כמה.
At the time, there was only one film **studio** in Israel; today there a few.

על פי המדרשים, **חֻרְבַּן** בית המקדש וירושלים נגרמו בשל שנאת חינם.
According to the Midrashim, the **destruction** of the Temple and of Jerusalem were caused by unjustified hatred.

העיקרון החשוב ביותר ביהדות הוא רדיפה אחר צדק חברתי ; ה**פֻּלְחָן** שני בחשיבותו.
The most important principle in Judaism is the pursuit of social justice; the **ritual** is secondary in importance.

Additional Examples in this Pattern

(male) model דֻּגְמָן   relief; vent פֻּרְקָן

---

861. *CoCCan*

our/your/their	my/your/his/her	const.	Gloss	sing/pl
אָבְדָנֵנוּ/**אָבְדַּנְ**כֶם/כֶן/**אָבְדָּ**נָם/נָן	**אָבְדָּ**נִי/נְךָ/נֵךְ/נוֹ/נָהּ	אָבְדַּן-	loss	אָבְדָּן ז'
אָבְדָנֵינוּ/**אָבְדְנֵי**כֶם/כֶן/הֶם/הֶן	**אָבְדָּ**נַי/נֶיךָ/נַיִךְ/נָיו/נֶיהָ	אָבְדְּנֵי-		אָבְדָּנִים

The suffix is *-an*, and it points to a noun or verb denoting a quality of the base. The first vowel is *kamats katan* [o].

Examples

אָבְדָּנוֹ של עמוס עוז היווה מכה קשה לעולם הספרות העברית.
The **loss** of Amos Oz constituted a major blow to Hebrew literature.

Special Expressions

אָבְדַּן דרך **loss** of way, losing one's way   **אָבְדַּן** חושים confusion, disorientation

Additional Examples in this Pattern

mink חָרְפָּן

---

862. ***CoCCan***, pl. *-ot*

our/your/their	my/your/his/her	const.	Gloss	sing/pl
קָרְבָּנֵנוּ/**קָרְבַּ**נְכֶם/נְכֶן/**קָרְבָּ**נָם/נָן	**קָרְבָּ**נִי/נְךָ/נֵךְ/נוֹ/נָהּ	קָרְבַּן-	sacrifice;	קָרְבָּן ז'
קָרְבְּנוֹתֵינוּ/תֵיכֶם/תֵיכֶן/תֵיהֶם/תֵיהֶן	**קָרְבְּנוֹ**תַי/תֶיךָ/תַיִךְ/תָיו/תֶיהָ	קָרְבְּנוֹת-	victim	קָרְבָּנוֹת

Like *CoCCan* above, but the plural suffix is *-ot.*

Examples

בישראל, מספר **קָרְבְּנוֹת** תאונות הדרכים עולה בהרבה על מספר כל חללי מלחמות ישראל.
In Israel, the number of **victims** in road accidents is much larger than the number of fallen soldiers in all of Israel's wars.

בספרו המרתק **אנטומיה של רצח עם** טוען ההיסטוריון עומר ברטוב שמבצעי רצח המוני של קבוצה אתנית ואלה המשתפים עימם פעולה רואים את עצמם כ**קָרְבְּנוֹת** של אותה קבוצה אתנית.
In his insightful book *Anatomy of Genocide* the historian Omer Bartov argues that perpetrators of genocide and their collaborators view themselves as **victims** of that ethnic group.

Special Expressions

perpetual daily sacrifice (at the Temple) **קָרְבַּן** התמיד

---

863. Noun + ***an*** linear derivation

Our/your/their	my/your/his/her	const.	Gloss	sing/pl
דוֹדָנֵנוּ/**דוֹדַנְ**כֶם/כֶן/**דוֹדָנָ**ם/ן	**דוֹדָ**נִי/נְךָ/נֵךְ/נוֹ/נָהּ	דוֹדַן-	cousin	דוֹדָן ז'
דוֹדָנֵינוּ/כֶם/כֶן/הֶם/הֶן	**דוֹדָ**נַי/נֶיךָ/נַיִךְ/נָיו/נֶיהָ	דוֹדָנֵי-		דוֹדָנִים

The suffix is *-an*. One can still argue that some of the occurrences may be assigned to subgroups of *mishkalim* (see below), but in most cases it appears that forms included in this pattern are linearly derived: אֶגְרוֹף 'fist' + *an* > אֶגְרוֹפָן 'boxer; brass knuckles.' As in the *CaCCan mishkal*, forms in this pattern also generally refer to an agent (a person controlling the action), especially when the action denoted by the base characterizes his/her occupation (אֶקְדְּחָן 'gunner,' אַבּוּבָן 'oboist'), but unlike *CaCCan* generally do not denote an instrument (except for עֲגוּרָן 'crane (construction),' and one of the meanings of אֶגְרוֹפָן 'brass knuckles' in the forms included here), nor an adjective denoting a characteristic quality of an agent.

Examples

למנשה אין אחים או אחיות בכלל, אבל יש לו הרבה **דוֹדָנִים**.
Menashe has no brother or sisters at all, but he has many **cousins**.

מי שמקבל מכה ב**אֶגְרוֹפָן** מעולם לא ישכח אותה.
Whoever is hit with a blow with **brass knuckles** never forgets it.

אבי היה ה**אַלְחוּטָן** של מפקד גדוד צנחנים בשירות החובה שלו.
Avi was the **wireless operator** of a paratroop battalion during his army service.

למנהיג המפלגה הנוכחי אין הרבה כריזמה, אבל הוא **בִּצּוּעָן** ממדרגה ראשונה.
The current party leader does not have much charisma, but he is first-rate **go-getter**.

רוב האנשים חושבים שמייקל ג'ורדן הוא ה**כַּדּוּרְסַלָּן** הטוב ביותר בעולם.
Most people think that Michael Jordan is the best **basketball player** ever.

רוב המראיינים הישראלים בטלוויזיה הם **חֲצְפָנִים**; תמיד משתדלים להוכיח למרואיין שהם מבינים בנושא הנדון יותר ממנו.
Most interviewers on Israeli TV are **cheeky (people)**; they always attempt to prove to the interviewee that they know about the subject under discussion more than s/he does.

Additional Examples in this Pattern

gunner אֶקְדְּחָן
oboist אַבּוּבָן
sprinter אָצָן
motorcyclist אוֹפַנּוֹעָן
achiever, go-getter Coll. בִּצּוּעָן
platypus בַּרְוָזָן
iron bender (constr.) בַּרְזִלָּן
roofer, tiler גַּגָּן
adventurer הַרְפַּתְקָן
recorder or flute player חֲלִילָן
snipe (bird) חַרְטוֹמָן
diamond dealer יַהֲלוֹמָן
soccer player כַּדּוּרַגְלָן
ticket seller, conductor כַּרְטִיסָן
milliner, hatter כּוֹבְעָן
juggler לַהֲטוּטָן
poultry farmer/worker לוּלָן
Peeping Tom מְצִיצָן
cloak room attendant מֶלְתְּחָן
switchboard operator מֶרְכְּזָן

---

864. Noun + *an/miCCeCan*

sing/pl	Gloss	const.	my/your/his/her	Our/your/their
מִשְׁפְּטָן/מִשְׁפָּטָן ז׳	jurist,	מִשְׁפְּטַן-	**מִשְׁפְּטָנִ**י/נְךָ/נֵךְ/נוֹ/נָהּ	מִשְׁפְּטָנֵנוּ/**מִשְׁפְּטַנְ**כֶם/כֶן/**מִשְׁפְּטָנָ**ם/ן
מִשְׁפְּטָנִים	lawyer	מִשְׁפְּטָנֵי-	**מִשְׁפְּטָנַ**י/נֶיךָ/נַיִךְ/נָיו/נֶיהָ	**מִשְׁפְּטָנֵי**נוּ/כֶם/כֶן/הֶם/הֶן

The suffix is *-an*, as in N + *an* above, with similar derived meanings, and the derivation is essentially linear מִשְׁפָּט + ◌ָן (with expected reduction of *kamats* to *shva*), but at the same time it can be regarded as derivation in the discontinuous *mishkal miCCeCan*. Note: the alternate articulation of the isolation form מִשְׁפָּטָן is less common today.

Examples

במערכת שלטונית טובה ומאוזנת שופטי בית המשפט העליון ממונים על פי כישוריהם כ**מִשְׁפְּטָנִים** ולא על פי שיקולים פוליטיים.
In a good, balanced governmental system supreme court judges are appointed based on their qualifications as **jurists** rather than according to political considerations.

אדוארד סעיד טען בזמנו שכל ה**מִזְרְחָנִים** המערביים אינם מבינים את העולם הערבי ומתייחסים לעולם הערבי ולאִסְלאם בהתנשאות מתוך דעות קדומות.
At the time, Edward Said argued that all Western **orientalists** do not understand the Arab world, and treat it and Islam with condescension, based on prejudice.

Additional Examples in this Pattern

telegrapher מִבְרְקָן	nursery worker (gardening) מִשְׁתְּלָן
milliner, hatter מִגְבְּעָן	

---

865. Noun + *an/miCCeCan* = *miCCaCan*, when the second root consonant is guttural

Our/your/their	my/your/his/her	const.	Gloss	sing/pl
מִסְעֲדָנֵנוּ/**מִסְעַדְנְ**כֶם/כֶן/**מִסְעֲדָנָ**ם/ן	**מִסְעֲדָנִ**י/נְךָ/נֵךְ/נוֹ/נָהּ	מִסְעֲדַן-	restaurateur	מִסְעֲדָן ז׳
מִסְעֲדָנֵינוּ/כֶם/כֶן/הֶם/הֶן	**מִסְעֲדָנַ**י/נֶיךָ/נַיִךְ/נָיו/נֶיהָ	מִסְעֲדָנֵי-		מִסְעֲדָנִים

Like Noun + *an/miCCeCan*, when the second root consonant is guttural, and where a *shva* it is replaced by *Hataf-pataH*, resulting in a *miCCeCan* > *miCCaCan*.

Examples

מעניין שאפילו בארץ קטנה כמו ישראל להרבה שֶׁפִים-**מִסְעֲדָנִים** יש מעמד של יְדוּעָנִים (״סֶלֶבְּרִיטָאִים״).

It is interesting that even in a small country such as Israel many chefs-**restaurateurs** have celebrity status.

Additional Examples in this Pattern

administrator מְנַהֲלָן

---

866. Noun + *an/miCCoCan*

Our/your/their	my/your/his/her	const.	Gloss	sing/pl
מִקְצוֹעֵנֵנוּ/**מִקְצוֹעַנְ**כֶם/כֶן/**מִקְצוֹעָנָ**ם/ן	**מִקְצוֹעָנִ**י/נְךָ/נֵךְ/נוֹ/נָהּ	מִקְצוֹעַן-	a	מִקְצוֹעָן ז׳
מִקְצוֹעָנֵינוּ/כֶם/כֶן/הֶם/הֶן	**מִקְצוֹעָנַ**י/נֶיךָ/נַיִךְ/נָיו/נֶיהָ	מִקְצוֹעֲנֵי-	professional	מִקְצוֹעָנִים

The suffix is *-an*, as in N + *an* above, with similar derived meanings, and the derivation is essentially linear מִקְצוֹעַ + ◌ָן, but at the same time it can be regarded as derivation in the discontinuous *mishkal miCCoCan*.

Examples

אחת הבעיות החמורות של מבנה הממשלה בישראל היא שהשרים הם מינויים מפלגתיים, ומשום כך רובם אינם **מִקְצוֹעָנִים**.

One of the serious problems with the structure of government in Israel is that ministers are party appointees, and consequently most of them are not **professionals**.

Additional Examples in this Pattern

weightlifter מִשְׁקוֹלָן

---

867. Noun + *an/maCCeCan*

Our/your/their	my/your/his/her	const.	Gloss	sing/pl
מַהְפְּכָנֵנוּ/מַהְפְּכַנְכֶם/כֶן/ מַהְפְּכָנָם/ן	מַהְפְּכָנִי/נְךָ/נֵךְ/נוֹ/נָהּ	מַהְפְּכַן-	a revolutionary	מַהְפְּכָן ז׳
מַהְפְּכָנֵינוּ/כֶם/כֶן/הֶם/הֶן	מַהְפְּכָנַי/נֶיךָ/נַיִךְ/נָיו/נֶיהָ	מַהְפְּכָנֵי-		מַהְפְּכָנִים

The suffix is *-an*, as in N + *an* above, with similar derived meanings, and the derivation is essentially linear ◌ָן + מַהְפֵּכָה (with expected reduction of *tsere* to *shva*), but at the same time it can be regarded as derivation in the discontinuous *mishkal maCCeCan*. Note: in daily speech מַהְפְּכָן *mahp(e)khan* is normally pronounced *mahapekhan* or *mahapkhan*; the normative pronounciation is rare.

Examples

רבים מן ה**מַהְפְּכָנִים** באירופה בסוף המאה התשע-עשרה ובתחילת המאה העשרים היו יהודים, מכיוון שיהודים האמינו תמיד ברדיפה אחר צדק חברתי.

Many of the **revolutionaries** in Europe at the end of the 19th Century and at the beginning of the 20th were Jews, because Jews have always believed in the pursuit of social justice.

Additional Examples in this Pattern

מַבְלְטָן one designing and creating dies

מַקְלְעָן machine gunner

מַרְזְחָן innkeeper, bartender Lit-Rare

---

868. Noun + *an/maCCiCan*

Our/your/their	my/your/his/her	const.	Gloss	sing/pl
מַחְלִיטָנֵנוּ/מַחְלִיטַנְכֶם/כֶן/ מַחְלִיטָנָם/ן	מַחְלִיטָנִי/נְךָ/נֵךְ/נוֹ/נָהּ	מַחְלִיטַן-	decision-maker Coll.	מַחְלִיטָן ז׳
מַחְלִיטָנֵינוּ/כֶם/כֶן/הֶם/הֶן	מַחְלִיטָנַי/נֶיךָ/נַיִךְ/נָיו/נֶיהָ	מַחְלִיטָנֵי-		מַחְלִיטָנִים

The suffix is *-an*, as in N + *an* above, with similar derived meanings, and the derivation is essentially linear ◌ָן+ מַחְלִיט, but at the same time it can be regarded as derivation in the discontinuous *mishkal maCCiCan*. Most forms belong to the colloquial register.

Examples

לא פעם, ה**מַחְלִיטָנִים** בבית הנשיא או בבית ראש הממשלה הם בעצם רעיותיהם.

It sometimes happens that the **decision-makers** in the President's or the Prime Minister's residence are actually their wives.

כשרונלד רייגן היה נשיא, היו שאמרו: למישהו כמו בוב הופ אנו קוראים **מַצְחִיקָן**, אבל ל**מַצְחִיקָן** אמיתי אנו קוראים "אדוני הנשיא".

When Ronald Reagan was president, some said: someone like Bob Hope we call **comedian**, but a real **comedian** we call "Mr. President."

בתחום של חברות ה״סְטַרְטַאפּ״ בישראל, על כל חברה אחת של **מַצְלִיחָנִים** יש תשע חברות של **מַפְסִידָנִים**.
Among startup companies in Israel, for every company of **successful people** there are nine companies of "**losers**."

Additional Examples in this Pattern

one who exaggerates מַגְזִימָן
one leaking information Coll. מַדְלִיפָן
nuisance, pest Coll. מַטְרִידָן
inventor, innovator Coll. מַמְצִיאָן
defamer Coll. מַשְׁמִיצָן
one who invests a lot מַשְׁקִיעָן

---

869. Noun + *an/maCCan*

Our/your/their	my/your/his/her	const.	Gloss	sing/pl
מַחְוָנֵנוּ/**מַחְוָנְ**כֶם/כֶן/**מַחְוָנָ**ם/ן	**מַחְוָנִ**י/נְךָ/נֵךְ/נוֹ/נָהּ	מַחְוַן-	indicator,	מַחְוָן ז׳
מַחְוָנֵינוּ/**מַחְוְנֵי**כֶם/כֶן/הֶם/הֶן	**מַחְוָנַ**י/נֶיךָ/נַיִךְ/נָיו/נֶיהָ	מַחְוְנֵי-	gauge	מַחְוָנִים

The suffix is *-an*, as in N + *an* above, and the derivation is essentially linear מַחְוֶה + ◌ָן (while eliding the *seghol* before an immediately-following *kamats*), but at the same time it can be regarded as derivation in the discontinuous *mishkal maCCan*. The third root consonant is a *y* that is not realized phonetically.

Examples

מַחְוָן הוא מתקן העשוי מצג, שעליו מחוג או זרוע הנעה ומספקת מידע.
An **indicator** is an instrument with display, on which a needle or pointer that provides information.

Additional Examples in this Pattern

equator מַשְׁוָן (קו המשוה)

---

870. Noun + *an/staCCan*

Our/your/their	my/your/his/her	const.	Gloss	sing/pl
סְתַגְלָנֵנוּ/**סְתַגְלַנְ**כֶם/כֶן/**סְתַגְלָנָ**ם/ן	**סְתַגְלָנִ**י/נְךָ/נֵךְ/נוֹ/נָהּ	סְתַגְלַן-	one easily adjusting to	סְתַגְלָן ז׳
סְתַגְלָנֵינוּ/כֶם/כֶן/הֶם/הֶן	**סְתַגְלָנַ**י/נֶיךָ/נַיִךְ/נָיו/נֶיהָ	סְתַגְלָנֵי-	change	סְתַגְלָנִים

The suffix is *-an*, as in N + *an* above, with similar derived meanings, and the derivation is essentially linear מִסְתַּגֵּל + ◌ָן (while deleting the prefix of the *hitpa`el* participle and the *tsere*), but at the same time it can be regarded as derivation in the discontinuous *mishkal staCCan*.

Examples

סְתַגְּלָנִים בדרך כלל מצליחים בפוליטיקה, מכיוון שהם יודעים לשנות את דיעותיהם בהתאם לנסיבות משתנות, אבל זה גם יוצר להם תדמית של חסרי אופי וחסרי מצפון.

People who easily adjust to changes generally do well in politics, since they know how to adapt their views to changing circumstances, but it also gives them an image of ones lacking in character and having no conscience.

Additional Examples in this Pattern

ascetic person סְתַגְּפָן	introverted, withdrawn, detached person סְתַגְּרָן

---

871. Noun + *an/shtaCCan*

sing/pl	Gloss	const.	my/your/his/her	Our/your/their
שְׁתַדְּלָן ז׳	lobbyist	שְׁתַדְּלַן-	**שְׁתַדְּלָנ**ִי/נְךָ/נֵךְ/נוֹ/נָהּ	שְׁתַדְּלָנֵנוּ/**שְׁתַדְּלַנְ**כֶם/כֶן/**שְׁתַדְּלָנָ**ם/ן
שְׁתַדְּלָנִים		שְׁתַדְּלָנֵי-	**שְׁתַדְּלָנַ**י/נֶיךָ/נַיִךְ/נָיו/נֶיהָ	**שְׁתַדְּלָנֵי**נוּ/כֶם/כֶן/הֶם/הֶן

The suffix is *-an*, as in N + *an* above, with similar derived meanings, and the derivation is essentially linear מִשְׁתַּדֵּל + ◌ָן (while deleting the prefix of the *hitpa`el* participle and the *tsere*), but at the same time it can be regarded as derivation in the discontinuous *mishkal shtaCCan*.

Examples

בוושינגטון כל **שְׁתַדְּלָן** חייב להירשם רשמית.

In Washington, any **lobbyist** must formally register as such.

Additional Examples in this Pattern

shirker שְׁתַמְּטָן

---

872. ?Noun + *an/C(e)CaCtan*

sing/pl	Gloss	const.	my/your/his/her	Our/your/their
פְּעַלְתָּן ז׳	active	פְּעַלְתַּן-	**פְּעַלְתָּנ**ִי/נְךָ/נֵךְ/נוֹ/נָהּ	פְּעַלְתָּנֵנוּ/**פְּעַלְתַּנְ**כֶם/כֶן/**פְּעַלְתָּנָ**ם/ן
פְּעַלְתָּנִים	person	פְּעַלְתָּנֵי-	**פְּעַלְתָּנַ**י/נֶיךָ/נַיִךְ/נָיו/נֶיהָ	**פְּעַלְתָּנֵי**נוּ/כֶם/כֶן/הֶם/הֶן

The suffix is *-an*, as in N + *an* above, with similar derived meanings. The derivation may be linear, פְּעוּלָּה + ◌ָן, with the suffix *+a* going back to *+t*, but the other required changes are a bit radical, so it is very likely that it should be regarded as derivation in the discontinuous *mishkal CCaCtan*.

Examples

פְּעַלְתָּנִים כמו יוסי אינם יכולים לשבת במנוחה לרגע.

Active people like Yossi cannot sit still for a moment.

---

873. Noun + *an/CCoCtan* = *CaCoCtan* when the first root consonant is guttural

Our/your/their	my/your/his/her	const.	Gloss	sing/pl
חֲרָשְׁתָּנֵנוּ/**חֲרָשְׁתַּנְ**כֶם/כֶן/**חֲרָשְׁתָּנָ**ם/ן	**חֲרָשְׁתָּ**נִי/נְךָ/נֵךְ/נוֹ/נָהּ	-חֲרָשְׁתַּן	industrialist	חֲרָשְׁתָּן ז׳
חֲרָשְׁתָּנֵינוּ/כֶם/כֶן/הֶם/הֶן	**חֲרָשְׁתָּ**נַי/נֶיךָ/נַיִךְ/נָיו/נֶיהָ	-חֲרָשְׁתָּנֵי	Arch.	חֲרָשְׁתָּנִים

The suffix is *-an*, as in N + *an* above, with similar derived meanings. The derivation may be linear, ◌ָן + חֲרֹשֶׁת, but it is equally plausible that it should be regarded as derivation in the discontinuous *mishkal CCoCtan* (the vowel following the ר׳ is *kamats katan*). When a *shva* is expected, it is replaced by *Hataf-pataH*, *CCoCtan* > *CaCoCtan*.

Examples

חֲרָשְׁתָּן הוא מונח שהשתמשו בו בעבר לתַּעֲשִׂיָּן.

Hasroshtan is an older term used for **industrialist**.

---

874. Noun + *an/C(e)CuCan*

Our/your/their	my/your/his/her	const.	Gloss	sing/pl
יְבוּאָנֵנוּ/**יְבוּאַנְ**כֶם/כֶן/**יְבוּאָנָ**ם/ן	**יְבוּאָ**נִי/נְךָ/נֵךְ/נוֹ/נָהּ	-יְבוּאַן	importer	יְבוּאָן ז׳
יְבוּאָנֵינוּ/כֶם/כֶן/הֶם/הֶן	**יְבוּאָ**נַי/נֶיךָ/נַיִךְ/נָיו/נֶיהָ	-יְבוּאָנֵי		יְבוּאָנִים

The suffix is *-an*, as in N + *an* above, with similar derived meanings, and the derivation is essentially linear ◌ָן + יְבוּא, but at the same time it can be regarded as derivation in the discontinuous *mishkal CCuCan*. *e* is inserted between the first two consonant when required to facilitate articulation.

Examples

מכיוון שישראל אינה מייצרת מכוניות, **יְבוּאָנֵי** המכוניות הישראלים, בעיקר מן המזרח הרחוק ומאירופה, עושים בה עסקים רווחיים ביותר.

Since Israel does not manufacture cars, Israeli car importers, mostly from the Far East and from Europe, conduct thriving businesses there.

בישראל, כמו בארה״ב, התקשורת עוסקת לא מעט בחייהם הפרטיים של **יְדוּעָנִים**.

In Israel, like in the US, the media deal a good deal with the private lives of **celebrities**.

Additional Examples in this Pattern

יְצוּאָן exporter   רְכוּשָׁן capitalist

---

875. Noun + *an/CiCan*

Our/your/their	my/your/his/her	const.	Gloss	sing/pl
טִיסָנֵנוּ/**טִיסַנְ**כֶם/כֶן/**טִיסָנָ**ם/ן	**טִיסָ**נִי/נְךָ/נֵךְ/נוֹ/נָהּ	-טִיסַן	model	טִיסָן ז׳
טִיסָנֵינוּ/כֶם/כֶן/הֶם/הֶן	**טִיסָ**נַי/נֶיךָ/נַיִךְ/נָיו/נֶיהָ	-טִיסָנֵי	plane	טִיסָנִים

The suffix is *-an*, as in N + *an* above, with similar derived meanings, and the derivation is essentially linear טִיסָה + ◌ָן, but at the same time it can be regarded as derivation in the discontinuous *mishkal CiCan*.

Examples

אביגדור בונה **טִיסָנִים** ומוכר אותם בסיטונות לחנויות צעצועים.
Avigdor builds **model airplanes** and sells them wholesale to toy stores.

הַבִּיתָן הישראלי בתערוכה עורר עניין רב בקרב המבקרים.
The Israeli **pavilion** in the exhibition aroused considerable interest among the visitors.

הַשִּׂיאָן הישראלי בהיאבקות חופשית עלה לארץ מגאורגיה.
The Israeli **record holder** in wrestling had immigrated to Israel from Georgia (in the Caucasus).

Additional Examples in this Pattern

calcium סִידָן	filled dumplings, kreplach, pierogi כִּיסָן	foxtail (plant) זִיפָן

---

876. Noun + *an/CeyCan*

Our/your/their	my/your/his/her	const.	Gloss	sing/pl
לֵיצָנֵנוּ/**לֵיצַנְכֶם**/כֶן/**לֵיצָנָם**/ן	**לֵיצָנִי**/נְךָ/נֵךְ/נוֹ/נָהּ	לֵיצַן-	clown,	לֵיצָן ז׳
לֵיצָנֵינוּ/כֶם/כֶן/הֶם/הֶן	**לֵיצָנַי**/נֶיךָ/נַיִךְ/נָיו/נֶיהָ	לֵיצָנֵי-	jester	לֵיצָנִים

The suffix is *-an*, as in N + *an* above, with similar derived meanings, and the derivation is essentially linear לֵ(י)ץ +◌ָן (the t*sere* expands to a "full" *tsere* with the glide *y*), but at the same time it can be regarded as derivation in the discontinuous *mishkal CeyCan*. Note: יֵינָן 'vintner' is derived from the construct state form of יַיִן 'wine': -יֵין.

Examples

לֵיצָנִים הם מרכיב חשוב בתוכנית של כל קרקס.
Clowns are an important component of the program in any circus.

משפחת אנטנורי היא משפחה מוערכת מאוד של **יֵינָנִים** באיטליה.
The Antenori family is a highly respected family of **vintners** in Italy.

Special Expressions

court **jester**, clown **לֵיצַן** החצר

Additional Examples in this Pattern

basil רֵיחָן	hydrogen מֵימָן
empty; ignorant person Lit. רֵיקָן	swordtail (fish) סֵיפָן

---

877. Noun + *an/CoCan*

Our/your/their	my/your/his/her	const.	Gloss	sing/pl
יוֹמָנֵנוּ/**יוֹמַנְ**כֶם/כֶן/**יוֹמָנָ**ם/ן	**יוֹמָ**נִי/נְךָ/נֵךְ/נוֹ/נָהּ	יוֹמַן-	diary;	יוֹמָן ז'
יוֹמָנֵינוּ/כֶם/כֶן/הֶם/הֶן	**יוֹמָ**נַי/נֶיךָ/נַיִךְ/נָיו/נֶיהָ	יוֹמָנֵי-	calendar	יוֹמָנִים

The suffix is *-an*, as in N + *an* above, with similar derived meanings, and the derivation is essentially linear ָן+ יוֹם, but at the same time it can be regarded as derivation in the discontinuous *mishkal CoCan*.

Examples

אנשי ציבור רבים כותבים ב**יוֹמָנָם** אודות מה שקורה בתקופת היותם בתפקיד – בשביל ההיסטוריה, ומסיבות אחרות.
Many public figures keep a **diary** of what happens while they serve – for history, and for other reasons.

האישה המוכה צלצלה למשטרה בלילה, אבל עד שהקצין ה**תּוֹרָן** בתחנה החליט לשלוח ניידת, היה כבר מאוחר מדיי.
The battered woman called the police at night, but until the **officer on duty** at the station decided to send a cruiser, it was too late.

Special Expressions

יוֹמַן חדשות daily news broadcast

יוֹמַן מבצעים (military) operations **log**

יוֹמַן מסע travel **diary**

Additional Examples in this Pattern

קוֹלָן tuning fork

קוֹצָן thistle

---

878. Noun + *an/CuCan*

Our/your/their	my/your/his/her	const.	Gloss	sing/pl
צוּרָנֵנוּ/**צוּרַנְ**כֶם/כֶן/**צוּרָנָ**ם/ן	**צוּרָ**נִי/נְךָ/נֵךְ/נוֹ/נָהּ	צוּרַן-	morpheme	צוּרָן ז'
צוּרָנֵינוּ/כֶם/כֶן/הֶם/הֶן	**צוּרָ**נַי/נֶיךָ/נַיִךְ/נָיו/נֶיהָ	צוּרָנֵי-		צוּרָנִים

The suffix is *-an*, as in N + *an* above, with similar derived meanings, and the derivation is essentially linear ָן + צוּרָה, but at the same time it can be regarded as derivation in the discontinuous *mishkal CuCan*.

Examples

ה**צוּרָן** היא יחידת המשמעות הבסיסית המינימלית בשפה.
The **morpheme** is the basic minimal unit of meaning in a language.

Additional Examples in this Pattern

זוּגָן zygophyllum (plant)

---

879. Noun + *an/taCCiCan*

Our/your/their	my/your/his/her	const.	Gloss	sing/pl
תַּכְשִׁיטָנֵנוּ/**תַּכְשִׁיטַנְ**כֶם/כֶן/**תַּכְשִׁיטָנָ**ם/ן	**תַּכְשִׁיטָ**נִי/נְךָ/נֵךְ/נוֹ/נָהּ	תַּכְשִׁיטַן-	jeweler	תַּכְשִׁיטָן ז׳
תַּכְשִׁיטָנֵינוּ/כֶם/כֶן/הֶם/הֶן	**תַּכְשִׁיטָנַ**י/נֶיךָ/נַיִךְ/נָיו/נֶיהָ	תַּכְשִׁיטָנֵי-		תַּכְשִׁיטָנִים

The suffix is *-an*, as in N + *an* above, with similar derived meanings, and the derivation is essentially linear תַּכְשִׁיט + ָן, but at the same time it can be regarded as derivation in the discontinuous *mishkal taCCiCan.*

Examples

הבאתי ל**תַּכְשִׁיטָן** האהוב עליי בארץ שרידי זהב מתכשיטים שלא ניתן לתקנם ושרידים משיני זהב, והוא יצק לי טבעת נישואין חדשה, נאה וכבדה מזהב ״מלא״, שלא יורדת מאצבעי כבר שנים רבות...
I brought my favorite **jeweler** in Israel gold remnants from broken jewelry and gold teeth, and he cast a new gold wedding ring, pretty and heavy, solid gold, which I have not removed from my finger for many years…

ה**תַּחְקִירָנִים** הטובים ביותר של סי בי אס עובדים עבור התוכנית ״ששים דקות״.
The best CBS **investigative reporters** work for the program "Sixty Minutes."

Additional Examples in this Pattern

relief (map) maker תַּבְלִיטָן　　DJ תַּקְלִיטָן
cost accountant תַּמְחִירָן

---

880. Noun + *an/taCCiCan* with reduplication

Our/your/their	my/your/his/her	const.	Gloss	sing/pl
תַּמְלִילָנֵנוּ/**תַּמְלִילַנְ**כֶם/כֶן/**תַּמְלִילָנָ**ם/ן	**תַּמְלִילָ**נִי/נְךָ/נֵךְ/נוֹ/נָהּ	תַּמְלִילַן-	lyricist; word processor	תַּמְלִילָן ז׳
תַּמְלִילָנֵינוּ/כֶם/כֶן/הֶם/הֶן	**תַּמְלִילָנַ**י/נֶיךָ/נַיִךְ/נָיו/נֶיהָ	תַּמְלִילָנֵי-		תַּמְלִילָנִים

The suffix is *-an*, as in N + *an/taCCiCan* above, with similar derived meanings, and the derivation is essentially linear תַּמְלִיל + ָן, but at the same time it can be regarded as derivation in the discontinuous *mishkal taCCiCan.* The second and third root consonants are identical (תַּקְטִיטָן).

Examples

באופרה העיקר הוא המוסיקה; כדי שאופרה תדבר גם לאינטלקט, נחוץ גם **תַּמְלִילָן** טוב.
The main draw of an opera is the music; for the opera to also appeal to the intellect, a good **librettist** is required.

Additional Examples in this Pattern

hobbyist תַּחְבִּיבָן　　tactician, trickster תַּכְסִיסָן

---

881. Noun + *an/taCCiCan*

Our/your/their	my/your/his/her	const.	Gloss	sing/pl
תַּצְפִּיתָנֵנוּ/**תַּצְפִּיתַנְ**כֶם/כֶן/**תַּצְפִּיתָנָ**ם/ן	**תַּצְפִּיתָ**נִי/נְךָ/נֵךְ/נוֹ/נָהּ	תַּצְפִּיתַן-	lookout	תַּצְפִּיתָן ז׳
תַּצְפִּיתָנֵינוּ/כֶם/כֶן/הֶם/הֶן	**תַּצְפִּיתָ**נַי/נֶיךָ/נַיִךְ/נָיו/נֶיהָ	תַּצְפִּיתָנֵי-		תַּצְפִּיתָנִים

The suffix is *-an*, as in N + *an/taCCiCan* above (no reduplication), with similar derived meanings, and the derivation is essentially linear ◌ָן+ תַּצְפִּית, but at the same time it can be regarded as derivation in the discontinuous *mishkal taCCitan*.

Examples

תַּצְפִּיתָן הוא אדם המשקיף מעמדת תצפית ועוקב אחר אויב, חשוד, אמצעי תחבורה בתנועה העלולים להתנגש זה בזה, וכו׳.

A lookout is a person observing from an observation point, tracking movement of an enemy, suspect, vehicles that may collide, etc.

Additional Examples in this Pattern

תַּדְמִיתָן image maker, public relations agent

תַּכְלִיתָן purposeful person

תַּסְכִּיתָן radio play producer

---

882. Noun + *an/taCCuCan*

Our/your/their	my/your/his/her	const.	Gloss	sing/pl
תַּפְאוּרָנֵנוּ/**תַּפְאוּרַנְ**כֶם/כֶן/**תַּפְאוּרָנָ**ם/ן	**תַּפְאוּרָ**נִי/נְךָ/נֵךְ/נוֹ/נָהּ	תַּפְאוּרַן-	set manager	תַּפְאוּרָן ז׳
תַּפְאוּרָנֵינוּ/כֶם/כֶן/הֶם/הֶן	**תַּפְאוּרָ**נַי/נֶיךָ/נַיִךְ/נָיו/נֶיהָ	תַּפְאוּרָנֵי-	(theater)	תַּפְאוּרָנִים

The suffix is *-an*, as in N + *an/taCCiCan* above, with similar derived meanings, and the derivation is essentially linear ◌ָן + תַּפְאוּרָה, but at the same time it can be regarded as derivation in the discontinuous *mishkal taCCuCan.*

Examples

יש **תַּפְאוּרָנִים** המעצבים תפאורות מורכבות ומפוארות ביותר, אבל יש גם המעדיפים תפאורה מינימלית/סמלית.

Some **set managers** design complex, majestic sets, but there are also others who prefer minimal/symbolic sets.

גיסי הוא **תַּחְזוּקָן** של בית ספר תיכון. זו עבודה לא קלה.

My brother-in-law is a high school **maintenance person**. It is not an easy job.

Additional Examples in this Pattern

תַּבְרוּאָן sanitation engineer

תַּמְרוּקָן cosmetician

תַּחְבּוּלָן trickster, tactician, wily person

---

883. Noun + *an/taCCuCan* = *taCaCuCan*, with reduplication, the first root consonant is guttural

sing/pl	Gloss	const.	my/your/his/her	Our/your/their
תַּעֲלוּלָן ז׳	prankster	תַּעֲלוּלַן-	**תַּעֲלוּלָ**נִי/נְךָ/נֵךְ/נוֹ/נָהּ	תַּעֲלוּלָנֵנוּ/**תַּעֲלוּלַנְ**כֶם/כֶן/**תַּעֲלוּלָנָ**ם/ן
תַּעֲלוּלָנִים		תַּעֲלוּלָנֵי-	**תַּעֲלוּלָ**נַי/נֶיךָ/נַיִךְ/נָיו/נֶיהָ	**תַּעֲלוּלָנֵי**נוּ/כֶם/כֶן/הֶם/הֶן

The base suffix is *-an*, as in N + *an/taCCiCan* above, with similar derived meanings, and the derivation is essentially linear תַּעֲלוּל +ָן, but at the same time it can be regarded as derivation in the discontinuous *mishkal taCCuCan* > *taCaCuCan*. The second and third consonants of the root are identical. When a *shva* is expected with a guttural, it is replaced by *Hataf-pataH* (תַּקְטוּטָן < תַּקֲטוּטָן).

Examples

קשה למורה כשיש **תַּעֲלוּלָן** בכיתה. מעשיו מפריעים לניהול תקין של השיעור.
It is difficult for a teacher to have a **prankster** in class. It interrupts the normal teaching process.

---

884. *CiCCon*

sing/pl	Gloss	const.	my/your/his/her	Our/your/their
גִּלְשׁוֹן ז׳	hang	גִּלְשׁוֹן-	**גִּלְשׁוֹ**נִי/נְךָ/נֵךְ/נוֹ/נָהּ	גִּלְשׁוֹנֵנוּ/**גִּלְשׁוֹנְ**כֶם/כֶן/**גִּלְשׁוֹנָ**ם/ן
גִּלְשׁוֹנִים	glider	גִּלְשׁוֹנֵי-	**גִּלְשׁוֹ**נַי/נֶיךָ/נַיִךְ/נָיו/נֶיהָ	**גִּלְשׁוֹנֵי**נוּ/כֶם/כֶן/הֶם/הֶן

The base suffix is *-on*, which in most other patterns denoted diminution, but generally not here. Some cases may be claimed to be derived linearly: טִפְּשׁוֹן < טִפֵּשׁ, after automatic *e*-deletion (in the of טִפְּשׁוֹן, diminution **is** involved…).

Examples

גִּלְשׁוֹן הוא כלי טיס קטן לא ממונע. הגולש תלוי ברתמה המחוברת לשלד הגלשון ושולט בו בעזרת הטיית גופו ימינה ושמאלה (לשלוט בכיוון) וקדימה אחורה (לשלוט במהירות).
Hang glider is small, unmotorized flying device. The glider is suspended with harness connected to the device, and controls it by tilting his body right or left to control direction, and up or down to control speed.

פִּזְמוֹנֶיהָ של נעמי שמר היו מן הפופולריים ביותר בתולדותיה הקרובות של מדינת ישראל.
Naomi Shemer's **songs** were some of the most popular in the recent history of Israel.

Additional Examples in this Pattern

correspondence text book אִגְּרוֹן
ravine, gorge בִּתְרוֹן
bunting (bird) גִּבְתּוֹן
wren גִּדְרוֹן
silly little fool טִפְּשׁוֹן
secret, mystery Lit. כִּבְשׁוֹן
short song, tune; refrain פִּזְמוֹן
pitchfork קִלְשׁוֹן
dome (architec.) קִמְרוֹן
armor שִׁרְיוֹן

---

885. ***CiCCon*** Plural *-ot*

Our/your/their	my/your/his/her	const.	Gloss	sing/pl
יִתְרוֹנֵנוּ/**יִתְרוֹנְ**כֶם/כֶן/**יִתְרוֹנָ**ם/ן	**יִתְרוֹ**נִי/נְךָ/נֵךְ/נוֹ/נָהּ	יִתְרוֹן-	advantage	יִתְרוֹן ז׳
יִתְרוֹנוֹתֵינוּ/כֶם/כֶן/הֶם/הֶן	**יִתְרוֹנוֹ**תַי/תֶיךָ/תַיִךְ/תָיו/תֶיהָ	יִתְרוֹנוֹת-		יִתְרוֹנוֹת

As in *CiCCon* above, but without diminution in any of the realizations, when the plural suffix is *-ot*.

Examples

יִתְרוֹנָן של בחירות אזוריות הוא שהן נותנות ייצוג מוגבר לאזורים שאינם מאוכלסים בצפיפות, אבל הניסיון מראה שיש בכך גם סכנה.
The **advantage** of regional elections is that it gives better representation to sparsely-populated regions, but experience shows that it also has its dangers.

שאלה מעניינת היא האם הירידה בקריאת ספרים על ידי ילדים ונוער והחלפתה באמצעים חזותיים משפיעה על התפתחות ה**דִּמְיוֹן**.
An interesting question is whether the decline in book reading by children and youth and its replacement by visual media affects the development of **imagination**.

קל מאוד לזהות את **סִגְנוֹנוֹ** של עגנון; הוא שונה מסגנונו של כל סופר עברי אחר.
It is very easy to identify Agnon's **style**; it is different from that of any other Hebrew writer.

Special Expressions

comparative **advantage** (econ.) **יִתְרוֹן** יחסי

creative **imagination** **דִּמְיוֹן** יוצר

(swimming) front crawl; (sport) free**style** wrestling **סִגְנוֹן** חופשי

redemption of Jewish captives by paying ransom (considered a requirement) **פִּדְיוֹן** שבויים

equal rights **שִׁוְיוֹן** זכויות

apathy, indifference **שִׁוְיוֹן** נפש

Additional Examples in this Pattern

imagination; resemblance דִּמְיוֹן

legion(s) לִגְיוֹן

redemption; ransom; proceeds פִּדְיוֹן

solution פִּתְרוֹן

equality שִׁוְיוֹן

regime; government שִׁלְטוֹן

sandbank, shoal שִׂרְטוֹן

---

886. ***CiCCon*** from segholate nouns

Our/your/their	my/your/his/her	const.	Gloss	sing/pl
סִפְרוֹנֵנוּ/**סִפְרוֹנְ**כֶם/כֶן/**סִפְרוֹנָ**ם/ן	**סִפְרוֹ**נִי/נְךָ/נֵךְ/נוֹ/נָהּ	סִפְרוֹן-	booklet	סִפְרוֹן ז׳
סִפְרוֹנֵינוּ/כֶם/כֶן/הֶם/הֶן	**סִפְרוֹ**נַי/נֶיךָ/נַיִךְ/נָיו/נֶיהָ	סִפְרוֹנֵי-		סִפְרוֹנִים

The suffix is *-on*, which generally denotes diminution. The base is segholate, */sifr/* (the base of *séfer* 'book') + *on* > *sifron*, and thus may possibly also be claimed to be derived linearly.

Examples

לפעמים יש ל**סִפְרוֹן** השפעה גדולה יותר גדולה על הציבור מאשר כרך עב-כרס: המניפסט הקומוניסטי של מרקס ואנגלס, ה**סִפְרוֹן** האדום של מאו...
Sometimes a **booklet** may have greater effect on the public than a thick volume would: Marx and Engels' Communist Manifesto, Mao's Red **Booklet**.

דני לא מסוגל לקום מן המיטה בבוקר ללא **סִפְלוֹן** (אחד לפחות) של אספרסו.
Danny is unable to get out of bed in the morning without at least one **small cup** of espresso.

כדי למשוך סטודנטים, מרצים רבים משתמשים היום ב**סִרְטוֹנִים** להמחשה.
In order to attract students, many professors use **film/video clips** to illustrate their presentations.

Additional Examples in this Pattern

small bridge גִּשְׁרוֹן
mistletoe (plant) דִּבְקוֹן
small flag, pennant דִּגְלוֹן
pin, small badge סִמְלוֹן
statuette, figurine פִּסְלוֹן
pimple פִּצְעוֹן
crayon צִבְעוֹן
quarter (of a year); quarterly (magazine, report) רִבְעוֹן
popsicle, ice lolly שִׁלְגּוֹן
distress; heartbreak (לב) שִׁבְרוֹן

---

887. ***CiCCon* = *CeCCon*** when the first root consonant is guttural

Our/your/their	my/your/his/her	const.	Gloss	sing/pl
עֶגְלוֹנֵנוּ/**עֶגְלוֹנְ**כֶם/כֶן/**עֶגְלוֹנָ**ם/ן	**עֶגְלוֹ**נִי/נְךָ/נֵךְ/נוֹ/נָהּ	עֶגְלוֹן-	carter	עֶגְלוֹן ז׳
עֶגְלוֹנֵינוּ/כֶם/כֶן/הֶם/הֶן	**עֶגְלוֹ**נַי/נֶיךָ/נַיִךְ/נָיו/נֶיהָ	עֶגְלוֹנֵי-		עֶגְלוֹנִים

The suffix is *-on* (no diminution involved in any occurrence). Since the first root consonant is guttural, *CiCCon* = *CeCCon (*with *seghol),* but *CeCCon* may also be regarded as an independent pattern.

Examples

בילדותי, **עֶגְלוֹנִים** היו מגיעים לרחובנו עם עגלותיהם ומוכרים נפט, קרח, ואפילו דברי מאפה טריים.
When I was a child, **carters** would come to our street with their carts/wagons, selling kerosene, ice blocks, and even fresh baked goods.

טבעונים מקבלים את ה**חֶלְבּוֹנִים** שגופם זקוק לו מקטניות, אגוזים שונים, וכד׳.
Vegans get the **proteins** their body needs from beans, nuts, etc.

Additional Examples in this Pattern

white of egg; protein חֶלְבּוֹן
yolk חֶלְמוֹן
median (stat.) חֶצְיוֹן

---

888. ***CiCCon* = *CeCCon*** when the first root consonant is guttural, plural suffix *-ot*

Our/your/their	my/your/his/her	const.	Gloss	sing/pl
עֶלְבּוֹנֵנוּ/**עֶלְבּוֹנְ**כֶם/כֶן/**עֶלְבּוֹנָ**ם/ן	**עֶלְבּוֹ**נִי/נְךָ/נֵךְ/נוֹ/נָהּ	עֶלְבּוֹן-	insult	עֶלְבּוֹן ז׳
עֶלְבּוֹנוֹתֵינוּ/כֶם/כֶן/הֶם/הֶן	**עֶלְבּוֹנוֹ**תַי/תֶיךָ/תַיִךְ/תָיו/תֶיהָ	עֶלְבּוֹנֵי-	N	עֶלְבּוֹנוֹת

The suffix is *-on* (no diminution involved in any occurrence). Since the first root consonant is guttural, *CiCCon* > *CeCCon*, but *CeCCon* may also be regarded as an independent pattern. The plural suffix is *-ot*.

Examples

אי אפשר לדעת מה יהיו תוצאותיו של **עֶלְבּוֹן**: לעתים לא כלום, לעתים אלימות, לעתים אפילו מלחמה.

One cannot tell what would result from an **insult**: sometimes nothing, sometimes violence, sometimes even war.

פוליטיקאים מושחתים תמיד דואגים שהכסף ששדדו מהעם יוחזק ב**חֶשְׁבּוֹנוֹת** אנונימיים במדינות כמו שוויצריה.

Corrupt politicians always make sure the money they pillaged from the people will be held in anonymous **accounts** in countries such as Switzerland.

Additional Examples in this Pattern

hiding place חֶבְיוֹן
disaster, disappointment Coll. חֶרְבּוֹן
math; arithmetic; bill, check; bank account חֶשְׁבּוֹן

---

889. ***CaCCon***

Our/your/their	my/your/his/her	const.	Gloss	sing/pl
קַנְיוֹנֵנוּ/**קַנְיוֹנְ**כֶם/כֶן/**קַנְיוֹנָ**ם/ן	**קַנְיוֹ**נִי/נְךָ/נֵךְ/נוֹ/נָהּ	קַנְיוֹן-	shopping	קַנְיוֹן ז׳
קַנְיוֹנֵינוּ/כֶם/כֶן/הֶם/הֶן	**קַנְיוֹ**נַי/נֶיךָ/נַיִךְ/נָיו/נֶיהָ	קַנְיוֹנֵי-	mall	קַנְיוֹנִים

The suffix is *-on*, which in most other patterns denoted diminution, but generally not here.

Examples

כנראה בהשפעת אמריקה, ה**קַנְיוֹנִים** הגדולים הם לא רק מרכזי קניות, אלא גם מרכזי בידור, בעיקר לצעירים.

Possibly because of American influence, the large **shopping malls** are not just shopping centers, but also entertainment centers, especially for the young.

עַרְמוֹנִים קלויים הם מעדן שישראלים אוהבים במיוחד – אולי מכיוון שקשה לגדלם בארץ.
Roasted **chestnuts** are a delicacy Israelis particularly like – perhaps because they are hard to grow in Israel.

Additional Examples in this Pattern

anise, sweet cumin כַּמְנוֹן	reed, bulrush אַגְמוֹן
bribe Lit. (pl. only) (...נִים) שַׁלְמוֹן	gable גַּמְלוֹן

---

890. ***CaCCon > CaCaCon*** when the 2nd root consonant is guttural

Our/your/their	my/your/his/her	const.	Gloss	sing/pl
פַּעֲמוֹנֵנוּ/**פַּעֲמוֹנְ**כֶם/כֶן/**פַּעֲמוֹנָ**ם/ן	**פַּעֲמוֹ**נִי/נְךָ/נֵךְ/נוֹ/נָהּ	-פַּעֲמוֹן	bell	פַּעֲמוֹן ז׳
פַּעֲמוֹנֵינוּ/כֶם/כֶן/הֶם/הֶן	**פַּעֲמוֹ**נַי/נֶיךָ/נַיִךְ/נָיו/נֶיהָ	-פַּעֲמוֹנֵי		פַּעֲמוֹנִים

The suffix is *-on*, which in most other patterns often denotes diminution, but not here. When a *shva* is expected with the guttural, it is replaced by a *Hataf-pataH*: *CaCCon* = *CaCaCon.*

Examples

אחד מספריו החשובים של המינגוויי הוא ״למי צלצלו ה**פַּעֲמוֹנִים**״.
One of Hemingway's important books is "To Whom the **Bell** Tolls" (in the Hebrew translation "To Whom the Bells Toll.")

בדרך כלל, כשנאלצים לפטר עובדים בתקופה כלכלית קשה, מפטרים קודם את מי שהצטרף לחברה **אַחֲרוֹן**.
Generally, when a company is forced to fire workers in a difficult economic period, they first fire the **last** person to have joined the company.

---

891. ***CaCCon = CaCaCon*** when the second root consonant is guttural, and the plural suffix is *-ot*

Our/your/their	my/your/his/her	const.	Gloss	sing/pl
רַעֲיוֹנֵנוּ/**רַעֲיוֹנְ**כֶם/כֶן/**רַעֲיוֹנָ**ם/ן	**רַעֲיוֹ**נִי/נְךָ/נֵךְ/נוֹ/נָהּ	-רַעֲיוֹן	idea,	רַעֲיוֹן ז׳
רַעֲיוֹנוֹתֵינוּ/כֶם/כֶן/הֶם/הֶן	**רַעֲיוֹנוֹ**תַי/תֶיךָ/תַיִךְ/תָיו/תֶיהָ	-רַעֲיוֹנוֹת	plan	רַעֲיוֹנוֹת

The suffix is *-on*, which in most other patterns often denotes diminution, but not here. When a *shva* is expected with the guttural, it is replaced by a *Hataf-pataH*. The plural suffix is *-ot*.

Examples

בתחילת דרכם, יזמי חברות הסְטַארְטַפּ חושבים שכל מה שנחוץ הוא **רַעֲיוֹן** חדש שאף אחד לא חשב עליו קודם; כשהם ״מתבגרים״ הם מבינים שרק אחוז קטן מן החברות האלה שורדות.
In the beginning, founders of startup companies believe that all it takes is a new **idea** that nobody thought of before; when they "grow up," they understand that only a small percentage of such enterprises survive.

---

892. ***CaCCon*** from segholate nouns

Our/your/their	my/your/his/her	const.	Gloss	sing/pl
דַּרְכּוֹנֵנוּ/**דַּרְכּוֹנְ**כֶם/כֶן/**דַּרְכּוֹנָ**ם/ן	**דַּרְכּוֹ**נִי/נְךָ/נֵךְ/נוֹ/נָהּ	דַּרְכּוֹן-	passport	דַּרְכּוֹן ז׳
דַּרְכּוֹנֵינוּ/כֶם/כֶן/הֶם/הֶן	**דַּרְכּוֹ**נַי/נֶיךָ/נַיִךְ/נָיו/נֶיהָ	דַּרְכּוֹנֵי-		דַּרְכּוֹנִים

The suffix is -on, which generally denotes diminution, and the base is segholate, */dark/* (the base of *dérekh* 'way') + *on* > *darkon.*

Examples

לישראלים רבים יש אזרחות כפולה, והם מחזיקים גם **דַּרְכּוֹן** של מדינה אחרת.
Many Israelis have dual citizenship, and they also have a different state's **passport**.

יַרְחוֹן הצבא הישראלי נקרא "מערכות".
The **monthly journal** of the Israeli army is called "Ma`arakhot" ("Wars/Campaigns")

המערות המפורסמות ביותר של האדם **הקַדְמוֹן** נתגלו בצרפת.
The most famous caves of **prehistoric** man were discovered in France.

Special Expressions

האדם **הקַדְמוֹן** **prehistoric** man
העולם **התַּחְתּוֹן** the **under**world, the world of crime

Additional Examples in this Pattern

גַּרְבּוֹן (...נִים) tights, pantyhose; socks (plural only)
חַדְרוֹן small room
יַלְדּוֹן small child
כַּלְבּוֹן small dog
קַרְחוֹן glacier; iceberg
תַּחְתּוֹן lower; lowest; underwear Coll.

---

893. ***CaCCon = CaCaCon*** from segholate nouns when the second root consonant is guttural

Our/your/their	my/your/his/her	const.	Gloss	sing/pl
סַהֲרוֹנֵנוּ/**סַהֲרוֹנְ**כֶם/כֶן/**סַהֲרוֹנָ**ם/ן	**סַהֲרוֹ**נִי/נְךָ/נֵךְ/נוֹ/נָהּ	סַהֲרוֹן-	crescent	סַהֲרוֹן ז׳
סַהֲרוֹנֵינוּ/כֶם/כֶן/הֶם/הֶן	**סַהֲרוֹ**נַי/נֶיךָ/נַיִךְ/נָיו/נֶיהָ	סַהֲרוֹנֵי-		סַהֲרוֹנִים

The suffix is *-on*, which generally denotes diminution, and the base is segholate, */sahr/* (the base of *sáhar* 'moon') + *on* > *saharon*. When a *shva* is expected with the guttural, it is replaced by *Hataf-pataH*.

Examples

הסַהֲרוֹן הוא מרכיב של מרבית הדגלים והסמלים הלאומיים של מדינות מוסלמיות.
The **crescent** is a component of most national flags and symbols in Muslim states.

---

894. **Noun** + ***on*** linear derivation

Our/your/their	my/your/his/her	const.	Gloss	sing/pl
סוּסוֹנֵנוּ/**סוּסוֹנְ**כֶם/כֶן/**סוּסוֹנָ**ם/ן	**סוּסוֹ**נִי/נְךָ/נֵךְ/נוֹ/נָהּ	סוּסוֹן-	pony,	סוּסוֹן ז'
סוּסוֹנֵינוּ/כֶם/כֶן/הֶם/הֶן	**סוּסוֹ**נַי/נֶיךָ/נַיִךְ/נָיו/נֶיהָ	סוּסוֹנֵי-	foal	סוּסוֹנִים

The suffix is *-on*. One can still argue that some of the occurrences may be assigned to subgroups of *mishkalim* (see below), but in most cases it appears that forms included in this pattern are linearly derived: סוּס 'horse' + *an* > סוּסוֹן 'pony; foal.' Most forms in this pattern denote diminution, but some refer to a collection of items bound together, חִידוֹן 'quiz,' מֵידָעוֹן 'info booklet,' נִיבוֹן 'anthology of sayings/expressions,' and to some other meanings such as papers, journals and periodicals published regularly, יוֹמוֹן 'daily paper,' יַרְחוֹן 'monthly publication,' or temporary structures made of…, like בַּדּוֹן 'temp. housing made of cloth,' פַּחוֹן 'tin shack.' Note: the base for דֻּבּוֹן 'baby bear, teddy bear; windproof/waterproof jacket with a hood' is -דֻּבּ, which remains throughout the declension, while the (stressed) isolation (masc. sing.) form is דֹּב 'bear.'

Examples

משה תולה תקוות רבות ב**סוּסוֹן** הזה. אביו ואמו היו סוסי מירוץ עטורי פרסים.
Moshe has great hopes for this **foal**. His father and mother were prize-winning race horses.

כשבאו גלי העלייה הגדולים מארצות ערב בשנות החמישים, לא הצליחה ממשלת ישראל לבנות מספיק בתים, וחלק מן העולים שוכנו זמנית ב**בַּדּוֹנִים** או ב**פַּחוֹנִים**.
With the major immigration waves from the Arab countries in in the fifties, the Israeli government could not manage to build enough housing, and some of the immigrants were housed in **residential units made of cloth** (or tents), or in **tin shacks**.

בובת **דֻּבּוֹן** היא אחד הצעצועים האהובים ביותר על ילדים.
A **teddy bear** doll is one of the most favorite children's toy.

בתקופת הרדיו בישראל, כשעוד לא הייתה טלוויזיה, אחת מתוכניות הבידור הפופולריות ביותר הייתה **חִידוֹן** הרדיו של שמואל רוזן.
In the radio era in Israel, before television, one of the most popular radio shows was Shmuel Rosen's radio **quiz**.

המילה **פִּילוֹן** מזכירה מייד לרוב הילדים את דַּמְבּוֹ של דיסני...
A reference to **young elephant** immediately reminds most children of Disney's Dumbo....

מכיוון שהיום כבר לא משתמשים הרבה ב**תֵּיוֹן**, הנטייה בדיבור היא לייחס את המונח לשקית תה.
Since today people do not use **teapots** much, the tendency in speech is to associate the term תֵּיוֹן with a **teabag**.

Special Expressions

in the dead of night **בְּאִישׁוֹן** לילה

Additional Examples in this Pattern

gosling אֲוָזוֹן
pupil (of eye) אִישׁוֹן
small bottle בַּקְבּוּקוֹן
daily newspaper יוֹמוֹן
information booklet מֵידָעוֹן
glossary מֻנָּחוֹן
portable terminal מְסוֹפוֹן
sprite, imp שֵׁדוֹן
lined sheet שׁוּרוֹן
quiz/game show שַׁעֲשׁוּעוֹן
date display; list of dates תַּאֲרִיכוֹן
teapot; tea bag Coll. תֵּיוֹן
duodenum תְּרֵיסַרְיוֹן

---

895. Noun + *on/C(e)CiCon*

Our/your/their	my/your/his/her	const.	Gloss	sing/pl
סְבִיבוֹנֵנוּ/**סְבִיבוֹנְ**כֶם/כֶן/**סְבִיבוֹנָ**ם/ן	**סְבִיבוֹ**נִי/נְךָ/נֵךְ/נוֹ/נָהּ	סְבִיבוֹן-	dreidel,	סְבִיבוֹן ז'
סְבִיבוֹנֵינוּ/כֶם/כֶן/הֶם/הֶן	**סְבִיבוֹ**נַי/נֶיךָ/נַיִךְ/נָיו/נֶיהָ	סְבִיבוֹנֵי-	spinning top	סְבִיבוֹנִים

The suffix is *-on*. This group can be regarded linearly derived, סָבִיב 'around' + *an* > סְבִיבוֹן (in this case following reduction of a *kamats* to *shva*), but it is equally plausible (if not more) that we are dealing here with a discontinuous *mishkal*, *CCiCon*. Most forms in this pattern denote diminution, but some refer to a collection of items bound together, יְדִיעוֹן 'bulletin, newsletter,' מְחִירוֹן 'price list,' and some other meanings. There are a few occurrences with the suffix *+on* that may be regarded as either linear derivation or a discontinuous *mishkal*, but almost all are one-member group, possibly two, so they were not assigned to separate patterns. The optional *e* is to facilitate articulation of some forms.

Examples

עבור הילדים, משחקי ה**סְבִיבוֹן** בחנוכה חשובים לא פחות מן הנרות...
For children, the **dreidel** game in Hanukkah is at least as important as the candles...

ה**דְּבִיבוֹנִים** נחמדים למראה, אבל נוברים בפחי אשפה ולעיתים נגועים בכלבת.
Raccoons are nice to look at, but they dig into trash cans and may be infected with rabies [Note the connection to דֹּב 'bear,' owing to similarity/relationship.]

גם בישראל יש חברה המפרסמת **מְחִירוֹנִים** למכוניות יד שנייה.
In Israel there is also a company that published second-hand car **price lists**.

כשמשתמשים בביטוי **פְּקִידוֹן**, תמיד הוא מלווה בקונוטציה שלילית ובזלזול.
When one uses the term **minor clerk** in Hebrew, it always carries negative connotation and suggests contemp.

Additional Examples in this Pattern

small cup גְּבִיעוֹן
small crystal גְּבִישׁוֹן
moustached warbler (bird) זְמִירוֹן
bulletin, newsletter יְדִיעוֹן
whiteout מְחִיקוֹן
light coat מְעִילוֹן
sub-clause סְעִיפוֹן
(very) young man צְעִירוֹן

small hut צְרִיפוֹן	small rug שְׁטִיחוֹן
entry רְשִׁימוֹן	Tertiary (geolog.) שְׁלִישׁוֹן

---

896. Noun + *on/CCiCon* = *CaCiCon*, the first root consonant is guttural

Our/your/their	my/your/his/her	const.	Gloss	sing/pl
אֲוִירוֹנֵנוּ/**אֲוִירוֹנְ**כֶם/כֶן/**אֲוִירוֹנָ**ם/ן	**אֲוִירוֹ**נִי/נְךָ/נֵךְ/נוֹ/נָהּ	אֲוִירוֹן-	airplane	אֲוִירוֹן ז׳
אֲוִירוֹנֵינוּ/כֶם/כֶן/הֶם/הֶן	**אֲוִירוֹ**נַי/נֶיךָ/נַיִךְ/נָיו/נֶיהָ	אֲוִירוֹנֵי-		אֲוִירוֹנִים

The suffix is *-on*. This group can also be regarded linearly derived, אֲוִיר 'air' + *an* > אֲוִירוֹן, but it is equally plausible that we are dealing with a discontinuous *mishkal*, *CCiCon* > *CaCiCon*. In a case like עֲפִיפוֹן 'kite' below, non-linear derivation makes more sense (no direct base). When a *shva* is expected with the guttural, it is replaced by *Hataf-pataH*.

Examples

המילה **אֲוִירוֹן** מיושנת היום ; במקומה משתמשים במָטוֹס.

The older word for **airplane**, אֲוִירוֹן, is hardly ever used today; מָטוֹס is used instead.

Additional Examples in this Pattern

cornetfish חֲלִילוֹן	kite עֲפִיפוֹן

---

897. Noun + *ónet* linear derivation

const.	Gloss	sing/pl
יַלְדֹּנֶת-	little	יַלְדֹּנֶת נ׳
יַלְדּוֹנוֹת-	girl	יַלְדּוֹנוֹת

The suffix is the feminine counterpart of *-on*, *-ónet*, and derivation is linear: *yalda* 'girl' + *-ónet* > *yaldónet*. Almost all forms in this pattern denote diminution, since any diminutive form with +*on* has a feminine alternant with +*ónet*, like *kalbon* 'doggy' ~ *kalbónet* 'small female dog' (usually associated with affectionate denotation), and any feminine ending with +*a* has a parallel diminutive form with +*ónet*, *Havila* 'package' ~ *Havilónet* 'small package,' but included here are only +*ónet* forms frequently used on their own, even when they have parallel +*on* forms in the masculine. There are no forms with possessive pronouns in actual use.

Examples

כשמשתמשים במילה **יַלְדֹּנֶת**, תמיד היא מלוּוָה בקונוטציה של חיבה.

When one uses the form **little girl** in Hebrew, it always has a connotation of affection.

יוסי רוצה לגור בתל אביב, אבל ידו אינה משגת לקנות, או לשכור, אפילו **דִּירֹנֶת** בת חדר שינה אחד בעיר.

Yossi would like to live in Tel Aviv, but he cannot afford to buy, or rent, even a one-bedroom **small apartment** in the city.

Additional Examples in this Pattern

small barrel חֲבִיּנֶת
silly (fem.) טִפְּשׁנֶת
small suitcase מִזְוָדנֶת
small crib עֲרִיסנֶת

---

898. *CiCaCon* (Plural *-ot*)

Our/your/their	my/your/his/her	const.	Gloss	sing/pl
זִכְרוֹנֵנוּ/**זִכְרוֹנְ**כֶם/כֶן/**זִכְרוֹנָ**ם/ן	**זִכְרוֹ**נִי/נְךָ/נֵךְ/נוֹ/נָהּ	זִכְרוֹן-	memory;	זִכָּרוֹן ז׳
זִכְרוֹנוֹתֵינוּ/כֶם/כֶן/הֶם/הֶן	**זִכְרוֹנוֹ**תַי/תֶיךָ/תַיִךְ/תָיו/תֶיהָ	זִכְרוֹנוֹת-	memoir	זִכְרוֹנוֹת

The plural suffix is *-ot*. Most occurrences are abstract nouns, some of which have no plural forms in actual use. Also included are some forms with gutturals behaving like regular forms, עִוָּרוֹן 'blindness' (pl. עִוְרוֹנִים), עִזָּבוֹן 'estate,' עִצָּבוֹן 'sorrow, pain,' and forms with gutturals without compensatory lengthening (in lieu of a *dagesh*), כִּהָיוֹן 'darkness.' In most cases the *dagesh forte* drops in the declension with the elision of the *kamats*.

Examples

כמעט כל מנהיג שסיים את כהונתו מקדיש את שארית ימיו לכתיבת **זִכְרוֹנוֹתָיו**. אם **זִכְרוֹנוֹ** כבר אינו מה שהיה פעם, הוא נעזר ביומנים שכתב, או שכתבו עבורו בזמן כהונתו.
Almost every leader who finished his term in office devotes the rest of his life to writing his **memoirs**. If his **memory** is not as good as it used to be, he is aided by the diaries he had kept, or that have been written of his behalf while in office.

במדינה כמו ישראל, משרד ה**בִּטָּחוֹן** הוא המשרד החשוב ביותר בממשלה.
In a state like Israel' the **defense/security** department is the most important one.

לא מעט מן האנשים שפרשו מעבודתם בגיל מבוגר ואינם מוצאים לעצמם עיסוק מְסַפֵּק שוקעים ב**דִּכָּאוֹן**.
A good number of people who retired at an advance age and are unable to find some new satisfying occupation may sink into **depression**.

לא קל היום למצוא עבודה, כשבכל מקום דורשים **נִסָּיוֹן** מאוד ספציפי.
It is not easy to find a job today, when everywhere they require very specific **experience**.

אצל אנשים מסוימים קשה לעיתים להבחין ביו גאונות ל**שִׁגָּעוֹן**.
In the case of some people, it is sometimes difficult to distinguish between genius and **madness**.

Special Expressions

spreadsheet **גִּלָּיוֹן** אלקטרוני
visual **memory** **זִכָּרוֹן** חזותי
short-term **memory** **זִכָּרוֹן** לטווח קצר
memory of an elephant **זִכָּרוֹן** של פיל

Additional Examples in this Pattern

disgrace, shame בִּזָּיוֹן
journal בִּטָּאוֹן
confidence; safety; security בִּטָּחוֹן
sheet of paper; newspaper גִּלָּיוֹן
edition, issue
concession, permit זִכָּיוֹן
pallor חִוָּרוֹן
annihilation, extinction כִּלָּיוֹן
attempt; trial, experiment; נִסָּיוֹן
experience
victory נִצָּחוֹן
cleaning; cleanliness נִקָּיוֹן
deposit פִּקָּדוֹן
bait, lure; temptation פִּתָּיוֹן
thirst צִמָּאוֹן
freeze קִפָּאוֹן
rotting רִקָּבוֹן
permit רִשָּׁיוֹן
flood N שִׁטָּפוֹן
drunkenness שִׁכָּרוֹן
amazement, wonder, surprise תִּמָּהוֹן

---

899. ***CiCaCon* (Plural -*ot*)** when the first root consonant is guttural

Our/your/their	my/your/his/her	const.	Gloss	sing/pl
חֶסְרוֹנֵנוּ/**חֶסְרוֹנְ**כֶם/כֶן/**חֶסְרוֹנָ**ם/ן	**חֶסְרוֹנִ**י/נְךָ/נֵךְ/נוֹ/נָהּ	חֶסְרוֹן-	disad-	חִסָּרוֹן ז׳
חֶסְרוֹנוֹתֵינוּ/כֶם/כֶן/הֶם/הֶן	**חֶסְרוֹנוֹ**תַי/תֶיךָ/תַיִךְ/תָיו/תֶיהָ	חֶסְרוֹנוֹת-	vantage	חֶסְרוֹנוֹת

Like זִכָּרוֹן above, but when the first root consonant is guttural, the *Hirik* is replaced by *seghol* in closed syllables in the declension, but not always – in occurrences like עִצָּבוֹן 'sorrow' (pl. עִצְּבוֹנוֹת) the *Hirik* is not replaced by *seghol* in the declension, following the regular forms above. Most occurrences are abstract nouns, some of which have no plural forms in actual use.

Examples

ירושלים היא עיר נהדרת, אבל יש לה **חִסָּרוֹן** אחד גדול: היא רחוקה מן הים...
Jerusalem is a wonderful city, but with one major **disadvantage**: it is far from the sea...

יש פוליטיקאים הנוהגים באימפולסיביות ככל העולה על דעתם ברגע מסוים, וקשה למצוא **הִגָּיוֹן** בהתנהגותם.
There are politicians who behave impulsively base on whatever occurs to them at any particular moment, and it is hard to find any **logic** in their behavior.

הצעת **חִסָּכוֹן**: אפשר לבנות **בְּחִפָּזוֹן** חומת-עץ עם גבול מקסיקו עם חומרים שייקנו בזול באייקיה.
A **savings** proposal: it is possible to build a wood wall in a rush on the Mexican border with materials bought inexpensively at Ikea.

הָעִקָּרוֹן החשוב ביותר בממשל תקין הוא הפרדה מוחלטת בין הרשויות השונות.
The most important **principle** in a good system of government is complete separation between the different arms of government.

Special Expressions

cold **logic** **הִגָּיוֹן** קר

light-and-sound **show** **חִזָּיוֹן** אור-קולי

Additional Examples in this Pattern

destruction, cessation Lit. חִדָּלוֹן
spectacle, show; vision חִזָּיוֹן
snail חִלָּזוֹן
swoon, fainting עִלָּפוֹן
pencil עִפָּרוֹן

---

900. ***CiCaCon*** when the first root consonant is guttural, pl. *-im*

Our/your/their	my/your/his/her	const.	Gloss	sing/pl
הֶזְיוֹנֵנוּ/**הֶזְיוֹנְ**כֶם/כֶן/**הֶזְיוֹנָ**ם/ן	**הֶזְיוֹנִ**י/נְךָ/נֵךְ/נוֹ/נָהּ	הֶזְיוֹן-	fantasy	הִזָּיוֹן ז׳
הֶזְיוֹנֵינוּ/כֶם/כֶן/הֶם/הֶן	**הֶזְיוֹנַ**י/תֶיךָ/תַיִךְ/תָיו/תֶיהָ	הֶזְיוֹנֵי-		הֶזְיוֹנִים

The plural suffix is *-im*. Like חִסָּרוֹן above, when the first root consonant is guttural, the *Hirik* is replaced by *seghol* in the declension in a closed syllable, but not always: עִוָּרוֹן ~ ר׳ עִוְרוֹנִים, עִצָּבוֹן ~ ר׳ עִצְבוֹנִים.

Examples

הִזָּיוֹן היא מילה ספרותית מילה גבוהה לפנטסיה.
hizayon is a high literary word for **fantasy**.

Additional Examples in this Pattern

wheat rust חִלָּדוֹן

---

901. ***CiCaCon = CeCaCon*** when the second root consonant is *r*, and in the declension *tesre > seghol*

Our/your/their	my/your/his/her	const.	Gloss	sing/pl
הֶרְיוֹנֵנוּ/**הֶרְיוֹנְ**כֶם/כֶן/**הֶרְיוֹנָ**ם/ן	**הֶרְיוֹנִ**י/נְךָ/נֵךְ/נוֹ/נָהּ	הֶרְיוֹן-	pregnancy	הֵרָיוֹן ז׳
הֶרְיוֹנוֹתֵינוּ/כֶם/כֶן/הֶם/הֶן	**הֶרְיוֹנוֹ**תַי/תֶיךָ/תַיִךְ/תָיו/תֶיהָ	הֶרְיוֹנוֹת-		הֶרְיוֹנוֹת

In the isolation form, the *Hirik* of *CiCaCon* is replaced by *tsere* (compensatory lengthening); in the declension the *tsere* is replaced by *seghol* (in a closed syllable).

Examples

ההֵרָיוֹן של חנה התקדם כשורה בשבעת החודשים הראשונים, אבל בחודשיים האחרונים היה עליה להישאר רוב הזמן במיטה.
Hannah's **pregnancy** progressed well during the first seven months, but in the last two she had to stay in bed most of the time.

Additional Examples in this Pattern

strong yearning, longing Lit. עֵרָגוֹן
trance (psych.) הֵרָגוֹן

---

902. ***CiCaCon* = *CaCaCon*** when the second root consonant is 'א, and in the declension a *pataH is* followed by *Hataf-pataH*

Our/your/their	my/your/his/her	const.	Gloss	sing/pl
רַאֲיוֹנֵנוּ/רַאֲיוֹנְכֶם/כֶן/רַאֲיוֹנָם/ן	רַאֲיוֹנִי/נְךָ/נֵךְ/נוֹ/נָהּ	רַאֲיוֹן-	interview	רֵאָיוֹן ז׳
רַאֲיוֹנוֹתֵינוּ/כֶם/כֶן/הֶם/הֶן	רַאֲיוֹנוֹתַי/תֶיךָ/תַיִךְ/תָיו/תֶיהָ	רַאֲיוֹנוֹת-		רַאֲיוֹנוֹת

In the isolation form, the *Hirik* of *CiCaCon* is replaced by *tsere* (compensatory lengthening); in the declension the first two vowels are *pataH* followed by *Hataf-pataH.*

Examples

בזמנו, כל מי שהיה חשוב בעיני עצמו שאף להגיע לפחות ל**רֵאָיוֹן** אחד עם ברברה וולטרס.
At the time, anybody who conceived of himself as important was eager for at least one **interview** with Barbara Walters.

Additional Examples in this Pattern

סֵאָבוֹן filth, dirt Lit.-Rare

תֵּאָבוֹן appetite

---

903. ***CiCaCon* = *CeCaCon*** when the second root consonant is *r*, and in the declension *tesre > Hirik*

Our/your/their	my/your/his/her	const.	Gloss	sing/pl
גִּרְעוֹנֵנוּ/גִּרְעוֹנְכֶם/כֶן/גִּרְעוֹנָם/ן	גִּרְעוֹנִי/נְךָ/נֵךְ/נוֹ/נָהּ	גִּרְעוֹן-	deficit	גֵּרָעוֹן ז׳
גִּרְעוֹנוֹתֵינוּ/כֶם/כֶן/הֶם/הֶן	גִּרְעוֹנוֹתַי/תֶיךָ/תַיִךְ/תָיו/תֶיהָ	גִּרְעוֹנוֹת-		גִּרְעוֹנוֹת

In the isolation form, the *Hirik* of *CiCaCon* is replaced by *tsere* (compensatory lengthening); in the declension the *tsere* is replaced by (or goes back to?) *Hirik.*

Examples

ה**גֵּרָעוֹן** במאזן התשלומים של ממשלת ארה״ב עולה באופן מדאיג בשנים האחרונות.
The **deficit** in the balance of payments of the US government has increased alarmingly in recent years.

Additional Examples in this Pattern

דֵּרָאוֹן disgrace, shame Lit.

פֵּרָעוֹן payment, paying off debt; redemption

---

904. ***CiCaCon* = *CeCaCon*** when the second root consonant is *r*, and in the declension there is only Sing. Construct State form

const.	Gloss	sing/pl
יֵרָקוֹן-	greensickness, chlorosis (plant disease)	יֵרָקוֹן ז׳

In the isolation form, the *Hirik* of *CiCaCon* is replaced by *tsere* (compensatory lengthening), and the *tsere* is replaced by *pataH* in the singular of the construct state.

---

905. ***CiCaCon* = *CeCaCon*** when the second root consonant is *r* or *h*, and the *tsere* is maintained in the declension

Our/your/their	my/your/his/her	const.	Gloss	sing/pl
עֵרְבוֹנֵנוּ/**עֵרְבוֹנְ**כֶם/כֶן/**עֵרְבוֹנָ**ם/ן	**עֵרְבוֹ**נִי/נְךָ/נֵךְ/נוֹ/נָהּ	עֵרְבוֹן-	security,	עֵרָבוֹן ז'
עֵרְבוֹנוֹתֵינוּ/כֶם/כֶן/הֶם/הֶן	**עֵרְבוֹנוֹ**תַי/תֶיךָ/תַיִךְ/תָיו/תֶיהָ	עֵרְבוֹנוֹת-	guarantee	עֵרְבוֹנוֹת

In the isolation form, the *Hirik* of *CiCaCon* is replaced by *tsere* (compensatory lengthening); in the declension the *tsere* is maintained (in קֵהָיוֹן only in the singular of the construct state).

Examples

כשהבנק מאשר משכנתא לרכישת דירה, הדירה עצמה מהווה **עֵרָבוֹן** אם הקונה אינו עומד בתשלומים.

When the bank approves a mortgage towards the purchase of an apartment, the apartment itself constitutes **security** in case of non-payment of mortgage obligations.

Additional Examples in this Pattern

dementia; insensitivity, apathy Lit. קֵהָיוֹן

W. Patterns with other, less common suffixes

906. ***CCay***

Our/your/their	my/your/his/her	const.	Gloss	sing/pl
תְּנָאֵנוּ/**תְּנַאֲ**כֶם/כֶן/**תְּנָאָ**ם/ן	**תְּנָאִ**י/אֲךָ/אֵךְ/אוֹ/אָהּ	תְּנַאי-	condition;	תְּנַאי ז'
תְּנָאֵינוּ/כֶם/כֶן/הֶם/הֶן	**תְּנָאַ**י/אֶיךָ/אַיִךְ/אָיו/אֶיהָ	תְּנָאֵי-	stipulation	תְּנָאִים

The א' was added as a transition to the following semi-vowel *y*, under the influence of Aramaic.

Examples

ה**תְּנָאִים** בבית הסוהר הזה הם כמו בבית מלון.

The **conditions** in this prison as are like in a hotel.

אני מוכן לקבל את העבודה, אבל ב**תְּנָאִים** מסוימים.

I am willing to take this job, but only under certain **conditions/stipulations**.

מס הכנסה מכיר ב**בְּלַאי** של ציוד הקשור בהכנסה כניכוי לצרכי מס.

Internal Revenue recognizes **wear and tear** (amortization) of equipment required for generating income as a deduction.

אני עסוק מאוד היום, אבל מחר יש לי **פְּנַאי**. נוכל להיפגש לארוחת צהריים?
I am very busy today, but I have **free time** tomorrow. Can we meet for lunch?

Special Expressions

בִּתְנַאי ש... **provided** that…
על-**תְּנַאי** **condition**al
צו על-**תְּנַאי** order nisi
תְּנַאי בל יעבור absolute **condition**
"**תְּנָאִים**" betrothal (traditional)
טְלַאי צהוב yellow badge/**patch**

Additional Examples in this Pattern

גְּלַאי décolletage; bare/exposed place Lit.
גְּנַאי shame, disgrace
טְלַאי patch
לְוַאי after- (aftertaste etc.); modifier
מְלַאי inventory
מְצַאי inventory

---

907. ***CCay*** = *CaCay* when the 1st root consonant is guttural

Our/your/their	my/your/his/her	const.	Gloss	sing/pl
הֲבָאֵנוּ/**הֲבָאֲ**כֶם/כֶן/**הֲבָאָ**ם/ן	**הֲבָ**אִי/אֲךָ/אֵךְ/אוֹ/אָהּ	הֲבַאי-	nonsense	הֲבַאי ז'

Like תְּנַאי above, but when a *shva* is expected with a guttural, it is replaced by *Hataf-pataH*. No plural.

Examples

בעברית ספרותית, במקום לומר "דברי שטות", או "שטויות", אומרים "(דברי) **הֲבַאי**".
In literary Hebrew one says הֲבַאי instead of colloquial שטויות **nonsense**.

Special Expressions

בַּחֲשַׁאי **secret**ly, **stealth**ily

Additional Examples in this Pattern

חֲשַׁאי stealth

---

908. ***CaCay***

Our/your/their	my/your/his/her	const.	Gloss	sing/pl
בַּנָּאֵנוּ/**בַּנָּאֲ**כֶם/כֶן/**בַּנָּאָ**ם/ן	**בַּנָּ**אִי/אֲךָ/אֵךְ/אוֹ/אָהּ	בַּנַּאי-	builder	בַּנַּאי ז'
בַּנָּאֵינוּ/כֶם/כֶן/הֶם/הֶן	**בַּנָּ**אַי/אֶיךָ/אַיִךְ/אָיו/אֶיהָ	בַּנָּאֵי-		בַּנָּאִים

The אי was added as a transition to the following semi-vowel *y*, under the influence of Aramaic. The second root consonant is always geminated. Most forms denote a professional/occupation or a parallel quality, and occasionally an instrument whose function is conveyed by the root.

Examples

רוב חלוצי העליות הראשונות לארץ ישראל בתחילת המאה העשרים היו (או בעצם למדו להיות) חקלאים, או **בַּנָּאִים**.
Most of the pioneers in Palestine in the early 20th Century were (or learned to be) agricultural workers, or **builders**.

גַּבַּאי בית הכנסת הוא מעין צירוף של מנהל וגזבר.
The “gabay” of the synagogue is a sort of combination of **manager and treasurer**.

לא תמיד ברור מה יותר חשוב להצלחה של סרט או מחזה: שחקנים טובים או **בַּמַּאי** טוב?
It is not always clear what more essential for a successful film or a play: good actors or a good **director**?

במספר רשתות טלוויזיה מנסים לעשות מן ה**חַזַּאי** שחקן-למחצה או מוקיון.
In some TV networks they try to turn the **meteorologist** into either a semi-actor or a clown.

Special Expressions

גַּלַּאי עשן **detector** smoke | **גַּלַּאי** מהירות **detector** of speed

Additional Examples in this Pattern

בַּדַּאי liar, fabricator Lit.
גַּלַּאי detector
הַגַּאי helmsman (ship)
זַכַּאי innocent (person); entitled (person)
זַנַּאי adulterer, lecher
חַוַּאי rancher, farmer
יַמַּאי seaman
כַּבַּאי fireman
מַסַּאי essayist
קַנַּאי zealot; jealous
רַמַּאי cheat N, crook
שַׁמַּאי assessor
שַׁנַּאי transformer

---

909. N +*ay*

sing/pl	Gloss	const.	my/your/his/her	Our/your/their
לְשׁוֹנַאי ז'	linguist	לְשׁוֹנַאי-	**לְשׁוֹנָא**ִי/אֲךָ/אֵךְ/אוֹ/אָהּ	לְשׁוֹנָאֵנוּ/**לְשׁוֹנָאֲ**כֶם/כֶן/**לְשׁוֹנָאָ**ם/ן
לְשׁוֹנָאִים		לְשׁוֹנָאֵי-	**לְשׁוֹנָא**ַי/אֶיךָ/אַיִךְ/אָיו/אֶיהָ	**לְשׁוֹנָאֵי**נוּ/כֶם/כֶן/הֶם/הֶן

The derivation is linear, ‘electrician’ חַשְׁמַלַּאי < ◌ַאי + חַשְׁמַל ‘electricity,’ occasionally with expected vowel change (usually reduction):
‘linguist’ לְשׁוֹנַאי < ◌ַאי + לָשׁוֹן ‘language.’ The א׳ was added as a glide to the following semi-vowel *y* (Aramaic influence). Most forms denote a professional or person with a certain occupation, occasionally some other noun related to the root.

Examples

לְשׁוֹנַאי, או בַּלְשָׁן, הוא מי שמתאר את מבנה הלשון, מנתח אותה ומסביר את תופעותיה.
A **linguist** is he who describes the structure of language, analyzes it and accounts for its phenomena.

היום מצב הַ**חַקְלָאִים** בעלי המשקים קטנים הוא קשה בשל התחרות עם משקי-ענק של חברות גדולות.
Today the condition of **farmers** with small farms is hard because of competition with large-scale farms of big companies.

אם מצאת **חַשְׁמַלַּאי** טוב, אשריך וטוב לך. אין בעל מקצוע חשוב מזה.
If you find a good **electrician**, you are lucky. No other professional is more important.

שֵׁיקספיר היה לא רק **מַחֲזַאי** גדול, אלא גם משורר מעולה.
Shakespeare was not just a great **playwright**; he was an excellent poet as well.

עִתּוֹנַאי טוב בודק היטב את מקורות המידע שלו לפני שהוא מביא "סְקוּפּ" לעורך לפרסום.
A good **journalist** checks his information sources well before bringing a "scoop" to his editor for publication.

Special Expressions

חַשְׁמַלַּאי רכב auto **electrician**

טוּרַאי ראשון **lance-corporal**

Additional Examples in this Pattern

philatelist בּוּלַאי
bass player בַּטְנוּנַאי
orchadist בֻּסְתְּנַאי
member of same age group גִּילַאי
portraitist דְּיוֹקְנַאי
accountant חֶשְׁבּוֹנַאי
private (military) טוּרַאי
legionnaire לְגְיוֹנַאי
snack bar owner/employee מִזְנוֹנַאי
storekeeper, stock keeper מַחְסְנַאי
mechanic מְכוֹנַאי
hotelier מְלוֹנַאי
lexicographer מִלּוֹנַאי
crane operator מְנוֹפַאי
pawnbroker מַשְׁכּוֹנַאי
songwriter (who writes lyrics) פִּזְמוֹנַאי
cashier קֻפַּאי

---

910. N +*ar*

Our/your/their	my/your/his/her	const.	Gloss	sing/pl
סַנְדְּלָרֵנוּ/**סַנְדְּלַרְ**כֶם/כֶן/**סַנְדְּלָרָ**ם/ן	**סַנְדְּלָ**רִי/רְךָ/רֵךְ/רוֹ/רָהּ	סַנְדְּלַר-	shoemaker	סַנְדְּלָר ז'
סַנְדְּלָרֵינוּ/כֶם/כֶן/הֶם/הֶן	**סַנְדְּלָ**רַי/רֶיךָ/רַיִךְ/רָיו/רֶיהָ	סַנְדְּלָרֵי-		סַנְדְּלָרִים

The derivation is linear, occasionally with expected vowel change (usually reduction): 'shoemaker' סַנְדְּלָר < סַנְדָּל + ◌ָר 'sandal.' Most forms denote a professional/occupation.

Examples

אימרה ביידיש: "כל הַ**סַּנְדְּלָרִים** הולכים יחפים".
A Yiddish saying: "All **shoemakers** go barefoot".

Additional Examples in this Pattern

falconer בַּזְיָר
warder, jailer גַּנְדָּר
bell-ringer פַּעֲמוֹנָר

---

911. N +*iya*

Our/your/their	my/your/his/her	const.	Gloss	sing/pl
סִפְרִיָּתֵנוּ/**סִפְרִיַּתְ**כֶם/כֶן/**סִפְרִיָּתָ**ם/ן	**סִפְרִיָּ**תִי/תְךָ/תֵךְ/תוֹ/תָהּ	סִפְרִיַּת-	library	סִפְרִיָּה נ'
סִפְרִיּוֹתֵינוּ/כֶם/כֶן/הֶם/הֶן	**סִפְרִיּוֹ**תַי/תֶיךָ/תַיִךְ/תָיו/תֶיהָ	סִפְרִיּוֹת-		סִפְרִיּוֹת

The derivation is linear, 'undershirt' גּוּפִיָּה < גּוּף +ִיָּה 'body,' (or where a segholate base is involved 'library' סִפְרִיָּה < סֵפֶר/סִפְר +ִיָּה 'book'), occasionally with expected vowel change (usually reduction). Some of the forms denote groups of items, זִמְרִיָּה 'singing festival,' כַּרְטִיסִיָּה 'multiple-entry ticket, תַּקְלִיטִיָּה 'record collection,' others locations in which products are made or sold, מַאֲפִיָּה 'bakery, מִגְדָּנִיָּה 'sweet shop,' מַסְגֵּרִיָּה 'locksmith shop,' and a few categories of limited scope, such as diminution, נַקְנִיקִיָּה 'hot dog' (=small נַקְנִיק 'sausage'), עוּגִיָּה 'cookie,' (small עוּגָה 'cake'), etc.

Examples

הַסִּפְרִיָּה הלאומית בירושלים היא הגדולה והטובה ביותר בישראל.
The National **Library** in Jerusalem is the largest and best in Israel.

כְּנֵסִיַּת הקבר הקדוש נמצאת בעיר העתיקה בירושלים, אבל הפרוטסטנטים מאמינים שישו נקבר בגן שמחוץ לחומות.
The **Church** of the Holy Sepulchre is in the Ancient City of Jerusalem, but the Protestants believe that Jesus was buried in the Garden Tomb outside the wall.

אתה מעדיף **גּוּפִיּוֹת** עם או בלי שרוולים?
Do you prefer **undershirts** with or without sleeves?

כשהייתי ילד, היה עובר מוכר **לַחְמָנִיּוֹת** טריות כל בוקר ברחובנו.
When I was a kid, a seller of **bread rolls** would pass through our street every morning.

אני מניח שכבר אין היום **מֶרְכָּזִיּוֹת** המופעלות ידנית על ידי מרכזניות.
I assume that today there are no longer **telephone exchanges** that are manually operated by human operators.

Special Expressions

סִפְרִיַּת השאלה lending **library**
סִפְרִיַּת יעץ/יען reference **library**
עוּגִיַּת מזל fortune **cookie**

Additional Examples in this Pattern

בַּרְוָזִיָּה duck hatchery
בַּרְזִיָּה set of connected faucets
בְּרֵכִיָּה mallard
גּוּמִיָּה rubber band
זִמְרִיָּה singing festival
חֶשְׁבּוֹנִיָּה abacus
יַמִּיָּה navy, fleet
כַּרְטִיסִיָּה multiple entry ticket
כְּרִיכִיָּה bookbinding shop
מַאֲפִיָּה bakery
מִגְדָּנִיָּה sweet shop
מַדְגֵּרִיָּה farm with a system of incubators
מַטְוִיָּה spinning mill
מִטְרִיָּה umbrella
מַסְגֵּרִיָּה locksmith shop
מַעֲשִׂיָּה tale

cracker מַצִּיָּה	cookie עוּגִיָּה
carpentry shop נַגָּרִיָּה	town hall עִירִיָּה
hot dog נַקְנִיקִיָּה	boarding school פְּנִימִיָּה
shoemaker's shop סַנְדְּלָרִיָּה	flora, vegetation צִמְחִיָּה

X. Patterns with the suffix *-i*

912. *CaCCuCi* Adj, with reduplication

f. sing/pl	m. sing/pl	Gloss
אֲדַמְדַּמִּית נ׳	אֲדַמְדַּמִּי ז׳	reddish
אֲדַמְדַּמִּיּוֹת	אֲדַמְדַּמִּיִּים	

The derivation is discontinuous; the second and third root consonants are identical (קְטַלְטַלִּי). Most forms denote diminution.

Examples

פנים **אֲדַמְדַּמִּיּוֹת** הן לעיתים תוצאה של שתייה רבה של אלכוהול.
Reddish face is often the result of excessive drinking of alcohol.

במשך חלק גדול מן השנה השמיים בלונדון **אַפְרוּרִיִּים**.
During a significant part of the year the sky in London is **grayish**.

יגאל **יַשְׁנוּנִי** היום; הוא לא ישן כראוי בלילה.
Yig'al is **sleepy** today; he did not sleep well last night.

מנהיגים אינם ממהרים לוותר, כדי שלא יחשבו שהם **רַכְרוּכִיִּים**.
Leaders do not give in easily, so that people do not think of them as **indecisive**.

Additional Examples in this Pattern

dim אַפְלוּלִי	porous נַקְבּוּבִי
bellied בַּטְנוּנִי	sad, forlorn עַגְמוּמִי
humped גַּבְנוּנִי	petty קַטְנוּנִי
match-like, thin גַּפְרוּרִי	(soil) containing humus רַקְבּוּבִי
whitish לַבְנוּנִי	oily שַׁמְנוּנִי

---

913. *CaCCuCi* Adj = *CaCaCuCi*, with reduplication, when the second root consonant is guttural

f. sing/pl	m. sing/pl	Gloss
סַהֲרוּרִית נ׳	סַהֲרוּרִי ז׳	somnambulant; dazed
סַהֲרוּרִיּוֹת	סַהֲרוּרִיִּים	

As in אֲדַמְדַּמִּי above, the derivation is discontinuous, the 2nd and 3rd root consonants are identical, and most forms denote diminution, but when a *shva* is expected with a guttural, it is replaced by *Hataf-pataH* (קַטֲלוּלִי).

Examples

משה כל כך מאושר שעדנה הסכימה להצעת הנישואין שלו, שהוא מסתובב כל היום כ**סַהֲרוּרִי**.
Moshe is so happy that Edna accepted his marriage proposal, that he is roaming about like a **dazed** person.

Additional Examples in this Pattern

shiny, radiant זַהֲרוּרִי
tiny זְעֵרוּרִי
concave, indented, sunken קַעֲרוּרִי

---

914. *CaCCiCi* Adj, with reduplication

f. sing/pl	m. sing/pl	Gloss
אַוְרִירִית נ׳ אַוְרִירִיּוֹת	אַוְרִירִי ז׳ אַוְרִירִיִּים	airy; light

The derivation is discontinuous, the second and third root consonants are identical (קַטְלִילִי), and forms denote diminution.

Examples

אם רוצים בצק **אַוְרִירִי** במיוחד ולחם שיישמר לתקופה ארוכה, כדאי להוסיף לבצק תפוחי אדמה.
If you wish to have particularly **airy** dough and bread that will keep for a long time, it is recommended that you add potatoes to the dough.

Additional Examples in this Pattern

wooly, fluffy צַמְרִירִי

---

915. N +*i* Adj linear derivation

f. sing/pl	m. sing/pl	Gloss
אֲחוֹרִית נ׳ אֲחוֹרִיּוֹת	אֲחוֹרִי ז׳ אֲחוֹרִיִּים	back Adj.

The derivation is linear, 'back Adj' אֲחוֹרִי < י + אָחוֹר 'back N,' occasionally with expected vowel changes. This is the simplest and commonest way of creating an adjective from a noun, when the speaker wishes to denote the very quality of that noun being a particular one and generally not beyond that. אֲחוֹרִי just means 'back Adj.,' and the possible connotation of 'of lower priority' indeed exists, but is not necessitated by the very existence of the +*i* suffix. Another example: in שֻׁלְחָנִי the meaning simply is 'of table,' as in 'table wine,' and the connotation of 'simple/basic wine' is possible, but is not necessary. As will be shown below, there are also, of course, instances of linear derivation with +*i* that may equally be attributed to discontinuous *mishkalim*.

Examples

ראוי לבדוק מדי פעם את לחץ האוויר בצמיגי המכונית, גם בקדמיים וגם ב**אֲחוֹרִיִּים**.
It is a good idea to occasionally check air pressure in your car's tires, front as well as **back** ones.

הופתעתי כשקיבלתי מכתב ברכה **אִישִׁי** ליום הולדתי ממנהל החברה.
I was surprised to receive a **personal** congratulatory note for my birthday from the company manager.

יש מנהיגים המאמינים שהם מתנת אלוהים לעמם, ושההשגחה ה**אֱלוֹהִית** מנחה אותם בכל מעשיהם.
Some leaders believe that they are god's gift to their people, and that **Divine** Providence guides them in all their activities.

האופן שבו עליזה ריהטה את דירתה מעיד על כך שיש לה חוש **אָמָּנוּתִי** אמיתי.
The manner in which Aliza furnished her apartment suggests that she has real **artistic** sense.

יש משהו כמעט **אֱנוֹשִׁי** במבט של הכלב הזה.
There is something almost **human** in the way this dog looks at you.

Special Expressions

הנעה **אֲחוֹרִית** **rear-wheel** drive

Additional Examples in this Pattern

אִכְפַּתִּי caring
אֱלוֹהִי divine, godly
אֲלַכְסוֹנִי diagonal
אֲנָכִי perpendicular
אַפְרִיקָאִי African
אַקְלִימִי related to climate
אַרְמֶנִי Armenian
אַתְלֵטִי athletic
בּוּלְגָּרִי Bulgarian
בִּלְבַדִּי unique
בְּעָיָתִי problematic
בְּרֵאשִׁיתִי primordial; primeval
גְּדוּדִי of a battalion
גּוֹרָלִי fatal
גַּלִּי wavy, undulating
דֻּבִּי bear-like
דָּתִי religious
הֲבָרָתִי syllabic
הוֹלַנְדִּי Dutch
הֲגַנָּתִי defensive
הֲמוֹנִי mass Adj; common, vulgar
הַנְדָּסִי of engineering
וִילוֹנִי velar
זְאֵבִי wolfish
זְגוּגִי glazed; glassy
זָוִיתִי angular
זִיפִי bristly
זְמַנִּי temporary
זְנוּתִי prostitution-like; (vulgar) unfair
חֲבֵרִי friendly
חֶבְרָתִי social

---

916. N +*i* Adj /*'eCCaCi*

f. sing/pl	m. sing/pl	Gloss
אֶזְרָחִית נ׳ אֶזְרָחִיּוֹת	אֶזְרָחִי ז׳ אֶזְרָחִיִּים	civil, civilian Adj.

As noted above, *i*-suffixation is the simplest and commonest way of creating an adjective from a noun, when the speaker wishes to denote the very quality of that noun being a particular one and generally not beyond that. The derivation is linear, אֶזְרָח+י, but may equally be attributed to the discontinuous *mishkal 'eCCaCi* with an initial א׳.

Examples

בכל מדינה דמוקרטית, הצבא כפוף לממשל **האֶזְרָחִי**.
In any democratic country, the army is subordinate to the **civilian** government.

Special Expressions

The end justifies the **means** המטרה מקדשת את **האֶמְצָעִים**

Additional Examples in this Pattern

middle Adj; means N אֶמְצָעִי

---

917. N +*i* Adj /*hitCaCCuti*

f. sing/pl	m. sing/pl	Gloss
הִתְיַשְּׁבוּתִית נ' הִתְיַשְּׁבוּתִיּוֹת	הִתְיַשְּׁבוּתִי ז' הִתְיַשְּׁבוּתִיִּים	relating to settlement in Israel

As noted above, the adding of +*i* denotes the very quality of a noun being a particular one and generally not beyond that. The derivation is linear, הִתְיַשְּׁבוּת+י, but may equally be attributed to the discontinuous *mishkal hitCaCCuti*.

Examples

המפעל **ההִתְיַשְּׁבוּתִי** בארץ ישראל החל בסוף המאה התשע-עשרה.
The (Jewish) **settlement** enterprise began at the end of the Nineteenth Century.

האם המסקנה שלך בעניין זה היא **הִתְרַשְּׁמוּתִית**, או (ש)היא מבוססת על נתוני מחקר?
Is your conclusion regarding this matter **impressionistic**, or is it based on research data?

Additional Examples in this Pattern

developmental הִתְפַּתְּחוּתִי volunteering Adj הִתְנַדְּבוּתִי

---

918. N +*i* Adj /*hitCaCCuti* = *histaCCuti*, the first root consonant is *s*

f. sing/pl	m. sing/pl	Gloss
הִסְתַּדְּרוּתִית נ' הִסְתַּדְּרוּתִיּוֹת	הִסְתַּדְּרוּתִי ז' הִסְתַּדְּרוּתִיִּים	relating to the Israeli workers' union

As in *hitCaCCuti* above, when the first root consonant is *s*, which in the *hitCaCeC* verb base metathesized with the prefixal *t*. The derivation is linear, הִסְתַּדְּרוּת+י, but may equally be attributed to the discontinuous *mishkal histaCCuti*.

Examples

מספר חברות **הִסְתַּדְּרוּתִיּוֹת** בישראל הופרטו במשך השנים.
A number of **workers' union** companies in Israel were privatized over the years.

Additional Examples in this Pattern

observative, observational הִסְתַּכְּלוּתִי probabilistic הִסְתַּבְּרוּתִי

---

919. N +*i* Adj /*heCeCi*

f. sing/pl	m. sing/pl	Gloss
הֶקֵּפִית נ׳ הֶקֵּפִיּוֹת	הֶקֵּפִי ז׳ הֶקֵּפִיִּים	peripheral; perimetric

As in all adjectives derived from noun with the suffix –*i*, the speaker wishes to denote the very quality of that noun being a particular one. The derivation is linear, הֶקֵּף+י, but may equally be attributed to the discontinuous *mishkal heCeCi*.

Examples

כאשר מדינה חוששת מחדירה של מחבלים מעבר לגבול, היא מקדישה משאבים ניכרים להגנה **הֶקֵּפִית**.
When a country is worried about penetration of terrorists across the border, it invests considerable resources in **perimetric** defense.

Additional Examples in this Pattern

discursive (philos.); analogous הֶקֵּשִׁי reactive (electricity) הֶגֵּבִי
accomplished; achieving הֶשֵּׂגִי

---

920. N +*i* Adj /*heCCeCi*

f. sing/pl	m. sing/pl	Gloss
הֶחְלֵטִית נ׳ הֶחְלֵטִיּוֹת	הֶחְלֵטִי ז׳ הֶחְלֵטִיִּים	decisive, determined

As in all adjectives derived from noun with the suffix –*i*, the speaker wishes to denote the very quality of that noun being a particular one. The derivation is linear, הֶחְלֵט+י, but may equally be attributed to the discontinuous *mishkal heCCeCi*.

Examples

הציבור מעדיף מנהיג **הֶחְלֵטִי**, אבל כזה המסוגל גם להגיע לפשרה במקרה הצורך.
The public prefers a **determined** leader, but one who is also capable of compromise if needed.

נגיד הבנק הודיע שהורדת שער הרבית היא צעד **הֶכְרֵחִי** בשלב זה כדי לקדם את הכלכלה.
The bank commissioner announced that lowering the interest rate at this stage is a **necessary** step to help the economy recover.

Additional Examples in this Pattern

habitual הֶרְגֵּלִי continuing, incomplete הֶמְשֵׁכִי
offensive Adj הֶתְקֵפִי contractual הֶסְכֵּמִי

---

921. N +*i* Adj /*haCaCati*

f. sing/pl	m. sing/pl	Gloss
הַכָּרָתִית נ' הַכָּרָתִיּוֹת	הַכָּרָתִי ז' הַכָּרָתִיִּים	conscious

As in all adjectives derived from noun with the suffix *–i*, the speaker wishes to denote the very quality of that noun being a particular one. The derivation is linear, הַכָּרָ(ת)+י, but may equally be attributed to the discontinuous *mishkal haCaCati*.

Examples

יש אנשים שבאופן שאינו **הַכָּרָתִי** אומרים לא לכל מה שמוצע להם, מחשש למניע נסתר מאחורי כל הצעה.
Some people who in an un**conscious** manner say no to whatever they are offered, for fear of hidden motives behind any offer.

Additional Examples in this Pattern

expressive הַבָּעָתִי

---

922. N +*i* Adj /*haCCaCati*

f. sing/pl	m. sing/pl	Gloss
הַדְרָגָתִית נ' הַדְרָגָתִיּוֹת	הַדְרָגָתִי ז' הַדְרָגָתִיִּים	gradual

As in all adjectives derived from noun with the suffix *–i*, the speaker wishes to denote the very quality of that noun being a particular one. The derivation is linear, הַדְרָגָ(ת)+י, but may equally be attributed to the discontinuous *mishkal haCCaCati*.

Examples

אחוזי מס ההכנסה עולים באופן **הַדְרָגָתִי** בהתאם לגודל ההכנסה.
The income tax rates go up in a **gradual** manner with the increase in income.

כשמקימים חברה חדשה הקושי הגדול הוא בדרך כלל בגיוס הון **הַתְחָלָתִי** להפעלתה הראשונית.
Generally, when starting a new company, the main difficulty is in mobilizing the **initial** capital for its launching.

Additional Examples in this Pattern

of training, instructive, guiding הַדְרָכָתִי
explanatory, propagandist הַסְבָּרָתִי
demonstrative הַפְגָּנָתִי
declarative הַצְהָרָתִי
comparative הַשְׁוָאָתִי
educational, academic הַשְׂכָּלָתִי

---

923. N +*i* Adj /*miCCaCti*

f. sing/pl	m. sing/pl	Gloss
מִשְׁטַרְתִּית נ' מִשְׁטַרְתִּיּוֹת	מִשְׁטַרְתִּי ז' מִשְׁטַרְתִּיִּים	of police

As in all adjectives derived from noun with the suffix –*i*, the speaker wishes to denote the very quality of that noun being a particular one. The derivation is linear, מִשְׁטָר(ת)+י, with automatic reduction of the *kamats* to zero, but may equally be attributed to the discontinuous *mishkal miCCaCti*.

Examples

כוח **מִשְׁטַרְתִּי** מוגבר הגיע כשהסתבר שפרצה קטטה בין המפגינים לקבוצת מחאה שהתאספה במקום.

A reinforced **police** force arrived when it turned out that a fight broke between the demonstrators and a group of protesters who gathered there.

התפלגות הקולות בהצבעה הייתה על פי השתייכות **מִפְלַגְתִּית** גְרֵידא.

The votes were split strictly according to **party** affiliation.

Additional Examples in this Pattern

of or related to war מִלְחַמְתִּי

---

924. N +*i* Adj /*miCCaCi*

f. sing/pl	m. sing/pl	Gloss
מִסְחָרִית נ׳ מִסְחָרִיּוֹת	מִסְחָרִי ז׳ מִסְחָרִיִּים	commercial

As in all adjectives derived from noun with the suffix –*i*, the speaker wishes to denote the very quality of that noun being a particular one. The derivation is linear, מִסְחָר+י, but may equally be attributed to the discontinuous *mishkal miCCaCi*.

Examples

בישראל משלמים פחות מסים על רכב **מִסְחָרִי**.

In Israel one pays less taxes on a **commercial** vehicle.

השפעת הפיקוח הפדרלי המוגבר על הגבול עם מקסיקו על הברחת הסמים לארה״ב היא **מִזְעָרִית**.

The effect of the increased federal control of the Mexican border on drug smuggling into the US has been **minimal**.

השתלטותו של היטלר על אירופה נבלמה לראשונה בסטאלינגרד, בחזית ה**מִּזְרָחִית**.

Hitler's taking over of Europe was first checked in Stalingrad, in the **Eastern** Front.

לחיים יש חנות מצליחה בתל-אביב למכירת ציוד **מִשְׂרָדִי**.

Hayyim has a successful store in Tel Aviv for sales of **office** equipment.

Additional Examples in this Pattern

operational מִבְצָעִי
of the desert מִדְבָּרִי
Midrashic מִדְרָשִׁי
eastern; Middle Eastern מִזְרָחִי
of the establishment מִמְסָדִי
administrative מִנְהָלִי

numerical מִסְפָּרִי legal מִשְׁפָּטִי
biblical מִקְרָאִי offensive מִתְקָפִי

---

925. N +*i* Adj /*miCCaCi* > *maCaCaCi* when the first root consonant is guttural

f. sing/pl	m. sing/pl	Gloss
מַעֲרָבִית נ׳ מַעֲרָבִיּוֹת	מַעֲרָבִי ז׳ מַעֲרָבִיִּים	western

As in מִסְחָרִי (מִקְטָלִי) above, but when the first root consonant is guttural, with a *shva*, that *shva* is converted to *Hataf-pataH*, and the preceding *Hiriq* is assimilated into a *pataH*. The derivation is linear, מַעֲרָב+י, but may equally be attributed to the discontinuous *mishkal miCCaCi > maCaCaCi*.

Examples

במזרח התיכון (פרט לישראל) תמיד מייחסים כל רעה חולה לקונספירציה **מַעֲרָבִית**.
In the Middle East (except for Israel) they always attribute everything bad that happens to **Western** conspiracy.

Additional Examples in this Pattern

circular מַעְגָּלִי of (social) class מַעֲמָדִי

---

926. N +*i* Adj /*meCCaCi*

f. sing/pl	m. sing/pl	Gloss
מֶרְכָּזִית נ׳ מֶרְכָּזִיּוֹת	מֶרְכָּזִי ז׳ מֶרְכָּזִיִּים	central

As in all adjectives derived from noun with the suffix –*i*, the speaker wishes to denote the very quality of that noun being a particular one. The derivation is linear, מֶרְכָּז+י, but may equally be attributed to the discontinuous *mishkal meCCaCi.*

Examples

תחנת האוטובוסים ה**מֶרְכָּזִית** בתל אביב הועתקה למקום אחר, שהציבור קורא לו תחנת האוטובוסים ה**מֶרְכָּזִית** החדשה...
The **central** bus station in Tel Aviv was moved to a new location, which the public calls the new **central** bus station...

Special Expressions

הגנה **מֶרְחָבִית** **territorial/home** defense

Additional Examples in this Pattern

of research מֶחְקָרִי spacial מֶרְחָבִי

---

927. N +*i* Adj */maCCeCi*

f. sing/pl	m. sing/pl	Gloss
מַכְתְּשִׁית נ׳ מַכְתְּשִׁיּוֹת	מַכְתְּשִׁי ז׳ מַכְתְּשִׁיִּים	alveolar (phonetics)

As in all adjectives derived from noun with the suffix *–i*, the speaker wishes to denote the very quality of that noun being a particular one. The derivation is linear, מַכְתֵּשׁ+י (with simultaneous reduction of the *tsere* to *shva*), but may equally be attributed to the discontinuous *mishkal maCCeCi.*

Examples

ת׳ ו-ד׳ בעברית הם עיצורים שִׁנִּיִּים ; באנגלית הם **מַכְתְּשִׁיִּים**.
t and *d* in Hebrew are dental; in English they are **alveolar**.

Additional Examples in this Pattern

of computer מַחְשְׁבִי
of cellar/basement מַרְתְּפִי
of crisis מַשְׁבְּרִי

---

928. N +*i* Adj */maCCaCti*

f. sing/pl	m. sing/pl	Gloss
מַחְתַּרְתִּית נ׳ מַחְתַּרְתִּיּוֹת	מַחְתַּרְתִּי ז׳ מַחְתַּרְתִּיִּים	underground Adj

As in all adjectives derived from noun with the suffix *–i*, the speaker wishes to denote the very quality of that noun being a particular one. The derivation is linear, מַחְתַּרְתּ+י from the segholate base of מַחְתֶּרֶת, but may equally be attributed to the discontinuous *mishkal maCCaCti.*

Examples

בתקופת המנדט הבריטי בארץ ישראל היו שלושה ארגונים צבאיים **מַחְתַּרְתִּיִּים** : ההגנה, האצ״ל ולח״י.
During the British mandate in Palestine there were two **underground** military organizations: the Hagannah, (Begin's) National Military Organization (the Irgun) and the Fighters for the Freedom of Israel (the Stern Gang).

Additional Examples in this Pattern

intellectual; of thought מַחְשַׁבְתִּי

---

929. N +*i* Adj */maCCaCi*

f. sing/pl	m. sing/pl	Gloss
מַלְאָכִית נ׳ מַלְאָכִיּוֹת	מַלְאָכִי ז׳ מַלְאָכִיִּים	angelic

As in all adjectives derived from noun with the suffix –*i*, the speaker wishes to denote the very quality of that noun being a particular one. The derivation is linear, מַלְאָךְ+י, but may equally be attributed to the discontinuous *mishkal maCCaCi.*

Examples

יש לה פנים **מַלְאָכִיּוֹת**, אך לִבָּהּ קשה כאבן.

She has an **angelic** face, but her heart is as hard as a rock.

Additional Examples in this Pattern

of, or pertaining to, meaning מַשְׁמָעִי

---

930. N +*i* Adj /*maCCani*

f. sing/pl	m. sing/pl	Gloss
מַשְׁוָנִית נ׳ מַשְׁוָנִיּוֹת	מַשְׁוָנִי ז׳ מַשְׁוָנִיִּים	equatorial

As in all adjectives derived from noun with the suffix –*i*, the speaker wishes to denote the very quality of that noun being a particular one. The derivation is linear, מַשְׁוֶה+(נ)י, with *seghol* > *kamats* and an *n* to separate the two consecutive vowels, but may equally be attributed to the discontinuous *mishkal maCCani.*

Examples

ישנם קלימטולוגים המגדירים את האקלים באזור קו־המשווה כ״**מַשְׁוָנִי**״ ולא טרופי.

Some climatologists define the climate in the equatorial region as "**equatorial**," not tropical.

Additional Examples in this Pattern

coniferous מַחְטָנִי

---

931. N +*i* Adj /*moCaCi*

f. sing/pl	m. sing/pl	Gloss
מוֹשָׁבִית נ׳ מוֹשָׁבִיּוֹת	מוֹשָׁבִי ז׳ מוֹשָׁבִיִּים	(of) seat Adj (one-seater, two-seater)

As in all adjectives derived from noun with the suffix –*i*, the speaker wishes to denote the very quality of that noun being a particular one. The derivation is linear, מוֹשָׁב 'seat' +י , but may equally be attributed to the discontinuous *mishkal moCaCi.*

Examples

המטוסים הקטנים הם בדרך כלל דו-**מוֹשָׁבִיִּים**.

Small planes are usually **two-seater** ones.

Additional Examples in this Pattern

institutional מוֹסָדִי

---

932. N +*i* Adj */staCCani*

f. sing/pl	m. sing/pl	Gloss
סְתַגְּלָנִית נ׳ סְתַגְּלָנִיּוֹת	סְתַגְּלָנִי ז׳ סְתַגְּלָנִיִּים	versatile, adaptive

As in all adjectives derived from noun with the suffix –*i*, the speaker wishes to denote the very quality of that noun being a particular one. The derivation is linear, סְתַגְּלָן+י, but may equally be attributed to the discontinuous *hitpa`el*-related *mishkal staCCani* (in *hitpa`el* a root-initial *s* metathesizes with the *t* of the prefix +*hit*, *hit*+*sagel* > *histagel* 'adapt').

Examples

הזיקית היא מבעלי החיים ה**סְתַגְּלָנִיִּים** ביותר, לפחות מבחינת הצבע...
The chameleon is one of the most **adaptive** animals, at least color-wise...

Additional Examples in this Pattern

introverted, withdrawn סְתַגְּרָנִי

---

933. N +*i* Adj /*CCiCi*

f. sing/pl	m. sing/pl	Gloss
בְּסִיסִית נ׳ בְּסִיסִיּוֹת	בְּסִיסִי ז׳ בְּסִיסִיִּים	basic

As in all adjectives derived from noun with the suffix –*i*, the speaker wishes to denote the very quality of that noun being a particular one. The derivation is linear (sometimes after automatic vowel reduction, בָּסִיס+ י > בְּסִיסִי), but may equally be attributed to the discontinuous *mishkal CCiCi*. In some cases, an *e* is inserted to facilitate the articulation of an initial cluster, e.g. /*ylidi*/ 'native' > *yelidi*.

Examples

ברוב האוניברסיטאות בעולם, על תלמידים לתואר ראשון לשמוע מספר מסוים של שיעורים **בְּסִיסִיִּים** כדי לוודא שרכשו השכלה כללית מינימלית.
In most universities in the world, students must take a certain number of **basic** courses, to ascertain that they have acquired minimal general education.

חיים לא נולד בארה״ב, אבל המיומנות שלו באנגלית מקבילה לזו של דובר **יְלִידִי**.
Hayyim was not born in the US, but his proficiency in English is equivalent to that of a **native** speaker.

הרבה חושבים שהנטיות ה**מְשִׁיחִיּוֹת** של חלק מן הציבור הישראלי מסכנות את שלום האומה.
Many think that the **messianic** inclinations of some of the Israeli public endanger the welfare of the nation.

כדי לפתור את בעיית הרעב בעולם, דני מציע הצעה לא-כל-כך **רְצִינִית**: לפתוח סניפים של מקדונלד בכל מקום בחצי מחיר...
To solve the problem of world hunger, Danny has made a not-so-**serious** proposal: to open McDonald branches everywhere, at half-price...

Special Expressions

ציוּן **שְׁלִילִי** **failing** grade (in educational system)

Additional Examples in this Pattern

גְּבִישִׁי crystalline	קְפִיצִי springy; retractable
גְּלִילִי cylindrical	רְבִיעִי fourth
וְרִידִי venous	שְׁבִיעִי seventh
נְזִירִי ascetic	שְׁלִילִי negative
סְלִילִי spiral	שְׁלִישִׁי third
פְּלִילִי criminal	שְׁרִירִי muscular
פְּנִימִי internal	תְּמִידִי constant, continuous
צְמִיגִי viscous	

---

934. N +*i* Adj /*CCiCi* = *CaCiCi* when the first root consonant is guttural

f. sing/pl	m. sing/pl	Gloss
חֲגִיגִית נ׳ חֲגִיגִיּוֹת	חֲגִיגִי ז׳ חֲגִיגִיִּים	festive

As in בְּסִיסִי above, but when the first root consonant is guttural and a *shva* is expected, that *shva* is replaced by *Hataf-pataH* (or occasionally by *Hataf-seghol*, as in אֱלִילִי 'idolatrous.') The derivation is linear, חֲגִיגָה+י, with the *a* automatically elided, but may equally be attributed to the discontinuous *mishkal CCiCi* > *CaCiCi*.

Examples

הנשיא החדש הושבע אתמול בטקס **חֲגִיגִי** במשכן הכנסת.
The new president was sworn in yesterday in a **festive** ceremony in the Knesset assembly hall.

במפגן **הָאֲוִירִי** השנתי קרתה תאונה: אחד המטוסים התרסק.
An accident occurred in the annual **aerial** display: one of the planes crashed.

ראש הממשלה החדש הוא בן למשפחה **אֲצִילִית** שאחד מאבותיה היה פעם דוכס...
The new prime minister is a member of a **noble** family one of whose ancestors was once a duke...

כדי לוודא שהסטייק שלי יישאר **עֲסִיסִי**, אני מבקש תמיד שיהיה בינוני-נא.
To make sure that my steak remain **juicy**, I always request that it be medium-rare.

Special Expressions

מִפְגַּן **אֲוִירִי** **aerial** display

Additional Examples in this Pattern

חֲלִיפִי alternative	עֲרִירִי alone; childless
חֲסִידִי Hassidic	עֲתִידִי future Adj
חֲרִישִׁי very quiet	

---

935. ?N +*i* Adj */C(e)CiCani*

f. sing/pl	m. sing/pl	Gloss
יְחִידָנִית נ׳ יְחִידָנִיּוֹת	יְחִידָנִי ז׳ יְחִידָנִיִּים	individual, distinct

The derivation may be argued to be linear, יְחִיד+נִי, but is more likely to be attributed to the discontinuous *mishkal C(e)CiCani*. The *e* is inserted to facilitate the articulation of the initial cluster: */yHidani/* > *yeHidani*.

Examples

בית הספר הזה מציג את עצמו כבית ספר **יְחִידָנִי**, שונה מבתי הספר הממלכתיים האחרים.
This school presents itself as a **distinct** school, different from all other state schools.

---

936. N +*i* Adj */CCiCani* = *CaCiCani* when the first root consonant is guttural

f. sing/pl	m. sing/pl	Gloss
עֲתִידָנִית נ׳ עֲתִידָנִיּוֹת	עֲתִידָנִי ז׳ עֲתִידָנִיִּים	futuristic

As in יְחִידָנִי above, but when the first root consonant is guttural and a *shva* is expected, that *shva* is replaced by *Hataf-pataH*. The derivation may be linear, עָתִיד+(נ)י ‘future’, but is more likely to be attributed to the discontinuous *mishkal CCiCani* > *CaCiCani*.

Examples

בתערוכה האלקטרונית הגדולה הוצגו מכשירים ותוכנות **עֲתִידָנִיִּים** שישנו את חיי היום-יום של כולנו בעשורים הקרובים.
In the great electronic exhibition, they demonstrated **futuristic** instruments and programs that will change our daily lives in the coming decades.

Additional Examples in this Pattern

aerobic אֲוִירָנִי

---

937. N +*i* Adj */CCiCati*

f. sing/pl	m. sing/pl	Gloss
יְצִירָתִית נ׳ יְצִירָתִיּוֹת	יְצִירָתִי ז׳ יְצִירָתִיִּים	creative

As in all adjectives derived from noun with the suffix *–i*, the speaker wishes to denote the very quality of that noun being a particular one. The derivation is linear, יְצִירָה/ת+י, but may equally be attributed to the discontinuous *mishkal CCiCati*. An *e* is inserted if required to facilitate the articulation of an initial cluster: */ytsirati/* > *yetsirati*.

Examples

מעניין שהרבה ילדים מגלים כישרונות **יְצִירָתִיִּים** של ממש, בעיקר בציור, אבל משום מה אינם מפתחים את הכישרונות הללו כשהם מתבגרים.

Interestingly, many children reveal real **creative** talents, especially in drawing/painting, but somehow do not develop these talents when they grow up.

מחלת הסרטן היא בחלק מן המקרים גנטית, ובמקרים אחרים **סְבִיבָתִית**.

In some cases, cancer is genetic; in others it is **environmental**.

Additional Examples in this Pattern

respiratory נְשִׁימָתִי

velvety קְטִיפָתִי

radiative, radiating קְרִינָתִי

related to hearing שְׁמִיעָתִי

perceptual תְּפִיסָתִי

---

938. N +*i* Adj /*CCiCati* = *CaCiCati* when the first root consonant is guttural

f. sing/pl	m. sing/pl	Gloss
חֲשִׁיבָתִית נ׳ חֲשִׁיבָתִיּוֹת	חֲשִׁיבָתִי ז׳ חֲשִׁיבָתִיִּים	of the thinking process

As in יְצִירָתִי above, but when the first root consonant is guttural and a *shva* is expected, that *shva* is replaced by *Hataf-pataH*. The derivation is linear, חֲשִׁיבָה/ת+י, but may equally be attributed to the discontinuous *mishkal CCiCati* > *CaCiCati*.

Examples

כדי לשחרר את עצמנו מדפוסי התנהגות, או הרגלים, שמפריעים לנו בחיי היום יום, עלינו להיות פתוחים לשינוי **חֲשִׁיבָתִי**.

In order to release ourselves from behavioral patterns, or habits, that make our daily life difficult, we should be open for changes in our **thinking** process.

---

939. N +*i* Adj /*CCiCuti*

f. sing/pl	m. sing/pl	Gloss
בְּטִיחוּתִית נ׳ בְּטִיחוּתִיּוֹת	בְּטִיחוּתִי ז׳ בְּטִיחוּתִיִּים	safe, secure, related to safety

As in all adjectives derived from noun with the suffix –*i*, the speaker wishes to denote the very quality of that noun being a particular one. The derivation is linear, בְּטִיחוּת+י, but may equally be attributed to the discontinuous *mishkal CCiCuti*.

Examples

גם בארה״ב מתחילים להבין שלבדיקת תיקים בכניסה למבנים ציבוריים יש חשיבות **בְּטִיחוּתִית** גדולה.

Even in the US they are beginning to understand that checking of bags at the entrance to public buildings is of great **security** importance.

Special Expressions

safety hazard מִפְגָּע **בְּטִיחוּתִי**

Additional Examples in this Pattern

clerical פְּקִידוּתִי

---

940. N +*i* Adj /*CCaCtani*

f. sing/pl	m. sing/pl	Gloss
שְׁאַפְתָּנִית נ׳ שְׁאַפְתָּנִיּוֹת	שְׁאַפְתָּנִי ז׳ שְׁאַפְתָּנִיִּים	ambitious

As in all adjectives derived from noun with the suffix –*i*, the speaker wishes to denote the very quality of that noun being a particular one. The derivation is linear, שְׁאַפְתָּן+י, but may equally be attributed to the discontinuous *mishkal CCaCtani*.

Examples

בזמנו, היעד ה**שְׁאַפְתָּנִי** ביותר נראה להנחית אנשים על הירח; היום זה נראה מובן מאליו.
At the time, the most **ambitious** goal was to land men on the moon; today it is taken for granted.

Additional Examples in this Pattern

gluttonous, voracious, greedy רַעַבְתָּנִי   domineering שְׁתַלְּטָנִי

---

941. N +*i* Adj /*CCaCati* = *CaCaCati* when the first root consonant is guttural

f. sing/pl	m. sing/pl	Gloss
חֲוָיָתִית נ׳ חֲוָיָתִיּוֹת	חֲוָיָתִי ז׳ חֲוָיָתִיִּים	experiential

When the first root consonant is guttural and a *shva* is expected, that *shva* is replaced by *Hataf-pataH*. The derivation is linear, חֲוָיָה/ת+י, but may equally be attributed to the discontinuous *mishkal CCaCati* > *CaCaCati*. Words in the *CCaCati mishkal* are rare (hypothetical סְבָרָתִי?), but one can reasonably assume that this is the base for the sub-*mishkal CaCaCati*.

Examples

למידה **חֲוָיָתִית** היא תמיד יותר אפקטיבית מלמידה תיאורטית, בעיקר אצל ילדים.
Experiential learning is always more effective than theoretical learning, particularly with children.

Additional Examples in this Pattern

experiential הֲוָיָתִי   hallucinatory, imaginary הֲזָיָתִי

---

942. N +*i* Adj /*CCaCi*

f. sing/pl	m. sing/pl	Gloss
כְּלָלִית נ׳ כְּלָלִיּוֹת	כְּלָלִי ז׳ כְּלָלִיִּים	general

As in all adjectives derived from noun with the suffix –*i*, the speaker wishes to denote the very quality of that noun being a particular one. The derivation is linear, כְּלָל+י (sometimes after automatic vowel reduction, בָּשָׂר+י > בְּשָׂרִי), but may equally be attributed to the discontinuous *mishkal CCaCi*.

Examples

הארגון הרפואי הגדול בישראל הוא "קופת (ה)חולים ה**כְּלָלִית**".
The largest health organization in Israel is the "**General** Health Maintenance Organization."

אין הרבה בתי ספר **פְּרָטִיִּים** בישראל.
There are few **private** schools in Israel.

בכל ארצות ערב קיים שלטון **צְבָאִי**, גם כאשר קיימת מערכת דמוקרטית כביכול.
All Arab countries are ruled by **military** government, even those that are nominal democracies.

בישראל שירות צבאי **קְרָבִי** עדיין נחשב ליוקרתי – יותר מאשר שירות שאינו **קְרָבִי**.
In Israel, **combatant** military service is still regarded as more prestigious than non-**combatant** service.

Special Expressions

קְדַם-**צְבָאִי** pre-**military**

חַד-**צְדָדִי** uni**lateral**

Additional Examples in this Pattern

בְּשָׂרִי related to meat, meat dish
זְכָרִי masculine, male Adj
יְמָנִי right-handed
סְתָמִי unclear, unspecified; meaningless; neuter

צְדָדִי of side (street, etc.); marginal
שְׂטָנִי satanical
שְׁרָבִי of or relating to a heat wave, hot and dry
תְּזָזִי frantic, frenetic Lit.

---

943. N +*i* Adj /*CCaCi* = *CaCaCi* when the first root consonant is guttural

f. sing/pl	m. sing/pl	Gloss
חֲלָבִית נ׳ חֲלָבִיּוֹת	חֲלָבִי ז׳ חֲלָבִיִּים	of dairy

As in כְּלָלִי above, but when the first root consonant is guttural and a *shva* is expected, that *shva* is replaced by *Hataf-pataH*. The derivation is linear, חָלָב+י (with the *kamats* reduced to *Hataf-pataH*), but may equally be attributed to the discontinuous *mishkal CCaCi* > *CaCaCi*.

Examples

בתקופה שלאחר קום המדינה, עם גלי העלייה הגדולים מארצות ערב, שוכנו חלק מן העולים החדשים במגורים **אֲרָעִיִּים** עד שהוקמו מספיק מבנים חדשים.

In the period after the establishment of the State of Israel, with the large immigration waves from the Arab countries, some of the new immigrants were housed in **temporary** housing until sufficient new buildings were erected.

אחד העקרונות המרכזיים בחיי הקהילות היהודיות בכל מקום היה תמיד עזרה **הֲדָדִית**: "כל ישראל ערבים זה לזה".

One of the central principles in the life of Jewish communities anywhere was **mutual** help: "All of Israel are responsible for each other".

התורכים אינם מכירים בכורדים שבתורכיה כעדה נפרדת. הם רואים בהם "תורכים **הֲרָרִיִּים**".

The Turks do not recognize the Kurds as a separate community. They regard them as "**Mountain** Turks."

Additional Examples in this Pattern

temporary אֲרָעִי
mutual הֲדָדִי
of mountain הֲרָרִי
related to outer space חֲלָלִי
giant, huge עֲנָקִי

---

944. N +*i* Adj */CCoCi*

f. sing/pl	m. sing/pl	Gloss
דְּרוֹמִית נ׳ דְּרוֹמִיּוֹת	דְּרוֹמִי ז׳ דְּרוֹמִיִּים	southern

As in all adjectives derived from noun with the suffix –*i*, the speaker wishes to denote the very quality of that noun being a particular one. The derivation is linear (sometimes after automatic vowel reduction, דָּרוֹם+י < דְּרוֹמִי), but may equally be attributed to the discontinuous *mishkal CCoCi*.

Examples

בגבול ה**דְּרוֹמִי** של ישראל הבעייה הביטחונית הגדולה היא רצועת עזה.

On Israel's **southern** border, the main security problem is the Gaza Strip.

הוא אינו איינשטיין, אך התובנות שלו נראות לי **גְּאוֹנִיּוֹת**.

He is no Einstein, but his insights appear to me **genius** (level).

בנייה **טְרוֹמִית** נפוצה למדיי היום בישראל.

Prefabricated construction is becoming commoner in Israel today.

מצב המשמעת בבתי הספר ה**יְסוֹדִיִּים** והתיכוניים בישראל היום הוא בכי רע.

The discipline situation in **elementary** and secondary schools in Israel today is pretty bad.

משה התנצל על התפרצותו; הוא הסביר שזו הייתה תגובה בלתי-**רְצוֹנִית** מצדו.

Moshe apologized for his outburst; he explained that it was an in**voluntary** reaction on his part.

Special Expressions

bi-**lingual** דו-**לְשׁוֹנִי** post-**primary** (education) עַל-**יְסוֹדִי**

Additional Examples in this Pattern

spongy סְפוֹגִי
northern צְפוֹנִי
abysmal, unfathomable תְּהוֹמִי
guttural, throaty גְּרוֹנִי
malicious זְדוֹנִי
linguistic; of language; of the tongue לְשׁוֹנִי

---

945. N +*i* Adj /*CCoCi* = *CaCoCi* when the first root consonant is guttural

f. sing/pl	m. sing/pl	Gloss
חֲלוֹמִית נ׳ חֲלוֹמִיּוֹת	חֲלוֹמִי ז׳ חֲלוֹמִיִּים	dream-like

As in דְּרוֹמִי above, but when the first root consonant is guttural and a *shva* is expected, that *shva* is replaced by *Hataf-pataH*. The derivation is linear, חֲלוֹם+י, but may equally be attributed to the discontinuous *mishkal CCoCi* > *CaCoCi*. Note: the base for אֲזוֹרִי is אֵזוֹר 'region,' and for עֲשׂוֹרִי it is עָשׂוֹר 'ten; decade,' and the *Hataf* was formed by reduction of the *tsere* and the *kamats*, respectively, but their declensions are the same as in other forms, and in this respect they may be regarded as belonging to the *CCoCi* > *CaCoCi mishkal*.

Examples

כששאלתי את דני אם נהנה מן הטיול שלו בקיץ באירופה, הוא ענה שזה היה נהדר, ממש **חֲלוֹמִי**.
When I asked Danny whether he enjoyed his trip to Europe in the summer, he responded that it was wonderful, truly **dream-like**.

Additional Examples in this Pattern

stupid, foolish; obstinate חֲמוֹרִי
decadal; decimal עֲשׂוֹרִי
regional אֲזוֹרִי
dream-like חֲלוֹמִי

---

946. N +*i* Adj /*CCuCi*

f. sing/pl	m. sing/pl	Gloss
גְּבוּלִית נ׳ גְּבוּלִיּוֹת	גְּבוּלִי ז׳ גְּבוּלִיִּים	border-line

As in all adjectives derived from noun with the suffix –*i*, the speaker wishes to denote the very quality of that noun being a particular one. The derivation is linear, גְּבוּל+י, but may equally be attributed to the discontinuous *mishkal CCuCi*.

Examples

זוהי בקשת קבלה **גְּבוּלִית**. קשה לנו כרגע להחליט אם לקבלו לתוכנית או לא.
This is a **border-line** application for admission. At the moment we cannot determine yet whether to approve his admission into the program.

עדיין לא ברור אם הגיע הזמן שגם מועמד **יְהוּדִי** יוכל להיבחר לנשיא ארה״ב.
It is not clear yet whether the time has come that a **Jewish** candidate will be able to be elected president of the US.

הקהילה ה**רְפוּאִית** מתחילה להאמין שאולי תפותח תוך כמה שנים תרופה למחלת הסרטן.
The **medical** community is beginning to believe that a cure for cancer may be developed within a few years.

Special Expressions

רב/בין-**תְּחוּמִי** multi/inter-**disciplinary**

Additional Examples in this Pattern

בְּתוּלִי virginal
נְבוּאִי prophetic
שְׁבוּעִי weekly Adj
תְּחוּמִי disciplinary (field of knowledge etc.)

---

947. N +*i* Adj /*CCuCi* = *CaCuCi*, when the first root consonant is guttural

f. sing/pl	m. sing/pl	Gloss
חֲלוּצִית נ׳ חֲלוּצִיּוֹת	חֲלוּצִי ז׳ חֲלוּצִיִּים	pioneering

As in גְּבוּלִי above, but when the first root consonant is guttural and a *shva* is expected, that *shva* is replaced by *Hataf-pataH*. The derivation is linear, חָלוּץ+י, but may equally be attributed to the discontinuous *mishkal CCuCi* > *CaCuCi*.

Examples

למרות היותה מדינה קטנה, ישראל היא מרכז חשוב של יוזמות **חֲלוּצִיּוֹת** בתחומים כמו מחקר רפואי, פיתוח תוכנות מתקדמות, מערכות הגנה, ועוד.
In spite of its small size, Israel is an important center for **pioneering** initiatives in areas such as medical research, development of advanced programming, defense systems, etc.

Additional Examples in this Pattern

אֲסוּפִי foundling, waif
חֲתוּלִי feline, cat-like

---

948. N/Adj +*i* Adj/*CiCCi*

f. sing/pl	m. sing/pl	Gloss
סִטְרִית נ׳ סִטְרִיּוֹת	סִטְרִי ז׳ סִטְרִיִּים	way (one-way, two-way)

The derivation is linear, from including borrowed bases: זִפְת+י from Arabic, סִטְרָא +י from Aramaic, Arabic *rasmi* > רִשְׁמִי, and from Hebrew Adj:
נִבְזִי 'despicable' < נִבְזֶה+י

Examples

נהיגה ברחוב חד-**סִטְרִי** נגד כיוון התנועה מסתיימת כמעט תמיד בתאונה.
Driving against the traffic in a one-**way** street almost always ends in an accident.

העמדה ה**רִשְׁמִית** של הממשלה הסעודית היא שאסור לנשים מוסלמיות לשיר בציבור.
The **official** position of the Saudi government is that Muslim women are not allowed to sing in public.

Special Expressions

חד-**סִטְרִי** one-way   דו-**סִטְרִי** two-way

Additional Examples in this Pattern

זִפְתִּי (Arabic) lousy, terrible, "shitty" Sl.   נִבְזִי despicable

---

949. N +*i* Adj /*CiCCi* from a segholate base

f. sing/pl	m. sing/pl	Gloss
טִבְעִית נ׳ טִבְעִיּוֹת	טִבְעִי ז׳ טִבְעִיִּים	natural

As in all adjectives derived from noun with the suffix *–i*, the speaker wishes to denote the very quality of that noun being a particular one. The derivation is linear, or semi-linear, from a segholate base, טִבְעִי < טֶבַע/טִבְע+י, but may equally be attributed to the discontinuous *mishkal CiCCi*.

Examples

בישראל מקבלים באופן **טִבְעִי** שאיש צבא בדרגה גבוהה יכול גם להיות פוליטיקאי טוב.
In Israel they regard it as **natural** that a high-ranking general can also be a good politician.

הזמן הוא מושג **נִצְחִי**, שאין בו כל שינוי, ואין לו התחלה ואין לו סוף.
Time is an **eternal** concept, which never changes; it has no beginning and no end.

פגשתי ניצולי שואה ששמרו על הטלאי הצהוב ונשאו אותו תמיד בארנקם, כאַקְט **סִמְלִי** של גאווה על היותם יהודים.
I met some Holocaust survivors who kept the yellow patch and always carried it in their wallets, as a **symbolic** act of pride in their being Jewish.

בישראל קוראים לארוחות צהריים מוזלות במסעדות "ארוחות **עִסְקִיּוֹת**".
In Israel they call lunch specials in restaurants "**business** lunches."

יש אנשים שלא מפסיקים לשקר, כדי להיות **עִקְבִיִּים**...
Some people never stop lying, so as to be **consistent**....

על ישמעאל נאמר שהיה ילד **פִּרְאִי** ("פרא אדם"), "ידו בכל ויד כל בו".
Of Ishmael it was said that he was a **wild** kid, "his hand was against every man, and every man's hand against him."

Special Expressions

pedigree dog כלב **גִּזְעִי**
super**natural** על-**טִבְעִי**
lunch special; **business** lunch ארוחה **עִסְקִית**

front wheel drive הנעה **קִדְמִית**
sub-**standard** תת-**תִּקְנִי**

Additional Examples in this Pattern

of pedigree; trendy Coll. גִּזְעִי
ceremonial טִקְסִי
inclinational, impulsive יִצְרִי
economic מִשְׁקִי
eagle-like נִשְׁרִי
-way סִטְרִי
Hebrew עִבְרִי
of plant, vegetal צִמְחִי
front Adj קִדְמִי
mealy, floury קִמְחִי

rhythmic קִצְבִּי
momentary רִגְעִי
emotional רִגְשִׁי
profitable רִוְחִי
tribal שִׁבְטִי
superficial שִׁטְחִי
mental שִׂכְלִי
false, untrue שִׁקְרִי
standard Adj; correct (language) תִּקְנִי

---

950. N +*i* Adj */CiCCani*

f. sing/pl	m. sing/pl	Gloss
גִּזְעָנִית נ׳ גִּזְעָנִיּוֹת	גִּזְעָנִי ז׳ גִּזְעָנִיִּים	racist

As in all adjectives derived from noun with the suffix –*i*, the speaker wishes to denote the very quality of that noun being a particular one. The derivation is linear, or semi-linear, since in the case of גִּזְעָן 'racist' we may be dealing with back-formation from גִּזְעָנִי 'racist Adj' or גִּזְעָנוּת, and thus one may assume derivation from a segholate base: גֶּזַע+ָן+ִי > גִּזְעָנִי. But such forms may also equally be attributed to the discontinuous *mishkal CiCCani*.

Examples

למרבית הצער, מספר האירועים ה**גִּזְעָנִיִּים** בארה״ב ובאירופה הולך ומתרבה לאחרונה.
Unfortunately, the number of **racist** incidents in the US and in Europe has been on the increase recently.

יש לטפל בבעייה באופן **עִנְיָנִי**, ולפתור אותה במהירות האפשרית.
The problem should be taken care of in a **matter-of-fact** manner, and solve it ASAP.

Additional Examples in this Pattern

furnace-like, very hot כִּבְשָׁנִי
possessory קִנְיָנִי

---

951. N +*i* Adj /*CiCCati*

f. sing/pl	m. sing/pl	Gloss
סִדְרָתִית נ׳ סִדְרָתִיּוֹת	סִדְרָתִי ז׳ סִדְרָתִיִּים	serial

As in all adjectives derived from noun with the suffix –*i*, the speaker wishes to denote the very quality of that noun being a particular one. The derivation is linear, סִדְרָה/ת+י 'series,' but may equally be attributed to the discontinuous *mishkal CiCCati*.

Examples

מדי פעם נחרדת ארה״ב כשנחשפות פרשות של רוצחים **סִדְרָתִיִּים**.
From time to time, the US is shocked when stories of **serial** murderers are exposed.

בבדיקה **שִׁגְרָתִית** של חדרים בבתי מלון בישראל נמצא כי התנאים הסניטריים ברבים מהם הם תת-תקניים.
In a **routine** inspection of hotel rooms in Israel it was discovered that the sanitary conditions in many of them are sub-standard.

Additional Examples in this Pattern

digital סִפְרָתִי	layered; of class שִׁכְבָתִי

---

952. N +*i* Adj /*CiCConi*

f. sing/pl	m. sing/pl	Gloss
כִּשְׁרוֹנִית נ׳ כִּשְׁרוֹנִיּוֹת	כִּשְׁרוֹנִי ז׳ כִּשְׁרוֹנִיִּים	talented

As in all adjectives derived from noun with the suffix –*i*, the speaker wishes to denote the very quality of that noun being a particular one. The derivation is linear, sometimes with vowel reduction, כִּשָּׁרוֹן + י > כִּשְׁרוֹנִי, but may equally be attributed to the discontinuous *mishkal CiCConi*.

Examples

אין ספק שהפסנתרן הזה **כִּשְׁרוֹנִי** ביותר, אבל חסר לו ניצוץ של השראה.
There is little doubt that this pianist is very **talented**, but he still lacks a spark of inspiration.

יותר ויותר אנשים מאמינים שדיאטה **טִבְעוֹנִית** אינה רק בריאה יותר באופן כללי, אלא גם מרפאת מחלות שונות.
More and more people believe not only that **vegan** diet is healthier in general, but that it also cures certain illnesses.

מטבע הדברים, הנושא ה**בִּטְחוֹנִי** הוא בראש מעייניו של הציבור בישראל.
Naturally, the **security** issue is primary in the Israeli public discourse.

זהו רק מודל **נִסְיוֹנִי** של המטוס החדש, אבל נראה שהוא ישנה את פני התעופה בעתיד.
This is just an **experimental** model of the new plane, but it appears that it will change the field of aviation in the future.

Special Expressions

science **fiction** מדע **בִּדְיוֹנִי**

Additional Examples in this Pattern

fictional בִּדְיוֹנִי
depressive דִּכְאוֹנִי
imaginary דִּמְיוֹנִי
floral פִּרְחוֹנִי
colorful צִבְעוֹנִי
vegetarian צִמְחוֹנִי
retail קִמְעוֹנִי
egalitarian שִׁוְיוֹנִי
governmental שִׁלְטוֹנִי

---

953. N +*i* Adj /*CiCCuCi*

f. sing/pl	m. sing/pl	Gloss
פִּרְסוּמִית נ׳ פִּרְסוּמִיּוֹת	פִּרְסוּמִי ז׳ פִּרְסוּמִיִּים	commercial

As in all adjectives derived from noun with the suffix –*i*, the speaker wishes to denote the very quality of that noun being a particular one. The derivation is linear, פִּרְסוּם+י, but may equally be attributed to the discontinuous *mishkal CiCCuCi*.

Examples

המרכיב ה**פִּרְסוּמִי** במהדורת החדשות הולך ומתרחב עם השנים. פשוט נורא!
The **commercial** component of the news broadcast keeps increasing with the years. Simply awful!

Additional Examples in this Pattern

organizational אִרְגּוּנִי

---

954. N +*i* Adj /*CiCCuCi*, with reduplication

f. sing/pl	m. sing/pl	Gloss
דִּקְדּוּקִית נ׳ דִּקְדּוּקִיּוֹת	דִּקְדּוּקִי ז׳ דִּקְדּוּקִיִּים	grammatical

As in all adjectives derived from noun with the suffix –*i*, the speaker wishes to denote the very quality of that noun being a particular one. The first and second root consonants are reduplicated in positions three and four, respectively. The derivation is linear, דִּקְדּוּק+י, but may equally be attributed to the discontinuous *mishkal CiCCuCi*.

Examples

אופיר הסביר לתלמידיו במה המבנה ה**דִּקְדּוּקִי** של המשפט בעברית שונה ממבנה המשפט באנגלית.
Ofir explained to his students how the **grammatical** structure of the Hebrew sentence is different from that of a compartable English sentence.

Additional Examples in this Pattern

casuistic פִּלְפּוּלִי

---

955. N +*i* Adj /*CiCCi*

f. sing/pl	m. sing/pl	Gloss
טִפְּשִׁית נ׳ טִפְּשִׁיּוֹת	טִפְּשִׁי ז׳ טִפְּשִׁיִּים	silly, stupid

As in all adjectives derived from noun with the suffix –*i*, the speaker wishes to denote the very quality of that noun being a particular one. The derivation is linear, with automatic vowel elision, טִפְּשִׁי < טִפֵּשׁ+י, but may equally be attributed to the discontinuous *mishkal CiCCi*.

Examples

רוב הפרסומות בטלוויזיה האמריקאית הן **טִפְּשִׁיּוֹת** לחלוטין; הנחת המפרסמים היא שהצופה הממוצע הוא בדרך כלל אדם פשוט וחסר אינטליגנציה.

Most of the commercials on American television are totally **stupid**; the advertisers' assumption is that the average viewer is generally simple and unintelligent.

Additional Examples in this Pattern

sharp, bright, quick-witted [Note: no *dagesh* in the *qof* here] פִּקְחִי

---

956. N +*i* Adj /*CiCuCi*

f. sing/pl	m. sing/pl	Gloss
חִיּוּבִית נ׳ חִיּוּבִיּוֹת	חִיּוּבִי ז׳ חִיּוּבִיִּים	positive

As in all adjectives derived from noun with the suffix –*i*, the speaker wishes to denote the very quality of that noun being a particular one. The derivation is linear, חִיּוּב+י, but may equally be attributed to the discontinuous *mishkal CiCuCi*.

Examples

רוב הרופאים מאמינים שגישה **חִיּוּבִית** ואופטימיות עוזרות לחולים להתגבר על חוליים – אפילו כשמדובר בסרטן.

Most doctors believe that **positive** attitude and optimism help patients overcome their illness – even in the case of cancer.

גם כאשר הממשלה מושבתת, עובדים **חִיּוּנִיִּים** חייבים להתייצב במקומות עבודתם.

Even when the government is shut down, **essential** workers must report to work.

דמויות **צִבּוּרִיּוֹת** שפעלו לטובת הכלל ולא עסקו רק בקידום האינטרסים הפרטיים שלהם צריכות לשמש כמודלים **חִנּוּכִיִּים** לדור הצעיר.

Public figures who have worked for the public good and have not engaged solely in promoting their private interests should serve as **educational** models for the young generation.

בחקר הסרטן היום עוסקים הרבה במציאת דרכים ללמד את המערכת **הַחִסּוּנִית** איך לתקוף ולחסל את תאי הסרטן.

In cancer research today, they vigorously study how to teach the **immunological** system to attack and destroy cancer cells.

בדורות האחרונים, ראש ממשלה **טִפּוּסִי** בישראל היה בדרך כלל איש-צבא לשעבר, בדרך כלל רמטכ״ל.

In recent generations, a **typical** prime minister in Israel was generally a former military officer, in most cases chief-of-staff.

Special Expressions

חשמל **חִיּוּבִי** **positive** charge

מספר **חִיּוּבִי** **positive** number

ציון **חִיּוּבִי** **positive/passing** grade

המערכת **הַחִסּוּנִית** **immune** system

תרגום **מִלּוּלִי** **verbatim** translation

Additional Examples in this Pattern

בִּדּוּרִי entertaining

בִּצּוּעִי executive related to implementation

דִּבּוּרִי colloquial

הִתּוּלִי humorous, comic

חִלּוּפִי alternative; commutative

חִשּׁוּבִי computational

טִפּוּלִי therapeutic, related to treatment

יִצּוּגִי representational

יִשּׁוּמִי applied

כִּוּוּנִי directional

לִמּוּדִי instructional

מִלּוּלִי literal

נִגּוּדִי conflicting, opposite, contradictory

סִדּוּרִי ordinal (number)

סִפּוּרִי narrative Adj

עִגּוּלִי round, circular

עִיּוּנִי theoretical

צִיּוּרִי picturesque

קִבּוּצִי collective

קִיּוּמִי existential

קִשּׁוּטִי decorative

רִגּוּשִׁי emotional, emotive

רִכּוּזִי centralized

---

957. N +*i* Adj /*CiCuCi*, no *dagesh*

f. sing/pl	m. sing/pl	Gloss
סִעוּדִית נ׳ סִעוּדִיּוֹת	סִעוּדִי ז׳ סִעוּדִיִּים	disabled, needing assistance

As in חִיּוּבִי above, but without a *dagesh forte*, owing to the presence of ה׳, ח׳ ע׳. The derivation is linear, סִעוּד+י׳, but may equally be attributed to the discontinuous *mishkal CiCuCi*.

Examples

לפחות בארה״ב, כל האוניברסיטאות מחויבות לסייע לכל סטודנט **סִעוּדִי**, בין אם מדובר בסטודנט פגוע פיסית או מנטלית.

At least in the US, all universities are obligated to assist any **disabled** student, regardless of whether s/he is **disabled** physically or mentally.

התרומה **הַיִּחוּדִית** של היהדות, ושל הנצרות בראשיתה, הייתה הרדיפה אחר צדק חברתי.

The **unique** contribution of Judaism, and of Christianity in its initial phase, was the pursuit of social justice.

הטלוויזיה הציבורית בארה"ב מפיקה הרבה סרטים **תִּעוּדִיִּים** חשובים.
Public television in the US produces many important **documentary** films.

Additional Examples in this Pattern

infective זִהוּמִי
referential יִחוּסִי
related to mission יִעוּדִי
managerial נִהוּלִי
[circular סִיבוּבִי]

---

958. N +*i* Adj /*CiCuCi* = *CeCuCi*, the second root consonant is 'א or 'ר

f. sing/pl	m. sing/pl	Gloss
תֵּאוּרִית נ׳ תֵּאוּרִיּוֹת	תֵּאוּרִי ז׳ תֵּאוּרִיִּים	descriptive

As in חִיּוּבִי above, but without a *dagesh forte*, owing to the presence of 'א', ר, and the *Hirik* is replaced by *tsere* as "compensatory lengthening." The derivation is linear, תֵּאוּר+י, but may equally be attributed to the discontinuous *mishkal CiCuCi* > *CeCuCi*.

Examples

בתחומי מחקר מסוימים בארץ מעודדים מחקר **תֵּאוּרִי** טהור, ומלמדים את הסטודנטים שאסור להניח הנחות מחקר העשויות להסביר את התופעה הנחקרת לפני שכל הנתונים נאספו ומוינו, כי זה "לא מדעי" להניח הנחות מראש.
In certain research areas in Israel they encourage only pure **descriptive** research, and teach the students that it is forbidden to make theoretical hypotheses that might explain the researched phenomenon before all data are gathered and classified, since it is "unscientific" to make any *a priori* assumptions.

Additional Examples in this Pattern

combinational צֵרוּפִי
intermittent, alternate סֵרוּגִי
explanatory בֵּאוּרִי

---

959. N +*i* Adj /*CiCi*

f. sing/pl	m. sing/pl	Gloss
גִּירִית נ׳ גִּירִיּוֹת	גִּירִי ז׳ גִּירִיִּים	chalky

As in all adjectives derived from noun with the suffix –*i*, the speaker wishes to denote the very quality of that noun being a particular one. The derivation is linear, גִּיר+י, but may equally be attributed to the discontinuous *mishkal CiCi*.

Examples

האדמה פה היא **גִּירִית**, ומתאימה רק לצמחים מסוימים.
The ground here is **chalky**, and suited only for certain plants.

Additional Examples in this Pattern

related to age גִּילִי

---

960. N +*i* Adj /*CeyCi*

f. sing/pl	m. sing/pl	Gloss
לֵילִית נ׳ לֵילִיּוֹת	לֵילִי ז׳ לֵילִיִּים	nocturnal

As in all adjectives derived from noun with the suffix –*i*, the speaker wishes to denote the very quality of that noun being a particular one. The derivation is linear, sometimes from a segholate base, לֵילִי < לַיִל/לֵיל+י, but may equally be attributed to the discontinuous *mishkal CeyCi*.

Examples

בעלי חיים **לֵילִיִּים** פיתחו כושר ראייה מעולה בחושך.
Nocturnal animals developed excellent night sight.

Additional Examples in this Pattern

egg-shaped בֵּיצִי
domestic בֵּיתִי
pertaining to corps (military) חֵילִי
wine-like יֵינִי
summery קֵיצִי

---

961. N +*i* Adj /*CeCCi*

f. sing/pl	m. sing/pl	Gloss
חֶלְקִית נ׳ חֶלְקִיּוֹת	חֶלְקִי ז׳ חֶלְקִיִּים	partial

As in all adjectives derived from noun with the suffix –*i*, the speaker wishes to denote the very quality of that noun being a particular one. The derivation is linear, or semi-linear, from a segholate base, חֶלְקִי < חֵלֶק/חֶלְק+י, but may equally be attributed to the discontinuous *mishkal CeCCi*.

Examples

אקדמאים לא מעטים מצליחים להשיג רק משרה **חֶלְקִית** באוניברסיטה.
Some academics only manage to obtain a **partial** position at the university.

טיסה ממזרח למערב נמשכת יותר זמן בשל הרוח **הַנֶּגְדִּית**.
A flight from east to west takes longer because of the **opposing** wind.

Additional Examples in this Pattern

herd-like עֶדְרִי
moral, ethical, principled עֶרְכִּי

---

962. N +*i* Adj /*CeCConi*

f. sing/pl	m. sing/pl	Gloss
חֶלְבּוֹנִית נ׳ חֶלְבּוֹנִיּוֹת	חֶלְבּוֹנִי ז׳ חֶלְבּוֹנִיִּים	of protein

As in all adjectives derived from noun with the suffix –*i*, the speaker wishes to denote the very quality of that noun being a particular one. The derivation is linear, חֶלְבּוֹן+י, but may equally be attributed to the discontinuous *mishkal CeCConi.*

Examples

המבנה ה**חֶלְבּוֹנִי** הראשון שפוענח היה של ההמוגלובין.
The first **protein** structure to be deciphered was that of hemoglobin.

במתמטיקה, שבר **עֶשְׂרוֹנִי** הוא שיטה לרישום מספרים ממשיים.
In math, a **decimal** fraction is a method of representing real numbers.

Additional Examples in this Pattern

bright yellow, yolk-like חֶלְמוֹנִי
arithmetic חֶשְׁבּוֹנִי
decimal עֶשְׂרוֹנִי

---

963. N +*i* Adj/*CeCConi* from *CiCaCon*

f. sing/pl	m. sing/pl	Gloss
הֶגְיוֹנִית נ׳ הֶגְיוֹנִיּוֹת	הֶגְיוֹנִי ז׳ הֶגְיוֹנִיִּים	reasonable, logical

As in all adjectives derived from noun with the suffix –*i*, the speaker wishes to denote the very quality of that noun being a particular one. The derivation is linear, with vowel changes, הִגָּיוֹן+י < הֶגְיוֹנִי, but may equally be attributed to the discontinuous *mishkal CeCConi.*

Examples

מבנה פרלמנטרי המבוסס על שתי מפלגות, כמו בארה״ב, נשמע **הֶגְיוֹנִי**, אבל ישראל עוד לא מוכנה לכך.
A parliamentary structure based on two parties, as in the US, sounds **logical**, but Israel is not ready for it yet.

בשל המחסור במים, על הישראלים להיות **חֶסְכוֹנִיִּים** ביותר בצריכתם.
Because of shortage of water, the Israelis need to be **frugal** in its consumption.

Additional Examples in this Pattern

apathetic אֶדְשׁוֹנִי
gestational הֶרְיוֹנִי
frugal חֶסְכוֹנִי
(matter of) principle Adj עֶקְרוֹנִי

---

964. N +*i* Adj /*CaCeCani*, with reduplication (קַטְטָנִי)

f. sing/pl	m. sing/pl	Gloss
בַּרְרָנִית נ בַּרְרָנִיּוֹת	בַּרְרָנִי ז בַּרְרָנִיִּים	choosy, selective

As in all adjectives derived from noun with the suffix –*i*, the speaker wishes to denote the very quality of that noun being a particular one. The second and third root consonants are identical. The derivation is linear, בַּרְרָן+י, but may equally be attributed to the discontinuous *mishkal CaCeCani*. *e* is inserted to facilitate articulation of a sequence of two identical consonants.

Examples

עזריאל **בַּרְרָנִי** מאוד, והוריו חוששים שלעולם לא ימצא לו חברה מתאימה לחיים.
Azriel is very **choosy**, and his parents are worried that he would never find a partner he likes.

יש לחנה שכנה **חַטְטָנִית**, שיושבת כל היום אצל החלון ויודעת הכל על כולם.
Hannah has a **prying** (fem.) neighbor, who sits at her window all they long and know everything about everybody.

Additional Examples in this Pattern

hesitant הַסְסָנִי
prying חַטְטָנִי
hesitant חַשְׁשָׁנִי
wailing, sobbing יַבְבָנִי
vibrating רַטְטָנִי

---

965. N +*i* Adj /*CaCCi*

f. sing/pl	m. sing/pl	Gloss
כַּסְפִּית נ' כַּסְפִּיּוֹת	כַּסְפִּי ז' כַּסְפִּיִּים	financial, monetary

As in all adjectives derived from noun with the suffix –*i*, the speaker wishes to denote the very quality of that noun being a particular one. The derivation is linear, or semi-linear, from a segholate base, כֶּסֶף/כַּסְפּ+י > כַּסְפִּי, but may equally be attributed to the discontinuous *mishkal CaCCi*.

Examples

מכללות פרטיות הממומנות על ידי שכר לימוד ותרומות בלבד נסגרות לעיתים מסיבות **כַּסְפִּיּוֹת**.
Private colleges that are dependent solely on tuition and gifts are sometimes closed for **financial** reasons.

למרות כל העדויות המדעיות, יש עדיין מי שמאמין שלשימוש בפחם יש השפעה **אַפְסִית** על הסביבה.
In spite of all the scientific evidence, some still believe that the use of coal has an **insignificant** effect on the environment.

עכבישים מסוימים ועקרבים לא פחות **אַרְסִיִּים** מנחשים.
Certain spiders and scorpions are no less **poisonous** than snakes.

נרקיסיות היא מחלה **נַפְשִׁית** – אולי לא חמורה, אבל בכל זאת מחלה.
Narcissism is a **mental** illness – perhaps not severe, but still an illness.

ביטחון **עַצְמִי** הוא תכונה חשובה, אבל עודף ביטחון **עַצְמִי** מרגיז לפעמים.
Self-confidence is an important quality, but excess of it can be annoying.

Additional Examples in this Pattern

national; down-to-earth, worldly אַרְצִי
masculine, male Adj גַּבְרִי
corporeal, materialistic גַּשְׁמִי
canine, dog-like כַּלְבִּי
rocky סַלְעִי
arched, bowed, carved קַשְׁתִּי
on foot; infantry Adj. (military) רַגְלִי
lower תַּחְתִּי

---

966. N +*i* Adj /*CaCCi* > *CaCaCi* when the second root consonant is guttural

f. sing/pl	m. sing/pl	Gloss
יַחֲסִית נ׳ יַחֲסִיּוֹת	יַחֲסִי ז׳ יַחֲסִיִּים	relative

As in כַּסְפִּי above, but when the first root consonant is guttural and a *shva* is expected, that *shva* is replaced by *Hataf-pataH*. The derivation is linear, יַחַס+י, but may equally be attributed to the discontinuous *mishkal CaCCi* > *CaCaCi*.

Examples

באופן **יַחֲסִי**, מחירי הטיפול בשיניים בישראל הרבה פחות גבוהים מאשר בארה״ב.
In a **relative** manner, costs of dental treatment in Israel are much lower than in the US.

למרות שהוא בן יותר מארבעים, ההופעה שלו היא ממש **נַעֲרִית**.
Although he is over forty, his appearance is truly **boyish**.

Additional Examples in this Pattern

volcanic גַּעֲשִׁי
equipped with caterpillar tracks זַחֲלִי
of the Israel Defense Forces צַהֲ״לִי
toxic, poisonous רַעֲלִי

---

967. N +*i* Adj /*CaCCiCi*

f. sing/pl	m. sing/pl	Gloss
גַּרְעִינִית נ׳ גַּרְעִינִיּוֹת	גַּרְעִינִי ז׳ גַּרְעִינִיִּים	nuclear

As in all adjectives derived from noun with the suffix –*i*, the speaker wishes to denote the very quality of that noun being a particular one. The derivation is linear, but may equally be attributed to the discontinuous *mishkal CaCCiCi*.

Examples

ב-1970 נכנס לתוקפו הסכם בינלאומי על אי-הפצה של נשק **גַּרְעִינִי**. מספר מדינות לא חתמו עליו (הודו, ישראל, פקיסטאן, דרום סודאן), וצפון קוריאה פרשה ממנו.
In 1970 an international agreement on non-proliferation of **nuclear** weapons went into effect. A few nations were non-signatories (India, Israel, Pakistan, South Sudan), and North Korea withdrew from it.

Additional Examples in this Pattern

containing a stone (fruit) גַּלְעִינִי

---

968. N +*i* Adj /*CaCCaCi*

f. sing/pl	m. sing/pl	Gloss
אַכְזָרִית נ׳ אַכְזָרִיּוֹת	אַכְזָרִי ז׳ אַכְזָרִיִּים	cruel

As in all adjectives derived from noun with the suffix –*i*, the speaker wishes to denote the very quality of that noun being a particular one. The derivation is linear, אַכְזָר+י, but may equally be attributed to the discontinuous *mishkal CaCCaCi*.

Examples

היפנים בדרך כלל **אַכְזָרִיִּים** במלחמותיהם, אבל מגלים פתיחות לדתות שונות.
The Japanese are generally **cruel** in their wars, but are open to different religions.

אין אדם **אַחְרָאִי** כמשה.
There is nobody as **responsible** as Moshe is.

Additional Examples in this Pattern

barbaric בַּרְבָּרִי duck-like בַּרְוָזִי mousy עַכְבָּרִי

---

969. N +*i* Adj /*CaCCani*

f. sing/pl	m. sing/pl	Gloss
הַרְסָנִית נ׳ הַרְסָנִיּוֹת	הַרְסָנִי ז׳ הַרְסָנִיִּים	destructive

As in all adjectives derived from noun with the suffix –*i*, the speaker wishes to denote the very quality of that noun being a particular one. Note: most forms in this *mishkal* have *CaCCan* counterparts, which denote agents (which also serve as the base for the *CaCCani* forms), but in the spoken register also adjectives. Thus, רַגְזָן is 'angry person' at any speech register, but in the spoken register is used for the adjective 'angry' as well. In the higher register, only רַגְזָנִי denotes the adjective 'angry.' The derivation is linear, הַרְסָן+י, but may equally be attributed to the discontinuous *mishkal CaCCani*.

Examples

להטלת מכסי מגן עלולה להיות השפעה **הַרְסָנִית** על הכלכלה בשל מכסים מקבילים שיוטלו על ידי המדינות שייפגעו.

Imposing protective tariffs might have **destructive** effect on the economy owing to parallel tariffs that will be imposed by the affected countries.

עד מלחמת העולם הראשונה, ארה״ב קיימה מדיניות **בַּדְלָנִית**, ולא התערבה בסכסוכים בינלאומיים.

Till WWI, the US conducted an **isolationist** policy, and did not intervene in international conflicts.

פרט למבצעים מיוחדים, צה״ל מתרכז בעיקר במניעת פעילות **חַבְּלָנִית**.

Except for special operations, the IDF generally concentrates on preventing **terroristic** activities.

חברות ההַי-טֶק הישראליות הן מן **הַחַדְשָׁנִיּוֹת** בעולם.

The Israeli hi-tech companies are some of the most **innovative** in the world.

כשאומרים על מישהו שהוא **חַסְכָנִי** לפעמים מתכוונים לומר שהוא קמצן/**קַמְצָנִי**...

When saying of someone that he is **frugal/economical** one sometimes means that he is **miserly**...

יש אנשים **סַלְחָנִים** בעולם, אבל רבים מהם **הַנַּקְמָנִים**...

There are some **forgiving** people in the world, but those that are **vindictive** are more numerous…

Additional Examples in this Pattern

בַּדְחָנִי amusing
בַּטְלָנִי careless, loafing
בַּיְשָׁנִי shy
בַּכְיָנִי weeping, crying, cry-baby
בַּלְשָׁנִי linguistic
דַּיְקָנִי punctilious, meticulous
דַּרְשָׁנִי homiletical
וַתְּרָנִי indulgent, conceding, lenient
זַלְלָנִי gluttonous
חַיְכָנִי smiling
חַמְדָנִי avaricious
חַמְקָנִי evasive
חַנְפָנִי fawning
חַשְׁדָנִי suspicious (person)
חַתְרָנִי subversive
טַרְחָנִי bothersome
יַצְרָנִי productive
מַרְדָנִי rebellious
נַצְחָנִי argumentative
נַצְלָנִי exploitative
סַבְלָנִי patient Adj
סַחְטָנִי extortive
סַפְקָנִי skeptic
סַקְרָנִי curious
סַרְבָנִי insubordinate
עַצְבָּנִי restless, nervous
עַקְשָׁנִי stubborn

---

970. N +*i* Adj /*CaCCani* > *CaCaCani*, when the second root consonant is guttural

f. sing/pl	m. sing/pl	Gloss
צַעֲקָנִית נ׳ צַעֲקָנִיּוֹת	צַעֲקָנִי ז׳ צַעֲקָנִיִּים	loud, noisy

As in הַרְסָנִי above, except that the second root consonant is guttural, and when a *shva* is expected with it, that *shva* is replaced by *Hataf-pataH*. The derivation is linear, צַעֲקָן+י, but may equally be attributed to the discontinuous *mishkal CaCCani* > *CaCaCani*.

Examples

המוסיקה ה**צַעֲקָנִית** מאוד בחתונות ישראליות מעבירה אותי על דעתי.
The very **loud** music in Israeli weddings drives me nuts.

נראה לי שקביעות **טַהֲרָנִיּוֹת** לעיתים נובעות מראיית תופעות של הלשון המדוברת כשגויות כאשר הן חורגות מן המקובל במשלב הגבוה.
It seems to me that **puristic** statements sometimes stem from seeing spoken phenomena as erroneous when they deviate from what is acceptable in the higher registers.

Additional Examples in this Pattern

(always) anxious, worried דַּאֲגָנִי
furious זַעֲפָנִי
angry, hot-tempered כַּעֲסָנִי
ridiculing לַעֲגָנִי
noisy רַעֲשָׁנִי

---

971. N +*i* Adj /*CaCCati*

f. sing/pl	m. sing/pl	Gloss
אַבְקָתִית נ׳ אַבְקָתִיּוֹת	אַבְקָתִי ז׳ אַבְקָתִיִּים	powdery

As in all adjectives derived from noun with the suffix –*i*, the speaker wishes to denote the very quality of that noun being a particular one. The derivation is linear, אַבְקָה/ת+י, but may equally be attributed to the discontinuous *mishkal CaCCati*.

Examples

לתת **אַבְקָתִי** משמש כתוספת או בסיס במתכונים רבים של בישול בירה.
Powdery malt serves as an additive or as base in many recipes for producing beer.

Additional Examples in this Pattern

carbonated פַּחְמָתִי

---

972. N +*i* Adj /*CaCConi*

f. sing/pl	m. sing/pl	Gloss
אַדְמוֹנִית נ׳ אַדְמוֹנִיּוֹת	אַדְמוֹנִי ז׳ אַדְמוֹנִיִּים	redheaded

As in all adjectives derived from noun with the suffix –*i*, the speaker wishes to denote the very quality of that noun being a particular one. The derivation is linear, אַדְמוֹן+י, but may equally be attributed to the discontinuous *mishkal CaCConi*.

Examples

״ליגת ה**אַדְמוֹנִיִּים** (או: אדומי השיער)״ הוא סיפור שרלוק הולמס קצר שכתב סר ארתור קונן דויל.
"The **Red-Headed** League" is a Sherlock Holmes short story written by Sir Arthur Conan Doyle.

ההבדלים ה**רַעְיוֹנִיִּים/רַעֲיוֹנִיִּים** בין סוציאליזם לקומוניזם הם הבדלים משמעותיים, אבל בארה״ב, למשל, אנשים רבים חושבים שהם היינו הך.
The **ideological** differences between socialism and communism are significant, but in the US, for instance, many people think of them as one and the same.

Additional Examples in this Pattern

ancient קַדְמוֹנִי chestnut (color) עַרְמוֹנִי lanky גַּמְלוֹנִי

---

973. N +*i* Adj /*CaCCuti*

f. sing/pl	m. sing/pl	Gloss
יַלְדוּתִית נ׳ יַלְדוּתִיּוֹת	יַלְדוּתִי ז׳ יַלְדוּתִיִּים	childish

As in all adjectives derived from noun with the suffix –*i*, the speaker wishes to denote the very quality of that noun being a particular one. The derivation is linear, יַלְדוּת+י, but may equally be attributed to the discontinuous *mishkal CaCCuti*.

Examples

יצחק הוא כבר בן שלוש-עשרה, אבל עדיין מאוד **יַלְדוּתִי**.
Yitzhak is already thirteen years old, but he is still very **childish**.

אם מורה אינו נוהג באופן **סַמְכוּתִי** בכיתה, אין לו הרבה סיכוי לקיים משמעת נאותה.
If a teacher does not behave in an **authoritative** manner in class, he has little chance of maintaining discipline.

Additional Examples in this Pattern

intrinsic עַצְמוּתִי infantile יַנְקוּתִי integrated; united אַחְדוּתִי

---

974. N +*i* Adj /*CaCCuti* > *CaCaCuti*, when the second root consonant is guttural

f. sing/pl	m. sing/pl	Gloss
יַהֲדוּתִית נ׳ יַהֲדוּתִיּוֹת	יַהֲדוּתִי ז׳ יַהֲדוּתִיִּים	of Judaism

As in יַלְדוּתִי above, except that the second root consonant is guttural, and when a *shva* is expected with it, that *shva* is replaced by *Hataf-pataH*. The derivation is linear, יַהֲדוּת+י, but may equally be attributed to the discontinuous *mishkal CaCCuti* > *CaCaCuti*.

Examples

חלק ניכר מן המצוות הן אוניברסליות, ואין בהן גוון **יַהֲדוּתִי** נפרד.
Some of the commandments are universal, and do not contain any "hue" **of Judaism** per se.

---

975. N +*i* Adj /*CaCCeCani, with reduplication*

f. sing/pl	m. sing/pl	Gloss
פַּטְפְּטָנִית נ׳ פַּטְפְּטָנִיּוֹת	פַּטְפְּטָנִי ז׳ פַּטְפְּטָנִיִּים	chatterbox Adj

As in all adjectives derived from noun with the suffix –*i*, the speaker wishes to denote the very quality of that noun being a particular one. The first and second root consonants are reduplicated in positions three and four, respectively. The derivation is linear, פַּטְפְּטָן+י, but may equally be attributed to the discontinuous *mishkal CaCCeCani* (קַטְקְטָנִי).

Examples

ברחוב שבו גדלתי בישראל הייתה לנו שכנה **פַּטְפְּטָנִית** שהתעקשה לדבר בלי סוף עם אימא מעבר לגדר ולא נתנה לה לעבוד.
In the street where I grew up in Israel there was a **chatterbox** neighbor who insists on talking to talk with Mom incessantly across the fence and would not let her work.

בישראל, וכן בקליפורניה, מזהירים בפני שימוש **בַּזְבְּזָנִי** במים, בעיקר בשנות בצורת.
In Israel, as well as in California, they warn against **wasteful** use of water, especially in years of drought.

היה לי באחת מכיתותיי סטודנט **נַמְנְמָנִי**, שהדרך היחידה להעיר אותו הייתה לזרוק עליו חתיכת גיר.
I had a **drowsy** student in one of my classes; the only way to wake him up was to throw a piece of chalk at him.

אני זוכר סיפור מילדותי על טיפוס **רַבְרְבָנִי** שסיפר שהרג חמישה במכה אחת. אח״כ הסתבר שהתכוון לחמישה זבובים במכת מצלף-זבובים אחת...
I remember a story from my childhood about a **boastful** character who reported that he killed five in one blow. It later turned out that he meant five flies in a single swat…

Additional Examples in this Pattern

noisy, clattering טַרְטְרָנִי
contentious סַכְסְכָנִי
cursory רַפְרְפָנִי
hesitant, stammering גַּמְגְּמָנִי
accurate, punctilious דַּקְדְּקָנִי
contemptuous, belittling זַלְזְלָנִי

---

976. N +*i* Adj /*CaCCaCi*, with reduplication, and *pataH* plus *dagesh*

f. sing/pl	m. sing/pl	Gloss
קַשְׂקַשִּׂית נ׳ קַשְׂקַשִּׂיּוֹת	קַשְׂקַשִּׂי ז׳ קַשְׂקַשִּׂיִּים	scaly, flaky

As in פִּטְפְּטָנִי above, but without the added *n*. The derivation is linear, קַשְׂקַשׂ+י, but may equally be attributed to the discontinuous *mishkal CaCCaCi*, with reduplication of the first and second root consonants in third and fourth position, respectively (קְטַקְטִי). The *pataH* of the third consonant is followed by a *dagesh forte* in the fourth.

Examples

סרטן העור מופיע בצורות שונות. לעיתים הוא נראה כמו רובד **קַשְׂקַשִּׂי** מקומי.
Skin cancer may have a few manifestations. Sometimes it looks like a **scaly** local layer.

Additional Examples in this Pattern

wheel-like, round גַּלְגַּלִּי

---

977. N +*i* Adj /*CaCiCi*

f. sing/pl	m. sing/pl	Gloss
טַפִּילִית נ׳ טַפִּילִיּוֹת	טַפִּילִי ז׳ טַפִּילִיִּים	parasitic

As in all adjectives derived from noun with the suffix –*i*, the speaker wishes to denote the very quality of that noun being a particular one. The derivation is linear, טַפִּיל+י, but may equally be attributed to the discontinuous *mishkal CaCiCi.*

Examples

קשה להאמין שצמח יפהפה כמו הסחלב (אורכידאה) הוא צמח **טַפִּילִי**.
It is hard to believe that a beautiful plant like the orchid is **parasitic**.

Additional Examples in this Pattern

chivalrous, gallant; knightly אַבִּירִי

---

978. N +*i* Adj /*CaCaCti*

f. sing/pl	m. sing/pl	Gloss
דַּלַּקְתִּית נ׳ דַּלַּקְתִּיּוֹת	דַּלַּקְתִּי ז׳ דַּלַּקְתִּיִּים	inflammatory

As in all adjectives derived from noun with the suffix –*i*, the speaker wishes to denote the very quality of that noun being a particular one. The derivation is linear, or quasi-linear, from a segholate base, דַּלֶּקֶת/דַּלַּק(ת) + י < דַּלַּקְתִּי, but may equally be attributed to the discontinuous *mishkal CaCaCti.*

Examples

הניתוח להסרת הגידול הממאיר התעכב בגלל התפתחות **דַּלַּקְתִּית** באזור המיועד לניתוח.
The operation of removing the malignant tumor was postponed owing to **inflammatory** development in the area of the proposed operation.

Additional Examples in this Pattern

humped דַּבַּשְׁתִּי   of land; continental יַבַּשְׁתִּי

---

979. N +*i* Adj /*CaCaCi*

f. sing/pl	m. sing/pl	Gloss
בַּלָּשִׁית נ׳ בַּלָּשִׁיּוֹת	בַּלָּשִׁי ז׳ בַּלָּשִׁיִּים	detective Adj

As in all adjectives derived from noun with the suffix –*i*, the speaker wishes to denote the very quality of that noun being a particular one. The derivation is linear, בַּלָּשׁ+י, but may equally be attributed to the discontinuous *mishkal CaCaCi.*

Examples

קשה לי להירדם לפני שאני קורא שעה/שעתיים במיטה, בד״כ רומן **בַּלָּשִׁי**.
It is hard for me to fall asleep before I read for an hour or two, generally a **detective** novel.

אומרים שההתנהגות ה**צַּבָּרִית** מתבטאת בעיקר באופן דיבור פתוח ולעיתים ישיר מדיי.
They say that the behavior of the **Israeli-born** expresses itself mainly in frank and overly direct fashion.

מספר לא קטן של דתיים **קַנָּאִיִּים** מדברים בניית בית מקדש שלישי והקרבת קורבנות בו.
A significant number of **fanatic** orthodox (believers) are talking of building a Third Temple and renewing offering sacrifices in it.

Special Expressions

young (**very small**) carrot גזר **גַּמָּדִי**

Additional Examples in this Pattern

legendary אַגָּדִי   soldier-like חַיָּלִי
tiny, miniscule גַּמָּדִי   primeval, ancient קַמָּאִי

---

980. N +*i* Adj /*CoCCi*

f. sing/pl	m. sing/pl	Gloss
חָדְשִׁית נ׳ חָדְשִׁיּוֹת	חָדְשִׁי ז׳ חָדְשִׁיִּים	monthly

As in all adjectives derived from noun with the suffix –*i*, the speaker wishes to denote the very quality of that noun being a particular one. The derivation is linear, or semi-linear, from a segholate base, חֹדֶשׁ/חָדְשׁ+י < חָדְשִׁי, but may equally be attributed to the discontinuous *mishkal CoCCi*. In a small number of forms the agentive suffix ָן+ is also added: חֹמֶר+ָן+י < חָמְרָנִי, גֹּלֶם+ָן+י < גָּלְמָנִי. They will not be treated as a separate (*CoCCani*) pattern here.

Examples

יש מוסדות המשלמים משכורת **חָדְשִׁית**, ואחרים משלמים פעם בשבועיים.
Some institutions pay a **monthly** salary, others pay on a biweekly basis.

מכיוון שאין בישראל הרבה אוצרות טבע, עליה לייבא כמויות גדולות של חומרים **גָּלְמִיִּים**.
Since Israel does not have a lot of natural resources, it must import large quantities of **raw** materials.

בדרך כלל, מצבו ה**חָמְרִי** של כל עובד משתפר עם הגיל ועם הוותק בעבודה.
Generally, the **material** condition of most workers improves with age and with seniority on the job.

חלק מן ההמנון הישראלי: "עוד לא אבדה תקוותנו להיות עם **חָפְשִׁי** בארצנו..."
Part of the Israeli national anthem: "We have not lost our hope to be a **free** nation in our country…"

מזג האוויר ה**חָרְפִּי** מקשה מאוד על החיים במערב התיכון השנה.
The **wintry** weather makes life quite difficult in the Mid-West this year.

Additional Examples in this Pattern

horizontal אָפְקִי	polar; opposite קָטְבִּי
foreign נָכְרִי	rooted; deep-seated שָׁרְשִׁי
rear Adj עָרְפִּי	content-related תָּכְנִי

---

981. N +*i* Adj /*CoCCi* = *CoCoCi*, when the second root consonant is guttural

f. sing/pl	m. sing/pl	Gloss
תָּאֳרִית נ׳	תָּאֳרִי ז׳	titular
תָּאֳרִיּוֹת	תָּאֳרִיִּים	

As in חָדְשִׁי above, except that the second root consonant is guttural, and when a *shva* is expected with it, that *shva* is replaced by *Hataf-kamats*. The derivation is linear, or semi-linear, from a segholate base, תֹּאַר/תָּאְר+י > תָּאֳר+י, but may equally be attributed to the discontinuous *mishkal CoCCi* > *CoCoCi*.

Examples

במשך שנים, תפקיד הנשיא בישראל נתפס כ**תָּאֳרִי** מעיקרו, אבל החל בכהונתו של שמעון פרס גדלה מעורבותו של הנשיא בפוליטיקה ובענייני מדינה אחרים.
For years, the role of the President in Israel was regarded as essentially **titular**, but starting with Shim`on Peres the President's involvement in politics and in other state matters has increased.

למיטב זכרוני, כשהיינו ילדים, במונח **גָּעֳלִי** השתמשו רק בנות – אף פעם לא בנים...
If I am not mistaken, when we were kids, the term גָּעֳלִי '**disgusting**' was only used by girls, never by boys.

Additional Examples in this Pattern

procedural נָהֳלִי of verb פָּעֳלִי

---

982. N +*i* Adj /*CaCuti*

f. sing/pl	m. sing/pl	Gloss
גָּלוּתִית נ׳ גָּלוּתִיּוֹת	גָּלוּתִי ז׳ גָּלוּתִיִּים	diasporic

As in all adjectives derived from noun with the suffix –*i*, the speaker wishes to denote the very quality of that noun being a particular one. The derivation is linear, גָּלוּת+י, but may equally be attributed to the discontinuous *mishkal CaCuCi*.

Examples

לחלוצים בוני המדינה היה חשוב שילדיהם יהיו שונים מן היהודים ה**גָּלוּתִיִּים** שאבותיהם היו במשך מאות שנים. אחת התוצאות הייתה שכאשר ניצולי שואה צעירים הגיעו ארצה, הדור הישראלי הצעיר לא תמיד התייחס אליהם כשווים.

For the pioneers who established the State of Israel it was important that their children be different from the **diasporic** Jews their fathers and forefathers had been for hundreds of years. One result was that when young Holocaust survivors arrived in Israel, the young Israeli generation did not always treat them as equals.

Additional Examples in this Pattern

contemplative הָגוּתִי

---

983. N +*i* Adj /*CoCeCani* with identical second and third consonants

f. sing/pl	m. sing/pl	Gloss
חוֹבְבָנִית נ׳ חוֹבְבָנִיּוֹת	חוֹבְבָנִי ז׳ חוֹבְבָנִיִּים	amateurish

As in all adjectives derived from noun with the suffix –*i*, the speaker wishes to denote the very quality of that noun being a particular one. The derivation is linear, חוֹבְבָן+י, but may equally be attributed to the discontinuous *mishkal CoCeCani*, in which the second and third root consonants are identical (קוֹטְטָנִי).

Examples

הכדורגל פופולרי מאוד בישראל, אך נבחרת ישראל מעולם לא הגיעה לשלב מתקדם בתחרויות ה״מונדיאל״. הסיבה: השחקנים **חוֹבְבָנִיִּים** ונהנתנים, ופשוט בקושי מתאמנים.

Soccer is very popular in Israel, but the Israeli team never reached any advanced stage in the World Cup games. The reason: the players are **amateurish** and hedonistic, and barely train.

Additional Examples in this Pattern

hesitant, indecisive חוֹשְׁשָׁנִי

---

984. N +*i* Adj /*CoCCi*

f. sing/pl	m. sing/pl	Gloss
נוֹזְלִית נ׳ נוֹזְלִיּוֹת	נוֹזְלִי ז׳ נוֹזְלִיִּים	liquid Adj

As in all adjectives derived from noun with the suffix –*i*, the speaker wishes to denote the very quality of that noun being a particular one. The derivation is linear, with automatic vowel elision, נוֹזְלִי < י + נוֹזֵל, but may equally be attributed to the discontinuous *mishkal CoCCi*.

Examples

כדי לעבד מתכות בצורות ותבניות שונות, יש לחממן בטמפרטורות גבוהות כדי לרככן או להביאן למצב **נוֹזְלִי**.
In order to shape metals in desired forms or molds, one needs to either subject them to high temperatures so as to soften them, or to transform them into **liquid** state.

המצב הכלכלי ה**נוֹכְחִי** של ונצואלה הוא בכי רע.
The **present** economic condition of Venezuela is catastrophic.

Additional Examples in this Pattern

arterial עוֹרְקִי	subjective (syntax) נוֹשְׂאִי	of jubilee יוֹבְלִי

---

985. N +*i* Adj /*CoCCani*

f. sing/pl	m. sing/pl	Gloss
חוֹלְמָנִית נ׳ חוֹלְמָנִיּוֹת	חוֹלְמָנִי ז׳ חוֹלְמָנִיִּים	dreamy

As in all adjectives derived from noun with the suffix –*i*, the speaker wishes to denote the very quality of that noun being a particular one. The derivation may be linear, with automatic vowel deletion, with an added *n* to split the vowel sequence, חוֹלֵם+ָנִי, but is more likely to be attributed to the discontinuous *mishkal CoCCani*.

Examples

יעקב פועל טוב, אבל בעבודה אומרים שכאשר אין לחץ הוא נעשה **חוֹלְמָנִי**.
Yaakov is a good worker, but at the job they say that if there is no pressure, he becomes **dreamy**.

אין כל ספק בנאמנותו של כלב לאדונו, אבל חתול עלול לעיתים להיות **בּוֹגְדָנִי**.
There is no doubt about the loyalty of a dog to his master, but a cat may be **treacherous** on occasion.

בנוסף לחומות, בתי סוהר בדרך כלל מוקפים גם בתַיִל **דּוֹקְרָנִי** בראש החומות.
In addition to walls, prisons are generally also surrounded by **barbed** wire on the top of the walls.

ראש הממשלה תקף את מפיקי הכתבה **החוֹשְׂפָנִית**, וטען כי היא נועדה לפגוע בסיכוייו להיבחר מחדש.
The Prime Minister attacked the producers of the **revealing** investigative report, claiming that it was intended to damage his prospects of winning re-election.

מעניין שחסידי קבוצה דתית פחות **סוֹבְלָנִיִּים** כלפי מאמיני קבוצה אחרת בתוך אותה חברה מאשר כלפי חברים של דת אחרת.
It is interesting that followers of one religious group are less **tolerant** towards followers of another group within the same society than they are towards members of a different religion.

Additional Examples in this Pattern

tearful, teary דוֹמְעָנִי
aggressive, destructive דוֹרְסָנִי
gluttonous זוֹלְלָנִי
penetrating; invasive חוֹדְרָנִי
swampy, marshy, boggy טוֹבְעָנִי
pestering, nagging טוֹרְדָנִי
predatory טוֹרְפָנִי
reproachful נוֹזְפָנִי
sarcastic עוֹקְצָנִי
harmful; offensive פּוֹגְעָנִי
intrusive, invasive פּוֹלְשָׁנִי
grating צוֹרְמָנִי
vivacious קוֹפְצָנִי
aggressive, belligerent, warring; combative תּוֹבְעָנִי

---

986. N +*i* Adj /*CoCCani* = *CoCaCani*, when the second root consonant is guttural

f. sing/pl	m. sing/pl	Gloss
לוֹחֲמָנִית נ׳ לוֹחֲמָנִיּוֹת	לוֹחֲמָנִי ז׳ לוֹחֲמָנִיִּים	aggressive, combative

As in חוֹלְמָנִי above, when the second root consonant is guttural; when a *shva* is expected with it, that *shva* is replaced by *Hataf-pataH*. The derivation may be linear, with automatic vowel change to a *Hataf-pataH* and an *n* splitting a two-vowel sequence, but is more likely to be attributed to the discontinuous *mishkal CoCCani* > *CoCaCani*.

Examples

אהוד הוא טיפוס **לוֹחֲמָנִי** ; אם אתה לא מסכים עם דעותיו הפוליטיות, הוא יוצא מגדרו.
Ehud is an **aggressive** person; if you do not agree with his views on political matters, he goes nuts.

Additional Examples in this Pattern

slow, crawling Lit. זוֹחֲלָנִי
crushing מוֹחֲצָנִי
sweeping סוֹחֲפָנִי

---

987. N +*i* Adj /*CoCi*, second root consonant is *y*

f. sing/pl	m. sing/pl	Gloss
חוֹזִית נ׳ חוֹזִיּוֹת	חוֹזִי ז׳ חוֹזִיִּים	contractual

As in all adjectives derived from noun with the suffix –*i*, the speaker wishes to denote the very quality of that noun being a particular one. The roots of these forms have a final *y*. The derivation is linear, חוֹזֶה+י with the *seghol* elided, but may equally be attributed to the discontinuous *mishkal CoCi*.

Examples

בימים אלה, כשאדם עשיר נושא בחורה הרבה יותר צעירה ממנו, יש ביניהם לעיתים קרובות התקשרות **חוֹזִית**.

These days, when a rich man marries a much younger woman, there often exists between them a **contractual** agreement.

Additional Examples in this Pattern

parental הוֹרִי	of scout צוֹפִי

---

988. N +*i* Adj /*CoCi*, middle root consonant is *w*

f. sing/pl	m. sing/pl	Gloss
יוֹמִית נ׳ יוֹמִיּוֹת	יוֹמִי ז׳ יוֹמִיִּים	daily

As in all adjectives derived from noun with the suffix –*i*, the speaker wishes to denote the very quality of that noun being a particular one. The roots of these forms have a middle *w*. The derivation is linear, יוֹם+י, but may equally be attributed to the discontinuous *mishkal CoCi*.

Examples

העיתון **היּוֹמִי** הנפוץ בארץ הוא ״ידיעות אחרונות״.

The **daily** newspaper with the highest distribution in Israel is "Yedioth Aharonot."

כאשר בונים בית על קרקע **חוֹלִית**, תמיד יש חשש אח״כ שייווצרו סדקים בקירות.

When one builds a house on **sandy** soil, there is always the worry about cracks being formed in the walls.

מנשה יצא בשליחות **סוֹדִית** לחו״ל, ועד היום לא מספר מה קרה שם.

Menashe went on a **secret** mission abroad, and to this day has never discussed what happened there.

ה״קונקורד״ היה מטוס הנוסעים הראשון שטס במהירות על-**קוֹלִית**, אבל לאחר תאונה רצינית הוצא מן השירות.

The "Concorde" was the first super-**sonic** passenger plane, after a serious accident it was taken out of service.

Additional Examples in this Pattern

generational דּוֹרִי	dermal עוֹרִי
coastal חוֹפִי	ape-like קוֹפִי
final סוֹפִי	thorny קוֹצִי

---

989. N +*i* Adj /*CoCani*

f. sing/pl	m. sing/pl	Gloss
קוֹלָנִית נ׳ קוֹלָנִיּוֹת	קוֹלָנִי ז׳ קוֹלָנִיִּים	loud

As in all adjectives derived from noun with the suffix –*i*, the speaker wishes to denote the very quality of that noun being a particular one. The roots of these forms have a middle *w*. The derivation may be linear, with an added *n* splitting a two-vowel sequence, קוֹל+ָני, but may equally be attributed to the discontinuous *mishkal CoCani*.

Examples

בשכונות מסוימות בניו יורק נשמעת לעיתים מוסיקה **קוֹלָנִית** מאוד ממכוניות חולפות.
In some neighborhoods in New York City, very **loud** music sometimes blares out of passing cars.

קשה מאוד למשפחות של חולים **סוֹפָנִיִּים**, כשכולם יודעים שלא נשאר הרבה זמן...
It is very difficult for families with **terminal** patients, when they all know that there is little time left...

Additional Examples in this Pattern

muddy בּוֹצָנִי　　　thorny, prickly קוֹצָנִי

---

990. N +*i* Adj /*CuCi*

f. sing/pl	m. sing/pl	Gloss
זוּגִית נ׳ זוּגִיּוֹת	זוּגִי ז׳ זוּגִיִּים	even (number); dual

As in all adjectives derived from noun with the suffix –*i*, the speaker wishes to denote the very quality of that noun being a particular one. The roots of these forms have a middle *w*. The derivation is linear, זוג+י, but may equally be attributed to the discontinuous *mishkal CuCi*.

Examples

באירופה ובישראל המספרים ה**זוּגִיִּים** של הבתים עולים בצדו הימני של הכביש; בארה״ב נראה שבמקרים מסוימים המספרים האי-**זוּגִיִּים** הם שעולים בצד ימין.
In Israel and in Europe the **even** house numbers of the houses rise on the right-hand side of the road; in the US, it seems that in certain cases it is the odd ("un**even**") numbers that rise on the right-hand side.

במכשיר הזה יש להכניס את הסוללות בסדר **טוּרִי**.
In this instrument one needs to insert the batteries **in a row**.

בבית הספר התיכון משה היה תלמיד **שׁוּלִי**, אבל כשהגיע לאוניברסיטה נתגלו בו כישורים מיוחדים, והיום הוא אחד מעורכי הדין המצליחים ביותר בישראל.
At high school Moshe was a **marginal** student, but when he got to the university some special talents surfaced in him, and today he is one of the most successful lawyers in Israel.

Additional Examples in this Pattern

dwarfish גּוּצִי
lumpy גּוּשִׁי
thread-like חוּטִי
categorial סוּגִי
equine סוּסִי

---

991. N +*i* Adj *tCuCati*

f. sing/pl	m. sing/pl	Gloss
תְּקוּפָתִית נ׳ תְּקוּפָתִיּוֹת	תְּקוּפָתִי ז׳ תְּקוּפָתִיִּים	periodic

As in all adjectives derived from noun with the suffix –*i*, the speaker wishes to denote the very quality of that noun being a particular one. The roots of these forms have a middle *w*. The derivation is linear, תְּקוּפָה/ת+י, with the silent *h* reverting to *t*, but may equally be attributed to the discontinuous *mishkal tCuCati*.

Examples

החלפת השמן ה**תְּקוּפָתִית** המומלצת למרבית המכוניות היא כל שלושה חודשים.
The **periodic** oil change recommended for most cars is every three months.

רוב הרופאים היום מסכימים אודות הערך ה**תְּזוּנָתִי** של גזר, רימון, סלק, תות-שדה שלא עברו ריסוס.
Most doctors today agree about the **nutritional** value of carrots, pomegranates, beets, strawberries that were organically grown (no pesticides).

אחת השאלות החשובות בהתפתחות תינוקות היא איך לטפל בילדים בעלי קשיים **תְּחוּשָׁתִיִּים** ומוטוריים.
One of the important questions in baby development is how to treat children with **sensory** and motor difficulties.

Additional Examples in this Pattern

rational, intellectual תְּבוּנָתִי
reactive תְּגוּבָתִי
fluctuating; volatile תְּנוּדָתִי
motor Adj; of a movement תְּנוּעָתִי
exhibitory תְּצוּגָתִי
formational תְּצוּרָתִי

---

992. N +*i* Adj /*tiCCoCti*

f. sing/pl	m. sing/pl	Gloss
תִּקְשָׁרְתִּית נ׳ תִּקְשָׁרְתִּיּוֹת	תִּקְשָׁרְתִּי ז׳ תִּקְשָׁרְתִּיִּים	communicative

As in all adjectives derived from noun with the suffix –*i*, the speaker wishes to denote the very quality of that noun being a particular one. The derivation is linear, or quasi-linear, from a segholate base, תִּקְשֹׁרֶת/תִּקְשָׁרְת+י > תִּקְשָׁרְתִּי, but may equally be attributed to the discontinuous *mishkal tiCCoCti*.

Examples

יכולות **תִּקְשָׁרְתִּיּוֹת** נמוכות עלולות לפגוע ביכולת התפקוד של האדם בחיי היום יום.
Insufficient **communicative** capabilities may negatively affect a person's ability to function in daily life.

Additional Examples in this Pattern

orchestral תִּזְמָרְתִּי

---

993. N +*i* Adj /*tiCCuCi*

f. sing/pl	m. sing/pl	Gloss
תִּפְעוּלִית נ׳ תִּפְעוּלִיּוֹת	תִּפְעוּלִי ז׳ תִּפְעוּלִיִּים	operational

As in all adjectives derived from noun with the suffix –*i*, the speaker wishes to denote the very quality of that noun being a particular one. The derivation is linear, תִּפְעוּל+י, but may equally be attributed to the discontinuous *mishkal tiCCuCi*.

Examples

רווח **תִּפְעוּלִי** הוא הרווח המתקבל מכלל הפעילות העסקית, לאחר שהופחתו כל ההוצאות בגין הפעלת העסק.
Operational profit is the profit generated by the total business activity, after all relevant expenses have been deducted.

Additional Examples in this Pattern

functional תִּפְקוּדִי

---

994. N +*i* Adj /*taCCiCi*

f. sing/pl	m. sing/pl	Gloss
תַּקְצִיבִית נ׳ תַּקְצִיבִיּוֹת	תַּקְצִיבִי ז׳ תַּקְצִיבִיִּים	budgetary

As in all adjectives derived from noun with the suffix –*i*, the speaker wishes to denote the very quality of that noun being a particular one. The derivation is linear, תַּקְצִיב+י, but may equally be attributed to the discontinuous *mishkal taCCiCi*.

Examples

לא פעם סוגרים חוגים באוניברסיטה בשל מספר נמוך של תלמידים וקשיים **תַּקְצִיבִיִּים**.
Occasionally they close down university departments owing to declining enrollments and **budgetary** difficulties.

המבנה ה**תַּחְבִּירִי** של המשפט בעברית שונה משמעותית ממבנהו באנגלית.
The **syntactic** structure of the sentence in Hebrew is significantly different from its structure in English.

Additional Examples in this Pattern

precedential תַּקְדִּימִי

---

995. N +*i* Adj /*taCCiti*

f. sing/pl	m. sing/pl	Gloss
תַּמְצִיתִית נ׳ תַּמְצִיתִיּוֹת	תַּמְצִיתִי ז׳ תַּמְצִיתִיִּים	concise, essential

As in all adjectives derived from noun with the suffix –*i*, the speaker wishes to denote the very quality of that noun being a particular one. The derivation is linear, תַּמְצִית+י, but may equally be attributed to the discontinuous *mishkal taCCiti*.

Examples

תקציר של הצעה להרצאה בכנס חייב להיות **תַּמְצִיתִי** וקצר, ובכל זאת להבהיר את התיזה ודרכי המחקר.
An abstract of a paper proposal for a conference needs to be **concise** and short, while still stating the main thesis and research methodology.

Additional Examples in this Pattern

purposeful; realistic תַּכְלִיתִי

---

996. N +*i* Adj *taCCuCati* = *taCaCuCati* when the first root consonant is guttural

f. sing/pl	m. sing/pl	Gloss
תַּעֲמוּלָתִית נ׳ תַּעֲמוּלָתִיּוֹת	תַּעֲמוּלָתִי ז׳ תַּעֲמוּלָתִיִּים	propagandic

As in all adjectives derived from noun with the suffix –*i*, the speaker wishes to denote the very quality of that noun being a particular one. The derivation is linear, with the silent *h* reverting to *t*, תַּעֲמוּלָה/ת+י, but may equally be attributed to the discontinuous *mishkal taCCuCati* > *taCaCuCati*. When the first root consonant is a guttural and a *shva* is expected with it, that *shva* is replaced by *Hataf-pataH*.

Examples

לקראת הבחירות, השידורים ה**תַּעֲמוּלָתִיִּים** באמצעי התקשורת יכולים להוציא כל אדם מדעתו.
Towards the elections, the **propagandic** podcasts in the media can drive anybody crazy.

Additional Examples in this Pattern

related to employment תַּעֲסוּקָתִי

Patterns with dual only or with plural only

997. Dual only

our/your/their	my/your/his/her	const.	Gloss	Plural
מִשְׁקָפֵינוּ/**מִשְׁקְפֵי**כֶם/כֶן/הֶם/הֶן	**מִשְׁקָ**פַי/פֶיךָ/פַיִךְ/פָיו/פֶיהָ	מִשְׁקְפֵי-	eyeglasses	מִשְׁקָפַיִם ז׳

The dual form in Hebrew is marked by the suffix *-áyim*. Theoretically, there exists a dual counterpart of any Hebrew noun, but unlike the dual category in Arabic, which is automatic-productive, the productivity of the dual category in Hebrew is limited in use (at least in spoken Hebrew) – especially to time terms (שָׁעָה 'hour' ~ שְׁעָתַיִם 'two hours,' יוֹם 'day' ~ יוֹמַיִם 'two days,' שָׁבוּעַ 'week' ~ שְׁבוּעַיִם 'two weeks, fortnight,' etc.), dual body parts (יָד 'hand' ~ יָדַיִם 'two hands,' עַיִן 'eye' ~ עֵינַיִם 'two eyes,' etc.), dual clothing items (נַעַל 'shoe' ~ נַעֲלַיִם 'pair of shoes,' גֶּרֶב 'sock' ~ גַּרְבַּיִם 'pair of socks'), and a few frequent isolated items that often require a dual counterpart (פַּעַם 'once' ~ פַּעֲמַיִם 'twice,' דֶּלֶת 'door' ~ דְּלָתַיִם 'two doors, as in 'closed doors at court,' etc.). Nevertheless, there are some dual forms, not many, that stand on their own and are not automatically derived from the singular. Even in an item like אוֹפַנַּיִם 'bicycle,' a form clearly derived from אוֹפַן 'wheel, cycle,' the item אוֹפַנַּיִם is not a simple combining of two wheels, but rather a vehicle having two wheels. It is possible to somehow sub-classify into *mishkalim* here as well, e.g., *miCCaCáyim* (מִגְזָזַיִם, מִכְנָסַיִם, מִסְפָּרַיִם, מִשְׁקָפַיִם etc.), but since the common meaning, if it exists at all, is not transparent or particularly important, we will not divide these forms into sub-*mishkalim*. An interesting phenomenon: sometimes "back formation" occurs in dual forms in spoken Hebrew, but even then, the meaning is not unambiguous: מִכְנָס can be an alternative form of מִכְנָסַיִם 'trousers,' or can mean part of it, 'trouser.' Alonside שׁוּלַיִם 'edge; margins,' שׁוּל has also become acceptable lately, particularly for one side of the road margin, or 'shoulder.' As for declension, when it is found in actual use, it follows the plural suffixes (one theory is that the plural and dual suffixes are etymologically-related anyway).

Examples

הראייה המשתנה עם הגיל מצריכה החלפת **מִשְׁקָפַיִם** מדי פעם.
With sight changing with age, new **eyeglasses** are required a few times.

ברוב הערים בארה״ב יש בכבישים מסלולים מיוחדים ל**אוֹפַנַּיִם**.
In most cities in the US there are special **bicycle** lanes in the streets.

היה לי תלמיד סקוטי קשוח שאפילו בקור הגדול בחורף הסתובב בחוץ עם **מִכְנָסַיִם** קצרים.
I had a tough Scottish student who even in the greatest cold in the winter would walk outside with short **pants**.

שכמכינים בשר על הגריל, רצוי מאוד להשתמש ב**מֶלְקָחַיִם**...
When preparing meat on the grill, it is a good idea to use **tongs**...

אני דואג תמיד שיהיו כמה זוגות **מִסְפָּרַיִם** בבית, לא רק במטבח אלא גם בחדרים אחרים.
I always make sure that there be a few pairs of **scissors** at home, not just in the kitchen, but in other rooms as well.

בישראל נהגו רוב האנשים לאכול את הארוחה העיקרית שלהם **בְּצָהֳרַיִם**. היום חלק גדול מהם כבר לא עושים זאת.

In Israel most people used to have their main meal **midday**; today a good number of them no longer do that.

Special Expressions

exercise **bike** **אוֹפַנֵּי** כושר
just/precise **scales** **מֹאזְנֵי** צדק
exercise **shorts** **מִכְנְסֵי** התעמלות
Bermuda **shorts** Sl. (Coll. *mikhnasey*) **מִכְנְסֵי** זלמן

goggles **מִשְׁקְפֵי** שחייה
safety **goggles** **מִשְׁקְפֵי** מגן
eye **glasses** **מִשְׁקְפֵי** ראייה
sun**glasses** **מִשְׁקְפֵי** שמש

Additional Examples in this Pattern

gums חֲנִיכַיִם   scales מֹאזְנַיִם   millstones רֵחַיִם

---

998. Plural only

our/your/their	my/your/his/her	const.	Gloss	Plural
כְּשׁוּרֵינוּ/כֶם/כֶן/הֶם/הֶן	**כְּשׁוּ**רַי/רֶיךָ/רַיִךְ/רָיו/רֶיהָ	כְּשׁוּרֵי-	qualifications	כְּשׁוּרִים ז'

Even if it seems that there exists a singular form of some of these forms, this is not the case. חַי 'alive' is not the masculine singular counterpart of חַיִּים 'life,' מַקְבִּיל 'parallel' is not the singular masculine singular counterpart of מַקְבִּילִים 'parallel bars (athletics),' נִפְלָא 'wonderful' is not the masculine singular counterpart of נִפְלָאוֹת 'wonders,' etc. A number of forms have no declensions at all in real use.

Examples

למרבית הצער, לא לכל מי שנבחר עלי ידי הבוחרים למשרה ציבורית יש **כְּשׁוּרִים** מתאימים למשרה.

Unfortunately, not everybody who is elected by voters to a public office has the right **qualifications** for that office.

מרטין ביטל ברגע האחרון את **אֵרוּסָיו**, אבל ארוסתו סירבה (בצדק) להחזיר לו את הטבעת היקרה שנתן לה.

Martin cancelled **his engagement** at the last minute, but his fiancé refused (justifiably) to return the expensive ring he had given her.

חג **הַבִּכּוּרִים** הוא אחד משלושה רגלים שנתיים שבהם היו בני ישראל עולים לרגל לירושלים.

Pentecost (or the Festival of **First Fruits**) was one of three yearly holidays on which the Children of Israel would go on pilgrimage to Jerusalem.

יש עדיין חברות שבהן מצופה ממשפחת הכלה שתציג לראווה סדין מוכתם בדם לאחר ליל **הַכְּלוּלוֹת** כדי להוכיח שאמנם הייתה עדיין **בִּבְתוּלֶיהָ** יום קודם לכן.

There are still some societies in which the bride's family is expected to display a blood-stained sheet after her **wedding** night so as to prove that she was in her **state of virginity** a day earlier.

הַחַיִּים הם לא פיקניק – במיוחד כשמזדקנים.

Life is no picnic – particularly not when one gets old.

כדי ששער ה**חֲלִיפִין** של המטבע הלאומי יהיה יציב במידת האפשר, על הבנק המרכזי של המדינה שמדובר בה להתערב בכלכלה מדי פעם.

In order to maintain the stability of the **exchange** rate of the national currency, the central bank of any country needs to occasional intervene in the economy.

לנהל מדינה זה לא פשוט כמו לנהל עסק **מְקַרְקְעִין** משפחתי...

To conduct the affairs of state is not as simple as running a family-based **real estate** business...

רובנו מתגעגעים לתקופת ה**נְעוּרִים** שלנו, ושוכחים שלמרות שהיינו אז בריאים יותר, זו הייתה לעיתים תקופה לא קלה, במיוחד לאלה מאיתנו שלא היו ילדים פופולריים.

Most of us miss the period of our **youth**, and forget that although we were healthier then, it may not have always been an easy period, particularly for those of us who were not popular children.

Special Expressions

insomnia, sleep disruptions **נְדוּדֵי** שינה

civil **marriage** **נִשּׂוּאִים** אזרחיים

Additional Examples in this Pattern

prostitution, adultery זְנוּנִים

wedding כְּלוּלוֹת

parallel bars (athletics) מַקְבִּילַיִם

wanderings נְדוּדִים

wonders נִפְלָאוֹת

marriage נִשּׂוּאִים/נִשּׂוּאִין

ancient times קְדוּמִים

mercy רַחֲמִים

ghosts רְפָאִים

yeast שְׁמָרִים

underwear תַּחְתּוֹנִים

source, reference; support תִּמּוּכִין

phylacteries (Judaism) תְּפִלִּין

idols תְּרָפִים

Indices

Index of Hebrew Nouns and Adjectives by Pattern

בְּגִידָה נ 1 betraying; betrayal; unfaithfulness = type of betrayal
בְּגִירָה נ 1 becoming adult; puberty; physical manifestation of adulthood [no pl.]
בְּדִיחָה נ 1 joke
בְּדִיקָה נ 1 checking, examining; examination, checkup especially medical
בְּזִיזָה נ 1 looting, plundering
בְּזִיקָה נ 1 sprinkling
בְּחִילָה נ 1 nausea
בְּחִינָה נ 1 examining; examination
בְּחִירָה נ 1 choosing; choice
בְּחִישָׁה נ 1 mixing, stirring
בְּטִישָׁה נ 1 trampling Lit
בְּלִיטָה נ 1 protrusion; bulge
בְּלִילָה נ 1 mixing; mixture
בְּלִימָה נ 1 braking, curbing; holding defense
בְּלִיעָה נ 1 swallowing
בְּלִישָׁה נ 1 detecting, tracking
בְּעִיטָה נ 1 kicking; a kick
בְּעִילָה נ 1 sexual intercourse
בְּעִירָה נ 1 burning
בְּצִיעָה נ 1 slicing bread
בְּקִיעָה נ 1 eruption, emergence
בְּרִיאָה נ 1 creation; universe
בְּרִיחָה נ 1 escaping; escape
בְּרִירָה נ 1 selecting, sorting
בְּשִׁילָה נ 1 ripening, maturing [no pl.]
גְּבִינָה נ 1 cheese
גְּדִילָה נ 1 growing [no pl.]
גְּדִיעָה נ 1 cutting down
גְּהִירָה נ 1 bending over Lit
גְּוִיעָה נ 1 dying Lit
גְּזִיזָה נ 1 cutting hair, shearing
גְּזִירָה נ 1 cutting; differentiation math
גְּחִינָה נ 1 bending over, prostrating Lit
גְּלִידָה נ 1 congealing rare; ice cream
גְּלִילָה נ 1 rolling up; rolling up of Torah scroll
גְּלִימָה נ 1 robe, gown, cloak
גְּלִיפָה נ 1 etching, engraving
גְּלִישָׁה נ 1 boiling over; surfing
גְּמִיאָה נ 1 drinking Lit; covering large distances fast
גְּמִילָה נ 1 weaning; withdrawal from drug addiction etc. = type of weaning
גְּמִיעָה נ 1 swallowing drink; a swallow of drink
גְּמִירָה נ 1 completing, finishing
גְּנִיזָה נ 1 archiving, storing; shelving
גְּנִיחָה נ 1 groaning; groan n
גְּסִיסָה נ 1 dying
גְּעִירָה נ 1 scolding
גְּרִידָה נ 1 scratching out; abortion = type of scratching out
גְּרִימָה נ 1 causing, causation
גְּרִיסָה נ 1 crushing, grinding
גְּרִיעָה נ 1 reduction, subtraction
גְּרִיפָה נ 1 sweeping away; collecting, esp. a lot of money in short time
גְּרִירָה נ 1 dragging; towing vehicle
דְּגִילָה נ 1 professing, asserting
דְּגִימָה נ 1 sampling; sample
דְּגִירָה נ 1 hatching; studying hard Coll.
דְּהִירָה נ 1 galloping
דְּחִיסָה נ 1 compressing; compression as in engine
דְּחִיפָה נ 1 push; stimulus
דְּחִיקָה נ 1 pushing, shoving aside
דְּלִיפָה נ 1 leaking; a leak
דְּלִיקָה נ 1 chasing Lit
דְּמִיעָה נ 1 crying, lacrimation
דְּעִיכָה נ 1 dying out, fading
דְּפִינָה נ 1 attaching, mounting
דְּפִיקָה נ 1 knock; failure Coll.; have intercourse Sl.
דְּקִירָה נ 1 prick N; stabbing = type of pricking
דְּרִיכָה נ 1 stepping on, treading; drawing bow, cocking weapon
דְּרִיסָה נ 1 running over, trampling; stepping on
דְּרִישָׁה נ 1 demanding; demand, requirement
וְעִידָה נ 1 conference, convention, congress
זְבִיחָה נ 1 slaughtering animal for sacrifice
זְהִירָה נ 1 radiance, brightness, luminescence [no pl.]
זְחִילָה נ 1 crawling
זְכִירָה נ 1 remembering
זְלִיגָה נ 1 dripping, trickling, esp. tears, sweat
זְלִילָה נ 1 overeating, gluttony
זְלִיפָה נ 1 leak, dripping, sprinkle n
זְמִירָה נ 1 pruning, trimming, clipping Lit
זְנִיחָה נ 1 abandonment, desertion [no pl.]
זְקִיפָה נ 1 standing upright; entering into account
זְקִירָה נ 1 pushing up, raising Lit
זְרִיחָה נ 1 sunrise
זְרִימָה נ 1 flow N
זְרִיעָה נ 1 sowing
זְרִיקָה נ 1 throwing, casting away; injection ("throwing") of vaccine etc. into body
טְבִיחָה נ 1 slaughtering
טְבִילָה נ 1 dipping; ritual immersion
טְבִיעָה נ 1 drowning; stamping
טְחִינָה נ 1 grinding, mincing
טְמִיעָה נ 1 assimilation, absorption
טְעִימָה נ 1 tasting; morsel
טְעִינָה נ 1 loading vehicle/weapon/battery
טְפִיחָה נ 1 slap, light blow
טְפִילָה נ 1 framing, false accusation
טְפִיפָה נ 1 mincing walk Lit
טְרִיפָה נ 1 beating, scrambling eggs; shuffling cards
טְרִיקָה נ 1 slamming door
יְגִיעָה נ 1 exertion, effort, pains
יְדִיעָה נ 1 knowing, awareness; news item
יְזִימָה נ 1 initiating
יְחִידָה נ 1 unit
יְנִיקָה נ 1 suckling, breast feeding; suction fluid
יְצִיאָה נ 1 exiting, leaving; exit
יְצִיבָה נ 1 posture
יְצִיקָה נ 1 pouring; casting
יְצִירָה נ 1 creation; work of art
יְקִידָה נ 1 burning; passion Lit
יְקִיצָה נ 1 waking up
יְרִידָה נ 1 descent; alighting; emigration from Israel
יְרִיעָה נ 1 sheet; description
יְרִיקָה נ 1 spitting
יְשִׁיבָה נ 1 sitting; meeting
כְּבִידָה נ 1 gravitation [no pl.]
כְּבִילָה נ 1 binding, chaining, handcuffing; restriction
כְּבִיסָה נ 1 laundering; laundry Coll.
כְּבִירָה נ 1 straining [no pl.]
כְּבִישָׁה נ 1 pressing; paving; suppressing emotion; preserving, pickling
כְּלִיאָה נ 1 imprisonment
כְּלִיבָה נ 1 sewing rough seams
כְּלִילָה נ 1 generalization Lit-rare [no pl.]
כְּמִיהָה נ 1 yearning Lit
כְּמִינָה נ 1 hiding, concealment Lit [no pl.]
כְּמִישָׁה נ 1 withering [no pl.]
כְּנִיסָה נ 1 entering; entrance; admission
כְּנִיעָה נ 1 surrender, submission
כְּסִיסָה נ 1 gnawing
כְּסִיפָה נ 1 yearning Lit-rare [no pl.]

כְּפִיפָה נ 1 bending
כְּפִירָה נ 1 heresy; denial
כְּפִיתָה נ 1 binding hands, feet; immobilizing
כְּרִיזָה נ 1 proclamation; pa system
כְּרִיכָה נ 1 bookbinding; binding of a book
כְּרִיעָה נ 1 bending, bowing; kneeling
כְּרִיתָה נ 1 tree-clearing; amputation
כְּתִיבָה נ 1 writing, recording
כְּתִישָׁה נ 1 pounding, crushing, grinding
כְּתִיתָה נ 1 pounding, crushing; cutlet, schnitzel
לְבִישָׁה נ 1 wearing
לְגִימָה נ 1 swallow, gulp, sip n
לְזִירָה נ 1 beaming of a laser, lasing [no pl.]
לְחִיכָה נ 1 lapping, licking Lit
לְחִימָה נ 1 fighting military
לְחִיצָה נ 1 pressing, pushing
לְחִישָׁה נ 1 whispering; whisper
לְטִיפָה נ 1 stroke, caress n
לְכִידָה נ 1 trapping, capturing
לְמִידָה נ 1 learning
לְעִיטָה נ 1 swallowing food or drink; overeating Lit
לְעִיסָה נ 1 chewing
לְפִיפָה נ 1 coiling, wrapping
לְפִיתָה נ 1 grasping, gripping tightly
לְקִיחָה נ 1 taking
לְקִיטָה נ 1 gathering, gleaning
לְקִיקָה נ 1 lapping; licking
מְאִיסָה נ 1 revulsion
מְדִידָה נ 1 measuring
מְהִילָה נ 1 dilution
מְזִיגָה נ 1 pouring
מְחִיאָה נ 1 clapping
מְחִיטָה נ 1 blowing one's nose
מְחִילָה נ 1 forgiving; forgiveness; relinquishing one's honor
מְחִיקָה נ 1 erasing; erasure; deletion
מְכִירָה נ 1 selling; sale
מְלִיאָה נ 1 plenum, general assembly
מְנִיעָה נ 1 preventing; prevention
מְסִירָה נ 1 delivery, transmission
מְעִידָה נ 1 stumbling
מְעִיכָה נ 1 squashing, mashing, crushing
מְעִילָה נ 1 embezzlement
מְצִיאָה נ 1 finding; bargain, find
מְצִיצָה נ 1 sucking
מְרִידָה נ 1 rebelling; rebellion, revolt
מְרִיחָה נ 1 spreading; smearing
מְרִיטָה נ 1 plucking feathers, hair
מְשִׁיחָה נ 1 anointing, spreading
מְשִׁיכָה נ 1 pulling, dragging
מְתִיחָה נ 1 stretching, pulling; practical joke Coll.
נְבִיחָה נ 1 barking; a bark
נְבִיטָה נ 1 germination, sprouting
נְבִילָה נ 1 withering, wilting
נְבִיעָה נ 1 gushing forth water; spring
נְבִירָה נ 1 searching, rummaging
נְגִיחָה נ 1 butt, gore N
נְגִינָה נ 1 music playing; accentuation grammar
נְגִיסָה נ 1 biting; a bite
נְגִיעָה נ 1 touching; a touch
נְגִיפָה נ 1 stroke, blow, push Lit
נְגִירָה נ 1 seepage, flow
נְגִישָׁה נ 1 malicious suit law
נְדִידָה נ 1 wandering, migrating
נְדִיפָה נ 1 evaporation, dissipation Lit [no pl.]
נְהִיגָה נ 1 driving a vehicle
נְהִימָה נ 1 growl, roar Lit; moan, groan Lit
נְהִירָה נ 1 thronging, upsurge, flow of people
נְזִילָה נ 1 leaking; a leak
נְזִיפָה נ 1 reproach, reprimand; discipline – (military)
נְחִירָה נ 1 snoring; snore N
נְחִיתָה נ 1 landing, touchdown
נְטִילָה נ 1 taking, receiving, obtaining; accepting responsibility
נְטִיעָה נ 1 planting trees; sapling
נְטִיפָה נ 1 dripping liquid
נְטִירָה נ 1 grudge-bearing; guarding
נְטִישָׁה נ 1 abandonment
נְסִיגָה נ 1 withdrawal, retreat
נְסִיעָה נ 1 journey, trip, ride, drive
נְסִיקָה נ 1 takeoff, climbing high plane
נְעִילָה נ 1 wearing/putting on shoes; closing, locking; adjournment
נְעִימָה נ 1 tune, melody
נְעִיצָה נ 1 insertion, sticking into, thrusting
נְעִירָה נ 1 braying
נְפִיחָה נ 1 flatulence
נְפִילָה נ 1 falling, fall, drop
נְקִיבָה נ 1 stipulation, announcement
נְקִיטָה נ 1 use measure, etc.; adoption of stance, etc.
נְקִיעָה נ 1 spraining
נְקִיפָה נ 1 passage of period of time; rare
נְקִישָׁה נ 1 knocking
נְשִׂיאָה נ 1 carrying; elevating; delivery of speech
נְשִׁיבָה נ 1 blowing
נְשִׁיכָה נ 1 biting; bite
נְשִׁילָה נ 1 shedding
נְשִׁימָה נ 1 breathing; breath
נְשִׁיפָה נ 1 exhalation; blow
נְשִׁיקָה נ 1 kiss n
נְשִׁירָה נ 1 molting, shedding; dropout from school
נְתִיחָה נ 1 dissection
נְתִינָה נ 1 giving
סְבִיאָה נ 1 guzzling mostly of wine/liquor
סְבִיבָה נ 1 surrounding; neighborhood; area
סְגִידָה נ 1 worship, honoring; adoration
סְגִירָה נ 1 closing, shutting
סְדִיקָה נ 1 cracking, splitting
סְחִיבָה נ 1 dragging, carrying; pilfering Coll.
סְחִיטָה נ 1 squeezing, extraction of juice; extortion
סְחִיפָה נ 1 sweeping away; erosion; captivation
סְטִירָה נ 1 a slap on face or cheek
סְכִירָה נ 1 damming, sluicing
סְלִידָה נ 1 disgust, revulsion
סְלִיחָה נ 1 forgiveness; pardon
סְלִילָה נ 1 paving
סְלִיקָה נ 1 payment; clearing in banking
סְמִיכָה נ 1 ordination, graduation
סְנִיטָה נ 1 teasing Lit
סְעִידָה נ 1 feasting, dining
סְפִיגָה נ 1 absorption
סְפִיחָה נ 1 adsorption Chem.
סְפִינָה נ 1 ship, boat
סְפִיקָה נ 1 flow rate
סְפִירָה נ 1 counting
סְקִילָה נ 1 stoning
סְקִירָה נ 1 survey; description, summary; study, poll
סְרִיגָה נ 1 knitting
סְרִיטָה נ 1 scratch n
סְרִיקָה נ 1 search; scan, perusal
סְתִימָה נ 1 sealing, plugging; filling in dentistry
סְתִירָה נ 1 contradiction; neutralization chemistry
פְּגִימָה נ 1 damage, disruption
פְּגִיעָה נ 1 blow; injury, damage; hit; insult
פְּגִישָׁה נ 1 meeting; appointment; meeting; reunion
פְּזִילָה נ 1 squint, sideways view
פְּחִיסָה נ 1 flattening, squashing
פְּחִיתָה נ 1 devaluation, depreciation; reduction
פְּטִירָה נ 1 death, passing; exemption

פְּלִיאָה נ 1 amazement, wonder, awe
פְּלִיטָה נ 1 ejection, emission; discharge; output
פְּלִישָׁה נ 1 invasion
פְּנִינָה נ 1 pearl
פְּסִילָה נ 1 disqualification; nullification
פְּסִיעָה נ 1 stepping; step
פְּסִיקָה נ 1 ruling law
פְּעִימָה נ 1 beat music; heart
פְּעִירָה נ 1 gape
פְּצִיעָה נ 1 wounding, injuring; wound, injury
פְּצִירָה נ 1 filing; file carpentry, metalwork
פְּקִיחָה נ 1 opening of eyes
פְּקִיעָה נ 1 expiration
פְּקִיקָה נ 1 corking, plugging; thrombosis
פְּרִיחָה נ 1 blooming; prosperity, development
פְּרִיטָה נ 1 cashing, breaking bill; strumming
פְּרִיכָה נ 1 breaking, crushing; pressing olives
פְּרִימָה נ 1 unraveling
פְּרִיסָה נ 1 spreading; deployment; distribution
פְּרִיעָה נ 1 redemption, payment; destruction, rampage
פְּרִיצָה נ 1 break-in; breach; breakthrough; outbreak; penetration
פְּרִיקָה נ 1 unloading; electric discharge
פְּרִישָׁה נ 1 retirement; seclusion
פְּשִׁיעָה נ 1 crime
פְּתִיחָה נ 1 opening; establishment; preface
פְּתִילָה נ 1 wick; fuse
פְּתִירָה נ 1 solving, deciphering
צְבִיטָה נ 1 pinch
צְבִיעָה נ 1 painting, coloring
צְבִירָה נ 1 accumulation
צְוִיחָה נ 1 shout, scream
צְלִיבָה נ 1 crucifixion
צְלִיחָה נ 1 crossing, traversing, fording
צְלִילָה נ 1 diving, a dive
צְלִיעָה נ 1 limp; lameness
צְלִיפָה נ 1 sniping; whipping
צְמִיחָה נ 1 growing, growth
צְנִיחָה נ 1 parachuting; descent; rapid decline/drop
צְנִיפָה נ 1 neigh, whinny
צְעִידָה נ 1 marching, walking, pacing
צְפִירָה נ 1 beeping, honking; siren
צְרִיבָה נ 1 burning, etching; burn
צְרִיחָה נ 1 scream
צְרִיכָה נ 1 consumption
צְרִימָה נ 1 grating sound; incompatibility
צְרִיפָה נ 1 refinement, purification
קְבִילָה נ 1 complaint
קְבִיעָה נ 1 decision; setting date, etc.; statement, declaration; determining; affixing
קְבִירָה נ 1 burying
קְדִיחָה נ 1 drilling
קְדִימָה נ 1 preference, precedence, priority
קְטִילָה נ 1 killing, extermination; critique Coll.
קְטִימָה נ 1 lopping, cutting off end
קְטִיעָה נ 1 interruption, disruption; amputation
קְטִיפָה נ 1 plucking, picking fruit, flowers
קְלִיחָה נ 1 flow, stream
קְלִיטָה נ 1 absorbing; absorption
קְלִיעָה נ 1 braiding, basket weaving; shooting, throwing
קְלִיפָה נ 1 peeling, skinning
קְמִילָה נ 1 withering, shriveling
קְמִיצָה נ 1 closing, pursing, clamping shut, ring finger
קְנִיסָה נ 1 fining
קְפִיאָה נ 1 freezing
קְפִיצָה נ 1 jumping; rise, increase
קְצִיפָה נ 1 mousse
קְצִיצָה נ 1 hamburger, cutlet
קְצִירָה נ 1 harvesting, reaping
קְרִיאָה נ 1 reading; call; shout; exclamation
קְרִינָה נ 1 radiation
קְרִיסָה נ 1 collapse; bankruptcy; bend
קְרִיעָה נ 1 tear
קְרִיצָה נ 1 wink
קְרִישָׁה נ 1 congelation, clotting
קְשִׁירָה נ 1 tying, knotting
רְבִיכָה נ 1 roux
רְבִיצָה נ 1 recumbence
רְגִימָה נ 1 stoning
רְגִיעָה נ 1 calm, quiet, restfulness
רְדִיפָה נ 1 chase, pursuit; persecution, oppression
רְחִיפָה נ 1 hovering, floating in air
רְחִיצָה נ 1 washing, wash; bathing
רְחִישָׁה נ 1 whisper, mumble, murmur
רְכִיבָה נ 1 riding
רְכִישָׁה נ 1 purchase, acquisition
רְמִיזָה נ 1 hinting
רְמִיסָה נ 1 trampling, crushing
רְעִידָה נ 1 rattling, shaking; trembling
רְפִידָה נ 1 insole; lining
רְצִיחָה נ 1 murder, murdering
רְקִיעָה נ 1 stamping of feet
רְשִׁימָה נ 1 list
רְתִיחָה נ 1 boiling
רְתִימָה נ 1 harnessing
רְתִיעָה נ 1 recoiling, withdrawing; hesitation
שְׁאִיבָה נ 1 pumping, drawing; extracting
שְׁאִילָה נ 1 borrowing; asking, querying
שְׁאִיפָה נ 1 aspiration, ambition; inhalation, breath
שְׁבִירָה נ 1 breaking
שְׁבִיתָה נ 1 strike, walkout
שְׁגִיאָה נ 1 error, mistake
שְׁדִידָה נ 1 robbery, burglary
שְׁזִירָה נ 1 interweaving
שְׁחִיטָה נ 1 slaughtering, slaughter
שְׁחִיקָה נ 1 wear, erosion; grinding; exhaustion
שְׁטִיחָה נ 1 spreading
שְׁטִיפָה נ 1 washing, rinsing
שְׁכִיבָה נ 1 lying down; reclining
שְׁכִינָה נ 1 divine spirit
שְׂכִירָה נ 1 rental; hiring
שְׁלִיחָה נ 1 sending
שְׁלִיטָה נ 1 control; command, knowledge
שְׁלִילָה נ 1 rejection; elimination; revocation
שְׁלִיפָה נ 1 pulling out; drawing, unsheathing
שְׁלִיקָה נ 1 poaching eggs etc.
שְׂמִיכָה נ 1 blanket
שְׁמִיעָה נ 1 hearing; listening
שְׁמִירָה נ 1 guarding, security; preserving
שְׁפִיטָה נ 1 judging; hearing (law), judgment
שְׁפִיכָה נ 1 pouring; ejaculation
שְׁפִיתָה נ 1 setting a pot on a fire
שְׁקִידָה נ 1 diligence
שְׁקִילָה נ 1 weighing, considering
שְׁקִיעָה נ 1 sunset; sinking; downfall
שְׂרִיטָה נ 1 scratch
שְׁרִיקָה נ 1 whistle
שְׁתִילָה נ 1 plant
שְׁתִיקָה נ 1 silence; unresponsiveness
תְּבִיעָה נ 1 demand; legal demand; prosecution law; insurance claim
תְּחִיבָה נ 1 insertion, sticking in, thrusting
תְּחִימָה נ 1 delineation, demarcation, delimitation
תְּלִישָׁה נ 1 pulling out, tearing off
תְּמִיהָה נ 1 surprise, wonder, amazement

support; 1 תְּמִיכָה נ stabilization; encouragement
fermentation; 1 תְּסִיסָה נ bubbling; agitation, discontent; unrest
swelling; lump; 1 תְּפִיחָה נ souffle
catching; grabbing; 1 תְּפִיסָה נ comprehension; perception; outlook
drumming esp fingers 1 תְּפִיפָה נ
sewing; dressmaking 1 תְּפִירָה נ
standardization, 1 תְּקִינָה נ establishing standards
blast of horn, trumpet 1 תְּקִיעָה נ
hoarding 2 אֲגִירָה נ
hold, grasp N 2 אֲחִיזָה נ
sealing; 2 אֲטִימָה נ opacification = sealing to light
eating 2 אֲכִילָה נ
enforcing, 2 אֲכִיפָה נ enforcement
saying, utterance, 2 אֲמִירָה נ expression
arresting; tying esp. 2 אֲסִירָה נ horse to carriage
cessation Lit.; 2 אֲפִיסָה נ exhaustion 'afisat koHot [no pl.]
keeping safe; 2 אֲצִירָה נ retention
weaving 2 אֲרִיגָה נ
packing, packaging; 2 אֲרִיזָה נ packing materials
migration, 2 הֲגִירָה נ immigration
thrust, push N 2 הֲדִיפָה נ
walking; a walk 2 הֲלִיכָה נ
knocking; adequacy 2 הֲלִימָה נ (latter no plural)
turning over; 2 הֲפִיכָה נ revolution
killing 2 הֲרִיגָה נ
destroying 2 הֲרִיסָה נ
beating, striking 2 חֲבִיטָה נ
parcel, package 2 חֲבִילָה נ
pudding; custard Lit 2 חֲבִיצָה נ
hug, embrace N 2 חֲבִיקָה נ
joining, link-up 2 חֲבִירָה נ military
bandaging; head- 2 חֲבִישָׁה נ covering
omelet 2 חֲבִיתָה נ
celebration; pleasure 2 חֲגִיגָה נ Coll.
strapping on safety 2 חֲגִירָה נ belt, girding
cessation, stopping 2 חֲדִילָה נ
penetration 2 חֲדִירָה נ
villa 2 חֲוִילָה נ
return N 2 חֲזִירָה נ
division of ; 2 חֲטִיבָה נ organization; brigade; felling of trees
snatching; 2 חֲטִיפָה נ kidnapping

leasing 2 חֲכִירָה נ
milking 2 חֲלִיבָה נ
brewing tea 2 חֲלִיטָה נ
dreaming 2 חֲלִימָה נ
suit; substitute Lit 2 חֲלִיפָה נ
taking off shoes; 2 חֲלִיצָה נ extraction; shoe removal under levirate law
pancake Lit 2 חֲמִיטָה נ
borscht 2 חֲמִיצָה נ
evasion, escape 2 חֲמִיקָה נ
embalming 2 חֲנִיטָה נ
pardoning, amnesty 2 חֲנִינָה נ
strangling, choking 2 חֲנִיקָה נ
stork 2 חֲסִידָה נ
blocking; blockade 2 חֲסִימָה נ
taking a handful 2 חֲפִינָה נ
packet 2 חֲפִיסָה נ
overlapping; 2 חֲפִיפָה נ shampooing hair
digging, excavating; 2 חֲפִירָה נ a dig, excavation; trench
quarrying, 2 חֲצִיבָה נ excavating; carving
division, separating; 2 חֲצִיצָה נ demarcation
legislating, 2 חֲקִיקָה נ legislation; engraving
investigation, 2 חֲקִירָה נ inquiry; research
deviation, exception 2 חֲרִיגָה נ
rhyming; threading, 2 חֲרִיזָה נ stringing
engraving, turning 2 חֲרִיטָה נ metal, chiseling
singeing, scorching 2 חֲרִיכָה נ
wintering of 2 חֲרִיפָה נ migratory birds [no pl.]
deciding, 2 חֲרִיצָה נ determining; slitting
screeching; mishap 2 חֲרִיקָה נ Coll.
plowing; digging up 2 חֲרִישָׁה נ info Sl.
engraving, turning 2 חֲרִיתָה נ metal, chiseling
thinking, thought 2 חֲשִׁיבָה נ process [no pl.]
exposure 2 חֲשִׂיפָה נ
pursing of lips 2 חֲשִׁיקָה נ
piece; item; 2 חֲתִיכָה נ attractive woman Coll.
signing, signature; 2 חֲתִימָה נ ending; conclusion
undermining; rowing 2 חֲתִירָה נ
flirtation Lit 2 עֲגִיבָה נ
anchoring; anchorage 2 עֲגִינָה נ
hoeing, tilling 2 עֲדִירָה נ
leaving, departure 2 עֲזִיבָה נ
wrapping, covering 2 עֲטִיפָה נ
a sneeze Lit 2 עֲטִישָׁה נ
plot, story; deeds, 2 עֲלִילָה נ tales, adventures

standing; sticking to 2 עֲמִידָה נ promise, schedule etc.; steadfastness
tie, cravat; noose 2 עֲנִיבָה נ
wearing, pinning, 2 עֲנִידָה נ decorating
punishing; 2 עֲנִישָׁה נ punishment
closing of eye(s) 2 עֲצִימָה נ
stopping; stop 2 עֲצִירָה נ
following, tracking 2 עֲקִיבָה נ
binding, tying 2 עֲקִידָה נ
twisting, bending, 2 עֲקִימָה נ curving
bypassing, 2 עֲקִיפָה נ circumventing
stinging; sting, bite 2 עֲקִיצָה נ
uprooting; 2 עֲקִירָה נ extraction; displacement, transfer
editing; arranging 2 עֲרִיכָה נ
cradle; crib 2 עֲרִיסָה נ
decapitation 2 עֲרִיפָה נ
desertion 2 עֲרִיקָה נ
exploitation Lit. [no 2 עֲשִׁיקָה נ pl.]
petition law; request, 2 עֲתִירָה נ plea Lit
coming; sexual 3 בִּיאָה נ intercourse
stage; forum 3 בִּימָה נ
understanding, sense, 3 בִּינָה נ wisdom
trip; sortie, flight 3 גִּיחָה נ
joy, happiness Lit. [no 3 גִּילָה נ pl.]
approach, access; 3 גִּישָׁה נ attitude
joy, happiness, 3 דִּיצָה נ rejoicing Lit
apartment, flat 3 דִּירָה נ
threshing; over- 3 דִּישָׁה נ involvement
gonorrhea; discharge 3 זִיבָה נ
feed (electr.) 3 זִינָה נ
affinity, bond 3 זִיקָה/זִקָּה נ
arena, sphere 3 זִירָה נ
riddle; mystery 3 חִידָה נ
sense, sensation; 3 חִישָׁה נ sense-measuring
grudge, bitterness 3 טִינָה נ
flight 3 טִיסָה נ
castle 3 טִירָה נ
sleeping arrangements, 3 לִינָה נ lodging
kneading 3 לִישָׁה נ
circumcision 3 מִילָה נ
death 3 מִיתָה נ
moving, wandering; 3 נִידָה נ menstruation
thread; tone, overtone; 3 נִימָה נ nap N
escape Lit-rare 3 נִיסָה נ
body movement; bend 3 נִיעָה נ
anointing; lubrication 3 סִיכָה נ

faction; group 3 סִיעָה נ
boat 3 סִירָה נ
double chin 3 פִּימָה נ
buoyancy [no pl.] 3 צִיפָּה נ
pulp, flesh of fruit 3 צִיפָּה נ
crest in heraldry 3 צִיצָה נ
arising; getting up 3 קִימָה נ
dirge, lamentation 3 קִינָה נ
running; a run 3 רִיצָה נ
return, homecoming 3 שִׁיבָה נ
conversation; talk; phone call; negotiation 3 שִׂיחָה נ
method 3 שִׁיטָה נ
placing, putting 3 שִׂימָה נ
phloem 3 שִׁיפָה נ
singing; poetry 3 שִׁירָה נ
bewilderment, stare, astonishment 4 בְּהִיָּה נ
crying, weeping 4 בְּכִיָּה נ
erosion 4 בְּלִיָּה נ
building, construction 4 בְּנִיָּה נ
creature 4 בְּרִיָּה נ
collection of taxes, dues 4 גְּבִיָּה נ
corpse, body 4 גְּוִיָּה נ
lowing, mooing, bellowing 4 גְּעִיָּה נ
stimulation 4 גְּרִיָּה נ
gliding 4 דְּאִיָּה נ
fading, becoming dull 4 דְּהִיָּה נ
postponement; rejection, rebuff 4 דְּחִיָּה נ
raising, dredging up; gleaning info 4 דְּלִיָּה נ
winning; win 4 זְכִיָּה נ
sprinkling, spreading all over Lit 4 זְרִיָּה נ
spinning thread 4 טְוִיָּה נ
erring, mistaking 4 טְעִיָּה נ
shot; shooting, firing 4 יְרִיָּה נ
extinguishment of fire Lit 4 כְּבִיָּה נ
burn 4 כְּוִיָּה נ
coercion, duress; compulsion 4 כְּפִיָּה נ
mining, quarrying, digging 4 כְּרִיָּה נ
stock, share 4 מְנָיָה נ
following Lit. [no pl.] 4 נְהִיָּה נ
leading, guiding 4 נְחִיָּה נ
tendency; trend; leaning ideological; inflection 4 נְטִיָּה נ
mongoose; ferret 4 נְמִיָּה נ
forgetfulness Lit 4 נְשִׁיָּה נ
deviation; digression; perversion 4 סְטִיָּה נ
redemption 4 פְּדִיָּה נ
turn; application; petition; facing 4 פְּנִיָּה נ
bleating; bleat 4 פְּעִיָּה נ
being fruitful 4 פְּרִיָּה נ
malice Lit-rare [no pl.] 4 צְדִיָּה נ
grilling, roasting, broiling 4 צְלִיָּה נ
viewing, watching 4 צְפִיָּה נ
toasting, roasting 4 קְלִיָּה נ
purchase, acquisition; shopping 4 קְנִיָּה נ
vision, eyesight; view; opinion 4 רְאִיָּה נ
reproduction, multiplying 4 רְבִיָּה נ
compress, bandage; eye-patch 4 רְטִיָּה נ
fraud, deception, cheating [no pl.] 4 רְמִיָּה נ
willfulness, forethought 4 רְצִיָּה נ
destruction Lit-rare 4 שְׁאִיָּה נ
capture 4 שְׁבִיָּה נ
staying; stay 4 שְׁהִיָּה נ
swimming; a swim 4 שְׂחִיָּה נ
drinking; a drink; beverage 4 שְׁתִיָּה נ
amazement, wonderment; pondering, considering 4 תְּהִיָּה נ
plotting, marking; sketching 4 תְּוִיָּה נ
hanging, suspending 4 תְּלִיָּה נ
wandering 4 תְּעִיָּה נ
baking 5 אֲפִיָּה נ
diction, pronunciation 5 הֲגִיָּה נ
parking 5 חֲנִיָּה נ
sheltering, taking refuge [no pl.] 5 חֲסִיָּה נ
overlapping Lit-rare [no pl.] 5 חֲפִיָּה נ
division, splitting; crossing 5 חֲצִיָּה נ
ascent; incline; increase; advance; immigration to Israel 5 עֲלִיָּה נ
making, doing; achievement, work 5 עֲשִׂיָּה נ
lost, missing 6 אוֹבֵד ז
copula (grammar) 6 אוֹגֵד ז
hamster; register (computing) 6 אוֹגֵר ז
enemy; opponent 6 אוֹיֵב ז
foster parent 6 אוֹמֵן ז
mourner Lit-rare 6 אוֹנֵן ז
curator 6 אוֹצֵר ז
someone lying in wait/ambush 6 אוֹרֵב ז
weaver 6 אוֹרֵג ז
packer, mover 6 אוֹרֵז ז
traitor 6 בּוֹגֵד ז
graduate 6 בּוֹגֵר ז
lonely; alone; isolated person; single person 6 בּוֹדֵד ז
examiner, inspector 6 בּוֹדֵק ז
looter, plunderer 6 בּוֹזֵז ז
prominent; outstanding; obvious; salient 6 בּוֹלֵט ז
person harvesting grapes 6 בּוֹצֵר ז
empty, fruitless; looter, plunderer Lit 6 בּוֹקֵק ז
cowboy 6 בּוֹקֵר ז
glittering, shiny, sparkling 6 בּוֹרֵק ז
arbitrator; sorter 6 בּוֹרֵר ז
sheep-shearer 6 גּוֹזֵז ז
burial stone; slab placed over body in grave 6 גּוֹלֵל ז
skater, skier; hang glider; surfer 6 גּוֹלֵשׁ ז
dying person 6 גּוֹסֵס ז
cause, factor; element; authority 6 גּוֹרֵם ז
sweeping, comprehensive 6 גּוֹרֵף ז
tow truck 6 גּוֹרֵר ז
spokesperson; speaker of a language 6 דּוֹבֵר ז
inanimate; still life in art; silent, still 6 דּוֹמֵם ז
fair; reasonable, fitting, appropriate 6 הוֹגֵן ז
hedonist, licentious person 6 הוֹלֵל ז
appropriate, suitable, fitting, adequate 6 הוֹלֵם ז
glutton 6 זוֹלֵל ז
amateur; fan 6 חוֹבֵב ז
sailor, naval officer 6 חוֹבֵל ז
medic; paramedic 6 חוֹבֵשׁ ז
one who celebrates, partygoer 6 חוֹגֵג ז
enlisted person 6 חוֹגֵר ז
one who returns; circular; recurrent; reflexive in grammar 6 חוֹזֵר ז
kidnapper 6 חוֹטֵף ז
fricative sound 6 חוֹכֵךְ ז
lessee, tenant 6 חוֹכֵר ז
milkman 6 חוֹלֵב/חַלְבָן ז
extractor, corkscrew Holets pkakim 6 חוֹלֵץ ז
coach, tutor 6 חוֹנֵךְ ז
quick, hurried Lit 6 חוֹפֵז ז
congruent; identical; overlapping 6 חוֹפֵף ז
hewer, stonecutter 6 חוֹצֵב ז
divider 6 חוֹצֵץ ז
investigator; researcher, interrogator 6 חוֹקֵר ז
step- father etc.; extra- wide load, on vehicle 6 חוֹרֵג ז
wintering birds 6 חוֹרֵף ז
plowman 6 חוֹרֵשׁ ז
serious, thinking, smart Coll. 6 חוֹשֵׁב ז
definitive; sharp; transverse, secant 6 חוֹתֵךְ ז
signatory 6 חוֹתֵם ז
father-in-law 6 חוֹתֵן ז
rower, oarsman 6 חוֹתֵר ז
carnivore; carnivorous 6 טוֹרֵף ז
ram's horn Lit; jubilee 6 יוֹבֵל ז
farmer Lit-rare 6 יוֹגֵב ז
initiator, promoter 6 יוֹזֵם ז
commuter Lit 6 יוֹמֵם ז
mammal; infant 6 יוֹנֵק ז

יוֹצֵר ז 6 creator, maker, producer
יוֹקֵד ז 6 blazing, burning
יוֹרֵד ז 6 emigrant from Israel
יוֹרֵשׁ ז 6 heir; successor
יוֹשֵׁב ז 6 inhabitant, dweller, resident
כּוֹבֵל ז 6 restrictive, limiting
כּוֹבֵשׁ ז 6 conqueror
כּוֹזֵב ז 6 false
כּוֹלֵל ז 6 comprehensive, inclusive; advanced Jewish studies program for the married
כּוֹנֵס ז 6 kones nekhasim overseer of company dismantling
כּוֹפֵל ז 6 multiplier math
כּוֹפֵר ז 6 heretic
כּוֹרֵךְ ז 6 bookbinder
כּוֹרֵם ז 6 winegrower
כּוֹשֵׁל ז 6 failing
כּוֹתֵב ז 6 writer, author
מוֹדֵד ז 6 surveyor; gauge
מוֹזֵג ז 6 bartender
מוֹכֵס ז 6 customs official
מוֹכֵר ז 6 seller
מוֹסֵר ז 6 Informer
מוֹצֵץ ז 6 pacifier, dummy
מוֹרֵד ז 6 rebel, revolutionary
מוֹשֵׁךְ ז 6 attractive
מוֹשֵׁל ז 6 ruler, governor
נוֹבֵל ז 6 dry, withered, wilted
נוֹגֵד ז 6 opposing, contradictory
נוֹגֵשׂ ז 6 oppressor; taskmaster Lit
נוֹדֵד ז 6 wondering, migrant
נוֹזֵל ז 6 liquid, fluid; liquid adj
נוֹטֵר ז 6 Jewish guard in British police; guard Lit
נוֹכֵל ז 6 crook, swindler
נוֹפֵשׁ ז 6 vacationer
נוֹצֵץ ז 6 sparkling, shining
נוֹקֵב ז 6 profound, fundamental
נוֹקֵד ז 6 shepherd, sheep farmer
נוֹקֵר ז 6 firing pin
נוֹתֵב ז 6 tracer bullet
סוֹבֵב ז 6 surrounding, environment
סוֹגֵר ז 6 sphincter (muscle); bracket
סוֹדֵר ז 6 ordinal number
סוֹכֵךְ ז 6 canopy, awning
סוֹכֵן ז 6 agent
סוֹלֵד ז 6 retracting, turned back; 'af soled 'upturned nose'
סוֹמֵךְ ז 6 support, post; second word in a construct state
סוֹפֵג ז 6 absorbent
סוֹפֵר ז 6 author, writer
סוֹרֵק ז 6 scanner
סוֹרֵר ז 6 rebellious
סוֹתֵר ז 6 contradictory, inconsistent
עוֹבֵד ז 6 worker, employee
עוֹבֵר ז 6 moving, passing; temporary; passing in the education system
עוֹדֵף ז 6 leftover; surplus; redundant
עוֹזֵר ז 6 assistant, aide
עוֹיֵן ז 6 hostile
עוֹכֵר ז 6 one who causes trouble; destroyer
עוֹלֵב ז 6 insulting Lit
עוֹמֵד ז 6 standing, stationary; fixed, stable
עוֹצֵר ז 6 regent
עוֹקֵב ז 6 sequential
עוֹקֵף ז 6 bypassing
עוֹרֵב ז 6 crow, raven
עוֹרֵג ז 6 yearning, longing Lit
עוֹרֵךְ ז 6 editor
עוֹרֵק ז 6 artery; vein
עוֹרֵר ז 6 appealer
עוֹתֵר ז 6 petitioner
פּוֹזֵל ז 6 cross-eyed
פּוֹחֵז ז 6 irresponsible, reckless Lit
פּוֹלֵשׁ ז 6 invader; intruder, trespasser
פּוֹסֵק ז 6 adjudicator in Jewish law; normative
פּוֹצֵץ ז 6 plosive (phonetics)
פּוֹרֵץ ז 6 burglar
פּוֹרֵשׁ ז 6 dissident, seceder; separatist
פּוֹשֵׁט ז 6 forager; invading, incursive; spreading
פּוֹשֵׁר ז 6 lukewarm
צוֹדֵק ז 6 just, fair; correct, right
צוֹלֵב ז 6 cross- crossfire, etc
צוֹלֵל ז 6 diver; pochard diving duck
צוֹנֵן ז 6 cool, chilly
צוֹרֵב ז 6 burning; stinging; cd burner
צוֹרֵם ז 6 strident, grating
צוֹרֵף ז 6 goldsmith, silversmith
צוֹרֵר ז 6 bitter enemy
קוֹדֵם ז 6 preceding; preferable to
קוֹדֵר ז 6 gloomy, dark
קוֹלֵט ז 6 solar collector
קוֹסֵם ז 6 magician; enticing, captivating
קוֹפֵץ ז 6 interested customer Coll.
קוֹצֵב ז 6 one who allots; kotsev lev 'pacemaker'
קוֹצֵר ז 6 harvester, reaper
קוֹרֵן ז 6 radiant, joyful
קוֹשֵׁר ז 6 rebel, conspirator
רוֹגֵז ז 6 angry, furious
רוֹגֵן ז 6 complaining, grumbling
רוֹגֵשׁ ז 6 choppy, sea etc.
רוֹטֵט ז 6 trembling; tremulous, quavering
רוֹכֵב ז 6 rider
רוֹכֵל ז 6 peddler, hawker
רוֹפֵס ז 6 weak, limp, feeble
רוֹפֵף ז 6 loose, unstable
שׁוֹבֵת ז 6 striker
שׁוֹדֵד ז 6 robber, burglar
שׁוֹטֵף ז 6 continuous; current; fluent
שׁוֹטֵר ז 6 policeman
שׂוֹכֵר ז 6 renter, tenant
שׁוֹלֵל ז 6 opposer, nay-sayer
שׁוֹמֵם ז 6 desolate, empty, abandoned
שׁוֹמֵר ז 6 guard
שׁוֹפֵט ז 6 judge; referee, umpire
שׁוֹקֵק ז 6 teeming, bustling
שׂוֹרֵק ז 6 choice vine
תּוֹכֵן ז 6 astronomer Lit
תּוֹמֵךְ ז 6 supporter; supportive
תּוֹסֵס ז 6 effervescent
תּוֹפֵר ז 6 seamster
תּוֹרֵם ז 6 donor
אוֹהֵב ז 7 lover; friend
אוֹהֵד ז 7 supporter, adherent; fan
בּוֹאֵשׁ ז 7 skunk
בּוֹהֵק ז 7 glittery, shining, gleaming
בּוֹחֵן ז 7 examiner, inspector, tester
בּוֹחֵר ז 7 voter, selector
בּוֹעֵר ז 7 burning; urgent Coll.
גּוֹאֵל ז 7 savior, redeemer
גּוֹעֵשׁ ז 7 raging, stormy
דּוֹאֵב ז 7 painful Lit
דּוֹאֵג ז 7 worried, anxious; caring, concerned
דּוֹהֵר ז 7 galloping, racing
זוֹהֵר ז 7 shining, glowing
זוֹחֵל ז 7 reptile
זוֹעֵם ז 7 angry, furious
זוֹעֵף ז 7 angry, irate
טוֹחֵן ז 7 miller
טוֹעֵן ז 7 pleader; claimant, contender e.g., to throne
יוֹעֵץ ז 7 consultant, adviser
כּוֹאֵב ז 7 painful
כּוֹהֵן/כֹּהֵן ז 7 priest
לוֹהֵב ז 7 blazing, burning Lit
לוֹהֵט ז 7 burning hot; intense
לוֹחֵם ז 7 fighter, soldier
לוֹעֵז ז 7 foreign, strange, not Hebrew Lit
מוֹהֵל ז 7 circumciser
מוֹחֵץ ז 7 crushing, smashing; decisive (victory)
מוֹחֵק ז 7 eraser
מוֹעֵן ז 7 sender of letter, package, etc.
נוֹאֵם ז 7 speaker
נוֹאֵף ז 7 adulterer
סוֹאֵן ז 7 noisy
סוֹהֵר ז 7 prison guard
סוֹחֵף ז 7 stirring; sweeping
סוֹחֵר ז 7 merchant, trader
סוֹעֵר ז 7 stormy
פּוֹעֵל ז 7 worker, laborer

צוֹהֵל ז 7 joyful
צוֹעֵר ז 7 cadet; intern
רוֹעֵץ ז 7 calamity; obstacle
רוֹעֵשׁ ז 7 loud, noisy
שׁוֹאֵב ז 7 vacuum cleaner
שׁוֹאֵל ז 7 questioner, inquirer
שׁוֹחֵט ז 7 slaughterer
שׁוֹחֵק ז 7 causing extensive wear
שׁוֹחֵר ז 7 proponent; supporter; cadet
שׁוֹעֵר ז 7 goalie; gatekeeper, guard
תּוֹאֵם ז 7 corresponding, matching
בּוֹרֵא ז 8 creator
חוֹטֵא ז 8 sinner
נוֹשֵׂא ז 8 carrier; subject (sent.)
סוֹבֵא ז 8 drunkard
קוֹרֵא ז 8 reader; type of desert bird
רוֹפֵא ז 8 doctor, physician
שׂוֹנֵא ז 8 hater, enemy
אוֹרֵחַ ז 9 guest, visitor
בּוֹרֵחַ ז 9 fugitive, escapee
מוֹנֵעַ ז 9 preventative
מוֹתֵחַ ז 9 thrilling, suspenseful
נוֹבֵעַ ז 9 gushing, flowing
נוֹכֵחַ ז 9 attendee
נוֹסֵעַ ז 9 passenger
פּוֹרֵעַ ז 9 rioter
פּוֹשֵׁעַ ז 9 criminal
צוֹלֵעַ ז 9 lame, limping
צוֹמֵחַ ז 9 plants, vegetation
קוֹלֵעַ ז 9 correct, on-the-mark
רוֹגֵעַ ז 9 calm, peaceful
רוֹוֵחַ ז 9 common, widespread
רוֹצֵחַ ז 9 murderer
רוֹקֵחַ ז 9 pharmacist
רוֹתֵחַ ז 9 boiling
תּוֹבֵעַ ז 9 prosecutor; plaintiff, complainant
תּוֹקֵעַ ז 9 shofar blower; trumpeter
אוֹפֶה ז 10 baker
בּוֹנֶה ז 10 builder, mason; beaver
גּוֹבֶה ז 10 collector esp. of taxes
גּוֹלֶה ז 10 exile
דּוֹחֶה ז 10 repulsive
הוֹגֶה ז 10 thinker, philosopher
הוֹוֶה ז 10 present; existing
הוֹזֶה ז 10 daydreamer
הוֹרֶה ז 10 parent
חוֹזֶה ז 10 contract; seer
חוֹלֶה ז 10 patient; sick person
חוֹצֶה ז 10 dissector
טוֹעֶה ז 10 mistaken
יוֹרֶה ז 10 shooter; first rain of the season
כּוֹרֶה ז 10 miner
לוֹוֶה ז 10 borrower
מוֹנֶה ז 10 diaper
נוֹשֶׁה ז 10 debtor
עוֹלֶה ז 10 immigrant to Israel

פּוֹרֶה ז 10 productive; fruitful
צוֹפֶה ז 10 scout, guard
קוֹנֶה ז 10 customer, buyer
רוֹאֶה ז 10 seer
רוֹבֶה ז 10 rifle
רוֹעֶה ז 10 shepherd
שׁוֹטֶה ז 10 a fool, an idiot; foolish; rabid (dog)
שׁוֹנֶה ז 10 different
שׁוֹסֶה ז 10 one who incites
תּוֹעֶה ז 10 lost; accidental; one who lost his way
אוֹמֶנֶת נ 11 nanny, nursemaid, nurse
גּוֹרֶרֶת נ 11 tugboat, tug
דּוֹגֶרֶת נ 11 brooder bird hatching eggs
יוֹלֶדֶת נ 11 woman giving birth
יוֹנֶקֶת נ 11 sucker; young shoot (botany)
עוֹפֶרֶת נ 11 lead (chemistry) [no pl.]
צוֹלֶלֶת נ 11 submarine
טוֹחֶנֶת נ 12 molar tooth
פּוֹעֶלֶת נ 12 worker bee
בּוֹלֶשֶׁת נ 13 secret police, undercover police
חוֹבֶרֶת נ 13 booklet
חוֹתֶלֶת נ 13 legging, calf-warmer
חוֹתֶמֶת נ 13 stamp, seal; postmark
כּוֹנֶרֶת נ 13 viola
כּוֹתֶפֶת נ 13 shoulder strap
כּוֹתֶרֶת נ 13 title of book, work; headline; petal
צוֹצֶלֶת נ 13 palm dove, wild pigeon
שׁוֹשֶׁלֶת נ 13 dynasty
שׁוֹשֶׁנֶת נ 13 rosette bot
אוֹיְבוּת נ 14 enmity, hatred, hostility
בּוֹלְטוּת נ 14 prominence, standing out
בּוֹקְרוּת נ 14 cattle raising [no pl.]
הוֹלֵלוּת נ 14 unruly conduct (*tsere* stable)
זוֹלְלוּת נ 14 gluttony Lit [no pl.]
חוֹבְלוּת נ 14 seamanship [no pl.]
חוֹבְשׁוּת נ 14 medic training course [no pl.]
חוֹנְכוּת נ 14 tutoring, coaching; mentoring
כּוֹנְנוּת נ 14 alertness, readiness
נוֹטְרוּת נ 14 Jewish guard unit in British police during British mandate [no pl.]
נוֹכְחוּת נ 14 presence, attendance
נוֹכְלוּת נ 14 fraud, swindle
סוֹכְנוּת נ 14 agency
עוֹיְנוּת נ 14 hostility
צוֹרְפוּת נ 14 gold and silver crafting [no pl.]
רוֹכְלוּת נ 14 peddling, hawking

רוֹקְחוּת נ 14 pharmacy science [no pl.]
שׁוֹפְטוּת נ 14 judging; refereeing [no pl.]
בָּאוּשׁ ז 15 smelly; spoilt esp. fruit Lit
בָּדוּל ז 15 isolated, alone Lit
בָּדוּק ז 15 confirmed, checked
בָּזוּי ז 15 despised
בָּחוּן ז 15 tested, proven Lit rare
בָּנוּי ז 15 built
בָּצוּר ז 15 fortified; picked grapes
בָּרוּא ז 15 created; creature
בָּרוּךְ ז 15 blessed
בָּרוּר ז 15 clear
בָּתוּל ז 15 virgin m.
גָּאוּל ז 15 emancipated, free Lit
גָּדוּם ז 15 amputated, truncated
גָּדוּר ז 15 fenced; restricted
גָּדוּשׁ ז 15 full, crammed, heaped
גָּהוּר ז 15 prostrate, bent over Lit
גָּזוּז ז 15 cut, shorn
גָּזוּל ז 15 stolen
גָּזוּם ז 15 pruned, clipped
גָּזוּר ז 15 cut; derived; decreed, ordained
גָּחוּן ז 15 bent over, prostrate
גָּלוּי ז 15 revealed, open; manifest
גָּלוּל ז 15 rolled up, wrapped
גָּלוּם ז 15 hidden, latent
גָּמוּד ז 15 tiny Lit-rare
גָּמוּל ז 15 weaned
גָּמוּר ז 15 finished; total
גָּנוּב ז 15 stolen
גָּנוּז ז 15 hidden, secreted
גָּעוּשׁ ז 15 raging, stormy Lit
גָּרוּב ז 15 wearing socks or stockings
גָּרוּם ז 15 thin, skinny; oversized
גָּרוּס ז 15 ground; crushed
גָּרוּף ז 15 raked, swept
גָּרוּר ז 15 dragged, towed; trailer
גָּרוּשׁ ז 15 divorced man
גָּשׁוּם ז 15 rainy
דָּאוּג ז 15 worried, concerned, anxious
דָּבוּק ז 15 firmly attached, glued, stuck
דָּגוּל ז 15 distinguished, outstanding
דָּגוּשׁ ז 15 geminate double length consonant
דָּהוּי ז 15 faded
דָּחוּי ז 15 rejected, spurned; deferred
דָּחוּס ז 15 compressed; tightly packed
דָּחוּף ז 15 urgent
דָּחוּק ז 15 hard-pressed, insufficient; squashed
דָּלוּי ז 15 drawn water – rare

lit; switched on 15 ז דָּלוּק
silent Lit 15 ז דָּמוּם
extinguished, fading Lit 15 ז דָּעוּךְ
laminated 15 ז דָּפוּף
terrible, bad; faulty; oppressed Sl. 15 ז דָּפוּק
terraced, stepped Lit 15 ז דָּרוּג
tensed; cocked; primed 15 ז דָּרוּךְ
trampled, run over 15 ז דָּרוּס
golden; gold coin archaic 15 ז זָהוּב
remembered 15 ז זָכוּר
muzzled Talmudic 15 ז זָמוּם
angry Lit; tiny, miniscule 15 ז זָעוּם
angry, furious 15 ז זָעוּף
tarred 15 ז זָפוּת
erect, straight; vertical, steep; upright 15 ז זָקוּף
in need of 15 ז זָקוּק
protruding, jutting out 15 ז זָקוּר
sprinkled 15 ז זָרוּי
thrown, discarded; slovenly Col. 15 ז זָרוּק
dipped, soaked 15 ז טָבוּל
woven 15 ז טָווּי
damp, musty 15 ז טָחוּב
ground, minced 15 ז טָחוּן
patched; spotted 15 ז טָלוּא
dewy, covered with dew 15 ז טָלוּל
solid, massive Lit 15 ז טָמוּם
hidden, concealed 15 ז טָמוּן
loaded, charged; requiring 15 ז טָעוּן
joined, attached Lit 15 ז טָפוּל
mincing walk; exact Lit-rare 15 ז טָפוּף
busy, occupied 15 ז טָרוּד
bleary-eyed 15 ז טָרוּט
disturbed; torn to pieces by beast; scrambled 15 ז טָרוּף
slammed door, etc. 15 ז טָרוּק
initiated 15 ז יָזוּם
child, infant, offspring Lit-bibl. 15 ז יָלוּד
appointed, determined, designated 15 ז יָעוּד
shaft of carriage, wagon 15 ז יָצוּל
poured, molded, cast 15 ז יָצוּק
created 15 ז יָצוּר
down, dejected, unwell; inferior 15 ז יָרוּד
shot; fired 15 ז יָרוּי
seated 15 ז יָשׁוּב
honorable, distinguished 15 ז כָּבוּד
extinguished 15 ז כָּבוּי
bound, chained; restricted 15 ז כָּבוּל

conquered; restrained; leveled ground; pickled, preserved 15 ז כָּבוּשׁ
gaunt, thin 15 ז כָּחוּשׁ
imprisoned; prisoner 15 ז כָּלוּא
included 15 ז כָּלוּל
hidden, concealed, secret 15 ז כָּמוּס
covered, concealed, hidden 15 ז כָּסוּי
silvery, silver-plated; longed for Lit 15 ז כָּסוּף
angry, irritated 15 ז כָּעוּס
forced, compelled 15 ז כָּפוּי
bent; subordinate 15 ז כָּפוּף
bound hands or feet 15 ז כָּפוּת
mined, dug 15 ז כָּרוּי
bound, wrapped; entailing; lust after 15 ז כָּרוּךְ
written 15 ז כָּתוּב
crushed, powdered 15 ז כָּתוּשׁ
dressed 15 ז לָבוּשׁ
enthusiastic, eager 15 ז לָהוּט
pressed, squeezed; very anxious 15 ז לָחוּץ
sharp, honed; bright, polished 15 ז לָטוּשׁ
captured, trapped 15 ז לָכוּד
well-versed, experienced 15 ז לָמוּד
chewed, gnawed 15 ז לָעוּס
wrapped, enveloped, bound, wound 15 ז לָפוּף
held tightly, grasped, clasped 15 ז לָפוּת
defective, deficient, inadequate 15 ז לָקוּי
repulsive, loathsome 15 ז מָאוּס
measured, moderate, unhurried 15 ז מָדוּד
diluted; circumcised 15 ז מָהוּל
poured 15 ז מָזוּג
forgiven; relinquished honor 15 ז מָחוּל
crushed, squeezed 15 ז מָחוּץ
erased, deleted 15 ז מָחוּק
sold; "fixed" sports; addicted Col. 15 ז מָכוּר
subscriber; subscribed to; counted 15 ז מָנוּי
devoted, loyal; given, granted; passed by tradition 15 ז מָסוּר
squashed, trapped 15 ז מָעוּךְ
found, located; common 15 ז מָצוּי
sucked 15 ז מָצוּץ
cliff, precipice 15 ז מָצוּק
serrated, notched, corrugated 15 ז מָרוּג
depressed Lit 15 ז מָרוּד
drawn; pulled 15 ז מָשׁוּךְ
moderate; level-headed; slow, measured 15 ז מָתוּן

hollow; empty; superficial, shallow 15 ז נָבוּב
sprouted, germinated 15 ז נָבוּט
withered, wilted, dried out 15 ז נָבוּל
gnawed, bitten into 15 ז נָגוּס
not relaxed, disturbed sleep Lit 15 ז נָדוּד
customary, acceptable; driven a vehicle 15 ז נָהוּג
rebuked; contrite, chastened 15 ז נָזוּף
necessary, required 15 ז נָחוּץ
inferior, lower in status 15 ז נָחוּת
slanted; bent; inflected 15 ז נָטוּי
devoid; lacking 15 ז נָטוּל
abandoned 15 ז נָטוּשׁ
short; low; of poor quality 15 ז נָמוּךְ
spread over 15 ז נָסוּךְ
locked 15 ז נָעוּל
attached, pinned; stuck, affixed 15 ז נָעוּץ
drooping 15 ז נָפוּל
locked weapon; hidden 15 ז נָצוּר
poked, perforated, punctured 15 ז נָקוּב
dotted, spotted 15 ז נָקוּד
taken, held action, precaution 15 ז נָקוּט
upturned eyes, gaze; predicate; object 15 ז נָשׂוּא
married 15 ז נָשׂוּי
bitten 15 ז נָשׁוּךְ
item of data; placed; liable to; given 15 ז נָתוּן
filthy Lit 15 ז סָאוּב
complicated, complex; tangled 15 ז סָבוּךְ
be of the opinion that 15 ז סָבוּר
tormented, tortured 15 ז סָגוּף
closed, shut; turned off 15 ז סָגוּר
split, cracked 15 ז סָדוּק
organized, arranged 15 ז סָדוּר
wrung; squeezed 15 ז סָחוּט
swept away; painful, anguished Lit 15 ז סָחוּף
slapped Lit 15 ז סָטוּר
leaf-covered 15 ז סָכוּךְ
dammed, sluiced 15 ז סָכוּר
paved 15 ז סָלוּל
hidden, concealed; latent 15 ז סָמוּי
adjacent, nearby; resting, leaning 15 ז סָמוּךְ
red, flushed 15 ז סָמוּק
straight, stiff, hard Lit 15 ז סָמוּר
story; agitated Lit 15 ז סָעוּר
soaked 15 ז סָפוּג
roofed; introverted Lit; concealed Lit 15 ז סָפוּן

counted; numbered, very few Lit 15 ז סָפוּר
stoned; cleared of stones Lit 15 ז סָקוּל
covered by media 15 ז סָקוּר
knitted, crocheted 15 ז סָרוּג
scratched 15 ז סָרוּט
drawn, dragged Lit 15 ז סָרוּךְ
combed; scanned 15 ז סָרוּק
blocked; vague 15 ז סָתוּם
unkempt, wild hair; contradictory 15 ז סָתוּר
faulty, defective, lacking 15 ז פָּגוּם
scattered; dispersed; loose 15 ז פָּזוּר
exempt 15 ז פָּטוּר
corridor; entrance door rare 15 ז פָּלוּשׁ
vacant; unoccupied; single unmarried 15 ז פָּנוּי
invalid, disqualified; improper 15 ז פָּסוּל
verse, phrase; decided, ordered law 15 ז פָּסוּק
gaping, wide open 15 ז פָּעוּר
corked, stoppered; blocked, jammed with traffic 15 ז פָּקוּק
separated 15 ז פָּרוּד
unwalled city 15 ז פָּרוּז
spread out; sliced 15 ז פָּרוּס
cracked, broken, breached 15 ז פָּרוּץ
disarmed weapon 15 ז פָּרוּק
recluse; ascetic 15 ז פָּרוּשׁ
simple; plain; extended, stretched out arms, legs 15 ז פָּשׁוּט
pinched 15 ז צָבוּט
accumulated, piled, heaped 15 ז צָבוּר
hostile Lit 15 ז צָהוּב
crucified; Christ 15 ז צָלוּב
grilled, roasted, broiled 15 ז צָלוּי
clear, transparent; lucid 15 ז צָלוּל
beside, next to; attached to; linked; close fitting (clothes); close to, close 15 ז צָמוּד
compact; compressed 15 ז צָמוּם
wizened, wrinkled 15 ז צָמוּק
lean, thin, gaunt; slim 15 ז צָנוּם
wrapped like turban; crumpled, folded 15 ז צָנוּף
dry, shriveled, wizened Lit 15 ז צָפוּד
expected, anticipated; liable, subject 15 ז צָפוּי
hidden, concealed 15 ז צָפוּן
crowded; dense, thick 15 ז צָפוּף
scorched, burned 15 ז צָרוּב
hoarse 15 ז צָרוּד
refined, purified; pure, absolute 15 ז צָרוּף

bound, wrapped up; buried emotion, memory 15 ז צָרוּר
collected, gathered Lit 15 ז קָבוּץ
buried 15 ז קָבוּר
ancient 15 ז קָדוּם
blurred, dull; lusterless, rough 15 ז קָהוּי
killed, exterminated 15 ז קָטוּל
trimmed, lopped 15 ז קָטוּם
harvested, plucked, cut, reaped 15 ז קָטוּף
unroofed Obs. 15 ז קָטוּר
recorded; absorbed; registered 15 ז קָלוּט
toasted, roasted 15 ז קָלוּי
peeled, skinned; blanched 15 ז קָלוּף
slim, slight; scant; vague 15 ז קָלוּשׁ
withered, shriveled 15 ז קָמוּל
tightly closed lips, fist, eyes 15 ז קָמוּץ
convex, domed, rounded, curved 15 ז קָמוּר
bought, purchased; acquired, achieved 15 ז קָנוּי
enchanting 15 ז קָסוּם
concave 15 ז קָעוּר
frozen 15 ז קָפוּא
tightly closed 15 ז קָפוּץ
rhythmic; limited, defined, measured 15 ז קָצוּב
diced, chopped; cropped; very short hair 15 ז קָצוּץ
harvested, reaped, cut 15 ז קָצוּר
invitee 15 ז קָרוּא
named 15 ז קָרוּי
crouched 15 ז קָרוּס
molded, shaped Lit 15 ז קָרוּץ
congealed 15 ז קָרוּשׁ
attentive 15 ז קָשׁוּב
tied, fastened; attached to; connected to 15 ז קָשׁוּר
fitting, appropriate; fit for, suitable for; deserving 15 ז רָאוּי
layered 15 ז רָבוּד
recumbent 15 ז רָבוּץ
angry 15 ז רָגוּז
shallow, superficial 15 ז רָדוּד
sleepy, drowsy; dormant; numb 15 ז רָדוּם
haunted, troubled; chased 15 ז רָדוּף
fluent 15 ז רָהוּט
hesitant, unsure Lit 15 ז רָהוּי
watered, saturated; replete 15 ז רָווּי
merciful 15 ז רָחוּם
washed, cleaned 15 ז רָחוּץ
wet 15 ז רָטֹב ~ רָטוּב
riding 15 ז רָכוּב
bent, hunched 15 ז רָכוּן
buttoned 15 ז רָכוּס
trampled, downtrodden 15 ז רָמוּס

veiled, masked 15 ז רָעוּל
relaxed, limp; loose 15 ז רָפוּי
weak, limp Lit 15 ז רָפוּס
desirable, wanted, welcome; advisable 15 ז רָצוּי
continuous; consecutive 15 ז רָצוּף
broken, smashed; fragmented 15 ז רָצוּץ
rotten, decaying; crooked, corrupt 15 ז רָקוּב
embroidered 15 ז רָקוּם
written; registered 15 ז רָשׁוּם
boiled 15 ז רָתוּחַ
harnessed, bridled; hitched; committed, devoted 15 ז רָתוּם
confined, stuck, "grounded" 15 ז רָתוּק
drawn, extracted; pumped 15 ז שָׁאוּב
borrowed 15 ז שָׁאוּל
finished, exhausted; depressed Sl. 15 ז שָׁבוּז
captive, prisoner; captured; ideologically entrenched 15 ז שָׁבוּי
broken; fractured; depressed 15 ז שָׁבוּר
wrong, mistaken, erroneous 15 ז שָׁגוּי
common, customary; routine 15 ז שָׁגוּר
robbed, burglarized, plundered 15 ז שָׁדוּד
blasted, emaciated; blighted; empty 15 ז שָׁדוּף
suntanned 15 ז שָׁזוּף
entwined; interwoven 15 ז שָׁזוּר
slaughtered; killed, butchered 15 ז שָׁחוּט
brownish, dark brown 15 ז שָׁחוּם
arid 15 ז שָׁחוּן
having tuberculosis; gaunt 15 ז שָׁחוּף
worn, eroded; exhausted; overused 15 ז שָׁחוּק
washed, rinsed; drenched 15 ז שָׁטוּף
lying, resting 15 ז שָׁכוּב
rented, hired 15 ז שָׂכוּר
integrated, interwoven; folded arms 15 ז שָׁלוּב
drawn weapon; extracted 15 ז שָׁלוּף
scalded with boiling water (food) Lit 15 ז שָׁלוּק
sloping, leaning forward/sideways 15 ז שָׁמוּט
guarded; kept; preserved, maintained; reserved, saved 15 ז שָׁמוּר
hated, loathed 15 ז שָׂנוּא
repeated, reviewed 15 ז שָׁנוּי
sharp, witty 15 ז שָׁנוּן

choked Lit 15 ז שָׁנוּק
slit, slashed, gashed 15 ז שָׁסוּף
sentenced to 15 ז שָׁפוּט
sane; moderate, restrained 15 ז שָׁפוּי
bent over; depressed Sl. 15 ז שָׁפוּף
food placed on fire/heat for cooking 15 ז שָׁפוּת
equal; reasonable; weighed; comparable; metered, rhyming 15 ז שָׁקוּל
transparent, clear 15 ז שָׁקוּף
scratched 15 ז שָׂרוּט
be in a state of mind etc.; soaked 15 ז שָׁרוּי
burnt, scorched 15 ז שָׂרוּף
drunk 15 ז שָׁתוּי
planted 15 ז שָׁתוּל
marked, sketched Lit 15 ז תָּווּי
defined, limited, delineated 15 ז תָּחוּם
frequent 15 ז תָּכוּף
hanging, hung; hanged; dependent; reliant upon 15 ז תָּלוּי
steep 15 ז תָּלוּל
picked, plucked; torn off; detached; unrealistic 15 ז תָּלוּשׁ
leaning, supported 15 ז תָּמוּךְ
fermented, aerated rare 15 ז תָּסוּס
abhorrent, detested Lit 15 ז תָּעוּב
caught; occupied; engaged 15 ז תָּפוּס
sewn; tailor-made 15 ז תָּפוּר
broken down, out of order 15 ז תָּקוּל
feeble, worn out 15 ז תָּשׁוּשׁ
lost; hopeless 16 ז אָבוּד
fattened animal 16 ז אָבוּס
bundles, combined 16 ז אָגוּד
accumulated 16 ז אָגוּר
religious; enthusiastic 16 ז אָדוּק
beloved; popular 16 ז אָהוּב
admired, cherished 16 ז אָהוּד
handcuffed, bound, chained 16 ז אָזוּק
girded Lit 16 ז אָזוּר
integral, complete, united 16 ז אָחוּד
percentage; percent; caught, held 16 ז אָחוּז
sealed; opaque 16 ז אָטוּם
eaten, devoured; corroded 16 ז אָכוּל
practiced, experienced 16 ז אָמוּן
supposed to; the above-mentioned 16 ז אָמוּר
forced, compelled; Marrano 16 ז אָנוּס
mortal, fatal 16 ז אָנוּשׁ
oil flask Lit 16 ז אָסוּךְ
gathered, collected, bundled 16 ז אָסוּף
forbidden; imprisoned 16 ז אָסוּר
baked 16 ז אָפוּי
pea 16 ז אָפוּן
wrapped, surrounded Lit 16 ז אָפוּף
stored, hoarded, put aside 16 ז אָצוּר
woven 16 ז אָרוּג
packed, packaged 16 ז אָרוּז
fiancé; engaged 16 ז אָרוּס
cursed, damned 16 ז אָרוּר
solid, hard Lit 16 ז אָשׁוּן
step; confirmed Lit-rare 16 ז אָשׁוּר
pronounced, articulated; thought of, considered Lit 16 ז הָגוּי
decent, fair; adequate, suitable 16 ז הָגוּן
pushed, shoved 16 ז הָדוּף
tight 16 ז הָדוּק
elegant, refined 16 ז הָדוּר
hallucinatory, imaginary 16 ז הָזוּי
smitten Lit 16 ז הָלוּם
shocked, stunned 16 ז הָמוּם
dead, killed person 16 ז הָרוּג
destroyed 16 ז הָרוּס
beaten; worn out 16 ז חָבוּט
hidden, unseen 16 ז חָבוּי
beaten, injured, battered 16 ז חָבוּל
embraced, hugged 16 ז חָבוּק
joined, attached, connected Lit 16 ז חָבוּר
bandaged, dressed; head-covered 16 ז חָבוּשׁ
belt-wearing 16 ז חָגוּר
imbued, saturated 16 ז חָדוּר
anticipated, predictable; forecast 16 ז חָזוּי
well-built, carved 16 ז חָטוּב
kidnapped; kidnapped person; fleeting, brief, momentary 16 ז חָטוּף
leased 16 ז חָכוּר
rusty, rusted 16 ז חָלוּד
soaked in hot water 16 ז חָלוּט
hollow 16 ז חָלוּל
pioneer, pioneering 16 ז חָלוּץ
gown, robe; antagonistic, contrary 16 ז חָלוּק
weak, feeble 16 ז חָלוּשׁ
cute; darling 16 ז חָמוּד
sour 16 ז חָמוּץ
serious, grave; severe 16 ז חָמוּר
armed 16 ז חָמוּשׁ
mummy; frozen, fossilized; embalmed 16 ז חָנוּט
favored, granted good Lit 16 ז חָנוּן
choked 16 ז חָנוּק
hypocritical; graceful Lit 16 ז חָסוּד
secret; protected 16 ז חָסוּי
blocked 16 ז חָסוּם
hasty, hurried; brief sexual encounter Sl. 16 ז חָפוּז
covered Lit 16 ז חָפוּי
washed, shampooed hair 16 ז חָפוּף
dug 16 ז חָפוּר
rolled up sleeve, etc. – Lit 16 ז חָפוּת
quarried; carved, etched 16 ז חָצוּב
halved, split, divided 16 ז חָצוּי
cheeky, rude, arrogant 16 ז חָצוּף
engraved, carved; statutory 16 ז חָקוּק
investigated, studied 16 ז חָקוּר
ruined Lit; carob 16 ז חָרוּב
bead; threaded, strung; rhyme, verse; rhyming 16 ז חָרוּז
engraved, chiseled; cone 16 ז חָרוּט
scorched, singed 16 ז חָרוּךְ
thorn Bibl. 16 ז חָרוּל
flat, snub, pug nose 16 ז חָרוּם
diligent, industrious; total, decided; wrinkled Lit; gulch, moat 16 ז חָרוּץ
rifled 16 ז חָרוּק
pierced 16 ז חָרוּר
plowed; furrowed, grooved 16 ז חָרוּשׁ
engraved; imprinted 16 ז חָרוּת
important; eminent, influential 16 ז חָשׁוּב
suspected; suspect 16 ז חָשׁוּד
dark 16 ז חָשׁוּךְ
exposed 16 ז חָשׂוּף
tight-lipped; desired 16 ז חָשׁוּק
sliced, chopped; cut 16 ז חָתוּךְ
cat 16 ז חָתוּל
signed, sealed 16 ז חָתוּם
sad, depressed 16 ז עָגוּם
crane (bird) 16 ז עָגוּר
adorned Lit 16 ז עָדוּי
hoed, tilled 16 ז עָדוּר
abandoned, neglected 16 ז עָזוּב
wrapped, covered Lit 16 ז עָטוּי
wrapped, covered 16 ז עָטוּף
decorated 16 ז עָטוּר
murky 16 ז עָכוּר
wretched, dismal; meager, worthless 16 ז עָלוּב
liable, likely 16 ז עָלוּל
secret, hidden 16 ז עָלוּם
dark; weak, unclear; blurry, hazy 16 ז עָמוּם
loaded, laden; busy, crowded 16 ז עָמוּס
wearing a tie 16 ז עָנוּב
adorned 16 ז עָנוּד
punishable Obs. 16 ז עָנוּשׁ
busy, occupied 16 ז עָסוּק

sad 16 עָצוּב ז
enormous; closed eyes 16 עָצוּם ז
constricted, restrained; imprisoned, detained; prisoner, detainee 16 עָצוּר ז
bound 16 עָקוּד ז
crooked 16 עָקוּם ז
stung, bitten 16 עָקוּץ ז
uprooted, extracted; displaced person 16 עָקוּר ז
crooked Lit 16 עָקוּשׁ ז
set table; arranged, prepared, organized; edited 16 עָרוּךְ ז
cunning 16 עָרוּם ז
decapitated 16 עָרוּף ז
ravine; channel radio, tv; track 16 עָרוּץ ז
made of; made, prepared; completed; liable, likely to 16 עָשׂוּי ז
exploited, oppressed 16 עָשׁוּק ז
amusing, entertaining 17 בָּדוּחַ ז
certain; safe 17 בָּטוּחַ ז
swallowed up 17 בָּלוּעַ ז
sliced bread 17 בָּצוּעַ ז
cracked, split 17 בָּקוּעַ ז
cut down, felled 17 גָּדוּעַ ז
shaven 17 גָּלוּחַ ז
being swallowed Lit 17 גָּמוּעַ ז
bad, inferior 17 גָּרוּעַ ז
tearful Lit 17 דָּמוּעַ ז
arrogant, haughty 17 זָחוּחַ ז
abandoned, deserted; trivial 17 זָנוּחַ ז
sown, seeded; scattered 17 זָרוּעַ ז
slaughtered 17 טָבוּחַ ז
drowned 17 טָבוּעַ ז
known; famous; certain 17 יָדוּעַ ז
bed, couch Lit 17 יָצוּעַ ז
submissive, docile, resigned 17 כָּנוּעַ ז
cut, mowed, trimmed 17 כָּסוּחַ ז
taken from, derived from 17 לָקוּחַ ז
salty, saline 17 מָלוּחַ ז
prevented from, precluded from; prohibited 17 מָנוּעַ ז
spread, smeared 17 מָרוּחַ ז
anointed; dipped 17 מָשׁוּחַ ז
stretched, taut; tense, nervous 17 מָתוּחַ ז
infected, contaminated 17 נָגוּעַ ז
swollen; inflated 17 נָפוּחַ ז
sprained, strained 17 נָקוּעַ ז
forgiven, pardoned 17 סָלוּחַ ז
flat, stretched out 17 סָרוּחַ ז
damaged, injured; hurt 17 פָּגוּעַ ז
wounded 17 פָּצוּעַ תו"ז
open eyes; watchful eye 17 פָּקוּחַ ז
split, cracked; invalid, void 17 פָּקוּעַ ז
unkempt; wild, unruly; redeemed 17 פָּרוּעַ ז
open 17 פָּתוּחַ ז
painted, colored; hypocrite; hypocritical 17 צָבוּעַ ז
tilted forward 17 צָנוּחַ ז
modest, humble 17 צָנוּעַ ז
leprous Lit 17 צָרוּעַ ז
routine; permanent, fixed; affixed 17 קָבוּעַ ז
braided, plaited 17 קָלוּעַ ז
torn 17 קָרוּעַ ז
stubborn; tough, hard; strict 17 קָשׁוּחַ ז
rickety, dilapidated; weak, unstable 17 רָעוּעַ ז
murdered 17 רָצוּחַ ז
beaten metal, hammered 17 רָקוּעַ ז
bent, hunched 17 שָׁחוּחַ ז
flat 17 שָׁטוּחַ ז
forgotten 17 שָׁכוּחַ ז
sent; spread out, stretched out hand 17 שָׁלוּחַ ז
split; torn, divided 17 שָׁסוּעַ ז
sunk, stuck; sunken 17 שָׁקוּעַ ז
recumbent, lying 17 שָׂרוּעַ ז
crumbled, loose earth 17 תָּחוּחַ ז
worm-eaten Lit 17 תָּלוּעַ ז
swollen, blown up 17 תָּפוּחַ ז
stuck, jammed 17 תָּקוּעַ ז
non-virgin woman; married woman 18 בְּעוּלָה נ
virgin f. 18 בְּתוּלָה נ
courage, bravery; fortitude; strength 18 גְּבוּרָה נ
postcard 18 גְּלוּיָה נ
tablet, pill 18 גְּלוּלָה נ
block, plate in printing 18 גְּלוּפָה נ
shavings 18 גְּרוּדָה נ
metastasis, secondary growth cancer 18 גְּרוּרָה נ
affix (grammar) 18 טְפוּלָה נ
basis Lit 18 יְסוּדָה נ
fund, segregated account; engaged 18 יְעוּדָה נ
the totality of an author's or artist's works 18 יְצוּרָה נ
salvation 18 יְשׁוּעָה נ
capsule medicine 18 כְּמוּסָה נ
clergy, priesthood 18 כְּמוּרָה נ
multiple (math.) 18 כְּפוּלָה נ
vest, waistcoat Lit 18 לְסוּטָה נ
compiled set of news items 18 לְקוּטָה נ
monarchy 18 מְלוּכָה נ
prophesy, prediction 18 נְבוּאָה נ
meal, dinner, feast 18 סְעוּדָה/סְעֻדָּה נ
dispersion, diaspora 18 פְּזוּרָה נ
down feathers, hair 18 פְּלוּמָה נ
grain of seed 18 פְּרוּדָה נ
small monetary unit; minute sum 18 פְּרוּטָה נ
slice 18 פְּרוּסָה נ
prostitute 18 פְּרוּצָה נ
march music 18 צְעוּדָה נ
set of items permanently fixed to a structure 18 קְבוּעָה נ
group 18 קְבוּצָה נ
burial 18 קְבוּרָה נ
trapezoid 18 קְטוּמָה נ
medicine; recovery, cure 18 רְפוּאָה נ
strap; strip 18 רְצוּעָה נ
record, listing 18 רְשׁוּמָה נ
oath, pledge 18 שְׁבוּעָה נ
neighborhood 18 שְׁכוּנָה נ
extension, branch 18 שְׁלוּחָה נ
rumor 18 שְׁמוּעָה נ
reservation; nature reserve 18 שְׁמוּרָה נ
torch 19 אֲבוּקָה נ
pea 19 אֲפוּנָה נ
meal 19 אֲרוּחָה נ
scab 19 אֲרוּכָה נ
band, small group of people 19 חֲבוּרָה נ
option; alternative 19 חֲלוּפָה נ
tripod 19 חֲצוּבָה נ
chained" woman " unable to get a divorce 19 עֲגוּנָה נ
neglect 19 עֲזוּבָה נ
leech 19 עֲלוּקָה נ
petition 19 עֲצוּמָה נ
flowerbed 19 עֲרוּגָה נ
reserve, store; provision 19 עֲתוּדָה נ
that can be brought before the high court of justice Coll./Sl. 20 בָּגִיץ ז
adult in legal sense n, adj 20 בָּגִיר ז
discrete math 20 בָּדִיד ז
light, pale; light, clear 20 בָּהִיר ז
vessel obs. 20 בָּזִיךְ ז
select, chosen, elite 20 בָּחִיר ז
senior; senior person 20 בָּכִיר ז
basis, foundation; base 20 בָּסִיס ז
flammable 20 בָּעִיר ז
grape harvest; harvested grapes 20 בָּצִיר ז
expert, knowledgeable, proficient 20 בָּקִיא ז
healthy 20 בָּרִיא ז
eyebrow Lit 20 גָּבִין ז
crystal 20 גָּבִישׁ ז
date harvest 20 גָּדִיד ז
stock, pile, stack of grain 20 גָּדִישׁ ז
small piece, snippet; that can be sheared 20 גָּזִיז ז
cuttable, easy to cut 20 גָּזִיר ז
cylinder; roll; region 20 גָּלִיל ז
flexible 20 גָּמִישׁ ז
sticky, adhesive 20 דָּבִיק ז
compressible 20 דָּחִיס ז

דָּלִיל ז 20 thin, sparse; watery, diluted
דָּלִיק ז 20 flammable
זָהִיר ז 20 careful, cautious
זָמִין ז 20 available
זָמִיר ז 20 nightingale
זָעִיר ז 20 small, tiny; miniature
זָקִיף ז 20 sentry; stalagmite
זָרִיז ז 20 quick, agile, nimble
זָרִים ז 20 flowing
טָמִיר ז 20 hidden, conceal
טָעִים ז 20 tasty
יָבִיל ז 20 transportable, movable
יָדִיד ז 20 friend
יָהִיר ז 20 arrogant
יָחִיד ז 20 alone, one; individual; singular (grammar)
יָלִיד ז 20 native of, born in
יָמִין ז 20 right
יָעִיל ז 20 efficient; effective
יָצִיג ז 20 representative
יָצִיק ז 20 liquefiable, moldable metal
יָרִיב ז 20 adversary
יָשִׂים ז 20 applicable
יָשִׁיר ז 20 direct
יָשִׁישׁ ז 20 very old; very old person
כָּבִיס ז 20 washable
כָּלִיל ז 20 complete, total, absolute
כָּפִיל ז 20 double
כָּפִיס ז 20 wooden beam, rafter
כָּפִיף ז 20 flexible, pliable; a subordinate
כָּרִיךְ ז 20 sandwich
כָּרִישׁ ז 20 shark
כָּשִׁיר ז 20 fit, qualified
לָבִיא ז 20 lion
לָבִישׁ ז 20 wearable
לָהִיט ז 20 hit song; fad, latest thing Coll.
לָכִיד ז 20 coherent
לָמִיד ז 20 learnable, teachable
לָעִיס ז 20 chewable
מָדִיד ז 20 measurable
מָהִיר ז 20 fast
מָחִיק ז 20 erasable
מָכִיר ז 20 sellable, marketable
מָסִיס ז 20 soluble, dissolvable
מָסִיק ז 20 olive harvest
מָעִיךְ ז 20 squashable, squeezable
מָרִישׁ ז 20 beam, joist
מָשִׁישׁ ז 20 tangible
נָבִיא ז 20 prophet, visionary; soothsayer
נָגִיד ז 20 governor, ruler; wealthy, influential person; philanthropist
נָגִישׁ ז 20 accessible
נָדִיב ז 20 generous, charitable; noble
נָדִיף ז 20 volatile
נָדִיר ז 20 rare
נָהִיר ז 20 clear, understood, lucid
נָזִיד ז 20 stew, broth
נָזִיל ז 20 liquid
נָזִיר ז 20 monk; nazirite; hermit
נָסִיךְ ז 20 prince
נָסִיר ז 20 sawable, cuttable
נָעִים ז 20 pleasant, nice
נָפִיל ז 20 giant Lit
נָפִיץ ז 20 explosive; volatile
נָצִיג ז 20 representative, delegate
נָשִׂיא ז 20 president; chairman; leader
נָשִׁיר ז 20 deciduous
נָתִיב ז 20 path, track; route; course, direction
נָתִיךְ ז 20 electrical fuse
נָתִין ז 20 subject, citizen
נָתִיק ז 20 detachable
סָבִיךְ ז 20 entangled, intertwined
סָבִיל ז 20 passive
סָבִיר ז 20 reasonable, logical
סָגִין ז 20 military coat Lit-rare
סָדִין ז 20 sheet
סָדִיר ז 20 regular, systematic
סָחִיט ז 20 squeezable
סָחִיר ז 20 negotiable, tradable (economics)
סָמִיךְ ז 20 thick
סָפִיג ז 20 absorbent
סָפִין/סְפִין ז 20 baseboard
סָפִיר ז 20 countable, numerable
סָרִיג ז 20 knit textile, clothing; dish rack, drainer
פָּזִיז ז 20 hasty, haphazard
פָּלִיט ז 20 refugee
פָּעִיל ז 20 active
פָּקִיד ז 20 clerk
פָּרִיד ז 20 divisible
פָּרִיךְ ז 20 crispy, crunchy, crumbly; brittle
פָּרִיק ז 20 collapsible; disintegrable
פָּתִיל ז 20 tied with a string Lit
פָּתִיר ז 20 solvable
פָּתִית ז 20 flake, alt. ptit
צָבִיר ז 20 cumulative
צָמִיג ז 20 viscous, sticky, adhesive
צָמִיד ז 20 bracelet
צָמִיר ז 20 wooly, hairy Lit
צָמִית ז 20 vassal; permanent, steady
צָנִיף ז 20 turban
צָעִיף ז 20 scarf
צָעִיר ז 20 young; young man
צָפִיד ז 20 tough; rigid, stiff
צָפִיר ז 20 goat
צָרִיךְ ז 20 required; essential
קָבִיל ז 20 acceptable; admissible (law)
קָטִין/קְטִין ז 20 minor, a minor person
קָטִיף ז 20 fruit-picking; fruit-picking season
קָלִיף ז 20 peelable
קָמִיט ז 20 wrinkly
קָצִין ז 20 officer; leader, ruler bibl.
קָצִיף ז 20 frothy, foamy
קָצִיץ ז 20 meat loaf alt ktsits
קָצִיר ז 20 harvest
קָרִיא ז 20 readable
קָרִישׁ/קְרִישׁ ז 20 gel; jelly; blood clot
קָשִׁישׁ ז 20 old, elderly; elderly person
רָבִיב ז 20 rain Lit
רָבִיד ז 20 necklace, choker
רָגִיז ז 20 irritable
רָגִיל ז 20 regular, usual, normal; used to
רָגִישׁ ז 20 sensitive; perceptive; allergic to
רָחִיץ ז 20 washable
רָכִיל ז 20 gossip
רָצִיף/רְצִיף ז 20 consecutive; platform train etc.
רָקִיד ז 20 danceable music
רָקִיק ז 20 cookie Lit
שָׂאִיר ז 20 survivor, surviving relative
שָׁבִיט ז 20 comet
שָׁבִיס ז 20 coif
שָׁבִיר ז 20 fragile, breakable
שָׁחִיף/שְׁחִיף ז 20 thin wood plank; thin person
שָׂכִיר ז 20 salaried employee
שָׁלִיף ז 20 that can easily be drawn
שָׁמִיר ז 20 dill; emery; guardable
שָׁמִישׁ ז 20 usable
שָׂעִיר ז 20 hairy; furry
שָׂעִיר ז 20 male goat Lit
שָׁפִיט ז 20 that can be judged/evaluated
שָׁפִיר ז 20 amnion
שָׁקִיל ז 20 equivalent; weighable
שָׂרִיד ז 20 remnant
שָׁרִיר ז 20 valid
שָׁרִיר/שְׁרִיר ז 20 muscle
שָׁתִיל ז 20 plant N
שָׁתִית נ 20 subsoil
תָּדִיר ז 20 frequent
תָּלִישׁ ז 20 detachable coupon, stub
תָּמִים ז 20 innocent; naive
תָּמִיר ז 20 tall, erect, upright
תָּפִיס ז 20 understandable, comprehensible
תָּקִין ז 20 in order, functioning well
תָּקִיף/תָּקֵף ז 20 valid, current, in force
אָבִיב ז 21 spring
אָבִיךְ ז 21 hazy

drain of sink, bath 21 אָבִיק ז
polite, courteous 21 אָדִיב ז
indifferent 21 אָדִישׁ ז
lampshade 21 אָהִיל ז
depletable, consumable; exhaustible 21 אָזִיל ז
uniform; constant; homogeneous 21 אָחִיד ז
impervious 21 אָטִים ז
edible 21 אָכִיל ז
enforceable 21 אָכִיף ז
wealthy, well to do, affluent 21 אָמִיד ז
authentic, true; reliable 21 אָמִין ז
tree top 21 אָמִיר ז
sensitive, delicate, refined 21 אָנִין ז
stalk of plant 21 אָנִיץ ז
harvest 21 אָסִיף ז
prisoner, convict 21 אָסִיר/אַסִּיר ז
late ripening fruit 21 אָפִיל ז
river bed, channel; route, channel 21 אָפִיק ז
noble, aristocratic; refined, honorable, magnanimous; nobleman 21 אָצִיל ז
fabric, woven material 21 אָרִיג ז
tenant farmer, sharecropper 21 אָרִיס ז
humid, muggy 21 הָבִיל ז
reproducible; revocable in banking 21 הָדִיר ז
reversible 21 הָפִיךְ ז
pleasant, friendly, likeable; favorite 21 חָבִיב ז
penetrable 21 חָדִיר ז
modern, up-to-date, novel, new 21 חָדִישׁ ז
flute; recorder 21 חָלִיל ז
alternative; substitute in law 21 חָלִיף ז
student; apprentice 21 חָנִיךְ ז
Hassid, follower of a Hassidic sect; follower of, devotee; devout person; righteous, pious, kind 21 חָסִיד ז
immune, resistant, -proof 21 חָסִין ז
eggplant 21 חָצִיל ז
hay 21 חָצִיר ז
exceptional, irregular; different person 21 חָרִיג ז
purse, handbag Lit 21 חָרִיט ז
sharp, spicy; bright, smart 21 חָרִיף ז
slit, slot; crack, chink; slice of cheese 21 חָרִיץ ז
rifling, groove in weaponry 21 חָרִיק ז
plowing; plowing season 21 חָרִישׁ ז
malleable metal 21 חָשִׁיל ז
hunk Coll. 21 חָתִיךְ ז

workable 21 עָבִיד ז
passable, navigable, traversable 21 עָבִיר ז
earring 21 עָגִיל ז
fine, delicate; fragile; refined 21 עָדִין ז
preferable 21 עָדִיף ז
udder 21 עָטִין ז
(perianth (botany 21 עָטִיף ז
durable 21 עָמִיד ז
agent, representative commerce 21 עָמִיל ז
sheaf, bundle of grain 21 עָמִיר ז
colleague, friend 21 עָמִית ז
juice, nectar 21 עָסִיס ז
astringent 21 עָפִיץ ז
intensified, intense, strenuous 21 עָצִים/עַצִּים ז
detainee 21 עָצִיר ז
consistent; sequential 21 עָקִיב ז
indirect 21 עָקִיף ז
bower Lit; pergola 21 עָרִיס ז
cloud Lit 21 עָרִיף ז
despot, dictator; tyrant 21 עָרִיץ ז
deserter 21 עָרִיק ז
rich; rich person 21 עָשִׁיר ז
future; planned (pl. `atidot) 21 עָתִיד, ר׳ עֲתִידוֹת ז
that can be split; fissionable 22 בָּקִיעַ ז
goblet, cup 22 גָּבִיעַ ז
negligible 22 זָנִיחַ ז
balcony, gallery 22 יָצִיעַ ז
herring; food preserved in salt 22 מָלִיחַ ז
messiah; redeemer 22 מָשִׁיחַ ז
flexible 22 מָתִיחַ ז
operable (medical) 22 נָתִיחַ ז
aftermath, derivative; self-seeding crop 22 סָפִיחַ ז
vulnerable; sensitive emotionally 22 פָּגִיעַ ז
preface, introduction, opening; that can be opened 22 פָּתִיחַ ז
crossable; able to succeed 22 צָלִיחַ ז
bullet 22 קָלִיעַ ז
tearable 22 קָרִיעַ ז
still, inflexible, hard, rigid; strict 22 קָשִׁיחַ ז
heavens, firmament 22 רָקִיעַ ז
carpet, rug 22 שָׁטִיחַ ז
common; frequent 22 שָׁכִיחַ ז
messenger 22 שָׁלִיחַ ז
tile 23 אָרִיחַ ז
adulthood, maturity [no pl.] 24 בְּגִירוּת נ
loneliness 24 בְּדִידוּת נ
fun, jocularity, hilarity 24 בְּדִיחוּת נ
isolation, insularity [no pl.] 24 בְּדִילוּת נ
haste, alarm, panic [no pl.] 24 בְּהִילוּת נ

brightness; clarity; lucidity 24 בְּהִירוּת נ
safety 24 בְּטִיחוּת נ
expertise, knowledge, familiarity 24 בְּקִיאוּת נ
fissionability 24 בְּקִיעוּת נ
health [no pl.] 24 בְּרִיאוּת נ
selectivity in telecommunications; clarity 24 בְּרִירוּת נ
flexibility 24 גְּמִישׁוּת נ
stickiness, adhesiveness 24 דְּבִיקוּת נ
compressibility 24 דְּחִיסוּת נ
urgency 24 דְּחִיפוּת נ
turbidity, murkiness [no pl.] 24 דְּלִיחוּת נ
sparseness, thinness 24 דְּלִילוּת נ
flammability 24 דְּלִיקוּת נ
thinness 24 דְּקִיקוּת נ
tension, preparedness 24 דְּרִיכוּת נ
caution, care 24 זְהִירוּת נ
arrogance, self-satisfaction; euphoria 24 זְחִיחוּת נ
availability 24 זְמִינוּת נ
being angry Lit [no pl.] 24 זְעִיפוּת נ
smallness, unimportance 24 זְעִירוּת נ
erectness, uprightness 24 זְקִיפוּת נ
nimbleness, promptness 24 זְרִיזוּת נ
flowingness [no pl.] 24 זְרִימוּת נ
concealment, hiddenness [no pl.] 24 טְמִירוּת נ
tastiness, savoriness 24 טְעִימוּת נ
friendship 24 יְדִידוּת נ
arrogance 24 יְהִירוּת נ
solitariness, privacy; uniqueness, oneness 24 יְחִידוּת נ
effectiveness; efficiency 24 יְעִילוּת נ
rivalry, competition 24 יְרִיבוּת נ
applicability 24 יְשִׂימוּת נ
old age [no pl.] 24 יְשִׁישׁוּת נ
restrictedness, bondage, confinement 24 כְּבִילוּת נ
gauntness, leanness Lit [no pl.] 24 כְּחִישׁוּת נ
moral perfection; integrity, completeness [no pl.] 24 כְּלִילוּת נ
submissiveness, acquiescence [no pl.] 24 כְּנִיעוּת נ
duplication 24 כְּפִילוּת נ
subordination; dependence 24 כְּפִיפוּת נ
divorce, separation Lit 24 כְּרִיתוּת נ
witness, worthiness 24 כְּשִׁירוּת נ
enthusiasm, passion 24 לְהִיטוּת נ
teachability 24 לְמִידוּת נ
speed 24 מְהִירוּת נ
saltiness, salinity 24 מְלִיחוּת נ

מְסִיסוּת נ 24 solubility, dissolvability
מְסִירוּת נ 24 devotion, dedication
מְצִיאוּת נ 24 reality
מְרִירוּת נ 24 bitterness
מְתִיחוּת נ 24 tension, anxiety
מְתִינוּת נ 24 moderation [no pl.]
מְתִיקוּת נ 24 sweetness
נְבִיאוּת נ 24 prophesy
נְבִיבוּת נ 24 hollowness; emptiness
נְגִידוּת נ 24 governorship; wealth Lit
נְגִישׁוּת נ 24 accessibility
נְדִיבוּת נ 24 generosity
נְדִיפוּת נ 24 volatility
נְדִירוּת נ 24 scarcity, rarity
נְהִירוּת נ 24 lucidity, clarity [no pl.]
נְזִילוּת נ 24 liquidity
נְזִירוּת נ 24 monasticism; asceticism
נְחִיצוּת נ 24 necessity, requirement, need
נְחִישׁוּת נ 24 firmness, insistence, decisiveness
נְחִיתוּת נ 24 inferiority
נְלִיזוּת נ 24 perversion, depravity
נְמִיכוּת נ 24 lowness, shortness
נְסִיכוּת נ 24 principality
נְעִימוּת נ 24 pleasantness
נְפִיחוּת נ 24 swelling, swollenness
נְפִיצוּת נ 24 explosiveness, volatility
נְצִיבוּת נ 24 commissionership
נְצִיגוּת נ 24 representation, representative
נְצִילוּת נ 24 efficiency
נְשִׂיאוּת נ 24 presidency, chairmanship
נְתִינוּת נ 24 citizenship
נְתִיקוּת נ 24 detachment, alienation [no pl.]
סְבִיכוּת נ 24 complexity
סְבִילוּת נ 24 tolerance, endurance; passivity
סְבִירוּת נ 24 probability; reasonableness
סְגִילוּת נ 24 adaptability, versatility [no pl.]
סְדִירוּת נ 24 regularity
סְחִירוּת נ 24 negotiability, tradability
סְמִיכוּת נ 24 proximity; construct state grammar
סְמִיכוּת נ 24 thickness, viscosity
סְמִיקוּת נ 24 redness, blush, flush rare [no pl.]
סְפִיגוּת נ 24 absorbency
סְתִימוּת נ 24 vagueness, ambiguity
פְּגִימוּת נ 24 defectiveness, incompleteness

פְּגִיעוּת נ 24 vulnerability; sensitivity emotional
פְּזִיזוּת נ 24 haste
פְּחִיסוּת נ 24 flatness
פְּחִיתוּת נ 24 unimportance, inferiority
פְּעִילוּת נ 24 activity
פְּקִידוּת נ 24 clerical work; office workers collectively
פְּרִיכוּת נ 24 crispness, crumbliness; brittleness
פְּרִישׁוּת נ 24 asceticism
פְּתִיחוּת נ 24 openness
צְבִיעוּת נ 24 hypocrisy
צְהִיבוּת נ 24 yellowness
צְחִיחוּת נ 24 dryness, aridity; barrenness
צְלִילוּת נ 24 clearness, clarity, lucidity
צְמִיגוּת נ 24 viscosity, stickiness
צְמִידוּת נ 24 proximity, closeness
צְמִיתוּת נ 24 vassalage
צְנִיעוּת נ 24 modesty, humility; simplicity
צְעִירוּת נ 24 youth, adolescence [no pl.]
צְפִיפוּת נ 24 crowdedness, density
צְרִידוּת נ 24 hoarseness
קְבִילוּת נ 24 acceptability; submissibility (law)
קְבִיעוּת נ 24 tenure; constancy
קְדִימוּת נ 24 preference, precedence, priority
קְטִינוּת נ 24 status of a minor law [no pl.]
קְלִילוּת נ 24 nimbleness; lightness; ease
קְלִישׁוּת נ 24 minimalness, scantness; weakness; vagueness [no pl.]
קְמִיחוּת נ 24 mealiness [no pl.]
קְמִיטוּת נ 24 wrinkledness [no pl.]
קְצִינוּת נ 24 officer status [no pl.]
קְרִיאוּת נ 24 legibility; readability [no pl.]
קְרִירוּת נ 24 coolness
קְשִׁיחוּת נ 24 toughness; strictness; rigidity
קְשִׁישׁוּת נ 24 age, elderliness [no pl.]
רְגִישׁוּת נ 24 sensitivity; perceptiveness; allergy
רְדִיפוּת נ 24 paranoia
רְהִיטוּת נ 24 fluency [no pl.]
רְטִיבוּת נ 24 wetness, dampness [no pl.]
רְכִילוּת נ 24 gossip
רְפִיסוּת נ 24 flaccidity; weakness
רְצִיפוּת נ 24 consecutiveness; continuity

שְׂבִיעוּת נ 24 being satiated, satisfied
שְׁבִירוּת נ 24 fragility
שְׁגִירוּת נ 24 regularity
שְׁחִיתוּת נ 24 corruption
שְׁטִיחוּת נ 24 flatness
שְׁכִיחוּת נ 24 frequency, commonness
שְׂכִירוּת נ 24 rent
שְׁלִיחוּת נ 24 mission
שְׁמִיעוּת נ 24 audibility [no pl.]
שְׁמִישׁוּת נ 24 usability; serviceability
שְׁנִינוּת נ 24 sharpness, wit
שְׂעִירוּת נ 24 hairiness [no pl.]
שְׁפִיטוּת נ 24 justiciability; capability to judge/evaluate
שְׁפִיכוּת נ 24 being poured/ejaculated
שְׁקִילוּת נ 24 equivalence
שְׁקִיפוּת נ 24 transparency
שְׂרִידוּת נ 24 survivability
שְׁרִירוּת נ 24 arbitrariness
תְּאִימוּת נ 24 compatibility computers
תְּדִירוּת נ 24 frequency
תְּחִיחוּת נ 24 looseness of soil [no pl.]
תְּכִיפוּת נ 24 frequency, repetition
תְּלִילוּת נ 24 steepness, gradient
תְּלִישׁוּת נ 24 detachment, remoteness
תְּמִיהוּת נ 24 strangeness Lit
תְּמִימוּת נ 24 innocence; naivete
תְּמִירוּת נ 24 tallness, erectness [no pl.]
תְּפִיחוּת נ 24 swelling
תְּשִׁישׁוּת נ 24 fatigue, frailty, infirmity
אֲבִיכוּת נ 25 haziness Lit [no pl.]
אֲדִיבוּת נ 25 politeness, courtesy
אֲדִיקוּת נ 25 devotion; piety
אֲדִישׁוּת נ 25 indifference
אֲחִידוּת נ 25 uniformity
אֲטִימוּת נ 25 impermeability; inflexibility, unperceptiveness
אֲמִידוּת נ 25 being wealthy [no pl.]
אֲמִינוּת נ 25 authenticity; reliability
אֲנִינוּת נ 25 sensitivity, refinement
אֲפִיצוּת נ 25 tolerance, variation engineering
אֲצִילוּת נ 25 nobility; aristocracy
אֲרִיכוּת נ 25 length, extent
אֲרִיסוּת נ 25 tenant farming, share cropping
הֲגִינוּת נ 25 decency, fairness
הֲלִימוּת נ 25 adequacy
הֲפִיכוּת נ 25 reversibility
חֲבִיבוּת נ 25 friendliness, pleasantness

חֲדִירוּת נ 25 penetrability
חֲלִישׁוּת נ 25 weakness, fatigue
חֲמִימוּת נ 25 warmth
חֲמִיצוּת נ 25 sourness
חֲנִיכוּת נ 25 apprenticeship
חֲסִידוּת נ 25 Hassidism; righteousness, piety
חֲסִינוּת נ 25 immunity; resistance
חֲצִיפוּת נ 25 cheek, audacity, arrogance [no pl.]
חֲרִיגוּת נ 25 irregularity, unusualness, exceptionality
חֲרִיפוּת נ 25 sharpness; severity; pungency
חֲרִיצוּת נ 25 cutting, sharpening; deciding [no pl.]
חֲשִׁיבוּת נ 25 importance, significance
חֲשִׂיפוּת נ 25 exposure
עֲבִירוּת נ 25 navigability, passability
עֲדִינוּת נ 25 gentleness, softness, sensibility
עֲדִיפוּת נ 25 preference
עֲכִירוּת נ 25 murkiness, cloudiness; turbidity
עֲלִיבוּת נ 25 forlornness, wretchedness, neglectedness
עֲלִיצוּת נ 25 happiness, joy, cheerfulness
עֲמִידוּת נ 25 durability, fastness
עֲמִילוּת נ 25 agency, representation
עֲמִימוּת נ 25 vagueness, ambiguousness; opacity
עֲפִיצוּת נ 25 astringency
עֲצִירוּת נ 25 constipation
עֲקִיבוּת נ 25 consistency
עֲקִימוּת נ 25 crookedness, twistedness, curvature
עֲרִיקוּת נ 25 desertion
עֲשִׁירוּת נ 25 wealth, affluence Lit [no pl.]
הִבָּדְלוּת נ 26 segregation, isolation
הִבָּדְקוּת נ 26 being tested, being examined
הִבָּלְמוּת נ 26 being braked, being blocked
הִבָּלְעוּת נ 26 being swallowed, being engulfed
הִבָּקְעוּת נ 26 splitting intr.
הִבָּרְאוּת נ 26 being created
הִגָּמְלוּת נ 26 weaning, withdrawal
הִגָּנְזוּת נ 26 being hidden, being secreted
הִגָּרְמוּת נ 26 being caused
הִגָּרְעוּת נ 26 being lessened, being diminished
הִגָּרְפוּת נ 26 being swept
הִגָּרְרוּת נ 26 being towed
הִדָּבְקוּת נ 26 sticking, adhering
הִדָּבְרוּת נ 26 agreeing, esp. to meet
הִדָּלְקוּת נ 26 being ignited, be lit; being turned on engine, light
הִדָּרְכוּת נ 26 becoming ready for action; becoming taut/tense; being cocked weapon [no pl.]
הִדָּרְסוּת נ 26 being run over, trampled
הִדָּרְשׁוּת נ 26 being required to, being made to; being necessary
הִוָּדְעוּת נ 26 becoming known
הִוָּכְחוּת נ 26 becoming convinced, becoming aware [no pl.]
הִוָּלְדוּת נ 26 being born
הִוָּסְפוּת נ 26 addition, accumulation
הִוָּצְרוּת נ 26 creation
הִוָּשְׁעוּת נ 26 being saved, being redeemed
הִוָּתְרוּת נ 26 remaining [no pl.]
הִזָּכְרוּת נ 26 recalling; being mentioned
הִזָּקְפוּת נ 26 being credited to into account; straightening back [no pl.]
הִזָּקְקוּת נ 26 necessity, requirement, need
הִזָּרְקוּת נ 26 being thrown
הִטָּמְעוּת נ 26 being assimilated
הִטָּפְלוּת נ 26 harassing; clinging to
הִטָּרְפוּת נ 26 being devoured
הִכָּבְלוּת נ 26 being bound, being fettered [no pl.]
הִכָּלְאוּת נ 26 being jailed, being incarcerated [no pl.]
הִכָּלְלוּת נ 26 being included; being generalized Lit
הִכָּלְמוּת נ 26 being ashamed, being embarrassed [no pl.]
הִכָּנְסוּת נ 26 entering
הִכָּנְעוּת נ 26 surrendering; submitting to [no pl.]
הִכָּרְתוּת נ 26 being cut off; being amputated [no pl.]
הִכָּשְׁלוּת נ 26 failing; faltering, stumbling
הִלָּכְדוּת נ 26 being caught, capture N.
הִמָּזְגוּת נ 26 being poured [no pl.]
הִמָּלְטוּת נ 26 escaping, fleeing
הִמָּלְכוּת נ 26 consulting someone Lit; regretting Lit
הִמָּנְעוּת נ 26 abstention; avoidance
הִמָּצְאוּת נ 26 being found; being located [no pl.]
הִמָּשְׁכוּת נ 26 continuation; being pulled; being attracted
הִמָּתְחוּת נ 26 being stretched
הִנָּגְעוּת נ 26 contagion [no pl.]
הִנָּדְפוּת נ 26 evaporating Lit-rare [no pl.]
הִנָּזְקוּת נ 26 being damaged; damage
הִנָּטְלוּת נ 26 being taken away from [no pl.]
הִנָּטְעוּת נ 26 planting [no pl.]
הִנָּטְשׁוּת נ 26 abandonment [no pl.]
הִנָּפְשׁוּת נ 26 vacationing, relaxing [no pl.]
הִנָּצְלוּת נ 26 being saved; surviving
הִנָּקְטוּת נ 26 being taken action, step [no pl.]
הִנָּתְזוּת נ 26 being sprayed [no pl.]
הִנָּתְקוּת נ 26 disengagement; being cut off
הִסָּדְקוּת נ 26 being cracked
הִסָּכְרוּת נ 26 being dammed river, lake [no pl.]
הִסָּלְחוּת נ 26 being forgiven [no pl.]
הִסָּלְלוּת נ 26 being paved [no pl.]
הִסָּמְכוּת נ 26 being based on; being leaned on, supported by [no pl.]
הִסָּפְגוּת נ 26 being absorbed; absorption
הִסָּפְחוּת נ 26 joining; agglomeration [no pl.]
הִסָּקְרוּת נ 26 being surveyed, being described [no pl.]
הִפָּגְמוּת נ 26 being impaired
הִפָּגְעוּת נ 26 being injured; being damaged; being offended
הִפָּגְשׁוּת נ 26 meeting
הִפָּטְרוּת נ 26 being rid of
הִפָּלְטוּת נ 26 being expelled/emitted; being discharged bullet; escaping words
הִפָּסְלוּת נ 26 being disqualified [no pl.]
הִפָּסְקוּת נ 26 cessation
הִפָּצְעוּת נ 26 being wounded; injury [no pl.]
הִפָּקְדוּת נ 26 being absent; being counted [no pl.]
הִפָּקְחוּת נ 26 being open eyes
הִפָּקְעוּת נ 26 exploding, bursting Lit-rare [no pl.]
הִפָּרְדוּת נ 26 separation
הִפָּרְטוּת נ 26 being changed large currency for small; being divided [no pl.]
הִפָּתְחוּת נ 26 opening; openness
הִצָּמְדוּת נ 26 adhering
הִצָּרְבוּת נ 26 burning, scorching
הִקָּבְעוּת נ 26 determination, setting
הִקָּבְרוּת נ 26 being buried, burial [no pl.]

הִקָּלְטוּת נ 26 absorption; assimilation
הִקָּלְעוּת נ 26 encountering
הִקָּרְעוּת נ 26 being torn
הִקָּשְׁרוּת נ 26 being tied/bound; being connected to; being emotionally attached to
הִשָּׁבְעוּת נ 26 swearing [no pl.]
הִשָּׁבְרוּת נ 26 breaking, being broken
הִשָּׁזְרוּת נ 26 becoming intertwined
הִשָּׁכְחוּת נ 26 being forgotten [no pl.]
הִשָּׁמְדוּת נ 26 destruction, annihilation
הִשָּׁמְטוּת נ 26 being dropped, falling [no pl.]
הִשָּׁמְעוּת נ 26 being heard; being obeyed; being voiced
הִשָּׁמְרוּת נ 26 being careful, safeguarded [no pl.]
הִשָּׁפְטוּת נ 26 being judged [no pl.]
הִשָּׁפְכוּת נ 26 being spilled, being poured
הִשָּׁקְלוּת נ 26 being weighed [no pl.]
הִשָּׂרְדוּת נ 26 survival [no pl.]
הִשָּׂרְטוּת נ 26 being scratched [no pl.]
הִשָּׂרְפוּת נ 26 being burnt; burning
הִתָּבְעוּת נ 26 being demanded to do something; being sued
הִתָּכְנוּת נ 26 feasibility, practicability
הִתָּלְשׁוּת נ 26 being torn off; being torn away from
הִתָּקְלוּת נ 26 encounter, bumping into
הִתָּקְעוּת נ 26 being thrust into; being stuck
הֵאָבְקוּת נ 27 wrestling; struggle N
הֵאָדְמוּת נ 27 going red, reddening
הֵאָזְרוּת נ 27 girding oneself Lit-rare
הֵאָחֲזוּת נ 27 holding on tightly; settlement
הֵאָטְמוּת נ 27 becoming sealed; insensitivity, hardening; becoming opaque
הֵאָכְלוּת נ 27 being eaten, consumption
הֵאָלְחוּת נ 27 becoming infected
הֵאָלְמוּת נ 27 being dumbstruck Lit
הֵאָלְצוּת נ 27 being forced to
הֵאָמְרוּת נ 27 being said
הֵאָנְחוּת נ 27 sighing
הֵאָנְסוּת נ 27 being raped/coerced
הֵאָנְקוּת נ 27 moaning, groaning

הֵאָסְרוּת נ 27 being jailed
הֵאָרְזוּת נ 27 being packed/wrapped
הֵאָרְכוּת נ 27 lengthening Rare [no pl.]
הֵהָפְכוּת נ 27 changing to; turning over; inversion [no pl.]
הֵהָרְסוּת נ 27 being destroyed
הֵחָלְצוּת נ 27 extricating oneself; being extricated; volunteering
הֵחָלְשׁוּת נ 27 Weakening
הֵחָנְקוּת נ 27 strangulation; being choked
הֵחָסְמוּת נ 27 blocking; being blocked [no pl.]
הֵחָפְזוּת נ 27 haste [no pl.]
הֵחָקְרוּת נ 27 being researched; being interrogated [no pl.]
הֵחָרְבוּת נ 27 destruction; being destroyed [no pl.]
הֵחָשְׁבוּת נ 27 being considered [no pl.]
הֵחָשְׁדוּת נ 27 being suspected [no pl.]
הֵחָשְׁלוּת נ 27 hardening Lit; being forged (metal) [no pl.]
הֵחָשְׂפוּת נ 27 being exposed; exposure
הֵחָתְכוּת נ 27 being cut/gashed; being decided/ruled [no pl.]
הֵעָגְנוּת נ 27 anchoring, attachment [no pl.]
הֵעָדְרוּת נ 27 absence; missing in action
הֵעָזְבוּת נ 27 being abandoned [no pl.]
הֵעָזְרוּת נ 27 help, assistance; being helped [no pl.]
הֵעָטְפוּת נ 27 being wrapped/covered [no pl.]
הֵעָכְרוּת נ 27 being marred; being muddied, being tainted [no pl.]
הֵעָלְבוּת נ 27 being insulted/offended
הֵעָלְמוּת נ 27 disappearance
הֵעָמְדוּת נ 27 rising, standing up [no pl.]
הֵעָנְשׁוּת נ 27 being punished; punishment [no pl.]
הֵעָצְמוּת נ 27 eyes becoming shut, closed
הֵעָצְרוּת נ 27 stopping
הֵעָקְמוּת נ 27 becoming bent [no pl.]
הֵעָקְרוּת נ 27 being uprooted; uprooting [no pl.]
הֵעָרְכוּת נ 27 deployment; organization; arranging
הֵעָרְמוּת נ 27 being piled up
הֵעָתְקוּת נ 27 being relocated
הֵעָתְרוּת נ 27 acceding to, acquiescing to [no pl.]

הֵרָגְעוּת נ 27 being calmed; calming down
הֵרָדְמוּת נ 27 falling asleep
הֵרָטְבוּת נ 27 getting wet
הֵרָמְסוּת נ 27 being crushed, being trampled [no pl.]
הֵרָפְאוּת נ 27 healing, being healed
הֵרָצְחוּת נ 27 being murdered [no pl.]
הֵרָקְבוּת נ 27 decomposition, rotting
הֵרָקְמוּת נ 27 being planned, being formed, being developed [no pl.]
הֵרָשְׁמוּת נ 27 being registered; registration
הֵרָתְמוּת נ 27 undertaking, devotion
הֵרָתְעוּת נ 27 reluctance [no pl.]
הִבָּהֲלוּת נ 28 being frightened, alarmed
הִבָּחֲנוּת נ 28 being examined
הִבָּחֲרוּת נ 28 being selected, being elected
הִבָּעֲתוּת נ 28 being terrified Lit [no pl.]
הִגָּאֲלוּת נ 28 being saved, being redeemed; being stained esp. w/ blood
הִדָּחֲסוּת נ 28 being compressed, being squeezed
הִדָּחֲפוּת נ 28 being pushed, being shoved; pushing one's way in
הִדָּחֲקוּת נ 28 being squeezed in; being pushed aside; forcing one's way in
הִוָּאֲשׁוּת נ 28 considering to be hopeless [no pl.]
הִוָּעֲדוּת נ 28 meeting
הִוָּעֲצוּת נ 28 consultation
הִזָּהֲרוּת נ 28 caution, care
הִכָּחֲדוּת נ 28 being annihilated, becoming extinct
הִלָּחֲצוּת נ 28 being squeezed in; being pressured, "stressed out" [no pl.]
הִמָּאֲסוּת נ 28 becoming boring, repulsive [no pl.]
הִמָּחֲצוּת נ 28 being crushed
הִמָּחֲקוּת נ 28 being erased [no pl.]
הִמָּעֲטוּת נ 28 diminishing, decrease [no pl.]
הִמָּעֲכוּת נ 28 being mashed/squashed [no pl.]
הִנָּעֲלוּת נ 28 locking; closure, adjournment [no pl.]
הִנָּעֲצוּת נ 28 being thrust into [no pl.]
הִסָּחֲבוּת נ 28 being dragged; being prolonged col
הִסָּחֲטוּת נ 28 being squeezed [no pl.]

being carried away 28 הִסָּחֲפוּת נ
being agitated [no pl.] 28 הִסָּעֲרוּת נ
depreciation, devaluation 28 הִפָּחֲתוּת נ
being excited, enthused 28 הִפָּעֲמוּת נ
opening wide mouth, gap [no pl.] 28 הִפָּעֲרוּת נ
gathering, assembling Lit 28 הִקָּהֲלוּת נ
being drawn/pumped [no pl.] 28 הִשָּׁאֲבוּת נ
staying, being, remaining 28 הִשָּׁאֲרוּת נ
being eroded, worn away [no pl.] 28 הִשָּׁחֲקוּת נ
leaning on 28 הִשָּׁעֲנוּת נ
accommodation, adjustment, adaptation 28 הִתָּאֲמוּת נ
being built/established 29 הִבָּנוּת נ
postponement 29 הִדָּחוּת נ
being burned 29 הִכָּווּת נ
accompanying [no pl.] 29 הִלָּווּת נ
being obliterated [no pl.] 29 הִמָּחוּת נ
being counted/a member of [no pl.] 29 הִמָּנוּת נ
cleansing oneself [no pl.] 29 הִנָּקוּת נ
redeeming, being redeemed [no pl.] 29 הִפָּדוּת נ
roasting, being roasted [no pl.] 29 הִצָּלוּת נ
narrowing; stenosis Med 29 הִצָּרוּת נ
pooling of water 29 הִקָּווּת נ
occurrence 29 הִקָּרוּת נ
repetition, recurrence 29 הִשָּׁנוּת נ
dependence, reliance [no pl.] 29 הִתָּלוּת נ
being halved/divided [no pl.] 30 הֵחָצוּת נ
response [no pl.] 30 הֵעָנוּת נ
being carried out; becoming [no pl.] 30 הֵעָשׂוּת נ
visibility, appearance [no pl.] 30 הֵרָאוּת נ
betrayed 31 נִבְגָּד ז
separate, different; offside (soccer) 31 נִבְדָּל ז
subject, examinee 31 נִבְדָּק ז
alarmed, frightened 31 נִבְהָל ז
examinee 31 נִבְחָן ז
choice, top quality; chosen; elected 31 נִבְחָר ז
illiterate, uneducated 31 נִבְעָר ז
robbed, burglarized 31 נִגְזָל ז
pulled, drawn, dragged 31 נִגְרָר ז
layer, level 31 נִדְבָּךְ ז

adorned, magnificent Lit 31 נִדְגָּל ז
astonished 31 נִדְהָם ז
required; be in demand 31 נִדְרָשׁ ז
angry, furious Lit 31 נִזְעָם ז
angry, furious, enraged Lit 31 נִזְעָף ז
muzzle-loading rifle, gun 31 נִטְעָן ז
painful 31 נִכְאָב ז
respected, important; substantial; a notable person 31 נִכְבָּד ז
disappointed 31 נִכְזָב ז
extinct; endangered 31 נִכְחָד ז
ashamed, embarrassed Lit 31 נִכְלָם ז
yearning; depressed Lit 31 נִכְמָר ז
longed for, yearned for Lit 31 נִכְסָף ז
angry, furious, enraged Lit 31 נִכְעָס ז
multiplicand math 31 נִכְפָּל ז
one who failed; failing, esp. grade 31 נִכְשָׁל ז
enthusiastic 31 נִלְהָב ז
ridiculous, preposterous, ludicrous 31 נִלְעָג ז
despised, loathed 31 נִמְאָס ז
hasty, hurried 31 נִמְהָר ז
flowery, poetic 31 נִמְלָץ ז
avoidable; improbable; one who abstains 31 נִמְנָע ז
addressee 31 נִמְעָן ז
energetic; lively; intensive 31 נִמְרָץ ז
moral, lesson 31 נִמְשָׁל ז
flexible, elastic 31 נִמְתָּח ז
tolerated 31 נִסְבָּל ז
the first component in a construct state, smikhut 31 נִסְמָךְ ז
agitated, excited; uneasy 31 נִסְעָר ז
appendix, addendum; attaché; adjunct 31 נִסְפָּח ז
hidden; invisible; occult 31 נִסְתָּר ז
injured, wounded; killed 31 נִפְגָּע ז
frightened, terrified, alarmed 31 נִפְחָד ז
deceased, departed 31 נִפְטָר ז
wonderful 31 נִפְלָא ז
horrifying 31 נִפְלָץ ז
indecent Lit; faulty Lit 31 נִפְסָד ז
the one acted upon 31 נִפְעָל ז
excited, thrilled 31 נִפְעָם ז
absentee 31 נִפְקָד ז
separate 31 נִפְרָד ז
exaggerated Lit 31 נִפְרָז ז
common Lit 31 נִפְרָץ ז
criminal; atrocious 31 נִפְשָׁע ז
needy person; pauper 31 נִצְרָךְ ז

chased, persecuted 31 נִרְדָּף ז
spectacular Lit 31 נִרְהָב ז
widespread 31 נִרְחָב ז
excited, agitated 31 נִרְעָשׁ ז
murdered person 31 נִרְצָח ז
31 נִרְצָע ז indentured/submissive slave
person participating in questionnaire 31 נִשְׁאָל ז
the remaining one 31 נִשְׁאָר ז
broken, destroyed 31 נִשְׁבָּר ז
sublime, lofty; strong, solid 31 נִשְׂגָּב ז
consignee in commerce 31 נִשְׁגָּר ז
forgotten 31 נִשְׁכָּח ז
that can be drawn, pulled out 31 נִשְׁלָף ז
needy, supported person 31 נִתְמָךְ ז
despicable 31 נִתְעָב ז
one being attacked, attackee 31 נִתְקָף ז
nice, pleasant, lovely 32 נֶחְמָד ז
decisive, final, firm (decision, opinion) 32 נֶחְרָץ ז
faltering, lagging 32 נֶחְשָׁל ז
great, exalted, glorious Lit. 33 נֶאֱדָר/נֶאְדָּר ז
beloved Lit. 33 נֶאֱהָב ז
full, replete; strengthened, girded Lit. 33 נֶאֱזָר ז
abominable, despicable, loathsome, vile 33 נֶאֱלָח ז
trustee, trusted ally; loyal, faithful, devoted 33 נֶאֱמָן ז
noble, lofty, exalted 33 נֶאֱצָל ז
accused (person) 33 נֶאֱשָׁם ז
magnificent, beautiful, impressive; wonderful, great 33 נֶהֱדָר/נֶהְדָּר ז
missing, excluded, absent; lacking 33 נֶעֱדָר/נֶעְדָּר ז
abandoned, forgotten, forsaken 33 נֶעֱזָב ז
insulted, offended 33 נֶעֱלָב ז
unknown (esp. in algebra); concealed, hidden 33 נֶעֱלָם/נֶעְלָם ז
admired, respected Lit. (coll. ne`erats) 34 נַעֲרָץ ז
leaking, spilling 35 נִגָּר ז
scattered, fallen leaf 35 נִדָּף ז
very dry (throat) 35 נִחָר ז
noticeable, recognizable; substantial, significant 35 נִכָּר ז
perpendicular; hilt, sword handle; extra (cinema) 35 נִצָּב ז
lofty, exalted; portable, mobile 35 נִשָּׂא ז
despicable, loathsome 36 נִבְזֶה ז
revealed, visible, unconcealed 36 נִגְלֶה ז
it seems, it is as if 36 נִדְמֶה ז
epileptic 36 נִכְפֶּה ז

tired 36 נִלְאֶה ז

accompanying 36 נִלְוֶה ז

despicable 36 נִקְלֶה ז

visible 36 נִרְאֶה ז

repeated 36 נִשְׁנֶה ז

twisted, distorted Lit. 37 נַעֲוֶה ז

lofty, exalted 37 נַעֲלֶה ז

idiotic, foolish 38 נוֹאָל ז

desperate, hopeless 38 נוֹאָשׁ ז

famous, well-known 38 נוֹדָע ז

additional 38 נוֹסָף ז

daring 38 נוֹעָז ז

terrible 38 נוֹרָא ז

settled, populated 38 נוֹשָׁב ז

very old 38 נוֹשָׁן ז

remaining 38 נוֹתָר ז

enlightened, cultured; intelligent 39 נָאוֹר ז

fitting, proper, suitable 39 נָאוֹת ז

embarrassed, perplexed [note possible alternants with u: nevukha etc.] 39 נָבוֹךְ ז

wise, intelligent 39 נָבוֹן ז

the topic under discussion/sentenced person 39 נָדוֹן ז

banal, commonplace 39 נָדוֹשׁ ז

correct, true; right, fitting 39 נָכוֹן ז

corrupt, deviant 39 נָלוֹז ז

evaporated, dissipated 39 נָמוֹג ז

retreating 39 נָסוֹג ז

common, widespread 39 נָפוֹץ ז

the topic under discussion; sentenced person 40 נִדּוֹן ז

injured person 40 נִזּוֹק ז

circumcised person 40 נִמּוֹל ז

survivor 40 נִצּוֹל ז

calm, relaxed 41 נִנּוֹחַ ז

difference, dissimilarity 42 נִבְדָּלוּת נ

illiteracy, ignorance [no pl.] 42 נִבְעָרוּת נ

shame, embarrassment Lit [no pl.] 42 נִכְלָמוּת נ

submissiveness [no pl.] 42 נִכְנָעוּת נ

friendliness, pleasantness [no pl.] 42 נִלְבָּבוּת נ

enthusiasm, excitement [no pl.] 42 נִלְהָבוּת נ

ludicrousness [no pl.] 42 נִלְעָגוּת נ

haste, hurriedness [no pl.] 42 נִמְהָרוּת נ

being energetic; vigor, decisiveness [no pl.] 42 נִמְרָצוּת נ

tolerability [no pl.] 42 נִסְבָּלוּת נ

agitation, excitement [no pl.] 42 נִסְעָרוּת נ

absenteeism (military) 42 נִפְקָדוּת נ

crookedness, twistedness 42 נִפְתָּלוּת נ

need; poverty [no pl.] 42 נִצְרָכוּת נ

anger, annoyance, furiousness [no pl.] 42 נִרְגָּזוּת נ

excitement, agitation [no pl.] 42 נִרְגָּשׁוּת נ

oppression, persecution; synonymity [no pl.] 42 נִרְדָּפוּת נ

enslavement, submission [no pl.] 42 נִרְצָעוּת נ

obliteration [no pl.] 42 נִשְׁכָּחוּת נ

abomination, vileness [no pl.] 43 נֶאֱלָחוּת נ

loyalty, faithfulness 43 נֶאֱמָנוּת נ

abandonment [no pl.] 43 נֶעֱזָבוּת נ

insult, effrontery 43 נֶעֱלָבוּת נ

loveliness, pleasantness 44 נֶחְמָדוּת נ

decisiveness, finality 44 נֶחְרָצוּת נ

slowness, backwardness 44 נֶחְשָׁלוּת נ

loss, disappearance 45 אִבּוּד ז

fossilization [no pl.] 45 אִבּוּן ז

galvanization [no pl.] 45 אִבּוּץ ז

powdering; dusting [no pl.] 45 אִבּוּק ז

organization, union 45 אִגּוּד ז

collection of water into a lake; pooling of resources 45 אִגּוּם ז

outflanking 45 אִגּוּף ז

vaporization, evaporation; simmering 45 אִדּוּי ז

passivization [no pl.] 45 אִדּוּשׁ ז

desire, yearning Lit 45 אִוּוּי ז

balance N 45 אִזּוּן ז

handcuffing [no pl.] 45 אִזּוּק ז

sealing, impermeability 45 אִטּוּם ז

evaporation 45 אִיּוּד ז

qualification, modifying 45 אִיּוּךְ ז

threat 45 אִיּוּם ז

negation, nullification 45 אִיּוּן ז

illustration 45 אִיּוּר ז

manning 45 אִיּוּשׁ ז

corrosion [no pl.] 45 אִכּוּל ז

location; pinpointing 45 אִכּוּן ז

shoemaker's last 45 אִמּוּם ז

training, exercise, practice 45 אִמּוּן ז

adopting/adoption, fostering of child, idea, plan 45 אִמּוּץ ז

verification; authentication 45 אִמּוּת ז

compulsion, coercion; rape 45 אִנּוּס ז

collection, gathering 45 אִסּוּף ז

prohibition, ban 45 אִסּוּר ז

blackout 45 אִפּוּל ז

zeroing, calibration 45 אִפּוּס ז

restraint 45 אִפּוּק ז

confirmation; acceptance 45 אִשּׁוּר ז

reinforcement, strengthening 45 אִשּׁוּשׁ ז

locating, identifying 45 אִתּוּר ז

clothing, apparel 45 בִּגּוּד ז

isolation; solitary confinement; insulation 45 בִּדּוּד ז

fabrication [no pl.] 45 בִּדּוּי ז

separation; differentiation 45 בִּדּוּל ז

security check 45 בִּדּוּק ז

entertainment; amusement 45 בִּדּוּר ז

humiliation, debasement 45 בִּזּוּי ז

decentralization 45 בִּזּוּר ז

expression, saying 45 בִּטּוּי ז

cancellation 45 בִּטּוּל ז

concreting 45 בִּטּוּן ז

sewage 45 בִּיּוּב ז

stamping, affixing of stamp 45 בִּיּוּל ז

staging; stage-managing 45 בִּיּוּם ז

spying, intelligence services [no pl.] 45 בִּיּוּן ז

mourning, lamentation [no pl.] 45 בִּכּוּי ז

spending time; recreation; a good time 45 בִּלּוּי ז

braking [no pl.] 45 בִּלּוּם ז

deception Sl. 45 בִּלּוּף ז

sleuthing, detection 45 בִּלּוּשׁ ז

stage-managing, direction of play, film 45 בִּמּוּי ז

building, development [no pl.] 45 בִּנּוּי ז

intoxication 45 בִּסּוּם ז

establishment, strengthening; support 45 בִּסּוּס ז

fortification; support 45 בִּצּוּר ז

visiting; visit 45 בִּקּוּר ז

demand N 45 בִּקּוּשׁ ז

cooking 45 בִּשּׁוּל ז

perfuming [no pl.] 45 בִּשּׂוּם ז

cleaving, splitting 45 בִּתּוּק ז

cutting up, bisecting, cutting into pieces 45 בִּתּוּר ז

piling, heaping; accumulation 45 גִּבּוּב ז

backup, support 45 גִּבּוּי ז

cheese making [no pl.] 45 גִּבּוּן ז

plastering 45 גִּבּוּס ז

consolidation, integration, forging "team spirit;" crystallization 45 גִּבּוּשׁ ז

abrasion geology 45 גִּדּוּד ז

growth; upbringing; tumor 45 גִּדּוּל ז

cursing, swearing 45 גִּדּוּף ז

fencing, enclosure 45 גִּדּוּר ז

variety, variation 45 גִּוּוּן ז

carbonating Coll. [no pl.] 45 גִּזּוּז ז

pruning 45 גִּזּוּם ז

gasification [no pl.] 45 גִּיּוּז ז

enlistment; recruitment; raising money 45 גִּיּוּס ז
conversion to Judaism 45 גִּיּוּר ז
embodiment, playing the role; grossing up taxation 45 גִּלּוּם ז
carving, etching, engraving 45 גִּלּוּף ז
belittling, curtailing, shrinking, minimization 45 גִּמּוּד ז
pitting (metallurgy) 45 גִּמּוּם ז
finish of furniture, building 45 גִּמּוּר ז
denunciation, condemnation 45 גִּנּוּי ז
gardening 45 גִּנּוּן ז
fondling, cuddling 45 גִּפּוּף ז
sulphurization; vulcanization 45 גִּפּוּר ז
bridging; mediation law 45 גִּשּׁוּר ז
groping, feeling; initial contact 45 גִּשּׁוּשׁ ז
encouraging one to talk; dubbing 45 דִּבּוּב ז
debugging (computing) 45 דִּבּוּג ז
dybbuk, spirit 45 דִּבּוּק ז
speaking, speech 45 דִּבּוּר ז
raising a flag 45 דִּגּוּל ז
modeling 45 דִּגּוּם ז
marking a dagesh 45 דִּגּוּשׁ ז
hopping, skipping 45 דִּדּוּי ז
mailing 45 דִּוּוּר ז
pedaling 45 דִּוּוּשׁ ז
postponement 45 דִּחוּי ז
phishing (internet) 45 דִּיּוּג ז
discussion, deliberation 45 דִּיּוּן ז
grouting [no pl.] 45 דִּיּוּס ז
accuracy, precision; punctuality 45 דִּיּוּק ז
housing 45 דִּיּוּר ז
transpiration; retouching [no pl.] 45 דִּיּוּת ז
subjugation, oppression 45 דִּכּוּי ז
jumping over; skipping over 45 דִּלּוּג ז
dilution; thinning out agriculture 45 דִּלּוּל ז
imagery; comparison; image 45 דִּמּוּי ז
bleeding 45 דִּמּוּם ז
thickening, reinforcement of wall, fence; lining 45 דִּפּוּן ז
puncture; acupuncture 45 דִּקּוּר ז
fertilization agricultural 45 דִּשּׁוּן ז
pronunciation 45 הִגּוּי ז
steering 45 הִגּוּי ז
interaction 45 הִדּוּד ז
hopping 45 הִדּוּס ז
tightening 45 הִדּוּק ז
praising; elegance 45 הִדּוּר ז
capitalization 45 הִוּוּן ז
gear (automotive); gait 45 הִלּוּךְ ז
stun N 45 הִמּוּם ז
gamble, bet N 45 הִמּוּר ז
quietening, hushing 45 הִסּוּי ז
hesitation; doubt N 45 הִסּוּס ז
reversal; opposite; inversion 45 הִפּוּךְ ז
melting metal; fusion 45 הִתּוּךְ ז
jesting 45 הִתּוּל ז
confirmation [no pl.] 45 וִדּוּא ז
confession 45 וִדּוּי ז
velarization [no pl.] 45 וִלּוּן ז
adjustment, regulation 45 וִסּוּת ז
meeting, convening Lit 45 וִעוּד ז
concession 45 וִתּוּר ז
fertilization, manuring 45 זִבּוּל ז
glazing 45 זִגּוּג ז
pairing, matching; matching of a couple 45 זִוּוּג ז
fitting out, equipping 45 זִוּוּד ז
arming, supplying weapons; reinforcement of concrete; sexual intercourse Sl.; adornments of letters in Jewish religious texts 45 זִיּוּן ז
forgery; being off-key (music) 45 זִיּוּף ז
acquittal; credit (monetary) 45 זִכּוּי ז
catharsis; cleansing 45 זִכּוּךְ ז
spraying 45 זִלּוּף ז
summons, assignment 45 זִמּוּן ז
pruning 45 זִמּוּר ז
attacking the rear - (military), picking off stragglers 45 זִנּוּב ז
pouncing; jump-off, start 45 זִנּוּק ז
tarring 45 זִפּוּת ז
standing erect Lit 45 זִקּוּף ז
distillation; purification; refining; flare 45 זִקּוּק ז
raising up Lit 45 זִקּוּר ז
fondness 45 חִבּוּב ז
beating, flagellation 45 חִבּוּט ז
sabotaging Rare 45 חִבּוּל ז
churning milk 45 חִבּוּץ ז
embrace, hug 45 חִבּוּק ז
sharpening; joke 45 חִדּוּד ז
innovation; new idea; renewal, renovation 45 חִדּוּשׁ ז
statement, expression 45 חִוּוּי ז
forecasting; prediction 45 חִזּוּי ז
strengthening, reinforcement 45 חִזּוּק ז
courting, wooing; cultivation of relationship 45 חִזּוּר ז
carving Lit; body-building 45 חִטּוּב ז
searching, groping; pick nose, etc 45 חִטּוּט ז
disinfection 45 חִטּוּי ז
reducing a vowel to a shva 45 חִטּוּף ז
obligation; debit; positivity; conviction 45 חִיּוּב ז
dialing phone number 45 חִיּוּג ז
smile 45 חִיּוּךְ ז
enlistment to the military, drafting [no pl.] 45 חִיּוּל ז
partitioning; extrapolation math 45 חִיּוּץ ז
friction; disagreement 45 חִכּוּךְ ז
forfeiture, confiscation, seizure 45 חִלּוּט ז
imploring Lit-rare [no pl.] 45 חִלּוּי ז
desecration, defilement 45 חִלּוּל ז
converting from holy to secular, profanation [no pl.] 45 חִלּוּן ז
division math; partition, division; difference Lit 45 חִלּוּק ז
heating; stimulation; warming up Coll. 45 חִמּוּם ז
arming - military; munition 45 חִמּוּשׁ ז
education 45 חִנּוּךְ ז
impunity; confidentiality 45 חִסּוּי ז
extermination, elimination, liquidation 45 חִסּוּל ז
hardening, tempering metal, glass 45 חִסּוּם ז
immunization; strengthening 45 חִסּוּן ז
subtraction math; absence 45 חִסּוּר ז
covering fire; cover-up; covering 45 חִפּוּי ז
carelessness, shoddiness Sl. 45 חִפּוּף ז
searching; search N 45 חִפּוּשׂ ז
quarrying, excavating 45 חִצּוּב ז
imitation 45 חִקּוּי ז
statute; etching 45 חִקּוּק ז
investigation, inquiry 45 חִקּוּר ז
calculation 45 חִשּׁוּב ז
strengthening 45 חִשּׁוּל ז
exposure; clearing, stripping 45 חִשּׂוּף ז
hoop 45 חִשּׁוּק ז
spoke; radius anatomy 45 חִשּׁוּר ז
cutting; intersection geometry; articulation - phonetics 45 חִתּוּךְ ז
diaper 45 חִתּוּל ז
underwriting 45 חִתּוּם ז
marrying off 45 חִתּוּן ז
dipping, immersion 45 טִבּוּל ז
frying 45 טִגּוּן ז
ranging - military 45 טִוּוּחַ ז
improvement; improvement of soil, reclamation 45 טִיּוּב ז

טִיּוּחַ ז 45 plastering wall; cover up Coll.
טִיּוּל ז 45 hike, trip, journey
טִלּוּף ז 45 hoof trimming
טִנּוּף ז 45 dirtying
טִפּוּל ז 45 care, treatment
טִפּוּס ז 45 climbing
יִבּוּא ז 45 import N
יִבּוּב ז 45 wailing, whimpering
יִבּוּם ז 45 levirate marriage
יִבּוּשׁ ז 45 drying
יִדּוּי ז 45 throwing, esp. stones
יִזּוּם ז 45 initiating
יִלּוּד ז 45 midwifery, obstetrics
יִלּוּל ז 45 wailing, lamenting
יִנּוּן ז 45 ionization (physics)
יִסּוּד ז 45 founding, establishment
יִסּוּף ז 45 revaluation (economics)
יִסּוּר ז 45 tormenting, causing pain
יִצּוּא ז 45 exporting, export
יִצּוּב ז 45 stabilization; strengthening
יִצּוּג ז 45 giving expression to; representation, acting on behalf of
יִצּוּר ז 45 manufacture, production; industry
יִקּוּר ז 45 increasing price, making expensive
יִשּׁוּב ז 45 settling, populating; settlement; population
יִשּׂוּם ז 45 applying; application
יִשּׁוּן ז 45 aging of meat, wine, cheese
יִשּׁוּר ז 45 straightening
יִתּוּר ז 45 excess, surplus
כִּבּוּד ז 45 honoring; refreshment
כִּבּוּס ז 45 washing, laundering
כִּבּוּשׁ ז 45 conquering; conquest, occupation; suppressing; leveling/paving road
כִּוּוּן ז 45 direction; point of view; adjustment, tuning
כִּוּוּץ ז 45 shrinking
כִּיּוּל ז 45 calibration
כִּיּוּס ז 45 pickpocketing
כִּיּוּף ז 45 ,enjoyment, pleasure sl
כִּיּוּר ז 45 modeling, molding
כִּלּוּל ז 45 integration, inclusion [no pl.]
כִּמּוּי ז 45 quantification
כִּמּוּת ז 45 quantification
כִּנּוּי ז 45 nickname
כִּנּוּן ז 45 establishment, founding; aiming, pointing - military
כִּנּוּס ז 45 assembling; conference, convention
כִּסּוּי ז 45 coverage
כִּפּוּר ז 45 atonement
כִּשּׁוּף ז 45 magic, sorcery, witchcraft
כִּתּוּב ז 45 captioning, from kitev 'write, inscribe'
כִּתּוּר ז 45 siege, encirclement
כִּתּוּת ז 45 beating; crushing, pulverizing
לִבּוּב ז 45 endearment Lit
לִבּוּב ז 45 making pancakes
לִבּוּי ז 45 fanning of flame; arousal of emotion
לִבּוּן ז 45 clarification, elucidation
לִוּוּי ז 45 escort; accompanying
לִטּוּן ז 45 Latinization [no pl.]
לִטּוּף ז 45 petting, stroking, caressing
לִטּוּשׁ ז 45 polishing; final touch-up; refinement
לִכּוּד ז 45 unification
לִמּוּד ז 45 studying, learning; teaching
לִפּוּף ז 45 coiling, wrapping
לִקּוּט ז 45 compilation, assembling
לִקּוּי ז 45 defect, shortcoming; eclipse
לִקּוּק ז 45 licking
מִגּוּן ז 45 protection, defense
מִגּוּר ז 45 defeat, destruction, eradication [no pl.]
מִדּוּד ז 45 benchmarking, gauging
מִדּוּף ז 45 shelving
מִדּוּר ז 45 compartmentalization [no pl.]
מִזּוּג ז 45 merging; air-conditioning
מִטּוּב ז 45 optimization
מִכּוּן ז 45 mechanization
מִלּוּט ז 45 escape, rescue, extrication
מִלּוּי/מִלּוּא ז 45 filling; refill
מִמּוּן ז 45 financing, funding
מִמּוּשׁ ז 45 realization, implementation, execution
מִנּוּי ז 45 appointing; appointment
מִנּוּן ז 45 dosage
מִסּוּד ז 45 institutionalization
מִסּוּי ז 45 taxation
מִסּוּךְ ז 45 shielding; screening, separating
מִפּוּי ז 45 mapping
מִצּוּב ז 45 positioning (marketing)
מִצּוּי ז 45 utilization; summarization; extraction
מִקּוּד ז 45 focusing
מִקּוּד ז 45 postal code, zip code
מִקּוּם ז 45 location
מִקּוּף ז 45 hyphenation
מִקּוּשׁ ז 45 laying mines
מִשּׁוּשׁ ז 45 feeling, touching
מִתּוּג ז 45 branding
מִתּוּג ז 45 operating electrical switch
מִתּוּךְ ז 45 plating, metallization
מִתּוּן ז 45 recession economics
נִבּוּי ז 45 prediction
נִבּוּל ז 45 coarseness, ugliness
נִגּוּב ז 45 drying, wiping
נִגּוּד ז 45 opposition, contradiction, difference
נִגּוּן ז 45 playing music; tune, melody; inflection
נִדּוּי ז 45 banishment, excommunication
נִדּוּף ז 45 evaporation
נִוּוּט ז 45 navigation
נִוּוּל ז 45 dismallness, ugliness Lit [no pl.]
נִוּוּן ז 45 atrophy, degeneration
נִטּוּל ז 45 handling [no pl.]
נִטּוּר ז 45 monitoring
נִיּוּד ז 45 fluctuation (exchange rate); mobility
נִכּוּי ז 45 deduction
נִכּוּר ז 45 alienation
נִכּוּשׁ ז 45 weeding
נִמּוּק ז 45 reason, explanation
נִסּוּי ז 45 experiment
נִסּוּךְ ז 45 libation (religious ritual)
נִסּוּר ז 45 sawing, cutting
נִפּוּט ז 45 beating of flax [no pl.]
נִפּוּי ז 45 sifting
נִפּוּץ ז 45 smashing; explosion
נִצּוּל ז 45 utilization; exploitation [no pl.]
נִצּוּר ז 45 Christianization [no pl.]
נִקּוּב ז 45 piercing, perforating, punching holes
נִקּוּד ז 45 vocalization (grammar)
נִקּוּז ז 45 drainage
נִקּוּי ז 45 cleaning
נִקּוּר ז 45 pecking, poking
נִקּוּשׁ ז 45 knocking, hitting
נִשּׁוּל ז 45 expulsion, disinheritance
נִשּׁוּף ז 45 aspirating
נִשּׁוּק ז 45 kissing
נִתּוּב ז 45 guiding, directing, routing
נִתּוּץ ז 45 smashing
נִתּוּק ז 45 severing, cutoff; disconnecting
נִתּוּר ז 45 jumping, hopping
סִבּוּךְ ז 45 complication
סִבּוּן ז 45 soaping
סִבּוּר ז 45 explanation, interpretation Lit
סִגּוּל ז 45 adaptation, adjustment
סִגּוּף ז 45 mortification, self-denial
סִדּוּק ז 45 cracking, fissuring

organizing, tidying; order, arrangement; prayer book with “ordered” prayers 45 סִדּוּר ז

classification, categorization 45 סִוּוּג ז

restriction, regulation, qualification 45 סִיּוּג ז

whitewashing 45 סִיּוּד ז

nightmare 45 סִיּוּט ז

end, ending, completion, conclusion 45 סִיּוּם ז

fencing sports 45 סִיּוּף ז

tour; patrol, reconnaissance 45 סִיּוּר ז

chance; probability 45 סִכּוּי ז

covering of a Sukkah 45 סִכּוּךְ ז

foiling, thwarting 45 סִכּוּל ז

summation, summary; total 45 סִכּוּם ז

risk 45 סִכּוּן ז

distortion, falsification 45 סִלּוּף ז

removal, clearing away 45 סִלּוּק ז

support Lit-rare, simukhin support; reference 45 סִמּוּךְ ז

symbolization 45 סִמּוּל ז

drugging; sedation 45 סִמּוּם ז

signal; marking, sign 45 סִמּוּן ז

the standing on end of hair; nailing [no pl.] 45 סִמּוּר ז

sifting, filtering; purification; sorting 45 סִנּוּן ז

affiliation 45 סִנּוּף ז

story, tale; affair, matter 45 סִפּוּר ז

clearing/removal of stones 45 סִקּוּל ז

coverage by media 45 סִקּוּר ז

masonry, chiseling 45 סִתּוּת ז

processing; arrangement, adaptation 45 עִבּוּד ז

thickening 45 עִבּוּי ז

intercalation (chemistry); pregnancy Lit., `ibur hashana ‘adding a month to a Jewish year’ 45 עִבּוּר ז

circle; rounding 45 עִגּוּל ז

anchoring 45 עִגּוּן ז

refinement 45 עִדּוּן ז

hoeing, tilling 45 עִדּוּר ז

distortion, falsification 45 עִוּוּת ז

hoeing, tilling (biblical) [no pl.] 45 עִזּוּק ז

wrapping, covering 45 עִטּוּף ז

decorating, ornamenting; decoration, ornament 45 עִטּוּר ז

sneeze Lit 45 עִטּוּשׁ ז

putting in, entering; recording 45 עִיּוּל ז

study N; consideration 45 עִיּוּן ז

urbanization [no pl.] 45 עִיּוּר ז

delay, hindrance 45 עִכּוּב ז

digestion [no pl.] 45 עִכּוּל ז

genius; prodigy 45 עִלּוּי ז

concealing [no pl.] 45 עִלּוּם ז

lovemaking Lit-rare 45 עִלּוּס ז

layout publishing 45 עִמּוּד ז

training Rare [no pl.] 45 עִמּוּל ז

dimming a light [no pl.] 45 עִמּוּם ז

shutting of eye Lit-rare [no pl.] 45 עִמּוּץ ז

confrontation; debate 45 עִמּוּת ז

pleasure, delight 45 עִנּוּג ז

torment N 45 עִנּוּי ז

massage N 45 עִסּוּי ז

task, activity; vocation; job 45 עִסּוּק ז

reek, stench 45 עִפּוּשׁ ז

design 45 עִצּוּב ז

sanction 45 עִצּוּם ז

consonant 45 עִצּוּר ז

bending, twisting; distortion 45 עִקּוּם ז

bypass 45 עִקּוּף ז

sterilization; neutering 45 עִקּוּר ז

weeding 45 עִשּׂוּב ז

smoking N 45 עִשּׁוּן ז

tithing 45 עִשּׂוּר ז

provision - military [no pl.] 45 עִתּוּד ז

timing 45 עִתּוּי ז

marshalling; relocation 45 עִתּוּק ז

abomination; denaturation of alcohol 45 פִּגּוּל ז

scaffolding 45 פִּגּוּם ז

backwardness; arrears; delay 45 פִּגּוּר ז

soft singing 45 פִּזּוּם ז

scattering 45 פִּזּוּר ז

fattening of animals 45 פִּטּוּם ז

firing from post, discharging 45 פִּטּוּר(ים/ין) ז

liturgical poem; poetry ~ piyet write poetry 45 פִּיּוּט ז

placation, appeasement, reconciliation 45 פִּיּוּס ז

explosion; demolition 45 פִּיצּוּץ ז

split, rift, separation 45 פִּלּוּג ז

wish, entreaty; prayer Lit 45 פִּלּוּל ז

clearing path, road; levelling 45 פִּלּוּס ז

evacuation 45 פִּנּוּי ז

pampering; indulgence 45 פִּנּוּק ז

sculpting, sculpture 45 פִּסּוּל ז

punctuation; opening wide 45 פִּסּוּק ז

compensation 45 פִּצּוּי ז

division, splitting; branching; split, rift 45 פִּצּוּל ז

command, authority - military 45 פִּקּוּד ז

corking 45 פִּקּוּק ז

simplification; spreading, sprawling 45 פִּשּׁוּט ז

spread of legs, etc 45 פִּשּׂוּק ז

conciliating, reaching compromise 45 פִּשּׁוּר ז

temptation 45 פִּתּוּי ז

mixing, blending 45 פִּתּוּךְ ז

bend, twist, turn 45 פִּתּוּל ז

public, population; community 45 צִבּוּר ז

siding with, supporting; lateral movement 45 צִדּוּד ז

justification 45 צִדּוּק ז

order, directive; imperative (grammar) 45 צִוּוּי ז

quoting; quotation 45 צִטּוּט ז

equipment; equipping 45 צִיּוּד ז

mark, grade; noting, mentioning 45 צִיּוּן ז

twittering, chirping 45 צִיּוּץ ז

drawing, picture; art, painting; depiction 45 צִיּוּר ז

obedience 45 צִיּוּת ז

clarification, purification Lit [no pl.] 45 צִלּוּל ז

photography; photograph; filmimg; photocopying; X-ray 45 צִלּוּם ז

association, attachment; coupling 45 צִמּוּד ז

shrinking, wizening; raisin 45 צִמּוּק ז

agglutination; subjugation 45 צִמּוּת ז

cooling, chilling 45 צִנּוּן ז

covering, coating 45 צִפּוּי ז

volume, capacity 45 קִבּוּל ז

collection; ingathering; kibbutz, collective settlement 45 קִבּוּץ ז

reaming, boring, marking 45 קִדּוּד ז

advancement; promotion 45 קִדּוּם ז

sanctification/blessing over wine etc. 45 קִדּוּשׁ ז

deduction; offset N 45 קִזּוּז ז

polarization 45 קִטּוּב ז

lopping, cutting off end 45 קִטּוּם ז

plucking, picking [no pl.] 45 קִטּוּף ז

incense burning 45 קִטּוּר ז

encoding 45 קִידּוּד ז

existence; fulfillment; subsistence; obserevance 45 קִיּוּם ז

peeling; scraping 45 קִלּוּף ז

wrinkling 45 קִמּוּט ז

reduction, cutting expenses 45 קִמּוּץ ז

curvature; curve 45 קִמּוּר ז

nesting 45 קִנּוּן ז

skimming 45 קִפּוּי ז

קפול ז 45 folding; collapsing; a fold

קפוץ ז 45 hopping, skipping

קצוב ז 45 budgeting

קצוץ ז 45 cut; cutback

קצור ז 45 shortening, reducing; summary; abbreviation

קשוט ז 45 decoration, ornament; decorating

קשוי ז 45 hardening, stiffening

קשור ז 45 connection, liaison; communication

רבוב ז 45 multiplexing

רבוד ז 45 stratification

רבוי ז 45 multiplicity; increase; plural (grammar)

רבוץ ז 45 sprinkling; depositing [no pl.]

רגול ז 45 spying, espionage; tailing, shadowing

רגוש ז 45 excitement; emotion

רדוד ז 45 flattening, making shallow

רווי ז 45 saturation [no pl.]

רטוט ז 45 vibration

רטון ז 45 grumbling

רטוש ז 45 hacking to pieces

רטוש ז 45 retouching (photography)

רכוז ז 45 concentration; assemblage

רכוך ז 45 softening; weakening - military

רנון ז 45 singing Lit; gossip

רסון ז 45 restraint; restraining

רפוד ז 45 upholstery lining, padding

רפוי ז 45 treatment, therapy

רצוד ז 45 flickering

רצוי ז 45 placation; serving a prison sentence

רצוף ז 45 paving, flooring

רקוד ז 45 dance; dancing

רקון ז 45 emptying

רשוי ז 45 licensing

רתוי ז 45 favor, equanimity Lit [no pl.]

רתוק ז 45 confinement - military

שבוב ז 45 chipping

שבוט ז 45 cloning

שבוץ ז 45 placement, assignment; setting of gemstone

שבוש ז 45 disruption; mistake, error

שגום ז 45 tenoning

שגור ז 45 launching; sending

שדוד ז 45 crumbling/loosening of soil

שדוך ז 45 matchmaking; pairing Coll.

שדול ז 45 lobbying, pressuring, persuasion; deduction

שדור ז 45 broadcast, transmission

שווט ז 45 systematization [no pl.]

שווי ז 45 giving, creating a look, atmosphere

שווק ז 45 marketing

שוור ז 45 alignment

שזוף ז 45 suntanning

שחור ז 45 seeking, reaching out

שטוי ז 45 mocking, practical joke Lit [no pl.]

שטור ז 45 policing

שיוב ז 45 recovery ecology

שיוט ז 45 sailing

שיוך ז 45 belonging, attribution

שיום ז 45 naming

שיוף ז 45 filing, planing

שיור ז 45 residue

שכוך ז 45 quietening, relieving pain, etc.

שכול ז 45 crossing one's legs or hands

שכון ז 45 housing; housing complex

שלוב ז 45 combination; integration; crossing one's legs or hands

שלוט ז 45 signposting

שלום ז 45 payment; reparations

שלוש ז 45 tripling; trinity

שמון ז 45 lubricating; lubrication

שמור ז 45 preservation; preserving; conservation

שמוש ז 45 use, utilization; purpose

שנוי ז 45 change

שנון ז 45 repetition; memorization

שנוס ז 45 girding

שנוק ז 45 stifling, throttling Lit

שסוי ז 45 incitement, urging to attack

שסוף ז 45 slitting, slashing, gashing

שפוד ז 45 skewering, piercing

שפוט ז 45 jurisdiction; judging; judgment

שפוי ז 45 compensation, damages insurance

שפול ז 45 bottom, edge, lower part

שפוץ ז 45 renovation; repairing, renovating; refurbishment; overhaul

שפור ז 45 improvement

שקוי ז 45 beverage, potion; elixir

שקול ז 45 consideration

שקום ז 45 rehabilitation

שקוף ז 45 reflection, reflecting; mirroring; X-ray screening

שתוך ז 45 corrosion [no pl.]

שתוף ז 45 participation, inclusion; sharing; cooperation

שתוק ז 45 paralysis; silencing - military

תבול ז 45 adding spice, flavoring, seasoning

תגור ז 45 bargaining, haggling Lit

תווי ז 45 notation music

תווך ז 45 mediation, arbitration; brokerage, negotiation [no pl.]

תיוג ז 45 tagging, labeling

תיול ז 45 wiring together

תיוק ז 45 filing documents

תיור ז 45 touring, sightseeing

תלוי ז 45 raising, lifting Lit [no pl.]

תלול ז 45 heaping soil around plant

תלום ז 45 furrowing

תמוך ז 45 support

תמור ז 45 rising sun, smoke Lit [no pl.]

תנוי ז 45 tale of woe [no pl.]

תסוף ז 45 re-evaluation

תפור ז 45 stitching

תקון ז 45 repair; correction; improvement, rehabilitation; reform

תקוף ז 45 validation statistics

ככוב ז 46 performing a leading role, starring

נכוס ז 46 appropriating, assimilating

סבוב/סיבוב ז 47 rotation; turn; cycle

עדוד/עידוד ז 47 encouragement, cheering up; promoting

רצוץ/ריצוץ ז 47 shattering, crushing

רקוק/ריקוק ז 47 spitting

תפוף/תיפוף ז 47 drumming

איתות ז 48 signaling

מיטוט ז 48 caving; breakdown, collapse

ציתות ז 48 eavesdropping [no pl.]

קימום ז 48 re-establishment [no pl.]

נימוס ז 49 politeness, manners

סיקוס ז 49 knot/node on a plant

אחוד ז 50 unification; merger, unity

אחוי ז 50 union, fusion

אחול ז 50 wish; wishes

אחור ז 50 delay N

בעור ז 50 elimination, destruction, extermination

בעות ז 50 terror, horror

גהוץ ז 50 ironing

גהוק ז 50 burp, belch N

גחוך ז 50 giggle, chuckle N

זהוי ז 50 identification

זהום ז 50 contamination, pollution; infection

פִּתּוּחַ ז 53 developing, development
צִמּוּחַ ז 53 plant growth [no pl.]
קִבּוּעַ ז 53 affixing, reinforcing, stabilizing [no pl.]
קִדּוּחַ ז 53 drilling, boring < kideaH 'drill and re-drill,' Lit-rare
קִטּוּעַ ז 53 amputation, cutting off, fragmentation
קִמּוּחַ ז 53 flouring [no pl.]
קִנּוּחַ ז 53 wiping, drying; dessert
קִפּוּחַ ז 53 discrimination, deprivation
רִבּוּעַ ז 53 square
רִוּוּחַ ז 53 spacing
רִקּוּעַ ז 53 flattening/hammering out of metal
שִׁגּוּעַ ז 53 driving someone crazy Coll.
שִׁטּוּחַ ז 53 flattening
שִׁלּוּחַ ז 53 launching; release; sending
שִׂמּוּחַ ז 53 cheering up [no pl.]
שִׁמּוּעַ ז 53 hearing (law)
שִׁנּוּעַ ז 53 transportation of goods, shipping and handling
שִׁסּוּעַ ז 53 splitting, tearing; interruption, disruption
שִׁפּוּעַ ז 53 slope, incline
שִׁקּוּעַ ז 53 draught (shipping); sedimentation; settling
תִּחוּחַ ז 53 loosening, breaking up earth [no pl.]
תִּלּוּעַ ז 53 deworming [no pl.]
אִגְרוּף ז 54 boxing
אִכְלוּס ז 54 populating, colonizing, settling
אִכְסוּן ז 54 accommodation, hosting
אִלְחוּט ז 54 wireless broadcasting [no pl.]
אִלְחוּשׁ ז 54 Anesthesia
אִלְמוּן ז 54 causing one to become a widower [no pl.]
אִלְתּוּר ז 54 improvisation
אִפְיוּן ז 54 characterization
אִפְסוּן ז 54 storage, setting aside [no pl.]
אִפְשׁוּר ז 54 enabling, making possible
אִקְלוּם ז 54 acclimatization
אִרְגּוּן ז 54 organizing; organization
אִשְׁפּוּז ז 54 hospitalization
בִּנְאוּם ז 54 internationalization [no pl.]
גִּלְווּן ז 54 galvanization
גִּלְעוּן ז 54 stoning/pitting fruit [no pl.]
גִּמְלוּן ז 54 scale-up [no pl.]
גִּנְדּוּר ז 54 adornment, beautification
גִּרְעוּן ז 54 producing nuclear material; making granular, irregular [no pl.]
דִּסְקוּס ז 54 discussion Coll.
דִּקְלוּם ז 54 recitation, declamation
דִּרְבּוּן ז 54 goading, spurring
הִפְנוּט ז 54 hypnotizing
חִבְרוּת ז 54 socialization
חִמְצוּן ז 54 oxydization
חִסְפּוּס ז 54 roughness, unevenness
חִצְצוּר ז 54 trumpeting
חִשְׁמוּל ז 54 electrification
כִּפְתּוּר ז 54 buttoning
כִּרְטוּס ז 54 card cataloguing
כִּרְסוּם ז 54 gnawing; metal cutting; gradual reduction
מִגְנוּט ז 54 magnetization
מִדְרוּג ז 54 building of terraces; television rating
מִדְרוּן ז 54 modernization [no pl.]
מִנְהוּר ז 54 tunneling
מִקְסוּם ז 54 maximization
מִרְכּוּז ז 54 centralization
מִשְׁטוּר ז 54 disciplining [no pl.]
מִשְׁכּוּן ז 54 mortgaging, using as collateral
נִטְרוּל ז 54 neutralization
נִרְמוּל ז 54 normalization
סִגְנוּן ז 54 styling, fashioning
סִנְגּוּר ז 54 defense, advocacy law [no pl.]
סִנְדּוּל ז 54 immobilizing vehicle in violation
סִנְווּר ז 54 temporary blindness, dazzle
סִנְתּוּז ז 54 synthesization
סִרְטוּן ז 54 carcinogenesis [no pl.]
סִרְכּוּז ז 54 centrifugation
עִדְכּוּן ז 54 update N
עִכְשׁוּו ז 54 actualization [no pl.]
עִרְבּוּל ז 54 mixing; whirling
עִרְגּוּל ז 54 rolling (metallurgy)
עִרְטוּל ז 54 exposing, revealing
עִרְפּוּל ז 54 blurring [no pl.]
פִּחְלוּץ ז 54 taxidermy
פִּחְמוּן ז 54 carbonization [no pl.]
פִּטְרוּל ז 54 patrolling
פִּלְבּוּל ז 54 rolling one's eyes
פִּנְטוּז ז 54 fantasizing Coll.
פִּסְטוּר ז 54 pasteurization [no pl.]
פִּרְזוּל ז 54 affixing metal fixtures; shoeing a horse
פִּרְכּוּס ז 54 fluttering, convulsing Lit
פִּרְכּוּס/פִּרְקוּס ז 54 cosmetic; embellishment Lit
פִּרְנוּס ז 54 supporting, maintaining [no pl.]
פִּרְסוּם ז 54 publicity; publication; advertising
פִּרְצוּל ז 54 parcellation of land
פִּרְקוּן ז 54 releasing emotional stress [no pl.]
צִנְזוּר ז 54 censoring
צִנְתּוּר ז 54 catheterization
קִטְלוּג ז 54 cataloguing
קִטְרוּג ז 54 accusation; testimony against an accused
קִלְטוּר ז 54 tilling, cultivation of soil [no pl.]
קִנְטוּר ז 54 spite, provocativeness
קִרְזוּל ז 54 curl
קִרְצוּף ז 54 scrubbing
רִטְפּוּשׁ ז 54 becoming fatter; obesity Rare [no pl.]
רִמְזוּר ז 54 installation of traffic lights
רִעְנוּן ז 54 refreshing, invigorating
שִׂכְלוּן ז 54 intellectualization [no pl.]
שִׁרְבּוּט ז 54 scribble, doodle N
שִׁרְיוּן ז 54 armoring; safeguarding
תִּבְלוּן ז 54 spicing, flavoring, seasoning [no pl.]
תִּחְמוּן ז 54 trickery, scheme Coll.
תִּכְנוּת ז 54 computer programming
תִּמְצוּת נ 54 summary, precis
תִּמְרוּן ז 54 maneuvering
תִּרְבּוּת נ 54 domesticating; causing to acquiring culture [no pl.]
תִּרְגּוּם ז 54 translating; translation
פִּעְנוּחַ ז 55 deciphering; solving; decoding
אִבְחוּן ז 56 diagnosis
אִזְכּוּר ז 56 reference, citation
אִחְזוּר ז 56 retrieval (computing)
אִחְסוּן ז 56 storage
אִחְצוּן ז 56 coming out of the closet [no pl.]
אִכְזוּב ז 56 disappointing [no pl.]
אִכְלוּל ז 56 induction [no pl.]
אִפְרוּט ז 56 deduction [no pl.]
אִשְׁפּוּר ז 56 finishing off textile materials
אִתְחוּל ז 56 initialization; booting (computing)
אִבְטוּחַ ז 57 guarding, securing [no pl.]
אִזְרוּחַ ז 57 naturalization [no pl.]
אִצְבּוּעַ ז 57 fingering (music) [no pl.]
מִזְעוּר ז 58 miniaturization, minimization
מִחְזוּר ז 58 recycling
מִחְשׁוּב ז 58 computerization

מִכְשׁוּר ז 58 equipping; equipment
מִלְכּוּד ז 58 booby-trapping
מִסְגּוּר ז 58 framing
מִסְחוּר ז 58 commercialization [no pl.]
מִסְמוּר ז 58 nailing
מִסְפּוּר ז 58 numbering
מִקְלוּט ז 58 making shelters [no pl.]
מִפְתּוּחַ ז 59 indexing
שִׁדְרוּג ז 60 upgrade N
שִׁחְבּוּר ז 60 change one type of syntactic structure to another
שִׁחְזוּר ז 60 reconstruction, restoration
שִׁחְלוּף ז 60 exchange; recombination genetics
שִׁטְעוּן ז 60 transshipment; reloading
שִׁכְפּוּל ז 60 reduplication; copying
שִׁכְתּוּב ז 60 revision, rewriting
שִׁלְהוּב ז 60 inciting, inflaming
שִׁעְבּוּד ז 60 slavery; enslaving; subjugation
שִׁעְבּוּר ז 60 Hebraizing [no pl.]
שִׁעְתּוּק ז 60 reproducing; transcribing
שִׁפְעוּל ז 60 activation [no pl.]
שִׁפְרוּט ז 60 elaboration
שִׁתְחוּל ז 60 restart (computing) [no pl.]
שִׁעֲרוּךְ ז 61 revaluation
שִׁזְרוּעַ ז 62 reseeding
שִׁכְנוּעַ ז 62 convincing, persuading
שִׁנְטוּעַ ז 62 replanting
שִׁחְרוּר ז 63 release, liberation; liberating; exemption
שִׁכְלוּל ז 63 enhancement, improvement; enhancing, improving
שִׁעֲמוּם ז 64 boredom [no pl.]
תִּבְנוּת ז 65 patterning
תִּבְרוּג ז 65 threading, screw-cutting
תִּגְבּוּר ז 65 reinforcing
תִּגְמוּל ז 65 compensation, reward
תִּדְלוּק ז 65 refueling
תִּדְרוּךְ ז 65 briefing
תִּזְמוּן ז 65 timing
תִּזְמוּר ז 65 orchestration
תִּחְבּוּל ז 65 machination, plot
תִּחְבּוּר ז 65 arranging words in a certain syntactic relationship
תִּחְזוּק ז 65 maintaining; maintenance
תִּחְלוּב ז 65 emulsification
תִּחְלוּף ז 65 subrogation, providing substitute [no pl.]
תִּחְמוּשׁ ז 65 arming [no pl.]
תִּחְקוּר ז 65 investigation, inquiry
תִּחְשׁוּב ז 65 calculating; calculation [no pl.]
תִּמְרוּץ ז 65 providing incentive
תִּסְבּוּךְ ז 65 complication Coll.
תִּסְכּוּל ז 65 frustration
תִּסְרוּט ז 65 producing a screenplay
תִּפְעוּל ז 65 operation, handling; management
תִּפְקוּד ז 65 functioning, function
תִּקְנוּן ז 65 standardization
תִּקְצוּב ז 65 budgeting
תִּקְשׁוּב ז 65 teleprocessing
תִּקְשׁוּר ז 65 communication system
תִּרְגּוּל ז 65 exercise, training, drilling
תִּרְכּוּב ז 65 preparation of vaccine [no pl.]
תִּשְׁאוּל ז 65 preliminary inquiry
בִּזְבּוּז ז 66 wasting, waste N
בִּלְבּוּל ז 66 confusion, mix-up
בִּצְבּוּץ ז 66 poking out, sprouting
בִּקְבּוּק ז 66 bottling
גִּלְגּוּל ז 66 rolling; somersault; metamorphosis; reincarnation
גִּמְגּוּם ז 66 stuttering
גִּרְגּוּר ז 66 gargling
דִּגְדּוּג ז 66 tickling
דִּכְדּוּךְ ז 66 depression, despondency
דִּלְדּוּל ז 66 depletion, diminution
דִּמְדּוּם ז 66 confusion; glowing of dim light
דִּנְדּוּן ז 66 pealing, ringing Lit
דִּפְדּוּף ז 66 leafing, turning pages
דִּקְדּוּק ז 66 grammar; being precise, punctilious
דִּרְדּוּר ז 66 roling down a slope; deterioration
דִּשְׁדּוּשׁ ז 66 stamping, treading
הִבְהוּב ז 66 flashing, blinking
הִדְהוּד ז 66 reverberation, echoing
הִמְהוּם ז 66 humming; mumbling
הִנְהוּן ז 66 nodding in agreement
הִרְהוּר ז 66 passing thought
זִלְזוּל ז 66 disrespect, contempt
זִמְזוּם ז 66 buzz, hum N
חִלְחוּל ז 66 trickling, percolation
חִרְחוּר ז 66 grunting
חִרְחוּר ז 66 provocation
טִאטוּא ז 66 sweeping
טִלְטוּל ז 66 moving, shaking, rolling
טִמְטוּם ז 66 stupidity
טִפְטוּף ז 66 dripping
טִקְטוּק ז 66 ticking
טִרְטוּר ז 66 rattle, din, clatter
טִשְׁטוּשׁ ז 66 confusion; effacement
כִּלְכּוּל ז 66 upkeep, maintenance, providing for
כִּרְכּוּר ז 66 wild dancing
כִּשְׁכּוּשׁ ז 66 wagging
לִבְלוּב ז 66 budding, blooming
לִגְלוּג ז 66 ridicule
לִכְלוּךְ ז 66 dirt, mess; dirtying
לִקְלוּק ז 66 licking, lapping
מִזְמוּז ז 66 ”caress, “necking
מִלְמוּל ז 66 mumbling
מִסְמוּס ז 66 melting, softening, dissolving
מִצְמוּץ ז 66 blinking
נִדְנוּד ז 66 swinging; nuisance Sl.
נִמְנוּם ז 66 nap N
נִפְנוּף ז 66 waving; fluttering
נִצְנוּץ ז 66 sparkling, twinkling; sparkle, twinkle
נִשְׁנוּשׁ ז 66 nosh, snacking, Sl.
סִבְסוּד ז 66 subsidization
סִגְסוּג ז 66 alloying
סִכְסוּךְ ז 66 dispute; conflict
סִלְסוּל ז 66 curl; trill N
סִפְסוּר ז 66 profiteering, speculation
עִלְעוּל ז 66 leafing, browsing
עִמְעוּם ז 66 dimming; dulling; blurring
עִפְעוּף ז 66 blinking
עִרְעוּר ז 66 appeal; objection
פִּטְפּוּט ז 66 chatter, prattle
פִּכְפּוּךְ ז 66 trickling; trickle
פִּלְפּוּל ז 66 in-depth study/debate
פִּלְפּוּל ז 66 peppering
פִּצְפּוּץ ז 66 smashing
פִּקְפּוּק ז 66 doubt N
פִּרְפּוּר ז 66 fluttering
פִּשְׁפּוּשׁ ז 66 rummaging; checking well
צִלְצוּל ז 66 chime, ring
צִמְצוּם ז 66 reduction, decrease
צִפְצוּף ז 66 beep; chirping
צִרְצוּר ז 66 chirping of cricket
קִוְקוּו ז 66 filling in with lines
קִלְקוּל ז 66 malfunction, spoiling
קִרְקוּר ז 66 crowing; cawing
קִשְׁקוּשׁ ז 66 scribble Coll.; idle chatter Coll.; rattle
רִפְרוּף ז 66 fluttering; cursory glance, scan
רִשְׁרוּשׁ ז 66 rustling
שִׂגְשׂוּג ז 66 prosperity
שִׁכְשׁוּךְ ז 66 wading; splashing
שִׁפְשׁוּף ז 66 rubbing; abrasion
שִׁקְשׁוּק ז 66 rattling, jingling
שִׁרְשׁוּר ז 66 concatenation
תִּלְתּוּל ז 66 curling hair
תִּקְתּוּק ז 66 ticking; typing Coll.
בִּעְבּוּעַ ז 67 bubbling
גִּעְגּוּעַ ז 67 cackling of geese

כִּעְכּוּעַ ז 67 coughing, clearing of throat
לִחְלוּחַ ז 67 dampening, moistening [no pl.]
נִעְנוּעַ ז 67 movement; shaking; swaying
פִּעְפּוּעַ ז 67 bubbling; seeping, infusion
צִחְצוּחַ ז 67 brushing, polishing
קִעְקוּעַ ז 67 tattooing
קִרְקוּעַ ז 67 grounding
רִחְרוּחַ ז 67 sniffing, smelling
זִעְזוּעַ ז 68 shaking
גַּעְגּוּעַ ז 69 longing, missing
זַעֲזוּעַ ז 69 shock, turbulence; turmoil; crisis, upheaval
שַׁעֲשׁוּעַ ז 69 entertainment, game
אִוְרוּר ז 70 ventilation
אִוְשׁוּשׁ ז 70 murmur, rustle
אִמְלוּל ז 70 making miserable
אִנְפּוּף ז 70 nasal speech, nasalization
אִפְנוּן ז 70 modulation – electronics
אִפְרוּר ז 70 incineration [no pl.]
אִשְׁרוּר ז 70 ratification
גִּוְנוּן ז 70 shading, variation
דִּבְלוּל ז 70 ruffling, thinning out
דִּקְרוּר ז 70 tingling, pricking lightly
כִּדְרוּר ז 70 dribble a ball
כִּוְנוּן ז 70 adjustment, tuning
נִקְבּוּב ז 70 perforation [no pl.]
סִחְרוּר ז 70 spin; dizziness
סִמְרוּר ז 70 shuddering
סִפְרוּר ז 70 numbering
סִרְטוּט/שִׂרְטוּט ז 70 drafting, drawing
עִצְבּוּב ז 70 innervation
עִקְצוּץ ז 70 stinging, itching
עִרְבּוּב ז 70 mixing; shuffling
צִחְקוּק ז 70 giggling
שִׂפְתּוּת ז 70 labialization [no pl.]
שִׁקְלוּל ז 70 weight (statistics); adjusted calculation
שִׁרְבּוּב ז 70 insertion in wrong place
תִּכְנוּן ז 70 planning; designing
תִּמְרוּר ז 70 placing road signs
מְאַיֵּד ז 71 carburetor
מְאַיֵּךְ ז 71 adjunct, modifier (grammar)
מְבַשֵּׁל ז 71 cook
מְבַשֵּׂר ז 71 herald, messenger; harbinger
מְדַכֵּא ז 71 depressing
מְחַבֵּל ז 71 destroyer, one causing damage
מְחַיֵּב ז 71 obligatory, binding
מְחַלֵּק ז 71 distributor (person); divisor (math)
מְחַנֵּךְ ז 71 home room teacher; educator
מְחַסֵּר ז 71 subtrahend (math)
מְחַשֵּׁב ז 71 calculator

מְטַיֵּל ז 71 tourist, hiker, traveler
מְטַפֵּל ז 71 caregiver; therapist
מְטַפֵּס ז 71 climber (person; plant)
מְיַבֵּשׁ ז 71 dryer
מְיַלֵּד ז 71 doctor who delivers babies
מְיַנֵּן ז 71 ionizer
מְיַסֵּד ז 71 founder
מְיַצֵּב ז 71 stabilizer
מְיַצֵּג ז 71 representative Adj
מְכַשֵּׁף ז 71 sorcerer, magician
מְלַבֵּב ז 71 heartwarming
מְלַטֵּף ז 71 soft, velvety
מְלַמֵּד ז 71 teacher, educator, Heder teacher
מְמַיֵּן ז 71 sorter, selector
מְמַכֵּר ז 71 addictive
מְנַגֵּן ז 71 player (music)
מְנַצֵּל ז 71 exploiter
מְנַקֵּב ז 71 hole puncher, perforator
מְנַקֵּד ז 71 vowelizer
מְנַקֵּר ז 71 purger, remover of thigh tendon from slaughtered animal
מְסַכֵּם ז 71 summarizing
מְסַפֵּק ז 71 satisfactory
מְסַפֵּר ז 71 narrator
מְסַתֵּת ז 71 stonemason
מְעַבֵּד ז 71 adapter, arranger (music); processor (food, words)
מְעַוֵּל ז 71 abuser
מְעַיֵּף ז 71 tiring, exhausting
מְעַצֵּב ז 71 designer
מְעַקֵּר ז 71 antiseptic, sterilizing
מְעַשֵּׁן ז 71 smoker
מְפַגֵּר ז 71 someone with a mental handicap
מְפַקֵּד ז 71 commander
מְפַשֵּׁר ז 71 conciliatory
מְקַדֵּם ז 71 coefficient (math)
מְקַשֵּׁר ז 71 liaison officer
מְרַגֵּל ז 71 spy
מְרַכֵּז ז 71 coordinator
מְרַכֵּךְ ז 71 softener
מְרַתֵּק ז 71 fascinating
מְשַׁכֵּר ז 71 intoxicating
מְתַוֵּךְ ז 71 agent; mediator
מְתַקֵּן ז 71 reformer
מְאַהֵב ז 72 lover
מְיַעֵץ ז 72 advisory
מְנַהֵל ז 72 manager, principal
מְנַחֵשׁ ז 72 diviner, fortune teller
מְרַחֵף ז 72 daydreaming Sl.
מְפָרֵךְ ז 73 exhausting, fatiguing
מְפָרֵק ז 73 liquidator
מְפָרֵשׁ ז 73 commentator; exegete
מְקָרֵר ז 73 refrigerator
מְשָׁרֵת ז 73 servant
מְתָאֵם ז 73 coordinator; coordinating Adj
מְיַגֵּעַ ז 74 tiring, exhausting
מְכַיֵּחַ ז 74 expectorant

מְנַצֵּחַ ז 74 victor; winner; conductor (music)
מְנַתֵּחַ ז 74 surgeon; analyst; analyzer
מְסַיֵּעַ ז 74 supporting, contributive
מְפַגֵּעַ ז 74 terrorist who carried out an attack
מְפַקֵּחַ ז 74 supervisor, inspector
מְפַתֵּחַ ז 74 developer
מְרַצֵּחַ ז 74 murderer
מְשַׁגֵּעַ ז 74 wonderful, terrific, gorgeous Sl.
מְהַנֶּה ז 75 enjoyable
מְזַהֶה ז 75 used as means of identification
מְכַנֶּה ז 75 denominator
מְלַוֶּה ז 75 escort
מְמַצֶּה ז 75 exhaustive, comprehensive
מְנַקֶּה ז 75 cleaner, janitor
מְעַבֶּה ז 75 condenser
מְפַתֶּה ז 75 enticing, tempting
מְגָרֶה ז 76 stimulating, arousing
מְאוֹתֵת ז 77 signaler
מְבוֹדֵד ז 77 insulating
מְחוֹלֵל ז 77 generator
מְחוֹקֵק ז 77 legislator
מְכוֹנֵן ז 77 founder; founding, establishing; constitutive
מְעוֹדֵד ז 77 encouraging
מְעוֹפֵף ז 77 flying, airborne
מְעוֹרֵר ז 77 arousing, stimulating
מְקוֹמֵם ז 77 outrageous
מְקוֹנֵן ז 77 mourner
מְשׁוֹטֵט ז 77 wanderer; wandering
מְשׁוֹרֵר ז 77 poet
מְתוֹפֵף ז 77 drummer
מְאַכְזֵב ז 78 disappointing
מְאַלְחֵשׁ ז 78 anesthetic
מְאַרְגֵּן ז 78 organizer
מְהַנְדֵּס ז 78 engineer
מְהַפְּנֵט ז 78 hypnotist; hypnotizing
מְחַצְצֵר ז 78 bugler, trumpeter
מְכַרְסֵם ז 78 rodent
מְסַגְנֵן ז 78 one who edits text for style
מְסַנְוֵר ז 78 blinding; dazzling
מְסַרְטֵן ז 78 carcinogenic
מְעַנְיֵן ז 78 interesting
מְעַרְבֵּל ז 78 cement mixer; blender
מְפַרְנֵס ז 78 breadwinner, wage earner
מְתַרְגֵּם ז 78 translator
מְרַאְיֵן/מְרַאֲיֵן ז 79 interviewer
מְמַסְפֵּר ז 80 numerator
מְשַׁעֲמֵם ז 81 boring
מְתַדְלֵק ז 82 gas station attendant
מְתַכְנֵת ז 82 computer programmer

מְחֻיָּץ ז 92 partitioned
מְחֻכָּךְ ז 92 rubbed, chafed
מְחֻכָּם ז 92 wise, clever, shrewd
מְחֻלָּל ז 92 desecrated, defiled
מְחֻלָּק ז 92 divided; compartmentalized
מְחֻמָּם ז 92 heated; angry Sl.
מְחֻמָּשׁ ז 92 armed
מְחֻמָּשׁ ז 92 pentagon; pentamerous, quintuple
מְחֻנָּךְ ז 92 polite, well-mannered
מְחֻסָּל ז 92 cancelled, eliminated
מְחֻסָּם ז 92 tempered - glass, metal
מְחֻסָּן ז 92 immunized; immune; impervious
מְחֻסָּר ז 92 lacking
מְחֻפָּר ז 92 entrenched
מְחֻפָּשׂ ז 92 costumed, dressed up
מְחֻצָּף ז 92 impertinent, insolent, cheeky
מְחֻשָּׁב ז 92 calculated
מְחֻשָּׁל ז 92 stolid, even-tempered; forged
מְחֻתָּד ז 92 articulate Adj; sharp, intense
מְחֻתָּל ז 92 diapered
מְחֻתָּן ז 92 in-law
מְטֻגָּן ז 92 fried
מְטֻוָּח ז 92 aimed, targeted
מְטֻיָּח ז 92 whitewashed; plastered
מְטֻיָּט ז 92 covered with mud
מְטֻלָּא ז 92 patched
מְטֻמָּא ז 92 contaminated, impure Lit
מְטֻנָּף ז 92 filthy, dirty
מְטֻפָּח ז 92 well-kept, nurtured, cultivated
מְטֻפָּל ז 92 patient N
מְטֻפָּשׁ ז 92 stupid, unwise
מְיֻבָּא ז 92 imported
מְיֻבָּל ז 92 callused, warty, horny, corned
מְיֻבָּשׁ ז 92 dried; desiccated
מְיֻגָּע ז 92 exhausted, worn out
מְיֻדָּד ז 92 friendly
מְיֻדָּע ז 92 acquaintance; definite - Gramm
מְיֻזָּע ז 92 sweaty
מְיֻחָד ז 92 special, extraordinary; unique
מְיֻחָל ז 92 awaited, longed for
מְיֻחָם ז 92 in heat - animal
מְיֻחָס ז 92 of distinguished lineage; attributed to
מְיֻמָּן ז 92 skilled, proficient
מְיֻנָּן ז 92 ionized
מְיֻסָּר ז 92 suffering, troubled, tormented
מְיֻצָּא ז 92 exported
מְיֻצָּב ז 92 stabilized, reinforced
מְיֻצָּג ז 92 represented by
מְיֻשָּׁב ז 92 populated, settled; level-headed; solved - dispute

מְיֻשָּׁן ז 92 obsolete, old-fashioned; aged, matured
מְיֻשָּׁר ז 92 straightened, leveled
מְיֻתָּם ז 92 orphaned; abandoned, neglected
מְיֻתָּר ז 92 extra, superfluous; redundant
מְכֻבָּד ז 92 esteemed, respected; worthy person, notable person
מְכֻבָּל ז 92 connected to cable
מְכֻבָּס ז 92 laundered, washed
מְכֻדָּן ז 92 bayonetted
מְכֻדָּר ז 92 balled, spherical
מְכֻוָּן ז 92 directed; tuned, adjusted; deliberate
מְכֻוָּץ ז 92 shrunken; cramped - muscle
מְכֻיָּס ז 92 pickpocketed
מְכֻמָּת ז 92 quantified
מְכֻנָּם ז 92 lousy
מְכֻנָּס ז 92 collected, compiled; gathered
מְכֻנָּף ז 92 winged
מְכֻסָּח ז 92 mowed, cut
מְכֻפָּל ז 92 double; multiplicand
מְכֻשָּׁף ז 92 enchanted; spellbound
מְכֻתָּב ז 92 recipient, addressee
מְכֻתָּף ז 92 shouldered - rifle, etc.
מְכֻתָּר ז 92 surrounded, besieged
מְלֻבָּן ז 92 white-hot; clarified; resolved
מְלֻבָּשׁ ז 92 dressed, attired
מְלֻטָּשׁ ז 92 polished
מְלֻכָּד ז 92 united, unified
מְלֻמָּד ז 92 scholar; scholarly, educated
מְלֻפָּף ז 92 wound, wrapped; coiled
מְלֻקָּט ז 92 collected, gathered
מְלֻקָּק ז 92 licked; clean, spotless Sl.
מְמֻגָּל ז 92 pussy, suppurated
מְמֻגָּן ז 92 protected, armor protected
מְמֻגָּף ז 92 wearing boots
מְמֻדָּר ז 92 departmentalized
מְמֻזָּג ז 92 air-conditioned; temperate; merged
מְמֻזָּל ז 92 lucky, fortunate
מְמֻיָּם ז 92 reconstituted
מְמֻיָּן ז 92 sorted
מְמֻכָּן ז 92 mechanized
מְמֻלָּא ז 92 filled, stuffed
מְמֻלָּח ז 92 seasoned, experienced, sophisticated, smart
מְמֻמָּן ז 92 financed
מְמֻמָּשׁ ז 92 realized - plan etc.
מְמֻנָּע ז 92 motorized
מְמֻסָּד ז 92 established, institutionalized
מְמֻסָּךְ ז 92 jammed - radio signal

מְמֻצָּע ז 92 average, mean - both Adj and N
מְמֻקָּד ז 92 focused, centered
מְמֻקָּם ז 92 situated, located, placed
מְמֻקָּשׁ ז 92 mined
מְמֹרָק ז 92 polished
מְמֻשָּׁךְ ז 92 extended - period of time
מְמֻתָּן ז 92 restrained
מְמֻתָּק ז 92 sweetened
מְנֻגָּב ז 92 dried, wiped dry
מְנֻגָּד ז 92 opposing, opposite
מְנֻגָּן ז 92 accented; tuneful Lit
מְנֻדָּב ז 92 donated; nominated, volunteered
מְנֻוָּל ז 92 evil Adj, contemptible; ugly, disgusting
מְנֻוָּן ז 92 withered, atrophied
מְנֻזָּל ז 92 having a runny nose
מְנֻחָם ז 92 comforted, consoled
מְנֻכָּר ז 92 alienated; estranged
מְנֻמָּס ז 92 polite, well-mannered
מְנֻמָּק ז 92 explained, reasoned
מְנֻמָּר ז 92 speckled, splotched
מְנֻמָּשׁ ז 92 freckled
מְנֻסָּח ז 92 worded
מְנֻסָּר ז 92 sawn, cut
מְנֻפָּח ז 92 inflated, blown up
מְנֻפָּט ז 92 carded - raw wool, cotton
מְנֻפָּץ ז 92 shattered, broken; carded, combed - textiles
מְנֻצָּח ז 92 vanquished, defeated
מְנֻצָּל ז 92 utilized, exploited
מְנֻקָּב ז 92 perforated, punctured
מְנֻקָּד ז 92 vowelized; dotted
מְנֻקָּר ז 92 pierced, punctured; purged - meat
מְנֻשָּׁל ז 92 dispossessed, disinherited; banished, exiled
מְנֻשָּׁף ז 92 aspirated - phonetics
מְנֻשָּׁק ז 92 kissed
מְנֻתָּב ז 92 directed, guided; demarcated into lanes
מְנֻתָּח ז 92 person who has undergone an operation
מְנֻתָּץ ז 92 shattered, broken, destroyed
מְנֻתָּק ז 92 cut, disconnected
מְסֻבָּךְ ז 92 complicated, complex; entangled
מְסֻבָּן ז 92 soaped, soapy; tricked, "fixed" Sl.
מְסֻגָּל ז 92 capable, able
מְסֻגָּף ז 92 tormented, tortured by absence of physical pleasures
מְסֻגָּר ז 92 closed, shut; introspective
מְסֻדָּר ז 92 tidy, neat, organized; taken care of Coll.; established Coll.
מְסֻוָּג ז 92 sorted, categorized; classified, confidential

hesitant, restrained 92 מְסֻיָּג ז
whitewashed 92 מְסֻיָּד ז
nightmarish 92 מְסֻיָּט ז
specific, defined, certain 92 מְסֻיָּם ז
decided, agreed; summarized 92 מְסֻכָּם ז
dangerous; risky 92 מְסֻכָּן ז
sugar-coated, glazed 92 מְסֻכָּר ז
stony, rocky 92 מְסֻלָּע ז
distorted, deceptive, untrue 92 מְסֻלָּף ז
removed; paid; cleared 92 מְסֻלָּק ז
symbolized 92 מְסֻמָּל ז
drugged, groggy 92 מְסֻמָּם ז
marked, indicated; signposted 92 מְסֻמָּן ז
nailed; glued, stuck 92 מְסֻמָּר ז
filtered, strained 92 מְסֻנָּן ז
incorporated, annexed, affiliated 92 מְסֻנָּף ז
annexed 92 מְסֻפָּח ז
doubtful, uncertain 92 מְסֻפָּק ז
supplied, provided 92 מְסֻפָּק ז
have had a haircut 92 מְסֻפָּר ז
related, recounted - story 92 מְסֻפָּר ז
cleared of stones 92 מְסֻקָּל ז
chiseled 92 מְסֻתָּת ז
processed; adapted, altered 92 מְעֻבָּד ז
intercalary 92 מְעֻבָּר ז
rounded 92 מְעֻגָּל ז
based on; fixed tightly 92 מְעֻגָּן ז
refined, sophisticated; elegant; genteel, delicate 92 מְעֻדָּן ז
distorted, twisted; distortion 92 מְעֻוָּת ז
decorated, adorned 92 מְעֻטָּר ז
rhombus 92 מְעֻיָּן ז
delayed; restrained - law 92 מְעֻכָּב ז
digested 92 מְעֻכָּל ז
unconscious 92 מְעֻלָּף ז
laid out in pages - publishing 92 מְעֻמָּד ז
while standing 92 מְעֻמָּד ז
dim, dull, vague 92 מְעֻמָּם ז
confronted 92 מְעֻמָּת ז
wearing a tie 92 מְעֻנָּב ז
cloudy, overcast 92 מְעֻנָּן ז
rotten, stinking, moldy 92 מְעֻפָּשׁ ז
designed 92 מְעֻצָּב ז
cubic 92 מְעֻקָּב ז
bent, curved; attached by lien, confiscated 92 מְעֻקָּל ז
curved, bent, twisted 92 מְעֻקָּם ז
sterilized, sterile, germ-free 92 מְעֻקָּר ז
weeded 92 מְעֻשָּׂב ז
smoked - meat etc. 92 מְעֻשָּׁן ז
tithed 92 מְעֻשָּׂר ז

postdated 92 מְעֻתָּד ז
denatured - alcohol 92 מְפֻגָּל ז
scattered; scatterbrained, absent-minded 92 מְפֻזָּר ז
afraid, frightened, scared 92 מְפֻחָד ז
charred, burnt 92 מְפֻחָם ז
fattened - goose etc. 92 מְפֻטָּם ז
fired, laid off 92 מְפֻטָּר ז
sooty 92 מְפֻיָּח ז
written like a liturgical poem; poetic, lyrical 92 מְפֻיָּט ז
placated 92 מְפֻיָּס ז
realistic, sober 92 מְפֻכָּח ז
divided, split, factious 92 מְפֻלָּג ז
sectioned, segmented 92 מְפֻלָּח ז
open at both ends - passageway, corridor 92 מְפֻלָּשׁ ז
spoiled, pampered 92 מְפֻנָּק ז
sculpted 92 מְפֻסָּל ז
punctuated - Gramm 92 מְפֻסָּק ז
split, divided 92 מְפֻצָּל ז
full to capacity Sl. 92 מְפֻצָּץ ז
supervised 92 מְפֻקָּח ז
focused Coll. 92 מְפֻקָּס ז
simplified 92 מְפֻשָּׁט ז
spread apart - arms etc. 92 מְפֻשָּׂק ז
developed, advanced 92 מְפֻתָּח ז
twisting, winding; complicated 92 מְפֻתָּל ז
quoted 92 מְצֻטָּט ז
equipped 92 מְצֻיָּד ז
excellent; marked 92 מְצֻיָּן ז
fringed - garment; crested - bird 92 מְצֻיָּץ ז
drawn; illustrated 92 מְצֻיָּר ז
crossed 92 מְצֻלָּב ז
photographed, photocopied 92 מְצֻלָּם ז
polygon; polygonal 92 מְצֻלָּע ז
scarred 92 מְצֻלָּק ז
wrinkled, withered; gaunt 92 מְצֻמָּק ז
suffering from a cold 92 מְצֻנָּן ז
accepted, popular; customary 92 מְקֻבָּל ז
kabbalist 92 מְקֻבָּל ז
collected 92 מְקֻבָּץ ז
holy, sacred 92 מְקֻדָּשׁ ז
deducted, offset 92 מְקֻזָּז ז
polarized 92 מְקֻטָּב ז
broken, fragmented 92 מְקֻטָּע ז
showered 92 מְקֻלָּח ז
cursed 92 מְקֻלָּל ז
peeled 92 מְקֻלָּף ז
floured 92 מְקֻמָּח ז
wrinkled, crumpled 92 מְקֻמָּט ז
curved 92 מְקֻמָּר ז
wiped (nose etc.) Lit 92 מְקֻנָּח ז
deprived 92 מְקֻפָּח ז
folded 92 מְקֻפָּל ז
chopped; cut, shortened; trimmed 92 מְקֻצָּץ ז

shortened, abbreviated 92 מְקֻצָּר ז
adorned, decorated 92 מְקֻשָּׁט ז
connected; tied; cohesive; well-connected 92 מְקֻשָּׁר ז
arched 92 מְקֻשָּׁת ז
stained, dirty Lit 92 מְרֻבָּב ז
layered 92 מְרֻבָּד ז
thickened with roux 92 מְרֻבָּךְ ז
quadrangular; square 92 מְרֻבָּע ז
angry, annoyed 92 מְרֻגָּז ז
excited; inflamed 92 מְרֻגָּשׁ ז
flattened, rolled out 92 מְרֻדָּד ז
spacious 92 מְרֻוָּח ז
distant, far off; estranged, alienated 92 מְרֻחָק ז
hacked to pieces, dismembered 92 מְרֻטָּשׁ ז
centralized; focused; concentrated 92 מְרֻכָּז ז
softened 92 מְרֻכָּךְ ז
hinted, implied 92 מְרֻמָּז ז
restrained; moderate 92 מְרֻסָּן ז
sprayed 92 מְרֻסָּס ז
mashed; smashed 92 מְרֻסָּק ז
upholstered; padded 92 מְרֻפָּד ז
tattered, worn out 92 מְרֻפָּט ז
floored, paved 92 מְרֻצָּף ז
beaten, hammered out - metal 92 מְרֻקָּע ז
sloppy, unkempt 92 מְרֻשָּׁל ז
evil, wicked; offensive 92 מְרֻשָּׁע ז
impoverished 92 מְרֻשָּׁשׁ ז
netted; meshed; webbed; interconnected 92 מְרֻשָּׁת ז
welded, soldered 92 מְרֻתָּךְ ז
fascinated, glued to one's seat; restricted, confined 92 מְרֻתָּק ז
high quality, choice; excellent, praiseworthy 92 מְשֻׁבָּח ז
checkered; placed in schedule; set with gems 92 מְשֻׁבָּץ ז
faulty, defective 92 מְשֻׁבָּשׁ ז
crazy; crazy person 92 מְשֻׁגָּע ז
flattened 92 מְשֻׁטָּח ז
polished, smoothed, filed 92 מְשֻׁיָּף ז
marbled 92 מְשֻׁיָּשׁ ז
cross-legged, cross-handed 92 מְשֻׁכָּל ז
combined; integrated 92 מְשֻׁלָּב ז
signposted 92 מְשֻׁלָּט ז
lacking, bereft Lit 92 מְשֻׁלָּל ז
triangle; triangular; triple 92 מְשֻׁלָּשׁ ז
convert N from Judaism Lit 92 מְשֻׁמָּד ז
oiled, greased 92 מְשֻׁמָּן ז
preserved, canned 92 מְשֻׁמָּר ז
used 92 מְשֻׁמָּשׁ ז
serrated, toothed 92 מְשֻׁנָּן ז
belted Lit 92 מְשֻׁנָּס ז
marked with lines to indicate grade 92 מְשֻׁנָּת ז

split, torn, rented 92 מְשֻׁסָּע ז
slit, slashed, gashed 92 מְשֻׁסָּף ז
moustached 92 מְשֻׂפָּם ז
having an abundance (of) Lit 92 מְשֻׁפָּע ז
sloped, slanted 92 מְשֻׁפָּע ז
renovated 92 מְשֻׁפָּץ ז
improved 92 מְשֻׁפָּר ז
rehabilitated 92 מְשֻׁקָּם ז
common, shared, joint 92 מְשֻׁתָּף ז
paralyzed 92 מְשֻׁתָּק ז
seasoned, spiced; spicy 92 מְתֻבָּל ז
tagged 92 מְתֻיָּג ז
filed 92 מְתֻיָּק ז
furrowed Lit 92 מְתֻלָּם ז
grubby; worm-eaten 92 מְתֻלָּע ז
octagon; octagonal 92 מְתֻמָּן ז
repaired; corrected; revised; improved; reformed 92 מְתֻקָּן ז
powdered - cheeks etc. 92 מְפֻדָּר ז
in love with 93 מְאֹהָב ז
engaged to be married 93 מְאֹרָס ז
event, incident 93 מְאֹרָע ז
depressed 93 מְבֹאָס ז
annotated 93 מְבֹאָר ז
frightened, terrified 93 מְבֹהָל ז
kindled, lit, burning 93 מְבֹעָר ז
terrified, horrified 93 מְבֹעָת ז
blessed; praiseworthy 93 מְבֹרָךְ ז
clear-cut, examined, investigated 93 מְבֹרָר ז
filthy, contaminated 93 מְגֹאָל ז
ironed, pressed 93 מְגֹהָץ ז
socked, stockinged – feet 93 מְגֹרָב ז
scraped; grated 93 מְגֹרָד ז
greased 93 מְגֹרָז ז
boneless; deboned 93 מְגֹרָם ז
grated 93 מְגֹרָר ז
exiled person 93 מְגֹרָשׁ ז
terraced; graduated; ranked 93 מְדֹרָג ז
dirty, filthy, polluted 93 מְזֹהָם ז
accelerated, expedited 93 מְזֹרָז ז
rhymed; strung - beads 93 מְחֹרָז ז
grooved, furrowed 93 מְחֹרָץ ז
rifled 93 מְחֹרָק ז
perforated 93 מְחֹרָר ז
purified 93 מְטֹהָר ז
crazy, insane 93 מְטֹרָף ז
in despair, desperate, hopeless 93 מְיֹאָשׁ ז
Judaized 93 מְיֹהָד ז
designate; appointed 93 מְיֹעָד ז
streamlined, made more efficient 93 מְיֹעָל ז
forested, wooded 93 מְיֹעָר ז
ugly, unattractive 93 מְכֹעָר ז
bound - a book 93 מְכֹרָךְ ז
white-hot; inflamed 93 מְלֹהָט ז
mashed 93 מְמֹעָךְ ז
shaken out - carpet etc. 93 מְנֹעָר ז
corrupt, despicable 93 מְסֹאָב ז
branched 93 מְסֹעָף ז
barred - window; alternating, discontinuous 93 מְסֹרָג ז
castrated, emasculated 93 מְסֹרָס ז
combed, coiffed 93 מְסֹרָק ז
mixed; involved 93 מְעֹרָב ז
magnificent, splendid, fancy 93 מְפֹאָר ז
boring, dull; bored; yawning, sleepy 93 מְפֹהָק ז
dispersed, scattered 93 מְפֹרָד ז
demilitarized 93 מְפֹרָז ז
detailed 93 מְפֹרָט ז
full of bays - coastline 93 מְפֹרָץ ז
dismantled, disassembled 93 מְפֹרָק ז
crumbled; disintegrated 93 מְפֹרָר ז
explicit; interpreted, annotated 93 מְפֹרָשׁ ז
unclear, foggy, blurry, veiled 93 מְצֹעָף ז
leprous 93 מְצֹרָע ז
attached 93 מְצֹרָף ז
close associate, crony 93 מְקֹרָב ז
cooled, chilled 93 מְקֹרָר ז
furnished 93 מְרֹהָט ז
expected, approximated 93 מְשֹׁעָר ז
entangled, interwoven 93 מְשֹׂרָג ז
coordinated, matched 93 מְתֹאָם ז
described 93 מְתֹאָר ז
horrible; disgusting, revolting 93 מְתֹעָב ז
documented 93 מְתֹעָד ז
industrialized 93 מְתֹעָשׁ ז
event, incident [pl. - ot] 94 מְאֹרָע ז
ridiculed, belittled 95 מְבֻזֶּה ז
exposed, uncovered, visible 95 מְגֻלֶּה ז
disgusting, offensive, indecent 95 מְגֻנֶּה ז
fictitious, bogus; virtual - computing 95 מְדֻמֶּה ז
hushed, silenced Lit 95 מְהֻסֶּה ז
covered 95 מְחֻפֶּה ז
mimicked, imitated 95 מְחֻקֶּה ז
beautified, decorated; authorized agent meyupe koaH 95 מְיֻפֶּה ז
called, known as, nicknamed 95 מְכֻנֶּה ז
covered 95 מְכֻסֶּה ז
fanned - flame; inflamed, impassioned 95 מְלֻבֶּה ז
supervisor, person in charge 95 מְמֻנֶּה ז
exiled, banished, excommunicated 95 מְנֻדֶּה ז
experienced 95 מְנֻסֶּה ז
sifted, sieved; screened, selected 95 מְנֻפֶּה ז
feathery 95 מְנֻצֶּה ז
cleaned; cleared, acquitted 95 מְנֻקֶּה ז
thickened 95 מְעֻבֶּה ז
excellent, terrific, wonderful 95 מְעֻלֶּה ז
tortured 95 מְעֻנֶּה ז
woody - (botany) 95 מְעֻצֶּה ז
affected, artificial, false, unnatural 95 מְעֻשֶּׂה ז
vacated; evacuated; evacuee 95 מְפֻנֶּה ז
covered 95 מְצֻפֶּה ז
expected, forecasted, predicted 95 מְצֻפֶּה ז
great, many, multiple, numerous 95 מְרֻבֶּה ז
deceived 95 מְרֻמֶּה ז
satisfied 95 מְרֻצֶּה ז
strange, unusual, weird 95 מְשֻׁנֶּה ז
sharpened; polished, smoothed Lit-rare 95 מְשֻׁפֶּה ז
isolated 96 מְבוֹדָד ז
rolled up, scrolled 96 מְגוֹלָל ז
gifted, highly intelligent; talented 96 מְחוֹנָן ז
starry, star-studded 96 מְכוֹכָב ז
outcome, result, consequence 96 מְסוֹבָב ז
encouraged, reassured, emboldened 96 מְעוֹדָד ז
festive, gay, happy 96 מְרוֹמָם ז
emptied 96 מְרוֹקָן ז
impoverished 96 מְרוֹשָׁשׁ ז
lacking, bereft Lit 96 מְשׁוֹלָל ז
nested 96 מְתוֹכָךְ ז
buckled 97 מְאֻבְזָם ז
accessorized 97 מְאֻבְזָר ז
clenched into a fist 97 מְאֻגְרָף ז
naturalized; civilanized 97 מְאֻזְרָח ז
populated 97 מְאֻכְלָס ז
hooked 97 מְאֻנְקָל ז
characterized 97 מְאֻפְיָן ז
haltered, tethered 97 מְאֻפְסָר ז
acclimatized, acclimated 97 מְאֻקְלָם ז
organized; methodical 97 מְאֻרְגָּן ז
internationalized Lit 97 מְבֻנְאָם ז
reinforced with iron rods, iron-plated 97 מְבֻרְזָל ז
galvanized 97 מְגֻלְוָן ז
be stoned-pitted - fruit 97 מְגֻלְעָן ז
seeded, deseeded - fruit; granulated 97 מְגֻרְעָן ז

הִתְאַפְּרוּת נ 108 making oneself up, putting on makeup
הִתְבַּגְּרוּת נ 108 maturation; adolescence
הִתְבַּדְּחוּת נ 108 joking
הִתְבַּדְּלוּת נ 108 being aloof; being separated
הִתְבַּדְּרוּת נ 108 having fun, being entertained; divergence - math
הִתְבַּטְּאוּת נ 108 self-expression; remark
הִתְבַּטְּלוּת נ 108 being canceled; being self-deprecating; being idle
הִתְבַּיְּשׁוּת נ 108 being ashamed, feeling ashamed; being shy
הִתְבַּיְּתוּת נ 108 domestication; homing
הִתְבַּלְּטוּת נ 108 standing out, being prominent; conspicuousness
הִתְבַּסְּמוּת נ 108 being drunk, getting drunk
הִתְבַּסְּסוּת נ 108 being based on; becoming established
הִתְבַּצְּעוּת נ 108 being carried out, being executed
הִתְבַּצְּרוּת נ 108 fortifying; fortification
הִתְבַּקְּעוּת נ 108 splitting, cracking
הִתְבַּשְּׁלוּת נ 108 being cooked; cooking
הִתְבַּשְּׂמוּת נ 108 perfuming oneself; inhaling perfume
הִתְבַּשְּׂרוּת נ 108 being notified, getting good news
הִתְגַּבְּרוּת נ 108 overcoming; strengthening
הִתְגַּבְּשׁוּת נ 108 consolidation, integration; crystallization
הִתְגַּיְּסוּת נ 108 induction - military; being recruited; volunteering
הִתְגַּיְּרוּת נ 108 converting to Judaism
הִתְגַּלְּחוּת נ 108 shaving oneself
הִתְגַּלְּמוּת נ 108 embodiment
הִתְגַּלְּשׁוּת נ 108 sliding, gliding
הִתְגַּמְּשׁוּת נ 108 being more flexible
הִתְגַּנְּבוּת נ 108 stealing into, sneaking into
הִתְגַּשְּׁמוּת נ 108 being realized; realization
הִתְהַדְּקוּת נ 108 tightening, fastening
הִתְהַפְּכוּת נ 108 somersault, flip; turning over, rolling over
הִתְוַדְּעוּת נ 108 making acquaintance
הִתְוַסְּפוּת נ 108 the addition of
הִתְחַבְּטוּת נ 108 difficulties in making a decision, misgivings
הִתְחַבְּקוּת נ 108 hugging, embracing
הִתְחַבְּרוּת נ 108 becoming friends Coll.
הִתְחַבְּרוּת נ 108 joining, combining, connection
הִתְחַדְּדוּת נ 108 sharpening; clarification; acuteness, severity - pain
הִתְחַדְּשׁוּת נ 108 renewal, revival
הִתְחַזְּקוּת נ 108 strengthening
הִתְחַיְּבוּת נ 108 commitment; obligation
הִתְחַכְּכוּת נ 108 rubbing against something
הִתְחַכְּמוּת נ 108 wisecracking; wisecrack
הִתְחַלְּפוּת נ 108 changing; exchanging
הִתְחַלְּקוּת נ 108 segmentation, division; splitting
הִתְחַמְּמוּת נ 108 warming, heating up
הִתְחַמְּקוּת נ 108 evasion, escape; getting out of doing something
הִתְחַמְּשׁוּת נ 108 arming
הִתְחַנְּכוּת נ 108 being educated [no pl.]
הִתְחַנְּנוּת נ 108 imploring, begging
הִתְחַנְּפוּת נ 108 flattery
הִתְחַסְּדוּת נ 108 sanctimoniousness, hypocrisy
הִתְחַסְּנוּת נ 108 immunization; strengthening
הִתְחַפְּשׂוּת נ 108 masquerading
הִתְחַצְּפוּת נ 108 being impudent, being insolent
הִתְחַשְּׁבוּת נ 108 consideration; thoughtfulness
הִתְחַתְּנוּת נ 108 marrying
הִתְיַבְּשׁוּת נ 108 drying out, drying up; dehydration
הִתְיַדְּדוּת נ 108 befriending
הִתְיַוְּנוּת נ 108 taking on the values and customs of Hellenism [no pl.]
הִתְיַמְּרוּת נ 108 pretending; pretentiousness
הִתְיַסְּרוּת נ 108 suffering
הִתְיַפְּחוּת נ 108 weeping, sobbing
הִתְיַצְּבוּת נ 108 stabilizing; stabilization; being called up to army
הִתְיַקְּרוּת נ 108 price increase
הִתְיַשְּׁבוּת נ 108 settling; settlement; sitting down
הִתְיַשְּׁנוּת נ 108 becoming obsolete; limitation - statute of limitation
הִתְיַשְּׁרוּת נ 108 straightening
הִתְיַתְּמוּת נ 108 becoming an orphan [no pl.]
הִתְכַּוְּנוּת נ 108 intending, meaning
הִתְכַּוְּצוּת נ 108 contraction; shrinking
הִתְכַּנְּסוּת נ 108 assembling, gathering; assembly; convergence
הִתְכַּתְּבוּת נ 108 corresponding; correspondence
הִתְכַּתְּשׁוּת נ 108 struggling, clashing, brawling
הִתְלַבְּטוּת נ 108 indecision; having doubts
הִתְלַבְּשׁוּת נ 108 dressing oneself
הִתְלַטְּפוּת נ 108 mutual caressing
הִתְלַכְּדוּת נ 108 unifying, consolidating
הִתְלַמְּדוּת נ 108 learning, studying, apprenticing
הִתְלַקְּחוּת נ 108 catching fire; erupting - war; immolation
הִתְלַקְּטוּת נ 108 congregating, assembling
הִתְלַקְּקוּת נ 108 licking oneself, preening - animal
הִתְמַזְּגוּת נ 108 merging; melding, blending in
הִתְמַכְּרוּת נ 108 addiction
הִתְמַלְּאוּת נ 108 becoming full
הִתְמַלְּחוּת נ 108 salinization [no pl.]
הִתְמַמְּשׁוּת נ 108 realization
הִתְמַסְּדוּת נ 108 establishing, institutionalizing
הִתְמַסְּרוּת נ 108 devotion, dedication
הִתְמַצְּאוּת נ 108 orientation, knowing one's way around; familiarity
הִתְמַקְּדוּת נ 108 focusing
הִתְמַקְּחוּת נ 108 bargaining
הִתְמַקְּמוּת נ 108 taking one's place
הִתְמַשְּׁכוּת נ 108 continuation, prolonging
הִתְמַתְּחוּת נ 108 stretching oneself
הִתְמַתְּנוּת נ 108 moderation, becoming moderate
הִתְנַבְּאוּת נ 108 prophesying, predicting
הִתְנַגְּבוּת נ 108 drying oneself
הִתְנַגְּדוּת נ 108 objection, opposition; resistance; defiance
הִתְנַגְּחוּת נ 108 arguing aggressively, wrangling
הִתְנַגְּנוּת נ 108 playing - music
הִתְנַגְּשׁוּת נ 108 crash, collision; clash, contradiction
הִתְנַדְּבוּת נ 108 volunteering
הִתְנַדְּפוּת נ 108 evaporating; dissipating
הִתְנַוְּנוּת נ 108 degeneration
הִתְנַזְּרוּת נ 108 abstaining from doing something

congealing; coagulating 109 הִתְקָרְשׁוּת נ
falling in love 110 הִתְאַהֲבוּת נ
unification, unionization; association, organization 110 הִתְאַחֲדוּת נ
being clarified 110 הִתְבָּאֲרוּת נ
becoming brutalized, becoming bestialized 110 הִתְבַּהֲמוּת נ
becoming clear 110 הִתְבַּהֲרוּת נ
despairing, giving up 110 הִתְיָאֲשׁוּת נ
converting to Judaism 110 הִתְיַהֲדוּת נ
arrogance 110 הִתְיַהֲרוּת נ
isolation, seclusion; being alone with 110 הִתְיַחֲדוּת נ
attitude, treatment; reference; relationship 110 הִתְיַחֲסוּת נ
re-organization, streamlining 110 הִתְיַעֲלוּת נ
consultation 110 הִתְיַעֲצוּת נ
denial 110 הִתְכַּחֲשׁוּת נ
enthusiasm 110 הִתְלַהֲבוּת נ
excitement 110 הִתְלַהֲטוּת נ
harsh words, criticism 110 הִתְלַהֲמוּת נ
whispering to each other 110 הִתְלַחֲשׁוּת נ
diminishing, reduction, decrease 110 הִתְמַעֲטוּת נ
behavior 110 הִתְנַהֲגוּת נ
conducting; advancing Lit 110 הִתְנַהֲלוּת נ
settling, inhabiting 110 הִתְנַחֲלוּת נ
shirking, shaking off 110 הִתְנַעֲרוּת נ
boasting 110 הִתְפָּאֲרוּת נ
wonder, excitement, enthusiasm 110 הִתְפַּעֲלוּת נ
wonder, excitement, enthusiasm 110 הִתְפַּעֲמוּת נ
crowd, gathering 110 הִתְקַהֲלוּת נ
becoming concave 110 הִתְקַעֲרוּת נ
expanding, widening 110 הִתְרַחֲבוּת נ
washing, bathing oneself 110 הִתְרַחֲצוּת נ
distancing 110 הִתְרַחֲקוּת נ
happening, event 110 הִתְרַחֲשׁוּת נ
becoming angry, becoming annoyed 110 הִתְרַעֲמוּת נ
entangling; entanglement 111 הִסְתַּבְּכוּת נ
soaping oneself 111 הִסְתַּבְּנוּת נ
probability 111 הִסְתַּבְּרוּת נ
adaptation, acclimation 111 הִסְתַּגְּלוּת נ
abstaining from physical pleasures 111 הִסְתַּגְּפוּת נ
seclusion; withdrawal from society; introversion 111 הִסְתַּגְּרוּת נ
union; getting along; organizing oneself 111 הִסְתַּדְּרוּת נ
reservation, hesitation, doubt 111 הִסְתַּיְּגוּת נ
calcification - medic 111 הִסְתַּיְּדוּת נ
ending, completion 111 הִסְתַּיְּמוּת נ
being aided by 111 הִסְתַּיְּעוּת נ
looking, observing; observation 111 הִסְתַּכְּלוּת נ
totaling; being summed up 111 הִסְתַּכְּמוּת נ
endangering oneself; taking a risk 111 הִסְתַּכְּנוּת נ
being distorted - words 111 הִסְתַּלְּפוּת נ
leaving, making an escape 111 הִסְתַּלְּקוּת נ
being temporarily blinded, being dazed [no pl.] 111 הִסְתַּמְּאוּת נ
relying on 111 הִסְתַּמְּכוּת נ
appearing, beginning to show signs, being apparent 111 הִסְתַּמְּנוּת נ
infiltration 111 הִסְתַּנְּנוּת נ
joining, becoming attached to [no pl.] 111 הִסְתַּפְּחוּת נ
being satisfied with 111 הִסְתַּפְּקוּת נ
having one's hair cut 111 הִסְתַּפְּרוּת נ
becoming entangled, becoming intertwined 111 הִסְתָּרְגוּת נ
combing, hairdressing 111 הִסְתָּרְקוּת נ
being blocked, being closed 111 הִסְתַּתְּמוּת נ
hiding oneself 111 הִסְתַּתְּרוּת נ
moral corruption 112 הִסְתָּאֲבוּת נ
branching out, splitting; bifurcation 112 הִסְתַּעֲפוּת נ
attack, assault, storming 112 הִסְתַּעֲרוּת נ
refraction; being broken, being refracted 113 הִשְׁתַּבְּרוּת נ
disruption; confusion 113 הִשְׁתַּבְּשׁוּת נ
going crazy, losing one's mind 113 הִשְׁתַּגְּעוּת נ
making efforts; lobbying 113 הִשְׁתַּדְּלוּת נ
suntanning 113 הִשְׁתַּזְּפוּת נ
prostrating; sprawling 113 הִשְׁתַּטְּחוּת נ
belonging 113 הִשְׁתַּיְּכוּת נ
settling, establishing residence 113 הִשְׁתַּכְּנוּת נ
earning 113 הִשְׂתַּכְּרוּת נ
getting drunk 113 הִשְׁתַּכְּרוּת נ
becoming integrated; integration 113 הִשְׁתַּלְּבוּת נ
tongue-lashing 113 הִשְׁתַּלְּחוּת נ
gaining control; taking over 113 הִשְׁתַּלְּטוּת נ
continuing education course or program 113 הִשְׁתַּלְּמוּת נ
shirking, evading 113 הִשְׁתַּמְּטוּת נ
implication 113 הִשְׁתַּמְּעוּת נ
choking 113 הִשְׁתַּנְּקוּת נ
expressing one's feelings 113 הִשְׁתַּפְּכוּת נ
improvement 113 הִשְׁתַּפְּרוּת נ
rehabilitation 113 הִשְׁתַּקְּמוּת נ
settling down 113 הִשְׁתַּקְּעוּת נ
reflection 113 הִשְׁתַּקְּפוּת נ
participation; participating 113 הִשְׁתַּתְּפוּת נ
becoming silent 113 הִשְׁתַּתְּקוּת נ
lumbering; being dragged; extending (a queue) 114 הִשְׁתָּרְכוּת נ
sprawling 114 הִשְׂתָּרְעוּת נ
enrooting [no pl.] 114 הִשְׁתָּרְשׁוּת נ
prostration, bowing down 115 הִשְׁתַּחֲווּת נ
coughing 115 הִשְׁתַּעֲלוּת נ
accumulation 116 הִצְטַבְּרוּת נ
self-justification 116 הִצְטַדְּקוּת נ
equipping oneself 116 הִצְטַיְּדוּת נ
excellence 116 הִצְטַיְּנוּת נ
being portrayed, being described; being perceived 116 הִצְטַיְּרוּת נ
intersecting; intersection, junction; making the sign of the cross 116 הִצְטַלְּבוּת נ
shriveling; becoming reduced, shrinking 116 הִצְטַמְּקוּת נ
cold, catching cold; cooling 116 הִצְטַנְּנוּת נ
being modest 116 הִצְטַנְּעוּת נ
being curled up 116 הִצְטַנְּפוּת נ
needing, requiring; having to do something 117 הִצְטָרְכוּת נ
joining 117 הִצְטָרְפוּת נ
being sorry; regretting 118 הִצְטַעֲרוּת נ
mating, sexual intercourse 119 הִזְדַּוְּגוּת נ
having sexual intercourse Sl.; arming 119 הִזְדַּיְּנוּת נ
purification, cleansing from sin; catharsis 119 הִזְדַּכְּכוּת נ
opportunity, occasion 119 הִזְדַּמְּנוּת נ
following, tagging along; lining up, queuing 119 הִזְדַּנְּבוּת נ
aging 119 הִזְדַּקְּנוּת נ

הִשְׁתּוֹלְלוּת נ 138 wild, unruly behavior
הִשְׁתּוֹמְמוּת נ 138 amazement, astonishment, wonder, incredulity
הִשְׁתּוֹקְקוּת נ 138 longing, yearning
הִצְטוֹפְפוּת נ 139 crowding
הִתְפַּטְּרוּת נ 140 being forced to resign Sl.
הִתְאַגְרְפוּת נ 141 boxing
הִתְאַזְרְחוּת נ 141 naturalization, becoming a citizen
הִתְאַכְלְסוּת נ 141 becoming populated [no pl.]
הִתְאַכְסְנוּת נ 141 staying as a guest
הִתְאַלְמְנוּת נ 141 becoming widowed
הִתְאַסְלְמוּת נ 141 converting to Islam
הִתְאַקְלְמוּת נ 141 acclimatation, acclimatization
הִתְאַרְגְּנוּת נ 141 becoming organized
הִתְאַשְׁפְּזוּת נ 141 being hospitalized; hospitalization
הִתְבַּכְיְנוּת נ 141 tendency to feel sorry for oneself, complaining Sl.
הִתְבַּרְגְּנוּת נ 141 bourgeoisifying
הִתְגַּנְדְּרוּת נ 141 coquetry, foppishness, dandyism
הִתְחַמְצְנוּת נ 141 oxygenating; oxygenation
הִתְחַשְׁבְּנוּת נ 141 making an accounting; settling a score Sl.
הִתְחַשְׁמְלוּת נ 141 electrocution
הִתְכַּרְבְּלוּת נ 141 bundling oneself; snuggling
הִתְלַכְסְנוּת נ 141 slanting [no pl.]
הִתְמַסְכְּנוּת נ 141 pretending to be miserable Coll.
הִתְמַקְצְעוּת נ 141 professionalization
הִתְעַדְכְּנוּת נ 141 updating, informing
הִתְעַנְיְנוּת נ 141 interest
הִתְעַצְבְּנוּת נ 141 becoming annoyed, getting angry, getting irritated
הִתְעַרְטְלוּת נ 141 stripping; undressing completely; exposing oneself emotionally
הִתְעַרְפְּלוּת נ 141 blurring, becoming foggy, becoming misty
הִתְפַּלְמְסוּת נ 141 debate N; debating
הִתְפַּלְסְפוּת נ 141 philosophizing
הִתְפַּרְנְסוּת נ 141 earning a living
הִתְפַּרְסְמוּת נ 141 becoming known, becoming published
הִתְפַּרְקְדוּת נ 141 reclining, lying on one's back [no pl.]

הִתְקַמְצְנוּת נ 141 stinginess, miserliness Coll.
הִתְקַרְנְפוּת נ 141 becoming inured, becoming indifferent
הִתְאַכְזְבוּת נ 142 disappointment; being disappointed
הִתְאַכְזְרוּת נ 142 being cruel
הִתְמַסְחְרוּת נ 143 commercializing, commercialization Coll.
הִתְמַעַרְבוּת נ 144 westernizing, westernization [no pl.]
הִתְרַעַנְנוּת נ 144 refreshing, refreshing oneself
הִתְבַּזְבְּזוּת נ 145 being wasted, being squandered
הִתְבַּלְבְּלוּת נ 145 getting confused; confusion
הִתְבַּרְבְּרוּת נ 145 getting lost Sl.
הִתְגַּעְגְּעוּת נ 145 missing, longing for, yearning for
הִתְיַפְיְפוּת נ 145 beautification
הִתְלַחְלְחוּת נ 145 becoming damp, becoming moist [no pl.]
הִתְלַכְלְכוּת נ 145 becoming dirty, becoming soiled
הִתְלַקְלְקוּת נ 145 licking oneself - animal
הִתְמַהְמְהוּת נ 145 tarrying, dawdling
הִתְמַסְמְסוּת נ 145 dissipating; melting, dissolving
הִתְמַרְמְרוּת נ 145 bitterness, anger, resentment; complaining
הִתְנַדְנְדוּת נ 145 wobbling, swaying, wavering; fluctuating; vacillating
הִתְנַמְנְמוּת נ 145 nap N
הִתְקַלְקְלוּת נ 145 breaking down, being damaged; becoming spoiled (food)
הִתְרַבְרְבוּת נ 145 arrogance, boastfulness
הִתְחַלְחֲלוּת נ 146 being shocked, being horrified
הִתְחַנְחֲנוּת נ 146 coquetry, self ingratiation
הִתְעַמְעֲמוּת נ 146 dimming, lowering of light; dulling of shininess
הִתְרַעַרְעוּת נ 146 weakening; loosening
הִתְאַוְרְרוּת נ 147 getting some fresh air; becoming refreshed
הִתְעַרְבְּבוּת נ 147 becoming mixed up; being mixed into
הִסְתַּנְוְרוּת נ 148 being temporarily blinded, being dazed
הִסְתַּקְרְנוּת נ 148 becoming curious
הִסְתַּעַרְבוּת נ 149 dressing as, or pretending to be, Arab

הִסְתַּכְסְכוּת נ 150 arguing; getting into conflict with someone
הִסְתַּלְסְלוּת נ 150 becoming curled
הִשְׁתַּחְצְנוּת נ 151 boasting Coll.
הִשְׁתַּכְנְעוּת נ 151 being convinced
הִשְׁתַּעְבְּדוּת נ 151 becoming enslaved
הִשְׁתַּלְשְׁלוּת נ 152 descending; lowering oneself; development
הִשְׁתַּעַשְׁעוּת נ 152 having fun, being entertained
הִשְׁתַּפְשְׁפוּת נ 152 rubbing (against something); being worn away; gaining experience Sl.
הִשְׁתַּחְרְרוּת נ 153 being freed, being released
הִשְׁתַּכְלְלוּת נ 153 enhancement, improvement; technological advancement
הִשְׁתַּרְבְּבוּת נ 153 being put in the wrong place; sticking out
הִשְׁתַּעַמְמוּת נ 154 being bored, boredom (no pl.)
הִצְטַמְצְמוּת נ 155 being reduced, being limited
הִצְטַעַצְעוּת נ 156 adorning oneself, glorifying oneself, trying to impress
הִזְדַּעַזְעוּת נ 157 being shocked; shock, agitation, distress
הִדַּלְדְּלוּת נ 158 shriveling, decline N, waning, weakening
הִדַּרְדְּרוּת נ 158 rolling down; deterioration; lapsing; going downhill
הִטַּלְטְלוּת נ 159 wandering; being tossed from side to side
הִטַּשְׁטְשׁוּת נ 159 blurring, fading
מִתְאַבֵּד ז 160 one who has committed suicide
מִתְאַבֵּק ז 160 wrestler
מִתְאַמֵּן ז 160 trainee (sports)
מִתְבַּגֵּר ז 160 adolescent
מִתְגַּיֵּס ז 160 recruit, conscript
מִתְחַכֵּם ז 160 smart aleck, wise "guy"
מִתְחַסֵּד ז 160 self-righteous
מִתְיַוֵּן ז 160 Hellenist
מִתְיַשֵּׁב ז 160 settler
מִתְלַמֵּד ז 160 apprentice, trainee
מִתְנַגֵּד ז 160 opposer, opponent; opposer of Hassidism
מִתְנַדֵּב ז 160 volunteer
מִתְנַחֵל ז 160 settler
מִתְנַשֵּׂא ז 160 arrogant, patronizing, condescending
מִתְעַמֵּל ז 160 gymnast
מִתְפַּלֵּל ז 160 worshiper
מִתְקַדֵּם ז 160 advanced, progressive
מִתְקַפֵּל ז 160 folding, collapsible

מִסְתַּבֵּר ז 161 reasonable, probable; it turns out that…
מִסְתַּגֵּף ז 161 one who abstains from physical pleasures
מִסְתַּיֵּג ז 161 dissenter, one who expresses doubts
מִסְתַּנֵּן ז 161 infiltrator
מִשְׁתַּכֵּן ז 162 resident of a new housing complex
מִשְׁתַּלֵּם ז 162 one attending a continuing education program
מִשְׁתַּלֵּם ז 162 worthwhile
מִשְׁתַּמֵּט ז 162 shirker
מִשְׁתַּמֵּשׁ ז 162 user, operator
מִשְׁתַּתֵּף ז 162 participant
מִתְחַזֶּה ז 163 pretender, impersonator
מִתְחַלֶּה ז 163 one who pretends to be sick
מִתְחָרֶה ז 163 competitor, contestant; adversary
מִתְכַּלֶּה ז 163 perishable
מִתְמַחֶה ז 163 one who concluded his general training and is now specializing
מִתְבּוֹדֵד ז 164 recluse
מִתְבּוֹלֵל ז 164 one who has assimilated, lost his cultural identity
מִתְגּוֹשֵׁשׁ ז 164 wrestler
מִתְלוֹנֵן ז 164 complainant
מִתְקוֹמֵם ז 164 insurrectionist, mutineer
מִתְאַגְרֵף ז 165 boxer
מִתְפַּלְסֵף ז 165 philosopher; one who "philosophizes" (derogatory)
מִתְכַּוְנֵן ז 166 adjustable
מִטַּלְטֵל ז 167 portable
הַבְאָשָׁה נ 168 denigration, vilification, defamation Lit.
הַבְדָּלָה נ 168 differentiating; differentiation; Havdalah ceremony at termination of Sabbath or festival
הַבְהָלָה נ 168 scaring, frightening N; urgent summon or transfer Lit.
הַבְהָקָה נ 168 shining, polishing
הַבְהָרָה נ 168 clarification; bleaching, lightening
הַבְזָקָה נ 168 flash, burst N; spreading N
הַבְחָלָה נ 168 artificially-enhanced ripening of fruit
הַבְחָנָה נ 168 differentiation, distinguishing; distinction; perception; observation
הַבְטָחָה נ 168 promise N, assurance
הַבְלָגָה נ 168 restraint, self-restraint
הַבְלָחָה נ 168 flickering
הַבְלָטָה נ 168 making prominent; prominence
הַבְלָעָה נ 168 allusion, hint, cover up; slurring
הַבְנָיָה נ 168 structuring
הַבְעָרָה נ 168 kindling, burning
הַבְקָעָה נ 168 breaking through, breaching
הַבְרָאָה נ 168 recuperation, convalescence; recovery
הַבְרָגָה נ 168 screwing, screwing on; screw thread
הַבְרָזָה נ 168 shirking, evasion - of duty, responsibility Sl; tapping
הַבְרָחָה נ 168 smuggling; getting someone to escape
הַבְרָכָה נ 168 making a camel kneel; bending branch over to strike new roots
הַבְרָקָה נ 168 polishing
הַבְרָשָׁה נ 168 brushing
הַבְשָׁלָה נ 168 ripening; maturation
הַגְבָּהָה נ 168 raising
הַגְבָּלָה נ 168 limiting; limitation, curtailment, restraint
הַגְבָּרָה נ 168 strengthening; amplification
הַגְדָּלָה נ 168 enlargement; magnification
הַגְדָּרָה נ 168 defining; definition; characterization
הַגְדָּשָׁה נ 168 filling to overflowing
הַגְזָמָה נ 168 exaggerating; exaggeration
הַגְחָכָה נ 168 ridiculing, making ridiculous
הַגְלָדָה נ 168 forming of a scab
הַגְלָיָה נ 168 deportation, exile N
הַגְמָאָה נ 168 giving to someone to drink Lit.
הַגְמָדָה נ 168 belittling, disparaging, minimizing
הַגְמָעָה נ 168 giving animals to drink
הַגְמָשָׁה נ 168 moderation, toning down; making more elastic
הַגְנָבָה נ 168 moving someone/something stealthily; sneaking something in
הַגְעָלָה נ 168 making dishes kosher by immersing in boiling water
הַגְעָשָׁה נ 168 enraging someone Lit.
הַגְרָלָה נ 168 lottery; chance, luck
הַגְרָעָה נ 168 degradation Lit. [no pl.]
הַגְשָׁמָה נ 168 realization, fulfillment; personification
הַדְאָגָה נ 168 causing concern, causing worry
הַדְבָּקָה נ 168 pasting, gluing; contagion, spreading infectious disease; keeping up with
הַדְבָּרָה נ 168 pest control; overcoming harmful entities
הַדְגָּמָה נ 168 demonstrating, illustrating; demonstration, illustration
הַדְגָּרָה נ 168 incubation, hatching
הַדְגָּשָׁה נ 168 stressing; stress, accentuation, emphasis; highlighting
הַדְהָיָה נ 168 causing to fade; fading, discoloration
הַדְהָרָה נ 168 causing to gallop
הַדְחָסָה נ 168 compressing, squeezing [no pl.]
הַדְחָקָה נ 168 repression - psychoanalysis
הַדְלָחָה נ 168 mudding, tainting, opacifying Lit.
הַדְלָיָה נ 168 trellising a vine
הַדְלָפָה נ 168 leak of information; causing a leak
הַדְלָקָה נ 168 lighting, kindling; turning on instrument, light etc.
הַדְמָיָה נ 168 simulation; imaging; virtualization
הַדְמָמָה נ 168 shutting down, silencing, turning off
הַדְמָעָה נ 168 lacrimation
הַדְפָּסָה נ 168 printing
הַדְרָגָה נ 168 progression, gradation, gradualness
הַדְרָכָה נ 168 guidance, leadership; teaching; advice; training
הַדְרָמָה נ 168 going southward
הַוְרָדָה נ 168 becoming pink; coloring pink [no pl.]
הַזְהָבָה נ 168 gilding [no pl.]
הַזְהָרָה נ 168 warning
הַזְכָּרָה נ 168 mentioning; mention N
הַזְלָפָה נ 168 sprinkling, splashing; intravenous infusion
הַזְמָנָה נ 168 invitation; order
הַזְנָחָה נ 168 neglect N
הַזְנָקָה נ 168 starting a race; tasking off fast
הַזְעָמָה נ 168 angering, annoying Lit. [no pl.]
הַזְעָפָה נ 168 frowning
הַזְעָקָה נ 168 calling, summoning, calling into action
הַזְעָרָה נ 168 miniaturization; microfilming
הַזְקָפָה נ 168 making someone stand erect
הַזְרָמָה נ 168 pouring, causing to flow; transfer of large quantities
הַזְרָעָה נ 168 insemination of animals

injecting; injection 168 נ הַזְרָקָה
hiding, concealing; concealment 168 נ הַחְבָּאָה
inserting; insertion, penetration; introduction 168 נ הַחְדָּרָה
going pale; becoming dull [no pl.] 168 נ הַחְוָרָה
visualization 168 נ הַחְזָיָה
holding on, grasping; storing; incarceration 168 נ הַחְזָקָה
return N, replacement; reinstatement; paying back 168 נ הַחְזָרָה
missing target; failing to chieve an aim 168 נ הַחְטָאָה
resuscitation; revitalization, reinvigoration 168 נ הַחְיָאָה
becoming wise, acquiring knowledge; imparting knowledge, making wise 168 נ הַחְכָּמָה
leasing 168 נ הַחְכָּרָה
rusting 168 נ הַחְלָדָה
decision; resolution 168 נ הַחְלָטָה
recuperation, recovery 168 נ הַחְלָמָה
exchanging, swapping; changing, replacing 168 נ הַחְלָפָה
skiing, skating, sliding; skid N; straightening hair; smoothing out 168 נ הַחְלָקָה
Weakening 168 נ הַחְלָשָׁה
souring; pickling; missing opportunity 168 נ הַחְמָצָה
worsening, deterioration; increased rigorousness or severity 168 נ הַחְמָרָה
parking 168 נ הַחְנָיָה
flattery 168 נ הַחְנָפָה
choking N [no pl.] 168 נ הַחְנָקָה
storing 168 נ הַחְסָנָה
subtraction; omission, missing out 168 נ הַחְסָרָה
externalization, giving expression openly 168 נ הַחְצָנָה
destroying; destruction [no pl.] 168 נ הַחְרָבָה
confiscation; boycott N; excommunication 168 נ הַחְרָמָה
worsening, deterioration 168 נ הַחְרָפָה
silencing; shouting down [no pl.] 168 נ הַחְרָשָׁה
taking into account; ascribing importance [no pl.] 168 נ הַחְשָׁבָה
casting suspicion [no pl.] 168 נ הַחְשָׁדָה
making dark, blacking out [no pl.] 168 נ הַחְשָׁכָה
diaper changing 168 נ הַחְתָּלָה
obtaining a signature; stamping, sealing 168 נ הַחְתָּמָה

dipping; immersing; immersion; baptism 168 נ הַטְבָּלָה
drowning someone or something; sealing, minting 168 נ הַטְבָּעָה
patching 168 נ הַטְלָאָה
hiding; burying 168 נ הַטְמָנָה
assimilating; assimilation 168 נ הַטְמָעָה
misleading N, deceiving, deception 168 נ הַטְעָיָה
emphasis, accentuation 168 נ הַטְעָמָה
loading 168 נ הַטְעָנָה
harassing; harassment, bothering 168 נ הַטְרָדָה
bothering, annoying, causing unnecessary work 168 נ הַטְרָחָה
debridgement, - removing damaged matter 168 נ הַטְרָיָה
anticipation; priming 168 נ הַטְרָמָה
declaring food to be non-kosher 168 נ הַטְרָפָה
causing pain [no pl.] 168 נ הַכְאָבָה
making heavier; being a burden, weighing heavily on one [no pl.] 168 נ הַכְבָּדָה
heaping up; increasing [no pl.] 168 נ הַכְבָּרָה
directing; guiding, advising 168 נ הַכְוָנָה
disappointing 168 נ הַכְזָבָה
extinction, obliteration, eradication 168 נ הַכְחָדָה
turning blue [no pl.] 168 נ הַכְחָלָה
denial 168 נ הַכְחָשָׁה
grafting; crossbreeding, hybridization 168 נ הַכְלָאָה
basting – sewing 168 נ הַכְלָבָה
generalization 168 נ הַכְלָלָה
shaming, humiliating, embarrassing Lit. 168 נ הַכְלָמָה
chlorination of water 168 נ הַכְלָרָה
hiding; burying Lit. 168 נ הַכְמָנָה
bringing in, entry, insertion; income, revenue 168 נ הַכְנָסָה
surrender; subservience 168 נ הַכְנָעָה
silver-plating; silvering, graying [no pl.] 168 נ הַכְסָפָה
whitening, paling [no pl.] 168 נ הַכְסָפָה
angering, irking, irritating 168 נ הַכְעָסָה
multiplying, doubling; duplication 168 נ הַכְפָּלָה
subjugating 168 נ הַכְפָּפָה
mudslinging, slander 168 נ הַכְפָּשָׁה

announcement, declaration; proclamation 168 נ הַכְרָזָה
forcing 168 נ הַכְרָחָה
decision; ruling 168 נ הַכְרָעָה
destroying, eliminating 168 נ הַכְרָתָה
causing failure 168 נ הַכְשָׁלָה
preparation; training; rendering kosher 168 נ הַכְשָׁרָה
dictating; dictation 168 נ הַכְתָּבָה
staining 168 נ הַכְתָּמָה
shouldering 168 נ הַכְתָּפָה
coronation 168 נ הַכְתָּרָה
nationalizing; nationalization 168 נ הַלְאָמָה
whitening, bleaching; laundering money 168 נ הַלְבָּנָה
dressing someone; clothing, apparel 168 נ הַלְבָּשָׁה
exciting, arousing [no pl.] 168 נ הַלְהָבָה
inciting, inflaming, exciting N [no pl.] 168 נ הַלְהָטָה
loan 168 נ הַלְוָאָה
funeral 168 נ הַלְוָיָה
welding, soldering 168 נ הַלְחָמָה
composing 168 נ הַלְחָנָה
mockery, ridiculing Lit. 168 נ הַלְעָגָה
slandering, libeling 168 נ הַלְעָזָה
fattening, overfeeding 168 נ הַלְעָטָה
lashing, whipping 168 נ הַלְקָאָה
informing 168 נ הַלְשָׁנָה
causing disgust, causing loathing [no pl.] 168 נ הַמְאָסָה
check, cheque; transfer or assignment of assets etc. 168 נ הַמְחָאָה
dramatizing 168 נ הַמְחָזָה
costing, pricing 168 נ הַמְחָרָה
illustration, demonstration 168 נ הַמְחָשָׁה
irrigation, raining, pouring, inundation 168 נ הַמְטָרָה
containerization 168 נ הַמְכָּלָה
salinating; salting of meat to make it kosher 168 נ הַמְלָחָה
giving birth - mammals, whelping, calving, foaling 168 נ הַמְלָטָה
coronation, crowning 168 נ הַמְלָכָה
recommendation; advice; credential 168 נ הַמְלָצָה
tripping up, causing to fall 168 נ הַמְעָדָה
lessening, reduction, decrease, diminution 168 נ הַמְעָטָה
invention; concept idea; fabrication; proffering 168 נ הַמְצָאָה
takeoff, lift-off; sublimation - Chem. 168 נ הַמְרָאָה

introduction, 168 הַקְדָּמָה נ preface; bringing forward (appt. etc.)
dedication; 168 הַקְדָּשָׁה נ allocating, designating; sanctifying, consecrating, dedicating to God
diminution, 168 הַקְטָנָה נ reduction
burning incense 168 הַקְטָרָה נ
typing, keying in 168 הַקְלָדָה נ
recording 168 הַקְלָטָה נ
teasing, mocking 168 הַקְנָטָה נ
instilling; 168 הַקְנָיָה נ imbuing; providing; causing to acquire
charming, 168 הַקְסָמָה נ enchanting
freezing 168 הַקְפָּאָה נ
meticulousness, 168 הַקְפָּדָה נ strictness, preciseness
bouncing (ball 168 הַקְפָּצָה נ etc.); sauntering; rousting - Milt. Sl.
allocating, 168 הַקְצָאָה נ allotting
allocation of 168 הַקְצָבָה נ funds, budgeting
radicalization 168 הַקְצָנָה נ
planing; polishing 168 הַקְצָעָה נ (speech etc.)
whipping (cream, 168 הַקְצָפָה נ etc.)
reading aloud 168 הַקְרָאָה נ
self-sacrifice; 168 הַקְרָבָה נ sacrificing
crusting over, 168 הַקְרָמָה נ browning
radiation; 168 הַקְרָנָה נ screening
solidifying, 168 הַקְרָשָׁה נ coagulating; congealing
listening, being 168 הַקְשָׁבָה נ attentive
hardening, 168 הַקְשָׁחָה נ toughening, strengthening
hardening, 168 הַקְשָׁיָה נ stiffening
showing 168 הַרְאָיָה נ
mating, breeding 168 הַרְבָּעָה נ
beating, hitting; 168 הַרְבָּצָה נ causing to lie down Lit.
annoying, 168 הַרְגָּזָה נ angering; bothering
habituation 168 הַרְגָּלָה נ
calming, 168 הַרְגָּעָה נ quietening; relieving (pain etc.)
feeling 168 הַרְגָּשָׁה נ
putting to sleep; 168 הַרְדָּמָה נ anesthetizing; anesthetization
saturation, satiation 168 הַרְוָיָה נ [no pl.]
slimming, 168 הַרְזָיָה נ becoming thinner, losing weight

broadening, 168 הַרְחָבָה נ widening; expansion; expanding on a topic
fluidization - 168 הַרְחָפָה נ chemistry
distancing; 168 הַרְחָקָה נ removal, expulsion
wetting 168 הַרְטָבָה נ
assembling; 168 הַרְכָּבָה נ grafting (botany)
bowing head, body 168 הַרְכָּנָה נ Lit.; bending Lit.
acquisition, 168 הַרְכָּשָׁה נ procurement
starving someone 168 הַרְעָבָה נ
shaking 168 הַרְעָדָה נ something; trembling Lit.; vibrating Lit.
poisoning 168 הַרְעָלָה נ
heaping (praise, 168 הַרְעָפָה נ gifts), inundating, showering upon
shelling, bombing 168 הַרְעָשָׁה נ (military); noisemaking
relaxation 168 הַרְפָּיָה נ
lecture N 168 הַרְצָאָה נ
rotting, 168 הַרְקָבָה נ decomposition [no pl.]
dancing, causing 168 הַרְקָדָה נ to dance
authorization 168 הַרְשָׁאָה נ
registration; 168 הַרְשָׁמָה נ impressing
conviction 168 הַרְשָׁעָה נ
boiling 168 הַרְתָּחָה נ
deterring; 168 הַרְתָּעָה נ intimidating
lending; 168 הַשְׁאָלָה נ borrowing - Coll. only; metaphor
leaving; keeping, 168 הַשְׁאָרָה נ causing to remain
enhancement; 168 הַשְׁבָּחָה נ betterment, improvement; capital gain
swearing in; being 168 הַשְׁבָּעָה נ sworn in
striking, closure; 168 הַשְׁבָּתָה נ stoppage
supervising 168 הַשְׁגָּחָה נ
routinizing, 168 הַשְׁגָּרָה נ conventionalization Lit.; running in Lit.
delaying, 168 הַשְׁהָיָה נ postponing; delay, postponement
comparison; 168 הַשְׁוָאָה נ equalization
sharpening, 168 הַשְׁחָזָה נ grinding, whetting
threading, 168 הַשְׁחָלָה נ beading, stringing
browning 168 הַשְׁחָמָה נ
blackening; 168 הַשְׁחָרָה נ tarnishing

vandalizing, 168 הַשְׁחָתָה נ damaging, destroying; corrupting
lying down; 168 הַשְׁכָּבָה נ causing to lie down; putting to bed
causing to forget 168 הַשְׁכָּחָה נ
education, 168 הַשְׂכָּלָה נ knowledge; the Enlightenment movement
wake-up call; 168 הַשְׁכָּמָה נ reveille; getting up in the morning
renting out, hiring 168 הַשְׂכָּרָה נ
imposing - order, 168 הַשְׁלָטָה נ rules
throwing; 168 הַשְׁלָכָה נ disposing; implication, ramification, consequence; projection psychology
completion; 168 הַשְׁלָמָה נ acceptance; making peace
depositing with a 168 הַשְׁלָשָׁה נ third party
destruction, 168 הַשְׁמָדָה נ eradication
omitting, 168 הַשְׁמָטָה נ omission
gaining weight, 168 הַשְׁמָנָה נ becoming fatter; obesity; fattening
voicing; playing 168 הַשְׁמָעָה נ of music, recording
slander, 168 הַשְׁמָצָה נ defamation
making one hate, 168 הַשְׂנָאָה נ loathe
suspension 168 הַשְׁעָיָה נ
leaning of 168 הַשְׁעָנָה נ something against something else
assumption, 168 הַשְׁעָרָה נ guess; conjecture
humiliation; 168 הַשְׁפָּלָה נ lowering
influence 168 הַשְׁפָּעָה נ
quietening 168 הַשְׁקָטָה נ
watering, 168 הַשְׁקָיָה נ irrigating; irrigation
submerging; 168 הַשְׁקָעָה נ investment
observation, view, 168 הַשְׁקָפָה נ opinion, conception
inspiration; 168 הַשְׁרָאָה נ induction
soaking 168 הַשְׁרָיָה נ
spawning 168 הַשְׁרָצָה נ
taking root; 168 הַשְׁרָשָׁה נ implanting; infusing
transplant; 168 הַשְׁתָּלָה נ transplantation; implant; plant
urinating 168 הַשְׁתָּנָה נ
silencing 168 הַשְׁתָּקָה נ
matching; 168 הַתְאָמָה נ suitability, compatibility;

הוֹרָדָה נ 171 lowering; dropping off passengers; removal; reduction; downloading - computing

הוֹרָקָה נ 171 going green; painting green

הוֹרָשָׁה נ 171 bequeathing, handing down

הוֹשָׁבָה נ 171 seating, placing

הוֹשָׁטָה נ 171 stretching out, reaching out

הוֹתָרָה נ 171 leaving behind

הוֹבָרָה נ 172 leaving land uncultivated

הוֹזָלָה/הֲזָלָה נ 172 lowering prices, making cheaper

הַבָּטָה נ 173 looking, observation

הַבָּעָה נ 173 facial expression; expression - of feelings etc.

הַגָּדָה נ 173 telling, recounting; saga, chronicle; Haggadah

הַגָּהָה נ 173 proofreading

הַגָּעָה נ 173 arrival; reaching, attending

הַגָּרָה נ 173 pouring, dribbling, spilling Lit.

הַגָּשָׁה נ 173 serving or service, esp. of food; submitting, handing in (e.g., report); presenting, delivering

הַדָּחָה נ 173 ousting, dismissal from employment, removal; seduction

הַדָּפָה נ 173 shedding, emission, giving off

הַדָּרָה נ 173 exclusion

הַזָּחָה נ 173 movement, shifting

הַזָּיָה/הַזָּאָה נ 173 sprinkling, splashing

הַזָּלָה נ 173 shedding tears; secretion

הַזָּעָה/הֲזָעָה נ 173 perspiring, sweating

הַטָּיָה נ 173 turning, diversion, bending; declension, inflection, conjugation (grammar); deviation (statistics)

הַטָּלָה/הֲטָלָה נ 173 placing, imposing

הַטָּפָה נ 173 preaching

הַכָּאָה נ 173 beating

הַכָּרָה נ 173 consciousness; recognition; acquaintance

הַכָּשָׁה נ 173 bite of snake or sting of scorpion

הַלָּנָה נ 173 complaining Lit.

הַנָּחָה/הֲנָחָה נ 173 placing; assumption; presumption, premise, postulation; hypothesis

הַסָּגָה נ 173 moving or withdrawing from one place to another

הַסָּחָה נ 173 removal, turning aside, deflection, deviation

הַסָּעָה נ 173 transportation

הַסָּקָה נ 173 heating; concluding, deducing, inferring

הַפָּלָה נ 173 causing to fall; abortion, miscarriage; downing plane

הַצָּבָה נ 173 positioning, stationing, posting

הַצָּגָה נ 173 showing; show, performance, play; display; presentation

הַצָּלָה נ 173 saving, rescuing

הַצָּעָה נ 173 suggestion; proposal; offer

הַצָּתָה נ 173 igniting, setting fire; arson; inflaming

הַקָּזָה נ 173 blood-letting

הַקָּפָה/הֲקָפָה נ 173 encirclement; inclusion; credit, deferred payment

הַקָּשָׁה/הֲקָשָׁה נ 173 knocking, striking; percussion; playing a keyboard instrument; typing on a keyboard

הַשָּׂאָה נ 173 marrying off, officiating at a wedding

הַשָּׁאָה נ 173 suggestion, seduction, persuasion Lit.

הַשָּׂגָה נ 173 obtaining, achieving; comprehension; doubt, disagreement, criticism

הַשָּׁלָה נ 173 shedding

הַשָּׁקָה נ 173 launching boat, product etc.; overlapping, interfacing; bringing together; touching (geometry)

הַתָּזָה נ 173 spraying; severing Lit.; hissing a word or sound

הַתָּכָה נ 173 melting, fusing, fusion

הַתָּקָה נ 173 translocation, displacement

הַתָּרָה נ 173 loosening knot etc.; release from chain etc.; granting permission; annulling vow, marriage etc.

הַתָּשָׁה נ 173 weakening, attrition

הֲבָאָה נ 174 bringing, conveying; reference, quotation; causing

הֲבָכָה נ 174 embarrassing; embarrassment; shaming

הֲבָנָה נ 174 understanding, comprehension; knowledge; awareness; appreciation

הֲבָסָה נ 174 vanquishing, defeat

הֲגָבָה נ 174 responding; response, reply

הֲגָחָה נ 174 bursting out, bursting forth

הֲגָפָה נ 174 closing, locking (doors, windows, shutters)

הֲדָחָה נ 174 rinsing

הֲזָזָה נ 174 moving tr., shifting, displacement

הֲזָחָה נ 174 movement, shifting

הֲזָיָה נ 174 hallucination; delirium

הֲזָנָה נ 174 feeding, nourishing; providing raw materials for engine, equipment

הֲטָבָה נ 174 improvement; benefit; bonus

הֲטָחָה נ 174 hurling, flinging, throwing; reviling, offending someone to their face

הֲטָלָה נ 174 throwing, dropping; laying eggs; projection

הֲטָסָה נ 174 flying an aircraft; air transport

הֲכָלָה נ 174 containing, including

הֲכָנָה נ 174 preparation

הֲלָטָה נ 174 covering, hiding face Lit.

הֲלָנָה נ 174 hosting overnight; delaying, postponing

הֲלָצָה נ 174 joke, jest

הֲמָטָה נ 174 causing, bringing about (something negative)

הֲמָרָה נ 174 exchange, changing, converting

הֲמָתָה נ 174 killing, putting to death

הֲנָבָה נ 174 yielding, producing; flourishing, prospering

הֲנָחָה נ 174 discount, reduction

הֲנָסָה נ 174 driving away, causing to flee; expulsion [no pl.]

הֲנָעָה נ 174 ignition of engine, propulsion; motivation (psychology)

הֲנָפָה נ 174 raising, usually of flag

הֲסָטָה נ 174 moving, shifting; removal, turning aside

הֲסָרָה נ 174 removal, withdrawal

הֲסָתָה נ 174 inciting; incitement

הֲפָצָה נ 174 distribution, spreading

הֲפָקָה נ 174 production

הֲצָפָה נ 174 flooding

הֲצָצָה נ 174 peeking; glancing

הֲצָקָה נ 174 bothering, annoying

הֲקָאָה נ 174 vomiting

הֲקָמָה נ 174 establishing, building; establishment

הֲרָחָה נ 174 smelling, sniffing [no pl.]

הֲרָמָה נ 174 lifting, raising

הֲרָצָה נ 174 test-run, trial run; running, operating

הֲרָקָה נ 174 emptying

הֲשָׁבָה נ 174 returning something

הֲשָׂמָה נ 174 placement, assigning

הֲשָׁתָה נ 174 imposing Rare

shining, glowing 187 מַזְהִיר ז
secretary 187 מַזְכִּיר ז
inviting 187 מַזְמִין ז
starter - sports 187 מַזְנִיק ז
informative 187 מַחְכִּים ז
lessor, landlord 187 מַחְכִּיר ז
convalescent 187 מַחְלִים ז
substitute 187 מַחְלִיף ז
strict, meticulous; stringent 187 מַחְמִיר ז
shameful, humiliating, disgraceful 187 מַחְפִּיר ז
destroyer 187 מַחְרִיב ז
awful, frightening, shocking, terrifying 187 מַחְרִיד ז
baptizer - Christianity 187 מַטְבִּיל ז
wonderful, exciting, beautiful Sl. 187 מַטְרִיף ז
painful 187 מַכְאִיב ז
profitable, lucrative 187 מַכְנִיס ז
silvery; greying hair 187 מַכְסִיף ז
multiplier (economics) 187 מַכְפִּיל ז
appliance, apparatus; instrument, device 187 מַכְשִׁיר ז
whitening, bleaching 187 מַלְבִּין ז
rousing, exciting 187 מַלְהִיב ז
composer of music 187 מַלְחִין ז
informer 187 מַלְשִׁין ז
cancerous, malignant; fatal, incurable; prickly 187 מַמְאִיר ז
inventor 187 מַמְצִיא ז
successor 187 מַמְשִׁיךְ ז
sweetener 187 מַמְתִּיק ז
leader 187 מַנְהִיג ז
inflaming, inciteful 187 מַסְעִיר ז
enough, sufficient 187 מַסְפִּיק ז
cinema projectionist 187 מַסְרִיט ז
illegal immigrant during the British Mandate period 187 מַעְפִּיל ז
demonstrator 187 מַפְגִּין ז
frightening, scary 187 מַפְחִיד ז
last person called up to the Torah or verses read then 187 מַפְטִיר ז
incriminating 187 מַפְלִיל ז
a cantillation mark denoting a break 187 מַפְסִיק ז
operator 187 מַפְעִיל ז
bomber 187 מַפְצִיץ ז
depositor (banking) 187 מַפְקִיד ז
dividing line 187 מַפְרִיד ז
military leader 187 מַצְבִּיא ז
declarant; person giving an affidavit 187 מַצְהִיר ז
smelly, stinky 187 מַצְחִין ז
funny, amusing 187 מַצְחִיק ז

party whip (who keeps a watchful eye over elected members) 187 מַצְלִיף ז
parallel; comparable; matching 187 מַקְבִּיל ז
preliminary, introductory 187 מַקְדִּים ז
charming, enchanting; wonderful, terrific 187 מַקְסִים ז
freezing 187 מַקְפִּיא ז
frothy, foamy, sudsy 187 מַקְצִיף ז
projectionist 187 מַקְרִין ז
causing sleepiness; anesthetic 187 מַרְדִּים ז
spectacular, breathtaking 187 מַרְהִיב ז
exciting; moving 187 מַרְטִיט ז
component, constituent; ingredient; assembler 187 מַרְכִּיב ז
enjoyable, exciting, joyous 187 מַרְנִין ז
dance instructor 187 מַרְקִיד ז
impressive 187 מַרְשִׁים ז
angel of denunciation and accusation Lit.-archaic 187 מַשְׂטִין ז
intelligent, educated; member of the Enlightenment movement in the 187 מַשְׂכִּיל ז
early riser 187 מַשְׁכִּים ז
renter (to a tenant) 187 מַשְׂכִּיר ז
complementary; complement noun 187 מַשְׁלִים ז
boring, dull Lit. 187 מַשְׁמִים ז
fattening 187 מַשְׁמִין ז
degrading, humiliating 187 מַשְׁפִּיל ז
observer 187 מַשְׁקִיף ז
fitting, suitable, appropriate; matching 187 מַתְאִים ז
beginning Adj.; beginner 187 מַתְחִיל ז
continuous, constant; diligent, studious 187 מַתְמִיד ז
provoking, inciting 187 מַתְסִיס ז
attacker 187 מַתְקִיף ז
fundraiser 187 מַתְרִים ז
Mars - proper name of planet 188 מַאְדִּים ז
listener 188 מַאֲזִין ז
believer; religious 188 מַאֲמִין ז
biblical cantillation symbol; extending (e.g. cable) 188 מַאֲרִיךְ ז
employer 188 מַעֲבִיד ז
crowning; decorated, glorified Lit. 188 מַעֲטִיר ז
insulting 188 מַעֲלִיב ז
deep; insightful; intensive 188 מַעֲמִיק ז
employer 188 מַעֲסִיק ז
saddening; unfortunate 188 מַעֲצִיב ז

Jewish evening prayer service 188 מַעֲרִיב ז
assessor, adjuster, appraiser 188 מַעֲרִיךְ ז
admirer, fan 188 מַעֲרִיץ ז
copyist 188 מַעֲתִיק ז
promising 189 מַבְטִיחַ ז
smuggler 189 מַבְרִיחַ ז
person who raises the Torah scroll 189 מַגְבִּיהַ ז
tear-causing, lacrimatory 189 מַדְמִיעַ ז
shocking, frightening, horrible 189 מַזְוִיעַ ז
decisive, deciding 189 מַכְרִיעַ ז
stinking, smelly, odious 189 מַסְרִיחַ ז
disturber, disrupter 189 מַפְרִיעַ ז
surprising 189 מַפְתִּיעַ ז
voter 189 מַצְבִּיעַ ז
successful 189 מַצְלִיחַ ז
balding 189 מַקְרִיחַ ז
soothing, calming, placating; analgesic 189 מַרְגִּיעַ ז
deterring 189 מַרְתִּיעַ ז
satisfying, filling 189 מַשְׂבִּיעַ ז
supervisor 189 מַשְׁגִּיחַ ז
influential 189 מַשְׁפִּיעַ ז
investor 189 מַשְׁקִיעַ ז
surprising; amazing, astounding 189 מַתְמִיהַּ ז
gutter; eaves 190 מַזְחִילָה נ
parallel N, equivalent N 190 מַקְבִּילָה נ
rolling pin; roller 191 מַעֲגִילָה/מַעְגִּילָה נ
leading; shipper, mover, transporter; aqueduct, conduit; leader 192 מוֹבִיל ז
conductor (electricity) 192 מוֹלִיךְ ז
informer 193 מוֹדִיעַ ז
reprover, preacher 193 מוֹכִיחַ ז
rescuer, savior 193 מוֹשִׁיעַ ז
misleading, deceptive 194 מַטְעֶה ז
exhausting, boring, tiring 194 מַלְאֶה ז
lender 194 מַלְוֶה ז
disobedient, rebellious Lit. 194 מַמְרֶה ז
moderator, discussion leader; show host; MC; advisor (academics) 194 מַנְחֶה ז
thirst-quenching 194 מַרְוֶה ז
lecturer 194 מַרְצֶה ז
client (in law) 194 מַרְשֶׁה ז
equalizing, equating; (ha)kav hamashve 'the equator' 194 מַשְׁוֶה ז
leading astray 194 מַתְעֶה ז
preacher; part of Passover Seder; messenger (Bibl.) 195 מַגִּיד ז

מֻפְגָּן ז 200 demonstrated, exhibited, expressed
מֻפְחָד ז 200 frightened, scared, terrified
מֻפְלָא ז 200 wonderful, exceptional; beyond one's comprehension
מֻפְלָג ז 200 grand, exalted, exaggerated
מֻפְנָם ז 200 introverted; internalized; suppressed (emotions)
מֻפְסָד ז 200 defeated, beaten Coll.; with a financial loss Coll.
מֻפְסָק ז 200 stopped, terminated
מֻפְעָל ז 200 activated, implemented
מֻפְצָץ ז 200 bombed, bombarded
מֻפְקָד ז 200 deposited; responsible for
מֻפְקָע ז 200 expropriated, appropriated, seized; exaggerated (price, etc.)
מֻפְקָר ז 200 wanton, reckless; wanton person; abandoned
מֻפְרָד ז 200 separated
מֻפְרָז ז 200 exaggerated
מֻפְרָךְ ז 200 unfounded, baseless
מֻפְרָע ז 200 disturbed psychology; wild, disruptive Sl.
מֻפְשָׁט ז 200 abstract, intangible; unrealistic
מֻפְשָׁל ז 200 rolled up, rolled back
מֻפְתָּע ז 200 surprised, amazed
מֻצְהָב ז 200 colored yellow, yellowed, yellowish
מֻצְהָר ז 200 declared, announced
מֻצְלָב ז 200 crossed; cross-bred
מֻצְלָח ז 200 successful, accomplished
מֻצְלָל ז 200 shaded (painting, drawing)
מֻצְנָח ז 200 parachuted
מֻצְנָע ז 200 hidden, concealed
מֻצְפָּן ז 200 encoded, encrypted; concealed, hidden
מֻצְרָךְ ז 200 required - linguistics
מֻקְדָּם ז 200 early
מֻקְדָּשׁ ז 200 dedicated, devoted
מֻקְטָן ז 200 reduced in size, small scale
מֻקְלָט ז 200 recorded
מֻקְסָם ז 200 enchanted, enthralled
מֻקְצָף ז 200 whipped (cream etc.)
מֻקְרָב ז 200 sacrificed
מֻקְרָם ז 200 browned, grilled, crusted
מֻקְרָן ז 200 irradiated; screened (film etc.)
מֻקְרָשׁ ז 200 congealed

מֻרְגָּשׁ ז 200 felt, sensed, perceived, noticeable
מֻרְוָח ז 200 with a profit Sl.
מֻרְחָב ז 200 widened, broadened, extended
מֻרְחָק ז 200 distanced, removed, banished
מֻרְטָב ז 200 wetted
מֻרְכָּב ז 200 made of, composed of; assembled; complex
מֻרְעָב ז 200 starved, famished
מֻרְעָד ז 200 vibrated
מֻרְעָל ז 200 poisoned; "is dying for" Sl.
מֻרְשָׁע ז 200 convicted person, guilty party
מֻרְתָּח ז 200 boiled; angered, irritated, agitated
מֻשְׁאָל ז 200 borrowed; metaphoric
מֻשְׁבָּע ז 200 Juror
מֻשְׁחָז ז 200 sharpened, honed
מֻשְׁחָל ז 200 threaded, strung, laced
מֻשְׁחָם ז 200 browned
מֻשְׁחָר ז 200 blackened
מֻשְׁחָת ז 200 corrupt, immoral; defaced, marred, destroyed
מֻשְׂכָּל ז 200 rational, intelligent; idea, concept Phil.
מֻשְׂכָּר ז 200 rented, let, leased
מֻשְׁלָג ז 200 snowy, snow-covered
מֻשְׁלָךְ ז 200 discarded, thrown away
מֻשְׁלָם ז 200 perfect; wonderful; complete, total
מֻשְׁמָץ ז 200 slandered, libeled
מֻשְׁפָּע ז 200 affected, influenced
מֻשְׁקָע ז 200 invested; sunk; immersed; absorbed
מֻשְׁרָשׁ ז 200 rooted, firmly established
מֻתְאָם ז 200 adapted, conformed, tailored, suited
מֻתְסָס ז 200 fermented, cultured
מֻתְקָן ז 200 installed, affixed
מְאֻגָּד ז 201 incorporated
מְאֻחָד ז 201 united, unified
מְאֻמָּן ז 201 credentialed
מְאֻפָּל ז 201 darkened, blacked out
מְאֻרָּךְ ז 201 elongated, extended
מְאֻרָק ז 201 grounded (elect.), ground
מְחֻרָב ז 201 destroyed, demolished
מֻחְרָם/מְחֻרָם ז 201 confiscated; excommunicated
מְעֻדָּף ז 201 preferred, favored
מְעֻמָּד/מֻעֲמָד ז 201 candidate, nominee, contender
מְעֻסָּק ז 201 employee
מְעֻצָּם ז 201 intensified; nominalized - linguistics

מְעֻשָּׁר ז 201 enriched, fortified (food)
מְעֻתָּק ז 201 copied, duplicated; shifted
מֻבְלַעַת נ 202 enclave
מֻסְכָּמָה נ 203 convention, consensus
מֻבְנֶה ז 204 structured; built in
מֻטְעֶה ז 204 mistaken, erroneous
מֻמְחֶה ז 204 expert, specialist
מֻנְחֶה ז 204 directed, guided, supervised; moderated, chaired
מֻסְוֶה ז 204 camouflaged, hidden, concealed
מֻפְלֶה ז 204 discriminated against
מֻפְנֶה ז 204 directed (towards)
מֻפְרֶה ז 204 fertilized
מֻקְנֶה ז 204 acquired
מֻקְצֶה ז 204 outcast; forbidden for use by Jewish law
מֻקְשֶׁה ז 204 solidified, hardened; perplexing, incomprehensible
מֻרְשֶׁה ז 204 person with power of attorney
מֻשְׁוֶה ז 204 compared to; comparable, on par with
מֻשְׁעֶה ז 204 suspended from office
מֻשְׁקֶה ז 204 watered
מֻתְוֶה ז 204 sketched, outlined
מֻתְנֶה ז 204 conditional, stipulated; automatic, involuntary
מֻבָּע ז 205 expressed
מֻגָּהּ ז 205 proofread
מֻגָּר ז 205 spilled, flowing Lit.
מֻגָּשׁ ז 205 served, presented, submitted
מֻדָּח ז 205 ousted
מֻדָּר ז 205 excluded
מֻכָּר ז 205 familiar, known; recognized
מֻסָּק ז 205 heated, fired
מֻפָּק ז 205 stressed, accented; articulated
מֻצָּב ז 205 military post or position
מֻצָּל ז 205 saved, rescued
מֻצָּע ז 205 offered, proffered; suggested
מֻצָּת ז 205 ignited, lit
מֻקָּף ז 205 surrounded, encircled, enclosed
מֻשָּׂג ז 205 concept, idea
מֻתָּז ז 205 sprayed, sprinkled; beheaded, severed
מֻתָּר ז 205 permitted, allowed; loose, loosened
מֻטֶּה ז 206 slanted; biased
מֻכֶּה ז 206 beaten, battered
מוּדָע ז 207 aware of; conscious
מוּכָח ז 207 proven, verified

רַב ז 221 much, great, vast, numerous; multi-; important; rabbi; teacher
רַךְ ז 221 soft
שַׁח ז 221 bent, hunched
שַׁי ז 221 gift, present
גַּג ז 222 roof; top, maximum
כַּף נ 222 hand, palm; foot; spoon
קַת נ 222 butt of weapon; handle
מַס ז 223 tax; fee, dues
סַף ז 223 threshold, doorstep; limen psychology
צַד, ר' צְדָדִים/צִדִּים ז 223 side; aspect; party (pl. tsdadim/tsidim)
גַּת ר' גִּתִּים/גִּתּוֹת נ 224 wine press (pl. gitim/gitot)
כַּת ר' כַּתּוֹת/כִּתּוֹת/כִּתִּים נ 224 sect, faction (pl. katot/kitot/kitim)
פַּת, ר' פִּתִּים נ 224 bread; meal Lit. (pl. pitim)
בַּת, ר' בָּנוֹת נ 225 daughter (pl. banot)
בַּר ז 226 pure, clean
דַּר ז 226 mother-of-pearl
הַר ז 226 mountain
כַּר ז 226 pillow, cushion
כַּר ז 226 plain, pasture, meadow
מַר ז 226 bitter
סַר ז 226 angry, sad, despondent Lit.
פַּר ז 226 bull
צַר ז 226 narrow; enemy
קַר ז 226 cold, chilly
רַע ז 226 bad, nasty; malicious; wrong; bad N, evil N
שַׂר ז 226 minister; ruler, commander (older usage)
אֹם ז 227 nation Lit.
אֹם ז 227 nut of a bolt
בֹּץ ז 227 mud [no pl.]
גֹּב ז 227 lair, den [no pl.]
דֹּב ז 227 bear
דֹּק ז 227 thin film, veil Lit. [no decl.] [no pl.]
זֹךְ ז 227 clarity, purity [no pl.]
חֹב ז 227 interior, inside Lit. [no pl.]
חֹד ז 227 sharp tip; spearhead
חֹל ז 227 weekday
חֹם ז 227 heat [no pl.]
כֹּד ז 227 rounded, somewhat pointed end, e.g., of egg Lit.
לֹג ז 227 biblical liquid measure
עֹל ז 227 burden; yoke [no pl.]
פֹּת, ר' פֹּתּוֹת נ 227 female genitalia [pl. putot]
רֹב ז 227 most; majority; abundance (Bibl.) [no pl.]
רֹךְ ז 227 softness, delicateness; gentleness [no pl.]
רֹק ז 227 saliva, spittle
שֹׁד ז 227 robbery, burglary [no pl.]
תֹּם ז 227 end, completion [no pl.]
תֹּם ז 227 innocence, simplicity, naivete [no pl.]
תֹּף ז 227 drum (musical instr.); middle ear; drum (machinery); cylinder (of revolver)
חֹק ז 228 law, statute
עֹז ז 228 might, strength
רֹן ז 228 joy, gladness, elation; singing
חֹר ז 229 hole
מֹר ז 229 myrrh [no pl.]
צֹר ז 229 flint
קֹר ז 229 cold N; coldness [no pl.]
כֹּחַ/כּוֹחַ ז 230 energy, strength; ability, power; force; authority
לֹעַ ז 230 pharynx
נֹהַּ ז 230 lamentation, bemoaning, wailing [no pl.]
נֹהַּ ז 230 strong yearning, longing; following Lit. [no pl.]
רֹעַ ז 230 evil, wickedness [no pl.]
אֵד ז 231 vapor, fume, steam; mist
אֵל ז 231 god
אֵת ז 231 spade, shovel
גֵּא ז 231 proud, haughty, arrogant
גֵּב? ז 231 cistern
גֵּר ז 231 convert, proselyte; alien resident
הֵד ז 231 echo; response
זֵד ז 231 evil person Bibl.
זֵר ז 231 wreath, bouquet, garland
כֵּן ז 231 honest, sincere
כֵּף ז 231 cape, point, headland
לֵץ ז 231 clown, jester, joker
מֵץ? ז 231 oppressor Bibl.
מֵת ז 231 deceased person
נֵד ז 231 wall of water Lit.
נֵף ז 231 halyard, halliard
נֵר ז 231 candle
עֵד ז 231 witness N
עֵט ז 231 pen
עֵר ז 231 awake; active; alert; aware of
שֵׁד ז 231 demon, genie, fiend
לֵחַ ז 232 freshness, vitality [no pl.]
מֵחַ/מוֹחַ, ר' מֵחִים/מֵחוֹת ז 232 marrow [pl. -im or -ot]
רֵעַ ז 232 friend, colleague, comrade; neighbor
גֵּו ז 233 trunk, torso, back
עֵץ ז 233 tree; wood
בֵּן, ר' בָּנִים ז 234 son; boy; member of group (pl. banim)
שֵׁם ז 234 name; noun; reputation (pl. shemot)
אֵב ז 235 bud, young shoot Lit.
אֵשׁ נ 235 fire; passion
גֵּז ז 235 fleece N
גֵּט ז 235 divorce certificate (Jewish law)
גֵּץ ז 235 spark
חֵךְ ז 235 palate
חֵן ז 235 grace, charm, attractiveness
חֵץ ז 235 arrow
נֵס ז 235 miracle; flag, pennant, standard
נֵץ ז 235 hawk
עֵז נ 235 goat
עֵת נ 235 time, season; era, epoch, age
צֵל ז 235 shadow; shade; iota, trace
קֵן ז 235 nest
קֵץ ז 235 end, finish, stop; death
שֵׂךְ ז 235 prickle (botany)
שֵׁן נ 235 tooth; cog
תֵּל ז 235 mound
אֵם, ר' אִמָּהוֹת/אִמּוֹת נ 236 mother; matriarch (pl. 'imahot/'imot)
לֵב ר' לְבָבוֹת/לִבּוֹת ז 236 heart (pl. levavot/libot)
שֶׂה זו"נ 237 lamb
פֶּה ז 238 mouth; opening, orifice, entrance
אִי ז 239 island
נִי ז 239 lamentation, bemoaning, wailing Lit.-rare [no pl.]
עִי ז 239 heap or mound of ruins Lit.
צִי ז 239 fleet; navy; marine corps
אוֹג ז 240 sumac
אוֹן ז 240 power, strength, vitality; sexual potency
גּוֹי ז 240 gentile, non-Jew; nation, people (Bibl.)
דּוֹד ז 240 uncle
דּוֹם ז 240 doum (type of palm tree)
הוֹד ז 240 glory, spledour, majesty [no pl.]
הוֹן ז 240 capital; fortune Coll. [no pl.]
זוֹב ז 240 secretion, discharge [no pl.]
זוֹג ז 240 body of bell outer part
זוֹל ז 240 cheap, inexpensive
זוֹם ז 240 gravy (Talmudic)
חוֹף ז 240 shore, coast
טוֹב ז 240 good, kind; pleasant; appropriate
יוֹם, ר' יָמִים ז 240 day [pl. yamim]
יוֹן ז 240 male pigeon, male dove
כּוֹשׁ ז 240 spindle stick
לוֹט ז 240 covering, wrapping

city; town (pl. 251 עִיר ר׳ עָרִים נ `arim)
disaster, trouble (Bibl.) 251 פִּיד ז
elephant 251 פִּיל ז
pin; penis 251 פִּין ז
tassel, fringe Lit. 251 פִּיף ז
pit, shaft 251 פִּיר ז
bud 251 צִיץ ז
legate, envoy, 251 צִיר ז representative; delegate; hinge; axle; contraction; sauce, gravy
vomit N [no pl.] 251 קִיא ז
castor oil seed [no 251 קִיק ז pl.?]
quiche 251 קִישׁ ז
251 רִיב, ר׳ רִיבִים/רִיבוֹת ז quarrel, argument, dispute (pl. rivim or rivot)
eyelash 251 רִיס ז
reef 251 רִיף ז
vacuum [no pl.] 251 רִיק ז
saliva; mucus 251 רִיר ז
poverty Lit. [no pl.] 251 רִישׁ ז
peak, zenith; 251 שִׂיא ז ultimate, best; highlight; record (sports)
song; poem 251 שִׁיר ז
bag, satchel; 251 תִּיק ז portfolio; file
flutter, tremor [no pl.] 252 זִיעַ ז
plaster N [no pl.] 252 טִיחַ ז
spittle, mucus, 252 כִּיחַ ז phlegm [no pl.]
movement Lit. 252 נִיעַ ז
soot [no pl.] 252 פִּיחַ ז
bush 252 שִׂיחַ ז
conversation; 252 שִׂיחַ ז discourse
pit (Talmudic) 252 שִׁיחַ ז
wall (pl. 253 קִיר, ר׳ קִירוֹת ז kirot)
misfortune; gentile 254 אֵיד ז holiday
bosom; lap 254 חֵיק ז
great, terrific; fun (no 254 כֵּיף ז pl., no decl.) Coll.
smell (pl. 255 רֵיחַ, ר׳ רֵיחוֹת ז reyHot)
fresh 256 טָרִי ז
clean 256 נָקִי ז
pauper; poor 256 עָנִי ז
roast (beef, lamb) 256 צָלִי ז
toast N; toasted grain 256 קָלִי ז Bibl.
scarlet, crimson Lit. 256 שָׁנִי ז [no pl.]
crying [no pl.] 257 בְּכִי/בֶּכִי ז
kid, young male goat 257 גְּדִי ז
bucket, pail; Aquarius 257 דְּלִי ז
dropper, narrow- 257 טְפִי ז necked bottle
tool, 257 כְּלִי, ר׳ כֵּלִים ז instrument; vessel (pl. kelim)
pile of produce 257 כְּרִי ז (Talmudic)

rebellion; 257 מְרִי ז disobedience
silk [no pl.] 257 מֶשִׁי ז
fruit; product, 257 פְּרִי, ר׳ פֵּרוֹת ז result; profit (pl. perot)
a gullible, 257 פֶּתִי, ר׳ פְּתָאִים ז naïve person (pl. pta'im)
deer, 257 צְבִי, ר׳ צְבָאִים ז gazelle (pl. tsva'im)
forecast [no pl.] 257 צֶפִי ז
accidental ejection of 257 קְרִי ז sperm [no pl.]
disobedience, 257 קֶרִי ז rebellion [no pl.]
captivity, 257 שְׁבִי ז imprisonment [no pl.]
secret, quiet manner 257 שְׁלִי ז Bibl. [no pl.]
bare hill Bibl. 257 שְׁפִי ז
warp (weaving) [no 257 שְׁתִי ז pl.]
hanger; quiver 257 תְּלִי/תֶּלִי ז (of arrows)
lion 258 אֲרִי, ר׳ אֲרָיוֹת (אֲרָיִים) ז Lit. (pl. 'arayot, less commonly 'arayim)
adornment, ornament 258 חֲלִי ז Bibl.
flap of envelope; flap 258 חֲפִי ז
258 חֲצִי/חֵצִי, ר׳ חֲצָאִים/חֲצָיִים ז half (pl. Hastsa'im/Hatsayim)
adornment, ornament 258 עֲדִי ז
pestle; pistil (botany) 258 עֱלִי ז
failure, 259 דְּחִי/(דֶּחִי) ז collapse, breakdown Bibl. [no pl.]
cheek; jaw 259 לְחִי/לֶחִי נו״ז
clap, stroke, blow 259 מְחִי ז Lit. [no pl.]
intestine, bowel 259 מְעִי ז
lamentation, 259 נְהִי ז bemoaning Bibl. [no pl.]
filth, contamination 259 סְחִי ז [no pl.]
mirror [no pl.] 259 רְאִי ז
grazing cattle 259 רְעִי ז
armpit 259 שֶׁחִי ז
proud; proud, 260 גֵּאֶה ז conceited person; gay
Identical 260 זֵהֶה ז
dark 260 כֵּהֶה ז
tired, exhausted, 260 לֵאֶה ז fatigued
tired, exhasted, 260 לֵהֶה ז fatigued Lit.
blunt, dull 260 קֵהֶה ז
hesitant, unsure, shy 260 רֵהֶה ז Lit.
lamb (pl. 261 טָלֶה ר׳ טְלָאִים ז tla'im)
shovel, dustpan 261 יָעֶה ז
house, 261 נָוֶה, ר׳ נָווֹת/נָאוֹת ז hostel, home; oasis (pl. navot/na'ot)

handicapped person, 261 נָכֶה ז cripple, invalid
stem, cane, stalk; 261 קָנֶה ז barrel; reed; windpipe, trachea
bract (botany) 262 חָפָה ז
leaf 262 עָלֶה ז
sacrum 262 עָצֶה ז
edge, 263 קָצֶה, ר׳ קְצָוֹת/קָצִים ז end, extremity (pl. ktsavot/katsim)
field 263 שָׂדֶה ז
chest; breast(s); 264 חָזֶה ז bosom
worn out, old Lit. 265 בָּלֶה ז
painful, aching, 265 דָּוֶה ז anguished; very sick
befitting, becoming; 265 יָאֶה ז suitable, right, proper
pretty, beautiful, nice 265 יָפֶה ז
newly extinguished; 265 כָּבֶה ז lifeless Lit.
temporary, short- 265 כָּלֶה ז lived; yearning, longing
handsome, pleasant, 265 נָאֶה ז good looking; substantial, high
swollen, distended 265 צָבֶה ז
hard, solid, stiff; 265 קָשֶׁה ז difficult; strict, severe
quenched, satiated 265 רָוֶה ז (with water)
thin, slim, skinny; 265 רָזֶה ז low-fat
weak, limp; lax 265 רָפֶה ז
equal, identical; 265 שָׁוֶה ז worth
thick, broad; rough, 266 עָבֶה ז course
a small piece 267 בָּדָל/בְּדָל ז
lightning; flash 267 בָּזָק ז message
onion 267 בָּצָל ז
cattle; beef 267 בָּקָר ז
hail (only construct, 267 בָּרָד ז no declension) [no pl.]
lightning; sparkle, 267 בָּרָק ז gleam, shine
flesh; meat 267 בָּשָׂר ז
barrel; large jar Lit- 267 גָּרָב ז rare
object, thing; speech, 267 דָּבָר ז word
cereal; grain 267 דָּגָן ז
marten 267 דָּלָק ז
male; mam; 267 זָכָר ז masculine (grammar)
beard 267 זָקָן ז
something sickening 267 זָרָא ז (no declension) [no pl.]
blade (botany) 267 טָרָף ז
brother-in-law Lit. 267 יָבָם ז
dear; expensive 267 יָקָר ז
old; longstanding 267 יָשָׁן ז
straight; honest, 267 יָשָׁר ז decent
lie N, illusion, tall tale 267 כָּזָב ז

glazier (fem. zagagit) 275 זַגָּג ז

singer (fem. zameret) 275 זַמָּר ז

tar-worker, pitch-worker 275 זַפָּת ז

one who does wiring (fem. Havetet) 275 חַוָּט ז

marlstone (no declension) 275 חַוָּר ז

cantor (fem. Hazanit) 275 חַזָּן ז

carver, sculptor (esp. using wood) (fem. Hatevet) 275 חַטָּב ז

obliged, required; owe; must 275 חַיָּב ז

tailor (fem. Hayetet) 275 חַיָּט ז

soldier (fem. Hayelet) 275 חַיָּל ז

butcher's knife (Talmudic) 275 חַלָּף ז

donkey driver (fem. Hameret) 275 חַמָּר ז

javelin sand boa 275 חַנָּק ז

tourniquet 275 חַסָּם ז

sapper, digger 275 חַפָּר ז

engraver 275 חַקָּק ז

accountant 275 חַשָּׁב ז

underwriter (insurance) 275 חַתָּם ז

cook, chef 275 טַבָּח ז

peacock (fem. taveset) 275 טַוָּס ז

plasterer (fem. TayaHat) 275 טַיָּח ז

hiker (fem. tayelet) 275 טַיָּל ז

pilot (aircraft) (fem. tayeset) 275 טַיָּס ז

entrepreneur ; initiator, promoter (fem. *yazemet*, Coll. *yazamit*) 275 יַזָּם ז

gunlayer, gunner; device adjusting instrument 275 כַּוָּן ז

liar, teller of tall tale 275 כַּזָּב ז

calibrator 275 כַּיָּל ז

pickpocket (fem. kayeset) 275 כַּיָּס ז

violinist (fem. kaneret, Coll. kanarit) 275 כַּנָּר ז

reporter, journalist, correspondent (fem. katevet) 275 כַּתָּב ז

porter, carrier (Talmudic) 275 כַּתָּף ז

sickle 275 מַגָּל ז

measure; index (economics); consumer price index 275 מַדָּד ז

shelf, ledge 275 מַדָּף ז

sailor (fem. malaHit) 275 מַלָּח ז

really, truly; precisely 275 מַמָּשׁ ז

cockroach (fem. makakit) 275 מַקָּק ז

NCO (Non-Commissioned Officer) (fem. nagedet) 275 נַגָּד ז

resistor (elect.) 275 נַגָּד ז

musician, player (fem. nagenet, Coll. naganit) 275 נַגָּן ז

carpenter (fem. nageret, Coll. nagarit) 275 נַגָּר ז

wanderer, vagabond, nomad (fem. navedet) 275 נַוָּד ז

navigator; scout (fem. navetet) 275 נַוָּט ז

portable, mobile, movable 275 נַיָּד ז

stationary 275 נַיָּח ז

dwarf, midget (fem. naneset, Coll. nanasit) 275 נַנָּס ז

drafter, formulator (fem. nasaHit) 275 נַסָּח ז

smith, blacksmith (fem. napaHit???) 275 נַפָּח ז

detonator 275 נַפָּץ ז

woodpecker (bird) 275 נַקָּר ז

carrier (medicine) (fem. nasa'it) 275 נַשָּׂא ז

breather pipe (vehicle); breather valve (industry) 275 נַשָּׁם ז

armorer; weaponeer (fem. nashakit) 275 נַשָּׁק ז

navigator (shipping); router (computing) (fem. natevet) 275 נַתָּב ז

analyzer; analyst (fem. nataHat) 275 נַתָּח ז

porter; carrier (fem. sabalit) 275 סַבָּל ז

anvil 275 סַדָּן ז

typesetter, compositor (fem. sadarit) 275 סַדָּר ז

longshoreman, stevedore, dockworker (fem. saveret, Coll. savarit) 275 סַוָּר ז

whitewasher (fem. sayedet?) 275 סַיָּד ז

groom (of horses) (fem. sayeset) 275 סַיָּס ז

assistant, helper (fem. saya`at) 275 סַיָּע ז

fencer (sports) (fem. sayefet) 275 סַיָּף ז

patrolman, inspector; scout (military) (fem. sayarit?) 275 סַיָּר ז

sergeant (military) (fem. samelet) 275 סַמָּל ז

cursor (computing); indicator (elect.); in (military) soldier who marks the beginning of a row (fem. samanit?) 275 סַמָּן ז

sailor, deck hand (fem. sapanit) 275 סַפָּן ז

supplier, provider (fem. sapakit) 275 סַפָּק ז

barber, hairdresser (fem. saparit) 275 סַפָּר ז

stonemason (fem. satatit?) 275 סַתָּת ז

buzzard (bird) 275 עַקָּב ז

farmer (fem. falaHit) 275 פַּלָּח ז

sapper (military) (fem. palasit?) 275 פַּלָּס ז

sculptor (fem. paselet) 275 פַּסָּל ז

commander (police), chief inspector; controller (computing) (fem. pakedet) 275 פַּקָּד ז

inspector (fem. pakaHit) 275 פַּקָּח ז

(house) painter (fem. tsaba`it) 275 צַבָּע ז

prickly pear cactus; native Israeli Coll. (fem. tsabarit) 275 צַבָּר ז

hunter (fem. tsayedet) 275 צַיָּד ז

artist, painter (fem. tsayeret) 275 צַיָּר ז

photographer (fem. tsalemet) 275 צַלָּם ז

sniper, marksman (fem. tsalafit) 275 צַלָּף ז

encoder; telegraph operator (fem. tsapanit) 275 צַפָּן ז

ornithologist (fem. tsaparit) 275 צַפָּר ז

capacitor, condenser (elect.) 275 קַבָּל ז

potter (fem. kadarit) 275 קַדָּר ז

linesman (sports); lineman (telecom., elec.) (fem. kavanit) 275 קַוָּן ז

engine (of train), locomotive 275 קַטָּר ז

existent, alive; binding, valid 275 קַיָּם ז

one with large testicles (Talmudic) 275 קַיָּן ז

marksman (fem. kala`it) 275 קַלָּע ז

butcher (fem. katsevet, Coll. katsavit) 275 קַצָּב ז

person relaying information between different bodies; signaler, signal operator (military) (fem. kasharit) 275 קַשָּׁר ז

archer (fem. kashatit) 275 קַשָּׁת ז

mortarman (fem. ragamit???) 275 רַגָּם ז

bachelor, unmarried (male) (fem. ravaka) 275 רַוָּק ז

coachman 275 רַכָּב ז

coordinator (fem. rakezet) 275 רַכָּז ז

upholsterer (fem. rapedet) 275 רַפָּד ז

floorer (fem. ratsafit) 275 רַצָּף ז

registrar (fem. rashemet) 275 רַשָּׁם ז

welder (fem. ratakhit) 275 רַתָּךְ ז

broadcaster (radio, TV) (fem. shaderet, Coll., shadarit) 275 שַׁדָּר ז

yachtsman, oarsman, rower, sailor (fem. shayetet) 275 שַׁיָּט ז

belonging to; relevant 275 שַׁיָּךְ ז

remote control Coll. (normative shalat raHak) 275 שַׁלָּט ז

bursar (fem. shalemet) 275 שַׁלָּם ז

limb, organ; wing Lit. pl. 'avarim/'eyvarim 287 אֵבֶר/אֵיבָר (כמו הֵיכָל) ז
clay (only constr., Hemar w pataH, no declension, no pl.) 287 חֵמָר ז
heart Lit. (pl. levavot) 287 לֵבָב, ר' לְבָבוֹת ז
foreign country, diaspora (only nekhar constr., no declension, no pl.) 287 נֵכָר ז
grape (pl. `anavim, constr. `invey) 287 עֵנָב, ר' עֲנָבִים ז
liquor (only constr., with pataH, no declension, no pl.) 287 שֵׁכָר ז
hair (pl. se`arot) 287 שֵׂעָר, ר' שְׂעָרוֹת ז
belly, underbelly 288 גָּחוֹן ז
south (only drom, constr., no declension, no pl.) 288 דָּרוֹם ז
orphan (pl. yetomim, fem. yetoma) 288 יָתוֹם ז
honor, respect; dignity [no pl.] 288 כָּבוֹד ז
something repulsive Bibl. (only me'os constr, no declension, no pl.) 288 מָאוֹס ז
corset, girdle 288 מָחוֹךְ ז
north (only tsfon constr., no declension, no pl.) 288 צָפוֹן ז
relative, family member 288 קָרוֹב ז
peace; wellbeing (pl. shlomot/shlomim) 288 שָׁלוֹם, ר' שְׁלוֹמוֹת/שְׁלוֹמִים ז
master, lord; Mr. 289 אָדוֹן ז
back (N) (pl./dual 'aHorayim); declension only of pl. 289 אָחוֹר, ר' זוגי אֲחוֹרַיִם ז
African wild ass (pl. `arodim/`arodot) 289 עָרוֹד, ר' עֲרוֹדִים/עֲרוֹדוֹת ז
decade 289 עָשׂוֹר ז
larynx; throat 290 גָּרוֹן ז
tongue; language 290 לָשׁוֹן זו"נ
district, sate, province, territory, region 290 מָחוֹז ז
car (of train); wagon 290 קָרוֹן ז
disaster 291 אָסוֹן ז
cupboard, closet 291 אָרוֹן ז
she-ass 291 אָתוֹן נ
greatness, glory; genius 292 גָּאוֹן ז
glider; drone 292 דָּאוֹן ז
wickedness, malice (pl. zdonot/zdonim) 292 זָדוֹן ר' זְדוֹנוֹת/זְדוֹנִים ז
grief, sorrow Lit. (pl. yegonim/yegonot) 292 יָגוֹן, ר' יְגוֹנִים/יְגוֹנוֹת ז
shame, disgrace N. (pl. klonim/klonot) 292 קָלוֹן, ר' קְלוֹנִים/קְלוֹנוֹת ז
thinness, gauntness [no pl.] 292 רָזוֹן ז
crowd, mob; tumult, noise Lit. 293 הָמוֹן ז
anger, wrath, indignation 293 חָרוֹן ז
leaflet, brochure, pamphlet 293 עָלוֹן ז
will, wish 294 רָצוֹן ז
tumult, noise Lit. 294 שָׁאוֹן ר' שְׁאוֹנִים ז
vision 295 חָזוֹן ז
sin, transgression; misdemeanor 295 עָווֹן ז
probe, tester 296 בָּחוֹן ז
probe (esp. in dentistry); calipers 296 גָּשׁוֹשׁ ז
ferret 296 חָמוֹס ז
herald, announcer (pl. karozim/karozot) 296 כָּרוֹז, ר' כָּרוֹזִים/כָּרוֹזוֹת ז
customer 297 לָקוֹחַ ז
money, capital 297 מָמוֹן ז
bumper (of car) 297 פָּגוֹשׁ ז
candlestick 297 פָּמוֹט ז
toddler 297 פָּעוֹט ז
big, large 298 גָּדוֹל ז
able 298 יָכוֹל ז
holy; holy man 298 קָדוֹשׁ ז
near, close; relative 298 קָרוֹב ז
far 298 רָחוֹק ז
bent, hunched 298 שָׁחוֹחַ ז
strong, powerful 299 חָסוֹן ז
sweet 300 מָתוֹק ז
pink 301 וָרֹד ז
golden 301 זָהֹב ז
green; verdant; unripe (fruit); inexperienced Sl. 301 יָרֹק ז
blue 301 כָּחֹל ז
orange 301 כָּתֹם ז
spotted, speckled, flecked Lit. 301 נָקֹד ז
purple; violet 301 סָגֹל ז
yellow 301 צָהֹב ז
brown, cinnamon-color 301 קָנֹם ז
wet 301 רָטֹב/רָטוֹב ז
brownish, dark brown 301 שָׁחֹם/שָׁחוּם ז
red 302 אָדֹם ז
terrible; threatening 302 אָיֹם ז
blackish Lit.-rare 302 אָכֹם ז
gray Lit. 302 אָמֹץ ז
smelling like gall (botany parasite) Lit. 302 אָפֹץ/עָפֹץ ז
long (physically or time-wise) 302 אָרֹךְ ז
dense, entangled, bushy 302 עָבֹת/עָבוֹת ז
round 302 עָגֹל ז
deep 302 עָמֹק ז
soft, delicate, refined Lit. 302 עָנֹג ז
crooked, twisted 302 עָקֹב ז
with stripes (animal), as if it had been bound Lit.-rare 302 עָקֹד ז
curved, twisted 302 עָקֹל ז
curved, twisted 302 עָקֹם ז
naked, nude; bereft 302 עָרֹם ז
gray 303 אָפֹר ז
of the color of earth, of dirt Lit. 303 עָפֹר ז
white, pure 303 צָחֹר ז
black 303 שָׁחֹר ז
saddle 304 אֻכָּף ז
craftsman, artisan 304 אֻמָּן ז
the five books of the Pentateuch 304 חֻמָּשׁ ז
French fried potato chip 304 טֻגָּן ז
fetus 304 עֻבָּר ז
fennel (plant) 304 שֻׁמָּר ז
partner 304 שֻׁתָּף ז
ladder; scale 305 סֻלָּם ז
artist 306 אָמָּן ז
wolf 307 זְאֵב ז
wailing, howling (no pl. or declension) 307 יְלֵל ז
pain 307 כְּאֵב ז
magnificence, splendor [no pl.] 307 פְּאֵר ז
oryx 307 רְאֵם ז
relative, family member; flesh, meat 307 שְׁאֵר ז
strength; majesty [no pl.] 307 שְׂאֵת ז
eye mask Lit. 308 אֲפֵר ז
well 309 בְּאֵר נ
sentence, judgment Lit. [no pl.] 310 גְּזָר ז
end, completion, termination [no pl.] 310 גְּמָר/גֶּמֶר ז
bedpan 310 גְּרָף ז
graph, pl. only 310 גְּרָף ז
tow truck [no pl.] 310 גְּרָר ז
pattern, design 310 דְּגָם ז
social stress [no pl.] 310 דְּחָק ז
homiletic interpretation of the Bible; homiletic exegesis [no pl.] 310 דְּרָשׁ ז
kit, equipment, package [no pl.] 310 זְוָד ז
muzzle 310 זְמָם ז
range; extent, bounds 310 טְוָח ז
moss 310 טְחָב ז
hope Lit.-rare; burden Lit.-rare 310 יְהָב ז
flight; path of a ball [no pl.] 310 יְעָף ז
honor, glory, respect [no pl.] 310 יְקָר ז
cow's udder 310 כְּחָל ז
law, basic rule; all 310 כְּלָל ז
copy 310 כְּפָל ז
village 310 כְּפָר ז
fallow, green fallow 310 כְּרָב ז
writing; handwriting 310 כְּתָב ז
rotation, revolution - astronomy 310 סְבָב ז

סְגָן ז 310 deputy; vice-president
סְדָר ז 310 composition (in typography and printing)
סְוָאר/סְוָר ז 310 stack (of boxes)
סְטָו ז 310 colonnade, portico
סְיָג ז 310 restriction, condition; border, fence, safeguard
סְיָח ז 310 foal, colt
סְכָךְ ז 310 the covering of a sukkah [no pl.]
סְפָר ז 310 border, edge, frontier [no pl.]
סְרָק ז 310 futility, fruitlessness [no pl.]
סְתָו ז 310 autumn, fall
סְתָם ז 310 unclear, unspecific; purposelessly [no pl.]
פְּגָם ז 310 damage, defect, fault, deficiency
פְּחָת ז 310 depreciation; waste, loss; reduction; amortization [no pl.]
פְּטָם ז 310 fattened livestock or poultry
פְּסָד ז 310 wastage [no pl.]
פְּסָק ז 310 ruling, decision
פְּקָק ז 310 cork, stopper, plug; traffic jam
פְּרָט ז 310 detail, particular; individual
פְּרָס ז 310 prize; award; reward
פְּשָׁט ז 310 simple explanation; literal meaning [no pl.]
צְלָב ז 310 cross
קְדָל ז 310 back of neck Lit.
קְלָף ז 310 card; parchment
רְבָב ז 310 spot, stain; fault, stain on one's reputation
רְקָק ז 310 swamp, bog, marsh [no pl.]
שְׁאָט ז 310 despising [no pl.]
שְׁאָר ז 310 remainder; others [no pl.]
שְׁבָב ז 310 sliver, shaving, chip
שְׁוָא ז 310 the central minimal short vowel
שְׁיָר ז 310 remainder, leftover
שְׂלָו ז 310 quail, pheasant
שְׁלָל ז 310 seam Lit. [no pl.]
שְׁלָשׁ ז 310 one of three identical objects
שְׁמָד ז 310 forced conversion from Judaism; religious persecution
שְׂרָד ז 310 service, official, formal [no pl.]
שְׂרָף ז 310 resin
תְּגָר ז 310 challenge [no pl.]
תְּמָד ז 310 mead [no pl.]
אֲוָז ז 311 goose; gander
אֱיָל ז 311 power, strength Lit.
אֲנָךְ ז 311 vertical, perpendicular N.; plumb line
אֲפָר ז 311 meadow, grazing area Lit.
אֲתָר ז 311 site
חֲטָף ז 311 Hataf (shortened vowel in Classical Hebrew)
חֲמָם/חֲמָם ז 311 cardamom [no pl.!]
חֲצָץ ז 311 a closed-off, fenced area Lit.
חֲשָׁד ז 311 suspicion; impression, suggestion
חֲשָׁשׁ ז 311 fear, concern, worry
חֲתָךְ ז 311 cut, incision, slash; section, cross-section
עֲנָק ז 311 giant; huge; necklace
עֲרָר ז 311 appeal
גְּבָב ז 312 pile, heap Lit. [no pl.]
מְנָת = מָנָה, ר׳ מְנָאוֹת/מְנָיוֹת נ 312 portion, pl. mena'ot/menayot
נְיָר ז 312 paper
צְבָת נ 312 pliers, pincer; vise-grip
קְנָס ז 312 fine N
קְרָב ז 312 battle, combat; struggle; race
שְׁטָר ז 312 bill, banknote
שְׁנָת = שֵׁנָה נ 312 sleep, slumber
זְמַן/זְמָן ז 313 time; period of time; tense (grammar)
כְּרַךְ ז 313 large city
לְשַׁד ז 313 juice, essence
מְעַט ז 313 little, few; a little
אֲגַם ז 314 lake
אֲגַף ז 314 wing, department, branch; flank
אֲטַב ז 314 frame holding walls of carriage together
הֲדַס ז 314 myrtle
חֲשַׁשׁ ז 314 fodder, straw (no pl.) [no pl.]
דְּבַשׁ ז 315 honey [no pl.]
סְבַךְ ז 315 entanglement, complicated situation; thicket
לְאֹם ז 316 nation, people
בֶּגֶד ז 317 article of clothing, garment
בֶּדֶק ז 317 repair, maintenance
בֶּזֶק ז 317 telecommunication; spark [no pl.]
בֶּטֶן נ 317 abdomen, belly; stomach
בֶּלֶט ז 317 prominence (topography)
בֶּלֶם ז 317 brake N
בֶּצֶר ז 317 ore
בֶּרֶז ז 317 faucet, tap
בֶּתֶר ז 317 piece, chunk, fragment (usually of animal or body)
גֶּבֶס ז 317 gypsum; plaster (no declension except construct) [no pl.]
גֶּדֶם ז 317 stump (of tree, etc.)
גֶּזֶל ז 317 robbery, theft [no pl.]
גֶּזֶם ז 317 pruned branches [no pl.]
גֶּזֶר ז 317 carrot
גֶּזֶר ז 317 piece, shred, fragment
גֶּלֶד ז 317 crust, scab; scale leaf
גֶּלֶם ז 317 (raw) material [no pl.]
גֶּשֶׁם ז 317 rain
גֶּשֶׁר ז 317 bridge; connection, association
דֶּבֶק ז 317 glue
דֶּבֶר ז 317 plague (no declension except construct, no pl.)
דֶּגֶל ז 317 flag, banner
דֶּגֶם ז 317 model, replica
דֶּלֶף ז 317 trickle N; dripping; shunt Med. [no pl.]
דֶּלֶק ז 317 fuel; petrol; gas
דֶּמֶם ז 317 bleeding, hemorrhage (no declension except construct, no pl.)
דֶּפֶק ז 317 disaster, catastrophe Sl. (no declension except construct, no pl.)
דֶּקֶל ז 317 palm tree
דֶּקֶר ז 317 pick N; probe (military); epee (fencing)
דֶּשֶׁן ז 317 fertilizer, manure; rich food Lit.
וֶשֶׁט ז 317 esophagus, gullet
וֶתֶק ז 317 seniority [no pl.]
זֶבֶד ז 317 gift Bibl.
זֶבֶל ז 317 manure, fertilizer; garbage, rubbish, junk
זֶמֶר ז 317 songs, singing
זֶפֶק ז 317 crop (of bird)
זֶרֶד ז 317 twig, tendril
זֶרֶם ז 317 flow; electric current flow; ideological or religious movement
טֶקֶס ז 317 ceremony; ritual
טֶרֶד ז 317 thrush (bird) - rare
יֶלֶק ז 317 locust; larva
יֶקֶב ז 317 winery
יֶתֶר ז 317 remainder, rest; excess, surplus [no pl.]
יֶתֶר ז 317 rope, cord, string; hypotenuse
כֶּבֶשׁ ז 317 ramp, gangway
כֶּבֶשׂ ז 317 sheep; mutton
כֶּלַח ז 317 freshness, vitality ??? (only in 'avad `alav kelaH (.‘outdated’ (no declension, no pl
כֶּנֶס ז 317 assembly, conference
כֶּסֶל ז 317 ilium; flank, loin (of meat)
כֶּסֶל/כְּסֶל ז 317 foolishness, stupidity Lit. [no pl.]
כֶּפֶל ז 317 multiplication; double
כֶּרֶךְ ז 317 volume
כֶּשֶׁל ז 317 failure, mistake; malfunction
כֶּשֶׁף ז 317 magic, witchcraft, wizardry
כֶּתֶם ז 317 stain; patch of color
כֶּתֶר ז 317 crown N
לֶבֶד ז 317 felt

לֶבֶט ז 317 difficulty in making a decision, misgiving (mostly in pl. levatim)
לֶבֶן ז 317 cultured milk [no pl.]
לֶקֶט ז 317 anthology, collection; wheat left for the poor to collect
לֶקֶשׁ ז 317 plants growing after the last rain, late crops [no pl.]
לֶשֶׁם ז 317 opal, jacinth
לֶתֶת ז 317 malt
מֶגֶד ז 317 precious, pleasant thing; goodness; sweet delicacy (declension in pl. only?)
מֶדֶד ז 317 measurement Lit. [no pl.]
מֶזֶג ז 317 temperament, demeanor
מֶכֶס ז 317 customs, import tax
מֶכֶר ז 317 sale; price, value, worth Lit.
מֶלֶט ז 317 cement (no declension, constr. only, no pl.)
מֶלֶל ז 317 talk, wording, idle chat [no pl.]
מֶמֶל ז 317 crushing stone (in olive press)
מֶסֶר ז 317 message; theme
מֶצֶר ז 317 border, limit
מֶרֶד ז 317 rebellion, insurrection; uprising
מֶרֶץ ז 317 vigor, energy [no pl.]
מֶרֶק ז 317 putty
מֶשֶׁךְ ז 317 duration [no pl.]
מֶשֶׁק ז 317 farm; economy; kibbutz, agricultural settlement Coll.
מֶתֶג ז 317 switch (elec.); bit (of bridle); Hebrew accent symbol
מֶתֶק ז 317 sweetness [no pl.]
נֶבֶג ז 317 spore
נֶבֶט ז 317 sprout, shoot, seedling
נֶגֶן ז 317 tune; playing Lit. [no pl.]
נֶגֶף ז 317 obstacle, hindrance
נֶגֶר ז 317 run-off (water)
נֶדֶר/נֵדֶר ז 317 vow, oath, promise
נֶזֶם ז 317 nose ring
נֶזֶק/נֵזֶק ז 317 damage, harm
נֶטַע ז 317 sapling
נֶכֶס ז 317 asset, property
נֶמֶק ז 317 necrosis; gangrene [no pl.]
נֶמֶשׁ ז 317 freckle
נֶסֶךְ/נֵסֶךְ ז 317 pouring out (water, wine, in religious ritual)
נֶסֶר ז 317 board, plank
נֶפֶץ ז 317 explosion, blast [no pl.]
נֶקֶב ז 317 pinhole, aperture
נֶקֶז ז 317 drain N [no pl.]
נֶקֶר ז 317 puncture; pick, chisel
נֶשֶׁךְ ז 317 interest (banking) Bibl. [no pl.]
נֶשֶׁל ז 317 slough - zoology [no pl.]
נֶשֶׁף ז 317 ball, party, reception
נֶשֶׁק ז 317 weapon
נֶשֶׁר ז 317 vulture; coll. eagle
נֶתֶז ז 317 spray N; ricochet
נֶתֶךְ ז 317 alloy
נֶתֶק ז 317 disconnection; rift; fuse (elec.)
סֶגֶל ז 317 personnel; senior staff
סֶגֶן ז 317 first lieutenant
סֶגֶר ז 317 curfew, closure
סֶדֶק ז 317 crack, fissure; fracture; slit
סֶכֶם ז 317 total N [no pl.]
סֶכֶר ז 317 dam, floodgate
סֶלֶק ז 317 beet
סֶמֶךְ ז 317 basis, foundation, reliable source [no pl.]
סֶקֶר ז 317 survey, study
סֶרֶט ז 317 ribbon, streamer; movie, film; film (photog.); tape
סֶרֶךְ ז 317 regulation, custom Arch.
סֶתֶם ז 317 blockage
פֶּגֶר ז 317 corpse, carcass
פֶּדֶר ז 317 omentum - anatomy
פֶּטֶל ז 317 raspberry [no pl.]
פֶּטֶר ז 317 first-born Bibl.
פֶּלֶא ז 317 wonder, miracle
פֶּלֶד ז 317 steel Lit. [no pl.]
פֶּלֶךְ ז 317 region, zone, area
פֶּלֶךְ ז 317 spindle
פֶּלֶס ז 317 level (instr.)
פֶּסֶל ז 317 sculpture, statue; idol
פֶּסֶק ז 317 break N
פֶּרֶג/פָּרָג ז 317 poppy seed
פֶּרֶד ז 317 mule
פֶּרֶט ז 317 odd number; itemized list [no pl.]
פֶּרֶךְ ז 317 travail, forced labor Lit. [no pl.]
פֶּרֶץ ז 317 outburst, gush; breach, crack; impulse, urge
פֶּרֶק ז 317 chapter; episode; period, era; joint, segment
פֶּרֶשׁ ז 317 excretion, bodily waste (no pl.) [no pl.]
פֶּשֶׁט ז 317 flood plain
פֶּתֶן ז 317 cobra, mamba
פֶּתֶק ז 317 note, message; scrap of paper
צֶבֶר ז 317 heap; spore
צֶבֶת ז 317 handful, bundle, sheaf (of grain, flowers)
צֶבֶת ז 317 pincers
צֶדֶף ז 317 seashell; shell
צֶדֶק ז 317 justice, fairness, righteousness; integrity [no pl.]
צֶוֶת ז 317 staff, team, crew
צֶמֶג ז 317 caoutchouc, rubber [no pl.]
צֶמֶד ז 317 duo, pair, team
צֶמֶל ז 317 ripe fig (Talmudic) [no pl.]
צֶפֶק ז 317 peritoneum (anatomy) [no pl.]
קֶבֶס ז 317 nausea Lit. [no pl.]
קֶבֶר ז 317 grave; tomb
קֶדֶם ז 317 ancient times; east Lit. [no pl.]
קֶטֶל ז 317 death, slaughter [no pl.]
קֶלֶט ז 317 input (computing) [no pl.]
קֶלֶס ז 317 mockery, ridiculing Lit. [no pl.]
קֶמֶט ז 317 wrinkle, crease; fold
קֶמֶר ז 317 dome, arch
קֶסֶם ז 317 magic, enchantment, spell; sorcery
קֶפֶל ז 317 fold, crease; pleat
קֶצֶב ז 317 pace, speed; tempo; rhythm
קֶצֶף ז 317 foam, froth, suds
קֶצֶר ז 317 short circuit; misunderstanding Coll.
קֶרֶב, ר' קְרָבַיִם ז 317 interior, inside (pl. kravayim 'innards, intestines')
קֶשֶׁב ז 317 attentiveness [no pl.]
קֶשֶׁר ז 317 knot; connection, contact; communication
רֶגֶב ז 317 lump, clod (of earth)
רֶטֶט ז 317 trembling, quaking, quivering [no pl.]
רֶכֶב ז 317 vehicle, car; upper grindstone
רֶכֶס ז 317 ridge, range (of hills, mountains)
רֶכֶשׁ ז 317 purchasing, acquisitions, procurement [no pl.]
רֶמֶז ז 317 hint, clue; indication
רֶמֶץ ז 317 ember (no pl.) [no pl.]
רֶמֶשׂ ז 317 insect, bug, crawling creatures
רֶסֶן ז 317 bridle; rein
רֶסֶק ז 317 puree; paste
רֶפֶד ז 317 padding, pad; layer, bed [no pl.]
רֶפֶשׁ ז 317 mud, mire
רֶצֶף ז 317 sequence; continuity; continuum
רֶשֶׁף ז 317 flash, flare; spark
רֶתֶק ז 317 holding force (military)
רֶתֶת ז 317 clonus (medicine) [no pl.]
שֶׁבֶר ז 317 break, fracture; fragment, piece; rift; fraction (math)
שֶׂגֶב ז 317 supremacy, greatness, exaltedness [no pl.]
שֶׁגֶם ז 317 tenon, connector, joint, key
שֶׁגֶר ז 317 litter (zoology)

סֵדֶר ז 322 order, organization; arrangement
סֵמֶל ז 322 symbol; badge; epitome
סֵפֶל ז 322 mug
סֵפֶר ז 322 book; literary work; scroll
סֵתֶר ז 322 hideaway; secret, mystery
פֵּשֶׁר ז 322 meaning, intent [no pl.]
שֵׁבֶט ז 322 tribe, clan; rod, staff; switch, thin branch; scepter
שֵׂכֶל ז 322 intelligence, wit; brains, common sense
שֵׁפֶל ז 322 ebb, low tide; low point [no pl.]
אֵבֶל ז 323 mourning, sadness [no pl.]
אֵבֶר ז 323 limb, organ; wing Lit.
אֵגֶל ז 323 droplet
אֵדֶר ז 323 hide of stuffed animal
אֵדֶר ז 323 hide of stuffed animal
אֵלֶם ז 323 silence, speechlessness Lit. [no pl.]
אֵסֶל ז 323 pole; lever; yoke
אֵפֶר ז 323 ash [no pl.]
אֵשֶׁל ז 323 tamarisk tree
הֵלֶךְ ז 323 wanderer, nomad Lit.
חֵבֶל ז 323 pang, pain, trial
חֵבֶל ז 323 pang, trial, pain
חֵטְא ז 323 sin; offense, misdemeanor
חֵלֶב ז 323 animal fat; candle wax; the best part Lit.
חֵלֶף ז 323 replacement, replacement part, alternative
חֵלֶק ז 323 part, portion
חֵלֶק ז 323 part, portion
חֵפֶץ ז 323 object, article; desire, want, wish Lit.
חֵפֶת ז 323 cuff link; cuff
חֵרֶם ז 323 excommunication; boycott, embargo, ban
חֵרֶם ז 323 fishing net (biblical)
עֵבֶר ז 323 side, direction, way
עֵגֶל ז 323 calf (male)
עֵדֶן ז 323 Eden, paradise; pleasure Lit.
עֵדֶר ז 323 flock, herd, drove
עֵדֶר ז 323 herd, flock, drove
עֵזֶר ז 323 aid, assistance; aid(s), accessory
עֵקֶד ז 323 collection (of books, articles) Lit.
עֵקֶל ז 323 basket used for pressing olives (arch.)
עֵרֶב ז 323 mixture; rabble [no pl.]
עֵרֶב ז 323 woof (in weaving) [no pl.]
עֵרֶךְ ז 323 value, worth; principle; order; dictionary entry
עֵשֶׂב ז 323 weed [constr. pl. `isvey/`esvey]
מֵצַח ז 324 forehead
נֵצַח/נֶצַח ז 324 eternity
סֵבֶל ז 325 suffering, pain, hardship
גֶּבֶר ז 326 male, man
גֶּפֶן ז 326 grapevine
גֶּרֶד ז 326 itch; erasure
גֶּרֶז ז 326 mortise (carpentry)
גֶּרֶם ז 326 bone Lit.; basis, framework, skeleton
גֶּרֶשׂ ז 326 groats (biblical and Talmudic) [no pl.]
דֶּרֶג ז 326 scale, rank, grade, echelon
דֶּרֶךְ זו"נ 326 road, path; route; method, way
דֶּרֶן ז 326 grub, larva
וֶרֶד ז 326 rose (plant, flower)
טֶנֶא ז 326 basket, pannier, fruit basket
טֶרֶף ז 326 prey
טֶרֶשׁ ז 326 rock Lit., mostly in plural, 'admat trashim 'rocky ground'
יֶלֶד ז 326 son, boy; child, kid
כֶּבֶל ז 326 fetter, chain; cable, wire
כֶּלֶב ז 326 dog, hound
כֶּסֶף ז 326 money; silver
כֶּרֶם ז 326 vineyard; olive grove, almond grove
כֶּרֶץ ז 326 ascarid, roundworm (parasite)
לֶחֶם ז 326 bread [note: pl. constr. laHamey]
מֶלֶךְ ז 326 king
נֶתֶר ז 326 sodium carbonate [no pl.]
סֶרֶן ז 326 (military) captain; Philistine ruler/governor Bibl.
סֶרֶן ז 326 axle
פֶּלֶג ז 326 brook, rivulet, creek, tributary; part, half
פֶּלֶט ז 326 (computer) output
פֶּרֶס ז 326 vulture
צֶלֶם ז 326 image; idol
צֶמֶר ז 326 wool
קֶרֶס ז 326 hook
קֶרֶשׁ ז 326 plank, board
רֶגֶל נ 326 time, occasion; one of the three pilgrimages (biblical)
רֶחֶם ז 326 womb, uterus
שֶׁמֶן ז 326 oil
תֶּלֶם ז 326 furrow
אֶבֶן נ 327 stone
אֶגֶד ז 327 bandage; bundle, bunch Lit.
אֶדֶן ז 327 windowsill; base (for column or wall)
אֶדֶר ז 327 maple tree; acer
אֶטֶב ז 327 clothes peg, clothespin; clip N
אֶטֶם ז 327 seal, gasket
אֶלֶף ז 327 thousand
אֶפֶס ז 327 zero; nothing
אֶרֶג ז 327 weaving N Lit.; fabric, makeup Lit. [no pl.]
אֶרֶז ז 327 cedar
אֶרֶס ז 327 venom, poison
אֶשֶׁד ז 327 rapid, cascade
אֶשֶׁךְ ז 327 testis, testicle
אֶתֶר ז 327 ether [no declension, no pl.]
הֶדֶף ז 327 shock wave; thrust, impetus [no pl.]
הֶדֶק ז 327 trigger; terminal (electricity); clip, clasp
הֶלֶם ז 327 shock, trauma [no pl.]
הֵפֶךְ/הֶפֶךְ ז 327 opposite, contrary N
הֶרֶג ז 327 killing, murder, slaughter, massacre [contr. only, no pl.]
הֶרֶס ז 327 destruction [contr. only, no pl.]
חֶבֶל ז 327 rope
חֶבֶק ז 327 label wrapped around item
חֶבֶר ז 327 group; league [no pl.]
חֶדֶר ז 327 room
חֶמֶר ז 327 wine Lit. [no pl.]
חֶנֶק ז 327 strangulation, choking; asphyxia [no pl.]
חֶסֶד ז 327 kindness, benevolence; goodness, charity, grace
חֶסֶם ז 327 block, obstruction; jam (in weapon)
חֶסֶר ז 327 absence, lack; deficit, shortage [no pl.]
חֶרֶט ז 327 stylus, pen
חֶרֶס ז 327 clay, earthenware; shard, potsherd
חֶרֶק ז 327 insect
חֶרֶשׁ ז 327 secret N (also adv. 'secretly')
חֶתֶךְ/חֲתָךְ ז 327 cut N
חֶתֶף ז 327 disaster Lit.; robbery; snatching
עֶבֶד ז 327 slave
עֶכֶן ז 327 snake, ringed snake
עֶכֶס ז 327 anklet (biblical)
עֶלֶם ז 327 young, young man
עֶצֶב ז 327 sadness, sorrow, grief
עֶצֶם ז 327 thing, object; essence, core, gist
עֶצֶר ז 327 stopper, stop
עֶרֶב ז 327 evening
בַּהַט ז 328 alabaster [no declension, no pl.]
בַּחַן ז 328 watch tower Lit.-rare
בַּעַל ז 328 owner, possessor; husband; Baal (Canaanite god)
בַּעַר ז 328 ignoramus, boor Lit.; fool, idiot, dimwit (biblical)

הֶבֶל ז 337 steam, vapor; breath; foolishness, nonsense [constr. pl. havley]
חֶלֶד ז 337 universe, world Lit. [no pl.]
חֶמֶד ז 337 grace, charm, beauty, loveliness [no pl.]
הֶגֶה ר׳ הֶגָאִים ז 338 steering wheel, helm; rudder; control, leadership [pl. haga'im]
הֶגֶה ר׳ הֶגָאִים/הֲגָיִים ז 338 utterance, spoken sound; sound [pl. haga'im/hagayim]
חֵקֶר ז 339 study, research [no pl.]
חֵשֶׁק ז 339 desire [no pl.]
עֵמֶק ז 339 valley, glen, dale
עֵסֶק ז 339 business
חֵמֶת נ 340 gourd, vessel containing liquid Lit.
בֹּסֶר ז 341 unripe fruit [no pl.]
בֹּקֶר ז 341 morning
בֹּרֶג ז 341 screw N
בֹּשֶׂם ז 341 perfume; scent
גֹּדֶל ז 341 size; magnitude, enormity
גֹּדֶשׁ ז 341 abundance, surplus; congestion [no pl.]
גֹּלֶם ז 341 pupa; inchoate object; dummy
גֹּמֶד ז 341 ulna; cubit
גֹּפֶר ז 341 gopher (tree; biblical) [no pl.?]
דֹּלֶב ז 341 plane-tree
דֹּמֶן ז 341 dung, excrement Lit. [no pl.]
דֹּפֶק ז 341 pulse [no pl.]
זֹקֶן ז 341 old age [no pl.]
טֹפֶס ז 341 form, blank; copy (of book)
טֹפֶר ז 341 claw
יֹבֶשׁ ז 341 dryness; monotony, sameness [no pl.]
יֹקֶר ז 341 high price, expensiveness, costliness [no pl.]
יֹשֶׁן ז 341 oldness, age [no pl.]
יֹשֶׁר ז 341 honesty, integrity, uprightness [no pl.]
כֹּבֶד ז 341 mass, heaviness; weight; gravity [no pl.]
כֹּמֶר ז 341 priest, minister, parson
כֹּסֶף ז 341 yearning, longing Lit. [no pl.]
כֹּפֶר ז 341 ransom [no pl.]
כֹּשֶׁר ז 341 ability, fitness, capability; capacity [no pl.]
כֹּתֶל/קֹתֶל ז 341 wall; side; fat piece of meat (latter generally spelled w qof)
לֹבֶן ז 341 whiteness [no pl.]
לֹטֶם ז 341 cistus (plant)
מֹרֶךְ ז 341 weakness, cowardice Lit. [no pl.]
מֹתֶק ז 341 sweetness [no pl.]
נֹמֶךְ ז 341 shortness, lowness [no pl.]
נֹפֶךְ ז 341 touch, shade, characteristic; garnet (biblical)
נֹפֶשׁ ז 341 vacation, holiday [no pl.]
נֹפֶת ז 341 honey Lit. [no pl.]
סֹבֶךְ ז 341 thicket, lair Lit.
צֹבֶר ז 341 accumulation, heap, pile; bulk
צֹמֶת ז 341 intersection, crossroads
צֹפֶן ז 341 code, cipher
צֹרֶךְ ז 341 need; necessity; requirement
קֹבֶץ ז 341 collection, anthology; computer file
קֹדֶשׁ, ר׳ קֳדָשִׁים/קֺדָשִׁים ז 341 holiness, sanctity, sacredness, pl. kodashim
קֹטֶב ז 341 pole, magnetic pole
קֹטֶן ז 341 smallness; pinky (biblical) [no pl.]
קֹטֶר ז 341 diameter
קֹצֶר ז 341 shortness; insufficiency, deficiency [no pl.]
קֹרֶט ז 341 pinch, smidgen [no pl.]
רֹבֶד ז 341 level, layer, stratum; echelon
רֹגֶז ז 341 anger, ire, wrath
רֹגֶם ז 341 tumulus
רֹטֶב ז 341 sauce, gravy, dressing
רֹשֶׁם ז 341 impression
רֹתֶם ז 341 retama, broom (plant)
שֹׁבֶל ז 341 train (of clothing); tab (philately); trail, wake
שֹׁמֶן ז 341 fat, fatness [no pl.]
שֹׁרֶשׁ, ר׳ שֳׁרָשִׁים/שָׁרָשִׁים ז 341 root, pl. shorashim
תֹּכֶן ז 341 contents; gist, substance
תֹּמֶר/תָּמָר ז 341 palm tree
תֹּפֶת ז 341 inferno; hell [no pl.]
תֹּקֶף ז 341 validity, legality; force; power [no pl.]
תֹּרֶן ז 341 mast; flagpole
תֹּרֶף ז 341 blank part of document
תֹּרֶף ז 341 pudenda, female external genitalia [no pl.]
אֹבֶךְ ז 342 haze, haziness [no pl.]
אֹגֶן ז 342 flange
אֹדֶם ז 342 red; ruby [no pl.]
אֹהֶל ז 342 tent
אֹטֶם ז 342 sealing; sealed structure; infarction (medicine) [no pl.?]
אֹכֶל ז 342 food; dining, meal [no pl.]
אֹמֶד ז 342 estimation, assessment [no pl.]
אֹמֶץ ז 342 bravery, courage, valor [no declension, no pl.]
אֹמֶר, ר׳ אֲמָרִים, אִמְרֵי ז 342 utterance, word, saying Lit., pl. 'amarim, 'imrey
אֹנֶס ז 342 rape N; coercion
אֹסֶף ז 342 collection, assortment; anthology
אֹפֶל ז 342 darkness, blackness Lit. [no pl.]
אֹפֶן ז 342 method, mode, technique
אֹפֶק ז 342 horizon; perspective
אֹרֶז ז 342 rice [no pl.]
אֹרֶךְ ז 342 length; duration
אֹרֶן ז 342 pine
אֹשֶׁר ז 342 happiness, bliss [no pl.]
חֹדֶשׁ ז 342 month
חֹזֶק ז 342 strength, power [no pl.]
חֹטֶם ז 342 nose Lit.
חֹטֶר ז 342 shoot, twig, branch; scion, descendant, esp. of a notable family
חֹמֶד ז 342 grace, charm, beauty Lit. (also Coll. darling) [no pl.]
חֹמֶט ז 342 lizard, skink
חֹמֶר ז 342 material, substance; raw material; matter
חֹסֶן ז 342 strength, power, might Lit. [no pl.]
חֹסֶר ז 342 absence, lack [no pl.]
חֹפֶן ר׳ זוגי חָפְנַיִם ז 342 handful, pl. dual Hofnayim
חֹפֶשׁ ז 342 freedom, liberty [no poss. clitics?]
חֹצֶן ז 342 lap of garment (biblical)
חֹקֶן ז 342 enema
חֹרֶב ז 342 dryness, aridity, heat Lit. [no pl.]
חֹרֶף ז 342 winter
חֹרֶשׁ ז 342 thicket, grove
חֹשֶׁךְ ז 342 darkness; evil, forces of darkness [no pl.]
חֹשֶׁן ז 342 breastplate (of High Priest) [no pl.]
עֹבֶשׁ ז 342 mold; mildew [no pl.]
עֹגֶן ז 342 anchor
עֹדֶף ז 342 change; surplus, excess, extra
עֹלֶשׁ ז 342 chicory, endive
עֹמֶס ז 342 load, burden [no pl.]
עֹמֶק ז 342 depth, `omko/`umko, `omkey/`umkey
עֹמֶר ז 342 sheaf, bundle of grain (biblical)
עֹנֶג ז 342 pleasure [no pl.]
עֹנֶשׁ ז 342 punishment
עֹפֶל ז 342 fortified hill (biblical)
עֹפֶר ז 342 fawn
עֹצֶר ז 342 curfew [no pl.]
עֹקֶץ ז 342 sting N, `oktso/`uktso, `oktsey/`uktsey
עֹרֶף ז 342 nape; home front; (military) rear

כּוֹנָן ז 366 disk drive (computers); stand, rack
כּוֹפָח ז 366 small cooking stove (Talmudic)
כּוֹתָר ז 366 title (of book, etc.)
לוֹלָב ז 366 bolt
עוֹלָל ז 366 babe, suckling infant, toddler Lit.
צוֹפָר ז 366 siren
קוֹלָב ז 366 hanger; rack
קוֹלָר ז 366 collar
שׁוֹבָב ז 366 mischievous; naughty
שׁוֹבָךְ ז 366 dovecote
שׁוֹשָׁן ז 366 lily
תּוֹלָע ז 366 red, scarlet (biblical) [no pl.]
תּוֹתָב ז 366 prosthetic, artificial Adj; prosthetic implant; bushing
תּוֹתָח ז 366 cannon (weaponry)
עוֹלָם ז 367 world; eternity
גּוֹרָל ז 368 fate; casting lots
חוֹתָל ז 368 wrapper, envelope; sack; container (Talmudic)
חוֹתָם ז 368 seal, impression; influence, effect; status, validity
שׁוֹפָר ז 368 shofar, ram's horn; the voice of
תּוֹבָר ז 368 belt loop; rosette
דּוֹנַג ז 369 beeswax; ear wax [no pl.]
כּוֹבַע ז 369 hat, cap; helmet (biblical)
מוֹרַג, ר' מוֹרִגִּים ז 369 ancient threshing implement [pl. morigim, morigey]
קוֹבַע ז 369 helmet, steel helmet (archaic)
דּוּכָן ז 370 stand, stall; dais, platform, podium; lectern, pulpit
כּוּמָז ז 370 female ornament (biblical)
לוּלָב ז 370 lulav, ceremonial palm frond
נוּפָר ז 370 water lily
סוּדָר ז 370 sweater Rare; headkerchief, scarf, shawl
עוּגָב ז 370 pipe organ
שׁוּמָן ז 370 fat [no /a/ reduction in pl. constr., shumaney, prob. because the original form was shuman w kubuts and a dagesh in the m]
דּוּחָל ז 371 chat (bird)
שׁוּעָל ז 371 fox
יוּבַל ז 372 river, tributary, creek
סוּגַר ז 373 cage
אֵיבָר ז 374 limb, organ; member (syntax)
אֵיתָן ז 374 strong, solid
בֵּיבָר ז 374 zoo, menagerie Lit.

הֵיכָל ר' הֵיכָלִים/לוֹת ז 374 palace; temple [plural: heykhalim/heykhalot]
פֵּיגָם ז 374 common rue (plant)
קֵיסָם ז 374 sliver; toothpick
שֵׁיזָף ז 374 jujube (tree, fruit)
כֵּילָף ז 375 hatchet (biblical)
חָרוּב ז 376 carob
שָׁבוּעַ ז 377 week
אַבּוּב ז 378 oboe
אַלּוּף ז 378 champion, record holder; major-general
בַּלּוּט ז 378 acorn
דַּבּוּר ז 378 hornet Coll.
חַבּוּשׁ ז 378 quince
חַלּוּק ז 378 smooth stone, pebble
חַמּוּק ז 378 curve (of body)
חַנּוּן ז 378 merciful, compassionate
טַבּוּר ז 378 navel, belly button, umbilicus; center, hub
יַתּוּךְ ז 378 tongs (Talmudic)
יַתּוּשׁ ז 378 mosquito
כַּדּוּר ז 378 ball, sphere; pill; bullet
מַבּוּל ז 378 flood, deluge, downpour
נַטּוּף ז 378 stalactite
סַמּוּר ז 378 weasel
עַכּוּז ז 378 buttocks, posterior
עַמּוּד ז 378 post, pole, pillar, column; lectern, pulpit
עַתּוּד ז 378 billy-goat (biblical)
שַׁכּוּל ז 378 bereaved
שַׁפּוּד ז 378 skewer; pin
תַּנּוּר ז 378 oven, stove
תַּפּוּד ז 378 potato
תַּפּוּז ז 378 orange
אַשּׁוּחַ ז 379 fir (tree)
מַדּוּחַ ז 379 temptation, seduction Lit.
מַלּוּחַ ז 379 orache (plant)
תַּפּוּחַ ז 379 apple; ball, knob
אַלּוֹן ז 380 oak (tree)
כַּמּוֹן ז 380 cumin (plant, spice)
רַתּוֹק ז 380 chain, cable
חַלּוֹן ז 381 window
גִּבּוֹר ז 382 hero; central figure, protagonist
גִּיּוֹר ז 382 convert to Judaism
יִלּוֹד ז 382 newborn
כִּיּוֹר ז 382 sink; basin
נִצּוֹל ז 382 survivor (of crash, tragedy, war)
צִפּוֹר נ 382 bird [plural also spelled w Hataf-kamats]
קִפּוֹד ז 382 hedgehog
רִמּוֹן ז 382 pomegranate; grenade
שִׁכּוֹר ז 382 drunk, drunkard
שִׁפּוֹן/שִׁיפּוֹן ז 382 rye [no pl.]
כִּנּוֹר ז 383 violin; stringed musical instrument (biblical)
צִנּוֹר ז 383 pipe, tube, channel

נִמּוֹל ז 384 circumcised
נִשּׁוֹם ז 384 assessee, tax-payer
מִלּוֹן ז 385 dictionary; lexicon; glossary
עִתּוֹן ז 385 newspaper; periodical
צִדּוֹן ז 385 broadside of ship
רִבּוֹן ז 385 ruler, overlord; sovereign; master [no possessive pronouns?]
אֵזוֹב ז 386 hyssop
אֵזוֹר ז 386 zone, region; belt
אֵפוֹד ז 386 vest of Jewish high priest; short coat (biblical); bullet-proof vest
דִּישׁוֹן ז 387 antelope, addax
טִירוֹן ז 387 recruit (military); beginner, greenhorn
כִּידוֹד ז 387 spark (biblical)
כִּידוֹן ז 387 spear; bayonet; javelin
כִּישׁוֹר ז 387 spindle, distaff
לִימוֹן ז 387 lemon
פִּיתוֹם ז 387 ventriloquist
צִינוֹק ז 387 solitary confinement
קִיטוֹר ז 387 steam; smoke, column of smoke [no pl.]
קִינוֹף ז 387 bed canopy frame (for mosquito netting)
קִיסוֹס ז 387 ivy (plant)
קִיפוֹן ז 387 mullet (fish)
קִיפוֹף ז 387 prosimian
שִׁיחוֹר/שְׁחוֹר ז 387 coal (Talmudic) [no pl.]
שִׁיפוֹן ז 387 rye [coll. shipon] [no pl.]
תִּירוֹשׁ ז 387 grape juice, must [no pl.]
וִילוֹן ז 388 curtain, drape, blind, shade ; soft palate
נִיצוֹץ ז 388 spark; flash; glimmer; talent, ability
סִילוֹן/סִלּוֹן ז 388 stream; outburst; jet
קִיטוֹן, ר' קִיטוֹנִיּוֹת ז 388 small bedchamber Lit. [pl. kitoniyot]
קִיתוֹן ז 388 ewer, large jar (Talmudic)
מִישׁוֹר ז 389 plain, plateau; area, level, field; plane (geometry)
תִּינוֹק ז 390 baby
אֵבוּס ז 391 stall, manger, feeding trough
אֵמוּן ז 392 faith, confidence, trust
בְּכוֹר ז 393 firstborn
בְּרוֹךְ ז 393 failure, disaster, foul-up Sl.
בְּרוֹשׁ ז 393 cypress
דְּרוֹר ז 393 freedom, liberty Lit. [no declension, no pl.]
דְּרוֹר ז 393 sparrow
טְחוֹל ז 393 spleen

גְּזִיר ז 405 faggot, piece of wood
גְּלִיד ז 405 icicle
גְּלִיף ז 405 glyph; carved figure
גְּרִיס ז 405 portion of a grain of wheat or other product; groats, grits
דְּבִיר ז 405 Holy of Holies (in the Temple); inner sanctum
וְרִיד ז 405 vein
זְבִיל ז 405 cylindrical container for transporting rockets, bombs etc.
טְרִיז ז 405 wedge
יְצִיר ז 405 creature, product Lit.
יְרִיד/יָרִיד ז 405 fair, exhibition, market
יְתִיב ז 405 biblical cantillation symbol [no declension, no pl.?]
כְּבִיר ז 405 thick fabric; woolen or fur blanket Lit.
כְּבִישׁ ז 405 roadway, paved road
כְּלִיב ז 405 staple
כְּלִיל ז 405 crown, garland; total, perfect (from constr. of kalil) Coll. [no pl.]
כְּסִיל ז 405 fool, idiot, imbecile, moron Lit.
כְּפִיר ז 405 young lion Lit.
כְּתִיב ז 405 spelling [no pl.]
לְחִיץ ז 405 button, switch
מְחִיר ז 405 price
מְטִיל ז 405 ingot, bar
מְעִיל ז 405 coat, cloak
מְרִיא ז 405 fatling; buffalo??? Bibl.
נְגִיף ז 405 virus
נְחִיל ז 405 swarm (of insects); group of animals
נְטִיף ז 405 stalactite
נְצִיב ז 405 governor, commissioner; pillar; pile, support
נְצִיץ ז 405 mica
נְקִיק ז 405 crevice, cranny
נְשִׁיק ז 405 light kiss Lit.
סְגִיר ז 405 shackle
סְלִיל ז 405 spool, reel, coil
סְלִיק ז 405 hiding place (esp. for weapons)
סְנִיף ז 405 branch (in banking, commerce)
סְעִיף ז 405 paragraph; clause (in law)
פְּנִים ז 405 inside, interior [no pl.]
פְּסִיג ז 405 cotyledon (botany)
פְּסִיס ז 405 lath, molding (carpentry)
פְּסִיק ז 405 comma; something small, insignificant Coll.
פְּעִים ז 405 pip, short high-pitched sound
פְּרִיט ז 405 item, object
פְּתִיל ז 405 wick; fuse (explosives)

צְלִיל ז 405 sound, tone; resonance
צְמִיג ז 405 tire (of a vehicle)
צְנִים ז 405 rusk
צְנִין ז 405 thorn, sting Lit.
צְנִיר ז 405 notch (geology)
צְרִיף ז 405 shed, shack
צְרִיר ז 405 dissonance
קְלִיד ז 405 key (of piano, organ)
קְפִיץ ז 405 spring, coil
רְדִיד ז 405 scarf, shawl Lit.
רְדִיד ז 405 sheet (of dough)
רְכִיב ז 405 component
רְסִיס ז 405 shard, sliver; shrapnel; shred, trace
רְצִיף ז 405 platform (at train/bus station), quay
רְקִיק ז 405 cookie, biscuit Lit.
שְׁבִיב ז 405 spark, flash; scrap, fragment
שְׁבִיל ז 405 path, trail
שְׁבִיס/שָׁבִיס ז 405 coif
שְׁזִיף ז 405 plum
שְׁזִיר ז 405 ply
שְׁחִין ז 405 boils (skin disease) [no pl.]
שְׁלִיל ז 405 fetus
שְׁלִיף ז 405 long bag placed on load-carrying animal
שְׁלִישׁ ז 405 third; trimester
שְׁקִיל ז 405 equivalent N
שְׁרִיר ז 405 muscle
שְׁתִיל/שָׁתִיל ז 405 seedling, young plant
תְּלִישׁ ז 405 detachable (coupon, stub)
תְּרִיס ז 405 shield, cover
תְּרִיס ז 405 shutter, blind
אֲבִיר/אַבִּיר ז 406 knight, nobleman; hero (biblical); warhorse (biblical)
אֱוִיל ז 406 fool, stupid person
אֲוִיר ז 406 air [no pl.]
אֱלִיל ז 406 idol; deity
הֲלִיךְ ז 406 proceeding (law), procedure; step
חֲזִיז ז 406 lightening (biblical); firecracker
חֲזִיר ז 406 pig
חֲטִיף ז 406 snack
חֲלִיף ז 406 alternative, substitute
חֲפִיר ז 406 moat; ditch
חֲרִיר ז 406 hole, aperture
חֲשִׂיף ז 406 small flock (biblical)
חֲשִׁישׁ ז 406 hashish [no pl.]
עֲוִיל ז 406 evil person, wrongdoer (biblical)
עֲטִיף ז 406 perianth (botany)
עֲלִיל ז 406 deed; fact [no pl.]
עֲצִיץ ז 406 flowerpot, planter
בְּקִיעַ ז 407 crack, breach, cleft
בְּרִיחַ ז 407 bolt, bar (of gate); dead bolt; bolt (of gun)

יְגִיעַ ז 407 hard work, travail, exertion Lit.
צְרִיחַ ז 407 tower, turret, castle; rook (chess)
רְבִיעַ ז 407 quarter Lit.; quarter of circle
נְחִיר ז 408 nostril
אַבְגָּר ז 409 agrimony (plant)
אַבְזָם ז 409 buckle (of belt)
אַבְזָר ז 409 accessory
אַבְרָשׁ ז 409 heather (plant)
אַכְזָר ז 409 cruel person, cruel Adj [declension only as Adj.]
אַלְמָן ז 409 widower
אַמְבָּט ז 409 bath (tub)
אַמְבָּר ז 409 granary (Talmudic)
אַפְסָר ז 409 halter
אַרְגָּז ז 409 crate, box, case
אַרְנָב ז 409 hare (male)
אַרְנָק ז 409 pocketbook, handbag, wallet
בַּלְדָּר ז 409 courier, messenger
בַּרְדָּס ז 409 hood, cowl
בַּרְוָז ז 409 duck N
בַּרְחָשׁ ז 409 mite
בַּרְנָשׁ ז 409 person; guy, chap, bloke
דַּרְבָּן ז 409 porcupine
דַּרְגָּשׁ ז 409 bench, board
דַּרְדָּס ז 409 sandal, slipper Lit.
זַחְלָ"ם = זַחֲלִי לְמֶחְצָה ז 409 half-track
חַרְדָּל ז 409 mustard plant [no pl.]
טַפְסָר ז 409 fireman officer; dignitary, official Lit.; angel (in liturgical poetry)
מַדְחָ"ן = מַד חֲנִיָּה ז 409 parking meter
מַזְלָט = מָטוֹס זָעִיר לְלֹא טַיָּס ז 409 drone
מַנְכָּ"ל = מְנַהֵל כְּלָלִי ז 409 genreral manager
סַחְלָב/שַׁחְלָב ז 409 orchid
סַנְדָּל ז 409 sandal
סַנְדָּק ז 409 godfather
סַפְסָל ז 409 bench
סַפְסָר ז 409 profiteer, ”speculator, ”scalper
סַרְבָּל ז 409 overall; coverall
סַרְעָף/שַׂרְעָף ז 409 (passing) thought
עַכְבָּר ז 409 mouse
עַרְבָּל ז 409 frequency mixer; cement mixer (rare); whirlpool
עַרְדָּל ז 409 overshoe
עַרְסָל ז 409 hammock
עַרְפָּד ז 409 vampire bat; vampire
עַרְצָב ז 409 mole cricket
פַּכְסָם ז 409 rusk, cracker, toast Lit.
פַּרְוָר/פַּרְבָּר ז 409 suburb
פַּרְנָס ז 409 community leader, community elder

catheter 409 צַנְתָּר ז
pencil case 409 קַלְמָר ז
small cupboard, chest Lit. 409 קַמְטָר ז
ratchet; bell (Talmudic) 409 קַרְקָשׁ ז
kingfisher 409 שַׁלְדָּג ז
night jar (bird of prey) 409 תַּחְמָס ז
large kitchen spoon 409 תַּרְוָד ז
seasonal (only for stream, river) [no declension, no pl.] 410 אַכְזָב ז
potash [no pl.] 410 אַשְׁלָג ז
vent, ventilation opening 411 אַוְרָר ז
draftsman 411 סַרְטָט/שַׂרְטָט ז
darkness; grave; naked-bellied tomb bat 412 אַשְׁמָן ז
stone, pit, pip (of fruit) 412 חַרְצָן ז
cardinal 412 חַשְׁמָן ז
scorpion; thorn (biblical) 412 עַקְרָב ז
tranquil; complacent 413 שַׁאֲנָן ז
archive N 414 גַּנְזָךְ ז
young child 414 דַּרְדַּק ז
bacterium 414 חַיְדַּק ז
aizoon (plant) 414 חַיְעַד ז
electricity; electric current; amber (biblical) [no pl.] 414 חַשְׁמַל ז
celery [no pl.] 414 כַּרְפַּס ז
food; delicacy Lit. 414 פַּתְבַּג ז
soldier, trooper (derog.) Lit. 414 קַלְגַּס ז
rhinoceros 414 קַרְנַף ז
mint 415 נַעֲנַע נ
earth, soil; ground, land; floor, bed (of sea, river) 415 קַרְקַע נ
wheel 416 גַּלְגַּל ז
sprig, young shoot, tendril, thin branch Lit. 416 זַלְזַל ז
buzzer 416 זַמְזַם ז
connecting rod 416 טַלְטַל ז
pancreas 416 לַבְלַב ז
limonium 416 עַדְעַד ז
leaflet (botany) 416 עַלְעַל ז
dimmer, rheostat 416 עַמְעַם ז
juniper 416 עַרְעַר ז
aperture adjuster (photography) 416 צַמְצַם ז
clog 416 קַבְקַב ז
jar, jug, flask 416 קַנְקַן ז
tattoo 416 קַעֲקַע/קַעְקַע ז
fish scale; dandruff 416 קַשְׂקַשׂ ז
hawk-moth, sphinx moth 416 רַפְרַף ז
curl (of hair) 416 תַּלְתַּל ז
thistle 417 דַּרְדַּר ז
butterfly 417 פַּרְפַּר ז
eyelid 418 עַפְעַף ז
sash, girdle 419 אַבְנֵט ז
Yeshiva student; young man 419 אַבְרֵךְ ז
athlete 419 אַתְלֵט ז
monument; memorial 419 גַּלְעֵד ז
bastard 419 מַמְזֵר ז
chin 419 סַנְטֵר ז
ruler, yardstick 419 סַרְגֵּל ז
pullover 419 פַּקְרֵס ז
orchard 419 פַּרְדֵּס ז
men's wig, toupee 419 קַפְלֵט ז
yard (surrounded by a fence) Lit. 419 קַרְפֵּף/קַרְפִּיף ז
cress (botany) 420 גַּרְגֵּר ז
frame, ledge, rim, edging strip, mantlepiece 421 לַזְבֵּז ז
iron 422 בַּרְזֶל ז
axe, hatchet 422 גַּרְזֶן ז
fertile agricultural area (biblical) [no pl.] 422 כַּרְמֶל ז
toasted young wheat (biblical) [no pl.] 422 כַּרְמֶל ז
sandalwood 423 אַלְגֹּם ז
coral; sandalwood 423 אַלְמֹג/אַלְגֹּם ז
gallows 423 גַּרְדֹּם (גַּרְדּוֹם) ז
ancient Egyptian priest or magician 423 חַרְטֹם ז
jacinth, ruby Bibl. 423 כַּדְכֹּד ז
border, edge; cornice; rim (architecture) 423 כַּרְכֹּב ז
crocus; saffron 423 כַּרְכֹּם ז
milling/metal cutting machine 423 כַּרְסֹם ז
thermometer 423 מַדְחֹם ז
ankle 424 קַרְסֹל ז
axe, hatchet; pickaxe 425 קַרְדֹּם ז
dispatch 426 אֶשְׁגָּר ז
challenge 426 אֶתְגָּר ז
citizen; civilian 427 אֶזְרָח ז
pistol, handgun; red precious stone Bibl. 427 אֶקְדָּח ז
small window, hatch 428 אֶשְׁנָב ז
pause; a pause cantillation mark 428 אֶתְנָח ז
prostitute's fee 428 אֶתְנָן ז
ivory 428 שֶׁנְהָב ז
center, middle 429 אֶמְצַע ז
finger; index finger 430 אֶצְבַּע נ
hazelnut tree/bush 431 אִלְסָר ז
casserole, stew-pot 431 אִלְפָּס ז
treasurer 431 גִּזְבָּר ז
notebook Lit.-rare 431 דִּפְתָּר ז
bamboo 431 חִזְרָן ז
fireman 431 טִפְסָר/טַפְסָר ז
officer; official; dignitary Lit.; angel (in liturgical poetry)
oil (especially high quality) Bibl. [no pl.] 431 יִצְהָר ז
bobbin housing (of sawing machine) 431 כִּרְכָּר ז
zigzag 431 סִכְסָךְ ז
nettle 431 סִרְפָּד ז
clapper, tongue of bell; uvula 431 עִנְבָּל ז
amber [no pl.] 431 עִנְבָּר ז
notepad, small notebook; account book; registry 431 פִּנְקָס ז
whippersnapper, street urchin 431 פִּרְחָח ז
wicket, small/narrow gate or door 431 פִּשְׁפָּשׁ ז
idiom, proverb, saying 431 פִּתְגָּם ז
ancient cymbals-like instrument 431 צִלְצָל ז
harpoon, fishing spear 431 צִלְצָל ז
circus 431 קִרְקָס ז
tree mentioned in the bible whose identity is unclear 431 תִּדְהָר ז
crocodile 431 תִּמְסָח ז
chisel; scalpel 432 אִזְמֵל ז
artichoke 432 קִנְרֵס ז
scythe 433 חֶרְמֵשׁ ז
434 בָּטְנָה/בָּטְנָה (בֹּטֶן) ז pistachio; peanut Coll. (alt. boten)
ebony (tree) [no decl., pl. only?] 434 הָבְנֶה ז
unfortunate, wretched, miserable 435 אֻמְלָל ז
eriobolus (plant, rose family) 435 חֻזְרָר ז
artichoke 435 חֻרְשָׁף ז
a type of citrus, used for grafting and its fruit for jam 435 חֻשְׁחָשׁ ז
coriander 435 כֻּסְבָּר ז
eolianite (a type of sandstone) [no declension, no pl.] 435 כֻּרְכָּר ז
crab apple 435 עֻזְרָד/עֻזְרָר ז
stuffed animal 435 פֻּחְלָץ ז
inn, hostel, motel 435 פֻּנְדָּק ז
prankster; mischief 435 קֻנְדָּס ז
sledgehammer, mallet 435 קֻרְנָס ז
sock Lit. 436 פֻּזְמָק ז
table 436 שֻׁלְחָן ז
nascent fruit [no pl.] 437 סְמָדַר ז
a type of locust Bibl. 437 צְלָצַל ז
cricket 437 צְרָצַר ז
vase 438 אֲגַרְטָל ז
impresario, agent 438 אֲמַרְגָּן ז
administrator 438 אֲמַרְכָּל ז
pepper 439 פִּלְפֵּל ז
bug, cimex; flea 439 פִּשְׁפֵּשׁ ז
spadix (botany) 440 אֶשְׁבּוֹל ז
citron, etrog 440 אֶתְרוֹג ז
hooligan, thug, ruffian 440 בִּרְיוֹן ז
stalk, stem 440 גִּבְעוֹל ז
multi-layered stalk/stem 440 גִּזְעוֹל ז
treasury (Talmudic) [no declension, no pl.] 440 טִמְיוֹן ז
dagger 441 פִּגְיוֹן ז
bag, sack Lit. 441 צִקְלוֹן ז

אֶבְיוֹן ז 442 pauper Lit.
אֶגְרוֹף ז 442 fist; punch
אֶפְרוֹחַ ז 443 chick
אֶקְדּוֹחַ ז 443 pistol, handgun (variant of 'ekdaH)
אַלְבּוֹם ז 444 album
אַנְקוֹל ז 444 hook
אַנְקוֹר ז 444 sparrow
אַרְכּוֹף ז 444 stapes, stirrup
דַּחְפּוֹר ז 444 bulldozer
דַּלְפּוֹן ז 444 pauper Coll.
זַרְקוֹר ז 444 spotlight, floodlight
חַרְגּוֹל ז 444 grasshopper
חַרְדּוֹן ז 444 starred agama lizard
חַרְטוֹם ז 444 bow (of boat), nose (of vehicle, ship); beak, nose
יַרְאוֹר ז 444 spotlight trainer/projector
כַּפְתּוֹר ז 444 button; switch
מַדְאוֹר ז 444 light meter
נַהֲלוֹל ז 444 thorn (biblical)
נַחְשׁוֹל ז 444 breaker, large wave
נַחְתּוֹם ז 444 baker Lit.
סַבְיוֹן ז 444 dandelion
עַלְעוֹל ז 444 storm; whirlwind Lit.
פַּסְקוֹל ז 444 soundtrack
פַּרְגּוֹד ז 444 screen, divider
פַּרְגּוֹל ז 444 whip, lash Lit.
פַּרְעוֹשׁ ז 444 flea
רַמְזוֹר ז 444 traffic light
רַמְקוֹל ז 444 loudspeaker
שַׁסְתּוֹם ז 444 valve
תַּרְכּוֹס ז 444 chest, trunk, large suitcase Lit.
יַהֲלוֹם ז 445 diamond
אַרְמוֹן ז 446 palace [in Bibl. 'armenot, but today reg.]
הַרְמוֹן ז 446 harem
אַלְחוּט ז 447 wireless N [no pl.]
אַלְחוּשׁ ז 447 Anesthesia
גַּלְמוּד ז 447 lonesome, lonely
זַרְנוּק ז 447 hose, nozzle
טַנְבּוּר ז 447 side drum
יַבְחוּשׁ ז 447 gnat, midge; a type of mosquito
יַזְנוּב ז 447 rat-tailed bat
יַחְמוּר ז 447 fallow deer
יַחְנוּק ז 447 cistanche (parasitic desert plant)
יַלְקוּט ז 447 bag; collection
יַנְבּוּט ז 447 prosopis (plant)
יַנְשׁוּף ז 447 owl
יַסְעוּר ז 447 petrel, puffin
יַפְרוּק ז 447 glasswort (plant)
יַרְבּוּז ז 447 amaranth (plant)
יַרְעוּד ז 447 bustard (a large crane-like bird)
נַסְיוּב ז 447 serum, blood serum
נַפְתּוּל ז 447 curve N, bend N
נַשְׁדּוּר ז 447 ammonia water [no declension, no pl.]
עַכְשׁוּב ז 447 solifuge, sun spider
עַרְקוּב ז 447 knee of an animal (Talmudic)
פַּלְצוּר ז 447 lasso
פַּרְצוּף ז 447 face, facial expression
שַׁלְחוּף ז 447 vesicle
שַׁרְתּוּעַ ז 448 strut
בַּזְבּוּז ז 449 serin (bird)
בַּקְבּוּק ז 449 bottle
בַּרְבּוּר ז 449 swan
חַלְחוּל ז 449 percolator
חַסְחוּס/סְחוּס ז 449 cartilage
סַרְסוּר ז 449 pimp, pander; broker
צַרְצוּר ז 449 a clay jug containing water or wine (Talmudic)
שַׁרְשׁוּר ז 449 tapeworm
בַּטְנוּן ז 450 double bass, contrabass
גַּבְלוּל ז 450 lump (of dough, mud) Talmudic
גַּבְנוּן ז 450 hunchback, hunch, hump; knoll, hillock
גַּבְשׁוּשׁ ז 450 bump, lump, protuberance
גַּוְנוּן ז 450 shading, variation
גַּפְרוּר ז 450 match (for lighting flame)
דַּבְלוּל ז 450 frayed thread ends, hair ends
לַבְנוּן ז 450 bleak (fish)
לַחְשׁוּשׁ ז 450 whisper, murmur
נַכְלוּל ז 450 deception, white lie Lit.
סַפְלוּל ז 450 small cup; cupule (botany)
קַמְטוּט ז 450 tiny wrinkle
קַמְצוּץ ז 450 pinch, smidgen
רַחְשׁוּשׁ/רַחֲשׁוּשׁ ז 450 whisper, silent murmur; rustle
שַׁבְלוּל ז 450 snail; cochlea
שַׁחְרוּר/שַׁחֲרוּר ז 450 merle, blackbird
תַּמְרוּר ז 450 road sign, traffic sign
זַאֲטוּט ז 451 infant, tiny child, toddler
לַהֲטוּט ז 451 juggling trick; magic trick, sleight of hand
פַּעֲלוּל ז 451 effect (in film, radio etc.)
אַקְלִים ז 452 climate
גַּלְעִין ז 452 pit, kernel, stone (of fruit)
גַּרְעִין ז 452 seed, kernel; nucleus; grain
זַרְזִיף ז 452 drizzle
זַרְנִיךְ ז 452 arsenic (archaic) [no pl.]
חַמְשִׁיר ז 452 limerick
יַסְמִין ז 452 jasmine
כַּרְטִיס ז 452 ticket; card
נַרְקִיס ז 452 daffodil (plant)
נַרְתִּיק ז 452 pouch, holster; vagina
עַרְפִּיחַ (ג״ג) ז 452 smog [no pl.]
שַׁרְבִיט ז 452 scepter; wand; baton
תַּבְלִין ז 452 spice
גַּרְגִּיר ז 453 grain; crumb, tiny particle
זַרְזִיר ז 453 starling (bird)
שַׁרְשִׁיר ז 453 teal (small duck)
דַּחְלִיל ז 454 scarecrow
זַחְלִיל ז 454 stair climbing aid attached to a wheelchair; caterpillar track
חַכְלִיל ז 454 red Lit. (in BH only adj., Hakhlili)
חַמְצִיץ ז 454 oxalis, wood sorrel (plant)
כַּפְרִיר ז 454 light frost
לַבְנִין ז 454 cabbage butterfly
סַגְרִיר ז 454 heavy rain
עַבְטִיט ז 454 thick mud Lit. [no pl.]
צַפְרִיר ז 454 zephyr (flowery); pleasant morning breeze or light rays
קַרְפִּיף ז 454 yard (surrounded by a fence) Lit.
קַשְׁרִיר ז 454 nodule
שַׁבְרִיר ז 454 shred, trace; fraction
שַׁגְרִיר ז 454 ambassador; delegate, representative
שַׁפְרִיר ז 454 canopy Lit.-rare
תַּכְסִיס/טַכְסִיס ז 454 trick, tactics
בְּצַלְצוּל ז 455 bulbil, small bulb, small onion, shallot
חֲלַבְלוּב ז 456 wolf's milk, spurge (plant)
חֲתַלְתּוּל ז 456 kitten
חֲזַרְזִיר ז 457 piglet
בְּהַרְהַר ז 458 slightly pale
בְּצַלְצַל ז 458 small onion, pickling onion
גְּבַרְבַּר/גְּבַרְבַר ז 458 young person trying to act "grown up" (Coll.)
וְרַדְרַד ז 458 pinkish
זְהַבְהַב ז 458 golden, golden-brown
זְנַבְנַב ז 458 small tail
זְעַרְעַר ז 458 very tiny
זְקַנְקַן ז 458 small beard
יְרַקְרַק ז 458 greenish
כְּחַלְחַל ז 458 bluish
כְּלַבְלַב ז 458 puppy
כְּתַמְתַּם ז 458 orangish, yellow-orange
כְּתַמְתַּם ז 458 small spot
לְבַנְבַּן ז 458 whitish
מְתַקְתַּק ז 458 sweetish
סְגַלְגַּל ז 458 mauve, lavender, purplish
סְגַלְגַּל ז 458 oval, elliptical
סְחַרְחַר ז 458 excited, agitated Lit.; dizzy
סְמַרְמַר ז 458 shuddering, quivering, trembling Lit.

dance 478 מָחוֹל ז
hotel, inn 478 מָלוֹן ז
residence; day care center; dorm 478 מָעוֹן ז
place; space; spot, position; seat 478 מָקוֹם ז
source, origin; spring 478 מָקוֹר ז
mortar; canister launcher 479 מְדוֹכָה נ
machine; mechanism Coll. 479 מְכוֹנָה נ
homeland, native land 479 מְכוֹרָה נ
light fixture; lamp 479 מְנוֹרָה נ
residence Lit.-rare 479 מְעוֹנָה נ
nothing, anything Lit. [no pl.] 480 מְאוּמָה נ
den, lair 480 מְאוּרָה נ
embarrassment; confusion 480 מְבוּכָה נ
lid, plug, cork, stopper 480 מְגוּפָה נ
(botany) loculus ; (shipping) compartment; (BH) granary 480 מְגוּרָה נ
bonfire 480 מְדוּרָה נ
commotion; riot, disturbance 480 מְהוּמָה נ
mezuzah (small scroll in box on doorpost); doorpost 480 מְזוּזָה נ
pair of compasses (geometry) 480 מְחוּגָה נ
shipping container 480 מְכוּלָה נ
kennel, doghouse; lodge (BH) 480 מְלוּנָה נ
rest N 480 מְנוּחָה נ
flight, escape, retreat 480 מְנוּסָה נ
fortress, stronghold 480 מְצוּדָה נ
depth, deep water 480 מְצוּלָה נ
trouble, distress 480 מְצוּקָה נ
running 480 מְרוּצָה נ
mischief, mischievousness 480 מְשׁוּבָה נ
hedgerow Lit.; hurdle (sports) 480 מְשׂוּכָה נ
scouring pad 480 מְשׁוּפָה נ
measuring cup 480 מְשׂוּרָה נ
state 481 מְדִינָה נ
preparatory program 481 מְכִינָה נ
flowery phrase, poetic phrase 481 מְלִיצָה נ
hand-held fan 481 מְנִיפָה נ
dispute, argument 481 מְרִיבָה נ
wheelbarrow 481 מְרִיצָה נ
mission, assignment, task 481 מְשִׂימָה נ
shipyard 482 מִבְדּוֹק ז
range, diapason (music; rare) 482 מִגְבּוֹל ז
(electricity) high tension wire pylon 482 מִגְדּוֹל ז

slope, incline, gradient 482 מִדְרוֹן ז
psalm; song, chorus Lit. 482 מִזְמוֹר ז
snack bar, kiosk; buffet 482 מִזְנוֹן ז
mattress Coll., normative form mizran 482 מִזְרוֹן/מִזְרָן ז
paintbrush, brush 482 מִכְחוֹל ז
whole; entirety 482 מִכְלוֹל ז
obstacle, impediment 482 מִכְשׁוֹל ז
hiding place; refuge 482 מִסְתּוֹר ז
stockpile, accumulation, cache 482 מִצְבּוֹר ז
tone (music), sound quality 482 מִצְלוֹל ז
mountain viewpoint, bird's eye view 482 מִצְפּוֹר ז
consignment 482 מִשְׁגּוֹר ז
path, pass, trail Lit. 482 מִשְׁעוֹל ז
escarpment 482 מִתְלוֹל ז
hybrid 483 מִכְלוֹא ז
animal feed [no pl.] 483 מִסְפּוֹא ז
electric shocker 484 מַהֲלוֹם ז
mental block, inhibition; jam (in weapon); brakes 484 מַעֲצוֹר ז
rolling pin 484 מַעֲרוֹךְ ז
incarceration (military) [no pl.] 485 מַחְבּוֹשׁ ז
cycle; cycled program; volume of trade; menstrual period; Jewish holiday prayer book 485 מַחְזוֹר ז
barrier; obstacle; muzzle 485 מַחְסוֹם ז
shortage, lack; poverty 485 מַחְסוֹר ז
cleavage 485 מַחְשׂוֹף ז
hiding place, cache 486 מַחְבּוֹא ז
delivery; shipment 487 מִשְׁלוֹחַ ז
buried treasure 488 מַטְמוֹן ז
pain, grief, suffering 488 מַכְאוֹב ז
shoulder pad 488 מַכְתּוֹף ז
last rain at the end of the rainy season 488 מַלְקוֹשׁ ז
supermarket 488 מַרְכּוֹל ז
fuze (fuse) (in (weaponry) 488 מַרְעוֹם ז
pledge, collateral 488 מַשְׁכּוֹן ז
lintel; doorpost 488 מַשְׁקוֹף ז
recipe 488 מַתְכּוֹן ז
rest, peace, relaxation 489 מַרְגּוֹעַ ז
monitor 489 מַשְׁגּוֹחַ ז
retractable tape measure 490 מַגְלוֹל ז
clothing, garment 490 מַלְבּוּשׁ ז
lock N 490 מַנְעוּל ז
path, track, course; lane; runway; orbit 490 מַסְלוּל ז
conscience 490 מַצְפּוּן ז

disappointing, depressing; disappointed, depressed Sl. 491 מַבְאוּס ז
happy, satisfied 491 מַבְסוּט ז
great, superb Sl. 491 מַגְנוּב ז
disgusting Sl. 491 מַגְעוּל ז
excited by, interested in, turned on by, enamored of Sl. 491 מַדְלוּק ז
miserable, wretched Sl. 491 מַדְרוּב ז
stupid Sl. 491 מַהְבּוּל ז
neglected; ugly Sl. 491 מַחְלוּא/מַחְלוּעַ ז
hollow-headed Sl. 491 מַחְלוּל(ה) ז
ugly; shriveled Sl. 491 מַחְנוּט(ה) ז
stupid Sl. 491 מַלְטוּף ז
cursed; unlucky Sl. 491 מַנְחוּס ז
overly muscular Sl. 491 מַנְפוּחַ ז
exhausted Sl. 491 מַסְחוּט ז
poor, miserable Sl. 491 מַסְכּוּן ז
puny, miserable, ,neglected Sl 491 מַסְרוּחַ ז
monstrous; ugly; disgusting Sl. 491 מַפְלוּצ(ה) ז
no longer a virgin Sl. 491 מַפְתּוּח(ה) ז
spring Lit. 492 מַבּוּעַ ז
bellows 492 מַפּוּחַ ז
pick, pick-axe 493 מַכּוֹשׁ ז
conveyor belt 493 מַסּוֹעַ ז
helicopter 493 מַסּוֹק ז
saw 493 מַסּוֹר ז
district, borough 493 מַקּוֹף ז
beak 493 מַקּוֹר ז
drumstick, hammer 493 מַקּוֹשׁ ז
favoritism; bias 493 מַשּׂוֹא (פָּנִים) ז
cache, subterranean granary 494 מַטְמוּרָה נ
granary, grain elevator, silo 494 מַמְגּוּרָה נ
plane (carpentry) 494 מַקְצוּעָה נ
edition; newscast 495 מַהֲדוּרָה נ
examination, test 496 מִבְדָּק ז
news flash 496 מִבְזָק ז
fortress, stronghold 496 מִבְצָר ז
spillway 496 מִבְרָץ ז
telegram 496 מִבְרָק ז
hilly area 496 מִבְתָּר ז
jumbled heap (Lit.) th century 496 מִגְבָּב ז
conglomeration 496 מִגְבָּשׁ ז
tower 496 מִגְדָּל ז
gender; erecting a fence 496 מִגְדָּר ז
variety, assortment; color range, shade 496 מִגְוָן ז
sector 496 מִגְזָר ז
weir; ski 496 מִגְלָשׁ ז
plot of land; empty lot, yard; field, court (sports) 496 מִגְרָשׁ ז
desert, wilderness 496 מִדְבָּר ז

מִרְקָע ז 498 television/home movie screen
מִרְתָּח ז 498 decoction [no pl.]
מִשְׁטָח ז 498 flat place; surface; smear, swab (medicine)
מִשְׁלָח (יָד) ז 498 occupation, profession (final vowel pataH in constr.)
מִשְׂפָּח ז 498 distortion of justice [no pl.]
מִשְׁקָע ז 498 sediment; residue
מִחְיָה נ 499 sustenance, living
מִכְוָה נ 499 burn, burning Lit.
מִכְסָה נ 499 ceiling, limit, allotment, ration; quota
מִצְוָה נ 499 commandment; decree; good deed, act of kindness
מִקְוָה/מִקְוֶה נ 499 ritual bath
מִקְנָה נ 499 purchase, acquisition Bibl.
מִקְשָׁה נ 499 field (esp. of watermelons); beaten work; solidity
מִרְמָה נ 499 fraud, deception
מִשְׁנָה נ 499 Mishna (Jewish oral law); doctrine, theory
מִשְׂרָה נ 499 job, position
מִשְׁרָה נ 499 juice, syrup, cordial Lit.; (pharmacy) tincture Lit.
מִתְוָה נ 499 draft, sketch; layout
מִצָּב ז 500 status
מִשָּׁק ז 500 join (carpentry)
מִכְמָן ז 501 hidden thing; treasure Lit.
מִשְׁמָן ז 501 being fat; being fertile; big, strong person Lit.
מִסְכֵּן ז 502 poor person
מִסְפֵּד ז 502 eulogy
מִשְׁמֵשׁ ז 502 apricot
מִזְבֵּחַ ז 503 altar
מִבְנֶה ז 504 building; structure
מִדְאֶה ז 504 gliding field
מִדְגֶּה ז 504 fishing farm
מִדְחֶה ז 504 error Lit.-rare
מִכְסֶה ז 504 cover, lid
מִכְרֶה, ר׳ מִכְרוֹת ז 504 mine (coal, gold, etc.) (pl. mikhrot)
מִלְוֶה ז 504 loan
מִלְקֶה ז 504 ecliptic, eclipse (astronomy)
מִפְנֶה ז 504 turning point; change
מִצְפֶּה ז 504 lookout; observatory; hilltop settlement
מִקְוֶה ז 504 ritual bath; small basin of collected water
מִקְנֶה ז 504 livestock, cattle Bibl.
מִקְצֶה ז 504 heat (sports)
מִקְרֶה ז 504 incident; chance; case
מִרְדֶּה ז 504 honey harvest; bread shovel
מִרְעֶה ז 504 pasture

מִשְׁגֶּה ז 504 error Lit.-rare
מִשְׂחֶה ז 504 heat (swimming)
מִשְׁנֶה ז 504 deputy; twice as much Bibl.
מִשְׁתֶּה, ר׳ מִשְׁתָּאוֹת ז 504 feast (pl. mishta'ot)
מִתְלֶה ז 504 hanger, hook, rack
מִבְרָקָה נ 505 telegraph station at a post office
מִבְשָׁלָה נ 505 brewery
מִגְבָּלָה נ 505 limitation
מִגְנָזָה נ 505 archive N
מִגְנָנָה נ 505 (military) defensive fighting; defense
מִגְרָרָה נ 505 sled, sledge, sleigh
מִדְרָכָה נ 505 sidewalk
מִדְרָשָׁה נ 505 college
מִזְבָּלָה נ 505 garbage dump, landfill
מִזְגָּגָה נ 505 glass factory
מִזְוָדָה נ 505 suitcase
מִזְקָקָה נ 505 distillery
מִזְרָקָה נ 505 fountain
מִטְבָּעָה נ 505 mint
מִטְמָנָה נ 505 landfill
מִכְבָּסָה נ 505 laundry facility
מִכְלָלָה נ 505 college
מִכְתָּבָה נ 505 writing desk
מִלְטָשָׁה נ 505 polishing workshop
מִמְסָרָה נ 505 gear (mech.)
מִנְבָּטָה נ 505 nursery (horticulture)
מִנְסָרָה נ 505 prism
מִסְדָּרָה נ 505 typesetting shop
מִסְלָקָה נ 505 clearing house (banking)
מִסְפָּנָה נ 505 shipping dock
מִסְפָּרָה נ 505 barber shop, hairdresser shop
מִפְטָמָה נ 505 place for fattening animals
מִפְלָגָה נ 505 (political) party
מִפְקָדָה נ 505 headquarters
מִפְרָדָה נ 505 divider, barrier
מִקְדָּמָה נ 505 advance (payment) N
מִרְקָקָה נ 505 spittoon
מִשְׁטָרָה נ 505 police
מִשְׂרָפָה נ 505 incinerator; crematorium
מִשְׁתָּלָה נ 505 nursery (gardening)
מִשְׁתָּנָה נ 505 urinal
מִתְפָּרָה נ 505 sewing workshop
מִתְקָפָה נ 505 offensive N
מִגְהָצָה נ 506 pressing/ironing room
מִזְחָלָה נ 506 sled, sledge, sleigh
מִלְחָמָה נ 506 war
מִמְחָטָה נ 506 handkerchief
מִנְהָלָה נ 506 administration
מִנְהָרָה נ 506 tunnel
מִסְעָדָה נ 506 restaurant
מִצְהָלָה נ 506 cry of joy Lit.

מִשְׁאָלָה נ 506 wish N
מִשְׁחָטָה נ 506 slaughterhouse
מִמְלָחָה נ 507 salt shaker
מִסְלָעָה נ 507 rockery (gardening)
מִפְרָעָה נ 507 payment on account (of past debt)
מִפְשָׂעָה נ 507 crotch, groin
מִשְׁפָּחָה נ 507 family
מִדְשָׁאָה נ 508 lawn
מִטְוָאָה נ 508 spinning mill
מִכְלָאָה נ 508 corral, paddock, enclosure; temporary prison camp
מִסְבָּאָה נ 508 pub
מִקְרָאָה נ 508 reader, anthology of readings
מִרְפָּאָה נ 508 clinic
מִשְׁוָאָה נ 508 equation
מִבְרֶשֶׁת נ 509 brush
מִגְזֶרֶת נ 509 stenciled cutout
מִגְרֶרֶת נ 509 grater; sled, sledge, sleigh
מִדְרֶכֶת נ 509 sidewalk Lit.
מִזְנֶבֶת נ 509 shtreimel
מִסְגֶּרֶת נ 509 frame; framework
מִסְכֶּרֶת נ 509 sugar bowl
מִסְנֶנֶת נ 509 strainer; colander
מִסְפֶּרֶת נ 509 scissor kick (soccer)
מִפְלֶצֶת נ 509 monster
מִפְרֶצֶת נ 509 aneurism
מִצְנֶפֶת נ 509 miter (ritual clothing); conical hat
מִצְרֶפֶת נ 509 leotard
מִקְטֶרֶת נ 509 (smoking) pipe
מִקְלֶדֶת נ 509 keyboard
מִקְצֶפֶת נ 509 meringue
מִרְכֶּזֶת נ 509 telephone exchange
מִרְפֶּסֶת נ 509 balcony, veranda
מִרְצֶפֶת נ 509 tiles (flooring, wall); pavement
מִשְׁבֶּצֶת נ 509 square; (jewelry) setting; rubric
מִשְׁוֶרֶת נ 509 stapes, stirrup
מִשְׁלֶבֶת נ 509 monogram
מִשְׁמֶרֶת נ 509 shift N; post, position
מִשְׁקֶפֶת נ 509 binoculars
מִזְחֶלֶת נ 510 sled, sledge, sleigh
מִזְעֶרֶת נ 510 miniature (painting, portrait) Lit.
מִשְׁאֶרֶת נ 510 large bowl for dough to rise
מִשְׁעֶנֶת נ 510 back rest
מִגְבַּעַת נ 511 brimmed hat
מִגְרַעַת נ 511 deficiency, defect
מִטְבַּעַת נ 511 die N, swage
מִטְפַּחַת נ 511 kerchief, handkerchief
מִצְלַעַת נ 511 hogback (geomorphology)
מִקְלַחַת נ 511 shower
מִקְלַעַת נ 511 braid; plexus

מַרְזֶפֶת נ 531 sledgehammer, mallet Rare
מַרְחֶשֶׁת נ 531 deep-fryer
מַשְׁחֶלֶת נ 531 needle threader
מַשְׁחֶתֶת נ 531 destroyer (navy)
מַאֲכֶלֶת נ 532 slaughtering/carving knife Lit.
מַעֲטֶפֶת נ 532 mantle; casing; surround; dura
מַעֲרֶכֶת נ 532 set; editorial staff; system
מַעֲרֶפֶת נ 532 guillotine (Rare)
מַטְבַּעַת נ 533 die, swage
מַרְדַּעַת נ 533 saddlecloth
מַחְלֹקֶת/מַחֲלֹקֶת נ 534 controversy, disagreement
מַחְפֹּרֶת נ 534 trench; mine, shaft; tunnel
מַחְרֹזֶת/מַחֲרֹזֶת נ 534 beaded necklace; medley
מַחְרֹקֶת/מַחֲרֹקֶת נ 534 screw-die
מַטְמֹרֶת נ 534 granary, cache Lit.
מַלְכֹּדֶת נ 534 trap
מַעְבֹּרֶת נ 534 ferry
מַשְׂכֹּרֶת נ 534 salary
מַתְכֹּנֶת נ 534 structure, format, framework
מַדְוֶה ז 535 ailment, affliction Lit
מַדְלֶה ז 535 crane, derrick
מַדְמֶה ז 535 simulator
מַחְוֶה/מַחֲוֶה ז 535 pointer
מַחְסֶה/מַחֲסֶה ז 535 cover, shelter
מַטְוֶה ז 535 spun wool, yarn
מַטְפֶּה ז 535 fire extinguisher
מַמְחֶה ז 535 blender
מַסְוֶה ז 535 mask, guise
מַקְלֶה ז 535 toaster
מַשְׁקֶה ז 535 server of drinks
מַתְלֶה ז 535 loop on clothing to hang on hook
מַרְאֶה ז 536 view, sight
מַשְׁקֶה ז 537 beverage, drink
מַאֲפֶה ז 538 pastry
מַעֲבֶה ז 538 thick N Lit.
מַעֲטֶה ז 538 cover; cloak
מַעֲנֶה (ר׳ -ים/-ות) ז 538 response
מַעֲצֶה ז 538 woodwork (in weapons)
מַעֲקֶה (ר׳ -ים/-ות) ז 538 banister, railing
מַעֲשֶׂה ז 538 deed
מַחֲזֶה ז 539 play; show
מַחֲנֶה ז 539 camp
מַעֲלֶה ז 539 incline, slope; rise, ascent
מַטֶּה ז 540 rod, staff; headquarters
מַבְדֵּד ז 541 electrical insulator
מַבְזֵק ז 541 flash (photog.)
מַבְלֵט ז 541 die (technology, engineering)
מַבְלֵל ז 541 jammer (radio, radar)
מַבְרֵג ז 541 screwdriver
מַבְרֵז ז 541 screw-tap
מַגְבֵּר ז 541 amplifier
מַגְלֵב ז 541 whip
מַגְלֵל ז 541 bobbin winder; paint roller
מַגְרֵד ז 541 scraper
מַדְגֵּשׁ ז 541 marker
מַדְפֵּס ז 541 printer (photography)
מַזְלֵג ז 541 fork
מַזְלֵף ז 541 watering can
מַזְנֵק ז 541 fire-hose nozzle; trigger
מַזְרֵק ז 541 syringe
מַחְבֵּט ז 541 bat, baseball bat
מַחְגֵּר ז 541 ratchet lock
מַחְדֵּד ז 541 pencil sharpener
מַחְדֵּר ז 541 feeding or gastric tube
מַחְזֵק/מַחֲזֵק ז 541 holder
מַחְזֵר ז 541 reflector
מַחְלֵף ז 541 commutator; exchanger
מַחְלֵץ ז 541 corkscrew
מַחְפֵּר ז 541 digger, bulldozer, excavator
מַחְשֵׁב ז 541 computer
מַחְשֵׂף ז 541 camera shutter release
מַטְמֵן ז 541 tea cozy
מַטְרֵף ז 541 beater, whisk
מַכְבֵּד ז 541 panicle (botany)
מַכְבֵּשׁ ז 541 steamroller
מַכְוֵן ז 541 tuner, regulator
מַכְלֵב ז 541 stapler
מַכְתֵּשׁ ז 541 crater
מַלְבֵּן ז 541 rectangle
מַלְגֵּז ז 541 fork-like agricultural implement
מַלְמֵד ז 541 shepherd's staff Rare
מַנְפֵּק ז 541 dispenser
מַסְגֵּר ז 541 locksmith
מַסְכֵּת ז 541 stethoscope
מַסְמֵר ז 541 nail
מַסְנֵן ז 541 filter
מַסְפֵּג ז 541 blotter
מַסְרֵק ז 541 comb
מַסְתֵּם ז 541 stopper, plug, valve
מַפְלֵג ז 541 distributor
מַפְלֵט ז 541 exhaust pipe
מַפְסֵק ז 541 switch
מַפְרֵט ז 541 pick, plectrum (music)
מַפְרֵם ז 541 seam ripper, "quick unpick" (sewing)
מַצְבֵּט ז 541 pincer
מַצְבֵּר ז 541 battery
מַצְמֵד ז 541 clutch
מַצְנֵם ז 541 toaster
מַצְנֵן ז 541 cooler
מַצְפֵּן ז 541 compass
מַקְבֵּל ז 541 collimator
מַקְדֵּד ז 541 ream (engineering)
מַקְלֵט ז 541 (radio) receiver
מַקְלֵף ז 541 vegetable peeler
מַקְצֵף ז 541 whisk; beater (of an electric mixer)
מַקְצֵץ ז 541 chopper (kitchen appliance)
מַקְרֵן ז 541 projector
מַקְרֵר ז 541 refrigerator
מַקְשֵׁר ז 541 intercom
מַרְבֵּק (עֵגֶל) ז 541 fattened calf
מַרְזֵב ז 541 eaves trough, gutter, drainpipe
מַרְטֵט ז 541 vibrator (construction)
מַרְסֵס ז 541 atomizer, sprayer
מַרְסֵק ז 541 masher, press (kitchen utensil)
מַרְפֵּד ז 541 pad
מַרְפֵּס ז 541 fontanel
מַרְפֵּק ז 541 elbow
מַרְתֵּף ז 541 cellar, basement
מַשְׁבֵּר ז 541 crisis
מַשְׁבֵּת ז 541 immobilizer
מַשְׁגֵּר ז 541 launcher
מַשְׁדֵּר ז 541 transmitter
מַשְׁנֵק ז 541 choke
מַשְׁפֵּךְ ז 541 watering can
מַשְׁפֵּת ז 541 burner (of as stove)
מַשְׁקֵט/מַשְׁתֵּק/מַשְׁתִּיק קוֹל ז 541 silencer
מַשְׂרֵט ז 541 scriber (for marking metal before working on it)
מַתְבֵּן ז 541 hayloft
מַתְמֵר ז 541 transducer
מַתְנֵד ז 541 oscillator
מַהֲדֵק/מְהַדֵּק ז 542 paper clip; stapler
מַעְדֵּר/מַעֲדֵר ז 542 hoe
מַעֲשֵׂר ז 543 tithing
מַבְחֵשׁ ז 544 mixing spoon; cocktail stick
מַבְעֵר ז 544 burner; lighter
מַגְהֵץ ז 544 iron
מַדְחֵס ז 544 compressor
מַדְחֵף ז 544 propeller
מַטְעֵן ז 544 charger
מַלְחֵם ז 544 soldering iron; blowtorch
מַלְחֵץ ז 544 presser foot (in sewing)
מַנְחֵת ז 544 absorber, attenuator, damper
מַפְחֵת ז 544 reducer (of noise etc.)
מַשְׁאֵף ז 544 inhaler
מַשְׂאֵת, ר׳ מַשְׂאוֹת ז 544 gift (pl. mas'ot)
מַשְׁחֵז ז 544 knife sharpener
מַתְאֵם ז 544 adapter (electronics)
מַקְפֵּא ז 545 freezer, deep freeze
מַרְפֵּא ז 545 cure [no pl.]
מַגְבֵּהַּ ז 546 jack
מַטְבֵּחַ ז 546 slaughter Rare
מַפְצֵחַ ז 546 nutcracker

תַּרְגִּיל ז 558 exercise, drill, training, practice
תַּרְחִיב ז 558 excursus
תַּרְחִיף ז 558 suspension (chemistry)
תַּרְחִיץ ז 558 lotion Rare
תַּרְחִישׁ ז 558 scenario
תַּרְטִיט ז 558 vibrato (music) [no pl.]
תַּרְכִּיב ז 558 vaccine
תַּרְכִּיז ז 558 concentrate
תַּרְמִיל (אין שורש...) ז 558 satchel, bag; pod; bullet casing
תַּרְסִיס ז 558 spray, aerosol
תַּרְשִׁים ז 558 diagram, sketch, chart
תַּרְשִׁישׁ ז 558 precious stone (aquamarine?) Biblical
תַּשְׁדִּיר ז 558 commercial
תַּשְׁטִיף ז 558 leachate (geology); gargle
תַּשְׁלִיב ז 558 guilloche (architecture)
תַּשְׁלִיךְ ז 558 tashlich (prayer recited on Rosh Hashana) [no pl.]
תַּשְׁלִיל ז 558 negative (photography)
תַּשְׁמִישׁ ז 558 use, utilization; object (usually religious); sexual intercourse
תַּשְׁנִיק ז 558 asphyxia; choking [no pl.]
תַּשְׁקִיף ז 558 forecast (weather); prospectus (stock exchange)
תַּשְׁרִיט ז 558 blueprint, land use scheme
תַּשְׁרִיר ז 558 validation [no pl.]
תַּאֲגִיד ז 559 corporation
תַּאֲרִיךְ ז 559 date
תַּהֲלִיךְ ז 559 process
תַּעֲרִיף ז 559 tariff, rate, cost
תַּעֲתִיק/תַּעְתִּיק ז 559 transcription
תַּאֲחִיזָה נ 560 adhesion (physics); linkage (genetics) [no pl.]
תַּבְנִית נ 561 pattern, form; baking dish
תַּגְלִית נ 561 discovery
תַּדְמִית נ 561 image, perception
תַּכְלִית נ 561 purpose
תַּמְנִית נ 561 token (linguistics)
תַּמְצִית נ 561 extract; summary, abstract; essence
תַּפְנִית נ 561 turn-about, change in direction
תַּצְפִּית נ 561 observation, observation point
תַּקְרִית נ 561 incident
תַּרְבִּית נ 561 tissue culture; culture (microbiology)
תַּרְמִית נ 561 deceit, fraud
תַּשְׁרִית נ 561 maceration
תַּשְׁתִּית נ 561 infrastructure

תַּחֲזִית נ 562 forecast
תַּעֲנִית נ 562 fast (usually religious)
תַּגְמוּל ז 563 remuneration, recompense; retribution
תַּחְלוּא/תַּחֲלוּא ז 563 disease, illness (pl. only)
תַּלְמוּד ז 563 Talmud, Oral law
תַּמְלוּג ז 563 royalties (pl. only)
תַּמְרוּק ז 563 cosmetics, perfumes
תַּנְחוּם ז 563 condolences (pl. only)
תַּפְנוּק ז 563 delights, pampering, indulgences (pl. only)
תַּצְלוּם ז 563 photograph
תַּצְרוּם ז 563 cacophony
תַּקְבּוּל ז 563 receipt, intake
תַּרְבּוּשׁ ז 563 fez
תַּשְׁלוּם ז 563 payment
תַּאֲחוּז ז 564 percentage
תַּחֲנוּן ז 564 supplicatory prayer; plea, entreaty
תַּעֲלוּל ז 564 prank, mischief, practical joke
תַּעֲנוּג ר׳ תַּעֲנוּגוֹת ז 564 pleasure (pl. ta`anugot)
תַּעֲצוּם ר׳ תַּעֲצוּמוֹת ז 564 strength (lit.) (pl. ta`atsumot)
תַּבְרוּאָה נ 565 sanitation [no pl.]
תַּחְבּוּלָה נ 565 trick, ruse, stratagem
תַּחְבּוּרָה נ 565 transportation [no pl.]
תַּחְזוּקָה/תַּחֲזוּקָה נ 565 maintenance
תַּחְלוּאָה/תַּחֲלוּאָה נ 565 morbidity
תַּחְלוּפָה/תַּחֲלוּפָה נ 565 turnover; changeover, substitution
תַּלְאוּבָה נ 565 intense heat (biblical); suffering
תַּפְאוּרָה נ 565 set (theater), decoration, decor
תַּהֲלוּכָה נ 566 procession, parade
תַּעֲבוּרָה נ 566 traffic [no pl.]
תַּעֲמוּלָה נ 566 propaganda
תַּעֲסוּקָה נ 566 employment
תַּעֲצוּמָה נ 566 strength, force, power Lit.
תַּעֲרוּבָה נ 566 warranty Lit.
תַּעֲרוּכָה נ 566 exhibition
תּוֹסָף ז 567 additive
תּוֹצָא ז 567 effect
תּוֹצָר ז 567 product, goods, commodity; outcome
תּוֹשָׁב ז 567 resident
תּוֹבָלָה נ 568 transport
תּוֹלָדָה נ 568 outcome
תּוֹרָשָׁה נ 568 heredity [no pl.]
תּוֹדָעָה נ 569 consciousness [no pl.]
תּוֹכָחָה/תּוֹכַחַת נ 569 reproof, rebuke, admonishment
תּוֹפָעָה נ 569 phenomenon

תּוֹצָאָה נ 569 outcome
תּוֹבָנָה נ 570 insight
תּוֹחֶלֶת נ 571 expectation, hope; expectancy Lit. [no pl.]
תּוֹלֶדֶת = תּוֹלָדָה נ 571 outcome, result, consequence
תּוֹסֶפֶת נ 571 addition, increase, increment
תּוֹעֶלֶת נ 571 benefit, use, value
תּוֹצֶרֶת נ 571 output, production, output [no pl.]
תּוֹשֶׁבֶת נ 571 base, seating
תְּאוּטָה נ 572 deceleration
תְּאוּנָה נ 572 accident
תְּאוּצָה נ 572 acceleration
תְּאוּרָה נ 572 lighting
תְּבוּאָה נ 572 produce, crops; cereals, grains
תְּבוּנָה נ 572 understanding, wisdom; intelligence; reason
תְּבוּסָה נ 572 defeat
תְּגוּבָה נ 572 reaction
תְּהוּדָה נ 572 resonance
תְּזוּזָה נ 572 movement, motion
תְּזוּנָה נ 572 nutrition
תְּחוּלָה נ 572 inception, incidence (law), application [no pl.]
תְּחוּשָׁה נ 572 sensation; feeling
תְּכוּלָה נ 572 capacity; contents
תְּכוּנָה/תְּכֻנָּה נ 572 quality
תְּלוּנָה נ 572 complaint
תְּמוּנָה נ 572 picture, photograph
תְּמוּרָה נ 572 return, compensation; value; change; permutation
תְּמוּתָה נ 572 mortality
תְּנוּבָה נ 572 produce, crop; yield, output
תְּנוּדָה נ 572 fluctuation; movement, rocking; oscillation
תְּנוּחָה נ 572 posture, position of body
תְּנוּמָה נ 572 nap, sleep
תְּנוּעָה נ 572 movement
תְּנוּפָה נ 572 momentum; drive, movement, push
תְּסוּגָה נ 572 regression (psychology)
תְּעוּדָה נ 572 document
תְּעוּזָה נ 572 daring
תְּעוּפָה נ 572 flight; aviation
תְּעוּקָה נ 572 pressure
תְּפוּגָה נ 572 expiry
תְּפוּסָה נ 572 capacity; occupancy
תְּפוּצָה נ 572 distribution
תְּפוּקָה נ 572 production, output
תְּצוּגָה נ 572 exhibit, display
תְּצוּרָה נ 572 formation, form; configuration
תְּקוּמָה נ 572 resurrection, revival
תְּקוּפָה נ 572 period, era; season
תְּקוּרָה נ 572 overhead

halo; corona; areola 586 הִלָּה נ
lechery, prostitution 586 זִמָּה נ
affinity, attachment; linkage 586 זִקָּה נ
affection 586 חִבָּה נ
henna [no pl.] 586 חִנָּה נ
terror, fear Lit. 586 חִתָּה נ
mosquito net hung over bed 586 כִּלָּה נ
skullcap; cupola, dome 586 כִּפָּה נ
class, grade; classroom; section (military) 586 כִּתָּה נ
core; kernel 586 לִבָּה נ
measurement; size; extent 586 מִדָּה נ
menstruating woman 586 נִדָּה נ
bud (botany) 586 נִצָּה נ
reason 586 סִבָּה נ
pin; brooch; hair clip; staple 586 סִכָּה נ
excuse 586 עִלָּה נ
dough 586 עִסָּה נ
corner 586 פִּנָּה נ
snippet; slice 586 פִּסָּה נ
cap (weaponry); knee cap 586 פִּקָּה נ
pita bread 586 פִּתָּה נ
desert, wilderness; wasteland 586 צִיָּה נ
chill, coldness; shield (biblical) 586 צִנָּה נ
comforter cover 586 צִפָּה נ
slight bow, nod, salutation 586 קִדָּה נ
jam, jelly 586 רִבָּה נ
larva; maggot 586 רִמָּה נ
joy; singing with joy 586 רִנָּה נ
dresser, chest of drawers 586 שִׁדָּה נ
woman (pl. nashim) 587 אִשָּׁה, ר' נָשִׁים נ
wheat 587 חִטָּה נ
flea 587 כִּנָּה נ
word 587 מִלָּה נ
acacia 587 שִׁטָּה נ
terebinth (tree) 588 אֵלָה נ
health, healing, wellbeing [no pl.] 588 גֵּהָה נ
cud 588 גֵּרָה נ
sweat [no pl.] 588 זֵעָה נ
wrath, fury Lit. 588 חֵמָה נ
feast, banquet Lit. 588 כֵּרָה נ
birth 588 לֵדָה נ
mucus, phlegm 588 לֵחָה נ
stomach 588 קֵבָה נ
lung 588 רֵאָה נ
chest, box; (written) word; bar (music) 588 תֵּבָה נ
wig; sidelock; corner 589 פֵּאָה נ
sleep [no pl.] 589 שֵׁנָה נ
ethnic group; group 590 עֵדָה נ
advice, counsel 590 עֵצָה נ
opinion 591 דֵּעָה נ
nation, people 592 אֻמָּה נ

lobe (anatomy) 592 אֻנָּה נ
puppet 592 בֻּבָּה נ
sludge 592 בֻּצָּה נ
small ball; marble (game of marbles) 592 גֻּלָּה נ
pit, hole, dimple 592 גֻּמָּה/א נ
bustard (bird) 592 חֻבָּה נ
canopy; canopy used at Jewish wedding 592 חֻפָּה נ
constitution 592 חֻקָּה נ
span, extent 592 מֻטָּה נ
sukkah (Jewish ritual); hut; tabernacle 592 סֻכָּה נ
lenience 592 קֻלָּה נ
money box; cash register; box office; treasury 592 קֻפָּה נ
hull (ship); body (tank etc.) 592 תֻּבָּה נ
innocence; honesty [no pl.] 592 תֻּמָּה נ
bright light, radiance Lit. 593 אוֹרָה נ
exile 593 גּוֹלָה נ
prostitute 593 זוֹנָה נ
duty 593 חוֹבָה נ
wall 593 חוֹמָה נ
good N; favor N 593 טוֹבָה נ
cauldron, large pot (Talmudic) 593 יוֹרָה נ
feather 593 נוֹצָה נ
burnt offering (Jewish law, in Temple) 593 עוֹלָה נ
season 593 עוֹנָה נ
vagina; sleeve for hinge 593 פּוֹתָה נ
excrement 593 צוֹאָה נ
height, stature; story, floor 593 קוֹמָה נ
beam 593 קוֹרָה נ
holocaust 593 שׁוֹאָה נ
branch Lit. 593 שׂוֹכָה נ
tibia (long leg bone) 593 שׁוֹקָה נ
thanks, gratitude 593 תּוֹדָה נ
Torah; theory; doctrine 593 תּוֹרָה נ
pigeon, dove 594 יוֹנָה נ
lobe (anatomy) 595 אוּנָה/אֻנָּה נ
bubble 595 בּוּעָה נ
shame, disgrace 595 בּוּשָׁה נ
(dead) body, cadaver 595 גּוּפָה נ
grave; afterworld [no pl.] 595 דּוּמָה נ
sorghum 595 דּוּרָה נ
small, minor thing 595 זוּטָה/א נ
dial N (telephone) 595 חוּגָה נ
hut 595 חוּשָׁה נ
sponge gourd, luffa plant 595 לוּפָה נ
light bulb 595 נוּרָה נ
genre 595 סוּגָה נ
storm, tempest 595 סוּפָה נ
cake 595 עוּגָה נ
sump 595 עוּקָה נ
rest, break Lit. 595 פּוּגָה נ
shape 595 צוּרָה נ

trench 595 שׁוּחָה נ
tax assessment; evaluation 595 שׁוּמָה/א נ
line; series 595 שׁוּרָה נ
sadness 595 תּוּגָה נ
enmity, hatred 596 אֵיבָה נ
horror, terror 596 אֵימָה ר' -וֹת/-ים נ
ancient volume measure 596 אֵיפָה/א נ
each space between staff lines (music) 596 בֵּינָה נ
ash tree 596 מֵילָה נ
end, final section; final clause 596 סֵיפָה/א נ
supplies [no pl.] 596 צֵידָה אין ר' נ
introduction, preface; beginning; initial clause 596 רֵישָׁה/א נ
old age; white hair 596 שֵׂיבָה נ
egg 597 בֵּיצָה נ
lining (of clothing) 598 בִּטְנָה נ
young female camel 598 בִּכְרָה נ
valley 598 בִּקְעָה נ
shack, hut 598 בִּקְתָּה נ
food (biblical) [no pl.] 598 בִּרְיָה נ
hill 598 גִּבְעָה נ
area, sector; figure, shape 598 גִּזְרָה נ
siphon 598 גִּשְׁתָּה נ
word Lit. 598 דִּבְרָה נ
molasses 598 דִּבְשָׁה נ
tear N 598 דִּמְעָה נ
cream Lit. 598 זִבְדָּה נ
singing 598 זִמְרָה נ
old age [no pl.] 598 זִקְנָה נ
semen; flow Lit. 598 זִרְמָה נ
rafter (building) 598 טִפְחָה נ
trouble, bother, nuisance 598 טִרְדָּה נ
trouble, bother, effort 598 טִרְחָה נ
splendor, brilliance Lit. [no pl.] 598 יִפְעָה נ
obedience; face wrinkles Lit-rare [no pl.] 598 יִקְהָה נ
awe, fear [no pl.] 598 יִרְאָה נ
balance, remainder 598 יִתְרָה נ
a certain distance [no pl.] 598 כִּבְרָה נ
kidney 598 כִּלְיָה נ
whiteness, pallor [no pl.] 598 לִבְנָה נ
office, bureau, department 598 לִשְׁכָּה נ
afternoon prayer service (Jewish); gift 598 מִנְחָה נ
ointment 598 מִשְׁחָה נ
safety catch 598 נִצְרָה נ
tunnel, aqueduct 598 נִקְבָּה נ
cave, grotto 598 נִקְרָה נ
series 598 סִדְרָה נ
digit 598 סִפְרָה נ

terror, horror 620 נ בַּלָּהָה
control 620 נ בַּקָּרָה
request 620 נ בַּקָּשָׁה
sabotage 620 נ חַבָּלָה
sin Lit. 620 נ חַטָּאָה
intention, aim 620 נ כַּוָּנָה
atonement 620 נ כַּפָּרָה
report, article 620 נ כַּתָּבָה
danger 620 נ סַכָּנָה
inhibition 620 נ עַכָּבָה
(last) will 620 נ צַוָּאָה
(written) receipt 620 נ קַבָּלָה
mishap, hitch 620 נ תַּקָּלָה
regulation 620 נ תַּקָּנָה
dry land Bibl. 621 נ חָרָבָה
affair; separation, section 621 נ פָּרָשָׁה
panic; rush 622 נ בֶּהָלָה
dry land 623 נ יַבָּשָׁה
caravan 623 נ שַׁיָּרָה
division (military) 624 נ אֻגְדָּה
steak 624 נ אֻמְצָה
stable N 624 נ אֻרְוָה
piston 624 נ בֻּכְנָה
niche, alcove 624 נ גֻּמְחָה
military unit (battalion/regiment) Arch. 624 נ גֻּנְדָּה
buttermilk 624 נ חֻבְצָה
rat 624 נ חֻלְדָּה
link; part; vertebra 624 נ חֻלְיָה
shirt, blouse 624 נ חֻלְצָה
weakness 624 נ חֻלְשָׁה
rumex, sorrel (plant) 624 נ חֻמְעָה
acid N 624 נ חֻמְצָה
severity, rigidity 624 נ חֻמְרָה
vacation, holiday 624 נ חֻפְשָׁה
cheek, insolence, impertinence 624 נ חֻצְפָּה
ruin (building) 624 נ חֻרְבָּה
cutting edge (of knife, ax, etc.) 624 נ חֻרְפָּה
grove, small forest 624 נ חֻרְשָׁה
defilement, impurity 624 נ טֻמְאָה
pretension 624 נ יֻמְרָה
prestige 624 נ יֻקְרָה
beret 624 נ כֻּמְתָּה
cotton 624 נ כֻּתְנָה
pus 624 נ מֻגְלָה
abscess 624 נ מֻרְסָה/א
issue, matter 624 נ סֻגְיָה
sole 624 נ סֻלְיָה
fact 624 נ עֻבְדָּה/א
formation (military) 624 נ עֻצְבָּה
question, problem 624 נ קֻשְׁיָה
anger, fury 624 נ רֻגְזָה
weakness 624 נ תֻּרְפָּה
pulp, oil cake (agriculture) 625 נ כֻּסְפָּה
filth, dirt 626 נ זֻהֲמָה
arrogance 626 נ יֻהֲרָה/יָהֳרָה
exaggeration, hyperbole 627 נ גֻּזְמָה/א
example 627 נ דֻּגְמָה/א

dumpling, matzo ball 627 נ כֻּפְתָּה
armchair 627 נ כֻּרְסָה
formula 627 נ נֻסְחָה
box 627 נ קֻפְסָה
caravan 628 נ אוֹרְחָה
fostering (a child) [no pl.] 628 נ אָמְנָה
fashion 628 נ אָפְנָה
foundation; prominent person 628 נ אָשְׁיָה
pistachio (tree) 628 נ בָּטְנָה
pirated software Sl. 628 נ גָּנְבָה
sulfate 628 נ גָּפְרָה
barge; raft 628 נ דּוֹבְרָה
partridge 628 נ חָגְלָה
strength, firmness [no pl.] 628 נ חָזְקָה
wisdom 628 נ חָכְמָה
hardware [no pl.?] 628 נ חָמְרָה
haste [no pl.] 628 נ חָפְזָה
destruction, annihilation [no pl.] 628 נ חָרְמָה
grove, small forest 628 נ חָרְשָׁה/חֻרְשָׁה
initiative 628 נ יָזְמָה
warfare, military tactics 628 נ לָחְמָה
courseware 628 נ לָמְדָה
lead of a pencil 628 נ עָפְרָה
strength, power 628 נ עָצְמָה
foreskin 628 נ עָרְלָה
cunning; act of cheating 628 נ עָרְמָה
satiation Lit. [no pl.] 628 נ שָׂבְעָה
computer program 628 נ תָּכְנָה
urethra 629 נ שָׁפְכָה
destruction, desolation, ruin 630 נ חָרְבָּה/חֻרְבָּה
purity, purification 631 נ טָהֳרָה
joy, rejoicing; cry of joy 631 נ צָהֳלָה
lie, fabrication 632 נ בְּדָיָה
weathering [no pl.] 632 נ בְּלָיָה
problem 632 נ בְּעָיָה
items of inferior quality (usually fruit) 632 נ בְּרָרָה
straw, stubble [no pl.] 632 נ גְּבָבָה/א
Gemara, Talmud 632 נ גְּמָרָא/ה
attraction (linguistics); sleigh 632 נ גְּרָרָה
wall shelves 632 נ דְּפָפָה
homily 632 נ דְּרָשָׁה
extinction, annihilation, extermination [no pl.] 632 נ כְּלָיָה
glove 632 נ כְּסָיָה
glove 632 נ כְּפָפָה
poster, placard 632 נ כְּרָזָה
uvula Rare 632 נ לְהָאָה
lizard 632 נ לְטָאָה
protest 632 נ מְחָאָה
stock, share 632 נ מְנָיָה
cave 632 נ מְעָרָה

fortress 632 נ מְצָדָה
hypothesis, opinion; conjecture 632 נ סְבָרָה/א
rag 632 נ סְחָבָה
shed 632 נ סְכָכָה
steel 632 נ פְּלָדָה
specification, inventory 632 נ פְּרָטָה
compromise N 632 נ פְּשָׁרָה
quarrel, altercation 632 נ קְטָטָה
evidence 632 נ רְאָיָה
satiation (of thirst) [no pl.] 632 נ רְוָיָה
veil, scarf 632 נ רְעָלָה
louver, slat 632 נ רְפָפָה
trio, group of three 632 נ שְׁלָשָׁה
authority, rulership 632 נ שְׂרָרָה
channel 632 נ תְּעָלָה
treaty 633 נ אֲמָנָה
being 633 נ הֲוָיָה
hallucination 633 נ הֲזָיָה
pleasure 633 נ הֲנָאָה
blow, thump 633 נ חֲבָטָה
trauma 633 נ חֲבָלָה
experience 633 נ חֲוָיָה
repeat; rehearsal 633 נ חֲזָרָה
greenhouse 633 נ חֲמָמָה
parking 633 נ חֲנָיָה
crossing 633 נ חֲצָיָה
regret 633 נ חֲרָטָה
grimace N 633 נ עֲוָיָה
small town 633 נ עֲיָרָה
berry; grape Lit. 633 נ עֲנָבָה
blessing 634 נ בְּרָכָה
silence [no pl.] 634 נ דְּמָמָה
parakeet 634 נ דְּרָרָה
wail N 634 נ יְבָבָה
childless widow awaiting Levirate marriage 634 נ יְבָמָה
wail N 634 נ יְלָלָה
24-hour period 634 נ יְמָמָה
sieve, sifter 634 נ כְּבָרָה
moon Lit. 634 נ לְבָנָה
funeral 634 נ לְוָיָה
despicable act, villainy 634 נ נְבָלָה
donation, contribution; alms 634 נ נְדָבָה
revenge 634 נ נְקָמָה
soul, spirit 634 נ נְשָׁמָה
net, lattice, grille 634 נ סְבָכָה
charity 634 נ צְדָקָה
scream 634 נ צְוָחָה
scream 634 נ צְרָחָה
curse 634 נ קְלָלָה
ten thousand 634 נ רְבָבָה
singing; joy Lit. 634 נ רְנָנָה
net, lattice, grille 634 נ שְׂבָכָה
(unintentional) error 634 נ שְׁגָגָה
wilderness, emptiness 634 נ שְׁמָמָה
palm tree, date (Talmudic) 634 נ תְּמָרָה
Jewish law 635 נ הֲלָכָה
bomb 636 נ פְּצָצָה

בְּשׂוֹרָה נ 671 news, tidings; Gospel

דְּיוֹטָה נ 671 floor, story (Talmudic)

דְּיוֹתָה נ 671 inkwell

זְמוֹרָה נ 671 branch (esp. of grapevine)

יְרוֹקָה נ 671 pond scum; patina Lit.

לְבוֹנָה נ 671 frankincense

מְשׁוֹשָׁה נ 671 antenna

סְחוֹרָה נ 671 merchandise

תְּמוֹכָה נ 671 supporting beam

אֲגוֹרָה נ 672 smallest Israeli coin

חֲגוֹרָה נ 672 belt

עֲבוֹדָה נ 672 work; job

דְּבוֹרָה נ 673 bee

שְׂעוֹרָה נ 673 barley

דָּלִיָּה נ 674 tendril

אַסְקֻפָּה נ 675 threshold, doorsill Lit.

חַרְצֻבָּה נ 675 knot, chain, fetter Lit.

מַהֲלֻמָּה נ 676 blow

קֻבְלָנָה נ 677 complaint

תְּבֻעָנָה נ 677 action, complaint, proceeding (law)

גְּלֻסְקָה נ 678 roll, bun, cake Lit.

כְּנֻפְיָה נ 678 gang

נְדוּנְיָה/נְדֻנְיָה נ 678 dowry

אֲלֻנְקָה נ 679 stretcher

טַלְטֵלָה נ 680 flinging, shaking, hurling

נַדְנֵדָה נ 680 swing, seesaw

צַפְצֵפָה נ 680 whistle

עַרְכָּאָה נ 681 proceeding (law); court (law)

פַּרְנָסָה נ 681 livelihood

קַיְטָנָה נ 681 summer day camp

קַרְפָּדָה נ 681 (female) toad

חַלְחָלָה נ 682 horror, fear, aversion

כַּלְכָּלָה נ 682 economy, economics

סַלְסָלָה נ 682 type of fabric Lit.-Rare

צַפְצָפָה נ 682 poplar

קַלְקָלָה נ 682 failure, iniquity, corruption

מַגֶּבֶת נ 683 towel

מַסֶּכֶת נ 683 tractate (of the Mishna); revue, review

מַצֶּבֶת נ 683 tombstone Rare; position Lit.

מַצֶּגֶת נ 683 presentation (computing)

מַצֶּקֶת נ 683 ladle

מַקֶּבֶת נ 683 sledgehammer Lit.

מַתֶּכֶת נ 683 metal

מַגַּעַת נ 684 contact (elec.)

אַדֶּמֶת נ 685 rubella, German measles [no pl.]

אַדֶּרֶת נ 685 robe, cloak

בַּזֶּלֶת נ 685 basalt [no pl.]

בַּסֶּסֶת נ 685 alkalosis (medicine) [no pl.]

בַּצֶּקֶת נ 685 edema

גַּזֶּזֶת נ 685 scalp ringworm [no pl.]

גַּמֶּלֶת נ 685 camel caravan

גַּנֶּנֶת נ 685 kindergarten teacher (fem.)

גַּשֶּׁשֶׁת נ 685 unmanned probe

דַּבֶּרֶת נ 685 garrulousness, "verbal diarrhea" Coll. [no pl.]

דַּבֶּשֶׁת נ 685 camel's hump

דַּלֶּקֶת נ 685 inflammation

דַּמֶּמֶת נ 685 hemophilia [no pl.]

זַפֶּקֶת נ 685 goiter [no pl.]

חַזֶּרֶת נ 685 mumps [no pl.]

חַטֶּטֶת נ 685 acne [no pl.]

חַמֶּצֶת נ 685 acidosis [no pl.]

חַצֶּבֶת נ 685 measles, rubeola [no pl.]

חַצֶּצֶת נ 685 lithiasis [no pl.]

טַיֶּלֶת נ 685 promenade, esplanade

טַיֶּסֶת נ 685 squadron (military)

יַבֶּלֶת נ 685 wart

יַבֶּשֶׁת נ 685 continent

יַלֶּפֶת נ 685 lichen

יַצֶּקֶת נ 685 cast iron [no pl.]

כַּוֶּנֶת נ 685 sight (of rifle etc.)

כַּוֶּרֶת נ 685 beehive

כַּלֶּבֶת נ 685 rabies [no pl.]

כַּנֶּנֶת נ 685 winch, crank

כַּסֶּפֶת נ 685 safe; deposit box

לַיֶּפֶת נ 685 fibrosis [no pl.]

מַיֶּמֶת נ 685 edema [no pl.]

מַתֶּנֶת נ 685 lumbago [no pl.]

נַזֶּלֶת נ 685 runny nose

נַיֶּדֶת נ 685 police cruiser

נַיֶּרֶת נ 685 paperwork (usually derog.) [no pl.]

סַיֶּרֶת נ 685 commando unit; battle cruiser

עַגֶּבֶת נ 685 syphilis [no pl.]

עַלֶּקֶת נ 685 orobanche (plant); trematode (worm)

עַקֶּמֶת נ 685 scoliosis [no pl.]

עַשֶּׁשֶׁת נ 685 caries (dentistry) [no pl.]

פַּטֶּרֶת נ 685 fungal infection [no pl.]

פַּצֶּלֶת נ 685 feldspar

פַּקֶּקֶת נ 685 thrombosis [no pl.]

צַלֶּקֶת נ 685 scar

צַמֶּקֶת נ 685 cirrhosis [no pl.]

צַמֶּרֶת נ 685 tree-top, top

צַנֶּרֶת נ 685 pipe system, pipeline

צַפֶּדֶת נ 685 tetanus [no pl.]

צַפֶּקֶת נ 685 peritonitis [no pl.]

קַטֶּפֶת נ 685 picking machine

קַלֶּטֶת נ 685 cassette

קַפֶּצֶת נ 685 trampoline

קַצֶּפֶת נ 685 whipped cream

קַצֶּרֶת נ 685 asthma [no pl.]

רַדֶּמֶת נ 685 lethargy [no pl.]

רַכֶּבֶת נ 685 train

רַכֶּזֶת נ 685 Ethernet hub

רַקֶּפֶת נ 685 cyclamen

שַׁיֶּטֶת נ 685 flotilla

שַׁלֶּכֶת נ 685 fall (of autumn leaves)

שַׁמֶּנֶת נ 685 cream [no pl.]

שַׁתֶּקֶת נ 685 aphasia [no pl.]

בַּהֶקֶת נ 686 vitiligo (medicine) [no pl.]

בַּהֶרֶת נ 686 freckle

נַחֶתֶת נ 686 landing craft

סַחֶבֶת נ 686 foot-dragging [no pl.]

סַעֶפֶת נ 686 manifold [no pl.]

צַהֶבֶת נ 686 jaundice [no pl.]

רַחֶפֶת נ 686 hovercraft

רַעֶלֶת נ 686 toxemia [no pl.]

שַׁחֶמֶת נ 686 cirrhosis [no pl.]

שַׁחֶפֶת נ 686 tuberculosis [no pl.]

שַׁעֶלֶת נ 686 whooping cough [no pl.]

גַּחֶלֶת נ 687 ember; glowing ember; remnant (pl. geHalim)

בָּאֶשֶׁת נ 688 halitosis, bad breath [no pl.]

בָּרֶקֶת נ 688 agate; emerald

גָּרֶדֶת נ 688 scabies [no pl.]

וָרֶדֶת נ 688 erysipelas (medicine) [no pl.]

טָרֶשֶׁת נ 688 sclerosis [no pl.]

נָאֶמֶת נ 688 tendency to deliver non-stop speeches [no pl.]

צָרֶבֶת נ 688 heartburn

קָרֶמֶת נ 688 diphtheria [no pl.]

שָׂרֶטֶת נ 688 scratch, cut

גַּבַּחַת נ 689 frontal baldness Lit.

גַּנַּחַת נ 689 asthma [no pl.]

נַפַּחַת נ 689 emphysema [no pl.]

סַפַּחַת נ 689 psoriasis; "tag-along," nuisance Coll.

פַּדַּחַת נ 689 forehead Lit.

צַלַּחַת נ 689 plate

צַפַּחַת נ 689 flask, bottle, jug

קַדַּחַת נ 689 fever, malaria [no pl.]

קַלַּחַת נ 689 turmoil; cauldron (biblical)

טַבַּעַת נ 690 ring

שַׁסַּעַת נ 690 schizophrenia [no pl.]

שַׁפַּעַת נ 690 influenza [no pl.]

קָרַחַת נ 691 bald spot

צָרַעַת נ 692 leprosy [no pl.]

תַּרְדֵּמַת נ 693 coma [no pl.]

אִגֶּרֶת נ 694 letter, missive

אִוֶּלֶת נ 694 stupidity, foolishness [no pl.]

גִּבֶּנֶת נ 694 hump

כִּנֶּמֶת נ 694 pediculosis, presence of lice on head/body [no pl.]

בַּצֹּרֶת נ 695 drought

כַּדֹּרֶת נ 695 bowling

כַּפֹּרֶת נ 695 covering of the holy ark (biblical)

חָלוּת נ 733 validity; being applied (law, etc.) [no pl.]
חָסוּת (ר׳?) נ 733 protection; sponsorship
טָעוּת נ 733 error
מָרוּת נ 733 authority [no pl.]
נָאוּת נ 733 being handsome [no pl.]
נָכוּת נ 733 disability, handicap [no pl.]
סָכוּת נ 733 prognosis [no pl.]
צָרוּת נ 733 narrowness [no pl.]
רָאשׁוּת נ 733 chairmanship, leadership, presidency [no pl.]
רָשׁוּת נ 733 authority (lands, port, etc.)
בְּדוּת נ 734 legend, fabrication
גְּנוּת נ 734 disgrace, defamation
דְּמוּת נ 734 figure, image; character
זְכוּת נ 734 right N
זְנוּת ר׳ זְנוּתִים? נ 734 prostitution (pl. znutim?)
כְּסוּת נ 734 clothing; cover
כְּשׁוּת נ 734 hop (plant) [no pl.]
לְקוּת נ 734 impairment, disability, deficiency
פְּדוּת נ 734 salvation, liberation Lit.
רְאוּת נ 734 visibility [no pl.]
רְשׁוּת נ 734 permission
שְׁבוּת נ 734 return N [no pl.]
שְׁהוּת נ 734 stay N, sojourn [no pl.]
שְׁטוּת נ 734 nonsense
תְּלוּת נ 734 dependence [no pl.]
חֲנוּת נ 735 store, shop
עֲלוּת נ 735 cost, expense
אַדְנוּת נ 736 authority, rule N, reign [no pl.]
אַחְדוּת נ 736 unity
אַפְסוּת נ 736 nothingness [no pl.]
בַּגְרוּת נ 736 maturity, maturation
גַּבְהוּת נ 736 egotism; pride Lit. [no pl.]
גַּבְרוּת נ 736 masculinity [no pl.]
גַּדְלוּת נ 736 greatness, eminence [no pl.]
גַּשְׁמוּת נ 736 corporeality, worldliness [no pl.]
דַּמְיוּת נ 736 resemblance, likeness [no pl.]
הַבְלוּת נ 736 folly, unimportance
הַדְרוּת נ 736 glory, majesty Lit. [no pl.]
הַלְמוּת נ 736 beat N [no pl.]
זַכְרוּת נ 736 masculinity; penis Lit.
חַשְׁכוּת נ 736 darkness; illiteracy, cultural void [no pl.]
יַוְנוּת נ 736 Hellenism [no pl.]
יַלְדוּת נ 736 childhood [no pl.]
יַנְקוּת נ 736 infancy, babyhood [no pl.]
יַרְקוּת נ 736 greenness Lit. [no pl.]
יַשְׁנוּת נ 736 oldness Lit. [no pl.]
יַשְׁרוּת נ 736 honesty, integrity Lit. [no pl.]
יַתְמוּת נ 736 orphanhood; loneliness; sense of loss [no pl.]
כַּשְׁרוּת נ 736 Jewish dietary law; validity, legality
מַלְכוּת נ 736 kingdom
מַלְקוּת נ 736 lash, whip (punishment) (Talmudic)
מַרְדוּת נ 736 rebellion, mutiny Lit. [no pl.]
נַבְלוּת נ 736 villainousness Lit.
נַוְלוּת נ 736 dismalness; despicableness Lit. [no pl.]
נַצְרוּת נ 736 Christianity [no pl.]
סַמְכוּת נ 736 authority
עַבְדוּת נ 736 slavery [no pl.]
עַמְקוּת נ 736 depth [no pl.]
עַצְבוּת נ 736 sadness [no pl.]
עַצְלוּת נ 736 laziness [no pl.]
עַצְמוּת נ 736 identity, self-concept Lit. [no pl.]
עַרְבוּת נ 736 guarantee; collateral
פַּשְׁטוּת נ 736 simplicity [no pl.]
קַדְמוּת נ 736 beginning, outset [no pl.]
קַדְרוּת נ 736 darkness; gloom [no pl.]
קַטְנוּת נ 736 childhood; smallness; pettiness
קַשְׁיוּת נ 736 hardness [no pl.]
תַּרְבּוּת נ 736 culture
בַּחֲרוּת נ 737 adolescence [no pl.]
בַּעֲלוּת נ 737 ownership [no pl.?]
בַּעֲרוּת נ 737 ignorance [no pl.]
יַהֲדוּת נ 737 Judaism [no pl.]
יַחֲסוּת נ 737 relativity
יַחֲפוּת נ 737 being barefoot Lit. [no pl.]
נַעֲרוּת נ 737 youth, adolescence [no pl.]
תַּחֲרוּת נ 737 competition
זִקְנוּת נ 738 old age [no pl.]
חִבְרוּת נ 738 socialization [no pl.]
טִפְלוּת נ 738 being subordinate, of second importance [no pl.]
נִבְזוּת נ 738 despicableness
נִכְפּוּת נ 738 being epileptic [no pl.]
נִקְלוּת נ 738 inferiority [no pl.] curved, bent, twisted Lit.
נִרְפּוּת נ 738 indolence; weariness [no pl.]
נִשְׁנוּת נ 738 repeatability [no pl.]
סִכְלוּת נ 738 stupidity, naivete [no pl.]
סִפְרוּת נ 738 literature
עִבְרוּת נ 738 Hebraization [no pl.]
פִּרְאוּת נ 738 wildness, savagery [no pl.]
צִדְקוּת נ 738 righteousness, piety [no pl.]
רִשְׁעוּת נ 738 wickedness
שִׁכְרוּת נ 738 drunkenness [no pl.]
שִׁפְלוּת נ 738 baseness, despicableness [no pl.]
תִּפְלוּת נ 738 tastelessness, rubbish [no pl.]
אִטְמוּת נ 739 atresia (pathol.) [no pl.]
אִטְרוּת נ 739 left-handedness [no pl.]
אִלְּמוּת נ 739 muteness [no pl.]
גִּבְּנוּת נ 739 hunchbackness [no pl.]
גִּדְּמוּת נ 739 amputatedness [no pl.]
חִגְּרוּת נ 739 lameness [no pl.]
חִוְּרוּת נ 739 being pale [no pl.]
טִפְּשׁוּת נ 739 stupidity, foolishness
עִוְּרוּת נ 739 blindness [no pl.]
עִלְּגוּת נ 739 stammering, mumbling [no pl.]
עִקְּשׁוּת נ 739 stubbornness [no pl.]
פִּסְּחוּת נ 739 being a cripple, lameness [no pl.]
פִּקְּחוּת נ 739 brilliance, intelligence [no pl.]
אַבְהוּת/אֲבָהוּת נ 740 paternity, fatherhood; paternalism
אֶבְיוֹנוּת נ 740 poverty Lit. [no pl.]
אֶגְרוֹפָנוּת נ 740 boxing [no pl.]
אַדְרִיכָלוּת/אַרְדִיכָלוּת נ 740 architecture [no pl.]
אֱוִילוּת נ 740 stupidity, foolishness [no pl.]
אֶזְרָחוּת נ 740 citizenship
אַחְרָיוּת נ 740 responsibility; liability [no pl.]
אֵיכוּת נ 740 quality
אֵימְתָנוּת נ 740 terror, intimidation [no pl.]
אֵינוּת נ 740 absence, non-existence [no pl.]
אֵיתָנוּת נ 740 steadfastness, resolution, firmness [no pl.]
אִכָּרוּת נ 740 farming, peasantry [no pl.]
אֱלוֹהוּת נ 740 divinity
אַלְחוּטָנוּת נ 740 radio operation [no pl.]
אֱלִילוּת נ 740 idolatry
אִמָּהוּת נ 740 motherhood [no pl.]
אֲמוֹדָאוּת נ 740 diving [no pl.]
אֻמְלָלוּת נ 740 misery
אָמָּנוּת נ 740 art
אֻמָּנוּת נ 740 craft

שַׁאֲנַנּוּת נ 751 complacence; serenity [no pl.]
אַגְרָנוּת נ 752 hoarding [no pl.]
אַכְלָנוּת נ 752 gluttony [no pl.]
אַלְמָנוּת נ 752 widowhood [no pl.]
אַסְפָנוּת נ 752 collecting, hoarding [no pl.]
בַּדְחָנוּת נ 752 joking, telling jokes [no pl.]
בַּדְלָנוּת נ 752 isolationism, separatism [no pl.]
בַּדְקָנוּת נ 752 pedantry, fussiness
בַּדְרָנוּת נ 752 entertainment [no pl.]
בַּטְלָנוּת נ 752 idleness, laziness [no pl.]
בַּיְשָׁנוּת נ 752 shyness [no pl.]
בַּכְיָנוּת נ 752 tendency to be a cry-baby [no pl.]
בַּלְעָנוּת נ 752 gluttony Lit. [no pl.]
בַּלְשָׁנוּת נ 752 linguistics [no pl.]
בַּקְרָנוּת נ 752 criticality [no pl.]
בַּרְרָנוּת נ 752 selectiveness [no pl.]
בַּשְׂרָנוּת נ 752 fleshiness, meatiness [no pl.]
גַּדְפָנוּת נ 752 abusing, cursing, reviling
גַּזְלָנוּת נ 752 robbery, theft [no pl.]
גַּחְמָנוּת/גַּחֲמָנוּת נ 752 capriciousness [no pl.]
גַּלְשָׁנוּת נ 752 surfing [no pl.]
דַּבְּרָנוּת נ 752 chattering babbling [no pl.]
דַּוְקָנוּת נ 752 literality, literalness [no pl.]
דַּיְקָנוּת נ 752 precision [no pl.]
דַּרְשָׁנוּת נ 752 exegesis, preaching, sermonizing [no pl.]
הַסְסָנוּת נ 752 vacillation, hesitancy, irresolution [no pl.]
הַרְסָנוּת נ 752 destructiveness [no pl.]
וַכְּחָנוּת נ 752 argumentativeness [no pl.]
וַתְּרָנוּת נ 752 lenience, concession, indulgence [no pl.]
זַחְלָנוּת נ 752 sluggishness, slowness [no pl.]
זַחְתָנוּת נ 752 arrogance, hautiness Lit.-Rare [no pl.]
זַיְּפָנוּת נ 752 forgery; insincerity [no pl.]
זַכְיָנוּת נ 752 franchising [no pl.]
זַלְלָנוּת נ 752 gluttony, greed [no pl.]
חַבְּלָנוּת נ 752 destructiveness; sabotage [no pl.]
חַבְתָנוּת נ 752 the cooper's profession
חַדְרָנוּת נ 752 housekeeping (hotel) [no pl.]

חַדְשָׁנוּת נ 752 inventiveness, innovativeness; innovation [no pl.]
חַטְטָנוּת נ 752 prying, interference [no pl.]
חַיְכָנוּת נ 752 smilingness [no pl.]
חַיְשָׁנוּת נ 752 hesitation, uncertainty, vacillation Lit. [no pl.]
חַלְבָּנוּת/חַלְבָנוּת נ 752 dairying
חַלְפָנוּת נ 752 money changing [no pl.]
חַמְדָנוּת נ 752 greediness, avarice, covetousness [no pl.]
חַמְסָנוּת נ 752 robbery with violence, theft [no pl.]
חַמְקָנוּת נ 752 evasiveness [no pl.]
חַנְפָנוּת נ 752 flattery, sycophancy [no pl.]
חַסְכָנוּת נ 752 frugality [no pl.]
חַצְרָנוּת נ 752 janitoring [no pl.]
חַקְיָנוּת נ 752 mimicry [no pl.]
חַקְרָנוּת נ 752 inquisitiveness [no pl.]
חַרְדָנוּת נ 752 anxiousness, apprehension
חַרְזָנוּת נ 752 rhyming [no pl.]
חַרְמָנוּת נ 752 being randy, lustful Col. [no pl.]; sexual lust
חַשְׁדָנוּת נ 752 wariness, suspicion [no pl.]
חַשְׂפָנוּת נ 752 striptease [no pl.]
חַשְׁקָנוּת נ 752 lust, desire
חַשְׁשָׁנוּת נ 752 apprehension, hesitation, fear [no pl.]
חַתְרָנוּת נ 752 subversion, undermining, sabotage [no pl.]
טַפְסָנוּת נ 752 building casts, making moulds [no pl.]
טַרְדָנוּת נ 752 pestering, annoyance, nagging, badgering [no pl.]
טַרְזָנוּת נ 752 dandyism
טַרְחָנוּת נ 752 troubling, bothering, annoying, pestering [no pl.]
יַבְבָנוּת נ 752 [no pl.] tendency to whimper
יַדְעָנוּת נ 752 erudition, know-how, expertise, knowledge, knowledgeableness [no pl.]
יַחְסָנוּת נ 752 haughtiness, family pride, snobbishness [no pl.]
יַחְפָנוּת נ 752 hooliganism, barefootedness, vagrancy [no pl.]
יַחְצָנוּת נ 752 public relations services [no pl.]
יַלְלָנוּת נ 752 howling, wailing [no pl.]
יַצְאָנוּת נ 752 prostitution [no pl.]
יַצְרָנוּת נ 752 manufacturing; productivity [no pl.]

יַקְרָנוּת נ 752 expensiveness, dearness, high price [no pl.]
יַרְקָנוּת נ 752 greengrocery [no pl.]
כַּוְרָנוּת נ 752 beekeeping [no pl.]
כַּזְבָנוּת נ 752 habitual lying, fabrication [no pl.]
כַּלְבָנוּת נ 752 dog handling, dog training [no pl.]
כַּרְסָנוּת נ 752 being wide, cumbersome; being big-bellied
כַּתְבָנוּת נ 752 typing [no pl.]
לַבְקָנוּת נ 752 albinism [no pl.]
לַחְשָׁנוּת נ 752 (theater) prompting [no pl.]
לַמְדָנוּת נ 752 erudition, scholarliness [no pl.]
לַקְקָנוּת נ 752 sweet tooth, craving after sweet foods; obsequiousness, ingratiation Col. [no pl.]
מַדְעָנוּת נ 752 Scientism [no pl.]
מַרְדָנוּת נ 752 rebelliousness [no pl
נַגְחָנוּת נ 752 argumentativeness, contentiousness, tendency to gore [no pl.]
נַדְבָנוּת נ 752 philanthropy, charitableness, generosity [no pl.]
נַטְרָנוּת נ 752 vengefulness, begrudging
נַצְחָנוּת נ 752 contentiousness, argumentativeness [no pl.]
נַצְלָנוּת נ 752 exploitation [no pl.]
נַקְבָנוּת נ 752 (computing) key-punching [no pl.]
נַקְמָנוּת נ 752 revengefulness, vindictiveness [no pl.]
נַקְרָנוּת נ 752 prying; fussiness [no pl.]
נַשְׁכָנוּת נ 752 tendency to bite
סַבְלָנוּת נ 752 patience [no pl.]
סַגְפָנוּת נ 752 asceticism [no pl.]
סַדְרָנוּת נ 752 stewarding, ushering [no pl.]
סַחְטָנוּת נ 752 extortion, blackmail [no pl.]
סַלְחָנוּת נ 752 forgivingness, mercifulness [no pl.]
סַלְפָנוּת נ 752 falsification, prevarication [no pl.]
סַפְדָנוּת נ 752 eulogizing [no pl.]
סַפְקָנוּת נ 752 doubt, uncertainty, skepticism [no pl.]
סַפְרָנוּת נ 752 librarianship [no pl.]
סַקְרָנוּת נ 752 curiosity, inquisitiveness [no pl.]
סַרְבָנוּת נ 752 insubordination, refusal to follow orders [no pl.]
עַגְבָנוּת נ 752 flirtation Lit. [no pl.]
עַמְלָנוּת נ 752 working, laboring [no pl.]

גַּמָּדוּת נ 757 short stature, nanism [no pl.]
גַּנָּנוּת נ 757 gardening [no pl.]
גַּשָּׁשׁוּת נ 757 tracking, scouting [no pl.]
דַּיָּלוּת נ 757 airline stewarding [no pl.]
דַּיָּנוּת נ 757 judgeship [no pl.]
חַיָּלוּת נ 757 being a soldier [no pl.]
כַּיָּסוּת נ 757 pickpocketing [no pl.]
אֻמְדָּנוּת נ 758 assessment, evaluation [no pl.]
בַּרְגָּנוּת נ 758 bourgeoisie [no pl.]
דֻּגְמָנוּת נ 758 modeling [no pl.]
קֻנְדָּסוּת נ 758 mischievousness [no pl.]
אוֹרְיָנוּת נ 759 literacy [no pl.]
בּוֹגְדָנוּת נ 759 treachery [no pl.]
בּוֹלְעָנוּת נ 759 big entity swallowing a small one [no pl.]
דּוֹקְרָנוּת נ 759 prickliness, spikiness [no pl.]
דּוֹרְסָנוּת נ 759 recklessness, destructiveness [no pl.]
חוֹלְמָנוּת נ 759 dreaming, daydreaming [no pl.]
טוֹבְעָנוּת נ 759 swampiness, bogginess [no pl.]
פּוֹסְקָנוּת נ 759 normativism [no pl.]
כּוֹחָנוּת/כֹּחָנוּת נ 760 belligerence, aggressiveness [no pl.]
אוֹנוּת נ 761 sexual potency [no pl.]
גּוֹיוּת נ 761 non-Jewishness [no pl.]
הוֹרוּת נ 761 parenthood [no pl.]
זוֹלוּת נ 761 cheapness; vulgarity [no pl.]
שׁוֹנוּת נ 761 difference, variance [no pl.]
אַגָּבִיּוּת נ 762 being incidental (no declension, no pl.)
אִטִּיּוּת נ 762 slowness [no pl.]
אֵינְסוֹפִיּוּת נ 762 infiniteness [no pl.]
אִישִׁיּוּת נ 762 personality [no pl.]
אִכְפַּתִּיּוּת נ 762 caring [no pl.]
אַלְמוֹנִיּוּת נ 762 anonymity [no pl.]
אָמָּנוּתִיּוּת נ 762 artistry (no declension, no pl.)
אֶמְצָעִיּוּת נ 762 centrality [no pl.]
אֲמִתִּיּוּת נ 762 veracity, truth [no pl.]
אָנֹכִיּוּת נ 762 egotism [no pl.]
אֱנוֹשִׁיּוּת נ 762 humaneness, compassion [no pl.]
אַנְטִישֵׁמִיּוּת נ 762 antisemitism [no pl.]
אַקְרָאִיּוּת נ 762 randomality [no pl.]
בֵּינוֹנִיּוּת נ 762 mediocrity [no pl.]
בֵּינְלְאֻמִּיּוּת נ 762 internationality [no pl.]
בֵּיתִיּוּת נ 762 domestication; house-loving [no pl.]
בִּלְבַדִּיּוּת נ 762 exclusivity [no pl.]
בַּלְבַּתִּיּוּת נ 762 being gentlemanlike, bourgoiserie (no decl., no pl.)
בֻּלְמוּסִיּוּת נ 762 overwhelming desire, ravenousness (no decl., no pl.)
בִּלְעָדִיּוּת נ 762 exclusivity; uniqueness [no pl.]
בְּעָיָתִיּוּת נ 762 problematicalness [no pl.]
בַּעַלְבַּתִּיּוּת נ 762 bourgeoiseri (no decl., no pl.)
בִּצְקִיּוּת נ 762 doughtiness [no pl.]
בִּקָּרְתִּיּוּת נ 762 criticism, being critical [no pl.]
בַּרְבָּרִיּוּת נ 762 barbarism [no pl.]
גּוּפָנִיּוּת נ 762 corporeality, materiality [no pl.]
גּוֹרָלִיּוּת נ 762 criticalness [no pl.]
גָּלוּתִיּוּת נ 762 ghetto manner [no pl.]
גַּלִּיּוּת נ 762 waviness, undulation [no pl.]
גַּלְמוּדִיּוּת נ 762 loneliness Lit. [no pl.]
גַּמְלוֹנִיּוּת נ 762 lankiness [no pl.]
גַּרְעִינִיּוּת נ 762 essence, kernel, basis Rare [no pl.]
דַּוְקָאִיּוּת נ 762 doing things deliberately to annoy [no pl.]
הֶגְיוֹנִיּוּת נ 762 logicality [no pl.]
הֶשֵּׂגִיּוּת נ 762 ambitiousness [no pl.]
וַדָּאִיּוּת נ 762 certainty [no pl.]
זֶהוּתִיּוּת נ 762 similar identity (no decl., no pl.)
זוּגִיּוּת נ 762 relationship of a couple [no pl.]
זְמַנִּיּוּת נ 762 temporariness [no pl.]
חַדְגּוֹנִיּוּת נ 762 monotony [no pl.]
חַדְפַּעֲמִיּוּת נ 762 one-time occurrence [no pl.]
חַדְצְדָדִיּוּת נ 762 singlesidedness [no pl.]
חוֹלָנִיּוּת נ 762 sickness [no pl.]
חִיצוֹנִיּוּת נ 762 external appearance [no pl.]
חַיָּתִיּוּת נ 762 beastiality [no pl.]
חֲלוּצִיּוּת נ 762 pioneering; initiative, originality [no pl.]
חֲמִצִיּוּת נ 762 acidity [no pl.]
חִנָּנִיּוּת נ 762 attractiveness, affability [no pl.]
חֻקִּיּוּת נ 762 legality; constancy, regularity [no pl.]
חֻקָּתִיּוּת נ 762 constitutionality [no pl.]
חֲרֵדִיּוּת נ 762 ultra-orthodoxy [no pl.]
טִיפּוּסִיּוּת נ 762 typicalness [no pl.]
טְרִיּוּת נ 762 freshness [no pl.]
יְהוּדִיּוּת נ 762 Jewishness [no pl.]
יוֹמְיוֹמִיּוּת נ 762 everyday life occurrence [no pl.]
יִחוּדִיּוּת נ 762 uniqueness [no pl.]
יְחִידִיּוּת נ 762 singlehood [no pl.]
יְצִירָתִיּוּת נ 762 creativity [no pl.]
יֶקִּיּוּת נ 762 behaving with the pedantry of a German Jew [no pl.]
יִשְׂרְאֵלִיּוּת נ 762 Israeliness [no pl.]
כּוֹחָנִיּוּת/כֹּחָנִיּוּת נ 762 belligerence, aggression [no pl.]
כְּלוּמִיּוּת נ 762 nothingness, insignificance [no pl.]
כְּנַעֲנִיּוּת נ 762 Canaanism (Israeli school of thought) [no pl.]
כְּפִיָּתִיּוּת נ 762 compulsiveness (no decl., no pl.)
כִּשְׁרוֹנִיּוּת נ 762 talentedness [no pl.]
כִּתָּתִיּוּת נ 762 factionalism [no pl.]
לְאֻמִּיּוּת נ 762 nationalism [no pl.]
לְבַדִּיּוּת נ 762 loneliness, isolation Lit. [no pl.]
לוֹעֲזִיּוּת נ 762 foreignness (of non-Hebrew word, lang.) [no pl.]
מְגַמָּתִיּוּת נ 762 tendentiousness [no pl.]
מַגְנֶטִיּוּת נ 762 magnetism [no pl.]
מִדְבָּרִיּוּת נ 762 desolateness, barrenness [no pl.]
מַדָּעִיּוּת נ 762 scientific method [no pl.]
מַהוּתִיּוּת נ 762 essentiality [no pl.]
מוֹפְתִיּוּת נ 762 examplariness [no pl.]
מוֹקְדִיּוּת נ 762 focalization, centrality [no pl.]
מִזְרָחִיּוּת נ 762 Middle Eastern characteristicalness [no pl.]
מַחְזוֹרִיּוּת/מַחֲזוֹרִיּוּת נ 762 cyclicality [no pl.]
מִיָּדִיּוּת נ 762 immediacy, promptness [no pl.]
מִינִיּוּת נ 762 sexuality [no pl.]
מִישׁוֹרִיּוּת נ 762 flatness, planarity [no pl.]
מֶכָנִיּוּת נ 762 mechanicalness [no pl.]
מְלָאכוּתִיּוּת נ 762 artificiality [no pl.]

יִצְרִיּוּת נ 776 following one's urges [no pl.]
נִבְזִיּוּת נ 776 despicability, contemptibleness [no pl.]
נִצְחִיּוּת נ 776 eternity [no pl.]
סִמְלִיּוּת נ 776 symbolism [no pl.]
עִבְרִיּוּת נ 776 being Hebrew [no pl.]
עִקְבִיּוּת נ 776 consistency [no pl.]
קִצְבִּיּוּת נ 776 rhythm [no pl.]
רִגְעִיּוּת נ 776 temporariness [no pl.]
רִגְשִׁיּוּת נ 776 emotionality [no pl.]
רִוְחִיּוּת נ 776 profitability [no pl.]
רִשְׁמִיּוּת נ 776 formality [no pl.]
שִׁטְחִיּוּת נ 776 superficiality [no pl.]
שִׂכְלִיּוּת נ 776 rationalism [no pl.]
שִׁקְרִיּוּת נ 776 falseness [no pl.]
עִנְיָנִיּוּת נ 777 matter-of-factness [no pl.]
שִׁגְרָתִיּוּת נ 778 routineness [no pl.]
נִסְיוֹנִיּוּת נ 779 experimentalness [no pl.]
צִבְעוֹנִיּוּת נ 779 colorfulness [no pl.]
שִׁוְיוֹנִיּוּת נ 779 equality [no pl.]
חִלּוֹנִיּוּת נ 780 secularity [no pl.]
צִיּוֹנִיּוּת נ 780 Zionism [no pl.]
קִפּוֹדִיּוּת נ 780 prickliness [no pl.]
רִבּוֹנִיּוּת נ 780 sovereignty [no pl.]
הִיּוּלִיּוּת נ 781 primeval state, primariness [no pl.]
חִיּוּבִיּוּת נ 781 positiveness [no pl.]
חִיּוּנִיּוּת נ 781 vitality [no pl.]
מִלּוּלִיּוּת נ 781 literalness; verbosity [no pl.]
נִגּוּדִיּוּת נ 781 difference, oppositeness [no pl.]
נִגּוּנִיּוּת נ 781 musicalness, melodiousness [no pl.]
סִבּוּכִיּוּת נ 781 complexity [no pl.]
צִבּוּרִיּוּת נ 781 public nature, universality; public [no pl.]
צִיּוּרִיּוּת נ 781 picturesequeness [no pl.]
קִבּוּצִיּוּת נ 781 collectivity; collectivism [no pl.]
רִכּוּזִיּוּת נ 781 centralization [no pl.]
שִׁמּוּשִׁיּוּת נ 781 usefulness [no pl.]
שִׁתּוּפִיּוּת נ 781 cooperativeness; collectiveness [no pl.]
קִיצוֹנִיּוּת נ 782 extremism [no pl.]
חֶלְקִיּוּת נ 783 incompleteness, partialness [no pl.]
נֶגְדִּיּוּת נ 783 contradiction, opposition [no pl.]
עֶרְכִּיּוּת נ 783 moral standard; valence, valency [no pl.]
עֶקְרוֹנִיּוּת נ 784 behavior by principle [no pl.]
אַבְנִיּוּת נ 785 stoniness [no pl.]
אַפְסִיּוּת נ 785 nothingness [no pl.]
אַרְסִיּוּת נ 785 poisonousness; malice [no pl.]
אַרְצִיּוּת נ 785 earthliness [no pl.]
גַּבְרִיּוּת נ 785 manhood, manliness [no pl.]
גַּרְמִיּוּת נ 785 boniness [no pl.]
גַּשְׁמִיּוּת נ 785 corporeality; materialism [no pl.]
טַרְשִׁיּוּת נ 785 rockiness [no pl.]
כַּלְבִּיּוּת נ 785 doggishness [no pl.]
כַּפְרִיּוּת נ 785 country life [no pl.]
נַחְצִיּוּת נ 785 emphaticness (phonetics) [no pl.]
נַפְשִׁיּוּת נ 785 spirituality Lit. [no pl.]
סַלְעִיּוּת נ 785 rockiness [no pl.]
עַצְמִיּוּת נ 785 identity, self-concept [no pl.]
בַּהֲמִיּוּת נ 786 brutishness, vulgarity, beastiality [no pl.]
גַּעֲשִׁיּוּת נ 786 volcanism [no pl.]
יַחֲסִיּוּת נ 786 relativity [no pl.]
אַוְרִירִיּוּת נ 787 lightness, airiness [no pl.]
חַכְלִילִיּוּת נ 787 redness, reddishness Lit. [no pl.]
שַׁבְרִירִיּוּת נ 787 fragility [no pl.]
אַכְזָרִיּוּת נ 788 cruelty [no pl.]
גַּלְוָנִיּוּת נ 788 galvanism [no pl.]
עַדְכָּנִיּוּת נ 788 being updated [no pl.]
עַסְקָנִיּוּת נ 788 wheeling-dealing (esp. in politics) [no pl.]
קַדְמוֹנִיּוּת נ 789 antiquity [no pl.]
אַדְמוּמִיּוּת נ 790 redness, ruddiness [no pl.]
אַפְלוּלִיּוּת נ 790 dimness, vagueness [no pl.]
אַפְרוּרִיּוּת נ 790 grayness [no pl.]
גַּבְנוּנִיּוּת נ 790 hunch, protrusiveness [no pl.]
לַבְנוּנִיּוּת נ 790 whiteness, paleness, pallor [no pl.]
לַחְלוּחִיּוּת נ 790 moistness [no pl.]
נַכְלוּלִיּוּת נ 790 deceptiveness, fraudulence Lit. [no pl.]
נַקְבּוּבִיּוּת נ 790 porousness [no pl.]
עַגְמוּמִיּוּת נ 790 sadness, forlornness [no pl.]
עַקְמוּמִיּוּת נ 790 being crooked, twisted [no pl.]
עַרְמוּמִיּוּת נ 790 cunning [no pl.]
קַטְנוּנִיּוּת נ 790 pettiness [no pl.]
רַכְרוּכִיּוּת נ 790 spinelessness, wimpishness [no pl.]
שַׁמְנוּנִיּוּת נ 790 oiliness [no pl.]
זַעֲרוּרִיּוּת נ 791 tininess [no pl.]
סַהֲרוּרִיּוּת נ 791 somnambulism; daydreaming [no pl.]
חַבְרוּתִיּוּת נ 792 friendliness, sociability [no pl.]
יַלְדוּתִיּוּת נ 792 childishness [no pl.]
סַמְכוּתִיּוּת נ 792 authoritarianism [no pl.]
סִפְרוּתִיּוּת נ 792 literariness [no pl.]
כַּדּוּרִיּוּת נ 793 roundness [no pl.]
כַּמּוּתִיּוּת נ 793 quantitativeness [no pl.]
אָפְקִיּוּת נ 794 horizontality; horizontalness [no pl.]
גָּלְמִיּוּת נ 794 rawness, amorphousness [no pl.]
חָמְרִיּוּת נ 794 materialism [no pl.]
חָפְשִׁיּוּת נ 794 freedom; ease [no pl.]
נָכְרִיּוּת נ 794 foreignness [no pl.]
קָטְבִּיּוּת נ 794 polarity [no pl.]
שָׁרְשִׁיּוּת נ 794 rootedness [no pl.]
גֹּעֲלִיּוּת נ 795 disgustingness, loathsomeness Col. [no pl.]
כֹּהֳלִיּוּת נ 795 alcohol content [no pl.]
אָפְנָתִיּוּת נ 796 being fashionable [no pl.]
דָּלִיּוּת נ 797 varicosity [no pl.]
דָּתִיּוּת נ 797 religiosity [no pl.]
חוֹלְמָנִיּוּת נ 798 dreaminess [no pl.]
סוֹדִיּוּת נ 799 secrecy [no pl.]
סוֹפִיּוּת נ 799 finality [no pl.]
קוֹצָנִיּוּת נ 800 thorniness [no pl.]
חוּצָנִיּוּת נ 801 extraterritoriality [no pl.]
חוּשָׁנִיּוּת נ 801 sensuality [no pl.]
תְּנוּדָתִיּוּת נ 802 fluctuation [no pl.]
תְּנוּעָתִיּוּת נ 802 mobility [no pl.]
תַּרְבּוּתִיּוּת נ 803 culture, sophistication [no pl.]
תּוֹעַלְתִּיּוּת נ 804 usefulness; practicability [no pl.]
תּוֹרַשְׁתִּיּוּת נ 804 heritability, heredity [no pl.]
בְּרִית נ 805 treaty; covenant; circumcision
טְרִית נ 805 sardine (it is not a suffix here)
חֲנִית נ 806 spear, javelin (is it not a suffix here?)
עֲוִית נ 806 spasm
מְחִית נ 807 puree
מְלִית נ 807 filling (in cooking/baking)
אַבְנִית נ 808 scale (in kettle, etc.) [no pl.]
אַלְפִּית נ 808 a thousandth (part)
בַּרְקִית נ 808 glaucoma [no pl.]

לִילִית נ 814 night owl; queen of evil spirits (Jewish mysticism) (is it a suffix here?)
לִכְלוּכִית נ 814 Cinderella
לִפְתִּית נ 814 rape (plant); canola
לְשׁוֹנִית נ 814 tongue of a lock; reed (music); tab
מֵאִית נ 814 a hundred's part
מוּלִית נ 814 mullus (fish)
מוֹנִית נ 814 taxicab
מוּסָפִית נ 814 affix
מוֹעֲדוֹנִית נ 814 small club
מַחְסָנִית נ 814 magazine (weaponry)
מַטְרוֹנִית נ 814 matron
מָיוֹנִית נ 814 mayonnaise
מִלִּית נ 814 function word, grammatical word
מַפּוּחִית נ 814 harmonica
מַפִּית נ 814 napkin
מְצָדִית נ 814 pillbox (guard post)
מַקְבִּילִית נ 814 parallelogram
מַרְגָּלִית נ 814 gem, pearl (is it a suffix here?)
מַרְגָּנִית נ 814 pimpernel (plant) (is it a suffix here?)
מָרִית נ 814 spatula
מַרְקוּלִית נ 814 mercurialis (plant)
מַשְׁכּוּכִית נ 814 farm animal leading the flock/herd; bellwether (is it a suffix here?)
נאדית נ 814 alveolus (anatomy)
נַהֲרוֹנִית נ 814 potamogeton (plant)
נוּרִית נ 814 buttercup (plant)
נִימִית נ 814 capillary (anatomy)
סוֹפִית נ 814 suffix
סִיבִית נ 814 particle board, chip board (carpentry)
סִימָנִית נ 814 ideogram, ideograph
סִירוֹנִית נ 814 siren, mermaid Lit.
סַלְתָּנִית נ 814 kind of edible fish (Talmudic)
סְנוּנִית נ 814 swallow (bird)
סְנַפִּירִית נ 814 hydrofoil
סָפִית נ 814 nut of violin, guitar
סְפָרָדִית נ 814 Spanish [no pl.]
סִתְוָנִית נ 814 colchicum, autumn crocus
עִדִּית נ 814 best, choicest; good soil (is it a suffix here?)
עֵינִית נ 814 eyepiece (of microscope, etc.)
עִירִית נ 814 chives; asphodel (is it a suffix here?)
עַכּוּבִית נ 814 gundelia (plant) (is it a suffix here?)
עַרְמוֹנִית נ 814 buckeye (tree); castanet(s); prostate
עֲשָׁשִׁית נ 814 oil lamp
פּוּמִית נ 814 mouthpiece (music)
פַּחִית נ 814 small can

פִּיוּנִית נ 814 pore (botany)
פְּנִימִית נ 814 inner tube; internal medicine ward
פַּעֲמוֹנִית נ 814 bellflower (plant)
פַּרְגִּית נ 814 young chicken
פַּשְׁטִידִית נ 814 patty
צְבוּרִית נ 814 slop bowl
צֵידָנִית נ 814 picnic cooler, food hamper
צִיצִית נ 814 tuft of hair
צְלוֹחִית נ 814 saucer; phial, vial Lit.
צִנּוֹרִית נ 814 narrow pipe, narrow tube
צַפִּיחִית נ 814 sweet baked good Lit.
צָרְפָתִית נ 814 French [no pl.]
קוּלִית נ 814 thigh; femur, thigh-bone
קוֹנְכִית נ 814 nasal concha (anatomy); shell
קוֹרְנִית נ 814 cornet (music)
קוֹרָנִית נ 814 thyme (plant, herb)
קִיסוֹסִית נ 814 smilax aspera (plant)
קְלוּמִית נ 814 peel of straw (Talmudic)
קֻפְסִית נ 814 small box, small container
קְרוֹנִית נ 814 rail-cart
קַרְקָעִית נ 814 bottom
קַשִּׁית נ 814 drinking straw
רִירִית נ 814 mucosa, mucous membrane
שְׁאֵרִית נ 814 remainder
שׁוּנִית/שֵׁנִית נ 814 reef
שְׂמָמִית נ 814 gecko (is it a suffix here?)
שַׁפִּירִית נ 814 dragonfly
שַׂקִּית נ 814 small bag
שַׁרְווּלִית נ 814 wristband
תָּאִית נ 814 cellulose
תָּוִית נ 814 label; characterization
תּוֹלַעֲנִית נ 814 helminthia (plant)
תַּחְתּוֹנִית נ 814 petticoat, slip
תְּרִיסָנִית נ 814 ray (cartilaginous fish)
מְחוֹלִית נ 815 chorea, St. Vitus' dance (medicine)
מְכוֹנִית נ 815 car
מְטַעֲנִית נ 816 covered pickup truck
מִפְרָשִׂית נ 816 sailboat
מִשְׁטָחִית נ 816 pad
מַגָּשִׁית נ 817 small tray
מַצָּעִית נ 817 receptacle (botany); placemat
מַשָּׂאִית נ 817 truck
מַסּוֹרִית נ 818 hacksaw
מַקּוֹשִׁית נ 818 xylophone
מַרְכּוֹלִית נ 819 minimarket
מַשְׁרוֹקִית נ 819 whistle (instr.) (is it a suffix here?)
רְבִיעִית נ 820 a fourth (part)

שְׁבִיעִית נ 820 a seventh (part)
שְׁלִישִׁית נ 820 a third (part)
שְׁמִינִית נ 820 an eighth (part)
תְּשִׁיעִית נ 820 a ninth (part)
אֲפִיפִית נ 821 wafer, waffle
חֲזִירִית נ 821 scrofula (medicine)
חֲמִישִׁית נ 821 a fifth (part)
עֲשִׂירִית נ 821 a tenth (part)
זְהָבִית נ 822 gagea (plant)
צְלָלִית נ 822 silhouette; shadow (puppet theater)
רְבָבִית נ 822 basis point
תְּזָזִית נ 822 craziness, hysteria; squall (meteorology)
אֲדָנִית נ 823 planter, window box
חֲזָזִית נ 823 lichen (botany)
חֲלָלִית נ 823 spaceship
זְהוֹרִית נ 824 rayon; crimson, crimson cloth Lit.
שְׁעוֹנִית נ 824 passionflower
דּוּגִית נ 825 small fishing boat
דְּמוּמִית נ 825 adonis (plant)
זְגוּגִית נ 825 glass panel, glass sheet
זְכוּכִית נ 825 glass
כְּתוּבִית נ 825 subtitle
פְּסוּקִית נ 825 clause (syntax)
צְדוּדִית נ 825 profile, side view
קְרוּמִית נ 825 very thin cover, membrane
שְׁלוּגִית נ 825 slush
שְׁלוּלִית נ 825 puddle
שְׁנוּנִית נ 825 acanthodactylus (type of lizard)
שְׁעוּעִית נ 825 beans
שְׁקוּפִית נ 825 transparency, slide
תְּלוּלִית נ 825 mound, small heap
כְּרוּכִית נ 825 strudel; (Internet) at
פִּשְׁתָּנִית נ 826 linaria (plant)
שְׂמָלָנִית נ 826 skirt Lit.
חִדְקוֹנִית נ 827 weevil
שִׁרְיוֹנִית נ 827 armored car
עִלִּית נ 828 elite; top quality; superstructure (of seacraft)
צִנִּית נ 828 podagra, gout
צִפִּית נ 828 pillowcase, cushion cover
רִבִּית נ 828 interest (banking)
שִׁשִּׁית נ 828 sixth (part)
חִנָּנִית נ 829 daisy (flower)
שִׁנָּנִית נ 829 dental hygienist (fem.)
אִתּוּרִית נ 830 beeper, pager
חִלּוּפִית נ 830 ameba
תִּיּוּרִית נ 830 tour bus
בַּרְזִלִּית נ 831 steel wool
עַרְפִלִּית נ 831 nebula
גַּחְלִילִית נ 832 firefly
חַכְלִילִית נ 832 redstart (bird)
פַּחְזָנִית נ 833 cream puff, profiterole
שַׁלְהָבִית נ 833 phlomis (plant)
שַׁעֲוָנִית נ 834 oilcloth

לַמְדָן ז 846 diligent scholar; erudite, learned
לַקְקָן ז 846 person with "sweet tooth"
מַזְגָן ז 846 air conditioner
מַלְשִׁן ז 846 rat, informer Sl.
מַרְדָן ז 846 rebel N
נַבְחָן ז 846 barker
נַבְלָן ז 846 harpist
נַבְרָן ז 846 vole, field mouse
נַגְחָן ז 846 a goring animal Lit.
נַדְבָן ז 846 philanthropist
נַחְרָן ז 846 snorer
נַטְרָן ז 846 begrudging, spiteful person Lit.
נַסְיָן ז 846 experimenter
נַצְחָן ז 846 a contentious person
נַצְלָן ז 846 exploiter
נַקְבָן ז 846 key-puncher (computing)
נַקְמָן ז 846 vindictive person
נַקְרָן ז 846 prying, nosy person
נַקְשָׁן ז 846 percussionist
נַשְׁכָן ז 846 biting (dog, child, etc.)
נַשְׁפָן ז 846 player of wind instrument
נַשְׁקָן ז 846 kisser Coll.
נַתְרָן ז 846 sodium
סַבְכָן ז 846 one who tends to make matters worse
סַבְלָן ז 846 patient, tolerant person
סַגְפָן ז 846 ascetic person
סַדְרָן ז 846 usher, steward
סַוְגָן ז 846 binder
סַחְבָן/סַחֲבָן ז 846 pilferer, petty thief Coll.
סַחְטָן ז 846 extortionist, blackmailer
סַיְעָן ז 846 collaborator
סַלְחָן ז 846 a forgiving person
סַלְפָן ז 846 liar, prevaricator
סַמְמָן ז 846 characteristic N
סַפְדָן ז 846 professional mourner
סַפְקָן ז 846 doubter, skeptic
סַפְרָן ז 846 librarian
סַקְרָן ז 846 curious (person)
סַרְבָן ז 846 refuser, insubordinate (person)
סַרְחָן ז 846 malodorous person Lit.
סַרְטָן ז 846 crab; cancer
עַגְבָן ז 846 flirter Lit.
עַדְשָׁן ז 846 freckled person Lit.
עַכְסָן ז 846 rattlesnake
עַמְלָן ז 846 workaholic Rare
עַמְקָן ז 846 profound, astute person
עַסְקָן ז 846 go-getter, politico, wheeler-dealer
עַפְיָן ז 846 anchovy
עַצְלָן ז 846 lazy (person)
עַקְמָן ז 846 crooked, twisted, dishonest person
עַקְשָׁן ז 846 stubborn (person)
פַּזְרָן ז 846 squanderer, spendthrift
פַּחְדָן ז 846 coward
פַּחְמָן ז 846 carbon
פַּיְטָן ז 846 poet
פַּיְסָן ז 846 appeaser
פַּלְגָן ז 846 separatist, divisive person
פַּלְשָׁן ז 846 one who often invades (privacy etc.)
פַּצְחָן ז 846 hacker (computing)
פַּרְשָׁן ז 846 commentator
פַּשְׁטָן ז 846 literalist
פַּשְׁרָן ז 846 compromiser
פַּתְיָן ז 846 seducer
צַוְחָן ז 846 screamer
צַחְקָן/צַחֲקָן ז 846 cheerful person
צַיְקָן ז 846 miser Lit.
צַיְתָן ז 846 obedient person
צַלְבָן ז 846 crusader
צַלְיָן ז 846 pilgrim
צַנְחָן ז 846 parachutist, paratrooper
צַרְחָן ז 846 screamer
צַרְכָן ז 846 consumer
קַטְלָן ז 846 deadly, lethal
קַיְטָן ז 846 summer vacationer
קַלְדָן ז 846 typist
קַלְלָן ז 846 cursing, swearing
קַלְפָן ז 846 card player, gambler
קַמְטָן ז 846 anguidae (lizard fam.); type of legless lizard
קַמְצָן ז 846 miser
קַנְיָן ז 846 purchaser, buyer
קַפְצָן ז 846 jumpy, bouncy
קַצְרָן ז 846 stenographer
קַרְיָן ז 846 announcer, newscaster
קַרְתָן ז 846 bumpkin, provincial
רַגְזָן ז 846 grumpy, irritable
רַגְשָׁן ז 846 emotional person
רַדְיָן ז 846 radian
רַחְמָן/רַחֲמָן ז 846 merciful
רַטְנָן ז 846 grumbler
רַכְלָן ז 846 gossipmonger
רַפְתָן ז 846 dairy farmer
רַצְחָן ז 846 murderer
רַצְעָן ז 846 leather worker, belt maker, cobbler
רַקְדָן ז 846 dancer
רַשְׁלָן ז 846 negligent (person)
רַתְחָן ז 846 hot-tempered, irascible
שַׁדְכָן ז 846 matchmaker
שַׂחְיָן ז 846 swimmer
שַׁחְצָן/שַׁחֲצָן ז 846 arrogant (person)
שַׂחְקָן/שַׂחֲקָן ז 846 player; actor
שַׁכְחָן ז 846 forgetful, absent-minded
שַׁמְרָן ז 846 conservative
שַׁקְדָן ז 846 diligent
שַׁקְרָן ז 846 liar
שַׂרְדָן ז 846 survivalist
שַׁרְקָן ז 846 guinea pig
שַׁרְקָן ז 846 whistler
שַׁתְיָן ז 846 habitual drinker
שַׁתְקָן ז 846 tight-lipped, reticent, taciturn
תַּבְעָן ז 846 clamorer; claimant
תַּגְרָן ז 846 dealer, merchant; haggler Lit.
תַּדְמָן ז 846 modelist
תַּוְיָן ז 846 plotter (computing)
תַּחְמָן ז 846 trickster, schemer, manipulator Sl.
תַּכְכָן ז 846 intriguer, quarrel-monger
תַּלְיָן ז 846 hangman
תַּפְרָן ז 846 down-and-out, derelict, pauper Sl.
תַּתְרָן ז 846 anosmic, lacking sense of smell
דַּבְּרָן ז 847 a talkative person
וַכְּחָן ז 847 argumentative person
חַבְּלָן ז 847 sapper; saboteur
קַבְּלָן ז 847 contractor
קַבְּצָן ז 847 beggar
קַבְּרָן/קַבְרָן ז 847 gravedigger
קַפְּדָן/קַפְדָן ז 847 strict, meticulous (person) (kafdan is a less frequent option)
חַלְבָּן/חַלְבָן ז 848 milkman (Halvan is a less frequent option)
טַלְפָן ז 848 switchboard operator, telephonist
בַּחֲשָׁן ז 849 interferer, meddler, stirrer
בַּעֲטָן ז 849 kicker, rebel, dissenter
גַּהֲצָן ז 849 ironer
גַּעֲרָן ז 849 one who often castigates, scolds
דַּאֲגָן ז 849 one who worries a lot
זַעֲמָן ז 849 coluber (type of snake)
זַעֲמָן ז 849 quick-tempered person
זַעֲפָן ז 849 quick-tempered
טַהֲרָן ז 849 purist
יַעֲרָן ז 849 forest ranger; forester
כַּעֲסָן ז 849 hot-headed, hot tempered person
לַהֲגָן ז 849 prattler
לַעֲגָן ז 849 ridiculer, belittler
נַאֲפָן ז 849 adulterer
צַעֲקָן ז 849 shouter
רַעֲנָן ז 849 fresh
רַעֲשָׁן ז 849 rattle, noise maker
גַּנְדְּרָן ז 850 dandy
זַבְלְגָן ז 850 bleary-eyed person
כַּרְסְמָן ז 850 rodent
עַבְדְּקָן ז 850 thick-bearded (man)
קַנְטְרָן ז 850 spiteful, annoying
תַּחְבְּלָן ז 850 wily, crafty, cunning

שַׁבַּתְיָן ז 863 Seventh Day Adventist
שְׁדַלָּן ז 863 lobbyist
שִׁנָּן ז 863 dental hygienist
שְׁעָן ז 863 watchmaker
שְׁקִיטָן ז 863 flamingo Rare
תַּאַוְתָן ז 863 lustful person, lecher
תְּבוּסְתָן ז 863 defeatist
תּוֹסֶפְתָּן ז 863 appendix (anatomy)
תּוֹעַלְתָּן ז 863 utilitarian (person)
תּוֹעַמְלָן ז 863 propagandist, advertiser
תּוֹתְחָן ז 863 gunner
תַּיָּרָן ז 863 tour operator, tour agent
תָּכְנִיתָן ז 863 computing programmar
תַּנּוּרָן ז 863 furnace operator
תַּעַמְלָן ז 863 propagandist, advertiser
תַּעֲשִׂיָּן ז 863 industrialist
תֻּרְגְּמָן ז 863 translator Rare
מִבְרְקָן ז 864 telegrapher
מִגְבְּעָן ז 864 milliner, hatter
מִזְרְחָן ז 864 orientalist
מִשְׁפְּטָן/מִשְׁפָּטָן ז 864 jurist, lawyer
מִשְׁתְּלָן ז 864 nursery worker (gardening)
מִנְהֲלָן ז 865 administrator
מִסְעֲדָן ז 865 restaurateur
מִקְצוֹעָן ז 866 a professional
מִשְׁקוֹלָן ז 866 weightlifter
מַבְלְטָן ז 867 one designing and creating dies
מַהְפְּכָן ז 867 revolutionary
מַקְלְעָן ז 867 machine gunner
מַרְזְחָן ז 867 innkeeper, bartender Rare
מַגְזִימָן ז 868 one who exaggerates
מַדְלִיפָן ז 868 one leaking information Coll.
מַחְלִיטָן ז 868 decision-maker Coll.
מַטְרִידָן ז 868 nuisance, pest Coll.
מַמְצִיאָן ז 868 inventor, innovator Coll.
מַפְסִידָן ז 868 loser" Coll."
מַצְחִיקָן ז 868 comedian Coll.
מַצְלִיחָן ז 868 successful person Coll.
מַשְׁמִיצָן ז 868 defamer Coll.
מַשְׁקִיעָן ז 868 one who invests a lot
מַחְוָן/מַחֲוָן ז 869 indicator, gauge
מַשְׁוָן ז 869 equator
סְתַגְּלָן ז 870 one who easily adjusts to changes
סְתַגְּפָן ז 870 ascetic person
סְתַגְּרָן ז 870 introverted, withdrawn, detached person
שְׁתַדְּלָן ז 871 lobbyist
שְׁתַלְּטָן ז 871 domineering, imperious
שְׁתַמְּטָן ז 871 shirker
פְּעַלְתָּן ז 872 active person
חֲרָשְׁתָּן ז 873 manufacturer, industrialist Arch.
יְבוּאָן ז 874 importer
יְדוּעָן ז 874 celebrity
יְצוּאָן ז 874 exporter
רְכוּשָׁן ז 874 capitalist
בִּיתָן ז 875 pavilion, stand; booth
זִיפָן ז 875 foxtail (plant)
טִיסָן ז 875 model airplane
כִּיסָן ז 875 filled dumplings, kreplach, pierogi, wontons
סִידָן ז 875 calcium
שִׂיאָן ז 875 record holder
יֵינָן ז 876 winemaker, vintner
לֵיצָן ז 876 clown, jester
מֵימָן ז 876 hydrogen
סֵיפָן ז 876 swordtail (fish)
רֵיחָן ז 876 basil
רֵיקָן ז 876 empty; ignorant person Lit.
יוֹמָן ז 877 diary; calendar
קוֹלָן ז 877 tuning fork
קוֹצָן ז 877 thistle
תּוֹרָן ז 877 person on duty, duty officer
זוּגָן ז 878 zygophyllum (plant)
צוּרָן ז 878 morpheme
תַּבְלִיטָן ז 879 relief (map) maker
תַּחְקִירָן ז 879 investigator, investigative reporter
תַּכְשִׁיטָן ז 879 jeweler
תַּמְחִירָן ז 879 cost accountant
תַּקְלִיטָן ז 879 disc jockey, DJ
תַּחְבִּיבָן ז 880 hobbyist
תַּכְסִיסָן ז 880 tactician, trickster
תַּמְלִילָן ז 880 librettist, lyricist; word processor
תַּדְמִיתָן ז 881 image maker, public relations agent
תַּכְלִיתָן ז 881 purposeful person
תַּסְכִּיתָן ז 881 radio play producer
תַּצְפִּיתָן ז 881 lookout
תַּבְרוּאָן ז 882 sanitation engineer, sanitary officer, sanitation inspector
תַּחְבּוּלָן ז 882 trickster, tactician, wily person
תַּחְזוּקָן/תַּחֲזוּקָן ז 882 maintenance person
תַּמְרוּקָן ז 882 cosmetician
תַּפְאוּרָן ז 882 set manager (theater)
תַּעֲלוּלָן ז 883 prankster, mischief-maker
אִגְּרוֹן ז 884 letter writing manual, correspondence text book
בִּדְיוֹן ז 884 fiction [no pl.]
בִּתְרוֹן ז 884 ravine, gorge
גִּבְתּוֹן ז 884 bunting (bird)
גִּדְרוֹן ז 884 wren
גִּלְשׁוֹן ז 884 hang glider
טִפְּשׁוֹן ז 884 silly little fool
כִּבְשׁוֹן ז 884 secret, mystery Lit.
פִּזְמוֹן ז 884 short song, tune; refrain
פִּרְיוֹן ז 884 fertility [no pl.]
צִבְיוֹן ז 884 unique style, character [no pl.]
קִלְשׁוֹן (ל׳ דגושה) ז 884 pitchfork
קִמְרוֹן ז 884 dome (architec.); anticlinorium (geology)
רִפְיוֹן ז 884 weakness; limpness [no pl.]
שִׁרְיוֹן ז 884 armor
תִּלְיוֹן ז 884 pendant
דִּמְיוֹן ז 885 imagination; resemblance
יִתְרוֹן ז 885 advantage
כִּפְיוֹן ז 885 epilepsy
לִגְיוֹן ז 885 legion(s)
סִגְנוֹן ז 885 style
סִרְחוֹן ז 885 stench, foul odor
פִּדְיוֹן ז 885 redemption; ransom; proceeds
פִּרְקוֹן ז 885 abreaction (psychoanalysis)
פִּתְרוֹן ז 885 solution
שִׁוְיוֹן ז 885 equality
שִׁלְטוֹן ז 885 regime; government
שִׂרְטוֹן ז 885 sandbank, shoal
גִּשְׁרוֹן ז 886 small bridge
דִּבְקוֹן ז 886 mistletoe (plant)
דִּגְלוֹן ז 886 small flag, pennant
סִמְלוֹן ז 886 pin, small badge
סִפְלוֹן ז 886 demitasse, small cup
סִפְרוֹן ז 886 booklet
סִרְטוֹן ז 886 short film; video clip
פִּסְלוֹן ז 886 statuette, figurine
פִּצְעוֹן ז 886 pimple
צִבְעוֹן ז 886 crayon
רִבְעוֹן ז 886 quarter (of a year); quarterly (magazine, report)
שִׁבְרוֹן ז 886 distress; heartbreak [no pl.]
שִׁלְגּוֹן ז 886 popsicle, ice lolly
חֶלְבּוֹן ז 887 white of egg; protein
חֶלְמוֹן ז 887 yolk
חֶצְיוֹן ז 887 median (statistics)
עֶגְלוֹן ז 887 carter, coachman
חֶבְיוֹן ז 888 hiding place, secret place
חֶרְבּוֹן ז 888 disaster, disappointment Coll.
חֶשְׁבּוֹן ז 888 math; arithmetic; bill, check; bank account
עֶלְבּוֹן ז 888 insult N
אַגְמוֹן ז 889 reed, bulrush
גַּמְלוֹן ז 889 gable

deltoid, kite-shaped 889 דַּלְתּוֹן ז
anise, sweet cumin 889 כַּמְנוֹן ז
chestnut 889 עַרְמוֹן ז
shopping center, mall 889 קַנְיוֹן ז
bribe Lit. (plural only) 889 שַׁלְמוֹן (...נִים) ז
last 890 אַחֲרוֹן ז
bell 890 פַּעֲמוֹן ז
idea, plan, proposal; theme 891 רַעֲיוֹן/רַעְיוֹן ז
alphabetical index 892 אַלְפּוֹן (אין דגש) ז
tights, pantyhose; socks (plural only) 892 גַּרְבּוֹן (...נִים) ז
passport 892 דַּרְכּוֹן ז
small room 892 חַדְרוֹן ז
small child 892 יַלְדּוֹן ז
monthly magazine 892 יַרְחוֹן ז
greenfinch (bird) 892 יַרְקוֹן ז
small dog 892 כַּלְבּוֹן ז
ear stick 892 צַמְרוֹן ז
ancient; ancient person 892 קַדְמוֹן ז
glacier; iceberg 892 קַרְחוֹן ז
lower; lowest; underwear Coll. 892 תַּחְתּוֹן ז
crescent 893 סַהֲרוֹן/שַׂהֲרוֹן ז
delightful, cute - esp. infant 894 חֲמוּדוֹן ז
gosling 894 אֲוָזוֹן ז
islet 894 אִיּוֹן ז
pupil (of eye) 894 אִישׁוֹן ז
thimble 894 אֶצְבָּעוֹן ז
small pistol/revolver 894 אֶקְדָּחוֹן ז
tetrahedron (geometry) 894 אַרְבָּעוֹן ז
temporary housing/shelter covered with cloth 894 בַּדּוֹן ז
young lad, stripling 894 בַּחוּרוֹן ז
small bottle 894 בַּקְבּוּקוֹן ז
duckling 894 בַּרְוָזוֹן ז
small roof, awning 894 גַּגּוֹן ז
cartwheel (athletics) 894 גַּלְגַּלּוֹן ז
roller, guide pulley 894 גַּלְגִּלּוֹן ז
pre-kindergarten 894 גַּנּוֹן ז
teddy bear 894 דֻּבּוֹן ז
small fly 894 זְבוּבוֹן ז
try-square (building, carpentry) 894 זָוִיתוֹן ז
dovetail 894 זְנַבְיוֹן ז
quiz 894 חִידוֹן ז
daily newspaper 894 יוֹמוֹן ז
small hat 894 כּוֹבָעוֹן ז
small star 894 כּוֹכָבוֹן ז
filled dumpling, pierogi, wonton 894 כִּיסוֹן ז
small dog 894 כְּלַבְלַבּוֹן ז
percentile 894 מֵאוֹן ז
cerebellum (anatomy) 894 מֹחוֹן ז
kitchenette 894 מִטְבָּחוֹן ז

information booklet 894 מֵידָעוֹן ז
glossary 894 מֻנָּחוֹן ז
portable terminal 894 מְסוֹפוֹן ז
paper napkin dispenser 894 מַפִּיּוֹן ז
parallelepiped (geometry) 894 מַקְבִּילוֹן ז
local newspaper 894 מְקוֹמוֹן ז
representative body (of association) 894 מֻרְשׁוֹן ז
small cellar 894 מַרְתְּפוֹן ז
answering machine 894 מְשִׁיבוֹן ז
anthology of sayings/expressions 894 נִיבוֹן ז
pony, foal 894 סוּסוֹן ז
little mouse 894 עַכְבָּרוֹן ז
polyhedron (geometry) 894 פֵּאוֹן ז
percussion mallet (music), hammer drill 894 פַּטִּישׁוֹן ז
young elephant 894 פִּילוֹן ז
pepper tree 894 פִּלְפְּלוֹן ז
nursery school 894 פָּעוֹטוֹן ז
poinciana (plant) 894 צֶאֱלוֹן ז
collar 894 צַוָּארוֹן ז
small crucifix (jewelry) 894 צְלָבוֹן ז
multi-sided geometrical form 894 רַבְצַלְעוֹן ז
questionnaire 894 שְׁאֵלוֹן ז
weekly magazine 894 שְׁבוּעוֹן ז
sabbatical 894 שַׁבָּתוֹן ז
sprite, imp 894 שֵׁדוֹן ז
flagellum (biology) 894 שׁוֹטוֹן ז
lined sheet 894 שׁוּרוֹן ז
conversation book/manual 894 שִׂיחוֹן ז
song book 894 שִׁירוֹן ז
clock, watch 894 שָׁעוֹן ז
quiz show, game show 894 שַׁעֲשׁוּעוֹן ז
radicle (botany) 894 שָׁרְשׁוֹן ז
joy, happiness 894 שָׂשׂוֹן ז
small cell 894 תָּאוֹן ז
date display; list of dates 894 תַּאֲרִיכוֹן ז
teapot; tea bag Coll. 894 תֵּיוֹן ז
periodical 894 תְּקוּפוֹן ז
diskette (computing) 894 תַּקְלִיטוֹן ז
articles of association, statute 894 תַּקָּנוֹן ז
duodenum 894 תְּרֵיסַרְיוֹן ז
very small satchel; silique (botany) 894 תַּרְמִילוֹן ז
booklet of crossword puzzles 894 תַּשְׁבְּצוֹן ז
icosahedron 894 עֶשְׂרִימוֹן ז
small cup 895 גְּבִיעוֹן ז
small crystal 895 גְּבִישׁוֹן ז
racoon 895 דְּבִיבוֹן ז
moustached warbler (bird) 895 זְמִירוֹן ז

stingray (fish) 895 טְרִיגוֹן ז
bulletin, newsletter 895 יְדִיעוֹן ז
correcting fluid, white-out 895 מְחִיקוֹן ז
price list 895 מְחִירוֹן ז
small/light coat 895 מְעִילוֹן ז
spinning top, dreidel 895 סְבִיבוֹן ז
sub-clause 895 סְעִיפוֹן ז
minor clerk (negative connotation) 895 פְּקִידוֹן ז
felt tipped pen 895 פְּתִילוֹן ז
young man 895 צְעִירוֹן ז
small hut 895 צְרִיפוֹן ז
entry 895 רְשִׁימוֹן ז
small rug 895 שְׁטִיחוֹן ז
Tertiary (geology) 895 שְׁלִישׁוֹן ז
pseudocerastes (a poisonous snake) 895 שְׁפִיפוֹן ז
airplane 896 אֲוִירוֹן ז
cornetfish 896 חֲלִילוֹן ז
kite 896 עֲפִיפוֹן ז
small apartment 897 דִּירָנֶת נ
small barrel 897 חֲבִיָּנֶת נ
silly (fem.) 897 טִפְּשֹׁנֶת נ
affectionate manner of referring to a girl 897 יַלְדֹּנֶת נ
small suitcase 897 מִזְוָדֹנֶת נ
small crib 897 עֲרִיסֹנֶת נ
disgrace, shame 898 בִּזָּיוֹן ז
journal, mouthpiece, organ 898 בִּטָּאוֹן ז
confidence; safety; security 898 בִּטָּחוֹן ז
sheet of paper; newspaper edition, issue 898 גִּלָּיוֹן ז
depression 898 דִּכָּאוֹן ז
concession, permit 898 זִכָּיוֹן ז
memory; memoirs; memory chip (computing) 898 זִכָּרוֹן ז
pallor [no pl.] 898 חִוָּרוֹן ז
waiting, expectation [no pl.] 898 חִכָּיוֹן ז
darkness, being dark Lit. (no comp. lengthening, no pl.) 898 כִּהָיוֹן ז
cyanosis (no comp. lengthening, no pl.) 898 כִּחָלוֹן ז
annihilation, extinction [no pl.] 898 כִּלָּיוֹן ז
blight [no pl.] 898 כִּמָּשׁוֹן ז
failure 898 כִּשָּׁלוֹן ז
talent 898 כִּשָּׁרוֹן ז
discount (banking, finances) 898 נִכָּיוֹן ז
attempt; trial, experiment; experience 898 נִסָּיוֹן ז
victory 898 נִצָּחוֹן ז
quarrel, struggle Lit. 898 נִצָּיוֹן ז
cleaning; cleanliness 898 נִקָּיוֹן ז
blindness (pl. suffix - im) 898 עִוָּרוֹן ז
estate, inheritance 898 עִזָּבוֹן ז
lien (law) 898 עִכָּבוֹן ז

עִצָּבוֹן ז 898 sorrow, grief Lit.; toil, pain Lit.
פִּכָּחוֹן ז 898 sobriety
פִּקָּדוֹן ז 898 deposit
פִּקָּחוֹן ז 898 realistic observation; vision, eyesight Lit.
פִּתָּיוֹן ז 898 bait, lure; temptation
צִחָיוֹן ז 898 dehydration (no comp. lengthening, no pl.)
צִמָּאוֹן ז 898 thirst
קִבָּעוֹן ז 898 fixation
קִמָּחוֹן ז 898 mildew (plant disease caused by fungi) [no pl.]
קִפָּאוֹן ז 898 freeze [no pl.]
רִקָּבוֹן ז 898 decomposition, rotting [no pl.]
רִשָּׁיוֹן ז 898 permit N
שִׁגָּעוֹן ז 898 madness
שִׁגָּרוֹן ז 898 rheumatism [no pl.]
שִׁדָּפוֹן ז 898 blight, blast
שִׁזָּפוֹן ז 898 suntan [no pl.]
שִׁטָּפוֹן ז 898 flood N
שִׁכָּחוֹן ז 898 amnesia, forgetfulness [no pl.]
שִׁכָּרוֹן ז 898 drunkenness [no pl.]
שִׁמָּמוֹן ז 898 emptiness, dreariness Lit. [no pl.]
תִּמָּהוֹן ז 898 amazement, wonder, surprise [no pl.]
הִגָּיוֹן ז 899 logic
חִדָּלוֹן ז 899 destruction, cessation Lit. [no pl.]
חִזָּיוֹן ז 899 spectacle, sight, show; vision
חִלָּדוֹן ז 899 wheat rust
חִלָּזוֹן ז 899 snail
חִסָּיוֹן ז 899 privilege, immunity (law)
חִסָּכוֹן ז 899 saving(s)
חִסָּרוֹן ז 899 disadvantage
חִפָּזוֹן ז 899 rush N [no pl.]
חִשָּׁכוֹן ז 899 blackout
עִלָּפוֹן ז 899 swoon, fainting [no pl.]
עִפָּרוֹן ז 899 pencil
עִקָּרוֹן ז 899 principle
הִזָּיוֹן ז 900 fantasy
הֵרָיוֹן ז 901 pregnancy
חֵרָגוֹן ז 901 trance (psych.) [no pl.]
עֵרָגוֹן ז 901 strong yearning, longing Lit.
סֵאָבוֹן ז 902 filth, dirt Lit.-Rare [no pl.]
רֵאָיוֹן ז 902 interview
תֵּאָבוֹן ז 902 appetite [no pl.]
גֵּרָעוֹן ז 903 deficit
דֵּרָאוֹן ז 903 disgrace, shame Lit. [no pl.]
פֵּרָעוֹן ז 903 payment, paying off debt; redemption
יֵרָקוֹן ז 904 greensickness, chlorosis (plant disease) [no pl.]

עֵרָבוֹן ז 905 security, guarantee, deposit
קֵהָיוֹן ז 905 dementia; insensitivity, apathy Lit. (only constr., no pl.)
בְּלַאי ז 906 wear and tear, physical deterioration (no decl., no pl.)
גְּלַאי ז 906 decolletage; bare/exposed place Lit.
גְּנַאי ז 906 shame, disgrace (no decl., only constr. sg., no pl.)
טְלַאי ז 906 patch
לְוַאי ז 906 after- (aftertaste etc.); modifier, attribute
מְלַאי ז 906 inventory
מְצַאי ז 906 inventory
פְּנַאי ז 906 leisure
תְּנַאי ז 906 condition
הֲבַאי ז 907 nonsense [no pl.]
חֲשַׁאי ז 907 stealth (no decl., no pl.)
בַּדַּאי ז 908 liar, fabricator Lit.
בַּמַּאי ז 908 director
בַּנַּאי ז 908 builder
גַּבַּאי ז 908 manager of synagogue
גַּלַּאי ז 908 detector
הַגַּאי ז 908 helmsman (shipping)
וַדַּאי ז 908 certainty; certainly
זַכַּאי/זַכַּי ז 908 innocent (person); entitled (person)
זַנַּאי ז 908 adulterer, lecher
חַוַּאי ז 908 rancher, farmer
חַזַּאי ז 908 meteorologist
טַוַּאי ז 908 weaver Lit.-Rare
יַמַּאי ז 908 seaman
כַּבַּאי ז 908 fireman
מַסַּאי ז 908 essayist
קַנַּאי ז 908 zealot; jealous
רַמַּאי ז 908 cheat N, crook
שַׁמַּאי ז 908 assessor
שַׁנַּאי ז 908 transformer
אֲמוֹדַאי ז 909 Diver
אַשְׁרַאי ז 909 credit
בּוּלַאי ז 909 philatelist
בַּטְנוּנַאי ז 909 bass player
בִּימַאי ז 909 director (stage, theater)
בֻּסְתְּנַאי ז 909 orchardist
בַּרְקַאי ז 909 morning star (Talmudic)
גִּילַאי ז 909 member of the same age group
דְּיוֹקְנַאי ז 909 portraitist
דִּקְלַאי/דִּקְלַי ז 909 palm grower
הֲוַי ז 909 way of life, atmosphere, local color
חַקְלַאי ז 909 farmer, agronomist
חֶשְׁבּוֹנַאי ז 909 accountant
חַשְׁמַלַּאי ז 909 electrician
טוּרַאי ז 909 private (military)
טִיסָנַאי ז 909 model airplane enthusiast
טֶכְנַאי ז 909 technician

יוֹמָנַאי ז 909 duty officer (police), desk sergeant
כִּילַי ז 909 miser Lit.
לִגְיוֹנַאי ז 909 legionnaire
לְשׁוֹנַאי ז 909 linguist
מְדִינַאי ז 909 statesman, diplomat
מִזְנוֹנַאי ז 909 snack bar owner/employee
מַחֲזַאי ז 909 playwright
מַחְסְנַאי ז 909 storekeeper, stock-keeper
מְכוֹנַאי ז 909 mechanic
מִלְגַאי ז 909 one who gets a scholarship
מְלוֹנַאי ז 909 hotelier
מִלּוֹנַאי ז 909 lexicographer
מָמוֹנַאי ז 909 financier
מִנְהֲלַאי ז 909 administrator
מְנוֹפַאי ז 909 crane operator
מַסּוֹקַאי ז 909 helicopter pilot
מְסִלַּאי ז 909 platelayer
מְשׁוֹטַאי ז 909 oarsman
מַשְׁכּוֹנַאי ז 909 pawnbroker
נִבְלַאי ז 909 harpist
נַחְלַאי ז 909 soldier in a Nahal unit (Israeli army)
סִיטוֹנַאי ז 909 wholesaler
סַכִּינַאי ז 909 stabber, knifer
עוּגָבַאי ז 909 organist
עֲתוּדַאי ז 909 soldier-student (military)
עִתּוֹנַאי ז 909 journalist
פִּזְמוֹנַאי ז 909 songwriter (who writes lyrics)
פֻּנְדְּקַאי ז 909 innkeeper
פְּנִימַאי ז 909 internist, specialist in internal medicine
קִמְעוֹנַאי ז 909 retailer
קֻפַּאי ז 909 cashier
רוֹבַאי ז 909 rifleman, infantryman
רְכִילַאי ז 909 gossip column writer
רַפְסוֹדַאי ז 909 raft operator
שַׁקְנַאי ז 909 pelican
שִׁרְיוֹנַאי ז 909 soldier in the armored corps
תַּסְרִיטַאי ז 909 script writer
בַּזְיָר ז 910 falconer
גֻּנְדָּר ז 910 warder, jailer
סַנְדְּלָר ז 910 shoemaker
פַּעֲמוֹנָר ז 910 bell-ringer
אֲוָזִיָּה נ 911 goose pen
אִטְרִיָּה נ 911 noodle
אֻכְלוּסִיָּה נ 911 population
אֳנִיָּה נ 911 boat, ship
אִפַּרְכִיָּה נ 911 district, region (Talmudic)
בֵּיצִיָּה נ 911 fried egg
בַּרְוָזִיָּה נ 911 duck hatchery
בִּרְזִיָּה נ 911 drinking fountain or set of connected faucets for common use
בְּרֵכִיָּה נ 911 mallard

גּוּמִיָּה נ 911 rubber band
גּוּפִיָּה נ 911 undershirt
דּוּמִיָּה נ 911 silence
זִכְרִיָּה נ 911 forget-me-not (plant)
זִמְרִיָּה נ 911 singing festival
חֲזִיָּה נ 911 bra, brassiere
חֲמִישִׁיָּה נ 911 quintet
חֲנֻכִּיָּה נ 911 Hanukkah lamp
חֶשְׁבּוֹנִיָּה נ 911 abacus
טוּרִיָּה נ 911 Middle Eastern spade with broad blade and short handle
יַמִּיָּה נ 911 navy, fleet, flotilla
כְּנֵסִיָּה נ 911 church
כַּרְטִיסִיָּה נ 911 multiple entry ticket
כְּרִיכִיָּה נ 911 bookbinding shop
כְּתֵפִיָּה נ 911 shoulder strap
לַחְמָנִיָּה נ 911 bread roll
מֵאִיָּה נ 911 hundred-note (money) Sl.
מַאֲפִיָּה נ 911 bakery
מִגְדָּנִיָּה נ 911 sweet shop, bakery shop
מַדְגֵּרִיָּה נ 911 farm with a system of incubators
מַטְוִיָּה נ 911 spinning mill
מַטְעַמִּיָּה נ 911 deli
מִטְרִיָּה נ 911 umbrella
מֵימִיָּה נ 911 water canteen
מַכַּבִּיָּה נ 911 Jewish sports competition event
מִכְתָּבִיָּה נ 911 writing case, portfolio
מִלְחִיָּה נ 911 salt shaker
מַמְתַּקִּיָּה נ 911 sweet shop
מַסְגְּרִיָּה נ 911 locksmith shop
מַעֲדַנִּיָּה נ 911 deli
מַעֲשִׂיָּה נ 911 tale
מִצְחִיָּה נ 911 (cap) visor
מַצִּיָּה נ 911 cracker
מֶרְכָּזִיָּה נ 911 telephone exchange
מַרְפֵּדִיָּה נ 911 upholstery shop
מְרָקִיָּה נ 911 soup tureen
מָתְנִיָּה נ 911 vest, waistcoat
נַגָּרִיָּה נ 911 carpentry shop
נַפָּחִיָּה נ 911 blacksmith shop
נַקְנִיקִיָּה נ 911 hot dog, wiener, frankfurter
נִשְׁפִּיָּה נ 911 small or limited ball/party
סַבּוֹנִיָּה נ 911 soap holder
סִימָנִיָּה נ 911 bookmark
סֻכָּרִיָּה נ 911 candy
סַנְדְּלָרִיָּה נ 911 shoemaker's shop
סֻפְגָּנִיָּה נ 911 doughnut
סִפְרִיָּה נ 911 library
סִרְטִיָּה נ 911 film library
עַגְבָנִיָּה נ 911 tomato
עוּגִיָּה נ 911 cookie
עָזְנִיָּה נ 911 black vulture
עִירִיָּה נ 911 town hall
עֲשִׂירִיָּה נ 911 group of ten

פַּחָחִיָּה/פֶּחָחִיָּה נ 911 car body shop
פִּטְרִיָּה נ 911 mushroom
פִּיָּה נ 911 opening, spout; mouthpiece (music)
פֻּמְפִּיָּה נ 911 grater
פְּנִימִיָּה נ 911 boarding school
פְּתִילִיָּה נ 911 kerosene burner
צִמְחִיָּה נ 911 flora, vegetation
צְמִיגִיָּה נ 911 tire repair shop
צִפִּיָּה נ 911 expectation; hope, aspiration
צַרְכָנִיָּה נ 911 discount supermarket
קֻבִּיָּה נ 911 cube
קְהִלִּיָּה נ 911 commonwealth, community
קוֹנְכִיָּה נ 911 shell
קוּקִיָּה נ 911 cuckoo
רֹאשִׁיָּה נ 911 harness on working animal; head kick
רְבִיעִיָּה נ 911 quartet
שְׁבִיעִיָּה נ 911 group of seven
שִׁכְמִיָּה נ 911 cape, shawl
שְׁלִישִׁיָּה נ 911 trio
שְׁמִינִיָּה נ 911 group of eight
שִׁמְשִׁיָּה נ 911 parasol
שַׁעֲרוּרִיָּה נ 911 scandal
שְׁפַנִּיָּה נ 911 pen for rabbits
שְׁקֵדִיָּה נ 911 almond tree
שִׁשִּׁיָּה נ 911 group of six
תַּאֲנִיָּה נ 911 mourning, sorrow Lit.
תּוּשִׁיָּה נ 911 resourcefulness
תִּינוֹקִיָּה נ 911 creche, day nursery
תִּיקִיָּה נ 911 filing cabinet; folder (computing)
תָּכְנִיָּה נ 911 printed program (theater, concert, etc.)
תַּמְרוּקִיָּה נ 911 perfumery
תַּעֲשִׂיָּה נ 911 industry
תַּקְלִיטִיָּה נ 911 record collection
תְּשִׁיעִיָּה נ 911 group of nine
אַדְמוּמִי ז 912 reddish
אַפְלוּלִי ז 912 dim
אַפְרוּרִי ז 912 grayish
בַּטְנוּנִי ז 912 bellied
גַּבְנוּנִי ז 912 humped, protuberant; hunch-backed
גַּבְשׁוּשִׁי ז 912 lumpy, bumpy
גַּפְרוּרִי ז 912 match-like, thin
יַבְשׁוּשִׁי ז 912 dryish Lit.
יַשְׁנוּנִי ז 912 sleepy
לַבְנוּנִי ז 912 whitish, pallid
לַחְלוּחִי ז 912 damp, moist
מַסְלוּלִי ז 912 relating to a path, lane, track, orbit
נַכְלוּלִי ז 912 deceptive, fraudulent Lit.
נַקְבּוּבִי ז 912 porous; perforated
עַגְמוּמִי ז 912 sad, forlorn
עַכְרוּרִי ז 912 slightly murky Lit.
עַקְמוּמִי ז 912 crooked, twisted
עַרְמוּמִי ז 912 cunning

קַטְנוּנִי ז 912 petty
רַטְנוּנִי ז 912 grouchy, grumbling Lit.
רַכְרוּכִי ז 912 spineless, indecisive
רַקְבּוּבִי ז 912 (soil) containing humus
שַׁמְנוּנִי ז 912 oily
זַהֲרוּרִי ז 913 shiny, radiant
זַעֲרוּרִי ז 913 tiny
סַהֲרוּרִי ז 913 somnambulant; daydreaming; dazed
קַעֲרוּרִי ז 913 concave, indented, sunken
אַוְרִירִי ז 914 airy, delicate; light, fluffy
צַמְרִירִי ז 914 wooly, fluffy
אָבְדָנִי ז 915 suicidal
אַבָּהִי ז 915 paternal
אַבְחָנָתִי ז 915 diagnostic
אֶבְיוֹנִי ז 915 beggarly Lit.
אֻגְדָּתִי ז 915 divisional (military)
אַגָּדָתִי ז 915 legendary, fabled
אֲגֻדָּתִי ז 915 societal
אֲגַפִּי ז 915 flanking
אֱדוֹמִי ז 915 Edomite
אַדְרִיכָלִי ז 915 architectural
אֱוִילִי ז 915 foolish, stupid Lit.
אוּנָתִי ז 915 lobar
אוֹסְטְרִי ז 915 Austrian
אוֹסְטְרָלִי ז 915 Australian
אוּקְרָאִינִי ז 915 Ukranian
אוֹרְקוֹלִי ז 915 audio-visual
אַזְהָרָתִי ז 915 warning Adj
אֲחוֹרִי ז 915 back Adj
אִטִּי ז 915 slow Adj
אִידִישָׁאִי ז 915 (of) Yiddish Adj, Yiddisher
אִיטַלְקִי ז 915 Italian
אֵיכוּתִי ז 915 qualitative
אֵיכוּתָנִי ז 915 of high standard, quality
אֵימְתָנִי ז 915 terrifying, intimidating
אִינְדּוֹנֶזִי ז 915 Indonesian
אִינְדְּיָאנִי ז 915 (American) Indian
אֵינְסוֹפִי ז 915 infinite
אִיסְלַנְדִּי ז 915 Icelandic
אִישִׁי ז 915 personal
אִישִׁיּוּתִי ז 915 related to personality, character
אִכְפַּתִּי ז 915 caring
אִכָּרִי ז 915 farm Adj, farming
אַלְבָּנִי ז 915 Albanian
אַלְגִּ'ירִי ז 915 Algerian
אֱלֹהִי ז 915 divine, godly
אֱלוֹקִי ז 915 divine, godly
אַלְחוּטִי ז 915 wireless Adj
אֲלַכְסוֹנִי ז 915 diagonal
אַלְמוֹתִי ז 915 immortal
אַלְמַתַּכְתִּי ז 915 non-metallic
אָלֶפְבֵּיתִי ז 915 alphabetical
אַמְגּוּשִׁי ז 915 magician, sorcerer (Talmudic); Magus

motherly 915 אִמָּהִי ז
Amharic 915 אַמְהָרִי ז
religious, faithful, believing 915 אֱמוּנִי ז
artistic 915 אָמָּנוּתִי ז
American 915 אַמֶרִיקָאִי ז
American 915 אַמֶרִיקָנִי ז
administrative 915 אֲמַרְכָּלִי ז
real, true 915 אֲמִתִּי ז
Angolan 915 אַנְגּוֹלִי ז
English 915 אַנְגְּלִי ז
Anglican 915 אַנְגְּלִיקָנִי ז
androgynous, hermaphroditic 915 אַנְדְּרוֹגִינִי ז
egotistic, self-centered 915 אָנוֹכִי ז
human 915 אֱנוֹשִׁי ז
antisemitic 915 אַנְטִישֵׁמִי ז
perpendicular 915 אֲנָכִי ז
lobar 915 אֻנָּתִי ז
Asian 915 אַסְיָנִי ז
Asian 915 אַסְיָתִי ז
rabble-like, mob-like 915 אֲסַפְסוּפִי ז
Afghani 915 אַפְגָּנִי ז
915 אַפּוֹטְרוֹפְּסִי/אֶפִּיטְרוֹפְּסִי ז guardian-like
nasal 915 אַפִּי ז
agnostic, heretic 915 אֶפִּיקוֹרְסִי ז
fashionable 915 אָפְנָתִי ז
African 915 אַפְרִיקָאִי ז
African 915 אַפְרִיקָנִי ז
Ephraimite; inhabitant of Efrat 915 אֶפְרָתִי ז
possible 915 אֶפְשָׁרִי ז
tiny, dwarfish 915 אֶצְבְּעוֹנִי ז
acorn-like 915 אִצְטְרֻבָּלִי ז
Equadoran 915 אֶקְוָדוֹרִי ז
related to climate 915 אַקְלִימִי ז
accidental 915 אַקְרָאִי ז
purple Lit. 915 אַרְגְּוָנִי ז
purple 915 אַרְגְּמָנִי ז
Argentinian 915 אַרְגֶּנְטִינִי ז
Aramaic 915 אֲרַמִּי ז
Armenian 915 אַרְמֶנִי ז
Israeli 915 אַרְצִיִשְׂרְאֵלִי ז
Assyrian 915 אַשּׁוּרִי ז
Ashkenazi 915 אַשְׁכְּנַזִּי ז
illusional 915 אַשְׁלָיָתִי ז
sinner, wrongdoer, libertine 915 אַשְׁמַאי ז
Ethiopian 915 אֶתְיוֹפִּי ז
athletic 915 אַתְלֵטִי ז
etheric 915 אֶתֶרִי ז
Babylonian 915 בָּבְלִי/בַּבְלִי ז
puppeteer 915 בֻּבָּנַאי ז
doll-like 915 בֻּבָּתִי ז
Bedouin 915 בֶּדְוִי ז
brutish, animal-like, stupid 915 בְּהֵמִי ז
Buddhist 915 בּוּדְהִיסְטִי ז
Bukhari 915 בּוּכָרִי ז
related to philately 915 בּוּלָאִי ז
Bulgarian 915 בּוּלְגָּרִי ז
Bolivian 915 בּוֹלִיבִי ז
Bolivian 915 בּוֹלִיבְיָאנִי ז
frothy, bubbly 915 בּוּעָתִי ז
Burmese 915 בּוּרְמֶזִי ז
Burmese 915 בּוּרְמִי ז
basaltic 915 בַּזַּלְתִּי ז
theatrical 915 בִּימָתִי ז
medium; mediocre 915 בֵּינוֹנִי ז
medieval 915 בֵּינַיְמִי ז
international 915 בֵּינְלְאֻמִּי ז
egg-shaped, ovoid 915 בֵּיצָתִי ז
unique; exclusive 915 בִּלְבַדִּי ז
Belgian 915 בֶּלְגִּי ז
exclusive 915 בִּלְעָדִי ז
Begali 915 בֶּנְגָּלִי ז
problematic 915 בְּעָיָתִי ז
bourgeois, genteel Coll. 915 בַּעַלְבָּתִּי ז
doughy, dough-like 915 בְּצֵקִי ז
swollen, edematous 915 בַּצַּקְתִּי ז
swampy 915 בִּצָּתִי ז
critical, fault-finding 915 בִּקָּרְתִּי ז
primordial; primeval 915 בְּרֵאשִׁיתִי ז
bourgeois 915 בֻּרְגָּנִי ז
ferrous, iron-like 915 בַּרְזִלִּי ז
British 915 בְּרִיטִי ז
arrogant 915 גַּאַוְתָנִי ז
egotist Lit. 915 גְּאֵיוֹנִי ז
back Adj, dorsal 915 גַּבִּי ז
tough, strong, brutish 915 גְּבַרְתָּנִי ז
regimental, of a battalion 915 גְּדוּדִי ז
member of youth battalions (military) 915 גַּדְנָ"עִי ז
non-Jewish 915 גּוֹיִי ז
bodily 915 גּוּפָנִי ז
fatal 915 גּוֹרָלִי ז
gaseous 915 גַּזִּי ז
Guinean 915 גִּינֵאִי ז
cranial, related to the skull 915 גֻּלְגָּלְתִּי ז
leathery Rare 915 גִּלְדָּנִי ז
wavy, undulating 915 גַּלִּי ז
Galician 915 גָּלִיצָאִי ז
foppish, coquettish 915 גַּנְדְּרָנִי ז
sulfurous, sulfuric 915 גָּפְרִיתִי ז
sulfate Adj 915 גָּפְרָתִי ז
granular 915 גַּרְגִּירִי ז
Girgashite 915 גִּרְגָּשִׁי ז
Georgian 915 גְּרוּזִי ז
Georgian 915 גְּרוּזִינִי ז
German 915 גֶּרְמָנִי ז
cherry-like 915 דֻּבְדְּבָנִי ז
bear-like 915 דֻּבִּי ז
honey-like Lit. 915 דִּבְשָׁנִי ז
waxy 915 דּוֹנַגִּי ז
religious Sl. 915 דּוֹסִי ז
looks like a scarecrow 915 דַּחְלִילִי ז
of apartment 915 דִּירָתִי ז
hemorrhagic 915 דָּמִי ז
knowing, resolute; assertive 915 דַּעֲתָנִי/דַּעְתָנִי ז
religious 915 דָּתִי ז
syllabic 915 הֲבָרָתִי ז
phonetic Rare 915 הֲגָאִי ז
defensive 915 הֲגַנָּתִי/הֲגָנָתִי ז
foolish, stupid (archaic) 915 הֶדְיוֹטִי ז
Hawaiian 915 הָוָאִי ז
Indian 915 הוֹדִי ז
Hottentot Adj 915 הוֹטֶנְטוֹטִי ז
Dutch 915 הוֹלַנְדִּי ז
Hungarian 915 הוּנְגָּרִי ז
coincidental 915 הִזְדַּמְּנוּתִי ז
Hindu Adj 915 הִינְדִּי ז
cognitive 915 הַכָּרָתִי ז
Halachic, pertaining to Jewish law; legal 915 הִלְכָתִי ז
mass Adj; common, vulgar 915 הֲמוֹנִי ז
of engineering 915 הַנְדָּסִי ז
adventurous 915 הַרְפַּתְקָנִי ז
behavioral 915 הִתְנַהֲגוּתִי ז
certain 915 וַדָּאִי ז
Wahabi 915 וָהַבִּי ז
Vietnamese 915 וְיֶטְנָמִי ז
velar (phonetics) 915 וִילוֹנִי ז
Welsh 915 וֶלְשִׁי ז
wolfish 915 זְאֵבִי ז
bleary-eyed 915 זַבְלְגָנִי נ
glazed, vitreous; glassy 915 זְגוּגִי ז
glazed, vitreous; glassy 915 זְגוּגִיתִי ז
identical 915 זֶהוּתִי ז
angular 915 זָוִיתִי ז
apart from, other than, beside 915 זוּלָתִי ז
altruistic 915 זוּלָתָנִי ז
terrible 915 זַוְעָתִי ז
zigzag Adj 915 זִיגְזָגִי ז
bright, radiant, shining 915 זִיוָנִי ז
radiant, shiny Lit. 915 זִיוְתָנִי ז
bristly 915 זִיפִי ז
bristly (botany) 915 זִיפָנִי ז
lousy, terrible, "shitty" (from Arabic; Sl.) 915 זִיפְתִּי ז
glazed, vitreous; glassy 915 זְכוּכִי ז
glazed, vitreous; glassy 915 זְכוּכִיתִי ז
temporary 915 זְמַנִּי ז
lewd, lustful 915 זִמָּתִי ז
prostitution-like; (vulgar) unfair, dirty 915 זְנוּתִי ז
phosphorescent 915 זַרְחוּרִי ז
phosphate Adj 915 זַרְחָתִי ז
traumatic, injurious 915 חַבָּלָתִי ז
friendly, sociable 915 חַבְרוּתִי ז
friendly, affable 915 חֲבֵרִי ז
social 915 חֶבְרָתִי ז
monotonous 915 חַדְגּוֹנִי ז
unilateral 915 חַדְצְדָדִי ז

watery 915 מֵימִי ז
hydrous, of hydrogen 915 מֵימָנִי ז
sexual 915 מִינִי ז
sexist 915 מִינָנִי ז
level, flat, planar 915 מִישׁוֹרִי ז
Maccabi (world Zionist sports club) 915 מַכַּבִּי ז
artificial 915 מְלָאכוּתִי ז
rectangular 915 מַלְבֵּנִי ז
royalist 915 מְלוּכָנִי ז
hotelier 915 מְלוֹנָאִי ז
lexicographer 915 מִלּוֹנָאִי ז
lexical 915 מִלּוֹנִי ז
flowery, poetic 915 מְלִיצִי ז
regal, royal 915 מַלְכוּתִי ז
transdermal 915 מִלְּעוֹרִי ז
having penultimate stress 915 מִלְּעֵילִי ז
having final stress 915 מִלְּרָעִי ז
dimensional 915 מְמַדִּי ז
financial 915 מָמוֹנִי ז
bastardly, sly, crafty Sl. 915 מַמְזֵרִי ז
state Adj, national; official 915 מַמְלַכְתִּי ז
real 915 מַמָּשִׁי ז
governmental 915 מֶמְשַׁלְתִּי ז
organizational 915 מַנְגְּנוֹנִי ז
motorized 915 מְנוֹעִי ז
prismatic 915 מִנְסַרְתִּי ז
of, or related to, essay 915 מַסָּאִי ז
Muslim 915 מֻסְלְמִי ז
traditional 915 מָסָרְתִּי ז
mysterious 915 מִסְתּוֹרִי ז
of laboratory 915 מַעְבַּדְתִּי ז
systemic 915 מַעַרַכְתִּי ז
practical 915 מַעֲשִׂי ז
monstrous 915 מִפְלַצְתִּי ז
retroactive 915 מִפְּרָעִי ז
situational 915 מַצָּבִי ז
realistic 915 מְצִיאוּתִי ז
voyeuristic 915 מְצִיצָנִי ז
conscientious 915 מַצְפּוּנִי ז
Egyptian 915 מִצְרִי ז
adjacent Lit. 915 מִצְרָנִי ז
choral 915 מַקְהֵלָתִי ז
local 915 מְקוֹמִי ז
original 915 מְקוֹרִי ז
clownish 915 מֻקְיוֹנִי ז
rhythmic 915 מִקְצָבִי ז
professional 915 מִקְצוֹעִי ז
professional 915 מִקְצוֹעָנִי ז
accidental 915 מִקְרִי ז
maximal 915 מְרַבִּי ז
Maronite 915 מָרוֹנִי ז
Moroccan 915 מָרוֹקָאִי ז
Moroccan 915 מָרוֹקָנִי ז
centralist 915 מִרְכּוּזִי ז
conceptual 915 מֻשָּׂגִי ז
silky 915 מִשְׁיִי ז
mission-driven, mission-based 915 מְשִׁימָתִי ז
of register 915 מִשְׁלַבִּי ז
significant, important 915 מַשְׁמָעוּתִי ז
of discipline 915 מִשְׁמַעְתִּי/מִשְׁמֶעְתִּי ז
Mishnaic 915 מִשְׁנָאִי ז
secondary (in importance, rank) 915 מִשְׁנִי ז
of the family 915 מִשְׁפַּחְתִּי ז
permissive 915 מַתִּירָנִי ז
proportional 915 מַתְכֻּנְתִּי ז
metallic 915 מַתַּכְתִּי ז
Nazi 915 נָאצִי ז
luminescent Lit. 915 נְהוֹרָנִי ז
hedonistic 915 נֶהֱנְתָנִי ז
nomadic 915 נַוָּדִי ז
notary Adj 915 נוֹטַרְיוֹנִי ז
feather-like 915 נוֹצִי ז
horrible 915 נוֹרָאִי ז
Norwegian 915 נוֹרְבֶגִי ז
pioneering; daring 915 נַחְשׁוֹנִי ז
cuprous; cupreous, coppery 915 נְחֻשְׁתִּי ז
cupreous 915 נְחֻשְׁתָּנִי ז
idiomatic 915 נִיבִי ז
Nigerian 915 נִיגֶרִי ז
fragrant 915 נִיחוֹחִי ז
polite 915 נִימוּסִי ז
very thin/fine; very narrow; capillaceous 915 נִימִי ז
of, or related to, port 915 נְמֵלִי ז
sleepy, drowsy 915 נִמְנוּמִי ז
tiger-like 915 נְמֵרִי ז
tiny, miniature Adj 915 נַנָּסִי ז
circumstantial 915 נְסִבָּתִי ז
formulary 915 נֻסְחָתִי ז
miraculous 915 נִסִּי ז
hawkish 915 נִצִּי ז
female Adj., feminine 915 נְקֵבִי ז
vaginal 915 נַרְתִּיקִי ז
feminine 915 נָשִׁי ז
presidential 915 נְשִׂיאוּתִי ז
grandfatherly 915 סַבָּאִי ז
causative, causal 915 סִבָּתִי ז
segholate 915 סֶגּוֹלִי ז
(Aramaic) much, great; enough, sufficiently 915 סַגִּי ז
special, unique; specific (physics) 915 סְגֻלִּי ז
stylistic 915 סִגְנוֹנִי ז
wintry, cold, rainy 915 סַגְרִירִי ז
of or related to the Jewish Agency 915 סוֹכְנוּתִי ז
stormy Lit. 915 סוֹפָתִי ז
Syrian 915 סוּרִי ז
Palestinian Aramaic (Arch.) 915 סוּרְסִי ז
chummy Sl. 915 סַחְבָּקִי ז
cartilaginous 915 סְחוּסִי ז
dizzying Lit. 915 סְחַרְחֲרָנִי ז
Siamese 915 סִיאָמִי ז
fibrous; stringy 915 סִיבִי ז
nightmarish 915 סִיּוּטִי ז
wholesale Adj 915 סִיטוֹנָאִי ז
wholesale Adj 915 סִיטוֹנִי ז
jet Adj 915 סִילוֹנִי ז
Chinese 915 סִינִי ז
factional 915 סִיעָתִי ז
Sikh 915 סִיקִי ז
Slavic 915 סְלָבִי ז
Slovenian 915 סְלוֹבֵנִי ז
ragged, tattered 915 סְמַרְטוּטִי ז
colorful, variegated 915 סַסְגּוֹנִי ז
spongy 915 סְפוֹגִי ז
containing an element of profiteering 915 סַפְסָרִי ז
Spanish 915 סְפָרַדִּי ז
literary 915 סִפְרוּתִי ז
Spartan 915 סְפַּרְטָנִי ז
Scottish 915 סְקוֹטִי ז
resembling a ruler 915 סַרְגֵּלִי ז
cancerous 915 סַרְטָנִי ז
autumnal 915 סְתָוִי ז
autumnal 915 סִתְוָנִי ז
factual 915 עֻבְדָּתִי ז
up-to-date 915 עַדְכָּנִי ז
ethnic 915 עֲדָתִי ז
spasmodic, spastic 915 עֲוִיתִי ז
world-wide 915 עוֹלָמִי ז
seasonal 915 עוֹנָתִי ז
of lead 915 עוֹפַרְתִּי ז
Ottoman 915 עוֹתְמָנִי ז
municipal 915 עִירוֹנִי ז
townish 915 עֲיָרָתִי ז
idolatrous, heathen, pagan 915 עַכּוּמִי ז
current, contemporary 915 עַכְשָׁוִי ז
lofty, exalted, supreme 915 עִלָּאִי ז
upper 915 עִלִּי ז
th of plot/story 915 עֲלִילָתִי ז
year land fallow debts canceled
Ammonite 915 עַמּוֹנִי ז
starchy 915 עֲמִילָנִי ז
Amalekite 915 עֲמָלֵקִי ז
popular; inexpensive; folk (music, art) 915 עֲמָמִי ז
giant, huge Lit. 915 עֲנָקְמוֹנִי ז
neural 915 עֲצַבִּי ז
woody Lit. 915 עֵצִי ז
slothful, slow 915 עַצְלְתָנִי ז
independent 915 עַצְמָאִי ז
spontaneous (medicine) 915 עַצְמוֹנִי ז
main, principal 915 עִקָּרִי ז
Arab 915 עֲרָבִי/עַרְבִי ז
of or pertaining to desert 915 עַרְבָתִי ז
tyrannical 915 עָרִיצִי ז
alert, awake 915 עֵרָנִי ז
foggy, misty; murky, dim 915 עַרְפִּלִּי ז
tenth 915 עֲשִׂירִי ז
journalistic 915 עִתּוֹנָאִי ז
related to time; periodic 915 עִתִּי ז
pagan 915 פַּגָּנִי ז
Polish 915 פּוֹלָנִי ז
oral 915 פּוּמִי ז

frantic, frenetic; 915 תְּזָזִיתִי ז hyperactive, restless
orchestrative 915 תִּזְמוּרִי ז
tricky, wily, 915 תַּחְבּוּלָנִי ז crafty, cunning
tricky, wily, 915 תַּחְבְּלָנִי ז crafty, cunning
initial; prosthetic 915 תְּחִלִּי ז (linguistics)
legislative 915 תְּחִקָּתִי ז
competitive 915 תַּחֲרוּתִי ז
central, middle; 915 תִּיכוֹנִי ז high school
Yemenite 915 תֵּימָנִי ז
childish 915 תִּינוֹקִי ז
touristic 915 תַּיָּרוּתִי ז
planned, 915 תָּכְנִיתִי ז programmed
tactical 915 תַּכְסִיסִי ז
dependent 915 תְּלוּתִי ז
Talmudic 915 תַּלְמוּדִי ז
clover-shaped 915 תִּלְתָּנִי ז
of the Hebrew Bible 915 תָּנָ״כִי ז
secondary 915 תִּנְיָנִי ז
mischievous 915 תַּעֲלוּלָנִי ז
industrial 915 תַּעֲשִׂיָּתִי ז
confusing, 915 תַּעֲתָעָנִי/תַּעְתְּעָנִי ז delusive, deceptive
apple-like 915 תַּפּוּחִי ז
terrifying, horrible 915 תִּפְלַצְתִּי ז
regulatory 915 תַּקָּנוֹנִי ז
cultured, 915 תַּרְבּוּתִי ז cultivated; cultural
translational 915 תַּרְגּוּמִי ז
lofty, noble, 915 תְּרוּמִי ז distinguished
medicinal 915 תְּרוּפָתִי ז
Turkish 915 תֻּרְכִּי ז
fowl-like; 915 תַּרְנְגוֹלִי ז conceited, haughty
from Tishb (Elijah) 915 תִּשְׁבִּי ז
civil, civilian Adj 916 אֶזְרָחִי ז
middle Adj; 916 אֶמְצָעִי ז means N
of or relating to 917 הִתְיַשְּׁבוּתִי ז the settlement of Israel
volunteering 917 הִתְנַדְּבוּתִי ז
developmental 917 הִתְפַּתְּחוּתִי ז
impressionistic 917 הִתְרַשְּׁמוּתִי ז
probabilistic 918 הִסְתַּבְּרוּתִי ז
related to the 918 הִסְתַּדְּרוּתִי ז largest workers organization in Israel
observative 918 הִסְתַּכְּלוּתִי ז
reactive (electricity) 919 הֶגֵּבִי ז
peripheral; 919 הֶקֵּפִי ז circumferential; perimetric
discursive 919 הֶקֵּשִׁי ז (philosophy); analogous
accomplished; 919 הֶשֵּׂגִי ז achieving
decisive, 920 הֶחְלֵטִי ז determined
necessary 920 הֶכְרֵחִי ז
continuing, 920 הֶמְשֵׁכִי ז incomplete
contractual 920 הֶסְכֵּמִי ז
habitual 920 הֶרְגֵּלִי ז
offensive 920 הֶתְקֵפִי/הַתְקָפִי ז Adj
expressive 921 הַבָּעָתִי ז
conscious 921 הַכָּרָתִי ז
gradual 922 הַדְרָגָתִי ז
training, 922 הַדְרָכָתִי ז instructive, guiding
explanatory, 922 הַסְבָּרָתִי ז propagandist
demonstrative 922 הַפְגָּנָתִי ז
declarative 922 הַצְהָרָתִי ז
deterring 922 הַרְתָּעָתִי ז
comparative 922 הַשְׁוָאָתִי ז
educational, 922 הַשְׂכָּלָתִי ז academic
initial 922 הַתְחָלָתִי ז
of or related to 923 מִלְחַמְתִּי ז war
of (political) party 923 מִפְלַגְתִּי ז
of police 923 מִשְׁטַרְתִּי ז
operational 924 מִבְצָעִי ז
of the desert 924 מִדְבָּרִי ז
sample Adj 924 מִדְגָּמִי ז
Midrashic, of 924 מִדְרָשִׁי ז Talmudic homiletic literature
minimal, negligible 924 מִזְעָרִי ז
eastern; Middle 924 מִזְרָחִי ז Eastern
of the 924 מִמְסָדִי ז establishment
administrative 924 מִנְהָלִי ז
commercial 924 מִסְחָרִי ז
numerical 924 מִסְפָּרִי ז
story (one-story, 924 מִפְלָסִי ז two-story)
of or relating to a 924 מִפְעָלִי ז factory
articular 924 מִפְרָקִי ז (anatomy); articulated
aggregate 924 מִצְרָפִי ז (economics)
preliminary 924 מִקְדָּמִי ז
biblical 924 מִקְרָאִי ז
game-like 924 מִשְׂחָקִי ז
legal 924 מִשְׁפָּטִי ז
prosodic 924 מִשְׁקָלִי ז
of the office 924 מִשְׂרָדִי ז
aggressive, 924 מִתְקָפִי ז offensive
circular 925 מַעֲגָלִי/מַעְגָּלִי ז
of (social) class 925 מַעֲמָדִי ז
western 925 מַעֲרָבִי ז
of research 926 מֶחְקָרִי ז
spacial 926 מֶרְחָבִי ז
central 926 מֶרְכָּזִי ז
of computer 927 מַחְשְׁבִי ז
alveolar 927 מַכְתְּשִׁי ז (phonetics)
of cellar/basement 927 מַרְתְּפִי ז
of or pertaining to 927 מַשְׁבְּרִי ז a crisis
מַחְשַׁבְתִּי/מַחֲשַׁבְתִּי ז 928 intellectual; of thought
underground Adj 928 מַחְתַּרְתִּי ז
angelic 929 מַלְאָכִי ז
of, or pertaining 929 מַשְׁמָעִי ז to, meaning
coniferous 930 מַחְטָנִי ז
equatorial 930 מַשְׁוָנִי ז
institutional 931 מוֹסָדִי ז
seater (one-seater, 931 מוֹשָׁבִי ז two seater)
versatile, adaptive 932 סְתַגְּלָנִי ז
introverted, 932 סְתַגְּרָנִי ז withdrawn
basic 933 בְּסִיסִי ז
cup-like; sepaloid 933 גְּבִיעִי ז (botany)
crystalline 933 גְּבִישִׁי ז
cylindrical 933 גְּלִילִי ז
venous 933 וְרִידִי ז
native 933 יְלִידִי ז
of the tribe of 933 יְמִינִי ז Benjamin
coronary 933 כְּלִילִי ז
silly, dumb 933 כְּסִילִי ז
spelling-related, 933 כְּתִיבִי ז orthographical
messianic 933 מְשִׁיחִי ז
prophetic 933 נְבִיאִי ז
viral 933 נְגִיפִי ז
of damages, of torts 933 נְזִיקִי ז (law)
ascetic; isolationist 933 נְזִירִי ז
princely 933 נְסִיכִי ז
giant, enormous 933 נְפִילִי ז
spiral 933 סְלִילִי ז
criminal 933 פְּלִילִי ז
internal 933 פְּנִימִי ז
pearly 933 פְּנִינִי ז
viscous, sticky 933 צְמִיגִי ז
retractable (tape 933 קְפִיצִי ז measure, etc.)
fourth 933 רְבִיעִי ז
serious 933 רְצִינִי ז
seventh 933 שְׁבִיעִי ז
negative 933 שְׁלִילִי ז
third 933 שְׁלִישִׁי ז
eighth 933 שְׁמִינִי ז
muscular 933 שְׁרִירִי ז
constant, 933 תְּמִידִי ז continuous
ninth 933 תְּשִׁיעִי ז
spring-like 934 אֲבִיבִי ז
aerial 934 אֲוִירִי ז
idolatrous 934 אֱלִילִי ז
noble 934 אֲצִילִי ז
festive; serious, 934 חֲגִיגִי ז formal
alternative, 934 חֲלִיפִי ז substitute Adj
Hassidic 934 חֲסִידִי ז
very quiet 934 חֲרִישִׁי ז
good-looking; sexy 934 חֲתִיכִי ז
juicy 934 עֲסִיסִי ז
alone; childless 934 עֲרִירִי ז

silly, stupid 955 טִפְּשִׁי ז
sharp, bright, quick-witted 955 פִּקְחִי ז
entertaining, amusing 956 בִּדּוּרִי ז
related to insurance 956 בִּטּוּחִי ז
executive related to implementation 956 בִּצּוּעִי ז
exploratory 956 גִּשּׁוּשִׁי ז
colloquial, vernacular 956 דִּבּוּרִי ז
interactive 956 הִדּוּדִי ז
primal; raw; amorphous 956 הִיּוּלִי ז
humorous, comic 956 הִתּוּלִי ז
of argument 956 וִכּוּחִי ז
innovative, inventive, modern 956 חִדּוּשִׁי ז
positive 956 חִיּוּבִי ז
essential; vital 956 חִיּוּנִי ז
exchangeable; commutative (mathematics) 956 חִלּוּפִי ז
educational 956 חִנּוּכִי ז
immunological 956 חִסּוּנִי ז
computational 956 חִשּׁוּבִי ז
therapeutic, related to treatment 956 טִפּוּלִי ז
typical 956 טִפּוּסִי/טִיפּוּסִי ז
representational 956 יִצּוּגִי ז
applied 956 יִשּׂוּמִי ז
directional 956 כִּוּוּנִי ז
integrative, inclusive 956 כִּלּוּלִי ז
instructional, educational 956 לִמּוּדִי ז
literal 956 מִלּוּלִי ז
tactile 956 מִשּׁוּשִׁי ז
conflicting, opposite, contradictory 956 נִגּוּדִי ז
musical, tuneful, melodic 956 נִגּוּנִי ז
wording Adj 956 נִסּוּחִי ז
experimental, trial Adj 956 נִסּוּיִי ז
surgical 956 נִתּוּחִי ז
ascetic, mortifying, self-denying 956 סִגּוּפִי ז
ordinal (number) 956 סִדּוּרִי ז
foiling, thwarting 956 סִכּוּלִי ז
narrative Adj 956 סִפּוּרִי ז
round, circular 956 עִגּוּלִי ז
ornamental 956 עִטּוּרִי ז
theoretical 956 עִיּוּנִי ז
digestive 956 עִכּוּלִי ז
ingenious, extraordinarily smart 956 עִלּוּיִי ז
poetic, lyrical 956 פִּיּוּטִי ז
sculptural 956 פִּסּוּלִי ז
public Adj 956 צִבּוּרִי ז
picturesque 956 צִיּוּרִי ז
photographic 956 צִלּוּמִי ז
capacitive 956 קִבּוּלִי ז
collective 956 קִבּוּצִי ז
existential 956 קִיּוּמִי ז

decorative, ornamental 956 קִשּׁוּטִי ז
square (mathematics) 956 רִבּוּעִי ז
emotional, emotive 956 רִגּוּשִׁי ז
centralized 956 רִכּוּזִי ז
relating to dance 956 רִקּוּדִי ז
residual 956 שִׁיּוּרִי ז
applied 956 שִׁמּוּשִׁי ז
judicial; judgmental 956 שִׁפּוּטִי ז
rehabilitative 956 שִׁקּוּמִי ז
cooperative 956 שִׁתּוּפִי ז
infective 957 זְהוּמִי ז
special, unique 957 יְחוּדִי ז
referential 957 יְחוּסִי ז
relation to a mission/task/assignment 957 יְעוּדִי ז
managerial 957 נְהוּלִי ז
circular 957 סִיבוּבִי ז
disabled, handicapped 957 סְעוּדִי ז
documentary 957 תְּעוּדִי ז
explanatory, exegetical 958 בֵּאוּרִי ז
intermittent, alternate 958 סֵרוּגִי ז
combinatorial 958 צֵרוּפִי ז
descriptive 958 תֵּאוּרִי ז
related to age 959 גִּילִי ז
chalky 959 גִּירִי ז
egg-shaped, ovoid 960 בֵּיצִי ז
domestic 960 בֵּיתִי ז
pertaining to corps (military) 960 חֵילִי ז
wine-like 960 יֵינִי ז
nocturnal 960 לֵילִי ז
summery 960 קֵיצִי ז
partial 961 חֶלְקִי ז
opposing, contradictory 961 נֶגְדִּי ז
herd-like (mentality, behavior) 961 עֶדְרִי ז
moral, ethical, principled 961 עֶרְכִּי ז
of protein, proteinaceous 962 חֶלְבּוֹנִי ז
bright yellow, yolk-like 962 חֶלְמוֹנִי ז
courtly Lit. 962 חֶצְרוֹנִי ז
arithmetic 962 חֶשְׁבּוֹנִי ז
of insult 962 עֶלְבּוֹנִי ז
leafy 962 עֶשְׂבּוֹנִי ז
decimal 962 עֶשְׂרוֹנִי ז
apathetic 963 אֲדִשׁוֹנִי ז
reasonable, logical 963 הֶגְיוֹנִי ז
gestational 963 הֶרְיוֹנִי ז
spiral (arch.) 963 חֶלְזוֹנִי ז
frugal, economical 963 חֶסְכוֹנִי ז
(matter of) principle Adj 963 עֶקְרוֹנִי ז
tiny, insignificant 964 אַפְסִי ז
poisonous 964 אַרְסִי ז
national; down-to-earth, worldly 964 אַרְצִי ז

choosy, selective 964 בַּרְרָנִי ז
the quality of one who tends to heap up things Adj 964 גַּבְבָנִי ז
hesitant, tentative 964 גַּשְׁשָׁנִי ז
hesitant 964 הַסְסָנִי ז
prying, interfering 964 חַטְטָנִי ז
hesitant 964 חַשְׁשָׁנִי ז
wailing, sobbing 964 יַבְבָנִי ז
related to howling, wailing 964 יַלְלָנִי ז
vibrating 964 רַטְטָנִי ז
always grumbling 964 רַטְנָנִי ז
stony 965 אַבְנִי ז
masculine, male Adj 965 גַּבְרִי ז
bony 965 גַּרְמִי ז
corporeal, materialistic 965 גַּשְׁמִי ז
useless, unimportant, worthless Lit.-Rare 965 הַבְלִי ז
rocky, stony 965 טַרְשִׁי ז
child-like 965 יַלְדִּי ז
canine, dog-like 965 כַּלְבִּי ז
financial, monetary 965 כַּסְפִּי ז
rural, rustic (like segholites) 965 כַּפְרִי ז
emphatic (phonetics) 965 נַחְצִי ז
spiritual, mental; emotional, psychological 965 נַפְשִׁי ז
rocky 965 סַלְעִי ז
self- (self-confidence, etc.) 965 עַצְמִי ז
carbonaceous; coaly 965 פַּחְמִי ז
costal (medicine) 965 צַלְעִי ז
wooly, furry 965 צַמְרִי ז
icy 965 קַרְחִי ז
horny 965 קַרְנִי ז
arched, bowed, carved 965 קַשְׁתִּי ז
on foot; infantry Adj. (military) 965 רַגְלִי ז
uterine 965 רַחְמִי ז
lower Adj 965 תַּחְתִּי ז
volcanic 966 גַּעֲשִׁי ז
equipped with caterpillar tracks 966 זַחֲלִי ז
relative 966 יַחֲסִי ז
wooded, forest-like 966 יַעֲרִי ז
youthful; boyish 966 נַעֲרִי ז
of the Israel Defense Forces 966 צַהֲ"לִי ז
poisonous, toxic 966 רַעֲלִי ז
containing a stone (fruit) 967 גַּלְעִינִי ז
nuclear 967 גַּרְעִינִי ז
responsible 968 אַחְרָאִי ז
cruel 968 אַכְזָרִי ז
barbaric 968 בַּרְבָּרִי ז
duck-like 968 בַּרְוָזִי ז
mousy 968 עַכְבָּרִי ז
staminate (botany) 969 אַבְקָנִי ז
long-winded, verbose 969 אַרְכָנִי ז
amusing, entertaining 969 בַּדְחָנִי ז

noisy, loud; vocal, vociferous 970 רַעֲשָׁנִי ז
powdery, dusty 971 אַבְקָתִי ז
carbonated 971 פַּחְמָתִי ז
redheaded 972 אַדְמוֹנִי ז
Anonymous 972 אַלְמוֹנִי ז
lanky, gangling 972 גַּמְלוֹנִי ז
chestnut (color) 972 עַרְמוֹנִי ז
ancient 972 קַדְמוֹנִי ז
ideological 972 רַעְיוֹנִי/רַעֲיוֹנִי ז
ruling, sovereign; exuding authority 973 אַדְנוּתִי ז
integrated; united, unified 973 אַחְדוּתִי ז
useless, unimportant, worthless Lit. 973 הַבְלוּתִי ז
childish 973 יַלְדוּתִי ז
infantile, babyish 973 יַנְקוּתִי ז
authoritative 973 סַמְכוּתִי ז
intrinsic 973 עַצְמוּתִי ז
of Judaism 974 יַהֲדוּתִי ז
squandering, wasteful 975 בַּזְבְּזָנִי ז
wasteful 975 בַּזְבְּזָנִי ז
hesitant, stammering 975 גַּמְגְּמָנִי ז
gluttonous, voracious 975 גַּרְגְּרָנִי ז
tickling 975 דַּגְדְּגָנִי ז
accurate, punctilious 975 דַּקְדְּקָנִי ז
contemptuous, disparaging, belittling 975 זַלְזְלָנִי ז
buzzing 975 זַמְזְמָנִי ז
noisy, clattering 975 טַרְטְרָנִי ז
vague, blurred, wishy-washy 975 טַשְׁטְשָׁנִי ז
mocking 975 לַגְלְגָנִי ז
drowsy, dreamy, groggy 975 נַמְנְמָנִי ז
argumentative, contentious 975 סַכְסְכָנִי ז
chatterbox, prattler 975 פַּטְפְּטָנִי ז
hair-splitting, casuistic 975 פַּלְפְּלָנִי ז
hesitant, irresolute, skeptical 975 פַּקְפְּקָנִי ז
parsimonious Lit. 975 צַמְצְמָנִי ז
noisy, shrieking 975 צַפְצְפָנִי ז
chattering, prattling 975 קַשְׁקְשָׁנִי ז
arrogant, boastful, pretentious 975 רַבְרְבָנִי ז
snooping, sniffing Adj 975 רַחְרְחָנִי ז
cursory 975 רַפְרְפָנִי ז
wheel-like, round 976 גַּלְגַּלִּי ז
scaly, flaky (skin) 976 קַשְׂקַשִּׂי ז
chivalrous, gallant; knightly 977 אַבִּירִי ז
parasitic 977 טַפִּילִי ז
humped 978 דַּבַּשְׁתִּי ז
inflammatory 978 דַּלַּקְתִּי ז
of land; continental 978 יַבַּשְׁתִּי ז
incidental 979 אַגָּבִי ז
fanciful, mythical; renown; legendary 979 אַגָּדִי ז
liar, fabricator Lit. 979 בַּדָּאִי ז
detective Adj 979 בַּלָּשִׁי ז
tiny, miniscule 979 גַּמָּדִי ז
Ethiopian (archaic) 979 חַבָּשִׁי ז
soldier-like, soldierly 979 חַיָּלִי ז
Israel-born 979 צַבָּרִי ז
primeval, ancient 979 קַמָּאִי ז
fanatic 979 קַנָּאִי ז
characteristic Adj 980 אָפְיָנִי ז
horizontal 980 אָפְקִי ז
longitudinal, lengthwise 980 אָרְכִּי ז
immature, unripe 980 בָּסְרִי ז
spiral, screw-like 980 בָּרְגִי ז
fragrant, scented, perfumed Lit. 980 בָּשְׂמִי ז
raw (material) 980 גָּלְמִי ז
awkward, clumsy 980 גָּלְמָנִי ז
sulfide 980 גָּפְרִי ז
contradictory; inverse 980 הָפְכִּי ז
monthly 980 חָדְשִׁי ז
nasal 980 חָטְמִי ז
material Adj, physical 980 חָמְרִי ז
materialistic 980 חָמְרָנִי ז
free 980 חָפְשִׁי ז
wintry 980 חָרְפִּי ז
alcoholic 980 כָּהֳלִי ז
lumbar 980 מָתְנִי ז
foreign 980 נָכְרִי ז
rear Adj; arranged one behind the other 980 עָרְפִּי ז
polar; opposite 980 קָטְבִּי ז
layered 980 רָבְדִּי ז
widthwise 980 רָחְבִּי ז
rooted; deep-seated 980 שָׁרְשִׁי ז
content-related 980 תָּכְנִי ז
infernal, hellish Lit. 980 תָּפְתִּי ז
disgusting 981 גָּעֳלִי ז
procedural 981 נָהֳלִי ז
of verb 981 פָּעֳלִי ז
titular 981 תָּאֳרִי ז
diasporic 982 גָּלוּתִי ז
contemplative 982 הָגוּתִי ז
amateurish 983 חוֹבְבָנִי ז
hesitant, indecisive 983 חוֹשְׁשָׁנִי ז
of jubilee 984 יוֹבְלִי ז
liquid Adj 984 נוֹזְלִי ז
present 984 נוֹכְחִי ז
subjective (syntax) 984 נוֹשְׂאִי ז
arterial 984 עוֹרְקִי ז
treacherous 985 בּוֹגְדָנִי ז
lustful, greedy 985 בּוֹלְעָנִי ז
gliding Lit.-Rare 985 גּוֹלְשָׁנִי ז
tearful, teary 985 דּוֹמְעָנִי ז
prickly 985 דּוֹקְרָנִי ז
aggressive, destructive 985 דּוֹרְסָנִי ז
destructive Rare 985 הוֹרְסָנִי ז
gluttonous 985 זוֹלְלָנִי ז
malicious, crafty 985 זוֹמְמָנִי ז
destructive (Talmudic); traumatic 985 חוֹבְלָנִי ז
piercing, penetrating; invasive 985 חוֹדְרָנִי ז
dreamy 985 חוֹלְמָנִי ז
evasive, slippery Lit. 985 חוֹמְקָנִי ז
hasty, quick Lit. 985 חוֹפְזָנִי ז
inquiring, searching, probing Rare 985 חוֹקְרָנִי ז
squeaky 985 חוֹרְקָנִי ז
suspicious 985 חוֹשְׁדָנִי ז
revealing 985 חוֹשְׂפָנִי ז
lustful Lit. 985 חוֹשְׁקָנִי ז
sharp, cutting Lit. 985 חוֹתְכָנִי ז
swampy, marshy, boggy 985 טוֹבְעָנִי ז
lashing Lit. 985 טוֹפְחָנִי ז
pestering, annoying, nagging 985 טוֹרְדָנִי ז
predatory, vicious 985 טוֹרְפָנִי ז
of initiative; initiatory 985 יוֹזְמָנִי/יָזְמָנִי ז
introverted, keeps his own counsel Lit. 985 כּוֹמְסָנִי ז
petting, stroking, caressing 985 לוֹטְפָנִי ז
nibbly, biting Lit. 985 נוֹגְסָנִי ז
reproachful 985 נוֹזְפָנִי ז
piercing, penetrating Lit. 985 נוֹקְבָנִי ז
vengeful, vindictive 985 נוֹקְמָנִי ז
tolerant, open-minded 985 סוֹבְלָנִי ז
ascetic Lit. 985 סוֹגְפָנִי ז
forgiving, merciful (arch.) 985 סוֹלְחָנִי ז
absorbent 985 סוֹפְגָנִי ז
flirtatious, salacious Lit. 985 עוֹגְבָנִי ז
sarcastic 985 עוֹקְצָנִי ז
harmful; offensive 985 פּוֹגְעָנִי ז
cross-eyed 985 פּוֹזְלָנִי ז
intrusive, invasive 985 פּוֹלְשָׁנִי ז
adjudicative; normative (linguistics) 985 פּוֹסְקָנִי ז
stinging, nippy 985 צוֹבְטָנִי ז
sniping, stinging 985 צוֹלְפָנִי ז
burning, stinging; insulting, scathing 985 צוֹרְבָנִי ז
irritating, grating 985 צוֹרְמָנִי ז
complaining, complainful Lit. 985 קוֹבְלָנִי ז
vivacious, lively 985 קוֹפְצָנִי ז
dominant 985 שׁוֹלְטָנִי ז
demanding 985 תּוֹבְעָנִי ז
aggressive 985 תּוֹקְפָנִי ז
slow, crawling Lit. 986 זוֹחֲלָנִי ז
aggressive, belligerent, warring; combative 986 לוֹחֲמָנִי ז
whispering, hushed, rustling 986 לוֹחֲשָׁנִי ז
crushing, smashing 986 מוֹחֲצָנִי ז

Index of Hebrew Nouns and Adjectives in Alphabetical Order

fishbone; fish skeleton 599 אִדְרָה נ
architecture [no pl.] 740 אַדְרִיכָלוּת/אַרְדִיכָלוּת נ
architectural 915 אַדְרִיכָלִי ז
robe, cloak 685 אַדֶּרֶת נ
apathetic 963 אֲדִשׁוֹנִי ז
love 613 אַהֲבָה נ
sympathy 613 אַהֲדָה נ
beloved; popular 16 אָהוּב ז
admired, cherished 16 אָהוּד ז
lampshade 21 אָהִיל ז
tent 342 אֹהֶל ז
aloe (plant), alt. plural 'ahalot 268 אָהָל, ר' אֲהָלִים/וֹת ז
spirit raised from the dead 242 אוֹב ז
lost, missing 6 אוֹבֵד ז
sumac 240 אוֹג ז
copula (grammar) 6 אוֹגֵד ז
ring binder; folder (computing) 855 אוֹגְדָן ז
hamster; register (computing) 6 אוֹגֵר ז
firebrand, partly burned wood 246 אוּד ז
lust, passion Lit. 585 אַוָּה נ
lover; friend 7 אוֹהֵב ז
supporter, adherent; fan 7 אוֹהֵד ז
desire, yearning Lit 45 אִוּוּי ז
goose; gander 311 אֲוָז ז
goose; gander 275 אַוָּז/אֲוָז ז
gosling 894 אֲוָזוֹן ז
goose pen 911 אֲוָזִיָּה נ
round, haunch (cut of meat) 814 אֲוָזִית נ
enemy; opponent 6 אוֹיֵב ז
enmity, hatred, hostility 14 אוֹיְבוּת נ
fool, stupid person 406 אֱוִיל ז
stupidity, foolishness [no pl.] 740 אֱוִילוּת נ
foolish, stupid Lit. 915 אֱוִילִי ז
air [no pl.] 406 אֲוִיר ז
airplane 896 אֲוִירוֹן ז
aerial 934 אֲוִירִי ז
aerobic 936 אֲוִירָנִי ז
penknife, pocket knife 366 אוֹלָר ז
stupidity, foolishness [no pl.] 694 אִוֶּלֶת נ
foster parent 6 אוֹמֵן ז
nanny, nursemaid, nurse 11 אוֹמֶנֶת נ
power, strength, vitality; sexual potency 240 אוֹן ז
evil; affliction [no pl.] 354 אָוֶן ז
lobe (anatomy) 595 אוּנָה/אֻנָּה נ
sexual potency [no pl.] 761 אוֹנוּת נ
one who masturbates Lit. (coll. me'onen) 366 אוֹנָן ז
mourner Lit-rare 6 אוֹנֵן ז
lobar 915 אוּנָתִי ז

Austrian 915 אוֹסְטְרִי ז
Australian 915 אוֹסְטְרָלִי ז
baker 10 אוֹפֶה ז
motorcyclist, biker 863 אוֹפַנּוֹעָן ז
bicycle 997 אוֹפַנַּיִם ז
treasure 366 אוֹצָר ז
curator 6 אוֹצֵר ז
Ukranian 915 אוּקְרָאִינִי ז
light, sunlight 242 אוֹר ז
fire, blaze; heat 246 אוּר ז
someone lying in wait/ambush 6 אוֹרֵב ז
weaver 6 אוֹרֵג ז
bright light, radiance Lit. 593 אוֹרָה נ
ventilation 70 אִוְרוּר ז
packer, mover 6 אוֹרֵז ז
guest, visitor 9 אוֹרֵחַ ז
caravan 628 אוֹרְחָה נ
literacy [no pl.] 759 אוֹרְיָנוּת נ
airy, delicate; light, fluffy 914 אַוְרִירִי ז
lightness, airiness [no pl.] 787 אַוְרִירִיּוּת נ
audio-visual 915 אוֹרְקוֹלִי ז
vent, ventilation opening 411 אַוְרָר ז
murmur, undertone 600 אִוְשָׁה נ
murmur, rustle 70 אִוְשׁוּשׁ ז
sign, signal 242 אוֹת ז
warning (cf. hazhara) 170 אַזְהָרָה, ראו הַזְהָרָה נ
warning Adj 915 אַזְהָרָתִי ז
hyssop 386 אֵזוֹב ז
balance N 45 אִזּוּן ז
handcuffed, bound, chained 16 אָזוּק ז
handcuffing [no pl.] 45 אִזּוּק ז
girded Lit 16 אָזוּר ז
zone, region; belt 386 אֵזוֹר ז
regional 945 אֵזוֹרִי ז
depletable, consumable; exhaustible 21 אָזִיל ז
reference, citation 56 אִזְכּוּר ז
memorial, commemoration (cf. hazkara) 170 אַזְכָּרָה, ראו הַזְכָּרָה נ
chisel; scalpel 432 אִזְמֵל ז
ear 348 אֹזֶן נ
earphone, headphone 813 אָזְנִית נ
alarm (cf. haz`aka) 170 אַזְעָקָה, ראו הַזְעָקָה נ
handcuffs 998 אֲזִקִּים (אֲזֵק?) ז
naturalization [no pl.] 57 אִזְרוּחַ ז
citizen; civilian 427 אֶזְרָח ז
citizenship 740 אֶזְרָחוּת נ
civil, civilian Adj 916 אֶזְרָחִי ז
fireplace 214 אָח ז
brother; male nurse; compatriot; close friend 219 אָח ז
unity 736 אַחְדוּת נ
integrated; united, unified 973 אַחְדוּתִי ז

integral, complete, united 16 אָחוּד ז
unification; merger, unity 50 אִחוּד ז
brotherhood 611 אַחְוָה/אַחֲוָה נ
percentage; percent; caught, held 16 אָחוּז ז
union, fusion 50 אִחוּי ז
wish; wishes 50 אִחוּל ז
delay N 50 אִחוּר ז
back (N) (pl./dual 'aHorayim); declension only of pl. 289 אָחוֹר, ר' זוגי אֲחוֹרַיִם ז
back Adj 915 אֲחוֹרִי ז
estate 659 אֲחֻזָּה נ
retrieval (computing) 56 אִחְזוּר ז
maintenance; holding (cf. haHzaka) 170 אַחְזָקָה, ראו הַחְזָקָה נ
uniform; constant; homogeneous 21 אָחִיד ז
uniformity 25 אֲחִידוּת נ
hold, grasp N 2 אֲחִיזָה נ
nephew 846 אַחְיָן ז
storage 56 אִחְסוּן ז
storage, storing (cf. haHsana) 170 אַחְסָנָה, ראו הַחְסָנָה נ
coming out of the closet [no pl.] 56 אִחְצוּן ז
responsible 968 אַחְרַאי ז
stern (of ship) 611 אַחְרָה נ
last 890 אַחֲרוֹן ז
responsibility; liability [no pl.] 740 אַחְרָיוּת נ
end Lit. 809 אַחֲרִית נ
frame holding walls of carriage together 314 אֵטָב ז
clothes peg, clothespin; clip N 327 אֶטֶב ז
sealed; opaque 16 אָטוּם ז
sealing, impermeability 45 אִטּוּם ז
slow Adj 915 אִטִּי ז
slowness [no pl.] 762 אִטִּיּוּת נ
impervious 21 אָטִים ז
sealing; opacification = sealing to light 2 אֲטִימָה נ
impermeability; inflexibility, unperceptiveness 25 אֲטִימוּת נ
seal, gasket 327 אֶטֶם ז
sealing; sealed structure; infarction (medicine) [no pl.?] 342 אֹטֶם ז
atresia (pathol.) [no pl.] 739 אַטְמוּת נ
left-handed person 283 אִטֵּר ז
left-handedness [no pl.] 739 אִטְּרוּת נ
noodle 911 אִטְרִיָּה נ
island 239 אִי ז
enmity, hatred 596 אֵיבָה נ
limb, organ; member (syntax) 374 אֵיבָר ז
misfortune; gentile holiday 254 אֵיד ז

(of) Yiddish Adj, 915 ז אִידִישָׁאִי
Yiddisher
buzzard 585 אַיָּה נ
evaporation 45 אִיּוּד ז
qualification, 45 אִיּוּךְ ז
modifying
threat 45 אִיּוּם ז
negation, nullification 45 אִיּוּן ז
islet 894 אִיּוֹן ז
illustration 45 אִיּוּר ז
manning 45 אִיּוּשׁ ז
position [no pl.] 731 אַיּוּת נ
Italian 915 אִיטַלְקִי ז
Italian [no pl.] 814 אִיטַלְקִית נ
quality 740 אֵיכוּת נ
qualitative 915 אֵיכוּתִי ז
of high standard, 915 אֵיכוּתָנִי ז
quality
deer (fem. ’ayala) 275 אַיָּל ז
power, strength Lit. 311 אֱיָל ז
ram (male sheep); 357 אַיִל ז
mogul
tree frog 814 אִילָנִית נ
terrible; threatening 302 אָיֹם ז
horror, 596 אֵימָה ר׳ -ות/-ים נ
terror
terror, 740 אֵימְתָנוּת נ
intimidation [no pl.]
terrifying, 915 אֵימְתָנִי ז
intimidating
Indonesian 915 אִינְדּוֹנֶזִי ז
(American) 915 אִינְדְּיָאנִי ז
Indian
absence, non- 740 אֵינוּת נ
existence [no pl.]
infinite 915 אֵינְסוֹפִי ז
infiniteness [no 762 אֵינְסוֹפִיּוּת נ
pl.]
Icelandic 915 אִיסְלַנְדִּי ז
ancient volume 596 אֵיפָה/א נ
measure
man, 251 אִישׁ, ר׳ אֲנָשִׁים ז
person; husband, spouse (pl.
’anashim)
pupil (of eye) 894 אִישׁוֹן ז
wedlock; marital 748 אִישׁוּת נ
relations [no pl.]
personal 915 אִישִׁי ז
personality [no pl.] 762 אִישִׁיּוּת נ
related to 915 אִישִׁיּוּתִי ז
personality, character
signaling 48 אִיתּוּת ז
strong, solid 374 אֵיתָן ז
steadfastness, 740 אֵיתָנוּת נ
resolution, firmness [no pl.]
eaten, devoured; 16 אָכוּל ז
corroded
corrosion [no pl.] 45 אִכּוּל ז
location; pinpointing 45 אִכּוּן ז
seasonal (only for 410 אַכְזָב ז
stream, river) [no declension, no
pl.]
אַכְזָבָה, ראו הַכְזָבָה נ 170
disappointment (cf. hakhzava)
disappointing [no pl.] 56 אִכְזוּב ז

cruel person, cruel 409 אַכְזָר ז
Adj [declension only as Adj.]
cruel 968 אַכְזָרִי ז
cruelty [no pl.] 788 אַכְזָרִיּוּת נ
edible 21 אָכִיל ז
eating 2 אֲכִילָה נ
enforceable 21 אָכִיף ז
enforcing, 2 אֲכִיפָה נ
enforcement
food; dining, meal 342 אֹכֶל ז
[no pl.]
induction [no pl.] 56 אִכְלוּל ז
populating, 54 אִכְלוּס ז
colonizing, settling
population 911 אֻכְלוּסִיָּה נ
glutton 846 אַכְלָן ז
gluttony [no pl.] 752 אַכְלָנוּת נ
blackish Lit.-rare 302 אָכֹם ז
comedo, 814 אַכְמוּמִית נ
blackhead (is it a suffix here?)
blueberry 814 אֻכְמָנִית נ
vestibule, 460 אַכְסַדְרָה נ
corridor
accommodation, 54 אִכְסוּן ז
hosting
hostel; hotel, 460 אַכְסַנְיָה/א נ
inn; lodging
saddle 304 אֻכָּף ז
yoke (clothing) 814 אֻכָּפִית נ
caring 915 אִכְפַּתִּי ז
caring [no pl.] 762 אִכְפַּתִּיּוּת נ
farmer, peasant (fem. 286 אִכָּר ז
’ikarit)
farming, peasantry 740 אִכָּרוּת נ
[no pl.]
formal 170 אַכְרָזָה, ראו הַכְרָזָה נ
public announcement,
proclamation (cf. hakhraza)
farm Adj, farming 915 אִכָּרִי ז
170 אַכְשָׁרָה, ראו הַכְשָׁרָה נ
qualification - insurance (cf.
hakhshara)
god 231 אֵל ז
album 444 אַלְבּוֹם ז
Albanian 915 אַלְבָּנִי ז
Algerian 915 אַלְג'ִירִי ז
sandalwood 423 אַלְגֹּם ז
curse, oath, covenant 582 אָלָה נ
Bibl.
club, cudgel 585 אַלָּה נ
terebinth (tree) 588 אֵלָה נ
divinity 740 אֱלוֹהוּת נ
divine, godly 915 אֱלוֹהִי ז
sepsis, infection [no 53 אִלּוּחַ ז
pl.]
oak (tree) 380 אַלּוֹן ז
champion, record 378 אַלּוּף ז
holder; major-general
divine, godly 915 אֱלוֹקִי ז
wireless 54 אַלְחוּט ז
broadcasting [no pl.]
wireless N [no pl.] 447 אַלְחוּט ז
wireless Adj 915 אַלְחוּטִי ז
wireless operator 863 אַלְחוּטָן ז

radio operation 740 אַלְחוּטָנוּת נ
[no pl.]
Anesthesia 54 אִלְחוּשׁ ז
Anesthesia 447 אַלְחוּשׁ ז
fat tale of sheep 611 אַלְיָה נ
idol; deity 406 אֱלִיל ז
idolatry 740 אֱלִילוּת נ
idolatrous 934 אֱלִילִי ז
violent; virulent 402 אַלִּים ז
violence 754 אַלִּימוּת נ
championship 754 אַלִּיפוּת נ
diagonal 915 אֲלַכְסוֹנִי ז
mute 283 אִלֵּם ז
silence, 323 אֵלֶם ז
speechlessness Lit. [no pl.]
coral; 423 אַלְמֹג/אַלְגֹּם ז
sandalwood
sheaf (of wheat) 659 אֲלֻמָּה נ
causing one to 54 אִלְמוּן ז
become a widower [no pl.]
Anonymous 972 אַלְמוֹנִי ז
anonymity [no 762 אַלְמוֹנִיּוּת נ
pl.]
muteness [no pl.] 739 אִלְּמוּת נ
immortal 915 אַלְמוֹתִי ז
widower 409 אַלְמָן ז
widowhood [no 752 אַלְמָנוּת נ
pl.]
non-metallic 915 אַלְמַתַּכְתִּי ז
stretcher 679 אֲלֻנְקָה נ
hazelnut tree/bush 431 אִלְסָר ז
thousand 327 אֶלֶף ז
alphabetical 915 אַלְפְבֵּיתִי ז
892 אַלְפוֹן (אין דגש) ז
alphabetical index
a thousandth (part) 808 אַלְפִּית נ
studio (recording, 860 אֻלְפָּן ז
TV etc.); intensive Hebrew
school
casserole, stew-pot 431 אִלְפָּס ז
improvisation 54 אִלְתּוּר ז
salmon (is it a 814 אִלְתִּית נ
suffix here?)
nation Lit. 227 אֹם ז
nut of a bolt 227 אֹם ז
236 אֵם, ר׳ אִמָּהוֹת/אִמּוֹת נ
mother; matriarch (pl.
’imahot/’imot)
bath (tub) 409 אַמְבָּט ז
bath; bathroom 460 אַמְבַּטְיָה נ
granary (Talmudic) 409 אַמְבָּר ז
magician, 915 אַמְגּוּשִׁי ז
sorcerer (Talmudic); Magus
estimation, 342 אֹמֶד ז
assessment [no pl.]
assessment, 758 אֻמְדָּנוּת נ
evaluation [no pl.]
female servant Lit. 584 אָמָה נ
forearm; cubit; 585 אַמָּה נ
middle finger
nation, people 592 אֻמָּה נ
586 אִמָּה, ר׳ אִמָּהוֹת/אֲמָהוֹת נ
matrix (in printing) pl.
(’imahot/’amahot

אֲפִיפִית נ 821 wafer, waffle
אֲפִיצוּת נ 25 tolerance, variation engineering
אָפִיק ז 21 river bed, channel; route, channel
אֶפִּיקוֹרְסוּת נ 740 heresy; non-belief [no pl.]
אֶפִּיקוֹרְסִי ז 915 agnostic, heretic
אָפֵל ז 280 dark; shady, fishy
אֹפֶל ז 342 darkness, blackness Lit. [no pl.]
אֲפֵלָה נ 650 darkness
אַפְלוּלִי ז 912 dim
אַפְלוּלִיּוּת נ 790 dimness, vagueness [no pl.]
אַפְלוּלִית נ 836 dimness, obscurity [no pl.]
אַפְלָיָה, ראו הַפְלָיָה נ 170 discrimination, favoritism, inequity (cf. haflaya)
אֹפֶן ז 342 method, mode, technique
אָפְנָה נ 628 fashion
אִפְנוּן ז 70 modulation – electronics
אָפְנָתִי ז 915 fashionable
אָפְנָתִיּוּת נ 796 being fashionable [no pl.]
אֶפֶס ז 327 zero; nothing
אִפְסוּן ז 54 storage, setting aside [no pl.]
אַפְסוּת נ 736 nothingness [no pl.]
אַפְסִי ז 964 tiny, insignificant
אַפְסִיּוּת נ 785 nothingness [no pl.]
אַפְסָר ז 409 halter
אֶפַע ז 331 emptiness, nothingness Lit.-rare [no pl.]
אֶפְעֶה ז 609 adder (snake)
אָפֵץ/עָפֵץ ז 302 smelling like gall (botany parasite) Lit.
אֹפֶק ז 342 horizon; perspective
אָפְקִי ז 980 horizontal
אָפְקִיּוּת נ 794 horizontality; horizontalness [no pl.]
אָפֹר ז 303 gray
אֲפֵר ז 308 eye mask Lit.
אָפָר ז 311 meadow, grazing area Lit.
אֵפֶר ז 323 ash [no pl.]
אֶפְרוֹחַ ז 443 chick
אִפְרוּט ז 56 deduction [no pl.]
אִפְרוּר ז 70 incineration [no pl.]
אַפְרוּרִי ז 912 grayish
אַפְרוּרִיּוּת נ 790 grayness [no pl.]
אַפְרוּרִית נ 836 gray N [no pl.]
אַפְרִיקָאִי ז 915 African
אַפְרִיקָנִי ז 915 African
אַפַּרְכְיָה נ 911 district, region (Talmudic)
אֲפַרְפַּר ז 459 grayish
אֲפַרְפָּרוּת נ 744 grayness [no pl.]
אֶפְרָתִי ז 915 Ephraimite; inhabitant of Efrat

אִפְשׁוּר ז 54 enabling, making possible
אֶפְשָׁרוּת נ 740 possibility
אֶפְשָׁרִי ז 915 possible
אִצְבּוּעַ ז 57 fingering (music) [no pl.]
אֶצְבַּע נ 430 finger; index finger
אֶצְבָּעוֹן ז 894 thimble
אֶצְבְּעוֹנִי ז 915 tiny, dwarfish
אָצוּר ז 16 stored, hoarded, put aside
אִצְטַגְנִינוּת נ 740 astrology Lit. [no pl.]
אִצְטְרֻבָּלִי ז 915 acorn-like
אָצִיל ז 21 noble, aristocratic; refined, honorable, magnanimous; nobleman
אַצִּיל ז 402 armpit or elbow Lit.
אֲצִילוּת נ 25 nobility; aristocracy
אֲצִילִי ז 934 noble
אֲצִירָה נ 2 keeping safe; retention
אֲצֻלָּה נ 659 aristocracy
אָצָן ז 863 sprinter
אֶקְדּוֹחַ ז 443 pistol, handgun (variant of 'ekdaH)
אֶקְדָּח ז 427 pistol, handgun; red precious stone Bibl.
אֶקְדָּחוֹן ז 894 small pistol/revolver
אֶקְדָּחָן ז 863 gunman
אַקְדָּמָה, ראו הַקְדָּמָה נ 170 introduction (cf. hakdama)
אֶקְוָדוֹרִי ז 915 Equadoran
אִקְלוּם ז 54 acclimatization
אַקְלִים ז 452 climate
אַקְלִימִי ז 915 related to climate
אַקְרָאִי ז 915 accidental
אַקְרָאִיּוּת נ 762 randomality [no pl.]
אַקָּרִית נ 814 acarid, acarina (is it a suffix here?)
אַרְבָּה נ 614 barge
אֲרֻבָּה נ 659 chimney
אַרְבָּעוֹן ז 894 tetrahedron (geometry)
אֶרֶג ז 327 weaving N Lit.; fabric, makeup Lit. [no pl.]
אִרְגּוּן ז 54 organizing; organization
אַרְגְּוָנִי ז 915 purple Lit.
אִרְגּוּנִי ז 953 organizational
אַרְגָּז ז 409 crate, box, case
אַרְגְּמָנִי ז 915 purple
אַרְגֶּנְטִינִי ז 915 Argentinian
אַרְגָּעָה, ראו הַרְגָּעָה נ 170 relief, calm, respite; all-clear (cf. harga`a)
אָרָד ז 268 bronze (only construct, no declension, no pl.)
אָרוּג ז 16 woven
אֻרְוָה נ 624 stable N
אָרוּז ז 16 packed, packaged
אֲרוּחָה נ 19 meal

אֲרוּכָה נ 19 scab
אָרוֹן ז 291 cupboard, closet
אֲרוֹנִית נ 814 small cupboard, chest
אָרוּס ז 16 fiancé; engaged
אֵרוּסִין ז 998 betrothal, engagement
אָרוּר ז 16 cursed, damned
אֶרֶז ז 327 cedar
אֹרֶז ז 342 rice [no pl.]
אֲרִי, ר' אֲרָיוֹת (אֲרָיִים) ז 258 lion Lit. (pl. 'arayot, less commonly 'arayim)
אָרִיג ז 21 fabric, woven material
אֲרִיגָה נ 2 weaving
אֲרִיזָה נ 2 packing, packaging; packing materials
אָרִיחַ ז 23 tile
אֲרִיכוּת נ 25 length, extent
אָרִיס ז 21 tenant farmer, sharecropper
אֲרִיסוּת נ 25 tenant farming, share cropping
אָרֹךְ ז 302 long (physically or time-wise)
אֹרֶךְ ז 342 length; duration
אַרְכָּה נ 611 extension of time
אַרְכּוֹף ז 444 stapes, stirrup
אָרְכִּי ז 980 longitudinal, lengthwise
אַרְכִיוֹנָאוּת נ 740 study and management of archives [no pl.]
אַרְכָן ז 846 long-winded person, verbose person
אַרְכָנִי ז 969 long-winded, verbose
אַרְמוֹן ז 446 palace [in Bibl. 'armenot, but today reg.]
אֲרַמִּי ז 915 Aramaic
אַרְמֶנִי ז 915 Armenian
אֹרֶן ז 342 pine
אַרְנָב ז 409 hare (male)
אַרְנֶבֶת נ 715 rabbit, hare (fem.)
אַרְנָק ז 409 pocketbook, handbag, wallet
אֶרֶס ז 327 venom, poison
אַרְסִי ז 964 poisonous
אַרְסִיּוּת נ 785 poisonousness; malice [no pl.]
אַרְעִי ז 943 temporary
אַרְעִיּוּת נ 772 transience, temporariness [no pl.]
אֶרֶץ נ 331 land, country; earth, world
אַרְצִי ז 964 national; down-to-earth, worldly
אַרְצִיּוּת נ 785 earthliness [no pl.]
אַרְצִישְׂרְאֵלִי ז 915 Israeli
אַרְקָה נ 611 earth, ground (elect.)
אֲרֶשֶׁת נ 703 expression, appearance [no pl.]
אֵשׁ נ 235 fire; passion
אֶשְׁבּוֹל ז 440 spadix (botany)
אֶשְׁגָּר ז 426 dispatch

בּוֹגְדָנִי ז 985 treacherous
בּוֹגֵר ז 6 graduate
בּוֹדֵד ז 6 lonely; alone; isolated person; single person
בּוּדְהִיסְטִי ז 915 Buddhist
בּוֹדֵק ז 6 examiner, inspector
בּוֹהֵק ז 7 glittery, shining, gleaming
בּוּז ז 246 scorn, contempt; disdain [no pl.]
בּוֹזֵז ז 6 looter, plunderer
בּוֹחֵן ז 7 examiner, inspector, tester
בּוֹחֵר ז 7 voter, selector
בּוּכָרִי ז 915 Bukhari
בּוּל ז 246 stamp (usually postage)
בּוּלָאוּת נ 740 philately [no pl.]
בּוּלַאי ז 909 philatelist
בּוּלָאִי ז 915 related to philately
בּוּלְגָרִי ז 915 Bulgarian
בּוֹלֵט ז 6 prominent; outstanding; obvious; salient
בּוֹלְטוּת נ 14 prominence, standing out
בּוֹלִיבִי ז 915 Bolivian
בּוֹלִיבְיָאנִי ז 915 Bolivian
בּוֹלְעָן ז 855 sinkhole; phagocyte (biol.)
בּוֹלְעָנוּת נ 759 big entity swallowing a small one [no pl.]
בּוֹלְעָנִי ז 985 lustful, greedy
בּוֹלֶשֶׁת נ 13 secret police, undercover police
בּוֹנֶה ז 10 builder, mason; beaver
בּוּעָה נ 595 bubble
בּוּעִית נ 814 vesicle, globule
בּוֹעֵר ז 7 burning; urgent Coll.
בּוּעָתִי ז 915 frothy, bubbly
בּוּץ ז 246 fine linen, byssus [no pl.]
בּוּצִית נ 814 canoe
בּוּצָנִי ז 989 muddy
בּוֹצֵר ז 6 person harvesting grapes
בּוֹקֵק ז 6 empty, fruitless; looter, plunderer Lit
בּוֹקֵר ז 6 cowboy
בּוֹקְרוּת נ 14 cattle raising [no pl.]
בּוֹר ז 242 pit, hole
בּוּר ז 246 ignoramus; ignorant; fallow land, uncultivated land
בּוֹרֵא ז 8 creator
בּוּרוּת נ 740 ignorance [no pl.]
בּוֹרֵחַ ז 9 fugitive, escapee
בּוֹרִית נ 814 saponaria (plant used in making soap)
בּוּרְמֶזִי ז 915 Burmese
בּוּרְמִי ז 915 Burmese
בּוֹרֵק ז 6 glittering, shiny, sparkling
בּוֹרֵר ז 6 arbitrator; sorter
בּוּשָׁה נ 595 shame, disgrace

בַּז ז 221 booty, spoils Lit.
בַּז ז 221 falcon
בַּזְבּוּז ז 449 serin (bird)
בִּזְבּוּז ז 66 wasting, waste N
בַּזְבְּזָן ז 851 squanderer, lavish spender
בַּזְבְּזָנוּת נ 749 squandering, wasting money [no pl.]
בַּזְבְּזָנִי ז 975 squandering, wasteful
בַּזְבְּזָנִי ז 975 wasteful
בִּזָּה נ 586 plundering, robbery
בָּזוּי ז 15 despised
בִּזּוּי ז 45 humiliation, debasement
בִּזּוּר ז 45 decentralization
בִּזָּיוֹן ז 898 disgrace, shame
בִּזְיוֹנִי ז 952 embarrassing, contemptible, despicable
בְּזִיזָה נ 1 looting, plundering
בָּזִיךְ ז 20 vessel obs.
בְּזִיקָה נ 1 sprinkling
בַּזְיָר ז 910 falconer
בַּזֶּלֶת נ 685 basalt [no pl.]
בַּזַּלְתִּי ז 915 basaltic
בָּזָק ז 267 lightning; flash message
בֶּזֶק ז 317 telecommunication; spark [no pl.]
בָּחוּן ז 15 tested, proven Lit rare
בָּחוֹן ז 296 probe, tester
בַּחוּרוֹן ז 894 young lad, stripling
בְּחִילָה נ 1 nausea
בְּחִינָה נ 1 examining; examination
בָּחִיר ז 20 select, chosen, elite
בְּחִירָה נ 1 choosing; choice
בְּחִישָׁה נ 1 mixing, stirring
בַּחַן ז 328 watch tower Lit.-rare
בֹּחַן ז 343 test, quiz N; criterion
בַּחֲרוּת נ 737 adolescence [no pl.]
בַּחֲשָׁה נ 612 wooden spoon for stirring food
בַּחֲשָׁן ז 849 interferer, meddler, stirrer
בִּטָּאוֹן ז 898 journal, mouthpiece, organ
בָּטוּחַ ז 17 certain; safe
בִּטּוּחַ ז 53 insurance
בְּטוּחָה נ 668 collateral, security (for loan)
בִּטּוּחִי ז 956 related to insurance
בִּטּוּי ז 45 expression, saying
בִּטּוּל ז 45 cancellation
בִּטּוּן ז 45 concreting
בֶּטַח ז 319 peace, security Lit.; colloq. 'sure, of course' [no pl.]
בִּטָּחוֹן ז 898 confidence; safety; security
בִּטְחוֹנִי ז 952 of security
בְּטִיחוּת נ 24 safety
בְּטִיחוּתִי ז 939 safe, secure, related to safety
בַּטִּישׁ ז 402 (manual) roller for pressing roadways in paving

בְּטִישָׁה נ 1 trampling Lit
בָּטֵל ז 279 invalid, void; worthless; idle
בַּטָּלָה נ 620 idleness
בַּטְלָן ז 846 loafer
בַּטְלָנוּת נ 752 idleness, laziness [no pl.]
בַּטְלָנִי ז 969 negligent, careless, loafing
בֶּטֶן נ 317 abdomen, belly; stomach
בִּטְנָה נ 598 lining (of clothing)
בָּטְנָה נ 628 pistachio (tree)
בָּטְנֶה/בָּטְנָה (בֹּטֶן) ז 434 pistachio; peanut Coll. (alt. boten)
בַּטְנוּן ז 450 double bass, contrabass
בַּטְנוּנַאי ז 909 bass player
בַּטְנוּנִי ז 912 bellied
בַּטְנוּנִית נ 814 cello
בִּיאָה נ 3 coming; sexual intercourse
בִּיב ז 251 sewer, drain
בֵּיבָר ז 374 zoo, menagerie Lit.
בִּיּוּב ז 45 sewage
בִּיּוּל ז 45 stamping, affixing of stamp
בִּיּוּם ז 45 staging; stage-managing
בִּיּוּן ז 45 spying, intelligence services [no pl.]
בִּימַאי ז 909 director (stage, theater)
בִּימָה נ 3 stage; forum
בִּימָתִי ז 915 theatrical
בִּינָה נ 3 understanding, sense, wisdom
בֵּינָה נ 596 each space between staff lines (music)
בֵּינוֹנִי ז 915 medium; mediocre
בֵּינוֹנִיּוּת נ 762 mediocrity [no pl.]
בֵּינַיִם ז 997 intermediate, middle
בֵּינַיְמִי ז 915 medieval
בִּינִית נ 814 barbel (fish)
בֵּינְלְאֻמִּי ז 915 international
בֵּינְלְאֻמִּיּוּת נ 762 internationality [no pl.]
בֵּיצָה נ 597 egg
בֵּיצִי ז 960 egg-shaped, ovoid
בֵּיצִיָּה נ 911 fried egg
בֵּיצִית נ 814 ovum (biol.); ovule (botany)
בֵּיצָתִי ז 915 egg-shaped, ovoid
בַּיָּר ז 275 cistern digger
בֵּיר ז 358 cistern Lit.-Rare
בִּירִית נ 814 garter, suspender (is it a suffix here?)
בִּירָנִית נ 814 fortress, stronghold (bibl.)
בַּיְשָׁן ז 846 shy person
בַּיְשָׁנוּת נ 752 shyness [no pl.]
בַּיְשָׁנִי ז 969 shy

swollen, edematous 915 בַּצַּקְתִּי ז
ore 317 בֶּצֶר ז
drought 695 בַּצֹּרֶת נ
swampy 915 בִּצָּתִי ז
bottle 449 בַּקְבּוּק ז
bottling 66 בִּקְבּוּק ז
small bottle 894 בַּקְבּוּקוֹן ז
a type of mosquito 585 בַּקָּה נ
cracked, split 17 בָּקוּעַ ז
splitting 53 בִּקּוּעַ ז
visiting; visit 45 בִּקּוּר ז
demand N 45 בִּקּוּשׁ ז
expert, knowledgeable, proficient 20 בָּקִיא ז
expertise, knowledge, familiarity 24 בְּקִיאוּת נ
that can be split; fissionable 22 בָּקִיעַ ז
crack, breach, cleft 407 בְּקִיעַ ז
eruption, emergence 1 בְּקִיעָה נ
fissionability 24 בְּקִיעוּת נ
crack, split; split section; hernia 319 בֶּקַע ז
valley 598 בִּקְעָה נ
cattle; beef 267 בָּקָר ז
inspector; supervisor, controller 275 בַּקָּר ז
morning 341 בֹּקֶר ז
control 620 בַּקָּרָה נ
fault-finding, nit-picking person 846 בַּקְרָן ז
criticality [no pl.] 752 בַּקְרָנוּת נ
fault finding, nit-picking 969 בַּקְרָנִי ז
criticism; review 697 בִּקֹּרֶת נ
critical, fault-finding 915 בִּקָּרְתִּי ז
criticism, being critical [no pl.] 762 בִּקָּרְתִּיּוּת נ
request 620 בַּקָּשָׁה נ
shack, hut 598 בִּקְתָּה נ
pure, clean 226 בַּר ז
primordial; primeval 915 בְּרֵאשִׁיתִי ז
swan 449 בַּרְבּוּר ז
barbaric 968 בַּרְבָּרִי ז
barbarism [no pl.] 762 בַּרְבָּרִיּוּת נ
chatterbox, babbler 851 בַּרְבְּרָן ז
blab, prattle, blather, jabber Sl. [no pl.] 749 בַּרְבְּרָנוּת נ
chatter, babble Sl. [no pl.] 717 בַּרְבֶּרֶת נ
screw N 341 בֹּרֶג ז
spiral, screw-like 980 בָּרְגִּי ז
bourgeoisie [no pl.] 758 בֻּרְגָּנוּת נ
bourgeois 915 בֻּרְגָּנִי ז
hail (only construct, no declension) [no pl.] 267 בָּרָד ז
hood, cowl 409 בַּרְדָּס ז
created; creature 15 בָּרוּא ז
deforestation [no pl.] 51 בֵּרוּא ז
duck N 409 בַּרְוָז ז
duckling 894 בַּרְוָזוֹן ז
duck-like 968 בַּרְוָזִי ז
duck hatchery 911 בַּרְוָזִיָּה נ
platypus 863 בַּרְוָזָן ז
blessed 15 בָּרוּךְ ז
failure, disaster, foul-up Sl. 393 בְּרוֹךְ ז
overflow 51 בֵּרוּץ ז
clear 15 בָּרוּר ז
investigation, clarification, inquiry 51 בֵּרוּר ז
cypress 393 בְּרוֹשׁ ז
diet [no pl.] 733 בָּרוּת נ
faucet, tap 317 בֶּרֶז ז
drinking fountain or set of connected faucets for common use 911 בֶּרְזִיָּה נ
iron 422 בַּרְזֶל ז
ferrous, iron-like 915 בַּרְזִלִּי ז
steel wool 831 בַּרְזִלִּית נ
iron bender (construction) 863 בַּרְזְלָן ז
iron bending (construction) [no pl.] 740 בַּרְזְלָנוּת נ
deserter, runaway 846 בַּרְחָן ז
mite 409 בַּרְחָשׁ ז
healthy 20 בָּרִיא ז
creation; universe 1 בְּרִיאָה נ
health [no pl.] 24 בְּרִיאוּת נ
creature 4 בְּרִיָּה נ
food (biblical) [no pl.] 598 בִּרְיָה נ
hooligan, thug, ruffian 440 בִּרְיוֹן ז
hooliganism [no pl.] 747 בִּרְיוֹנוּת נ
related to hooliganism 952 בִּרְיוֹנִי ז
bolt, bar (of gate); dead bolt; bolt (of gun) 407 בְּרִיחַ ז
escaping; escape 1 בְּרִיחָה נ
British 915 בְּרִיטִי ז
selecting, sorting 1 בְּרִירָה נ
selectivity in telecommunications; clarity 24 בְּרִירוּת נ
treaty; covenant; circumcision 805 בְּרִית נ
knee 320 בֶּרֶךְ נ
blessing 634 בְּרָכָה נ
pool 649 בְּרֵכָה נ
mallard 911 בְּרֵכִיָּה נ
person; guy, chap, bloke 409 בַּרְנָשׁ ז
tanning (leather) [no pl.] 740 בֻּרְסְקָאוּת נ
lightning; sparkle, gleam, shine 267 בָּרָק ז
morning star (Talmudic) 909 בַּרְקַאי ז
glaucoma [no pl.] 808 בַּרְקִית נ
thistle, briar, thorn 846 בַּרְקָן ז
agate; emerald 688 בָּרֶקֶת נ
items of inferior quality (usually fruit) 632 בְּרָרָה נ
choice, selection 649 בְּרֵרָה נ
choosy, fussy person 846 בַּרְרָן ז
selectiveness [no pl.] 752 בַּרְרָנוּת נ
choosy, selective 964 בַּרְרָנִי ז
cooking 45 בִּשּׁוּל ז
perfuming [no pl.] 45 בִּשּׂוּם ז
news, tidings; Gospel 671 בְּשׂוֹרָה נ
ripening, maturing [no pl.] 1 בְּשִׁילָה נ
ripe 279 בָּשֵׁל ז
perfumer, spice manufacturer (fem. basemet) 275 בַּשָּׂם ז
perfume; scent 341 בֹּשֶׂם ז
fragrant, scented, perfumed Lit. 980 בָּשְׂמִי ז
aroma [no pl.?] 708 בְּשֹׂמֶת נ
flesh; meat 267 בָּשָׂר ז
related to meat, meat dish 942 בְּשָׂרִי ז
fleshiness, meatiness [no pl.] 752 בַּשְׂרָנוּת נ
meaty, fleshy 969 בַּשְׂרָנִי ז
shame, disgrace Lit. pl. from busha 'shame' > bushot 346 בֹּשֶׁת נ
daughter (pl. banot) 225 בַּת, ר׳ בָּנוֹת נ
scrubland, undergrowth 582 בָּתָה נ
virgin m. 15 בָּתוּל ז
virgin f. 18 בְּתוּלָה נ
virginal 946 בְּתוּלִי ז
virginity, purity [no pl.] 775 בְּתוּלִיּוּת נ
virginity; purity, chasteness 998 בְּתוּלִים ז
cleaving, splitting 45 בִּתּוּק ז
cutting up, bisecting, cutting into pieces 45 בִּתּוּר ז
piece, chunk, fragment (usually of animal or body) 317 בֶּתֶר ז
ravine, gorge 884 בִּתְרוֹן ז
proud, haughty, arrogant 231 גֵּא ז
proud; proud, conceited person; gay 260 גֵּאֶה ז
pride 612 גַּאֲוָה נ
emancipated, free Lit 15 גָּאוּל ז
greatness, glory; genius 292 גָּאוֹן ז
genius [no pl.] 740 גְּאוֹנוּת נ
genius Adj 944 גְּאוֹנִי ז
genius [no pl.] 773 גְּאוֹנִיּוּת נ
arrogant, conceited person 863 גַּאַוְתָן ז
arrogance [no pl.] 746 גַּאַוְתָנוּת נ
arrogant 915 גַּאַוְתָנִי ז
egotist Lit. 915 גְּאֵיוֹנִי ז
redemption, salvation 658 גְּאֻלָּה נ
lair, den [no pl.] 227 גֹּב ז
cistern 231 גֵּב? ז
office of synagogue manager [no pl.] 756 גַּבָּאוּת נ
manager of synagogue 908 גַּבַּאי ז
pile, heap Lit. [no pl.] 312 גְּבָב ז

גְּבָבָה/א נ 632 straw, stubble [no pl.]

גַּבְבָן ז 846 one who tends to heap up things

גַּבְבָנִי ז 964 the quality of one who tends to heap up things Adj

גֹּבַהּ ז 344 height; extent, level

גַּבָּה נ 585 eyebrow

גַּבְהוּת נ 736 egotism; pride Lit. [no pl.]

גִּבּוּב ז 45 piling, heaping; accumulation

גִּבּוּי ז 45 backup, support

גְּבוּל (ר׳ גם גְּבוּלִים) ז 401 border; borderline; extreme, limit [occ. plural gvulim]

גְּבוּלִי ז 946 border-line

גִּבּוּן ז 45 cheese making [no pl.]

גִּבּוּס ז 45 plastering

גִּבּוּעַ ז 53 swell [no pl.]

גִּבּוֹר ז 382 hero; central figure, protagonist

גְּבוּרָה נ 18 courage, bravery; fortitude; strength

גִּבּוּשׁ ז 45 consolidation, integration, forging "team spirit;" crystallization

גִּבֵּחַ ז 284 bald; with anterior baldness

גַּבַּחַת נ 689 frontal baldness Lit.

גַּבִּי ז 915 back Adj, dorsal

גְּבִיָּה נ 4 collection of taxes, dues

גָּבִין ז 20 eyebrow Lit

גְּבִינָה נ 1 cheese

גָּבִיעַ ז 22 goblet, cup

גְּבִיעוֹן ז 895 small cup

גְּבִיעוֹנִית נ 814 fritillary (plant)

גְּבִיעִי ז 933 cup-like; sepaloid (botany)

גְּבִיר ז 405 master, lord; rich man

גָּבִישׁ ז 20 crystal

גְּבִישׁוֹן ז 895 small crystal

גְּבִישִׁי ז 933 crystalline

גְּבִישִׁיּוּת נ 768 crystallization [no pl.]

גַּבְלוּל ז 450 lump (of dough, mud) Talmudic

גַּבְלִית נ 808 oriel

גַּבָּן ז 275 cheese maker (fem. gabenet)

גִּבֵּן ז 283 hunchback; hunchbacked

גַּבְנוּן ז 450 hunchback, hunch, hump; knoll, hillock

גַּבְנוּנִי ז 912 humped, protuberant; hunch-backed

גַּבְנוּנִיּוּת נ 790 hunch, protrusiveness [no pl.]

גַּבְנוּנִית נ 836 hump, protuberance

גִּבְנוּת נ 739 hunchbackness [no pl.]

גַּבֶּנֶת נ 694 hump

גֶּבֶס ז 317 gypsum; plaster (no declension except construct) [no pl.]

גִּבְסִי ז 949 gypsum, plaster Adj

גֶּבַע ר׳ גְּבָעִים/גְּבָעוֹת ז 319 small hill, low mountain Lit (pl. gva`im/gva`ot)

גִּבְעָה נ 598 hill

גִּבְעוֹל ז 440 stalk, stem

גִּבְעוֹלִי ז 952 stalk-like, stem-like

גֶּבֶר ז 326 male, man

גְּבַרְבַּר/גְּבַרְבַר ז 458 young person trying to act "grown up" (Coll.)

גַּבְרוּת נ 736 masculinity [no pl.]

גַּבְרִי ז 965 masculine, male Adj

גַּבְרִיּוּת נ 785 manhood, manliness [no pl.]

גְּבֶרֶת נ 702 Mrs., madam

גְּבַרְתָּן ז 852 tough guy, brute

גְּבַרְתָּנוּת נ 745 muscular strength, toughness [no pl.]

גְּבַרְתָּנִי ז 915 tough, strong, brutish

גַּבְשׁוּשׁ ז 450 bump, lump, protuberance

גַּבְשׁוּשִׁי ז 912 lumpy, bumpy

גַּבְשׁוּשִׁית נ 836 bump N; wart, lump, irregularity

גִּבְתּוֹן ז 884 bunting (bird)

גַּג ז 222 roof; top, maximum

גַּגּוֹן ז 894 small roof, awning

גַּגָּן ז 863 roofer, tiler

גָּדָה נ 583 bank (of river)

גְּדוּד ז 399 battalion, regiment

גִּדּוּד ז 45 abrasion geology

גְּדוּדִי ז 915 regimental, of a battalion

גְּדוּדִית נ 814 bed, flowerbed; ridge

גָּדוֹל ז 298 big, large

גִּדּוּל ז 45 growth; upbringing; tumor

גָּדוּם ז 15 amputated, truncated

גָּדוּעַ ז 17 cut down, felled

גִּדּוּף ז 45 cursing, swearing

גָּדוּר ז 15 fenced; restricted

גִּדּוּר ז 45 fencing, enclosure

גָּדוּשׁ ז 15 full, crammed, heaped

גְּדִי ז 257 kid, young male goat

גָּדִיד ז 20 date harvest

גְּדִיל ז 405 tassel, fringe; strand

גְּדִילָה נ 1 growing [no pl.]

גְּדִילָן ז 863 thistle

גְּדִיעָה נ 1 cutting down

גָּדִישׁ ז 20 stock, pile, stack of grain

גֹּדֶל ז 341 size; magnitude, enormity

גְּדֻלָּה נ 658 greatness

גַּדְלוּת נ 736 greatness, eminence [no pl.]

גִּדֵּם ז 283 one whose hand has been amputated to the elbow

גֶּדֶם ז 317 stump (of tree, etc.)

גִּדְמוּת נ 739 amputatedness [no pl.]

גַּדְנָ״עִי ז 915 member of youth battalions (military)

גִּדֵּעַ ז 284 one whose hand has been amputated to the shoulder; an animal whose antlers have been chopped off

גֶּדַע ז 319 stump (of tree)

גַּדְפָן ז 846 foul-mouth

גַּדְפָנוּת נ 752 abusing, cursing, reviling

גַּדְפָנִי ז 969 foul-mouthed

גָּדֵר ר׳ גְּדֵרוֹת/גְּדֵרִים נ 281 fence, border (pl. gderot/gderim)

גְּדֵרָה נ 649 enclosure; paddock

גִּדְרוֹן ז 884 wren

גֹּדֶשׁ ז 341 abundance, surplus; congestion [no pl.]

גֵּהָה נ 588 health, healing, wellbeing [no pl.]

גִּהוּץ ז 50 ironing

גִּהוּק ז 50 burp, belch N

גָּהוּר ז 15 prostrate, bent over Lit

גְּהִירָה נ 1 bending over Lit

גַּהֲצָן ז 849 ironer

גֵּו ז 233 trunk, torso, back

גּוֹאֵל ז 7 savior, redeemer

גּוֹבֶה ז 10 collector esp. of taxes

גִּוּוּן ז 45 variety, variation

גּוֹזֵז ז 6 sheep-shearer

גּוֹזָל ז 366 young bird, chick, fledgling

גּוֹי ז 240 gentile, non-Jew; nation, people (Bibl.)

גְּוִיָּה נ 4 corpse, body

גּוֹיוּת נ 761 non-Jewishness [no pl.]

גּוֹיִי ז 915 non-Jewish

גְּוִיל ז 405 parchment; yellowing page of old books

גְּוִיעָה נ 1 dying Lit

גּוֹלֶה ז 10 exile

גּוֹלָה נ 593 exile

גּוֹלֵל ז 6 burial stone; slab placed over body in grave

גּוֹלֵשׁ ז 6 skater, skier; hang glider; surfer

גּוֹלְשָׁנִי ז 985 gliding Lit.-Rare

גּוּמִיָּה נ 911 rubber band

גָּוֶן ז 356 color; hue; nuance

גַּוְנוּן ז 450 shading, variation

גִּוְנוּן ז 70 shading, variation

גּוֹנִית נ 844 nuance

גּוֹסֵס ז 6 dying person

גּוֹעֵשׁ ז 7 raging, stormy

גּוּף ז 246 body; object; group; person (grammar)

גּוּפָה נ 595 (dead) body, cadaver

גּוּפִיָּה נ 911 undershirt

גּוּפִיף ז 250 (biology) cell, corpuscle

גּוֹפָן ז 366 font (in printing)

גּוּפָנִי ז 915 bodily

גּוּפָנִיּוּת נ 762 corporeality, materiality [no pl.]
גּוּץ ז 246 dwarf
גּוּצִי ז 990 dwarfish
גּוּר ז 246 cub, whelp, pup
גּוֹרָל ז 368 fate; casting lots
גּוֹרָלִי ז 915 fatal
גּוֹרָלִיּוּת נ 762 criticalness [no pl.]
גּוֹרֵם ז 6 cause, factor; element; authority
גּוֹרֵף ז 6 sweeping, comprehensive
גּוֹרֵר ז 6 tow truck
גּוֹרֶרֶת נ 11 tugboat, tug
גּוּשׁ ז 246 lump, chunk; group of houses; bloc, coalition
גּוּשִׁי ז 990 lumpy
גֵּז ז 235 fleece N
גִּזְבָּר ז 431 treasurer
גִּזְבָּרוּת נ 740 accounts department [no pl.]
גָּזוּז ז 15 cut, shorn
גִּזּוּז ז 45 carbonating Coll. [no pl.]
גָּזוּל ז 15 stolen
גָּזוּם ז 15 pruned, clipped
גִּזּוּם ז 45 pruning
גָּזוּר ז 15 cut; derived; decreed, ordained
גַּזֶּזֶת נ 685 scalp ringworm [no pl.]
גַּזִּי ז 915 gaseous
גָּזִיז ז 20 small piece, snippet; that can be sheared
גְּזִיזָה נ 1 cutting hair, shearing
גָּזִיר ז 20 cuttable, easy to cut
גְּזִיר ז 405 faggot, piece of wood
גְּזִירָה נ 1 cutting; differentiation math
גָּזִית נ 814 hewn (smooth) stone
גֶּזֶל ז 317 robbery, theft [no pl.]
גְּזֵלָה נ 649 theft; stolen object
גַּזְלָן ז 846 robber
גַּזְלָנוּת נ 752 robbery, theft [no pl.]
גַּזְלָנִי ז 969 thieving, robbing - Adj
גֶּזֶם ז 317 pruned branches [no pl.]
גֻּזְמָה/א נ 627 exaggeration, hyperbole
גֶּזַע ז 319 trunk (of tree); race (anthropology); stem (grammar)
גִּזְעוֹל ז 440 multi-layered stalk/stem
גִּזְעִי ז 949 of pedigree; trendy Coll.
גִּזְעִיּוּת נ 776 pedigree [no pl.]
גִּזְעָן ז 857 racist
גִּזְעָנוּת נ 740 racism [no pl.]
גִּזְעָנִי ז 950 racist
גְּזַר ז 310 sentence, judgment Lit. [no pl.]
גֶּזֶר ז 317 carrot
גֶּזֶר ז 317 piece, shred, fragment
גִּזְרָה נ 598 area, sector; figure, shape
גְּזֵרָה נ 649 decree
גִּזְרוֹנִי ז 952 etymological, derivational
גַּזָּרָן ז 846 cutter (clothing)
גִּחוּךְ ז 50 giggle, chuckle N
גָּחוּן ז 15 bent over, prostrate
גָּחוֹן ז 288 belly, underbelly
גְּחִינָה נ 1 bending over, prostrating Lit
גַּחְכָן ז 846 one who giggles a lot
גַּחְכָנִי ז 969 giggling Adj
גַּחַל ז 328 coal, amber Lit. [no pl.]
גַּחְלִילִית נ 832 firefly
גַּחֲלִית נ 809 carbuncle
גַּחֶלֶת נ 687 ember; glowing ember; remnant (pl. geHalim)
גַּחְמָן/גַּחֲמָן ז 846 capricious person
גַּחְמָנוּת/גַּחֲמָנוּת נ 752 capriciousness [no pl.]
גַּחְמָנִי/גַּחֲמָנִי ז 969 capricious
גַּחַר ז 328 crevice, cranny (Talmudic)
גֵּט ז 235 divorce certificate (Jewish law)
גַּיְא/גַּי, ר׳ גֵּיאָיוֹת ז 358 valley, gorge, ravine, gulch [plural gey'ayot]
גִּיגִית/גִּגִית נ 814 tub (is it a suffix here?)
גִּיד ז 251 tendon
גִּיּוּז ז 45 gasification [no pl.]
גִּיּוּס ז 45 enlistment; recruitment; raising money
גִּיּוֹר ז 382 convert to Judaism
גִּיּוּר ז 45 conversion to Judaism
גִּיחָה נ 3 trip; sortie, flight
גִּיל ז 251 age, period of life
גִּיל ז 251 joy, happiness
גִּילַאי ז 909 member of the same age group
גִּילָה נ 3 joy, happiness Lit. [no pl.]
גִּילִי ז 959 related to age
גִּינֵאִי ז 915 Guinean
גִּיס ז 251 brother-in-law
גַּיָּס ז 275 enlistment officer, recruitment officer (arch.)
גַּיִס ז 360 corps (military); large body of soldiers
גִּיר ז 251 lime, calcite; chalk
גִּירִי ז 959 chalky
גִּירִית נ 814 badger
גִּישָׁה נ 3 approach, access; attitude
גְּלַאי ז 906 decolletage; bare/exposed place Lit.
גַּלַּאי ז 908 detector
גַּלָּב ז 275 barber, hairdresser Lit.
גִּלְגּוּל ז 66 rolling; somersault; metamorphosis; reincarnation
גַּלְגַּל ז 416 wheel
גַּלְגַּלּוֹן ז 894 cartwheel (athletics)
גַּלְגִּלּוֹן ז 894 roller, guide pulley
גַּלְגַּלִּי ז 976 wheel-like, round
גַּלְגִּלִּית נ 814 skate N
גַּלְגֶּלֶת נ 717 pulley block
גֻּלְגֹּלֶת נ 724 skull
גֻּלְגָּלְתִּי ז 915 cranial, related to the skull
גֶּלֶד ז 317 crust, scab; scale leaf
גִּלְדָּנִי ז 915 leathery Rare
גֻּלָּה נ 592 small ball; marble (game of marbles)
גִּלְוּוּן ז 54 galvanization
גָּלוּחַ ז 17 shaven
גִּלּוּחַ ז 53 shaving
גָּלוּי ז 15 revealed, open; manifest
גְּלוּיָה נ 18 postcard
גָּלוּל ז 15 rolled up, wrapped
גְּלוּלָה נ 18 tablet, pill
גָּלוּם ז 15 hidden, latent
גִּלּוּם ז 45 embodiment, playing the role; grossing up taxation
גַּלְוָנִיּוּת נ 788 galvanism [no pl.]
גִּלּוּף ז 45 carving, etching, engraving
גְּלוּפָה נ 18 block, plate in printing
גָּלוּת נ 733 exile
גָּלוּתִי ז 982 diasporic
גָּלוּתִיּוּת נ 762 ghetto manner [no pl.]
גַּלָּח ז 275 priest Lit.
גַּלִּי ז 915 wavy, undulating
גְּלִיד ז 405 icicle
גְּלִידָה נ 1 congealing rare; ice cream
גִּלָּיוֹן ז 898 sheet of paper; newspaper edition, issue
גַּלִּיּוּת נ 762 waviness, undulation [no pl.]
גָּלִיל ז 20 cylinder; roll; region
גְּלִילָה נ 1 rolling up; rolling up of Torah scroll
גְּלִילִי ז 933 cylindrical
גְּלִילִיּוּת נ 769 cylindricalness [no pl.]
גְּלִימָה נ 1 robe, gown, cloak
גְּלִיף ז 405 glyph; carved figure
גְּלִיפָה נ 1 etching, engraving
גְּלִיצָאִי ז 915 Galician
גְּלִישָׁה נ 1 boiling over; surfing
גֶּלֶם ז 317 (raw) material [no pl.]
גֹּלֶם ז 341 pupa; inchoate object; dummy
גַּלְמוּד ז 447 lonesome, lonely
גַּלְמוּדִיּוּת נ 762 loneliness Lit. [no pl.]
גָּלְמִי ז 980 raw (material)
גָּלְמִיּוּת נ 794 rawness, amorphousness [no pl.]
גָּלְמָנִי ז 980 awkward, clumsy
גְּלֶסְקָה נ 678 roll, bun, cake Lit.

גְּרוּר ז 51 grating vegetables, cheese [no pl.]
גְּרוּרָה נ 18 metastasis, secondary growth cancer
גָּרוּשׁ ז 15 divorced man
גְּרוּשׁ ז 399 grush (obsolete Israeli currency); virtually valueless amount Sl.
גֵּרוּשׁ ז 51 driving out; expulsion
גֶּרֶז ז 326 mortise (carpentry)
גַּרְזֶן ז 422 axe, hatchet
גְּרִידָה נ 1 scratching out; abortion = type of scratching out
גְּרִיָּה נ 4 stimulation
גְּרִימָה נ 1 causing, causation
גַּרְיָן ז 846 teaser (advertising)
גְּרִיס ז 405 portion of a grain of wheat or other product; groats, grits
גְּרִיסָה נ 1 crushing, grinding
גְּרִיעָה נ 1 reduction, subtraction
גְּרִיפָה נ 1 sweeping away; collecting, esp. a lot of money in short time
גְּרִירָה נ 1 dragging; towing vehicle
גֶּרֶם ז 326 bone Lit.; basis, framework, skeleton
גַּרְמִי ז 965 bony
גַּרְמִיּוּת נ 785 boniness [no pl.]
גֶּרְמָנִי ז 915 German
גֶּרְמָנִית נ 814 German [no pl.]
גֹּרֶן נ 346 thrashing floor; open space
גִּרְסָה/א נ 602 version
גִּרְעוּן ז 54 producing nuclear material; making granular, irregular [no pl.]
גֵּרָעוֹן ז 903 deficit
גֵּרְעוֹנִי ז 952 of deficit Adj.
גַּרְעִין ז 452 seed, kernel; nucleus; grain
גַּרְעִינִי ז 967 nuclear
גַּרְעִינִיּוּת נ 762 essence, kernel, basis Rare [no pl.]
גַּרְעֶנֶת נ 715 trachoma
גְּרָף ז 310 bedpan
גְּרָף ז 310 graph, pl. only
גְּרֹפֶת נ 708 silt, alluvium, sediment
גְּרָר ז 310 tow truck [no pl.]
גְּרָרָה נ 632 attraction (linguistics); sleigh
גֶּרֶשׂ ז 326 groats (biblical and Talmudic) [no pl.]
גֶּרֶשׁ/גֵּרֶשׁ ר׳ גֵּרְשַׁיִם ז 320 apostrophe pl. dual gershayim 'inverted commas' [no other inflection]
גָּשׁוּם ז 15 rainy
גִּשּׁוּר ז 45 bridging; mediation law
גַּשּׁוֹשׁ ז 296 probe (esp. in dentistry); calipers
גִּשּׁוּשׁ ז 45 groping, feeling; initial contact
גִּשּׁוּשִׁי ז 956 exploratory
גֶּשֶׁם ז 317 rain
גַּשְׁמוּת נ 736 corporeality, worldliness [no pl.]
גַּשְׁמִי ז 965 corporeal, materialistic
גַּשְׁמִיּוּת נ 785 corporeality; materialism [no pl.]
גֶּשֶׁר ז 317 bridge; connection, association
גִּשְׁרוֹן ז 886 small bridge
גִּשְׁרִית נ 812 bridge (of string instrument)
גַּשָּׁשׁ ז 275 tracker, scout (fem. gashashit)
גַּשָּׁשׁוּת נ 757 tracking, scouting [no pl.]
גַּשְׁשָׁנִי ז 964 hesitant, tentative
גַּשָּׁשֶׁת נ 685 unmanned probe
גִּשְׁתָּה נ 598 siphon
גַּת ר׳ גִּתִּים/גִּתּוֹת נ 224 wine press (pl. gitim/gitot)
גִּתִּית נ 814 musical instrument (bibl.)
דְּאָבָה נ 640 grief, anguish
דְּאָגָה נ 640 worry
דַּאֲגָן ז 849 one who worries a lot
דַּאֲגָנוּת נ 753 anxiety, worrying [no pl.]
דַּאֲגָנִי ז 970 anxious, worried
דָּאָה נ 582 kite (bird)
דָּאוּג ז 15 worried, concerned, anxious
דָּאוֹן ז 292 glider; drone
דְּאִיָּה נ 4 gliding
דֹּאַר ז 343 mail, postal service [no pl.]
דֹּב ז 227 bear
דֻּבְדְּבָנִי ז 915 cherry-like
דִּבָּה נ 586 badmouthing, libel, gossip
דִּבּוּב ז 45 encouraging one to talk; dubbing
דִּבּוּג ז 45 debugging (computing)
דֻּבּוֹן ז 894 teddy bear
דָּבוּק ז 15 firmly attached, glued, stuck
דִּבּוּק ז 45 dybbuk, spirit
דַּבּוּר ז 378 hornet Coll.
דִּבּוּר ז 45 speaking, speech
דְּבוֹרָה נ 673 bee
דִּבּוּרִי ז 956 colloquial, vernacular
דְּבוֹרָנִית נ 814 ophrys (plant)
דֻּבִּי ז 915 bear-like
דְּבִיבוֹן ז 895 racoon
דָּבִיק ז 20 sticky, adhesive
דְּבִיקוּת נ 24 stickiness, adhesiveness
דְּבִיר ז 405 Holy of Holies (in the Temple); inner sanctum
דְּבֵלָה נ 649 bunch of dried figs
דִּבְלוּל ז 450 frayed thread ends, hair ends
דִּבְלוּל ז 70 ruffling, thinning out
דָּבֵק ז 279 attached, adherent
דֶּבֶק ז 317 glue
דִּבְקוֹן ז 886 mistletoe (plant)
דִּבְקִי ז 949 sticky, gluey
דָּבָר ז 267 object, thing; speech, word
דַּבָּר ז 275 leader Lit.
דֶּבֶר ז 317 plague (no declension except construct, no pl.)
דִּבֵּר ר׳ דִּבְּרוֹת ז 283 commandment; faculty of speech, articulation (pl. dibrot)
דִּבְרָה נ 598 word Lit.
דַּבְּרָן ז 847 a talkative person
דַּבְּרָנוּת נ 752 chattering babbling [no pl.]
דַּבְּרָנִי ז 969 talkative
דַּבֶּרֶת נ 685 garrulousness, "verbal diarrhea" Coll. [no pl.]
דְּבַשׁ ז 315 honey [no pl.]
דִּבְשָׁה נ 598 molasses
דִּבְשִׁי ז 949 honey-like
דֻּבְשָׁן ז 860 honey (term of endearment for male)
דֻּבְשָׁנִי ז 915 honey-like Lit.
דֻּבְשָׁנִית נ 814 honey cookie
דַּבֶּשֶׁת נ 685 camel's hump
דַּבַּשְׁתִּי ז 978 humped
דָּג ז 216 fish
דַּגְדְּגָן ז 851 clitoris
דַּגְדְּגָנִי ז 975 tickling
דִּגְדּוּג ז 66 tickling
דָּגָה נ 583 fish (general) [no pl.]
דּוּגִית נ 825 small fishing boat
דָּגוּל ז 15 distinguished, outstanding
דִּגּוּל ז 45 raising a flag
דִּגּוּם ז 45 modeling
דָּגוּשׁ ז 15 geminate double length consonant
דִּגּוּשׁ ז 45 marking a dagesh
דְּגִילָה נ 1 professing, asserting
דְּגִימָה נ 1 sampling; sample
דְּגִירָה נ 1 hatching; studying hard Coll.
דַּגָּל ז 275 flag-bearer, standard bearer (obs.) (fem. dagelet)
דֶּגֶל ז 317 flag, banner
דִּגְלוֹן ז 886 small flag, pennant
דַּגְלָן ז 846 flag bearer
דֶּגֶם ז 310 pattern, design
דֶּגֶם ז 317 model, replica
דֻּגְמָה/א נ 627 example
דֻּגְמָן ז 860 model
דֻּגְמָנוּת נ 758 modeling [no pl.]
דָּגָן ז 267 cereal; grain
דַּגְרָן ז 846 bookish, studious person, nerd Coll.
דָּגֵשׁ ז 279 dagesh (gemination sign); emphasis, stress
דִּדּוּי ז 45 hopping, skipping
דָּהוּי ז 15 faded

דְּהִיָּה נ 4 fading, becoming dull
דְּהִירָה נ 1 galloping
דֹּהַן ז 343 pomade, hair oil; grease Lit. [no pl.]
דַּהֲרָה נ 640 gallop N
דּוֹאֵב ז 7 painful Lit
דּוֹאֵג ז 7 worried, anxious; caring, concerned
דּוֹבֵר ז 6 spokesperson; speaker of a language
דּוֹבְרָה נ 628 barge; raft
דּוּגִית נ 845 dinghy, skiff
דּוֹגֶרֶת נ 11 brooder bird hatching eggs
דּוֹד ז 240 uncle
דּוּד ז 249 vat; water tank; boiler, tank for heating water
דּוֹדָן ז 863 cousin
דָּוֶה ז 265 painful, aching, anguished; very sick
דּוֹהֵר ז 7 galloping, racing
דִּוּוּחַ ז 53 report N
דִּוּוּר ז 45 mailing
דִּוּוּשׁ ז 45 pedaling
דּוּחַ ז 248 report; traffic ticket
דּוֹחֶה ז 10 repulsive
דּוּחַל ז 371 chat (bird)
דּוּכָן ז 370 stand, stall; dais, platform, podium; lectern, pulpit
דּוּם ז 240 doum (type of palm tree)
דּוּמָה נ 595 grave; afterworld [no pl.]
דּוּמִיָּה נ 911 silence
דּוֹמֵם ז 6 inanimate; still life in art; silent, still
דּוֹמְעָנִי ז 985 tearful, teary
דּוֹנַג ז 369 beeswax; ear wax [no pl.]
דּוֹנַגִּי ז 915 waxy
דּוֹסִי ז 915 religious Sl.
דַּוְקָאִיּוּת נ 762 doing things deliberately to annoy [no pl.]
דַּוְקָן ז 846 one who does things deliberately to annoy or to anger
דַּוְקָנוּת נ 752 literality, literalness [no pl.]
דַּוְקָנִי ז 969 literal (law)
דּוֹקְרָן ז 855 spike, prong; sear (weaponry)
דּוֹקְרָן ז 863 pitchfork
דּוֹקְרָנוּת נ 759 prickliness, spikiness [no pl.]
דּוֹקְרָנִי ז 985 prickly
דּוֹר ז 242 generation
דּוּר ז 246 whorl, virticil (botany)
דַּוָּר/דַּוָּאר ז 275 postman (fem. daveret, Coll. davarit)
דּוּרָה נ 595 sorghum
דּוֹרִי ז 988 generational
דּוֹרְסָנוּת נ 759 recklessness, destructiveness [no pl.]
דּוֹרְסָנִי ז 985 aggressive, destructive
דַּוְשָׁה נ 610 pedal
דּוּת נ 247 cellar (Talmudic); cistern
דָּחוּי ז 15 rejected, spurned; deferred
דִּחוּי ז 45 postponement
דָּחוּס ז 15 compressed; tightly packed
דָּחוּף ז 15 urgent
דָּחוּק ז 15 hard-pressed, insufficient; squashed
דְּחִי/(דֶּחִי) ז 259 failure, collapse, breakdown Bibl. [no pl.]
דְּחִיָּה נ 4 postponement; rejection, rebuff
דָּחִיס ז 20 compressible
דְּחִיסָה נ 1 compressing; compression as in engine
דְּחִיסוּת נ 24 compressibility
דְּחִיפָה נ 1 push; stimulus
דְּחִיפוּת נ 24 urgency
דְּחִיקָה נ 1 pushing, shoving aside
דַּחְלִיל ז 454 scarecrow
דַּחְלִילִי ז 915 looks like a scarecrow
דֹּחַן ז 343 millet [no pl.]
דַּחַס ז 328 crowding, pressure, Lit. [no pl.]
דַּחַף ז 328 urge, compulsion, impact, desire [no declemsion?]
דַּחְפּוֹר ז 444 bulldozer
דְּחָק ז 310 social stress [no pl.]
דַּחַק ז 328 stress, depression, pressure [no pl.]
דֹּחַק ז 343 crowding, congestion [no pl.]
דַּי ז 221 sufficient amount
דַּיָּג ז 275 fisherman (fem. dayeget)
דַּיִג ז 357 fishing; fish breeding [no pl.]
דַּיָּה נ 585 kite (bird)
דִּיּוּג ז 45 phishing (internet)
דְּיוֹטָה נ 671 floor, story (Talmudic)
דִּיּוּן ז 45 discussion, deliberation
דִּיּוּס ז 45 grouting [no pl.]
דִּיּוּק ז 45 accuracy, precision; punctuality
דְּיוֹקְנַאי ז 909 portraitist
דִּיּוּר ז 45 housing
דִּיּוּת ז 45 transpiration; retouching [no pl.]
דַּיּוּת נ 740 sufficiency [no pl.]
דְּיוֹתָה נ 671 inkwell
דַּיָּל ז 275 host, steward, cabin attendant (fem. dayelet)
דַּיָּלוּת נ 757 airline stewarding [no pl.]
דִּין ז 251 law; legal system; sentence, judgment
דַּיָּן ז 275 rabbinical judge
דַּיָּנוּת נ 757 judgeship [no pl.]
דַּיְסָה/א נ 614 porridge
דִּיצָה נ 3 joy, happiness, rejoicing Lit
דָּיֵק ז 279 dyke, barrier, fortification
דַּיְקָן ז 846 punctual, punctilious person
דַּיְקָנוּת נ 752 precision [no pl.]
דַּיְקָנִי ז 969 punctilious, meticulous
דִּיר ז 251 pen (for animals)
דַּיָּר ז 275 tenant; inhabitant (fem. dayeret)
דִּירָה נ 3 apartment, flat
דִּירוֹנֶת נ 897 small apartment
דִּירָתִי ז 915 of apartment
דַּיִשׁ ז 357 threshing [no pl.]
דִּישָׁה נ 3 threshing; over-involvement
דִּישׁוֹן ז 387 antelope, addax
דַּךְ ז 221 depressed, disadvantaged
דִּכָּאוֹן ז 898 depression
דִּכְאוֹנִי ז 952 depressive
דַּכְאָנִי ז 969 depressing
דִּכְדּוּךְ ז 66 depression, despondency
דַּכְדֶּכֶת נ 723 depression [no pl.]
דִּכּוּי ז 45 subjugation, oppression
דֳּכִי ז 349 breaking of waves, surge Lit.
דֳּכִי/דֹּכִי ז 349 breaking of waves, surge Lit.
דֻּכָּסוּת נ 740 dukedom; duchy
דַּל ז 221 poor, little, meager; pauper, indigent
דֹּלֶב ז 341 plane-tree
דַּלְגִּית נ 808 skipping rope
דַּלְגָן ז 846 springbuck (type of antelope)
דִּלְדּוּל ז 66 depletion, diminution
דִּלּוּג ז 45 jumping over; skipping over
דָּלוּי ז 15 drawn water – rare
דִּלּוּל ז 45 dilution; thinning out agriculture
דָּלוּק ז 15 lit; switched on
דַּלּוּת נ 731 poverty Lit. [no pl.]
דְּלִי ז 257 bucket, pail; Aquarius
דְּלִיָּה נ 4 raising, dredging up; gleaning info
דָּלִיָּה נ 674 tendril
דַּלִּיּוּת נ 797 varicosity [no pl.]
דְּלִיחוּת נ 24 turbidity, murkiness [no pl.]
דָּלִיל ז 20 thin, sparse; watery, diluted
דְּלִילוּת נ 24 sparseness, thinness
דְּלִיפָה נ 1 leaking; a leak
דָּלִיק ז 20 flammable
דְּלִיקָה נ 1 chasing Lit
דְּלִיקוּת נ 24 flammability

דָּלִית נ 842 tendril (esp. of grape vine)
דְּלַעַת נ 707 pumpkin
דֶּלֶף ז 317 trickle N; dripping; shunt Med. [no pl.]
דַּלְפוֹן ז 444 pauper Coll.
דָּלָק ז 267 marten
דֶּלֶק ז 317 fuel; petrol; gas
דְּלֵקָה נ 649 fire
דַּלֶּקֶת נ 685 inflammation
דַּלַּקְתִּי ז 978 inflammatory
דֶּלֶת נ 330 door, doorway
דַּלְתּוֹן ז 889 deltoid, kite-shaped
דָּם ז 216 blood; life, existence
דִּמְדּוּם ז 66 confusion; glowing of dim light
דֻּמְדְּמָנִית נ 843 red currant, ribes
דִּמּוּי ז 45 imagery; comparison; image
דָּמוּם ז 15 silent Lit
דִּמּוּם ז 45 bleeding
דְּמוּמִית נ 825 adonis (plant)
דָּמוּעַ ז 17 tearful Lit
דְּמוּת נ 734 figure, image; character
דֳּמִי ז 349 silence, stillness Lit. [no pl.]
דָּמִי ז 915 hemorrhagic
דִּמְיוֹן ז 885 imagination; resemblance
דִּמְיוֹנִי ז 952 imaginary, fictional
דְּמִיּוּת נ 736 resemblance, likeness [no pl.]
דְּמִיעָה נ 1 crying, lacrimation
דָּמִית נ 842 choroid (anatomy) [no pl.]
דֶּמֶם ז 317 bleeding, hemorrhage (no declension except construct, no pl.)
דְּמָמָה נ 634 silence [no pl.]
דַּמֶּמֶת נ 685 hemophilia [no pl.]
דֹּמֶן ז 341 dung, excrement Lit. [no pl.]
דֶּמַע ז 319 tearful crying, lacrimation Lit. [no pl.]
דִּמְעָה נ 598 tear N
דִּנְדּוּן ז 66 pealing, ringing Lit
דִּסְקָה נ 601 disk, disc
דִּסְקוּס ז 54 discussion Coll.
דִּסְקִית נ 812 dog tag, identity disc; washer
דֵּעָה נ 591 opinion
דָּעוּךְ ז 15 extinguished, fading Lit
דְּעִיכָה נ 1 dying out, fading
דַּעַץ ז 328 Paleo-Hebrew alphabet [no pl.]
דַּעַת ז 328 knowledge; wisdom; intelligence, understanding [no pl.]
דַּעְתָן/דַּעֲתָן ז 863 know-all, smugly knowledgeable; assertive
דַּעֲתָנוּת/דַּעְתָנוּת נ 740 smugness; aggressiveness; assertiveness [no pl.]
דַּעֲתָנִי/דַּעְתָנִי ז 915 knowing, resolute; assertive
דִּפְדּוּף ז 66 leafing, turning pages
דַּפְדְּפָן ז 851 browser (internet)
דַּפְדֶּפֶת נ 717 loose-leaf folder
דִּפּוּן ז 45 thickening, reinforcement of wall, fence; lining
דְּפוּס ז 399 printing; template, pattern; mold
דָּפוּף ז 15 laminated
דָּפוּק ז 15 terrible, bad; faulty; oppressed Sl.
דֹּפִי ז 349 blemish, fault, defect [no pl.]
דְּפִינָה נ 1 attaching, mounting
דְּפִיקָה נ 1 knock; failure Coll.; have intercourse Sl.
דֹּפֶן זו"נ 346 side, side wall, side panel; wall
דַּפָּס ז 275 printer (person) (fem. dapasit)
דַּפָּפָה נ 632 wall shelves
דֶּפֶק ז 317 disaster, catastrophe Sl. (no declension except construct, no pl.)
דֹּפֶק ז 341 pulse [no pl.]
דַּפָּר ז 275 fool, idiot, thickhead (military slang)
דַּפְתָּר ז 431 notebook Lit.-rare
דַּק ז 221 thin; skinny; small
דֹּק ז 227 thin film, veil Lit. [no decl.] [no pl.]
דִּקְדּוּק ז 66 grammar; being precise, punctilious
דִּקְדּוּקִי ז 954 grammatical
דַּקְדְּקָן ז 851 punctilious, pedantic (person)
דַּקְדְּקָנוּת נ 749 pedantry, fussiness [no pl.]
דַּקְדְּקָנִי ז 975 accurate, punctilious
דַּקָּה נ 585 minute
דִּקּוּר ז 45 puncture; acupuncture
דַּקּוּת נ 731 thinness, fineness
דָּקִיק ז 402 very thin, paper-thin [perhaps dimin. sub-pattern, CaCiC?]
דַּקִּיק ז 404 very thin, paper-thin
דַּקִּיקוּת נ 24 thinness
דַּקִּיקוּת נ 754 thinness [no pl.]
דְּקִירָה נ 1 prick N; stabbing = type of pricking
דֶּקֶל ז 317 palm tree
דַּקְלַאי/דַּקְלַי ז 909 palm grower
דִּקְלוּם ז 54 recitation, declamation
דַּקָּר ז 275 grouper (fish), Jaffa cod
דֶּקֶר ז 317 pick N; probe (military); epee (fencing)
דִּקְרוּר ז 70 tingling, pricking lightly
דַּר ז 226 mother-of-pearl
דֵּרָאוֹן ז 903 disgrace, shame Lit. [no pl.]
דִּרְבּוּן ז 54 goading, spurring
דַּרְבָּן ז 409 porcupine
דָּרְבָן/דָּרְבָּן ז 862 spur
דָּרְבָנִית נ 814 delphinium (plant)
דֶּרֶג ז 326 scale, rank, grade, echelon
דַּרְגָּה נ 610 rank; position; level
דַּרְגָּשׁ ז 409 bench, board
דִּרְדּוּר ז 66 roling down a slope; deterioration
דַּרְדָּס ז 409 sandal, slipper Lit.
דַּרְדַּק ז 414 young child
דַּרְדַּר ז 417 thistle
דַּרְדֶּרֶת נ 717 rockfall
דָּרוּג ז 15 terraced, stepped Lit
דֵּרוּג ז 51 classification, grading
דָּרוּךְ ז 15 tensed; cocked; primed
דָּרוֹם ז 288 south (only drom, constr., no declension, no pl.)
דְּרוֹמִי ז 944 southern
דָּרוּס ז 15 trampled, run over
דְּרוֹר ז 393 freedom, liberty Lit. [no declension, no pl.]
דְּרוֹר ז 393 sparrow
דְּרוּשׁ ז 399 homiletic literature
דְּרִיכָה נ 1 stepping on, treading; drawing bow, cocking weapon
דְּרִיכוּת נ 24 tension, preparedness
דְּרִיסָה נ 1 running over, trampling; stepping on
דְּרִישָׁה נ 1 demanding; demand, requirement
דֶּרֶךְ זו"נ 326 road, path; route; method, way
דַּרְכּוֹן ז 892 passport
דַּרְכְּמוֹנִית נ 814 hartwort (plant)
דֶּרֶן ז 326 grub, larva
דְּרָרָה נ 634 parakeet
דָּרָשׁ ז 310 homiletic interpretation of the Bible; homiletic exegesis [no pl.]
דְּרָשָׁה נ 632 homily
דַּרְשָׁן ז 846 preacher, sermonizer
דַּרְשָׁנוּת נ 752 exegesis, preaching, sermonizing [no pl.]
דַּרְשָׁנִי ז 969 homiletical
דֶּשֶׁא ז 319 grass
דִּשְׁדּוּשׁ ז 66 stamping, treading
דִּשּׁוּן ז 45 fertilization agricultural
דָּשֵׁן ז 279 fertile, rich (land); rich (food); full-bodied
דֶּשֶׁן ז 317 fertilizer, manure; rich food Lit.

הֶגְבֵּל ז 179 limitation, restraint, curtailment
הַגְבָּלָה נ 168 limiting; limitation, curtailment, restraint
הֶגְבֵּר ז 179 amplification
הַגְבָּרָה נ 168 strengthening; amplification
הֶגֵּד ז 182 statement; dictum; axiom
הַגָּדָה נ 173 telling, recounting; saga, chronicle; Haggadah
הַגְדָּלָה נ 168 enlargement; magnification
הַגְדָּרָה נ 168 defining; definition; characterization
הַגְדָּשָׁה נ 168 filling to overflowing
הֶגֶה ר' הֲגָאִים ז 338 steering wheel, helm; rudder; control, leadership [pl. haga'im]
הֶגֶה ר' הֲגָאִים/הֲגָיִים ז 338 utterance, spoken sound; sound [pl. haga'im/hagayim]
הַגָּהָה נ 173 proofreading
הָגוּי ז 16 pronounced, articulated; thought of, considered Lit
הִגּוּי ז 45 pronunciation
הִגּוּי ז 45 steering
הָגוּן ז 16 decent, fair; adequate, suitable
הָגוּת נ 733 meditation, contemplation
הָגוּתִי ז 982 contemplative
הַגְזָמָה נ 168 exaggerating; exaggeration
הֲגָחָה נ 174 bursting out, bursting forth
הַגְחָכָה נ 168 ridiculing, making ridiculous
הֲגִיָּה נ 5 diction, pronunciation
הִגָּיוֹן ז 899 logic
הֶגְיוֹנִי ז 963 reasonable, logical
הֶגְיוֹנִיּוּת נ 762 logicality [no pl.]
הֲגִינוּת נ 25 decency, fairness
הֲגִירָה נ 2 migration, immigration
הַגְלָדָה נ 168 forming of a scab
הַגְלָיָה נ 168 deportation, exile N
הַגְמָאָה נ 168 giving to someone to drink Lit.
הַגְמָדָה נ 168 belittling, disparaging, minimizing
הִגָּמְלוּת נ 26 weaning, withdrawal
הַגְמָעָה נ 168 giving animals to drink
הַגְמָשָׁה נ 168 moderation, toning down; making more elastic
הַגְנָבָה נ 168 moving someone/something stealthily; sneaking something in
הֲגַנָּה/הֲגָנָה נ 177 defense; protection

הִגָּנְזוּת נ 26 being hidden, being secreted
הֲגַנָּתִי/הֲגָנָתִי ז 915 defensive
הַגָּעָה נ 173 arrival; reaching, attending
הַגְעָלָה נ 168 making dishes kosher by immersing in boiling water
הַגְעָשָׁה נ 168 enraging someone Lit.
הֲגָפָה נ 174 closing, locking (doors, windows, shutters)
הַגָּרָה נ 173 pouring, dribbling, spilling Lit.
הַגְרָלָה נ 168 lottery; chance, luck
הִגָּרְמוּת נ 26 being caused
הַגְרָעָה נ 168 degradation Lit. [no pl.]
הִגָּרְעוּת נ 26 being lessened, being diminished
הִגָּרְפוּת נ 26 being swept
הִגָּרְרוּת נ 26 being towed
הַגָּשָׁה נ 173 serving or service, esp. of food; submitting, handing in (e.g., report); presenting, delivering
הַגְשָׁמָה נ 168 realization, fulfillment; personification
הֵד ז 231 echo; response
הַדְאָגָה נ 168 causing concern, causing worry
הַדְבָּקָה נ 168 pasting, gluing; contagion, spreading infectious disease; keeping up with
הִדַּבְּקוּת נ 123 contagion
הִדָּבְקוּת נ 26 sticking, adhering
הַדְבָּרָה נ 168 pest control; overcoming harmful entities
הִדַּבְּרוּת נ 123 parleying, negotiating
הִדָּבְרוּת נ 26 agreeing, esp. to meet
הֶדְגֵּם ז 179 demonstration Rare
הַדְגָּמָה נ 168 demonstrating, illustrating; demonstration, illustration
הַדְגָּרָה נ 168 incubation, hatching
הֶדְגֵּשׁ ז 179 emphasis, accentuation
הַדְגָּשָׁה נ 168 stressing; stress, accentuation, emphasis; highlighting
הֲדָדִי ז 943 mutual
הֲדָדִיּוּת נ 772 reciprocity [no pl.]
הִדְהוּד ז 66 reverberation, echoing
הַדְהָיָה נ 168 causing to fade; fading, discoloration
הַדְהָרָה נ 168 causing to gallop
הִדּוּד ז 45 interaction
הִדּוּדִי ז 956 interactive
הֲדוֹם ז 395 foot-rest, stool
הִדּוּס ז 45 hopping

הָדוּף ז 16 pushed, shoved
הָדוּק ז 16 tight
הִדּוּק ז 45 tightening
הָדוּר ז 16 elegant, refined
הִדּוּר ז 45 praising; elegance
הֲדוּרִים ז 998 uneven, twisted area or road
הֲדָחָה נ 173 ousting, dismissal from employment, removal; seduction
הֲדָחָה נ 174 rinsing
הִדָּחוּת נ 29 postponement
הַדְחָסָה נ 168 compressing, squeezing [no pl.]
הִדָּחֲסוּת נ 28 being compressed, being squeezed
הִדָּחֲפוּת נ 28 being pushed, being shoved; pushing one's way in
הֶדְחֵק ז 179 displacement
הַדְחָקָה נ 168 repression - psychoanalysis
הִדָּחֲקוּת נ 28 being squeezed in; being pushed aside; forcing one's way in
הֶדְיוֹטוּת נ 740 state of being a layman [no pl.]
הֶדְיוֹטִי ז 915 foolish, stupid (archaic)
הִדַּיְּנוּת נ 123 litigation; contentiousness
הֲדִיפָה נ 2 thrust, push N
הָדִיר ז 21 reproducible; revocable in banking
הִדַּלְדְּלוּת נ 158 shriveling, decline N, waning, weakening
הַדְלָחָה נ 168 mudding, tainting, opacifying Lit.
הַדְלָיָה נ 168 trellising a vine
הַדְלָפָה נ 168 leak of information; causing a leak
הַדְלָקָה נ 168 lighting, kindling; turning on instrument, light etc.
הִדָּלְקוּת נ 26 being ignited, be lit; being turned on engine, light
הִדַּמּוּת נ 134 modeling oneself on, copying; assimilation - phonetics
הַדְמָיָה נ 168 simulation; imaging; virtualization
הַדְמָמָה נ 168 shutting down, silencing, turning off
הַדְמָעָה נ 168 lacrimation
הֲדַס ז 314 myrtle
הֶדֶף ז 327 shock wave; thrust, impetus [no pl.]
הֲדָפָה נ 173 shedding, emission, giving off
הֶדְפֵּס ז 179 print N
הַדְפָּסָה נ 168 printing
הִדַּפְּקוּת נ 123 knocking on a door repeatedly
הֶדֶק ז 327 trigger; terminal (electricity); clip, clasp
הָדָר ז 268 citrus

הֲזָמָה/הַזָּמָה נ 177 refutation of a witness, proving a witness to be perjurious
הַזְמָנָה נ 168 invitation; order
הֲזָנָה נ 174 feeding, nourishing; providing raw materials for engine, equipment
הַזְנָחָה נ 168 neglect N
הַזְנָקָה נ 168 starting a race; tasking off fast
הֲזָעָה/הַזָּעָה נ 173 perspiring, sweating
הַזְעָמָה נ 168 angering, annoying Lit. [no pl.]
הַזְעָפָה נ 168 frowning
הַזְעָקָה נ 168 calling, summoning, calling into action
הַזְעָרָה נ 168 miniaturization; microfilming
הֶזֵּק ז 182 damage, harm Lit.; property damage law
הַזְקָפָה נ 168 making someone stand erect
הִזָּקְפוּת נ 26 being credited to into account; straightening back [no pl.]
הִזָּקְקוּת נ 26 necessity, requirement, need
הַזְרָמָה נ 168 pouring, causing to flow; transfer of large quantities
הַזְרָעָה נ 168 insemination of animals
הַזְרָקָה נ 168 injecting; injection
הִזָּרְקוּת נ 26 being thrown
הַחְבָּאָה נ 168 hiding, concealing; concealment
הַחְדָּרָה נ 168 inserting; insertion, penetration; introduction
הַחְוָרָה נ 168 going pale; becoming dull [no pl.]
הַחְזָיָה נ 168 visualization
הַחְזָקָה נ 168 holding on, grasping; storing; incarceration
הֶחְזֵר ז 179 refund; return; reflection
הַחְזָרָה נ 168 return N, replacement; reinstatement; paying back
הַחְטָאָה נ 168 missing target; failing to chieve an aim
הַחְיָאָה נ 168 resuscitation; revitalization, reinvigoration
הַחְכָּמָה נ 168 becoming wise, acquiring knowledge; imparting knowledge, making wise
הֶחְכֵּר ז 179 leasing
הַחְכָּרָה נ 168 leasing
הַחְלָדָה נ 168 rusting
הֲחָלָה נ 175 application of law, coming into force [no pl.]
הֶחְלֵט ז 179 essentially only in beheHlet ‘definitely’

הַחְלָטָה נ 168 decision; resolution
הֶחְלֵטִי ז 920 decisive, determined
הֶחְלֵטִיּוּת נ 763 determination [no pl.]
הַחְלָמָה נ 168 recuperation, recovery
הַחְלָפָה נ 168 exchanging, swapping; changing, replacing
הֵחָלְצוּת נ 27 extricating oneself; being extricated; volunteering
הַחְלָקָה נ 168 skiing, skating, sliding; skid N; straightening hair; smoothing out
הַחְלָשָׁה נ 168 Weakening
הֵחָלְשׁוּת נ 27 Weakening
הַחְמָצָה נ 168 souring; pickling; missing opportunity
הַחְמָרָה נ 168 worsening, deterioration; increased rigorousness or severity
הַחְנָיָה נ 168 parking
הַחְנָפָה נ 168 flattery
הַחְנָקָה נ 168 choking N [no pl.]
הֵחָנְקוּת נ 27 strangulation; being choked
הֵחָסְמוּת נ 27 blocking; being blocked [no pl.]
הַחְסָנָה נ 168 storing
הַחְסָרָה נ 168 subtraction; omission, missing out
הֵחָפְזוּת נ 27 haste [no pl.]
הֵחָצוּת נ 30 being halved/divided [no pl.]
הַחְצָנָה נ 168 externalization, giving expression openly
הֵחָקְרוּת נ 27 being researched; being interrogated [no pl.]
הַחְרָבָה נ 168 destroying; destruction [no pl.]
הֵחָרְבוּת נ 27 destruction; being destroyed [no pl.]
הַחְרָמָה נ 168 confiscation; boycott N; excommunication
הַחְרָפָה נ 168 worsening, deterioration
הַחְרָשָׁה נ 168 silencing; shouting down [no pl.]
הַחְשָׁבָה נ 168 taking into account; ascribing importance [no pl.]
הֵחָשְׁבוּת נ 27 being considered [no pl.]
הַחְשָׁדָה נ 168 casting suspicion [no pl.]
הֵחָשְׁדוּת נ 27 being suspected [no pl.]
הֲחָשָׁה נ 175 speeding up; moving something rapidly
הַחְשָׁכָה נ 168 making dark, blacking out [no pl.]
הֵחָשְׁלוּת נ 27 hardening Lit; being forged (metal) [no pl.]

הֵחָשְׂפוּת נ 27 being exposed; exposure
הֵחָתְכוּת נ 27 being cut/gashed; being decided/ruled [no pl.]
הַחְתָּלָה נ 168 diaper changing
הַחְתָּמָה נ 168 obtaining a signature; stamping, sealing
הֲטָבָה נ 174 improvement; benefit; bonus
הַטְבָּלָה נ 168 dipping; immersing; immersion; baptism
הַטְבָּעָה נ 168 drowning someone or something; sealing, minting
הִטַּגְּנוּת נ 124 being fried, frying [no pl.]
הִטַּהֲרוּת נ 125 purification
הֲטָחָה נ 174 hurling, flinging, throwing; reviling, offending someone to their face
הַטָּיָה נ 173 turning, diversion, bending; declension, inflection, conjugation (grammar); deviation (statistics)
הֶטֵּל ז 182 tax, levy, excise
הֶטֵּל ז 184 projection (geometry)
הַטְלָאָה נ 168 patching
הֲטָלָה נ 174 throwing, dropping; laying eggs; projection
הַטָּלָה/הֲטָלָה נ 173 placing, imposing
הִטַּלְטְלוּת נ 159 wandering; being tossed from side to side
הִטַּמְּאוּת נ 124 contamination [no pl.]
הַטְמָנָה נ 168 hiding; burying
הַטְמָעָה נ 168 assimilating; assimilation
הִטַּמְּעוּת נ 124 assimilation, being assimilated
הִטָּמְעוּת נ 26 being assimilated
הִטַּנְּפוּת נ 124 getting dirty
הֶטֵּס ז 184 airlift
הֲטָסָה נ 174 flying an aircraft; air transport
הַטְעָיָה נ 168 misleading N, deceiving, deception
הַטְעָמָה נ 168 emphasis, accentuation
הֶטְעֵן ז 179 cathexis
הַטְעָנָה נ 168 loading
הַטָּפָה נ 173 preaching
הִטָּפְלוּת נ 26 harassing; clinging to
הֶטְפֵּס ז 179 stereotype
הַטְרָדָה נ 168 harassing; harassment, bothering
הַטְרָחָה נ 168 bothering, annoying, causing unnecessary work
הַטְרָיָה נ 168 debridgement, - removing damaged matter
הֶטְרֵם ז 179 anticipation

הֲמָטָה נ 174 causing, bringing about (something negative)
הַמְטָרָה נ 168 irrigation, raining, pouring, inundation
הֶמְיָן ז 863 sash (Talmudic)
הַמְכָּלָה נ 168 containerization
הֲמֻלָּה נ 659 commotion
הַמְלָחָה נ 168 salinating; salting of meat to make it kosher
הַמְלָטָה נ 168 giving birth - mammals, whelping, calving, foaling
הִמָּלְטוּת נ 26 escaping, fleeing
הַמְלָכָה נ 168 coronation, crowning
הִמָּלְכוּת נ 26 consulting someone Lit; regretting Lit
הַמְלָצָה נ 168 recommendation; advice; credential
הִמָּנוּת נ 29 being counted/a member of [no pl.]
הִמָּנְעוּת נ 26 abstention; avoidance
הֲמַסָּה נ 177 melting, dissolving
הַמְעָדָה נ 168 tripping up, causing to fall
הַמְעָטָה נ 168 lessening, reduction, decrease, diminution
הִמָּעֲטוּת נ 28 diminishing, decrease [no pl.]
הִמָּעֲכוּת נ 28 being mashed/squashed [no pl.]
הַמְצָאָה נ 168 invention; concept idea; fabrication; proffering
הִמָּצְאוּת נ 26 being found; being located [no pl.]
הַמְרָאָה נ 168 takeoff, lift-off; sublimation - Chem.
הַמְרָדָה נ 168 bringing about mutiny, rebellion; sedition - law
הֲמָרָה נ 174 exchange, changing, converting
הַמְרָצָה נ 168 motivation, goading, urging, encouraging
הַמְשָׂגָה נ 168 conceptualization
הֶמְשֵׁךְ ז 179 continuation, continuance
הַמְשָׁכָה נ 168 continuation, prolonging
הִמָּשְׁכוּת נ 26 continuation; being pulled; being attracted
הֶמְשֵׁכִי ז 920 continuing, incomplete
הֶמְשֵׁכִיּוּת נ 763 continuity [no pl.]
הַמְשָׁלָה נ 168 appointment of a ruler
הַמְשָׁלָה נ 168 comparing, equating
הֲמָתָה נ 174 killing, putting to death
הִמָּתְחוּת נ 26 being stretched
הַמְתָּנָה נ 168 waiting
הַמְתָּקָה נ 168 sweetening; desalination of sea water
הֲנָאָה נ 633 pleasure
הֲנָבָה נ 174 yielding, producing; flourishing, prospering
הַנְבָּטָה נ 168 germination, sprouting
הַנְגָּדָה נ 168 comparing, contrasting
הַנְגָּנָה נ 168 intonation
הִנָּגְעוּת נ 26 contagion [no pl.]
הֶנֵּד ז 184 movement, nod Lit.
הַנְדָּסִי ז 915 of engineering
הִנָּדְפוּת נ 26 evaporating Lit-rare [no pl.]
הַנְהָגָה נ 168 leadership; leading; introducing; imposing; instituting
הִנְהוּן ז 66 nodding in agreement
הַנְהָלָה נ 168 management, administration
הַנְהָרָה נ 168 explication - Phil.
הִנָּזְקוּת נ 26 being damaged; damage
הֲנָחָה נ 174 discount, reduction
הַנָּחָה/הֲנָחָה נ 173 placing; assumption; presumption, premise, postulation; hypothesis
הַנְחָיָה נ 168 guidance, instruction; guiding, directing; officiating
הַנְחָלָה נ 168 endowing, bequeathing
הַנְחָתָה נ 168 landing airplane etc.; sudden command or assignment Coll.; reduction - physics
הִנָּטְלוּת נ 26 being taken away from [no pl.]
הִנָּטְעוּת נ 26 planting [no pl.]
הִנָּטְשׁוּת נ 26 abandonment [no pl.]
הַנְמָכָה נ 168 lowering; quieting; diminution in importance
הַנְמָקָה נ 168 explanation, reasoning, substantiation
הֲנָסָה נ 174 driving away, causing to flee; expulsion [no pl.]
הֶנֵּעַ ז 185 movement; motion, gesture; drive
הֲנָעָה נ 174 ignition of engine, propulsion; motivation (psychology)
הַנְעָלָה נ 168 footwear; providing with shoes; putting shoes on someone
הִנָּעֲלוּת נ 28 locking; closure, adjournment [no pl.]
הַנְעָמָה נ 168 making pleasant
הִנָּעֲצוּת נ 28 being thrust into [no pl.]
הֶנֵּף ז 184 wave N, flutter N
הֲנָפָה נ 174 raising, usually of flag
הַנְפָּקָה נ 168 issue, issuing of stocks, coins etc.; stock issue
הַנְפָּשָׁה נ 168 animation
הִנָּפְשׁוּת נ 26 vacationing, relaxing [no pl.]
הֶנֵּץ ז 186 blossoming [no pl.]
הֲנֵצָה/הֲנָצָה נ 177 flowering, blossoming; budding
הַנְצָחָה נ 168 memorialization; perpetuation; immortalization
הִנָּצְלוּת נ 26 being saved; surviving
הִנָּקוּת נ 29 cleansing oneself [no pl.]
הִנָּקְטוּת נ 26 being taken action, step [no pl.]
הַנְשָׁמָה נ 168 artificial respiration
הַנְשָׁרָה נ 168 expulsion, dismissal
הִנָּתְזוּת נ 26 being sprayed [no pl.]
הִנָּתְקוּת נ 26 disengagement; being cut off
הֶסֵּב ז 186 turn, rotation; endorsement, signature [no pl.]
הֲסַבָּה/הֲסָבָה נ 177 turning; altering, converting; endorsement of check, etc.; career change
הֶסְבֵּר ז 179 explanation
הַסְבָּרָה נ 168 propaganda, publicity, information; explaining; explanation
הַסְבָּרָתִי ז 922 explanatory, propagandist
הֲסָגָה נ 173 moving or withdrawing from one place to another
הַסְגָּלָה נ 168 modification, adaptation for another purpose
הֶסְגֵּר ז 179 confinement, detention; quarantine; embargo, blockade
הַסְגָּרָה נ 168 extradition , handing over; giving away, revealing
הִסָּדְקוּת נ 26 being cracked
הֶסְדֵּר ז 179 agreement, arrangement, settlement; military service combining army service with Jewish Studies
הַסְדָּרָה נ 168 arrangement; resolution; regularization [no pl.]
הַסְוָאָה נ 168 camouflage N
הִסּוּי ז 45 quietening, hushing
הִסּוּס ז 45 hesitation; doubt N
הֶסַּח ז 183 distractedness, distraction
הִסָּחֲבוּת נ 28 being dragged; being prolonged col

loading 169 הַעֲמָסָה נ

deepening 169 הַעֲמָקָה נ

response [no pl.] 30 הֵעָנוּת נ

awarding; 169 הַעֲנָקָה נ granting, providing

punishing 169 הַעֲנָשָׁה נ

being punished; 27 הֵעָנְשׁוּת נ punishment [no pl.]

employing 169 הַעֲסָקָה נ

illegal immigration 169 הַעְפָּלָה נ to Palestine during British mandate; climbing, ascending; progressing, rising

saddening [no pl.] 169 הַעֲצָבָה נ

intensification, 169 הַעֲצָמָה נ - amplification; empowerment hour period

eyes becoming 27 הֵעָצְמוּת נ shut, closed

stopping 27 הֵעָצְרוּת נ

becoming bent [no 27 הֵעָקְמוּת נ pl.]

being uprooted; 27 הֵעָקְרוּת נ uprooting [no pl.]

remark, comment; 175 הֶעָרָה נ note

estimation; 169 הַעֲרָכָה נ appraisal; evaluation; appreciation

deployment; 27 הֵעָרְכוּת נ organization; arranging

deceiving 169 הַעֲרָמָה נ

raising obstacle; 169 הַעֲרָמָה נ piling up, heaping

being piled up 27 הֵעָרְמוּת נ

admiration 169 הַעֲרָצָה נ

being carried out; 30 הֵעָשׂוּת נ becoming [no pl.]

enriching 169 הַעֲשָׁרָה נ

copy N 180 הֶעֱתֵק/הֶעְתֵּק ז

copying; 169 הַעְתָּקָה/הַעֲתָקָה נ moving, shifting

being relocated 27 הֵעָתְקוּת נ

acceding to, 27 הֵעָתְרוּת נ acquiescing to [no pl.]

shelling - 168 הַפְגָּזָה נ (military); fission - physics

being impaired 26 הִפָּגְמוּת נ

acting out Psych 179 הֶפְגֵּן ז

demonstration, 168 הַפְגָּנָה נ rally; demonstrating, expressing

demonstrative 922 הַפְגָּנָתִי ז

הַפְגָּנָתִיּוּת נ 764 demonstrativeness (no decl., no pl.)

being injured; 26 הִפָּגְעוּת נ being damaged; being offended

meeting 26 הִפָּגְשׁוּת נ

redeeming, being 29 הִפָּדוּת נ redeemed [no pl.]

reversal; opposite; 45 הִפּוּךְ ז inversion

scaring, instilling 168 הַפְחָדָה נ fear; intimidating

reducing, 168 הַפְחָתָה נ diminishing; deduction

depreciation, 28 הִפָּחֲתוּת נ devaluation

Haftarah - section 168 הַפְטָרָה נ read from Prophets on Sabbath and festivals after Torah reading

being rid of 26 הִפָּטְרוּת נ

reversible 21 הָפִיךְ ז

turning over; 2 הֲפִיכָה נ revolution

reversibility 25 הֲפִיכוּת נ

opposite, 327 הֵפֶךְ/הֶפֶךְ ז contrary N

coup d'etat; 650 הֲפֵכָה נ upheaval

contradictory; 980 הָפְכִּי ז inverse

departure of ship; 168 הַפְלָגָה נ sailing, traveling by sea; exaggeration

causing to fall; 173 הַפָּלָה נ abortion, miscarriage; downing plane

ejecting 168 הַפְלָטָה נ

being 26 הִפָּלְטוּת נ expelled/emitted; being discharged bullet; escaping words

discriminating; 168 הַפְלָיָה נ discrimination

incriminating 168 הַפְלָלָה נ

fluorination [no pl.] 168 הַפְלָרָה נ

hypnotizing 54 הִפְּנוּט ז

turning one's body; 168 הַפְנָיָה נ directing, diverting; referring, referral; draw one's attention

internalizing 168 הַפְנָמָה נ (feelings, thoughts), internalization; absorbing, assimilating (knowledge, info)

loss; damage; 179 הֶפְסֵד ז failure

being disqualified 26 הִפָּסְלוּת נ [no pl.]

break, rest 179 הֶפְסֵק ז

break, recess, 168 הַפְסָקָה נ intermission; stopping, halting

cessation 26 הִפָּסְקוּת נ

activating; 168 הַפְעָלָה נ operating, running

being excited, 28 הִפָּעֲמוּת נ enthused

opening wide 28 הִפָּעֲרוּת נ mouth, gap [no pl.]

distribution, 174 הֲפָצָה נ spreading

being wounded; 26 הִפָּצְעוּת נ injury [no pl.]

bombing, 168 הַפְצָצָה נ bombardment; fission physics

insistent pleading 168 הַפְצָרָה נ

depositing 168 הַפְקָדָה נ

being absent; 26 הִפָּקְדוּת נ being counted [no pl.]

production 174 הֲפָקָה נ

being open eyes 26 הִפָּקְחוּת נ

expropriation 168 הַפְקָעָה נ

exploding, 26 הִפָּקְעוּת נ bursting Lit-rare [no pl.]

abandoned, 179 הֶפְקֵר ז ownerless entity [no pl.]

abandoning 168 הַפְקָרָה נ

הַפְרָאָה, ראו הַפְרָיָה נ 168 fertilization Lit.-rare - see hafraya

separating 168 הַפְרָדָה נ

separation 26 הִפָּרְדוּת נ

violating; violation 176 הֲפָרָה נ

exaggerating 168 הַפְרָזָה נ

causing to bloom; 168 הַפְרָחָה נ making arable

flying - a kite, 168 הַפְרָחָה נ balloon

privatization 168 הַפְרָטָה נ

being changed 26 הִפָּרְטוּת נ large currency for small; being divided [no pl.]

fertilization; 168 הַפְרָיָה נ fertilizing; pollination; inspiring, making more productive

refuting, 168 הַפְרָכָה נ disproving

disturbance; 168 הַפְרָעָה נ (interruption; disorder (medicine

difference 179 הֶפְרֵשׁ ז

secreting; 168 הַפְרָשָׁה נ separating, allocating

undressing 168 הַפְשָׁטָה נ someone; abstraction

thawing, melting 168 הַפְשָׁרָה נ

opening; openness 26 הִפָּתְחוּת נ

surprise N 168 הַפְתָּעָה נ

flocculation [no 168 הַפְתָּתָה נ pl.]

positioning, 173 הֲצָבָה נ stationing, posting

voting; pointing 168 הַצְבָּעָה נ at; raising one's hand

exposition 182 הֶצֵּג ז

showing; show, 173 הַצָּגָה נ performance, play; display; presentation

salute N; saluting 168 הַצְדָּעָה נ

justification; 168 הַצְדָּקָה נ justifying

declaration; 168 הַצְהָרָה נ affidavit

declarative 922 הַצְהָרָתִי ז

making someone 168 הַצְחָקָה נ laugh

accumulation 116 הִצְטַבְּרוּת נ

self-justification 116 הִצְטַדְּקוּת נ

crowding 139 הִצְטוֹפְפוּת נ

equipping 116 הִצְטַיְּדוּת נ oneself

excellence 116 הִצְטַיְּנוּת נ

הַרְחָבָה נ 168 broadening, widening; expansion; expanding on a topic
הֲרָחָה נ 174 smelling, sniffing [no pl.]
הַרְחָפָה נ 168 fluidization - chemistry
הַרְחָקָה נ 168 distancing; removal, expulsion
הַרְטָבָה נ 168 wetting
הֵרָטְבוּת נ 27 getting wet
הֲרִיגָה נ 2 killing
הֵרָיוֹן ז 901 pregnancy
הֶרְיוֹנִי ז 963 gestational
הֲרִיסָה נ 2 destroying
הֶרְכֵּב ז 179 make-up, ingredients; set, arrangement, line-up; panel; ensemble; composition
הַרְכָּבָה נ 168 assembling; grafting (botany)
הַרְכָּנָה נ 168 bowing head, body Lit.; bending Lit.
הַרְכָּשָׁה נ 168 acquisition, procurement
הֲרָמָה נ 174 lifting, raising
הַרְמוֹן ז 446 harem
הֵרָמְסוּת נ 27 being crushed, being trampled [no pl.]
הֶרֶס ז 327 destruction [contr. only, no pl.]
הַרְסָן ז 846 destructive person
הַרְסָנוּת נ 752 destructiveness [no pl.]
הַרְסָנִי ז 969 destructive
הַרְעָבָה נ 168 starving someone
הַרְעָדָה נ 168 shaking something; trembling Lit.; vibrating Lit.
הֲרָעָה נ 176 worsening
הַרְעָלָה נ 168 poisoning
הַרְעָפָה נ 168 heaping (praise, gifts), inundating, showering upon
הַרְעָשָׁה נ 168 shelling, bombing (military); noisemaking
הֵרָפְאוּת נ 27 healing, being healed
הַרְפָּיָה נ 168 relaxation
הַרְפַּתְקָן ז 863 adventurer
הַרְפַּתְקָנוּת נ 740 adventurousness [no pl.]
הַרְפַּתְקָנִי ז 915 adventurous
הַרְצָאָה נ 168 lecture N
הֲרָצָה נ 174 test-run, trial run; running, operating
הֵרָצְחוּת נ 27 being murdered [no pl.]
הַרְקָבָה נ 168 rotting, decomposition [no pl.]
הֵרָקְבוּת נ 27 decomposition, rotting
הַרְקָדָה נ 168 dancing, causing to dance
הֲרָקָה נ 174 emptying

הֵרָקְמוּת נ 27 being planned, being formed, being developed [no pl.]
הֲרָרִי ז 943 mountainous
הֲרָרִיּוּת נ 772 mountainousness [no pl.]
הַרְשָׁאָה נ 168 authorization
הַרְשָׁמָה נ 168 registration; impressing
הֵרָשְׁמוּת נ 27 being registered; registration
הַרְשָׁעָה נ 168 conviction
הֶרֶת נ 331 thymus (anatomy) [no pl.]
הַרְתָּחָה נ 168 boiling
הֵרָתְמוּת נ 27 undertaking, devotion
הַרְתָּעָה נ 168 deterring; intimidating
הֵרָתְעוּת נ 27 reluctance [no pl.]
הַרְתָּעָתִי ז 922 deterring
הִשָּׁאֲבוּת נ 28 being drawn/pumped [no pl.]
הַשָּׂאָה נ 173 marrying off, officiating at a wedding
הַשָּׁאָה נ 173 suggestion, seduction, persuasion Lit.
הַשְׁאָלָה נ 168 lending; borrowing - Coll. only; metaphor
הַשְׁאָרָה נ 168 leaving; keeping, causing to remain
הִשָּׁאֲרוּת נ 28 staying, being, remaining
הֲשָׁבָה נ 174 returning something
הַשְׁבָּחָה נ 168 enhancement; betterment, improvement; capital gain
הַשְׁבָּעָה נ 168 swearing in; being sworn in
הִשָּׁבְעוּת נ 26 swearing [no pl.]
הִשָּׁבְרוּת נ 26 breaking, being broken
הַשְׁבָּתָה נ 168 striking, closure; stoppage
הֶשֵּׂג ז 182 achievement, accomplishment
הַשָּׂגָה נ 173 obtaining, achieving; comprehension; doubt, disagreement, criticism
הַשְׁגָּחָה נ 168 supervising
הֶשֵּׂגִי ז 919 accomplished; achieving
הֶשֵּׂגִיּוּת נ 762 ambitiousness [no pl.]
הַשְׁגָּרָה נ 168 routinizing, conventionalization Lit.; running in Lit.
הַשְׁהָיָה נ 168 delaying, postponing; delay, postponement
הַשְׁוָאָה נ 168 comparison; equalization
הַשְׁוָאָתִי ז 922 comparative

הִשָּׁזְרוּת נ 26 becoming intertwined
הַשְׁחָזָה נ 168 sharpening, grinding, whetting
הַשְׁחָלָה נ 168 threading, beading, stringing
הַשְׁחָמָה נ 168 browning
הִשָּׁחֲקוּת נ 28 being eroded, worn away [no pl.]
הַשְׁחָרָה נ 168 blackening; tarnishing
הַשְׁחָתָה נ 168 vandalizing, damaging, destroying; corrupting
הֶשֵּׁט ז 184 sea transport, movement by sea
הַשְׁכָּבָה נ 168 lying down; causing to lie down; putting to bed
הַשְׁכָּחָה נ 168 causing to forget
הִשָּׁכְחוּת נ 26 being forgotten [no pl.]
הַשְׂכָּלָה נ 168 education, knowledge; the Enlightenment movement
הַשְׂכָּלָתִי ז 922 educational, academic
הַשְׁכָּמָה נ 168 wake-up call; reveille; getting up in the morning
הַשְׂכָּרָה נ 168 renting out, hiring
הַשָּׁלָה נ 173 shedding
הַשְׁלָטָה נ 168 imposing - order, rules
הַשְׁלָכָה נ 168 throwing; disposing; implication, ramification, consequence; projection psychology
הַשְׁלָמָה נ 168 completion; acceptance; making peace
הַשְׁלָשָׁה נ 168 depositing with a third party
הַשְׁמָדָה נ 168 destruction, eradication
הִשָּׁמְדוּת נ 26 destruction, annihilation
הֲשָׂמָה נ 174 placement, assigning
הַשְׁמֵט ז 179 ellipsis
הַשְׁמָטָה נ 168 omitting, omission
הִשָּׁמְטוּת נ 26 being dropped, falling [no pl.]
הַשְׁמָנָה נ 168 gaining weight, becoming fatter; obesity; fattening
הַשְׁמָעָה נ 168 voicing; playing of music, recording
הִשָּׁמְעוּת נ 26 being heard; being obeyed; being voiced
הַשְׁמָצָה נ 168 slander, defamation
הִשָּׁמְרוּת נ 26 being careful, safeguarded [no pl.]

הִתְאַפְּסוּת נ 108 being calibrated, being zeroed; regaining one's senses sl
הִתְאַפְּקוּת נ 108 self-restraint
הִתְאַפְּרוּת נ 108 making oneself up, putting on makeup
הִתְאַקְלְמוּת נ 141 acclimatation, acclimatization
הִתְאַרְגְּנוּת נ 141 becoming organized
הִתְאָרְחוּת נ 109 staying as guest, being hosted
הִתְאָרְכוּת נ 109 lengthening
הִתְאָרְסוּת נ 109 becoming engaged
הִתְאַשְׁפְּזוּת נ 141 being hospitalized; hospitalization
הִתְבָּאֲרוּת נ 110 being clarified
הִתְבַּגְּרוּת נ 108 maturation; adolescence
הִתְבַּדּוּת נ 126 falsification, being proven false
הִתְבַּדְּחוּת נ 108 joking
הִתְבַּדְּלוּת נ 108 being aloof; being separated
הִתְבַּדְּרוּת נ 108 having fun, being entertained; divergence - math
הִתְבַּהֲמוּת נ 110 becoming brutalized, becoming bestialized
הִתְבַּהֲרוּת נ 110 becoming clear
הִתְבּוֹדְדוּת נ 135 seclusion
הִתְבּוֹלְלוּת נ 135 assimilation
הִתְבּוֹנְנוּת נ 135 observing, watching
הִתְבּוֹסְסוּת נ 135 wallowing
הִתְבַּזְבְּזוּת נ 145 being wasted, being squandered
הִתְבַּזּוּת נ 126 making a mockery of oneself; humiliation
הִתְבַּטְּאוּת נ 108 self-expression; remark
הִתְבַּטְּלוּת נ 108 being canceled; being self-deprecating; being idle
הִתְבַּיְּשׁוּת נ 108 being ashamed, feeling ashamed; being shy
הִתְבַּיְּתוּת נ 108 domestication; homing
הִתְבַּכְיְנוּת נ 141 tendency to feel sorry for oneself, complaining Sl.
הִתְבַּלְבְּלוּת נ 145 getting confused; confusion
הִתְבַּלּוּת נ 126 being worn out
הִתְבַּלְּטוּת נ 108 standing out, being prominent; conspicuousness
הִתְבַּסְּמוּת נ 108 being drunk, getting drunk
הִתְבַּסְּסוּת נ 108 being based on; becoming established
הִתָּבְעוּת נ 26 being demanded to do something; being sued

הִתְבַּצְּעוּת נ 108 being carried out, being executed
הִתְבַּצְּרוּת נ 108 fortifying; fortification
הִתְבַּקְּעוּת נ 108 splitting, cracking
הִתְבַּרְבְּרוּת נ 145 getting lost Sl.
הִתְבָּרְגוּת נ 109 screwing, unscrewing of screw
הִתְבַּרְגְּנוּת נ 141 bourgeoisifying
הִתְבָּרְרוּת נ 109 becoming clear
הִתְבַּשְּׁלוּת נ 108 being cooked; cooking
הִתְבַּשְּׂמוּת נ 108 perfuming oneself; inhaling perfume
הִתְבַּשְּׂרוּת נ 108 being notified, getting good news
הִתְגָּאוּת נ 128 being proud, bragging
הִתְגַּבְּרוּת נ 108 overcoming; strengthening
הִתְגַּבְּשׁוּת נ 108 consolidation, integration; crystallization
הִתְגּוֹדְדוּת נ 135 gathering, assembling, congregating
הִתְגּוֹנְנוּת נ 135 self-defense
הִתְגּוֹרְרוּת נ 135 living, dwelling
הִתְגּוֹשְׁשׁוּת נ 135 wrestling match, violent struggle, brawl
הִתְגַּיְּסוּת נ 108 induction - military; being recruited; volunteering
הִתְגַּיְּרוּת נ 108 converting to Judaism
הִתְגַּלּוּת נ 126 revelation; epiphany
הִתְגַּלְּחוּת נ 108 shaving oneself
הִתְגַּלְּמוּת נ 108 embodiment
הִתְגַּלְּשׁוּת נ 108 sliding, gliding
הִתְגַּמְּשׁוּת נ 108 being more flexible
הִתְגַּנְּבוּת נ 108 stealing into, sneaking into
הִתְגַּנְדְּרוּת נ 141 coquetry, foppishness, dandyism
הִתְגַּעְגְּעוּת נ 145 missing, longing for, yearning for
הִתְגָּרוּת נ 128 teasing; arousal
הִתְגָּרְמוּת נ 109 ossification
הִתְגַּשְּׁמוּת נ 108 being realized; realization
הִתְהַדְּקוּת נ 108 tightening, fastening
הִתְהַוּוּת נ 126 coming into being, being created
הִתְהוֹלְלוּת נ 135 licentiousness, wild behavior
הִתְהַפְּכוּת נ 108 somersault, flip; turning over, rolling over
הִתְוַדּוּת נ 126 confessing; confession
הִתְוַדְּעוּת נ 108 making acquaintance
הַתְוָיָה נ 168 indication; laying out, setting out; marking

הִתּוּךְ ז 45 melting metal; fusion
הִתּוּל ז 45 jesting
הִתּוּלִי ז 956 humorous, comic
הִתְוַסְּפוּת נ 108 the addition of
הֶתֵּז ז 182 spray, mist
הַתָּזָה נ 173 spraying; severing Lit.; hissing a word or sound
הִתְחַבְּטוּת נ 108 difficulties in making a decision, misgivings
הִתְחַבְּקוּת נ 108 hugging, embracing
הִתְחַבְרוּת נ 108 becoming friends Coll.
הִתְחַבְּרוּת נ 108 joining, combining, connection
הִתְחַדְּדוּת נ 108 sharpening; clarification; acuteness, severity - pain
הִתְחַדְּשׁוּת נ 108 renewal, revival
הִתְחוֹלְלוּת נ 135 occurring, happening
הִתְחַזּוּת נ 126 impersonating
הִתְחַזְּקוּת נ 108 strengthening
הִתְחַיְּבוּת נ 108 commitment; obligation
הִתְחַכְּכוּת נ 108 rubbing against something
הִתְחַכְּמוּת נ 108 wisecracking; wisecrack
הַתְחָלָה נ 168 beginning, start, outset
הִתְחַלְחֲלוּת נ 146 being shocked, being horrified
הִתְחַלְּפוּת נ 108 changing; exchanging
הִתְחַלְּקוּת נ 108 segmentation, division; splitting
הַתְחָלָתִי ז 922 initial
הִתְחַמְּמוּת נ 108 warming, heating up
הִתְחַמְצְנוּת נ 141 oxygenating; oxygenation
הִתְחַמְּקוּת נ 108 evasion, escape; getting out of doing something
הִתְחַמְּשׁוּת נ 108 arming
הִתְחַנְחֲנוּת נ 146 coquetry, self ingratiation
הִתְחַנְּכוּת נ 108 being educated [no pl.]
הִתְחַנְּנוּת נ 108 imploring, begging
הִתְחַנְּפוּת נ 108 flattery
הִתְחַסְּדוּת נ 108 sanctimoniousness, hypocrisy
הִתְחַסְּנוּת נ 108 immunization; strengthening
הִתְחַפְּשׂוּת נ 108 masquerading
הִתְחַצְּפוּת נ 108 being impudent, being insolent
הִתְחַקּוּת נ 126 researching, investigating
הִתְחָרְדוּת נ 109 becoming ultra-orthodox Coll.

הִתְנַהֲלוּת נ 110 conducting; advancing Lit
הִתְנוֹדְדוּת נ 135 staggering, reeling, swaying
הִתְנַוְּנוּת נ 108 degeneration
הִתְנוֹסְסוּת נ 135 flying (of a flag); displaying [no pl.]
הִתְנוֹעֲעוּת נ 136 swaying [no pl.]
הִתְנוֹפְפוּת נ 135 waving, fluttering
הִתְנוֹצְצוּת נ 135 gleaming, shining Lit.
הִתְנַזְּרוּת נ 108 abstaining from doing something
הִתְנַחֲלוּת נ 110 settling, inhabiting
הַתְנָיָה נ 168 conditioning; stipulation
הִתְנַכְּלוּת נ 108 harassment; harassing
הִתְנַכְּרוּת נ 108 ignoring alienating
הִתְנַמְנְמוּת נ 145 nap N
הִתְנַסּוּת נ 126 experience; experiencing
הִתְנַסְּחוּת נ 108 wording; expressiveness
הַתְנָעָה נ 168 starting an engine
הִתְנַעֲרוּת נ 110 shirking, shaking off
הִתְנַפּוּת נ 126 being sifted; sifting [no pl.]
הִתְנַפְּחוּת נ 108 swelling, becoming inflated
הִתְנַפְּלוּת נ 108 attacking; attack, onslaught
הִתְנַפְּצוּת נ 108 shattering, crashing
הִתְנַצְּחוּת נ 108 wrangling, arguing
הִתְנַצְּלוּת נ 108 apology
הִתְנַצְּרוּת נ 108 conversion to Christianity
הִתְנַקּוּת נ 126 cleansing oneself [no pl.]
הִתְנַקְּזוּת נ 108 draining, flowing
הִתְנַקְּמוּת נ 108 avenging, taking revenge
הִתְנַקְּשׁוּת נ 108 assassination
הִתְנַשְּׂאוּת נ 108 arrogance, condescension
הִתְנַשְּׁמוּת נ 108 hyperventilating, breathing heavily
הִתְנַשְּׁפוּת נ 108 breathing heavily, panting
הִתְנַשְּׁקוּת נ 108 kissing each other
הִתְנַתְּקוּת נ 108 disengagement, separating from
הַתְסָסָה נ 168 fermentation
הִתְעַבּוּת נ 126 becoming thicker
הִתְעַבְּרוּת נ 108 conceiving, becoming pregnant

הִתְעַדְכְּנוּת נ 141 updating, informing
הִתְעַדְּנוּת נ 108 refinement, softening, moderation
הִתְעוֹדְדוּת נ 135 being encouraged
הִתְעוֹפְפוּת נ 135 flying, fluttering
הִתְעַוְּרוּת נ 108 becoming blind
הִתְעוֹרְרוּת נ 135 waking up, awakening; revival; liveliness
הִתְעַוְּתוּת נ 108 twisting, distorting
הִתְעַטְּפוּת נ 108 wrapping oneself
הִתְעַטְּשׁוּת נ 108 sneezing
הִתְעַיְּפוּת נ 108 becoming tired
הִתְעַכְּבוּת נ 108 being delayed
הִתְעַלּוּת נ 126 feeling of spiritual elevation
הִתְעַלְּלוּת נ 108 abusing; abuse
הִתְעַלְּמוּת נ 108 ignoring, disregarding
הִתְעַלְּפוּת נ 108 fainting
הִתְעַמְּלוּת נ 108 gymnastics
הִתְעַמְּמוּת נ 108 dimming of light; dulling of shininess [no pl.]
הִתְעַמְעֲמוּת נ 146 dimming, lowering of light; dulling of shininess
הִתְעַמְּקוּת נ 108 delving into, investigating; becoming engrossed in
הִתְעַמְּרוּת נ 108 being cruel, abusing
הִתְעַנְּגוּת נ 108 enjoying oneself
הִתְעַנּוּת נ 126 suffering
הִתְעַנְיְנוּת נ 141 interest
הִתְעַנְּנוּת נ 108 becoming cloudy
הִתְעַסְּקוּת נ 108 becoming involved with
הִתְעַצְּבוּת נ 108 being molded, being formed
הִתְעַצְּבוּת נ 108 being sad, becoming sad
הִתְעַצְבְּנוּת נ 141 becoming annoyed, getting angry, getting irritated
הִתְעַצּוּת נ 126 woodification [no pl.]
הִתְעַצְּלוּת נ 108 being lazy
הִתְעַצְּמוּת נ 108 becoming stronger
הִתְעַקְּלוּת נ 108 twisting, turning - of path, road
הִתְעַקְּמוּת נ 108 becoming bent, becoming crooked
הִתְעַקְּשׁוּת נ 108 insisting, stubbornness
הִתְעַרְבְּבוּת נ 147 becoming mixed up; being mixed into
הִתְעָרְבוּת נ 109 bet
הִתְעָרְבוּת נ 109 interfering, interference, intervention

הִתְעָרוּת נ 128 integrating, acclimatizing
הִתְעַרְטְלוּת נ 141 stripping; undressing completely; exposing oneself emotionally
הִתְעַרְעֲרוּת נ 146 weakening; loosening
הִתְעַרְפְּלוּת נ 141 blurring, becoming foggy, becoming misty
הִתְעַשְּׁרוּת נ 108 becoming rich
הִתְעַשְּׁתוּת נ 108 regaining one's composure
הִתְפָּאֲרוּת נ 110 boasting
הִתְפּוֹגְגוּת נ 135 waning, dissipating
הִתְפּוֹצְצוּת נ 135 explosion; exploding
הִתְפּוֹרְרוּת נ 135 crumbling; disintegrating
הִתְפַּזְּרוּת נ 108 scattering; dissipating
הִתְפַּטְּרוּת נ 108 resignation
הִתְפַּטְּרוּת נ 140 being forced to resign Sl.
הִתְפַּיְּסוּת נ 108 reconciling; reconciliation
הִתְפַּכְּחוּת נ 108 becoming sober
הִתְפַּלְּאוּת נ 108 amazement, astonishment, wonderment
הִתְפַּלְּגוּת נ 108 segmentation, division; distribution (stat.)
הַתְפָּלָה נ 168 desalination of water
הִתְפַּלְמְסוּת נ 141 debate N; debating
הִתְפַּלְסְפוּת נ 141 philosophizing
הִתְפַּלְּשׁוּת נ 108 wallowing
הִתְפַּנּוּת נ 126 vacating; evacuating
הִתְפַּנְּקוּת נ 108 self-indulging; pampering
הִתְפַּעֲלוּת נ 110 wonder, excitement, enthusiasm
הִתְפַּעֲמוּת נ 110 wonder, excitement, enthusiasm
הִתְפַּצְּלוּת נ 108 splitting, branching off
הִתְפַּקְּדוּת נ 108 being counted
הִתְפַּקְּעוּת נ 108 exploding, bursting
הִתְפָּרְדוּת נ 109 splitting, branching out
הִתְפַּרְנְסוּת נ 141 earning a living
הִתְפָּרְסוּת נ 109 spreading; deployment - military
הִתְפַּרְסְמוּת נ 141 becoming known, becoming published
הִתְפָּרְעוּת נ 109 wildness, unruliness; rampaging, running amok
הִתְפָּרְצוּת נ 109 break-in; outburst; outbreak; eruption; interruption

meeting, convening 45 וִעוּד ז Lit
conference, convention, congress 1 וְעִידָה נ
pink 301 וָרֹד ז
rose (plant, flower) 326 וֶרֶד ז
pinkish 458 וְרַדְרַד ז
erysipelas (medicine) [no pl.] 688 וֶרֶדֶת נ
vein 405 וְרִיד ז
venous 933 וְרִידִי ז
esophagus, gullet 317 וֶשֶׁט ז
concession 45 וִתּוּר ז
old-timer 403 וָתִיק ז
seniority Rare [no pl.] 755 וָתִיקוּת נ
seniority [no pl.] 317 וֶתֶק ז
one who gives up, conceder; lenient 846 וַתְּרָן ז
lenience, concession, indulgence [no pl.] 752 וַתְּרָנוּת נ
indulgent, conceding, lenient 969 וַתְּרָנִי ז
wolf 307 זְאֵב ז
wolfish 915 זְאֵבִי ז
infant, tiny child, toddler 451 זַאֲטוּט ז
a man rendered impure because of urethral secretion (Jewish law) 214 זָב ז
gift Bibl. 317 זֶבֶד ז
cream Lit. 598 זְבָדָה נ
woman who has intermenstrual bleeding 582 זָבָה נ
fly (insect) 399 זְבוּב ז
small fly 894 זְבוּבוֹן ז
celestial abode Lit. 399 זְבוּל ז
fertilization, manuring 45 זִבּוּל ז
ballast (is it a suffix here?) 814 זְבוֹרִית נ
worst quality land; inferior goods 814 זִבּוּרִית נ
sacrifice (animal) 319 זֶבַח ז
slaughtering animal for sacrifice 1 זְבִיחָה נ
cylindrical container for transporting rockets, bombs etc. 405 זְבִיל ז
one spreading manure/fertilizer in field; garbage collector 275 זַבָּל ז
manure, fertilizer; garbage, rubbish, junk 317 זֶבֶל ז
bleary-eyed person 850 זַבְלְגָן ז
being bleary-eyed 740 זַבְלְגָנוּת נ
bleary-eyed 915 זַבְלְגָנִי נ
scarab 808 זַבְלִית נ
salesperson, shop assistant (fem. zabanit) 275 זַבָּן ז
grape skin, peel, husk 214 זַג ז
glazier (fem. zagagit) 275 זַגָּג ז
one with dissimilar eyes (Talmudic) 846 זַגְדָן ז
glazing 45 זִגּוּג ז

glazed, vitreous; glassy 915 זְגוּגִי ז
glassiness [no pl.] 775 זְגוּגִיּוּת נ
glass panel, glass sheet 825 זְגוּגִית נ
glazed, vitreous; glassy 915 זְגוּגִיתִי ז
evil person Bibl. 231 זֵד ז
wickedness, malice (pl. zdonot/zdonim) 292 זָדוֹן ר׳ זְדוֹנוֹת/זְדוֹנִים ז
malicious, evil, wicked 944 זְדוֹנִי ז
wickedness, malice, evil [no pl.] 773 זְדוֹנִיּוּת נ
gold 269 זָהָב ז
golden 301 זָהֹב ז
golden, golden-brown 458 זְהַבְהַב ז
gilded Lit. 942 זְהָבִי ז
gagea (plant) 822 זְהָבִית נ
oriole (bird) 846 זַהֲבָן ז
Identical 260 זֶהֶה ז
golden; gold coin archaic 15 זָהוּב ז
identification 50 זִהוּי ז
contamination, pollution; infection 50 זִהוּם ז
infective 957 זִהוּמִי ז
rayon; crimson, crimson cloth Lit. 824 זְהוֹרִית נ
identical 915 זֶהוּתִי ז
similar identity (no decl., no pl.) 762 זֶהוּתִיּוּת נ
careful, cautious 20 זָהִיר ז
radiance, brightness, luminescence [no pl.] 1 זְהִירָה נ
caution, care 24 זְהִירוּת נ
filth, dirt 626 זֻהֲמָה נ
brightness, radiance 343 זֹהַר ז
shiny, radiant 913 זַהֲרוּרִי ז
radiance, glow Lit. 837 זַהֲרוּרִית נ
secretion, discharge [no pl.] 240 זוֹב ז
body of bell outer part 240 זוֹג ז
pair; couple 247 זוּג ז
even (number); dual 990 זוּגִי ז
relationship of a couple [no pl.] 762 זוּגִיּוּת נ
zygophyllum (plant) 878 זוּגָן ז
kit, equipment, package [no pl.] 310 זֶוֶד ז
shining, glowing 7 זוֹהֵר ז
pairing, matching; matching of a couple 45 זִוּוּג ז
fitting out, equipping 45 זִוּוּד ז
Zuz - ancient Jewish coin; ancient metric unit 246 זוּז ז
reptile 7 זוֹחֵל ז
slow, crawling Lit. 986 זוֹחֲלָנִי ז
small, minor thing 595 זוּטָה/א נ
angle (is it a suffix here?) 814 זָוִית נ

try-square (building, carpentry) 894 זָוִיתוֹן ז
angular 915 זָוִיתִי ז
cheap, inexpensive 240 זוֹל ז
cheapness; vulgarity [no pl.] 761 זוֹלוּת נ
glutton 6 זוֹלֵל ז
gluttony Lit [no pl.] 14 זוֹלְלוּת נ
glutton 855 זוֹלְלָן ז
gluttonous 985 זוֹלְלָנִי ז
apart from, other than, beside 915 זוּלָתִי ז
altruistic 915 זוּלָתָנִי ז
gravy (Talmudic) 240 זוֹם ז
malicious, crafty 985 זוֹמְמָנִי ז
prostitute 593 זוֹנָה נ
horror 638 זְוָעָה נ
angry, furious 7 זוֹעֵם ז
angry, irate 7 זוֹעֵף ז
terrible 915 זְוָעָתִי ז
arrogant, haughty 17 זָחוּחַ ז
arrogance, self-satisfaction; euphoria 24 זְחִיחוּת נ
crawling 1 זְחִילָה נ
caterpillar 328 זַחַל ז
half-track 409 זַחְלָ״ם = זַחֲלִי לְמֶחֱצָה ז
equipped with caterpillar tracks 966 זַחֲלִי ז
stair climbing aid attached to a wheelchair; caterpillar track 454 זַחְלִיל ז
tracked carrier (military) 809 זַחֲלִית נ
slowpoke Coll. 846 זַחְלָן ז
sluggishness, slowness [no pl.] 752 זַחְלָנוּת נ
sluggard 969 זַחְלָנִי ז
arrogant person 846 זַחְתָּן ז
arrogance, hautiness Lit.-Rare [no pl.] 752 זַחְתָּנוּת נ
arrogant 969 זַחְתָּנִי ז
gonorrhea; discharge 3 זִיבָה נ
blazer Lit.-rare 251 זִיג ז
zigzag Adj 915 זִיגְזָגִי ז
brightness, brilliance, radiance 251 זִיו ז
arming, supplying weapons; reinforcement of concrete; sexual intercourse Sl.; adornments of letters in Jewish religious texts 45 זִיּוּן ז
bright, radiant, shining 915 זִיוָנִי ז
forgery; being off-key (music) 45 זִיּוּף ז
radiant, shiny Lit. 915 זִיוְתָנִי ז
projection, protuberance 251 זִיז ז
contempt, disrespect [no pl.] 747 זִילוּת נ
gill 251 זִים ז
arms, weapons; penis (vulgar) [no pl.] 357 זַיִן ז
feed (electr.) 3 זִינָה נ

זִקְנוּת נ 738 old age [no pl.]
זְקַנְקַן ז 458 small beard
זָקֵף ז 279 perpendicular
זָקֵף ז 279 zakef (bilblical cantillation symbol)
זָר ז 214 stranger, outsider; foreigner; strange, foreign
זֵר ז 231 wreath, bouquet, garland
זָרָא ז 267 something sickening (no declension) [no pl.]
זַרְבּוּבִית נ 836 spout; snout (of animal)
זֶרֶד ז 317 twig, tendril
זֵרוּז ז 51 urging, goading; injection given for induction of labor
זָרוּי ז 15 sprinkled
זֵרוּי ז 51 sprinkling; powdering Lit [no pl.]
זָרוּעַ ז 17 sown, seeded; scattered
זְרוֹעַ נ 398 arm
זָרוּק ז 15 thrown, discarded; slovenly Col.
זָרוּת נ 733 alienage, strangeness
זַרְזִיף ז 452 drizzle
זַרְזִיר ז 453 starling (bird)
זַרְחָה נ 610 phosphate
זַרְחוֹרִי ז 915 phosphorescent
זַרְחָן ז 846 phosphorus
זַרְחָנִי ז 969 phosphorescent, phosphoric
זַרְחָתִי ז 915 phosphate Adj
זְרִיָּה נ 4 sprinkling, spreading all over Lit
זָרִיז ז 20 quick, agile, nimble
זְרִיזוּת נ 24 nimbleness, promptness
זְרִיחָה נ 1 sunrise
זָרִים ז 20 flowing
זְרִימָה נ 1 flow N
זְרִימוּת נ 24 flowingness [no pl.]
זְרִיעָה נ 1 sowing
זְרִיקָה נ 1 throwing, casting away; injection ("throwing") of vaccine etc. into body
זֶרֶם ז 317 flow; electric current flow; ideological or religious movement
זִרְמָה נ 598 semen; flow Lit.
זִרְמִי ז 949 flowing
זַרְנוּק ז 447 hose, nozzle
זַרְנִיךְ ז 452 arsenic (archaic) [no pl.]
זֶרַע ז 329 seed; semen; sperm
זַרְעִית נ 808 skylark
זַרְקוֹר ז 444 spotlight, floodlight
זֶרֶת נ 321 little finger, "pinkie"
חֹב ז 227 interior, inside Lit. [no pl.]
חִבָּה נ 586 affection
חֲבָה נ 592 bustard (bird)
חִבּוּב ז 45 fondness
חָבוּט ז 16 beaten; worn out
חִבּוּט ז 45 beating, flagellation
חָבוּי ז 16 hidden, unseen
חָבוּל ז 16 beaten, injured, battered
חִבּוּל ז 45 sabotaging Rare
חִבּוּץ ז 45 churning milk
חָבוּק ז 16 embraced, hugged
חִבּוּק ז 45 embrace, hug
חָבוּר ז 16 joined, attached, connected Lit
חֲבוּר ז 400 stub, butt (check, ticket)
חֲבוּרָה נ 19 band, small group of people
חַבּוּרָה נ 668 bruise, contusion
חָבוּשׁ ז 16 bandaged, dressed; head-covered
חַבּוּשׁ ז 378 quince
חֲבוּת נ 733 liability, indebtedness (formal) [no pl.]
חַבָּטָה נ 633 blow, thump
חָבִיב ז 21 pleasant, friendly, likeable; favorite
חֲבִיבוּת נ 25 friendliness, pleasantness
חֶבְיוֹן ז 888 hiding place, secret place
חֲבִיטָה נ 2 beating, striking
חֲבִילָה נ 2 parcel, package
חֲבִיֹּנֶת נ 897 small barrel
חֲבִיצָה נ 2 pudding; custard Lit
חֲבִיקָה נ 2 hug, embrace N
חֲבִירָה נ 2 joining, link-up military
חֲבִישָׁה נ 2 bandaging; head-covering
חָבִית נ 814 barrel
חֲבִיתָּה נ 2 omelet
חִבֵּל ז 283 rigging (shipping)
חֵבֶל ז 323 pang, pain, trial
חֶבֶל ז 323 pang, trial, pain
חֶבֶל ז 327 rope
חֲבַלְבַּל ז 459 bindweed, convulvulus (plant)
חַבָּלָה נ 620 sabotage
חֲבָלָה נ 633 trauma
חַבְּלָן ז 847 sapper; saboteur
חַבְּלָנוּת נ 752 destructiveness; sabotage [no pl.]
חַבְּלָנִי ז 969 destructive, damaging; terroristic
חֲבָלָתִי ז 915 traumatic, injurious
חֶבְצָה נ 624 buttermilk
חֶבֶק ז 327 label wrapped around item
חָבֵר ז 280 friend
חֶבֶר ז 327 group; league [no pl.]
חֲבַרְבַּר ז 459 striped (animal)
חֶבְרָה נ 606 company; society
חִבְרוּת ז 54 socialization
חַבְרוּת נ 738 socialization [no pl.]
חַבְרוּתִי ז 915 friendly, sociable
חַבְרוּתִיּוּת נ 792 friendliness, sociability [no pl.]
חֲבֵרִי ז 915 friendly, affable
חֶבְרָתִי ז 915 social
חַבַּשִׁי ז 979 Ethiopian (archaic)
חַבְתָּן ז 846 cooper
חַבְתָּנוּת נ 752 the cooper's profession
חָגָב ז 268 grasshopper
חָגוּר ז 16 belt-wearing
חֲגוֹר ז 395 webbing, load-bearing equipment (military)
חֲגוֹרָה נ 672 belt
חֲגִיגָה נ 2 celebration; pleasure Coll.
חֲגִיגִי ז 934 festive; serious, formal
חֲגִיגִיּוּת נ 770 ceremoniousness [no pl.]
חֲגִירָה נ 2 strapping on safety belt, girding
חָגְלָה נ 628 partridge
חִגֵּר ז 283 lame; lame person
חִגְּרוּת נ 739 lameness [no pl.]
חַד ז 221 sharp
חֹד ז 227 sharp tip; spearhead
חַדְגּוֹנִי ז 915 monotonous
חַדְגּוֹנִיּוּת נ 762 monotony [no pl.]
חִדּוּד ז 45 sharpening; joke
חֶדְוָה נ 607 joy
חָדוּר ז 16 imbued, saturated
חִדּוּשׁ ז 45 innovation; new idea; renewal, renovation
חִדּוּשִׁי ז 956 innovative, inventive, modern
חַדּוּת נ 731 sharpness [no pl.]
חֲדִילָה נ 2 cessation, stopping
חָדִיר ז 21 penetrable
חֲדִירָה נ 2 penetration
חֲדִירוּת נ 25 penetrability
חָדִישׁ ז 21 modern, up-to-date, novel, new
חִדָּלוֹן ז 899 destruction, cessation Lit. [no pl.]
חַדְפַּעֲמִיּוּת נ 762 one-time occurrence [no pl.]
חַדְצְדָדִי ז 915 unilateral
חַדְצְדָדִיּוּת נ 762 singlesidedness [no pl.]
חַדְקוֹלִי ז 915 single-voiced; monophonic
חִדְקוֹנִית נ 827 weevil
חִדְקָן ז 857 sturgeon
חֶדֶר ז 327 room
חַדְרוֹן ז 892 small room
חַדְרָן ז 846 chamber-man (male of chambermaid)
חַדְרָנוּת נ 752 housekeeping (hotel) [no pl.]
חָדָשׁ ז 268 new; unused
חֹדֶשׁ ז 342 month
חֲדָשָׁה נ 639 piece of news
חַדְשׁוּתִי ז 915 newsworthy
חָדְשִׁי ז 980 monthly
חַדְשָׁן ז 846 innovator

interferer, prying 846 ז חַטְטָן
person
prying, 752 נ חַטְטָנוּת
interference [no pl.]
prying, interfering 964 ז חַטְטָנִי
acne [no pl.] 685 נ חַטֶּטֶת
division of ; 2 נ חֲטִיבָה
organization; brigade; felling of
trees
regimental, of 915 ז חֲטִיבָתִי
brigade
snack 406 ז חֲטִיף
snatching; 2 נ חֲטִיפָה
kidnapping
nose Lit. 342 ז חֹטֶם
nasal 980 ז חָטְמִי
althea, hollyhock, 813 נ חָטְמִית
rose of Sharon
Hataf (shortened 311 ז חֲטַף
vowel in Classical Hebrew)
shoot, twig, branch; 342 ז חֹטֶר
scion, descendant, esp. of a
notable family
alive 221 ז חַי
obliged, required; 275 ז חַיָּב
owe; must
dialer 846 ז חַיְגָן
riddle; mystery 3 נ חִידָה
quiz 894 ז חִידוֹן
bacterium 414 ז חַיְדַּק
bacterial 915 ז חַיְדַּקִּי
mysterious, 915 ז חִידָתִי
cryptic, mystifying
animal 585 נ חַיָּה
obligation; debit; 45 ז חִיּוּב
positivity; conviction
positive 956 ז חִיּוּבִי
positiveness [no 781 נ חִיּוּבִיּוּת
pl.]
dialing phone number 45 ז חִיּוּג
smile 45 ז חִיּוּךְ
enlistment to the 45 ז חִיּוּל
military, drafting [no pl.]
essential; vital 956 ז חִיּוּנִי
vitality [no pl.] 781 נ חִיּוּנִיּוּת
partitioning; 45 ז חִיּוּץ
extrapolation math
liveliness, vitality 731 נ חִיּוּת
[no pl.]
tailor (fem. Hayetet) 275 ז חַיָּט
tailoring of clothes 363 ז חַיִט
Lit.
life 998 ז חַיִּים
smiler 846 ז חַיְכָן
smilingness [no pl.] 752 נ חַיְכָנוּת
smiling 969 ז חַיְכָנִי
terror, fear 251 ז חִיל
soldier (fem. Hayelet) 275 ז חַיָּל
strength; bravery; 363 ז חַיִל
force; wealth
being a soldier [no 757 נ חַיָּלוּת
pl.]
pertaining to corps 960 ז חֵילִי
(military)
soldier-like, soldierly 979 ז חַיָּלִי

aizoon (plant) 414 ז חַיְעַד
partition, barrier; rift, 357 ז חַיִץ
gap, division
external 915 ז חִיצוֹנִי
external 762 נ חִיצוֹנִיּוּת
appearance [no pl.]
bosom; lap 254 ז חֵיק
sense, sensation; 3 נ חִישָּׁה
sense-measuring
hesitant person 846 ז חַיְשָׁן
hesitation, 752 נ חַיְשָׁנוּת
uncertainty, vacillation Lit. [no
pl.]
vacillating, 969 ז חַיְשָׁנִי
hesitating, uncertain Lit.
sensory 915 ז חִישָׁתִי
animalistic, animal- 915 ז חַיָּתִי
like
beastiality [no pl.] 762 נ חַיָּתִיּוּת
palate 235 ז חֵךְ
fishing rod 585 נ חַכָּה
friction; disagreement 45 ז חִכּוּךְ
leased 16 ז חָכוּר
palatal 915 ז חִכִּי
waiting, expectation 898 ז חִכָּיוֹן
[no pl.]
leasing 2 נ חֲכִירָה
red Lit. (in BH only 454 ז חַכְלִיל
adj., Hakhlili)
redness, 740 נ חַכְלִילוּת
reddishness Lit. [no pl.]
redness, 787 נ חַכְלִילִיּוּת
reddishness Lit. [no pl.]
redstart (bird) 832 נ חַכְלִילִית
wise, intelligent, 268 ז חָכָם
smart
wisdom 628 נ חָכְמָה
midwife (Talmudic) 639 נ חֲכָמָה
tasty, palatable 915 ז חִכָּנִי
weekday 227 ז חֹל
scum 606 נ חֶלְאָה
milk (no plural, 268 ז חָלָב
constr. Halev)
animal fat; candle 323 ז חֵלֶב
wax; the best part Lit.
white of egg; 887 ז חֶלְבּוֹן
protein
of protein, 962 ז חֶלְבּוֹנִי
proteinaceous
of dairy (Jewish 943 ז חֲלָבִי
law); milky, lacteal Lit.
milkiness; 772 נ חֲלָבִיּוּת
whiteness [no pl.]
wolf's milk, 456 ז חַלַבְלוּב
spurge (plant)
milkman 848 ז חַלְבָן/חַלְבָּן
(Halvan is a less frequent option)
dairying 752 נ חַלְבָנוּת/חַלְבָּנוּת
universe, world Lit. 337 ז חֶלֶד
[no pl.]
mole 353 ז חֹלֶד
rat 624 נ חֻלְדָּה
rust 659 נ חֲלֻדָּה
wheat rust 899 ז חִלָּדוֹן
challah 585 נ חַלָּה

rusty, rusted 16 ז חָלוּד
halva [no pl.] 614 נ חַלְוָה
soaked in hot water 16 ז חָלוּט
forfeiture, 45 ז חִלּוּט
confiscation, seizure
imploring Lit-rare [no 45 ז חִלּוּי
pl.]
hollow 16 ז חָלוּל
desecration, 45 ז חִלּוּל
defilement
dream 397 ז חֲלוֹם
dream-like 945 ז חֲלוֹמִי
window 381 ז חַלּוֹן
converting from holy 45 ז חִלּוּן
to secular, profanation [no pl.]
secular 915 ז חִלּוֹנִי
secularity [no pl.] 780 נ חִלּוֹנִיּוּת
computing pane; 814 נ חַלּוֹנִית
photography frame
passage of time [no 395 ז חֲלוֹף
declension, no pl.]
option; alternative 19 נ חֲלוּפָה
alternative 915 ז חֲלוּפִי
exchangeable; 956 ז חִלּוּפִי
commutative (mathematics)
ameba 830 נ חִלּוּפִית
pioneer, pioneering 16 ז חָלוּץ
pioneering 947 ז חֲלוּצִי
pioneering; 762 נ חֲלוּצִיּוּת
initiative, originality [no pl.]
gown, robe; 16 ז חָלוּק
antagonistic, contrary
smooth stone, 378 ז חַלּוּק
pebble
division math; 45 ז חִלּוּק
partition, division; difference
Lit
weak, feeble 16 ז חָלוּשׁ
validity; being 733 נ חָלוּת
applied (law, etc.) [no pl.]
snail 899 ז חִלָּזוֹן
spiral (arch.) 963 ז חֶלְזוֹנִי
percolator 449 ז חַלְחוּל
trickling, percolation 66 ז חִלְחוּל
horror, fear, 682 נ חַלְחָלָה
aversion
rectum 721 נ חַלְחֹלֶת
adornment, ornament 258 ז חֲלִי
Bibl.
disease, illness 350 ז חֳלִי/חֹלִי
Lit.
milking 2 נ חֲלִיבָה
link; part; vertebra 624 נ חֻלְיָה
brewing tea 2 נ חֲלִיטָה
flute; recorder 21 ז חָלִיל
cornetfish 896 ז חֲלִילוֹן
recorder (musical 814 נ חֲלִילִית
instrument)
recorder or flute 863 ז חַלִּילָן
player
dreaming 2 נ חֲלִימָה
alternative; substitute 21 ז חָלִיף
in law
alternative, 406 ז חֲלִיף
substitute

חַנְפָנִי ז 969 flattering, fawning
חַנָּק ז 275 javelin sand boa
חֶנֶק ז 327 strangulation, choking; asphyxia [no pl.]
חַנְקָה נ 611 nitrate
חַנְקָן ז 846 nitrogen
חַנְקָנִי ז 969 nitrogenous
חַנְקָתִי ז 915 nitrous
חֶסֶד ז 327 kindness, benevolence; goodness, charity, grace
חַסָּה/א נ 585 lettuce
חָסוּד ז 16 hypocritical; graceful Lit
חָסוּי ז 16 secret; protected
חִסּוּי ז 45 impunity; confidentiality
חִסּוּל ז 45 extermination, elimination, liquidation
חָסוּם ז 16 blocked
חִסּוּם ז 45 hardening, tempering metal, glass
חָסוֹן ז 299 strong, powerful
חִסּוּן ז 45 immunization; strengthening
חִסּוּנִי ז 956 immunological
חִסּוּר ז 45 subtraction math; absence
חָסוּת (ר׳?) נ 733 protection; sponsorship
חַסְחוּס/סְחוּס ז 449 cartilage
חָסִיד ז 21 Hassid, follower of a Hassidic sect; follower of, devotee; devout person; righteous, pious, kind
חֲסִידָה נ 2 stork
חֲסִידוּת נ 25 Hassidism; righteousness, piety
חֲסִידִי ז 934 Hassidic
חֲסִיָּה נ 5 sheltering, taking refuge [no pl.]
חִסָּיוֹן ז 899 privilege, immunity (law)
חֲסִימָה נ 2 blocking; blockade
חָסִין ז 21 immune, resistant, -proof
חֲסִינוּת נ 25 immunity; resistance
חִסָּכוֹן ז 899 saving(s)
חֶסְכוֹנִי ז 963 frugal, economical
חַסְכָן ז 846 frugal person
חַסְכָנוּת נ 752 frugality [no pl.]
חַסְכָנִי ז 969 frugal, economical
חַסָּם ז 275 tourniquet
חֶסֶם ז 327 block, obstruction; jam (in weapon)
חֹסֶן ז 342 strength, power, might Lit. [no pl.]
חִסְפּוּס ז 54 roughness, unevenness
חַסְפֶּסֶת נ 715 German madwort (plant); pellagra (pathol.)
חָסֵר ז 280 deficient, lacking
חֶסֶר ז 327 absence, lack; deficit, shortage [no pl.]
חֹסֶר ז 342 absence, lack [no pl.]
חִסָּרוֹן ז 899 disadvantage
חָף ז 214 sprocket, tooth, stud (of a machine)
חַף ז 221 innocent, free of
חָפֶה ז 262 bract (botany)
חֻפָּה נ 592 canopy; canopy used at Jewish wedding
חָפוּז ז 16 hasty, hurried; brief sexual encounter Sl.
חָפוּי ז 16 covered Lit
חִפּוּי ז 45 covering fire; cover-up; covering
חָפוּף ז 16 washed, shampooed hair
חִפּוּף ז 45 carelessness, shoddiness Sl.
חָפוּר ז 16 dug
חִפּוּשׂ ז 45 searching; search N
חִפּוּשִׁית נ 814 beetle (is it a suffix here?)
חָפוּת ז 16 rolled up sleeve, etc. – Lit
חַפּוּת נ 731 innocence, guiltlessness [no pl.]
חִפָּזָה נ 628 haste [no pl.]
חִפָּזוֹן ז 899 rush N [no pl.]
חֲפִי ז 258 flap of envelope; flap
חֲפִיָּה נ 5 overlapping Lit-rare [no pl.]
חֲפִינָה נ 2 taking a handful
חֲפִיסָה נ 2 packet
חֲפִיפָה נ 2 overlapping; shampooing hair
חֲפִיר ז 406 moat; ditch
חֲפִירָה נ 2 digging, excavating; a dig, excavation; trench
חָפִית נ 842 bract, bracteole (botany)
חֹפֶן ר׳ זוגי חָפְנַיִם ז 342 handful, pl. dual Hofnayim
חֵפֶץ ז 323 object, article; desire, want, wish Lit.
חַפָּר ז 275 sapper, digger
חַפָּרִית נ 840 European spadefoot toad
חֲפַרְפֶּרֶת נ 729 mole
חֹפֶשׁ ז 342 freedom, liberty [no poss. clitics?]
חֻפְשָׁה נ 624 vacation, holiday
חָפְשִׁי ז 980 free
חָפְשִׁיּוּת נ 794 freedom; ease [no pl.]
חֵפֶת ז 323 cuff link; cuff
חֵץ ז 235 arrow
חֲצָאִית נ 841 skirt
חָצָב ז 268 squill (plant)
חַצֶּבֶת נ 685 measles, rubeola [no pl.]
חָצוּב ז 16 quarried; carved, etched
חִצּוּב ז 45 quarrying, excavating
חֲצוּבָה נ 19 tripod
חָצוּי ז 16 halved, split, divided
חָצוּף ז 16 cheeky, rude, arrogant
חֲצוֹצְרָן ז 863 trumpeter
חִצִּי ז 915 arrow-like
חֲצִי/חֵצִי, ר׳ חֲצָאִים/חֲצָיִים ז 258 half (pl. Hastsa'im/Hatsayim)
חֲצִיבָה נ 2 quarrying, excavating; carving
חֲצִיָּה נ 5 division, splitting; crossing
חֲצָיָה נ 633 crossing
חֶצְיוֹן ז 887 median (statistics)
חָצִיל ז 21 eggplant
חֲצִיפוּת נ 25 cheek, audacity, arrogance [no pl.]
חֲצִיצָה נ 2 division, separating; demarcation
חָצִיר ז 21 hay
חֹצֶן ז 342 lap of garment (biblical)
חֻצְפָּה נ 624 cheek, insolence, impertinence
חֻצְפָּן ז 863 insolent, impertinent, cheeky (person)
חֻצְפָּנִי ז 915 cheeky
חָצָץ ז 268 gravel
חֲצָץ ז 311 a closed-off, fenced area Lit.
חִצְצוּר ז 54 trumpeting
חַצֶּצֶת נ 685 lithiasis [no pl.]
חָצֵר, ר׳ חֲצֵרוֹת/חֲצֵרִים נ 282 yard; court (pl. Hatserot/Hatserim)
חֶצְרוֹנִי ז 962 courtly Lit.
חַצְרָן ז 846 janitor, caretaker
חַצְרָנוּת נ 752 janitoring [no pl.]
חֹק ז 228 law, statute
חֻקָּה נ 592 constitution
חִקּוּי ז 45 imitation
חָקוּק ז 16 engraved, carved; statutory
חִקּוּק ז 45 statute; etching
חָקוּר ז 16 investigated, studied
חִקּוּר ז 45 investigation, inquiry
חֻקִּי ז 915 legal
חֻקִּיּוּת נ 762 legality; constancy, regularity [no pl.]
חַקְיָן ז 846 imitator, mimic
חַקְיָנוּת נ 752 mimicry [no pl.]
חַקְיָנִי ז 969 imitative, mimetic
חֲקִיקָה נ 2 legislating, legislation; engraving
חֲקִיקָתִי ז 915 legislative
חֲקִירָה נ 2 investigation, inquiry; research
חַקְלַאי ז 909 farmer, agronomist
חַקְלָאִי ז 915 agricultural
חֹקֶן ז 342 enema
חַקָּק ז 275 engraver
חֵקֶר ז 339 study, research [no pl.]
חַקְרָן ז 846 inquisitive, inquiring
חַקְרָנוּת נ 752 inquisitiveness [no pl.]
חַקְרָנִי ז 969 inquiring, searching, probing
חֻקָּתִי ז 915 constitutional

exposure; clearing, stripping 45 חִשּׂוּף ז
tight-lipped; desired 16 חָשׂוּק ז
hoop 45 חִשּׁוּק ז
spoke; radius anatomy 45 חִשּׁוּר ז
a type of citrus, used for grafting and its fruit for jam 435 חֻשְׁחָשׁ ז
thinking, thought process [no pl.] 2 חֲשִׁיבָה נ
importance, significance 25 חֲשִׁיבוּת נ
of the thinking process 938 חֲשִׁיבָתִי ז
malleable metal 21 חָשִׁיל ז
small flock (biblical) 406 חָשִׂיף ז
exposure 2 חֲשִׂיפָה נ
exposure 25 חֲשִׂיפוּת נ
pursing of lips 2 חֲשִׂיקָה נ
hashish [no pl.] 406 חָשִׁישׁ ז
darkness; evil, forces of darkness [no pl.] 342 חֹשֶׁךְ ז
darkness [no pl.] 654 חֲשֵׁכָה נ
partial darkness, dimness Lit. [no pl.] 836 חֲשַׁכּוּכִית נ
blackout 899 חִשְׁכוֹן ז
darkness; illiteracy, cultural void [no pl.] 736 חֶשְׁכוּת נ
electrification 54 חִשְׁמוּל ז
electricity; electric current; amber (biblical) [no pl.] 414 חַשְׁמַל ז
electrician 909 חַשְׁמַלַּאי ז
photoelectric 915 חַשְׁמַלּוֹרִי ז
electric 915 חַשְׁמַלִּי ז
tramcar, trolley car 814 חַשְׁמַלִּית נ
torpedo (fish) 863 חַשְׁמַלָּן ז
cardinal 412 חַשְׁמָן ז
breastplate (of High Priest) [no pl.] 342 חֹשֶׁן ז
striptease artist; stripper 846 חַשְׂפָן ז
striptease [no pl.] 752 חַשְׂפָנוּת נ
desire [no pl.] 339 חֵשֶׁק ז
lustful person 846 חַשְׁקָן ז
lust, desire 752 חַשְׁקָנוּת נ
lustful, lascivious 969 חַשְׁקָנִי ז
gathering of thick clouds [no pl.] 614 חַשְׁרָה נ
fear, concern, worry 311 חֲשָׁשׁ ז
fodder, straw (no pl.) [no pl.] 314 חֲשַׁשׁ ז
hesitant, apprehensive person 846 חַשְׁשָׁן ז
apprehension, hesitation, fear [no pl.] 752 חַשְׁשָׁנוּת נ
hesitant 964 חַשְׁשָׁנִי ז
terror, fear Lit. 586 חִתָּה נ
sliced, chopped; cut 16 חָתוּךְ ז
cutting; intersection - geometry; articulation - phonetics 45 חִתּוּךְ ז
cat 16 חָתוּל ז
diaper 45 חִתּוּל ז
feline, cat-like 947 חֲתוּלִי ז
signed, sealed 16 חָתוּם ז
underwriting 45 חִתּוּם ז
marrying off 45 חִתּוּן ז
bumps (in road), irregularities; obstacles 998 חַתְחַתִּים ז
Hittite 915 חִתִּי ז
hunk Coll. 21 חָתִיךְ ז
piece; item; attractive woman Coll. 2 חֲתִיכָה נ
good-looking; sexy 934 חֲתִיכִי ז
signing, signature; ending; conclusion 2 חֲתִימָה נ
undermining; rowing 2 חֲתִירָה נ
cut, incision, slash; section, cross-section 311 חֲתָךְ ז
cut N 327 חֶתֶךְ/חֲתָךְ ז
kitten 456 חֲתַלְתּוּל ז
underwriter (insurance) 275 חַתָּם ז
bridegroom, groom; son-in-law; guest of honor 268 חָתָן ז
wedding 659 חֲתֻנָּה נ
disaster Lit.; robbery; snatching 327 חֶתֶף ז
subversive person 846 חַתְרָן ז
subversion, undermining, sabotage [no pl.] 752 חַתְרָנוּת נ
subversive 969 חַתְרָנִי ז
sweeping Lit 51 טֵאוּט ז
sweeping 66 טְאַטוּא ז
slaughtered 17 טָבוּחַ ז
dipped, soaked 15 טָבוּל ז
dipping, immersion 45 טִבּוּל ז
drowned 17 טָבוּעַ ז
sinking; submersion 53 טִבּוּעַ ז
navel, belly button, umbilicus; center, hub 378 טַבּוּר ז
umbilical 915 טַבּוּרִי ז
navelwort (plant) 814 טַבּוּרִית נ
cook, chef 275 טַבָּח ז
slaughter, massacre [no pl.] 319 טֶבַח ז
slaughtering 1 טְבִיחָה נ
dipping; ritual immersion 1 טְבִילָה נ
drowning; stamping 1 טְבִיעָה נ
table, tabulation 619 טַבְלָה/א נ
tablet; pill 808 טַבְלִית נ
grebe, loon (bird) 846 טַבְלָן ז
nature; character, temperament [no pl.] 319 טֶבַע ז
being vegan [no pl.] 747 טִבְעוֹנוּת נ
vegan 915 טִבְעוֹנִי ז
vegan 952 טִבְעוֹנִי ז
natural 949 טִבְעִי ז
naturalness [no pl.] 776 טִבְעִיּוּת נ
ring 690 טַבַּעַת נ
ring-shaped 915 טַבַּעְתִּי/טַבַּעַתִּי ז
resident of Tiberias 915 טְבֶרְיָנִי ז
Tiberian (esp. a Masorah scholars) 969 טַבְרָנִי ז
frying 45 טִגּוּן ז
French fried potato chip 304 טֶגֶן ז
purification; purging 50 טִהוּר ז
purity; righteousness [no pl.] 343 טֹהַר ז
purity, purification 631 טָהֳרָה נ
purist 849 טַהֲרָן ז
purism (language) [no pl.] 753 טַהֲרָנוּת נ
purist 970 טַהֲרָנִי ז
weaver Lit.-Rare 908 טַוַּאי ז
good, kind; pleasant; appropriate 240 טוֹב ז
goodness [no pl.] 246 טוּב ז
good N; favor N 593 טוֹבָה נ
swampiness, bogginess [no pl.] 759 טוֹבְעָנוּת נ
swampy, marshy, boggy 985 טוֹבְעָנִי ז
ranging - military 45 טִוּוּחַ ז
woven 15 טָווּי ז
range; extent, bounds 310 טְוָח ז
miller 7 טוֹחֵן ז
molar tooth 12 טוֹחֶנֶת נ
spinning thread 4 טְוִיָּה נ
peacock (fem. taveset) 275 טַוָּס ז
mistaken 10 טוֹעֶה ז
pleader; claimant, contender e.g., to throne 7 טוֹעֵן ז
lashing Lit. 985 טוֹפְחָנִי ז
row, line; queue; column (in newspaper); series (math) 246 טוּר ז
private (military) 909 טוּרַאי ז
pestering, nagging 855 טוֹרְדָן ז
pestering, annoying, nagging 985 טוֹרְדָנִי ז
in line, arranged in a row 990 טוּרִי ז
Middle Eastern spade with broad blade and short handle 911 טוּרִיָּה נ
carnivore; carnivorous 6 טוֹרֵף ז
predatory, vicious 985 טוֹרְפָנִי ז
Turkish 915 טוּרְקִי ז
moss 310 טְחָב ז
mustiness, moisture, dampness [no pl.] 328 טַחַב ז
damp, musty 15 טָחוּב ז
spleen 393 טְחוֹל ז
ground, minced 15 טָחוּן ז
grinding, mincing 1 טְחִינָה נ
mill 612 טַחֲנָה נ
quality, standard [no pl.] 251 טִיב ז
improvement; improvement of soil, reclamation 45 טִיּוּב ז
plastering wall; cover up Coll. 45 טִיּוּחַ ז
hike, trip, journey 45 טִיּוּל ז
plaster N [no pl.] 252 טִיחַ ז
plasterer (fem. TayaHat) 275 טַיָּח ז
mortar; mud [no pl.] 251 טִיט ז

food ritually unfit for eating (Jewish law) 649 טְרֵפָה נ
rock Lit., mostly in plural, 'admat trashim 'rocky ground' 326 טֶרֶשׁ ז
rocky, stony 965 טַרְשִׁי ז
rockiness [no pl.] 785 טַרְשִׁיּוּת נ
sclerosis [no pl.] 688 טָרֶשֶׁת נ
confusion; effacement 66 טִשְׁטוּשׁ ז
vague, blurred, wishy-washy 975 טַשְׁטְשָׁנִי ז
befitting, becoming; suitable, right, proper 265 יָאֶה ז
despair [no pl.] 51 יֵאוּשׁ ז
yuppie 915 יָאפִּי ז
wail N 634 יְבָבָה נ
whimperer, lamenter, wailer 846 יַבְבָן ז
[no pl.] tendency to whimper 752 יַבְבָנוּת נ
wailing, sobbing 964 יַבְבָנִי ז
import, importation; imports [no pl.] 399 יְבוּא ז
import N 45 יִבּוּא ז
importer 874 יְבוּאָן ז
wailing, whimpering 45 יִבּוּב ז
produce, crop; yield 399 יְבוּל ז
levirate marriage 45 יִבּוּם ז
Jebusite 915 יְבוּסִי ז
drying 45 יִבּוּשׁ ז
gnat, midge; a type of mosquito 447 יַבְחוּשׁ ז
transportable, movable 20 יָבִיל ז
couch grass, couch grass plant 808 יַבְּלִית נ
wart 685 יַבֶּלֶת נ
brother-in-law Lit. 267 יָבָם ז
childless widow awaiting Levirate marriage 634 יְבָמָה נ
dry 279 יָבֵשׁ ז
dryness; monotony, sameness [no pl.] 341 יֹבֶשׁ ז
dry land 623 יַבָּשָׁה נ
dryish Lit. 912 יַבְשׁוּשִׁי ז
dryness, indifference [no pl.] 708 יַבֶּשֶׁת נ
continent 685 יַבֶּשֶׁת נ
of land; continental 978 יַבַּשְׁתִּי ז
grief, sorrow Lit. (pl. yegonim/yegonot) 292 יָגוֹן, ר' יְגוֹנִים/יְגוֹנוֹת ז
hard work, travail, exertion Lit. 407 יְגִיעַ ז
exertion, effort, pains 1 יְגִיעָה נ
labor, effort [no pl.] 319 יֶגַע ז
arm; hand 217 יָד נ
throwing, esp. stones 45 יִדּוּי ז
muff, handwarmer 814 יְדוֹנִית נ
known; famous; certain 17 יָדוּעַ ז
informing, making aware; making indefinite into definite (grammar); definiteness [no pl.] 53 יִדּוּעַ ז
celebrity 874 יְדוּעָן ז
friend 20 יָדִיד ז
friendship 24 יְדִידוּת נ
friendly 915 יְדִידוּתִי ז
knowing, awareness; news item 1 יְדִיעָה נ
bulletin, newsletter 895 יְדִיעוֹן ז
handle 814 יָדִית נ
manual 915 יָדְנִי ז
knowledge [no pl.] 319 יֶדַע ז
soothsayer, magician, necromancer 952 יִדְּעוֹנִי ז
erudite, knowledgeable person 846 יַדְעָן ז
erudition, know-how, expertise, knowledge, knowledgeableness [no pl.] 752 יַדְעָנוּת נ
erudite, knowledgeable 969 יַדְעָנִי ז
hope Lit.-rare; burden Lit.-rare 310 יְהָב ז
Judaism [no pl.] 737 יַהֲדוּת נ
of Judaism 974 יַהֲדוּתִי ז
Judaization [no pl.] 50 יִהוּד ז
Jewish 946 יְהוּדִי ז
Jewishness [no pl.] 762 יְהוּדִיּוּת נ
Hebrew language (biblical) [no pl.] 814 יְהוּדִית נ
arrogant 20 יָהִיר ז
arrogance 24 יְהִירוּת נ
diamond 445 יַהֲלוֹם ז
diamond dealer 863 יַהֲלוֹמָן ז
arrogance 626 יֶהֱרָה/יָהֳרָה נ
river, tributary, creek 372 יוּבַל ז
ram's horn Lit; jubilee 6 יוֹבֵל ז
of jubilee 984 יוֹבְלִי ז
farmer Lit-rare 6 יוֹגֵב ז
initiator, promoter 6 יוֹזֵם ז
of initiative; initiatory 985 יוֹזְמָנִי/יָזְמָנִי ז
woman giving birth 662 יוֹלֵדָה נ
woman giving birth 11 יוֹלֶדֶת נ
day [pl. yamim] 240 יוֹם, ר' יָמִים ז
daily newspaper 894 יוֹמוֹן ז
daily 988 יוֹמִי ז
(occurring) every day 915 יוֹמְיוֹמִי ז
everyday life occurrence [no pl.] 762 יוֹמְיוֹמִיּוּת נ
commuter Lit 6 יוֹמֵם ז
diary; calendar 877 יוֹמָן ז
duty officer (police), desk sergeant 909 יוֹמָנַאי ז
male pigeon, male dove 240 יוֹן ז
mud, dirt, filth Bibl. 279 יָוֵן ז
pigeon, dove 594 יוֹנָה נ
Hellenism [no pl.] 736 יַוְנוּת נ
Greek 915 יְוָנִי ז
dovish 988 יוֹנִי ז
Greek [no pl.] 814 יְוָנִית נ
mammal; infant 6 יוֹנֵק ז
sucker; young shoot (botany) 11 יוֹנֶקֶת נ
consultant, adviser 7 יוֹעֵץ ז
creator, maker, producer 6 יוֹצֵר ז
blazing, burning 6 יוֹקֵד ז
emigrant from Israel 6 יוֹרֵד ז
shooter; first rain of the season 10 יוֹרֶה ז
cauldron, large pot (Talmudic) 593 יוֹרָה נ
conformist, "square" Sl. 915 יוֹרַמִּי ז
heir; successor 6 יוֹרֵשׁ ז
inhabitant, dweller, resident 6 יוֹשֵׁב ז
initiated 15 יָזוּם ז
initiating 45 יִזּוּם ז
initiating 1 יְזִימָה נ
entrepreneur ; initiator, promoter (fem. *yazemet*, Coll. *yazamit*) 275 יָזָם ז
initiative 628 יָזְמָה נ
rat-tailed bat 447 יַזְנוּב ז
sweat, perspiration Lit. [no pl.] 319 יֶזַע ז
uniqueness; being alone with someone of the opposite sex (orthodox term) 50 יִחוּד ז
special, unique 957 יִחוּדִי ז
uniqueness [no pl.] 762 יִחוּדִיּוּת נ
anticipation, expectation, hope 50 יִחוּל ז
female animal being in "heat"; sexual excitement 50 יִחוּם ז
pedigree; attribution 50 יִחוּס ז
referential 957 יִחוּסִי ז
cutting (botany), shoot, twig 50 יִחוּר ז
alone, one; individual; singular (grammar) 20 יָחִיד ז
unique, hapax legomenon (occurring only once in a specific text) 915 יְחִידָאִי ז
unit 1 יְחִידָה נ
solitariness, privacy; uniqueness, oneness 24 יְחִידוּת נ
singlehood [no pl.] 762 יְחִידִיּוּת נ
individuality, uniqueness [no pl.] 740 יְחִידָנוּת נ
individual, distinct, discreet 935 יְחִידָנִי ז
fallow deer 447 יַחְמוּר ז
cistanche (parasitic desert plant) 447 יַחְנוּק ז
attitude, relation; ratio; pedigree Lit. 328 יַחַס/יַחַשׂ ז
case (syntax) 612 יַחֲסָה נ
relativity 737 יַחֲסוּת נ
relative 966 יַחֲסִי ז
relativity [no pl.] 786 יַחֲסִיּוּת נ
member of distinguished family; one who puts on airs, snob 846 יַחְסָן ז

prestige 624 נ יְקָרָה
cerambycid 814 נ יַקְרוּנִית (beetle)
expensive, charging 846 ז יַקְרָן high prices
expensiveness, 752 נ יַקְרָנוּת dearness, high price [no pl.]
prestigious 915 ז יֻקְרָתִי
God-fearing person; 279 ז יְרֵא fearful Lit.
awe, fear [no pl.] 598 נ יִרְאָה
spotlight 444 ז יַרְאוֹר trainer/projector
amaranth (plant) 447 ז יַרְבּוּז
Jordanian 915 ז יַרְדֵּנִי
down, dejected, 15 ז יָרוּד unwell; inferior
interception of plane, 51 ז יֵרוּט ship, shoot down
shot; fired 15 ז יָרוּי
pond scum; patina 671 נ יְרוֹקָה Lit.
Jerusalemite 915 ז יְרוּשַׁלְמִי
moon 279 ז יָרֵחַ
month Lit. 329 ז יֶרַח
monthly magazine 892 ז יַרְחוֹן
lunar; moon-like 915 ז יַרְחִי
adversary 20 ז יָרִיב
rivalry, competition 24 נ יְרִיבוּת
fair, exhibition, 405 ז יְרִיד/יָרִיד market
descent; alighting; 1 נ יְרִידָה emigration from Israel
shot; shooting, firing 4 נ יְרִיָּה
sheet; description 1 נ יְרִיעָה
spitting 1 נ יְרִיקָה
thigh 279 ז יָרֵךְ
loin meat [no pl.] 614 נ יַרְכָּה
tunic 808 נ יַרְכִּית
bustard (a large 447 ז יַרְעוּד crane-like bird)
vegetable 270 ז יָרָק
green; verdant; 301 ז יָרֹק unripe (fruit); inexperienced Sl.
vegetation, herbage, 330 ז יֶרֶק greenery
greenfinch (bird) 892 ז יַרְקוֹן
greensickness, 904 ז יֵרָקוֹן chlorosis (plant disease) [no pl.]
greenness Lit. [no 736 נ יַרְקוּת pl.]
greengrocer 846 ז יַרְקָן
greengrocery [no 752 נ יַרְקָנוּת pl.]
greenish 458 ז יְרַקְרַק
greenishness [no 743 נ יְרַקְרַקּוּת pl.]
scum (stagnant 708 נ יָרֹקֶת water); patina [no pl.]
inheritance 658 נ יְרֻשָּׁה
buttocks 846 ז יַשְׁבָן
seated 15 ז יָשׁוּב
settling, populating; 45 ז יִשּׁוּב settlement; population
applying; application 45 ז יִשּׂוּם

applied 956 ז יִשּׂוּמִי
aging of meat, wine, 45 ז יִשּׁוּן cheese
salvation 18 נ יְשׁוּעָה
straightening 45 ז יִשּׁוּר
existential 915 ז יֵשׁוּתִי
sitting; meeting 1 נ יְשִׁיבָה
applicable 20 ז יָשִׂים
applicability 24 נ יְשִׂימוּת
direct 20 ז יָשִׁיר
very old; very old 20 ז יָשִׁישׁ person
old age [no pl.] 24 נ יְשִׁישׁוּת
Ishmaelite, Arab 915 ז יִשְׁמְעֵאלִי Lit.
old; longstanding 267 ז יָשָׁן
oldness, age [no pl.] 341 ז יֹשֶׁן
sleepy 912 ז יַשְׁנוּנִי
oldness Lit. [no pl.] 736 נ יַשְׁנוּת
straight; honest, 267 ז יָשָׁר decent
honesty, integrity, 341 ז יֹשֶׁר uprightness [no pl.]
Israeli 915 ז יִשְׂרְאֵלִי
Israeliness [no 762 נ יִשְׂרְאֵלִיּוּת pl.]
honesty, integrity 736 נ יַשְׁרוּת Lit. [no pl.]
stake, peg 279 ז יָתֵד
tongs (Talmudic) 378 ז יַתּוּךְ
orphan (pl. 288 ז יָתוֹם yetomim, fem. yetoma)
excess, surplus 45 ז יִתּוּר
mosquito 378 ז יַתּוּשׁ
mosquito-like; 915 ז יַתּוּשִׁי small, insignificant, annoying
biblical cantillation 405 ז יְתִיב symbol [no declension, no pl.?]
redundant, 402 ז יַתִּיר superfluous
redundancy 754 נ יַתִּירוּת (electronic systems) [no pl.]
orphanhood; 736 נ יַתְמוּת loneliness; sense of loss [no pl.]
large, excessive, 279 ז יָתֵר abundant
remainder, rest; 317 ז יֶתֶר excess, surplus [no pl.]
rope, cord, string; 317 ז יֶתֶר hypotenuse
balance, remainder 598 נ יִתְרָה
advantage 885 ז יִתְרוֹן
pain 307 ז כְּאֵב
fireman 908 ז כַּבַּאי
fire engine, fire 840 נ כַּבָּאִית truck
heavy 279 ז כָּבֵד
liver 279 ז כָּבֵד
mass, heaviness; 341 ז כֹּבֶד weight; gravity [no pl.]
luggage; belongings 658 נ כְּבֻדָּה
newly extinguished; 265 ז כָּבֶה lifeless Lit.
honorable, 15 ז כָּבוּד distinguished

honor, respect; 288 ז כָּבוֹד dignity [no pl.]
honoring; refreshment 45 ז כִּבּוּד
extinguished 15 ז כָּבוּי
bound, chained; 15 ז כָּבוּל restricted
washing, laundering 45 ז כִּבּוּס
conquered; 15 ז כָּבוּשׁ restrained; leveled ground; pickled, preserved
conquering; 45 ז כִּבּוּשׁ conquest, occupation; suppressing; leveling/paving road
gravitation [no pl.] 1 נ כְּבִידָה
gravitational 915 ז כְּבִידָתִי
extinguishment of fire 4 נ כְּבִיָּה Lit
binding, chaining, 1 נ כְּבִילָה handcuffing; restriction
restrictedness, 24 נ כְּבִילוּת bondage, confinement
washable 20 ז כָּבִיס
laundering; laundry 1 נ כְּבִיסָה Coll.
tremendous, 402 ז כַּבִּיר enormous, mighty
thick fabric; woolen 405 ז כְּבִיר or fur blanket Lit.
straining [no pl.] 1 נ כְּבִירָה
roadway, paved road 405 ז כְּבִישׁ
pressing; paving; 1 נ כְּבִישָׁה suppressing emotion; preserving, pickling
fetter, chain; cable, 326 ז כֶּבֶל wire
a certain distance 598 נ כִּבְרָה [no pl.]
sieve, sifter 634 נ כְּבָרָה
ramp, gangway 317 ז כֶּבֶשׁ
sheep; mutton 317 ז כֶּבֶשׂ
secret, mystery Lit. 884 ז כִּבְשׁוֹן
furnace 857 ז כִּבְשָׁן
furnace-like, very 950 ז כִּבְשָׁנִי hot
rounded, somewhat 227 ז כַּד pointed end, e.g., of egg Lit.
worthwhile 915 ז כְּדָאִי
worthwhileness, 771 נ כְּדָאִיּוּת profitability [no pl.]
ball, sphere; pill; 378 ז כַּדּוּר bullet
soccer player 863 ז כַּדּוּרַגְלָן
round spherical 915 ז כַּדּוּרִי
roundness [no pl.] 793 נ כַּדּוּרִיּוּת
corpuscle, blood 814 נ כַּדּוּרִית cell; spherule; pompon
basketball player 863 ז כַּדּוּרְסַלָן
jacinth, ruby Bibl. 423 ז כַּדְכֹּד
hyacinth 863 ז כַּדָּן
dribble a ball 70 ז כִּדְרוּר
bowling 695 נ כַּדֹּרֶת
dark 260 ז כֵּהֶה

כְּלִיאָה נ 1 imprisonment
כְּלִיב ז 405 staple
כְּלִיבָה נ 1 sewing rough seams
כִּלְיָה נ 598 kidney
כְּלָיָה נ 632 extinction, annihilation, extermination [no pl.]
כִּלָּיוֹן ז 898 annihilation, extinction [no pl.]
כָּלִיל ז 20 complete, total, absolute
כְּלִיל ז 405 crown, garland; total, perfect (from constr. of kalil) Coll. [no pl.]
כְּלִילָה נ 1 generalization Lit-rare [no pl.]
כְּלִילוּת נ 24 moral perfection; integrity, completeness [no pl.]
כְּלִילִי ז 933 coronary
כִּלְכּוּל ז 66 upkeep, maintenance, providing for
כַּלְכָּלָה נ 682 economy, economics
כַּלְכָּלִי ז 915 economic
כַּלְכְּלָן ז 851 economist
כְּלָל ז 310 law, basic rule; all
כְּלָלִי ז 942 general
כְּלָלִיּוּת נ 771 generalness [no pl.]
כְּלִמָּה נ 646 shame Lit.
כַּלָּנִית נ 814 anemone (poppy-like flower)
כָּמֵהַּ ז 279 longing, yearning
כְּמֵהָה ר' כְּמֵהִין נ 649 truffle, pl. kmehin
כִּמּוּי ז 45 quantification
כַּמּוֹן ז 380 cumin (plant, spice)
כָּמוּס ז 15 hidden, concealed, secret
כְּמוּסָה נ 18 capsule medicine
כְּמוּרָה נ 18 clergy, priesthood
כִּמּוּת ז 45 quantification
כַּמּוּת נ 731 quantity
כַּמּוּתִי ז 915 quantitative
כַּמּוּתִיּוּת נ 793 quantitativeness [no pl.]
כְּמִיהָה נ 1 yearning Lit
כְּמִינָה נ 1 hiding, concealment Lit [no pl.]
כְּמִישָׁה נ 1 withering [no pl.]
כַּמְנוֹן ז 889 anise, sweet cumin
כֹּמֶר ז 341 priest, minister, parson
כָּמֵשׁ ז 279 wilted, withered Lit.
כִּמָּשׁוֹן ז 898 blight [no pl.]
כֻּמְתָּה נ 624 beret
כֵּן ז 231 honest, sincere
כַּנָּה נ 585 mounting, bracket; stock of plant on which a shoot is grafted
כִּנָּה נ 587 flea
כִּנּוּי ז 45 nickname
כִּנּוּן ז 45 establishment, founding; aiming, pointing - military

כִּנּוּס ז 45 assembling; conference, convention
כָּנוּעַ ז 17 submissive, docile, resigned
כִּנּוֹר ז 383 violin; stringed musical instrument (biblical)
כְּנִיסָה נ 1 entering; entrance; admission
כְּנִיעָה נ 1 surrender, submission
כְּנִיעוּת נ 24 submissiveness, acquiescence [no pl.]
כִּנֶּמֶת נ 694 pediculosis, presence of lice on head/body [no pl.]
כַּנֶּנֶת נ 685 winch, crank
כֶּנֶס ז 317 assembly, conference
כְּנֵסִיָּה נ 911 church
כְּנֵסִיָּתִי ז 915 of the church
כְּנֶסֶת נ 702 assembly; Knesset (Israeli parliament)
כְּנַעֲנִי ז 915 Canaanite
כְּנַעֲנִיּוּת נ 762 Canaanism (Israeli school of thought) [no pl.]
כָּנָף, ר' כְּנָפַיִם/כְּנָפוֹת נ 267 wing; edge (esp. of garment) (pl. knafayim/knafot)
כְּנָפִי ז 915 winged
כְּנֻפְיָה נ 678 gang
כְּנָפִית נ 808 samara, winged seed/dried fruit
כְּנֻפְיָתִי ז 915 gang-style
כַּנָּר ז 275 violinist (fem. kaneret, Coll. kanarit)
כִּסֵּא, ר' כִּסְאוֹת ז 283 chair (pl. kis'ot)
כֻּסְבָּר ז 435 coriander
כָּסוּחַ ז 17 cut, mowed, trimmed
כִּסּוּחַ ז 53 cutting, mowing
כָּסוּי ז 15 covered, concealed, hidden
כִּסּוּי ז 45 coverage
כָּסוּף ז 15 silvery, silver-plated; longed for Lit
כְּסוּת נ 734 clothing; cover
כְּסָיָה נ 632 glove
כְּסִיל ז 405 fool, idiot, imbecile, moron Lit.
כְּסִילִי ז 933 silly, dumb
כְּסִיסָה נ 1 gnawing
כְּסִיפָה נ 1 yearning Lit-rare [no pl.]
כֶּסֶל ז 317 ilium; flank, loin (of meat)
כֶּסֶל/כִּסֶל ז 317 foolishness, stupidity Lit. [no pl.]
כֻּסֶּמֶת נ 700 buckwheat, kasha
כֶּסֶף ז 326 money; silver
כֹּסֶף ז 341 yearning, longing Lit. [no pl.]
כֻּסְפָּה נ 625 pulp, oil cake (agriculture)
כַּסְפִּי ז 965 financial, monetary
כַּסְפִּית נ 808 mercury [no pl.]
כַּסְפִּיתִי ז 915 mercurial

כַּסֶּפֶת נ 685 safe; deposit box
כֶּסֶת נ 321 down comforter, duvet
כָּעוּס ז 15 angry, irritated
כִּעוּר ז 50 ugliness
כַּעַךְ ז 328 bagel
כִּעְכּוּעַ ז 67 coughing, clearing of throat
כַּעַס ז 328 anger, wrath, fury
כַּעֲסָן ז 849 hot-headed, hot tempered person
כַּעֲסָנוּת נ 753 hot-headedness, impetuousness [no pl.]
כַּעֲסָנִי ז 970 angry, hot-tempered
כֵּף ז 231 cape, point, headland
כַּף נ 222 hand, palm; foot; spoon
כַּפָּה נ 585 paw
כִּפָּה נ 586 skullcap; cupola, dome
כָּפוּי ז 15 forced, compelled
כְּפוּלָה נ 18 multiple (math.)
כָּפוּף ז 15 bent; subordinate
כְּפוֹר ז 393 frost; very cold weather
כִּפּוּר ז 45 atonement
כָּפוּת ז 15 bound hands or feet
כְּפִיָּה נ 4 coercion, duress; compulsion
כִּפְיוֹן ז 885 epilepsy
כָּפִיל ז 20 double
כְּפִילוּת נ 24 duplication
כָּפִיס ז 20 wooden beam, rafter
כָּפִיף ז 20 flexible, pliable; a subordinate
כְּפִיפָה נ 1 bending
כְּפִיפוּת נ 24 subordination; dependence
כְּפִיר ז 405 young lion Lit.
כְּפִירָה נ 1 heresy; denial
כַּפִּית נ 814 teaspoon
כְּפִיתָה נ 1 binding hands, feet; immobilizing
כְּפִיָּתִי ז 915 compulsive
כְּפִיָּתִיּוּת נ 762 compulsiveness (no decl., no pl.)
כֶּפֶל ז 310 copy
כֶּפֶל ז 317 multiplication; double
כָּפָן ז 267 hunger Lit.-rare (only construct, no declension, no pl.)
כַּפָּן ז 863 spoonbill (bird)
כְּפָפָה נ 632 glove
כְּפָר ז 310 village
כֹּפֶר ז 341 ransom [no pl.]
כַּפָּרָה נ 620 atonement
כַּפְרִי ז 965 rural, rustic (like segholites)
כַּפְרִיּוּת נ 785 country life [no pl.]
כְּפָרִיר ז 454 light frost
כַּפֹּרֶת נ 695 covering of the holy ark (biblical)
כֻּפְתָּה נ 627 dumpling, matzo ball
כִּפְתּוּר ז 54 buttoning

making pancakes 45 לִבּוּב ז
fanning of flame; arousal of emotion 45 לִבּוּי ז
clarification, elucidation 45 לִבּוּן ז
frankincense 671 לְבוֹנָה נ
dressed 15 לָבוּשׁ ז
clothing, attire, dress 399 לְבוּשׁ ז
difficulty in making a decision, misgiving (mostly in pl. levatim) 317 לֶבֶט ז
lion 20 לָבִיא ז
wearable 20 לָבִישׁ ז
wearing 1 לְבִישָׁה נ
pancreas 416 לַבְלָב ז
budding, blooming 66 לִבְלוּב ז
white; white man 267 לָבָן ז
cultured milk [no pl.] 317 לֶבֶן ז
whiteness [no pl.] 341 לֹבֶן ז
whitish 458 לְבַנְבַּן ז
whiteness, paleness, pallor [no pl.] 743 לְבַנְבַּנוּת נ
birch (tree) 608 לִבְנֶה ז
whiteness, pallor [no pl.] 598 לַבְנָה נ
moon Lit. 634 לְבָנָה נ
brick 653 לְבֵנָה נ
bleak (fish) 450 לַבְנוּן ז
whitish, pallid 912 לַבְנוּנִי ז
whiteness, paleness, pallor [no pl.] 790 לַבְנוּנִיּוּת נ
whiteness, paleness, pallor [no pl.] 836 לַבְנוּנִית נ
cabbage butterfly 454 לַבְנִין ז
albino 846 לַבְקָן ז
albinism [no pl.] 752 לַבְקָנוּת נ
biblical liquid measure 227 לֹג ז
legion(s) 885 לִגְיוֹן ז
legionnaire 909 לִגְיוֹנַאי ז
swallow, gulp, sip n 1 לְגִימָה נ
ridiculing, belittling; ridiculer, belittler 851 לַגְלְגָן ז
ridiculing, belittling [no pl.] 749 לַגְלְגָנוּת נ
mocking 975 לַגְלְגָנִי ז
ridicule 66 לִגְלוּג ז
birth 588 לֵדָה נ
natal (prenatal, post natal) 915 לֵדָתִי ז
uvula Rare 632 לְהָאָה נ
blade; tongue of flame 328 לַהַב ז
flame 644 לֶהָבָה נ
prattle, chatter; dialect 328 לַהַג ז
prattler 849 לַהֲגָן ז
prattle, chatter, blather, jabber [no pl.] 753 לַהֲגָנוּת נ
prattling, . chattering, blithering, jabbering Lit 970 לַהֲגָנִי ז
tired, exhausted, fatigued Lit. 260 לָהֶה ז
enthusiastic, eager 15 לָהוּט ז

casting in film, theater 50 לִהוּק ז
intense heat, blaze; enthusiasm; passion 328 לַהַט ז
juggling trick; magic trick, sleight of hand 451 לַהֲטוּט ז
juggler 863 לַהֲטוּטָן ז
hit song; fad, latest thing Coll. 20 לָהִיט ז
enthusiasm, passion 24 לְהִיטוּת נ
flock (birds), school (fish); military squadron, group 328 לַהַק ז
choir, band, troupe; flock (birds), school (fish) 612 לַהֲקָה נ
after- (aftertaste etc.); modifier, attribute 906 לְוַאי ז
blazing, burning Lit 7 לוֹהֵב ז
burning hot; intense 7 לוֹהֵט ז
borrower 10 לֹוֶה ז
tabulation 53 לִוּוּחַ ז
escort; accompanying 45 לִוּוּי ז
almond Bibl.; hazelnut 246 לוּז ז
blackboard; board, plank; playing board; control panel; calendar; table, list; plate (in printing); tablet 248 לוּחַ ז
plate, sign 814 לוּחִית נ
fighter, soldier 7 לוֹחֵם ז
aggressive, belligerent, warring; combative 986 לוֹחֲמָנִי ז
whispering, hushed, rustling 986 לוֹחֲשָׁנִי ז
covering, wrapping 240 לוֹט ז
covered; enclosed; enclosure 246 לוּט ז
petting, stroking, caressing 985 לוֹטְפָנִי ז
funeral 634 לְוָיָה נ
satellite 846 לַוְיָן ז
satellitic 969 לַוְיָנִי ז
chicken coop; playpen; shaft, pit Bibl. 246 לוּל ז
bolt 366 לוֹלָב ז
lulav, ceremonial palm frond 370 לוּלָב ז
poultry farmer/worker 863 לוּלָן ז
foreign, strange, not Hebrew Lit 7 לוֹעֵז ז
of a foreign (non-Hebrew) language 915 לוֹעֲזִי ז
foreignness (of non-Hebrew word, lang.) [no pl.] 762 לוֹעֲזִיּוּת נ
foreign (non-Hebrew) language [no pl.] 814 לוֹעֲזִית נ
arum (botany) [no pl.] 246 לוּף ז
sponge gourd, luffa plant 595 לוּפָה נ
arisarum (plant) 814 לוּפִית נ
frame, ledge, rim, edging strip, mantlepiece 421 לִזְבֵּז ז
gunwale 715 לַזְבֶּזֶת נ
beaming of a laser, lasing [no pl.] 1 לְזִירָה נ

damp, moist; humid 221 לַח ז
freshness, vitality [no pl.] 232 לֵחַ ז
mucus, phlegm 588 לֵחָה נ
pressed, squeezed; very anxious 15 לָחוּץ ז
whispering Lit 50 לִחוּשׁ ז
dampness, humidity [no pl.] 732 לַחוּת נ
cheek; jaw 259 לְחִי/לֶחִי נו״ז
lapping, licking Lit 1 לְחִיכָה נ
fighting military 1 לְחִימָה נ
button, switch 405 לְחִיץ ז
pressing, pushing 1 לְחִיצָה נ
whispering; whisper 1 לְחִישָׁה נ
dampening, moistening [no pl.] 67 לִחְלוּחַ ז
damp, moist 912 לַחְלוּחִי ז
moistness [no pl.] 790 לַחְלוּחִיּוּת נ
moisture; freshness, vitality [no pl.] 838 לַחְלוּחִית נ
bread [note: pl. constr. laHamey] 326 לֶחֶם ז
solder N 328 לַחַם ז
warfare, military tactics 628 לָחְמָה נ
conjuctiva (of eye) 808 לַחְמִית נ
bread roll 911 לַחְמָנִיָּה נ
tune, melody 328 לַחַן ז
pressure, force; stress; oppression Lit. 328 לַחַץ ז
button, switch Coll. 846 לַחְצָן ז
press stud, snap Coll. 814 לַחְצָנִית נ
whisper, murmur; incantation, spell 328 לַחַשׁ ז
whisper, murmur 450 לַחְשׁוּשׁ ז
prompter (theater) 846 לַחְשָׁן ז
(theater) prompting [no pl.] 752 לַחְשָׁנוּת נ
whispered, murmured 969 לַחְשָׁנִי ז
lizard 632 לְטָאָה נ
Latinization [no pl.] 45 לִטּוּן ז
petting, stroking, caressing 45 לִטּוּף ז
sharp, honed; bright, polished 15 לָטוּשׁ ז
polishing; final touch-up; refinement 45 לִטּוּשׁ ז
Latin 915 לָטִינִי ז
Latin [no pl.] 814 לָטִינִית נ
stroke, caress n 1 לְטִיפָה נ
cistus (plant) 341 לֹטֶם ז
caressing 969 לַטְפָנִי ז
Lithuanian 915 לִיטָאִי ז
night, Lit. alternant of *layla* 358 לַיִל ז
night, see *layil* (suffix is not fem.!) 358 לַיְלָה ז
nocturnal 960 לֵילִי ז
night owl; queen of evil spirits (Jewish mysticism) (is it a suffix here?) 814 לִילִית נ

מְאֻכְזָב ז 98 disappointed
מַאֲכָל ז 519 food item; dish
מְאֻכָּל ז 92 consumed, corroded
מְאֻכְלָס ז 97 populated
מַאֲכֶלֶת נ 532 slaughtering/carving knife Lit.
מְאֻכָּף ז 92 saddled
מְאַלְחֵשׁ ז 78 anesthetic
מַאֲלֵמַת נ 89 combine harvester
מְאֻלָּף ז 92 trained
מְאֻלָּץ ז 92 forced, unnatural
מַאֲמִין ז 188 believer; religious
מָאֳמָן ז 201 credentialed
מְאֻמָּן ז 92 trained, skilled
מַאֲמָץ ז 525 effort
מְאֻמָּץ ז 92 adopted; strained
מַאֲמָר ז 519 article
מְאֻמָּת ז 92 verified, authenticated
מְאֻנָּךְ ז 92 vertical, perpendicular
מְאֻנָּס ז 92 forced Lit
מְאֻנְקָל ז 97 hooked
מַאֲסָר ז 519 imprisonment, incarceration
מַאֲפֶה ז 538 pastry
מַאֲפִיָּה נ 911 bakery
מְאֻפְיָן ז 97 characterized
מָאֳפָל ז 201 darkened, blacked out
מְאֻפָּס ז 92 zeroed; adjusted
מְאֻפְסָר ז 97 haltered, tethered
מְאֻפָּק ז 92 restrained
מְאֻפָּר ז 92 made up - cosmetics
מַאֲפֵרָה נ 551 ashtray
מְאֻקְלָם ז 97 acclimatized, acclimated
מַאֲרָב ז 519 ambush
מַאֲרָג ז 519 fabric, tapestry, weave, web [no pl.]
מְאַרְגֵּן ז 78 organizer
מְאֻרְגָּן ז 97 organized; methodical
מְאֵרָה נ 649 curse Lit.
מַאֲרָז ז 519 package
מַאֲרִיךְ ז 188 biblical cantillation symbol; extending (e.g. cable)
מָאֳרָךְ ז 201 elongated, extended
מְאֹרָס ז 93 engaged to be married
מְאֹרָע ז 93 event, incident
מְאֹרָע ז 94 event, incident [pl. - ot]
מָאֳרָק ז 201 grounded (elect.), ground
מְאֻשָּׁר ז 92 happy, contented
מְאֻשְׁרָר ז 105 ratified
מְאֻשָּׁשׁ ז 92 well-founded, proven
מְאֻתָּר ז 92 located
מְבָאוּס ז 491 disappointing, depressing; disappointed, depressed Sl.

מַבְאִישׁ ז 187 rotten, stinking, putrid
מְבֹאָס ז 93 depressed
מְבֹאָר ז 93 annotated
מֻבְאָשׁ ז 200 odious, rotted, putrid
מְבֻגָּר ז 92 adult, mature; older than
מַבְדֵּד ז 541 electrical insulator
מְבֻדָּד ז 92 insulated – elec.
מִבְדּוֹק ז 482 shipyard
מְבֻדָּח ז 92 happy; amused
מַבְדִּיל ז 187 distinguishing, separating
מֻבְדָּל ז 200 differentiated, separated, distinguished
מִבְדָּק ז 496 examination, test
מַבְהִיל ז 187 terrifying, shocking
מַבְהִיק ז 187 radiant, shining
מְבֹהָל ז 93 frightened, terrified
מֻבְהָק ז 200 typical, characteristic; clear; significant (statistics)
מִבְהָק ז 497 highlight (photography)
מֻבְהָקוּת נ 211 typicalness, characteristicalness; significance (statistics)
מֻבְהָר ז 200 clarified, explained; lighted, bleached
מָבוֹא ז 478 preface, introduction
מְבוֹדָד ז 96 isolated
מְבוֹדֵד ז 77 insulating
מָבוֹךְ ז 477 maze, labyrinth
מְבוּכָה נ 480 embarrassment; confusion
מַבּוּל ז 378 flood, deluge, downpour
מַבּוּעַ ז 492 spring Lit.
מְבֻזֶּה ז 95 ridiculed, belittled
מִבְזָק ז 496 news flash
מַבְזֵק ז 541 flash (photog.)
מְבֻזָּר ז 92 decentralized
מַבְחִיל ז 187 nauseating, sickening
מֻבְחָן ז 200 distinct, distinguished
מִבְחָן ז 497 test, exam
מַבְחֵנָה נ 550 test tube
מֻבְחָר ז 200 choice, selected, top quality
מִבְחָר ז 497 choice
מַבְחֵשׁ ז 544 mixing spoon; cocktail stick
מַבָּט ז 520 glance, look, gaze
מִבְטָא ז 498 accent
מֻבְטָח ז 200 promised
מִבְטָח ז 498 safe haven Lit.
מְבֻטָּח ז 92 insured; insured person
מַבְטִיחַ ז 189 promising
מֻבְטָל ז 200 unemployed
מְבֻטָּל ז 92 cancelled; insignificant
מְבֻטָּן ז 92 lined - clothing

מְבֻטָּן ז 92 reinforced with concrete
מִבְטָשָׁה נ 550 fulling mill
מֵבִיךְ ז 197 embarrassing
מְבֻיָּל ז 92 stamped - envelope
מְבֻיָּם ז 92 staged
מֵבִין ז 197 expert
מְבֻיָּץ ז 92 ovulated Coll.
מֵבִישׁ ז 197 shameful, embarrassing
מְבֻיָּשׁ ז 92 embarrassed
מְבֻיָּת ז 92 domesticated
מֻבְלָט ז 200 highlighted; prominent
מַבְלֵט ז 541 die (technology, engineering)
מַבְלְטָן ז 867 one designing and creating dies
מַבְלֵל ז 541 jammer (radio, radar)
מֻבְלָע ז 200 concealed, hidden; intermingled
מֻבְלַעַת נ 202 enclave
מְבֻלָּק ז 92 cracked, smashed Lit
מְבֻנְאָם ז 97 internationalized Lit
מֻבְנֶה ז 204 structured; built in
מִבְנֶה ז 504 building; structure
מִבְנִי ז 915 structural
מַבְסוּט ז 491 happy, satisfied
מְבֻסָּם ז 92 tipsy, slightly drunk
מְבֻסָּס ז 92 established, proven, based
מֻבָּע ז 205 expressed
מַבָּע ז 521 expression, look; utterance
מַבְעִית ז 187 horrifying, terrifying
מַבְעֵר ז 544 burner; lighter
מְבֹעָר ז 93 kindled, lit, burning
מְבֹעָת ז 93 terrified, horrified
מִבְצָע ז 498 operation
מְבֻצָּע ז 92 executed, completed, realized
מִבְצָעִי ז 924 operational
מִבְצָר ז 496 fortress, stronghold
מְבֻצָּר ז 92 fortified
מְבֻקָּע ז 92 cracked, fissured
מְבֻקָּר ז 92 controlled; supervised
מְבֻקָּשׁ ז 92 in demand; wanted
מֻבְרָג ז 200 screwed on; screwed in
מַבְרֵג ז 541 screwdriver
מַבְרֵגָה נ 550 electric screwdriver
מַבְרֵז ז 541 screw-tap
מְבֻרְזָל ז 97 reinforced with iron rods, iron-plated
מֻבְרָח ז 200 smuggled
מַבְרִיחַ ז 189 smuggler
מַבְרִיק ז 187 sparkling, shiny; brilliant
מֻבְרָךְ ז 200 kneeling
מְבֹרָךְ ז 93 blessed; praiseworthy
מִבְרָץ ז 496 spillway

מִגְרָשׁ ז 496 plot of land; empty lot, yard; field, court (sports)
מְגֹרָשׁ ז 93 exiled person
מֻגָּשׁ ז 205 served, presented, submitted
מַגָּשׁ ז 520 tray
מַגְשִׁים ז 187 one who fulfills his dreams
מַגָּשִׁית נ 817 small tray
מְגֻשָּׁם ז 92 cumbersome, clumsy, awkward
מְגֻשָּׁמוּת נ 107 clumsiness, awkwardness [no pl.]
מְגֻשָּׁר ז 92 bridged
מֻדְאָג ז 200 worried, concerned, anxious
מֻדְאָגוּת נ 211 being worried [no pl.]
מִדְאָה ז 504 gliding field
מַדְאוֹר ז 444 light meter
מַדְאִיג ז 187 worrisome, perturbing, disturbing
מְדֻבָּב ז 92 dubbed - cinema, TV
מְדֻבְלָל ז 105 unkempt, tangled, snarled
מֻדְבָּק ז 200 glued, attached, stuck
מַדְבֵּקָה נ 550 sticker
מִדְבָּר ז 496 desert, wilderness
מְדֻבָּר ז 92 talked about; subject of discussion
מִדְבָּרִי ז 924 of the desert
מִדְבָּרִיּוּת נ 762 desolateness, barrenness [no pl.]
מִדְגֶּה ז 504 fishing farm
מֻדְגָּם ז 200 demonstrated
מִדְגָּם ז 496 sample N
מְדֻגָּם ז 92 patterned - fabric; done perfectly Sl.
מִדְגָּמִי ז 924 sample Adj
מַדְגֵּרָה נ 550 hatchery, incubator
מַדְגֵּרִיָּה נ 911 farm with a system of incubators
מֻדְגָּשׁ ז 200 emphasized, stressed; accentuated
מַדְגֵּשׁ ז 541 marker
מַדָּד ז 275 measure; index (economics); consumer price index
מֶדֶד ז 317 measurement Lit. [no pl.]
מִדָּה נ 586 measurement; size; extent
מַדְהֵבָה נ 550 oppression (biblical)
מַדְהִים ז 187 amazing, astonishing, dumbfounding
מָדוּד ז 15 measured, moderate, unhurried
מִדּוּד ז 45 benchmarking, gauging
מַדְוֶה ז 535 ailment, affliction Lit
מַדּוּחַ ז 379 temptation, seduction Lit.
מְדֻוָּח ז 92 reported
מָדוֹךְ ז 477 retinal cone (anatomy) (resembles pestle)
מְדוֹכָה נ 479 mortar; canister launcher
מָדוֹן ז 477 strife, dispute, contention, quarrel Lit.
מִדּוּף ז 45 shelving
מִדּוּר ז 45 compartmentalization [no pl.]
מָדוֹר ז 477 department; section; compartment; housing Talmudic
מְדֻוָּר ז 92 mailed, posted
מְדוּרָה נ 480 bonfire
מֻדָּח ז 205 ousted
מַדְחָ"ן = מַד חֲנִיָּה ז 409 parking meter
מִדְחֶה ז 504 error Lit.-rare
מַדְחֹם ז 423 thermometer
מַדְחֵס ז 544 compressor
מַדְחֵף ז 544 propeller
מֻדְחָק ז 200 repressed (psychoanalysis)
מָדִיד ז 20 measurable
מַדִּיד ז 402 gauge
מְדִידָה נ 1 measuring
מֵדִיחַ ז 196 instigator, agitator, inciter
מֵדִיחַ ז 198 dishwashing machine, dishwasher
מְדִינַאי ז 909 statesman, diplomat
מְדִינָאִי ז 915 of a diplomat/statesman
מְדִינָה נ 481 state
מִדְיָנִי ז 915 Midianite
מְדִינִי ז 915 political
מְדִינִיּוּת נ 768 policy [no pl.]
מְדִינָתִי ז 915 of the state
מְדֻיָּק ז 92 exact, accurate, precise
מְדַכֵּא ז 71 depressing
מְדֻכָּא ז 92 depressed, oppressed
מְדַכְדֵּךְ ז 83 discouraging, depressing
מַדְלֶה ז 535 crane, derrick
מִדְלוֹק ז 491 excited by, interested in, turned on by, enamored of Sl.
מַדְלִיף ז 187 one who leaks information
מַדְלִיפָן ז 868 one leaking information Coll.
מַדְלִיק ז 187 wonderful, terrific, great Sl.
מֻדְלָף ז 200 leaked (information)
מֻדְלָק ז 200 inflamed (medical)
מַדְמֶה ז 535 simulator
מְדֻמֶּה ז 95 fictitious, bogus; virtual - computing
מְדֻמְיָן ז 97 imaginary, fanciful, unreal
מַדְמִיעַ ז 189 tear-causing, lacrimatory
מַדְמֵנָה נ 550 swamp, bog, mire Lit.
מַדָּע ז 523 science
מַדָּעִי ז 915 scientific
מַדָּעִיּוּת נ 762 scientific method [no pl.]
מַדְעָן ז 863 scientist
מַדְעָנוּת נ 752 Scientism [no pl.]
מַדָּף ז 275 shelf, ledge
מַדְפִּיס ז 187 printer - person; print-shop owner
מְדֻפְלָם ז 97 certified, qualified
מֻדְפָּס ז 200 printed
מַדְפֵּס ז 541 printer (photography)
מַדְפֶּסֶת נ 550 printer
מְדַקְדֵּק ז 83 grammarian
מְדֻקְלָם ז 97 declaimed, recited
מֻדָּר ז 205 excluded
מֻדְרָג ז 200 terraced; graduated; ranked
מִדְרָג ז 496 echelon, rank, level, hierarchy
מְדֹרָג ז 93 terraced; graduated; ranked
מַדְרֵגָה נ 550 step, stair
מִדְרוּב ז 491 miserable, wretched Sl.
מִדְרוּג ז 54 building of terraces; television rating
מִדְרוּן ז 54 modernization [no pl.]
מִדְרוֹן ז 482 slope, incline, gradient
מִדְרוֹנִי ז 915 slope Adj, slanting
מַדְרִיךְ ז 187 guide; counselor; instructor; mentor; guidebook
מֻדְרָךְ ז 200 guided (esp. tour)
מִדְרָךְ ז 496 foothold, footplate, footboard
מִדְרָכָה נ 505 sidewalk
מִדְרֶכֶת נ 509 sidewalk Lit.
מִדְרָס ז 496 insole
מִדְרָשׁ ז 496 Talmudic legend based on a biblical verse; homiletical exegesis of the bible
מִדְרָשָׁה נ 505 college
מִדְרָשִׁי ז 924 Midrashic, of Talmudic homiletic literature
מְדֻשָּׁא ז 92 grassy Lit
מִדְשָׁאָה נ 508 lawn
מְדֻשָּׁן ז 92 plump; fertilized
מַדְשֵׁנֶת נ 89 fertilizing machine
מְהַבְהֵב ז 83 flashing, flickering; flashing light
מְהֻבּוֹל ז 491 stupid Sl.
מַהְבִּיל ז 187 piping hot, steaming
מְהֻגָּן ז 92 fair, honest; decent
מַהֲדוּרָה נ 495 edition; newscast
מַהְדִּיר ז 187 editor; one who republishes
מְהֻדָּק ז 92 stapled; held tightly together

model Adj 915 מוֹפְתִי ז
examplariness [no pl.] 762 מוֹפְתִיּוּת נ
outlet; way out; origin 473 מוֹצָא ז
shaded 208 מוּצָל ז
flooded 209 מוּצָף ז
pacifier, dummy 6 מוֹצֵץ ז
solid N & Adj; firm 207 מוּצָק ז
solidity; firmness 212 מוּצָקוּת נ
product 207 מוּצָר ז
focus, center; bonfire, pyre 552 מוֹקֵד ז
focal, central; localized (medicine) 915 מוֹקְדִי ז
focalization, centrality [no pl.] 762 מוֹקְדִיּוּת נ
telephone receptionist 863 מוֹקְדָן ז
clowning [no pl.] 740 מוּקְיוֹנוּת נ
clownish 915 מוּקְיוֹנִי ז
denunciated 207 מוּקְעָ ז
mine (military); obstacle 552 מוֹקֵשׁ ז
fear, fright, terror Lit. 473 מוֹרָא ז
fear, dread Lit. 476 מוֹרָאָה ז
ancient threshing implement [pl. morigim, morigey] 369 מוֹרַג, ר׳ מוֹרִגִּים ז
off-loaded, taken down 207 מוּרָד ז
slope, hillside 463 מוֹרָד ז
rebel, revolutionary 6 מוֹרֵד ז
raised, elevated 209 מוּרָם ז
inherited; bequeathed 207 מוֹרָשׁ ז
heritage, legacy 474 מוֹרָשָׁה ז
seated 207 מוּשָׁב ז
returned, restored 209 מוּשָׁב ז
seat, chair; session; cooperative settlement in Israel 461 מוֹשָׁב ז
farming community of private farms in Israel; colony 474 מוֹשָׁבָה ז
seater (one-seater, two seater) 931 מוֹשָׁבִי ז
extended (hand, etc.) 207 מוּשָׁט ז
floated, sailed 209 מוּשָׁט ז
rescuer, savior 193 מוֹשִׁיעַ ז
attractive 6 מוֹשֵׁךְ ז
rein 660 מוֹשְׁכָה נ
ruler, governor 6 מוֹשֵׁל ז
sung, chanted 209 מוּשָׁר ז
death [no pl.] 354 מָוֶת ז
formal panel of judges, consultants, etc. 461 מוֹתָב ז
thrilling, suspenseful 9 מוֹתֵחַ ז
thriller (book, movie) 855 מוֹתְחָן ז
advantage, superiority; leftover, extra Lit. 463 מוֹתָר ז
exhausted 208 מוּתָשׁ ז
altar 503 מִזְבֵּחַ ז

garbage dump, landfill 505 מִזְבָּלָה נ
temperament, demeanor 317 מֶזֶג ז
glazed 92 מְזֻגָּג ז
glass factory 505 מִזְגָּגָה נ
zigzagged Coll. 103 מְזֻגְזָג ז
air conditioner 846 מַזְגָן ז
gilded, gold-plated 200 מֻזְהָב ז
used as means of identification 75 מְזֻהֶה ז
shining, glowing 187 מַזְהִיר ז
dirty, filthy, polluted 93 מְזֹהָם ז
poured 15 מָזוּג ז
merging; air-conditioning 45 מִזּוּג ז
paired, coupled, matched 92 מְזֻוָּג ז
luggage, baggage, hand luggage 496 מִזְוָד ז
suitcase 505 מִזְוָדָה נ
small suitcase 897 מִזְוָדֹנֶת נ
mezuzah (small scroll in box on doorpost); doorpost 480 מְזוּזָה נ
shocking, frightening, horrible 189 מַזְוִיעַ ז
food 478 מָזוֹן ז
cure, medicine, relief Lit. 477 מָזוֹר ז
pointed, angular 92 מְזֻוָּת ז
gutter; eaves 190 מַזְחִילָה נ
sled, sledge, sleigh 506 מִזְחָלָה נ
sled, sledge, sleigh 510 מִזְחֶלֶת נ
pouring 1 מְזִיגָה נ
willful wrongdoer (Talmudic) 197 מֵזִיד ז
nutritious, nourishing 197 מֵזִין ז
armed 92 מְזֻיָּן ז
forged, fake 92 מְזֻיָּף ז
damager (law); pest, harmful insect; demon Lit.; damaging 195 מַזִּיק ז
secretary 187 מַזְכִּיר ז
secretariat, office 741 מַזְכִּירוּת נ
purified, refined 92 מְזֻכָּךְ ז
mentioned, cited 200 מֻזְכָּר ז
memorandum. memo 496 מִזְכָּר ז
souvenir, memento 531 מַזְכֶּרֶת נ
luck, good fortune; fate; zodiac sign 278 מַזָּל ז
fork 541 מַזְלֵג ז
belittled, disparaged 103 מְזֻלְזָל ז
drone 409 מַזְלָט = מָטוֹס זָעִיר לְלֹא טַיָּס ז
sprayed, sprinkled 200 מֻזְלָף ז
watering can 541 מַזְלֵף ז
sprayed, sprinkled 92 מְזֻלָּף ז
plot, intrigue, conspiracy 466 מְזִמָּה נ
"caress, "necking 66 מִזְמוּז ז
psalm; song, chorus Lit. 482 מִזְמוֹר ז
psalmic 915 מִזְמוֹרִי ז

one who loves to "caress, "playboy 851 מְזַמְזֵן ז
inviting 187 מַזְמִין ז
cash N 92 מְזֻמָּן ז
sung, chanted 92 מְזֻמָּר ז
pruning shears 550 מַזְמֵרָה נ
tailed - animal 92 מְזֻנָּב ז
shtreimel 509 מִזְנֶבֶת נ
snack bar, kiosk; buffet 482 מִזְנוֹן ז
snack bar owner/employee 909 מִזְנוֹנַאי ז
neglected; derelict, dilapidated 200 מֻזְנָח ז
neglect; dilapidation 211 מֻזְנָחוּת נ
starter - sports 187 מַזְנִיק ז
rapid deployment force (esp. firefighters) 496 מִזְנָק ז
fire-hose nozzle; trigger 541 מַזְנֵק ז
miniaturization, minimization 58 מִזְעוּר ז
shocking, terrifying 84 מְזַעְזֵעַ ז
minimal, negligible 924 מִזְעָרִי ז
miniature (painting, portrait) Lit. 510 מִזְעֶרֶת נ
tarred; lousy Coll. 92 מְזֻפָּת ז
bearded 92 מְזֻקָּן ז
refined, purified 92 מְזֻקָּק ז
distillery 505 מִזְקָקָה נ
distillery, refinery 550 מַזְקֵקָה נ
mattress Coll., normative form mizran 482 מִזְרוֹן/מִזְרָן ז
accelerated, expedited 93 מְזֹרָז ז
east [no pl.] 498 מִזְרָח ז
eastern; Middle Eastern 924 מִזְרָחִי ז
Middle Eastern characteristicalness [no pl.] 762 מִזְרָחִיּוּת נ
orientalist 864 מִזְרְחָן ז
seeding, sowing ; sown seed 498 מִזְרָע ז
seeder 550 מַזְרֵעָה נ
injected (medicine, drugs) 200 מֻזְרָק ז
syringe 541 מַזְרֵק ז
fountain 505 מִזְרָקָה נ
marrow [pl. -im or -ot] 232 מֹחַ/מוֹחַ, ר׳ מֹחִים/מֹחוֹת ז
protest 632 מְחָאָה נ
hidden, concealed 200 מֻחְבָּא ז
hiding place, cache 486 מַחְבּוֹא ז
incarceration (military) [no pl.] 485 מַחְבּוֹשׁ ז
bat, baseball bat 541 מַחְבֵּט ז
destroyer, one causing damage 71 מְחַבֵּל ז
churned (butter, cheese) 92 מְחֻבָּץ ז
butter churn 550 מַחְבֵּצָה נ
hugged, embraced 92 מְחֻבָּק ז
ramp, connecting road 513 מֶחְבָּר ז

partition, divider, screen 466 מְחִצָּה נ
half Lit. 516 מַחֲצָה/מֶחֱצָה נ
half 811 מַחֲצִית נ
mat 531 מַחְצֶלֶת נ
extrovert 200 מֻחְצָן ז
impertinent, insolent, cheeky 92 מְחֻצָּף ז
toothpick Lit. 550 מַחְצֵצָה נ
bugler, trumpeter 78 מְחַצְצֵר ז
eraser, rubber 328 מַחַק ז
mimicked, imitated 95 מְחֻקֶּה ז
research 513 מֶחְקָר ז
of research 926 מֶחְקָרִי ז
latrine, privy 529 מַחְרָאָה/מַחֲרָאָה נ
destroyed, demolished 201 מָחֳרָב ז
rhymed; strung - beads 93 מְחֹרָז ז
beaded necklace; medley 534 מַחְרֹזֶת/מַחֲרֹזֶת נ
gurgled 103 מְחֻרְחָר ז
instigator, trouble-maker, agitator 83 מְחַרְחֵר ז
lathe shop 526 מַחְרָטָה/מַחֲרָטָה נ
lathe 550 מַחְרֵטָה/מַחֲרֵטָה נ
destroyer 187 מַחְרִיב ז
awful, frightening, shocking, terrifying 187 מַחְרִיד ז
accursed, annoying - vulgar 97 מְחֻרְיָן ז
confiscated; excommunicated 201 מֻחְרָם/מָחֳרָם ז
grooved, furrowed 93 מְחֹרָץ ז
rifled 93 מְחֹרָק ז
screw-die 534 מַחְרֹקֶת/מַחֲרֹקֶת נ
perforated 93 מְחֹרָר ז
plow (or plough) 550 מַחְרֵשָׁה/מַחֲרֵשָׁה נ
computer 541 מַחְשֵׁב ז
calculator 71 מְחַשֵּׁב ז
calculated 92 מְחֻשָּׁב ז
thought 526 מַחְשָׁבָה/מַחֲשָׁבָה נ
of computer 927 מַחְשְׁבִי ז
craftsmanship 531 מַחְשֶׁבֶת/מַחֲשֶׁבֶת נ
intellectual; of thought 928 מַחְשַׁבְתִּי/מַחֲשַׁבְתִּי ז
computerization 58 מִחְשׁוּב ז
cleavage 485 מַחְשׂוֹף ז
darkened 200 מֻחְשָׁךְ ז
deep darkness Lit. 524 מַחְשָׁךְ ז
stolid, even-tempered; forged 92 מְחֻשָּׁל ז
electrified 97 מְחֻשְׁמָל ז
camera shutter release 541 מַחְשֵׂף ז
hashish den 526 מַחְשָׁשָׁה נ
firepan; brazier 615 מַחְתָּה נ
bumpy, rough Lit. 103 מְחֻתְחָת ז
articulate Adj; sharp, intense 92 מְחֻתָּד ז
diapered 92 מְחֻתָּל ז
in-law 92 מְחֻתָּן ז

underground organization 531 מַחְתֶּרֶת נ
underground Adj 928 מַחְתַּרְתִּי ז
broom 549 מַטְאֲטֵא ז
kitchen 498 מִטְבָּח ז
slaughter Rare 546 מַטְבֵּחַ ז
kitchenette 894 מִטְבָּחוֹן ז
baptizer - Christianity 187 מַטְבִּיל ז
dip N, sauce 496 מַטְבֵּל ז
impressed, stamped 200 מֻטְבָּע ז
coin 547 מַטְבֵּעַ ז
mint 505 מִטְבָּעָה נ
die N, swage 511 מַטְבַּעַת נ
die, swage 533 מִטְבַּעַת נ
fried 92 מְטֻגָּן ז
slanted; biased 206 מֻטֶּה ז
rod, staff; headquarters 540 מַטֶּה ז
span, extent 592 מֻטָּה נ
purified 93 מְטֹהָר ז
spinning mill 508 מַטְוָאָה נ
optimization 45 מִטּוּב ז
spun wool, yarn 535 מַטְוֶה ז
shooting practice; firing range, shooting gallery 498 מִטְוָח ז
aimed, targeted 92 מְטֻוָּח ז
spinning mill 911 מַטְוִיָּה נ
overhead projector; rocket/missile launcher 477 מַטּוֹל ז
airplane 477 מָטוֹס ז
swab 477 מַטּוֹשׁ ז
salvo; barrage 521 מַטָּח ז
food grinder 550 מַטְחֵנָה נ
beneficent; benefactor 197 מֵטִיב/מֵיטִיב ז
whitewashed; plastered 92 מְטֻיָּח ז
covered with mud 92 מְטֻיָּט ז
ingot, bar 405 מֵטִיל ז
tourist, hiker, traveler 71 מְטַיֵּל ז
preacher 195 מַטִּיף ז
of or related to the General Staff (military) 915 מַטְכָּ"לִי ז
patched 200 מֻטְלָא ז
patched 92 מְטֻלָּא ז
task, mission, assignment 471 מַטָּלָה נ
portable, mobile 103 מְטֻלְטָל ז
portable 167 מִטַּלְטֵל ז
rag 810 מַטְלִית נ
contaminated, impure Lit 92 מְטֻמָּא ז
buried treasure 488 מַטְמוֹן ז
cache, subterranean granary 494 מַטְמוּרָה נ
stupid, foolish 103 מְטֻמְטָם ז
amazing Sl. 83 מְטַמְטֵם ז
buried, hidden, concealed 200 מֻטְמָן ז
tea cozy 541 מַטְמֵן ז
landfill 505 מִטְמָנָה נ
assimilated 200 מֻטְמָע ז
granary, cache Lit. 534 מַטְמֹרֶת נ
filthy, dirty 92 מְטֻנָּף ז

flyover, aerial demonstration 523 מַטָּס ז
grove, orchard 521 מַטָּע ז
misleading, deceptive 194 מַטְעֶה ז
mistaken, erroneous 200 מֻטְעֶה ז
mistaken, erroneous 204 מֻטְעֶה ז
stressed, accented; recited 200 מֻטְעָם ז
delicacy 524 מַטְעָם ז
deli 911 מַטְעַמִּיָּה נ
loaded, laden 200 מֻטְעָן ז
load N 497 מִטְעָן ז
charger 544 מַטְעֵן ז
digger-loader (construction) 550 מַטְעֵנָה נ
covered pickup truck 816 מִטְעֲנִית נ
fire extinguisher 535 מַטְפֶּה ז
well-kept, nurtured, cultivated 92 מְטֻפָּח ז
kerchief, handkerchief 511 מִטְפַּחַת נ
drip (medicine) 83 מְטַפְטֵף ז
caregiver; therapist 71 מְטַפֵּל ז
patient N 92 מְטֻפָּל ז
climber (person; plant) 71 מְטַפֵּס ז
stupid, unwise 92 מְטֻפָּשׁ ז
rain, shower Lit. 270 מָטָר ז
troubled, worried 200 מֻטְרָד ז
nuisance, annoyance 496 מִטְרָד ז
purpose, goal, objective; target 471 מַטָּרָה נ
matron 814 מֶטְרוֹנִית נ
metropolitan 915 מֶטְרוֹפּוֹלִיטָנִי ז
foppish, dandified Lit 97 מְטֻרְזָן ז
nuisance, pest Coll. 868 מִטְרְדָן ז
umbrella 911 מִטְרִיָּה נ
wonderful, exciting, beautiful Sl. 187 מַטְרִיף ז
crazy, "nuts" Sl. 105 מְטֻרְלָל ז
crazy, wild; driven nuts 200 מֻטְרָף ז
beater, whisk 541 מַטְרֵף ז
crazy, insane 93 מְטֹרָף ז
blurry, unclear; confused, groggy, dazed Sl. 103 מְטֻשְׁטָשׁ ז
in despair, desperate, hopeless 93 מְיֹאָשׁ ז
imported 92 מְיֻבָּא ז
callused, warty, horny, corned 92 מְיֻבָּל ז
dryer 71 מְיַבֵּשׁ ז
dried; desiccated 92 מְיֻבָּשׁ ז
tiring, exhausting 74 מְיַגֵּעַ ז
exhausted, worn out 92 מְיֻגָּע ז
friendly 92 מְיֻדָּד ז
immediate 915 מִיָּדִי ז
immediacy, promptness [no pl.] 762 מִיָּדִיּוּת נ
information [no pl.] 465 מֵידָע ז

acquaintance; 92 מְיֻדָּע ז definite - Gramm
information 894 מֵידָעוֹן ז booklet
information/data- 863 מֵידָעָן ז base manager/scientist
Judaized 93 מְיֹהָד ז
identity (formal) 740 מִיהוּת נ [no pl.]
mayonnaise 814 מְיוֹנִית נ
project, initiative, 465 מֵיזָם ז plan
sweater, sweatshirt 465 מֵיזָע ז
sweaty 92 מְיֻזָּע ז
special, 92 מְיֻחָד ז extraordinary; unique
specialty, 107 מְיֻחָדוּת נ uniqueness [no dagesh] [no pl.]
awaited, longed for 92 מְיֻחָל ז
in heat - animal 92 מְיֻחָם ז
of distinguished 92 מְיֻחָס ז lineage; attributed to
utmost, best [no pl.] 465 מֵיטָב ז
optimal 915 מֵיטָבִי ז
caving; breakdown, 48 מִיטוּט ז collapse
smallest coin used in 251 מִיל ז Israel during the British mandate period (thousandth part of large monetary unit)
doctor who delivers 71 מְיַלֵּד ז babies
obstetrics [no decl.] 91 מְיַלְּדוּת נ
circumcision 3 מִילָה נ
ash tree 596 מֵילָה נ
watery 915 מֵימִי ז
water canteen 911 מֵימִיָּה נ
hydrogen 876 מֵימָן ז
skilled, proficient 92 מְיֻמָּן ז
skill, expertise, 107 מְיֻמָּנוּת נ proficiency
hydrous, of 915 מֵימָנִי ז hydrogen
edema [no pl.] 685 מַיֶּמֶת נ
kind, species; gender; 251 מִין ז type, sort
heresy [no pl.] 740 מִינוּת נ
sexual 915 מִינִי ז
sexuality [no pl.] 762 מִינִיּוּת נ
ionizer 71 מְיַנֵּן ז
ionized 92 מְיֻנָּן ז
sexist 915 מִינָנִי ז
founder 71 מְיַסֵּד ז
suffering, troubled, 92 מְיֻסָּר ז tormented
designate; appointed 93 מְיֹעָד ז
streamlined, made 93 מְיֹעָל ז more efficient
advisory 72 מְיַעֵץ ז
forested, wooded 93 מְיֹעָר ז
beautified, 95 מְיֻפֶּה ז decorated; authorized agent meyupe koaH
dandyish Sl. 103 מְיֻפְיָף ז
juice 251 מִיץ ז
exported 92 מְיֻצָּא ז
installation (art); 465 מֵיצָב ז status [no pl.]
stabilizer 71 מְיַצֵּב ז
stabilized, reinforced 92 מְיֻצָּב ז
performance, 465 מֵיצָג ז display N
representative Adj 71 מְיַצֵּג ז
represented by 92 מְיֻצָּג ז
nettle tree 357 מֵישׁ ז
populated, settled; 92 מְיֻשָּׁב ז level-headed; solved - dispute
plain, plateau; 389 מִישׁוֹר ז area, level, field; plane (geometry)
level, flat, planar 915 מִישׁוֹרִי ז
flatness, 762 מִישׁוֹרִיּוּת נ planarity [no pl.]
obsolete, old- 92 מְיֻשָּׁן ז fashioned; aged, matured
straight place; 465 מֵישָׁר ז straightness, honesty
straightened, leveled 92 מְיֻשָּׁר ז
screw anchor; dowel 465 מֵיתָד ז
death 3 מִיתָה נ
orphaned; 92 מְיֻתָּם ז abandoned, neglected
string, cord 465 מֵיתָר ז
extra, superfluous; 92 מְיֻתָּר ז redundant
superfluousness 107 מְיֻתָּרוּת נ [no pl.]
pain, grief, 488 מַכְאוֹב ז suffering
painful 187 מַכְאִיב ז
panicle (botany) 541 מַכְבֵּד ז
esteemed, respected; 92 מְכֻבָּד ז worthy person, notable person
Maccabi (world 915 מַכַּבִּי ז Zionist sports club)
Jewish sports 911 מַכַּבִּיָּה נ competition event
connected to cable 92 מְכֻבָּל ז
hat pin, hair pin 550 מַכְבֵּנָה נ
laundered, washed 92 מְכֻבָּס ז
laundry facility 505 מִכְבָּסָה נ
steamroller 541 מַכְבֵּשׁ ז
bayonetted 92 מְכֻדָּן ז
balled, spherical 92 מְכֻדָּר ז
beaten, battered 206 מֻכֶּה ז
blow 585 מַכָּה נ
burn, burning Lit. 499 מִכְוָה נ
starry, star-studded 96 מְכוֹכָב ז
shipping container 480 מְכוּלָה נ
directed, oriented 200 מֻכְוָן ז towards
mechanization 45 מִכּוּן ז
institute; any place 477 מָכוֹן ז specializing in…; foundation, base
tuner, regulator 541 מַכְוֵן ז
directed; tuned, 92 מְכֻוָּן ז adjusted; deliberate
mechanic 909 מְכוֹנַאי ז
machine; 479 מְכוֹנָה נ mechanism Coll.
car 815 מְכוֹנִית נ
adjusted, tuned 105 מְכֻוְנָן ז
founder; founding, 77 מְכוֹנֵן ז establishing; constitutive
shrunken; cramped - 92 מְכֻוָּץ ז muscle
sold; “fixed” sports; 15 מָכוּר ז addicted Col.
homeland, native 479 מְכוֹרָה נ land
pick, pick-axe 493 מַכּוֹשׁ ז
paintbrush, brush 482 מִכְחוֹל ז
colored bluish; 200 מֻכְחָל ז bluish
denied, deniable 200 מֻכְחָשׁ ז
expectorant 74 מְכַיֵּחַ ז
preparatory 481 מְכִינָה נ program
pickpocketed 92 מְכֻיָּס ז
acquaintance 195 מַכִּיר ז
sellable, marketable 20 מָכִיר ז
selling; sale 1 מְכִירָה נ
tank 557 מְכָל/מֵיכָל ז
hybrid 200 מֻכְלָא ז
corral, paddock, 508 מִכְלָאָה נ enclosure; temporary prison camp
stapler 541 מַכְלֵב ז
hybrid 483 מִכְלוֹא ז
whole; entirety 482 מִכְלוֹל ז
included; 200 מֻכְלָל ז generalized,; conglomerated
system, assembly 496 מִכְלָל ז
college 505 מִכְלָלָה נ
shamed, 200 מֻכְלָם ז embarrassed
chlorinated 200 מֻכְלָר ז
grocery, 695 מַכֹּלֶת נ convenience store < ’-k-l
hidden, concealed, 200 מֻכְמָן ז latent
hidden thing; 501 מִכְמָן ז treasure Lit.
speed trap 512 מַכְמֹנֶת נ
fishing net 512 מִכְמֹרֶת נ
quantified 92 מְכֻמָּת ז
denominator 75 מְכַנֶּה ז
called, known as, 95 מְכֻנֶּה ז nicknamed
mechanicalness 762 מֶכָנִיּוּת נ [no pl.]
profitable, lucrative 187 מַכְנִיס ז
lousy 92 מְכֻנָּם ז
collected, compiled; 92 מְכֻנָּס ז gathered
496 מִכְנָס, ר׳ זוגי מִכְנָסַיִם ז trouser, pant leg (pl. dual mikhnasayim)
pair of pants, pair 997 מִכְנָסַיִם ז of trousers
subdued, defeated, 200 מֻכְנָע ז beaten, humiliated
tailcoat [no pl.?] 496 מִכְנָף ז

winged 92 מְכֻנָּף ז
customs, import tax 317 מֶכֶס ז
cover, lid 504 מִכְסֶה ז
covered 95 מְכֻסֶּה ז
ceiling, limit, 499 מִכְסָה נ allotment, ration; quota
mowed, cut 92 מְכֻסָּח ז
lawn mower 550 מַכְסֵחָה נ
lawn mower 90 מְכַסַּחַת נ
silvery; greying 187 מַכְסִיף ז hair
silver-plated; 200 מֻכְסָף ז silvery, shining
ugly, unattractive 93 מְכֹעָר ז
multiplier 187 מַכְפִּיל ז (economics)
doubled; multiplied 200 מֻכְפָּל ז
double; multiplicand 92 מְכֻפָּל ז
product (math) 550 מַכְפֵּלָה נ
familiar, known; 205 מֻכָּר ז recognized
sale; price, value, 317 מֶכֶר ז worth Lit.
acquaintance 520 מַכָּר ז
mine 504 מִכְרֶה, ר׳ מִכְרוֹת ז (coal, gold, etc.) (pl. mikhrot)
declared, announced 200 מֻכְרָז ז
tender, bid; auction 496 מִכְרָז ז
compelled to do 200 מֻכְרָח ז something; must
decisive, deciding 189 מַכְרִיעַ ז
bound - a book 93 מְכֹרָךְ ז
rodent 78 מְכַרְסֵם ז
gnawed, chewed; 97 מְכֻרְסָם ז engraved
decided, settled; 200 מֻכְרָע ז defeated, beaten
obstacle, 482 מִכְשׁוֹל ז impediment
equipping; 58 מִכְשׁוּר ז equipment
appliance, 187 מַכְשִׁיר ז apparatus; instrument, device
mechanic, 863 מַכְשִׁירָן ז technician
obstacle, 550 מַכְשֵׁלָה נ hinderance
sorcerer, magician 71 מְכַשֵּׁף ז
enchanted; 92 מְכֻשָּׁף ז spellbound
sorcery [no decl.] 91 מְכַשְּׁפוּת נ
talented; trained, 200 מֻכְשָׁר ז qualified; prepared; koshered
talent, aptitude; 211 מֻכְשָׁרוּת נ capability
dictated 200 מֻכְתָּב ז
letter 496 מִכְתָּב ז
recipient, addressee 92 מְכֻתָּב ז
writing desk 505 מִכְתָּבָה נ
writing case, 911 מִכְתָּבִיָּה נ portfolio
shard, fragment Lit. 466 מְכִתָּה נ
shoulder pad 488 מַכְתּוֹף ז
stained, dirty 200 מֻכְתָּם ז
epigram 496 מִכְתָּם ז

shouldered - rifle, 92 מְכֻתָּף ז etc.
crowned, 200 מֻכְתָּר ז coronated; head of Arab town or village
surrounded, besieged 92 מְכֻתָּר ז
crater 541 מַכְתֵּשׁ ז
alveolar 927 מַכְתְּשִׁי ז (phonetics)
pothole 531 מַכְתֶּשֶׁת נ (geography)
full 279 מָלֵא ז
exhausting, boring, 194 מַלְאֶה ז tiring
inventory 906 מְלַאי ז
artificial 915 מְלָאכוּתִי ז
artificiality [no 762 מְלָאכוּתִיּוּת נ pl.]
angelic 929 מַלְאָכִי ז
nationalized 200 מֻלְאָם ז
heartwarming 71 מְלַבֵּב ז
fanned - flame; 95 מְלֻבֶּה ז inflamed, impassioned
clothing, garment 490 מַלְבּוּשׁ ז
whitening, 187 מַלְבִּין ז bleaching
rectangle 541 מַלְבֵּן ז
white-hot; clarified; 92 מְלֻבָּן ז resolved
rectangular 915 מַלְבֵּנִי ז
worn, dressed, 200 מֻלְבָּשׁ ז attired
dressed, attired 92 מְלֻבָּשׁ ז
one who gets a 909 מִלְגַּאי ז scholarship
fellowship 602 מִלְגָּה נ
fork-like agricultural 541 מַלְגֵּז ז implement
forklift 550 מַלְגֵּזָה נ
forklift operator 863 מַלְגְּזָן ז
ludicrous Lit. 103 מְלֻגְלָג ז
word 587 מִלָּה נ
white-hot; inflamed 93 מְלֹהָט ז
rousing, exciting 187 מַלְהִיב ז
fullness Lit. [no pl.] 393 מְלוֹא ז
bezel (bibl.); panel 670 מִלּוּאָה נ (arch.); inlay, onlay (dental)
the right to use 393 מְלוֹג ז profits or interest, but not the principal or the asset [no declension, no pl.]
lender 194 מַלְוֶה ז
loan 504 מִלְוֶה ז
escort 75 מְלַוֶּה ז
salty, saline 17 מָלוּחַ ז
orache (plant) 379 מַלּוּחַ ז
escape, rescue, 45 מִלּוּט ז extrication
filling; refill 45 מִלּוּי/מִלּוּא ז
monarchy 18 מְלוּכָה נ
monarchist, royalist 863 מְלוּכָן ז
royalist 915 מְלוּכָנִי ז
literal 956 מִלּוּלִי ז
literalness; 781 מִלּוּלִיּוּת נ verbosity [no pl.]

dictionary; lexicon; 385 מִלּוֹן ז glossary
hotel, inn 478 מָלוֹן ז
hotelier 909 מְלוֹנַאי ז
lexicographer 909 מִלּוֹנַאי ז
hotelier 915 מְלוֹנָאִי ז
lexicographer 915 מִלּוֹנָאִי ז
kennel, doghouse; 480 מְלוּנָה נ lodge (BH)
lexicography [no 740 מִלּוֹנוּת נ pl.]
lexical 915 מִלּוֹנִי ז
kneading machine; 477 מָלוֹשׁ ז mixing bowl
sailor (fem. malaHit) 275 מַלָּח ז
salt 319 מֶלַח ז
salt flat (geog.) 649 מְלֵחָה נ
salty, saline 949 מִלְחִי ז
salt shaker 911 מִלְחִיָּה נ
composer of music 187 מַלְחִין ז
damp, moist 103 מְלַחְלָח ז
welded, soldered 200 מֻלְחָם ז
soldering iron; 544 מַלְחֵם ז blowtorch
war 506 מִלְחָמָה נ
of or related to 923 מִלְחַמְתִּי ז war
belligerence 765 מִלְחַמְתִּיּוּת נ (no decl., no pl.)
presser foot (in 544 מַלְחֵץ ז sewing)
vise (also: vice), 997 מֶלְחָצַיִם ז clamp
clamp (carpentry) 531 מַלְחֶצֶת נ
saltpeter 705 מְלַחַת נ
cement (no 317 מֶלֶט ז declension, constr. only, no pl.)
stupid Sl. 491 מַלְטוּךְ ז
soft, velvety 71 מְלַטֵּף ז
polished 92 מְלֻטָּשׁ ז
polishing 505 מִלְטָשָׁה נ workshop
polishing machine 531 מַלְטֶשֶׁת נ
plenum, general 1 מְלִיאָה נ assembly
herring; food 22 מָלִיחַ ז preserved in salt
saltiness, salinity 24 מְלִיחוּת נ
interceder, 197 מֵלִיץ ז advocate; translator, interpreter Bibl.
flowery phrase, 481 מְלִיצָה נ poetic phrase
flowery, poetic 915 מְלִיצִי ז
using flowery 768 מְלִיצִיּוּת נ language [no pl.]
filling (in 807 מְלִית נ cooking/baking)
function word, 814 מִלִּית נ grammatical word
king 326 מֶלֶךְ ז
united, unified 92 מְלֻכָּד ז
trap 534 מַלְכֹּדֶת נ
booby-trapping 58 מִלְכּוּד ז
kingdom 736 מַלְכוּת נ

manager, principal 72 ז מְנַהֵל
administrator 909 ז מְנַהֲלַאי
administration 506 נ מִנְהָלָה
administrative 924 ז מִנְהָלִי
administrator 865 ז מִנְהָלָן
tunnel 506 נ מִנְהָרָה
terminology 53 ז מִנּוּחַ
calm, serenity, peace Lit. 477 ז מָנוֹחַ ל״ג
rest N 480 נ מְנוּחָה
subscriber; subscribed to; counted 15 ז מָנוּי
appointing; appointment 45 ז מִנּוּי
evil Adj, contemptible; ugly, disgusting 92 ז מְנֻוָּל
dosage 45 ז מִנּוּן
withered, atrophied 92 ז מְנֻוָּן
escape, flight, refuge Lit. 477 ז מָנוֹס
flight, escape, retreat 480 נ מְנוּסָה
prevented from, precluded from; prohibited 17 ז מָנוּעַ
motorization [no pl.] 53 ז מִנּוּעַ
motorized 915 ז מְנוֹעִי
crane; lever; impetus 477 ז מָנוֹף
crane operator 909 ז מְנוֹפַאי
weaver's beam; boom (sailing) 477 ז מָנוֹר
light fixture; lamp 479 נ מְנוֹרָה
having a runny nose 92 ז מְנֻזָּל
monastery 496 ז מִנְזָר
position (music) 523 ז מַנָּח
moderator, discussion leader; show host; MC; advisor (academics) 194 ז מַנְחֶה
directed, guided, supervised; moderated, chaired 204 ז מֻנְחֶה
afternoon prayer service (Jewish); gift 598 נ מִנְחָה
glossary 894 ז מִנְחוֹן
cursed; unlucky Sl. 491 ז מְנַחוּס
bequeathed, bestowed 200 ז מֻנְחָל
comforted, consoled 92 ז מְנֻחָם
diviner, fortune teller 72 ז מְנַחֵשׁ
landed (aircraft, etc.) 200 ז מֻנְחָת
landing pad, landing strip 497 ז מִנְחָת
absorber, attenuator, damper 544 ז מְנַחֵת
neutralized 97 ז מְנֻטְרָל
stock, share 4 נ מְנָיָה
stock, share 632 נ מְנָיָה
wrapped in plastic 97 ז מְנֻיְלָן
number amount; quorum for Jewish public prayer 858 ז מִנְיָן
motive, motivation 198 ז מֵנִיעַ
preventing; prevention 1 נ מְנִיעָה
hand-held fan 481 נ מְנִיפָה
מַנְכָּ״ל = מְנַהֵל כְּלָלִי ז 409 genreral manager
alienated; estranged 92 ז מְנֻכָּר

sleepy, drowsy, groggy 103 ז מְנֻמְנָם
polite, well-mannered 92 ז מְנֻמָּס
explained, reasoned 92 ז מְנֻמָּק
speckled, splotched 92 ז מְנֻמָּר
freckled 92 ז מְנֻמָּשׁ
experienced 95 ז מְנֻסֶּה
worded 92 ז מְנֻסָּח
sawn, cut 92 ז מְנֻסָּר
prism 505 נ מִנְסָרָה
prismatic 915 ז מִנְסַרְתִּי
prevention [no pl.] 319 ז מֶנַע
range, diapason (music) 497 ז מִנְעָד
lock N 490 ז מַנְעוּל
locksmith 863 ז מַנְעוּלָן
footwear Lit. 497 ז מִנְעָל
key in musical instrument 84 ז מַנְעֲנֵעַ
shaken out - carpet etc. 93 ז מְנֹעָר
sifted, sieved; screened, selected 95 ז מְנֻפֶּה
overly muscular Sl. 491 ז מְנַפּוּחַ
inflated, blown up 92 ז מְנֻפָּח
carded - raw wool, cotton 92 ז מְנֻפָּט
cotton gin 550 נ מַנְפֵּטָה
waved 103 ז מְנֻפְנָף
shattered, broken; carded, combed - textiles 92 ז מְנֻפָּץ
issued, distributed 200 ז מֻנְפָּק
dispenser 541 ז מַנְפֵּק
feathery 95 ז מְנֻצֶּה
victor; winner; conductor (music) 74 ז מְנַצֵּחַ
vanquished, defeated 92 ז מְנֻצָּח
exploiter 71 ז מְנַצֵּל
utilized, exploited 92 ז מְנֻצָּל
hole puncher, perforator 71 ז מְנַקֵּב
perforated, punctured 92 ז מְנֻקָּב
vowelizer 71 ז מְנַקֵּד
vowelized; dotted 92 ז מְנֻקָּד
cleaner, janitor 75 ז מְנַקֶּה
cleaned; cleared, acquitted 95 ז מְנֻקֶּה
purger, remover of thigh tendon from slaughtered animal 71 ז מְנַקֵּר
pierced, punctured; purged - meat 92 ז מְנֻקָּר
carrier, sling for babies 498 ז מַנְשָׂא
bite (dentistry) 496 ז מִנְשָׁךְ
dispossessed, disinherited; banished, exiled 92 ז מְנֻשָּׁל
aspirated - phonetics 92 ז מְנֻשָּׁף
kissed 92 ז מְנֻשָּׁק
manifest, platform (politics) 496 ז מִנְשָׁר
מְנָת = מָנָה, ר׳ מְנָאוֹת/מְנָיוֹת נ 312 portion, pl. mena'ot/menayot
directed, guided; demarcated into lanes 92 ז מְנֻתָּב

mint, peppermint 600 נ מִנְתָּה
surgeon; analyst; analyzer 74 ז מְנַתֵּחַ
person who has undergone an operation 92 ז מְנֻתָּח
surgery - profession [no decl.] 91 נ מְנַתְּחוּת
shattered, broken, destroyed 92 ז מְנֻתָּץ
cut, disconnected 92 ז מְנֻתָּק
tax; fee, dues 223 ז מַס
corrupt, despicable 93 ז מְסֹאָב
essayist 908 ז מַסָּאִי
of, or related to, essay 915 ז מַסָּאִי
endorser (banking) 199 ז מֵסֵב
bearing (mechanics) 467 ז מֵסַב
pub 508 נ מִסְבָּאָה
party; getting together; circumstance 466 נ מְסִבָּה
support, truss (construction) 496 ז מִסְבָּךְ
complicated, complex; entangled 92 ז מְסֻבָּךְ
soaped, soapy; tricked, "fixed" Sl. 92 ז מְסֻבָּן
subsidized (normative: mesuvsad) 97 ז מְסֻבְסָד
mosque 496 ז מִסְגָּד
framing 58 ז מִסְגּוּר
capable, able 92 ז מְסֻגָּל
capability, fitness, suitability [no pl.] 107 נ מְסֻגָּלוּת
one who edits text for style 78 ז מְסַגְנֵן
stylized, well-written; stylish 97 ז מְסֻגְנָן
tormented, tortured by absence of physical pleasures 92 ז מְסֻגָּף
turned in to the authorities; parenthetical 200 ז מֻסְגָּר
locksmith 541 ז מַסְגֵּר
closed, shut; introspective 92 ז מְסֻגָּר
locksmith shop 911 נ מַסְגֵּרִיָּה
frame; framework 509 נ מִסְגֶּרֶת
formation, parade, roll call; order (monks, etc.) 496 ז מִסְדָּר
tidy, neat, organized; taken care of Coll.; established Coll. 92 ז מְסֻדָּר
typesetting shop 505 נ מִסְדָּרָה
typesetting machine 531 נ מַסְדֶּרֶת
essay; despair, great sorrow Lit. 585 נ מַסָּה
one round trip of a service vehicle (bus, etc.) 477 ז מָסוֹב
outcome, result, consequence 96 ז מְסוֹבָב
sorted, categorized; classified, confidential 92 ז מְסֻוָּג
institutionalization 45 ז מִסּוּד
camouflaged, hidden, concealed 204 ז מֻסְוֶה

mask, guise 535 מַסְוֶה ז
switch, turnout (in railway tracks) 477 מְסוֹט ז
taxation 45 מִסּוּי ז
shielding; screening, separating 45 מִסּוּךְ ז
rot Lit-rare [no pl.] 393 מְסוֹס ז
conveyor belt 493 מַסּוֹעַ ז
terminal 477 מָסוֹף ז
portable terminal 894 מְסוֹפוֹן ז
helicopter 493 מַסּוֹק ז
helicopter pilot 909 מַסּוֹקַאי ז
devoted, loyal; given, granted; passed by tradition 15 מָסוּר ז
saw 493 מַסּוֹר ז
Masorah (notations on the exact traditional text of the bible) 667 מָסוֹרָה נ
hacksaw 818 מַסּוֹרִית נ
exhausted Sl. 491 מַסְחוּט ז
commercialization [no pl.] 58 מִסְחוּר ז
juice extractor, juicer 550 מַסְחֵטָה נ
trade [no pl.] 497 מִסְחָר ז
commercial 924 מִסְחָרִי ז
commercialism [no pl.] 762 מִסְחָרִיּוּת נ
spinning, dizzy; dazed, confused 103 מְסֻחְרָר ז
dizzying 85 מְסַחְרֵר ז
hesitant, restrained 92 מְסֻיָּג ז
whitewashed 92 מְסֻיָּד ז
nightmarish 92 מְסֻיָּט ז
specific, defined, certain 92 מְסֻיָּם ז
soluble, dissolvable 20 מָסִיס ז
solubility, dissolvability 24 מְסִיסוּת נ
supporting, contributive 74 מְסַיֵּעַ ז
fire stoker 195 מַסִּיק ז
olive harvest 20 מָסִיק ז
delivery, transmission 1 מְסִירָה נ
devotion, dedication 24 מְסִירוּת נ
inciter, instigator 197 מֵסִית ז
screen; curtain 274 מָסָךְ ז
mask, disguise; face mask (cosmetics) 470 מַסֵּכָה נ
poor, miserable Sl. 491 מַסְכּוּן ז
agreed, agreed upon; accepted, customary, common 200 מֻסְכָּם ז
summarizing 71 מְסַכֵּם ז
decided, agreed; summarized 92 מְסֻכָּם ז
convention, consensus 203 מֻסְכָּמָה נ
poor person 502 מִסְכֵּן ז
dangerous; risky 92 מְסֻכָּן ז
sugar-coated, glazed 92 מְסֻכָּר ז
sugar bowl 509 מִסְכֶּרֶת נ
stethoscope 541 מַסְכֵּת ז
tractate (of the Mishna); revue, review 683 מַסֶּכֶת נ
platelayer 909 מְסִלַּאי ז
railroad track; track; orbit 466 מְסִלָּה נ
path, track, course; lane; runway; orbit 490 מַסְלוּל ז
relating to a path, lane, track, orbit 912 מַסְלוּלִי ז
Muslim 915 מֻסְלְמִי ז
curly 103 מְסֻלְסָל ז
stony, rocky 92 מְסֻלָּע ז
rockery (gardening) 507 מִסְלָעָה נ
distorted, deceptive, untrue 92 מְסֻלָּף ז
removed; paid; cleared 92 מְסֻלָּק ז
clearing house (banking) 505 מִסְלָקָה נ
melting, softening, dissolving 66 מִסְמוּס ז
nailing 58 מִסְמוּר ז
authorized; certified 200 מֻסְמָךְ ז
document; certificate, diploma 496 מִסְמָךְ ז
symbolized 92 מְסֻמָּל ז
drugged, groggy 92 מְסֻמָּם ז
marked, indicated; signposted 92 מְסֻמָּן ז
nail 541 מַסְמֵר ז
nailed; glued, stuck 92 מְסֻמָּר ז
rivet 531 מַסְמֶרֶת נ
blinding; dazzling 78 מְסַנְוֵר ז
dazzled, dazed, blinded 97 מְסֻנְוָר ז
filter 541 מַסְנֵן ז
filtered, strained 92 מְסֻנָּן ז
strainer; colander 509 מִסְנֶנֶת נ
strainer Coll 89 מְסַנֶּנֶת נ
incorporated, annexed, affiliated 92 מְסֻנָּף ז
syncopated 97 מְסֻנְקָף ז
hike, march; journey, voyage 522 מַסָּע (ר' -וֹת/-ים) ז
backrest; armrest 497 מִסְעָד ז
restaurant 506 מִסְעָדָה נ
restaurateur 865 מִסְעֲדָן ז
inflaming, inciteful 187 מַסְעִיר ז
fork (in a road); intersection; branching; bifurcation 497 מִסְעָף ז
branched 93 מְסֹעָף ז
stormy; enraged Lit. 200 מֻסְעָר ז
blotter 541 מַסְפֵּג ז
eulogy 502 מִסְפֵּד ז
animal feed [no pl.] 483 מִסְפּוֹא ז
numbering 58 מִסְפּוּר ז
annexed 92 מְסֻפָּח ז
enough, sufficient 187 מַסְפִּיק ז
docking area in a shipyard; division in the Israeli navy 496 מִסְפָּן ז
shipping dock 505 מִסְפָּנָה נ
satisfactory 71 מְסַפֵּק ז
doubtful, uncertain 92 מְסֻפָּק ז
supplied, provided 92 מְסֻפָּק ז
number 496 מִסְפָּר ז
narrator 71 מְסַפֵּר ז
have had a haircut 92 מְסֻפָּר ז
related, recounted - story 92 מְסֻפָּר ז
barber shop, hairdresser shop 505 מִסְפָּרָה נ
numerical 924 מִסְפָּרִי ז
scissors 997 מִסְפָּרַיִם ז
scissor kick (soccer) 509 מִסְפֶּרֶת נ
heated, fired 205 מֻסָּק ז
cleared of stones 92 מְסֻקָּל ז
conclusion 529 מַסְקָנָה נ
curious 97 מְסַקְרָן ז
message; theme 317 מֶסֶר ז
barred - window; alternating, discontinuous 93 מְסֹרָג ז
knitting needle 550 מַסְרֵגָה נ
puny, miserable, ,neglected Sl 491 מַסְרוּחַ ז
film, videoed 200 מֻסְרָט ז
video camera 550 מַסְרֵטָה נ
carcinogenic 78 מְסַרְטֵן ז
stinking, smelly, odious 189 מַסְרִיחַ ז
cinema projectionist 187 מַסְרִיט ז
castrated, emasculated 93 מְסֹרָס ז
comb 541 מַסְרֵק ז
combed, coiffed 93 מְסֹרָק ז
combing machine, carder (textiles) 550 מַסְרֵקָה נ
tradition 696 מָסֹרֶת נ
traditional 915 מָסָרְתִּי ז
traditionalism [no pl.] 762 מָסָרְתִּיּוּת נ
reasonable, probable; it turns out that… 161 מִסְתַּבֵּר ז
one who abstains from physical pleasures 161 מִסְתַּגֵּף ז
hiding place; refuge 482 מִסְתּוֹר ז
mysterious 915 מִסְתּוֹרִי ז
mystery [no pl.] 766 מִסְתּוֹרִיּוּת נ
dissenter, one who expresses doubts 161 מִסְתַּיֵּג ז
stopper, plug, valve 541 מַסְתֵּם ז
infiltrator 161 מִסְתַּנֵּן ז
hidden, concealed 200 מֻסְתָּר ז
stonemason 71 מְסַתֵּת ז
chiseled 92 מְסֻתָּת ז
adapter, arranger (music); processor (food, words) 71 מְעַבֵּד ז
processed; adapted, altered 92 מְעֻבָּד ז
laboratory 526 מַעְבָּדָה נ
of laboratory 915 מַעְבַּדְתִּי ז
thick N Lit. 538 מַעֲבֶה ז
condenser 75 מְעַבֶּה ז

thickened 95 מְעֻבֶּה ז
employer 188 מַעֲבִיד ז
passageway; passage; transition 519 מַעֲבָר ז
intercalary 92 מְעֻבָּר ז
transit camp 526 מַעְבָּרָה נ
Hebraized 97 מְעֻבְרָת ז
ferry 534 מַעְבֹּרֶת נ
rolling pin; roller 191 מַעֲגִילָה/מַעְגִּילָה נ
rounded 92 מְעֻגָּל ז
circle; cycle; range, scope 519 מַעְגָּל/מַעֲגָל ז
circular 925 מַעְגָּלִי/מַעֲגָלִי ז
harbor, anchorage, marina 519 מַעֲגָן ז
based on; fixed tightly 92 מְעֻגָּן ז
delicacy 525 מַעֲדָן ז
refined, sophisticated; elegant; genteel, delicate 92 מְעֻדָּן ז
deli 911 מַעֲדַנִּיָּה נ
preferred, favored 201 מֻעֲדָף ז
hoe 542 מַעְדֵּר/מַעֲדֵר ז
coin Lit. 583 מָעָה נ
encouraged, reassured, emboldened 96 מְעוֹדָד ז
encouraging 77 מְעוֹדֵד ז
catapult 477 מָעוֹט ז
minority; small quantity; diminution 50 מִעוּט ז
squashed, trapped 15 מָעוּךְ ז
abuser 71 מְעַוֵּל ז
residence; day care center; dorm 478 מָעוֹן ז
residence Lit.-rare 479 מְעוֹנָה נ
imagination, vision; flight, hovering 477 מָעוֹף ז
flying, airborne 77 מְעוֹפֵף ז
arousing, stimulating 77 מְעוֹרֵר ז
distorted, twisted; distortion 92 מְעֻוָּת ז
refuge, fortress; stronghold 555 מָעוֹז ז
little, few; a little 313 מְעַט ז
cover; cloak 538 מַעֲטֶה ז
crowning; decorated, glorified Lit. 188 מַעֲטִיר ז
wrapping 519 מַעֲטָף ז
envelope 527 מַעֲטָפָה נ
mantle; casing; surround; dura 532 מַעֲטֶפֶת נ
decorated, adorned 92 מְעֻטָּר ז
intestine, bowel 259 מְעִי ז
stumbling 1 מְעִידָה נ
squashable, squeezable 20 מָעִיךְ ז
squashing, mashing, crushing 1 מְעִיכָה נ
coat, cloak 405 מְעִיל ז
embezzlement 1 מְעִילָה נ
small/light coat 895 מְעִילוֹן ז
rhombus 92 מְעֻיָּן ז
tiring, exhausting 71 מְעַיֵּף ז

troublesome, burdensome 197 מֵעִיק ז
delayed; restrained - law 92 מְעֻכָּב ז
digested 92 מְעֻכָּל ז
embezzlement [no pl.] 328 מַעַל ז
raising, lifting Lit. [no pl.] 343 מֹעַל ז
incline, slope; rise, ascent 539 מַעֲלֶה ז
excellent, terrific, wonderful 95 מְעֻלֶּה ז
advantage; degree; step 616 מַעֲלָה נ
insulting 188 מַעֲלִיב ז
elevator 811 מַעֲלִית נ
inequity, misdeed 519 מַעֲלָלִים) ז
unconscious 92 מְעֻלָּף ז
position; status; class; occasion 519 מַעֲמָד ז
laid out in pages - publishing 92 מְעֻמָּד ז
while standing 92 מְעֻמָּד ז
candidate, nominee, contender 201 מֻעֲמָד/מֻעֳמָד ז
candidacy 211 מֻעֲמָדוּת נ
of (social) class 925 מַעֲמָדִי ז
deep; insightful; intensive 188 מַעֲמִיק ז
starched 97 מְעֻמְלָן ז
dim, dull, vague 92 מְעֻמָּם ז
load, capacity 519 מַעֲמָס ז
burden 527 מַעֲמָסָה נ
dim, dull, vague, blurry 103 מְעֻמְעָם ז
depth 525 מַעֲמָק ז
confronted 92 מְעֻמָּת ז
address 328 מַעַן ז
sling 519 מַעֲנָב ז
wearing a tie 92 מְעֻנָּב ז
response 538 מַעֲנֶה (ר׳ -ים/-וֹת) ז
tortured 95 מְעֻנֶּה ז
interesting 78 מְעַנְיֵן ז
interested 97 מְעֻנְיָן ז
furrow Lit. 809 מַעֲנִית נ
cloudy, overcast 92 מְעֻנָּן ז
grant 519 מַעֲנָק ז
employer 188 מַעֲסִיק ז
employee 201 מֻעֲסָק ז
illegal immigrant during the British Mandate period 187 מַעְפִּיל ז
a daring action Lit. 518 מַעְפָּל ז
rotten, stinking, moldy 92 מְעֻפָּשׁ ז
ganglion 519 מַעֲצָב ז
designer 71 מְעַצֵּב ז
designed 92 מְעֻצָּב ז
neglect, aimlessness Lit. [no pl.] 551 מַעֲצֵבָה נ
draw-knife 519 מַעֲצָד ז
woodwork (in weapons) 538 מַעֲצֶה ז
woody - (botany) 95 מְעֻצֶּה ז

mental block, inhibition; jam (in weapon); brakes 484 מַעְצוֹר ז
saddening; unfortunate 188 מַעֲצִיב ז
intensified; nominalized - linguistics 201 מֻעֲצָם ז
(world) power 527 מַעֲצָמָה נ
arrest 519 מַעֲצָר/מַעְצָר ז
surveillance; tracking; follow-up 519 מַעֲקָב ז
cubic 92 מְעֻקָּב ז
banister, railing 538 מַעֲקֶה (ר׳ -ים/-וֹת) ז
bent, curved; attached by lien, confiscated 92 מְעֻקָּל ז
curved, bent, twisted 92 מְעֻקָּם ז
bypass 519 מַעֲקָף ז
antiseptic, sterilizing 71 מְעַקֵּר ז
sterilized, sterile, germ-free 92 מְעֻקָּר ז
obstacle, difficulty Lit. 525 מַעֲקָשׁ ז
west [no pl.] 519 מַעֲרָב ז
mixed; involved 93 מְעֹרָב ז
western 925 מַעֲרָבִי ז
western character [no pl.] 762 מַעֲרָבִיּוּת נ
cement mixer; blender 78 מְעַרְבֵּל ז
cave 632 מְעָרָה נ
rolling pin 484 מַעֲרוֹךְ ז
naked, nude, exposed, revealed 97 מְעֻרְטָל ז
Jewish evening prayer service 188 מַעֲרִיב ז
assessor, adjuster, appraiser 188 מַעֲרִיךְ ז
admirer, fan 188 מַעֲרִיץ ז
alignment, arrangement, array 519 מַעֲרָךְ ז
war, battle; campaign; system; act 527 מַעֲרָכָה נ
set; editorial staff; system 532 מַעֲרֶכֶת נ
systemic 915 מַעַרְכְתִּי ז
unstable, disturbed 103 מְעֹרְעָר ז
guillotine (Rare) 532 מַעֲרֶפֶת נ
weeded 92 מְעֻשָּׂב ז
deed 538 מַעֲשֶׂה ז
affected, artificial, false, unnatural 95 מְעֻשֶּׂה ז
practical 915 מַעֲשִׂי ז
tale 911 מַעֲשִׂיָּה נ
practicality [no pl.] 762 מַעֲשִׂיּוּת נ
smoker 71 מְעַשֵּׁן ז
smoked - meat etc. 92 מְעֻשָּׁן ז
meat smoker; chimney (arch.) 551 מַעֲשֵׁנָה נ
enriched, fortified (food) 201 מֻעֲשָׁר ז
tithing 543 מַעֲשֵׂר ז
tithed 92 מְעֻשָּׂר ז
postdated 92 מְעֻתָּד ז
copyist 188 מַעְתִּיק ז

disturbed 200 מְפֹרָע ז
psychology; wild, disruptive Sl.
payment on account (of past debt) 507 מִפְרָעָה נ
disturbed state (psych.) 211 מְפֹרָעוּת נ
retroactive 915 מִפְרַעִי ז
gulf, bay, inlet 496 מִפְרָץ ז
full of bays - coastline 93 מְפֹרָץ ז
aneurism 509 מִפְרֶצֶת נ
joint 496 מִפְרָק ז
liquidator 73 מְפָרֵק ז
dismantled, disassembled 93 מְפֹרָק ז
recumbent 97 מְפֻרְקָד ז
articular (anatomy); articulated 924 מִפְרָקִי ז
neck 531 מַפְרֶקֶת נ
crumbled; disintegrated 93 מְפֹרָר ז
sail 496 מִפְרָשׂ ז
commentator; exegete 73 מְפָרֵשׁ ז
explicit; interpreted, annotated 93 מְפֹרָשׁ ז
sailboat 816 מִפְרָשִׂית נ
abstract, intangible; unrealistic 200 מֻפְשָׁט ז
simplified 92 מְפֻשָּׁט ז
abstractness 211 מֻפְשָׁטוּת נ
rolled up, rolled back 200 מֻפְשָׁל ז
crotch, groin 507 מִפְשָׂעָה נ
spread; split 496 מִפְשָׂק ז
spread apart - arms etc. 92 מְפֻשָּׂק ז
conciliatory 71 מְפַשֵּׁר ז
enticing, tempting 75 מְפַתֶּה ז
indexing 59 מִפְתּוּחַ ז
no longer a virgin Sl. 491 מְפֻתּוּח(ה) ז
opening; aperture; span 498 מִפְתָּח ז
developer 74 מְפַתֵּחַ ז
developed, advanced 92 מְפֻתָּח ז
key; index; spanner 547 מַפְתֵּחַ ז
surprising 189 מַפְתִּיעַ ז
twisting, winding; complicated 92 מְפֻתָּל ז
threshold 496 מִפְתָּן ז
surprised, amazed 200 מֻפְתָּע ז
oppressor Bibl. 231 מֵץ ז
inventory 906 מְצַאי ז
military post or position 205 מֻצָּב ז
status 500 מִצָּב ז
situation 520 מַצָּב ז
tombstone, gravestone; memorial monument 470 מַצֵּבָה נ
workforce; (military) strength; inventory 471 מַצָּבָה נ
stockpile, accumulation, cache 482 מִצְבּוֹר ז

pincer 541 מַצְבֵּט ז
pair of pincers; pince nez 997 מִצְבָּטַיִם ז
situational 915 מַצָּבִי ז
military leader 187 מַצְבִּיא ז
voter 189 מַצְבִּיעַ ז
marker pen 546 מַצְבֵּעַ ז
battery 541 מַצְבֵּר ז
in a bad mood Sl. 97 מְצֻבְרָח ז
tombstone Rare; position Lit. 683 מַצֶּבֶת נ
presentation, display 520 מֻצָּג ז
presentation (computing) 683 מַצֶּגֶת נ
stronghold 557 מְצָד ז
fortress 632 מְצָדָה נ
pillbox (guard post) 814 מִצְדִּית נ
Matzah 585 מַצָּה נ
colored yellow, yellowed, yellowish 200 מֻצְהָב ז
declarant; person giving an affidavit 187 מַצְהִיר ז
cry of joy Lit. 506 מִצְהָלָה נ
declared, announced 200 מֻצְהָר ז
customs declaration 497 מִצְהָר ז
positioning (marketing) 45 מִצּוּב ז
chase, hunt, pursuit 477 מָצוֹד ז
fortress, stronghold 480 מְצוּדָה נ
commandment; decree; good deed, act of kindness 499 מִצְוָה נ
found, located; common 15 מָצוּי ז
utilization; summarization; extraction 45 מִצּוּי ז
depth, deep water (alt. of *metsula*) 399 מְצוֹל ז
depth, deep water 480 מְצוּלָה נ
reaching a compromise; averaging 53 מִצּוּעַ ז
float, buoy 477 מָצוֹף ז
sucked 15 מָצוּץ ז
cliff, precipice 15 מָצוּק ז
cliff, precipice, bluff 477 מָצוֹק/מָצוּק ז
trouble, distress 480 מְצוּקָה נ
siege, blockade [no pl.] 477 מָצוֹר ז
forehead 324 מֵצַח ז
(cap) visor 911 מִצְחִיָּה נ
smelly, stinky 187 מַצְחִין ז
funny, amusing 187 מַצְחִיק ז
comedian Coll. 868 מַצְחִיקָן ז
codex 497 מִצְחָף ז
brushed, polished, sparkling clean 103 מְצֻחְצָח ז
stand-up comedy Lit. 497 מִצְחָק ז
quoted 92 מְצֻטָּט ז
finding; bargain, find 1 מְצִיאָה נ
reality 24 מְצִיאוּת נ
realistic 915 מְצִיאוּתִי ז

realism, realistic conduct [no pl.] 762 מְצִיאוּתִיּוּת נ
presenter, exhibitor 195 מַצִּיג ז
equipped 92 מְצֻיָּד ז
cracker 911 מַצִּיָּה נ
lifeguard 195 מַצִּיל ז
excellent; marked 92 מְצֻיָּן ז
fringed - garment; crested - bird 92 מְצֻיָּץ ז
sucking 1 מְצִיצָה נ
Peeping Tom, voyeur; busybody 863 מְצִיצָן ז
voyeuristic 915 מְצִיצָנִי ז
bothersome, troublesome, annoying 197 מֵצִיק ז
drawn; illustrated 92 מְצֻיָּר ז
lighter, cigarette lighter 195 מַצִּית ז
saved, rescued 205 מֻצָּל ז
crossed; cross-bred 200 מֻצְלָב ז
crossed 92 מְצֻלָּב ז
Christian church or monastery 550 מִצְלֶבֶת נ
small bell; cymbal 466 מְצִלָּה נ
tone (music), sound quality 482 מִצְלוֹל ז
successful, accomplished 200 מֻצְלָח ז
successful 189 מַצְלִיחַ ז
successful person Coll. 868 מַצְלִיחָן ז
party whip (who keeps a watchful eye over elected members) 187 מַצְלִיף ז
shaded (painting, drawing) 200 מֻצְלָל ז
photographed, photocopied 92 מְצֻלָּם ז
camera 550 מַצְלֵמָה נ
polygon; polygonal 92 מְצֻלָּע ז
hogback (geomorphology) 511 מִצְלַעַת נ
scarred 92 מְצֻלָּק ז
clutch 541 מַצְמֵד ז
blinking 66 מִצְמוּץ ז
limited, small, reduced 103 מְצֻמְצָם ז
wrinkled, withered; gaunt 92 מְצֻמָּק ז
hair-raising, horrifying 85 מְצַמְרֵר ז
junction (electronics) 496 מִצְמָת ז
censored 97 מְצֻנְזָר ז
parachuted 200 מֻצְנָח ז
parachute N 498 מִצְנָח ז
parachute 546 מַצְנֵחַ ז
toaster 541 מַצְנֵם ז
cooler 541 מַצְנֵן ז
suffering from a cold 92 מְצֻנָּן ז
hidden, concealed 200 מֻצְנָע ז
miter (ritual clothing); conical hat 509 מִצְנֶפֶת נ
offered, proffered; suggested 205 מֻצָּע ז

chopped; cut, 92 מְקֻצָּץ ז
shortened; trimmed
shortened, 92 מְקֻצָּר ז
abbreviated
grain harvester 550 מַקְצֵרָה נ
a few, some, a little 496 מִקְצָת ז
[no pl.]
cockroach (fem. 275 מַקָּק ז
makakit)
legend, key; the 498 מִקְרָא ז
Bible (hamikra)
reader, anthology 508 מִקְרָאָה נ
of readings
light table; 550 מַקְרָאָה נ
teleprompter
biblical 924 מִקְרָאִי ז
sacrificed 200 מֻקְרָב ז
close associate, 93 מְקֹרָב ז
crony
incident; chance; 504 מִקְרֶה ז
case
accidental 915 מִקְרִי ז
coincidence [no 762 מִקְרִיּוּת נ
pl.]
balding 189 מַקְרִיחַ ז
projectionist 187 מַקְרִין ז
browned, grilled, 200 מֻקְרָם ז
crusted
irradiated; screened 200 מֻקְרָן ז
(film etc.)
projector 541 מַקְרֵן ז
movie projector 550 מַקְרֵנָה נ
scrubbed 97 מְקֻרְצָף ז
grounded 97 מְקֻרְקָע ז
land, real estate 998 מְקַרְקְעִין ז
scalped 97 מְקֻרְקָף ז
refrigerator 541 מַקְרֵר ז
refrigerator 73 מְקָרֵר ז
cooled, chilled 93 מְקֹרָר ז
congealed 200 מֻקְרָשׁ ז
key (on a keyboard) 520 מַקָּשׁ ז
solidified, 204 מֻקְשֶׁה ז
hardened; perplexing,
incomprehensible
field (esp. of 499 מִקְשָׁה נ
watermelons); beaten work;
solidity
adorned, decorated 92 מְקֻשָּׁט ז
covered with 103 מְקֻשְׂקָשׂ ז
scales
scribbled on 103 מְקֻשְׁקָשׁ ז
intercom 541 מַקְשֵׁר ז
liaison officer 71 מְקַשֵּׁר ז
connected; tied; 92 מְקֻשָּׁר ז
cohesive; well-connected
arched 92 מְקֻשָּׁת ז
bitter 226 מַר ז
myrrh [no pl.] 229 מֹר ז
view, sight 536 מַרְאֶה ז
mirror 615 מַרְאָה נ
interviewer 79 מְרַאְיֵן/מְרַאֲיֵן ז
vision; view; 810 מַרְאִית נ
point of view [no pl.]
maximum [no pl.] 467 מֵרַב ז
stained, dirty Lit 92 מְרֻבָּב ז

carpet, rug 524 מַרְבָד ז
layered 92 מְרֻבָּד ז
great, many, 95 מְרֻבֶּה ז
multiple, numerous
maximal 915 מְרַבִּי ז
most, the majority 810 מַרְבִּית נ
[no pl.]
thickened with roux 92 מְרֻבָּךְ ז
quadrangular; square 92 מְרֻבָּע ז
being square; 107 מְרֻבָּעוּת נ
acting strictly by the rule Col.
[no pl.]
deposit, stratum 496 מִרְבָּץ ז
(geology)
fattened calf 541 מַרְבֵּק (עֵגֶל) ז
rest, peace, 489 מַרְגּוֹעַ ז
relaxation
angry, annoyed 92 מְרֻגָּז ז
soothing, calming, 189 מַרְגִּיעַ ז
placating; analgesic
spy 71 מְרַגֵּל ז
foot (of a bed, hill, 998 מַרְגְּלוֹת נ
mountain)
gem, pearl (is it a 814 מַרְגָּלִית נ
suffix here?)
mortar (weaponry) 550 מַרְגֵּמָה נ
pimpernel (plant) 814 מַרְגָּנִית נ
(is it a suffix here?)
felt, sensed, 200 מֻרְגָּשׁ ז
perceived, noticeable
mood, general 518 מַרְגָּשׁ ז
feeling Coll. [no pl.]
excited; inflamed 92 מְרֻגָּשׁ ז
rebellion, 317 מֶרֶד ז
insurrection; uprising
flattened, rolled out 92 מְרֻדָּד ז
honey harvest; 504 מִרְדֶּה ז
bread shovel
rebellion, mutiny 736 מַרְדּוּת נ
Lit. [no pl.]
causing 187 מַרְדִּים ז
sleepiness; anesthetic
rebel N 846 מַרְדָּן ז
rebelliousness [no 752 מַרְדָּנוּת נ
pl
rebellious 969 מַרְדָּנִי ז
shepherd's staff 546 מַרְדֵּעַ ז
Rare
saddlecloth 533 מַרְדַּעַת נ
chase N 496 מִרְדָּף ז
gall, bile 582 מָרָה נ
furnished 93 מְרֹהָט ז
spectacular, 187 מַרְהִיב ז
breathtaking
maximization [no pl.] 51 מֵרוּב ז
serrated, notched, 15 מָרוּג ז
corrugated
depressed Lit 15 מָרוּד ז
thirst-quenching 194 מַרְוֶה ז
spread, smeared 17 מָרוּחַ ז
with a profit Sl. 200 מֻרְוָח ז
space 498 מִרְוָח ז
spacious 92 מְרֻוָּח ז
height, peak; 477 מָרוֹם ז
heavens, sky

festive, gay, happy 96 מְרוֹמָם ז
Maronite 915 מָרוֹנִי ז
running 480 מְרוּצָה נ
polishing; 51 מֵרוּק ז
absolution, cleansing, erasure of
sins
Moroccan 915 מָרוֹקָאִי ז
emptied 96 מְרוֹקָן ז
Moroccan 915 מָרוֹקָנִי ז
embitterment 51 מֵרוּר ז
impoverished 96 מְרוֹשָׁשׁ ז
authority [no pl.] 733 מָרוּת נ
eaves trough, gutter, 541 מַרְזֵב ז
drainpipe
pub, tavern 546 מַרְזֵחַ ז
innkeeper, 867 מַרְזְחָן ז
bartender Rare
sledgehammer, 531 מַרְזֶפֶת נ
mallet Rare
widened, 200 מֻרְחָב ז
broadened, extended
wide open space, 514 מֶרְחָב ז
spaciousness; space, room
spacial 926 מֶרְחָבִי ז
daydreaming Sl. 72 מְרַחֵף ז
public bath house 513 מֶרְחָץ ז
distanced, 200 מֻרְחָק ז
removed, banished
distance 515 מֶרְחָק ז
distant, far off; 92 מְרֻחָק ז
estranged, alienated
deep-fryer 531 מַרְחֶשֶׁת נ
wetted 200 מֻרְטָב ז
vibrator 541 מַרְטֵט ז
(construction)
exciting; moving 187 מַרְטִיט ז
hacked to pieces, 92 מְרֻטָּשׁ ז
dismembered
rebellion; 257 מְרִי ז
disobedience
fatling; buffalo??? 405 מְרִיא ז
Bibl.
dispute, argument 481 מְרִיבָה נ
rebelling; rebellion, 1 מְרִידָה נ
revolt
spreading; smearing 1 מְרִיחָה נ
plucking feathers, 1 מְרִיטָה נ
hair
wheelbarrow 481 מְרִיצָה נ
(somewhat) bitter 404 מָרִיר ז
bitterness 24 מְרִירוּת נ
beam, joist 20 מָרִישׁ ז
spatula 814 מָרִית נ
weakness, cowardice 341 מֹרֶךְ ז
Lit. [no pl.]
made of, composed 200 מֻרְכָּב ז
of; assembled; complex
body (of a vehicle 513 מֶרְכָּב ז
etc.); fuselage of plane
carriage, chariot 517 מֶרְכָּבָה נ
complexity 211 מֻרְכָּבוּת נ
centralization 54 מִרְכּוּז ז
centralist 915 מִרְכּוּזִי ז
supermarket 488 מַרְכּוֹל ז
minimarket 819 מַרְכּוֹלִית נ

מְשֻׁחְזָר ז 100 reconstructed; reconstituted
מִשְׁחָטָה נ 506 slaughterhouse
מְשֻׁחָל ז 200 threaded, strung, laced
מִשְׁחוֹלֶת נ 512 device for cleaning rifle barrel
מַשְׁחֶלֶת נ 531 needle threader
מֻשְׁחָם ז 200 browned
מִשְׂחָק ז 497 game; acting; play
מִשְׂחָקִי ז 924 game-like
מֻשְׁחָר ז 200 blackened
מְשֻׁחְרָר ז 101 freed; loosened; dismissed; exempt
מְשַׁחְרֵר ז 86 liberator
מֻשְׁחָת ז 200 corrupt, immoral; defaced, marred, destroyed
מַשְׁחֶתֶת נ 531 destroyer (navy)
מִשְׁטוּר ז 54 disciplining [no pl.]
מִשְׁטָח ז 498 flat place; surface; smear, swab (medicine)
מְשֻׁטָּח ז 92 flattened
מִשְׁטָחִית נ 816 pad
מַשְׂטִין ז 187 angel of denunciation and accusation Lit.-archaic
מַשְׂטֵמָה נ 550 hatred, loathing Lit.
מִשְׁטָר ז 496 regime
מִשְׁטָרָה נ 505 police
מִשְׁטַרְתִּי ז 923 of police
מֶשִׁי ז 257 silk [no pl.]
מְשִׁיבוֹן ז 894 answering machine
מָשִׁיחַ ז 22 messiah; redeemer
מְשִׁיחָה נ 1 anointing, spreading
מְשִׁיחִי ז 933 messianic
מְשִׁיחִיּוּת נ 762 messianism [no pl.]
מָשִׁיט ז 197 rower, oarsman, sailor
מִשְׁיִי ז 915 silky
מְשִׁיכָה נ 1 pulling, dragging
מְשִׂימָה נ 481 mission, assignment, task
מְשִׂימָתִי ז 915 mission-driven, mission-based
מְשֻׁיָּף ז 92 polished, smoothed, filed
מַשִּׁיק ז 195 tangent
מָשִׁישׁ ז 20 tangible
מְשֻׁיָּשׁ ז 92 marbled
מֶשֶׁךְ ז 317 duration [no pl.]
מִשְׁכָּב ז 496 couch, bed Lit.; sexual intercourse
מִשְׁכּוֹכִית נ 814 farm animal leading the flock/herd; bellwether (is it a suffix here?)
מִשְׁכּוּן ז 54 mortgaging, using as collateral
מַשְׁכּוֹן ז 488 pledge, collateral
מַשְׁכּוֹנַאי ז 909 pawnbroker
מַשְׂכִּיל ז 187 intelligent, educated; member of the Enlightenment movement in the

מַשְׁכִּים ז 187 early riser
מַשְׂכִּיר ז 187 renter (to a tenant)
מַשְׂכִּית נ 810 image; ornament, locket Lit.
מֻשְׂכָּל ז 200 rational, intelligent; idea, concept Phil.
מִשְׂכָּל ז 496 intelligence [no pl.]
מְשֻׂכָּל ז 92 cross-legged, cross-handed
מְשֻׁכְלָל ז 101 enhanced, advanced, sophisticated
מִשְׁכָּן ז 496 dwelling, residence; the Tabernacle
מְשֻׁכְנָע ז 100 convinced
מֻשְׂכָּר ז 200 rented, let, leased
מְשַׁכֵּר ז 71 intoxicating
מַשְׂכֹּרֶת נ 534 salary
מָשָׁל ז 267 proverb, fable, allegory
מִשְׁלָב ז 496 register (sociolinguistics)
מְשֻׁלָּב ז 92 combined; integrated
מִשְׁלַבִּי ז 915 of register
מִשְׁלֶבֶת נ 509 monogram
מֻשְׁלָג ז 200 snowy, snow-covered
מְשֻׁלְהָב ז 100 excited, riled up, impassioned, inflamed
מִשְׁלוֹחַ ז 487 delivery; shipment
מִשְׁלַח (יָד) ז 498 occupation, profession (final vowel pataH in constr.)
מִשְׁלַחַת נ 511 delegation
מִשְׁלָט ז 496 military post (obsolete?)
מְשֻׁלָּט ז 92 signposted
מַשְׁלִים ז 187 complementary; complement noun
מֻשְׁלָךְ ז 200 discarded, thrown away
מְשֻׁלָּל ז 92 lacking, bereft Lit
מֻשְׁלָם ז 200 perfect; wonderful; complete, total
מֻשְׁלָמוּת נ 211 perfection
מִשְׁלָשׁ ז 496 dead letter box, dead drop (espionage)
מְשֻׁלָּשׁ ז 92 triangle; triangular; triple
מְשַׁלְשֵׁל ז 83 laxative
מְשֻׁמָּד ז 92 convert N from Judaism Lit
מַשְׁמִים ז 187 boring, dull Lit.
מַשְׁמִין ז 187 fattening
מַשְׁמִיצָן ז 868 defamer Coll.
מִשְׁמָן ז 501 being fat; being fertile; big, strong person Lit.
מְשֻׁמָּן ז 92 oiled, greased
מַשְׁמָע ז 518 meaning
מַשְׁמָעוּתִי ז 915 significant, important
מַשְׁמָעִי ז 929 of, or pertaining to, meaning
מִשְׁמַעַת נ 511 discipline [no pl.]
מִשְׁמַעְתִּי/מִשְׁמַעְתִּי ז 915 of discipline

מֻשְׁמָץ ז 200 slandered, libeled
מִשְׁמָר ז 496 guard
מְשֻׁמָּר ז 92 preserved, canned
מִשְׁמֶרֶת נ 509 shift N; post, position
מִשְׁמֹרֶת נ 512 guardianship, custody
מִשְׁמֵשׁ ז 502 apricot
מְשֻׁמָּשׁ ז 92 used
מִשְׁנָאִי ז 915 Mishnaic
מִשְׁנֶה ז 504 deputy; twice as much Bibl.
מְשֻׁנֶּה ז 95 strange, unusual, weird
מִשְׁנָה נ 499 Mishna (Jewish oral law); doctrine, theory
מִשְׁנִי ז 915 secondary (in importance, rank)
מִשְׁנִיּוּת נ 762 subsidiarity [no pl.]
מִשְׁנָן ז 857 dentition (dentistry)
מְשֻׁנָּן ז 92 serrated, toothed
מְשֻׁנָּס ז 92 belted Lit
מַשְׁנֵק ז 541 choke
מְשֻׁנָּת ז 92 marked with lines to indicate grade
מְשִׁסָּה נ 466 plundering, booty; destruction Lit.
מְשֻׁסָּע ז 92 split, torn, rented
מְשֻׁסָּף ז 92 slit, slashed, gashed
מֻשְׁעֶה ז 204 suspended from office
מִשְׁעוֹל ז 482 path, pass, trail Lit.
מְשֻׁעֲמָם ז 106 bored, uninterested
מְשַׁעֲמֵם ז 81 boring
מִשְׁעָן ז 497 rest, support
מִשְׁעֶנֶת נ 510 back rest
מְשֹׁעָר ז 93 expected, approximated
מְשֻׁעֲשָׁע ז 104 amused, entertained
מְשַׁעֲשֵׁעַ ז 84 amusing, entertaining
מְשֻׁפֶּה ז 95 sharpened; polished, smoothed Lit-rare
מִשְׂפָּח ז 498 distortion of justice [no pl.]
מִשְׁפָּחָה נ 507 family
מִשְׁפַּחְתִּי ז 915 of the family
מִשְׁפַּחְתִּיּוּת נ 765 family feeling/conduct (no decl., no pl.)
מִשְׁפָּט ז 496 trial; law; sentence (syntax)
מִשְׁפָּטִי ז 924 legal
מִשְׁפְּטָן/מִשְׁפָּטָן ז 864 jurist, lawyer
מַשְׁפִּיל ז 187 degrading, humiliating
מַשְׁפִּיעַ ז 189 influential
מִשְׁפָּךְ ז 496 garbage dump
מַשְׁפֵּךְ ז 541 watering can
מְשֻׁפָּם ז 92 moustached
מֻשְׁפָּע ז 200 affected, influenced
מְשֻׁפָּע ז 92 having an abundance (of) Lit

support (structure) 496 מִתְמָךְ ז
octagon; octagonal 92 מְתֻמָּן ז
transducer 541 מַתְמֵר ז
waist, hip 345 מֹתֶן ז
giving; gift Lit. 520 מַתָּן ז
opposer, opponent; 160 מִתְנַגֵּד ז opposer of Hassidism
oscillator 541 מַתְנֵד ז
volunteer 160 מִתְנַדֵּב ז
conditional, 204 מֻתְנֶה ז stipulated; automatic, involuntary
gift 471 מַתָּנָה נ
settler 160 מִתְנַחֵל ז
lumbar 980 מָתְנִי ז
vest, waistcoat 911 מָתְנִיָּה נ
filet, porterhouse 813 מָתְנִית נ steak; belt, sash; battledress
starter (of car) 546 מַתְנֵעַ ז
arrogant, 160 מִתְנַשֵּׂא ז patronizing, condescending
lumbago [no pl.] 685 מַתֶּנֶת נ
provoking, inciting 187 מַתְסִיס ז
fermented, cultured 200 מֻתְסָס ז
horrible; disgusting, 93 מְתֹעָב ז revolting
documented 93 מְתֹעָד ז
leading astray 194 מַתְעֶה ז
gymnast 160 מִתְעַמֵּל ז
industrialized 93 מְתֹעָשׂ ז
worshiper 160 מִתְפַּלֵּל ז
philosopher; one 165 מִתְפַּלְסֵף ז who "philosophizes" (derogatory)
sewing workshop 505 מִתְפָּרָה נ
sweetness [no pl.] 317 מֶתֶק ז
sweetness [no pl.] 341 מֹתֶק ז
advanced, 160 מִתְקַדֵּם ז progressive
insurrectionist, 164 מִתְקוֹמֵם ז mutineer
attacker 187 מַתְקִיף ז
installed, affixed 200 מֻתְקָן ז
apparatus, device; 496 מִתְקָן ז facility
reformer 71 מְתַקֵּן ז
repaired; corrected; 92 מְתֻקָּן ז revised; improved; reformed
standardized 105 מְתֻקְנָן ז
offensive N 505 מִתְקָפָה נ
aggressive, 924 מִתְקָפִי ז offensive
folding, 160 מִתְקַפֵּל ז collapsible
highly mentioned 102 מְתֻקְשָׁר ז in the media; highly connected
sweetish 458 מְתַקְתַּק ז
permitted, allowed; 205 מֻתָּר ז loose, loosened
cultured, refined, 97 מְתֻרְבָּת ז civilized
translator 78 מְתַרְגֵּם ז
translator 863 מְתֻרְגְּמָן ז
fundraiser 187 מַתְרִים ז
barricade 496 מִתְרָס ז
gift, present Lit. [no pl.] 520 מַתָּת ז
wineskin, waterskin; 245 נֹאד ז fart - coarse slang
alveolus (anatomy) 814 נֹאדִית נ
great, exalted, 33 נֶאְדָר/נֶאְדָּר ז glorious Lit.
handsome, pleasant, 265 נָאֶה ז good looking; substantial, high
beloved Lit. 33 נֶאֱהָב ז
speech, address 399 נְאוּם ז
adultery 51 נִאּוּף/נִאוּף ז
adultery 52 נִאוּף/נִאּוּף ז
cursing, swearing 51 נִאּוּץ/נִאוּץ ז
cursing, swearing 52 נִאוּץ/נִאּוּץ ז
enlightened, cultured; 39 נָאוֹר ז intelligent
enlightenment, 742 נְאוֹרוּת נ progressiveness [no pl.]
fitting, proper, 39 נָאוֹת ז suitable
being handsome [no pl.] 733 נָאוּת נ
propriety, being 742 נְאוֹתוּת נ proper or suitable [no pl.]
full, replete; 33 נֶאְזָר ז strengthened, girded Lit.
abominable, 33 נֶאֱלָח ז despicable, loathsome, vile
abomination, 43 נֶאֱלָחוּת נ vileness [no pl.]
trustee, trusted ally; 33 נֶאֱמָן ז loyal, faithful, devoted
loyalty, faithfulness 43 נֶאֱמָנוּת נ
tendency to deliver 688 נָאֶמֶת נ non-stop speeches [no pl.]
adulterer 849 נַאֲפָן ז
invective; 640 נְאָצָה נ blasphemy
Nazi 915 נָאצִי ז
noble, lofty, exalted 33 נֶאֱצָל ז
moan, groan N Lit. 328 נַאַק ז
moan, groan Lit. 640 נְאָקָה נ
accused (person) 33 נֶאֱשָׁם ז
spore 317 נֶבֶג ז
betrayed 31 נִבְגָּד ז
sporal 949 נִבְגִּי ז
separate, different; 31 נִבְדָּל ז offside (soccer)
difference, 42 נִבְדָּלוּת נ dissimilarity
subject, examinee 31 נִבְדָּק ז
alarmed, frightened 31 נִבְהָל ז
prophesy, prediction 18 נְבוּאָה נ
prophetic 946 נְבוּאִי ז
hollow; empty; 15 נָבוּב ז superficial, shallow
sprouted, germinated 15 נָבוּט ז
prediction 45 נִבּוּי ז
embarrassed, 39 נָבוֹךְ ז perplexed [note possible alternants with u: nevukha etc.]
withered, wilted, 15 נָבוּל ז dried out
coarseness, ugliness 45 נִבּוּל ז
wise, intelligent 39 נָבוֹן ז
wisdom, wit [no pl.] 742 נְבוֹנוּת נ
despicable, loathsome 36 נִבְזֶה ז
despicableness 738 נִבְזוּת נ
despicable 948 נִבְזִי ז
despicability, 776 נִבְזִיּוּת נ contemptibleness [no pl.]
examinee 31 נִבְחָן ז
barker 846 נַבְחָן ז
bark-like, throaty (a cough) 969 נַבְחָנִי ז
choice, top quality; 31 נִבְחָר ז chosen; elected
team (usually in sports) 712 נִבְחֶרֶת נ
sprout, shoot, 317 נֶבֶט ז seedling
prophet, visionary; 20 נָבִיא ז soothsayer
prophesy 24 נְבִיאוּת נ
prophetic 933 נְבִיאִי ז
hollowness; 24 נְבִיבוּת נ emptiness
barking; a bark 1 נְבִיחָה נ
germination, 1 נְבִיטָה נ sprouting
withering, wilting 1 נְבִילָה נ
gushing forth water; 1 נְבִיעָה נ spring
searching, rummaging 1 נְבִירָה נ
depth Lit.; nadir 322 נֶבֶךְ ז
vile person, villain 267 נָבָל ז
harp, lyre 322 נֵבֶל/נֶבֶל ז
harpist 909 נִבְלַאי ז
despicable act, 634 נְבָלָה נ villainy
carcass 652 נְבֵלָה נ
villainousness Lit. 736 נַבְלוּת נ
harpist 846 נַבְלָן ז
illiterate, uneducated 31 נִבְעָר ז
illiteracy, ignorance 42 נִבְעָרוּת נ [no pl.]
vole, field mouse 846 נַבְרָן ז
chandelier 713 נִבְרֶשֶׁת נ
NCO (Non- 275 נַגָּד ז Commissioned Officer) (fem. nagedet)
resistor (elect.) 275 נַגָּד ז
against; 336 נֶגֶד מ"י או ז' opposite; versus Prep; counter-N [no pl.]
wife, woman Lit. [no pl.!] 607 נֶגְדָּה נ
opposing, 961 נֶגְדִּי ז contradictory
contradiction, 783 נֶגְדִּיּוּת נ opposition [no pl.]
344 נֹגַהּ, ר' נְגָהִים/נְגוֹהִים/ נְגֹהוֹת ז brightness, gleam, glow, pl. negahim, negohim, negohot
drying, wiping 45 נִגּוּב ז
opposition, 45 נִגּוּד ז contradiction, difference
conflicting, 956 נִגּוּדִי ז opposite, contradictory

נִגּוּדִיּוּת נ 781 difference, oppositeness [no pl.]
נִגּוּחַ ז 53 goading, taunting; goring [no pl.]
נִגּוּן ז 45 playing music; tune, melody; inflection
נִגּוּנִי ז 956 musical, tuneful, melodic
נִגּוּנִיּוּת נ 781 musicalness, melodiousness [no pl.]
נָגוּס ז 15 gnawed, bitten into
נָגוּעַ ז 17 infected, contaminated
נִגּוּעַ ז 53 infection, contamination
נִגְזָל ז 31 robbed, burglarized
נִגְזֶרֶת נ 711 derivative; by-product
נַגְחָן ז 846 a goring animal Lit.
נַגְחָנוּת נ 752 argumentativeness, contentiousness, tendency to gore [no pl.]
נָגִיד ז 20 governor, ruler; wealthy, influential person; philanthropist
נְגִידוּת נ 24 governorship; wealth Lit
נְגִיחָה נ 1 butt, gore N
נְגִינָה נ 1 music playing; accentuation grammar
נְגִינָתִי ז 937 musical, tuneful
נְגִיסָה נ 1 biting; a bite
נְגִיעָה נ 1 touching; a touch
נְגִיף ז 405 virus
נְגִיפָה נ 1 stroke, blow, push Lit
נְגִיפִי ז 933 viral
נְגִירָה נ 1 seepage, flow
נָגִישׁ ז 20 accessible
נְגִישָׁה נ 1 malicious suit law
נְגִישׁוּת נ 24 accessibility
נִגְלֶה ז 36 revealed, visible, unconcealed
נַגָּן ז 275 musician, player (fem. nagenet, Coll. naganit)
נֶגֶן ז 317 tune; playing Lit. [no pl.]
נֶגַע ז 319 problem, negative phenomenon; affliction, damage
נֶגֶף ז 317 obstacle, hindrance
נַגָּר ז 275 carpenter (fem. nageret, Coll. nagarit)
נֶגֶר ז 317 run-off (water)
נִגָּר ז 35 leaking, spilling
נַגָּרִיָּה נ 911 carpentry shop
נִגְרָר ז 31 pulled, drawn, dragged
נִגְרֶרֶת נ 711 trailer
נָד ז 214 wandering
נֵד ז 231 wall of water Lit.
נְדָבָה נ 634 donation, contribution; alms
נִדְבָּךְ ז 31 layer, level
נַדְבָן ז 846 philanthropist
נַדְבָנוּת נ 752 philanthropy, charitableness, generosity [no pl.]
נַדְבָנִי ז 969 philanthropic, charitable, generous
נִדְגָּל ז 31 adorned, magnificent Lit
נִדָּה נ 586 menstruating woman
נִדְהָם ז 31 astonished
נָדוּד ז 15 not relaxed, disturbed sleep Lit
נְדוּד/נְדֻד ז 393 wandering, migration [no pl.]
נְדוּדִים ז 998 wanderings, travels
נִדּוּי ז 45 banishment, excommunication
נָדוֹן ז 39 the topic under discussion/sentenced person
נִדּוֹן ז 40 the topic under discussion; sentenced person
נְדוּנְיָה/נְדֻנְיָה נ 678 dowry
נִדּוּף ז 45 evaporation
נָדוֹשׁ ז 39 banal, commonplace
נָדִיב ז 20 generous, charitable; noble
נְדִיבוּת נ 24 generosity
נְדִידָה נ 1 wandering, migrating
נָדִיף ז 20 volatile
נְדִיפָה נ 1 evaporation, dissipation Lit [no pl.]
נְדִיפוּת נ 24 volatility
נָדִיר ז 20 rare
נְדִירוּת נ 24 scarcity, rarity
נָדָל ז 267 centipede
נִדְמֶה ז 36 it seems, it is as if
נָדָן/נְדָן ז 267 scabbard, sheath
נַדְנֵדָה נ 680 swing, seesaw
נַדְנְדָנוּת נ 749 bothersomeness Sl. [no pl.]
נִדְנוּד ז 66 swinging; nuisance Sl.
נִדָּף ז 35 scattered, fallen leaf
נֶדֶר/נֵדֶר ז 317 vow, oath, promise
נִדְרָשׁ ז 31 required; be in demand
נֹהַּ ז 230 lamentation, bemoaning, wailing [no pl.]
נֹהַּ ז 230 strong yearning, longing; following Lit. [no pl.]
נֹהַג ז 343 custom, habit, practice [no pl.]
נַהָג/נֶהָג ז 276 driver (fem. naheget)
נֶהְדָּר/נֶהֱדָר ז 33 magnificent, beautiful, impressive; wonderful, great
נָהוּג ז 15 customary, acceptable; driven a vehicle
נִהוּג ז 50 piloting, navigation
נִהוּל ז 50 management; administration [no pl.]
נִהוּלִי ז 957 managerial
נְהוֹרָנִי ז 915 luminescent Lit.
נְהִי ז 259 lamentation, bemoaning Bibl. [no pl.]
נְהִיגָה נ 1 driving a vehicle
נְהִיָּה נ 4 following Lit. [no pl.]
נְהִימָה נ 1 growl, roar Lit; moan, groan Lit
נָהִיר ז 20 clear, understood, lucid
נְהִירָה נ 1 thronging, upsurge, flow of people
נְהִירוּת נ 24 lucidity, clarity [no pl.]
נֹהַל ז 343 regulation, accepted practice; procedure
נַהֲלוֹל ז 444 thorn (biblical)
נַהֲלִי ז 981 procedural
נְהָמָה נ 640 growl(ing), roar(ing) N
נֶהֱנְתָן ז 863 hedonist
נֶהֱנְתָנוּת נ 740 hedonism [no pl.]
נֶהֱנְתָנִי ז 915 hedonistic
נְהָקָה נ 640 braying
נָהָר ז 271 river
נְהָרָה נ 640 brightness, illumination [no pl.]
נַהֲרוֹנִית נ 814 potamogeton (plant)
נוֹאָל ז 38 idiotic, foolish
נוֹאֵם ז 7 speaker
נוֹאֵף ז 7 adulterer
נוֹאָשׁ ז 38 desperate, hopeless
נוֹבֵל ז 6 dry, withered, wilted
נוֹבֵעַ ז 9 gushing, flowing
נוֹגֵד ז 6 opposing, contradictory
נוֹגְדָן ז 855 antibody (medicine)
נוֹגְסָנִי ז 985 nibbly, biting Lit.
נוֹגֵשׂ ז 6 oppressor; taskmaster Lit
נוֹד ז 240 wandering [no pl.]
נַוָּד ז 275 wanderer, vagabond, nomad (fem. navedet)
נוֹדֵד ז 6 wondering, migrant
נַוָּדִי ז 915 nomadic
נוֹדָע ז 38 famous, well-known
נָוֶה, ר' נָווֹת/נְאוֹת ז 261 house, hostel, home; oasis (pl. navot/na'ot)
נִוּוּט ז 45 navigation
נִוּוּל ז 45 dismallness, ugliness Lit [no pl.]
נִוּוּן ז 45 atrophy, degeneration
נוֹזֵל ז 6 liquid, fluid; liquid adj
נוֹזְלִי ז 984 liquid Adj
נוֹזְפָנִי ז 985 reproachful
נוֹחַ ז 241 comfortable, convenient easy
נוֹחוּת נ 740 comfort
נוֹחִיּוּת נ 762 comfort [no pl.]
נַוָּט ז 275 navigator; scout (fem. navetet)
נוֹטֵר ז 6 Jewish guard in British police; guard Lit
נוֹטְרוּת נ 14 Jewish guard unit in British police during British mandate [no pl.]
נוֹטַרְיוֹנִי ז 915 notary Adj
נוֹי ז 240 beauty, ornamentation
נוֹכֵחַ ז 9 attendee
נוֹכְחוּת נ 14 presence, attendance

present 984 נוֹכְחִי ז
crook, swindler 6 נוֹכֵל ז
fraud, swindle 14 נוֹכְלוּת נ
loom 246 נוֹל ז
dismalness; despicableness Lit. [no pl.] 736 נַוְלוּת נ
passenger 9 נוֹסֵעַ ז
additional 38 נוֹסָף ז
movement, wandering Lit. [no pl.] 241 נוֹעַ ז
daring 38 נוֹעָז ז
view, scenery, landscape 240 נוֹף ז
water lily 370 נוּפָר ז
vacationer 6 נוֹפֵשׁ ז
feather 593 נוֹצָה נ
feather-like 915 נוֹצִי ז
sparkling, shining 6 נוֹצֵץ ז
profound, fundamental 6 נוֹקֵב ז
piercing, penetrating Lit. 985 נוֹקְבָנִי ז
shepherd, sheep farmer 6 נוֹקֵד ז
punctilious person, pedant Rare 855 נוֹקְדָן ז
vengeful, vindictive 985 נוֹקְמָנִי ז
firing pin 6 נוֹקֵר ז
fire; flare Lit. 246 נוּר ז
terrible 38 נוֹרָא ז
horrible 915 נוֹרָאִי ז
Norwegian 915 נוֹרְבֶגִי ז
light bulb 595 נוּרָה נ
buttercup (plant) 814 נוּרִית נ
carrier; subject (sent.) 8 נוֹשֵׂא ז
subjective (syntax) 984 נוֹשְׂאִי ז
settled, populated 38 נוֹשָׁב ז
debtor 10 נוֹשֶׁה ז
very old 38 נוֹשָׁן ז
tracer bullet 6 נוֹתֵב ז
remaining 38 נוֹתָר ז
rebuked; contrite, chastened 15 נָזוּף ז
injured person 40 נִזּוֹק ז
stew, broth 20 נָזִיד ז
liquid 20 נָזִיל ז
leaking; a leak 1 נְזִילָה נ
liquidity 24 נְזִילוּת נ
reproach, reprimand; discipline – (military) 1 נְזִיפָה נ
of damages, of torts (law) 933 נְזִיקִי ז
monk; nazirite; hermit 20 נָזִיר ז
monasticism; asceticism 24 נְזִירוּת נ
ascetic; isolationist 933 נְזִירִי ז
runny nose 685 נַזֶּלֶת נ
nose ring 317 נֶזֶם ז
lamium (plant) 812 נִזְמִית נ
angry, furious Lit 31 נִזְעָם ז
angry, furious, enraged Lit 31 נִזְעָף ז
reproachful 969 נַזְפָנִי ז
damage, harm 317 נֶזֶק/נֵזֶק ז
crown, wreath 322 נֵזֶר ז

mute (letter, vowel sign) 214 נָח ז
condolence, consolation 50 נִחוּם ז
necessary, required 15 נָחוּץ ז
guess, conjecture 50 נִחוּשׁ ז
inferior, lower in status 15 נָחוּת ז
leading, guiding 4 נְחִיָּה נ
swarm (of insects); group of animals 405 נְחִיל ז
necessity, requirement, need 24 נְחִיצוּת נ
nostril 408 נְחִיר ז
snoring; snore N 1 נְחִירָה נ
firmness, insistence, decisiveness 24 נְחִישׁוּת נ
landing, touchdown 1 נְחִיתָה נ
inferiority 24 נְחִיתוּת נ
stream, brook 328 נַחַל ז
soldier in a Nahal unit (Israeli army) 909 נַחְלָאִי ז
estate; heritage, inheritance 618 נַחֲלָה נ
consolation, comfort; remorse, regret Lit. [no pl.] 343 נֹחַם ז
nice, pleasant, lovely 32 נֶחְמָד ז
loveliness, pleasantness 44 נֶחְמָדוּת נ
consolation 645 נֶחָמָה נ
emphatic (phonetics) 965 נַחְצִי ז
emphaticness (phonetics) [no pl.] 785 נַחְצִיּוּת נ
snore N, snoring 328 נַחַר ז
very dry (throat) 35 נִחָר ז
snore N 612 נַחֲרָה נ
snorer 846 נַחְרָן ז
snoring Adj 969 נַחְרָנִי ז
decisive, final, firm (decision, opinion) 32 נֶחְרָץ ז
decisiveness, finality 44 נֶחְרָצוּת נ
snake, serpent 269 נָחָשׁ ז
magic, sorcery, witchcraft, divination Lit. 328 נַחַשׁ ז
breaker, large wave 444 נַחְשׁוֹל ז
pioneering; daring N [no pl.] 740 נַחְשׁוֹנוּת נ
pioneering; daring 915 נַחְשׁוֹנִי ז
serpentine 942 נְחָשִׁי ז
faltering, lagging 32 נֶחְשָׁל ז
slowness, backwardness 44 נֶחְשָׁלוּת נ
copper [no pl.] 710 נְחֹשֶׁת נ
cuprous; cupreous, coppery 915 נְחֻשְׁתִּי ז
brass serpent (biblical) 863 נְחֻשְׁתָּן ז
cupreous 915 נְחֻשְׁתָּנִי ז
flat (music) 279 נָחֵת ז
satisfaction, pleasure [no pl.] 328 נַחַת ז
marine (military) (fem. naHetet???) 276 נַחָת/נֶחָת ז

baker Lit. 444 נַחְתּוֹם ז
landing craft 686 נַחֶתֶת נ
slanted; bent; inflected 15 נָטוּי ז
devoid; lacking 15 נָטוּל ז
handling [no pl.] 45 נִטּוּל ז
stalactite 378 נַטּוּף ז
monitoring 45 נִטּוּר ז
abandoned 15 נָטוּשׁ ז
tendency; trend; leaning ideological; inflection 4 נְטִיָּה נ
taking, receiving, obtaining; accepting responsibility 1 נְטִילָה נ
planting trees; sapling 1 נְטִיעָה נ
stalactite 405 נְטִיף ז
dripping liquid 1 נְטִיפָה נ
grudge-bearing; guarding 1 נְטִירָה נ
abandonment 1 נְטִישָׁה נ
burden, load [no pl.] 322 נֵטֶל ז
hand-washing cup in Jewish ritual 610 נַטְלָה נ
sapling 317 נֶטַע ז
sapling, plant 319 נֶטַע ז
muzzle-loading rifle, gun 31 נִטְעָן ז
drop 322 נֵטֶף ז
neutralization 54 נִטְרוּל ז
begrudging, spiteful person Lit. 846 נַטְרָן ז
vengefulness, begrudging 752 נַטְרָנוּת נ
begrudging, spiteful Lit. 969 נַטְרָנִי ז
lamentation, bemoaning, wailing Lit.-rare [no pl.] 239 נִי ז
canine, fang 251 נִיב ז
saying, idiom; dialect 251 נִיב ז
anthology of sayings/expressions 894 נִיבוֹן ז
idiomatic 915 נִיבִי ז
Nigerian 915 נִיגֶרִי ז
movement, waggling [no pl.] 251 נִיד ז
portable, mobile, movable 275 נַיָּד ז
moving, wandering; menstruation 3 נִידָה נ
police cruiser 685 נַיֶּדֶת נ
fluctuation (exchange rate); mobility 45 נִיּוּד ז
stationary 275 נַיָּח ז
fragrant 915 נִיחוֹחִי ז
comfort; satisfaction Lit. [no pl.] 740 נִיחוּת נ
indigo (plant) 251 נִיל ז
capillary 251 נִים ז
thread; tone, overtone; nap N 3 נִימָה נ
politeness, manners 49 נִימוּס ז
polite 915 נִימוּסִי ז
politeness, courtesy [no pl.] 762 נִימוּסִיּוּת נ

very thin/fine; very narrow; capillaceous 915 נִימִי ז
capillarity [no pl.] 762 נִימִיּוּת נ
capillary (anatomy) 814 נִימִית נ
great-grandson 251 נִין ז
escape Lit-rare 3 נִיסָה נ
movement Lit. 252 נִיעַ ז
body movement; bend 3 נִיעָה נ
mobility [no pl.] 740 נִיעוּת נ
spark; flash; glimmer; talent, ability 388 נִיצוֹץ ז
meadow, grazing area Lit. 251 נִיר ז
paper 312 נְיָר ז
paperwork (usually derog.) [no pl.] 685 נַיֶּרֶת נ
painful 31 נִכְאָב ז
sadness, gloom lit. 998 נְכָאִים ז
respected, important; substantial; a notable person 31 נִכְבָּד ז
grandson 336 נֶכֶד ז
grand-nephew 859 נֶכְדָּן ז
handicapped person, cripple, invalid 261 נָכֶה ז
deduction 45 נִכּוּי ז
correct, true; right, fitting 39 נָכוֹן ז
readiness, willingness 742 נְכוֹנוּת נ
appropriating, assimilating 46 נִכּוּס ז
alienation 45 נִכּוּר ז
weeding 45 נִכּוּשׁ ז
disability, handicap [no pl.] 733 נָכוּת נ
disappointed 31 נִכְזָב ז
extinct; endangered 31 נִכְחָד ז
discount (banking, finances) 898 נִכָּיוֹן ז
deception, white lie Lit. 450 נֵכֶל ז
deceptive, fraudulent Lit. 912 נַכְלוּלִי ז
deceptiveness, fraudulence Lit. [no pl.] 790 נַכְלוּלִיּוּת נ
ashamed, embarrassed Lit 31 נִכְלָם ז
shame, embarrassment Lit [no pl.] 42 נִכְלָמוּת נ
yearning; depressed Lit 31 נִכְמָר ז
submissiveness [no pl.] 42 נִכְנָעוּת נ
asset, property 317 נֶכֶס ז
longed for, yearned for Lit 31 נִכְסָף ז
angry, furious, enraged Lit 31 נִכְעָס ז
epileptic 36 נִכְפֶּה ז
being epileptic [no pl.] 738 נִכְפּוּת נ
multiplicand math 31 נִכְפָּל ז
foreign country, diaspora (only nekhar constr., no declension, no pl.) 287 נֵכָר ז
noticeable, recognizable; substantial, significant 35 נִכָּר ז
foreign 980 נָכְרִי ז
foreignness [no pl.] 794 נָכְרִיּוּת נ
one who failed; failing, esp. grade 31 נִכְשָׁל ז
tired 36 נִלְאֶה ז
friendliness, pleasantness [no pl.] 42 נִלְבָּבוּת נ
enthusiastic 31 נִלְהָב ז
enthusiasm, excitement [no pl.] 42 נִלְהָבוּת נ
accompanying 36 נִלְוֶה ז
corrupt, deviant 39 נָלוֹז ז
corruptedness, immorality [no pl.] 742 נְלוֹזוּת נ
perversion, depravity 24 נְלִיזוּת נ
ridiculous, preposterous, ludicrous 31 נִלְעָג ז
ludicrousness [no pl.] 42 נִלְעָגוּת נ
despised, loathed 31 נִמְאָס ז
hasty, hurried 31 נִמְהָר ז
haste, hurriedness [no pl.] 42 נִמְהָרוּת נ
evaporated, dissipated 39 נָמוֹג ז
short; low; of poor quality 15 נָמוּךְ ז
circumcised 384 נִמּוֹל ז
circumcised person 40 נִמּוֹל ז
reason, explanation 45 נִמּוּק ז
mongoose; ferret 4 נְמִיָּה נ
lowness, shortness 24 נְמִיכוּת נ
shortness, lowness [no pl.] 341 נֹמֶךְ ז
port, harbor, airport 279 נָמֵל ז
ant 637 נְמָלָה נ
of, or related to, port 915 נְמֵלִי ז
flowery, poetic 31 נִמְלָץ ז
nap N 66 נִמְנוּם ז
sleepy, drowsy 915 נִמְנוּמִי ז
slumberer 851 נַמְנְמָן ז
drowsy, dreamy, groggy 975 נַמְנְמָנִי ז
avoidable; improbable; one who abstains 31 נִמְנָע ז
addressee 31 נִמְעָן ז
necrosis; gangrene [no pl.] 317 נֶמֶק ז
necrotic 949 נִמְקִי ז
tiger 279 נָמֵר ז
tiger-like 915 נְמֵרִי ז
energetic; lively; intensive 31 נִמְרָץ ז
being energetic; vigor, decisiveness [no pl.] 42 נִמְרָצוּת נ
freckle 317 נֶמֶשׁ ז
moral, lesson 31 נִמְשָׁל ז
flexible, elastic 31 נִמְתָּח ז
calm, relaxed 41 נִנּוֹחַ ז
dwarf, midget (fem. naneset, Coll. nanasit) 275 נַנָּס ז
tiny, miniature Adj 915 נַנָּסִי ז
smallness [no pl.] 762 נַנָּסִיּוּת נ
miracle; flag, pennant, standard 235 נֵס ז
circumstance 648 נְסִבָּה נ
tolerated 31 נִסְבָּל ז
tolerability [no pl.] 42 נִסְבָּלוּת נ
circumstantial 915 נְסִבָּתִי ז
recessive (genetics) 969 נַסְגָּנִי ז
retreating 39 נָסוֹג ז
wording 53 נִסּוּחַ ז
wording Adj 956 נִסּוּחִי ז
experiment 45 נִסּוּי ז
experimental, trial Adj 956 נִסּוּיִי ז
spread over 15 נָסוּךְ ז
libation (religious ritual) 45 נִסּוּךְ ז
sawing, cutting 45 נִסּוּר ז
drafter, formulator (fem. nasaHit) 275 נַסָּח ז
344 נֹסַח/נֻסַּח, ר' נְסָחִים/נֻסָּחִים ז wording; version; style, pl. (nesaHim/nusaHim
formula 627 נֻסְחָה נ
formulary 915 נֻסְחָתִי ז
miraculous 915 נִסִּי ז
withdrawal, retreat 1 נְסִיגָה נ
serum, blood serum 447 נַסְיוּב ז
attempt; trial, experiment; experience 898 נִסָּיוֹן ז
experimental 952 נִסְיוֹנִי ז
experimentalness [no pl.] 779 נִסְיוֹנִיּוּת נ
prince 20 נָסִיךְ ז
principality 24 נְסִיכוּת נ
princely 933 נְסִיכִי ז
experimenter 846 נַסְיָן ז
journey, trip, ride, drive 1 נְסִיעָה נ
takeoff, climbing high plane 1 נְסִיקָה נ
sawable, cuttable 20 נָסִיר ז
pouring out (water, wine, in religious ritual) 317 נֶסֶךְ/נֵסֶךְ ז
the first component in a construct state, smikhut 31 נִסְמָךְ ז
agitated, excited; uneasy 31 נִסְעָר ז
agitation, excitement [no pl.] 42 נִסְעָרוּת נ
appendix, addendum; attaché; adjunct 31 נִסְפָּח ז
board, plank 317 נֶסֶר ז
rasping, grating (sound) 969 נַסְרָנִי ז
sawdust [no pl.] 708 נְסֹרֶת נ
hidden; invisible; occult 31 נִסְתָּר ז
moving, mobile 214 נָע ז
missing, excluded, absent; lacking 33 נֶעְדָּר/נֶעֱדָר ז
twisted, distorted Lit. 37 נַעֲוֶה ז
locked 15 נָעוּל ז
attached, pinned; stuck, affixed 15 נָעוּץ ז
shaking 50 נִעוּר ז

youth 998 נְעוּרִים ז
abandoned, forgotten, forsaken 33 נֶעֱזָב ז
abandonment [no pl.] 43 נֶעֱזָבוּת נ
wearing/putting on shoes; closing, locking; adjournment 1 נְעִילָה נ
pleasant, nice 20 נָעִים ז
tune, melody 1 נְעִימָה נ
pleasantness 24 נְעִימוּת נ
insertion, sticking into, thrusting 1 נְעִיצָה נ
braying 1 נְעִירָה נ
shoe [plural na`alayim, occ. ne`alim/ne`a lot] 328 נַעַל, ר׳ נַעֲלַיִם ז
insulted, offended 33 נֶעֱלָב ז
insult, effrontery 43 נֶעֱלָבוּת נ
lofty, exalted 37 נַעֲלֶה ז
unknown (esp. in algebra); concealed, hidden 33 נֶעְלָם/נֶעֱלָם ז
pleasantness [no pl.] 343 נֹעַם ז
movement; shaking; swaying 67 נִעְנוּעַ ז
mint 415 נַעְנָע נ
tack, thumbtack 328 נַעַץ ז
youth, youngster, adolescent; minor (law); servant (biblical) 328 נַעַר ז
youth, youngsters, teenagers [no declension, no pl.] 343 נֹעַר ז
bray N 640 נְעָרָה נ
youth, adolescence [no pl.] 737 נַעֲרוּת נ
youthful; boyish 966 נַעֲרִי ז
admired, respected Lit. (coll. ne`erats) 34 נַעֲרָץ ז
chaff [no pl.] 708 נְעֹרֶת נ
halyard, halliard 231 נֵף ז
injured, wounded; killed 31 נִפְגָּע ז
sifter, sieve 582 נָפָה נ
swollen; inflated 17 נָפוּחַ ז
inflating, blowing up 53 נִפּוּחַ ז
beating of flax [no pl.] 45 נִפּוּט ז
sifting 45 נִפּוּי ז
drooping 15 נָפוּל ז
common, widespread 39 נָפוֹץ ז
smashing; explosion 45 נִפּוּץ ז
smith, blacksmith (fem. napaHit???) 275 נַפָּח ז
volume; capacity; scope, extent 319 נֶפַח ז
frightened, terrified, alarmed 31 נִפְחָד ז
volumetric 949 נִפְחִי ז
blacksmith shop 911 נַפָּחִיָּה נ
emphysema [no pl.] 689 נַפַּחַת נ
deceased, departed 31 נִפְטָר ז
flatulence 1 נְפִיחָה נ
swelling, swollenness 24 נְפִיחוּת נ
giant Lit 20 נָפִיל ז
falling, fall, drop 1 נְפִילָה נ
giant, enormous 933 נְפִילִי ז
explosive; volatile 20 נָפִיץ ז
explosiveness, volatility 24 נְפִיצוּת נ
touch, shade, characteristic; garnet (biblical) 341 נֹפֶךְ ז
stillbirth; failure; dud (military) 322 נֵפֶל ז
wonderful 31 נִפְלָא ז
wonders 998 נִפְלָאוֹת נ
horrifying 31 נִפְלָץ ז
manufacturing waste; fallout [no pl.] 708 נְפֹלֶת נ
waving; fluttering 66 נִפְנוּף ז
indecent Lit; faulty Lit 31 נִפְסָד ז
the one acted upon 31 נִפְעָל ז
excited, thrilled 31 נִפְעָם ז
detonator 275 נַפָּץ ז
explosion, blast [no pl.] 317 נֶפֶץ ז
absentee 31 נִפְקָד ז
absenteeism (military) 42 נִפְקָדוּת נ
separate 31 נִפְרָד ז
exaggerated Lit 31 נִפְרָז ז
common Lit 31 נִפְרָץ ז
soul, spirit; person 330 נֶפֶשׁ נ
vacation, holiday [no pl.] 341 נֹפֶשׁ ז
spiritual, mental; emotional, psychological 965 נַפְשִׁי ז
spirituality Lit. [no pl.] 785 נַפְשִׁיּוּת נ
criminal; atrocious 31 נִפְשָׁע ז
honey Lit. [no pl.] 341 נֹפֶת ז
curve N, bend N 447 נַפְתּוּל ז
crookedness, twistedness 42 נִפְתָּלוּת נ
hawk 235 נֵץ ז
perpendicular; hilt, sword handle; extra (cinema) 35 נִצָּב ז
bud (botany) 586 נִצָּה נ
survivor (of crash, tragedy, war) 382 נָצוֹל ז
survivor 40 נִצּוֹל ז
utilization; exploitation [no pl.] 45 נִצּוּל ז
locked weapon; hidden 15 נָצוּר ז
Christianization [no pl.] 45 נִצּוּר ז
eternity 324 נֵצַח/נֶצַח ז
victory 898 נִצָּחוֹן ז
eternal 949 נִצְחִי ז
eternity [no pl.] 776 נִצְחִיּוּת נ
a contentious person 846 נַצְחָן ז
contentiousness, argumentativeness [no pl.] 752 נַצְחָנוּת נ
contentious, argumentative 969 נַצְחָנִי ז
hawkish 915 נִצִּי ז
governor, commissioner; pillar; pile, support 405 נְצִיב ז
commissionership 24 נְצִיבוּת נ
representative, delegate 20 נָצִיג ז
representation, representative 24 נְצִיגוּת נ
quarrel, struggle Lit. 898 נִצָּיוֹן ז
hawkishness [no pl.] 762 נִצִּיּוּת נ
efficiency 24 נְצִילוּת נ
mica 405 נְצִיץ ז
exploiter 846 נַצְלָן ז
exploitation [no pl.] 752 נַצְלָנוּת נ
exploitative 969 נַצְלָנִי ז
utilization 697 נִצֶּלֶת נ
manufacturing reusable waste; salvage [no pl.] 708 נְצֹלֶת נ
bud; beginning, first sign 286 נִצָּן ז
sparkling, twinkling; sparkle, twinkle 66 נִצְנוּץ ז
stem, shoot 322 נֵצֶר ז
safety catch 598 נִצְרָה נ
Christianity [no pl.] 736 נַצְרוּת נ
needy person; pauper 31 נִצְרָךְ ז
need; poverty [no pl.] 42 נִצְרָכוּת נ
pinhole, aperture 317 נֶקֶב ז
tunnel, aqueduct 598 נִקְבָּה נ
female 649 נְקֵבָה נ
perforation [no pl.] 70 נִקְבּוּב ז
porous; perforated 912 נַקְבּוּבִי ז
porousness [no pl.] 790 נַקְבּוּבִיּוּת נ
tiny hole; pore 836 נַקְבּוּבִית נ
female Adj., feminine 915 נְקֵבִי ז
key-puncher (computing) 846 נַקְבָן ז
(computing) key-punching [no pl.] 752 נַקְבָנוּת נ
spotted, speckled, flecked Lit. 301 נָקֹד ז
point; dot 658 נְקֻדָּה נ
poked, perforated, punctured 15 נָקוּב ז
piercing, perforating, punching holes 45 נִקּוּב ז
dotted, spotted 15 נָקוּד ז
vocalization (grammar) 45 נִקּוּד ז
drainage 45 נִקּוּז ז
taken, held action, precaution 15 נָקוּט ז
cleaning 45 נִקּוּי ז
sprained, strained 17 נָקוּעַ ז
pecking, poking 45 נִקּוּר ז
knocking, hitting 45 נִקּוּשׁ ז
drain N [no pl.] 317 נֶקֶז ז
clean 256 נָקִי ז
stipulation, announcement 1 נְקִיבָה נ
cleaning; cleanliness 898 נִקָּיוֹן ז
use measure, etc.; adoption of stance, etc. 1 נְקִיטָה נ
spraining 1 נְקִיעָה נ
passage of period of time; rare 1 נְקִיפָה נ

סְבִיאָה נ 1 guzzling mostly of wine/liquor
סְבִיבָה נ 1 surrounding; neighborhood; area
סְבִיבוֹן ז 895 spinning top, dreidel
סְבִיבָתִי ז 937 environmental
סְבִיוֹן ז 444 dandelion
סָבִיךְ ז 20 entangled, intertwined
סְבִיכוּת נ 24 complexity
סָבִיל ז 20 passive
סְבִילוּת נ 24 tolerance, endurance; passivity
סָבִיר ז 20 reasonable, logical
סְבִירוּת נ 24 probability; reasonableness
סְבָךְ ז 315 entanglement, complicated situation; thicket
סֹבֶךְ ז 341 thicket, lair Lit.
סְבָכָה נ 634 net, lattice, grille
סַבְכָן ז 846 one who tends to make matters worse
סַבָּל ז 275 porter; carrier (fem. sabalit)
סֵבֶל ז 325 suffering, pain, hardship
סַבְלָן ז 846 patient, tolerant person
סַבְלָנוּת נ 752 patience [no pl.]
סַבְלָנִי ז 969 patient Adj
סִבֹּלֶת נ 697 endurance
סַבֶּלֶת נ 708 tolerance, stamina Rare [no pl.]
סִבְסוּד ז 66 subsidization
סֵבֶר ז 322 facial expression; meaning Lit.; hope Lit. [no pl.]
סְבָרָה/א נ 632 hypothesis, opinion; conjecture
סִבָּתִי ז 915 causative, causal
סִבָּתִיּוּת נ 762 causality [no pl.]
סִגּוּל ז 45 adaptation, adjustment
סֶגּוֹלִי ז 915 segholate
סָגוּף ז 15 tormented, tortured
סִגּוּף ז 45 mortification, self-denial
סִגּוּפִי ז 956 ascetic, mortifying, self-denying
סָגוּר ז 15 closed, shut; turned off
סְגוֹר ז 393 closure, seal [no pl.]
סַגִּי ז 915 (Aramaic) much, great; enough, sufficiently
סְגִידָה נ 1 worship, honoring; adoration
סְגִיָּה נ 624 issue, matter
סְגִילוּת נ 24 adaptability, versatility [no pl.]
סָגִין ז 20 military coat Lit-rare
סְגִיר ז 405 shackle
סְגִירָה נ 1 closing, shutting
סֶגֶל ז 317 personnel; senior staff
סָגֹל ז 301 purple; violet

סְגַלְגַּל ז 458 mauve, lavender, purplish
סְגַלְגַּל ז 458 oval, elliptical
סְגַלְגַּלּוּת נ 743 ovalness, ellipticalness; violet (color) [no pl.]
סְגֻלָּה נ 658 unique quality; folk remedy
סְגֻלִּי ז 915 special, unique; specific (physics)
סְגֻלִּיּוּת נ 762 specialness, uniqueness Lit. [no pl.]
סֶגֶן ז 317 first lieutenant
סְגָן ז 310 deputy; vice-president
סִגְנוּן ז 54 styling, fashioning
סִגְנוֹן ז 885 style
סִגְנוֹנִי ז 915 stylistic
סַגְסֹגֶת נ 721 alloy
סִגְסוּג ז 66 alloying
סַגְּפָן ז 846 ascetic person
סַגְּפָנוּת נ 752 asceticism [no pl.]
סַגְּפָנִי ז 969 ascetic, mortifying, self-denying
סֶגֶר ז 317 curfew, closure
סַגְרִיר ז 454 heavy rain
סַגְרִירִי ז 915 wintry, cold, rainy
סָדוּק ז 15 split, cracked
סִדּוּק ז 45 cracking, fissuring
סָדוּר ז 15 organized, arranged
סִדּוּר ז 45 organizing, tidying; order, arrangement; prayer book with "ordered" prayers
סִדּוּרִי ז 956 ordinal (number)
סָדִין ז 20 sheet
סְדִיקָה נ 1 cracking, splitting
סָדִיר ז 20 regular, systematic
סְדִירוּת נ 24 regularity
סַדָּן ז 275 anvil
סַדְנָה נ 619 workshop
סֶדֶק ז 317 crack, fissure; fracture; slit
סִדְקִי ז 949 glottal (phonetics)
סִדְקִית נ 812 (sewing) notions, Fr. galanterie [no pl.]
סַדָּר ז 275 typesetter, compositor (fem. sadarit)
סְדָר ז 310 composition (in typography and printing)
סֵדֶר ז 322 order, organization; arrangement
סִדְרָה נ 598 series
סַדְרָן ז 846 usher, steward
סַדְרָנוּת נ 752 stewarding, ushering [no pl.]
סִדְרָתִי ז 951 serial
סַהַר ז 328 moon, crescent Lit. [no pl.]
סֹהַר ז 343 prison, jail [no declension, except in beyt sohar, no pl.]
סַהֲרוֹן/שַׂהֲרוֹן ז 893 crescent
סַהֲרוּרִי ז 913 somnambulant; daydreaming; dazed
סַהֲרוּרִיּוּת נ 791 somnambulism; daydreaming [no pl.]

סוֹאֵן ז 7 noisy
סְוָאר/סְוָר ז 310 stack (of boxes)
סוֹבֵא ז 8 drunkard
סוֹבֵב ז 6 surrounding, environment
סוֹבְלָנִי ז 985 tolerant, open-minded
סוּג ז 246 type, sort, kind; category, class; genus (Biol.)
סוּגָה נ 595 genre
סוּגִי ז 990 generic; categorial
סַוְגָן ז 846 binder
סוֹגְפָנִי ז 985 ascetic Lit.
סוּגַר ז 373 cage
סוֹגֵר ז 6 sphincter (muscle); bracket
סוֹדִי ז 988 secret Adj
סוֹדִיּוּת נ 799 secrecy [no pl.]
סוּדָר ז 370 sweater Rare; headkerchief, scarf, shawl
סוֹדֵר ז 6 ordinal number
סוֹהֵר ז 7 prison guard
סִוּוּג ז 45 classification, categorization
סוֹחֵף ז 7 stirring; sweeping
סוֹחֲפָנִי ז 986 forceful, inciteful, sweeping
סוֹחֵר ז 7 merchant, trader
סוֹכֵךְ ז 6 canopy, awning
סוֹכֵן ז 6 agent
סוֹכְנוּת נ 14 agency
סוֹכְנוּתִי ז 915 of or related to the Jewish Agency
סוֹלֵד ז 6 retracting, turned back; 'af soled 'upturned nose'
סוֹלְחָן ז 855 forgiving, pardoning
סוֹלְחָנִי ז 985 forgiving, merciful (arch.)
סוֹלְלָה נ 660 battery; embankment; rampart
סוֹלָן ז 863 soloist
סוֹמֵךְ ז 6 support, post; second word in a construct state
סוֹמְכָה נ 660 support, armrest Lit.
סוּס ז 246 horse
סְיָח/סוּסוֹן ז 894 pony, foal
סוּסִי ז 990 equine
סוֹעֵר ז 7 stormy
סוֹף ז 240 end; finish; death [no pl.]
סוּף ז 246 rush, bulrush, reed [no pl.]
סוֹפֵג ז 6 absorbent
סוֹפְגָנִי ז 985 absorbent
סוּפָה נ 595 storm, tempest
סוֹפִי ז 988 final
סוֹפִיּוּת נ 799 finality [no pl.]
סוֹפִית נ 814 suffix
סוֹפָנִי ז 989 terminal Adj
סוֹפֵר ז 6 author, writer
סוּפָתִי ז 915 stormy Lit.

סַוָּר ז 275 longshoreman, stevedore, dockworker (fem. saveret, Coll. savarit)
סוּרִי ז 915 Syrian
סוּרְסִי ז 915 Palestinian Aramaic (Arch.)
סוֹרֵק ז 6 scanner
סוֹרֵר ז 6 rebellious
סוּת נ 247 clothing, garments Bibl.-rare
סוֹתֵר ז 6 contradictory, inconsistent
סַחַב ז 328 thrust (aeronautics) [no pl.]
סְחָבָה נ 632 rag
סַחְבָן/סַחֲבָן ז 846 pilferer, petty thief Coll.
סַחְבָּקִי ז 915 chummy Sl.
סַחֶבֶת נ 686 foot-dragging [no pl.]
סָחוּט ז 15 wrung; squeezed
סְחוּס ז 399 cartilage
סְחוּסִי ז 915 cartilaginous
סָחוּף ז 15 swept away; painful, anguished Lit
סְחוֹרָה נ 671 merchandise
סַחְטָן ז 846 extortionist, blackmailer
סַחְטָנוּת נ 752 extortion, blackmail [no pl.]
סַחְטָנִי ז 969 extortive
סְחִי ז 259 filth, contamination [no pl.]
סְחִיבָה נ 1 dragging, carrying; pilfering Coll.
סָחִיט ז 20 squeezable
סְחִיטָה נ 1 squeezing, extraction of juice; extortion
סְחִיפָה נ 1 sweeping away; erosion; captivation
סָחִיר ז 20 negotiable, tradable (economics)
סְחִירוּת נ 24 negotiability, tradability
סַחְלָב/שַׁחְלָב ז 409 orchid
סַחַף ז 328 sediment; erosion [no pl.]
סְחֹפֶת נ 708 silt, alluvium, sediment [no pl.]
סַחַר ז 328 trade, commerce, negotiation, business [no pl.]
סְחְרוּר ז 70 spin; dizziness
סְחַרְחַר ז 458 excited, agitated Lit.; dizzy
סְחַרְחֲרָנִי ז 915 dizzying Lit.
סְחַרְחֹרֶת נ 730 vertigo, dizziness
סְטָו ז 310 colonnade, portico
סָטוּר ז 15 slapped Lit
סְטִיָּה נ 4 deviation; digression; perversion
סְטִירָה נ 1 a slap on face or cheek
סְטְרִי ז 948 way (one-way, two-way)
סִיאָמִי ז 915 Siamese
סִיב ז 251 fiber
סִיבוּבִי ז 957 circular
סִיבִי ז 915 fibrous; stringy
סִיבִית נ 814 particle board, chip board (carpentry)
סִיג ז 251 slag
סְיָג ז 310 restriction, condition; border, fence, safeguard
סִיד ז 251 lime; whitewash [no pl.]
סַיָּד ז 275 whitewasher (fem. sayedet?)
סִידָן ז 875 calcium
סִיּוּג ז 45 restriction, regulation, qualification
סִיּוּד ז 45 whitewashing
סִיּוּט ז 45 nightmare
סִיּוּטִי ז 915 nightmarish
סִיּוּם ז 45 end, ending, completion, conclusion
סִיּוּעַ ז 53 aid, assistance; help
סִיּוּף ז 45 fencing sports
סִיּוּר ז 45 tour; patrol, reconnaissance
סְיָח ז 310 foal, colt
סִיטוֹנַאי ז 909 wholesaler
סִיטוֹנָאִי ז 915 wholesale Adj
סִיטוֹנוּת נ 740 wholesale [no pl.]
סִיטוֹנִי ז 915 wholesale Adj
סִיכָה נ 3 anointing; lubrication
סִילוֹן/סִלּוֹן ז 388 stream; outburst; jet
סִילוֹנִי ז 915 jet Adj
סִימָנִיָּה נ 911 bookmark
סִימָנִית נ 814 ideogram, ideograph
סִיֹּמֶת נ 697 suffix
סִין ז 251 tenon
סִינִי ז 915 Chinese
סִיס ז 251 swallow, swift (bird)
סַיָּס ז 275 groom (of horses) (fem. sayeset)
סַיָּע ז 275 assistant, helper (fem. saya`at)
סִיעָה נ 3 faction; group
סַיְעָן ז 846 collaborator
סִיעָתִי ז 915 factional
סִיעָתִיּוּת נ 762 factionalism [no pl.]
סַיָּף ז 275 fencer (sports) (fem. sayefet)
סַיִף ז 359 foil, fencing sword; fencing (sports)
סֵיפָה/א נ 596 end, final section; final clause
סֵיפָן ז 876 swordtail (fish)
סִיקוּס ז 49 knot/node on a plant
סִיקִי ז 915 Sikh
סִיר ז 251 cooking pot; chamber pot
סַיָּר ז 275 patrolman, inspector; scout (military) (fem. sayarit?)
סִירָה נ 3 boat
סִירוֹנִית נ 814 siren, mermaid Lit.
סַיֶּרֶת נ 685 commando unit; battle cruiser
סַךְ ז 214 sum, total
סִכָּה נ 586 pin; brooch; hair clip; staple
סֻכָּה נ 592 sukkah (Jewish ritual); hut; tabernacle
סִכּוּי ז 45 chance; probability
סָכוּךְ ז 15 leaf-covered
סִכּוּךְ ז 45 covering of a Sukkah
סִכּוּל ז 45 foiling, thwarting
סִכּוּלִי ז 956 foiling, thwarting
סְכוּם ז 399 sum of money; sum, total
סִכּוּם ז 45 summation, summary; total
סִכּוּן ז 45 risk
סָכוּר ז 15 dammed, sluiced
סָכוּת נ 733 prognosis [no pl.]
סַכִּין/שַׂכִּין זו״נ 402 knife
סַכִּינַאי ז 909 stabber, knifer
סְכִירָה נ 1 damming, sluicing
סְכָךְ ז 310 the covering of a sukkah [no pl.]
סְכָכָה נ 632 shed
סָכָל ז 267 foolish, idiotic
סִכְלוּת נ 738 stupidity, naivete [no pl.]
סֶכֶם ז 317 total N [no pl.]
סַכָּנָה נ 620 danger
סִכְסוּךְ ז 66 dispute; conflict
סִכְסָךְ ז 431 zigzag
סַכְסְכָן ז 851 argumentative, contentious
סַכְסְכָנוּת נ 749 argumentativeness [no pl.]
סַכְסְכָנִי ז 975 argumentative, contentious
סֶכֶר ז 317 dam, floodgate
סֻכָּרִיָּה נ 911 candy
סֻכֶּרֶת נ 699 diabetes [no pl.]
סְלָבִי ז 915 Slavic
סְלוֹבֵנִי ז 915 Slovenian
סָלוּחַ ז 17 forgiven, pardoned
סָלוּל ז 15 paved
סִלּוּף ז 45 distortion, falsification
סִלּוּק ז 45 removal, clearing away
סַלְחָן ז 846 a forgiving person
סַלְחָנוּת נ 752 forgivingness, mercifulness [no pl.]
סַלְחָנִי ז 969 forgiving
סְלִידָה נ 1 disgust, revulsion
סֻלְיָה נ 624 sole
סְלִיחָה נ 1 forgiveness; pardon
סְלִיל ז 405 spool, reel, coil
סְלִילָה נ 1 paving
סְלִילִי ז 933 spiral
סְלִיק ז 405 hiding place (esp. for weapons)
סְלִיקָה נ 1 payment; clearing in banking
סֻלָּם ז 305 ladder; scale
סִלְסוּל ז 66 curl; trill N

type of fabric Lit.- 682 סַלְסָלָה נ
Rare
stone; rock 329 סֶלַע ז
rocky 965 סַלְעִי ז
rockiness [no pl.] 785 סַלְעִיּוּת נ
wheateater, 808 סַלְעִית נ
oenanthe (bird)
liar, prevaricator 846 סַלְפָן ז
falsification, 752 סַלְפָנוּת נ
prevarication [no pl.]
lying, prevaricating 969 סַלְפָנִי ז
beet 317 סֶלֶק ז
semolina; finely 346 סֹלֶת נ
sifted flour (bibl.)
kind of edible fish 814 סַלְתָּנִית נ
(Talmudic)
nascent fruit [no pl.] 437 סְמָדַר ז
hidden, concealed; 15 סָמוּי ז
latent
adjacent, nearby; 15 סָמוּךְ ז
resting, leaning
support Lit-rare, 45 סִמּוּךְ ז
simukhin support; reference
support, stake 667 סְמוֹכָה נ
support, 998 סְמוֹכִין ז
foundation, evidence; reference
symbolization 45 סִמּוּל ז
drugging; sedation 45 סִמּוּם ז
signal; marking, sign 45 סִמּוּן ז
red, flushed 15 סָמוּק ז
straight, stiff, hard Lit 15 סָמוּר ז
weasel 378 סָמוּר ז
the standing on end 45 סִמּוּר ז
of hair; nailing [no pl.]
alley 603 סִמְטָה נ
thick 20 סָמִיךְ ז
ordination, 1 סְמִיכָה נ
graduation
proximity; 24 סְמִיכוּת נ
construct state grammar
thickness, viscosity 24 סְמִיכוּת נ
redness, blush, 24 סְמִיקוּת נ
flush rare [no pl.]
basis, foundation, 317 סֶמֶךְ ז
reliable source [no pl.]
authority 736 סַמְכוּת נ
authoritative 973 סַמְכוּתִי ז
792 סַמְכוּתִיּוּת נ
authoritarianism [no pl.]
sergeant (military) 275 סַמָּל ז
(fem. samelet)
symbol; badge; 322 סֵמֶל ז
epitome
pin, small badge 886 סִמְלוֹן ז
symbolic 949 סִמְלִי ז
symbolism [no pl.] 776 סִמְלִיּוּת נ
characteristic N 846 סַמְמָן ז
cursor (computing); 275 סַמָּן ז
indicator (elect.); in (military)
soldier who marks the beginning
of a row (fem. samanit?)
redness, flush, blush 352 סֹמֶק ז
[no pl.]
juncus (a thorny 267 סָמָר ז
plant)

shuddering 70 סִמְרוּר ז
ragged, tattered 915 סְמַרְטוּטִי ז
762 סְמַרְטוּטִיּוּת נ
submissiveness [no pl.]
shuddering, 458 סְמַרְמַר ז
quivering, trembling Lit.
shuddering Lit. 730 סְמַרְמֹרֶת נ
defense, advocacy 54 סַנֵּגוֹר ז
law [no pl.]
immobilizing 54 סִנְדּוּל ז
vehicle in violation
sandal 409 סַנְדָּל ז
shoemaker 910 סַנְדְּלָר ז
shoemaker's shop 911 סַנְדְּלָרִיָּה נ
godfather 409 סַנְדָּק ז
temporary 54 סִנְווּר ז
blindness, dazzle
sifting, filtering; 45 סִנּוּן ז
purification; sorting
swallow (bird) 814 סְנוּנִית נ
affiliation 45 סִנּוּף ז
punch, sharp 725 סְנוֹקֶרֶת נ
blow Lit.
temporary 998 סַנְוֵרִים ז
blindness Lit.
visor 715 סַנֶּרֶת נ
chin 419 סַנְטֵר ז
teasing Lit 1 סְנִיטָה נ
branch (in banking, 405 סְנִיף ז
commerce)
hydrofoil 814 סְנַפִּירִית נ
synthesization 54 סִנְתּוּז ז
moth 216 סָס ז
colorful, variegated 915 סַסְגּוֹנִי ז
colorfulness [no 762 סַסְגּוֹנִיּוּת נ
pl.]
support, assistance, 328 סַעַד ז
aid [no pl.]
meal 658 סְעֻדָּה/סְעוּדָה נ
nursing [no pl.] 50 סִעוּד ז
meal, dinner, 18 סְעוּדָה/סְעֻדָּה נ
feast
disabled, 957 סִעוּדִי ז
handicapped
subdivision, 50 סִעוּף ז
branching
story; agitated Lit 15 סָעוּר ז
si`ur moHot 'brain 50 סִעוּר ז
storming'
feasting, dining 1 סְעִידָה נ
paragraph; clause 405 סְעִיף ז
(in law)
sub-clause 895 סְעִיפוֹן ז
thought Bibl. 279 סֵעֵף ז
distribution 328 סַעַף ז
(electronics and electricity) [no
pl.]
manifold [no pl.] 686 סַעֶפֶת נ
gale, storm, tempest 328 סַעַר ז
Lit. [no pl.]
storm 640 סְעָרָה נ
threshold, doorstep; 223 סַף ז
limen psychology
absorbent 969 סַפְגָנִי ז
doughnut 911 סֻפְגָּנִיָּה נ

professional 846 סַפְדָן ז
mourner
eulogizing [no pl.] 752 סַפְדָנוּת נ
sofa 585 סַפָּה נ
soaked 15 סָפוּג ז
sponge 393 סְפוֹג ז
spongy 944 סְפוֹגִי ז
sponginess [no pl.] 762 סְפוֹגִיּוּת נ
spongy 915 סְפוֹגָנִי ז
roofed; introverted 15 סָפוּן ז
Lit; concealed Lit
counted; numbered, 15 סָפוּר ז
very few Lit
story, tale; affair, 45 סִפּוּר ז
matter
narrative Adj 956 סִפּוּרִי ז
attachment, 319 סֶפַח ז
addendum, stub
psoriasis; "tag- 689 סַפַּחַת נ
along," nuisance Coll.
absorbent 20 סָפִיג ז
absorption 1 סְפִיגָה נ
absorbency 24 סְפִיגוּת נ
aftermath, 22 סָפִיחַ ז
derivative; self-seeding crop
adsorption Chem. 1 סְפִיחָה נ
baseboard 20 סְפִין/סַפִּין ז
ship, boat 1 סְפִינָה נ
flow rate 1 סְפִיקָה נ
countable, numerable 20 סָפִיר ז
sapphire 402 סַפִּיר ז
counting 1 סְפִירָה נ
nut of violin, guitar 814 סְפִית נ
mug 322 סֵפֶל ז
small cup; cupule 450 סִפְלוּל ז
(botany)
demitasse, small 886 סִפְלוֹן ז
cup
sailor, deck hand 275 סַפָּן ז
(fem. sapanit)
hold in a ship 614 סִפְנָה נ
profiteering, 66 סִפְסוּר ז
speculation
bench 409 סַפְסָל ז
profiteer, 409 סַפְסָר ז
"speculator, "scalper
containing an 915 סַפְסָרִי ז
element of profiteering
supplier, provider 275 סַפָּק ז
(fem. sapakit)
doubt 279 סָפֵק ז
doubter, skeptic 846 סַפְקָן ז
doubt, 752 סַפְקָנוּת נ
uncertainty, skepticism [no pl.]
skeptic 969 סַפְקָנִי ז
barber, hairdresser 275 סַפָּר ז
(fem. saparit)
border, edge, frontier 310 סְפָר ז
[no pl.]
book; literary work; 322 סֵפֶר ז
scroll
Spanish 915 סְפָרַדִּי ז
Spanish [no pl.] 814 סְפָרַדִּית נ
digit 598 סִפְרָה נ
booklet 886 סִפְרוֹן ז

סִפְרוּר ז 70 numbering
סִפְרוּת נ 738 literature
סִפְרוּתִי ז 915 literary
סִפְרוּתִיּוּת נ 792 literariness [no pl.]
סְפַּרְטָנִי ז 915 Spartan
סִפְרִיָּה נ 911 library
סַפְרָן ז 846 librarian
סַפְרָנוּת נ 752 librarianship [no pl.]
סִפֹּרֶת נ 697 fiction writing
סִפְרָתִי ז 951 digital
סְקוֹטִי ז 915 Scottish
סָקוּל ז 15 stoned; cleared of stones Lit
סִקּוּל ז 45 clearing/removal of stones
סָקוּר ז 15 covered by media
סִקּוּר ז 45 coverage by media
סְקִילָה נ 1 stoning
סְקִירָה נ 1 survey; description, summary; study, poll
סֶקֶר ז 317 survey, study
סִקְרָה/א נ 598 red paint (Talmudic) [no pl.]
סַקְרָן ז 846 curious (person)
סַקְרָנוּת נ 752 curiosity, inquisitiveness [no pl.]
סַקְרָנִי ז 969 curious
סַר ז 226 angry, sad, despondent Lit.
סַרְבָּל ז 409 overall; coverall
סַרְבָן ז 846 refuser, insubordinate (person)
סַרְבָנוּת נ 752 insubordination, refusal to follow orders [no pl.]
סַרְבָנִי ז 969 insubordinate, uncooperative
סַרְגֵּל ז 419 ruler, yardstick
סַרְגֵּלִי ז 915 resembling a ruler
סָרָה נ 582 ill N, slander [no pl.]
סֵרוּב ז 51 refusal, rejection
סָרוּג ז 15 knitted, crocheted
סֵרוּג ז 51 barring, gratin
סֵרוּגִי ז 958 intermittent, alternate
סָרוּחַ ז 17 flat, stretched out
סָרוּט ז 15 scratched
סָרוּךְ ז 15 drawn, dragged Lit
סֵרוּס ז 51 castration; distortion
סָרוּק ז 15 combed; scanned
סֵרוּק ז 51 combing, hairdressing
סֶרַח ז 319 surplus, excess; train (clothing)
סִרְחוֹן ז 885 stench, foul odor
סַרְחָן ז 846 malodorous person Lit.
סֶרֶט ז 317 ribbon, streamer; movie, film; film (photog.); tape
סִרְטוּט/שִׂרְטוּט ז 70 drafting, drawing
סַרְטוּן ז 54 carcinogenesis [no pl.]
סִרְטוֹן ז 886 short film; video clip
סַרְטָט/שַׂרְטָט ז 411 draftsman
סִרְטִיָּה נ 911 film library
סַרְטָן ז 846 crab; cancer
סַרְטָנִי ז 915 cancerous
סַרְטָנִי ז 969 carcinogenic
סְרִיג ז 20 knit textile, clothing; dish rack, drainer
סְרִיגָה נ 1 knitting
סְרִיטָה נ 1 scratch n
סָרִיס ז 403 eunuch
סְרִיקָה נ 1 search; scan, perusal
סֶרֶךְ ז 317 regulation, custom Arch.
סִרְכָה נ 602 fault, defect (esp. in lung of slaughtered animal)
סִרְכּוּז ז 54 centrifugation
סַרְכֶּזֶת נ 715 centrifuge
סֶרֶן ז 326 (military) captain; Philistine ruler/governor Bibl.
סֶרֶן ז 326 axle
סַרְסוּר ז 449 pimp, pander; broker
סַרְעַף/שַׂרְעַף ז 409 (passing) thought
סַרְעֶפֶת נ 715 diaphragm
סִרְפָּד ז 431 nettle
סַרְפֶּדֶת נ 713 urticaria, nettle rash
סָרָק ז 267 red paint (Talmudic) (only construct, no declension, no pl.)
סְרָק ז 310 futility, fruitlessness [no pl.]
סְתַגְלָן ז 870 one who easily adjusts to changes
סְתַגְלָנִי ז 932 versatile, adaptive
סְתַגְּפָן ז 870 ascetic person
סְתַגְּרָן ז 870 introverted, withdrawn, detached person
סְתַגְּרָנִי ז 932 introverted, withdrawn
סְתָו ז 310 autumn, fall
סְתָוִי ז 915 autumnal
סָתוּם ז 15 blocked; vague
סְתָוָנִי ז 915 autumnal
סְתָוָנִית נ 814 colchicum, autumn crocus
סָתוּר ז 15 unkempt, wild hair; contradictory
סִתּוּת ז 45 masonry, chiseling
סְתִימָה נ 1 sealing, plugging; filling in dentistry
סְתִימוּת נ 24 vagueness, ambiguity
סְתִירָה נ 1 contradiction; neutralization chemistry
סְתָם ז 310 unclear, unspecific; purposelessly [no pl.]
סֶתֶם ז 317 blockage
סְתָמִי ז 942 unclear, unspecified; meaningless; neuter
סְתָמִיּוּת נ 771 vagueness; impersonality [no pl.]
סֵתֶר ז 322 hideaway; secret, mystery
סַתָּת ז 275 stonemason (fem. satatit?)
עָב ז 214 cloud
עֶבֶד ז 327 slave
עֻבְדָּה/א נ 624 fact
עַבְדוּת נ 736 slavery [no pl.]
עַבְדְּקָן ז 850 thick-bearded (man)
עֻבְדָּתִי ז 915 factual
עֻבְדָּתִיּוּת נ 762 factualism [no pl.]
עָבֶה ז 266 thick, broad; rough, course
עִבּוּד ז 45 processing; arrangement, adaptation
עֲבוֹדָה נ 672 work; job
עֲבוֹט ז 395 pawn, pledge, deposit
עִבּוּי ז 45 thickening
עִבּוּר ז 45 intercalation (chemistry); pregnancy Lit., `ibur hashana ‘adding a month to a Jewish year’
עֲבוֹת ז 397 strong rope Lit. [alternant plural form `avotim]
עַבְטִיט ז 454 thick mud Lit. [no pl.]
עֳבִי ז 350 thickness
עָבִיד ז 21 workable
עָבִיר ז 21 passable, navigable, traversable
עֲבִירוּת נ 25 navigability, passability
עָבָר ז 268 past [no pl.]
עֻבָּר ז 304 fetus
עֵבֶר ז 323 side, direction, way
עֶבְרָה נ 606 anger, wrath Lit.
עֲבֵרָה נ 650 violation; transgression
עִבְרוּת נ 738 Hebraization [no pl.]
עִבְרִי ז 949 Hebrew Adj
עִבְרִיּוּת נ 776 being Hebrew [no pl.]
עֲבַרְיָן ז 863 criminal
עִבְרִית נ 812 Hebrew (no decl., no pl.)
עָבֵשׁ ז 280 moldy; boring, unoriginal
עֹבֶשׁ ז 342 mold; mildew [no pl.]
עָבֹת/עָבוֹת ז 302 dense, entangled, bushy
עֲגָבִים ז 998 flirtations Lit.
עַגְבָן ז 846 flirter Lit.
עַגְבָנוּת נ 752 flirtation Lit. [no pl.]
עַגְבָנִי ז 969 flirtatious, salacious
עַגְבָנִיָּה נ 911 tomato
עַגֶּבֶת נ 685 syphilis [no pl.]
עָגָה נ 582 slang; jargon
עִגּוּל ז 45 circle; rounding
עִגּוּלִי ז 956 round, circular
עָגוּם ז 16 sad, depressed

עִגּוּן ז 45 anchoring
עֲגוּנָה נ 19 "chained" woman unable to get a divorce
עָגוּר ז 16 crane (bird)
עֲגוּרָן ז 863 crane (construction)
עֲגִיבָה נ 2 flirtation Lit
עָגִיל ז 21 earring
עֲגִינָה נ 2 anchoring; anchorage
עָגֹל ז 302 round
עֵגֶל ז 323 calf (male)
עֲגַלְגַּל ז 459 rounded, roundish
עֲגָלָה נ 641 wagon
עֶגְלוֹן ז 887 carter, coachman
עַגְמוּמִי ז 912 sad, forlorn
עַגְמוּמִיּוּת נ 790 sadness, forlornness [no pl.]
עַגְמִימוּת נ 740 sadness, forlornness [no pl.]
עֹגֶן ז 342 anchor
עֵד ז 231 witness N
עֵדָה נ 590 ethnic group; group
עִדּוּד/עִידוּד ז 47 encouragement, cheering up; promoting
עָדוּי ז 16 adorned Lit
עִדּוּן ז 45 refinement
עָדוּר ז 16 hoed, tilled
עִדּוּר ז 45 hoeing, tilling
עֲדִי ז 258 adornment, ornament
עָדִין ז 21 fine, delicate; fragile; refined
עֲדִינוּת נ 25 gentleness, softness, sensibility
עָדִיף ז 21 preferable
עֲדִיפוּת נ 25 preference
עֲדִירָה נ 2 hoeing, tilling
עִדִּית נ 814 best, choicest; good soil (is it a suffix here?)
עִדְכּוּן ז 54 update N
עַדְכָּנוּת נ 740 being updated [no pl.]
עַדְכָּנִי ז 915 up-to-date
עַדְכָּנִיּוּת נ 788 being updated [no pl.]
עֵדֶן ז 323 Eden, paradise; pleasure Lit.
עֶדְנָה נ 606 gentleness, tenderness
עַדְעַד ז 416 limonium
עֹדֶף ז 342 change; surplus, excess, extra
עֵדֶר ז 323 flock, herd, drove
עֵדֶר ז 323 herd, flock, drove
עֶדְרִי ז 961 herd-like (mentality, behavior)
עֲדָשָׁה נ 639 lens
עַדְשָׁן ז 846 freckled person Lit.
עַדְשָׁנִי ז 969 freckled Lit.
עֲדָתִי ז 915 ethnic
עֲדָתִיּוּת נ 772 ethnicity [no pl.]
עוֹבֵד ז 6 worker, employee
עוֹבֵר ז 6 moving, passing; temporary; passing in the education system
עוּגָב ז 370 pipe organ
עוּגָבַאי ז 909 organist

עוֹגְבָנִי ז 985 flirtatious, salacious Lit.
עוּגָה נ 595 cake
עוּגִיָּה נ 911 cookie
עוּד ז 246 oud
עוֹדֵף ז 6 leftover; surplus; redundant
עָוֹן ז 295 sin, transgression; misdemeanor
עִוּוּת ז 45 distortion, falsification
עוֹזֵר ז 6 assistant, aide
עוֹטְפָן ז 855 folder
עֲוָיָה נ 633 grimace N
עֲוִיל ז 406 evil person, wrongdoer (biblical)
עוֹיֵן ז 6 hostile
עוֹיְנוּת נ 14 hostility
עֲוִית נ 806 spasm
עֲוִיתִי ז 915 spasmodic, spastic
עוֹכֵר ז 6 one who causes trouble; destroyer
עָוֶל ז 354 injustice [consonantal vav maintained in `avlo etc.; no pl]
עוֹלֵב ז 6 insulting Lit
עוֹלֶה ז 10 immigrant to Israel
עוֹלָה נ 593 burnt offering (Jewish law, in Temple)
עַוְלָה נ 614 injustice
עוֹלָל ז 366 babe, suckling infant, toddler Lit.
עוֹלֵלָה נ 663 gleaning (of grapes), secondary crops
עוֹלָם ז 367 world; eternity
עוֹלָמִי ז 915 world-wide
עוֹלָמִיּוּת נ 762 universality [no pl.]
עוֹמֵד ז 6 standing, stationary; fixed, stable
עוֹנָה נ 593 season
עוֹנָתִי ז 915 seasonal
עוֹנָתִיּוּת נ 762 being seasonal [no pl.]
עִוְעִים ז 998 craziness, freneticness Lit.
עוֹף ז 242 bird; poultry; chicken
עוֹפֶרֶת נ 11 lead (chemistry) [no pl.]
עוֹפַרְתִּי ז 915 of lead
עוֹצֵר ז 6 regent
עוֹקֵב ז 6 sequential
עוֹקְדָן ז 855 binder
עוּקָה נ 595 sump
עוֹקֵף ז 6 bypassing
עוֹקְצָנִי ז 985 sarcastic
עוֹר ז 242 skin; hide; leather
עִוֵּר ז 283 blind; blind person
עוֹרֵב ז 6 crow, raven
עוֹרֵג ז 6 yearning, longing Lit
עִוָּרוֹן ז 898 blindness (pl. suffix -im)
עִוְּרוּת נ 739 blindness [no pl.]
עוֹרִי ז 988 dermal
עוֹרֵךְ ז 6 editor
עוֹרֵק ז 6 artery; vein

עוֹרְקִי ז 984 arterial
עוֹרֵר ז 6 appealer
עוֹתְמָנִי ז 915 Ottoman
עוֹתֵר ז 6 petitioner
עַז ז 221 strong, mighty; intense
עֹז ז 228 might, strength
עֵז נ 235 goat
עִזָּבוֹן ז 898 estate, inheritance
עָזוּב ז 16 abandoned, neglected
עֲזוּבָה נ 19 neglect
עִזּוּק ז 45 hoeing, tilling (biblical) [no pl.]
עַזּוּת נ 731 cheek, audacity; power, strength Lit. [no pl.]
עֲזִיבָה נ 2 leaving, departure
עָזְנִיָּה נ 911 black vulture
עֵזֶר ז 323 aid, assistance; aid(s), accessory
עֻזְרָד/עֲזְרָר ז 435 crab apple
עֶזְרָה נ 606 help, aid [no pl.]
עֲזָרָה נ 641 separate section (e.g. women's in synagogue)
עֵט ז 231 pen
עָטוּי ז 16 wrapped, covered Lit
עָטוּף ז 16 wrapped, covered
עִטּוּף ז 45 wrapping, covering
עָטוּר ז 16 decorated
עִטּוּר ז 45 decorating, ornamenting; decoration, ornament
עִטּוּרִי ז 956 ornamental
עִטּוּשׁ ז 45 sneeze Lit
עָטִין ז 21 udder
עָטִיף ז 21 (perianth (botany
עֲטִיף ז 406 perianth (botany)
עֲטִיפָה נ 2 wrapping, covering
עֲטִישָׁה נ 2 a sneeze Lit
עֲטָרָה נ 642 crown, tiara; glans penis
עִטְרָן ז 857 tar [no pl.]
עִי ז 239 heap or mound of ruins Lit.
עִיּוּל ז 45 putting in, entering; recording
עִיּוּן ז 45 study N; consideration
עִיּוּנִי ז 956 theoretical
עִיּוּר ז 45 urbanization [no pl.]
עַיִט ז 357 eagle (not vulture, as popularly assumed)
עַיִן נ 361 spring, fountain
עַיִן נ 364 eye; shade, color; appearance
עֵינִית נ 814 eyepiece (of microscope, etc.)
עָיֵף ז 280 tired
עַיִר ז 365 young ass
עִיר ר׳ עָרִים נ 251 city; town (pl. `arim)
עֲיָרָה נ 633 small town
עִירוֹנִי ז 915 municipal
עִירִיָּה נ 911 town hall
עִירִית נ 814 chives; asphodel (is it a suffix here?)
עֲיָרָתִי ז 915 townish
עַכָּבָה נ 620 inhibition

עִכָּבוֹן ז 898 lien (law)
עַכְבָּר ז 409 mouse
עַכְבָּרוֹן ז 894 little mouse
עַכְבָּרִי ז 968 mousy
עִכּוּב ז 45 delay, hindrance
עַכּוּבִית נ 814 gundelia (plant) (is it a suffix here?)
עַכּוּז ז 378 buttocks, posterior
עִכּוּל ז 45 digestion [no pl.]
עִכּוּלִי ז 956 digestive
עַכּוּמִי ז 915 idolatrous, heathen, pagan
עָכוּר ז 16 murky
עֲכִירוּת נ 25 murkiness, cloudiness; turbidity
עֶכֶן ז 327 snake, ringed snake
עֶכֶס ז 327 anklet (biblical)
עַכְסָן ז 846 rattlesnake
עַכְרוּרִי ז 912 slightly murky Lit.
עַכְשׁוּב ז 447 solifuge, sun spider
עִכְשׁוּו ז 54 actualization [no pl.]
עַכְשָׁוִי ז 915 current, contemporary
עֹל ז 227 burden; yoke [no pl.]
עִלָּאִי ז 915 lofty, exalted, supreme
עֶלְבּוֹן ז 888 insult N
עֶלְבּוֹנִי ז 962 of insult
עִלֵּג ז 283 stuttered, stammered; incorrect language
עִלְּגוּת נ 739 stammering, mumbling [no pl.]
עָלֶה ז 262 leaf
עִלָּה נ 586 excuse
עָלוּב ז 16 wretched, dismal; meager, worthless
עַלְוָה נ 611 foliage
עִלּוּי ז 45 genius; prodigy
עִלּוּיִי ז 956 ingenious, extraordinarily smart
עָלוּל ז 16 liable, likely
עָלוּם ז 16 secret, hidden
עִלּוּם ז 45 concealing [no pl.]
עֲלוּמִים ז 998 youth, adolescence
עָלוֹן ז 293 leaflet, brochure, pamphlet
עַלְוָנִי ז 969 leafy
עִלּוּס ז 45 lovemaking Lit-rare
עֲלוּקָה נ 19 leech
עֲלוּת נ 735 cost, expense
עָלֵז ז 280 joyful, happy Lit.
עֲלָטָה נ 642 darkness, gloom Lit.
עֱלִי ז 258 pestle; pistil (botany)
עִלִּי ז 915 upper
עֲלִיבוּת נ 25 forlornness, wretchedness, neglectedness
עֲלִיָּה נ 5 ascent; incline; increase; advance; immigration to Israel
עֶלְיוֹנוּת נ 740 superiority [no pl.]
עַלִּיז ז 402 happy, cheerful; gay, delightful
עַלִּיזוּת נ 754 gaiety, cheerfulness [no pl.]
עֲלִיל ז 406 deed; fact [no pl.]

עֲלִילָה נ 2 plot, story; deeds, tales, adventures
עֲלִילָתִי ז 915 th of plot/story
year land fallow debts canceled
עֲלִיצוּת נ 25 happiness, joy, cheerfulness
עִלִּית נ 828 elite; top quality; superstructure (of seacraft)
עֶלֶם ז 327 young, young man
עָלֵס ז 280 joyful, happy Lit.
עֶלֶס ז 318 joy, cheerfulness Lit.
עַלְעוֹל ז 444 storm; whirlwind Lit.
עִלְעוּל ז 66 leafing, browsing
עַלְעַל ז 416 leaflet (botany)
עִלָּפוֹן ז 899 swoon, fainting [no pl.]
עַלֶּקֶת נ 685 orobanche (plant); trematode (worm)
עֹלֶשׁ ז 342 chicory, endive
עֶמְדָּה נ 606 position
עַמּוּד ז 378 post, pole, pillar, column; lectern, pulpit
עִמּוּד ז 45 layout publishing
עִמּוּל ז 45 training Rare [no pl.]
עָמוּם ז 16 dark; weak, unclear; blurry, hazy
עִמּוּם ז 45 dimming a light [no pl.]
עַמּוֹנִי ז 915 Ammonite
עָמוּס ז 16 loaded, laden; busy, crowded
עִמּוּץ ז 45 shutting of eye Lit-rare [no pl.]
עִמּוּת ז 45 confrontation; debate
עָמִיד ז 21 durable
עֲמִידָה נ 2 standing; sticking to promise, schedule etc.; steadfastness
עֲמִידוּת נ 25 durability, fastness
עָמִיל ז 21 agent, representative commerce
עֲמִילוּת נ 25 agency, representation
עֲמִילָן ז 863 starch
עֲמִילָנִי ז 915 starchy
עֲמִימוּת נ 25 vagueness, ambiguousness; opacity
עָמִיר ז 21 sheaf, bundle of grain
עָמִית ז 21 colleague, friend
עָמָל ז 268 labor, hard work [no pl.]
עָמֵל ז 280 worker, laborer
עַמְלָה נ 611 commission
עֲמָלָה נ 639 commission
עַמְלָן ז 846 workaholic Rare
עַמְלָנוּת נ 752 working, laboring [no pl.]
עַמְלָנִי ז 969 working hard, toiling
עֲמָלֵקִי ז 915 Amalekite
עֲמָמִי ז 915 popular; inexpensive; folk (music, art)
עֲמָמִיּוּת נ 772 simplicity, popularity [no pl.]

עֹמֶס ז 342 load, burden [no pl.]
עִמְעוּם ז 66 dimming; dulling; blurring
עַמְעַם ז 416 dimmer, rheostat
עָמֹק ז 302 deep
עֵמֶק ז 339 valley, glen, dale
עֹמֶק ז 342 depth, `omko/`umko, `omkey/`umkey
עַמְקוּת נ 736 depth [no pl.]
עַמְקָן ז 846 profound, astute person
עַמְקָנוּת נ 752 profundity, astuteness Lit. [no pl.]
עַמְקָנִי ז 969 profound, astute
עֹמֶר ז 342 sheaf, bundle of grain (biblical)
עֲמֻתָּה נ 659 non-profit organization
עֵנָב, ר׳ עֲנָבִים ז 287 grape (pl. `anavim, constr. `invey)
עֲנָבָה נ 633 berry; grape Lit.
עִנְבָּל ז 431 clapper, tongue of bell; uvula
עִנְבָּר ז 431 amber [no pl.]
עָנֹג ז 302 soft, delicate, refined Lit.
עֹנֶג ז 342 pleasure [no pl.]
עֶנֶד ז 318 decoration; knot
עָנָו ז 268 humble, modest, unpretentious
עָנוּב ז 16 wearing a tie
עִנּוּג ז 45 pleasure, delight
עָנוּד ז 16 adorned
עֲנָוָה נ 639 modesty [no pl.]
עִנּוּי ז 45 torment N
עָנוּשׁ ז 16 punishable Obs.
עַנְוְתָן ז 853 humble, modest (person)
עָנִי ז 256 pauper; poor
עֹנִי ז 350 poverty; suffering Bibl. [no pl.]
עֲנִיבָה נ 2 tie, cravat; noose
עֲנִידָה נ 2 wearing, pinning, decorating
עֲנִיּוּת נ 762 being poor [no pl.]
עִנְיָן ז 858 matter, issue; interest N
עִנְיָנִי ז 950 businesslike, matter-of-fact
עִנְיָנִיּוּת נ 777 matter-of-factness [no pl.]
עֲנִישָׁה נ 2 punishing; punishment
עָנָן ז 268 cloud
עֲנָנָה נ 639 gloom; cloud Lit.
עָנָף ז 268 branch; department
עָנֵף ז 280 branched; diverse, widespread
עֲנָפִי/עַנְפִּי ז 943 affiliated
עֲנָק ז 311 giant; huge; necklace
עֲנָקִי ז 943 giant, huge
עֲנָקִיּוּת נ 762 hugeness, enormity [no pl.]
עֲנַקְמוֹנִי ז 915 giant, huge Lit.
עֹנֶשׁ ז 342 punishment

dough 586 עִסָּה נ
massage N 45 עִסּוּי ז
busy, occupied 16 עָסוּק ז
task, activity; 45 עִסּוּק ז
vocation; job
juice, nectar 21 עָסִיס ז
juicy 934 עֲסִיסִי ז
juiciness; 770 עֲסִיסִיּוּת נ
vivaciousness [no pl.]
business 339 עֵסֶק ז
deal 601 עִסְקָה נ
of business 949 עִסְקִי ז
go-getter, politico, 846 עַסְקָן ז
wheeler-dealer
involvement in 752 עַסְקָנוּת נ
public business [no pl.]
related to 969 עַסְקָנִי ז
politico/wheeler-dealer
wheeling-dealing 788 עַסְקָנִיּוּת נ
(esp. in politics) [no pl.]
reek, stench 45 עִפּוּשׁ ז
branch Lit. 351 עֳפִי, ר׳ עֳפָאִים ז
[pl. `afa'im]
anchovy 846 עַפְיָן ז
kite 896 עֲפִיפוֹן ז
astringent 21 עָפִיץ ז
astringency 25 עֲפִיצוּת נ
fortified hill (biblical) 342 עֹפֶל ז
blinking 66 עִפְעוּף ז
eyelid 418 עַפְעַף ז
gall (botany) 268 עָפָץ ז
earth, dirt; dust (Lit.) 268 עָפָר ז
(alt. plural `afarot)
of the color of earth, 303 עָפֹר ז
of dirt Lit.
fawn 342 עֹפֶר ז
ore 611 עַפְרָה נ
lead of a pencil 628 עֻפְרָה נ
pencil 899 עִפָּרוֹן ז
tree; wood 233 עֵץ ז
nerve 274 עָצָב ז
sad, sorrowful Lit. 280 עָצֵב ז
sadness, sorrow, grief 327 עֶצֶב ז
formation (military) 624 עֻצְבָּה נ
innervation 70 עִצְבּוּב ז
sorrow, grief Lit.; 898 עִצָּבוֹן ז
toil, pain Lit.
sadness [no pl.] 736 עַצְבוּת נ
neural 915 עֲצַבִּי ז
restlessness, 752 עַצְבָּנוּת נ
anxiety, nervousness [no pl.]
restless, nervous, 969 עַצְבָּנִי ז
anxious; irritable, jumpy
sacrum 262 עָצֶה ז
advice, counsel 590 עֵצָה נ
sad 16 עָצוּב ז
design 45 עִצּוּב ז
enormous; closed 16 עָצוּם ז
eyes
sanction 45 עִצּוּם ז
petition 19 עֲצוּמָה נ
constricted, 16 עָצוּר ז
restrained; imprisoned,
detained; prisoner, detainee
consonant 45 עִצּוּר ז

woody Lit. 915 עֵצִי ז
intensified, 21 עָצִים/עֲצִים ז
intense, strenuous
closing of eye(s) 2 עֲצִימָה נ
intensity Lit. [no 754 עֲצִימוּת נ
pl.]
flowerpot, planter 406 עָצִיץ ז
detainee 21 עָצִיר ז
stopping; stop 2 עֲצִירָה נ
constipation 25 עֲצִירוּת נ
lazy, idle; loafer 280 עָצֵל ז
laziness [no pl.] 736 עַצְלוּת נ
lazy (person) 846 עַצְלָן ז
laziness, 752 עַצְלָנוּת נ
indolence, slothfulness [no pl.]
slothful, slow 915 עַצְלְתָּנִי ז
thing, object; 327 עֶצֶם ז
essence, core, gist
bone 331 עֶצֶם נ
independent 915 עַצְמָאִי ז
strength, power 628 עָצְמָה נ
spontaneous 915 עַצְמוֹנִי ז
(medicine)
identity, self- 736 עַצְמוּת נ
concept Lit. [no pl.]
intrinsic 973 עַצְמוּתִי ז
self- (self- 965 עַצְמִי ז
confidence, etc.)
identity, self- 785 עַצְמִיּוּת נ
concept [no pl.]
stopper, stop 327 עֶצֶר ז
curfew [no pl.] 342 עֹצֶר ז
assembly, rally; 703 עֲצֶרֶת נ
factorial (math)
buzzard (bird) 275 עַקָּב ז
crooked, twisted 302 עָקֹב ז
heel; 282 עָקֵב, ר׳ עֲקֵבוֹת/עֲקֵבִים ז
trace (pl. `akevot/`akevim)
trace; memory trace 599 עִקְבָה נ
consistent 949 עִקְבִי ז
consistency [no pl.] 776 עִקְבִיּוּת נ
with stripes (animal), 302 עָקֹד ז
as if it had been bound Lit.-rare
collection (of books, 323 עֶקֶד ז
articles) Lit.
binding 650 עֲקֵדָה נ
stress (psychology); 582 עָקָה נ
depression; pressure
bound 16 עָקוּד ז
crooked 16 עָקוּם ז
bending, twisting; 45 עִקּוּם ז
distortion
bypass 45 עִקּוּף ז
stung, bitten 16 עָקוּץ ז
uprooted, extracted; 16 עָקוּר ז
displaced person
sterilization; 45 עִקּוּר ז
neutering
crooked Lit 16 עָקוּשׁ ז
consistent; sequential 21 עָקִיב ז
following, tracking 2 עֲקִיבָה נ
consistency 25 עֲקִיבוּת נ
binding, tying 2 עֲקִידָה נ
twisting, bending, 2 עֲקִימָה נ
curving

crookedness, 25 עֲקִימוּת נ
twistedness, curvature
indirect 21 עָקִיף ז
bypassing, 2 עֲקִיפָה נ
circumventing
stinging; sting, bite 2 עֲקִיצָה נ
uprooting; 2 עֲקִירָה נ
extraction; displacement,
transfer
headband wound 268 עָקָל ז
around a kaffiyeh
curved, twisted 302 עָקֹל ז
basket used for 323 עֶקֶל ז
pressing olives (arch.)
twisting, winding; 459 עֲקַלְקַל ז
crooked, underhanded
being crooked 744 עֲקַלְקַלּוּת נ
[no pl.]
curved, twisted 302 עָקֹם ז
twistedness; 353 עֹקֶם ז
distortion [no pl.]
curve 659 עֲקֻמָּה נ
crooked, twisted 912 עֲקַמּוּמִי ז
being crooked, 790 עֲקַמּוּמִיּוּת נ
twisted [no pl.]
curvature [no pl.] 836 עֲקַמּוּמִית נ
curvature [no pl.] 750 עֲקַמִימוּת נ
crooked, twisted, 846 עַקְמָן ז
dishonest person
insincerity, 752 עַקְמָנוּת נ
dishonesty עַקְמָנִי ז
scoliosis [no pl.] 685 עַקֶּמֶת נ
sting N, 342 עֹקֶץ ז
`oktso/`uktso, `oktsey/`uktsey
stinging, itching 70 עִקְצוּץ ז
sterile, infertile, 268 עָקָר ז
barren; futile
essence, main part, 286 עִקָּר ז
gist; principle
scorpion; thorn 412 עַקְרָב ז
(biblical)
scorpion fish 863 עַקְרַבָּן ז
childless/barren 642 עֲקָרָה נ
woman
principle 899 עִקָּרוֹן ז
(matter of) 963 עֶקְרוֹנִי ז
principle Adj
behavior by 784 עֶקְרוֹנִיּוּת נ
principle [no pl.]
main, principal 915 עִקָּרִי ז
housewife 703 עֲקֶרֶת נ
stubborn 283 עִקֵּשׁ ז
stubbornness [no 739 עַקְשׁוּת נ
pl.]
stubborn (person) 846 עַקְשָׁן ז
stubbornness, 752 עַקְשָׁנוּת נ
obstinacy, intransigence;
persistence, tenacity [no pl.]
obstinate, stubborn 969 עַקְשָׁנִי ז
awake; active; alert; 231 עֵר ז
aware of
temporary 943 עֲרָאִי ז
temporariness [no 772 עֲרָאִיּוּת נ
pl.]
guarantor 280 עָרֵב ז

magnificence, 307 ז פְּאֵר
splendor [no pl.]
abomination; 45 ז פִּגּוּל
denaturation of alcohol
faulty, defective, 15 ז פָּגוּם
lacking
scaffolding 45 ז פִּגּוּם
damaged, injured; hurt 17 ז פָּגוּעַ
terrorist attack 53 ז פִּגּוּעַ
backwardness; 45 ז פִּגּוּר
arrears; delay
bumper (of car) 297 ז פָּגוֹשׁ
shell (munitions) 267 ז פָּגָז
dagger 441 ז פִּגְיוֹן
damage, disruption 1 נ פְּגִימָה
defectiveness, 24 נ פְּגִימוּת
incompleteness
vulnerable; sensitive 22 ז פָּגִיעַ
emotionally
blow; injury, 1 נ פְּגִיעָה
damage; hit; insult
vulnerability; 24 נ פְּגִיעוּת
sensitivity emotional
meeting; 1 נ פְּגִישָׁה
appointment; meeting; reunion
damage, defect, fault, 310 ז פְּגָם
deficiency
pagan; a rustic 273 ז פֶּגֶן
pagan 915 ז פַּגָנִי
paganism [no pl.] 762 נ פַּגָנִיּוּת
injury, mishap; 319 ז פֶּגַע
disaster
corpse, carcass 317 ז פֶּגֶר
recess, vacation 614 נ פַּגְרָה
salvation, liberation 734 נ פְּדוּת
Lit.
forehead Lit. 689 נ פַּדַּחַת
redemption 4 נ פְּדִיָּה
redemption; 885 ז פִּדְיוֹן
ransom; proceeds
omentum - anatomy 317 ז פֶּדֶר
mouth; opening, 238 ז פֶּה
orifice, entrance
yawn N 50 ז פִּהוּק
rest, break Lit. 595 נ פּוּגָה
harmful; offensive 985 ז פּוֹגְעָנִי
cross-eyed 6 ז פּוֹזֵל
cross-eyed 985 ז פּוֹזְלָנִי
irresponsible, reckless 6 ז פּוֹחֵז
Lit
fine feathers; blue 246 ז פּוּךְ
eye shadow Talm. [no pl.]
740 נ פּוּלְמוּסָנוּת/ פֻּלְמוּסָנוּת
controversialness [no pl.]
Polish 915 ז פּוֹלָנִי
invader; intruder, 6 ז פּוֹלֵשׁ
trespasser
intrusive, invasive 985 ז פּוֹלְשָׁנִי
oral 915 ז פּוּמִי
mouthpiece (music) 814 נ פּוּמִית
Punic 915 ז פּוּנִי
adjudicator in Jewish 6 ז פּוֹסֵק
law; normative
normativist 855 ז פּוֹסְקָן

normativism [no 759 נ פּוֹסְקָנוּת
pl.]
adjudicative; 985 ז פּוֹסְקָנִי
normative (linguistics)
worker, laborer 7 ז פּוֹעֵל
worker bee 12 נ פּוֹעֶלֶת
plosive (phonetics) 6 ז פּוֹצֵץ
lot, fate, luck 246 ז פּוּר
productive; fruitful 10 ז פּוֹרֶה
Portuguese 915 ז פּוֹרְטוּגְזִי
Portuguese 915 ז פּוֹרְטוּגָלִי
fertility [no pl.] 762 נ פּוֹרִיּוּת
of or related to 915 ז פּוּרִימִי
Purim
rioter 9 ז פּוֹרֵעַ
burglar 6 ז פּוֹרֵץ
dissident, seceder; 6 ז פּוֹרֵשׁ
separatist
forager; invading, 6 ז פּוֹשֵׁט
incursive; spreading
criminal 9 ז פּוֹשֵׁעַ
lukewarm 6 ז פּוֹשֵׁר
vagina; sleeve for 593 נ פּוֹתָה
hinge
bottle opener 855 ז פּוֹתְחָן
gold; something 218 ז פָּז
golden [no pl.]
soft singing 45 ז פִּזּוּם
scattered; dispersed; 15 ז פָּזוּר
loose
scattering 45 ז פִּזּוּר
dispersion, diaspora 18 נ פְּזוּרָה
hasty, haphazard 20 ז פָּזִיז
haste 24 נ פְּזִיזוּת
squint, sideways view 1 נ פְּזִילָה
short song, tune; 884 ז פִּזְמוֹן
refrain
songwriter (who 909 ז פִּזְמוֹנַאי
writes lyrics)
sock Lit. 436 ז פֻּזְמָק
squanderer, 846 ז פַּזְרָן
spendthrift
squanderousness, 752 נ פַּזְרָנוּת
spendthriftiness; philanthropy,
generosity [no pl.]
squanderous, 969 ז פַּזְרָנִי
spendthrifty
tin, can, garbage can; 221 ז פַּח
snare
fear, anxiety 328 ז פַּחַד
coward 846 ז פַּחְדָן
cowardice [no pl.] 752 נ פַּחְדָנוּת
fearful, cowardly 969 ז פַּחְדָנִי
province ruled by a 612 נ פֶּחָה
pasha
blackening with soot 50 ז פִּחוּם
[no pl.]
reduction, 50 ז פִּחוּת
diminution; devaluation (of a
currency)
haste; recklessness 328 ז פַּחַז
Lit. [no pl.]
cream puff, 833 נ פַּחְזָנִית
profiterole

tinsmith, metal 276 ז פַּחָח/פֶּחָח
worker; car body repairman
(fem. paHaHit)
car body 911 נ פַּחָחִיָּה/פֶּחָחִיָּה
shop
flattening, squashing 1 נ פְּחִיסָה
flatness 24 נ פְּחִיסוּת
small can 814 נ פַּחִית
devaluation, 1 נ פְּחִיתָה
depreciation; reduction
unimportance, 24 נ פְּחִיתוּת
inferiority
taxidermy 54 ז פִּחְלוּץ
stuffed animal 435 ז פֶּחְלָץ
carbonate 610 נ פַּחְמָה
carbonization [no 54 ז פִּחְמוּן
pl.]
carbonaceous; coaly 965 ז פַּחְמִי
hydrocarbon 863 ז פַּחְמֵימָן
carbon 846 ז פַּחְמָן
carbonaceous 969 ז פַּחְמָנִי
carbonated 971 ז פַּחְמָתִי
depreciation; waste, 310 ז פְּחָת
loss; reduction; amortization
[no pl.]
trap, snare, pit Lit. 328 ז פַּחַת
topaz 598 נ פִּטְדָה
fattening of animals 45 ז פִּטּוּם
exempt 15 ז פָּטוּר
exemption 393 ז פְּטוֹר
firing from 45 ז (פִּטּוּר(ים/ין
post, discharging
death, passing; 1 נ פְּטִירָה
exemption
hammer 402 ז פַּטִּישׁ
percussion mallet 894 ז פַּטִּישׁוֹן
(music), hammer drill
raspberry [no pl.] 317 ז פֶּטֶל
fattened livestock or 310 ז פְּטָם
poultry
nipple 598 נ פִּטְמָה
chatter, prattle 66 ז פִּטְפּוּט
chatterbox, prattler 851 ז פַּטְפְּטָן
chattering, 749 נ פַּטְפְּטָנוּת
babbling [no pl.]
chatterbox, prattler 975 ז פַּטְפְּטָנִי
first-born Bibl. 317 ז פֶּטֶר
patrolling 54 ז פִּטְרוּל
patronage [no pl.] 740 נ פַּטְרוֹנוּת
patronizing 915 ז פַּטְרוֹנִי
mushroom 911 נ פִּטְרִיָּה
fungal 915 ז פִּטְרִיָּתִי
fungal infection [no 685 נ פַּטֶּרֶת
pl.]
common rue (plant) 374 ז פֵּיגָם
disaster, trouble (Bibl.) 251 ז פִּיד
opening, spout; 911 נ פִּיָּה
mouthpiece (music)
blackening from soot 53 ז פִּיּוּחַ
liturgical poem; 45 ז פִּיּוּט
poetry ~ piyet write poetry
poetic, lyrical 956 ז פִּיּוּטִי
pore (botany) 814 נ פִּיּוֹנִית
placation, 45 ז פִּיּוּס
appeasement, reconciliation

decisiveness, 752 פַּסְקָנוּת נ
certainty [no pl.]
decisive 969 פַּסְקָנִי ז
part, parting 708 פִּסֹּקֶת נ
(hairdressing)
toddler 297 פָּעוֹט ז
nursery school 894 פָּעוֹטוֹן ז
gaping, wide open 15 פָּעוּר ז
bleating; bleat 4 פְּעִיָּה נ
active 20 פָּעִיל ז
activity 24 פְּעִילוּת נ
pip, short high- 405 פְּעִים ז
pitched sound
beat music; heart 1 פְּעִימָה נ
gape 1 פְּעִירָה נ
verb; activities, 343 פֹּעַל ז
achievements
action 658 פְּעֻלָּה נ
effect (in film, radio 451 פַּעֲלוּל ז
etc.)
of verb 981 פָּעֳלִי ז
active person 872 פַּעַלְתָּן ז
very active 915 פַּעַלְתָּנִי ז
time, occasion; 328 פַּעַם ז
once; pace; beat
beat 612 פְּעָמָה נ
bell 890 פַּעֲמוֹן ז
bellflower (plant) 814 פַּעֲמוֹנִית נ
bell-ringer 910 פַּעֲמוֹנָר ז
deciphering; 55 פִּעְנוּחַ ז
solving; decoding
bubbling; seeping, 67 פִּעְפּוּעַ ז
infusion
gap, rift 328 פַּעַר ז
cracking nuts, seeds; 53 פִּצּוּחַ ז
solving riddle etc.; molecular
fission
compensation 45 פִּצּוּי ז
division, splitting; 45 פִּצּוּל ז
branching; split, rift
wounded 17 תו"ז פָּצוּעַ
hacker (computing) 846 פַּצְחָן ז
wounding, injuring; 1 פְּצִיעָה נ
wound, injury
filing; file carpentry, 1 פְּצִירָה נ
metalwork
feldspar 685 פֶּצֶלֶת נ
wound, injury, sore 319 פֶּצַע ז
pimple 886 פִּצְעוֹן ז
smashing 66 פִּצְפּוּץ ז
bomb 636 פְּצָצָה נ
commander (police), 275 פַּקָּד ז
chief inspector; controller
(computing) (fem. pakedet)
command 658 פְּקֻדָּה נ
deposit 898 פִּקָּדוֹן ז
cap (weaponry); 586 פִּקָּה נ
knee cap
command, authority - 45 פִּקּוּד ז
military
open eyes; watchful 17 פָּקוּחַ ז
eye
supervision 53 פִּקּוּחַ ז
split, cracked; 17 פָּקוּעַ ז
invalid, void

mushroom 668 פְּקוּעָה נ
corked, stoppered; 15 פָּקוּק ז
blocked, jammed with traffic
corking 45 פִּקּוּק ז
inspector (fem. 275 פַּקָּח ז
pakaHit)
smart, bright 284 פִּקֵּחַ ז
realistic 898 פִּקְחוֹן ז
observation; vision, eyesight
Lit.
brilliance, 739 פִּקְחוּת נ
intelligence [no pl.]
sharp, bright, quick- 955 פִּקְחִי ז
witted
clerk 20 פָּקִיד ז
minor clerk 895 פְּקִידוֹן ז
(negative connotation)
clerical work; 24 פְּקִידוּת נ
office workers collectively
clerical 939 פְּקִידוּתִי ז
opening of eyes 1 פְּקִיחָה נ
Pakistani 915 פָּקִיסְטָנִי ז
expiration 1 פְּקִיעָה נ
corking, plugging; 1 פְּקִיקָה נ
thrombosis
bud (botany) 319 פֶּקַע ז
bulb 706 פְּקַעַת נ
bulbous 915 פְּקַעְתִּי ז
doubt N 66 פִּקְפּוּק ז
doubter, skeptic 851 פַּקְפְּקָן ז
suspicion, 749 פַּקְפְּקָנוּת נ
doubtfulness, hesitation,
skepticism [no pl.]
hesitant, 975 פַּקְפְּקָנִי ז
irresolute, skeptical
cork, stopper, plug; 310 פְּקָק ז
traffic jam
thrombosis [no pl.] 685 פַּקֶּקֶת נ
pullover 419 פַּקְרֵס ז
bull 226 פַּר ז
savage; wild ass 319 פֶּרֶא ז
wildness, savagery 738 פִּרְאוּת נ
[no pl.]
wild, unruly, cruel, 949 פִּרְאִי ז
unrefined, reckless
poppy, poppy seed 267 פֶּרֶג ז
poppy seed 317 פֶּרֶג/פָּרָג ז
screen, divider 444 פַּרְגּוֹד ז
whip, lash Lit. 444 פַּרְגּוֹל ז
young chicken 808 פַּרְגִּית נ
young chicken 814 פֻּרְגִּית נ
mule 317 פֶּרֶד ז
departing, departure 649 פְּרֵדָה נ
molecule 658 פְּרֻדָּה נ
orchard 419 פַּרְדֵּס ז
citrus grower 863 פַּרְדְּסָן ז
citrus growing 740 פַּרְדְּסָנוּת נ
[no pl.]
cow 582 פָּרָה נ
separated 15 פָּרוּד ז
divisiveness, schism 51 פֵּרוּד ז
grain of seed 18 פְּרוּדָה נ
fur 610 פַּרְוָה נ
unwalled city 15 פָּרוּז ז

demilitarization [no 51 פֵּרוּז ז
pl.]
detailing; details; 51 פֵּרוּט ז
breakdown
small monetary 18 פְּרוּטָה נ
unit; minute sum
spread out; sliced 15 פָּרוּס ז
slice 18 פְּרוּסָה נ
Prussian 915 פְּרוּסִי ז
unkempt; wild, 17 פָּרוּעַ ז
unruly; redeemed
cracked, broken, 15 פָּרוּץ ז
breached
prostitute 18 פְּרוּצָה נ
disarmed weapon 15 פָּרוּק ז
dismantling, 51 פֵּרוּק ז
disassembling
crumb, morsel 51 פֵּרוּר ז
suburb 409 פַּרְוָר/פַּרְבָּר ז
recluse; ascetic 15 פָּרוּשׁ ז
explanation; 51 פֵּרוּשׁ ז
interpretation; commentary
fruity 915 פֵּרוֹתִי ז
affixing metal 54 פִּרְזוּל ז
fixtures; shoeing a horse
flower, blossom; 319 פֶּרַח ז
apprentice
floral, flowered 952 פִּרְחוֹנִי ז
whippersnapper, 431 פִּרְחָח ז
street urchin
whippersnapperish 915 פִּרְחָחִי ז
detail, particular; 310 פְּרָט ז
individual
odd number; 317 פֶּרֶט ז
itemized list [no pl.]
specification, 632 פִּרְטָה נ
inventory
private 942 פְּרָטִי ז
privacy [no pl.] 771 פְּרָטִיּוּת נ
meticulousness, 752 פַּרְטָנוּת נ
detailedness [no pl
detailed 969 פַּרְטָנִי ז
fruit; product, 257 פְּרִי, ר' פֵּרוֹת ז
result; profit (pl. perot)
divisible 20 פָּרִיד ז
being fruitful 4 פְּרִיָּה נ
fertility [no pl.] 884 פִּרְיוֹן ז
blooming; 1 פְּרִיחָה נ
prosperity, development
item, object 405 פְּרִיט ז
cashing, breaking 1 פְּרִיטָה נ
bill; strumming
crispy, crunchy, 20 פָּרִיךְ ז
crumbly; brittle
breaking, crushing; 1 פְּרִיכָה נ
pressing olives
crispness, 24 פְּרִיכוּת נ
crumbliness; brittleness
unraveling 1 פְּרִימָה נ
spreading; 1 פְּרִיסָה נ
deployment; distribution
redemption, 1 פְּרִיעָה נ
payment; destruction, rampage

chromatic - monochromatic, colored - multicolored 949 צִבְעִי ז
pigment 857 צִבְעָן ז
prickly pear cactus; native Israeli Coll. (fem. tsabarit) 275 צַבָּר ז
heap; spore 317 צֶבֶר ז
accumulation, heap, pile; bulk 341 צֹבֶר ז
Israel-born 979 צַבָּרִי ז
handful, bundle, sheaf (of grain, flowers) 317 צֶבֶת ז
pincers 317 צֶבֶת ז
pliers, pincer; vise-grip 312 צְבָת נ
side; aspect; party (pl. tsdadim/tsidim) 223 צַד, ר׳ צְדָדִים/צִדִּים ז
of side (street, etc.); marginal, minor 942 צְדָדִי ז
marginality; sidedness [no pl.] 771 צְדָדִיּוּת נ
siding with, supporting; lateral movement 45 צִדּוּד ז
profile, side view 825 צְדוּדִית נ
broadside of ship 385 צִדּוֹן ז
justification 45 צִדּוּק ז
of side, lateral 915 צִדִּי ז
malice Lit-rare [no pl.] 4 צְדִיָּה נ
righteous; righteous/saintly person 402 צַדִּיק ז
righteousness [no pl.] 754 צַדִּיקוּת נ
temple (anatomy) 319 צֶדַע ז
seashell; shell 317 צֶדֶף ז
mollusk (clam, oyster, mussel) 598 צִדְפָּה נ
justice, fairness, righteousness; integrity [no pl.] 317 צֶדֶק ז
charity 634 צְדָקָה נ
righteousness, piety [no pl.] 738 צִדְקוּת נ
self-righteousness [no pl.] 752 צַדְקָנוּת נ
self-righteous 969 צַדְקָנִי/צִדְקָנִי ז
of the Israel Defense Forces 966 צַהַ"לִי ז
yellow 301 צָהֹב ז
the color yellow [no pl.] 343 צֹהַב ז
yellowish 458 צְהַבְהַב ז
yellowishness 743 צְהַבְהַבּוּת נ
equilateral triangle (faces [no pl.]
jaundice [no pl.] 686 צַהֶבֶת נ
hostile Lit 15 צָהוֹב ז
yellowness 24 צְהִיבוּת נ
joy, rejoicing; cry of joy 631 צָהֳלָה נ
small window, aperture; opening, opportunity 343 צֹהַר ז
noon, early afternoon; lunch 997 צָהֳרַיִם ז
excrement 593 צוֹאָה נ
(last) will 620 צַוָּאָה נ

collar 894 צַוָּארוֹן ז
fecal 915 צוֹאָתִי ז
stinging, nippy 985 צוֹבְטָנִי ז
just, fair; correct, right 6 צוֹדֵק ז
joyful 7 צוֹהֵל ז
order, directive; imperative (grammar) 45 צִוּוּי ז
scream 634 צְוָחָה נ
screamer 846 צַוְחָן ז
shouting, screaming [no pl.] 752 צַוְחָנוּת נ
loud, screeching 969 צַוְחָנִי ז
laughing, jolly, merry 986 צוֹחֲקָנִי ז
shout, scream 1 צְוִיחָה נ
cross- crossfire, etc 6 צוֹלֵב ז
diver; pochard diving duck 6 צוֹלֵל ז
submariner 855 צוֹלְלָן ז
submarine 11 צוֹלֶלֶת נ
lame, limping 9 צוֹלֵעַ ז
sniping, stinging 985 צוֹלְפָנִי ז
fast; fasting 242 צוֹם ז
plants, vegetation 9 צוֹמֵחַ ז
cool, chilly 6 צוֹנֵן ז
gypsy 915 צוֹעֲנִי ז
gypsyhood [no pl.] 762 צוֹעֲנִיּוּת נ
cadet; intern 7 צוֹעֵר ז
nectar 246 צוּף ז
scout, guard 10 צוֹפֶה ז
of scout 987 צוֹפִי ז
scouthood [no pl.] 762 צוֹפִיּוּת נ
honey-sucker, sunbird 845 צוּפִית נ
siren 366 צוֹפָר ז
palm dove, wild pigeon 13 צוּצֶלֶת נ
pressure, stress, trouble [no pl.] 240 צוֹק ז
cliff, precipice 246 צוּק ז
cliff, rock 246 צוּר ז
burning; stinging; cd burner 6 צוֹרֵב ז
burning, stinging; insulting, scathing 985 צוֹרְבָנִי ז
shape 595 צוּרָה נ
stonecrop, wall pepper, creeping jack (plant) 845 צוּרִית נ
strident, grating 6 צוֹרֵם ז
irritating, grating 985 צוֹרְמָנִי ז
morpheme 878 צוּרָן ז
formal, formative 915 צוּרָנִי ז
goldsmith, silversmith 6 צוֹרֵף ז
gold and silver crafting [no pl.] 14 צוֹרְפוּת נ
bitter enemy 6 צוֹרֵר ז
staff, team, crew 317 צֶוֶת ז
of or related to team or group 949 צֶוֶתִי ז
pure, clear, unblemished 221 צַח ז
laughter, giggling, chuckling [plural only in Coll.?] 393 צְחוֹק ז
whiteness; purity Lit. [no pl.] 393 צְחוֹר ז

cleanliness, purity, freshness 732 צַחוּת נ
dehydration (no comp. lengthening, no pl.) 898 צִחָיוֹן ז
dryness, aridity; barrenness 24 צְחִיחוּת נ
stench 612 צַחֲנָה נ
brushing, polishing 67 צִחְצוּחַ ז
giggling 70 צִחְקוּק ז
cheerful person 846 צַחְקָן/צַחֲקָן ז
laughing giggling 969 צַחְקָנִי/צַחֲקָנִי ז
white, pure 303 צָחֹר ז
whitish; pure white Lit. 458 צְחַרְחַר ז
quoting; quotation 45 צִטּוּט ז
fleet; navy; marine corps 239 צִי ז
hunter (fem. tsayedet) 275 צַיָּד ז
hunting; game; hunt [no pl.] 357 צַיִד ז
supplies [no pl.] 596 צֵידָה אין ר׳ נ
picnic cooler, food hamper 814 צֵידָנִית נ
desert, wilderness; wasteland 586 צִיָּה נ
equipment; equipping 45 צִיּוּד ז
mark, grade; noting, mentioning 45 צִיּוּן ז
Zionism [no pl.] 740 צִיּוֹנוּת נ
Zionist 915 צִיּוֹנִי ז
Zionism [no pl.] 780 צִיּוֹנִיּוּת נ
twittering, chirping 45 צִיּוּץ ז
drawing, picture; art, painting; depiction 45 צִיּוּר ז
picturesque 956 צִיּוּרִי ז
picturesequeness [no pl.] 781 צִיּוּרִיּוּת נ
obedience 45 צִיּוּת ז
solitary confinement 387 צִינוֹק ז
buoyancy [no pl.] 3 צִיפָה נ
pulp, flesh of fruit 3 צִיפָה נ
bud 251 צִיץ ז
crest in heraldry 3 צִיצָה נ
tuft of hair 814 צִיצִית נ
twittering, chirping 969 צַיְצָנִי ז
miser Lit. 846 צַיְקָן ז
miserliness, stinginess Lit. [no pl.] 752 צַיְקָנוּת נ
legate, envoy, representative; delegate; hinge; axle; contraction; sauce, gravy 251 צִיר ז
artist, painter (fem. tsayeret) 275 צַיָּר ז
legation, representation 747 צִירוּת נ
axial 915 צִירִי ז
eavesdropping [no pl.] 48 צִיתוּת ז
obedient person 846 צַיְתָן ז
typing [no pl.] 752 צַיְתָנוּת נ
obedient; submissive, subservient 969 צַיְתָנִי ז

shale, slate 598 צִפְחָה נ
flask, bottle, jug 689 צַפַּחַת נ
forecast [no pl.] 257 צְפִי ז
tough; rigid, stiff 20 צָפִיד ז
viewing, watching 4 צְפִיָּה נ
expectation; hope, aspiration 911 צִפִּיָּה נ
sweet baked good Lit. 814 צַפִּיחִית נ
crowdedness, density 24 צְפִיפוּת נ
goat 20 צָפִיר ז
beeping, honking; siren 1 צְפִירָה נ
pillowcase, cushion cover 828 צִפִּית נ
encoder; telegraph operator (fem. tsapanit) 275 צַפָּן ז
code, cipher 341 צֹפֶן ז
viper, adder 319 צֶפַע ז
poisonous snake, Lit. 952 צִפְעוֹנִי ז
beep; chirping 66 צִפְצוּף ז
whistle 680 צַפְצֵפָה נ
poplar 682 צַפְצָפָה נ
noisy, shrieking 975 צַפְצְפָנִי ז
peritoneum (anatomy) [no pl.] 317 צֶפֶק ז
peritonitis [no pl.] 685 צַפֶּקֶת נ
ornithologist (fem. tsaparit) 275 צַפָּר ז
zephyr (flowery); pleasant morning breeze or light rays 454 צַפְרִיר ז
bag, sack Lit. 441 צִקְלוֹן ז
narrow; enemy 226 צַר ז
flint 229 צֹר ז
heartburn 688 צָרֶבֶת נ
trouble, difficulty 582 צָרָה נ
scorched, burned 15 צָרוּב ז
hoarse 15 צָרוּד ז
leprous Lit 17 צָרוּעַ ז
refined, purified; pure, absolute 15 צָרוּף ז
joining; combination; phrase (linguistics) 51 צֵרוּף ז
combinatorial 958 צֵרוּפִי ז
package; bundle, bunch; burst (of gunfire) 396 צְרוֹר ז
bound, wrapped up; buried emotion, memory 15 צָרוּר ז
narrowness [no pl.] 733 צָרוּת נ
scream 634 צְרָחָה נ
screamer 846 צַרְחָן ז
screaming, shrieking [no pl.] 752 צַרְחָנוּת נ
screaming, shrieking 969 צַרְחָנִי ז
persimmon resin; balm Lit. [no pl.] 349 צֹרִי/צֳרִי ז
burning, etching; burn 1 צְרִיבָה נ
hoarseness 24 צְרִידוּת נ
tower, turret, castle; rook (chess) 407 צְרִיחַ ז
scream 1 צְרִיחָה נ
required; essential 20 צָרִיךְ ז
consumption 1 צְרִיכָה נ
grating sound; incompatibility 1 צְרִימָה נ
shed, shack 405 צְרִיף ז
refinement, purification 1 צְרִיפָה נ
small hut 895 צְרִיפוֹן ז
dissonance 405 צְרִיר ז
need; necessity; requirement 341 צֹרֶךְ ז
consumer 846 צַרְכָן ז
consumerism [no pl.] 752 צַרְכָנוּת נ
consumer Adj 969 צַרְכָנִי ז
discount supermarket 911 צַרְכָנִיָּה נ
silicon 863 צֹרָן ז
wasp 598 צִרְעָה נ
leprosy [no pl.] 692 צָרַעַת נ
French 915 צָרְפָתִי ז
French [no pl.] 814 צָרְפָתִית נ
a clay jug containing water or wine (Talmudic) 449 צַרְצוּר ז
chirping of cricket 66 צִרְצוּר ז
cricket 437 צְרָצַר ז
Circassian 915 צֶ'רְקֶסִי ז
jackdaw (bird) 269 קָאָק ז
stomach 588 קֵבָה נ
volume, capacity 45 קִבּוּל ז
capacitive 956 קִבּוּלִי ז
routine; permanent, fixed; affixed 17 קָבוּעַ ז
affixing, reinforcing, stabilizing [no pl.] 53 קִבּוּעַ ז
set of items permanently fixed to a structure 18 קְבוּעָה נ
collected, gathered Lit 15 קָבוּץ ז
collection; ingathering; kibbutz, collective settlement 45 קִבּוּץ ז
group 18 קְבוּצָה נ
collective 956 קִבּוּצִי ז
collectivity; collectivism [no pl.] 781 קִבּוּצִיּוּת נ
of the group 915 קְבוּצָתִי ז
buried 15 קָבוּר ז
burial 18 קְבוּרָה נ
cubic 915 קֻבִּי ז
cube 911 קֻבִּיָּה נ
acceptable; admissible (law) 20 קָבִיל ז
complaint 1 קְבִילָה נ
acceptability; submissibility (law) 24 קְבִילוּת נ
decision; setting date, etc.; statement, declaration; determining; affixing 1 קְבִיעָה נ
tenure; constancy 24 קְבִיעוּת נ
burying 1 קְבִירָה נ
cubic 915 קֻבִּיָּתִי ז
capacitor, condenser (elect.) 275 קַבָּל ז
(written) receipt 620 קַבָּלָה נ
Kabbalistic 915 קַבָּלִי ז
contractor 847 קַבְּלָן ז
complaint 677 קֻבְלָנָה נ
contract work [no pl.] 752 קַבְּלָנוּת נ
contractual 969 קַבְּלָנִי ז
capacity 697 קִבֹּלֶת נ
nausea Lit. [no pl.] 317 קֶבֶס ז
permanent; standing army (vs. reserve) [no pl.] 319 קֶבַע ז
fixation 898 קִבָּעוֹן ז
cup Lit.-Rare 701 קֻבַּעַת נ
collection, anthology; computer file 341 קֹבֶץ ז
beggar 847 קַבְּצָן ז
begging [no pl.] 752 קַבְּצָנוּת נ
beggarly 969 קַבְּצָנִי ז
clog 416 קַבְקַב ז
bran, course flour 286 קֵבָר ז
grave; tomb 317 קֶבֶר ז
gravedigger 847 קַבְּרָן/קַבְרָן ז
undertaking, gravedigging, burying [no pl.] 752 קַבְּרָנוּת נ
biceps; arm Lit. 697 קִבֹּרֶת נ
gastric 915 קֵבָתִי ז
slight bow, nod, salutation 586 קִדָּה נ
reaming, boring, marking 45 קִדּוּד ז
drilling, boring < kideaH 'drill and re-drill,' Lit-rare 53 קִדּוּחַ ז
ancient 15 קָדוּם ז
advancement; promotion 45 קִדּוּם ז
ancient times 998 קְדוּמִים ז
holy; holy man 298 קָדוֹשׁ ז
sanctification/blessing over wine etc. 45 קִדּוּשׁ ז
bore (weaponry); hole, well 319 קֶדַח ז
fever, malaria [no pl.] 689 קַדַּחַת נ
feverish; hectic, restless 915 קַדַּחְתָּנִי ז
drilling 1 קְדִיחָה נ
preference, precedence, priority 1 קְדִימָה נ
preference, precedence, priority 24 קְדִימוּת נ
back of neck Lit. 310 קֹדֶל ז
ancient times; east Lit. [no pl.] 317 קֶדֶם ז
progress [no pl.] 598 קִדְמָה נ
front 610 קִדְמָה נ
ancient; ancient person 892 קַדְמוֹן ז
antiquity [no pl.] 740 קַדְמוֹנוּת נ
ancient 972 קַדְמוֹנִי ז
antiquity [no pl.] 789 קַדְמוֹנִיּוּת נ

קַדְמוּת נ 736 beginning, outset [no pl.]
קְדָמִי ז 942 preliminary
קִדְמִי ז 949 front Adj
קִדֹּמֶת נ 697 telephone area code
קָדְקֳדִי ז 915 of the crown of the head
קַדָּר ז 275 potter (fem. kadarit)
קְדֵרָה נ 649 casserole, cauldron
קַדְרוּת נ 736 darkness; gloom [no pl.]
קָדֵשׁ ז 279 male prostitute (in pagan ritual)
קֹדֶשׁ, ר׳ קָדָשִׁים/קֳדָשִׁים ז 341 holiness, sanctity, sacredness, pl. kodashim
קְדֻשָּׁה נ 658 holiness
קֵהֶה ז 260 blunt, dull
קָהוּי ז 15 blurred, dull; lusterless, rough
קֵהָיוֹן ז 905 dementia; insensitivity, apathy Lit. (only constr., no pl.)
קָהָל ז 269 audience; public; community
קְהִלָּה נ 646 community
קְהִלִיָּה נ 911 commonwealth, community
קְהִלָּתִי ז 915 of a community; parochial
קְהִלָּתִיּוּת נ 762 community activity [no decl., no pl.]
קוּבְלָנִי ז 985 complaining, complainful Lit.
קוֹבַע ז 369 helmet, steel helmet (archaic)
קוֹדֵם ז 6 preceding; preferable to
קוֹדְמָן ז 855 antecedent
קוֹדֵר ז 6 gloomy, dark
קַוִּי ז 915 linear
קוֹל ז 242 voice; sound; opinion, vote
קוֹלָב ז 366 hanger; rack
קוֹלֵט ז 6 solar collector
קוֹלִי ז 988 of sound, audio Adj
קוֹלִית נ 814 thigh; femur, thigh-bone
קוֹלָן ז 877 tuning fork
קוֹלְנוֹעִי ז 915 cinematic
קוֹלְנוֹעָן ז 863 cinematographer, film maker
קוֹלָנִי ז 989 loud
קוֹלֵעַ ז 9 correct, on-the-mark
קוֹלָר ז 366 collar
קוֹמָה נ 593 height, stature; story, floor
קוֹמְמִיּוּת נ 762 independence [no pl.]
קַוָּן ז 275 linesman (sports); lineman (telecom., elec.) (fem. kavanit)
קוֹנֶה ז 10 customer, buyer
קוֹנְכִיָּה נ 911 shell

קוֹנְכִית נ 814 nasal concha (anatomy); shell
קוֹסֵם ז 6 magician; enticing, captivating
קוֹף ז 240 monkey, ape
קוּף ז 246 eye of a needle
קוּפְּטִי ז 915 Coptic
קוֹפִי ז 988 ape-like
קוֹפֵץ ז 6 interested customer Coll.
קוֹפְצָנִי ז 985 vivacious, lively
קוֹץ ז 240 thorn
קוֹצֵב ז 6 one who allots; kotsev lev 'pacemaker'
קְוֻצָּה נ 658 lock, hank of hair
קוֹצִי ז 988 thorny
קוֹצָן ז 877 thistle
קוֹצָנִי ז 989 thorny, prickly
קוֹצָנִיּוּת נ 800 thorniness [no pl.]
קוֹצֵר ז 6 harvester, reaper
קִוְקוּו ז 66 filling in with lines
קַוְקָזִי ז 915 Caucasian
קוּקִיָּה נ 911 cuckoo
קוֹקְנִי ז 915 Cockney
קוּר ז 246 cobweb; silk thread; webbing
קוֹרֵא ז 8 reader; type of desert bird
קוּרְדִּי ז 915 Kurdish
קוֹרָה נ 593 beam
קוֹרֵן ז 6 radiant, joyful
קוֹרְנִית נ 814 cornet (music)
קוֹרָנִית נ 814 thyme (plant, herb)
קוֹשֵׁר ז 6 rebel, conspirator
קִזּוּז ז 45 deduction; offset N
קֹטֶב ז 341 pole, magnetic pole
קָטְבִּי ז 980 polar; opposite
קָטְבִּיּוּת נ 794 polarity [no pl.]
קָטֵגוֹרִי ז 915 categorical; categorial
קִטּוּב ז 45 polarization
קָטוּל ז 15 killed, exterminated
קָטוּם ז 15 trimmed, lopped
קִטּוּם ז 45 lopping, cutting off end
קְטוּמָה נ 18 trapezoid
קִטּוּעַ ז 53 amputation, cutting off, fragmentation
קָטוּף ז 15 harvested, plucked, cut, reaped
קִטּוּף ז 45 plucking, picking [no pl.]
קָטוּר ז 15 unroofed Obs.
קִטּוּר ז 45 incense burning
קְטָטָה נ 632 quarrel, altercation
קְטִילָה נ 1 killing, extermination; critique Coll.
קְטִימָה נ 1 lopping, cutting off end
קָטִין/קְטִין ז 20 minor, a minor person
קְטִינוּת נ 24 status of a minor law [no pl.]
קְטִיעָה נ 1 interruption, disruption; amputation

קָטִיף ז 20 fruit-picking; fruit-picking season
קְטִיפָה נ 1 plucking, picking fruit, flowers
קְטִיפָתִי ז 937 velvety
קֶטֶל ז 317 death, slaughter [no pl.]
קִטְלוּג ז 54 cataloguing
קַטְלָן ז 846 deadly, lethal
קַטְלָנִי ז 969 lethal
קֹטֶן ז 341 smallness; pinky (biblical) [no pl.]
קָטָן/קָטֹן ז 274 small, little; young; minute
קַטְנוּנִי ז 912 petty
קַטְנוּנִיּוּת נ 790 pettiness [no pl.]
קַטְנוּת נ 736 childhood; smallness; pettiness
קְטַנְטַן/טֹן ז 458 tiny, wee, minute, miniature
קְטַנְתָּן ז 863 tiny
קֶטַע ז 319 section, part; segment; "riot" Sl.
קַטֶּפֶת נ 685 picking machine
קַטָּר ז 275 engine (of train), locomotive
קֹטֶר ז 341 diameter
קִטְרוּג ז 54 accusation; testimony against an accused
קְטֹרֶת נ 708 incense
קִיא ז 251 vomit N [no pl.]
קִידּוּד ז 45 encoding
קִיּוּם ז 45 existence; fulfillment; subsistence; obserevance
קִיּוּמִי ז 956 existential
קַיִט ז 357 summer vacation [no pl.]
קִיטוֹן, ר׳ קִיטוֹנִיּוֹת ז 388 small bedchamber Lit. [pl. kitoniyot]
קִיטוֹר ז 387 steam; smoke, column of smoke [no pl.]
קַיְטָן ז 846 summer vacationer
קַיְטָנָה נ 681 summer day camp
קַיָּם ז 275 existent, alive; binding, valid
קִימָה נ 3 arising; getting up
קִימוּם ז 48 re-establishment [no pl.]
קַיָּן ז 275 one with large testicles (Talmudic)
קַיִן ז 357 spear Lit-rare
קִינָה נ 3 dirge, lamentation
קִינוֹף ז 387 bed canopy frame (for mosquito netting)
קִיסוֹס ז 387 ivy (plant)
קִיסוֹסִית נ 814 smilax aspera (plant)
קֵיסָם ז 374 sliver; toothpick
קֵיסָרִי ז 915 Caesarean
קִיפוֹן ז 387 mullet (fish)
קִיפּוֹף ז 387 prosimian
קַיִץ ז 357 summer
קִיצוֹנִי ז 915 extreme

קִיצוֹנִיּוּת נ 782 extremism [no pl.]
קֵיצִי ז 960 summery
קִיק ז 251 castor oil seed [no pl.?]
קִיקְיוֹנִי ז 915 ephemeral, transitory, temporary
קִיר, ר׳ קִירוֹת ז 253 wall (pl. kirot)
קִישׁ ז 251 quiche
קִיתוֹן ז 388 ewer, large jar (Talmudic)
קַל ז 221 light; easy; slight
קַלְגַּס ז 414 soldier, trooper (derog.) Lit.
קַלְדָן ז 846 typist
קַלְדָנוּת נ 752 typing [no pl.]
קַלָּה נ 592 lenience
קָלוּט ז 15 recorded; absorbed; registered
קָלוּי ז 15 toasted, roasted
קְלוּמִית נ 814 peel of straw (Talmudic)
קָלוֹן, ר׳ קְלוֹנִים/קְלוֹנוֹת ז 292 shame, disgrace N. (pl. klonim/klonot)
קָלוּעַ ז 17 braided, plaited
קָלוּף ז 15 peeled, skinned; blanched
קִלּוּף ז 45 peeling; scraping
קָלוּשׁ ז 15 slim, slight; scant; vague
קַלּוּת נ 731 ease, easiness; lightness
קֶלַח ז 319 corncob
קַלַּחַת נ 689 turmoil; cauldron (biblical)
קֶלֶט ז 317 input (computing) [no pl.]
קִלְטוּר ז 54 tilling, cultivation of soil [no pl.]
קַלְטֶרֶת נ 715 cultivator (agr.)
קַלֶּטֶת נ 685 cassette
קָלִי ז 256 toast N; toasted grain Bibl.
קְלִיד ז 405 key (of piano, organ)
קְלִיָּה נ 4 toasting, roasting
קְלִיחָה נ 1 flow, stream
קְלִיטָה נ 1 absorbing; absorption
קַלִּיל ז 404 very light
קַלִּילוּת נ 24 nimbleness; lightness; ease
קְלִיעַ ז 22 bullet
קְלִיעָה נ 1 braiding, basket weaving; shooting, throwing
קָלִיף ז 20 peelable
קְלִיפָה נ 1 peeling, skinning
קְלִישׁוּת נ 24 minimalness, scantness; weakness; vagueness [no pl.]
קְלָלָה נ 634 curse
קַלְלָן ז 846 cursing, swearing

קַלְמִית נ 808 shawm (medieval musical instrument), shepherd's pipe
קַלְמָר ז 409 pencil case
קֶלֶס ז 317 mockery, ridiculing Lit. [no pl.]
קַלָּע ז 275 marksman (fem. kala`it)
קֶלַע ז 329 slingshot, sling, catapult
קְלָף ז 310 card; parchment
קְלִפָּה נ 646 shell
קַלְפָן ז 846 card player, gambler
קַלְפָנוּת נ 752 card playing [no pl.]
קְלִפָּתִי ז 915 cortical (anatomy)
קִלְקוּל ז 66 malfunction, spoiling
קַלְקָלָה נ 682 failure, iniquity, corruption
קְלַרְנִיתָן ז 863 clarinet player
קִלְּשׁוֹן (ל׳ דגושה) ז 884 pitchfork
קִלְּשׁוֹנִי ז 915 pitchfork-like, three-pronged
קַלַּת נ 330 fruit basket
קַלְתִּית נ 808 tartlet
קָם ז 214 hater, enemy Lit.
קַמָּאִי ז 979 primeval, ancient
קִמּוּחַ ז 53 flouring [no pl.]
קִמּוּט ז 45 wrinkling
קָמוּל ז 15 withered, shriveled
קָמוּץ ז 15 tightly closed lips, fist, eyes
קִמּוּץ ז 45 reduction, cutting expenses
קָמוּר ז 15 convex, domed, rounded, curved
קִמּוּר ז 45 curvature; curve
קֶמַח ז 319 flour [no pl.]
קִמָּחוֹן ז 898 mildew (plant disease caused by fungi) [no pl.]
קִמְחִי ז 949 mealy, floury
קֶמֶט ז 317 wrinkle, crease; fold
קִמְטוּט ז 450 tiny wrinkle
קְמַטְמַט ז 458 tiny wrinkle
קַמְטָן ז 846 anguidae (lizard fam.); type of legless lizard
קַמְטָר ז 409 small cupboard, chest Lit.
קְמִיחוּת נ 24 mealiness [no pl.]
קָמִיט ז 20 wrinkly
קְמִיטוּת נ 24 wrinkledness [no pl.]
קְמִילָה נ 1 withering, shriveling
קָמִין ז 403 fireplace
קְמִיצָה נ 1 closing, pursing, clamping shut, ring finger
קָמֵל ז 279 withered, wilted, shriveled
קָמֵעַ ז 279 talisman; amulet
קִמְעוֹנָאוּת נ 740 retailing [no pl.]
קִמְעוֹנַאי ז 909 retailer
קִמְעוֹנָאִי ז 915 retail Adj
קִמְעוֹנוּת נ 740 retailing [no pl.]
קִמְעוֹנִי ז 952 retail Adj

קֹמֶץ ז 352 handful
קֻמְצוּץ ז 450 pinch, smidgen
קַמְצָן ז 846 miser
קַמְצָנוּת נ 752 miserliness [no pl.]
קַמְצָנִי ז 969 miserly
קֶמֶר ז 317 dome, arch
קִמְרוֹן ז 884 dome (architec.); anticlinorium (geology)
קִמֹּרֶת נ 697 arch; anticlinorium (geol.)
קֵן ז 235 nest
קִנְאָה נ 598 jealousy
קַנַּאי ז 908 zealot; jealous
קַנָּאִי ז 979 fanatic
קֻנְדָּס ז 435 prankster; mischief
קֻנְדָּסוּת נ 758 mischievousness [no pl.]
קֻנְדָּסִי ז 915 mischievous
קָנֶה ז 261 stem, cane, stalk; barrel; reed; windpipe, trachea
קִנּוּחַ ז 53 wiping, drying; dessert
קָנוּי ז 15 bought, purchased; acquired, achieved
קִנּוּן ז 45 nesting
קָנוֹנִי ז 915 canonical
קְנוֹקֶנֶת נ 726 tendril
קִנְטוּר ז 54 spite, provocativeness
קַנְטְרָן ז 850 spiteful, annoying
קַנְטְרָנוּת נ 740 spite, vexation [no pl.]
קַנְטְרָנִי ז 915 annoying, irritating, vexing
קְנִיָּה נ 4 purchase, acquisition; shopping
קַנְיוֹן ז 889 shopping center, mall
קַנְיָן ז 846 purchaser, buyer
קִנְיָן ז 858 asset, property; ownership
קַנְיָנוּת נ 752 acquisitions, retailing [no pl.]
קִנְיָנִי ז 950 possessory
קְנִיסָה נ 1 fining
קְנִית נ 842 acrosephalus (bird)
קִנֹּם ז 301 brown, cinnamon-color
קְנָס ז 312 fine N
קַנְקַן ז 416 jar, jug, flask
קִנְרֵס ז 432 artichoke
קֶנֶת נ 330 butt; handle (Talmudic)
קַסְדָּה נ 610 helmet
קָסוּם ז 15 enchanting
קֶסֶם ז 317 magic, enchantment, spell; sorcery
קֶסֶת נ 330 inkstand
קָעוּר ז 15 concave
קִעוּר ז 50 concaving
קִעְקוּעַ ז 67 tattooing
קַעְקַע/קַעֲקַע ז 416 tattoo
קַעַר ז 328 crater, depression
קַעַר ז 343 concavity; keel [no pl.]

bowl 640 קְעָרָה נ
concave, indented, sunken 913 קַעֲרוּרִי ז
skullcap (flower) 837 קַעֲרוּרִית נ
small bowl 809 קַעֲרִית נ
freeze [no pl.] 898 קִפָּאוֹן ז
cashier 909 קֻפַּאי ז
strict, meticulous (person) (kafdan is a less frequent option) 847 קַפְּדָן/קַפְדָן ז
strictness, pedantry, severity; (talmudic) impatience, irascibility [no pl.] 752 קַפְּדָנוּת/קַפְדָנוּת נ
meticulous, strict; firm, uncompromising 969 קַפְּדָנִי/קַפְדָנִי ז
money box; cash register; box office; treasury 592 קֻפָּה נ
frozen 15 קָפוּא ז
hedgehog 382 קִפּוֹד ז
spiny, prickly 915 קִפּוֹדִי ז
prickliness [no pl.] 780 קִפּוֹדִיּוּת נ
spiny anteater 863 קִפּוֹדָן ז
discrimination, deprivation 53 קִפּוּחַ ז
skimming 45 קִפּוּי ז
folding; collapsing; a fold 45 קִפּוּל ז
tightly closed 15 קָפוּץ ז
hopping, skipping 45 קִפּוּץ ז
very tall Lit. 284 קִפֵּחַ ז
freezing 1 קְפִיאָה נ
spring, coil 405 קְפִיץ ז
jumping; rise, increase 1 קְפִיצָה נ
retractable (tape measure, etc.) 933 קְפִיצִי ז
springiness, elasticity [no pl.] 768 קְפִיצִיּוּת נ
fold, crease; pleat 317 קֶפֶל ז
men's wig, toupee 419 קֶפְלֶט ז
box 627 קֻפְסָה נ
small box, small container 814 קֻפְסִית נ
jumpy, bouncy 846 קַפְצָן ז
trampoline 685 קַפֶּצֶת נ
Kafkaesque 915 קַפְקָאִי ז
of Cyprus 915 קַפְרִיסָאִי ז
of Cyprus 915 קַפְרִיסִינִי ז
of cash register; successful at the box office 915 קֻפָּתִי ז
end, finish, stop; death 235 קֵץ ז
butcher (fem. katsevet, Coll. katsavit) 275 קַצָּב ז
pace, speed; tempo; rhythm 317 קֶצֶב ז
pension 602 קִצְבָּה נ
allowance, ration 658 קִצְבָּה נ
rhythmic 949 קִצְבִּי ז
rhythm [no pl.] 776 קִצְבִּיּוּת נ
edge, end, extremity (pl. ktsavot/katsim) 263 קָצֶה, ר' קְצָווֹת/קָצִים ז
rhythmic; limited, defined, measured 15 קָצוּב ז
budgeting 45 קִצּוּב ז
diced, chopped; cropped; very short hair 15 קָצוּץ ז
cut; cutback 45 קִצּוּץ ז
harvested, reaped, cut 15 קָצוּר ז
shortening, reducing; summary; abbreviation 45 קִצּוּר ז
nigella (spice plant) [no pl.] 319 קֶצַח ז
officer; leader, ruler bibl. 20 קָצִין ז
officer status [no pl.] 24 קְצִינוּת נ
frothy, foamy 20 קָצִיף ז
mousse 1 קְצִיפָה נ
meat loaf alt ktsits 20 קָצִיץ ז
hamburger, cutlet 1 קְצִיצָה נ
harvest 20 קָצִיר ז
harvesting, reaping 1 קְצִירָה נ
military officers (collec.); officer's rank 658 קְצֻנָּה נ
foam, froth, suds 317 קֶצֶף ז
whipped cream 685 קַצֶּפֶת נ
short, brief 267 קָצָר ז
short circuit; misunderstanding Coll. 317 קֶצֶר ז
shortness; insufficiency, deficiency [no pl.] 341 קֹצֶר ז
stenographer 846 קַצְרָן ז
stenography, shorthand [no pl.] 752 קַצְרָנוּת נ
very short, very brief 458 קְצַרְצַר ז
asthma [no pl.] 685 קַצֶּרֶת נ
cold, chilly 226 קַר ז
cold N; coldness [no pl.] 229 קֹר ז
Creole 915 קְרֵאוֹלִי ז
Karaite 915 קָרָאִי ז
battle, combat; struggle; race 312 קְרָב ז
interior, inside (pl. kravayim 'innards, intestines') 317 קֶרֶב, ר' קְרָבַיִם ז
proximity; relationship; similarity [no pl.] 598 קִרְבָה נ
combatant 942 קְרָבִי ז
being combatant [no pl.] 771 קְרָבִיּוּת נ
sacrifice; victim 862 קָרְבָּן ז
mite 808 קַרְדִּית נ
axe, hatchet; pickaxe 425 קַרְדֹּם ז
cold front 582 קָרָה נ
invitee 15 קָרוּא ז
Croatian 915 קְרוֹאָטִי ז
relative, family member 288 קָרוֹב ז
near, close; relative 298 קָרוֹב ז
bringing close; proximity 51 קֵרוּב ז
named 15 קָרוּי ז
roofing [no pl.] 51 קֵרוּי ז
skin, membrane; crust 399 קְרוּם ז
membranous 946 קְרוּמִי ז
very thin cover, membrane 825 קְרוּמִית נ
car (of train); wagon 290 קָרוֹן ז
rail-cart 814 קְרוֹנִית נ
crouched 15 קָרוּס ז
torn 17 קָרוּעַ ז
molded, shaped Lit 15 קָרוּץ ז
cooling; refrigeration [no pl.] 51 קֵרוּר ז
congealed 15 קָרוּשׁ ז
curl 54 קִרְזוּל ז
bald; bald person 285 קֵרֵחַ ז
ice 329 קֶרַח ז
glacier; iceberg 892 קַרְחוֹן ז
icy 965 קַרְחִי ז
bald spot 691 קָרַחַת נ
pinch, smidgen [no pl.] 341 קֹרֶט ז
accidental ejection of sperm [no pl.] 257 קֶרִי ז
disobedience, rebellion [no pl.] 257 קֶרִי ז
readable 20 קָרִיא ז
reading; call; shout; exclamation 1 קְרִיאָה נ
legibility; readability [no pl.] 24 קְרִיאוּת נ
city, town; campus 598 קִרְיָה נ
announcer, newscaster 846 קַרְיָן ז
radiation 1 קְרִינָה נ
(radio, television) announcing; narration [no pl.] 752 קַרְיָנוּת נ
radiative, radiating 937 קְרִינָתִי ז
collapse; bankruptcy; bend 1 קְרִיסָה נ
tearable 22 קָרִיעַ ז
tear 1 קְרִיעָה נ
wink 1 קְרִיצָה נ
cool 404 קָרִיר ז
coolness 24 קְרִירוּת נ
gel; jelly; blood clot 20 קָרִישׁ/קְרִישׁ ז
congelation, clotting 1 קְרִישָׁה נ
diphtheria [no pl.] 688 קָרֶמֶת נ
fund, foundation; capital 330 קֶרֶן נ
horn, antler; corner; free kick (soccer); ray, beam of light 334 קֶרֶן נ
horny 965 קַרְנִי ז
cornea 808 קַרְנִית נ
sledgehammer, mallet 435 קֻרְנָס ז
rhinoceros 414 קַרְנַף ז
hook 326 קֶרֶס ז
ankle 424 קַרְסֹל ז
tear, rip, hole; split, rift, separation 319 קֶרַע ז
(female) toad 681 קַרְפָּדָה נ
yard (surrounded by a fence) Lit. 454 קַרְפִּיף ז
yard (surrounded by a fence) Lit. 419 קַרְפֵּף/קַרְפִּיף ז
scrubbing 54 קִרְצוּף ז

tick (insect) 808 קַרְצִית נ
grounding 67 קִרְקוּעַ ז
crowing; cawing 66 קִרְקוּר ז
circus 431 קִרְקָס ז
of circus; circus-like 915 קִרְקָסִי ז
earth, soil; ground, land; floor, bed (of sea, river) 415 קַרְקַע נ
of/on the ground 915 קַרְקָעִי ז
bottom 814 קַרְקָעִית נ
scalp 715 קַרְקֶפֶת נ
ratchet; bell (Talmudic) 409 קַרְקַשׁ ז
refrigerant 277 קָרָר ז
plank, board 326 קֶרֶשׁ ז
city, town, settlement, province Lit. 330 קֶרֶת נ
bumpkin, provincial 846 קַרְתָּן ז
provinciality, conservativeness, naivete [no pl.] 752 קַרְתָּנוּת נ
provincial, conservative, naïve 969 קַרְתָּנִי ז
attentiveness [no pl.] 317 קֶשֶׁב ז
hard, solid, stiff; difficult; strict, severe 265 קָשֶׁה ז
attentive 15 קָשׁוּב ז
valve (botany); cup Arch. 610 קַשְׂוָה נ
stubborn; tough, hard; strict 17 קָשׁוּחַ ז
decoration, ornament; decorating 45 קִשּׁוּט ז
decorative, ornamental 956 קִשּׁוּטִי ז
hardening, stiffening 45 קִשּׁוּי ז
tied, fastened; attached to; connected to 15 קָשׁוּר ז
connection, liaison; communication 45 קִשּׁוּר ז
obstinate Lit. 284 קֶשַׁח ז
hardness; difficulty; obduracy 349 קֹשִׁי ז
straw-like 915 קַשִּׁי ז
question, problem 624 קֻשְׁיָה נ
hardness [no pl.] 736 קַשְׁיוּת נ
still, inflexible, hard, rigid; strict 22 קָשִׁיחַ ז
toughness; strictness; rigidity 24 קְשִׁיחוּת נ
tying, knotting 1 קְשִׁירָה נ
old, elderly; elderly person 20 קָשִׁישׁ ז
age, elderliness [no pl.] 24 קְשִׁישׁוּת נ
drinking straw 814 קַשִּׁית נ
scribble Coll.; idle chatter Coll.; rattle 66 קִשְׁקוּשׁ ז
fish scale; dandruff 416 קַשְׂקַשׂ ז
scaly, flaky (skin) 976 קַשְׂקַשִּׂי ז
chatterbox, prattler 851 קַשְׁקְשָׁן ז
chattering, prattling, nattering Sl. [no pl.] 749 קַשְׁקְשָׁנוּת נ
chattering, prattling 975 קַשְׁקְשָׁנִי ז
chatter, prattle [no pl.] 717 קַשְׁקֶשֶׁת נ
dandruff, ichtiosis; fish scales 717 קַשְׂקֶשֶׂת נ
person relaying information between different bodies; signaler, signal operator (military) (fem. kasharit) 275 קַשָּׁר ז
knot; connection, contact; communication 317 קֶשֶׁר ז
nodule 454 קַשְׁרִיר ז
archer (fem. kashatit) 275 קַשָּׁת ז
bow; rainbow; arc 330 קֶשֶׁת נ
arched, bowed, carved 965 קַשְׁתִּי ז
iris (of eye) 808 קַשְׁתִּית נ
butt of weapon; handle 222 קַת נ
Catholic 915 קָתוֹלִי ז
lung 588 רֵאָה נ
showcase, display 617 רַאֲוָה נ
fitting, appropriate; fit for, suitable for; deserving 15 רָאוּי ז
visibility [no pl.] 734 רְאוּת נ
show off 863 רַאַוְתָן ז
ostentatious, pretentious 915 רַאַוְתָנִי ז
mirror [no pl.] 259 רְאִי ז
vision, eyesight; view; opinion 4 רְאִיָּה נ
evidence 632 רְאָיָה נ
interview 902 רֵאָיוֹן ז
oryx 307 רְאֵם ז
head 244 רֹאשׁ ז
precedence, priority [no pl.] 740 רִאשׁוֹנוּת נ
initial; basic, elementary 915 רִאשׁוֹנִי ז
precedence, priority; freshness [no pl.] 762 רִאשׁוֹנִיּוּת נ
chairmanship, leadership, presidency [no pl.] 733 רָאשׁוּת נ
main 915 רָאשִׁי ז
harness on working animal; head kick 911 רֹאשִׁיָּה נ
initial 915 רֵאשִׁיתִי ז
tadpole 863 רֹאשָׁן ז
much, great, vast, numerous; multi-; important; rabbi; teacher 221 רַב ז
most; majority; abundance (Bibl.) [no pl.] 227 רֹב ז
spot, stain; fault, stain on one's reputation 310 רְבָב ז
ten thousand 634 רְבָבָה נ
basis point 822 רְבָבִית נ
variedness, colorfulness [no pl.] 740 רַבְגּוֹנוּת נ
varied, colorful 915 רַבְגּוֹנִי ז
variedness, colorfulness [no pl.] 762 רַבְגּוֹנִיּוּת נ
level, layer, stratum; echelon 341 רֹבֶד ז
layered 980 רְבָדִי ז
jam, jelly 586 רִבָּה נ
multiplexing 45 רִבּוּב ז
layered 15 רָבוּד ז
stratification 45 רִבּוּד ז
multiplicity; increase; plural (grammar) 45 רִבּוּי ז
ruler, overlord; sovereign; master [no possessive pronouns?] 385 רִבּוֹן ז
sovereignty [no pl.] 740 רִבּוֹנוּת נ
sovereign 915 רִבּוֹנִי ז
sovereignty [no pl.] 780 רִבּוֹנִיּוּת נ
square 53 רִבּוּעַ ז
square (mathematics) 956 רִבּוּעִי ז
recumbent 15 רָבוּץ ז
sprinkling; depositing [no pl.] 45 רִבּוּץ ז
majority Adj 915 רֻבִּי ז
rain Lit 20 רְבִיב ז
necklace, choker 20 רָבִיד ז
reproduction, multiplying 4 רְבִיָּה נ
roux 1 רְבִיכָה נ
quarter Lit.; quarter of circle 407 רְבִיעַ ז
fourth 933 רְבִיעִי ז
quartet 911 רְבִיעִיָּה נ
a fourth (part) 820 רְבִיעִית נ
recumbence 1 רְבִיצָה נ
interest (banking) 828 רִבִּית נ
rabbinic 915 רַבָּנִי ז
rhubarb 286 רַבָּס ז
great-grandson Bibl. 284 רִבֵּעַ ז
quarter, fourth 319 רֶבַע ז
quarter (of a year); quarterly (magazine, report) 886 רִבְעוֹן ז
quarterly Adj 952 רִבְעוֹנִי ז
multi-sided 915 רַבְצְדָדִי ז
multifacetedness [no pl.] 762 רַבְצְדָדִיּוּת נ
multi-sided geometrical form 894 רַבְצַלְעוֹן ז
multi-voiced/sound 915 רַבְקוֹלִי ז
having multiple voices [no pl.] 762 רַבְקוֹלִיּוּת נ
braggart 851 רַבְרְבָן ז
arrogance, boastfulness, pretentiousness [no pl.] 749 רַבְרְבָנוּת נ
arrogant, boastful, pretentious 975 רַבְרְבָנִי ז
large, broad; metropolitan 915 רַבָּתִי ז
lump, clod (of earth) 317 רֶגֶב ז
angry 15 רָגוּז ז
spying, espionage; tailing, shadowing 45 רִגּוּל ז
excitement; emotion 45 רִגּוּשׁ ז
emotional, emotive 956 רִגּוּשִׁי ז
anger, ire, wrath 341 רֹגֶז ז
anger, fury 624 רָגְזָה נ

רֶטֶט ז 317 trembling, quaking, quivering [no pl.]
רַטְטָנִי ז 964 vibrating
רְטִיבוּת נ 24 wetness, dampness [no pl.]
רְטִיָּה נ 4 compress, bandage; eye-patch
רַטְנוּנִי ז 912 grouchy, grumbling Lit.
רַטְנָן ז 846 grumbler
רַטְנָנִי ז 964 always grumbling
רִטְפּוּשׁ ז 54 becoming fatter; obesity Rare [no pl.]
רִיב, ר' רִיבִים/רִיבוֹת ז 251 quarrel, argument, dispute (pl. rivim or rivot)
רֵיחַ, ר' רֵיחוֹת ז 255 smell (pl. reyHot)
רֵיחָן ז 876 basil
רֵיחָנִי ז 915 fragrant
רֵיחָנִיּוּת נ 762 fragrance [no pl.]
רִיס ז 251 eyelash
רִיף ז 251 reef
רִיצָה נ 3 running; a run
רִיק ז 251 vacuum [no pl.]
רֵיקוּת נ 740 emptiness Lit. [no pl.]
רֵיקָן ז 876 empty; ignorant person Lit.
רֵיקָנִי ז 915 empty, vacuous
רִיר ז 251 saliva; mucus
רִירִי ז 915 mucous
רִירִית נ 814 mucosa, mucous membrane
רִישׁ ז 251 poverty Lit. [no pl.]
רֵישָׁה/א נ 596 introduction, preface; beginning; initial clause
רַךְ ז 221 soft
רֹךְ ז 227 softness, delicateness; gentleness [no pl.]
רַכָּב ז 275 coachman
רֶכֶב ז 317 vehicle, car; upper grindstone
רַכֶּבֶת נ 685 train
רְכוּב ז 15 riding
רִכּוּז ז 45 concentration; assemblage
רִכּוּזִי ז 956 centralized
רִכּוּזִיּוּת נ 781 centralization [no pl.]
רִכּוּךְ ז 45 softening; weakening - military
רָכוּן ז 15 bent, hunched
רָכוּס ז 15 buttoned
רְכוּשׁ ז 399 property, asset; possessions [no pl.]
רְכוּשָׁן ז 874 capitalist
רְכוּשָׁנִי ז 915 materialistic; possessive
רַכּוּת נ 731 softness [no pl.]
רַכָּז ז 275 coordinator (fem. rakezet)
רַכֶּזֶת נ 685 Ethernet hub
רְכִיב ז 405 component
רְכִיבָה נ 1 riding
רָכִיל ז 20 gossip
רְכִילַאי ז 909 gossip column writer
רְכִילוּת נ 24 gossip
רְכִישָׁה נ 1 purchase, acquisition
רַכְלָן ז 846 gossipmonger
רַכְלָנוּת נ 752 gossip, blather, prattle [no pl.]
רֶכֶס ז 317 ridge, range (of hills, mountains)
רֹכֶס/רֶכֶס ז 352 mountain range
רַכְרוּכִי ז 912 spineless, indecisive
רַכְרוּכִיּוּת נ 790 spinelessness, wimpishness [no pl.]
רֶכֶשׁ ז 317 purchasing, acquisitions, procurement [no pl.]
רַמַּאי ז 908 cheat N, crook
רָמָה נ 582 level; plateau
רִמָּה נ 586 larva; maggot
רִמּוֹן ז 382 pomegranate; grenade
רָמוּס ז 15 trampled, downtrodden
רֶמֶז ז 317 hint, clue; indication
רִמְזוּר ז 54 installation of traffic lights
רַמְזוֹר ז 444 traffic light
רֹמַח ז 344 spear, lance
רְמִיָּה נ 4 fraud, deception, cheating [no pl.]
רְמִיזָה נ 1 hinting
רְמִיסָה נ 1 trampling, crushing
רֶמֶץ ז 317 ember (no pl.) [no pl.]
רַמְקוֹל ז 444 loudspeaker
רֶמֶשׂ ז 317 insect, bug, crawling creatures
רַמְשִׁית נ 808 serenade
רֹן ז 228 joy, gladness, elation; singing
רִנָּה נ 586 joy; singing with joy
רִנּוּן ז 45 singing Lit; gossip
רְנָנָה נ 634 singing; joy Lit.
רִסּוּן ז 45 restraint; restraining
רְסִיס ז 405 shard, sliver; shrapnel; shred, trace
רֶסֶן ז 317 bridle; rein
רֶסֶק ז 317 puree; paste
רַע ז 226 bad, nasty; malicious; wrong; bad N, evil N
רֹעַ ז 230 evil, wickedness [no pl.]
רֵעַ ז 232 friend, colleague, comrade; neighbor
רָעָב ז 269 hunger; famine [no pl.]
רָעֵב ז 279 hungry
רַעַבְתָּן/רַעַבְתָן ז 852 glutton
רַעַבְתָנוּת נ 746 gluttony, voracity [no pl.]
רְעַבְתָנִי ז 940 gluttonous, voracious, greedy
רַעַד ז 328 shivering, trembling
רְעָדָה נ 640 shivering
רָעָה נ 582 evil
רָעוּל ז 15 veiled, masked
רָעוּעַ ז 17 rickety, dilapidated; weak, unstable
רְעִי ז 259 grazing cattle
רְעִידָה נ 1 rattling, shaking; trembling
רַעְיָה/רַעְיָה נ 612 wife; consort
רַעְיוֹן/רַעְיוֹן ז 891 idea, plan, proposal; theme
רַעְיוֹנִי/רַעְיוֹנִי ז 972 ideological
רַעַל ז 328 poison, toxin
רְעָלָה נ 632 veil, scarf
רַעֲלִי ז 966 poisonous, toxic
רַעֶלֶת נ 686 toxemia [no pl.]
רַעַם ז 328 thunder N
רַעֲמָה/רַעְמָה נ 612 mane
רִעְנוּן ז 54 refreshing, invigorating
רַעֲנָן ז 849 fresh
רַעֲנַנּוּת נ 751 freshness [no pl.]
רַעַף ז 328 roofing tile
רַעַשׁ ז 328 noise; sound; tumult; earthquake Lit.
רַעֲשָׁן ז 849 rattle, noise maker
רַעֲשָׁנוּת נ 752 loudness [no pl.]
רַעֲשָׁנִי ז 970 noisy, loud; vocal, vociferous
רְפָאִים ז 998 ghosts, spirits
רַפָּד ז 275 upholsterer (fem. rapedet)
רֶפֶד ז 317 padding, pad; layer, bed [no pl.]
רָפֶה ז 265 weak, limp; lax
רְפוּאָה נ 18 medicine; recovery, cure
רְפוּאִי ז 946 medical
רִפּוּד ז 45 upholstery lining, padding
רָפוּי ז 15 relaxed, limp; loose
רִפּוּי ז 45 treatment, therapy
רָפוּס ז 15 weak, limp Lit
רְפִידָה נ 1 insole; lining
רַפְיָה נ 614 raffia
רִפְיוֹן ז 884 weakness; limpness [no pl.]
רְפִיסוּת נ 24 flaccidity; weakness
רַפְסוֹדַאי ז 909 raft operator
רְפָפָה נ 632 louver, slat
רִפְרוּף ז 66 fluttering; cursory glance, scan
רַפְרָף ז 416 hawk-moth, sphinx moth
רַפְרְפָנִי ז 975 cursory
רַפְרֶפֶת נ 717 mousse, whip, dessert, custard
רֶפֶשׁ ז 317 mud, mire
רֶפֶת נ 321 dairy barn, cowshed
רְפָתָה נ 598 bee bread
רַפְתָן ז 846 dairy farmer
רַפְתָנוּת נ 752 dairy farming [no pl.]

tribal 949 ז שִׁבְטִי
captivity, 257 ז שְׁבִי
imprisonment [no pl.]
spark, flash; scrap, 405 ז שְׁבִיב
fragment
capture 4 נ שְׁבִיָּה
comet 20 ז שָׁבִיט
path, trail 405 ז שְׁבִיל
coif 20 ז שָׁבִיס
coif 405 ז שְׁבִיס/שָׁבִיס
being satiated, 24 נ שְׂבִיעוּת
satisfied
seventh 933 ז שְׁבִיעִי
group of seven 911 נ שְׁבִיעִיָּה
a seventh (part) 820 נ שְׁבִיעִית
fragile, breakable 20 ז שָׁבִיר
breaking 1 נ שְׁבִירָה
fragility 24 נ שְׁבִירוּת
strike, walkout 1 נ שְׁבִיתָה
net, lattice, grille 634 נ שְׂבָכָה
train (of clothing); 341 ז שֹׁבֶל
tab (philately); trail, wake
snail; cochlea 450 ז שַׁבְּלוּל
strong current (in 697 נ שִׁבֹּלֶת
river)
stalk (of grain) 698 נ שִׁבֹּלֶת
satiation [no pl.] 344 ז שֹׂבַע
satiation Lit. [no pl.] 628 נ שָׂבְעָה
stroke, 267 ז שָׁבָץ
cerebrovascular accident (only
construct, no decl. no pl.)
break, fracture; 317 ז שֶׁבֶר
fragment, piece; rift; fraction
(math)
distress; heartbreak 886 ז שִׁבָּרוֹן
[no pl.]
shred, trace; 454 ז שַׁבְרִיר
fraction
frail, feeble 915 ז שַׁבְרִירִי
fragility [no pl.] 787 נ שַׁבְרִירִיּוּת
weather vane 717 נ שַׁבְשֶׁבֶת
Sabbath; Saturday 278 נ שַׁבָּת
sabbatical 894 ז שַׁבָּתוֹן
of the Sabbath 915 ז שַׁבַּתִּי
Seventh Day 863 ז שַׁבְּתָן
Adventist
supremacy, 317 ז שֶׂגֶב
greatness, exaltedness [no pl.]
(unintentional) error 634 נ שְׁגָגָה
wrong, mistaken, 15 ז שָׁגוּי
erroneous
tenoning 45 ז שִׁגּוּם
driving someone 53 ז שִׁגּוּעַ
crazy Coll.
common, customary; 15 ז שָׁגוּר
routine
launching; sending 45 ז שִׁגּוּר
lofty, exalted, 402 ז שַׂגִּיא
supreme
error, mistake 1 נ שְׁגִיאָה
sublime, lofty, 402 ז שַׂגִּיב
exalted
regularity 24 נ שְׁגִירוּת
tenon, connector, 317 ז שֶׁגֶם
joint, key

madness 898 ז שִׁגָּעוֹן
crazy 952 ז שִׁגְעוֹנִי
litter (zoology) 317 ז שֶׁגֶר
routine 598 נ שִׁגְרָה
rheumatism [no pl.] 898 ז שִׁגָּרוֹן
rheumatic 952 ז שִׁגְרוֹנִי
ambassador; 454 ז שַׁגְרִיר
delegate, representative
embassy 750 נ שַׁגְרִירוּת
routine Adj 951 ז שִׁגְרָתִי
routineness [no 778 נ שִׁגְרָתִיּוּת
pl.]
prosperity 66 ז שִׂגְשׂוּג
robbery, burglary [no 227 ז שֹׁד
pl.]
demon, genie, fiend 231 ז שֵׁד
breast 217 ז שַׁד/שֹׁד
field 263 ז שָׂדֶה
dresser, chest of 586 נ שִׁדָּה
drawers
robbed, burglarized, 15 ז שָׁדוּד
plundered
crumbling/loosening 45 ז שִׂדּוּד
of soil
matchmaking; 45 ז שִׁדּוּךְ
pairing Coll.
lobbying, pressuring, 45 ז שִׁדּוּל
persuasion; deduction
sprite, imp 894 ז שֵׁדוֹן
devilish, demonic 915 ז שֵׁדוֹנִי
blasted, emaciated; 15 ז שָׁדוּף
blighted; empty
broadcast, 45 ז שִׁדּוּר
transmission
demonic, devilish, 915 ז שֵׁדִי
malicious
robbery, burglary 1 נ שְׁדִידָה
matchmaker 846 ז שַׁדְּכָן
matchmaking [no 752 נ שַׁדְּכָנוּת
pl.]
lobby 658 נ שְׁדֵלָה
lobbyist 863 ז שְׁדְּלָן
field, cultivated 656 נ שְׁדֵמָה
land Lit.
glareola (bird) 808 נ שְׁדֵמִית
blight, blast 898 ז שִׁדָּפוֹן
broadcaster (radio, 275 ז שַׁדָּר
TV) (fem. shaderet, Coll.,
shadarit)
message, dispatch 317 ז שֶׁדֶר
spine 602 נ שִׁדְרָה
avenue 649 נ שְׂדֵרָה
upgrade N 60 ז שִׁדְרוּג
keel 812 נ שִׁדְרִית
lamb 237 שֶׂה זו"נ
delay, lag Lit 50 ז שִׁהוּי
hiccup 50 ז שִׁהוּק
stay N, sojourn [no 734 נ שְׁהוּת
pl.]
staying; stay 4 נ שְׁהִיָּה
onyx 343 ז שֹׁהַם
the central minimal 310 ז שְׁוָא
short vowel
vacuum cleaner 7 ז שׁוֹאֵב
holocaust 593 נ שׁוֹאָה

questioner, inquirer 7 ז שׁוֹאֵל
mischievous; 366 ז שׁוֹבָב
naughty
mischievous; 915 ז שׁוֹבָבִי
youthful
mischievous 915 ז שׁוֹבְבָנִי
dovecote 366 ז שׁוֹבָךְ
striker 6 ז שׁוֹבֵת
robber, burglar 6 ז שׁוֹדֵד
Swedish 915 ז שְׁוֶדִי
equal, identical; 265 ז שָׁוֶה
worth
systematization [no 45 ז שִׁוּוּט
pl.]
giving, creating a 45 ז שִׁוּוּי
look, atmosphere
marketing 45 ז שִׁוּוּק
alignment 45 ז שִׁוּוּר
trench 595 נ שׁוּחָה
slaughterer 7 ז שׁוֹחֵט
causing extensive 7 ז שׁוֹחֵק
wear
proponent; supporter; 7 ז שׁוֹחֵר
cadet
whip 240 ז שׁוֹט
a fool, an idiot; 10 ז שׁוֹטֶה
foolish; rabid (dog)
flagellum (biology) 894 ז שׁוֹטוֹן
continuous; current; 6 ז שׁוֹטֵף
fluent
policeman 6 ז שׁוֹטֵר
value, worth [no pl.] 349 ז שׁוֹוִי
equality 885 ז שִׁוְיוֹן
egalitarian 952 ז שִׁוְיוֹנִי
equality [no pl.] 779 נ שִׁוְיוֹנִיּוּת
Swiss 915 ז שְׁוֵיצִי
branch Lit. 593 נ שׂוֹכָה
renter, tenant 6 ז שׂוֹכֵר
margin, rim; 246 ז שׁוּל
shoulder of paved road
dominant 985 ז שׁוֹלְטָנִי
marginal 990 ז שׁוּלִי
marginality [no 762 נ שׁוּלִיּוּת
pl.]
margins; brim, rim 997 ז שׁוּלַיִם
- now sg. shul too
opposer, nay-sayer 6 ז שׁוֹלֵל
garlic; any 246 ז שׁוּם
tax assessment; 595 נ שׁוּמָה/א
evaluation
desolate, empty, 6 ז שׁוֹמֵם
abandoned
fat [no /a/ reduction 370 ז שׁוּמָן
in pl. constr., shumaney, prob.
because the original form was
shuman w kubuts and a dagesh
in the m]
guard 6 ז שׁוֹמֵר
Samaritan 915 ז שׁוֹמְרוֹנִי
hater, enemy 8 ז שׂוֹנֵא
hater, enemy (fem.) 661 נ שׂוֹנְאָה
different 10 ז שׁוֹנֶה
difference, variance 761 נ שׁוֹנוּת
[no pl.]
reef 814 נ שׁוּנִית/שֻׁנִּית

marble [no pl.] 357 שַׁיִשׁ ז
prickle (botany) 235 שֵׂךְ ז
layer 598 שִׁכְבָה נ
layered; of class 951 שִׁכְבָתִי ז
lying, resting 15 שָׁכוּב ז
forgotten 17 שָׁכוּחַ ז
quietening, relieving pain, etc. 45 שִׁכּוּךְ ז
bereaved 378 שַׁכּוּל ז
bereavement [no pl.] 393 שְׁכוֹל ז
crossing one's legs or hands 45 שִׂכּוּל ז
housing; housing complex 45 שִׁכּוּן ז
neighborhood 18 שְׁכוּנָה נ
of the neighborhood 915 שְׁכוּנָתִי ז
rented, hired 15 שָׂכוּר ז
drunk, drunkard 382 שִׁכּוֹר ז
forgetfulness, absentmindedness [no pl.] 598 שִׁכְחָה נ
amnesia, forgetfulness [no pl.] 898 שִׁכָּחוֹן ז
forgetful, absent-minded 846 שַׁכְחָן ז
forgetfulness [no pl.] 752 שַׁכְחָנוּת נ
lying down; reclining 1 שְׁכִיבָה נ
common; frequent 22 שָׁכִיחַ ז
frequency, commonness 24 שְׁכִיחוּת נ
divine spirit 1 שְׁכִינָה נ
salaried employee 20 שָׂכִיר ז
rental; hiring 1 שְׂכִירָה נ
rent 24 שְׂכִירוּת נ
intelligence, wit; brains, common sense 322 שֵׂכֶל ז
enhancement, improvement; enhancing, improving 63 שִׁכְלוּל ז
intellectualization [no pl.] 54 שִׂכְלוּן ז
mental, intellectual 949 שִׂכְלִי ז
rationalism [no pl.] 776 שִׂכְלִיּוּת נ
rationalistic 915 שִׂכְלְתָנִי ז
upper back 317 שֶׁכֶם ז
shoulder blade 598 שִׁכְמָה נ
cape, shawl 911 שִׁכְמִיָּה נ
neighbor 279 שָׁכֵן ז
convincing, persuading 62 שִׁכְנוּעַ ז
reduplication; copying 60 שִׁכְפּוּל ז
wage, salary; payment; retribution [no pl.] 267 שָׂכָר ז
liquor (only constr., with pataH, no declension, no pl.) 287 שֵׁכָר ז
charter (plane, boat, bus) [no pl.] 317 שֶׂכֶר ז
drunkenness [no pl.] 898 שִׁכָּרוֹן ז
drunkenness [no pl.] 738 שִׁכְרוּת נ
wading; splashing 66 שִׁכְשׁוּךְ ז
revision, rewriting 60 שִׁכְתּוּב ז

rung, step; stage, phase 274 שָׁלָב ז
herpes 715 שַׁלְבֶּקֶת נ
snow 317 שֶׁלֶג ז
popsicle, ice lolly 886 שַׁלְגּוֹן ז
skeleton; outline; foundation (in construction) 317 שֶׁלֶד ז
kingfisher 409 שַׁלְדָּג ז
chassis 598 שִׁלְדָּה נ
skeletal 949 שִׁלְדִּי ז
phlomis (plant) 833 שַׁלְהָבִית נ
flame 715 שַׁלְהֶבֶת נ
inciting, inflaming 60 שִׁלְהוּב ז
calm, serene, peaceful 279 שָׁלֵו ז
quail, pheasant 310 שְׂלָו ז
integrated, interwoven; folded arms 15 שָׁלוּב ז
combination; integration; crossing one's legs or hands 45 שִׁלּוּב ז
slush 825 שְׁלוּגִית נ
calm, serenity 614 שַׁלְוָה נ
sent; spread out, stretched out hand 17 שָׁלוּחַ ז
launching; release; sending 53 שִׁלּוּחַ ז
extension, branch 18 שְׁלוּחָה נ
signposting 45 שִׁלּוּט ז
puddle 825 שְׁלוּלִית נ
payment; reparations 45 שִׁלּוּם ז
שָׁלוֹם, ר' שְׁלוֹמוֹת/שְׁלוֹמִים ז 288 peace; wellbeing (pl. shlomot/shlomim)
of, or related to, peace 915 שְׁלוֹמִי ז
clumsy, unlucky 915 שְׁלוּמִיאֵלִי ז
being clumsy or unlucky [no pl.] 762 שְׁלוּמִיאֵלִיּוּת נ
drawn weapon; extracted 15 שָׁלוּף ז
scalded with boiling water (food) Lit 15 שָׁלוּק ז
tripling; trinity 45 שִׁלּוּשׁ ז
dagger 319 שֶׁלַח ז
vesicle 447 שַׁלְחוּף ז
blister, vesicle (medicine) 835 שַׁלְחוּפִית נ
table 436 שֻׁלְחָן ז
of, or related to, a table 915 שֻׁלְחָנִי ז
remote control Coll. (normative shalat raHak) 275 שַׁלָּט ז
sign; placard; in Bibl. Shield 317 שֶׁלֶט ז
regime; government 885 שִׁלְטוֹן ז
governmental 952 שִׁלְטוֹנִי ז
dominant (genetics) 969 שַׁלְטָנִי ז
secret, quiet manner Bibl. [no pl.] 257 שֶׁלִי ז
placenta (anatomy) 598 שִׁלְיָה נ
messenger 22 שָׁלִיחַ ז
sending 1 שְׁלִיחָה נ
mission 24 שְׁלִיחוּת נ

ruler, leader; ruling, governing, controlling; dominant, influential 402 שַׁלִּיט ז
control; command, knowledge 1 שְׁלִיטָה נ
fetus 405 שָׁלִיל ז
rejection; elimination; revocation 1 שְׁלִילָה נ
negative 933 שְׁלִילִי ז
negativity [no pl.] 769 שְׁלִילִיּוּת נ
that can easily be drawn 20 שָׁלִיף ז
long bag placed on load-carrying animal 405 שְׁלִיף ז
pulling out; drawing, unsheathing 1 שְׁלִיפָה נ
poaching eggs etc. 1 שְׁלִיקָה נ
adjutant 403 שָׁלִישׁ ז
third; trimester 405 שְׁלִישׁ ז
Tertiary (geology) 895 שְׁלִישׁוֹן ז
tertiary (science); service-related (sector, branch) (economics) 915 שְׁלִישׁוֹנִי ז
adjutancy (military) [no pl.] 755 שָׁלִישׁוּת נ
third 933 שְׁלִישִׁי ז
trio 911 שְׁלִישִׁיָּה נ
a third (part) 820 שְׁלִישִׁית נ
osprey 267 שָׁלָךְ ז
fall (of autumn leaves) 685 שַׁלֶּכֶת נ
booty; plunder; bounty, treasure, catch, haul [no pl.] 267 שָׁלָל ז
seam Lit. [no pl.] 310 שְׁלָל ז
bursar (fem. shalemet) 275 שַׁלָּם ז
complete , whole 279 שָׁלֵם ז
dress (after metathesis) Arch. 610 שַׂלְמָה נ
bribe Lit. (plural only) 889 שַׁלְמוֹן (...נִים) ז
stubble (after reaping field) 317 שֶׁלֶף ז
blister, bladder, vesicle (medicine) 835 שַׁלְפּוּחִית נ
one of three identical objects 310 שְׁלָשׁ ז
trio, group of three 632 שְׁלָשָׁה נ
heavy chain; chain of events 718 שַׁלְשֶׁלֶת נ
name; noun; reputation (pl. shemot) 234 שֵׁם ז
assessor 908 שַׁמַּאי ז
left Adj 915 שְׂמָאלִי ז
being left - handed [no pl.] 762 שְׂמָאלִיּוּת נ
leftist 915 שְׂמָאלָנִי ז
forced conversion from Judaism; religious persecution 310 שְׁמָד ז
wilderness; destruction Lit. 585 שַׁמָּה נ
cheering up [no pl.] 53 שִׂמּוּחַ ז

שִׁפּוּץ ז 45 renovation; repairing, renovating; refurbishment; overhaul
שִׁפּוּר ז 45 improvement
שָׁפוּת ז 15 food placed on fire/heat for cooking
שִׁפְחָה נ 598 slave (female)
שְׁפִי ז 257 bare hill Bibl.
שָׁפִיט ז 20 that can be judged/evaluated
שְׁפִיטָה נ 1 judging; hearing (law), judgment
שְׁפִיטוּת נ 24 justiciability; capability to judge/evaluate
שְׁפִיכָה נ 1 pouring; ejaculation
שְׁפִיכוּת נ 24 being poured/ejaculated
שְׁפִיפוֹן ז 895 pseudocerastes (a poisonous snake)
שָׁפִיר ז 20 amnion
שַׁפִּיר ז 402 good, reasonable; benign (medicine)
שַׁפִּירִית נ 814 dragonfly
שָׁפִית נ 842 labellum (plant)
שְׁפִיתָה נ 1 setting a pot on a fire
שֶׁפֶךְ ז 317 estuary; spilling
שָׁפְכָה נ 629 urethra
שְׁפֹכֶת נ 708 debris [no pl.]
שָׁפְכָתִי ז 915 urethral
שָׁפָל ז 267 worthless; low; humble; despicable
שֵׁפֶל ז 322 ebb, low tide; low point [no pl.]
שְׁפֵלָה נ 649 plain
שִׁפְלוּת נ 738 baseness, despicableness [no pl.]
שָׂפָם ז 267 mustache
שָׁפָן ז 274 cony, hyrax; rabbit (coll. only)
שְׁפַנִּיָּה נ 911 pen for rabbits
שְׁפַנְפַּן ז 458 small rabbit, bunny
שֶׁפַע ז 319 abundance, profusion
שִׁפְעוּל ז 60 activation [no pl.]
שַׁפַּעַת נ 690 influenza [no pl.]
שֶׁפֶר ז 317 beauty, pleasantness, grace Lit. [no poss. pron.]
שִׁפְרוּט ז 60 elaboration
שַׁפְרִיר ז 454 canopy Lit.-rare
שִׁפְשׁוּף ז 66 rubbing; abrasion
שַׁפְשֶׁפֶת נ 717 jock itch; door mat
שִׂפְתּוּת ז 70 labialization [no pl.]
שְׂפָתִי ז 915 labial (phonetics)
שֶׁצֶף ז 317 flow, torrent; rage, fury [no pl.]
שָׁקֵד ז 279 almond (tree, fruit)
שְׁקֵדִי ז 915 almond-shaped, elliptical
שְׁקֵדִיָּה נ 911 almond tree
שַׁקְדָן ז 846 diligent
שַׁקְדָנוּת נ 752 diligence, industriousness, studiousness, perseverance [no pl.]
שַׁקְדָנִי ז 969 diligent, industrious, studious
שִׁקּוּי ז 45 beverage, potion; elixir
שָׁקוּל ז 15 equal; reasonable; weighed; comparable; metered, rhyming
שִׁקּוּל ז 45 consideration
שִׁקּוּם ז 45 rehabilitation
שִׁקּוּמִי ז 956 rehabilitative
שָׁקוּעַ ז 17 sunk, stuck; sunken
שִׁקּוּעַ ז 53 draught (shipping); sedimentation; settling
שָׁקוּף ז 15 transparent, clear
שִׁקּוּף ז 45 reflection, reflecting; mirroring; X-ray screening
שְׁקוּפִית נ 825 transparency, slide
שָׁקֵט ז 279 quiet; silent; calm
שֶׁקֶט ז 317 silence, quiet; peace, relaxation [no pl.]
שְׁקִידָה נ 1 diligence
שְׁקִיטָן ז 863 flamingo Rare
שָׁקִיל ז 20 equivalent; weighable
שְׁקִיל ז 405 equivalent N
שְׁקִילָה נ 1 weighing, considering
שְׁקִילוּת נ 24 equivalence
שְׁקִיעָה נ 1 sunset; sinking; downfall
שְׁקִיפוּת נ 24 transparency
שַׂקִּיק ז 402 small bag [perhaps dimin. sub-pattern, CaCiC?]
שַׂקִּית נ 814 small bag
שֶׁקֶל ז 317 shekel (Israeli currency); an old silver unit of weight
שִׁקְלוּל ז 70 weight (statistics); adjusted calculation
שִׁקְלִי ז 949 of shekel (value, basis, etc.)
שִׁקְמָה נ 605 sycamore
שַׁקְנַאי ז 909 pelican
שֶׁקַע ז 319 depression; electrical outlet; low pressure system
שֶׁקֶף ז 317 transparency, slide
שֶׁקֶץ ז 317 abomination; non-Jewish boy
שִׁקְצָה נ 600 gentile (fem.) Lit.
שֶׁקֶר ז 317 lie, untruth, falsehood
שִׁקְרִי ז 949 false, fraudulent, untrue
שִׁקְרִיּוּת נ 776 falseness [no pl.]
שַׁקְרָן ז 846 liar
שַׁקְרָנוּת נ 752 lying, mendacity [no pl.]
שַׁקְרָנִי ז 969 lying Adj
שִׁקְשׁוּק ז 66 rattling, jingling
שֹׁקֶת נ 346 water trough
שַׂר ז 226 minister; ruler, commander (older usage)
שָׁרָב ז 267 heat wave
שִׁרְבּוּב ז 70 insertion in wrong place
שִׁרְבּוּט ז 54 scribble, doodle N
שְׁרָבִי ז 942 of or relating to a heat wave, hot and dry
שַׁרְבִיט ז 452 scepter; wand; baton
שְׁרַבְרַב ז 458 plumber
שְׁרַבְרָבוּת נ 743 plumbing [no pl.]
שְׂרָד ז 310 service, official, formal [no pl.]
שַׂרְדָן ז 846 survivalist
שַׁרְווּלִית נ 814 wristband
שָׂרוּט ז 15 scratched
שָׁרוּי ז 15 be in a state of mind etc.; soaked
שְׂרוֹךְ ז 393 shoelace; lacing
שָׂרוּעַ ז 17 recumbent, lying
שָׂרוּף ז 15 burnt, scorched
שֵׁרוּשׁ ז 51 uprooting, eradication
שֵׁרוּת ז 51 service; help
שִׂרְטוֹן ז 885 sandbank, shoal
שָׂרֶטֶת נ 688 scratch, cut
שָׂרִיג ז 403 twig, shoot, tendril
שָׂרִיד ז 20 remnant
שְׂרִידוּת נ 24 survivability
שִׁרְיוּן ז 54 armoring; safeguarding
שִׁרְיוֹן ז 884 armor
שִׁרְיוֹנַאי ז 909 soldier in the armored corps
שִׁרְיוֹנִית נ 827 armored car
שְׂרִיטָה נ 1 scratch
שְׁרִיקָה נ 1 whistle
שָׁרִיר ז 20 valid
שְׁרִיר ז 405 muscle
שָׁרִיר/שְׁרִיר ז 20 muscle
שְׁרִירוּת נ 24 arbitrariness
שְׁרִירוּתִי ז 915 arbitrary
שְׁרִירוּתִיּוּת נ 762 arbitrariness [no pl.]
שְׁרִירִי ז 933 muscular
שָׂרָף ז 267 seraph, ministering angel Lit.; poisonous snake Lit.-rare
שְׂרָף ז 310 resin
שְׂרֵפָה נ 649 fire
שְׁרַפְרַף ז 458 stool, small seat
שֶׁרֶץ ז 317 insect, bug; vermin
שַׁרְקָן ז 846 guinea pig
שַׁרְקָן ז 846 whistler
שַׁרְקָנוּת נ 752 whistling N
שַׁרְקָנִי ז 969 whistling Adj
שְׁרַקְרַק ז 458 bee eater (bird)
שְׂרָרָה נ 632 authority, rulership
שֹׁרֶשׁ, ר׳ שֳׁרָשִׁים/שָׁרָשִׁים ז 341 root, pl. shorashim
שָׁרְשׁוֹן ז 894 radicle (botany)
שַׁרְשׁוּר ז 449 tapeworm
שִׁרְשׁוּר ז 66 concatenation
שָׁרְשִׁי ז 980 rooted; deep-seated
שָׁרְשִׁיּוּת נ 794 rootedness [no pl.]
שַׁרְשִׁיר ז 453 teal (small duck)
שַׁרְשֶׁרֶת נ 719 chain
שָׁרָת ז 277 janitor; server (comp.) (fem. of janitor sharatit?)
שַׁרְתּוּעַ ז 448 strut

תְּהוֹמִי ז 944 abysmal, unfathomable
תְּהוֹמִיּוּת נ 762 depth, fathomless deep Lit. [no pl.]
תְּהִיָּה נ 4 amazement, wonderment; pondering, considering
תְּהִלָּה נ 580 praise, adoration; biblical: glory, splendor
תַּהֲלוּכָה נ 566 procession, parade
תַּהֲלִיךְ ז 559 process
תָּו ז 214 musical note; score (music); mark, sign, brand; character Comp.
תּוֹאֵם ז 7 corresponding, matching
תּוֹאֲמָן ז 856 conformist
תּוֹבָלָה נ 568 transport
תּוֹבָנָה נ 570 insight
תּוֹבֵעַ ז 9 prosecutor; plaintiff, complainant
תּוֹבְעָנִי ז 985 demanding
תּוֹבָר ז 368 belt loop; rosette
תּוּגָה נ 595 sadness
תּוּגְרִי ז 915 Turkish Lit.-Rare
תּוֹדָה נ 593 thanks, gratitude
תּוֹדָעָה נ 569 consciousness [no pl.]
תָּווּי ז 15 marked, sketched Lit
תִּוּוּי ז 45 notation music
תִּוּוּךְ ז 45 mediation, arbitration; brokerage, negotiation [no pl.]
תּוֹחֶלֶת נ 571 expectation, hope; expectancy Lit. [no pl.]
תְּוִיָּה נ 4 plotting, marking; sketching
תַּוְיָן ז 846 plotter (computing)
תָּוִית נ 814 label; characterization
תּוֹךְ ז 240 inside, interior
תָּוֶךְ ז 355 center, middle; inside, interior
תּוֹכֵחָה נ 665 reproof, rebuke, admonishment
תּוֹכָחָה/תּוֹכַחַת נ 569 reproof, rebuke, admonishment
תּוֹכַחְתִּי ז 915 reproachful
תּוֹכִי ז 915 inside, internal
תּוֹכִיּוּת נ 762 internality [no pl.]
תּוֹכִית נ 844 infix
תּוֹכֵן ז 6 astronomer Lit
תּוֹלָדָה נ 568 outcome
תּוֹלֶדֶת = תּוֹלָדָה נ 571 outcome, result, consequence
תּוֹלָע ז 366 red, scarlet (biblical) [no pl.]
תּוֹלֵעָה נ 666 worm, maggot Lit-Rare
תּוֹלָעִי ז 915 vermiform, worm-like
תּוֹלַעֲנִית נ 814 helminthia (plant)
תּוֹלַעְתִּי/תּוֹלָעְתִּי ז 915 vermiform, worm-like
תּוֹמֵךְ ז 6 supporter; supportive

תּוּנִיסָאִי ז 915 Tunisian
תּוּנִיסִי ז 915 Tunisian
תּוֹסֵס ז 6 effervescent
תּוֹסָף ז 567 additive
תּוֹסֶפֶת נ 571 addition, increase, increment
תּוֹסֶפְתָּן ז 863 appendix (anatomy)
תּוֹעֵבָה נ 664 abomination
תּוֹעֶה ז 10 lost; accidental; one who lost his way
תּוֹעֶלֶת נ 571 benefit, use, value
תּוֹעַלְתִּי ז 915 practicable, utilitarian, profitable
תּוֹעַלְתִּיּוּת נ 804 usefulness; practicability [no pl.]
תּוֹעַלְתָּן ז 863 utilitarian (person)
תּוֹעַלְתָּנִי ז 915 practicable, utilitarian, profitable
תּוֹעַמְלָן ז 863 propagandist, advertiser
תּוֹעַמְלָנִי ז 915 propagandist
תּוֹפָעָה נ 569 phenomenon
תּוֹפֵר ז 6 seamster
תּוֹצָא ז 567 effect
תּוֹצָאָה נ 569 outcome
תּוֹצָר ז 567 product, goods, commodity; outcome
תּוֹצֶרֶת נ 571 output, production, output [no pl.]
תּוֹקֵעַ ז 9 shofar blower; trumpeter
תּוֹקְפָן ז 855 aggressive person
תּוֹקְפָנִי ז 985 aggressive
תּוֹר ז 240 queue, line; turn, time; succession; period, age (of)
תּוֹר ז 240 turtledove
תּוֹרָה נ 593 Torah; theory; doctrine
תּוֹרֵם ז 6 donor
תּוֹרָן ז 877 person on duty, duty officer
תּוֹרָנִי ז 915 pertaining to the Torah; religious, observant
תּוֹרָשָׁה נ 568 heredity [no pl.]
תּוֹרַשְׁתִּי ז 915 hereditary
תּוֹרַשְׁתִּיּוּת נ 804 heritability, heredity [no pl.]
תּוֹשָׁב ז 567 resident
תּוֹשָׁבוּת נ 740 residency [no pl.]
תּוֹשֶׁבֶת נ 571 base, seating
תּוּשִׁיָּה נ 911 resourcefulness
תּוּת ז 246 mulberry; strawberry
תּוֹתָב ז 366 prosthetic, artificial Adj; prosthetic implant; bushing
תּוֹתָח ז 366 cannon (weaponry)
תּוֹתְחָן ז 863 gunner
תּוּתִית נ 845 strawberry shortcake
תַּזְגִּיג ז 558 enamel [no pl.]
תְּזוּזָה נ 572 movement, motion
תְּזוּנָה נ 572 nutrition
תְּזוּנָתִי ז 991 nutritional

תְּזָזִי ז 942 frantic, frenetic Lit.
תְּזָזִית נ 822 craziness, hysteria; squall (meteorology)
תְּזָזִיתִי ז 915 frantic, frenetic; hyperactive, restless
תִּזְכִּיר ז 558 memorandum
תִּזְכֹּרֶת נ 576 reminder; memorandum
תִּזְמוּן ז 65 timing
תִּזְמוּר ז 65 orchestration
תִּזְמוּרִי ז 915 orchestrative
תִּזְמֹרֶת נ 576 orchestra
תִּזְמָרְתִּי ז 992 orchestral
תַּזְקִיק ז 558 distillate; product of refining
תַּזְרִים ז 558 flow chart
תַּזְרֹמֶת נ 576 flow volume [no pl.]
תִּחְבּוּל ז 65 machination, plot
תַּחְבּוּלָה נ 565 trick, ruse, stratagem
תַּחְבּוּלָן ז 882 trickster, tactician, wily person
תַּחְבּוּלָנִי ז 915 tricky, wily, crafty, cunning
תִּחְבּוּר ז 65 arranging words in a certain syntactic relationship
תַּחְבּוּרָה נ 565 transportation [no pl.]
תַּחְבִּיב ז 558 hobby
תַּחְבִּיבָן ז 880 hobbyist
תַּחְבִּיר ז 558 syntax
תַּחְבִּירִי ז 994 syntactic
תַּחְבְּלָן ז 850 wily, crafty, cunning
תַּחְבְּלָנוּת נ 740 cunning, inventiveness, wiliness, trickery [no pl.]
תַּחְבְּלָנִי ז 915 tricky, wily, crafty, cunning
תַּחְבֹּשֶׁת נ 577 dressing, bandage
תַּחְדִּישׁ ז 558 innovation
תָּחוּחַ ז 17 crumbled, loose earth
תִּחוּחַ ז 53 loosening, breaking up earth [no pl.]
תְּחוּלָה נ 572 inception, incidence (law), application [no pl.]
תָּחוּם ז 15 defined, limited, delineated
תְּחוּם ז 399 area, range, zone; discipline, field; limit; domain
תִּחוּם ז 50 delineation, demarcation
תְּחוּמִי ז 946 disciplinary (field of knowledge etc.)
תְּחוּשָׁה נ 572 sensation; feeling
תְּחוּשָׁתִי ז 991 sensory
תִּחְזוּק ז 65 maintaining; maintenance
תַּחְזוּקָה/ תַּחֲזוּקָה נ 565 maintenance
תַּחְזוּקָן/תַּחֲזוּקָן ז 882 maintenance person
תַּחֲזִית נ 562 forecast

Talmud, Oral law 563 תַּלְמוּד ז
Talmudic 915 תַּלְמוּדִי ז
student 558 תַּלְמִיד ז
digest N 558 תַּלְקִיט ז
curling hair 66 תַּלְתּוּל ז
curl (of hair) 416 תַּלְתַּל ז
clover [no pl.] 857 תִּלְתָּן ז
clover-shaped 915 תִּלְתָּנִי ז
honest; innocent; unsophisticated, naïve N & Adj 218 תָּם ז
end, completion [no pl.] 227 תֹּם ז
innocence, simplicity, naivete [no pl.] 227 תֹּם ז
mead [no pl.] 310 תֶּמֶד ז
amazed, astounded 279 תָּמֵהַּ ז
innocence; honesty [no pl.] 592 תֻּמָּה נ
amazement, wonder, surprise [no pl.] 898 תִּמָּהוֹן ז
weirdness, strangeness [no pl.] 747 תִּמְהוֹנוּת נ
strange, weird person 952 תִּמְהוֹנִי ז
weirdness, strangeness [no pl.] 762 תִּמְהוֹנִיּוּת נ
leaning, supported 15 תָּמוּךְ ז
support 45 תָּמוּךְ ז
supporting beam 671 תְּמוֹכָה נ
source, reference, backing, support; backup 998 תִּמּוּכִין ז
yesterday Lit.-rare 393 תְּמוֹל ז
picture, photograph 572 תְּמוּנָה נ
rising sun, smoke Lit [no pl.] 45 תִּמּוּר ז
return, compensation; value; change; permutation 572 תְּמוּרָה נ
naivete, innocence [no pl.] 731 תַּמּוּת נ
mortality 572 תְּמוּתָה נ
mixture, blend 576 תַּמְזֹגֶת נ
costing, pricing (accounting) 558 תַּמְחִיר ז
cost accountant 879 תַּמְחִירָן ז
collapse N [no pl.] 317 תֶּמֶט ז
constant, continuous 933 תְּמִידִי ז
constancy, continuity [no pl.] 768 תְּמִידִיּוּת נ
surprise, wonder, amazement 1 תְּמִיהָה נ
strangeness Lit 24 תְּמִיהוּת נ
support; stabilization; encouragement 1 תְּמִיכָה נ
innocent; naive 20 תָּמִים ז
innocence; naivete 24 תְּמִימוּת נ
tall, erect, upright 20 תָּמִיר ז
tallness, erectness [no pl.] 24 תְּמִירוּת נ
support N 317 תֶּמֶךְ ז
royalties (pl. only) 563 תַּמְלוּג ז
brine 575 תַּמְלַחַת נ
text, lyrics, libretto 558 תַּמְלִיל ז

librettist, lyricist; word processor 880 תַּמְלִילָן ז
token (linguistics) 561 תַּמְנִית נ
solution (chemistry) 580 תְּמִסָּה נ
crocodile 431 תִּמְסָח ז
handout 558 תַּמְסִיר ז
transmission (mechanics, engineering) 576 תִּמְסֹרֶת נ
summary, precis 54 תִּמְצוּת נ
extract; summary, abstract; essence 561 תַּמְצִית נ
concise, essential, succinct 995 תַּמְצִיתִי ז
essentiality [no pl.] 762 תַּמְצִיתִיּוּת נ
palm, date (tree); date (fruit) 267 תָּמָר ז
palm tree 341 תֹּמֶר/תֹּמֶר ז
palm tree, date (Talmudic) 634 תְּמָרָה נ
maneuvering 54 תִּמְרוּן ז
providing incentive 65 תִּמְרוּץ ז
cosmetics, perfumes 563 תַּמְרוּק ז
perfumery 911 תַּמְרוּקִיָּה נ
cosmetician 882 תַּמְרוּקָן ז
road sign, traffic sign 450 תַּמְרוּר ז
placing road signs 70 תִּמְרוּר ז
incentive 558 תַּמְרִיץ ז
fresco 558 תַּמְשִׁיחַ ז
of the Hebrew Bible 915 תַּנָ״כִי ז
teacher, rabbinic authority in time of Mishnah 275 תַּנָּא ז
condition 906 תְּנַאי ז
resistance Lit. [no pl.] 576 תְּנֻגֶּדֶת נ
produce, crop; yield, output 572 תְּנוּבָה נ
fluctuation; movement, rocking; oscillation 572 תְּנוּדָה נ
fluctuating; volatile 991 תְּנוּדָתִי ז
fluctuation [no pl.] 802 תְּנוּדָתִיּוּת נ
posture, position of body 572 תְּנוּחָה נ
tale of woe [no pl.] 45 תִּנּוּי ז
lobe (of ear) 399 תְּנוּךְ ז
nap, sleep 572 תְּנוּמָה נ
movement 572 תְּנוּעָה נ
motor Adj; related to a movement 991 תְּנוּעָתִי ז
mobility [no pl.] 802 תְּנוּעָתִיּוּת נ
momentum; drive, movement, push 572 תְּנוּפָה נ
oven, stove 378 תַּנּוּר ז
furnace operator 863 תַּנּוּרָן ז
condolences (pl. only) 563 תַּנְחוּם ז
crocodile 402 תַּנִּין ז
secondary 915 תַּנְיָנִי ז
barn owl 574 תִּנְשֶׁמֶת נ
complication Coll. 65 תִּסְבּוּךְ ז

complex (psychology) 558 תַּסְבִּיךְ ז
complication, complexity 576 תִּסְבֹּכֶת נ
format (in computing) 558 תַּסְדִּיר ז
regression (psychology) 572 תְּסוּגָה נ
fermented, aerated rare 15 תָּסוּס ז
re-evaluation 45 תִּסּוּף ז
embolism (medicine) 558 תַּסְחִיף ז
fermentation; bubbling; agitation, discontent; unrest 1 תְּסִיסָה נ
frustration 65 תִּסְכּוּל ז
radio play 558 תַּסְכִּית ז
radio play producer 881 תַּסְכִּיתָן ז
association (psychology) 558 תַּסְמִיךְ ז
symptom 558 תַּסְמִין ז
syndrome (medicine) 576 תִּסְמֹנֶת נ
filtrate 558 תַּסְנִין ז
ferment N 275 תַּסָּס ז
expendable supplies, combat supplies [no pl.] 576 תִּסְפֹּקֶת נ
haircut 576 תִּסְפֹּרֶת נ
survey, review 558 תַּסְקִיר ז
producing a screenplay 65 תִּסְרוּט ז
screenplay 558 תַּסְרִיט ז
script writer 909 תַּסְרִיטַאי ז
hair style, hairdo 576 תִּסְרֹקֶת נ
traffic [no pl.] 566 תַּעֲבוּרָה נ
abhorrent, detested Lit 15 תָּעוּב ז
disgust, abhorrence 50 תִּעוּב ז
documentation 50 תִּעוּד ז
document 572 תְּעוּדָה נ
documentary 957 תִּעוּדִי ז
daring 572 תְּעוּזָה נ
installing a canal system; channeling 50 תִּעוּל ז
flight; aviation 572 תְּעוּפָה נ
pressure 572 תְּעוּקָה נ
industrialization [no pl.] 50 תִּעוּשׁ ז
wandering 4 תְּעִיָּה נ
channel 632 תְּעָלָה נ
prank, mischief, practical joke 564 תַּעֲלוּל ז
prankster, mischief-maker 883 תַּעֲלוּלָן ז
mischievous 915 תַּעֲלוּלָנִי ז
propaganda 566 תַּעֲמוּלָה נ
propogandic 996 תַּעֲמוּלָתִי ז
propagandist, advertiser 863 תַּעַמְלָן ז
pleasure (pl. ta`anugot) 564 תַּעֲנוּג ר׳, תַּעֲנוּגוֹת ז

fast (usually religious) 562 תַּעֲנִית נ
employment 566 תַּעֲסוּקָה נ
related to employment 996 תַּעֲסוּקָתִי ז
strength (lit.) (pl. ta`atsumot) 564 תַּעֲצוּם ר׳ תַּעֲצוּמוֹת ז
strength, force, power Lit. 566 תַּעֲצוּמָה נ
razor; scabbard, sheath (biblical) 328 תַּעַר ז
mixture, blend 578 תַּעֲרֹבֶת נ
warranty Lit. 566 תַּעֲרוּבָה נ
exhibition 566 תַּעֲרוּכָה נ
tariff, rate, cost 559 תַּעֲרִיף ז
industry 911 תַּעֲשִׂיָּה נ
industrialist 863 תַּעֲשִׂיָּן ז
industrial 915 תַּעֲשִׂיָּתִי ז
transcription 559 תַּעֲתִיק/תַּעְתִּיק ז
confusing, delusive, deceptive 915 תַּעֲתְעָנִי/תַּעְתְּעָנִי ז
drum (musical instr.); middle ear; drum (machinery); cylinder (of revolver) 227 תֹּף ז
set (theater), decoration, decor 565 תַּפְאוּרָה נ
set manager (theater) 882 תַּפְאוּרָן ז
beauty, glory, splendor 574 תִּפְאֶרֶת נ
expiry 572 תְּפוּגָה נ
potato 378 תַּפּוּד ז
orange 378 תַּפּוּז ז
swollen, blown up 17 תָּפוּחַ ז
apple; ball, knob 379 תַּפּוּחַ ז
apple-like 915 תַּפּוּחִי ז
caught; occupied; engaged 15 תָּפוּס ז
capacity; occupancy 572 תְּפוּסָה נ
drumming 47 תִּפּוּף/תִּיפּוּף ז
distribution 572 תְּפוּצָה נ
production, output 572 תְּפוּקָה נ
sewn; tailor-made 15 תָּפוּר ז
stitching 45 תִּפּוּר ז
bulk 576 תִּפְזֹרֶת נ
mycelium (botany) 558 תַּפְטִיר ז
swelling; lump; souffle 1 תְּפִיחָה נ
swelling 24 תְּפִיחוּת נ
understandable, comprehensible 20 תָּפִיס ז
catching; grabbing; comprehension; perception; outlook 1 תְּפִיסָה נ
perceptual 937 תְּפִיסָתִי ז
drumming esp fingers 1 תְּפִיפָה נ
sewing; dressmaking 1 תְּפִירָה נ
bland, tasteless 279 תָּפֵל ז
tastelessness, frivolity Lit. [no pl.] 579 תִּפְלָה נ
prayer 580 תְּפִלָּה נ
tastelessness, rubbish [no pl.] 738 תְּפֵלוּת נ

effusion 558 תַּפְלִיט ז
phylacteries (Judaism) 998 תְּפִלִּין נ
horror, something horrible; monster 574 תִּפְלֶצֶת נ
terrifying, horrible 915 תִּפְלַצְתִּי ז
delights, pampering, indulgences (pl. only) 563 תַּפְנוּק ז
turn-about, change in direction 561 תַּפְנִית נ
clasp, catch, clip 317 תֶּפֶס ז
operation, handling; management 65 תִּפְעוּל ז
operative; operating, operational 993 תִּפְעוּלִי ז
rapid drumming Lit. [constr. only] [no pl.] 317 תֶּפֶף ז
functioning, function 65 תִּפְקוּד ז
functional 993 תִּפְקוּדִי ז
duty, task, job; function; part, role 558 תַּפְקִיד ז
shoemaker who makes the uppers (fem. taparit???) 275 תַּפָּר ז
stitch 317 תֶּפֶר ז
inflorescence (botany); flowering Lit. 575 תִּפְרַחַת נ
menu 558 תַּפְרִיט ז
down-and-out, derelict, pauper Sl. 846 תַּפְרָן ז
distribution [no pl.] 576 תִּפְרֹסֶת נ
inferno; hell [no pl.] 341 תֹּפֶת ז
infernal, hellish Lit. 980 תָּפְתִּי ז
concretion (geology) 558 תַּצְבִּיר ז
collection, heap, mound Lit.-Rare [no pl.] 576 תִּצְבֹּרֶת נ
declaration, affidavit 558 תַּצְהִיר ז
exhibit, display 572 תְּצוּגָה נ
exhibitory 991 תְּצוּגָתִי ז
formation, form; configuration 572 תְּצוּרָה נ
formational 991 תְּצוּרָתִי ז
intersection, crossing 576 תִּצְלֹבֶת נ
photograph 563 תַּצְלוּם ז
chord (music); onomatopoeia 558 תַּצְלִיל ז
complex (chemistry) 558 תַּצְמִיד ז
observation, observation point 561 תַּצְפִּית נ
lookout 881 תַּצְפִּיתָן ז
cacophony 563 תַּצְרוּם ז
etching 558 תַּצְרִיב ז
consumption, utilization [no pl.] 576 תִּצְרֹכֶת נ
jigsaw puzzle 581 תַּצְרֵף ז
combination Rare [no pl.?] 576 תִּצְרֹפֶת נ
receipt, intake 563 תַּקְבּוּל ז

parallelism; correspondence (poetry) 576 תִּקְבֹּלֶת נ
precedent 558 תַּקְדִּים ז
precedential 994 תַּקְדִּימִי ז
hope 579 תִּקְוָה נ
broken down, out of order 15 תָּקוּל ז
resurrection, revival 572 תְּקוּמָה נ
repair; correction; improvement, rehabilitation; reform 45 תִּקּוּן ז
stuck, jammed 17 תָּקוּעַ ז
validation statistics 45 תִּקּוּף ז
period, era; season 572 תְּקוּפָה נ
periodical 894 תְּקוּפוֹן ז
periodic 991 תְּקוּפָתִי ז
overhead 572 תְּקוּרָה נ
in order, functioning well 20 תָּקִין ז
standardization, establishing standards 1 תְּקִינָה נ
being in order; being undamaged [no pl.] 754 תְּקִינוּת נ
blast of horn, trumpet 1 תְּקִיעָה נ
decisive, resolute, tough 402 תַּקִּיף ז
valid, current, in force 20 תָּקִיף/תָּקֵף ז
firmness [no pl.] 754 תַּקִּיפוּת נ
mishap, hitch 620 תַּקָּלָה נ
record, album; disk (in computing) 558 תַּקְלִיט ז
diskette (computing) 894 תַּקְלִיטוֹן ז
record collection 911 תַּקְלִיטִיָּה נ
disc jockey, DJ 879 תַּקְלִיטָן ז
standard, norm 317 תֶּקֶן ז
regulation 620 תַּקָּנָה נ
standardization 65 תִּקְנוּן ז
articles of association, statute 894 תַּקָּנוֹן ז
regulatory 915 תַּקָּנוֹנִי ז
standard Adj; correct (language) 949 תִּקְנִי ז
electric plug 319 תֶּקַע ז
valid, current, in force 279 תָּקֵף ז
validity, legality; force; power [no pl.] 341 תֹּקֶף ז
validity [no pl.] 740 תְּקֵפוּת נ
budgeting 65 תִּקְצוּב ז
budget; allowance 558 תַּקְצִיב ז
budgetary 994 תַּקְצִיבִי ז
abstract 558 תַּקְצִיר ז
puncture 317 תֶּקֶר ז
refreshments Lit. 576 תִּקְרֹבֶת נ
ceiling 579 תִּקְרָה נ
gel 558 תַּקְרִישׁ ז
incident 561 תַּקְרִית נ
teleprocessing 65 תִּקְשׁוּב ז
communication system 65 תִּקְשׁוּר ז
civil service regulations (acronym) 558 תַּקְשִׁי"ר ז

communications, media 576 תִּקְשֹׁרֶת נ
communicative 992 תִּקְשָׁרְתִּי ז
ticking; typing Coll. 66 תִּקְתּוּק ז
fez 563 תַּרְבּוּשׁ ז
domesticating; causing to acquiring culture [no pl.] 54 תִּרְבּוּת נ
culture 736 תַּרְבּוּת נ
cultured, cultivated; cultural 915 תַּרְבּוּתִי ז
culture, sophistication [no pl.] 803 תַּרְבּוּתִיּוּת נ
ragout (dish) 558 תַּרְבִּיךְ ז
academy Lit. Rare 558 תַּרְבִּיץ ז
tissue culture; culture (microbiology) 561 תַּרְבִּית נ
exercise, training, drilling 65 תִּרְגּוּל ז
translating; translation 54 תִּרְגּוּם ז
translational 915 תִּרְגּוּמִי ז
exercise, drill, training, practice 558 תַּרְגִּיל ז
exercises, drill, repetitive practice 576 תִּרְגֹּלֶת נ
translator Rare 863 תֻּרְגְּמָן ז
spinach 317 תֶּרֶד ז
deep sleep; hibernation 573 תַּרְדֵּמָה נ
coma [no pl.] 693 תַּרְדֶּמֶת נ
large kitchen spoon 409 תַּרְוָד ז
donation, contribution 572 תְּרוּמָה נ
lofty, noble, distinguished 915 תְּרוּמִי ז
shout, cry; blast (of trumpet, shofar) 572 תְּרוּעָה נ
medication 572 תְּרוּפָה נ
medicinal 915 תְּרוּפָתִי ז
excuse 51 תֵּרוּץ ז
linden tree 598 תִּרְזָה נ
excursus 558 תַּרְחִיב ז
suspension (chemistry) 558 תַּרְחִיף ז
lotion Rare 558 תַּרְחִיץ ז
scenario 558 תַּרְחִישׁ ז
vibrato (music) [no pl.] 558 תַּרְטִיט ז
shield, cover 405 תְּרִיס ז
shutter, blind 405 תְּרִיס ז
ray (cartilaginous fish) 814 תְּרִיסָנִית נ
duodenum 894 תְּרֵיסַרְיוֹן ז
chemical compound 576 תִּרְכֹּבֶת נ
preparation of vaccine [no pl.] 65 תִּרְכּוּב ז
chest, trunk, large suitcase Lit. 444 תַּרְכּוֹס ז
concentration (the relative content of a component) [no pl.] 576 תִּרְכֹּזֶת נ
Turkish 915 תֻּרְכִּי ז
vaccine 558 תַּרְכִּיב ז
concentrate 558 תַּרְכִּיז ז
clues, hints 576 תִּרְמֹזֶת נ
satchel, bag; pod; bullet casing 558 תַּרְמִיל (אין שורש...) ז
backpacking [no pl.] 740 תַּרְמִילָאוּת נ
very small satchel; silique (botany) 894 תַּרְמִילוֹן ז
deceit, fraud 561 תַּרְמִית נ
mast; flagpole 341 תֹּרֶן ז
fowl-like; conceited, haughty 915 תַּרְנְגוֹלִי ז
spray, aerosol 558 תַּרְסִיס ז
poison Lit. 573 תַּרְעֵלָה נ
grudge, grievance, complaint 577 תַּרְעֹמֶת נ
blank part of document 341 תֶּרֶף ז
pudenda, female external genitalia [no pl.] 341 תֹּרֶף ז
weakness 624 תִּרְפָּה נ
idols, household gods 998 תְּרָפִים ז
diagram, sketch, chart 558 תַּרְשִׁים ז
precious stone (aquamarine?) Biblical 558 תַּרְשִׁישׁ ז
record, report, details 576 תִּרְשֹׁמֶת נ
preliminary inquiry 65 תִּשְׁאוּל ז
praise Lit. 575 תִּשְׁבַּחַת נ
from Tishb (Elijah) 915 תִּשְׁבִּי ז
crossword puzzle 581 תַּשְׁבֵּץ ז
booklet of crossword puzzles 894 תַּשְׁבְּצוֹן ז
commercial 558 תַּשְׁדִּיר ז
dispatch, communication, message 576 תִּשְׁדֹּרֶת נ
return, yield (economics) 572 תְּשׁוּאָה נ
answer, reply, response 572 תְּשׁוּבָה נ
input (economy) 572 תְּשׂוּמָה נ
salvation, help, rescue Lit. 572 תְּשׁוּעָה נ
desire 572 תְּשׁוּקָה נ
gift, present 572 תְּשׁוּרָה נ
feeble, worn out 15 תָּשׁוּשׁ ז
interlacing Lit. 576 תִּשְׁזֹרֶת נ
arrow crossword puzzle, Swedish crossword 581 תַּשְׁחֵץ ז
youth Lit. [no pl.] 576 תִּשְׁחֹרֶת נ
leachate (geology); gargle 558 תַּשְׁטִיף ז
ninth 933 תְּשִׁיעִי ז
group of nine 911 תְּשִׁיעִיָּה נ
a ninth (part) 820 תְּשִׁיעִית נ
fatigue, frailty, infirmity 24 תְּשִׁישׁוּת נ
concern, group, complex; gearing (mechanics) 576 תִּשְׁלֹבֶת נ
payment 563 תַּשְׁלוּם ז
guilloche (architecture) 558 תַּשְׁלִיב ז
tashlich (prayer recited on Rosh Hashana) [no pl.] 558 תַּשְׁלִיךְ ז
negative (photography) 558 תַּשְׁלִיל ז
use, utilization; object (usually religious); sexual intercourse 558 תַּשְׁמִישׁ ז
storage substance (biochemistry) [no pl.] 576 תִּשְׁמֹרֶת נ
asphyxia; choking [no pl.] 558 תַּשְׁנִיק ז
flow, pouring, spilling Lit. [no pl.] 576 תִּשְׁפֹּכֶת נ
forecast (weather); prospectus (stock exchange) 558 תַּשְׁקִיף ז
perspective 576 תִּשְׁקֹפֶת נ
tip, gratuity; gift Lit. 317 תֶּשֶׁר ז
blueprint, land use scheme 558 תַּשְׁרִיט ז
validation [no pl.] 558 תַּשְׁרִיר ז
maceration 561 תִּשְׁרִית נ
infrastructure 561 תַּשְׁתִּית נ
rim, brim 669 תִּתּוֹרָה נ
anosmic, lacking sense of smell 846 תַּתְרָן ז
lack of sense of smell [no pl] 752 תַּתְרָנוּת נ

Printed in Great Britain
by Amazon

84475837R00468